TOYOTA COROLLA 1600

Service Manual

1975/1976/1977/1978/1979

Robert Bentley Complete Service Manuals

Toyota Service Manuals

Toyota Celica Service Manual: 1978-1984. *Robert Bentley*

Toyota Corolla Service Manual: 1975-1979, all 1600 Models. *Robert Bentley*

Toyota Corolla Service Manual: 1980-1983, all 1.8 models. *Robert Bentley*

Toyota Tercel Service Manual: 1980-1984, including 4WD Wagon. *Robert Bentley*

Toyota Pickup, 4Runner Service Manual: 1978-1987, including Diesel and 4WD Models. *Robert Bentley*

Volkswagen Service Manuals

Volkswagen Beetle and Karmann Ghia Official Service Manual Type 1: 1966-1969. *Volkswagen United States*
VW Part No. LPV 997 169

Volkswagen Super Beetle, Beetle and Karmann Ghia Official Service Manual Type 1: 1970-1979. *Volkswagen United States*
VW Part No. LPV 997 109

Volkswagen Station Wagon/Bus Official Service Manual Type 2: 1968-1979. *Volkswagen United States*
VW Part No. LPV 997 288

Volkswagen Fastback and Squareback Official Service Manual Type 3: 1968-1973. *Volkswagen United States*
VW Part No. LPV 997 383

Volkswagen Dasher Service Manual: 1974-1981, including Diesel. *Robert Bentley*
VW Part No. LPV 997 335

Volkswagen Rabbit/Scirocco Service Manual: 1975-1979 Gasoline Models. *Robert Bentley*
VW Part No. LPV 997 174

Volkswagen Rabbit/Scirocco/Jetta Service Manual: 1980-1984 Gasoline Models, including Pickup Truck, Convertible and GTI. *Robert Bentley*
VW Part No. LPV 800 104

Volkswagen Rabbit/Jetta Diesel Service Manual: 1977-1984, including Pickup Truck and Turbo Diesel. *Robert Bentley*
VW Part No. LPV 800 122

Volkswagen Vanagon Official Factory Repair Manual: 1980-1987, including Air-cooled, and Water-cooled Gasoline Engines, Diesel Engine, Syncro, and Camper. *Volkswagen United States*
VW Part No. LPV 800 146

Volkswagen Quantum Official Factory Repair Manual: 1982-1986, Gasoline and Turbo Diesel, including Wagon and Syncro. *Volkswagen United States*
VW Part No. LPV 800 201

Volkswagen GTI, Golf, and Jetta Official Factory Repair Manual: 1985-1987 Gasoline, Diesel, and Turbo Diesel including Golf GT, Jetta GLI, and 16V models. *Volkswagen United States.*
VW Part No. LPV 800 107

Volkswagen Fox Official Factory Repair Manual: 1987 *Volkswagen United States*
VW Part No. LPV 800 501

Audi Service Manuals

Audi Fox Service Manual: 1973-1979. *Robert Bentley*
Audi Part No. LPA 997 082

Audi 4000, Coupe Official Factory Repair Manual: 1980-1983, Gasoline, Diesel, and Turbo Diesel. *Audi of America*
Audi Part No. LPV 800 422

Audi 4000S, 4000CS, and Coupe GT Official Factory Repair Manual: 1984-1987, including Quattro and Quattro Turbo. *Audi of America*
Audi Part No. LPV 800 423

Audi 5000, 5000S Official Factory Repair Manual: 1977-1983 Gasoline and Turbo Gasoline, Diesel and Turbo Diesel. *Audi of America*
Audi Part No. LPV 800 443

Audi 5000S, 5000CS Official Factory Repair Manual: 1984-1986 Gasoline, Turbo, and Turbo Diesel, including Wagon and Quattro. *Audi of America*
Audi Part No. LPV 800 444

British Leyland Service Manuals

Complete Official MGB: 1962-1974. *British Leyland Motors*

Complete Official MGB: 1975-1980. *British Leyland Motors*

The MG Workshop Manual, Complete Tuning and Maintenance for all models, form "M" Type to "T.F. 1500." *W.E. Blower*

Complete Official MG Midget 1500: 1975-1979. *British Leyland Motors*

Complete Official Triumph TR2 & TR3: 1953-1961. *British Leyland Motors*

Complete Official Triumph TR4 & TR4A: 1961-1968. *British Leyland Motors*

Complete Official Triumph GT6, GT6+, & GT6 Mk III: 1967-1973. *British Leyland Motors*

Complete Official Triumph TR6 & TR250: 1967-1976. *British Leyland Motors*

Complete Official Triumph TR7: 1975-1981. *British Leyland Motors*

Complete Official Triumph Spitfire Mk III, Mk IV, and 1500: 1968-1974. *British Leyland Motors*

Complete Official Triumph Spitfire 1500: 1975-1980. *British Leyland Motors*

Complete Official Jaguar "E." *British Leyland Motors*

Complete Official Austin-Healey 100-Six and 3000: 1956-1968. *British Leyland Motors*

Complete Official 948cc and 1098cc Sprite/Midget. *British Leyland Motors*

Complete Official 1275cc Sprite/Midget: 1967-1974. *British Leyland Motors*

TOYOTA COROLLA 1600

Service Manual

1975/1976/1977/1978/1979

Robert Bentley
Cambridge, Massachusetts

Published and distributed by:

Robert Bentley, Inc.
1000 Massachusetts Avenue
Cambridge, Massachusetts 02138

Copies of this manual may be purchased from selected booksellers and automotive accessories and parts dealers, or directly from the publlisher by mail.

NOTE TO USERS OF THIS MANUAL

The publisher encourages comments from the readers of this manual. These communications have been and will be carefully considered in preparation of this and other manuals. Please write to Robert Bentley, Inc., at the address on this page.

This manual is published by Robert Bentley, Inc., which has sole responsibility for its content. Toyota has not reviewed and does not vouch for the accuracy of the technical specifications and procedures described in this manual.

CAUTION

It is assumed that the reader is familiar with basic automotive repair procedures.

Before attempting any work on your Toyota, read the cautions and warnings on page ix and any caution or warning which may accompany a procedure in the service manual.

Special tools required in performing certain service operations are identified in the manual and recommended for use.

Use of tools or procedures other than those recommended in this service manual may be detrimental to the vehicle's safe operation as well as the safety of the person servicing the vehicle.

Part numbers listed in this manual are for reference only. Always check with your authorized dealer to verify part numbers.

Robert Bentley, Inc., the publisher, has made every effort to ensure the accuracy of this manual. The publisher cannot be responsible for the result of any error in this manual.

Library of Congress Catalog Card No. 79-53189
ISBN 0-8376-0242-4
Bentley Stock No. TCR9
90 89 88 87 10 9 8 7 6 5 4 3 2

Illustrations by Gretchen Bruno and Jane Haraway
Cover drawings by Jane Haraway

Manufactured in the United States of America

Foreword

Toyota Corollas are among the most widely sold cars in the world, and their outstanding reputation for economy, reliability, and low maintenance costs has done much to make Toyota the best-selling imported car make in North America. There is, however, considerable variety in the kinds of cars that carry the Corolla name, ranging from the standard sedans, which are inexpensive to buy and operate, to the SR-5 versions of the Sport Coupe and Liftback, which have luxury features usually found on more exotic and expensive automobiles.

This Toyota Corolla 1600 Service Manual covers all Corolla cars with the 1600 (2T-C) engine that have been sold in the United States and Canada for the Model Years 1975, 1976, 1977, 1978, and 1979. An absolutely certain way to determine whether your Corolla is a 1600 model is to check its model number, which is in the engine compartment on a metal plate near the center of the firewall, just to the rear of the engine's exhaust manifold. The model number is stamped into this metal plate, and will begin with the letters TE if the car is one of the 1975 through 1979 cars covered by this Manual. For example, the model number TE31L-MDFA indicates that the car is a 1600 DeLuxe Sedan built during the 1978 and 1979 model years. The Vehicle Identification Number, which is visible through the lower left-hand corner of the windshield, also begins with the letters TE on the cars that are covered by this Manual.

For the Corolla owner with mechanical skills and for independent garages, this Manual gives all the specifications that are available in a Toyota workshop. In addition, a Corolla owner who has no intention of working on his or her car will find that reading and owning this Manual will make it possible to discuss repairs intelligently with a professional mechanic.

The aim throughout has been simplicity, clarity, and completeness with step-by-step procedures and accurate specifications. Every human effort has been made to ensure the highest degree of accuracy possible. When the vast array of data presented in this Manual is taken into account, however, no claim to infallibility can be made.

We therefore cannot be responsible for the result of any errors that may have crept into the text or illustrations. The Publisher encourages comments from the readers of this Manual in regard to any errors and, also, suggestions for improvement in the presentation of the technical material. These communications have been and will be carefully considered in the preparation of this and other manuals. Please write to Robert Bentley, Inc., 872 Massachusetts Ave., Cambridge, Massachusetts 02139.

The Corolla owner intending to do maintenance and repairs should have a set of metric wrenches, a torque wrench, screwdrivers, and feeler gauges, since these basic hand tools will be used in accomplishing a majority of the repairs described in this Manual. Usually, there will be a caution in the text when a repair requires special tools or special skills.

If you are a professional mechanic already working on Toyotas, you may have the special tools that are shown in some of the illustrations in this Manual. If you have previously worked only on cars built to the old U.S. Standard of inch and foot measurements, you will not have to replace your expensive micrometers, vernier calipers, and other precision tools because specifications are given both in millimeters and in inches, except when special Toyota metric tools or adjustments to metric dimensions are indispensable (these measurements are given in millimeters only).

In keeping with the adoption of the SI *(Systeme International)* units of measure, which constitute the Modernized Metric System, torque wrench readings in Nm (newton meters) are used throughout. These Nm specifications are not direct conversions of the factory specifications, which are given in mkg (meter kilograms); rather, they are convenient Nm figures that fall within the range of mkg figures given by the factory. For example, a factory specification of 4.0 to 6.5 mkg would equal 39.22 to 63.73 Nm—an overly fussy specification for an instrument such as a torque wrench which is not usually calibrated in increments smaller than 5 Nm. So, in this Manual, the specification would be given as 40 to 60 Nm, which falls within the range of torques expressed by the factory specifications. In all instances this Manual includes in parentheses the conversion of torque specifications to ft. lb. (foot pounds). For example, 40 to 60 Nm (30 to 44 ft. lb.).

Toyota offers an extensive warranty. Therefore, before deciding to repair a Corolla that is covered by the new-car warranty, consult your Authorized Toyota Dealer. You may find that he can make the repair either free or at minimum cost. Should any repair ever be needed that you feel is too difficult to do yourself, a trained Toyota mechanic is ready to do the job for you

Robert Bentley, Inc.

Please read these warnings and cautions before proceeding with maintenance and repair work.

WARNING—

• Never work under a lifted car unless it is solidly supported on stands intended for the purpose. Do not support a car on cinder blocks, hollow tiles, or other props that may crumble under continuous load. Do not work under a car that is supported solely by a jack.

• If you are going to work under a car on the ground, make sure that the ground is level. Block the wheels to keep the car from rolling. Disconnect the battery ground strap to prevent others from starting the car while you are under it.

• Never run the engine unless the work area is well ventilated. Carbon monoxide kills.

• Friction materials such as brake and clutch linings or brake pads may contain asbestos fibers. Do not create dust by grinding, sanding or by cleaning with compressed air. Avoid breathing asbestos fibers and asbestos dust. Breathing asbestos may result in serious diseases, such as asbestosis or cancer, and cause severe injury and death.

• Tie long hair behind your head. Do not wear a necktie, scarf, loose clothing, or necklace when you work near machine tools or running engines. If your hair, clothing, or jewelry were to get caught in the machinery, severe injury could result.

• Disconnect the battery ground strap whenever you work on the fuel system or the electrical system. When you work around fuel, do not smoke or work near heaters or other fire hazards. Keep an approved fire extinguisher handy.

• Illuminate your work area adequately but safely. Use a portable safety light for working inside or under the car. Make sure its bulb is enclosed by a wire cage. The hot filament of an accidentally broken bulb can ignite spilled fuel or oil.

• Catch draining fuel, oil, or brake fluid in suitable containers. Do not use food or beverage containers that might mislead someone into drinking from them. Store flammable fluids away from fire hazards. Wipe up spills at once, but do not store the oily rags, which can ignite and burn spontaneously.

• Finger rings should be removed so that they cannot cause electrical shorts, get caught in running machinery, or be crushed by heavy parts.

• Keep sparks, lighted matches, and open flame away from the top of the battery. If hydrogen gas escaping from the cap vents is ignited, it will ignite gas trapped in the cells and cause the battery to explode.

• Always observe good workshop practices. Wear goggles when you operate machine tools or work with battery acid. Gloves or other protective clothing should be worn whenever the job requires it.

CAUTION—

• If you lack the skills, tools and equipment, or a suitable workshop for any procedure described in this Manual, we suggest you leave such repairs to an Authorized Toyota Dealer or other qualified shop. We especially urge you to consult your Authorized Toyota Dealer before attempting any repairs on a car still covered by the new-car warranty.

• Toyota is constantly improving its cars and sometimes these changes, both in parts and specifications, are made applicable to earlier models. Therefore parts numbers listed in this manual are for reference only. Always check with your Authorized Toyota Parts Department for the latest information.

• Before starting a job, make certain that you have all necessary tools and parts on hand. Read all instructions thoroughly; do not attempt shortcuts. Use tools appropriate to the work and use only replacement parts meeting Toyota specifications. Makeshift tools, parts, and procedures will not make good repairs.

• Use pneumatic and electric tools only to loosen threaded parts and fasteners. Never use such tools to tighten fasteners, especially on light alloy parts.

• Be mindful of the environment and ecology. Before you drain the crankcase, find out the proper way to dispose of the oil. Do not pour oil onto the ground, down a drain, or into a stream, pond, or lake. Consult local ordinances that govern the disposal of wastes.

Directions for using torque wrenches calibrated in meter kilograms

In adopting the SI *(Systeme International)* units of measure, which constitute the Modernized Metric System, the old metric unit of torque, the meter kilogram (mkg or kgf/m), is being replaced by a new unit of torque, the newton meter (Nm). Tool manufacturers are now making this change and if you purchase a new torque wrench we recommend that you obtain one calibrated in newton meters. As metrication proceeds, torque specifications given in foot pounds (ft. lb. or lbf/ft) and meter kilograms will be replaced by torque specifications given only in newton meters. However, throughout this Manual we have included in parentheses conversions to foot pounds which can be used by persons who own torque wrenches made to the obsolete U.S. system.

If you have an older metric torque wrench you must convert the newton meter specifications given in this Manual to meter kilograms. To do this, simply point off the last digit. For example, 35 Nm would become 3.5 mkg. To convert Nm to centimeter kilograms (cmkg), add a zero. For example, 5 Nm would become 50 cmkg. These conversions are not mathematically precise (35 Nm actually equals 3.57 mkg) but they are adequate for normal workshop purposes. The specifications given in this Manual have been developed so that using the simple system of conversion just described will not cause the tightening torques of nuts and bolts to fall outside the ranges given by the car manufacturer.

AUTOMATIC TRANSMISSION

Contents

TABLES

Automatic Transmission

The automatic transmission is housed in a cast aluminum alloy case that has the bellhousing and the ATF (automatic transmission fluid) pump bolted to the front of it and a cast aluminum alloy extension housing bolted to the rear. The transmission itself consists of an engine-driven torque converter coupled to a fully automatic three-speed planetary gear system. The design is unique in that all of its clutches and brakes are of the multiple-disc kind, with no contracting bands. In addition to providing smoother shifts and longer service life, this design makes unnecessary the periodic band adjustments that are required for correct maintenance of most automatic transmissions.

The automatic transmission eliminates the friction clutch and clutch pedal used with the manual transmission and makes manual changes unnecessary during normal driving in the forward gears. However, provision is made for the manual selection of first and second gears when special driving conditions demand it. Downshifts, kickdown, and throttle valve position are controlled by a cable that is connected to the accelerator pedal linkage. There is no vacuum unit to control these functions, as on some other kinds of automatic transmissions.

Cleanliness and careful workmanship are imperative when you repair the automatic transmission. Familiarize yourself with the instructions before you begin a job and make sure that you have the necessary tools—particularly for procedures given with metric specifications only. Specifications that lack U.S. equivalents require that the related work be carried out only with metric tools and instruments. It is also important that you have on hand all of the new gaskets and seals that are required for the job. The reuse of old gaskets and seals is almost certain to cause leaks and erratic shifting when a repaired transmission is returned to service.

Though you may not have the tools or the skills for carrying out actual repairs, you may be able to remove the transmission, which can help to reduce service time. In this case, we recommend that the transmission be thoroughly cleaned on the outside and then taken to the shop as is—partial disassembly will not make repairs easier and may indeed complicate them. We especially urge you to consult an Authorized Dealer before you attempt repairs on a car that is still covered by the new-car warranty.

1. GENERAL DESCRIPTION

A cross-section of the automatic transmission is given in Fig. 1-1. The torque converter and the bellhousing are at the left in the illustration. At the right end of the illustration is the extension housing, which contains the output shaft, the governor, and the speedometer drive. The extension housing has a bushing and a seal that receive the front end of the car's driveshaft. The driveshaft is internally splined so that it can slide forward and backward on the splined output shaft as the rear wheels move up and down on their springs.

The transmission case contains the ATF pump, the hydraulic controls, and the planetary gear system. The planetary gear system is lubricated solely by the ATF that is circulated through the transmission by the ATF pump. Because the ATF does not circulate unless the engine is running, it is important to remember that the transmission parts are only partially lubricated when the engine is turned off and the car is being towed.

***CAUTION* ——**
Never tow a car with an automatic transmission faster than 48 kph (30 mph) or farther than 80 km (50 mi.). Bearings can be damaged by lack of lubrication. If you must tow the car farther, either lift the rear wheels or disconnect the driveshaft at the rear end. The disconnected driveshaft should be left in place, wired to the car body. If it is fully removed, ATF will leak out of the transmission.

Torque Converter

The torque converter is a large doughnut-shaped assembly located between the engine and the transmission. The torque converter not only receives engine output and passes it on to the transmission, but also multiplies engine torque at low vehicle speeds and serves as a fluid coupling between the engine and the transmission. Curved impeller vanes inside the housing set up a flow of ATF that drives another vaned wheel called the turbine. The turbine drives the input shaft, which carries power to the planetary gear system. The central set of vanes in the torque converter is called the stator. At low speeds, a one-way clutch keeps the stator stationary so that its curved vanes will re-direct the flow of ATF in such a way that torque is multiplied. At higher speeds, when there is no longer a speed differential between the impeller vanes and the turbine, the stator begins to rotate with the mass of fluid and torque multiplication ceases.

ATF Pump

ATF must be circulated under pressure before the automatic transmission can function. The ATF pump that creates this pressure is located at the extreme front end of the transmission case. The pump is driven at engine rpm because it is connected mechanically to the torque converter's housing. Therefore, the pump circulates ATF whenever the engine is running, regardless of selector lever position.

Planetary Gear System

A torque converter alone cannot supply the torque multiplication needed for all driving conditions. The output of the torque converter is therefore routed into a planetary gear system. The planetary gear system consists of two multiple-disc clutches in the front part of the case, three multiple-disc brakes in the central and rear parts of the case, and two planetary gearsets—one gearset for forward operation of the vehicle and the other gearset for reverse.

The two hydraulically operated multiple-disc clutches control the delivery of the torque converter's turbine output to the planetary gearsets. The clutch at the front end of the transmission is called the forward clutch because it transfers power to the planetary gears in all forward gears. The clutch just to the rear of the forward clutch is called the direct and reverse clutch because it transfers power to the planetary gears only when the transmission is in direct (3rd gear) or in reverse.

For simplicity, and to avoid confusion, the three multiple-disc brakes will be referred to in this Manual as the No. 1 brake, the No. 2 brake, and the No. 3 brake—numbering the brakes from the front to the rear of the transmission. The No. 3 brake is a 1st/reverse gear brake. This brake is applied to obtain reverse operation and also when the selector lever is at **L**. In **L** it locks the 1st gear one-way clutch in both directions of rotation and thus provides additional engine braking. The No. 1 brake and the No. 2 brake divide the functions handled in most automatic transmissions by a 2nd gear brake, with a consequent improvement in transmission operation.

Hydraulic Controls

The hydraulic control system directs and regulates hydraulic pressure from the ATF pump, thereby controlling shifting of the planetary gear system. Shifts are produced by the ring-shaped pistons of the clutches and the brakes. The direct and reverse clutch and the No. 3 brake have dual (inner and outer) pistons. The force with which this clutch and this brake are applied can be varied depending on whether hydraulic pressure is delivered to the inner (larger) or the outer (smaller) piston.

Three primary control devices regulate the movement of the control valves in the automatic transmission's valve body assembly. One of these is the manual valve, which is connected to the selector lever by a rod. Moving the lever changes the setting of the valve and produces the necessary application of hydraulic pressure for the drive range selected. The second primary control

Fig. 1-1. Cross section of automatic transmission.

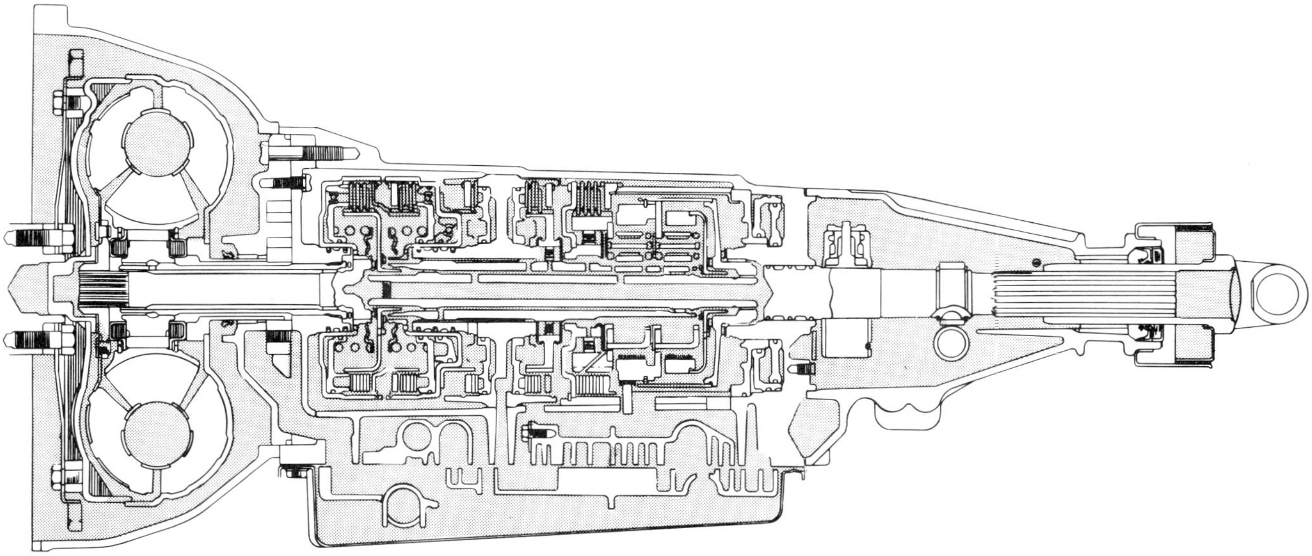

device is the downshift valve/throttle valve assembly, which is operated by the accelerator cable and makes the transmission responsive to variations in engine speed and load. A third primary control device, the governor, controls ATF pressure relative to the output shaft's rotational speed and makes the transmission responsive to variations in vehicle speeds.

2. MAINTENANCE

The following routine maintenance jobs should be performed at the time or mileage intervals prescribed in **LUBRICATION AND MAINTENANCE,** where you will also find the specifications and the quantities for the lubricants required. The actual work is fully described either in **LUBRICATION AND MAINTENANCE** or in this section of the Manual under the listed headings.

1. Checking automatic transmission fluid (ATF) level, checking condition of fluid, and if necessary, adding ATF
2. Replacing ATF
3. Checking that the kickdown operates correctly during a road test and, if necessary, adjusting the throttle cable. **4.1**, **3.1**.

3. SHIFT CONTROL LINKAGE

The shift control linkage consists of the selector lever, mounted to the driver's right, and the rod and lever that convey the selector lever's movement to the manual shaft lever on the transmission. In addition, there is the throttle cable that couples the movements of the accelerator pedal to the transmission's hydraulic controls.

3.1 Adjusting Linkages

The selector linkage should be adjusted if the pointer of the selector lever does not align itself correctly with the appropriate letter or number on the control position indicator. Adjust the throttle cable if the transmission does not shift at the correct speeds or if the transmission does not kickdown correctly.

To adjust selector linkage:

1. Working beneath the car, at the bottom of the selector lever, loosen the locknut (Fig. 3-1) so that the selector rod moves freely at the swivel pin.

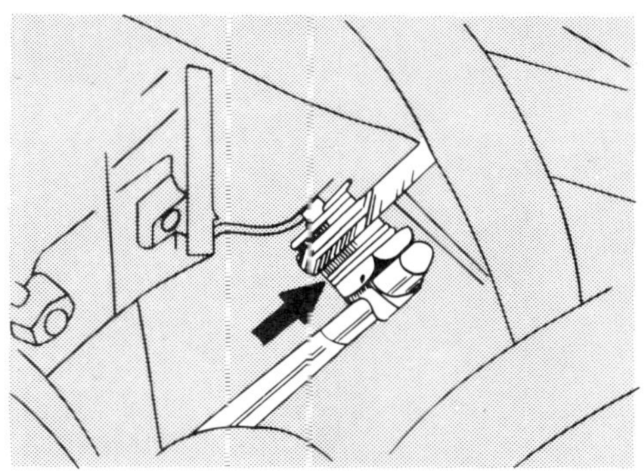

Fig. 3-1. Locknut (arrow) that holds rod to swivel pin.

2. Have someone inside the car hold the selector lever so that the pointer is aligned with the **N** on the control position indicator.
3. Working beneath the car, correctly position the manual shaft lever by first moving it fully toward the front of the car, and then returning it to its third detent notch, which is neutral (counting the foremost notch as "one"). See Fig. 3-2.

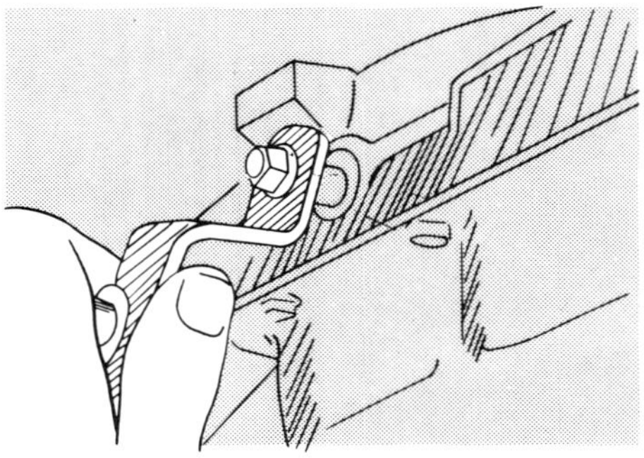

Fig. 3-2. Manual valve lever being moved to its neutral position.

4. With the selector lever at **N** and the manual valve lever at its neutral detent, tighten the locknut shown previously in Fig. 3-1. Then check that, in each of the selector lever positions, the pointer aligns itself with the correct numeral or letter on the control position indicator. Check also that the engine starts only in **N** or **P**; if not, adjust the neutral start switch.

To adjust throttle cable:

1. Remove the air cleaner as described in conjunction with removal of the cylinder head cover in **ENGINE**. If the cable is visibly worn or damaged, replace it.
2. With the engine stopped, have someone hold the accelerator pedal fully to the floor. Then measure the distance between the end of the cable conduit and the stopper collar of the throttle cable, as indicated in Fig. 3-3. The correct dimension is 52 mm (2.05 in., or 2 3/64 in.).

Fig. 3-3. Cable protrusion at full throttle being measured. Engine shown is not for car covered by this Manual.

3. If the dimension measured in the preceding step was not correct, loosen the locknuts (Fig. 3-4) that hold the cable conduit to the bracket.
4. By loosening and tightening the appropriate locknuts, reposition the cable conduit in the bracket until the cable protrusion at full throttle is correct. Then tighten the locknuts against the bracket.

***CAUTION* ——**
Overtightening the locknuts can damage the threaded end of the cable conduit.

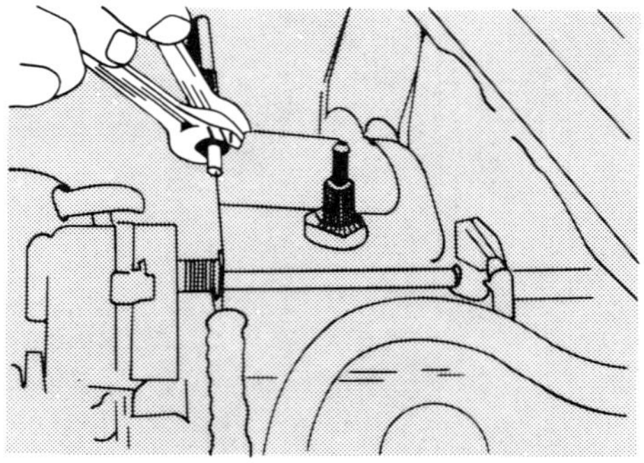

Fig. 3-4. Cable conduit position being adjusted by repositioning locknuts on threaded end of cable conduit.

5. Conduct a road test to see that the transmission shifts up and down at the correct speeds, and that the kickdown operates as it should. If not, either the adjustment is still incorrect or there is some other problem, such as low ATF or an out-of-tune engine.

3.2 Adjusting Neutral Start Switch

The neutral start switch is located on the selector lever assembly. For access, first remove the center console as described in **BODY AND INTERIOR.** You will then see the neutral start switch located at the right-hand side of the selector lever assembly, beneath the control position indicator panel. To adjust the switch, loosen the two screws that hold it to the selector lever mounting. Then move the switch forward or backward on its elongated screw holes until the starter operates only with the selector lever in **N** or **P**. Tighten the screws to hold the switch in this position, then reinstall the console. Switch replacement is covered in **ELECTRICAL SYSTEM.**

3.3 Removing and Installing Selector Lever

Before you can remove the selector lever assembly you must first remove the center console as described in **BODY AND INTERIOR.** Working beneath the car, detach the selector rod from the selector lever assembly by removing the nuts, the washer, the bushing, and the swivel pin. See Fig. 3-1 given earlier. Working in the passenger compartment, remove the screws that hold the selector lever assembly to the car body. Lift up the assembly—being careful not to tear or otherwise damage the weatherseal. Then disconnect the electrical wires for the neutral start switch and the control position indicator light so that the selector lever assembly can be removed from the car.

Installation is the reverse of removal. Following installation, adjust the selector linkage as described in **3.1 Adjusting Linkages.**

4. GENERAL TRANSMISSION SERVICE

The tests described under this heading can be carried out with the transmission installed in the car. Some of the repairs described can be made either with the transmission in the car or with the transmission removed.

4.1 Tests and Troubleshooting

Before diagnosing automatic transmission troubles, review the history of the unit. This review can offer important clues to present difficulties. Next, check the selector lever position and, if necessary, adjust the selector linkage. Also check and, if necessary, adjust the throttle cable. See **3.1 Adjusting Linkages.** If possible, you should then road test the car so that you have a first-hand knowledge of the automatic transmission's operating problems.

Road Testing

Before driving, check the engagement times with the engine idling. When the selector lever is moved from **N** to **D**, it should take no longer than 1.2 seconds for 1st gear to engage. When the selector lever is moved from **N** to **R**, it should take no longer than 1.5 seconds for reverse to engage. Slow engagement indicates low ATF pressure or sticking control valves.

Drive the car in all transmission ranges and under as many road conditions as possible. Note the shift points both up and down. They should take place quickly, without interrupting the power flow. **Table a** gives the approximate shift points for the automatic transmission. Owing to variations in tire size and speedometer accuracy, the speeds given in this table should be considered approximations only. 1

Listen for engine racing between gears, a possible indication of slipping clutches or brakes. Compare the operating characteristics that you observe with the problems named in the troubleshooting table given under the next heading.

Troubleshooting Table

The following preliminary checks should always be made before using the troubleshooting table:

1. Be sure that the engine is tuned up and running right.
2. Inspect the transmission for external damage, loose or missing screws, and obvious leaks.
3. Check the ATF level as described in **LUBRICATION AND MAINTENANCE.** Rub some ATF between your fingers and sniff it to detect the burned odor that means burned friction linings. If the ATF is dirty, it may be clogging the automatic controls. Carry out a stall speed test to determine if the clutches or brakes are slipping.
4. Check for water in the ATF (shown by a high fluid level or water beads on the dipstick). This is an indication of leakage in the ATF cooler portion of the radiator.
5. Check the adjustment of the selector linkage; check the adjustment of the throttle cable. See **3.1 Adjusting Linkages.** Additional information on checking for a faulty throttle cable is given later in **Troubleshooting Throttle Cable.**

The operating characteristics observed during the road test and during the five basic checks just described

Table a. Approximate Automatic Shift Speeds at Wide-open Throttle

Final drive gear ratio	Selector lever at D				Selector lever at L
	1st gear to 2nd gear	2nd gear to 3rd gear	3rd gear to 2nd gear	2nd gear to 1st gear	2nd gear to 1st gear
4.100	45 to 60 kph (28 to 37 mph)	86 to 101 kph (53 to 63 mph)	82 to 97 kph (51 to 60 mph)	38 to 51 kph (24 to 32 mph)	38 to 53 kph (24 to 33 mph)
3.909	47 to 62 kph (29 to 39 mph)	90 to 105 kph (56 to 65 mph)	86 to 101 kph (53 to 63 mph)	40 to 53 kph (25 to 33 mph)	41 to 56 kph (25 to 35 mph)

should give you an idea of the transmission's problems. **Table b** may suggest remedies for the transmission faults that you have observed. The numbers in bold type in the remedy column refer to numbered headings in this section.

CAUTION ——

Do not attempt adjustments or repairs until you have thoroughly read the procedures for making the adjustments or repairs. Otherwise, you may make adjustments or repairs unnecessarily or incorrectly.

Whenever you troubleshoot an automatic transmission, try to pin down the main component involved: torque converter, planetary gear system, or hydraulic controls. If **Table b** has failed to pinpoint the malfunction adequately, the tests that follow the table should help you to isolate the problem.

Table b. Automatic Transmission Troubleshooting

Problem	Probable cause	Remedy
1. Car does not move in any drive range (selector linkage correctly adjusted)	a. Parking lock stuck in engaged position	a. If engine operates under obvious load in drive ranges, but not in **N** or **P**, inspect and if necessary repair parking lock mechanism. See **5.4**.
	b. Line pressure incorrect	b. Measure line pressure and, if incorrect, remove and clean or repair valve body assembly; if no valve body fault is found, remove and repair ATF pump. See **4.1**, **5.2**, **5.3**, **5.5**.
	c. Transmission internal leakage	c. Remove, disassemble, and repair transmission. See **4.3**, **5.5**.
	d. Torque converter failing to drive ATF pump or failing to transmit power to planetary gear system owing to clogged ATF passages	d. Remove, inspect, and if necessary replace or clean torque converter. Clean ATF passages that supply converter. See **5.1**.
	e. Valve body dirty, possibly because of foreign matter from burned clutch or brake discs	e. Remove and clean valve body; repair damaged transmission components. See **5.2**, **5.3**, **5.5**.
	f. Clutch or brake discs badly burned or worn out	f. Remove, disassemble, and repair transmission. See **4.3**, **5.5**.
2. Car does not move in any forward drive range, but moves in **R**	a. Line pressure incorrect	a. Measure line pressure and, if incorrect, remove and clean or repair valve body assembly; if no valve body fault is found, remove and repair forward clutch, which probably has a leaking piston seal. See **4.1**, **5.2**, **5.3**, **5.5**.
	b. Valve body dirty, possibly because of foreign matter from burned clutch discs	b. Remove and clean valve body. Repair damaged transmission components. See **5.2**, **5.3**, **5.5**.
	c. Forward clutch faulty	c. Remove, disassemble, and repair transmission. See **4.3**, **5.5**.
	d. No. 3 brake one-way clutch faulty	d. Remove, disassemble, and repair transmission. See **4.3**, **5.5**.
3. Car does not move in **R**, but moves in forward drive ranges	a. Line pressure incorrect	a. Measure line pressure and, if incorrect, remove and clean or repair valve body assembly; if no valve body fault is found, remove and repair ATF pump, or direct and reverse clutch, or No. 3 brake (the last two probably have leaking pistons). See **4.1**, **5.2**, **5.3**, **5.5**.
	b. Valve body dirty, possibly because of foreign matter from burned clutch or brake discs	b. Remove and clean valve body. Repair damaged transmission components. See **5.2**, **5.3**, **5.5**.
	c. Direct and reverse clutch faulty	c. Remove, disassemble, and repair transmission. See **4.3**, **5.5**.
	d. No. 3 brake faulty	d. Remove, disassemble, and repair transmission. See **4.3**, **5.5**.
4. Harsh engagement when selector lever is moved into any drive range	a. Line pressure too high	a. Measure line pressure and, if incorrect, remove and clean or repair valve body assembly. See **4.1**, **5.2**, **5.3**.
	b. Accumulator faulty	b. Remove, inspect, and if necessary repair all three accumulators. See **5.5**.
	c. Valve body faulty	c. Remove and then clean or repair valve body. See **5.2**, **5.3**.
	d. Clutch or brake pistons faulty	d. Remove, disassemble, and repair transmission. See **4.3**, **5.5**.

Table b. Automatic Transmission Troubleshooting (continued)

Problem	Probable cause	Remedy
5. Screeching or whining noise fron transmission, whenever engine is running, that increases with engine speed	a. Torque converter drive plate broken b. ATF oil strainer clogged c. ATF pump faulty	a. Inspect drive plate. See **ENGINE** and **4.3**. b. Clean ATF strainer and if necessary, repair damaged transmission components that have caused contamination of the ATF. See **5.2**, **5.3**, **5.5**. c. Remove and repair ATF pump. See **5.5**.
6. Knocking or similar metallic noises, or a grinding sound	a. Torque converter drive plate broken b. Torque converter damaged or torque converter one-way clutch faulty c. Faulty or slipping one-way clutch in transmission d. Planetary gearset(s) faulty e. Transmission bearings faulty f. ATF pump faulty	a. Inspect drive plate. See **ENGINE** and **4.3**. b. Remove, inspect, and if necessary replace torque converter. See **5.1**. c. Remove, disassemble, and repair transmission. See **4.3**, **5.5**. d. Remove, disassemble, and repair transmission. See **4.3**, **5.5**. e. Inspect and if necessary, replace worn or damaged bearings. See **5.5**. f. Inspect and if necessary, repair or replace ATF pump. See **5.5**.
7. Delayed 1st gear/2nd gear upshift, delayed 2nd gear/3rd gear upshift, or transmission downshifts from 3rd to 2nd gear and then back to 3rd without changes in load, speed, or throttle position (throttle cable correctly adjusted)	a. Line pressure incorrect b. Governor pressure incorrect c. Valve body faulty	a. Measure line pressure and, if incorrect, remove and clean or repair valve body assembly. See **4.1**, **5.2**, **5.3**. b. Measure governor pressure and, if incorrect, remove and clean or repair governor. See **4.1**, **5.3**. c. Remove and clean or repair valve body. See **5.2**, **5.3**.
8. Slippage during 1st gear/2nd gear upshift (selector linkage and throttle cable correctly adjusted)	a. Line pressure incorrect b. Valve body faulty c. No. 2 brake or its one-way clutch faulty	a. Measure line pressure and, if incorrect, remove and clean or repair valve body assembly; if no valve body fault is found, remove and repair ATF pump. See **4.1**, **5.2**, **5.3**, **5.5**. b. Remove and clean or repair valve body. See **5.2**, **5.3**. c. Disassemble and repair transmission. See **4.3**, **5.5**.
9. Slippage during 2nd gear/3rd gear upshift (selector linkage and throttle cable correctly adjusted)	a. Line pressure incorrect b. Valve body faulty c. Direct and reverse clutch faulty	a. Measure line pressure and, if incorrect, remove and clean or repair valve body assembly; if no valve body fault is found, remove and repair ATF pump. See **4.1**, **5.2**, **5.3**, **5.5**. b. Remove and clean or repair valve body. See **5.2**, **5.3**. c. Remove, disassemble, and repair transmission. See **4.3**, **5.5**.
10. Drag, binding, or tie-up on 1st gear/2nd gear upshift (selector linkage correctly adjusted)	a. Line pressure incorrect b. Valve body faulty c. No. 3 brake or its one-way clutch faulty d. Accumulator faulty	a. Measure line pressure and, if incorrect, remove and clean or repair valve body assembly; if no valve body fault is found, remove and repair ATF pump or No. 3 brake. See **4.1**, **5.2**, **5.3**, **5.5**. b. Remove and clean or repair valve body. See **5.2**, **5.3**. c. Remove disassemble, and repair transmission. See **4.3**, **5.5**. d. Remove, inspect, and if necessary, repair all three accumulators. See **5.5**.
11. Drag, binding, or tie-up on 2nd gear/3rd gear upshift (selector linkage correctly adjusted)	a. Line pressure incorrect b. Valve body faulty c. No. 2 brake or its one-way clutch faulty	a. Measure line pressure and, if incorrect, remove and clean or repair valve body assembly; if no valve body fault is found, remove and repair ATF pump or direct and reverse clutch. See **4.1**, **5.2**, **5.3**, **5.5**. b. Remove and clean or repair valve body. See **5.2**, **5.3**. c. Remove, disassemble, and repair transmission. See **4.3**, **5.5**.

(continued on next page)

Table b. Automatic Transmission Troubleshooting (continued)

Problem	Probable cause	Remedy
	d. Direct and reverse clutch faulty	d. Remove, disassemble, and repair transmission. See **4.3**, **5.5**.
12. Slip, squawk, or shudder on full throttle take-off in forward drive ranges (selector linkage and throttle cable correctly adjusted)	a. Line pressure low b. Valve body faulty c. No. 3 brake one-way clutch faulty d. Forward clutch faulty	a. Measure line pressure and, if incorrect, remove and clean or repair valve body assembly; if no valve body fault is found, remove and repair ATF pump; if no ATF pump fault is found, correct transmission internal leakage. See **4.1**, **5.2**, **5.3**, **5.5**. b. Remove and clean or repair valve body. See **5.2**, **5.3**. c. Remove, disassemble, and repair transmission. See **4.3**, **5.5**. d. Remove, disassemble, and repair transmission. See **4.3**, **5.5**.
13. Slip, squawk, or shudder on take-off in **R** (selector linkage and throttle cable correctly adjusted)	a. Line pressure low b. Valve body faulty c. Direct and reverse clutch faulty d. No. 3 brake faulty	a. Measure line pressure and, if incorrect, remove and clean or repair valve body assembly; if no ATF pump fault is found, correct transmission internal leaks at direct and reverse clutch and at No. 3 brake pistons. See **4.1**, **5.2**, **5.3**, **5.5**. b. Remove and clean or repair valve body. See **5.2**, **5.3**. c. Remove, disassemble, and repair transmission. See **4.3**, **5.5**. d. Remove, disassemble, and repair transmission. See **4.3**, **5.5**.
14. Intermittent squawk from transmission during car operation	a. Torque converter drive plate broken b. Clutch or brake discs worn out or otherwise faulty	a. Inspect drive plate. See **ENGINE** and **4.3**. b. Remove, disassemble, and repair transmission. See **4.3**, **5.5**.
15. Harsh downshift (throttle cable correctly adjusted)	a. Line pressure incorrect b. Accumulator faulty c. Sequence valves faulty d. Valve body faulty	a. Measure line pressure and, if incorrect, remove and clean or repair valve body assembly, checking especially for faults in the primary regulator valve and the throttle valve. See **4.1**, **5.2**, **5.3**. b. Remove, inspect, and if necessary repair all three accumulators. See **5.5**. c. Remove and clean or repair valve body assembly, checking especially for faults in the throttle valve and the primary regulator valve. See **5.2**, **5.3**. d. Remove and clean or repair valve body assembly, checking especially for faults in the throttle valve and the primary regulator valve. See **5.2**, **5.3**.
16. No downshifts as car coasts to slower speeds, or no 3rd gear/2nd gear kickdown, or no 2nd gear/1st gear kickdown (throttle cable correctly adjusted)	a. Governor pressure incorrect b. Valve body faulty	a. Measure governor pressure and, if incorrect, remove and clean or repair governor. See **4.1**, **5.3**. b. Remove and clean or repair valve body assembly, checking especially for faults in the throttle valve, the downshift plug, and the detent regulator valve. See **5.2**, **5.3**.
17. No downshifts, or downshift to 1st gear occurs above specified maximum speed when **L** is manually selected	a. Throttle cable faulty or incorrectly adjusted b. Governor faulty	a. Inspect throttle cable, and if necessary adjust it or replace and then adjust it. See **3.1**, **4.1**, **5.2**. b. Remove and clean or repair governor. See **5.3**.
18. No engine braking with selector lever at **2**	a. Line pressure incorrect b. No. 1 brake faulty	a. Remove and clean or repair valve body assembly, checking especially for faults in the intermediate modulator valve. See **5.2**, **5.3**. b. Remove, disassemble, and repair transmission. See **4.3**, **5.5**.

Table b. Automatic Transmission Troubleshooting (continued)

Problem	Probable cause	Remedy
19. Downshift occurs above or below specified speed range during coasting to slower speeds	a. Throttle cable faulty or incorrectly adjusted b. Line pressure incorrect c. Governor faulty d. Valve body faulty e. Sticking clutch or brake pistons	a. Inspect throttle cable and, if necessary, adjust it or replace and then adjust it. See **3.1**, **4.1**, **5.2**. b. Measure line pressure and, if incorrect, remove and clean or repair valve body assembly, checking especially for faults in the throttle valve and the primary regulator valve; if no valve body fault is found, remove and repair the ATF pump; if no ATF pump fault is found, replace the ATF pump's ATF seal rings. See **4.1**, **5.2**, **5.3**, **5.5**. c. Remove and clean or repair governor. See **5.3**. d. Remove and clean or repair valve body assembly, checking especially for faults in the shift valves. See **5.2**, **5.3**. e. Remove, disassemble, and repair transmission. See **4.3**, **5.5**.
20. Parking lock does not engage	a. Selector linkage incorrectly adjusted b. Parking lock mechanism faulty	a. Inspect selector lever and selector linkage; if necessary, adjust or repair and then adjust selector linkage. See **3.1.** b. Remove valve body, then remove and repair parking lock components. See **5.2**, **5.4**.
21. Stall speed too high in stall speed test, with clutch or brake squawk with selector lever at **D** (throttle cable correctly adjusted)	a. Line pressure low b. Valve body faulty c. Forward clutch faulty	a. Measure line pressure and, if incorrect, remove and clean or repair valve body assembly, checking especially for faults in the throttle valve and the primary regulator valve; if no valve body fault is found, remove and repair the ATF pump; if no ATF pump fault is found, repair the forward clutch piston. See **4.1**, **5.2**, **5.3**, **5.5**. b. Remove and clean or repair valve body assembly. See **5.2**, **5.3**. c. Remove, disassemble, and repair transmission. See **4.3**, **5.5**.
22. Stall speed too high in stall speed test, with clutch or brake squawk with selector lever at **R** (throttle cable correctly adjusted)	a. Line pressure low b. Valve body faulty c. Direct and reverse clutch faulty d. No. 3 brake faulty	a. Measure line pressure and, if incorrect, remove and clean or repair valve body assembly, checking especially for faults in the throttle valve and the primary regulator valve; if no valve body fault is found, remove and repair the ATF pump; if no ATF pump fault is found, repair the direct and reverse clutch piston or repair the No. 3 brake. See **5.2**, **5.3**. b. Remove and clean or repair valve body assembly. See **5.2**, **5.3**. c. Remove, disassemble, and repair transmission. See **4.3**, **5.5**. d. Remove, disassemble, and repair transmission. See **4.3**, **5.5**.
23. Engagement time exceeds 1.2 seconds when selector lever is moved from **N** to **D** (selector linkage correctly adjusted)	a. Line pressure low b. Valve body faulty c. Accumulator faulty d. Forward clutch or ATF pump's ATF seal rings faulty	a. Measure line pressure and, if incorrect, remove and clean or repair valve body assembly, checking especially for faults in the primary regulator valve; if no valve body fault is found, remove and repair ATF pump or its ATF seal rings; if no ATF pump fault is found, repair the forward clutch piston. See **4.1**, **5.2**, **5.3**, **5.5**. b. Remove, clean, and repair valve body assembly. See **5.2**, **5.3**. c. Remove, inspect, and if necessary repair all three accumulators. See **5.5**. d. Remove, disassemble, and repair transmission. See **4.3**, **5.5**.
24. Engagement time exceeds 1.5 seconds when selector lever is moved from **N** to **R** (selector linkage correctly adjusted)	a. Line pressure low b. Valve body faulty	a. Measure line pressure and, if incorrect, remove and clean or repair valve body assembly, checking especially for faults in the primary regulator valve; if no fault is found, remove and repair ATF pump or its ATF seal rings; if no ATF pump fault is found, repair the No. 3 piston or the direct and reverse clutch piston. See **4.1**, **5.2**, **5.3**, **5.5**. b. Remove, clean, and repair valve body assembly. See **5.2**, **5.3**.

(continued on next page)

Table b. Automatic Transmission Troubleshooting (continued)

Problem	Probable cause	Remedy
	c. Direct and reverse clutch faulty d. No. 3 brake or ATF pump's ATF seal rings faulty	c. Remove, disassemble, and repair transmission. See **4.3**, **5.5**. d. Remove, disassemble, and repair transmission. See **4.3**, **5.5**.
25. Governor pressure or line pressure too high or too low during pressure test	Sticking hydraulic controls, blocked ATF passages, or transmission internal leaks	See **Table e. Pressure Testing Analysis** given later under **Pressure Testing**. See **4.1**.

Troubleshooting Throttle Cable

Because its length and condition have a vital influence on the accurate functioning of the automatic transmission's hydraulic controls, the condition of the throttle cable should be carefully checked whenever the transmission operates incorrectly despite apparent accurate adjustment of the throttle cable. To check the throttle cable for stretching, deterioration of its conduit, and other factors that can interfere with correct operation of the hydraulic controls, first remove the air cleaner. (This job is described in **ENGINE** in conjunction with removal and installation of the cylinder head cover.) Then detach the throttle cable from the carburetor's throttle arm by taking out the pin.

Pull the end of the throttle cable out to the limit of its travel as indicated in Fig. 4-1. In its extended position, the distance from the stopping collar on the cable to the threaded end of the cable conduit should be about 52 to 55 mm (about 2 to 2 5/32 in.). If this dimension is not correct, replace the cable as described in **5.2 Removing and Installing ATF Pan and Valve Body.** If the dimension is correct, allow the cable to retract slowly and as far as possible into its conduit. If the cable does not retract smoothly, or if when fully retracted the distance between the stopping collar and the end of the threaded part of the conduit is greater than 0.05 mm (.002 in.), the cable is faulty and should be replaced.

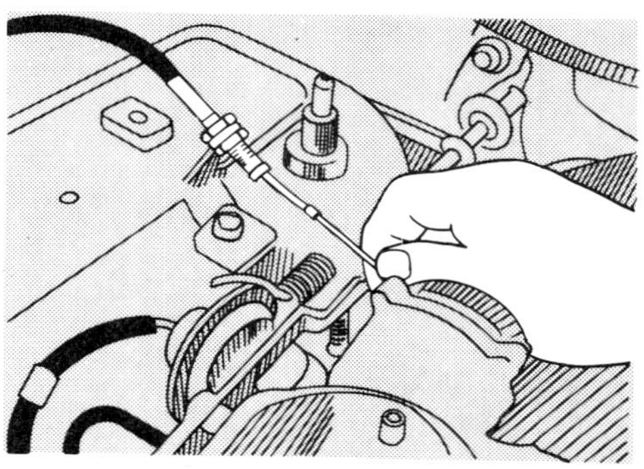

Fig. 4-1. Throttle cable being pulled out to limit of its travel. Engine shown here is not used in cars covered by this Manual.

Stall Speed Testing and Pressure Testing

A stall speed test provides a quick check of the torque converter and the planetary gear system. You should only test the stall speed if the car accelerates poorly despite a perfectly-tuned engine—or if the ATF is burnt-smelling, which could indicate the kind of brake or clutch slippage that a stall speed test will detect.

A line pressure test should be carried out simultaneously with the stall speed test so that it can be determined whether slippage in the planetary gear system is being caused by low line pressure. Use a precision electric tachometer for these tests as dashboard instruments are not calibrated with sufficient accuracy.

> ***CAUTION —***
> *Never extend the stall speed test beyond the time it takes to read the instruments—20 seconds maximum. Prolonging the test may overheat the transmission and damage the seals.*

To test:

1. Connect the tachometer according to the instrument manufacturer's instructions. Connect a pressure gauge with a 0 to 20 bar (or 0 to 300 psi) scale to the line pressure port of the transmission. Connect a pressure gauge with a 0 to 10 bar (or 0 to 100 psi) scale to the governor pressure port of the transmission. See Fig. 4-2.

   > **NOTE —**
   > You need not measure governor pressure during the stall speed test. The gauge connected to the governor pressure port is used later in this procedure for testing the governor pressure at different vehicle speeds.

2. Start the engine. Set the parking brake and depress the foot brake firmly to hold the car stationary.
3. Place the selector lever in **D** and floor the accelerator pedal. Instead of revving up, the engine

should run at a reduced rpm, known as stall speed. At stall speed, quickly read the tachometer and the line pressure gauge, then allow the engine to return to idle and place the selector lever at **N**. **Table c** gives the correct stall speed and line pressure specifications.

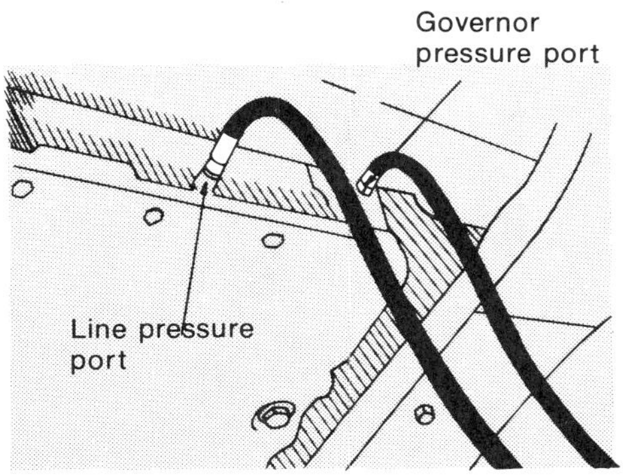

Fig. 4-2. Pressure gauge hoses connected to pressure testing ports of automatic transmission. Thread size is U.S. 5/16" × 24.

4. Repeat the stall speed test with the selector lever at **R**. The correct specifications are given in **Table c.**

Table c. Correct Line Pressures and RPM at Stall Speed

Drive range	Stall speed rpm	Line pressure
D	2050 ± 150 rpm	9.5 to 12.0 bar (135 to 171 psi)
R	2050 ± 150 rpm	14.0 to 17.0 bar (200 to 242 psi)

NOTE ——
If the stall speed is about 400 rpm below the specified range, or is above the specified range with no detectable clutch or brake slippage (squawking), something is wrong with the torque converter. If the stall speed is above the specified range with clutch or brake squawk, refer to items 21 and 22 in **Table b**, given earlier.

5. To determine whether the line pressure is in the correct range for proper transmission operation, again apply the brakes firmly and operate the engine at 1000 rpm with the selector lever at **D**. The line pressure should be 4.0 to 4.5 bar (57 to 64 psi). At 1000 rpm with the selector lever at **R** the line pressure should be 5.8 to 6.8 bar (82 to 97 psi). If the line pressure is incorrect, determine the cause with the help of **Table e,** which appears later. 1

6. To test the governor pressure, raise the rear wheels off the ground and chock the front wheels solidly. Then release the parking brake and start the engine. At the speeds listed, the governor pressure should be within the ranges given in **Table d** with the selector lever at **D**. Possible causes of incorrect governor pressures can be determined from **Table e.**

NOTE ——
The bold numbers in the Remedy column of **Table e** refer to the headings in this section of the Manual where the suggested repairs are described.

Table d. Correct Governor Pressures at Given Speeds

Transmission output shaft rpm and vehicle speed	Governor pressure
1000 output shaft rpm (about 27 kph or 17 mph)	0.9 to 1.5 bar (12.8 to 21.3 psi)
1800 output shaft rpm (about 48 kph or 30 mph)	1.6 to 2.2 bar (22.8 to 31.3 psi)
3500 output shaft rpm (about 96 kph or 60 mph)	4.1 to 5.3 bar (58.3 to 75.3 psi)

7. Disconnect the pressure gauges and install the pressure tap plugs with new seals. Torque the plugs to 6 to 8 Nm (53 to 71 in. lb.). Then disconnect the tachometer and the pressure gauges and lower the car to the ground.

Table e. Pressure Testing Analysis

Problem	Probable cause	Remedy
1. Governor pressure incorrect	a. Line pressure incorrect	a. Measure line pressure and, if incorrect, remove and clean or repair valve body assembly; if no valve body fault is found, remove and repair ATF pump or ATF pump's ATF seal rings. See **4.1**, **5.2**, **5.3**, **5.5**.
	b. Governor faulty	b. Remove, inspect, and if necessary repair or replace governor. See **5.2**, **5.3**.
	c. Valve body faulty	c. Remove and clean or repair valve body, checking especially for governor valve faults. See **5.2**, **5.3**.
	d. Transmission internal leakage	d. Remove, disassemble, and repair transmission. See **4.3**, **5.5**.

(continued on next page)

Table e. Pressure Testing Analysis (continued)

Problem	Probable cause	Remedy
2. Line pressure too high in both **D** and **R**	a. Throttle cable faulty or incorrectly adjusted b. Valve body faulty	a. Inspect throttle cable and, if necessary, adjust it or replace and then adjust it. See **3.1**, **4.1**, **5.2**. b. Remove and clean or repair valve body, checking especially for throttle valve and primary regulator valve faults. See **5.2**, **5.3**.
3. Line pressure too low in both **D** and **R**	a. Valve body faulty b. ATF pump faulty, or transmission leaking internally	a. Remove and clean or repair valve body, checking especially for throttle valve and primary regulator valve faults. See **5.2**, **5.3**. b. Remove, disassemble, and repair transmission. See **4.3**, **5.5**.
4. Line pressure too low in **D**, but correct in **R**	a. Valve body faulty b. Forward clutch faulty	a. Remove and clean or repair valve body, checking especially for a damaged or sticking manual valve and for foreign matter in the ports of the valve body lower part; check for obstructions in all ATF passages for the forward clutch circuit. See **5.2**, **5.3**. b. Remove, disassemble, and repair transmission. See **4.3**, **5.5**.
5. Line pressure too low in **R**, but correct in **D**	a. Valve body faulty b. ATF pump faulty or ATF pump's ATF seal rings faulty c. Direct and reverse clutch faulty or No. 3 brake faulty	a. Remove and clean or repair valve body, checking especially for faults in the direct and reverse clutch sequence valve or in the No. 3 brake sequence valve. See **5.2**, **5.3**. b. Remove transmission, then remove, inspect, and if necessary, repair ATF pump or ATF pump's ATF seal rings. See **4.3**, **5.5**. c. Remove, disassemble, and repair transmission. See **4.3**, **5.5**.

4.2 Locating and Stopping External ATF Leaks

Aside from a crack in the transmission case, extension housing, or ATF cooler lines, Fig. 4-3 indicates all of the possible locations for external ATF leaks. Usually, the source of external leaks will be evident by the presence of fresh, wet ATF. Tightening the bolts, plugs, or unions to the torque specifications given in the illustration will in some cases cure a leak. However, the maximum torque given should never be exceeded because it could distort the parts and cause greater leakage.

> ***CAUTION* ——**
> *Never tighten the pan bolts to more than 4 to 5 Nm (35 to 44 in. lb.) in an attempt to cure a leaking gasket. Overtightening will deform the pan and make it impossible to get a good seal. Always install a new gasket to correct a leak that persists after the bolts have been correctly torqued.*

Hard-to-find leaks, such as those caused by cracks in the transmission case, the extension housing, the torque converter, or the ATF cooler lines, can be pinpointed through the use of a fluorescent dye added to the ATF. After a short period of operation with the dye in the ATF, the sources of leakage will stand out clearly when they are examined with ultraviolet light (black light).

Except for the pump ATF seal and the pump O-ring, all the gaskets and O-rings indicated in Fig. 4-3 can be replaced without removing the transmission from the car. The necessary procedures for replacing the ATF pan gasket, the extension housing gasket, the pump O-ring, and the pump ATF seal are all given in **5. Transmission Repair.** Procedures for replacing the rear ATF seal and the manual shaft seals are given under the next two headings.

Replacing Rear ATF Seal

To prevent damage and incorrect ATF seal installation, you should have the tools shown in the illustrations under this heading, or similar tools that are correct for the purpose. The seal need only be replaced if it is leaking or if it has been removed for access to the extension housing bushing. The old seal is ruined by removal and cannot be reused.

To remove:

1. Raise the car on a hoist or support it on jack stands.
2. Using a file or a center punch, mark adjacent points on the rear axle's pinion flange and the rear universal joint so that the driveshaft can be reinstalled in its original position on the pinion flange. Then remove the driveshaft as described in **DRIVESHAFT AND REAR AXLE.**

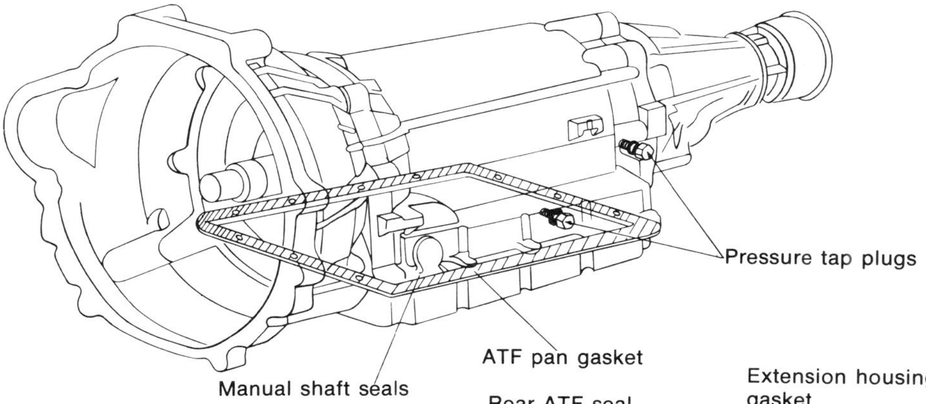

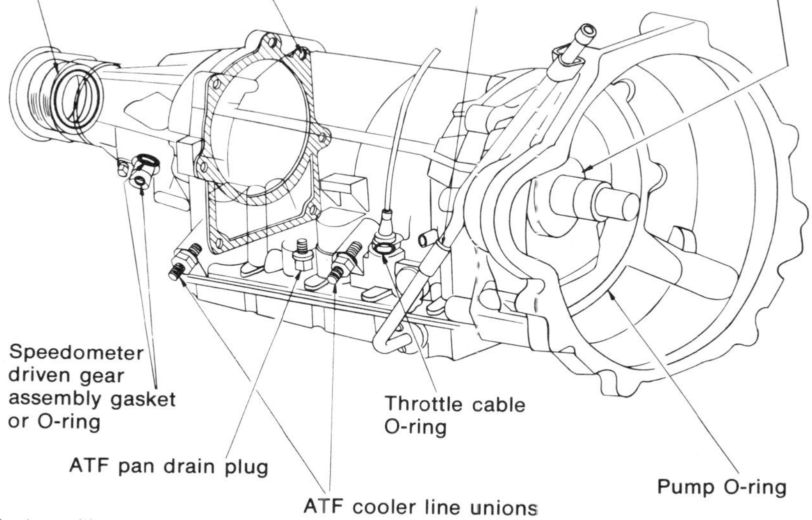

Tightening torques

ATF pan bolts, 4–5 Nm (35–44 in. lb.)
Pressure tap plugs, 6–8 Nm (53–71 in. lb.)
Speedometer driven gear assembly retainer, 14–15 Nm (10–11 ft. lb.)
Extension housing bolts, 30–40 Nm (22–30 ft. lb.)
ATF pan drain plug, 15–20 Nm (11–15 ft. lb.)
ATF cooler line unions, 20–30 Nm (15–22 ft.lb.)

Fig. 4-3. Potential locations of external ATF leaks, with specified torques for threaded components.

3. Using an expansion puller such as the one shown in Fig. 4-4, withdraw the rear ATF seal and the dust seal either in a single operation or by pulling out first the dust seal and then the ATF seal.

CAUTION ——

Before you pull out the seals, thoroughly clean the rear part of the extension housing and the inside of the deflector. Otherwise, abrasive dirt may find its way into the transmission where it will jam hydraulic controls and cause rapid wear.

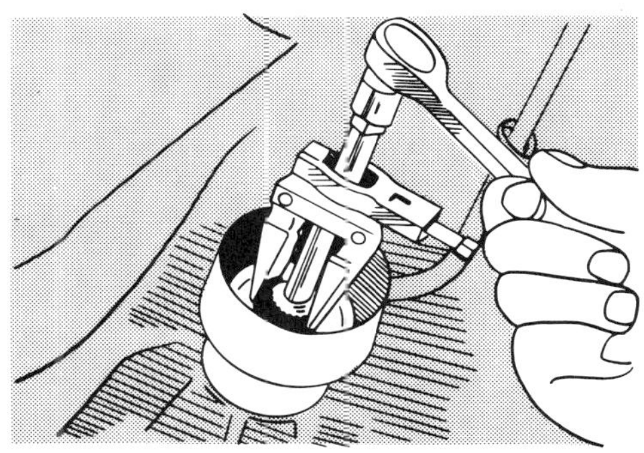

Fig. 4-4. Dust seal ard rear ATF seal being removed.

To install:

1. If the seal has been leaking, inspect the sealing surface of the driveshaft's front universal joint yoke. If it is scored or grooved, replace the yoke.

2. Thoroughly clean and inspect the seal recess in the transmission's extension housing. If it is rough or burred, smooth the recess with crocus cloth.
3. Use a seal driver, such as the Toyota special service tool 09325-20010 shown in Fig. 4-5, to install the new ATF seal. Drive in the ATF seal so that its lip points into the transmission's extension housing, and drive the seal in as far as it will go.
4. Drive in the new dust seal until its outer face is flush with the rear of the extension housing.

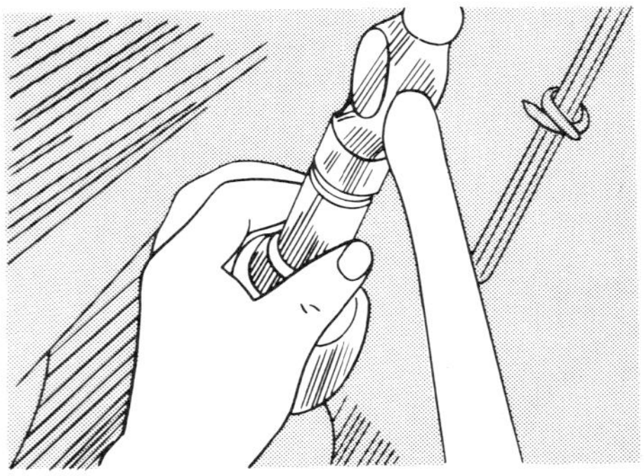

Fig. 4-5. Rear ATF seal being driven in.

5. With careful reference to the marks that you made prior to removal, install the driveshaft as described in **DRIVESHAFT AND REAR AXLE.** Torque the bolts that hold the driveshaft to the pinion flange to 35 to 40 Nm (26 to 30 ft. lb.). On cars with a two-piece driveshaft, torque the bolts that hold the center bearing to the body to 35 to 40 Nm (26 to 30 ft. lb.).
6. Lower the car to the ground. Check the ATF level as described in **LUBRICATION AND MAINTENANCE.** If necessary, correct the level using Type F ATF.

Replacing Manual Shaft ATF Seals

Thoroughly clean the outside of the transmission before you begin work. Otherwise, dirt may find its way into the transmission while you are making this repair.

To replace:

1. Detach the selector rod from the manual shaft lever by taking out the cotter pin and removing the washers, the grommet, and the bushing.
2. Remove the nut that holds the manual shaft lever to the manual shaft, as indicated in Fig. 4-6. Then remove the lever.
3. Remove the ATF pan and the valve body as described in **5.2 Removing and Installing ATF Pan and Valve Body.** Then remove the parking pawl assembly as described in **5.4 Disassembling and Assembling Internal Control Linkage.**

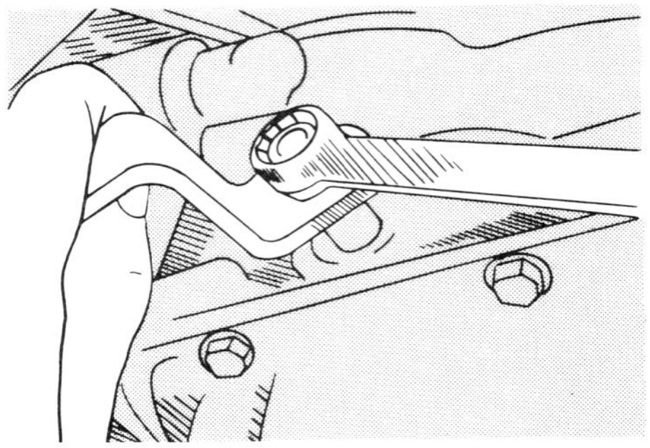

Fig. 4-6. Manual shaft lever being removed from manual shaft.

4. Using a hammer and a punch, as shown in Fig. 4-7, drive out the rolled pin that holds the manual shaft to the transmission's detent lever. Then pull the manual shaft partially out of the detent lever to the right—just far enough to withdraw the shaft fully from the left ATF seal.

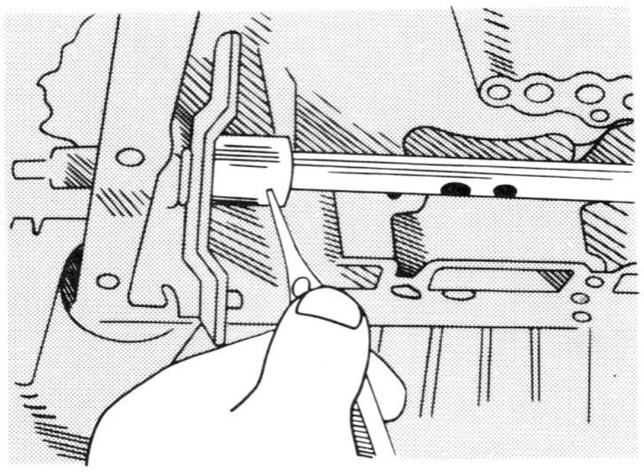

Fig. 4-7. Rolled pin being driven out of detent lever hub and manual shaft.

5. Being careful not to scratch or score the seal recess in the transmission case, use a screwdriver to pry out the right-side ATF seal, as indicated in Fig. 4-8. Then move the shaft to the left, just enough to withdraw it from the left ATF seal, and pry out the left-side ATF seal.

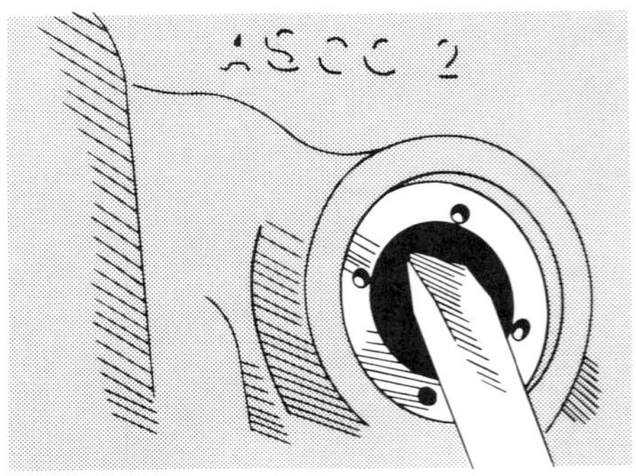

Fig. 4-8. Manual shaft ATF seal being pried out.

6. Make sure that the manual shaft is neither burred nor grooved in the seal contact areas. Replace faulty shafts. Then drive in the new ATF seals as indicated in Fig. 4-9. The seal lips must point into the transmission case.

NOTE ——

You should use a correctly fitting seal driver, such as Toyota special service tool 09361-30010. When installing the left-side seal, it is helpful to install a 19-mm deep socket wrench over the driver to increase the driver's length.

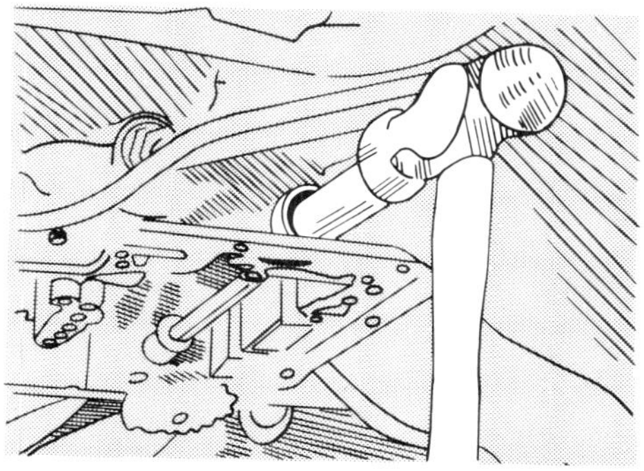

Fig. 4-9. New manual shaft ATF seal being driven in.

7. Reposition the manual shaft so that the hole in the shaft is aligned with the hole in the detent lever hub. Then drive in a new rolled pin so that the slot in the pin is at right angles to the shaft axis.

8. Install the parking pawl assembly as described in **5.4 Disassembling and Assembling Internal Control Linkage;** install the valve body and the ATF pan as described in **5.2 Removing and Installing ATF Pan and Valve Body.**

9. Install the manual shaft lever on the manual shaft, torquing the nut to 15 to 20 Nm (11 to 15 ft. lb.). Then reconnect the selector rod to the lever—using a new cotter pin and replacing worn or damaged rubber grommets.

4.3 Removing and Installing Transmission

Before you attempt to remove the automatic transmission, be sure that you have a safe means for supporting the car off the ground. You should also have a transmission jack so that you will not risk having the transmission fall or drop down at the rear, thereby placing an abnormal strain on the torque converter and related parts.

To remove:

1. Open the hood. Remove the ATF dipstick. Then disconnect the negative (−) battery cable from the battery.

CAUTION—

The battery must be disconnected in order to prevent accidental short circuits when you later remove the starter.

1

2. Remove the air cleaner as described in conjunction with cylinder head cover removal in **ENGINE.** Detach the transmission's throttle cable from the accelerator linkage by taking out the clip and then removing the washer and the pin.

3. Remove the starter's upper mounting bolt and unbolt the ATF dipstick tube from the engine. Remove the upper bolts that hold the transmission's bellhousing to the engine.

4. If you do not intend to support the rear of the engine with a jack after you have raised the car, install a support for the rear of the engine. To do this, place a steel bar or a length of 2″ × 4″ lumber across the rear of the engine compartment so that its ends rest solidly on the part of the body that is contacted by the hood when the hood is closed. Then, using a chain or strong rope, tie the rear engine-hoisting hook to the steel bar or two-by-four. The chain or rope may be slightly slack so that some downward engine movement will be possible.

5. Raise the car on a hoist or support it on stands designed for the purpose. Using a file or a centerpunch, mark adjacent points on the rear axle's pinion flange and the rear universal joint so that the driveshaft can be reinstalled in its original position on the pinion flange. Then remove the driveshaft as described in **DRIVESHAFT AND REAR AXLE.**

6. Place a drain pan under the transmission's ATF pan. Remove the drain plug and allow the ATF to drain out. When the pan is fully drained, reinstall the plug to a torque of 15 to 20 Nm (11 to 15 ft. lb.).

7. Detach the selector rod from the manual shaft lever by taking out the cotter pin and removing the washers, the grommet, and the bushing.

8. Unbolt the exhaust pipe support from the transmission's bellhousing.

9. Unbolt the clamps for the ATF cooler lines, both on the engine and on the transmission. Then detach the ATF cooler lines from the transmission by unscrewing the unions. Be prepared to catch any ATF that drains from the cooling lines.

10. Using water pump pliers, unscrew the knurled ferrule nut that holds the speedometer cable to the speedometer driven gear assembly. Then de-

tach the cable from the transmission, being careful not to bend the cable sharply. See Fig. 4-10.

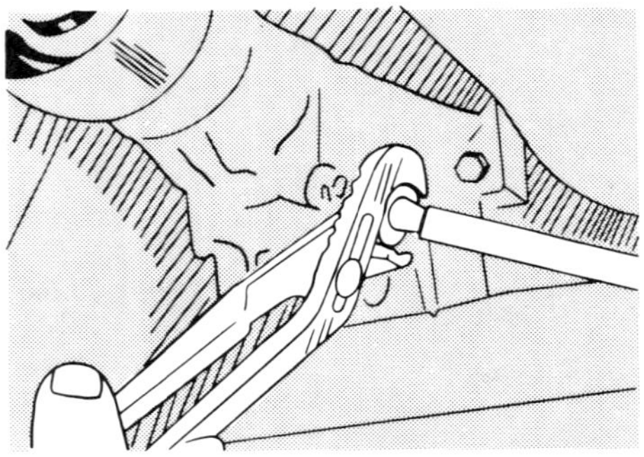

Fig. 4-10. Speedometer cable being detached from transmission.

11. Disconnect the wires and the battery positive (+) cable from the starter solenoid. Unbolt the starter from the engine, then withdraw the starter from the bellhousing.

NOTE ——
You can leave the starter lying atop the suspension crossmember and the steering tierods.

12. Remove the rubber plugs from the intermediate plate where it covers the front of the bellhousing. See Fig. 4-11.

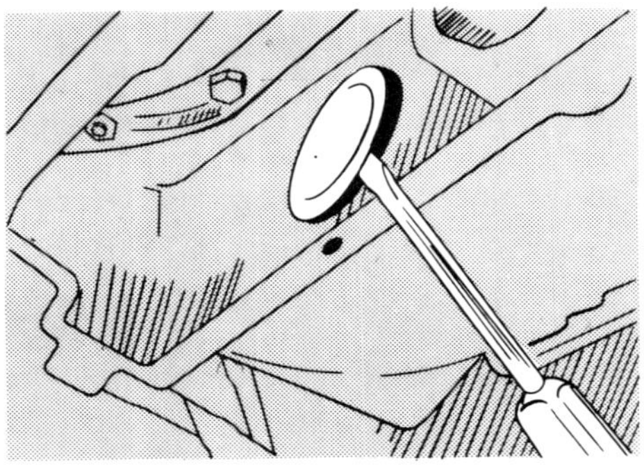

Fig. 4-11. Rubber plug being pried out of intermediate plate.

13. Remove the splash shield that is beneath the radiator. Then, using a wrench on the bolt that is in the center of the crankshaft pulley, hand-turn the crankshaft, thus positioning each of the six torque converter-to-drive plate bolts for removal as shown in Fig. 4-12.
14. Make a pin such as the one shown in Fig. 4-13. To do this, obtain a bolt that has the same size threads as do the torque converter-to-drive plate bolts. Then saw off the bolt head and saw a screwdriver slot into the end of the shank. Using a screwdriver, install the pin in place of the last torque converter-to-drive plate bolt that you removed.

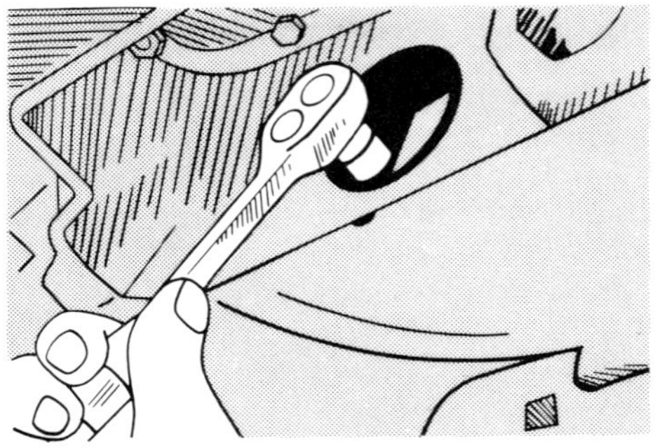

Fig. 4-12. Torque converter-to-drive plate bolt being removed. Turn crankshaft six times to place each bolt in position for removal.

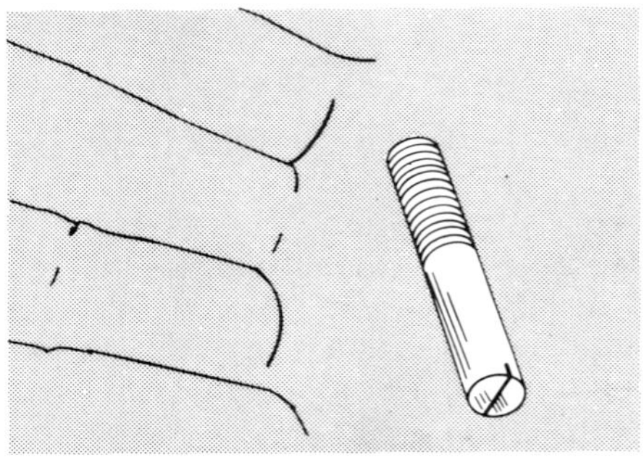

Fig. 4-13. Pin for installation in torque converter. Pin is later pushed on to ensure that torque converter is removed along with transmission instead of sticking to drive plate.

15. Install a wheeled transmission jack beneath the transmission, then raise the jack until the transmission is fully supported.
16. Remove the bolts that hold the rear transmission mount crossmember to the car body. Gradually lower the transmission jack until the slack is taken up in the engine rear support which you installed in step 4.

CAUTION ——
Lower the transmission and engine a little at a time, checking frequently to see that the engine's fan does not contact its shroud before the slack is removed from the engine rear support device. If you have not installed a rear support, place a jack beneath the rear of the engine to keep the engine from dropping too low.

17. With both the engine and the transmission firmly supported, remove the remaining bolts that hold the transmission's bellhousing to the engine.

18. Using a pry bar, as shown in Fig. 4-14, start the transmission moving rearward by pushing on the end of the pin you installed in step 14. Keep moving the transmission carefully rearward until the torque converter is completely away from the drive plate, then lower the transmission from the car.

19. Install a bar or wire across the mouth of the bellhousing in order to keep the torque converter from falling out.

CAUTION —

Be especially careful not to snag or damage the throttle cable. At no time should you allow the weight of the transmission or the engine to be supported by the torque converter or allow the torque converter to be pulled partially off its support on the transmission. Doing either may damage the pump seal or the torque converter.

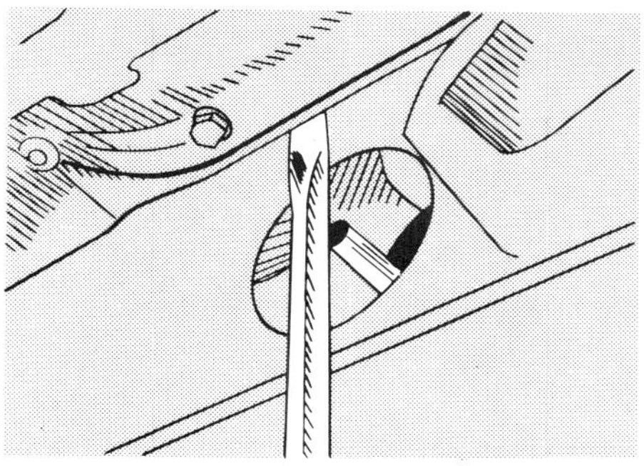

Fig. 4-14. Transmission being pushed rearward by prying against pin installed in torque converter bolt hole.

20. Remove the intermediate plate from the engine. If necessary, unbolt the rear transmission mount crossmember from the transmission.

To install:

1. Remove and check the torque converter as described in **5.1 Removing, Cleaning, Inspecting, and Installing Torque Converter.** Then reinstall the torque converter—making sure that it is fully engaged on the splined shafts and the ATF pump. See Fig. 4-15.

2. Check the drive plate for runout and damage as described in **5.1 Removing, Cleaning, Inspecting, and Installing Torque Converter.** Replace faulty drive plates as described in **ENGINE.**

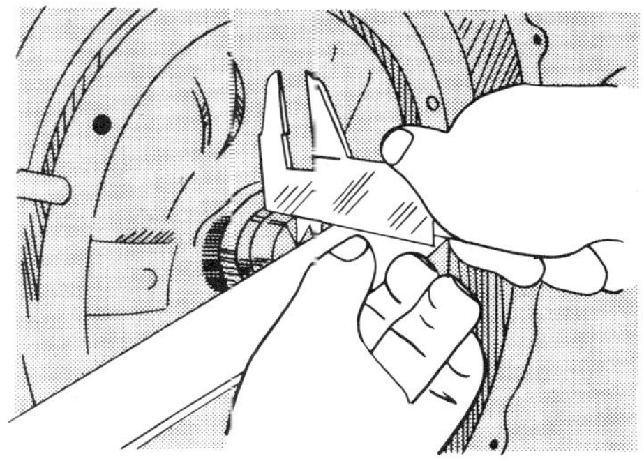

Fig. 4-15. Correct installation of torque converter being checked. With straightedge laid across transmission bel housing, distance to torque converter pilot should be 11.5 mm (29/64 in.).

3. Use multipurpose grease as an adhesive to hold the intermediate plate on the dowels on the rear of the engine block. Lightly lubricate the pilot recess in the crankshaft as indicated in Fig. 4-16.

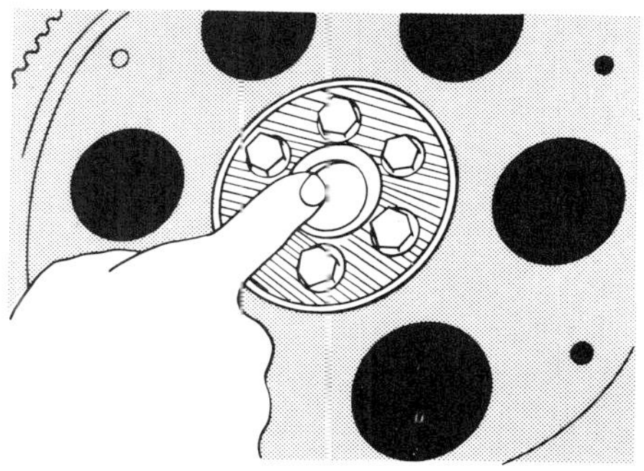

Fig. 4-16. Multipurpose grease being applied to pilot recess in center of crankshaft.

4. If necessary, install the rear transmission mount crossmember on the transmission, torquing the bolts to 20 to 25 Nm (15 to 18 ft. lb.). Place the transmission on the transmission jack.

5. With the transmission supported on the transmission jack, carefully align the bolt holes in the torque converter with the corresponding holes in the drive plate. Align the dowels in the engine block with the corresponding holes in the bellhousing, then move the transmission forward—making sure that the torque converter pilot enters the recess in the center of the crankshaft.

CAUTION —

To prevent damage when the car is returned to service, the torque converter must at this stage rest squarely against the drive plate. Its correct position is an indication that the pilot is not binding against the crankshaft.

6. With the transmission's bellhousing in firm contact with the intermediate plate, install finger-tight the bolts that hold the engine to the transmission.
7. Using the transmission jack, raise the transmission and engine until you can loosely install the bolts that hold the rear transmission mount crossmember to the car body.
8. Torque the engine-to-transmission bolts to 55 to 75 Nm (41 to 55 ft. lb.). Torque the bolts that hold the rear transmission mount crossmember to the body to 20 to 25 Nm (15 to 18 ft. lb.).
9. Install the six bolts that hold the torque converter to the drive plate. Using a wrench on the crankshaft pulley attaching bolt, turn the crankshaft to gain access to the bolts. Torque the bolts to 15 to 20 Nm (11 to 15 ft. lb.), then install the rubber plug in the intermediate plate.
10. Remove the transmission jack. Reinstall the starter and reconnect the exhaust pipe bracket. Torque the starter bolts to 55 to 75 Nm (41 to 55 ft. lb.).
11. Reinstall the splash shield that is beneath the radiator.
12. Make sure that the felt gasket and the collar washer are correctly installed on the end of the speedometer cable (Fig. 4-17). Then, being careful not to bend the cable sharply, reconnect the speedometer cable to the transmission and tighten the knurled ferrule nut to hold the cable in place.

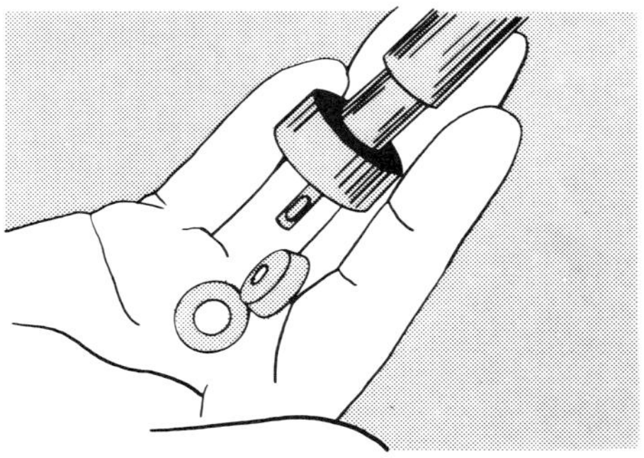

Fig. 4-17. Felt gasket and collar washer—which should be installed in that order inside ferrule nut.

13. Reconnect the ATF cooler lines, replacing the hoses if they are cracked, swollen, or stiff. Torque the unions to 20 to 30 Nm (15 to 22 ft. lb.). Reattach the cooler line clamps to the engine and to the transmission, torquing the bolts to 7 to 8 Nm (5 to 6 ft. lb. or 62 to 71 in. lb.).
14. With careful reference to the marks you made prior to removal, install the driveshaft as described in **DRIVESHAFT AND REAR AXLE.** Torque the four bolts that hold the driveshaft to the pinion flange to 35 to 40 Nm (26 to 30 ft. lb.). On cars with a two-piece driveshaft, torque the bolts that hold the center bearing to the body to 35 to 40 Nm (26 to 30 ft. lb.).
15. Reconnect the selector rod to the transmission's manual shaft lever—using a new cotter pin and replacing worn or damaged grommets. Then adjust the selector linkage as described in **3.1 Adjusting Linkages.**
16. Lower the car to the ground. Then, if installed in step 4 of the removal procedure, remove the engine rear support device.
17. Reconnect the transmission's throttle cable to the engine's accelerator linkage. Then adjust the throttle cable as described in **3.1 Adjusting Linkages.**
18. Install the air cleaner as described in conjunction with cylinder head cover installation in **ENGINE.** Install the ATF dipstick.
19. Refill the transmission with Type F ATF as described in **LUBRICATION AND MAINTENANCE.** Reconnect the battery's negative (−) cable.

5. TRANSMISSION REPAIR

Some of the repairs described under the following headings, such as removing and servicing the valve body, can be made with the transmission in the car. However, all repairs to the planetary gear system, including the clutches and the brakes, require that the transmission be removed.

5.1 Removing, Cleaning, Inspecting, and Installing Torque Converter

The torque converter usually requires removal only when you must replace the ATF pump's ATF seal or clean the torque converter after a transmission failure has contaminated the ATF. Since the torque converter is a welded assembly, you must replace it as a unit if it is leaky or noisy, if it has loose welds, if its stator or one-way clutch is worn-out or damaged, or if a stall speed test shows the unit to be faulty.

To remove:

1. Remove the transmission as described in **4.3 Removing and Installing Transmission.**
2. Remove the wire or the securing bar that you installed across the mouth of the bellhousing during transmission removal.
3. Grasp the torque converter with both hands. Remove it by pulling it with a twisting motion off its splined support tube on the ATF pump.

> *CAUTION* —
> *Do not rock or tilt the torque converter when you remove or install it. This could damage the ATF pump's ATF seal, the stator one-way clutch, or other components in the torque converter hub.*

4. Place the torque converter on the workbench with its open side up, then cover the hub to keep out dirt.
5. If the ATF has been contaminated by metal particles or composition material from the clutch or brake plates, clean the torque converter using a mechanically agitated cleaning machine, such as the Toyota Transmission Cleaner. You should also flush the ATF cooler and ATF cooler lines at this time.

> *CAUTION* —
> *Do not attempt to clean the torque converter with solvent and hand agitation. Doing this will not remove all of the contaminating particles. Residual contaminants are a major cause of recurring transmission troubles, and must be removed before the transmission is put back into service.*

To inspect:

1. Particularly if there have been unusual noises or abnormal ATF pump seal wear, check both the drive plate and the torque converter for excessive runout. To check drive plate runout, install a dial indicator as shown in Fig. 5-1. Then, after zeroing the dial indicator with a 1-mm (or .050-in.) preload, rotate the engine's crankshaft once. The indicated runout should not exceed 0.20 mm (.008 in.). Replace faulty drive plates as described in **ENGINE.**

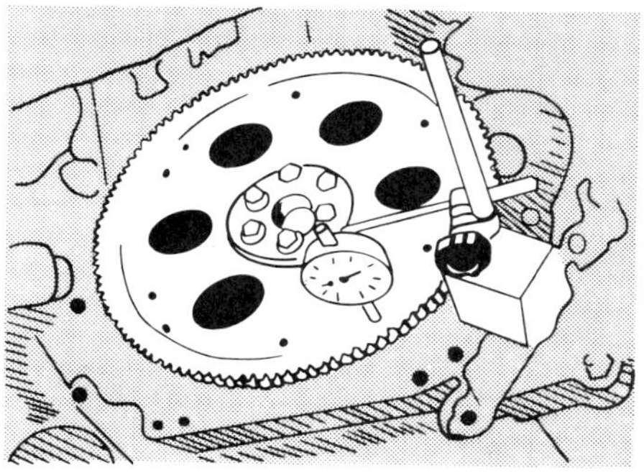

Fig. 5-1. Drive plate runout being measured.

2. To check the torque converter for excessive runout, temporarily install it on the drive plate, torquing the six bolts to 15 to 20 Nm (11 to 15 ft. lb.). Install a dial indicator as shown in Fig. 5-2. Then, after zeroing the dial indicator with a 1-mm (or .050-in.) preload, rotate the engine's crankshaft once. The indicated runout should not exceed 0.30 mm (.012 in.). Replace faulty torque converters.

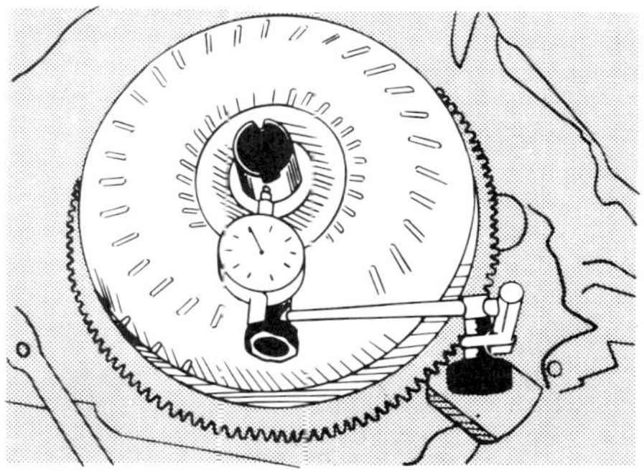

Fig. 5-2. Torque converter runout being measured.

3. Especially if the ATF pump's ATF seal has been leaking, inspect the ATF seal contact area on the torque converter's ATF pump drive sleeve. If the sleeve is noticeably grooved, replace the torque converter.
4. To check the operation of the one-way clutch, use the tools shown in Fig. 5-3. Install the tools as indicated in Fig. 5-4. Using the T-handled turning tool, rotate the clutch inner race. The clutch should lock when turned counterclockwise but should rotate with less than 2.5 Nm (22 in. lb.) of torque applied in the clockwise direction.

> **NOTE** —
> If the one-way clutch does not operate correctly, the malfunction may be caused by particles of foreign matter. Clean the torque converter as described earlier, then repeat the test to make sure that the torque converter is really faulty.

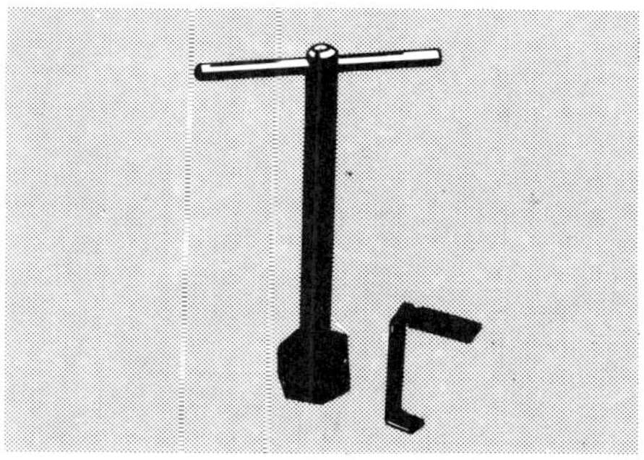

Fig. 5-3. Toyota special service toolset 09397-22020, for testing torque converter one-way clutch, consists of T-handled turning tool and flat metal locking tool.

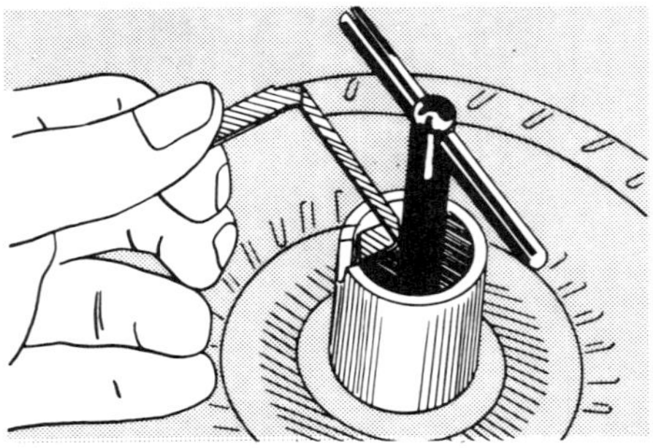

Fig. 5-4. One-way clutch testing toolset installation. T-handled turning tool is inserted into splines of one-way clutch inner race. Locking tool is inserted to engage one-way clutch outer race and ATF pump drive notch in torque converter's ATF pump drive sleeve.

5. To check the stator's axial play, use snap ring pliers to grip the stator splines and move the stator up and down. Measured with a vernier caliper, as indicated in Fig. 5-5, the axial play should not exceed 1.50 mm (.060 in.). If it does, replace the torque converter.

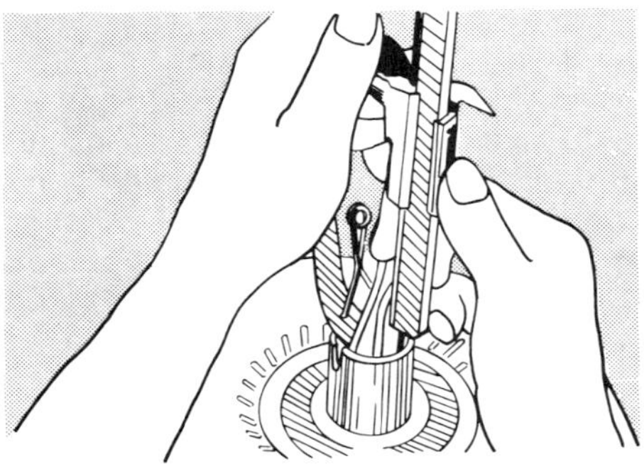

Fig. 5-5. Stator axial play being measured.

6. Especially if the ATF pump's ATF seal has been leaking, measure the ATF pump bushing (Fig. 5-6). If its inside diameter is greater than 38.188 mm (1.5035 in.), replace the ATF pump or the ATF pump body.

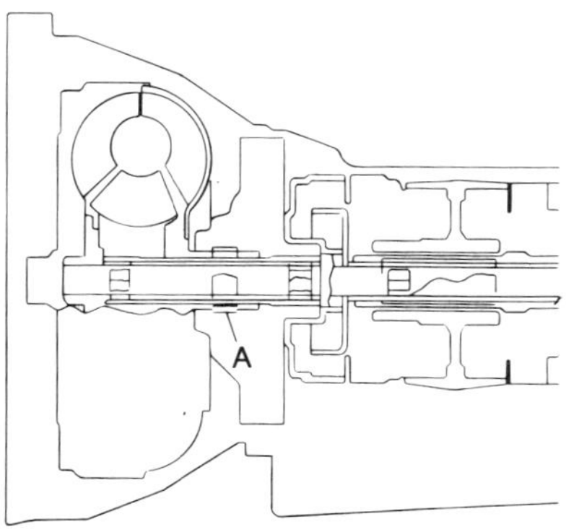

Fig. 5-6. Location of ATF pump bushing (**A**) inside assembled transmission.

To install:

1. If the torque converter has been cleaned, add half a liter or half a quart of ATF through the hub so that the internal parts will have lubrication when the engine is started.
2. Install the torque converter on the transmission by pushing it straight in. Then rotate the torque converter clockwise and counterclockwise until the stator splines and the turbine splines engage their respective shafts and the notches of the ATF pump drive sleeve engage the ATF pump's drivegear.
3. To check that the torque converter is correctly installed on the transmission, place a straightedge across the mouth of the transmission's bellhousing as indicated in Fig. 5-7. If the distance from the straightedge to the torque converter's pilot is less than 11.5 mm ($^{29}/_{64}$ in.), either the splines or the ATF pump drive is not correctly engaged.
4. With the torque converter correctly installed, place a bar of wire across the mouth of the bellhousing to prevent the torque converter from falling out during transmission installation.

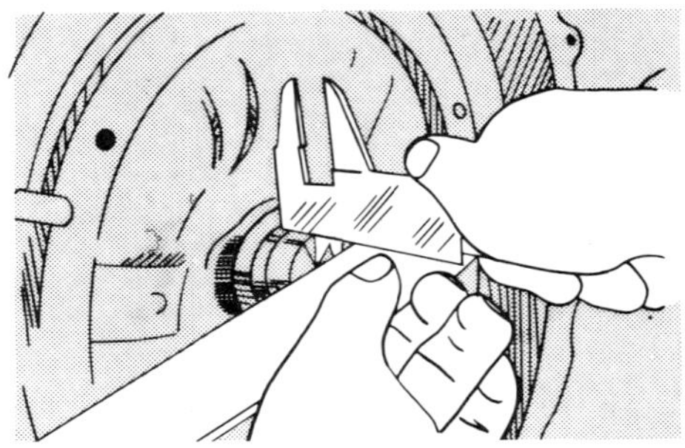

Fig. 5-7. Torque converter being checked for correct installation with straightedge and vernier caliper.

Replacing ATF Pump's ATF Seal

The ATF pump's ATF seal, which prevents the loss of ATF around the torque converter's ATF pump drive sleeve, can be replaced once the torque converter is removed. Though it is only necessary to replace the seal if it is worn or damaged, most experienced mechanics prefer to replace this seal routinely during any transmission repair in order to prevent its early failure.

Remove the old ATF seal as indicated in Fig. 5-8. Alternatively, you can pry out the seal with a screwdriver—being careful not to scratch the stator support or the seal recess.

Start a new seal in the recess so that its lip points into the transmission. Lightly coat the exposed periphery of the seal with adhesive sealer. Then drive the seal fully in as shown in Fig. 5-9. Wipe away all traces of surplus sealer so that it cannot accidentally enter the ATF.

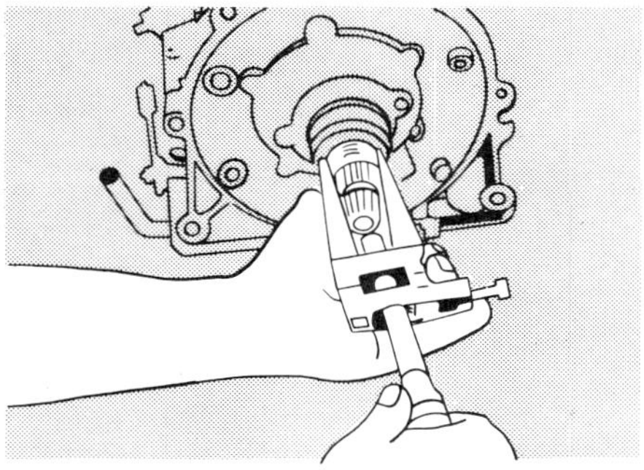

Fig. 5-8. ATF pump's ATF seal being removed with expansion puller.

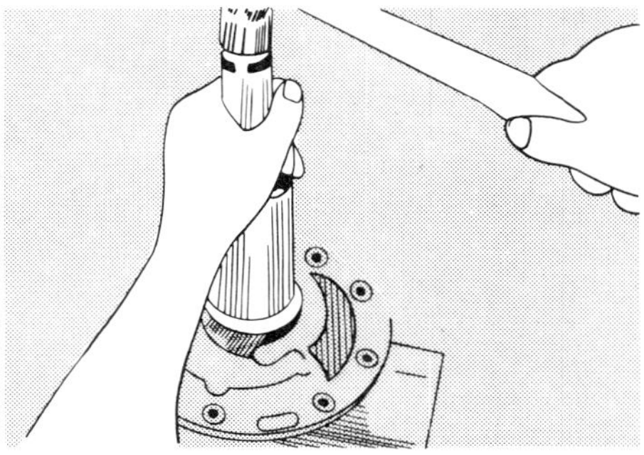

Fig. 5-9. ATF pump's ATF seal being driven in with Toyota special service tool 09214-60010 (crankshaft pulley installer). This can be done with the ATF pump either installed or removed as shown.

5.2 Removing and Installing ATF Pan and Valve Body

The valve body can be removed and installed with the transmission in the car. This job is usually done in order to clean the valve body. Before beginning any disassembly, thoroughly clean the outside of the transmission in order to keep dirt from entering the transmission's working parts.

To remove:

1. If the transmission has been removed, invert it on a repair stand or on a clean workbench; if the transmission is in the car, raise the car on a hoist or support it on stands designed for the purpose.

   NOTE ——
   Before you raise the car, remove the air cleaner as described in conjunction with cylinder head cover removal in **ENGINE.** Then disconnect the transmission's throttle cable from the accelerator linkage by taking out the clip and the pin.

2. If the transmission is in the car, place a drain pan under the transmission's ATF pan. Then remove the drain plug and allow the ATF to drain. With the ATF drained, reinstall the plug to a torque of 15 to 20 Nm (11 to 15 ft. lb.). 1
3. Using a 10-mm socket wrench on a suitable extension, remove the 14 bolts that hold the ATF pan to the transmission case (Fig. 5-10). Then remove the pan and discard the gasket.

   NOTE ——
   You will find a small rectangular magnet clinging to the inside of the ATF pan. If there are metal particles in the pan, wipe clean the magnet and try to pick up the particles with it. Steel (magnetic) particles indicate that there is bearing, gear, or clutch and brake plate wear; brass (non-magnetic) particles indicate bushing wear.

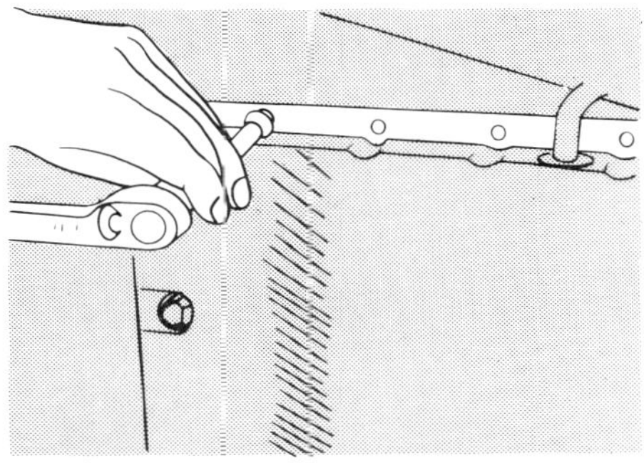

Fig. 5-10. ATF pan bolts being removed.

4. Using an 8-mm socket wrench, remove the five bolts that hold the ATF strainer to the valve body assembly. Then lift off the strainer (Fig. 5-11).

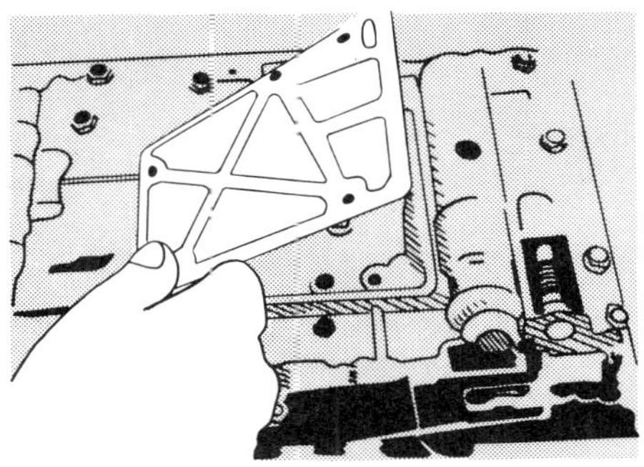

Fig. 5-11. ATF strainer being removed with transmission removed and inverted.

5. If the transmission is in the car, make a flat retainer for the accumulator pistons, as indicated in Fig. 5-12. The retainer can be made of wood, plastic, or metal.

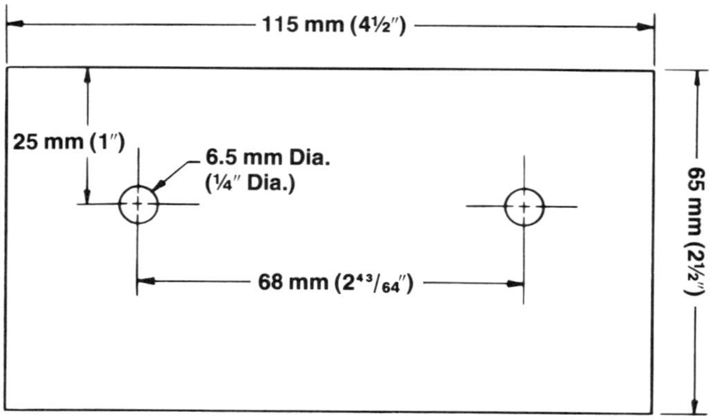

Fig. 5-12. Dimensions for accumulator piston retainer. This retainer must be used to keep accumulator pistons from falling out after valve body is removed from installed transmission.

6. Move the manual shaft lever so that the detent roller is on the center notch of the detent lever. This will keep the manual valve from falling out when the valve body is removed. See Fig. 5-13.

Fig. 5-13. Detent roller centered on detent segment of detent lever.

7. Using a 10-mm socket wrench, remove the 17 bolts indicated in Fig. 5-13. If the transmission is installed, support the valve body assembly as the last bolt is removed.

8. Partially remove the valve body assembly. If the transmission is installed, be ready to insert the accumulator piston retainer that you made in step 5. Temporarily mount the piston retainer using two of the ATF pan bolts. See Fig. 5-15.

NOTE ——

Removal and repair of the accumulator is covered in **5.5 Disassembling and Assembling Transmission.** The work described there can also be carried out with the transmission installed in the car.

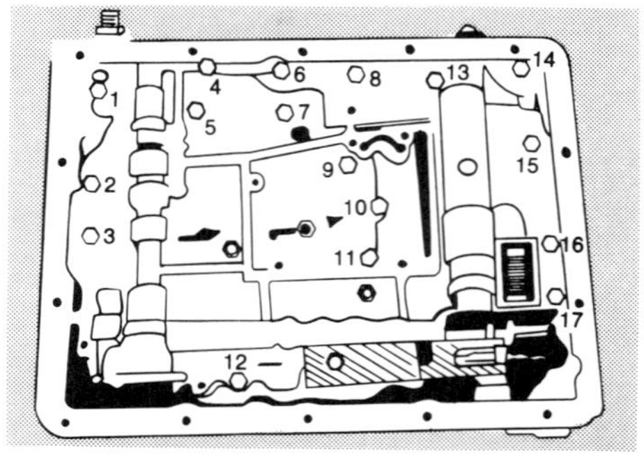

Fig. 5-14. Locations of the 17 bolts that hold valve body assembly to transmission case.

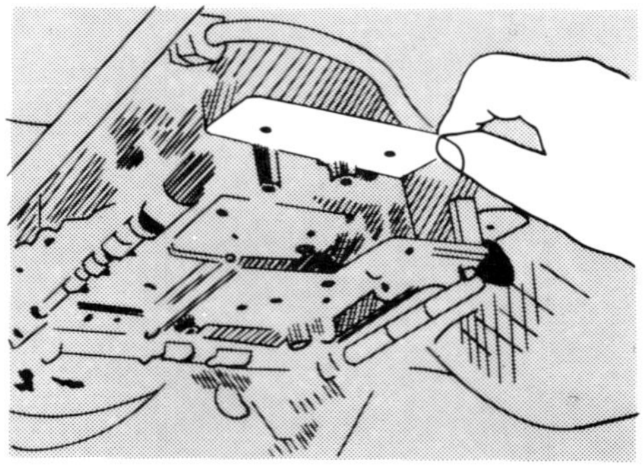

Fig. 5-15. Accumulator piston retainer prepared for immediate installation as valve body assembly is lowered from installed transmission.

9. Lower the valve body, then disconnect the throttle cable as indicated in Fig. 5-16 or Fig. 5-17. Then remove the valve body assembly and place it right side up on a clean workbench. If necessary, disassemble and clean the valve body assembly as described in **5.3 Disassembling and Assembling.**

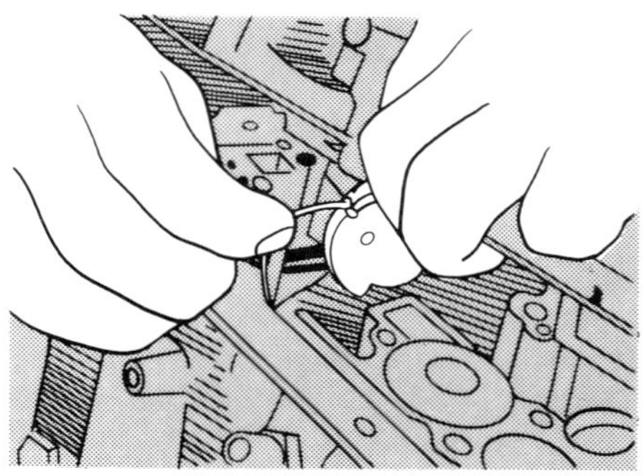

Fig. 5-16. Throttle cable being detached from cam on valve body assembly with transmission removed.

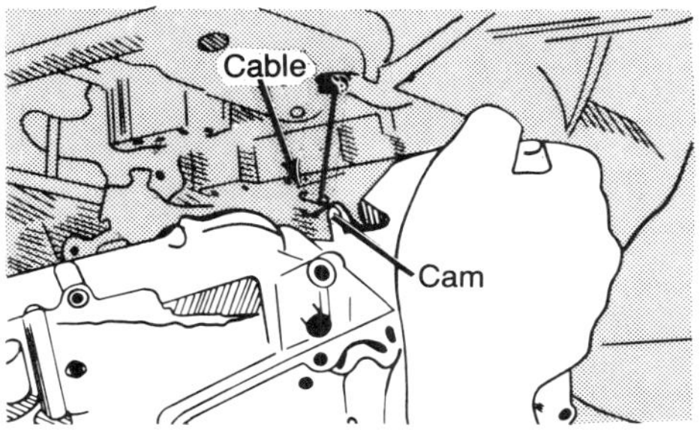

Fig. 5-17. Throttle cable being detached from cam on valve body assembly with transmission installed.

Fig. 5-19. Throttle cable being attached to cam with transmission removed.

To install:

1. Make sure that all removed components are washed in clean solvent and are dried with compressed air. Do not dry automatic transmission components with fluffy cloths that can leave lint behind to jam the hydraulic controls or clog the ATF strainer.

NOTE ——
Unless the ATF is very dirty or contaminated by solid particles, it usually is sufficient to immerse the complete assembly in clean solvent and dry it with moisture-free compressed air. However, be careful not to hold the air jet so close that it moves the valves violently. Doing this could damage the springs. Disassembly for thorough cleaning is covered later under the heading **5.3 Disassembling and Assembling Valve Body.**

2. Reconnect the throttle cable to the cam as indicated in Fig. 5-18 or Fig. 5-19.

NOTE ——
Throttle cable replacement is covered under the next heading.

3. Position the valve body on the transmission. If the transmission is installed, remove the accumulator piston retainer that you installed in step 8 of the removal procedure, then quickly position the valve body on the transmission. Make sure that the pin on the detent lever engages the manual valve, as indicated in Fig. 5-20.

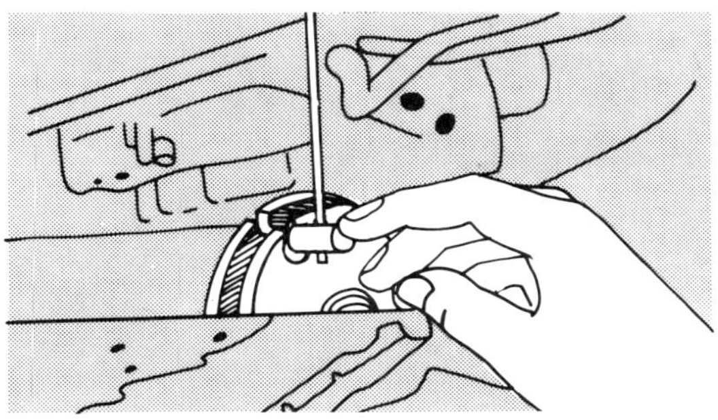

Fig. 5-18. Throttle cable being attached to cam with transmission in car.

4. Install several of the valve body bolts finger-tight to hold the valve body assembly in position.

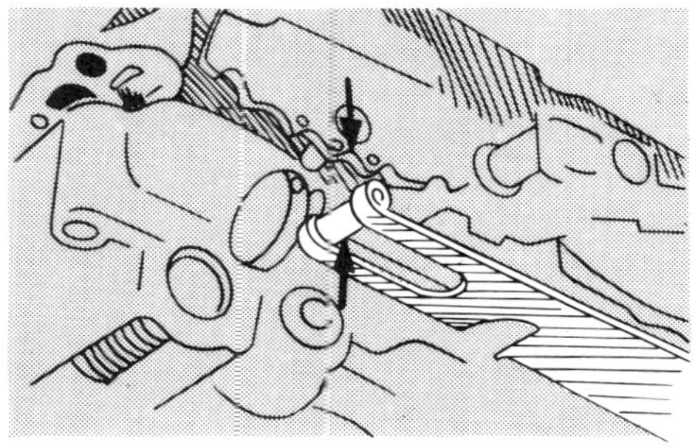

Fig. 5-20. Pin on detent lever (upper arrow) that must engage groove in manual valve. Position detent segment so that detent roller (lower arrow) engages a middle notch.

5. Install all of the bolts finger-tight—making sure that the correct length is used in each hole. See Fig. 5-21.

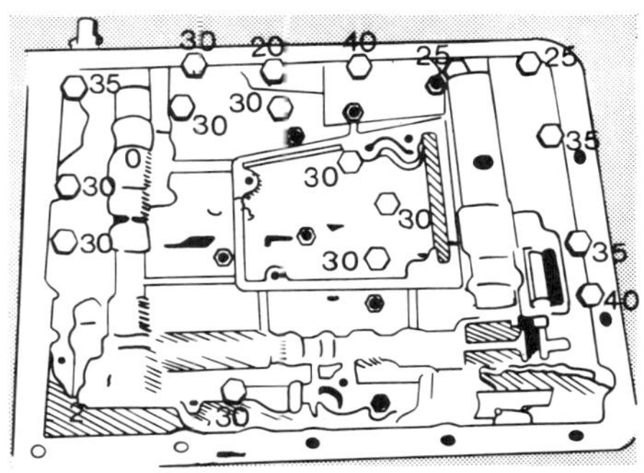

Bolt lengths: 20 mm (about 3/4 in.)
25 mm (about 1 in.)
30 mm (about 1 3/16 in.)
35 mm (about 1 3/8 in.)
40 mm (about 1 1/2 in.)

Fig. 5-21. Correct locations for bolts that hold valve body to transmission case. Numbers indicate bolt lengths in mm.

6. Working diagonally, torque all 17 bolts in stages to 8 to 11 Nm (71 to 97 in. lb.).
7. Install the ATF strainer and its five bolts. Then, using an 8-mm socket wrench, torque the strainer bolts and the detent spring bolt to 5 to 6 Nm (44 to 53 in. lb.).
8. Install a new ATF pan gasket without sealer, as indicated in Fig. 5-22. Place the small rectangular magnet in the bottom of the ATF pan where it will be beneath the ATF strainer when the transmission is installed. Then position the ATF pan on the transmission case and install all 14 bolts finger-tight.

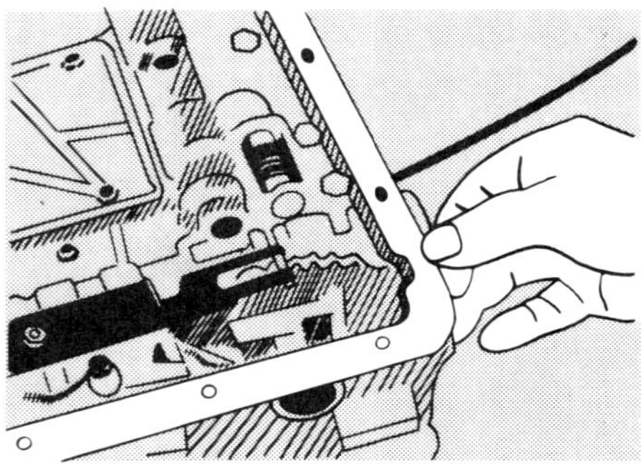

Fig. 5-22. ATF pan gasket correctly installed. Notch in gasket should be adjacent to detent lever as shown.

9. Using a 10-mm socket wrench and a suitable extension, torque the ATF pan bolts in stages to 4 to 5 Nm (35 to 44 in. lb.).
10. If the transmission is in the car, lower the car to the ground. Reconnect the transmission's throttle cable to the engine's accelerator linkage, then adjust the cable as described in **3.1 Adjusting Linkages.** Refill the transmission with ATF as described in **LUBRICATION AND MAINTENANCE.**

Replacing Throttle Cable

The throttle cable can be replaced with the transmission either in the car or removed. To replace the cable, first remove the valve body assembly as described under the preceding heading. Then use a 10-mm (or ⅜-in.) socket wrench on a long extension to push the cable's plastic end fitting out of the transmission case. See Fig. 5-23.

Make sure that the O-ring (included with replacement cables) is installed on the new cable as indicated in Fig. 5-24. Lubricate the cable's end fitting and the O-ring with ATF, then hand-press the cable end fitting into the transmission case, being careful not to damage the O-ring as it enters the bore.

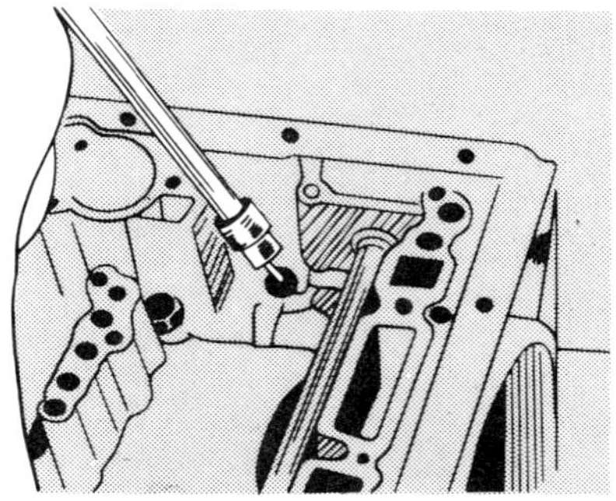

Fig. 5-23. Socket wrench being used to push throttle cable end fitting out of transmission case.

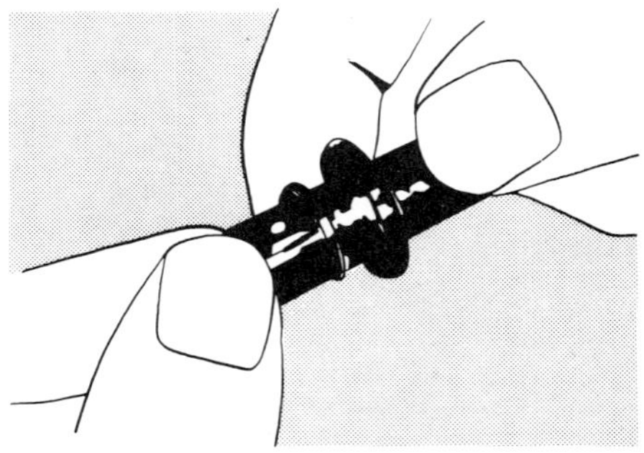

Fig. 5-24. O-ring being installed in groove on throttle cable end fitting.

5.3 Disassembling and Assembling Valve Body

As a rule, the valve body assembly is only taken apart for cleaning and inspection. However, most valve body components are available as replacement parts and can be replaced individually so long as clearances are not excessive owing to wear on adjacent surfaces, such as the control valve bores.

The valve body assembly consists of four main parts. The largest of these is the manual valve body, which is located on the bottom. Atop the manual valve body is the separator plate with its two gaskets. The remaining two main parts are the throttle valve body and the 2nd gear/3rd gear shift valve body, both of which are located on the upper side of the valve body assembly—the throttle valve body being the smaller of the two.

To avoid confusion and mixed-up components, it is best first to separate the valve body assembly into its main parts and then to disassemble and assemble each valve body one at a time. This is the way the work is described in the procedures that follow (which also makes it possible to disassemble and assemble one main part only, for example the 2nd gear/3rd gear shift valve body, leaving the remaining main parts untouched).

To separate main parts:

1. Place the valve body assembly right-side-up on a clean workbench covered with a clean sheet of paper. Then, using an 8-mm socket wrench as shown in Fig. 5-25, remove the ten bolts from the throttle valve body and the 2nd gear/3rd gear shift valve body.

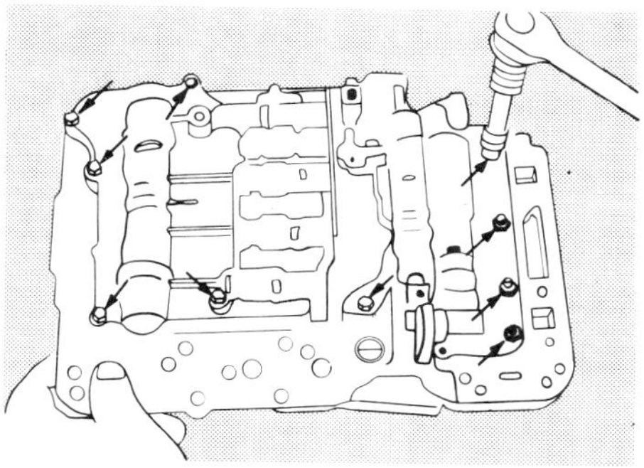

Fig. 5-25. Bolts (arrows) to be removed from top of valve body assembly.

2. Turn the valve body assembly upside down. Using an 8-mm socket wrench, remove the bolt that holds the detent spring, then remove the spring.
3. Carefully withdraw the manual valve from its bore.
4. Using an 8-mm socket wrench, remove the seven bolts indicated in Fig. 5-26. Lift off the small metal cover.

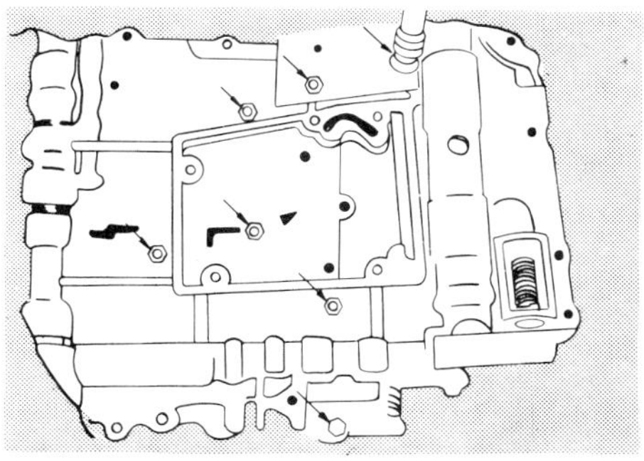

Fig. 5-26. Bolts (arrows) to be removed from bottom of valve body assembly. Socket wrench is shown on one of three bolts for small metal cover.

5. Carefully lift off the manual valve body and the separator plate and its gaskets as a single assembly, leaving the throttle valve body and the 2nd gear/3rd gear shift valve body on the workbench, as shown in Fig. 5-27.

> ***CAUTION —***
> *If you lift the manual valve body off the separator plate, or if you allow the throttle valve body or the 2nd gear/3rd gear shift valve body to stick to the separator plate gasket and then fall, you are likely to lose or mix up one or more of the ball valves.*

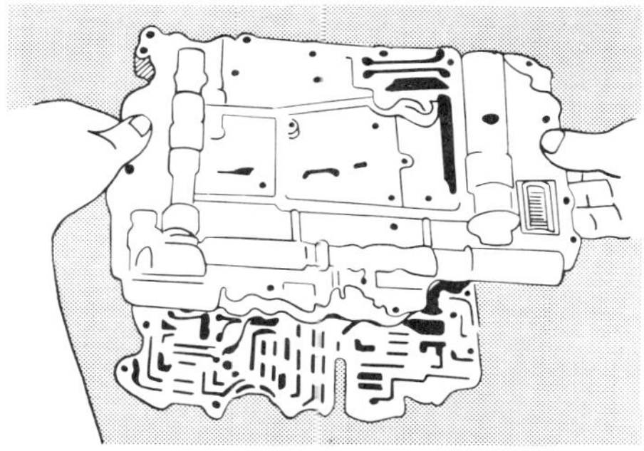

Fig. 5-27. Manual valve body, separator plate, and gaskets being lifted off throttle valve body and 2nd gear/3rd gear shift valve body.

6. Turn the manual valve body over and place it on the workbench right-side-up. Then lift off the separator plate and its gaskets—being careful not to lose the spring-loaded ATF cooler bypass valve or one of the ball valves.

To assemble main parts:

1. Make sure that all ball valves and the ATF cooler bypass valve are correctly in place. If necessary, consult the later procedures that describe the disassembly and assembly of the individual valve bodies.
2. Position the separator plate upper gasket atop the 2nd gear/3rd gear shift valve body, moving the throttle valve body out of the way to one side.

> ***CAUTION —***
> *The separator plate upper gasket (Part No. 35433) and the separator plate lower gasket (Part No. 35431) are not the same. Compare the new gasket to the old gasket or to the gasket shown in Fig. 5-28. If the gaskets are interchanged, the transmission will not shift properly.*

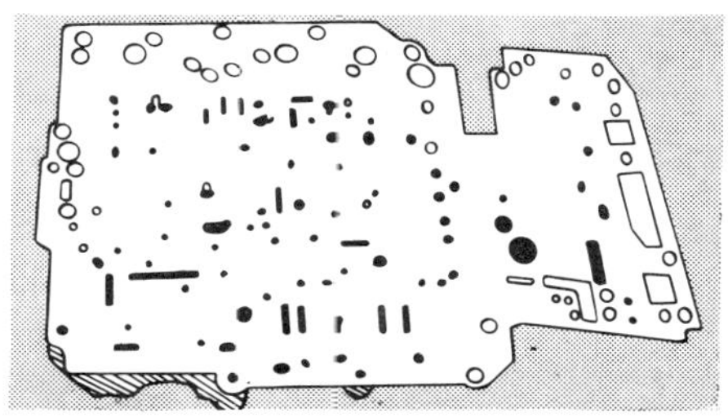

Fig. 5-28. Separator plate upper gasket positioned atop 2nd gear/3rd gear shift valve body.

3. Place the separator plate lower gasket and then the separator plate atop the manual valve body. Temporarily insert a bolt through the throttle valve body side of the assembly to keep the components aligned.
4. Holding the separator plate and its gasket firmly to the manual valve body, invert the manual valve body and place it atop the separator plate upper gasket and the 2nd gear/3rd gear shift valve body. Install the three bolts indicated in Fig. 5-29 finger-tight.

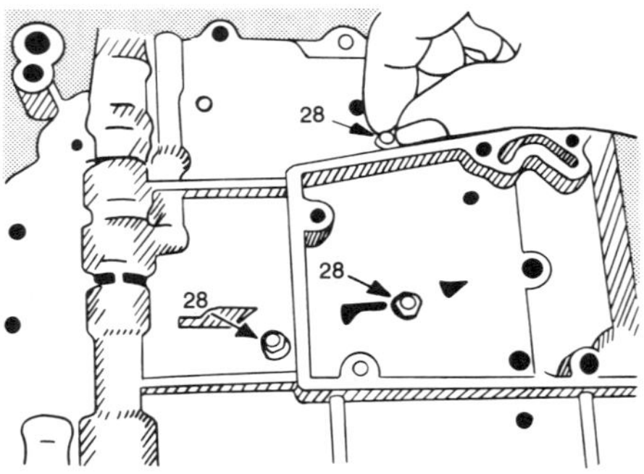

Fig. 5-29. Three 28-mm (about 1⅛-in.) long bolts used to align and loosely assemble manual valve body, separator plate, gaskets, and 2nd gear/3rd gear shift valve body.

5. Invert the assembly, check the gaskets and separator plate alignment, then install the five bolts indicated in Fig. 5-30 finger-tight.

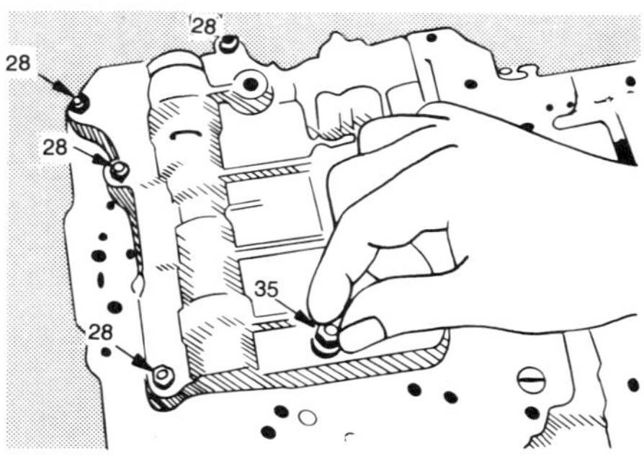

Fig. 5-30. 28-mm (about 1⅛-in.) long bolts and single 35-mm (about 1⅜-in.) long bolt used to mount 2nd gear/3rd gear shift valve body.

6. Making sure that the gaskets and the separator plate are still aligned, remove the temporary alignment bolt inserted in step 3.
7. After making sure that the rubber check valve ball is correctly in place in the throttle valve body, lower the main assembly onto the throttle valve body. Align the bolt holes, then loosely install the bolt indicated in Fig. 5-31.

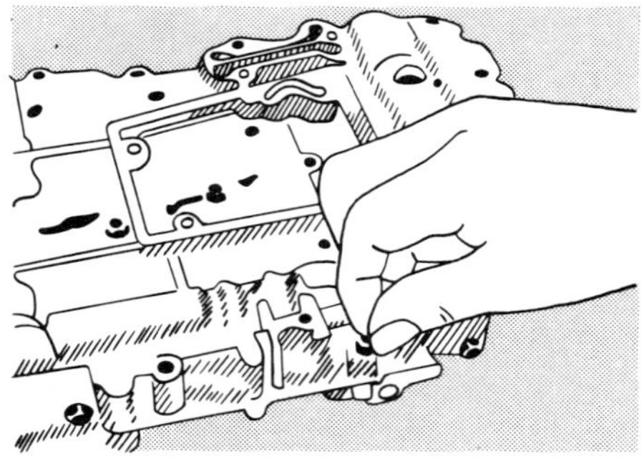

Fig. 5-31. One 22-mm (about ⅞-in.) long bolt used to hold throttle valve body to valve body assembly.

8. Position the small metal cover atop the manual valve body, then install its three 40-mm (about 1½-in.) long bolts finger-tight. Install the two remaining 28-mm (about 1⅛-in.) long bolts finger-tight.
9. Turn the valve body assembly right-side-up. Install the bolts indicated in Fig. 5-32 finger-tight.

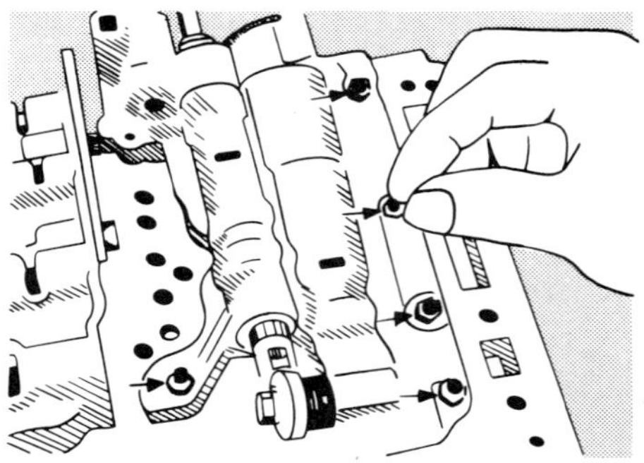

Fig. 5-32. Five 18-mm (about 11/16-in.) long bolts to be installed at periphery of throttle valve body.

10. After making sure that the gaskets are not kinked and that all components are correctly aligned, use an 8-mm socket wrench to torque all of the bolts on the upper side of the valve body assembly in stages to 5 to 6 Nm (44 to 53 in. lb.).
11. Invert the valve body assembly. Using an 8-mm socket wrench, torque all the bolts on the lower side of the valve body in stages to 5 to 6 Nm (44 to 53 in. lb.).
12. Lubricate the manual valve with clean ATF, then insert it into its bore in the valve body assembly.
13. Install the detent spring, torquing the bolt to 5 to 6 Nm (44 to 53 in. lb.).

Disassembling and Assembling Manual Valve Body

Fig. 5-33 is an exploded view of the manual valve body and the separator plate and its gaskets. The part numbers are given for the individual components. Because many parts in the valve body assembly look alike, it is easy to mix them up. Therefore, keep the parts in order while they are disassembled. If, during assembly, you are unsure of the correct location for a spring, it can be identified using the measurements given in **6. Automatic Transmission Technical Data.**

Fig. 5-34. Loose components atop manual valve body (circled). Cooler bypass valve is at top, No. 2 brake check ball at lower left, and regulator valve damping check ball at lower right.

To disassemble:

1. Remove the separator plate and its gaskets. Then remove the cooler bypass valve and its spring, the No. 2 brake check ball, and finally the regulator valve damping check ball and its spring. See Fig. 5-34.

> ***CAUTION —***
>
> *These are loose parts — be careful not to lose them. The regulator valve damping ball and its spring should be removed last, so that you can turn over the manual valve body and dump them into your hand.*

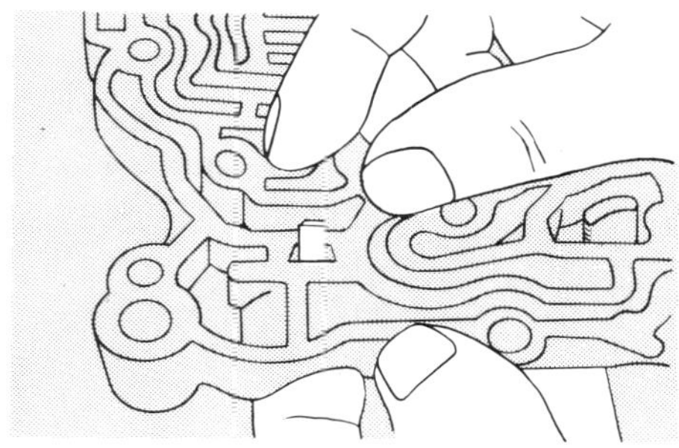

Fig. 5-35. Seat piece for 1st/2nd gear shift valve being removed. Push seat upward with finger, then grasp it with other hand and pull out.

2. Remove the seat piece for the 1st/2nd gear shift valve, as indicated in Fig. 5-35.

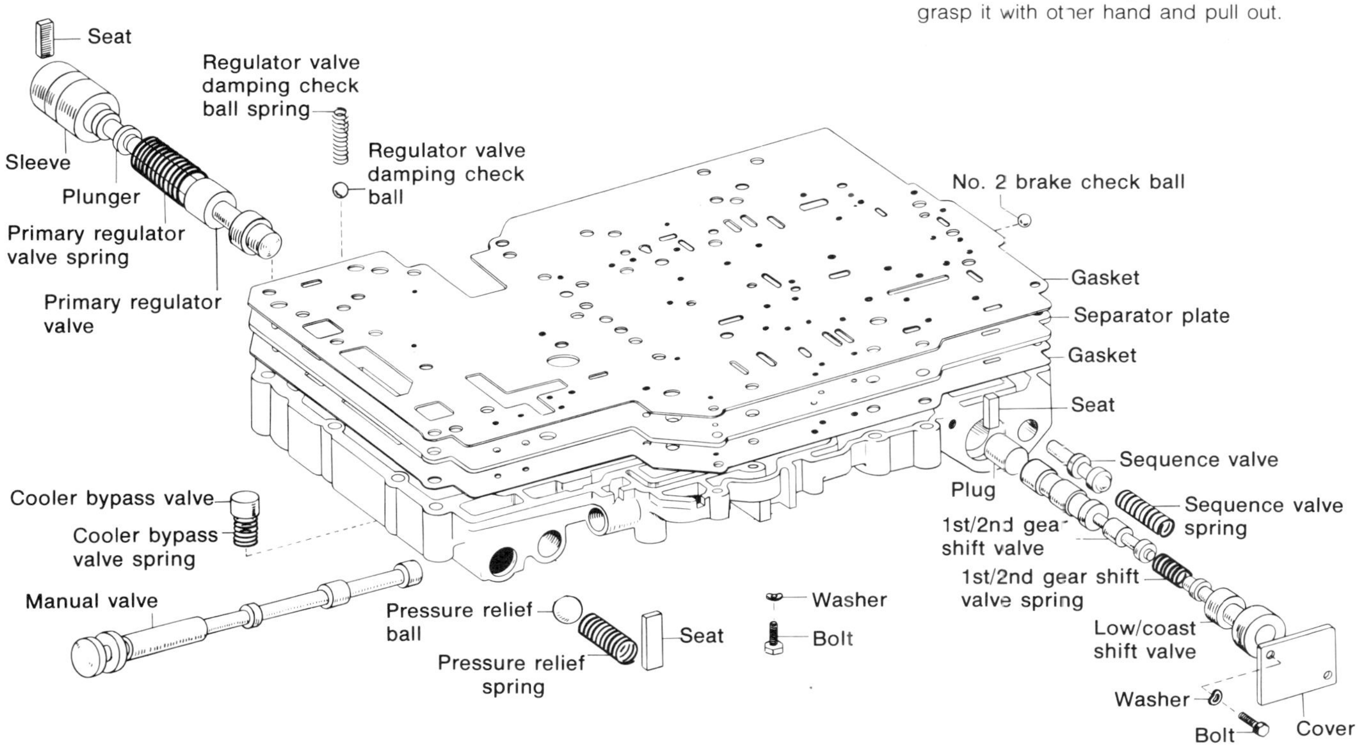

Fig. 5-33. Exploded view of manual valve body.

3. Remove the 1st/2nd gear shift valve and its spring by tilting the valve body and allowing these components to slide out. Keep the spring with the valve so that it will not be mixed up with some other spring.

NOTE —

In removing the 1st/2nd gear shift valve and its spring, you will be taking it out in the direction opposite that indicated earlier in Fig. 5-33. This will relieve spring pressure on the low/coast shift valve so that it will not fly out suddenly when it is removed in step 5.

4. Remove one bolt for the cover over the low/coast shift valve and the sequence valve; loosen the other bolt. Then pivot the cover so that you can take out the sequence valve spring and the sequence valve, as indicated in Fig. 5-36.

WARNING—

Keep your eyes and face away as you pivot the cover. The spring is under tension and could fly out suddenly if you are not prepared to catch it.

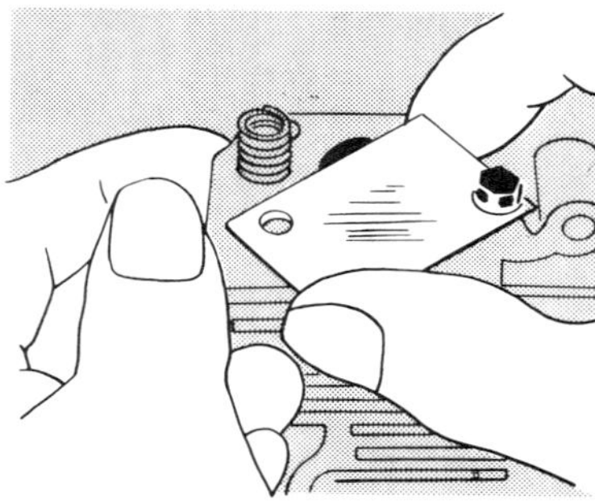

Fig. 5-36. Sequence valve spring and sequence valve being removed.

5. Fully remove the cover. Then take out the low/coast shift valve by tilting and gently shaking the valve body.
6. Remove the seat piece for the primary regulator valve, as indicated in Fig. 5-37. Then remove the sleeve, the plunger, the spring, and the primary regulator valve.

WARNING —

The spring is highly compressed. Do not point the valve sleeve toward your face or the sleeve and the spring may fly out and strike you. To remove the seat piece, hold the valve body face down while you press in on the valve sleeve. The seat piece will drop out. Slowly relieve the compressed spring, then gently shake out the parts that are to be removed.

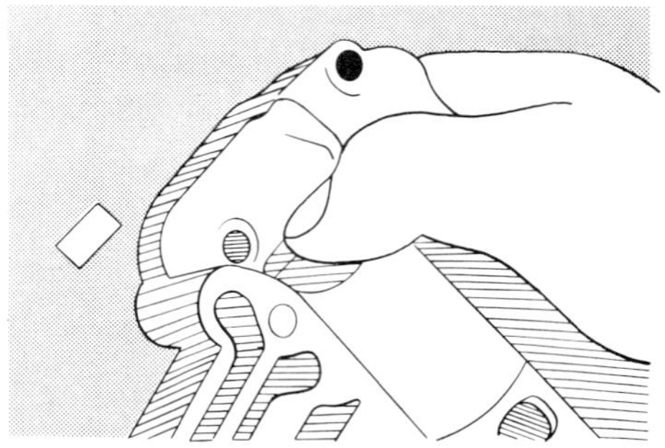

Fig. 5-37. Sleeve being pressed in with thumb so that seat piece (on workbench) drops out.

7. Remove the seat piece for the pressure relief ball and spring, as indicated in Fig. 5-38. Then tilt the valve body so that the spring and the ball fall into your hand.

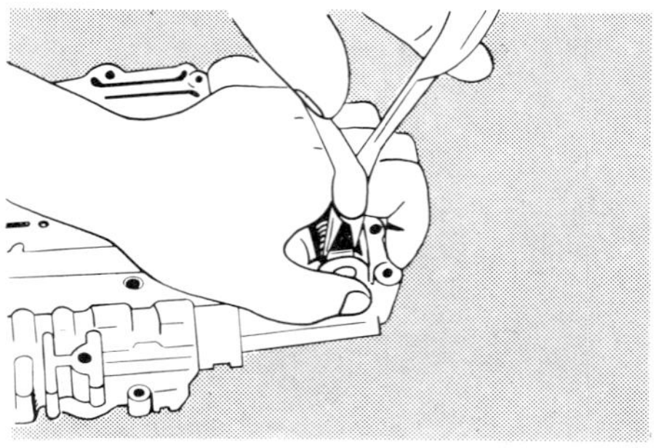

Fig. 5-38. Seat piece for pressure relief assembly being removed with needle nose pliers. Keep hand over spring as shown so that it cannot fly out and become lost. Be careful not to bend spring as you pull out seat piece.

8. Thoroughly wash all components in clean solvent, then dry them with moisture-free compressed air. If any valve or ball is worn or damaged, replace it. Unplug clogged ATF passages, and replace the separator plate or the valve body if either is not perfectly flat at its mating surface(s).

CAUTION —

Do not use a scraper to remove foreign matter as this can make scratches and gouges that will permit ATF leakage or jam the valves. Do not wipe parts with a soft fluffy cloth that can leave behind lint, which can cause the valves to stick.

9. Inspect the springs. Replace any that is rusted, no longer stands square, had distorted coils, or is otherwise damaged. Replace springs that are shorter than the dimensions given in Fig. 5-39.

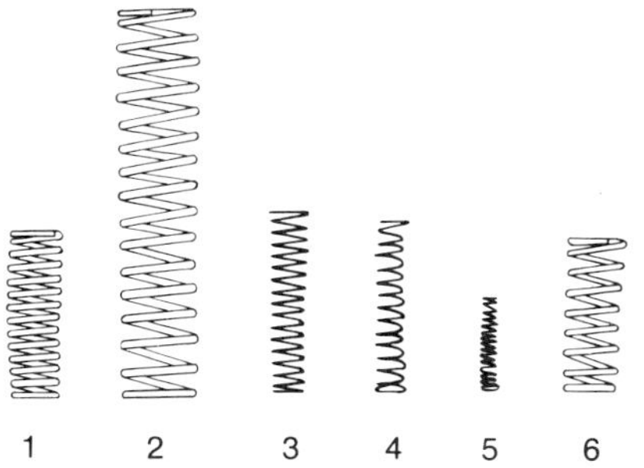

Spring	Minimum permissible length
1. Pressure relief ball spring	32.14 mm (1.265 in.)
2. Primary regulator valve spring (1975-1977)	81.48 mm (3.208 in.)
Primary regulator valve spring (1978 and later)	73.32 mm (2.887 in.)
3. Sequence valve spring	37.55 mm (1.478 in.)
4. 1st/2nd gear shift valve spring	34.62 mm (1.363 in.)
5. Regulator valve damping check ball spring	19.50 mm (.768 in.)
6. Cooler bypass valve spring	30.65 mm (1.207 in.)

Fig. 5-39. Correct minimum lengths for springs in manual valve body.

To assemble:

1. Make sure that all parts are still perfectly clean and dry. Insert the pressure relief ball in the valve body, then simultaneously install its spring and seat piece as indicated in Fig. 5-40.

NOTE ——

You should lightly lubricate each valve with clean ATF just before you insert it into the valve body. All other parts should be installed dry.

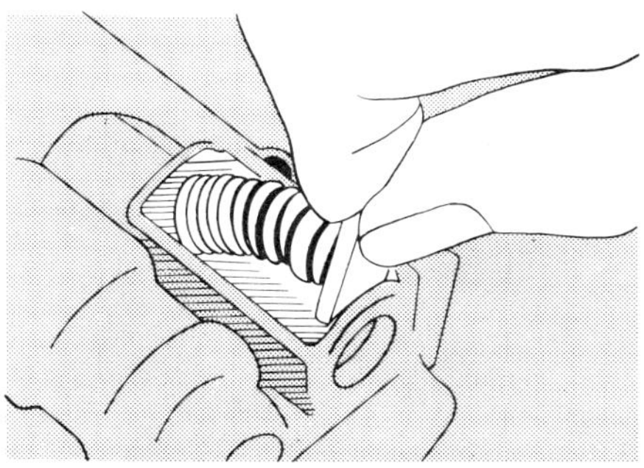

Fig. 5-40. Spring and seat piece for pressure relief ball being installed.

2. Install the primary regulator valve together with its spring. Push in the valve until its end enters the hole in the opposite end of the bore and is flush with the valve body on that end.

3. Insert the regulator valve plunger into the sleeve—rounded end first. When fully installed, the plunger should be recessed inside the sleeve.

4. Holding the valve body level so that the plunger does not fall out of the sleeve, push the sleeve and plunger into the valve body, compressing the primary regulator valve spring. Then install the seat piece as indicated in Fig. 5-41.

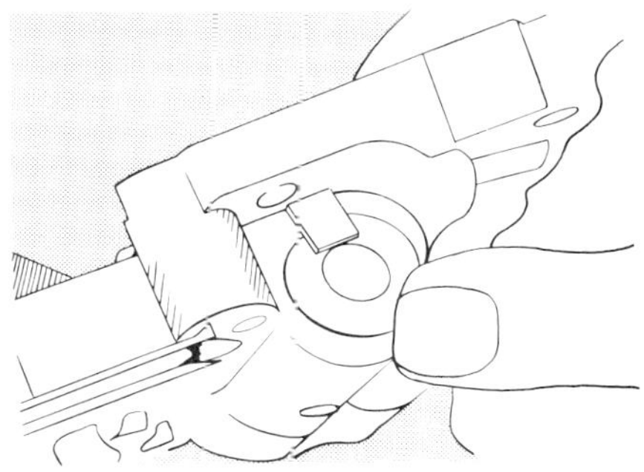

Fig. 5-41. Primary regulator valve spring seat piece correctly installed.

5. Install the low/coast shift valve—small end first. Then install the cover plate with one bolt, install the sequence valve and its spring as shown in Fig. 5-42, and fully install the cover plate. Torque the bolts to 5 to 6 Nm (44 to 53 in. lb.).

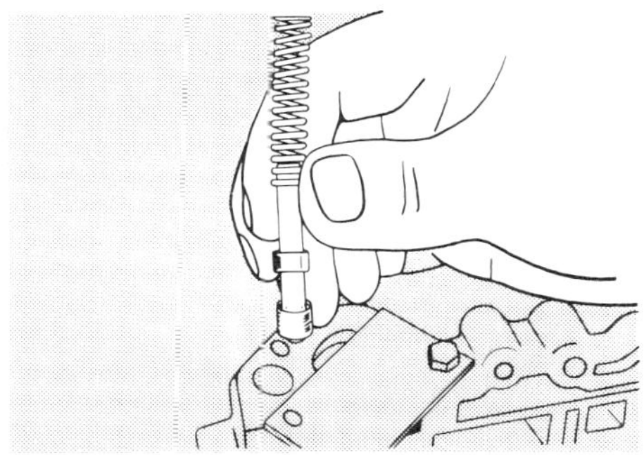

Fig. 5-42. Sequence valve and its spring being installed. Notice position of partially-installed cover plate. After installing sequence valve, swing cover over spring and install second bolt.

6. Insert first the 1st/2nd gear shift valve spring and then the 1st/2nd gear shift valve—small end first—into the valve body. Insert the plug, then install the seat piece.

7. Install the ball valves and the ATF cooler bypass valve as indicated in Fig. 5-43.

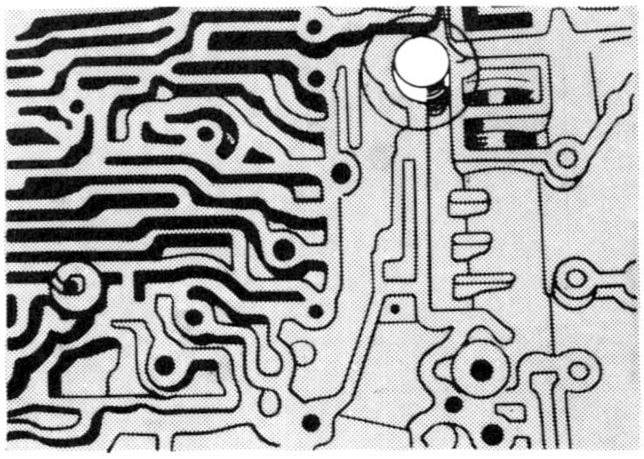

Fig. 5-43. Locations of ball valves and ATF cooler bypass valve (all circled). No. 2 brake check ball is at left of illustration, and is smallest of the two rubber ball valves. ATF cooler bypass valve and spring are at top. AT lower right is regulator valve damping check ball, which sits atop its spring.

8. Install the separator plate lower gasket and then the separator plate atop the manual valve body. Temporarily install one short bolt finger-tight to compress the separator plate against the tension of the spring-loaded ATF cooler bypass valve.

NOTE ——

The upper and lower separator plate gaskets are not the same. Be careful not to mix them up.

Disassembling and Assembling Throttle Valve Body

Fig. 5-44 is an exploded view of the throttle valve body. The part numbers are given for the individual components. If, during assembly, you are unsure of the correct location for a spring, it can be identified using the measurements given in **6. Automatic Transmission Technical Data.**

To disassemble:

1. Hold the throttle valve retainer with your thumb so that the retainer cannot fall out. Then invert the throttle valve body and dump out the check ball and the cut-back valve plug's seat piece into the palm of your hand. If necessary, shake the valve body gently to free the seat piece.
2. Remove the cut-back valve plug and the cut-back valve.
3. Using an 8-mm socket wrench, remove one bolt from the cover plate and loosen the other bolt. Then swing the plate aside until you can hold in the spring-loaded secondary regulator valve as indi-

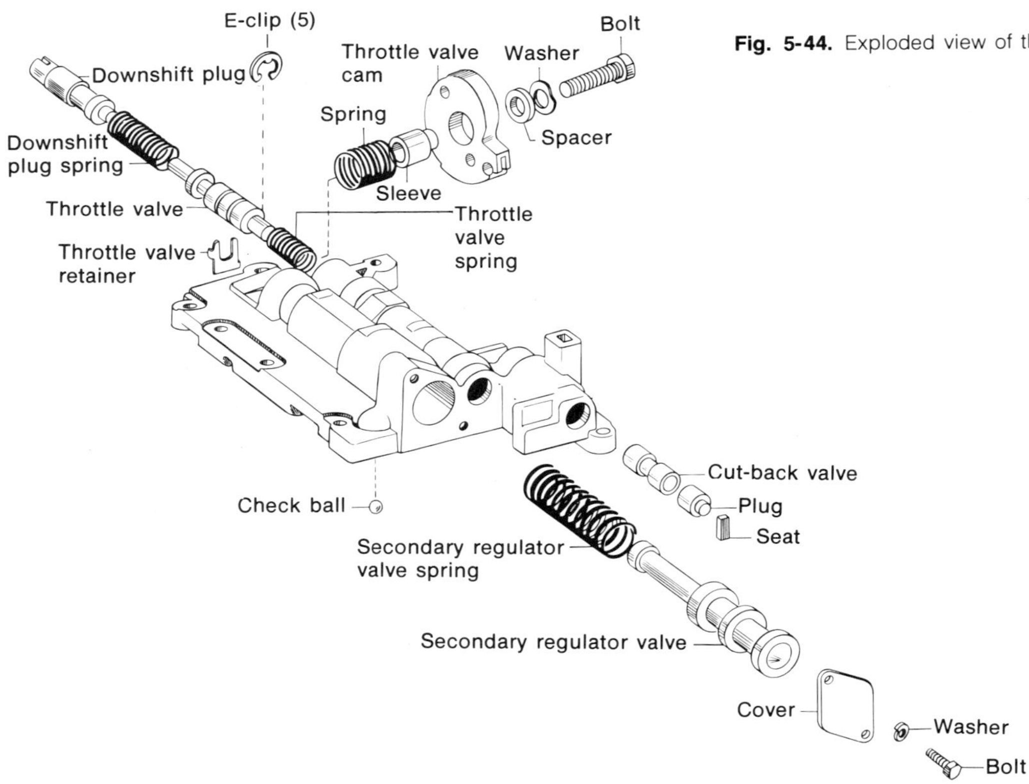

Fig. 5-44. Exploded view of throttle valve body.

cated in Fig. 5-45. Relieve the spring tension and remove the valve and its spring, keeping them together.

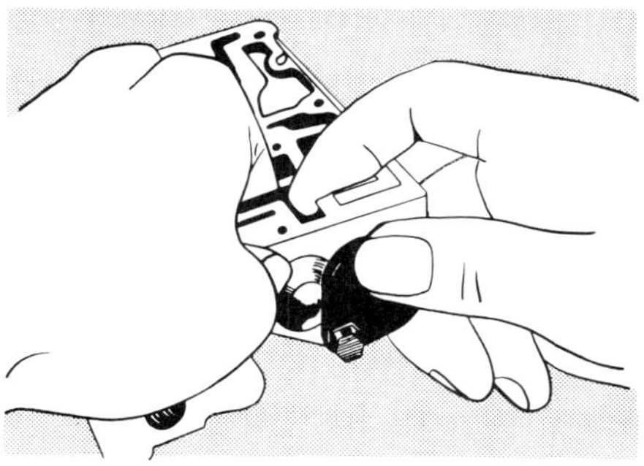

Fig. 5-45. Secondary regulator valve being removed.

4. Push the downshift plug into the valve body and temporarily retain it in this position by inserting the cut-back valve plug's seat piece, as indicated in Fig. 5-46. Then, using a 10-mm socket wrench, remove the throttle valve cam, the washers, the sleeve, and the thrust spring.

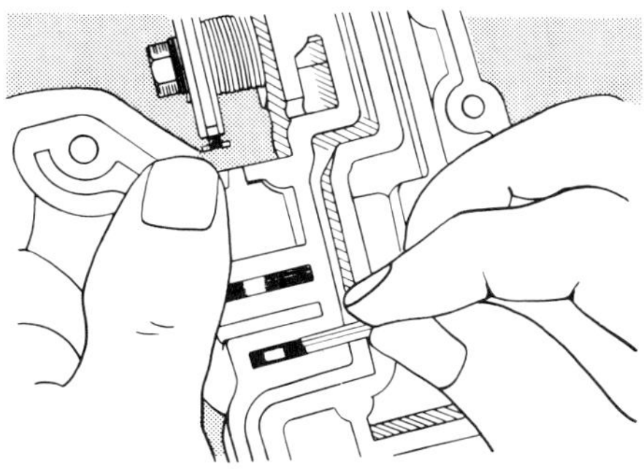

Fig. 5-46. Cut-back valve plug's seat piece being used to hold in downshift valve plug during cam removal.

5. Turn the valve body upside-down and press on the downshift plug so that the temporarily-installed seat piece will fall out. Then tilt the valve body and allow the downshift plug and its spring to fall out into the palm of your hand.
6. Using needle-nose pliers, pull out the throttle valve retainer. Then tilt the valve body and allow the throttle valve to fall out into your palm.
7. Remove the E-clip(s) and the throttle valve spring.

NOTE ——
Each E-clip is a shim of precise thickness. Make note of the number of E-clips installed. It is important to the operation of the transmission that the identical number of E-clips be installed during assembly.

8. Thoroughly wash all components in clean solvent, then dry them with moisture-free compressed air. If any valve or ball is worn or damaged, replace it. Unplug clogged ATF passages, and replace the valve body if its machined surface is gouged or distorted.

CAUTION ——
Do not use a scraper to remove foreign matter as this can make scratches and gouges that will permit ATF leakage or jam the valves. Do not wipe parts with a soft fluffy cloth that can leave behind lint, which can cause the valves to stick.

9. Inspect the springs. Replace any that is rusted, no longer stands square, has distorted coils, or is otherwise damaged. Replace springs that are shorter than the dimensions given in Fig. 5-47.

1 2 3

Spring	Minimum permissible length
1. Throttle valve spring	19.24 mm (.757 in.)
2. Downshift plug spring	43.00 mm (1.693 in.)
3. Secondary regulator valve spring	74.83 mm (2.946 in.)

Fig. 5-47. Correct minimum lengths for springs in throttle valve body.

To assemble:

1. Make sure that all parts are still perfectly clean and dry. Insert the throttle valve with its three closely-spaced lands first. If necessary, consult Fig. 5-44 given earlier. Install the throttle valve retainer as indicated in Fig. 5-48.

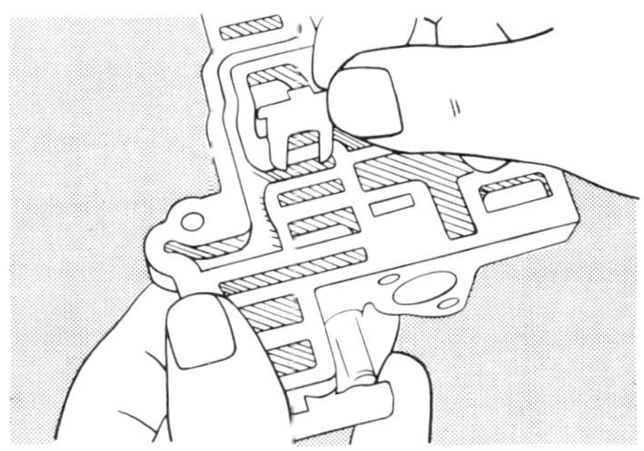

Fig. 5-48. Throttle valve retainer being installed. Notice orientation of tabs on retainer and retainer's position in valve body.

2. Install the original number of E-clips on the exposed end of the throttle valve, then install the throttle valve spring as shown in Fig. 5-49.

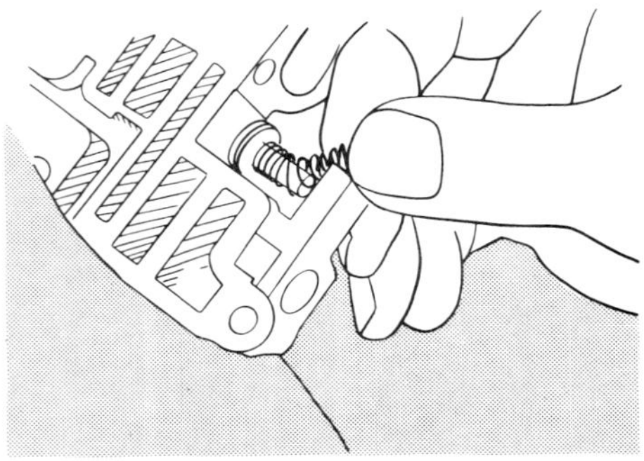

Fig. 5-49. Throttle valve spring being installed over end of throttle valve. Note position of E-clips between spring and valve body casting.

3. Insert the downshift plug spring so that it slips over the throttle valve. Install the downshift plug atop the spring—slotted end last. Then push the downshift plug in and temporarily keep it retracted by inserting the cut-back valve plug's seat piece. If necessary, refer to Fig. 5-46, given earlier.
4. Install the throttle cam assembly so that the spring engages the throttle valve body and the cam as indicated in Fig. 5-50. Torque the bolt to 6 to 8 Nm (53 to 71 in. lb.).

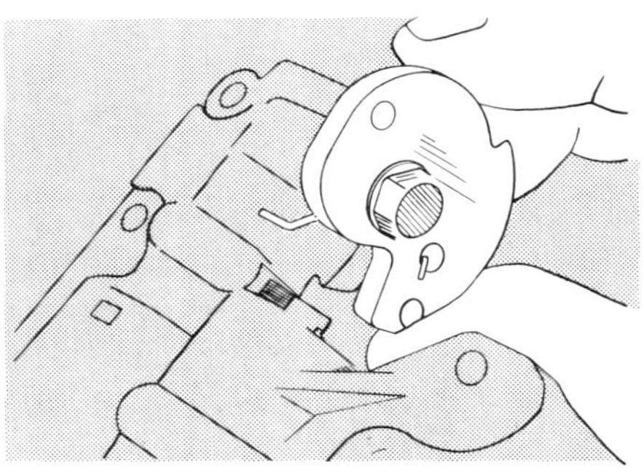

Fig. 5-50. Throttle valve cam spring correctly installed.

5. Remove the temporarily-installed seat piece. Then make sure that the roller of the downshift plug follows the smaller portion of the cam, as indicated in Fig. 5-51.
6. Loosely install the cover plate with one bolt. Insert the secondary regulator valve and its spring as shown in Fig. 5-52, then fully install the plate. Torque the bolts to 5 to 6 Nm (44 to 53 in. lb.).

Fig. 5-51. Downshift plug roller correctly oriented with throttle valve cam.

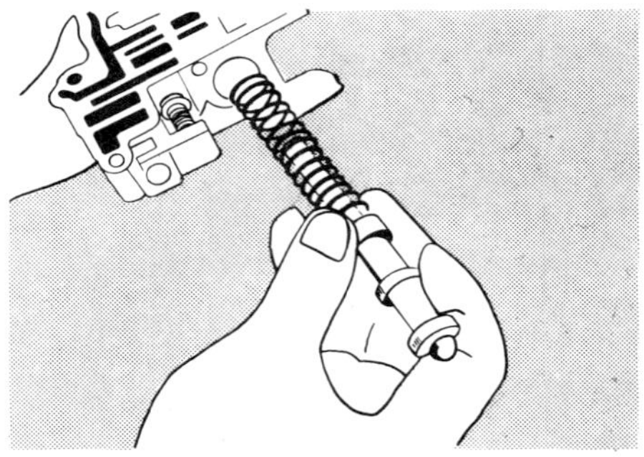

Fig. 5-52. Secondary regulator valve and spring being installed. Notice loosely-installed cover that can be pivoted into place to hold valve against spring tension while second bolt is installed.

7. Install the cut-back valve—small end first. Install the plug, protrusion outermost, then install the seat piece.

> **NOTE —**
>
> As an adhesive to hold the seat in place, coat the seat piece with Vaseline only.

8. Reserve the check ball for installation in the throttle valve body just before the full valve body assembly is reassembled.

Disassembling and Assembling 2nd Gear/3rd Gear Shift Valve Body

Fig. 5-53 is an exploded view of the 2nd gear/3rd gear shift valve body. The part numbers are given for the individual components. Keep the parts in order while they are disassembled, because many components of the valve body look alike and it is easy to mix them up. If, during assembly, you are unsure of the correct location for a spring, it can be identified using the measurements given in **6. Automatic Transmission Technical Data.**

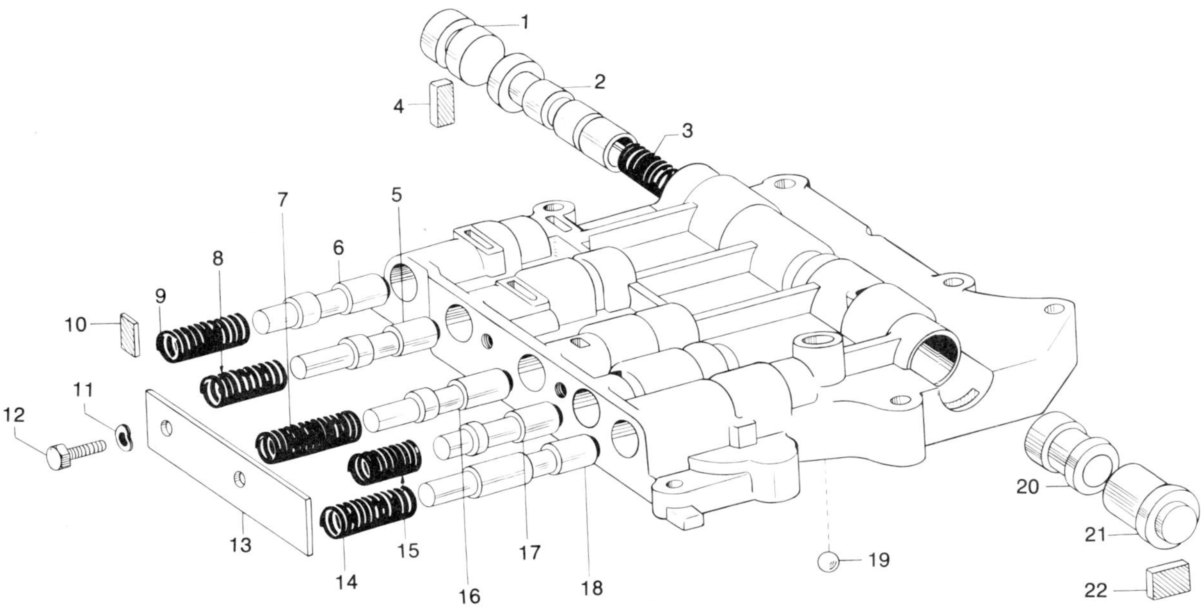

1. 2nd/3rd gear shift valve plug
2. 2nd/3rd gear shift valve
3. Intermediate shift valve spring
4. Seat
5. Intermediate modulator valve
6. Detent regulator valve
7. Reverse sequence valve spring
8. Intermediate modulator valve spring
9. Detent regulator valve spring
10. Seat
11. Washer
12. Bolt
13. Side cover
14. Low modulator valve spring
15. Governor modulator valve spring
16. Reverse sequence valve
17. Governor modulator valve
18. Low modulator valve
19. Ball (3)
20. Intermediate shift valve
21. Intermediate shift valve plug
22. Seat

Fig. 5-53. Exploded view of 2nd gear/3rd gear shift valve body.

To disassemble:

1. Make note of the ball valve locations in the 2nd gear/3rd gear shift valve body. Then place your hand over the valve body to cover all three check balls, as indicated in Fig. 5-54. Invert the valve body, catching the two rubber and one steel ball valves in your hand.

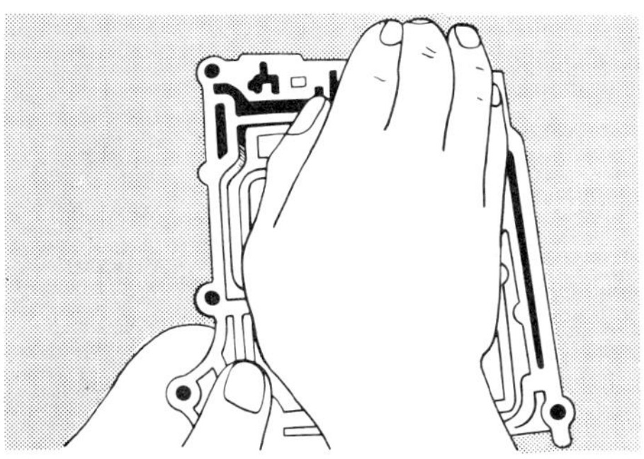

Fig. 5-54. Hand in position to catch ball valves as valve body is inverted.

2. Keeping the valve body inverted, press in on the intermediate shift valve plug so that the seat piece drops out. Then remove the plug, the intermediate shift valve, and its spring.
3. With the valve body still inverted, move the 2nd gear/3rd gear shift valve plug in and out with your fingertip until the seat piece for the plug drops out. Then remove the plug and the 2nd gear/3rd gear shift valve.
4. Using an 8-mm socket wrench, remove one bolt from the valve body's side cover. Loosen the other bolt, then slightly rotate the cover as shown in Fig. 5-55 so that you can lift out the low modulator valve spring and shake out the low modulator valve.

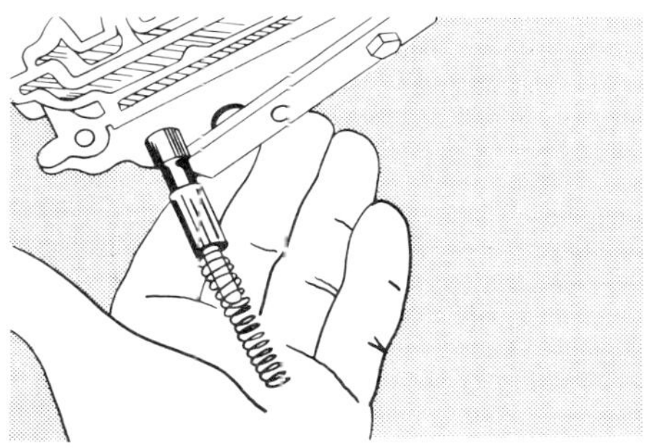

Fig. 5-55. Low modulator valve and spring being removed. Notice how side cover has been rotated. Always store each spring with its own valve to prevent mixups.

5. Rotate the side cover a bit more so that you can remove the governor modulator valve and its spring. Rotate the cover further and remove the reverse sequence valve and its spring.
6. Fully remove the side cover, then remove the intermediate modulator valve and its spring.
7. Remove the seat piece for the detent regulator valve, as shown in Fig. 5-56. Then remove the detent regulator valve and its spring.

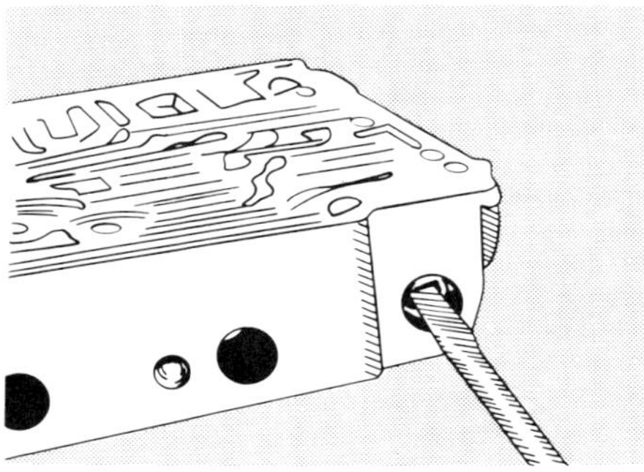

Fig. 5-56. Seat piece for detent regulator valve being lifted out with tip of screwdriver. Be careful not to damage spring or valve body.

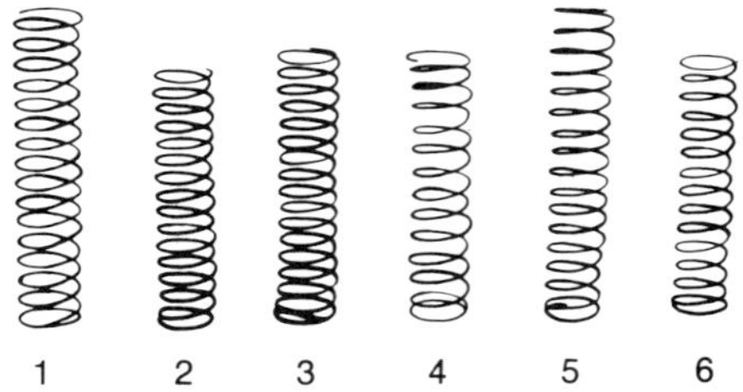

Spring	Minimum permissible length—mm (in.)
1. Detent regulator valve spring	
(1975-1977)	42.35 (1.667)
(1978 and later)	32.08 (1.263)
2. Intermediate modulator valve spring	35.43 (1.395)
3. Reverse sequence valve spring	36.83 (1.450)
4. Governor modulator valve spring	36.07 (1.420)
5. Low modulator valve spring	42.35 (1.667)
6. 2nd/3rd gear shift valve spring	35.10 (1.382)

Fig. 5-57. Correct minimum lengths for springs in 2nd gear/3rd gear shift valve body. Though same length is given for detent regulator valve spring on 1975 through 1977 cars and low modulator valve spring, the two are not identical and should not be interchanged.

8. Thoroughly wash all components in clean solvent, then dry them with moisture-free compressed air. If any valve or ball is worn or damaged, replace it. Unplug clogged ATF passages, and replace the valve body if its machined surface is gouged or distorted.

CAUTION —
Do not use a scraper to remove foreign matter as this can make scratches and gouges that will permit ATF leakage or jam the valves. Do not wipe parts with a soft fluffy cloth that can leave behind lint, which can cause the valve to stick.

9. Inspect the springs. Replace any that is rusted, no longer stands square, has distorted coils, or is otherwise damaged. Replace springs that are shorter than the dimensions given in Fig. 5-57.

To assemble:

1. Insert the detent regulator valve, round end first, into the valve body. Insert the detent regulator valve spring, then hold it down with the tip of a broad-bladed screwdriver while you install the seat piece (Fig. 5-58). After you have slipped the seat piece over the edge of the spring, you can use needle-nose pliers to hold the spring in—straddling the seat piece. Make sure that the seat piece fully covers the end of the spring.

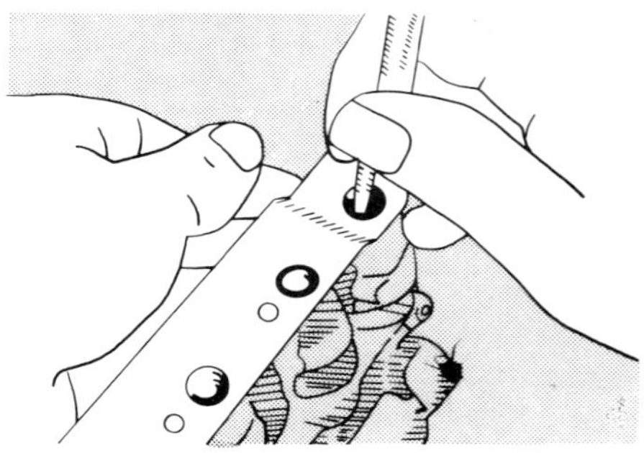

Fig. 5-58. Seat piece for detent regulator valve spring being inserted.

2. Loosely install the side cover with one bolt at its short end. Then insert the reverse sequence valve and its spring as indicated in Fig. 5-59, swinging the cover partially into place to hold the spring compressed in the bore.
3. Using the procedure described in the preceding step, install the governor modulator valve and its spring, and then the low modulator valve and its spring. Install the second side cover bolt. Using an 8-mm socket wrench, torque both bolts to 5 to 6 Nm (44 to 53 in. lb.).

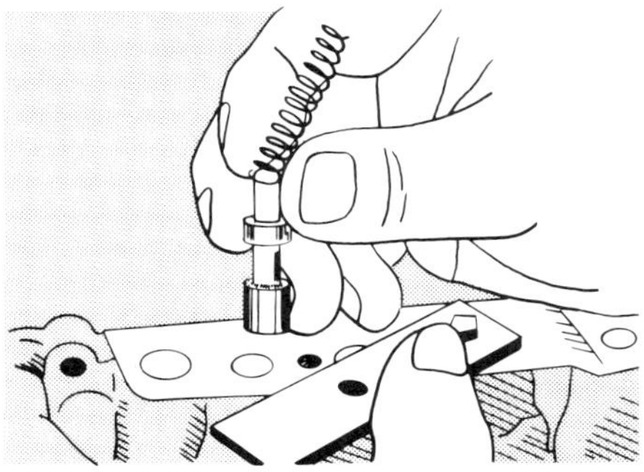

Fig. 5-59. Reverse sequence valve and its spring being installed. Notice how partially installed side cover can be rotated into position to hold in the compressed spring.

4. Insert the 2nd/3rd gear shift valve, small end first, into the valve body. Then install the 2nd/3rd gear shift valve plug and its seat piece—engaging the seat piece in the groove in the plug.
5. Insert the intermediate shift valve spring, the intermediate shift valve, and the intermediate shift valve plug, as indicated in Fig. 5-60. Press in the plug against spring tension and install its seat piece.

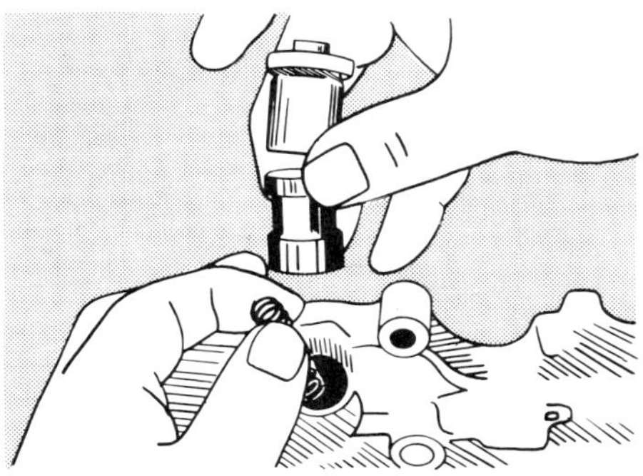

Fig. 5-60. Intermediate shift valve and related parts being installed.

6. Install one rubber check ball in the location shown in Fig. 5-61 and the other rubber check ball in the location shown in Fig. 5-62. The balls are identical and may be interchanged.

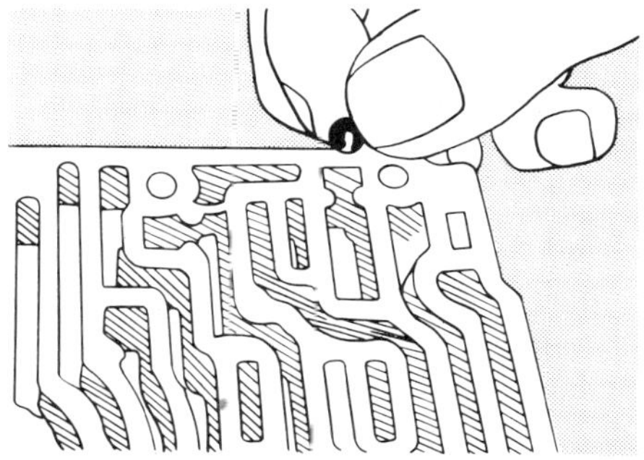

Fig. 5-61. Rubber check ball being installed in square recess near edge of valve body.

Fig. 5-62. Rubber check ball being installed in square recess in middle of valve body.

7. Install the steel check ball in the location shown in Fig. 5-63.

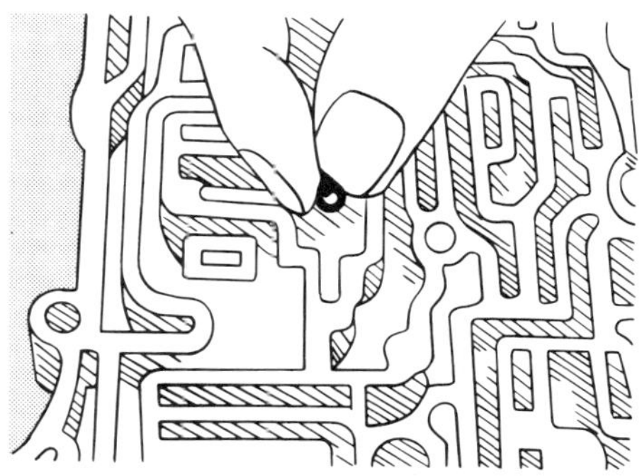

Fig. 5-63. Steel check ball being installed in square recess in middle of valve body, just a short way from the location for the rubber check ball shown in Fig. 5-62.

Removing and Installing Extension Housing and Governor

(transmission in car)

Very often, the governor must be cleaned, repaired, or replaced at the same time as the valve body assembly is cleaned, repaired, or replaced. As with valve body servicing, governor servicing can be done without removing the transmission from the car. The procedures given here can also be used to correct ATF leaks past a faulty extension housing gasket.

To remove governor:

1. Raise the car on a hoist or support it on stands designed for the purpose.
2. Using a file or a center punch, mark adjacent points on the rear axle's pinion flange and the rear universal joint so that the driveshaft can be reinstalled in its original position on the pinion flange. Then remove the driveshaft as described in **DRIVESHAFT AND REAR AXLE.**
3. Place a jack beneath the transmission, then raise the jack until the transmission/engine assembly is firmly supported. Unbolt the rear transmission mount crossmember and remove it.
4. Using water pump pliers, unscrew the knurled ferrule nut that holds the speedometer cable conduit to the speedometer driven gear assembly on the transmission's extension housing. Then detach the cable from the transmission, being careful not to bend the cable sharply. See Fig. 5-64.

Fig. 5-64. Speedometer cable being detached from transmission.

5. Using a 12-mm wrench, remove the retaining bolt for the speedometer driven gear assembly. Then, using a screwdriver as indicated in Fig. 5-65, carefully pry the speedometer driven gear assembly out of the transmission's extension housing.

Fig. 5-65. Speedometer driven gear assembly being pried out of extension housing.

6. Remove the bolts that hold the extension housing to the transmission case. Then remove the extension housing. See Fig. 5-66.

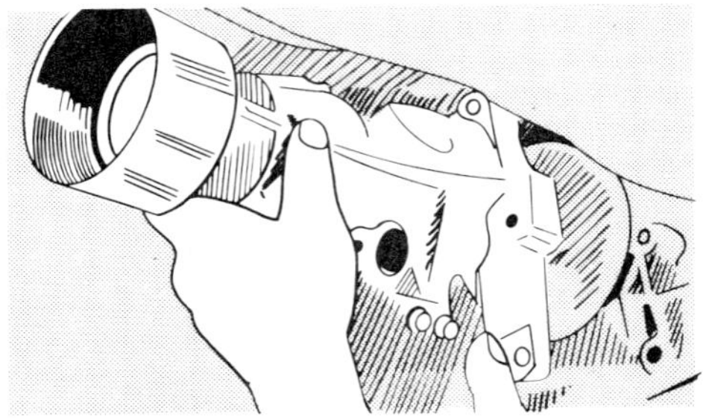

Fig. 5-66. Extension housing being removed.

7. To remove the speedometer drivegear, first remove the snap ring from the shaft, then slide off the drivegear (Fig. 5-67). If you intend to remove the governor, also remove the speedometer drivegear's Woodruff key and the second snap ring.

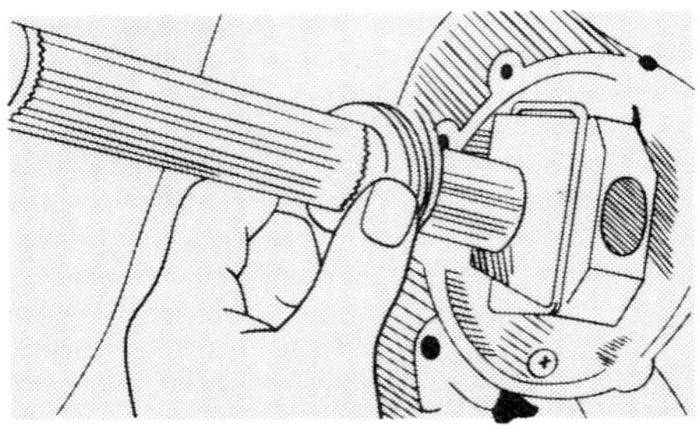

Fig. 5-67. Speedometer drivegear being removed from output shaft.

To remove, repair, and install governor:

1. Remove the extension housing. Remove the speedometer drive gear and its key and snap rings. This work is described in the preceding procedure.
2. Using a large screwdriver, as indicated in Fig. 5-68, lift the wire retaining clip that is on the flat side of the governor body. With the clip lifted, slide the governor off the shaft.

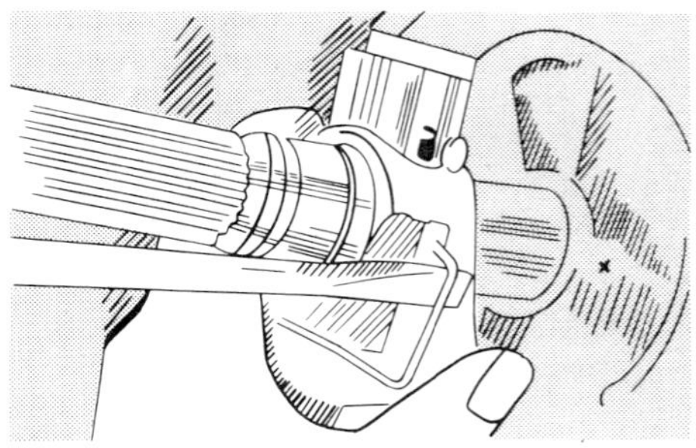

Fig. 5-68. Governor being removed. Notice how screwdriver is being used to keep clip lifted.

3. Remove the E-clip, as indicated in Fig. 5-69. Lift off the governor weight. Remove first the guide shaft and spring, as shown in Fig. 5-70, then remove the valve—taking these three components out through the center bore of the governor body.

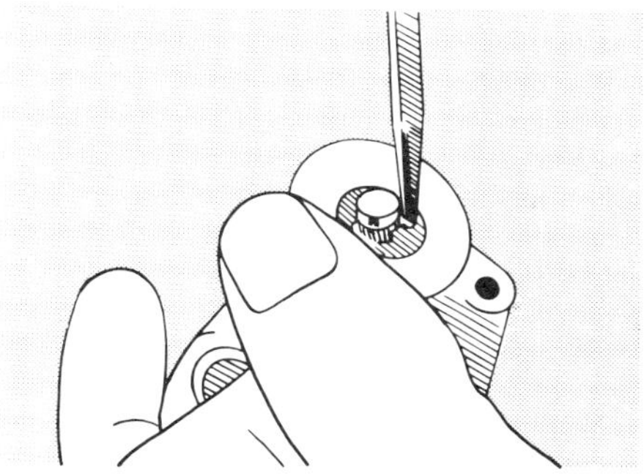

Fig. 5-69. E-clip being removed from end of guide shaft. Insert finger in governor body's center bore to keep the guide shaft from flying out suddenly under spring tension.

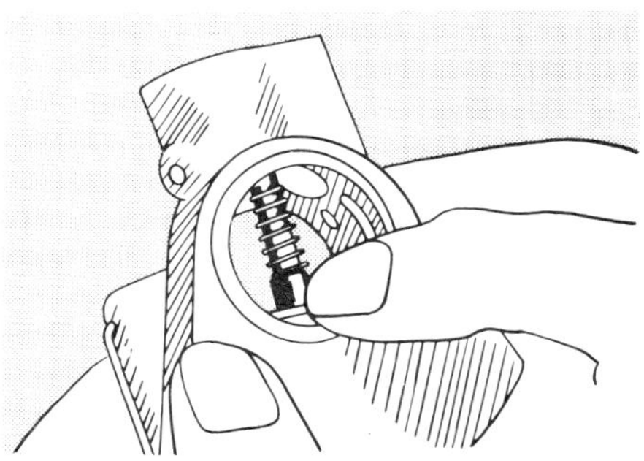

Fig. 5-70. Guide shaft and spring being removed through center bore of governor body. Once these two components are removed, you can remove the valve through the center bore.

4. Carefully inspect the governor body. If the body is cracked or if its valve bore is scored, replace the governor as a unit. Clean the governor body, checking especially that the ATF passages are clear.

5. Inspect the governor valve, the guide shaft, the weight, the spring, and the E-clip. Replace individual components that are worn, rusted, or otherwise damaged.

6. Thoroughly clean all parts in clean solvent, then dry them with moisture-free compressed air. Do not wipe the parts with a cloth that may leave behind bits of lint, which could cause the valve to jam.

7. Install the valve, small end first, in the governor body. See Fig. 5-71. Make sure that the valve both slides and rotates freely in its bore. If not, there is dirt or rust that should be cleaned away or the rusted component should be replaced. If the governor bore is distorted, replace the governor as a unit.

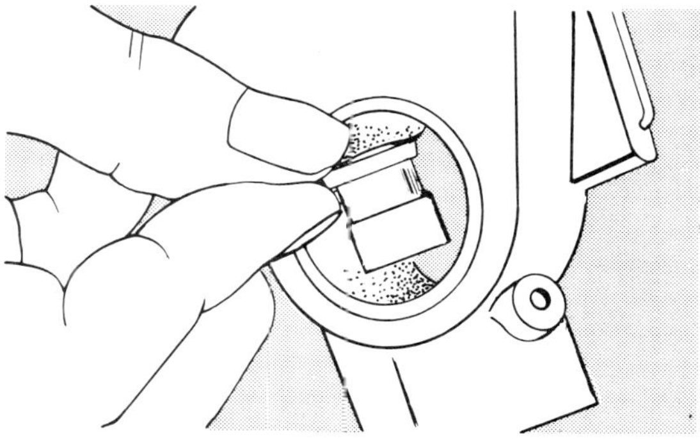

Fig. 5-71. Valve being installed in governor body.

8. Install the spring and then the guide shaft. Hold the guide shaft in against spring tension while you install the weight—recessed side outermost—and the E-clip.

9. Install the governor on the transmission's output shaft, holding the wire retainer up with the tip of a screwdriver until the governor is in position. Make certain that the retainer fully enters the hole in the shaft so that the governor is locked firmly in position.

NOTE ——

Be sure to install the governor so that the flat boss and the groove for the wire retainer are toward the rear of the car. If necessary, refer to Fig. 5-68, given earlier.

To install extension housing:

1. Thoroughly clean the extension housing in clean solvent, then dry it with moisture-free compressed air. Clean and inspect the speedometer gears and related parts. Replace worn or damaged components.

2. If the governor was removed, install the front snap ring for the speedometer drivegear and insert the Woodruff key into the shaft. Install the speedometer drivegear and its second snap ring.

3. Place a new extension housing gasket on the transmission, using Vaseline as an adhesive to hold it in place.

4. Install the extension housing, installing all six bolts finger-tight. The two short bolts go in the two bottom holes. Working diagonally, torque the bolts in stages to 30 to 40 Nm (22 to 30 ft. lb.).

5. Install the speedometer driven gear assembly. Using a 12-mm socket wrench, torque the bolt for the retainer to 14 to 15 Nm (10 to 11 ft. lb.).

6. Make sure that the felt gasket and the collar washer are correctly installed on the end of the speedometer cable (Fig. 5-72). Then, being careful not to bend the cable sharply, reconnect the speedometer cable to the transmission and tighten the knurled ferrule nut to hold the cable in place.

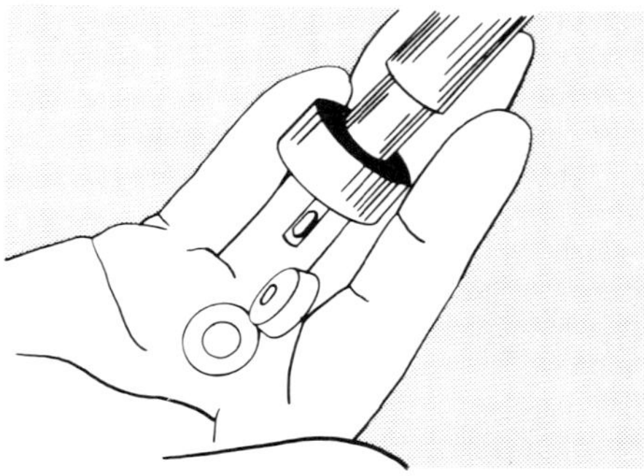

Fig. 5-72. Felt gasket and collar washer, which should be installed in that order inside ferrule nut.

7. Reinstall the rear transmission mount cross-member. Torque the bolts to 20 to 25 Nm (15 to 18 ft. lb.). Then remove the jack that has been supporting the transmission/engine assembly.
8. With careful reference to the marks you made prior to removal, install the driveshaft as described in **DRIVESHAFT AND REAR AXLE.** Torque the four bolts that hold the driveshaft to the pinion flange to 35 to 40 Nm (26 to 30 ft. lb.). On cars with a two-piece driveshaft, torque the bolts that hold the center bearing to the body to 35 to 40 Nm (26 to 30 ft. lb.).
9. Lower the car to the ground. Check and, if necessary, correct the ATF level as described in **LUBRICATION AND MAINTENANCE.**

5.4 Disassembling and Assembling Internal Control Linkage

The internal control linkage, connected to the manual valve shaft and operated by the selector lever in the passenger compartment, can be removed and repaired after the valve body has been removed. It is unnecessary to remove the transmission from the car.

To disassemble:

1. Using a 10-mm socket wrench, as shown in Fig. 5-73, unbolt and remove the parking lock pawl bracket.
2. Remove the spring from the parking lock pawl pivot pin, as shown in Fig. 5-74.
3. Remove the pivot pin as shown in Fig. 5-75, then remove the parking lock pawl.

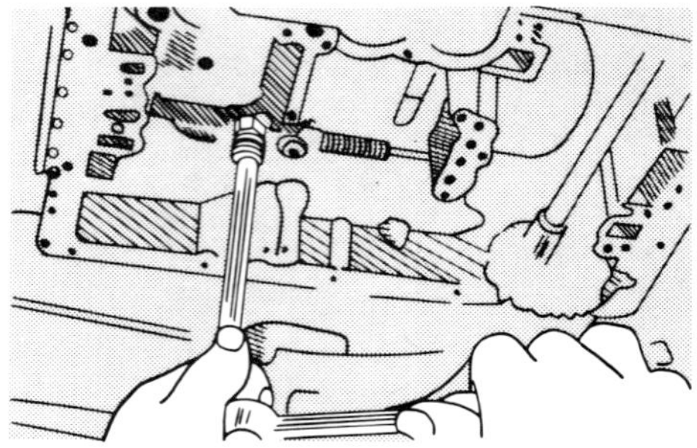

Fig. 5-73. Parking lock pawl bracket being unbolted. There are two bolts.

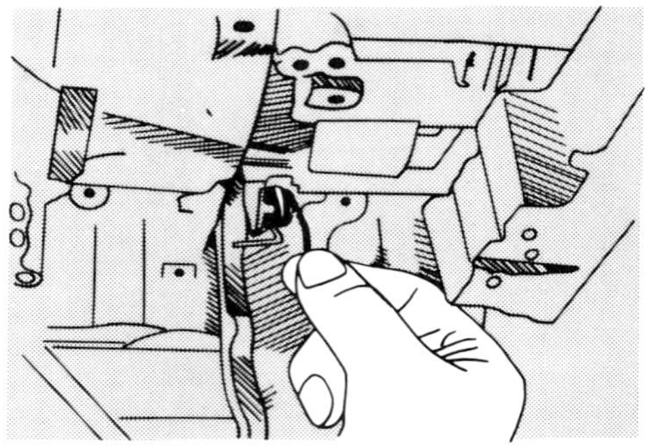

Fig. 5-74. Spring for parking lock pawl being removed.

Fig. 5-75. Pin for parking lock pawl being removed.

4. Disconnect the parking lock operating rod from the detent lever (Fig. 5-76).

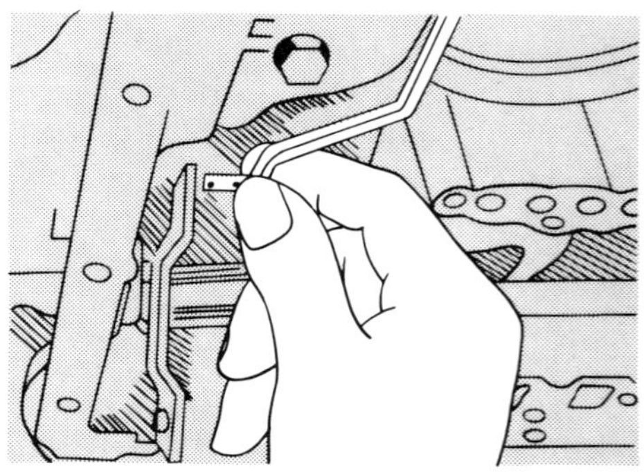

Fig. 5-76. Parking lock operating rod being disconnected from detent lever on manual shaft.

5. Remove the nut from the manual shaft as shown in Fig. 5-77. Then remove the manual shaft lever.

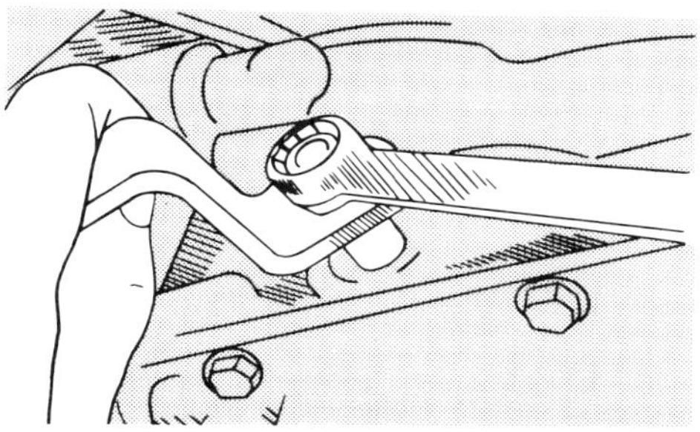

Fig. 5-77. Manual shaft lever being removed.

6. Using a hammer and a punch, drive out the rolled pin that holds the detent lever to the manual shaft. See Fig. 5-78. Slide the manual shaft out of the detent lever, as indicated in Fig. 5-79. Remove the detent lever, then slide the manual shaft fully out of the transmission case.

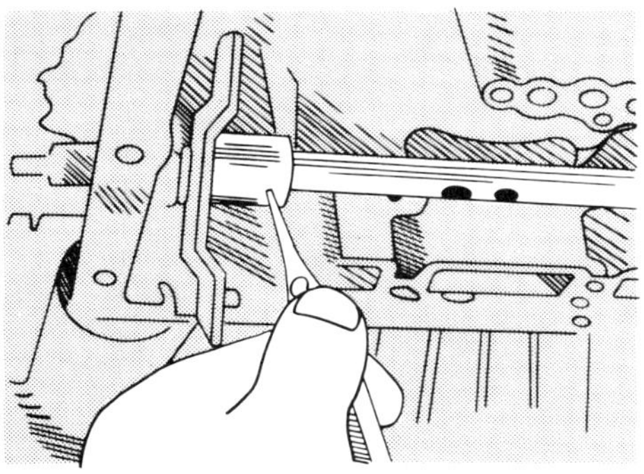

Fig. 5-78. Rolled pin being driven out of detent lever and manual shaft.

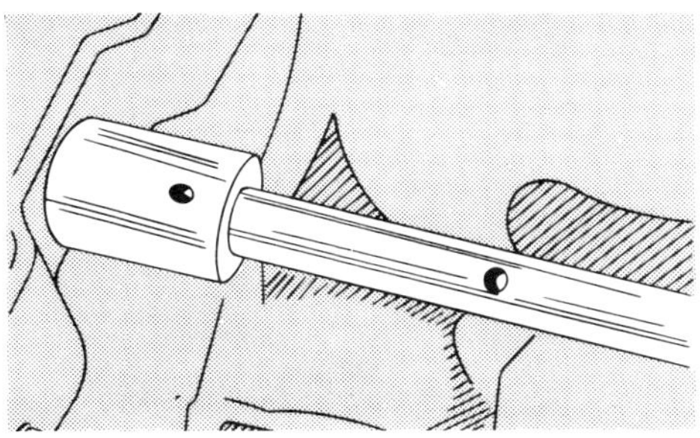

Fig. 5-79. Manual shaft being withdrawn from detent lever and transmission case.

To install:

1. Replace both manual shaft ATF seals as described in **4.2 Locating and Stopping External ATF Leaks.** Then position the detent lever inside the transmission and carefully insert the manual shaft until the rolled pin hole in the shaft is aligned with the hole in the hub of the detent lever.
2. Drive in a new rolled pin so that its slot is at right angles to the shaft axis.
3. Reconnect the parking lock operating rod to the detent lever.
4. Install the parking lock pawl and its pivot pin. Then install the spring over the end of the pivot pin so that the ends of the spring are in the positions shown in Fig. 5-80.

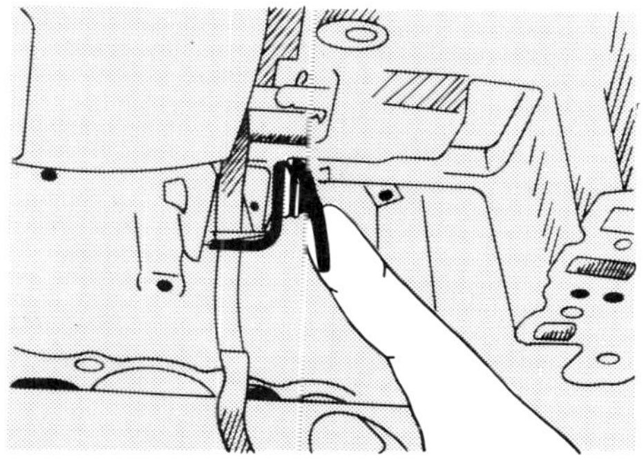

Fig. 5-80. Parking lock pawl spring correctly installed. Notice orientation of spring ends.

5. Make sure that the operating rod is fully forward. Then install the parking pawl bracket (Fig. 5-81), screwing the bolts in finger-tight. Push the bracket rearward and check that the pawl operates freely. After free operation is obtained, torque the bolts to 6 to 7 Nm (53 to 62 in. lb.). Check that the parking lock pawl still operates freely, then install the valve body and the ATF pan.

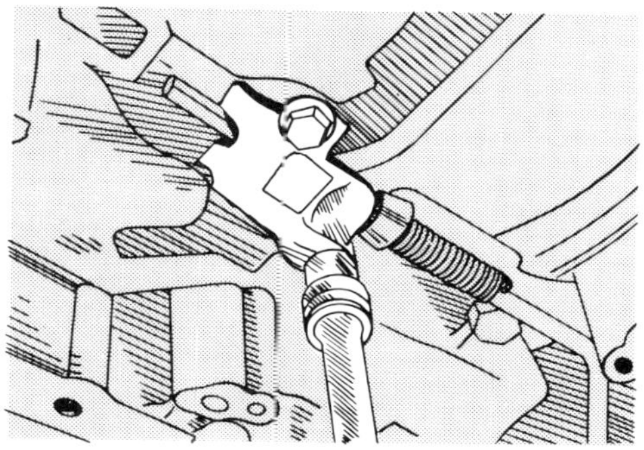

Fig. 5-81. Parking lock pawl bracket being installed.

5.5 Disassembling and Assembling Transmission

Thoroughly clean the outside of the transmission before you disassemble it so that dirt will not enter the hydraulic controls or the mechanical parts. Study the repair procedures on the following pages. If they require equipment that you do not have, the transmission should be turned over to a specialist before any disassembly.

> ***CAUTION —***
> *If you lack the skills, the tools, or a suitable workshop for automatic transmission work, we suggest you leave these repairs to an Authorized Dealer or other qualified shop. We especially urge you to consult an Authorized Dealer before attempting repairs on a car still covered by the new-car warranty.*

To disassemble transmission into main parts:

1. Using a 17-mm socket wrench, remove the two larger bolts that hold the bellhousing to the transmission. Use a 14-mm socket wrench to remove the four smaller bolts.
2. Using a suitable puller, remove the ATF pump's ATF seal. If necessary, consult **5.1 Removing, Cleaning, Inspecting, and Installing Torque Converter.**
3. Using a 13-mm wrench, remove the seven bolts that hold the ATF pump to the front of the transmission case. See Fig. 5-82.

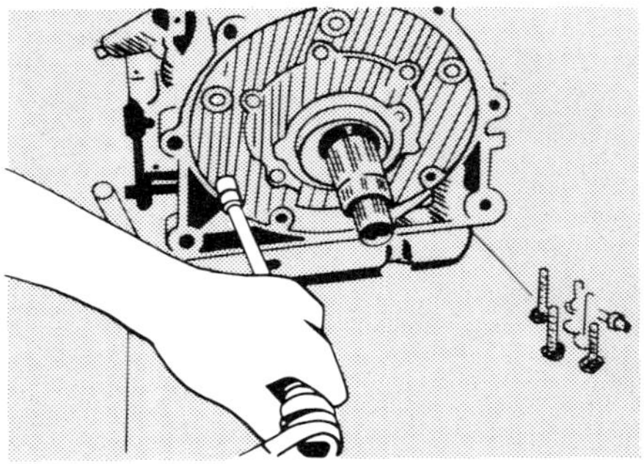

Fig. 5-82. ATF pump bolts being removed.

4. Using a puller (Fig. 5-83) that will grip the back of the spline on the ATF pump's stator support, pull the ATF pump free of the transmission case.

> ***CAUTION —***
> *Be careful not to damage the bushing contact surface that is between the splined part of the stator support and the ATF pump body.*

5. Grasp the ATF pump's stator support and pull the ATF pump off the transmission. Then grasp the input shaft and pull the forward clutch assembly out of the case.

> ***CAUTION —***
> *Be careful not to lose the needle-roller thrust bearing and the races (Fig. 5-84) that are between the forward clutch and the direct and reverse clutch.*

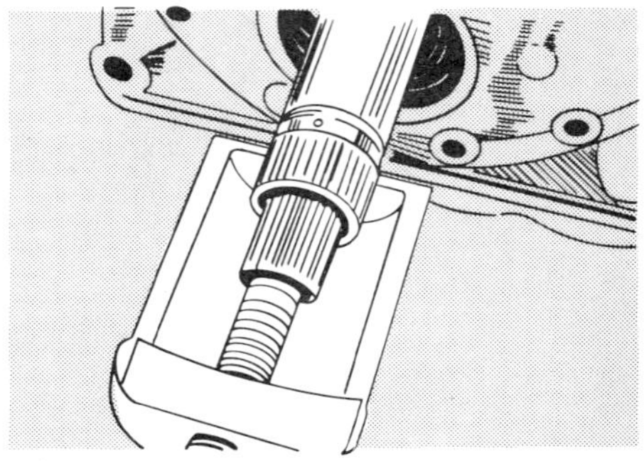

Fig. 5-83. Toyota special service tool 09610-20011 (steering pitman arm puller) being used to pull ATF pump free of transmission.

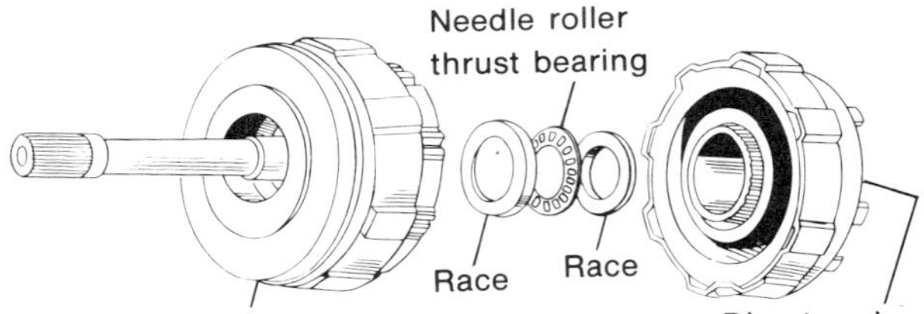

Fig. 5-84. Forward clutch shown in relation to thrust bearing and direct and reverse clutch. Once the ATF pump is removed, the forward clutch can easily be pulled out of the transmission case.

6. Remove the direct and reverse clutch, as shown in Fig. 5-85.

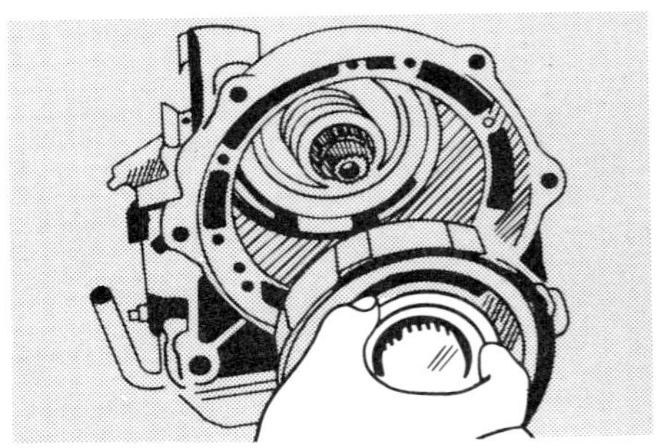

Fig. 5-85. Direct and reverse clutch being removed.

7. Using a 12-mm wrench, remove the bolt from the speedometer driven gear retainer. Then remove the speedometer driven gear assembly.

8. Using a suitable puller, remove the rear ATF seal and the dust seal from the transmission's extension housing. If necessary, consult **4.2 Locating and Stopping External ATF Leaks.**

9. Unbolt the extension housing from the transmission case. Then remove the extension housing as indicated in Fig. 5-86 and discard the gasket.

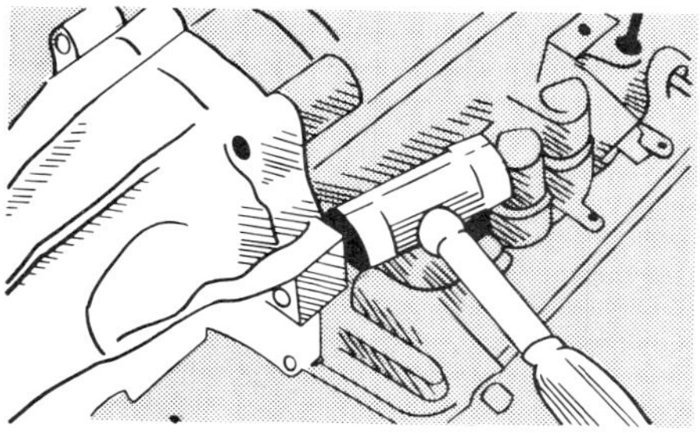

Fig. 5-86. Soft hammer being used to loosen extension housing. Once freed of the transmission case, the extension housing can easily be pulled off to the rear.

10. Remove the snap ring and then the speedometer drivegear from the transmission's output shaft. Remove the second snap ring and the Woodruff key.

11. Using a screwdriver as indicated in Fig. 5-87, lift the wire retainer for the governor. Then, keeping the retainer lifted, pull the governor off the output shaft.

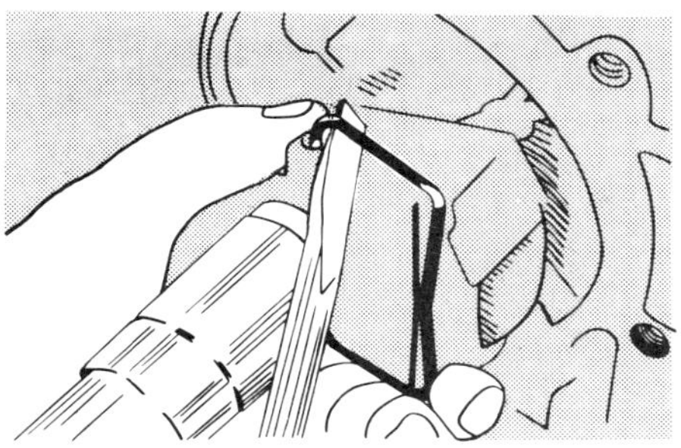

Fig. 5-87. Governor being removed from transmission's output shaft.

12. Remove the ATF pan and the valve body assembly as described in **5.2 Removing and Installing ATF Pan and Valve Body.**

13. Position a rag to catch each accumulator piston, then use low-pressure (1 bar or 14 psi) compressed air at the points indicated in Fig. 5-88 to expel the piston gently.

WARNING —

Keep your face away to avoid being struck, should a piston accidentally fly out. Do not use regular high-pressure compressed air.

Fig. 5-88. Accumulator piston being expelled. Inject low-pressure compressed air at points indicated by arrows.

14. Remove the internal control linkage as described in **5.4 Disassembling and Assembling Internal Control Linkage.**

15. Using a 14-mm socket wrench, remove the two center support bolts (Fig. 5-89). It is not abnormal for the second bolt to be loose after the other bolt has been removed.

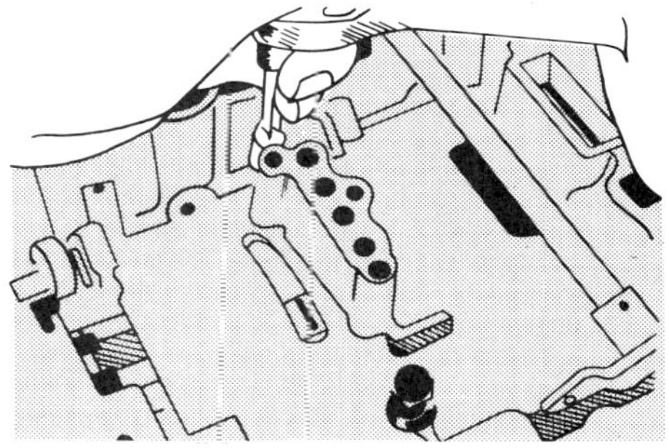

Fig. 5-89. Center support bolt being removed. Second bolt can be seen at bottom of illustration.

16. Remove the center support together with the sun gear assembly, taking it out through the front of the transmission case as indicated in Fig. 5-90.

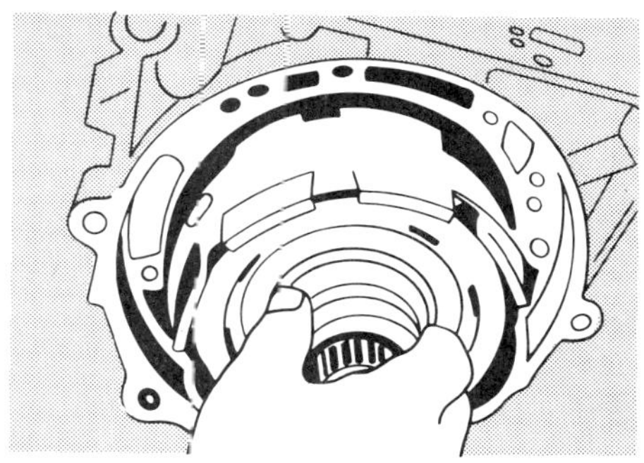

Fig. 5-90. Sun gear assembly and center support being removed.

1

17. Remove the retaining ring for the reaction plate, as indicated in Fig. 5-91.

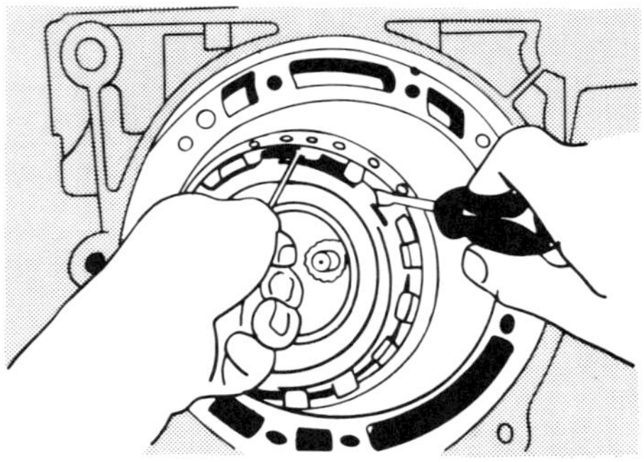

Fig. 5-91. Reaction plate retaining ring being removed. Use a very long screwdriver to compress the retaining ring, then lift it from its groove with a hook made from coat hanger wire.

18. Grasp the intermediate shaft and pull the remaining parts out of the transmission case. If the rear thrust bearing and races do not come out along with the rear parts group, remove the bearing components separately in order to prevent their loss.

NOTE ——
Assembly of the transmission is covered as the final part of each of the disassembly and assembly procedures given under the unnumbered headings that follow.

Disassembling and Assembling Accumulators, Transmission Case, and Rear Brake Pistons

The accumulators can be serviced without removing the transmission from the car. However, the work is much easier if the transmission has been removed. If the transmission is in the car, it may still be necessary to expel the accumulator pistons with compressed air as described earlier in Fig. 5-88. In the procedures that follow, it is assumed that the accumulator pistons and their springs were removed as part of initial transmission disassembly. An exploded view of the rear brake pistons is given in Fig. 5-92.

To disassemble:

1. To remove the return springs for the rear brake pistons, obtain Toyota special service tool 00002-00223-03 (Fig. 5-93). Install the special tool so that its ring is against the return spring seat, as shown in Fig. 5-94. Use a 17-mm wrench to tighten the bolts evenly—and just enough to compress the springs slightly.

CAUTION ——
Overtightening the bolts will damage the springs or the spring seat.

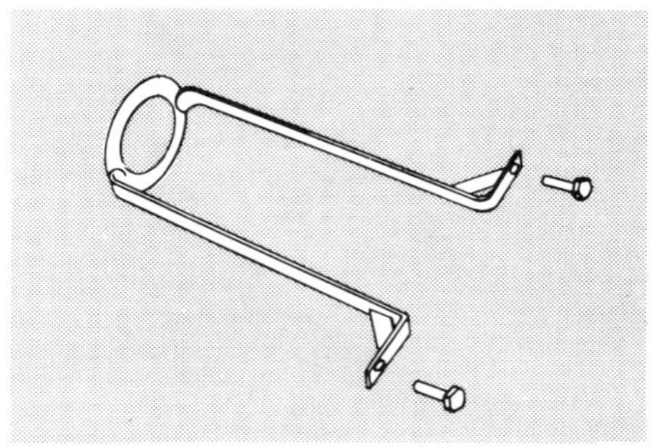

Fig. 5-93. Toyota special service tool used for compressing rear brake piston return springs.

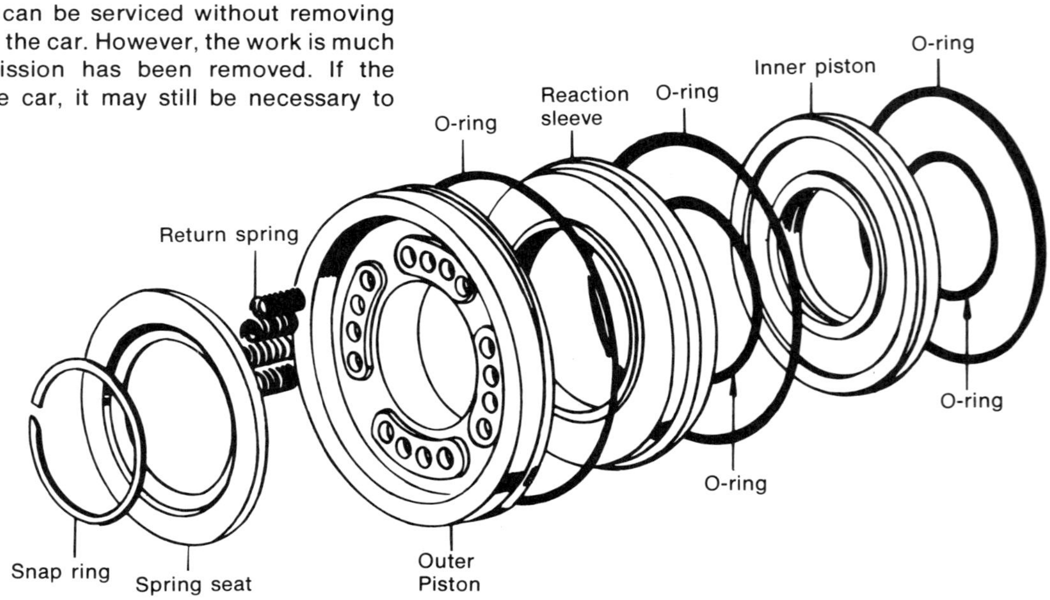

Fig. 5-92. Exploded view of rear brake pistons.

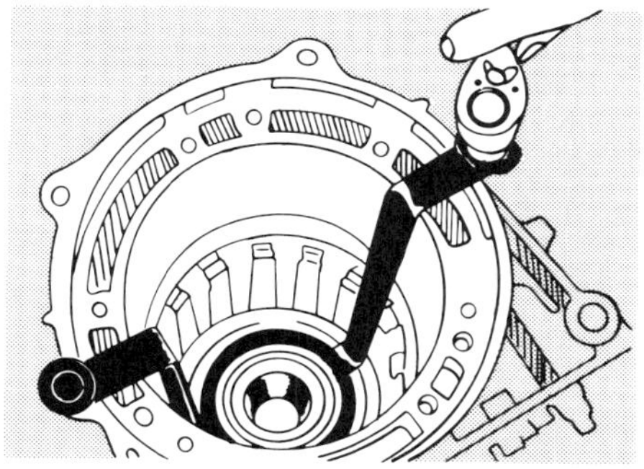

Fig. 5-94. Return springs being compressed. Notice position of ring part of tool against spring seat. Tighten bolts evenly in stages.

2. Using snap ring pliers, remove the snap ring for the spring seat. Then gradually unbolt the special service tool until the springs are no longer under tension. Remove the tool and lift out the spring seat.
3. Remove the 16 return springs, keeping them together to prevent loss.
4. Place several clean shop rags on the workbench. Then place the transmission case, front-end-down, atop the rags. Use compressed air to expel the rear brake outer piston and the reaction sleeve from the case. See Fig. 5-95.

> **NOTE ——**
> If the application of compressed air fails to pop the piston and the sleeve out of the case, so that they fall onto the rags, you will have to lift out the piston with needle-nose pliers, then lift out the reaction sleeve with two hooks made from coat hanger wire. Be careful not to damage the return spring bores as you grip them with pliers.

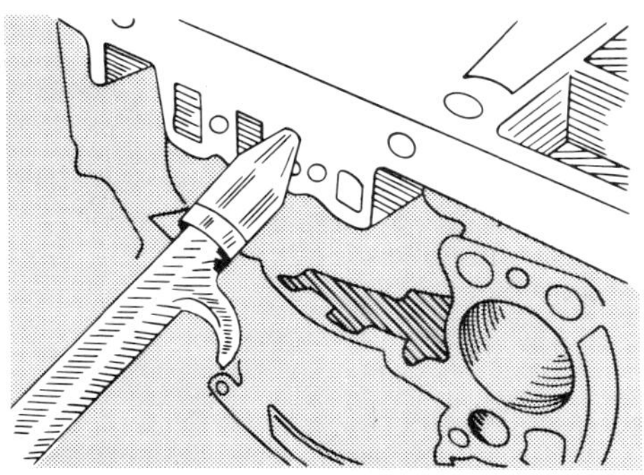

Fig. 5-95. Compressed air being injected into outer piston ATF hole.

5. Using a hook made from coat hanger wire, lift out the inner piston (Fig. 5-96).

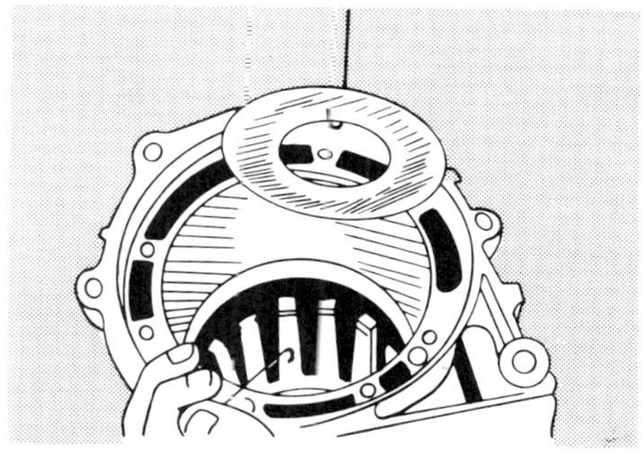

Fig. 5-96. Inner piston being lifted out of case.

6. Using your fingers only (to prevent scratches in the O-ring grooves), remove the O-rings from the pistons and the reaction sleeve.
7. Remove the rear cover from the transmission case by taking out the screws. Discard the gasket.
8. Remove the ATF cooler line fittings and the ATF pressure tap plugs. Discard the O-rings.
9. Thoroughly wash all components in clean solvent, then dry them with moisture-free compressed air. Unplug clogged ATF passages, especially in the case.

> ***CAUTION ——***
> *Do not use a scraper to remove foreign matter as this can make scratches and gouges that will permit ATF leakage or jam the valves. Do not wipe parts with a soft fluffy cloth that can leave behind lint. Lint can clog the ATF strainer or cause the control valves to stick.*

10. Carefully inspect the case for cracks and other damage. Check that the gasket surfaces are not warped or gouged. Check that the piston bores, the O-ring sliding surfaces, and the output shaft bushing are not gouged, grooved, or otherwise damaged.
11. Measure the inside diameter of the bushing in the transmission case. If it is worn to a diameter greater than 38.188 mm (1.5035 in.), replace the transmission case.
12. Check that all 16 return springs are of equal height. Replace broken or distorted springs. Full spring specifications appear in **6. Automatic Transmission Technical Data.**

To assemble:

1. Make sure that all parts are still perfectly clean and dry.

2. Install the pressure tap plugs and the ATF cooler line fittings with new O-rings. Torque the pressure tap plugs to 6 to 8 Nm (53 to 71 in. lb.); torque the ATF cooler line fittings to 20 to 30 Nm (15 to 22 ft. lb.).
3. Install the rear cover and a new gasket.
4. Install new O-rings on the inner piston, the outer piston, and the reaction sleeve. Then lightly lubricate the O-rings with clean ATF and push the inner piston into the cupped side of the reaction sleeve as indicated in Fig. 5-97.

NOTE ——
When installing the new O-rings on the reaction sleeve, be sure to install the thinner of the large-diameter O-rings on the outside of the sleeve.

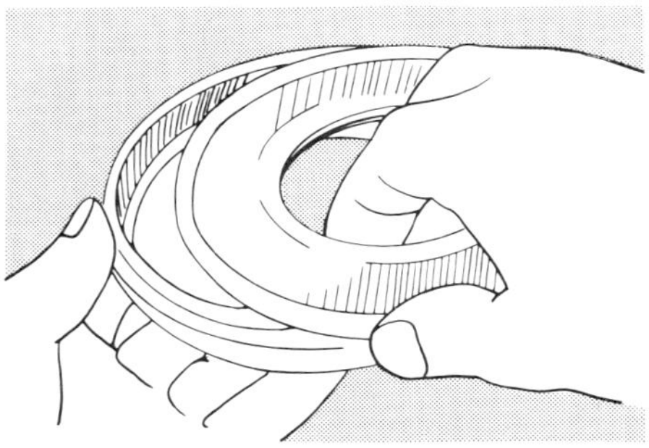

Fig. 5-97. Inner piston being inserted into reaction sleeve.

5. After lubricating the O-rings with clean ATF, install the outer piston in the reaction sleeve as indicated in Fig. 5-98.

Fig. 5-98. Outer piston being installed in reaction sleeve.

6. Lubricate the O-rings and the bores inside the transmission case with clean ATF. Orient the rear brake piston/reaction sleeve assembly so that the recesses for the return spring are up, then push the assembly into position in the case—being careful not to damage the O-rings.
7. Install the 16 piston return springs.
8. Carefully position the return spring seat atop the springs. Then look through the cutout in the bottom of the case to make sure that no spring has accidentally been knocked over.
9. Carefully position Toyota special service tool 00002-00223-03 on the spring seat. Tighten the bolts alternately and evenly—keeping the seat centered. Compress the springs only enough so that the snap ring can be installed.
10. Push the snap ring into place with your fingers. Then check visually that it is fully seated and centered by the three lugs on the spring retainer. With the snap ring correctly installed, remove the special tool.
11. Check the accumulator pistons for wear, cracks, and other damage. Check that the accumulator springs are neither broken nor distorted. Replace faulty components. Install new O-rings on the pistons (Fig. 5-99). Full spring specifications appear in **6. Automatic Transmission Technical Data.**

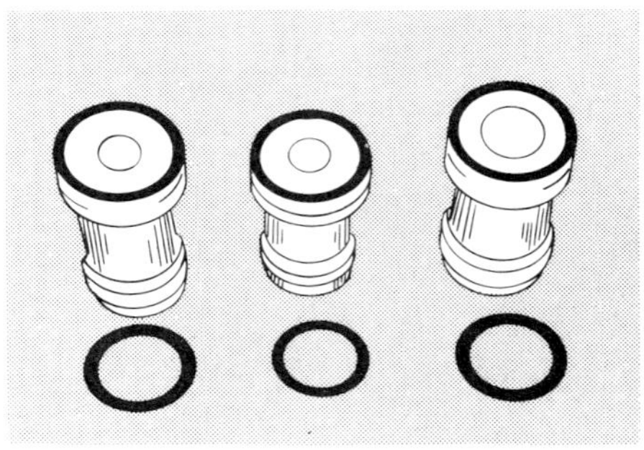

Fig. 5-99. New O-rings for installation on accumulator pistons.

12. Place the longest spring in the accumulator bore nearest the rear of the transmission case. Place the shortest spring in the middle bore, and the remaining spring in the front bore.
13. Lubricate the accumulator pistons with clean ATF. Then install them in the transmission case with the smallest piston in the middle. (The outer pistons are of different sizes and cannot be interchanged). See Fig. 5-100.
14. Install the temporary retaining plate to keep the accumulator pistons in their bores until you are ready to install the valve body assembly.

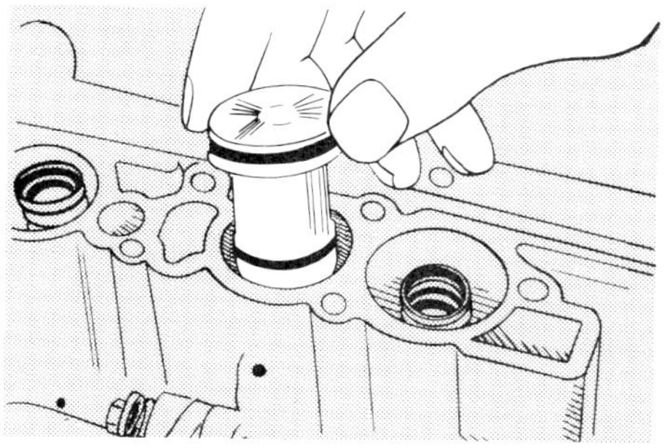

Fig. 5-100. Smallest piston being installed in central accumulator bore. Notice springs already installed on outer bores.

Disassembling and Assembling Output Shaft

Fig. 5-101 is an exploded view of the output shaft assembly, which includes the No. 3 brake discs and plates, a planetary gearset, the ntermediate shaft, and related parts. Become familiar with the part names given in the illustration. These names will be used frequently in the work procedures that follow.

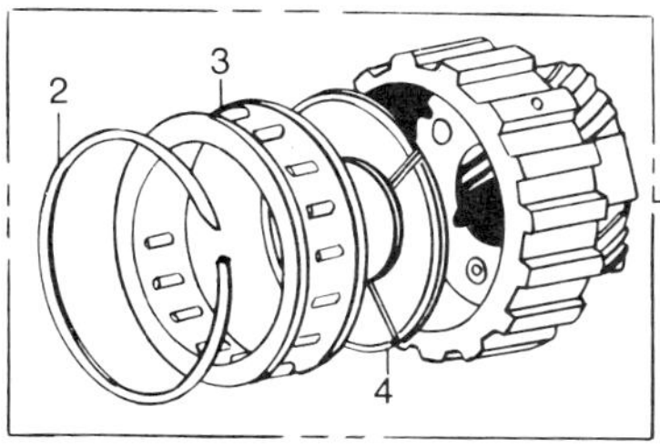

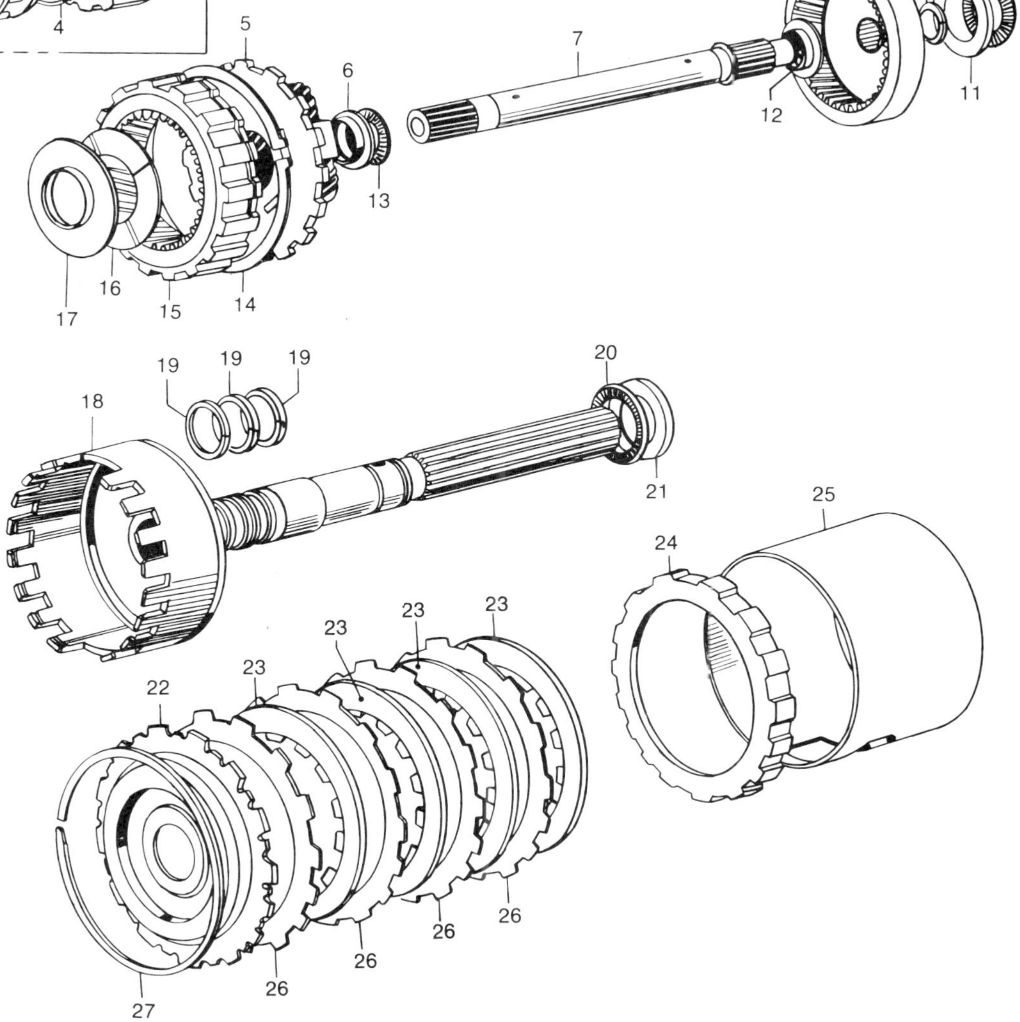

1. Front planetary gearset
2. Snap ring
3. Clutch with end bearings
4. No. 1 nylon thrust washer
5. Rear planetary gearset
6. No. 1 thrust bearing race
7. Intermediate shaft
8. Rear annulus gear
9. Set ring
10. No. 2 thrust bearing
11. No. 2 thrust bearing race
12. No. 1 thrust bearing race
13. No. 1 thrust bearing
14. Snap ring
15. Front annulus gear
16. No. 2 nylon thrust washer
17. No. 2 thrust washer
18. Output shaft
19. ATF seal ring (3)
20. No. 3 thrust bearing
21. No. 3 thrust bearing race
22. One-way clutch inner race
23. Disc (4)
24. Pressure plate
25. Apply tube
26. Plate (4)
27. Ring

Fig. 5-101. Exploded view of output shaft assembly.

To disassemble:

1. Remove the No. 3 brake disc/plate pack and the front planetary gearset as a unit (Fig. 5-102). Remove the No. 2 thrust washer and the No. 2 nylon thrust washer (which may be stuck to the rear planetary gearset).

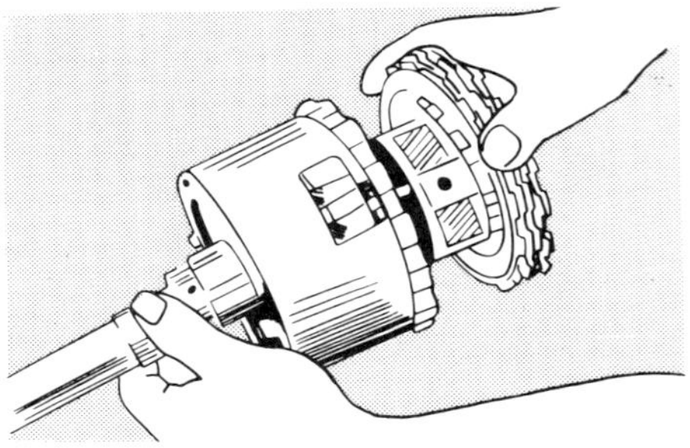

Fig. 5-102. No. 3 brake disc/plate pack and front planetary gearset being removed.

2. Remove the No. 3 brake disc/plate pack from the front planetary gearset—keeping the discs and plates in their exact assembled order.

NOTE —

Holding the disc/plate pack together with a wire loop will keep it in order. Used discs and plates must be reinstalled in their original positions and locations. The old disc/plate pack can also be used as a guide for correct installation of replacement discs and plates.

3. Remove the one-way clutch inner race from the front planetary gearset, pulling it out by hand.
4. Remove the snap rings from the front planetary gearset (Fig. 5-103).

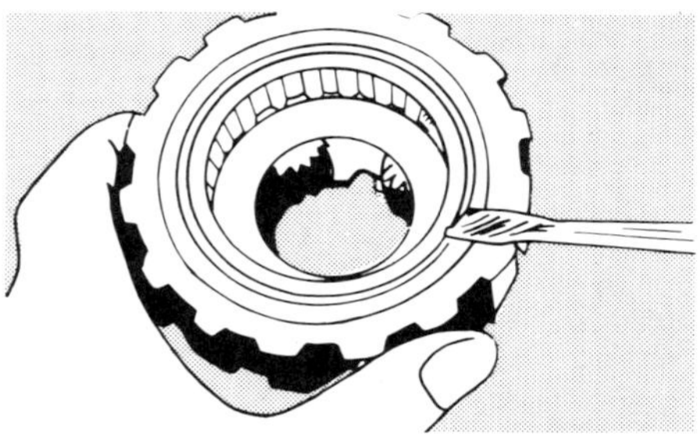

Fig. 5-103. Medium-size screwdriver being used to pry snap ring out of front planetary gearset.

5. Remove the one-way clutch with its end bearings from the front planetary gearset, noticing the orientation of the collared sides of the end bearings to the one-way clutch. Remove the No. 1 nylon thrust washer.
6. Remove first the pressure plate and then the apply tube from the output shaft assembly.
7. Using needle-nose pliers as indicated in Fig. 5-104, compress the snap ring that holds the front annulus gear inside the drum of the output shaft. With the ring compressed, pull off the front annulus gear.

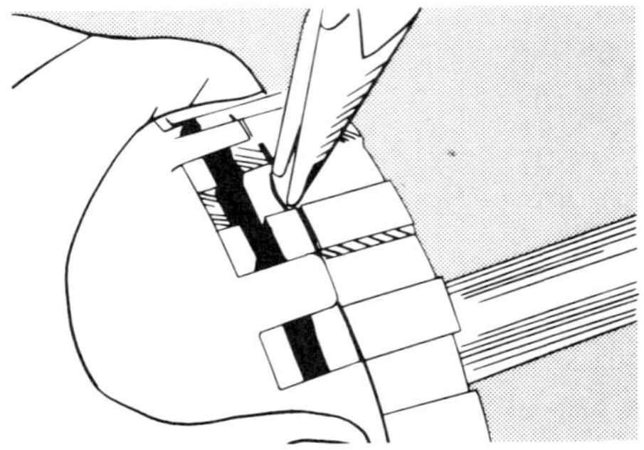

Fig. 5-104. Needle-nose pliers being used to compress snap ring for front annulus gear.

8. Separate the intermediate shaft assembly (including the rear planetary gearset and the rear annulus gear) from the output shaft assembly. Then remove the No. 2 thrust bearing and the No. 2 thrust bearing race, noticing the orientation of these parts.
9. Using your fingers only, unhook each of the three ATF seal rings, then pull it off over the splined end of the output shaft.
10. Lift out the rear planetary gearset as indicated in Fig. 5-105, then lift it off the intermediate shaft. Remove the No. 1 thrust bearing and its front race.

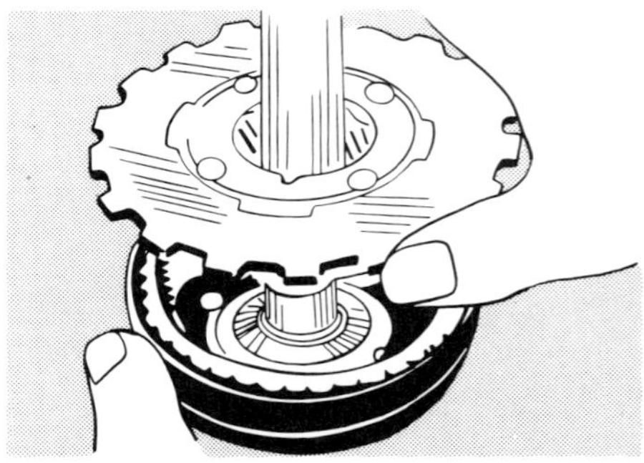

Fig. 5-105. Rear planetary gearset being lifted out of rear annulus gear.

11. Remove the set ring from the intermediate shaft as indicated in Fig. 5-106. Then remove the rear annulus gear from the intermediate shaft and take out the No. 1 thrust bearing's rear race.
12. Thoroughly wash all components—except the lined discs—in clean solvent, then dry them with moisture-free compressed air.

CAUTION —

Do not use high-pressure compressed air to clean the lined discs. Doing this can damage

***CAUTION (cont.)* ——**
the lining material. After cleaning and inspection, immediately place the disc/plate pack in a pan of clean ATF so that the lined discs will not dry out. If you intend to install new lined discs, they should be placed in clean ATF at this time so that they will be thoroughly saturated with ATF prior to installation.

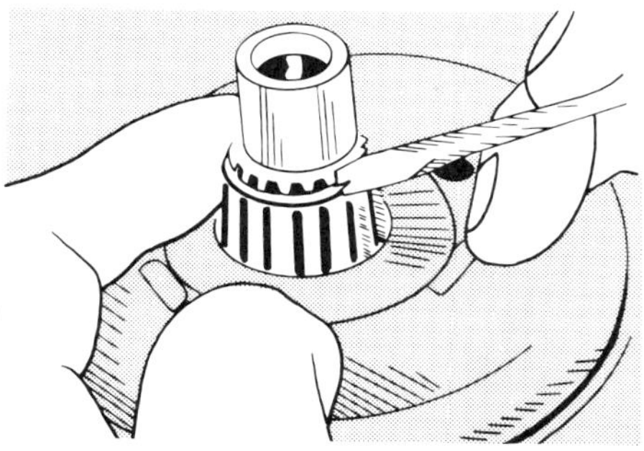

Fig. 5-106. Small screwdriver being used to remove set ring from groove in rear splines of intermediate shaft.

13. Carefully inspect the discs and plates. The lugs should not be worn or deformed and both discs and plates should be absolutely flat. Check for scoring, flaking, and debonding of the disc linings, and make sure that neither the discs nor the plates are blackened by burning. Replace damaged discs and plates and replace any disc that has worn to a thickness of less than 2.10 mm (.083 in.).
14. Check all thrust washers and thrust bearings and races. Replace any component that has visible wear or damage.
15. Inspect the one-way clutch with special attention to the sprags, ribbon springs, rollers, and cage side surfaces. Check that the one-way clutch inner race shows no wear or damage on its lugs, hub, or friction surface. Replace worn or damaged components.
16. Inspect the teeth of the annulus gears for wear and damage. Inspect the parking pawl lugs on the front annulus gear and the internal splines of the rear annulus gear. Replace worn or damaged gears.
17. Inspect the planetary gearsets. If the lugs or the pinion teeth are visibly worn or damaged, replace the gearset. Also replace gearsets that have any play between the pinion gears and their shafts.
18. Inspect the intermediate shaft and the output shaft, making sure that no ATF holes are clogged. Replace shafts that have damaged splines, worn or damaged bearing surfaces, or which prove to be bent when rolled on a flat surface.

NOTE ——
If the bushing inside the output shaft has worn to a diameter greater than 18.076 mm (.7117 in.), replace the output shaft.

19. Inspect the apply tube and the pressure plate. If either is worn or deformed, or if the reaction plate is burned, replace it.

1

To assemble:

1. Install the No. 1 thrust bearing's rear race on the rear of the intermediate shaft so that the collar on the race is toward the shoulder on the shaft. Then install the rear annulus gear as indicated in Fig. 5-107 and install the set ring to hold the gear in place on the shaft.

NOTE ——
Throughout the assembly procedure, you should lubricate each part thoroughly with clean ATF before you install the part in the output shaft assembly or the transmission case.

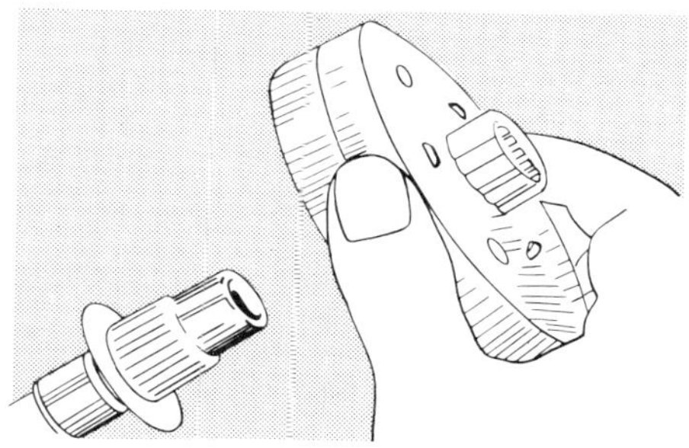

Fig. 5-107. Rear annulus gear being installed on intermediate shaft. Notice position of No. 1 thrust bearing race on shaft. Install set ring by pushing it down with your fingers and winding it into place.

2. Install the No. 1 thrust bearing and its front race inside the rear annulus gear, making sure that both are flat against the previously installed rear race. Then install the rear planetary gearset as indicated in Fig. 5-108.

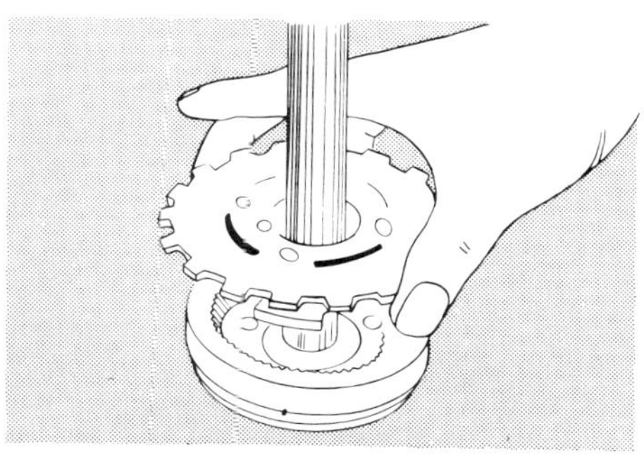

Fig. 5-108. Rear planetary gearset being installed over intermediate shaft. Rotate gearset to make sure all pinions mesh fully with annulus gear.

3. Install the No. 2 nylon thrust washer atop the rear planetary gearset so that the lugs of the washer engage the correct recesses in the gearset. The lugs are of different shapes and must engage appropriately shaped recesses.

4. Install the three ATF seal rings on the output shaft, sliding each ring into place in its groove and locking its overlapping ends. Then install the output shaft wrong-way round in the extension housing so that the extension housing can be used as an assembly stand (Fig. 5-109).

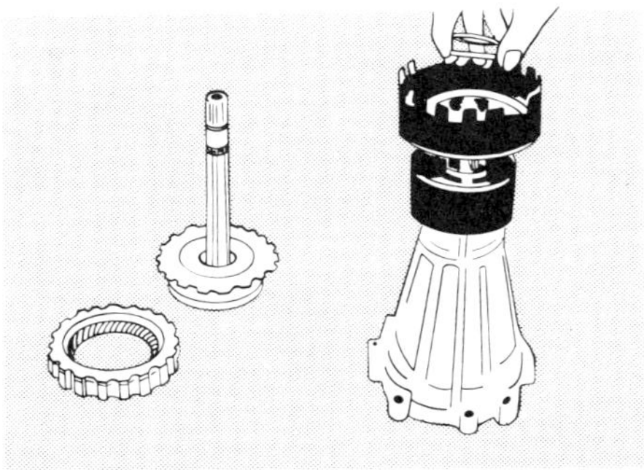

Fig. 5-109. Extension housing being used as assembly stand for output shaft.

5. Install the No. 2 thrust bearing and then its race inside the drum of the output shaft. Then install the intermediate shaft assembly as indicated in Fig. 5-110, making sure that the lugs interlock.

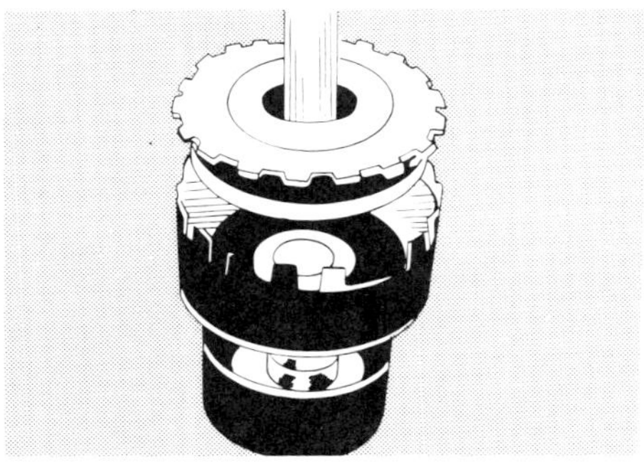

Fig. 5-110. Intermediate shaft assembly being installed on output shaft.

6. If previously removed, install the snap ring in the groove of the front annulus gear. Then install the front annulus gear—snap ring side first—in the output shaft drum, compressing the snap ring as indicated in Fig. 5-111 so that the annulus gear will slide fully into position. Make sure that when the snap ring is released it seats fully in the grooves all around the lugs of the output shaft drum.

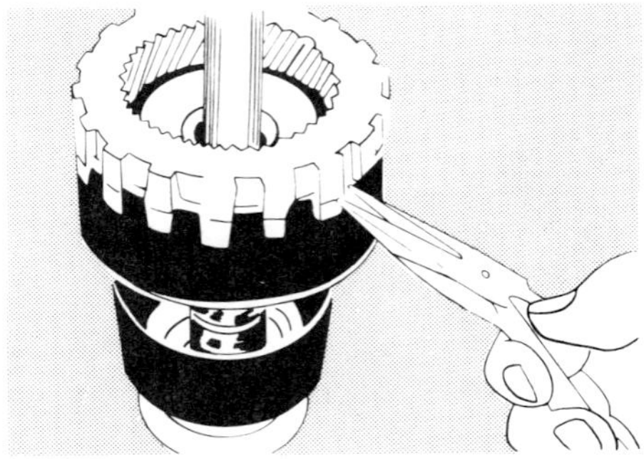

Fig. 5-111. Snap ring being compressed so that front annulus gear can be installed in output shaft drum. When snap ring is correctly seated in drum, gap in ring is the width of one lug on annulus gear.

7. Remove the output shaft assembly from the extension housing. Then, using Vaseline as an adhesive and a lubricant, install first the No. 3 thrust bearing and then the No. 3 thrust bearing's front race on the output shaft, flat against the rear of the drum.

8. Install the No. 3 thrust bearing's rear race in the transmission case so that the collar on the race is toward the rear of the case. Lubricate the face and the bore of the race with Vaseline.

9. Slip the apply tube onto the output shaft, then install the pressure plate as indicated in Fig. 5-112.

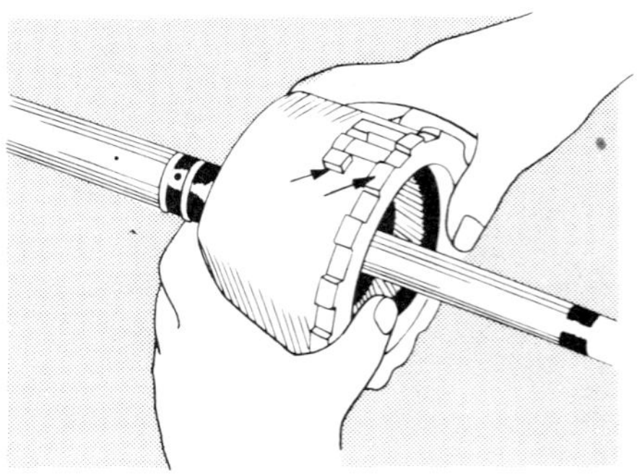

Fig. 5-112. Apply tube and pressure plate being installed. Align locking tab of apply tube with a tooth on the pressure plate, as indicated by arrows.

10. Making sure that the assembly goes straight in without damaging the case, partially insert the output shaft assembly into the transmission case. Then align the locking tab of the apply tube with the first notch in the case to the left of the parking pawl opening. See Fig. 5-113.

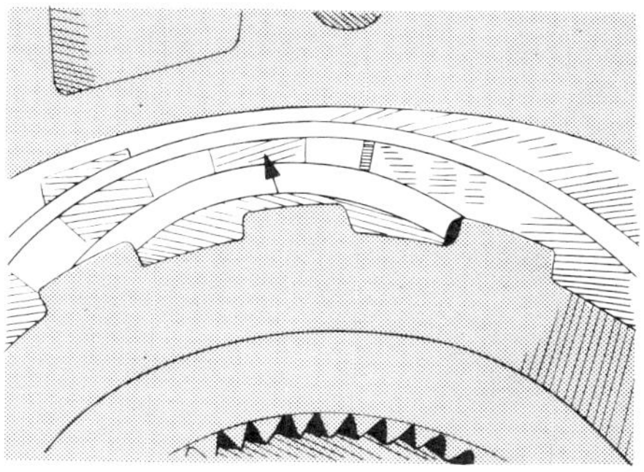

Fig. 5-113. Locking tab of apply tube (arrow) being aligned with first notch in case to left of parking pawl opening. Rotate apply tube as required to align tab correctly.

11. By looking through the bottom of the case, check the alignment of the apply tube's locking tab (Fig. 5-114). Then push and jiggle the output shaft assembly all the way into the transmission case until, when you look through the rear cutout in the bottom of the case, you can see that the apply tube is fully seated all the way against the rear brake outer piston.

Fig. 5-114. Correct alignment of apply tube tab (arrow) with notch (**A**) in case when viewed through cutout in bottom of transmission case.

12. Install the No. 1 nylon thrust washer inside the front planetary gearset, so that the lugs of the washer engage the cutouts in the gearset.

13. Install one end bearing for the one-way clutch—collar uppermost. Install the one-way clutch as indicated in Fig. 5-115. Install the other end bearing, collar down, then install the snap ring to hold the one-way clutch assembly inside the front planetary gearset.

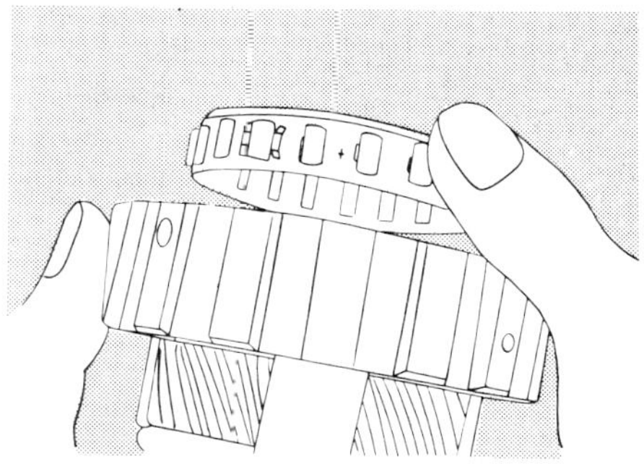

Fig. 5-115. One-way clutch being installed in front planetary gearset. Arrow between rollers of one-way clutch must point toward pinion gears as shown.

14. Temporarily install the one-way clutch inner race in the one-way clutch. Then check the operation of the one-way clutch as indicated in Fig. 5-116.

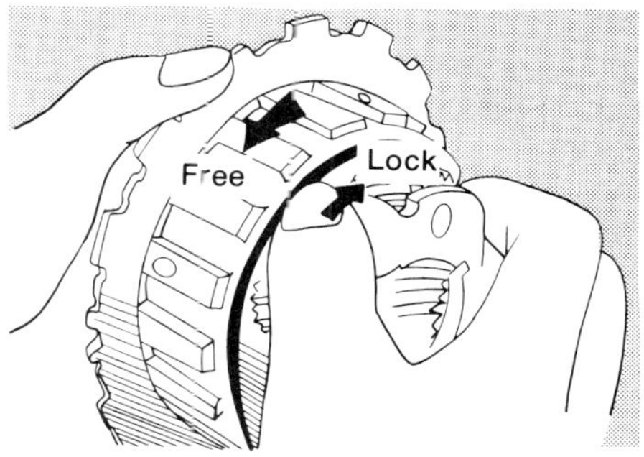

Fig. 5-116. One-way clutch being tested. Planetary gearset should rotate freely counterclockwise, but lock when turned clockwise.

15. Remove the one-way clutch inner race from the one-way clutch. Then, using Vaseline as an adhesive, install the No. 2 thrust washer on the front planetary gearset so that its lugs engage the recesses in the planetary gearset.

16. Install the front planetary gearset on the output shaft assembly, which is inside the transmission case. Rotate the gearset to make sure that its pinions mesh fully with the front annulus gear.

1

17. Install alternately four lined discs and four plates, as indicated in Fig. 5-117. The lugs of the discs must engage the grooves of the front planetary gearset and the lugs of the plates must engage the grooves in the transmission case.

> ***CAUTION —***
> *Do not install dry discs, as they can fail when the transmission is returned to service. Soak new lined discs for at least 15 minutes before installation. The clearance measurement to be made in the next step will be inaccurate if the discs and plates have excess ATF on them. Use low-pressure compressed air only to blow excess ATF off the discs and plates.*

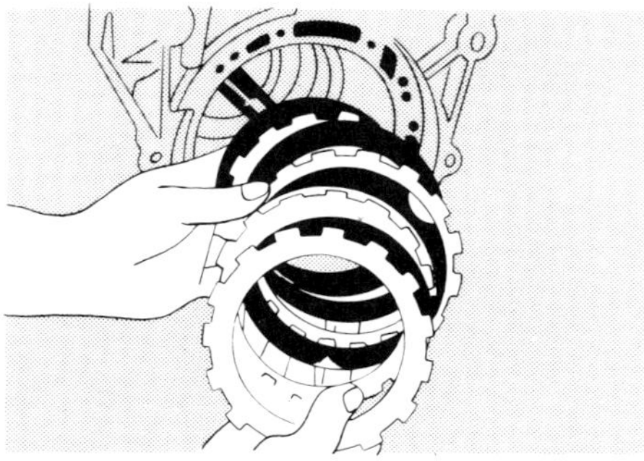

Fig. 5-117. No. 3 brake disc/plate pack being installed.

18. Measure the No. 3 brake disc/plate pack free clearance as indicated in Fig. 5-118. If the pack is not below the snap ring groove, either the discs and plates are incorrectly assembled or there is an extra plate or disc that has been mistakenly installed. The correct clearance is 0.80 to 1.80 mm (.032 to .071 in.).

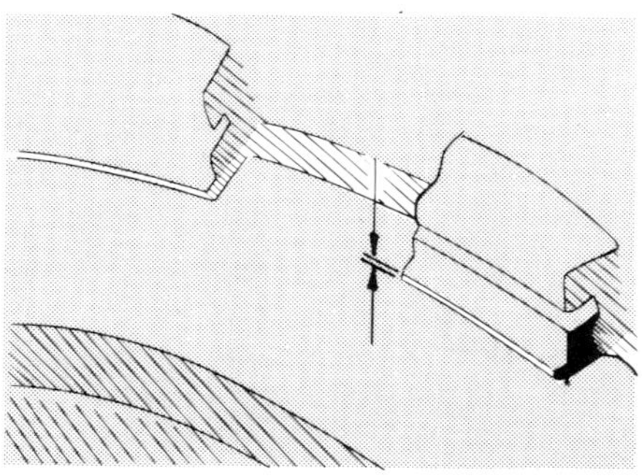

Fig. 5-118. Clearance (between arrows) that must exist between uppermost plate and lower edge of snap ring groove.

19. Install the one-way clutch inner race so that the notched tooth is toward the valve body side of the transmission case (Fig. 5-119). The inner race is correctly installed if the snap ring groove is fully visible all around.

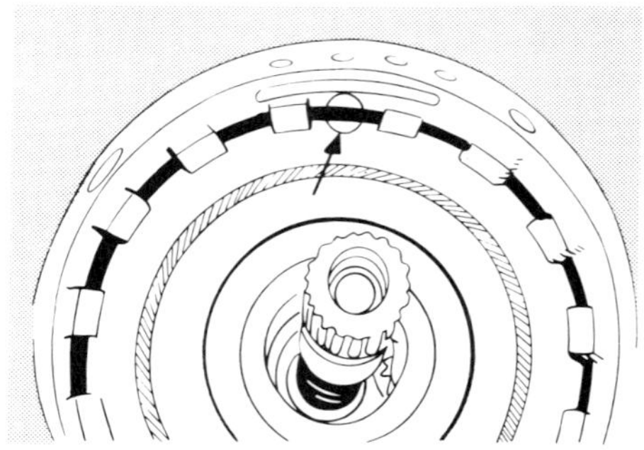

Fig. 5-119. Notched tooth of one-way clutch inner race that should be installed toward valve body (bottom of transmission case).

20. Using one or two large screwdrivers to compress the snap ring, install the large snap ring that holds the one-way clutch inner race in the transmission case.

21. Inject compressed air alternately into the ATF passages for the rear brake inner piston and the rear brake outer piston (Fig. 5-120). Listen to make sure that the pistons move and retract freely. If not, some part of the transmision case or the output shaft assembly has been assembled incorrectly.

Fig. 5-120. Compressed air being injected into ATF passage for rear brake outer piston. Hole above nozzle is for inner piston.

Disassembling and Assembling Center Support Assembly

Fig. 5-121 is an exploded view of the center support assembly, which includes the No. 1 brake, the No. 2 brake, the sun gear, and related components. Become familiar with the part names given in the illustration. These names will be used frequently in the work procedures that follow.

Fig. 5-121. Exploded view of center support assembly.

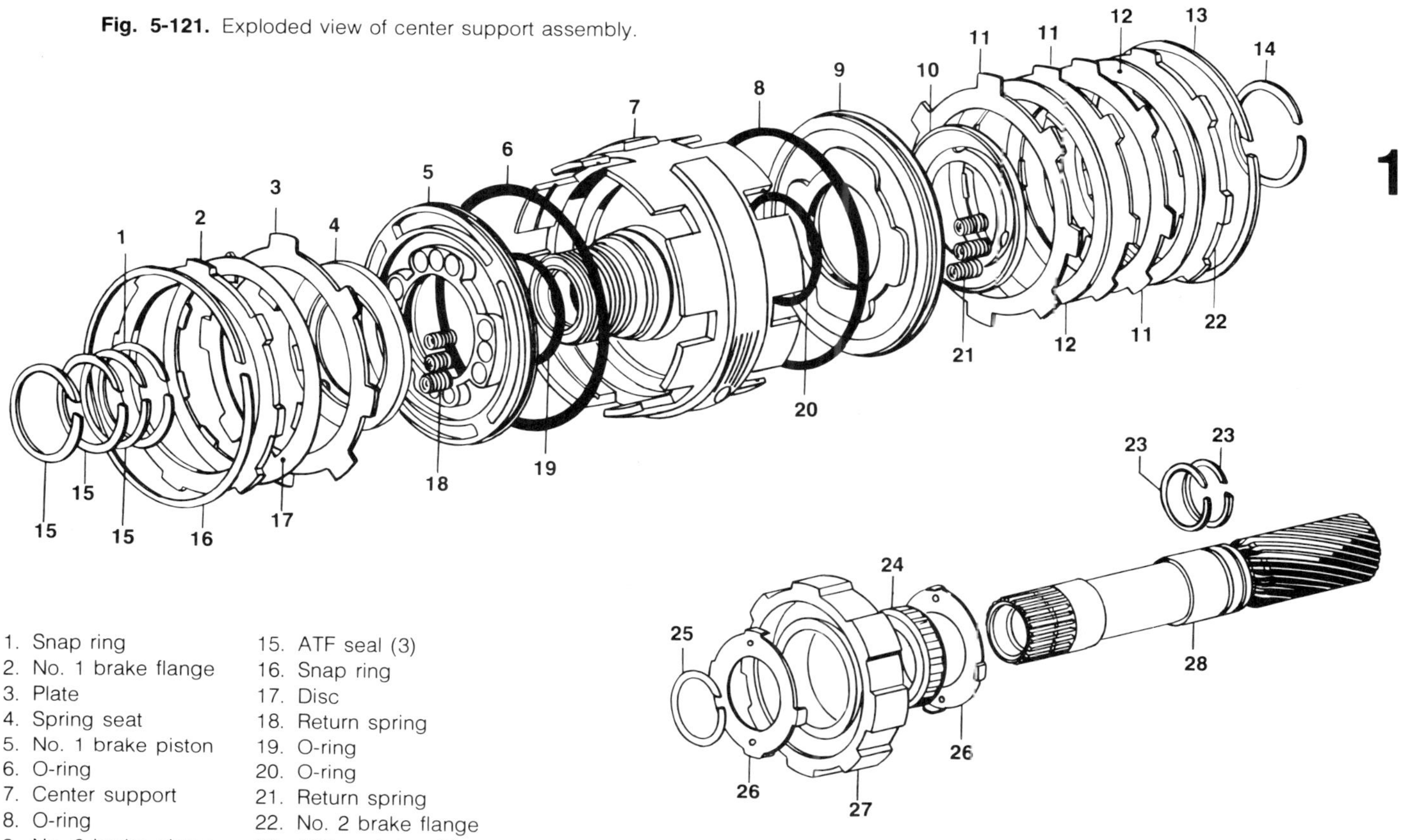

1. Snap ring
2. No. 1 brake flange
3. Plate
4. Spring seat
5. No. 1 brake piston
6. O-ring
7. Center support
8. O-ring
9. No. 2 brake piston
10. Spring seat
11. Plate (3)
12. Disc (2)
13. Snap ring
14. Snap ring
15. ATF seal (3)
16. Snap ring
17. Disc
18. Return spring
19. O-ring
20. O-ring
21. Return spring
22. No. 2 brake flange
23. ATF seal ring (2)
24. One-way clutch with end bearings
25. Snap ring
26. One-way clutch retainer (2)
27. No. 2 brake hub
28. Sun gear

To disassemble:

1. Remove the snap ring from the splined end of the sun gear, then lift the center support assembly off the sun gear assembly as indicated in Fig. 5-122.

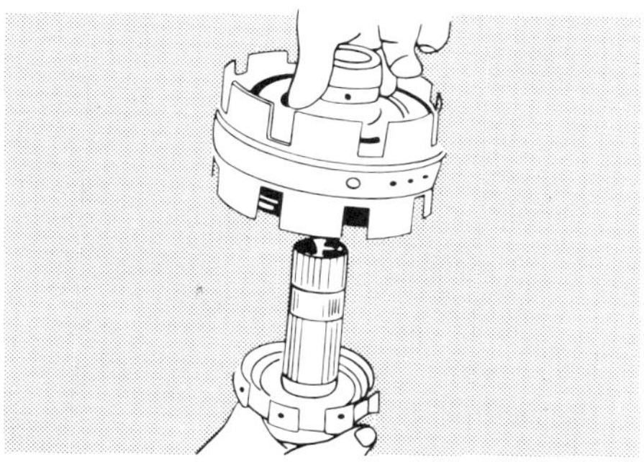

Fig. 5-122. Center support assembly being lifted off sun gear assembly.

2. Remove the large snap ring from the front of the center support assembly. Lift out the No. 1 brake flange, the No. 1 brake disc, and the No. 1 brake plate.
3. Using a repair press with a bridge mandrel, such as the Toyota special service tool 00002-00223-04 shown in Fig. 5-123, press down the spring seat for the No. 1 brake piston just enough to allow removal of the snap ring. Then gradually relieve the spring tension and remove the spring seat and the 12 return springs.

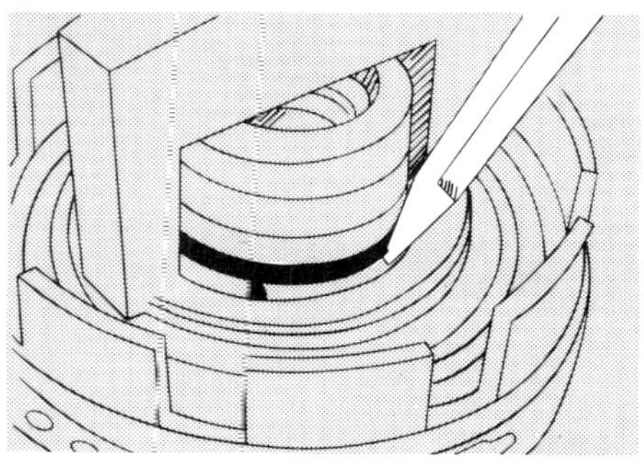

Fig. 5-123. Snap ring being removed with snap ring pliers. Notice bridge mandrel that is being used to hold down spring seat.

4. Place a clean shop rag on the workbench. Place the center support assembly on the rag so that the No. 1 brake piston is pointed down. Then use compressed air as indicated in Fig. 5-124 to blow the No. 1 brake piston out of the center support and down onto the rag.

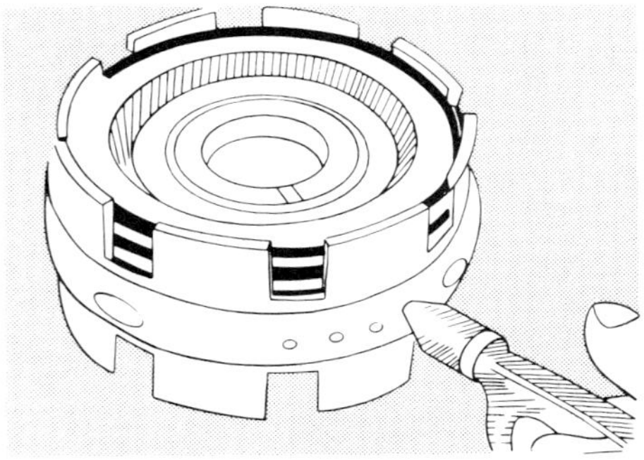

Fig. 5-124. Compressed air being injected into ATF port for No. 1 brake piston. If piston does not pop out, you can pull it out with needle-nose pliers—being careful not to damage the return spring recesses as you grip them.

5. Using your fingers only, remove and discard the O-rings that are on the No. 1 brake piston.
6. Using your fingers only, unhook each of the three ATF seal rings from the front of the center support, then pull the ring off the hub.
7. Remove the large snap ring from the rear of the center support assembly. Lift out the No. 2 brake flange and the No. 2 brake disc/plate pack—keeping the discs and plates in their exact assembled order.

NOTE ——

Holding the disc/plate pack together with a wire loop will keep it in order. Used discs and plates must be reinstalled in their original positions and locations. The old disc/plate pack can also be used as a guide for correct installation of replacement discs and plates.

8. Using the same tools and procedures that you used in disassembling the No. 1 brake, remove the snap ring, the spring seat, and the 12 return springs. Then apply compressed air at the point indicated in Fig. 5-125 to blow out the No. 2 brake piston.
9. Using your fingers only, remove and discard the O-rings that are on the No. 2 brake piston.
10. Pull the No. 2 brake hub/one-way clutch assembly off the sun gear. Then, using your fingers only, unhook each of the two ATF seal rings from the sun gear and pull the ring off over the spiral-cut gear teeth.

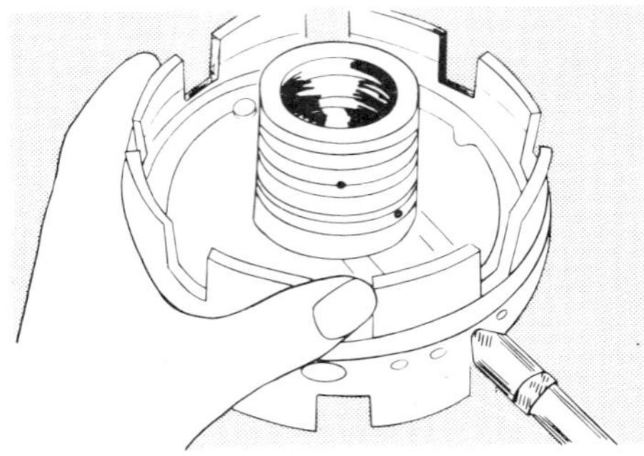

Fig. 5-125. Compressed air being used to blow No. 2 brake piston out of center support.

11. Clamp the No. 2 brake hub/one-way clutch assembly in a vise with soft jaws. Using a screwdriver as indicated in Fig. 5-126, bend back several of the tabs on one of the one-way clutch retainers. Then pry the retainer off, leaving the second retainer installed on the brake hub.

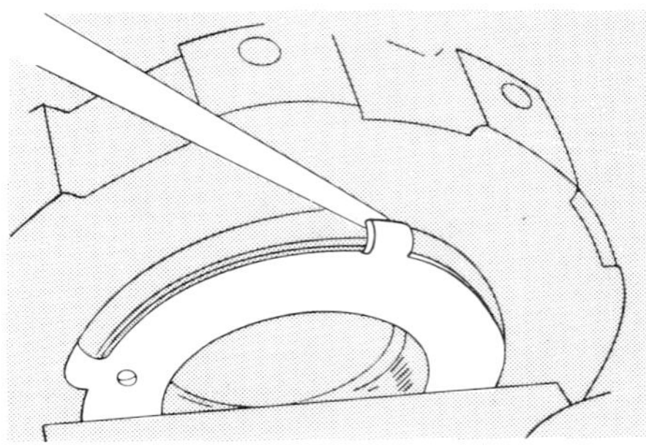

Fig. 5-126. One-way clutch retainer being pried off.

12. Remove the one-way clutch and its end bearings from the No. 2 brake hub.
13. Thoroughly wash all components—except the lined discs—in clean solvent. Then dry them with moisture-free compressed air.

CAUTION ——

Do not use high-pressure compressed air to clean the lined discs. Doing this can damage the lining material. After cleaning and inspection, immediately place the disc/plate pack in a pan of clean ATF so that the lined discs will not dry out. If you intend to install new lined discs, they should be placed in clean ATF at this time so that they will be thoroughly saturated with ATF prior to installation.

14. Carefully inspect the discs and plates. The lugs should not be worn or deformed and both discs and plates should be absolutely flat. Check for

scoring, flaking, and debonding of the disc linings, and make sure that neither the discs nor the plates are blackened by burning. Replace damaged discs and plates and replace any disc that has worn to a thickness of less than 2.10 mm (.083 in.).

15. Inspect the one-way clutch with special attention to the sprags, ribbon springs, rollers, and cage side surfaces. Check that the end bearings are not worn and that neither the lugs nor the inner friction surface of the No. 2 brake hub is worn or damaged. Replace faulty parts.

16. Inspect the teeth and the splines of the sun gear for wear and damage. Also check the ATF seal ring grooves and the bearing surfaces. Replace worn or damaged sun gears.

> **NOTE ——**
> You should also replace the sun gear if either of the two bushings inside the gear has worn to a diameter greater than 21. 577 mm (.8495 in.)

17. Inspect the center support and the brake pistons. Replace components that have damaged ATF seal or O-ring grooves, or which are cracked, distorted, burred, or otherwise worn or damaged.

> **NOTE ——**
> You should also replace the center support if the bushing in its center has worn to a diameter greater than 36.461 mm (1.4355 in.).

18. Inspect the return springs. Replace any spring that is broken or does not have the same length as the other springs in its group. Full spring specifications appear in **6. Automatic Transmission Technical Data.**

To assemble:

1. Install one end bearing for the one-way clutch in the No. 2 brake hub—collar uppermost. Then install the one-way clutch as indicated in Fig. 5-127. Install the other end bearing, collar down.

> **NOTE ——**
> Throughout the assembly procedure, you should lubricate each part thoroughly with clean ATF before you install the part in the sun gear assembly or the center support assembly.

2. Install a new one-way clutch retainer, then crimp its tabs over the bead on the No. 2 brake hub as indicated in Fig. 5-128.

3. Install two new ATF seal rings on the sun gear by slipping them over the gear and into their grooves, then locking them in place by overlapping the ring ends.

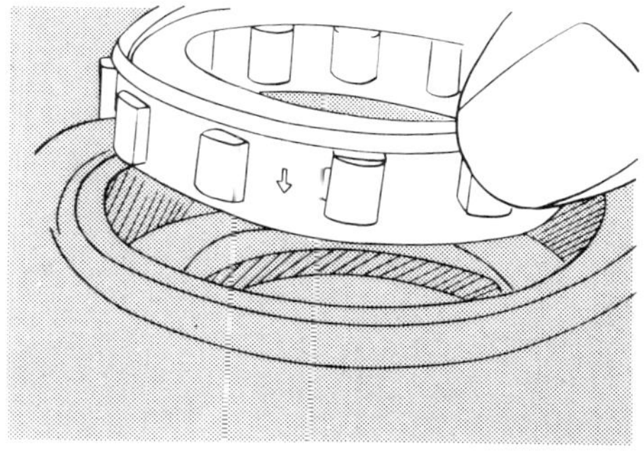

Fig. 5-127. One-way clutch being installed in No. 2 brake hub. Arrow between rollers of one-way clutch must point away from flat-faced end of hub.

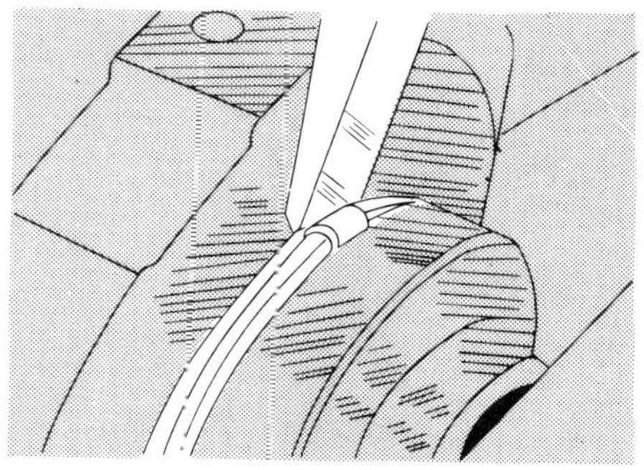

Fig. 5-128. Cold chisel being used to bend retainer tabs over bead on hub.

4. Install the one-way clutch/No. 2 brake hub assembly on the sun gear so that the smooth-faced side of the hub is toward the spiral cut teeth of the sun gear.

5. Check the operation of the one-way clutch as indicated in Fig. 5-129. The sun gear should turn freely counterclockwise and should lock when turned clockwise.

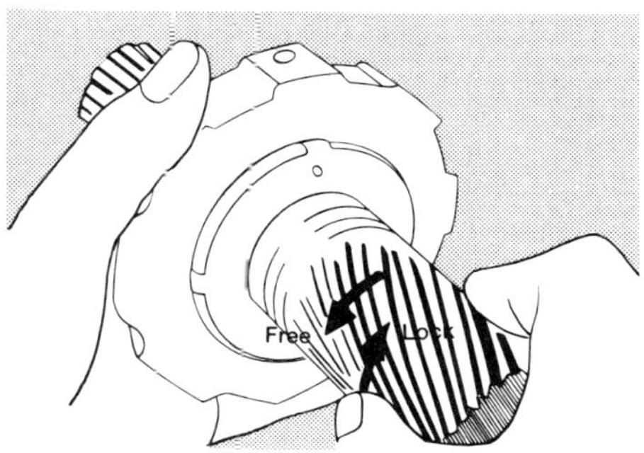

Fig. 5-129. Operation of one-way clutch being checked.

6. Install three new ATF seal rings on the hub of the center support, overlapping their ends to lock them in place.

7. Being careful not to damage the grooves, install new inner and outer O-rings on the brake pistons. (The two pistons are identical.)
8. Thoroughly lubricate the O-rings of the No. 1 brake piston with clean ATF. Then, being careful not to damage the O-rings or the ATF seal rings, work the No. 1 brake piston into place inside the center support.
9. Install the 12 return springs in the recesses of the No. 1 brake piston. Position the spring seat atop the springs, then loosely position the snap ring atop the spring seat. Using the repair press, compress the return springs so that you can install the snap ring as indicated in Fig. 5-130.

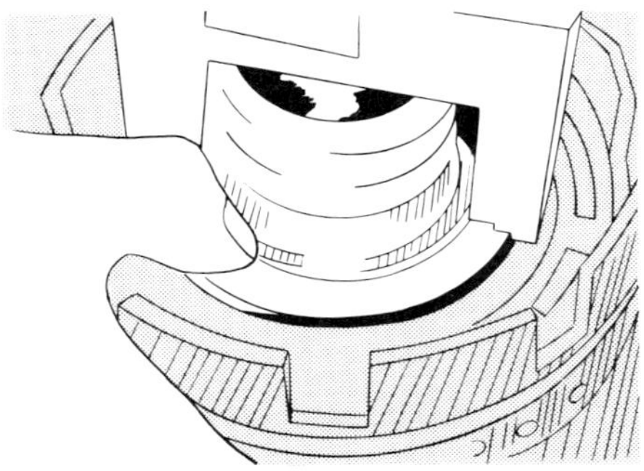

Fig. 5-130. Snap ring being pressed down into groove with thumb while spring seat is held down with repair press and bridge mandrel.

10. Using the same procedures that you used in installing the No. 1 brake piston, its return springs, the spring seat, and the snap ring, install the corresponding components of the No. 2 brake.
11. Install first the No. 1 brake plate and then the No. 1 brake lined disc. Install the No. 1 brake flange. Install the large snap ring as indicated in Fig. 5-131.

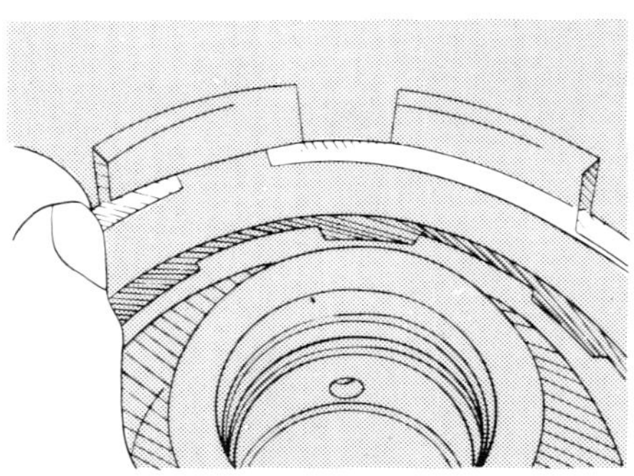

Fig. 5-131. Large snap ring for No. 1 brake flange correctly installed. Make sure that the gap in the snap ring is not exposed between the lugs of the center support.

12. Using feeler gauges of various thicknesses, determine the free clearance of the No. 1 brake, as shown in Fig. 5-132. The clearance should be between 0.30 and 1.00 mm (.012 and .040 in.). If it is less, the brake has been incorrectly assembled; if it is more, there is excessive wear on some brake component.

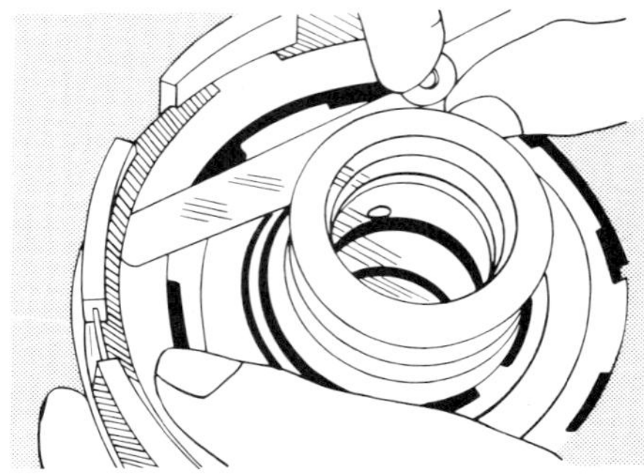

Fig. 5-132. No. 1 brake free clearance being determined with feeler gauge inserted between large snap ring and No. 1 brake flange.

13. Install the No. 2 brake disc/plate pack; the sequence is plate, disc, plate, plate, disc. Notice that two plates are installed adjacent to one another.
14. Install the No. 2 brake flange and the large snap ring, positioning the gap in the snap ring so that it is not exposed between lugs of the center support. Then, using the same procedure that you used with the No. 1 brake, determine the No. 2 brake free clearance, which should be between 0.30 and 1.20 mm (.012 and .047 in.).
15. Using the tip of a screwdriver, align the lugs of the No. 2 brake discs. Then install the sun gear assembly as indicated in Fig. 5-133, meshing the No. 2 brake hub with the lugs of the discs.

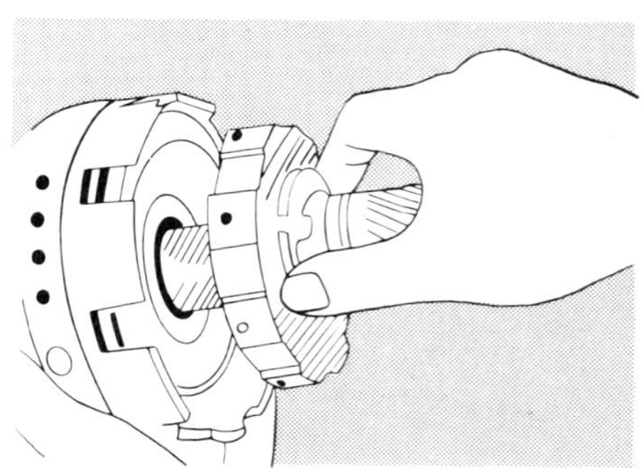

Fig. 5-133. Sun gear assembly being installed in center support assembly. Push sun gear assembly into center support.

16. Install the snap ring in the groove in the splines of the sun gear.

NOTE ——
The center support assembly will be installed later, together with the direct and reverse clutch assembly.

Disassembling and Assembling Direct and Reverse Clutch

Fig. 5-134 is an exploded view of the direct and reverse clutch. Counting from the front of the transmission, this is the second of the two hydraulically operated multiple-disc clutches. Become familiar with the part names given in the illustration. These names will be used frequently in the work procedures that follow.

To disassemble:

1. Remove the large snap ring from the front of the clutch drum. Lift out the clutch flange and the direct and reverse clutch disc/plate pack—keeping the discs and plates in their exact assembled order.

   NOTE ——
   Holding the disc/plate pack together with a wire loop will keep it in order. Used discs and plates must be reinstalled in their original positions and locations. The old disc/plate pack can also be used as a guide for correct installation of replacement discs and plates.

2. Using a repair press with a bridge mandrel, such as the Toyota special service tool 00002-00223-04 shown in Fig. 5-135, press down the spring seat just enough to allow removal of the snap ring. Then gradually relieve the spring tension and remove the spring seat and the spring.

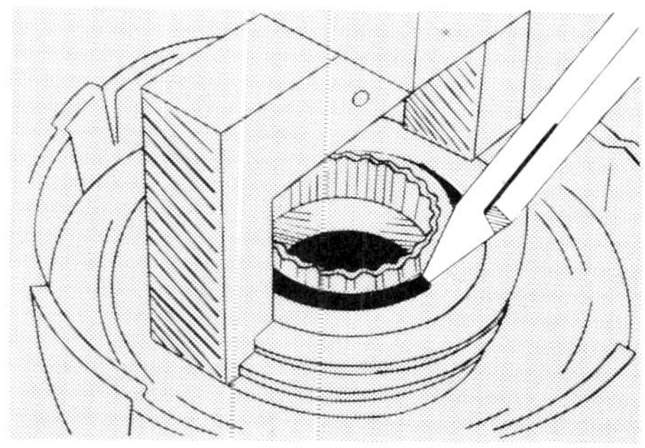

Fig. 5-135. Snap ring being removed with snap ring pliers. Notice bridge mandrel that is being used to hold down spring seat.

3. Hold the center support assembly so that the splined end of the sun gear is uppermost. Then install the direct and reverse clutch atop the center support assembly. Make sure that the ATF seal rings on the center support hub are not damaged during installation and that the rings fit tightly inside the clutch drum.

Fig. 5-134. Exploded view of direct and reverse clutch.

1. Snap ring
2. Disc (2)
3. Plate (3)
4. Snap ring
5. Piston return spring
6. O-ring
7. O-ring
8. Clutch flange
9. Spring seat
10. O-ring
11. Outer piston
12. O-ring
13. Inner piston
14. Drum

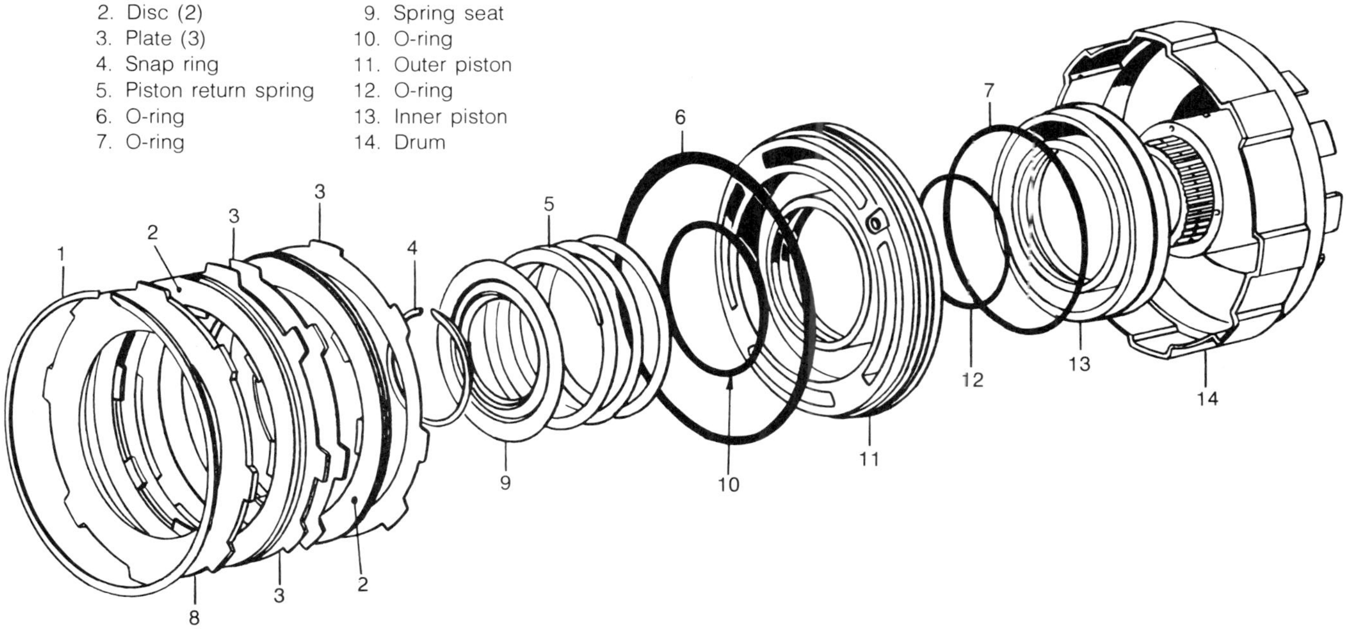

4. Place a clean shop rag on the workbench. Then invert the center support/direct and reverse clutch assembly and place it atop the rag so that the clutch pistons are pointed down. Use compressed air as indicated in Fig. 5-136 to blow the inner and outer pistons out of the clutch drum and down onto the rag.

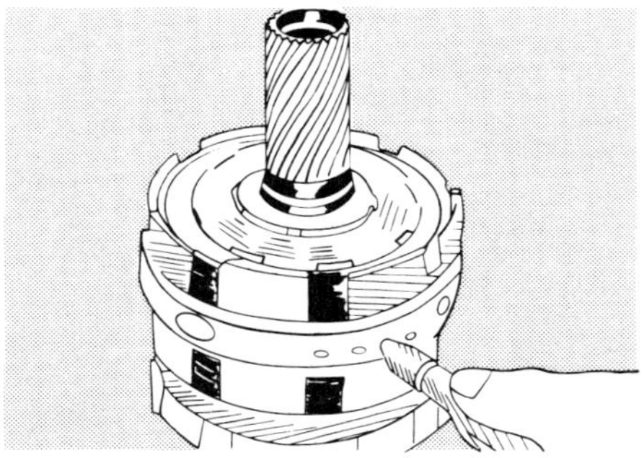

Fig. 5-136. Compressed air being injected into ATF port for inner piston, which will expel both pistons from the drum.

5. Using your fingers only, remove and discard the four O-rings that are on the direct and reverse clutch pistons.
6. Remove the direct and reverse clutch drum from the center support assembly. Thoroughly wash all direct and reverse clutch components—except the lined discs—in clean solvent, then dry them with moisture-free compressed air.

CAUTION —

Do not use high-pressure compressed air to clean the lined discs. Doing this can damage the lining material. After cleaning and inspection, immediately place the disc/plate pack in a pan of clean ATF so that the lined discs will not dry out. If you intend to install new lined discs, they should be placed in clean ATF at this time so that they will be thoroughly saturated with ATF prior to installation.

7. Carefully inspect the discs and plates. The lugs should not be worn or deformed and both discs and plates should be absolutely flat. Check for scoring, flaking, and debonding of the disc linings, and make sure that neither the discs nor the plates are blackened by burning. Replace damaged discs and plates and replace any disc that has worn to a thickness of less than 2.10 mm (.083 in.).
8. Inspect the inner and outer pistons. Replace pistons that have cracked or worn or damaged O-ring grooves or sliding surfaces.

NOTE —

Shake the pistons to make sure that the check balls are free. Blow low-pressure compressed air into the holes in the piston face to see that the balls do not leak.

9. Inspect the piston return spring. Replace it if there is any visible wear or damage. Full spring specifications appear in **6. Automatic Transmission Technical Data.**

To assemble:

1. Using your fingers only, install new O-rings on the inner and outer pistons. Then lubricate the O-rings and the piston sliding surfaces with clean ATF.

NOTE —

Throughout the assembly procedure, you should lubricate each part thoroughly with clean ATF before you install it in the clutch drum.

2. Install the inner (small) piston in the clutch drum so that the (flat-faced) side of the piston with the check valve hole in it is down. See Fig. 5-137.

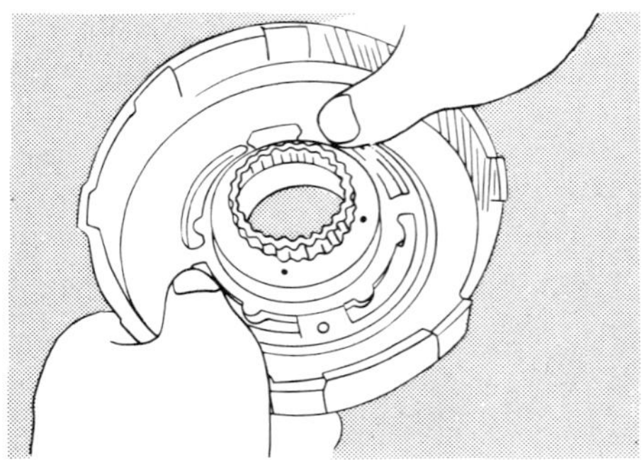

Fig. 5-137. Inner piston being installed, flat-face first, in clutch drum.

3. Install the outer piston in the clutch drum so that the (flat-faced) side of the piston with the check valve hole in it is down.
4. Install the return spring, position the spring seat atop the spring, then loosely position the snap ring atop the spring seat. Using the repair press, compress the return spring so that you can install the snap ring as indicated in Fig. 5-138.
5. Install the direct and reverse clutch disc/plate pack: the sequence is plate, disc, plate, plate, disc. Notice that two plates are installed adjacent to one another.
6. Install the clutch flange and the large snap ring, positioning the gap in the snap ring so that it is not exposed between lugs of the clutch drum.

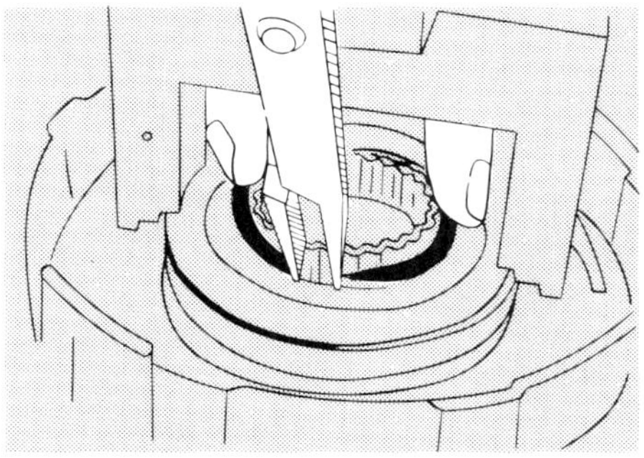

Fig. 5-138. Snap ring being installed with snap ring pliers while spring seat is held down with repair press and bridge mandrel.

7. Using feeler gauges of various thicknesses, determine the free clearance of the direct and reverse clutch, as shown in Fig. 5-139. The clearance should be between 0.40 and 1.20 mm (.016 and .047 in.). If it is less, the clutch has been incorrectly assembled; if it is more, there is excessive wear on some clutch component.

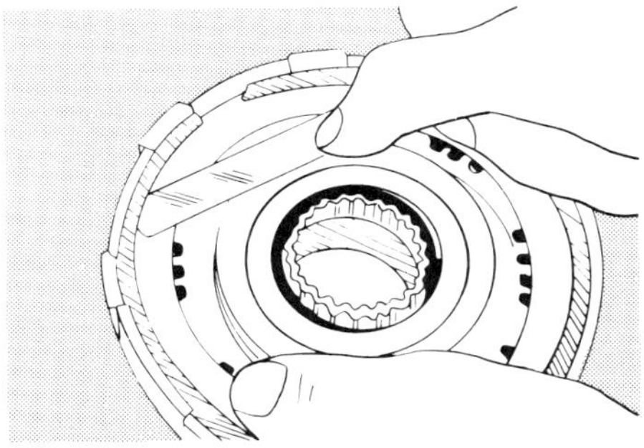

Fig. 5-139. Direct and reverse clutch clearance being determined with feeler gauge inserted between large snap ring and clutch flange.

8. While pulling outward on the sun gear, push the center support assembly into the transmission case as indicated in Fig. 5-140. Align the center support's bolt holes with the bolt holes in the case, then install the two bolts finger-tight. (The bolts will be torqued at a later stage of assembly.)

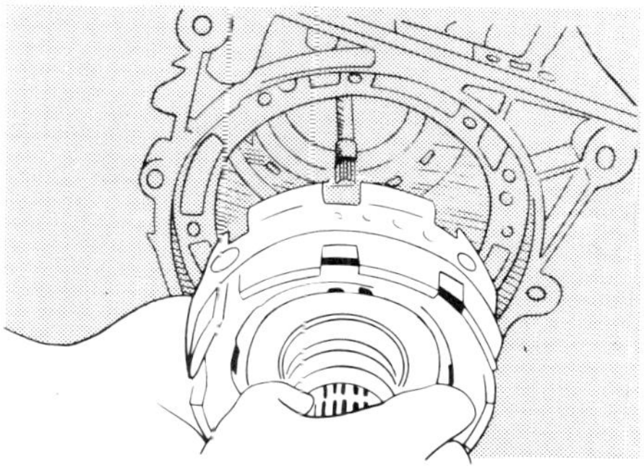

Fig. 5-140. Center support assembly being inserted into transmission case. Sun gear must mesh with pinions of both planetary gearsets. Before installation, make sure that No. 2 brake hub is fully meshed with its discs.

9. Install the direct and reverse clutch so that its splines are meshed with those of the sun gear and the drum is fully over the three ATF seal rings on the hub of the center support. When correctly installed, the splined hub of the clutch drum will be flush with the end of the sun gear. See Fig. 5-141.

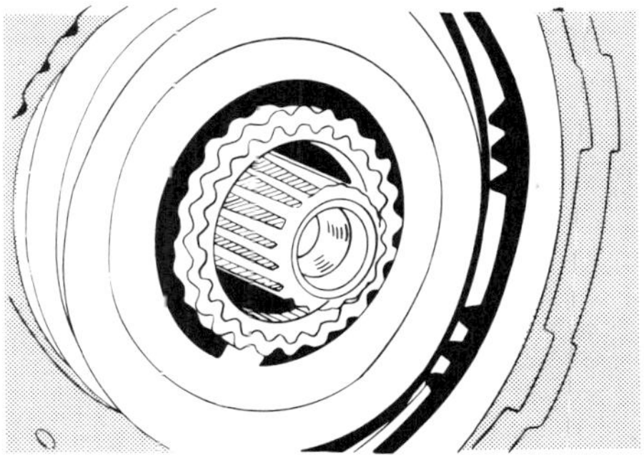

Fig. 5-141. Direct and reverse clutch correctly installed. Notice that splined hub of clutch drum is flush with end of sun gear.

Disassembling and Assembling Forward Clutch

Fig. 5-142 is an exploded view of the forward clutch, the front clutch assembly of the transmission. Become familiar with the part names given in the illustration. These names will be used frequently in the work procedures that follow.

1. Forward clutch
2. No. 2 thrust bearing race
3. No. 2 thrust bearing race
4. No. 2 thrust bearing
5. Direct and reverse clutch
6. Drum with input shaft
7. Forward clutch piston
8. O-ring
9. O-ring
10. Return spring seat
11. No. 1 thrust bearing
12. Plate (4)
13. Forward clutch hub
14. Snap ring
15. Direct and reverse clutch hub
16. Thin snap ring
17. Disc (3)
18. No. 1 thrust bearing race
19. No. 1 thrust bearing race
20. Snap ring
21. Piston return spring

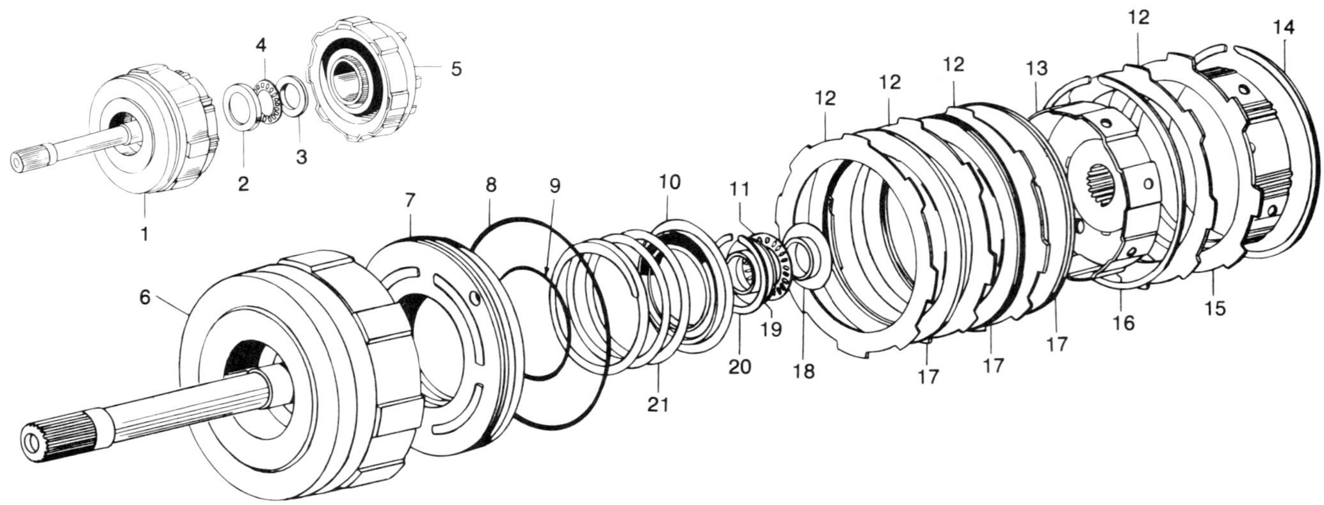

Fig. 5-142. Exploded view of forward clutch. Inset at upper left shows relationship of forward clutch to direct and reverse clutch.

To disassemble:

1. Remove the No. 2 thrust bearing and its races.
2. Install the forward clutch assembly on the extension housing, so that the extension housing can be used as a repair stand. See Fig. 5-143.

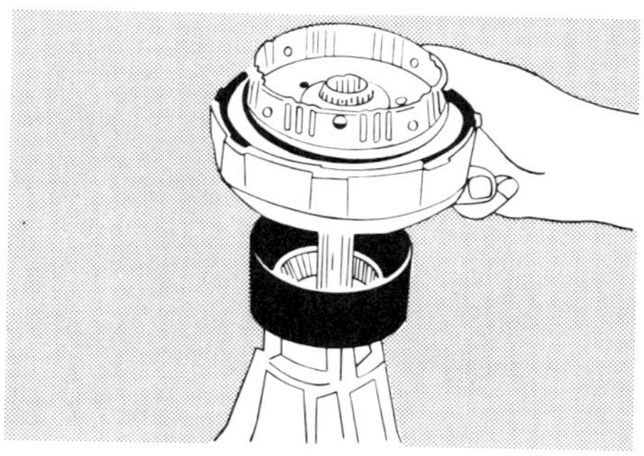

Fig. 5-143. Forward clutch being placed on extension housing so that extension housing can be used as a repair stand.

3. Remove the large snap ring from the front of the clutch drum. Lift out the direct and reverse clutch hub, the forward clutch hub, and then the No. 1 thrust bearing and its races. Notice that the collars of both races point toward the front of the transmission.
4. Remove the clutch plate and the clutch disc. Keep them in a place where they will not be mixed up with the discs and plates yet to be removed.
5. Using a screwdriver, compress and remove the thin snap ring.
6. Remove the remainder of the forward clutch discs and plates—keeping the discs and plates in their exact assembled order.

NOTE ——
Holding the disc/plate pack together with a wire loop will keep it in order. Used discs and plates must be reinstalled in their original positions and locations. The old disc/plate pack can also be used as a guide for correct installation of replacement discs and plates.

7. Using a repair press with a bridge mandrel, such as the Toyota special service tool 00002-00223-04 shown in Fig. 5-144, press down the spring seat just enough to allow removal of the snap ring. Then gradually relieve the spring tension and remove the spring seat and the piston return spring.

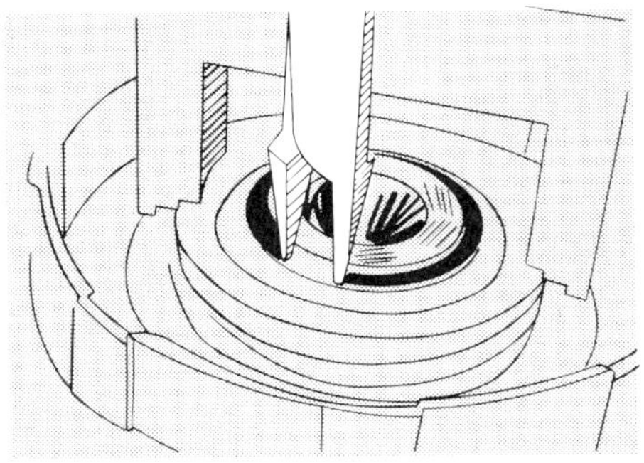

Fig. 5-144. Snap ring being removed with snap ring pliers. Notice bridge mandrel that is being used to hold down spring seat.

8. Temporarily install the forward clutch on the ATF pump, making sure that the drum is a tight fit on the ATF seal rings of the pump. Use compressed air as indicated in Fig. 5-145 to blow out the clutch piston.

NOTE ——

If the piston fails to come out, you can use needle-nose pliers to remove the piston if you are careful not to scratch the piston hub as you grip it.

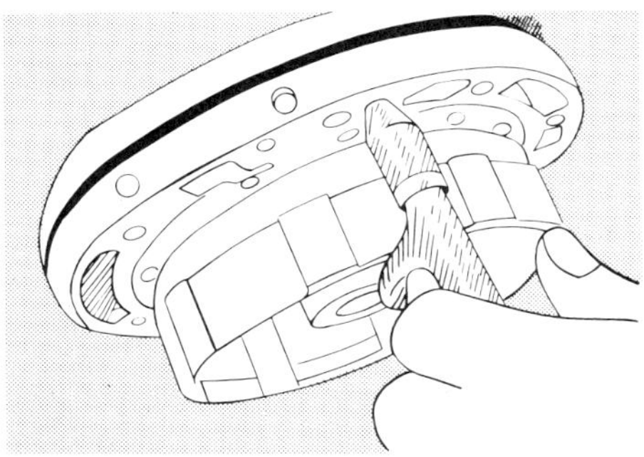

Fig. 5-145. Compressed air being injected into forward clutch ATF port of ATF pump cover.

9. Using your fingers only, remove the O-rings from the forward clutch piston.
10. Remove the forward clutch drum from the ATF pump. Thoroughly wash all forward clutch components—except the lined discs—in clean solvent, then dry them with moisture-free compressed air.

CAUTION ——

Do not use high-pressure compressed air to clean the lined discs. Doing this can damage the lining material. After cleaning and inspection, immediately place the disc/plate pack in a pan of clean ATF so that the lined discs will not dry out. If you intend to install new lined discs, they should be placed in clean ATF at this time so that they will be thoroughly saturated with ATF prior to installation.

11. Carefully inspect the discs and plates. The lugs should not be worn or deformed and both discs and plates should be absolutely flat. Check for scoring, flaking, and debonding of the disc linings, and make sure that neither the discs nor the plates are blackened by burning. Replace damaged discs and plates and replace any disc that has worn to a thickness of less than 2.10 mm (.083 in.).
12. Inspect the piston. Replace it if it is cracked, or if the sliding surfaces or O-ring grooves are worn.

NOTE ——

Shake the piston to make sure that the check ball is free. Blow low-pressure compressed air into the hole in the piston face to see that the ball does not leak.

13. Inspect the clutch drum for cracks and damage. Check the input shaft bearing surfaces for wear, burning, or damage, and check the splines for wear, grooves, and chipped teeth. Replace the clutch drum with input shaft if it is faulty.
14. Inspect the clutch hubs for wear and damage. Replace faulty components.
15. Inspect the piston return spring. Replace it if there is any visible wear or damage. Full spring specifications appear in **6. Automatic Transmission Technical Data.**

To assemble:

1. Using your fingers only, install new O-rings on the clutch piston. Then lubricate the O-rings and the piston sliding surfaces with clean ATF.

NOTE ——

Throughout the assembly procedure, you should lubricate each part thoroughly with clean ATF before you install it in the clutch drum.

2. Install the piston in the clutch drum so that the cupped side of the piston is pointing out of the drum and the check ball hole points into the drum.

3. Install the return spring. Position the spring seat atop the spring, then loosely position the snap ring atop the spring seat. Using the repair press, compress the return spring so that you can install the snap ring as indicated in Fig. 5-146.

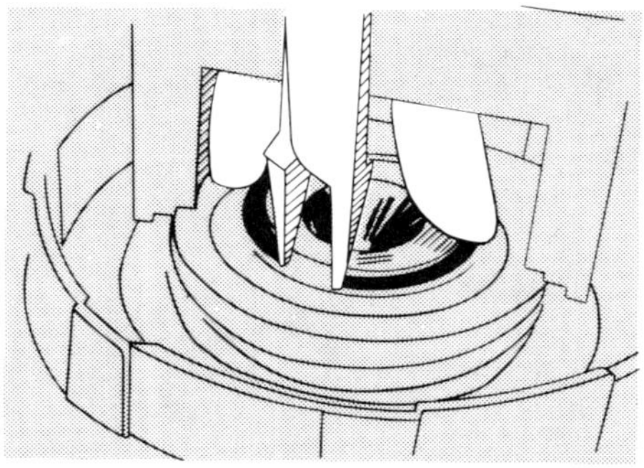

Fig. 5-146. Snap ring being installed with snap ring pliers while spring seat is held down with repair press and bridge mandrel.

4. Install the entire forward clutch disc/plate pack—including the single disc and plate that are beyond the thin snap ring. This installation is for measuring purposes only, so do not install the thin snap ring. The sequence is plate, disc, plate, disc, plate, (no snap ring), disc, plate.
5. Temporarily install the direct and reverse clutch hub and the large, thick snap ring.
6. Using feeler gauges of various thicknesses, determine the free clearance of the forward clutch, as shown in Fig. 5-147. The clearance should be between 0.40 and 1.40 mm (.016 and .055 in.). If it is less, the clutch has been incorrectly assembled; if it is more, there is excessive wear on some clutch component.

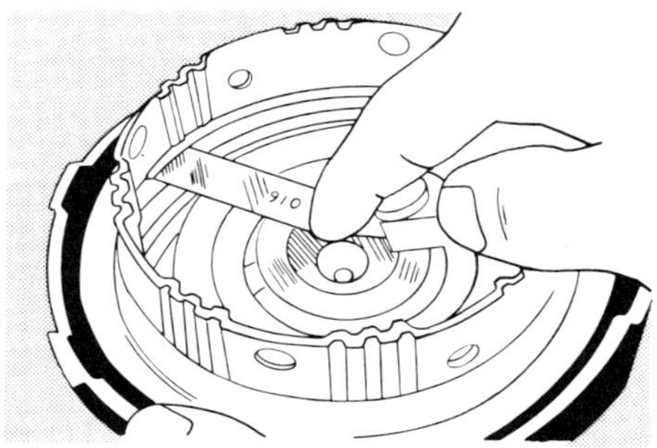

Fig. 5-147. Forward clutch clearance being determined with feeler gauge inserted between large snap ring and flange on direct and reverse clutch hub.

7. Remove the large, thick snap ring and the direct and reverse clutch hub. Remove one clutch plate and one clutch disc.
8. Install the thin snap ring, compressing it and inserting it into the groove of the clutch drum by hand. Make sure that the gap in the ring is not exposed in a groove of the drum.
9. Install first the one disc and then the one plate. Then, using Vaseline as an adhesive, stick the No. 1 thrust bearing and its races to the hub of the drum, as indicated in Fig. 5-148. Notice that the collars on both races point toward the input shaft.

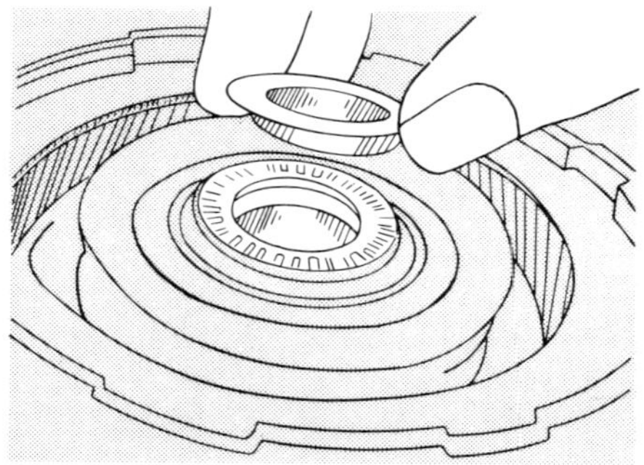

Fig. 5-148. No. 1 thrust bearing and races being installed. Install one race, the bearing, and then the second race, in that order.

10. Using the tip of a screwdriver, align the lugs of the clutch discs. Then install the forward clutch hub—splined end outermost. Make sure that the hub engages all of the discs, and that it seats fully against the No. 1 thrust bearing race.
11. Install the direct and reverse clutch hub. Using a screwdriver to compress the large snap ring, install the snap ring in the clutch drum. Make sure that the ring gap is not exposed in an open notch.
12. Using Vaseline as an adhesive, install the No. 2 thrust bearing's front race and then the No. 2 thrust bearing on the direct and reverse clutch hub. See Fig. 5-149.

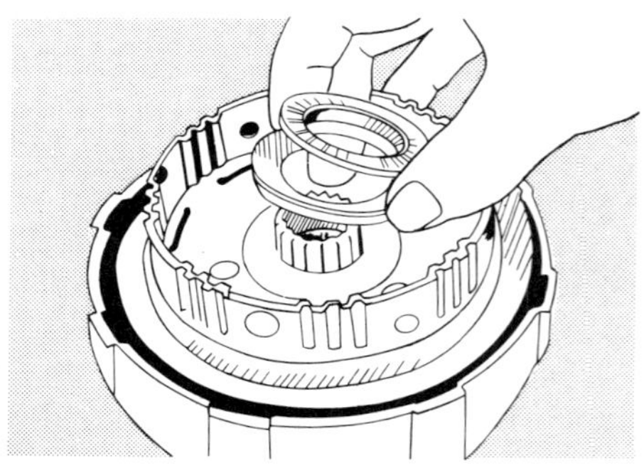

Fig. 5-149. No. 2 thrust bearing and its front race being installed.

13. Using Vaseline as an adhesive, install the No. 2 thrust bearing's rear race over the splined end of the direct and reverse clutch drum, inside the transmission case. The collar on the race should point to the rear of the transmission, toward the sun gear.

14. Reaching into the transmission with a screwdriver, align the lugs of the direct and reverse clutch discs. Then install the forward clutch assembly in the transmission case, meshing the direct and reverse clutch hub with the discs and engaging the splines.

> **NOTE ——**
> To check that the hub has fully engaged all of the discs, look through the ATF pump drain hole and sight across the case. The forward clutch drum should not be visible when it is correctly installed in the case.

Disassembling and Assembling ATF Pump and Completing Transmission Assembly

Fig. 5-150 is an exploded view of the ATF pump. If you have not already removed the pump's ATF seal, remove it as described in **5.1 Removing, Cleaning, Inspecting, and Installing Torque Converter** before you begin disassembling the ATF pump.

To disassemble ATF pump:

1. Place the torque converter open-side-up on the workbench, then install the ATF pump on the torque converter so that the splines on the pump's stator support engage those of the torque converter's stator. In this way, the torque converter can be used as a convenient repair stand for the ATF pump.

2. Remove the ATF pump's two ATF seal rings. These are plastic rings and should be discarded. Install new ATF seal rings during assembly.

3. Using a 10-mm wrench, remove the six bolts and washers that hold the ATF pump cover with stator support to the ATF pump body. Then lift off the cover—pulling the stator support out of the torque converter. The remaining pump parts will be supported by the torque converter's ATF pump drive sleeve.

4. Remove the O-ring and discard it. Then lift the pump body off the torque converter and take out the ATF pump's drivegear and the driven gear.

> ***CAUTION ——***
> *Mark the top side of each gear as you remove it so that later it can be reinstalled in its original position inside the pump body. If used gears are installed upside down, the pump may be noisy.*

Fig. 5-150. Exploded view of ATF pump.

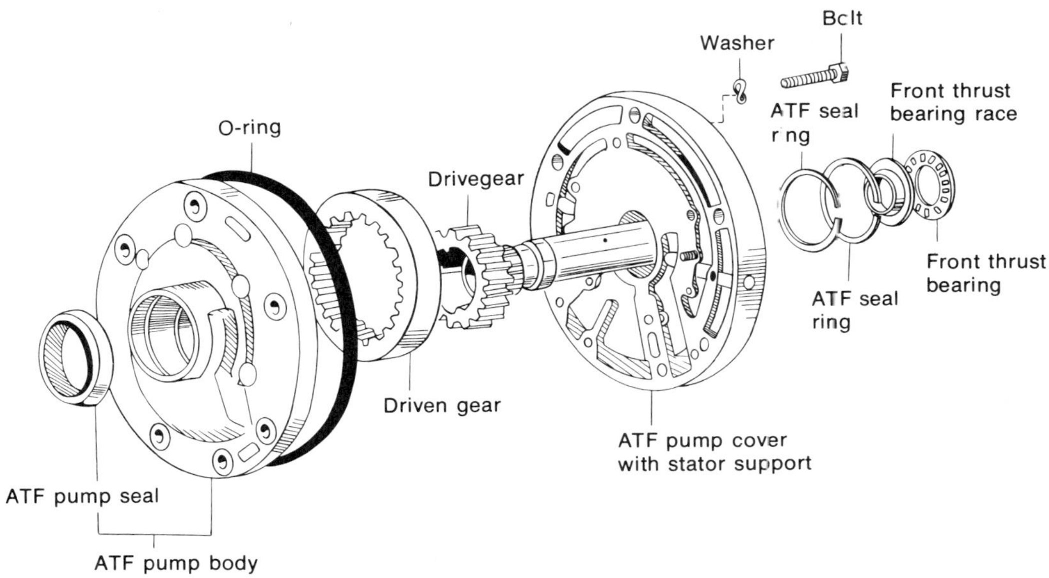

To inspect and assemble:

1. Thoroughly wash all ATF pump components in clean solvent, then dry them with moisture-free compressed air. Do not dry the parts with fluffy rags that can leave behind lint. Lint can jam the precision parts of the automatic transmission.
2. Inspect the ATF pump body and cover for cracks, scoring and other damage. The stator support and its splines should be neither worn nor damaged. Replace worn or damaged components.
3. Measure the inside diameters of the bushings indicated in Fig. 5-151. If any bushing exceeds the maximum permissible inside diameter given in the illustration, replace the component that contains the bushing.

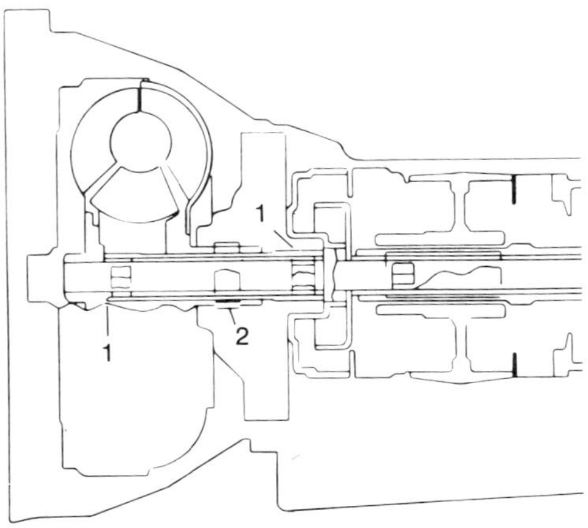

Bushing	Maximum permissible inside diameter
1. Bushings in stator support	21.577 mm (.8495 in.)
2. Bushing inside pump body	38.188 mm (1.5035 in.)

Fig. 5-151. Locations of bushings inside ATF pump.

4. Inspect the gears and replace any that has visible wear, cracks, scoring, or other damage.
5. Install the gears in the ATF pump body, making sure that the sides you marked "TOP" are uppermost.
6. Determine the clearance between the ATF pump driven gear and the ATF pump body as shown in Fig. 5-152. It should be possible to insert a 0.07-mm (.003-in.) feeler gauge, but it should not be possible to insert an 0.30-mm (.012-in.) feeler gauge. Replace worn or distorted components.
7. Determine the gear tip clearance as shown in Fig. 5-153. It should be possible to insert an 0.11-mm (.004-in.) feeler gauge, but it should not be possible to insert an 0.30-mm (.012-in.) feeler gauge. Replace worn or distorted parts.

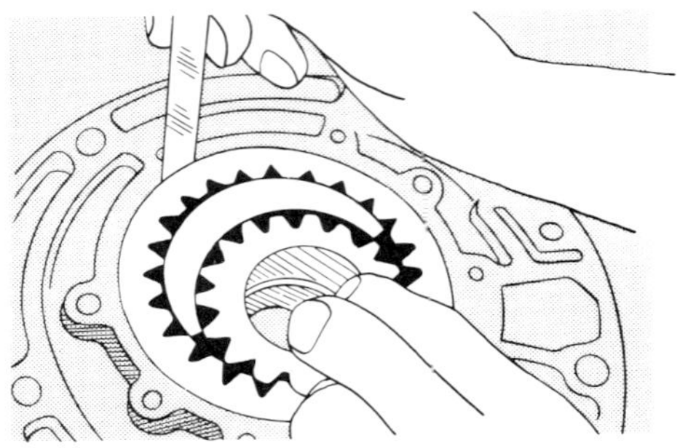

Fig. 5-152. Clearance between driven gear and pump body being checked with feeler gauge.

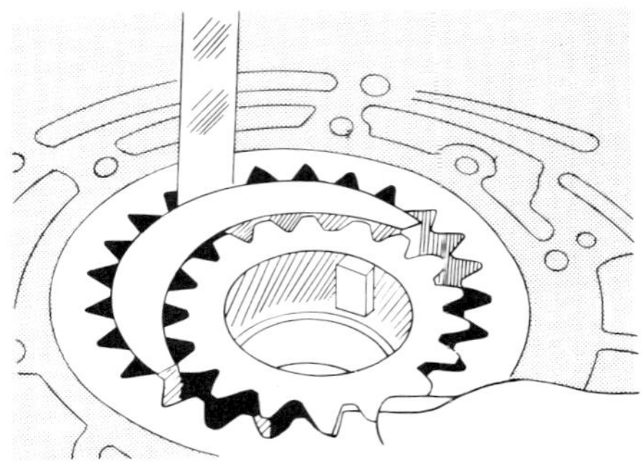

Fig. 5-153. Gear tip clearance being checked. With gears in tight engagement, insert feeler gauge between teeth of driven gear and crescent-shaped part of pump body.

8. Check the side clearance of the ATF pump gears as indicated in Fig. 5-154. You should be able to insert an 0.02-mm (.001-in.) feeler gauge between the straightedge and the gears, but you should not be able to insert an 0.10-mm (.004-in.) feeler gauge. Replace worn or distorted parts.

Fig. 5-154. Side clearance of gears being checked. Place straightedge across gears and pump body, then insert feeler gauge at several points between straightedge and gears.

9. Place the ATF pump body and the gears on the torque converter so that you can use the torque converter as a repair stand.

10. Lubricate the gears and adjacent areas of the pump body and the pump cover with clean ATF. Then install the pump cover with stator support and loosely install the six bolts and washers.

11. Install an alignment band as indicated in Fig. 5-155. Using a 10-mm socket wrench, torque the six bolts in stages to 6 to 8 Nm (53 to 71 in. lb.).

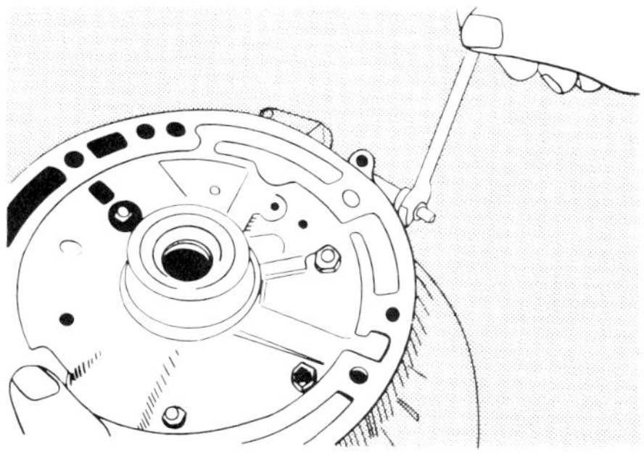

Fig. 5-155. Alignment band (Toyota special service tool 00002-00223-02) being installed around pump body and cover. A large hose clamp or duct clamp can be used if it is carefully installed.

12. Remove the alignment band. With a liberal application of Vaseline to hold them in place, install two new ATF seal rings on the pump cover. Press the rings into their grooves until the rings are flush with the surface, then wipe away the excess Vaseline.

13. Install a new O-ring on the ATF pump. Remove the pump from the torque converter and place it atop a block of wood. Then, using Toyota special service tool 09214-60010, or some other suitable seal driver, install a new ATF seal on the pump so that the seal lip points into the pump and the flat side of the seal is flush with the edge of the pump body.

14. Using Vaseline as an adhesive, install the front thrust bearing and its race as indicated in Fig. 5-156.

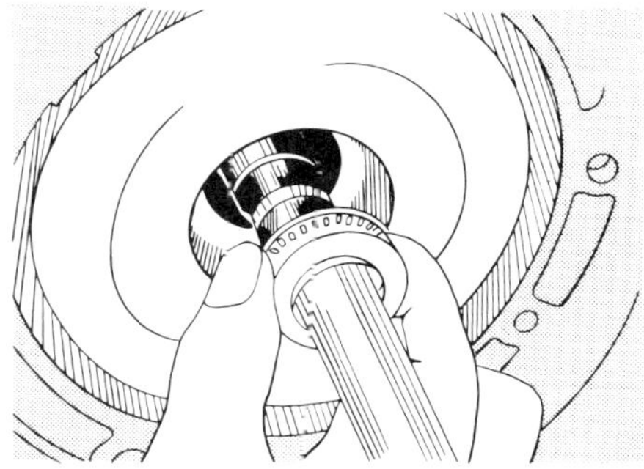

Fig. 5-156. Front thrust bearing and its race being installed over input shaft. Notice that collar on race points toward front of transmission.

15. Install two guide pins as indicated in Fig. 5-157. Lubricate the ATF pump's O-ring with clean ATF, then install the pump and five of the washers and bolts finger-tight. Remove the guide pins and then install the remaining two washers and bolts finger-tight.

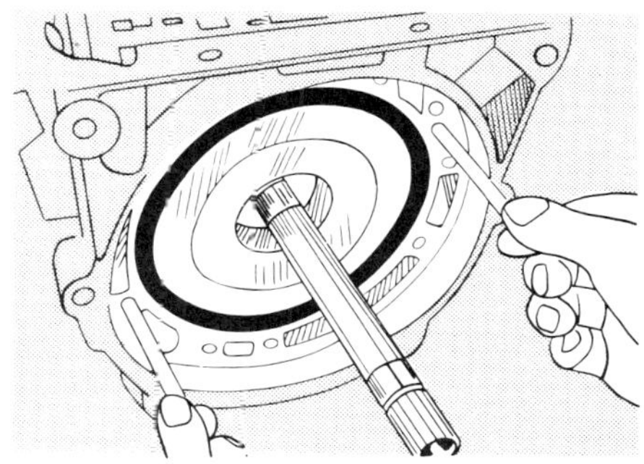

Fig. 5-157. Guide pins being installed in two opposed ATF pump bolt holes in transmission case. Pins can be made from long bolts that have had heads cut off and screwdriver slots sawn into the shanks.

16. Working diagonally with a 13-mm socket wrench, torque the bolts evenly to 20 to 25 Nm (15 to 18 ft. lb.)—pulling the ATF pump fully into the transmission case.

CAUTION —

Be careful not to damage the O-ring, making sure that it slips into the case and is not forced out of its groove. Hand-turn the input shaft while you tighten the bolts to make sure that it is not binding and that the pump is being drawn straight into the case.

17. Using a 14-mm socket wrench, torque the two center support bolts alternately in 7 Nm (5 ft. lb.) increments to 25 to 30 Nm (18 to 22 ft. lb.).

18. Measure the axial play of the input shaft as indicated in Fig. 5-158. The correct axial play is 0.33 to 0.97 mm (.013 to .038 in.). If it is more, excessively worn components have been installed in the transmission. If it is less, some part of the transmission has been incorrectly installed.

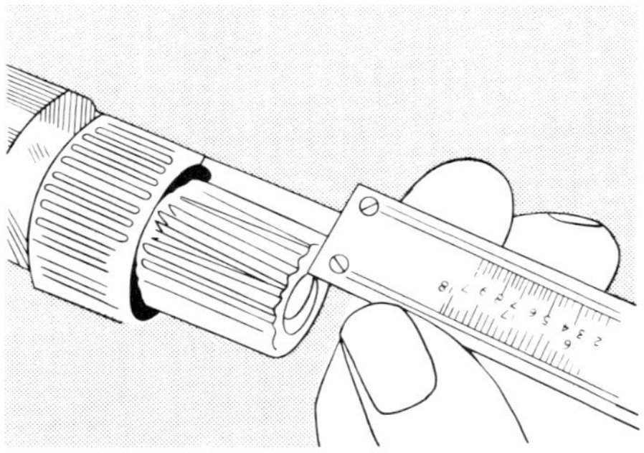

Fig. 5-158. Input axial play being measured. Push shaft in, then measure from tip of input shaft to edge of stator support with vernier caliper. Repeat measurement with input shaft pulled out. Difference in two measurements is axial play.

19. Using low-pressure compressed air, check the operation of the clutch and brake pistons. See Fig. 5-159. Listen for noise that indicates correct movement and retraction of each piston. If pistons fail to move or retract, some part of the transmission has been incorrectly assembled.

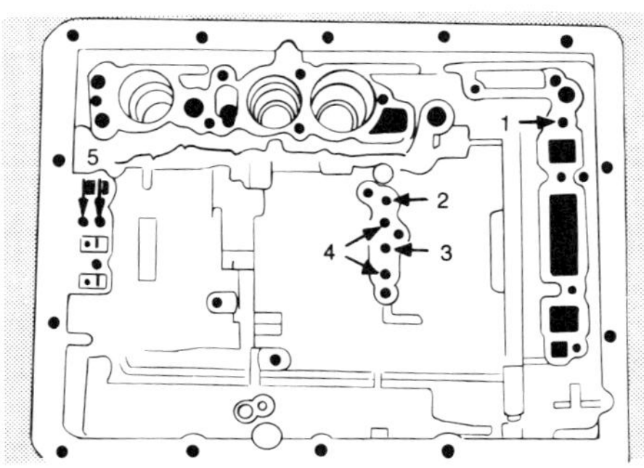

1. Forward clutch
2. No. 1 brake
3. No. 2 brake
4. Direct and reverse clutch
5. No. 3 brake

Fig. 5-159. Points where low-pressure compressed air should be applied to make an air pressure check of piston operations.

20. Install the internal control linkage as described in **5.4 Disassembling and Assembling Internal Control Linkage.** Install the valve body and the ATF pan as described in **5.2 Removing and Installing ATF Pan and Valve Body.**

21. Install the governor on the output shaft, as indicated in Fig. 5-160. Then, using the two snap rings and the Woodruff key, install the speedometer drivegear on the output shaft.

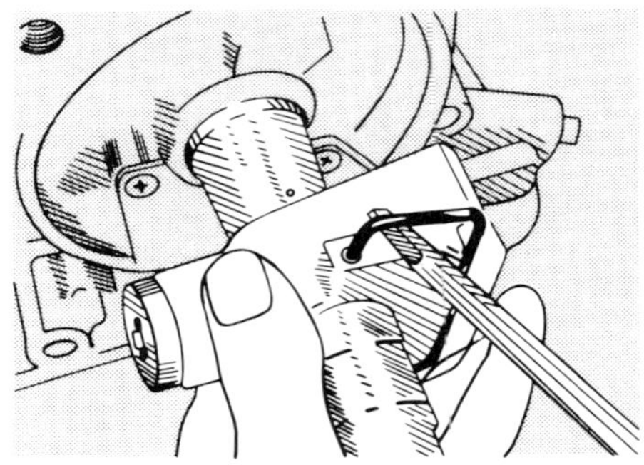

Fig. 5-160. Governor being installed. Hold wire retainer up until governor is in position. Notice that boss for retainer is on side of governor furthest from transmission case.

22. Measure the bushing inside the rear of the extension housing. If it has worn to a diameter greater than 38.075 mm (1.4990 in.), replace the extension housing.

23. Lubricate the output shaft, the governor, and the speedometer drivegear with clean ATF. Then, using a new gasket, install the extension housing on the transmission case. The two short bolts go at the bottom of the extension housing. Working diagonally, torque the six bolts in stages to 30 to 40 Nm (22 to 30 ft. lb.).

24. Install a new rear ATF seal and dust seal in the extension housing. If necessary, consult **4.2 Locating and Stopping External ATF Leaks.**

25. Using a new O-ring, install the speedometer driven gear assembly. Install the retainer. Using a 12-mm socket wrench, torque the bolt to 14 to 15 Nm (10 to 11 ft. lb.).

26. Install the bellhousing. Using a 17-mm socket wrench, torque the large bolts to 50 to 65 Nm (37 to 48 ft. lb.); using a 14-mm socket wrench, torque the small bolts to 30 to 40 Nm (22 to 30 ft. lb.).

6. AUTOMATIC TRANSMISSION TECHNICAL DATA

I. Tightening Torques

Location	Designation	Nm	Ft. lb. (In. lb.)
ATF pan to transmission case	bolt	4–5	(35–44)
Driveshaft rear universal joint to pinion flange or rear axle	bolt	35–40	26–30
Two-piece driveshaft center bearing to car body	bolt	35–40	26–30
Manual lever to transmission's manual shaft	nut	15–20	11–15
ATF drain plug in ATF pan	plug	15–20	11–15
Transmission rear mount to extension housing	bolt	20–25	15–18
Transmission rear mount crossmember to car body	bolt	20–25	15–18
Transmission bellhousing to engine block	bolt	55–75	41–55
Torque converter to drive plate	bolt	15–20	11–15
Starter to engine and bellhousing	bolt	55–75	41–55
ATF cooler line fitting in transmission case	fitting	20–30	15–22
ATF cooler line to fitting	union	20–30	15–22
ATF cooler line clamp to engine or transmission	bolt	7–8	5–6 (62–71)
Valve body assembly to transmission case	bolt	8–11	(71–97)
ATF strainer to valve body	bolt	5–6	(44–53)
Throttle valve body to manual valve body	bolt	5–6	(44–53)
2nd gear/3rd gear shift valve body to manual valve body	bolt	5–6	(44–53)
Detent spring to valve body assembly	bolt	5–6	(44–53)
Throttle cam assembly to throttle valve body	bolt	6–8	(53–71)
Cover plates to valve bodies	bolt	5–6	(44–53)
Extension housing to transmission case	bolt	30–40	22–30
Speedometer driven gear assembly retainer to transmission case	bolt	14–15	10–11
Parking pawl bracket to transmission case	bolt	6–7	(53–62)
Pressure tap plugs in transmission case	plug	6–8	(53–71)
ATF pump cover to ATF pump body	bolt	6–8	(53–71)
ATF pump to transmission case	bolt	20–25	15–18
Center support to transmission case (torque bolts alternately in 7 Nm (5 ft. lb.) increments	bolt	25–30	18–22
Bellhousing to transmission case	large bolt small bolt	50–65 30–40	37–48 22–30

II. ATF Pump Specifications

Designation	With new parts	Wear limit
Clearance between driven gear and pump body	0.07 to 0.15 mm (.003 to .006 in.)	0.30 mm (.012 in.)
Clearance between tip of driven gear tooth and pump body crescent, with drivegear installed	0.11 to 0.14 mm (.004 to .006 in.)	0.30 mm (.012 in.)
Clearance from sides of gears to cover (side clearance)	0.02 to 0.05 mm (.001 to .002 in.)	0.10 mm (.004 in.)

III. Dimensions Used During Transmission Assembly

Dimension	With new parts	Wear limit
No. 3 brake disc/plate pack free clearance	0.80 to 1.80 mm (.032 to .071 in.)	2.20 mm (.087 in.)
No. 2 brake disc/plate pack free clearance	0.30 to 1.20 mm (.012 to .047 in.)	1.20 mm (.047 in.)
No. 1 brake disc/plate pack free clearance	0.30 to 1.00 mm (.012 to .040 in.)	1.20 mm (.047 in.)
Direct and reverse clutch disc/plate pack free clearance	0.40 to 1.20 mm (.016 to .047 in.)	1.60 mm (.063 in.)
Forward clutch disc/plate pack free clearance	0.40 to 1.40 mm (.016 to .055 in.)	1.90 mm (.075 in.)
Input shaft axial play	0.33 to 0.97 mm (.013 to .038 in.)	—
Remaining thickness of lined discs	—	2.10 mm (.083 in.)

IV. Pressure Testing Data

Governor pressure	**Output shaft rpm**	**Pressure**	
	1000 (about 17 mph) 1800 (about 30 mph) 3500 (about 60 mph)	0.9–1.5 bar (12.8–21.3 psi) 1.6–2.2 bar (22.8–31.3 psi) 4.1–5.3 bar (58.3–75.4 psi)	
Line pressure	**Engine rpm**	**Pressure with selector lever at D**	**Pressure with selector lever at R**
	1000 at stall speed	4.0–4.5 bar (57–64 psi) 9.5–12.0 bar (135–171 psi)	5.8–6.8 bar (82–97 psi) 14.0–17.0 bar (200–242 psi)
Stall speed	2050 ± 150 rpm		
Time lag before gear engagement	Selector lever moved from **N** to **D** Selector lever moved from **N** to **R**	Less than 1.2 seconds Less than 1.5 seconds	
Throttle cable adjustment at wide-open throttle position	Cable conduit rubber end cap to throttle cable stop collar	52 mm (2.05 in. or 2 3/64 in.)	

V. Valve Body Spring Dimensions

Spring location	Outside diameter	Free height	Number of coils	Wire diameter
Springs in throttle valve body				
Throttle valve	8.58 mm (.338 in.)	19.24 mm (.757 in.)	8	0.71 mm (.028 in.)
Downshift plug	10.89 mm (.429 in.)	43.00 mm (1.693 in.)	15.5	1.19 mm (.047 in.)
Secondary regulator valve	16.84 mm (.663 in.)	74.83 mm (2.946 in.)	15	1.60 mm (.063 in.)
Springs in 1st gear/2nd gear shift valve body				
Intermediate modulator valve	8.76 mm (.345 in.)	35.43 mm (1.395 in.)	14	0.89 mm (.035 in.)
Reverse sequence valve	9.14 mm (.360 in.)	36.83 mm (1.450 in.)	15	1.14 mm (.045 in.)
Governor modulator valve	9.09 mm (.358 in.)	36.07 mm (1.420 in.)	12	0.71 mm (.028 in.)
Low modulator valve	9.24 mm (.364 in.)	42.35 mm (1.667 in.)	15	0.84 mm (.033 in.)
2nd/3rd gear shift valve	8.96 mm (.353 in.)	35.10 mm (1.382 in.)	12.5	0.76 mm (.030 in.)
1975 through 1977 model detent regulator valve	9.24 mm (.364 in.)	42.35 mm (1.667 in.)	15	0.84 mm (.033 in.)
1978 and later model detent regulator valve	8.85 mm (.348 in.)	32.08 mm (1.263 in.)	15	0.90 mm (.035 in.)
Springs in manual valve body				
Sequence valve	9.17 mm (.361 in.)	37.55 mm (1.478 in.)	14.5	1.17 mm (.046 in.)
1st/2nd gear shift valve	7.52 mm (.296 in.)	34.62 mm (1.363 in.)	13	0.56 mm (.022 in.)
Pressure relief ball	13.14 mm (.517 in.)	32.14 mm (1.265 in.)	9	2.03 mm (.080 in.)
Cooler bypass valve	13.82 mm (.544 in.)	30.65 mm (1.207 in.)	7	1.32 mm (.052 in.)
1975 through 1977 model primary regulator valve	17.72 mm (.698 in.)	81.48 mm (3.208 in.)	15	1.59 mm (.063 in.)
1978 and later model primary regulator valve	16.72 mm (.658 in.)	73.32 mm (2.887 in.)	15	1.59 mm (.063 in.)
Regulator valve damping check ball	—	19.50 mm (.768 in.)	—	—

VI. Approximate Automatic Shift Speeds at Wide-open Throttle

Final drive gear ratior	Selector lever at D				Selector lever at L
	1st gear to 2nd gear	2nd gear to 3rd gear	3rd gear to 2nd gear	2nd gear to 1st gear	2nd gear to 1st gear
4.100	45 to 60 kph (28 to 37 mph)	86 to 101 kph (53 to 63 mph)	82 to 97 kph (51 to 60 mph)	38 to 51 kph (24 to 32 mph)	38 to 53 kph (24 to 33 mph)
3.909	47 to 62 kph (29 to 39 mph)	90 to 105 kph (56 to 65 mph)	86 to 101 kph (53 to 63 mph)	40 to 53 kph (25 to 33 mph)	41 to 56 kph (25 to 35 mph)

VII. Transmission Bushing Dimensions

Location	Bushing length mm (in.)	Inside diameter when new mm (in.)	Inside diameter wear limit mm (in.)
Bushings inside stator support	9.70 (.382)	21.501 to 21.527 (.8465 to .8475)	21.577 (.8495)
Bushing inside ATF pump body	13.46 (.530)	38.113 to 38.138 (1.5005 to 1.5015)	38.188 (1.5035)
Bushings inside sun gear	9.70 (.382)	21.501 to 21.527 (.8465 to .8475)	21.577 (.8495)
Bushing inside center support	65.68 (2.586)	36.386 to 36.411 (1.4325 to 1.4335)	36.461 (1.4355)
Bushing in rear of transmission case	13.46 (.530)	38.113 to 38.138 (1.5005 to 1.5015)	38 188 (1.5035)
Bushing inside output shaft	9.70 (.382)	18.001 to 18.025 (.7087 to .7096)	18 076 (.7117)
Bushing inside rear of extension housing	30.00 (1.181)	38.000 to 38.025 (1.4961 to 1.4970)	38.075 (1.4990)

VIII. Clutch and Brake Piston Return Spring Specifications

Designation	New parts	Wear limit
Clutch piston return spring .... free height	33.30 mm (1.311 in.)	32.20 mm (1.268 in.)
.... installed height	22.30 mm (.878 in.)	—
.... installed load	37.29–41.23 kg (82.19–90.90 lb.)	—
.... coil inside diameter	65.50–66.36 mm (2.579–2.613 in.)	—
Brake piston return spring .... free height	16.12 mm (.625 in.)	15.70 mm (.618 in.)
load required to compress to height of 11.5 mm (29/64 in.)	2.15–2.38 kg (4.74–5.25 lb.)	—
.... coil outside diameter	8.00 mm (.315 in.)	—

IX. Accumulator Piston and Spring Specifications

Accumulator location	Piston outside diameter mm (in.)	Piston length mm (in.)	Piston bore (in case) mm (in.)	Spring free height mm (in.)
Front	34.80–34.85 (1.3701–1.3720)	48.50 (1.909)	34.97–35.00 (1.3768–1.3779)	63.50 (2.500)
Center	31.80–31.85 (1.2520–1.2539)	45.00 (1.772)	31.97–32.00 (1.2587–1.2598)	34.82 (1.371)
Rear	31.80–31.85 (1.2520–1.2539)	49.50 (1.949)	31.97–32.00 (1.2587–1.2598)	68.56 (2.698)

CLUTCH AND MANUAL TRANSMISSION

Contents

TABLE

Clutch and Manual Transmission

Both the four-speed manual transmission, standard on the cars covered by this Manual, and the optional five-speed manual transmission share the same basic design and have many interchangeable parts. The four-speed T40 transmission is, in fact, the five-speed T50 transmission with the fifth-gear gearset left out. These transmissions, used only with the 1600 engine, are completely different from the four-speed and five-speed manual transmissions used on Corolla models with smaller-displacement engines.

The T40/T50 transmission design is unique today because it has a split-type "clamshell" case. This design requires more careful engineering and a greater number of precision machining steps than the box-type cases commonly used in modern production cars, but the design also has several noteworthy advantages. First, the split-type case makes transmission repairs easier and eliminates the need for special tools and assembly jigs that are sometimes necessary when tunnel-type or box-type transmissions are being repaired or adjusted. Second, the split case permits the use of very robust ball and roller countergear bearings, instead of the small and awkward-to-assemble needle bearing sets that are commonly found in this location. Finally, the case is stronger because it lacks the large access openings found on most production car transmissions.

Another noteworthy feature of the Toyota T40 and T50 transmissions is that their gearshift linkage is contained entirely within the extension housing and the transmission case. This ensures better gearshift lever control and feel than is normally found with external linkages. It also prevents corrosion and deteriorating rubber bushings from interfering with transmission operation after several years of driving in wet or snowy conditions.

Though you may not have the tools or the skills for carrying out actual repairs, you may be able to remove the transmission, which can help reduce service time. In this case, we recommend that you thoroughly clean the transmission on the outside and then take it to the shop as is—partial disassembly will not make repairs easier and may indeed complicate them. We especially urge you to consult an Authorized Dealer before you attempt repairs on a car that is still covered by the new-car warranty.

Cleanliness and a careful approach are imperative when repairing either the clutch or the manual transmission. If necessary, mark the parts to show their proper assembly order or position. Also make sure that you have the necessary tools, particularly for procedures given only with metric specifications. Work that is designated by the lack of U.S. equivalents can be carried out correctly only with metric tools and instruments.

1. GENERAL DESCRIPTION

Fig. 1-1 shows cross-sections of both the four-speed and the five-speed manual transmissions that are used in the cars covered by this Manual. It can be seen from the illustration that the main difference between the two transmissions is the addition of the fifth-gear gearset at the rear of the T50 gear train, and the incorporation of two additional ball bearing races.

Transmission Case

The transmission case, as well as the bellhousing and the extension housing, is die cast in high-strength aluminum alloy. The bellhousing, bolted to the front of the split-type "clamshell" transmission case, houses the flywheel and the clutch. The extension housing, which is bolted to the rear of the transmission case, provides a mounting point for the gearshift lever and gives support to the output shaft and the driveshaft's front universal joint.

Transmission Gear Train

The transmission gears are of the constant-mesh type with balk ring synchronizers. All forward gears are synchronized, and all clutch gear/synchronizer assemblies are located on the transmission's mainshaft. The gears on the mainshaft can be replaced individually. The countershaft, however, consists of a one-piece cluster gear and, on five-speed models, a separate fifth-speed gear. On both four-speed and five-speed countershafts, the reverse gear is separate and fits on splines at the rear of the countershaft.

Clutch

The clutch is a conventional single dry plate unit bolted to the engine's flywheel. On both the four-speed and five-speed models, the clutch is operated hydraulically by a slave cylinder bolted to the bellhousing. Hydraulic pressure is generated by a master cylinder operated by the clutch pedal.

2. MAINTENANCE

The maintenance steps that must be performed at regular intervals are listed here and described either in **LUBRICATION AND MAINTENANCE** or in this section of the Manual under the heading listed.

1. Checking and, if necessary, adjusting clutch pedal freeplay. **3.1**
2. Checking clutch master cylinder fluid level, and adding fluid if necessary
3. Checking and, if necessary, correcting the transmission oil level
4. Changing transmission oil.

3. CLUTCH

The clutch hydraulic system can be serviced and repaired with no major disassembly of any part of the car. However, in order to service either the clutch disk and pressure plate or the clutch release bearing, you must remove the transmission from the car. You can also service the clutch with the engine removed, but you should consider this alternative only if the engine too requires extensive repairs.

Fig. 1-1. Cross-sections of four-speed and five-speed transmissions. Notice the large ball and roller bearings that support the countershaft (the lower shaft of the transmission).

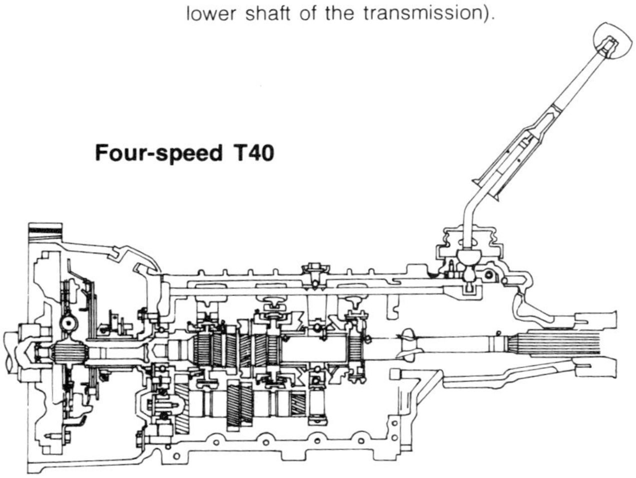

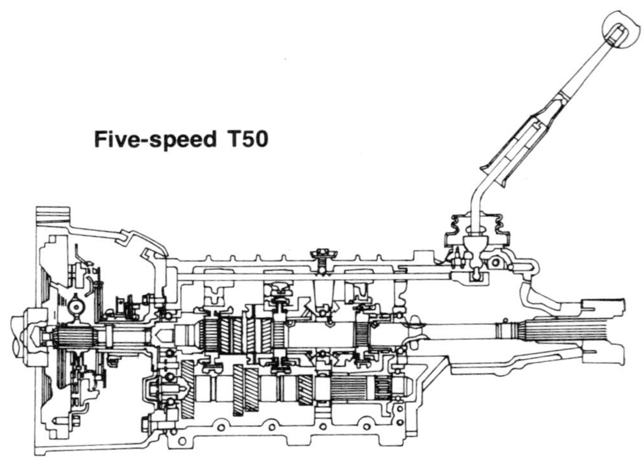

3.1 Adjusting Clutch Freeplay

Incorrect clutch freeplay is among the most frequent causes of clutch failure and may also be a contributing factor to some transmission failures. Check and adjust the clutch freeplay (1) at the regular mileage intervals prescribed in **LUBRICATION AND MAINTENANCE,** (2) whenever the clutch does not engage or disengage properly, and (3) following the installation of new clutch parts.

To adjust freeplay:

1. On 1978 and later cars only, check and, if necessary, adjust the pedal height and the pedal freeplay as indicated in Fig. 3-1. Because of a redesigned clutch release lever and slave cylinder, no further clutch adjustments are required on 1978 and later cars.
2. On 1975 through 1977 cars only, check and, if necessary, adjust the pedal height and the pedal freeplay as indicated in Fig. 3-1. Then carry out the remaining steps in this procedure.

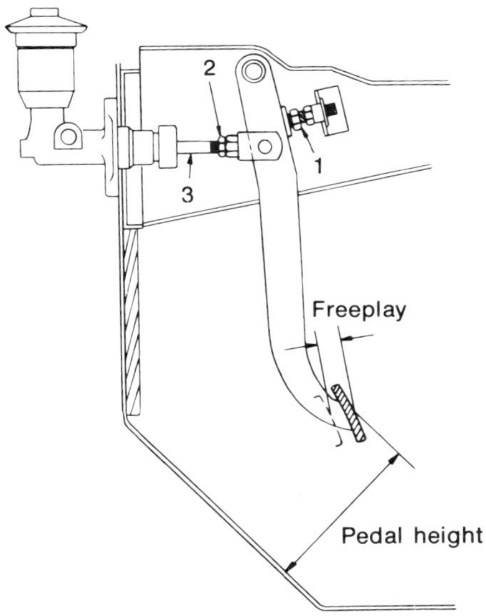

Dimension	1975–1977	1978 and later
Pedal height	169 mm ($6\,^{21}/_{32}$ in.)	169 mm ($6\,^{21}/_{32}$ in.)
Pedal freeplay	20 to 40 mm ($^{25}/_{32}$ to $1\,^{9}/_{16}$ in.)	5 to 15 mm ($^{13}/_{64}$ to $^{19}/_{32}$ in.)
Pushrod clearance	2 to 3.5 mm ($^{5}/_{64}$ to $^{9}/_{64}$ in.)	—

Fig. 3-1. Pedal adjustments. Pedal height, measured from pedal pad surface to floorboard insulation sheet (beneath carpet), is adjusted by turning bolt (**1**). Pedal freeplay (distance pedal travels before pushrod contacts master cylinder piston) is adjusted by loosening locknut (**2**) and turning pushrod (**3**), thereby changing pushrod clearance.

3. Working beneath the car, unhook the return spring from the lug on the slave cylinder. Then measure the distance that the clutch release lever can be pulled away from the slave cylinder pushrod's spherical seat. If this freeplay is not between 2 and 3.5 mm ($^{5}/_{64}$ and $^{9}/_{64}$ in.), adjust it as indicated in Fig. 3-2.

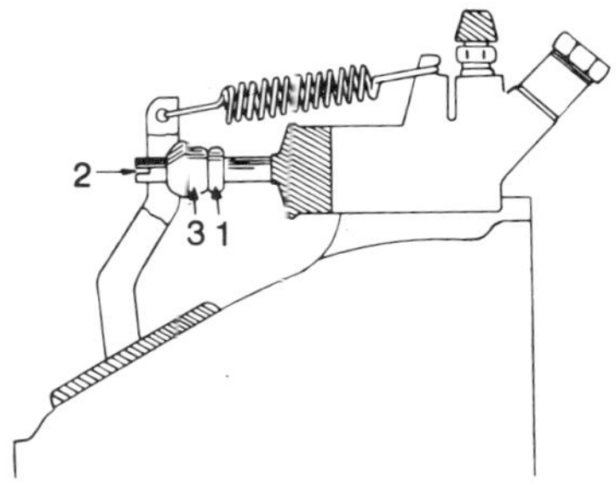

Fig. 3-2. Clutch freeplay adjustment. To adjust freeplay, loosen locknut (**1**), then use a screwdriver to turn pushrod (**2**) while holding nut (**3**) stationary with wrench. Tighten locknut and reconnect spring when freeplay is correct.

2

Bleeding Hydraulic System

After you have adjusted the clutch freeplay, have someone operate the clutch pedal while you observe the clutch release lever. If there is little movement of the release lever, or if there is a great deal of pedal travel before the release lever begins to move, bleed the hydraulic system as described in the next procedure. You should also bleed the system if depressing the pedal fails to disengage the clutch fully, as indicated by difficult gear shifting or clashing engagement of the gears.

To bleed hydraulic system:

1. Fill the clutch master cylinder reservoir with new, unused brake fluid that meets the DOT 3 standard. Then raise the car on a hoist or support it on stands designed for the purpose.
2. Remove the dust cap from the bleeder valve on the slave cylinder. Slip a 4-mm ($^{5}/_{32}$-in.) I.D. hose over the bleeder valve and immerse the other end in a jar partially filled with clean brake fluid. The jar must be clear so that you can see air bubbles coming out of the hose.

3. Using a wrench as indicated in Fig. 3-3, open the bleeder valve a half-turn. Have someone slowly depress the clutch pedal until it reaches the floor and keep it there while you close the bleeder valve.
4. Have your helper slowly release the pedal until it is completely up. Repeat the preceding step until no more air bubbles emerge from the hose. If the system contains a great deal of air, it will be necessary to add more fluid to the reservoir once or twice. Never let the reservoir be emptied completely, or you will have to begin bleeding the system all over again.

***WARNING* ——**
Do not use soft-drink bottles or other food containers to store brake fluid or to bleed the clutch. Brake fluid is poisonous and can also damage painted surfaces if you allow it to spill on the car body.

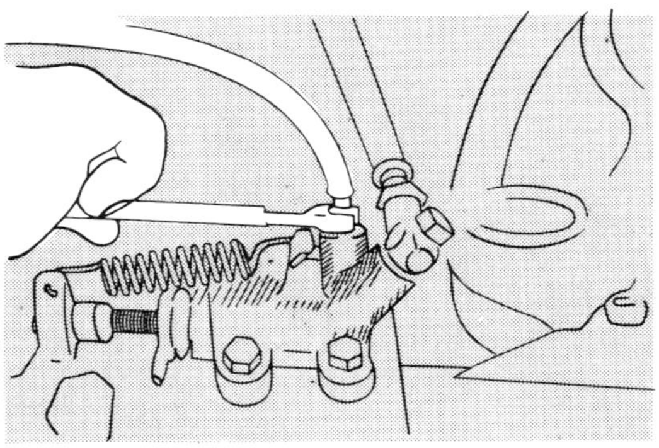

Fig. 3-3. Wrench being used to open bleeder valve on slave cylinder. Notice hose slipped over end of valve.

3.2 Removing and Installing Clutch Pedal

Fig. 3-4 is an exploded view that illustrates the removal of the clutch pedal and related components. To remove the pedal, first remove the pedal return spring. Remove the cotter pin and the clevis pin for the pushrod yoke. Remove the pedal mounting bolt, then remove the pedal and disassemble the bushing and the collars.

Installation is the reverse of removal. Replace the bushing or any collar, pin, or bolt that is worn. Worn pedal pads and pedals with worn bearing bores should likewise be replaced. Apply a thin coating of multipurpose grease to the bushing before you install it. Torque the nut for the pedal (mounting bolt to 30 to 40 Nm (22 to 30 ft. lb.).

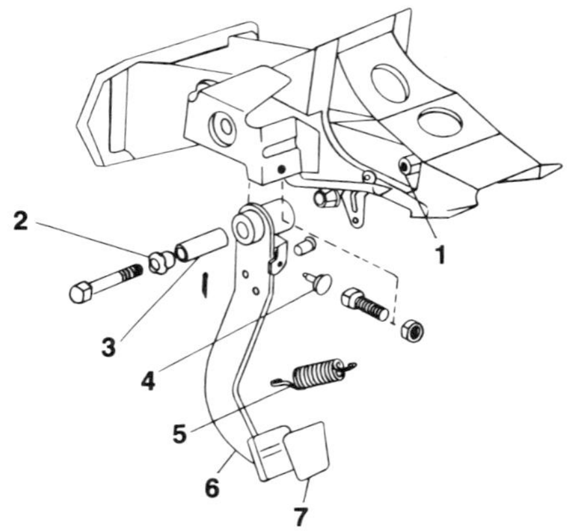

1. Nut
2. Collar (2)
3. Bushing
4. Stop cushion
5. Pedal return spring
6. Pedal
7. Pedal pad

Fig. 3-4. Exploded view of clutch pedal and related components.

3.3 Removing and Installing Clutch Master Cylinder

The clutch master cylinder is located in the engine compartment, to the left of the brake servo and brake master cylinder. To prevent getting fluid on the car body, which can damage the paint, use a clean syringe to remove as much fluid as possible from the reservoir before you remove the master cylinder.

To remove:

1. Working in the engine compartment, disconnect the hydraulic line from the clutch master cylinder.
2. Working beneath the dashboard, remove the cotter pin and the clevis pin from the clutch pedal, thus disconnecting the pedal from the master cylinder's pushrod yoke.
3. Beneath the dashboard, remove the two nuts that hold the clutch master cylinder to the car body.
4. Remove the master cylinder from the engine compartment.

To install:

1. Loosely position the clutch master cylinder on the car body, guiding the pushrod yoke into position on the clutch pedal.
2. Before you install the mounting nuts, attach the hydraulic line to the master cylinder. Torque the union to 13 to 15 Nm (9.5 to 11 ft. lb.).
3. Working beneath the dashboard, install the two mounting nuts to a torque of 6 to 10 Nm (53 to 89 in. lb.).
4. Install the clevis pin and a new cotter pin. Then adjust and bleed the clutch as described in **3.1 Adjusting Clutch Freeplay.**

Rebuilding Clutch Master Cylinder

Fig. 3-5 is an exploded view of the clutch master cylinder. All the necessary components for repairing or rebuilding the master cylinder are available in a rebuilding kit.

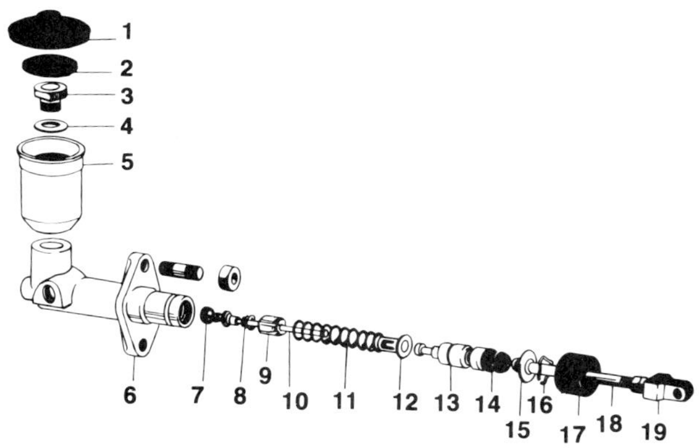

1. Reservoir filler cap
2. Float
3. Reservoir mounting bolt
4. Mounting bolt washer
5. Reservoir
6. Master cylinder body
7. Inlet valve
8. Conical spring
9. Inlet valve housing
10. Connecting rod
11. Piston return spring
12. Return spring retainer
13. Piston
14. Piston cup
15. Piston stop plate
16. Retaining ring
17. Boot
18. Pushrod
19. Pushrod yoke

Fig. 3-5. Exploded view of clutch master cylinder.

To rebuild:

1. Clamp the master cylinder in a vise that has soft jaws. Then, using a suitable socket wrench and an extension, remove the reservoir mounting bolt, being very careful not to damage any fluid sealing surfaces.
2. Pull back the boot. Then use the tip of a screwdriver to remove the retaining ring from its groove.
3. Withdraw the internal parts from the master cylinder.
4. Inspect the bore inside the master cylinder body. If the bore is visibly scored or worn—or if the clearance between the cylinder and the piston exceeds 0.15 mm (.0059 in.) even with a new piston—replace the master cylinder as a unit.
5. Inspect the remaining components. If the piston cup or any other part is visibly worn or damaged, replace all the parts with new parts from a clutch master cylinder rebuilding kit.
6. Wash all parts in clean brake fluid that meets the DOT 3 standard; then assemble the internal components as indicated in Fig. 3-6.
7. Apply silicone grease or brake cylinder paste at the points indicated in Fig. 3-6. Then install the internal parts in the master cylinder body.

CAUTION —

Do not use any lubricant other than brake cylinder paste, silicone grease, or some other lubricant that is marketed as a rubber grease suitable for use in brake and clutch hydraulic systems. Other lubricants will cause rapid deterioration of the rubber components of the hydraulic system.

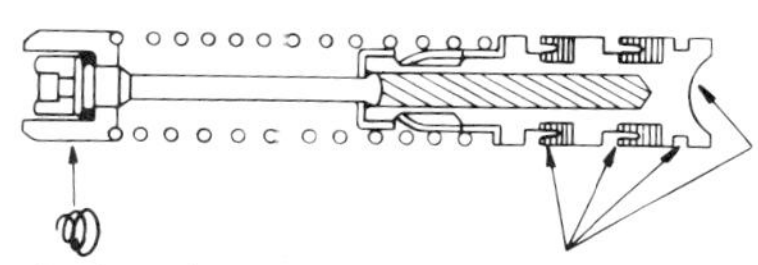

Fig. 3-6. Clutch master cylinder internal parts correctly assembled. Notice correct directions shown for lips on cups.

8. Install the retaining ring, the boot, and the pushrod.
9. With the master cylinder clamped in a vise with soft jaws, install the reservoir. Torque the reservoir mounting bolt to 20 to 25 Nm (15 to 18 ft. lb.).

3.4 Removing and Installing Clutch Slave Cylinder

The clutch slave cylinder is located on the right-hand side of the transmission's bellhousing. You need not disconnect the hydraulic line if the cylinder is being dismounted prior to removal of the transmission.

To remove:

1. Working beneath the car, disconnect the hydraulic line from the slave cylinder (item **A** in Fig. 3-7), and quickly plug the line.
2. On 1975 through 1977 cars, remove the coil spring (item **B** in Fig. 3-7).
3. Remove the two mounting bolts (items **C** in Fig. 3-7). Then remove the slave cylinder from the car.

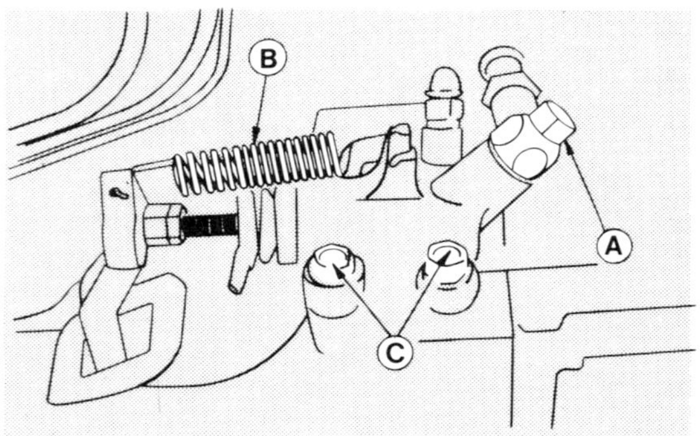

Fig. 3-7. Clutch slave cylinder removal. Hydraulic line connection is at **A**, coil spring at **B**, and mounting bolts at **C**.

Installation is the reverse of removal. Torque the mounting bolts to 10 to 15 Nm (7.5 to 11 ft. lb.). Torque the hydraulic line union bolt to 35 to 40 Nm (26 to 30 ft. lb.). Following installation adjust and bleed the clutch as described in **3.1 Adjusting Clutch Freeplay.**

Rebuilding Clutch Slave Cylinder

To disassemble the slave cylinder, first remove it. Then pull off the rubber boot that surrounds the pushrod and remove the pushrod. Using compressed air injected into the hydraulic line port, expel the internal parts from the slave cylinder. Alternatively, you can shake the internal parts out of the cylinder by tapping the cylinder against a piece of hard wood.

Wash all parts in clean brake fluid. Replace the clutch slave cylinder as a unit if its bore is visibly worn. Otherwise, assemble the cylinder as indicated in Fig. 3-8, using new components from a slave cylinder rebuilding kit. Be sure to install the cups so that their lips point in the directions indicated in the illustration.

CAUTION —
Do not use lubricants that are not prescribed for use in brake or clutch hydraulic cylinders. Incorrect lubricants will cause rapid deterioration of rubber components in the system.

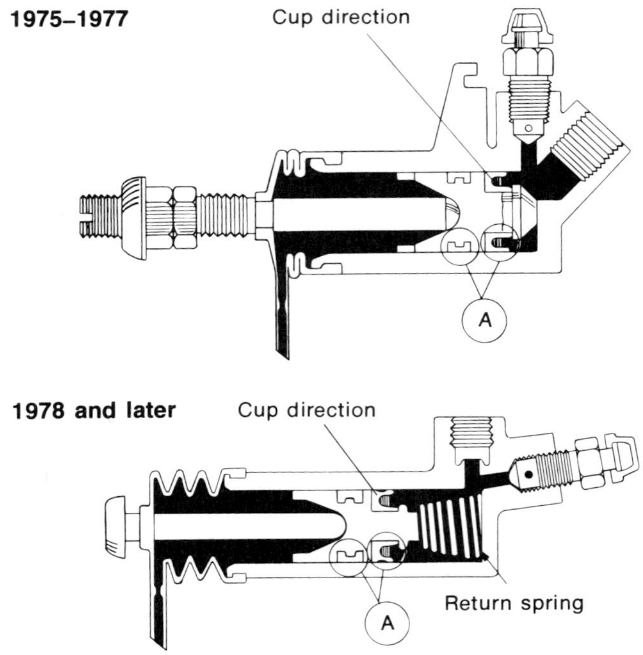

Fig. 3-8. Clutch slave cylinders correctly assembled. Notice positions of cups. Lubricate cups (**A**) with silicone grease, brake cylinder paste, or some other rubber lubricant recommended for hydraulic cylinder components. Notice return spring used only in later cylinder.

3.5 Removing and Installing Clutch

The flywheel and clutch assembly remain on the engine's crankshaft when you separate the transmission from the engine. The clutch release bearing and related parts stay in the transmission's bellhousing.

To remove:

1. Unless the engine has already been removed for repair, remove the transmission as described in **4.4 Removing and Installing Transmission.**
2. Mark the position of the pressure plate assembly so that you can install it in the exact original position on the flywheel. Loosen each bolt about a quarter-turn at a time (Fig. 3-9). Work around the flywheel until the pressure is relieved, then remove the bolts completely.
3. Remove the pressure plate assembly and the clutch disk from the flywheel.

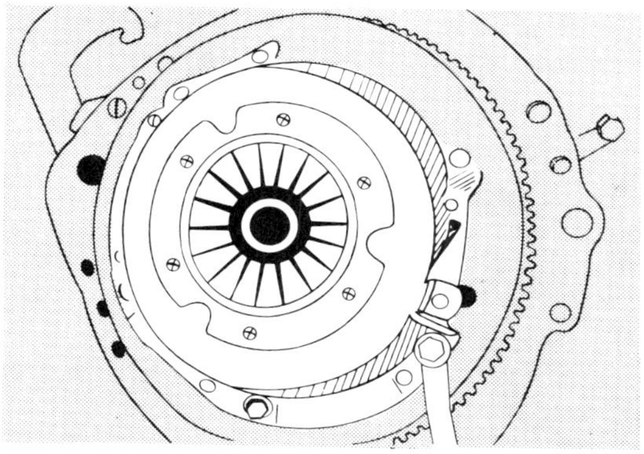

Fig. 3-9. Clutch pressure plate assembly being unbolted from flywheel.

To install:

1. Clean the friction surface of the flywheel and inspect it for wear, cracks, and grooves. Minor defects may be corrected by regrinding or machining at a specialty shop. If the flywheel is unserviceable, replace it as described in **ENGINE**.
2. Inspect the pressure plate for wear, cracks, and grooves. Alternately bright and dull areas indicate a warped plate. If the clutch has been slipping, compare the old pressure plate assembly with a new assembly. If the disengagement levers of the old assembly are noticeably lower than those of the new assembly, the diaphragm spring has lost tension and the pressure plate assembly should be replaced.
3. Inspect the clutch release bearing. If it feels gritty when you turn it, or if it has been making noise, replace it as indicated in Fig. 3-10. Never wash the bearing in solvent since doing this will remove the factory-installed lubricant. If the release bearing is unserviceable, replace it.

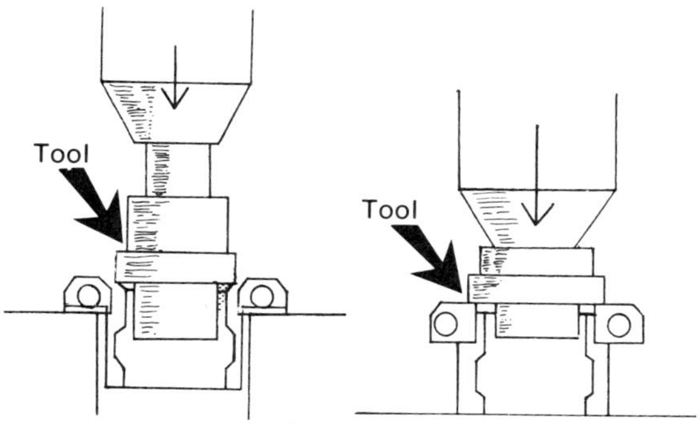

Fig. 3-10. Clutch release bearing being replaced. At left, release bearing hub is pressed out of old release bearing using a tool that will contact only the hub. At right, new release bearing is pressed onto hub using a tool that will contact only the release bearing's inner race. Pressing on outer race will damage bearing.

4. Use solvent to clean the pilot bearing, which is in the center of the engine's crankshaft. Check to see that the balls are not rough or flattened by wear. If necessary, replace the bearing as indicated in Fig. 3-11. Pack the bearing with just enough multipurpose grease to coat all the balls lightly.

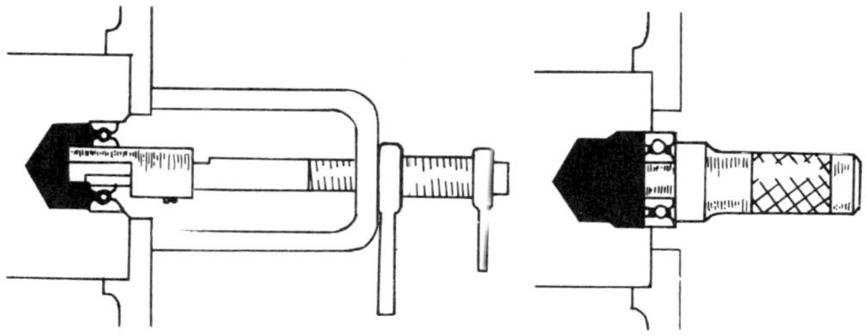

Fig. 3-11. Pilot bearing being replaced. At left, puller is being used to withdraw old bearing from recess in crankshaft. At right, new bearing is being driven in with tool that contacts bearing outer race and enters bearing's bore. Coat bearing with multipurpose grease before driving it in.

5. Inspect the clutch disk for wear. There should be at least 0.30 mm (.012 in.) of friction material remaining above the rivet heads. Any disk that has worn to this point—or nearly so—should be replaced.
6. Inspect the clutch disk splines and the transmission input shaft splines. The splines must not be broken or distorted. Lightly lubricate the splines with multipurpose grease. Then see that the clutch disk slides freely on the input shaft without undue radial play. If the disk is warped or in any way unserviceable, replace it.
7. Using a centering tool (Fig. 3-12) or a spare transmission input shaft, install the clutch disk against the flywheel with the raised side of its hub toward the transmission. Then install the pressure plate assembly on the flywheel according to the reference marks made earlier.

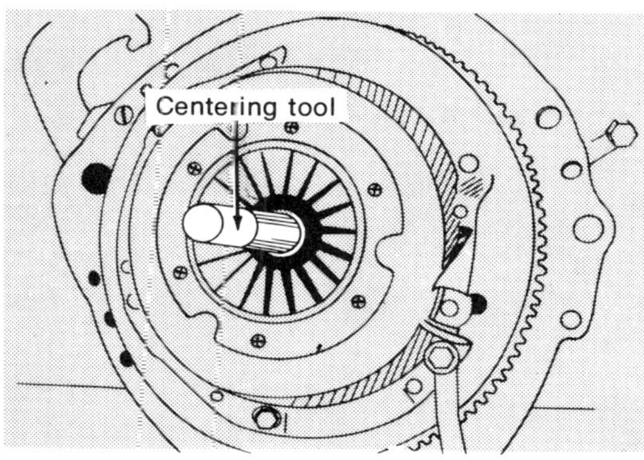

Fig. 3-12. Centering tool in position to hold clutch disk while pressure plate assembly is installed.

2

8. Loosely install all the mounting bolts. Working diagonally, tighten the mounting bolts a turn or two at a time until they are snug. Then torque the bolts to 15 to 20 Nm (11 to 15 ft. lb.).
9. Measure the outside diameter of the throwout bearing guide sleeve (Fig. 3-13). Replace the guide sleeve, which is bolted to the center of the bellhousing, if the guide sleeve is worn. Replace the seal indicated in Fig. 3-13 if gear oil has been leaking onto the clutch, or if gear oil is apparent on the inside of the bellhousing.

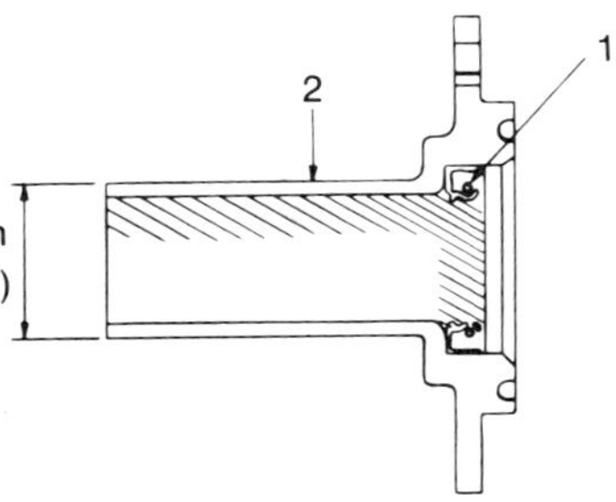

Fig. 3-13. Cross-section of throwout bearing guide sleeve. Measured at contact area (**2**), sleeve should not be worn to an outside diameter less than 32.90 mm (1.295 in.). Oil seal is at **1**. When installing guide sleeve, torque bolts to 12 to 15 Nm (9 to 11 ft. lb.).

10. Install the transmission as described in **4.4 Removing and Installing Transmission.** Adjust the clutch freeplay as described in **3.1 Adjusting Clutch Freeplay.** Recheck the freeplay adjustment after approximately 500 km (300 mi.) of driving.

4. GENERAL MANUAL TRANSMISSION SERVICE

The repairs described here can be carried out with the transmission installed in the car. Unless specified otherwise, the procedures apply equally to the four-speed T40 and the five-speed T50 transmissions.

4.1 Replacing Rear Oil Seal

The transmission rear oil seal need be replaced only if it is leaking or if it has been removed for access to the extension housing bushing. The old seal is ruined by removal and cannot be reused. The extension housing must be removed if the bushing is to be replaced.

To remove:

1. Raise the car on a hoist or support it on stands designed for the purpose.
2. Using a file or a center punch, mark the adjacent points on the rear axle's pinion flange and the rear universal joint so that the driveshaft can be reinstalled in its original position on the pinion flange. Then remove the driveshaft as described in **DRIVESHAFT AND REAR AXLE.**
3. Using a puller as indicated in Fig. 4-1, remove the old oil seal.

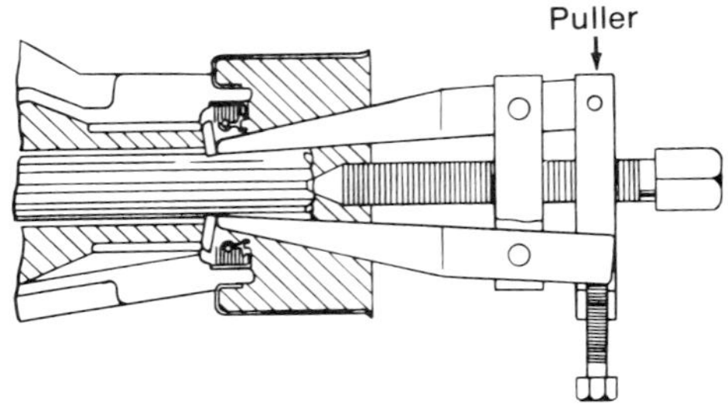

Fig. 4-1. Transmission rear oil seal being pulled out of extension housing.

To install:

1. Thoroughly clean the seal recess in the transmission's extension housing.
2. Hand-start the new seal—closed side outward—into the transmission's extension housing.
3. Using a seal driver such as the one illustrated in Fig. 4-2, drive the new seal squarely in until its closed side is flush with the edge of the extension housing.

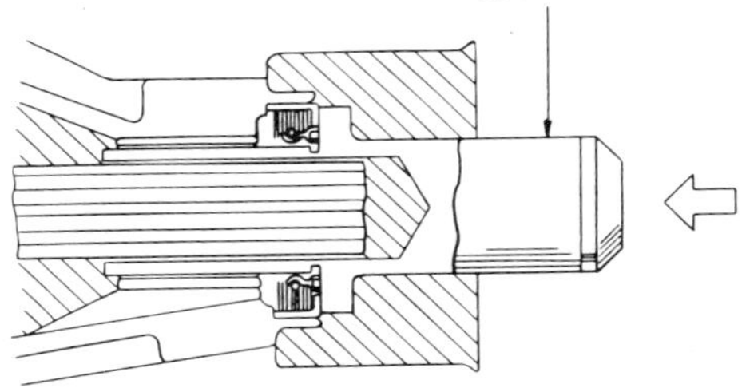

Fig. 4-2. Transmission rear oil seal being driven in.

4. With careful reference to the marks that you made prior to removal, install the driveshaft as described in **DRIVESHAFT AND REAR AXLE.** Torque the bolts that hold the driveshaft to the pinion flange to 35 to 40 Nm (26 to 30 ft. lb.). On cars with two-piece driveshafts, torque the bolts that hold the center bearing to the car body to 35 to 40 Nm (26 to 30 ft. lb.).
5. Check the transmission oil level and, if necessary, correct it as described in **LUBRICATION AND MAINTENANCE.** Lower the car to the ground.

4.2 Removing and Installing Extension Housing
(transmission in car)

Repairs to the speedometer drivegear and replacement of the extension housing bushing require that the extension housing be removed from the transmission. You can do this work without removing the transmission from the car. Speedometer driven gear repairs are covered in **ELECTRICAL SYSTEM** in conjunction with the dashboard instruments.

To remove:

1. Remove the center console. Then remove the four bolts that hold the gearshift lever assembly to the transmission. Remove the gearshift lever assembly as a unit. If necessary, consult **4.3 Removing and Installing Gearshift Lever Assembly.**
2. Raise the car on a hoist or support it on stands designed for the purpose. Drain the transmission.
3. Using a file or a center punch, mark adjacent points on the rear axle's pinion flange and the rear universal joint so that the driveshaft can be reinstalled in its original position on the pinion flange. Then remove the driveshaft as described in **DRIVESHAFT AND REAR AXLE.**
4. Place a jack beneath the transmission, then raise the jack until the transmission/engine assembly is firmly supported. Unbolt the rear transmission mount crossmember and remove it.
5. Using water pump pliers, unscrew the knurled ferrule nut that holds the speedometer cable conduit to the speedometer driven gear assembly on the transmission's extension housing. Then detach the cable from the transmission, being careful not to bend the cable sharply.
6. Using a 12-mm wrench, remove the retaining bolt for the speedometer driven gear assembly. Then, using a screwdriver, carefully pry the speedometer driven gear assembly out of the transmission's extension housing.
7. Disconnect the wires from any electrical switches on the extension housing.
8. Remove the bolts that hold the extension housing to the transmission case. Then remove the extension housing.
9. To remove the speedometer drivegear, first remove the snap ring from the output shaft, and then slide off the drivegear, being very careful not to lose the ball that is in a recess in the shaft, beneath the drivegear.

To install:

1. Thoroughly clean the extension housing in clean solvent, then dry it with compressed air. Clean and inspect the speedometer gears and related parts. Replace worn or damaged components.
2. Measure the inside diameter of the extension housing bushing. If it is worn to an inside diameter in excess of 32.075 mm (1.2628 in.), or if it is visibly scored or otherwise damaged, replace the bushing as described under the next unnumbered heading.
3. If the speedometer drivegear was removed, install the ball in the output shaft using multipurpose grease as an adhesive. Then install the drivegear and its rear snap ring.
4. Place a new extension housing gasket on the transmission, using multipurpose grease as an adhesive to hold it in place.
5. Install the extension housing; all six bolts should be finger-tight. Working diagonally, torque the bolts in stages to 40 to 45 Nm (30 to 33 ft. lb.).
6. Install the speedometer driven gear assembly. Using a 12-mm wrench, torque the bolt for the retainer to 14 to 15 Nm (10 to 11 ft. lb.).
7. Make sure that the felt gasket and the collar washer are correctly installed on the end of the speedometer cable (Fig. 4-3). Then, being careful not to bend the cable sharply, reconnect the speedometer cable to the transmission and tighten the knurled ferrule nut to hold the cable in place.

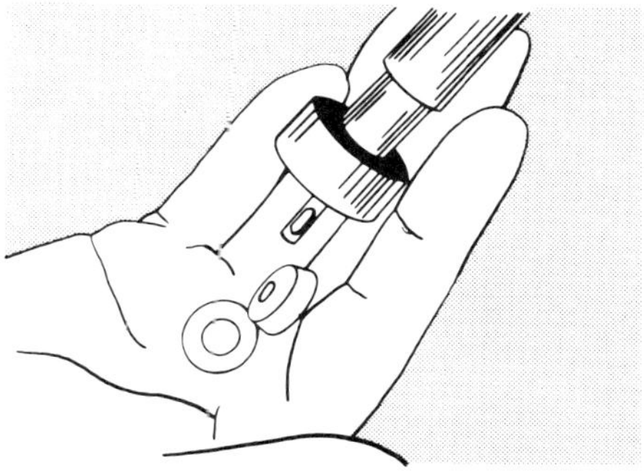

Fig. 4-3. Felt gasket and collar washer, which should be installed in that order inside ferrule nut.

8. Reinstall the rear transmission mount crossmember. Torque the bolts to 20 to 25 Nm (15 to 18 ft. lb.). Then remove the jack that has been supporting the transmission/engine assembly.
9. With careful reference to the marks you made prior to removal, install the driveshaft as described in **DRIVESHAFT AND REAR AXLE.** Torque

2

the four bolts that hold the driveshaft to the pinion flange to 35 to 40 Nm (26 to 30 ft. lb.). On cars with two-piece driveshafts, torque the bolts that hold the center bearing to the body to 35 to 40 Nm (26 to 30 ft. lb.).

10. Using a new gasket, install the gearshift assembly housing on the extension housing, torquing the bolts to 11 to 15 Nm (8 to 11 ft lb.). Make sure that all wires are correctly reconnected to any switches on the transmission's extension housing.
11. Refill the transmission with SAE 90, API GL-4 gear oil as described in **LUBRICATION AND MAINTENANCE.** Then lower the car to the ground.

Replacing Extension Housing Bushing

The transmission's extension housing must be removed before you can replace the extension housing bushing. The bushing should be replaced if it is scored or otherwise damaged, or if it has worn to an inside diameter in excess of 32.075 mm (1.2628 in.).

To replace:

1. With the extension housing removed, use a large screwdriver to pry out the rear oil seal, being careful not to scratch the seal recess.
2. Heat the rear of the extension housing to about 80° to 100°C (176° to 212°F) in a pan of oil placed in a larger pan of boiling water. Then, using a tool that will contact only the bushing (Fig. 4-4), drive the bushing out toward the front of the extension housing.
3. Reheat the extension housing to about 80° to 100°C (176° to 212°F). Then drive in the new bushing as indicated in Fig. 4-4, being sure that the 5-mm (about $^3/_{16}$-in.) hole in the bushing points toward the top of the extension housing.

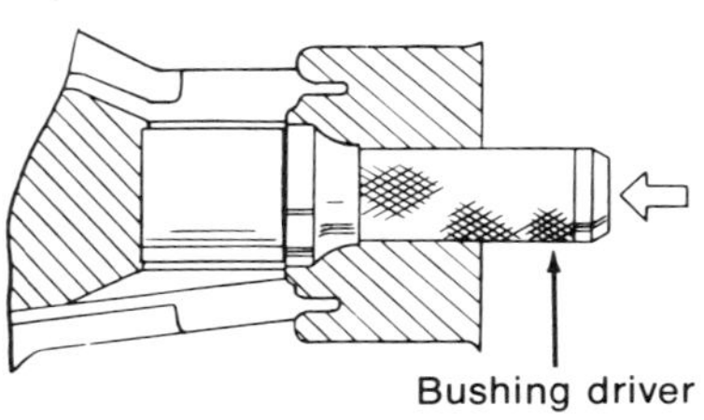

Fig. 4-4. Tool used for driving bushing in or out. Drive bushing in until it is flush with edge of oil seal recess.

4. Measure the newly installed bushing. The correct inside diameter with new parts is 32.000 to 32.025 mm (1.2598 to 1.2608 in.).
5. Install a new rear oil seal, as described in **4.1 Replacing Rear Oil Seal.**

4.3 Removing and Installing Gearshift Lever Assembly

The gearshift lever assembly must be removed before you can remove the extension housing from the transmission. During transmission removal, only the lever itself need be removed, as described in **4.4 Removing and Installing Transmission.**

To remove:

1. Remove the center console and the boot that surrounds the gearshift lever. If necessary, consult **BODY AND INTERIOR.**
2. Remove the four bolts that hold the gearshift lever assembly to the transmission's extension housing.
3. Remove the gearshift lever assembly as a unit. Cover the opening in the transmission to prevent the entry of dirt and foreign objects.
4. Inspect the gearshift lever assembly for wear and damage as indicated in Fig. 4-5. If necessary, disassemble the gearshift lever assembly to replace worn or damaged parts as described under the next unnumbered heading.

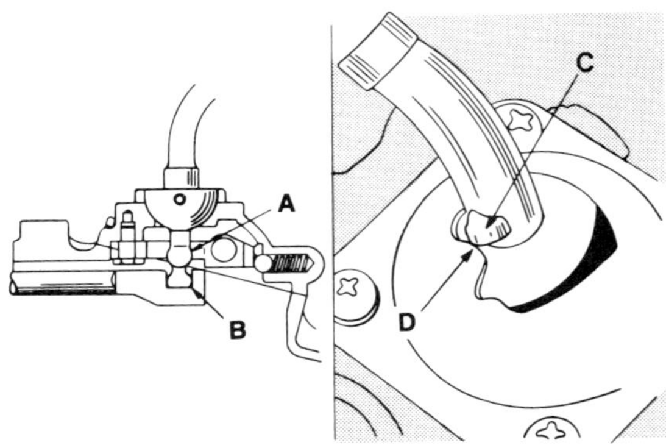

Fig. 4-5. Gearshift lever assembly inspection. With new parts, clearance at point **A** should be 0.50 to 1.00 mm (.020 to .040 in.) and clearance at point **B** should be 0.20 to 0.60 mm (.008 to .024 in.). On five-speed transmissions, reverse lock-out lug (**C**) and its contact surface (**D**) should not be noticeably worn.

To install:

1. Place a new gearshift lever assembly gasket atop the opening on the transmission's extension housing.
2. Install the gearshift lever assembly over the gasket so that the hollow dowel(s) and the bolt holes line up.
3. Install the four bolts to a torque of 11 to 15 Nm (8 to 11 ft. lb.). Then reinstall the console.

Disassembling and Assembling Gearshift Lever Assembly

Fig. 4-6 is an exploded view of the gearshift lever assembly. Each of the individual components shown is available as a replacement part.

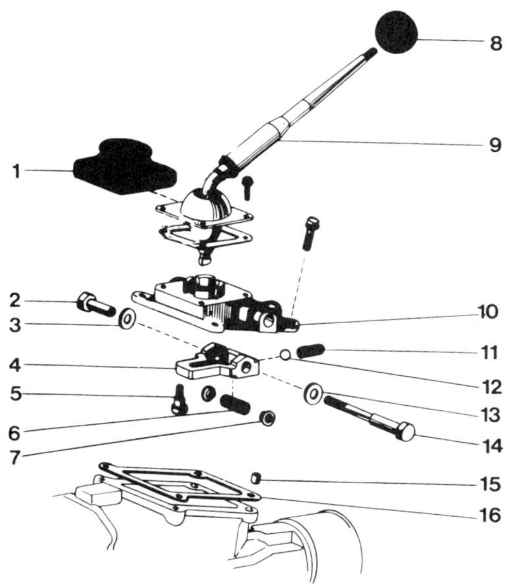

1. Boot (shape varies with model)
2. Shift return bushing
3. Shift return bushing gasket
4. Shift return plate
5. Shift return plate locknut
6. Shift return spring
7. Shift return spring seat
8. Gearshift knob
9. Gearshift lever
10. Gearshift assembly housing
11. Reverse detent spring
12. Reverse detent ball
13. Shift return shaft gasket
14. Shift return shaft
15. Hollow dowel
16. Gearshift lever assembly gasket

Fig. 4-6. Exploded view of gearshift lever assembly.

To disassemble:

1. Remove the Phillips head screws that hold the gearshift lever ball to the gearshift lever assembly housing. Then remove the gearshift lever from the housing.
2. Remove the shift return plate lockbolt.
3. Place a wrench on the head of the shift return shaft to hold the shaft stationary. Then use a second wrench to remove the shift return bushing and its gasket.
4. Remove the shift return shaft and its gasket, then remove the remaining internal parts from the housing, being careful not to lose the reverse detent ball.

Assembly is the reverse of disassembly. Replace all worn or damaged parts, and lubricate all friction surfaces with multipurpose grease during assembly. Torque the shift return bushing/shift return shaft to 7 to 9 Nm (5 to 7 ft. lb.). Torque the shift return plate lockbolt to 10 to 15 Nm (7.5 to 11 ft. lb.).

4.4 Removing and Installing Transmission

Before you attempt to remove the transmission, be sure that you have a safe means for supporting the car off the ground. You should also have a transmission jack so that you will not risk having the transmission fall or drop down at the rear, thereby placing an abnormal strain on the clutch and the input shaft.

To remove:

1. Open the hood. Disconnect the negative (–) battery cable from the battery.

> ***CAUTION —***
> *Disconnect the battery. Failure to do this may cause accidental short circuits when you later remove the starter.*

2. Remove the starter's upper mounting bolt and remove the upper bolts that hold the transmission's bellhousing to the engine.
3. If you do not intend to support the rear of the engine with a jack after you have raised the car, install a support for the rear of the engine. To do this, place a steel bar or a length of two-by-four lumber across the rear of the engine compartment so that its ends rest solidly on the part of the body that is contacted by the hood when the hood is closed. Then, using a chain or strong rope, tie the rear engine-hoisting hook to the steel bar or two-by-four. The chain or rope should be slightly slack so that some downward engine movement will be possible, improving access to the bellhousing upper bolts.

4. Working in the passenger compartment, remove the console. If necessary, consult **BODY AND INTERIOR.** Take out the four Phillips head screws indicated in Fig. 4-7, then remove the gearshift lever and its ball joint from the gearshift lever assembly housing.

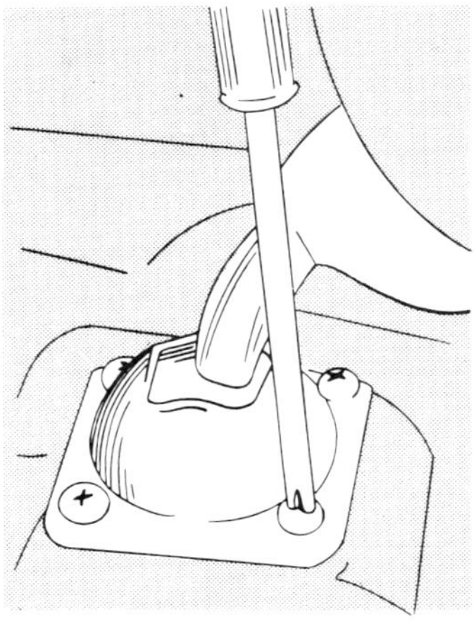

Fig. 4-7. Screw being removed from gearshift lever's ball joint.

5. Unbolt the exhaust pipe from the exhaust manifold.
6. Using water pump pliers, unscrew the knurled ferrule nut that holds the speedometer cable to the speedometer driven gear assembly. Then detach the cable from the transmission, being careful not to bend the cable sharply.
7. Disconnect the back-up light switch wire (on some cars, this is an in-line connector in the right-hand side of the engine compartment).

CAUTION —
If the hood must be lowered in order to raise the car because of a low ceiling, remove the engine's air cleaner as described in conjunction with cylinder head cover removal in **ENGINE**. *Doing this will keep the air cleaner from striking the hood as the rear of the engine is lowered.*

8. Raise the car on a hoist or support it on stands designed for the purpose. Using a file or a center punch, mark adjacent points on the rear axle's pinion flange and the rear universal joint so that you can reinstall the driveshaft in its original position on the pinion flange. Then remove the driveshaft as described in **DRIVESHAFT AND REAR AXLE.**
9. Unbolt the exhaust pipe from the transmission's bellhousing.
10. Disconnect the wires and the battery positive (+) cable from the starter solenoid. Unbolt the starter from the engine, then withdraw the starter from the bellhousing.

NOTE —
You can leave the starter lying atop the suspension crossmember and the steering tierods.

11. Disconnect any wires that may be attached to switches on the transmission, identifying the wires for correct reinstallation.
12. Unbolt the clutch slave cylinder from the transmission's bellhousing. Install a heavy rubber band over the pushrod end to prevent the internal parts of the hydraulic cylinder from popping out. Leave the slave cylinder hanging from the hydraulic line.
13. Install a wheeled transmission jack beneath the transmission, then raise the jack until the transmission is fully supported.
14. Remove the bolts that hold the rear transmission mount crossmember to the car body. Gradually lower the transmission jack until the transmission does not go down any more.

CAUTION —
Lower the transmission and engine a little at a time, checking frequently to see that the engine's fan does not contact its shroud before the slack is removed from the engine rear support device. If you have not installed a rear support, place a jack beneath the rear of the engine to keep the engine from dropping too low.

15. With both the engine and the transmission firmly supported, remove the remaining bolts that hold the transmission's bellhousing to the engine. This includes the bolts that hold the strengthening braces to the lower part of the bellhousing.
16. Insert a screwdriver between the engine's intermediate plate and the bellhousing to pry the bellhousing free of the dowels. Carefully move the transmission rearward until the transmission's input shaft is completely out of the clutch and flywheel assembly. Then lower the transmission from the car.

CAUTION —
At no time should you allow the weight of the transmission or the engine to be supported by the transmission's input shaft. Doing this may damage the clutch or the transmission.

17. If necessary, remove the bolts and then remove the rear transmission mount crossmember from the transmission.

To install:

1. Inspect the clutch release bearing and related parts. Replace worn parts. Using multipurpose grease, lubricate the transmission's input shaft, the pilot bearing in the crankshaft, and the clutch release mechanism. These operations are described in **3.5 Removing and Installing Clutch**.
2. If necessary, install the rear transmission mount crossmember on the transmission, torquing the bolts to 20 to 25 Nm (15 to 18 ft. lb.). Place the transmission on the transmission jack.
3. Put the transmission into gear (any gear). Then, with the transmission supported on the transmission jack, carefully align the transmission's input shaft with the splined bore in the clutch disk hub.
4. Carefully move the transmission forward so that the input shaft enters the clutch disk hub. Then, grasping the transmission's output shaft where it emerges from the rear of the transmission, hand-turn the output shaft one way and the other until the splines of the input shaft mesh with those in the clutch disk.
5. Being careful to align the holes in the bellhousing with the hollow dowels on the engine block, move the transmission forward until it firmly contacts the engine and the plate. Then install finger-tight the bolts that hold the engine to the transmission.
6. Torque the engine block-to-transmission bolts to 55 to 65 Nm (41 to 48 ft. lb.); torque the bellhousing-to-stiffening bracket bolts to 35 to 45 Nm (26 to 33 ft. lb.); torque the two small bolts at the bottom of the bellhousing to 20 Nm (15 ft. lb.)
7. Using the transmission jack, raise the transmission and the engine until you can install the bolts that hold the rear transmission mount crossmember to the car body. Torque the bolts to 20 to 25 Nm (15 to 18 ft. lb.).
8. Remove the transmission jack. Reinstall the starter and reconnect the exhaust pipe bracket. Torque the starter bolts to 55 to 75 Nm (41 to 55 ft. lb.).
9. Make sure that the felt gasket and the collar washer are correctly installed on the end of the speedometer cable (Fig. 4-8). Then, being careful not to bend the cable sharply, reconnect the speedometer cable to the transmission and tighten the knurled ferrule nut to hold the cable in place.

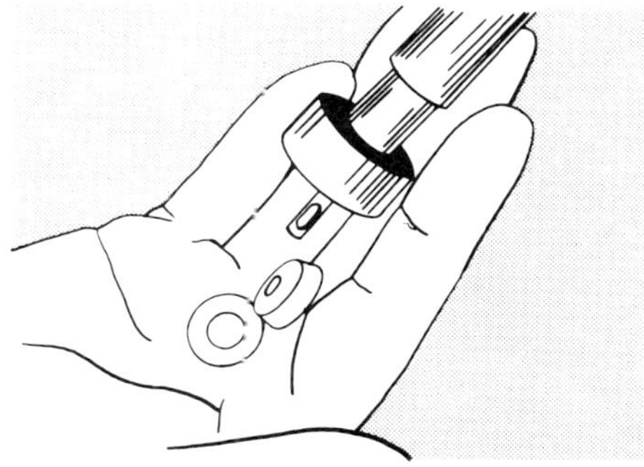

Fig. 4-8. Felt gasket and collar washer, which should be installed in that order inside ferrule nut.

10. Reinstall the clutch slave cylinder. Then adjust the clutch freeplay as described in **3.1 Adjusting Clutch Freeplay.** Torque the bolts that hold the slave cylinder to the bellhousing to 10 to 15 Nm (7.5 to 11 ft. lb.).
11. Reconnect any wires that go to switches installed on the transmission. Reconnect the exhaust pipe to the exhaust manifold. Torque the nuts to 30 to 45 Nm (22 to 33 ft. lb.).
12. With careful reference to the marks you made prior to removal, install the driveshaft as described in **DRIVESHAFT AND REAR AXLE.** Torque the four bolts that hold the driveshaft to the pinion flange to 35 to 40 Nm (26 to 30 ft. lb.). On cars with a two-piece driveshaft, torque the bolts that hold the center bearing to the body to 35 to 40 Nm (26 to 30 ft. lb.).
13. If you drained the transmission, or if any oil has leaked out, refill the transmission with SAE 90, API GL-4 gear oil as described in **LUBRICATION AND MAINTENANCE.** Torque the drain plug and the filler plug to 30 to 35 Nm (22 to 26 ft. lb.).
14. Lower the car to the ground. Then remove the engine rear support device if you installed it in step 3 of the removal procedure.
15. Where applicable, reconnect the back-up light switch wire at the in-line connector in the engine compartment. Reinstall the air cleaner, if necessary, as described in **ENGINE AND CLUTCH.**
16. Install the gearshift lever and then the console.
17. Reconnect the battery negative (−) cable. Then check that the clutch, the gearshift, and the back-up lights function correctly.

5. TRANSMISSION GEAR TRAIN REPAIRS

In disassembling the transmission, you will encounter a number of snap rings that must be removed. Once you remove them, it is advisable that you replace all these snap rings with new ones. Several of these snap rings are selective. That is, a number of similar rings of various thicknesses are available for use in assembly. The correct ring must be selected during assembly; otherwise, the transmission will be noisy and will wear rapidly.

***CAUTION* ——**
Please read the instructions thoroughly before you attempt transmission repairs. If you lack the necessary skills or tools, we suggest that you leave this work to an Authorized Dealer or other qualified shop. Before taking a removed transmission in for repair, thoroughly clean its exterior but do not undertake any disassembly.

5.1 Removing and Installing Gear Train

To remove the transmission gear train, it is necessary to disassemble the transmission case. Fig. 5-1 is an exploded view of the transmission case, the bellhousing, and the extension housing. Become familiar with the names of the components given in the illustration. You will encounter these names frequently in the procedure that follows.

To remove gear train:

1. Remove the oil drain plug and drain the gear oil from the transmission case.
2. Take out the six bolts that hold the bellhousing to the front of the transmission case. Then remove the bellhousing, its gasket, the two conical thrust springs, and the flat thrust washer. Leave the clutch throwout bearing, the clutch fork, the clutch throwout bearing guide sleeve, and related parts installed in the bellhousing.
3. Using a 12-mm wrench, remove the bolt for the speedometer driven gear assembly's retainer. Remove the retainer, then use a screwdriver to pry the speedometer driven gear assembly out of the extension housing.
4. If you did not do so previously, remove the gearshift assembly housing from the extension housing.

1. Shift rod detent cover
2. Detent cover gasket
3. Clutch guide sleeve
4. Clutch inspection plate
5. Ball for back-up light switch
6. Guide sleeve gasket
7. Mainshaft oil seal
8. Right-hand stiffening bracket
9. Left-hand stiffening bracket
10. Bellhousing
11. Bellhousing gasket
12. Alignment dowel
13. Right-hand half of transmission case
14. Left-hand half of transmission case
15. Oil drain and filler plugs
16. Extension housing gasket
17. Hollow alignment dowel
18. Extension housing
19. Extension housing bushing
20. Rear oil seal
21. Dust deflector

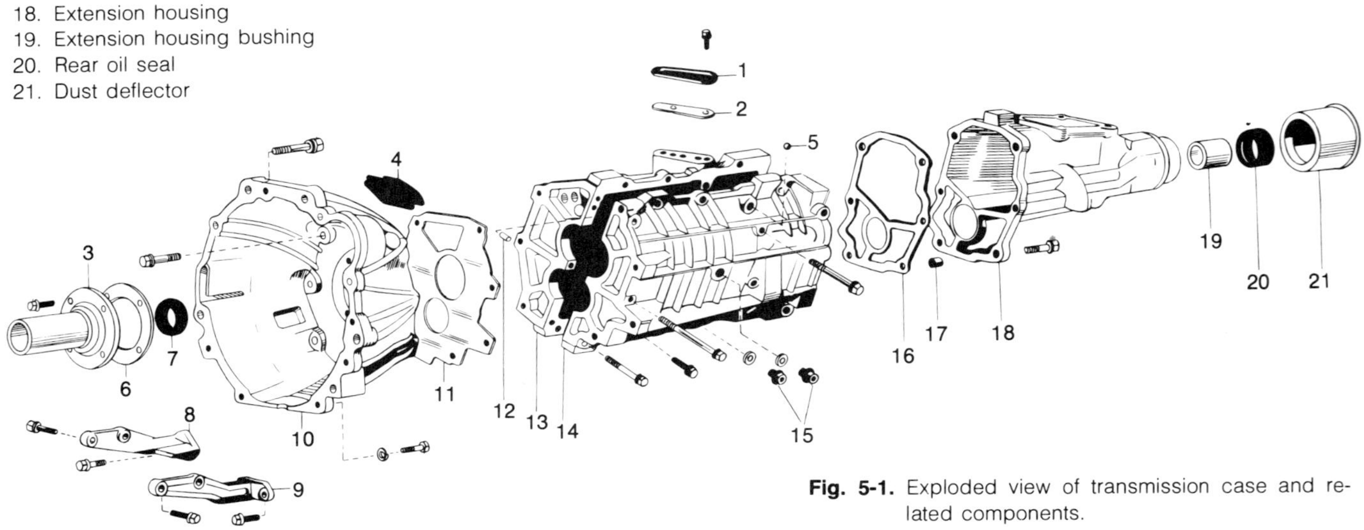

Fig. 5-1. Exploded view of transmission case and related components.

5. Remove the six bolts that hold the extension housing to the rear of the transmission case. Then remove the extension housing and its gasket, leaving the extension housing bushing, the extension housing oil seal, and the dust deflector installed on the extension housing.
6. Remove the back-up light switch and the ball for the back-up light switch.
7. Place the transmission right side down on a clean workbench covered with clean cardboard or clean wrapping paper. Remove the fourteen bolts that hold the right-hand half of the transmission case to the left-hand half.
8. Using a plastic hammer as indicated in Fig. 5-2, lightly tap the bosses on the right-hand half of the case in order to separate the halves of the case.

CAUTION —

Do not attempt to separate the halves of the transmission case by inserting a screwdriver or other tool between them. Prying the case halves apart will scratch the precision-machined mating surfaces or distort the case, causing oil leaks and possible gear problems.

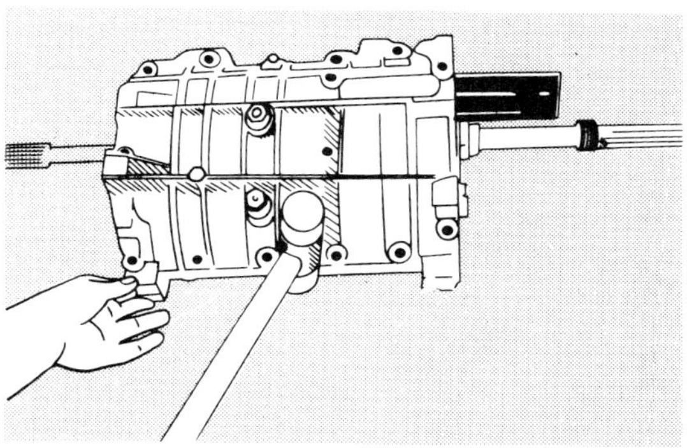

Fig. 5-2. Plastic hammer being used to separate halves of transmission case.

9. Carefully lift out the countergear assembly as indicated in Fig. 5-3, being careful not to lose the roller bearing locking ball. Remove the ball.
10. Take out the mainshaft assembly as a unit, keeping the input shaft portion and the output shaft portion together in a single unit (Fig. 5-4).
11. Using a punch ground to the dimensions given in Fig. 5-5, drive out the three rolled pins that hold the shift forks to the shift rods.

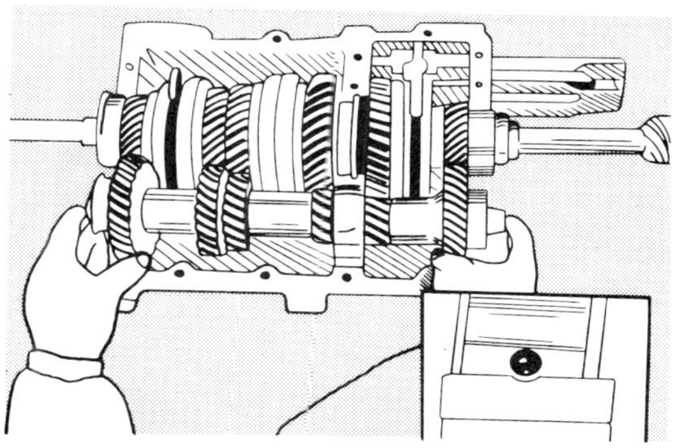

Fig. 5-3. Countergear assembly being removed. Inset shows roller bearing locking ball.

2

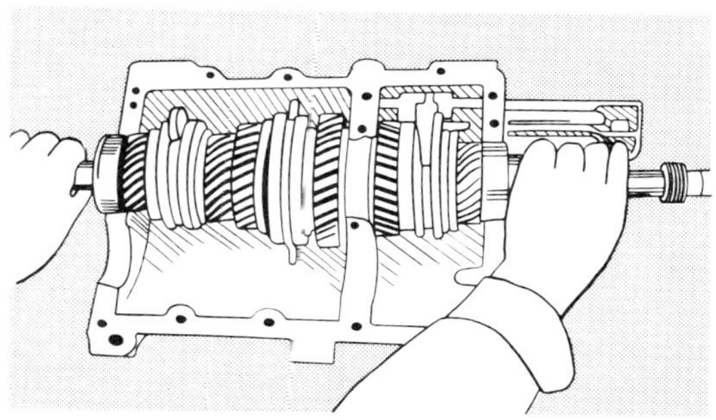

Fig. 5-4. Mainshaft assembly being lifted out of case. Assembly must be eased downward to disengage it from shift forks.

NOTE —

It may not be possible to drive out fully the rolled pin that holds the front shift fork to its shaft. However, leaving the pin partially engaged in the fork will not cause any difficulty in fork removal. Do not risk damage by hammering unnecessarily on this pin in an attempt to remove it completely.

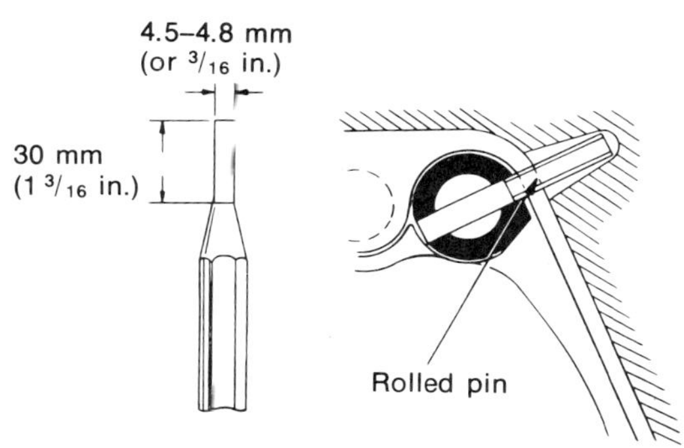

Fig. 5-5. Rolled pin removal. Correct dimensions for punch are given at left. Diagram at right indicates how pins are driven out into recess in right-hand half of case.

12. Remove the shift rod detent cover from the right-hand half of the transmission case. Then remove the three detent spring seats, the three detent ball springs, and the three detent balls (Fig. 5-6).

13. Remove the three shift rods one at a time, sliding each rod out of its shift fork and the case. Then lift out the shift fork.

NOTE ——

If it is not possible to withdraw a shift rod, make sure that the other two rods are in their centralized (neutral) positions.

14. Remove the two interlock pins (Fig. 5-6).

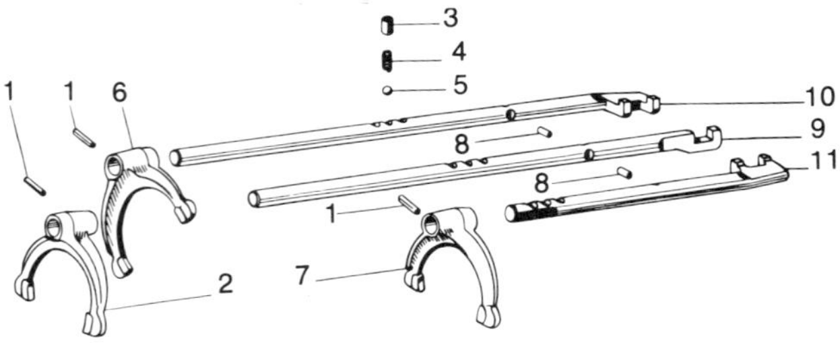

1. Rolled pin (3)
2. 1st/2nd gear shift fork
3. Detent spring seat (3)
4. Detent ball spring (3)
5. Detent ball (3)
6. 3rd/4th gear shift fork
7. Reverse (T40) or reverse/5th (T50) shift fork
8. Interlock pins (2)
9. 1st/2nd gear shift rod
10. 3rd/4th gear shift rod
11. Reverse (T40) or reverse/5th (T50) shift rod

Fig. 5-6. Exploded view of shift rods, shift forks, and detent system components.

15. Using feeler gauges of various thicknesses, as indicated in Fig. 5-7, determine the axial play of the reverse idler gear. Write down this measurement for use during transmission assembly.

16. Remove the retaining bolt and washer for the reverse idler gear. Drive the idler gear shaft out toward the rear of the case and remove the idler gear and its two thrust washers. See Fig. 5-7.

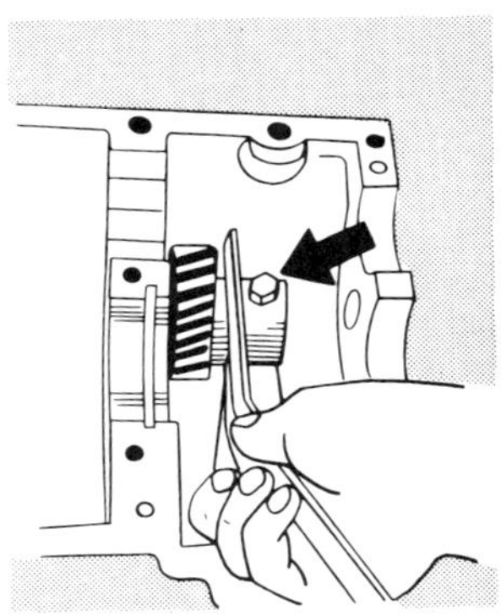

Fig. 5-7. Reverse idler gear axial play measurement. With new parts, the axial play should be between 0.05 and 0.50 mm (.0020 and .0197 in.). Wear limit is 1.00 mm (.040 in.). Arrow indicates retaining bolt for reverse idler gear's shaft.

To install:

1. If any parts of the gear train have been disassembled or cleaned, thoroughly lubricate all bearings and contact surfaces with SAE 90, API GL-4 gear oil.

2. If the reverse idler gear axial play exceeded the 1.00-mm (.040-in.) wear limit, replace the thrust washers and, if necessary, the gear—depending on the extent to which the gear is worn. Then install the idler gear as indicated in Fig. 5-8, torquing the bolt to 12 to 15 Nm (9 to 11 ft. lb.).

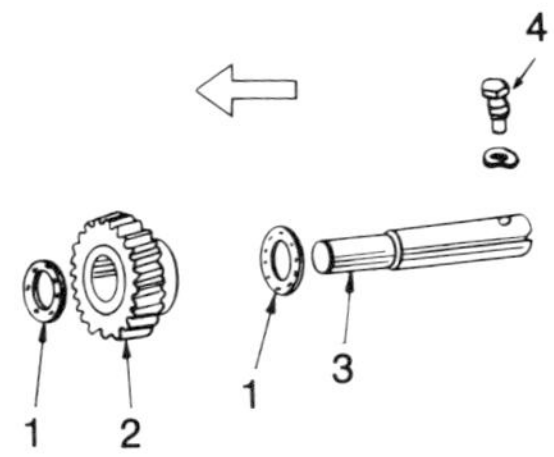

1. Thrust washer (2)
2. Idler gear
3. Shaft
4. Retaining bolt

Fig. 5-8. Reverse idler gear components. Make certain that protrusion on each thrust washer engages its recess in transmission case; then insert shaft in direction indicated by arrow.

3. Check the clearance between each shift fork and the groove in the corresponding clutch gear assembly. If the clearance exceeds 1.00 mm (.040 in.) but the groove in the clutch gear sleeve does not exceed the 8.5-mm (.335-in.) wear limit, the shift fork is worn excessively and should be replaced. If necessary, consult **5.2 Disassembling and Assembling Output Shaft.**

4. Using Fig. 5-9 as a guide, reinstall the shift forks, the shift rods, and the interlock pins in the case, making sure that the rolled pins are a tight fit. The shift rods are identified in Fig. 5-6, given earlier.

NOTE ——

Install one shift rod and shift fork at a time, starting with the 3rd/4th gear assembly. Before you install the 1st/2nd gear shift rod, install the first interlock pin. Install the second interlock pin before you install the reverse/5th shaft and fork. See Fig. 5-10.

5. Install the three detent balls, their springs, and their spring seats. Then install the shift rod detent cover with a new gasket, torquing the bolts to 12 to 15 Nm (9 to 11 ft. lb.).

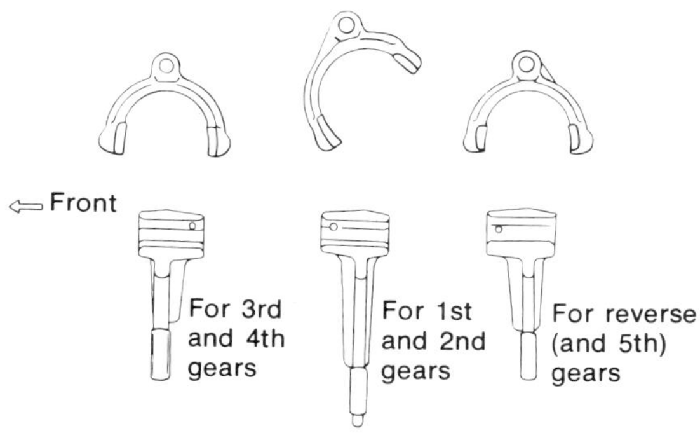

Fig. 5-9. Correct installed positions for shift forks.

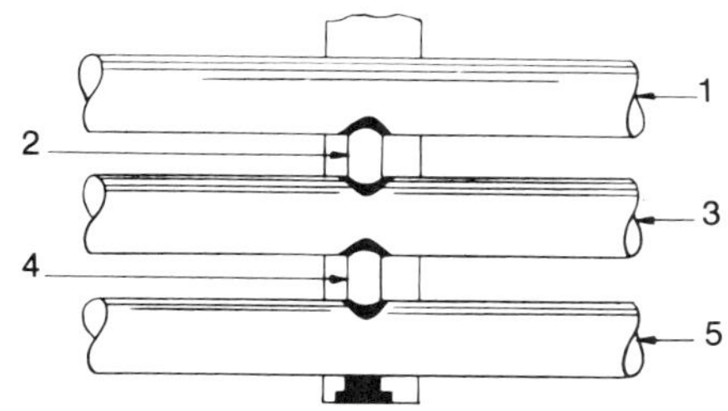

1. 3rd/4th gear shift rod
2. First interlock pin
3. 1st/2nd gear shift rod
4. Second interlock pin
5. Reverse (or reverse/5th) shift rod

Fig. 5-10. Arrangement of interlock pins in bore in transmission case. Components are numbered in installation sequence.

6. Reinstall the mainshaft assembly in the right-hand half of the transmission case (Fig. 5-11). The shift forks must engage the grooves of their respective clutch gear assembly sleeves, and the shoulder on the center bearing must engage the groove in the case's bearing saddle.

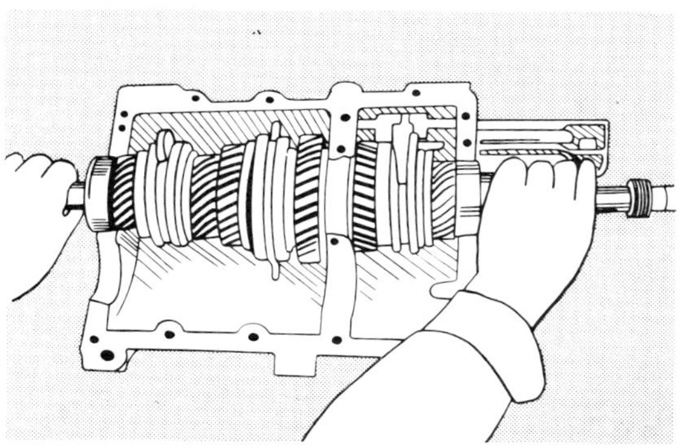

Fig. 5-11. Mainshaft assembly being installed in case.

7. Install the countershaft as indicated in Fig. 5-12, making sure that the locking ball is correctly engaged in both the recess in the roller bearing outer race and in the recess in the transmission case.

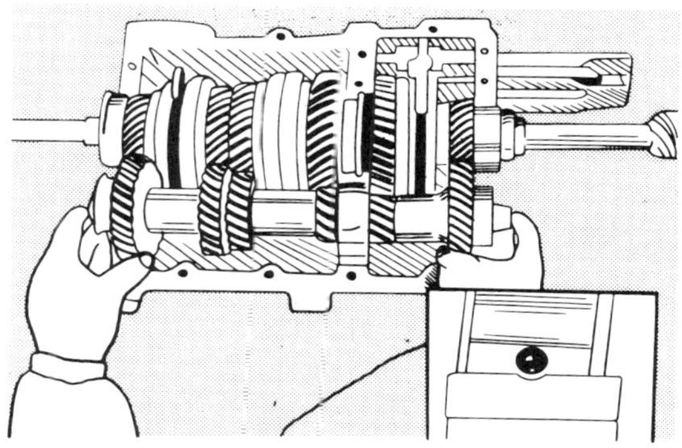

Fig. 5-12. Countershaft being installed. Inset shows locking ball in recess of roller bearing outer race. You can use multipurpose grease as an adhesive to hold ball in place during transmission assembly.

8. Place all three shift rods in their centralized (neutral) positions and see that the sleeves of all three clutch gear assemblies are centered on their hubs. Then check that the gear train can be shifted into all speeds and that the gears rotate freely in all speeds.
9. Using a clean rag dipped in solvent, wipe clean the mating surfaces of both halves of the transmission case. Then evenly and lightly coat the mating surface of each case half with oil-resistant liquid sealer.
10. Install the left-hand half of the transmission case on the right-hand half. Install the bolts in the locations indicated in Fig. 5-13. Then, working diagonally, torque the bolts in stages to 20 Nm (15 ft. lb.).

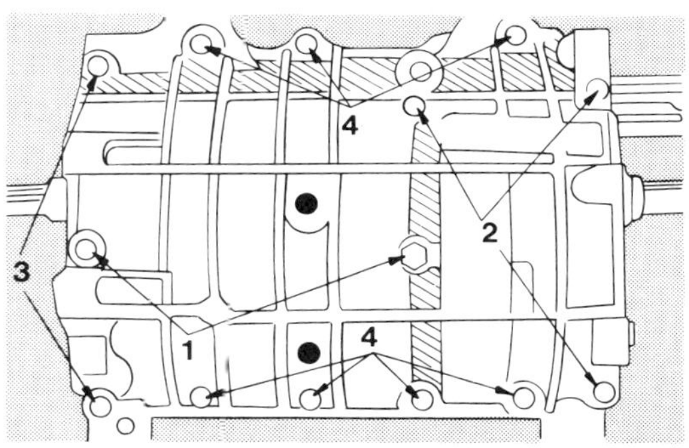

Bolt lengths

1. 90 mm (3½ in.)
2. 70 mm (2¾ in.)
3. 45 mm (1¾ in.)
4. 32 mm (1¼ in.)

Fig. 5-13. Correct locations for bolts of each length.

11. Install the ball for the back-up light switch. Then install the back-up light switch to a torque of 35 to 50 Nm (26 to 37 ft. lb.).

12. Using a new gasket, install the extension housing. Working diagonally, torque the six bolts in stages to 40 to 45 Nm (30 to 33 ft. lb.).
13. Install the speedometer driven gear assembly. Using a 12-mm wrench, torque the bolt for the retainer to 14 to 15 Nm (10 to 11 ft. lb.).
14. Install the gearshift lever assembly housing together with a new gasket. Torque the bolts to 11 to 15 Nm (8 to 11 ft. lb.).
15. Using multipurpose grease as an adhesive, install the two conical thrust springs and the thrust washer in the bellhousing locations indicated in Fig. 5-14.

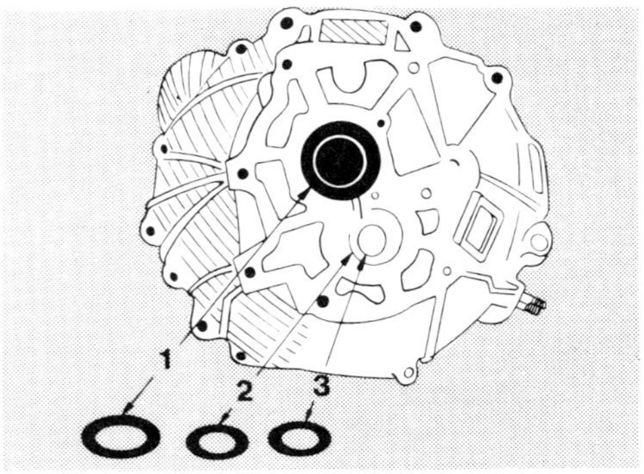

1. Large conical thrust spring
2. Flat thrust washer
3. Small conical thrust spring

Fig. 5-14. Correct locations for gear train thrust components in bellhousing recesses. Install components in sequence given in illustration. Convex sides of conical thrust springs should be toward bellhousing.

16. Using a new gasket, install the bellhousing on the transmission case. Working diagonally, torque the bolts in stages to 35 to 45 Nm (26 to 33 ft. lb.).
17. Be sure to refill the transmission with SAE 90, API GL-4 gear oil as described in **LUBRICATION AND MAINTENANCE.** (This can most easily be done after the transmission has been reinstalled in the car.)

5.2 Disassembling and Assembling Output Shaft

Fig. 5-15 is an exploded view of the output shafts used in the four-speed and the five-speed manual transmissions. The output shaft constitutes the rear, and largest, portion of the mainshaft assembly. Become familiar with the names of the various components, for you will encounter them frequently in the procedures that follow.

Fig. 5-15. Exploded view of output shaft. On cars with five-speed transmissions, components in lower box replace those in upper box.

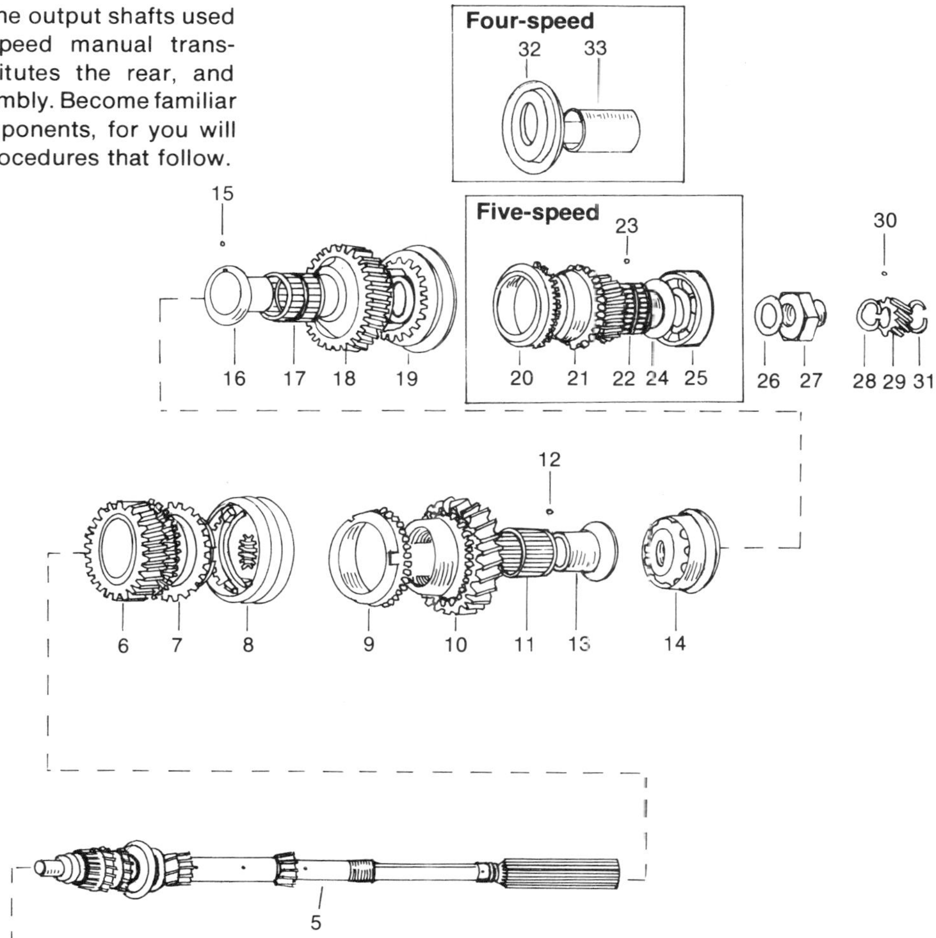

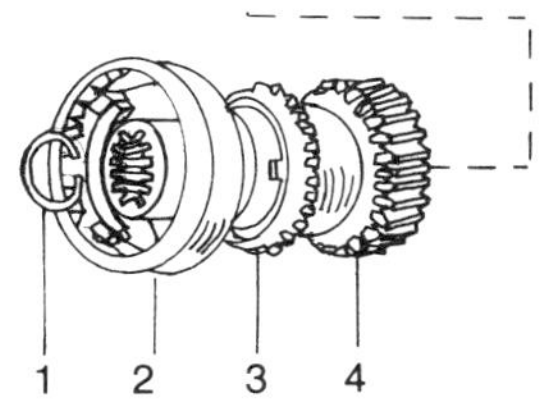

1. Output shaft front snap ring
2. 3rd/4th clutch gear assembly
3. 3rd gear synchronizer ring
4. 3rd gear
5. Output shaft
6. 2nd gear
7. 2nd gear synchronizer ring
8. 1st/2nd clutch gear assembly
9. 1st gear synchronizer ring
10. 1st gear
11. Needle roller bearing race
12. Inner bearing race locking ball
13. Needle bearing inner race
14. Ball bearing race
15. Inner bearing race locking ball
16. Needle bearing inner race
17. Needle roller bearing race
18. Reverse gear
19. Reverse (T40) or reverse/ 5th (T50) clutch gear assembly
20. 5th gear synchronizer ring
21. 5th gear
22. Needle roller bearing race
23. Inner bearing race locking ball
24. Needle bearing inner race
25. Ball bearing race
26. Shim
27. Locknut
28. Speedometer drive-gear front snap ring
29. Speedometer drivegear
30. Speedometer drivegear locking ball
31. Speedometer drive-gear rear snap ring
32. Stop plate
33. Tubular spacer

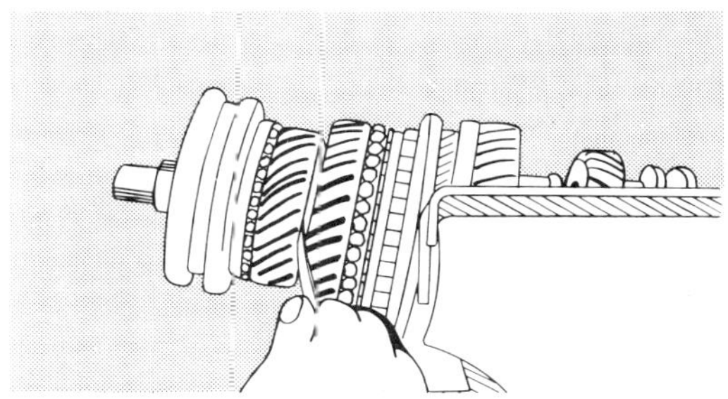

Thrust clearances with new parts		Wear limit
1st gear:	0.150 to 0.275 mm (.0059 to .0108 in.)	0.50 mm (.020 in.)
2nd gear:	0.150 to 0.250 mm (.0059 to .0098 in.)	0.50 mm (.020 in.)
3rd gear:	0.150 to 0.300 mm (.0059 to .0118 in.)	0.60 mm (.024 in.)
Reverse:	0.200 to 0.325 mm (.0079 to .0128 in.)	0.60 mm (.024 in.)
5th gear:	0.150 to 0.275 mm (.0059 to .0108 in.)	0.50 mm (.020 in.)

Fig. 5-16. Thrust clearance (axial play) of gears on output shaft being determined with feeler gauges.

To disassemble:

1. Using feeler gauges of various thicknesses, determine the thrust clearances (axial play) of all gears on the output shaft (Fig. 5-16). If the axial play of any gear is outside the ranges given in the illustration, the worn components will have to be replaced during assembly.

2. Working at the rear of the output shaft, remove the speedometer drivegear's rear snap ring. Remove the speedometer drivegear, being careful not to lose the drivegear locking ball. Then remove the speedometer drivegear's front snap ring.

3. Using a cape chisel as indicated in Fig. 5-17, release the staked part of the locknut. Then remove the locknut as indicated in Fig. 5-18.

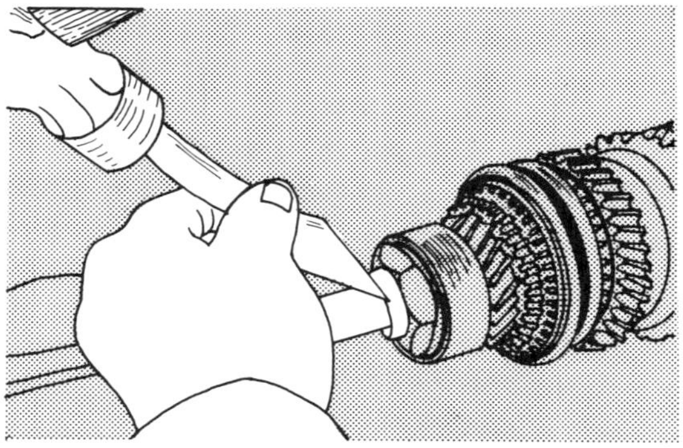

Fig. 5-17. Cape chisel being used to release staked part of locknut.

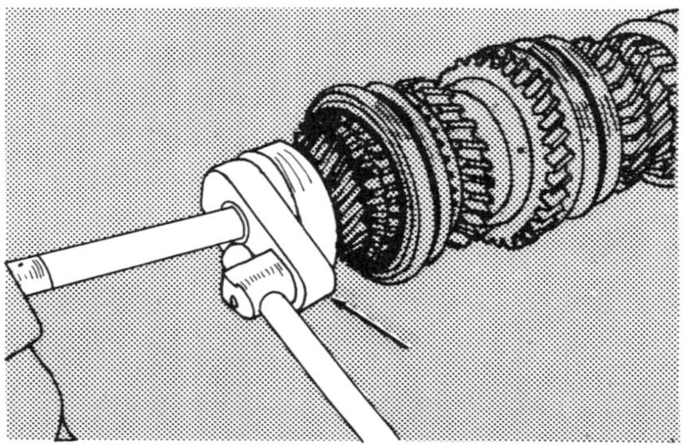

Fig. 5-18. Locknut being removed. Toyota special service tool 09326 is shown (arrow), but a suitable box wrench can be used.

4. Support the reverse gear on the repair press bed as indicated in Fig. 5-19. Then press the shaft out of the splines of the reverse (T40) or reverse/5th (T50) clutch gear assembly.

CAUTION —

Support the shaft with your hand so that it does not fall when the splined part of the shaft is clear of the clutch gear assembly hub. Store the gears and the synchronizer parts in order so that they will not be mixed up with other components prior to assembly. On T50 transmissions, be careful not to lose the locking ball for the 5th gear inner bearing race.

5. Remove the needle roller bearing for the reverse gear, the bearing inner race, its locking ball, the ball bearing race, 1st gear together with its needle roller bearing and inner race, and the 1st gear synchronizer ring. These are loose parts on the shaft.

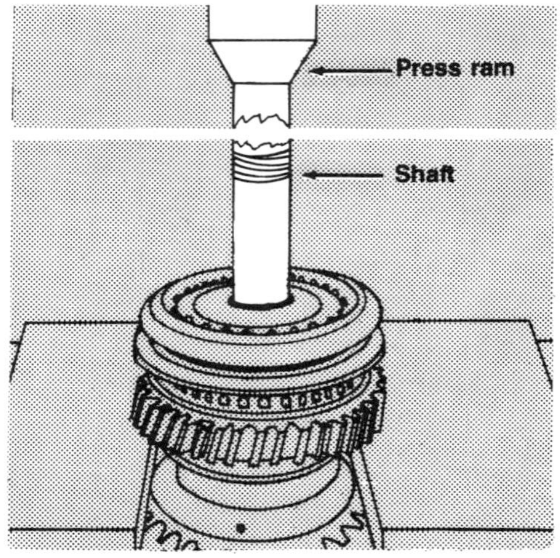

Fig. 5-19. Shaft being pressed out of components on rear of shaft with reverse gear supported. T40 shaft is shown. On T50, 5th gear components and ball bearing race will also be pressed off at this time.

6. Support 2nd gear on the repair press bed as indicated in Fig. 5-20. Then press the shaft out of the splines of the 1st/2nd clutch gear assembly.

CAUTION —

Support the shaft with your hand as you did in step 4 to prevent possible damage. Store removed components in order to prevent mixups.

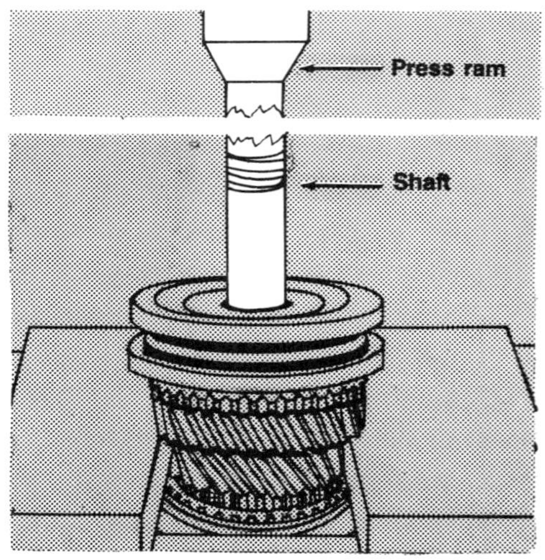

Fig. 5-20. Shaft being pressed out of components on rear of shaft, with 2nd gear supported.

7. Using snap ring pliers, remove the output shaft front snap ring. Then, with 3rd gear supported on the repair press bed as indicated in Fig. 5-21, press the shaft out of the splines of the 3rd/4th clutch gear assembly.

CAUTION —
Support the shaft with your hand as before to prevent damage. Store removed components in order to prevent mixups.

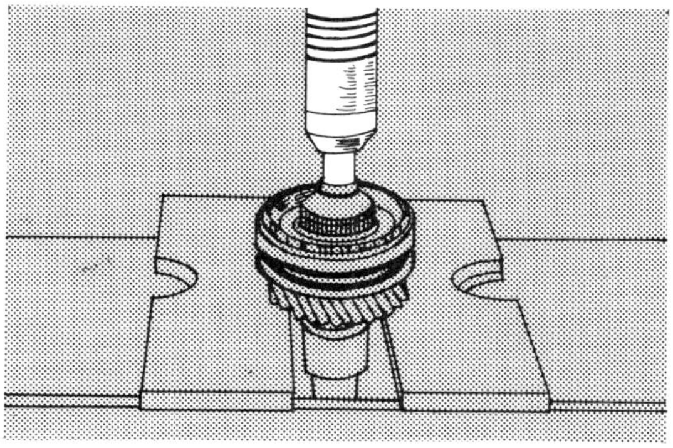

Fig. 5-21. Shaft being pressed out of components on front of shaft with 3rd gear supported.

8. If it is necessary to disassemble one or more of the clutch gear assemblies, do so by pushing the hub, keys, and key springs out of the sleeve as indicated in Fig. 5-22.

CAUTION —
Be careful that the keys do not fly out suddenly, owing to spring tension, and become lost. Keep the components of each clutch gear assembly separate so that they will not be mixed up with components from another clutch gear assembly.

Fig. 5-22. Hub, keys, and key springs being hand-pressed out of clutch gear assembly sleeve. Considerable pressure must be exerted on hub in order to do this.

To assemble:

1. Whether or not you have disassembled the clutch gear assemblies, check the clearance between each shift fork and its matching clutch gear assembly sleeve. See Fig. 5-23.

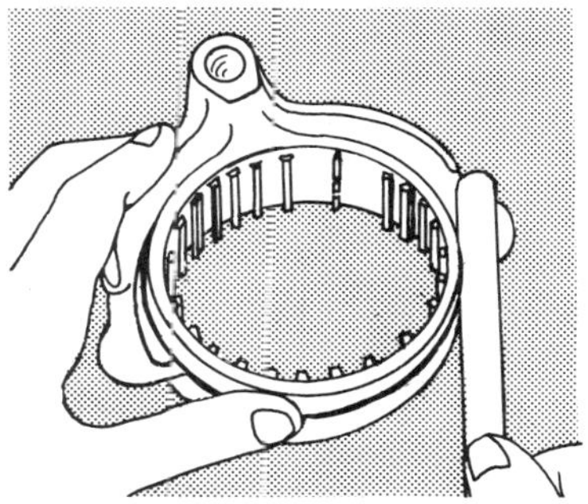

Maximum permissible clearance: 1.00 mm (.040 in.)
Maximum permissible groove width: 8.50 mm (.335 in.)

Fig. 5-23. Feeler gauge being used to determine side clearance between shift fork and groove in clutch gear assembly sleeve.

2. If necessary, reassemble the clutch gear assemblies as indicated in Fig. 5-24, thoroughly lubricating them with SAE 90, API GL-4 gear oil. During assembly, replace keys that are worn and springs that are distorted or worn at the points where they contact the keys. If either the sleeve or the hub is worn, replace the clutch gear assembly as a unit.

NOTE —
Throughout this assembly procedure, you should thoroughly lubricate each gear and bearing with SAE 90, API GL-4 gear oil as you install the component on the shaft.

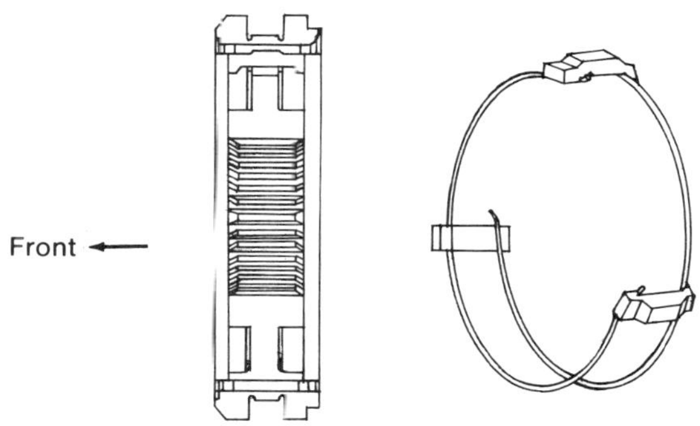

Fig. 5-24. Correct installation of parts of clutch gear assembly. Notice how springs overlap each other and how their hooked ends engage keys.

2

3. One at a time, install each synchronizer ring on its appropriate gear. Then measure the clearance between the ring and the gear as indicated in Fig. 5-25.

NOTE ——
You should also visually check the tapered faces of the synchronizer ring. If you see alternate bright and dull areas, which indicate a distorted ring, replace the ring. If the gear is scored, replace both the ring and the gear.

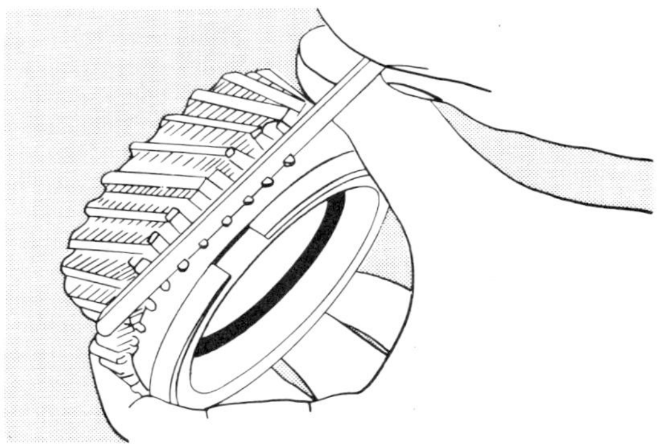

Clearance with new parts: 1.00 to 2.00 mm (.040 to .080 in.)
Minimum permissible clearance: 0.80 mm (.031 in.)

Fig. 5-25. Clearance between gear and synchronizer ring being measured.

4. Check the shaft for bending as indicated in Fig. 5-26. Replace bent shafts. Also replace shafts that have distorted splines or other damage.

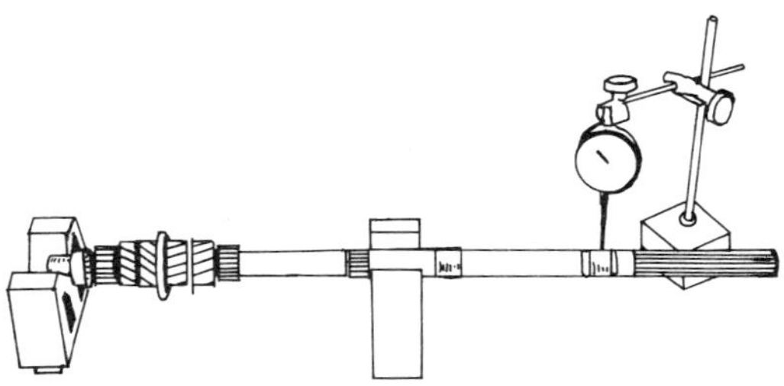

Fig. 5-26. Output shaft being checked for bending. Support shaft on V-blocks, then rotate against dial indicator. Maximum permissible bend is 0.06 mm (.0024 in.).

5. Install the needle roller bearing races and the needle bearing inner races in their matching gears. Then measure the oil clearance (radial play) as indicated in Fig. 5-27. Measure 5th gear, 1st gear, and reverse gear only.

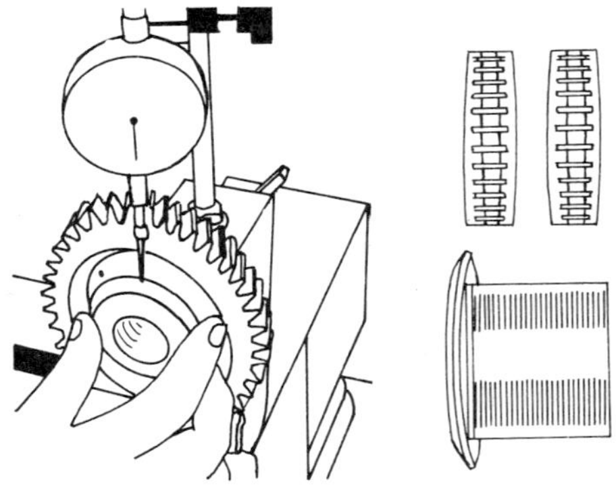

Play with new parts: 0.009 to 0.064 mm (.0004 to .0025 in.)
Wear limit: 0.064 mm (.0025 in.)

Fig. 5-27. Needle bearing radial play being measured. Gear is locked solidly in position. Bearing inner race is then moved up and down against gauge pin of dial indicator.

6. Measure the inside diameter of each gear. If at any point it exceeds the wear limit given in **Table a**, replace the gear.

Table a. Gear Inside Diameters

Gear	Wear limit
1st	42.15 mm (1.659 in.)
2nd and 3rd	38.15 mm (1.502 in.)
5th	36.06 mm (1.420 in.)
Reverse	42.15 mm (1.659 in.)

7. Measure the 2nd gear journal and the 3rd gear journal of the output shaft. If the diameter of either journal is less than 37.80 mm (1.4898 in.), replace the shaft. Also replace the shaft if the thickness of the shaft's center flange is less than 4.00 mm (.157 in.).

8. Install first the 2nd gear and then the 3rd gear on the output shaft. With the shaft stationary, move each gear up and down against a dial indicator in order to determine its oil clearance (radial play). The correct clearance for each gear is 0.101 mm (.0040 in.).

9. Install the 2nd gear and its synchronizer ring on the shaft. Then loosely install the 1st/2nd clutch gear assembly on the shaft, orienting the clutch gear assembly's sleeve as indicated in Fig. 5-28 and starting the hub onto the splines of the shaft.

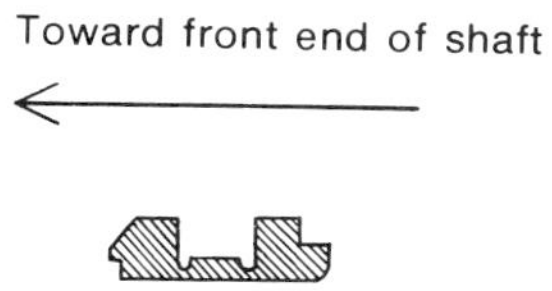

Fig. 5-28. Cross section of 1st/2nd clutch gear assembly's sleeve, showing correct orientation.

10. Support the clutch gear assembly on the repair press bed with a tool that will contact only the inner part of the clutch gear assembly's hub. Align the cutouts of the synchronizer ring with the keys of the clutch gear assembly as indicated in Fig. 5-29, then press the shaft down into the clutch gear assembly.

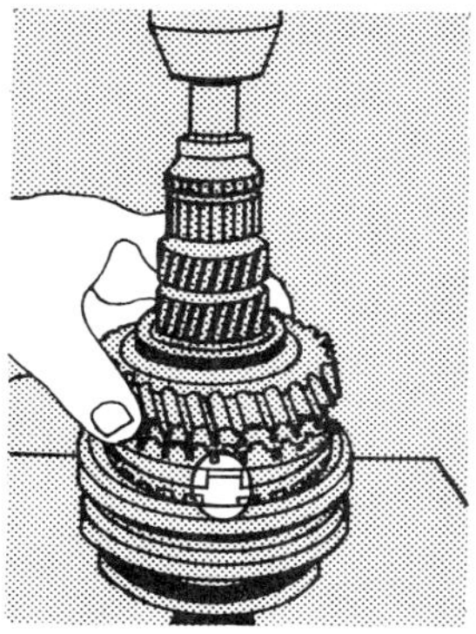

Fig. 5-29. Shaft being pressed into 1st/2nd clutch gear assembly. Circle indicates one of three cutouts in synchronizer ring that must be aligned with clutch gear keys.

11. Using multipurpose grease as an adhesive, install the inner bearing race locking ball in the shaft. Then install the 1st gear synchronizer ring and the 1st gear, carefully aligning the three cutouts in the synchronizer ring with the keys of the 1st/2nd clutch gear assembly.
12. Using multipurpose grease as an adhesive, install the locking ball for 1st gear bearing inner race. Install the needle roller bearing race and the needle bearing inner race for the 1st gear as a unit, making sure that the inner race correctly engages the locking ball.
13. Install the ball bearing race so that the shoulder on its periphery is away from 1st gear.
14. Using multipurpose grease as an adhesive, install the second inner bearing race locking ball. Assemble the reverse gear, its needle roller bearing race, and its needle bearing inner race. Then install these components as a unit, making sure that the inner race correctly engages the locking ball.
15. Loosely install the reverse (T40) or the reverse/5th (T50) clutch gear assembly on the shaft, orienting the clutch gear assembly's sleeve as indicated in Fig. 5-30 and starting the hub onto the splines of the shaft.

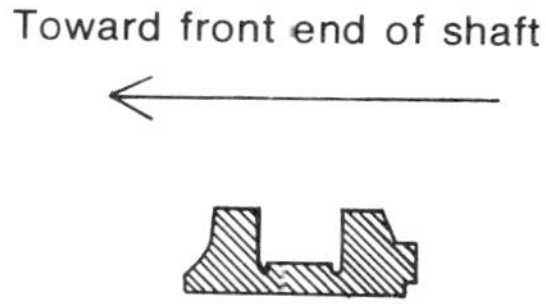

Fig. 5-30. Cross section of reverse (T40) or reverse/5th (T50) clutch gear assembly's sleeve, showing correct orientation. On the five-speed T50 transmission, the longer, protruding ends of the clutch gear assembly keys should be toward the front of the shaft.

16. Support the clutch gear assembly on the repair press bed with a tool that will contact only the inner part of the clutch gear assembly's hub. Then press the shaft down onto the clutch gear assembly as indicated in Fig. 5-31.

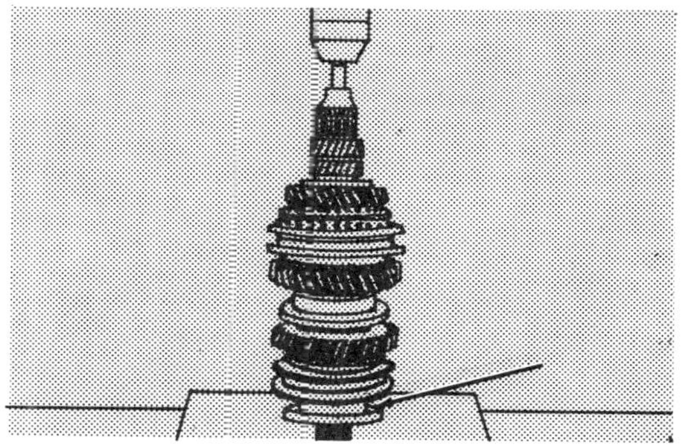

Fig. 5-31. Output shaft being pressed onto clutch gear assembly. Arrow indicates tool used to support hub of clutch gear assembly.

17. On the T50 five-speed transmission, use multipurpose grease as an adhesive to hold the inner bearing race locking ball in its recess in the shaft. Then install the 5th gear synchronizer ring, aligning the cutouts in the ring with the keys of the clutch gear assembly. Install 5th gear together with its needle roller bearing and bearing inner race, making sure that the inner race correctly engages the locking ball. Finally, install the ball bearing race with its shielded side toward the rear end of the shaft.
18. On the T40 four-speed transmission, install first the stop plate and then the tubular spacer. The crowned side of the stop plate should be toward the clutch gear assembly.
19. Install the shim, and then install the locknut to a torque of 60 to 70 Nm (44 to 52 ft. lb.).

NOTE ——
If the old locknut is to be reused, install an additional shim if this is necessary to reposition the locknut so that the old stake mark will be at a new point on the shaft. Do not, however, stake the locknut at this time.

20. Install the 3rd gear on the front end of the output shaft. Install the 3rd gear synchronizer ring.

21. Loosely install the 3rd/4th clutch gear assembly on the front of the shaft, orienting the clutch gear assembly's sleeve as indicated in Fig. 5-32 and starting the hub onto the splines of the shaft.

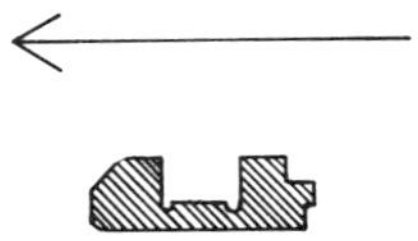

Fig. 5-32. Cross section of 3rd/4th clutch gear assembly's sleeve, showing correct orientation.

22. Support the 1st gear on the press bed as indicated in Fig. 5-33. Then place a tool atop the output shaft assembly that will contact only the inner part of the hub of the 3rd/4th clutch gear assembly. Align the cutouts in the 3rd gear synchronizer ring with the keys of the clutch gear assembly, then press the clutch gear assembly fully onto the shaft.

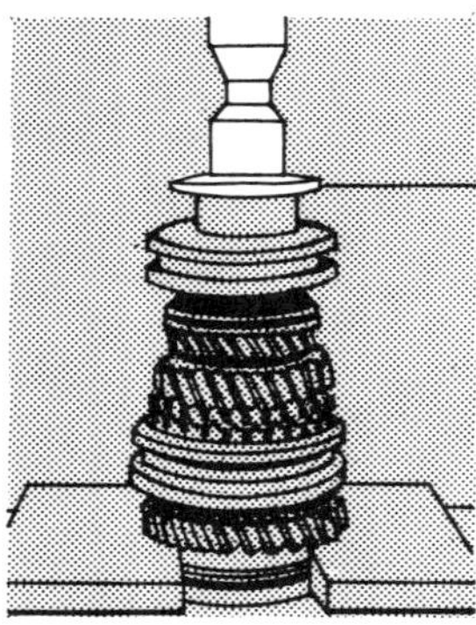

Fig. 5-33. 3rd/4th clutch gear assembly being pressed down onto output shaft splines. Make sure that cutouts in 3rd gear synchronizer ring are correctly aligned with keys of clutch gear assembly.

23. By trial and error, select a new output shaft front snap ring that will just fill the groove between the front part of the splines and the front surface of the clutch gear assembly hub. Then install the snap ring, making sure that there is no clearance at all between the ring and the hub. See Fig. 5-34.

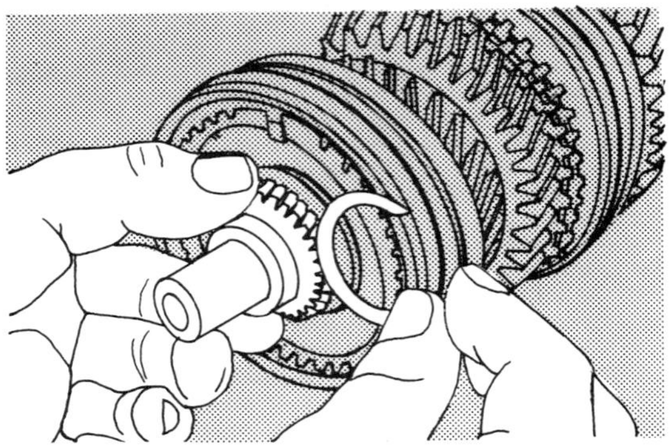

Available snap ring thicknesses
1.95 to 2.00 mm (.077 to .079 in.)
2.00 to 2.05 mm (.079 to .081 in.)
2.05 to 2.10 mm (.081 to .083 in.)
2.10 to 2.15 mm (.083 to .085 in.)
2.15 to 2.20 mm (.085 to .087 in.)

Fig. 5-34. Snap ring being tried in groove. Correct ring will fit tightly and permit absolutely no axial movement of clutch gear assembly's hub.

24. Using feeler gauges of various thicknesses, determine the thrust clearances (axial play) of all gears on the output shaft (Fig. 5-35). If the axial play of any gear is outside the ranges given in the illustration, either there are worn components or you have reassembled the output shaft incorrectly.

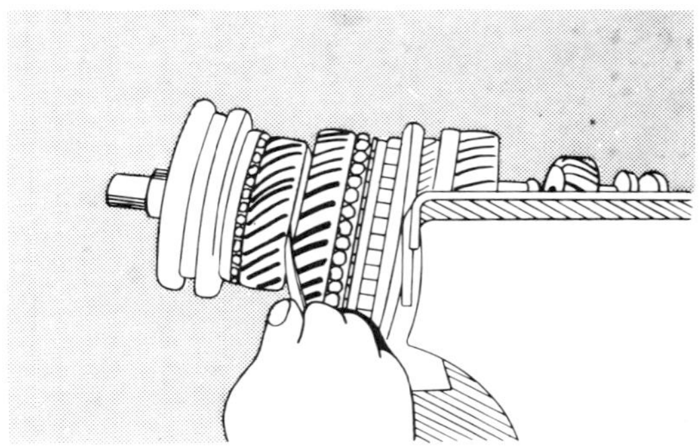

Thrust clearances with new parts		**Wear limit**
1st gear:	0.150 to 0.275 mm (.0059 to .0108 in.)	0.50 mm (.020 in.)
2nd gear:	0.150 to 0.250 mm (.0059 to .0098 in.)	0.50 mm (.020 in.)
3rd gear:	0.150 to 0.300 mm (.0059 to .0118 in.)	0.60 mm (.024 in.)
Reverse:	0.200 to 0.325 mm (.0079 to .0128 in.)	0.60 mm (.024 in.)
5th gear:	0.150 to 0.275 mm (.0059 to .0108 in.)	0.50 mm (.020 in.)

Fig. 5-35. Thrust clearance (axial play) of gears on output shaft being determined with feeler gauges.

25. With the gear clearances correct, as measured in the preceding step, use a cape chisel to stake the locknut, driving its locking collar partially into the recess of the output shaft.

26. Install the speedometer driven gear, using the locking ball and the two snap rings.

5.3 Disassembling and Assembling Input Shaft

Fig. 5-36 is an exploded view of the input shaft. The input shaft snap ring is a selective fit, with five snap ring thicknesses available. The correct snap ring must be selected by trial and error during input shaft assembly.

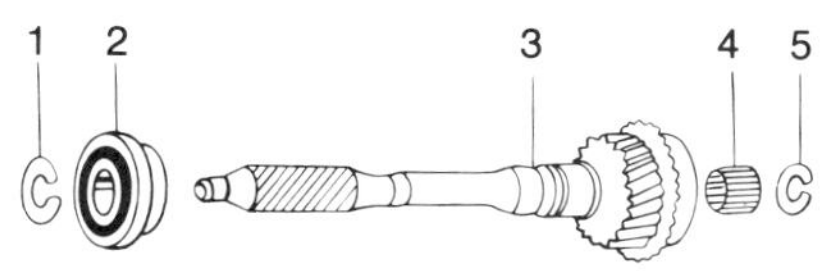

1. Input shaft snap ring
2. Ball bearing race with large snap ring
3. Input shaft
4. Needle roller bearings
5. Needle bearing snap ring

Fig. 5-36. Exploded view of input shaft.

To disassemble:

1. Check the input shaft visually for wear and damage. The splines and the gear teeth should be in perfect condition and the bearing should not be noisy when you turn it by hand. Replace faulty input shafts.

2. Remove the needle bearing snap ring and the needle roller bearings from the center of the input shaft so that they will not be lost. If the bearings are galled or flattened by wear, replace the needle bearings during assembly.

3. Using snap ring pliers as indicated in Fig. 5-37, remove the snap rings from the input shaft and from the periphery of the ball bearing race.

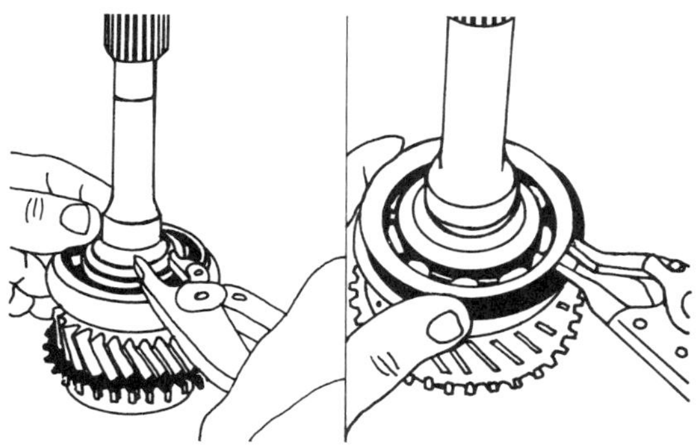

Fig. 5-37. Snap rings being removed from input shaft and ball bearing race.

4. Using a plate on the press bed that will support the ball bearing race, press the input shaft out of the ball bearing race as indicated in Fig. 5-38.

CAUTION —
Support the shaft with your hand while you press the shaft out of the bearing race. Otherwise, the shaft may fall suddenly, damaging the gear or the clutch splines and pilot. Once removed, the bearing race should be replaced because pressing out the shaft will damage the old bearing.

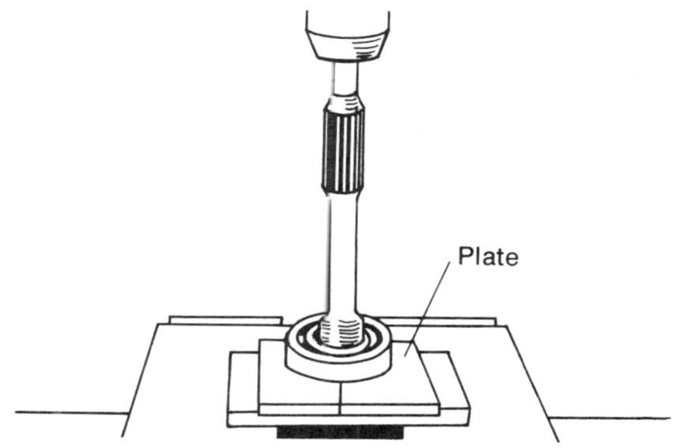

Fig. 5-38. Input shaft being pressed out of ball bearing race.

5. Loosely install the new ball bearing race on the output shaft, making sure that the snap ring groove in the periphery of the bearing race is toward the front end of the shaft. Then, using a tool on the press bed that will support only the bearing's inner race, press the input shaft into the new bearing as indicated in Fig. 5-39.

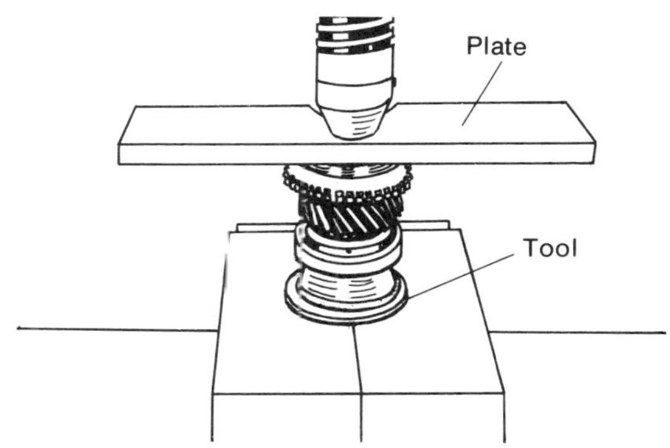

Fig. 5-39. Input shaft being pressed into new bearing. Notice plate interposed between press ram and shaft.

6. By trial and error, select a new input shaft snap ring that will just fill the groove ahead of the ball bearing's inner race. Then install the snap ring,

making sure that there is no clearance at all between the ring and the bearing. See Fig. 5-40.

Available snap ring thicknesses
1.95 to 2.00 mm (.077 to .079 in.)
2.00 to 2.05 mm (.079 to .081 in.)
2.05 to 2.10 mm (.081 to .083 in.)
2.10 to 2.15 mm (.083 to .085 in.)
2.15 to 2.20 mm (.085 to .087 in.)

Fig. 5-40. Snap ring being tried in groove. Correct ring will fit tightly and permit absolutely no axial movement of bearing.

7. Install a new snap ring in the periphery of the ball bearing race.
8. Using multipurpose grease as a lubricant and an adhesive, install the needle bearings in the center of the input shaft. Install the snap ring.
9. Lubricate the gear and the ball bearing race with SAE 90, API GL-4 gear oil before you install the shaft in the transmission.

Countershaft for four-speed transmission

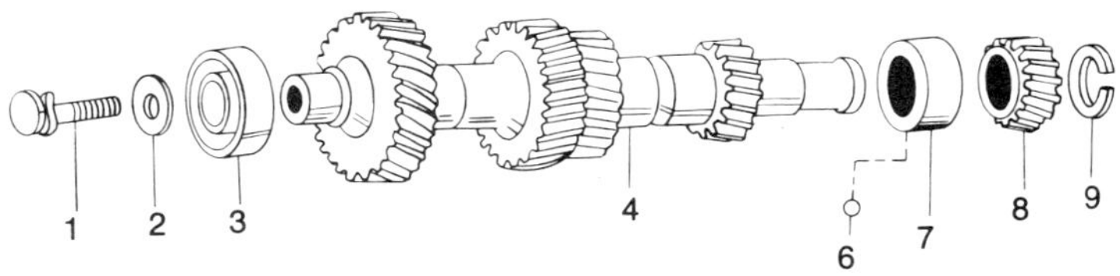

Countershaft for five-speed transmission

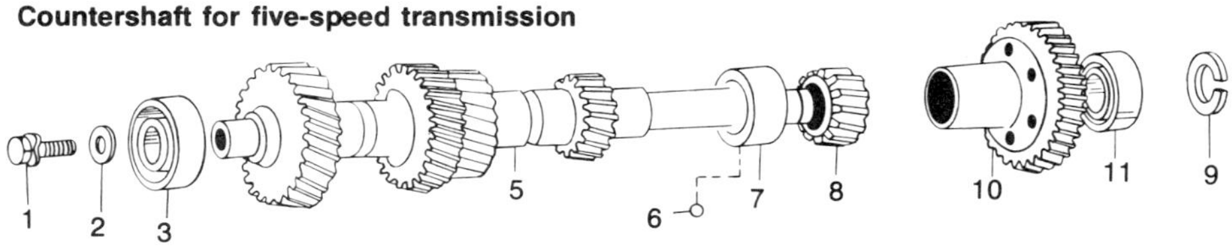

5.4 Disassembling and Assembling Countershaft and Reverse Idler Gear

Fig. 5-41 shows exploded views of the countershafts used in both the T40 four-speed transmission and the T50 five-speed transmission. Become familiar with the names of the various components, as you will encounter them frequently in the procedures that follow.

To disassemble:

1. Remove the special bolt and the bearing lock plate. Remove the large snap ring from the periphery of the front ball bearing race.
2. Using a puller as indicated in Fig. 5-42, remove the ball bearing race from the countershaft.

CAUTION —
Because the puller will exert abnormal pressure on the bearing's outer race, the bearing will be ruined by removal. A new bearing must be installed during assembly. Be sure that the center screw of the puller you use does not damage the threads in the center of the countershaft.

3. On four-speed countershafts only, remove the countershaft snap ring from the rear end of the shaft. Then remove the reverse gear and the roller bearing race.
4. On five-speed countershafts only, remove the countershaft snap ring from the rear end of the shaft. Then, using a puller as indicated in Fig. 5-43, remove the rear ball bearing race from the countershaft.

CAUTION —
Because the puller will exert abnormal pressure on the bearing's outer race, the bearing will be ruined by removal. A new bearing must be installed during assembly.

Fig. 5-41. Exploded views of countershafts for T40 (top) and T50 (bottom) transmissions.

1. Special bolt
2. Bearing lock plate
3. Front ball bearing race with snap ring
4. Countershaft (T40)
5. Countershaft (T50)
6. Roller bearing locking ball
7. Roller bearing race
8. Reverse gear
9. Countershaft snap ring
10. 5th gear (T50)
11. Rear ball bearing race (T50)

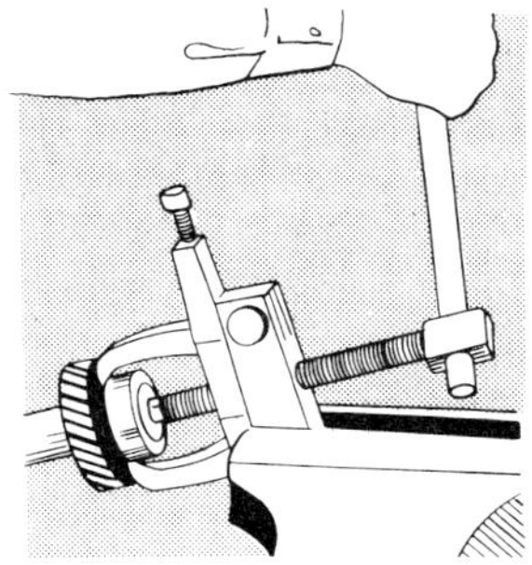

Fig. 5-42. Front ball bearing race being pulled off countershaft.

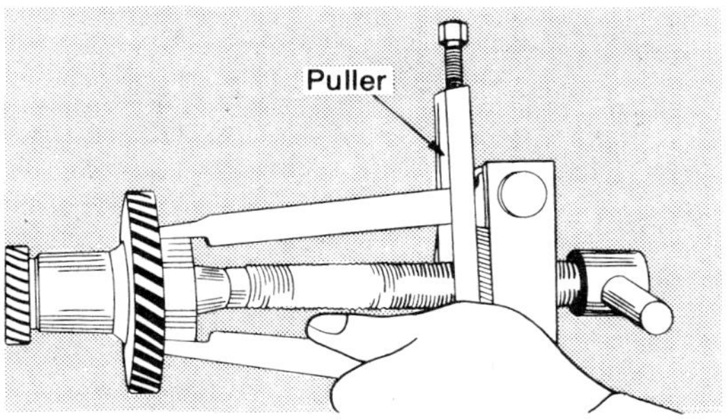

Fig. 5-43. Rear ball bearing race being pulled off rear end of countershaft for T50 transmission.

5. On five-speed countershafts only, support the 5th gear on the press bed as indicated in Fig. 5-44. Then press the countershaft out of the 5th gear. Remove the reverse gear and the roller bearing race.

> ***CAUTION —***
> *Be prepared to catch the countershaft when it is pressed free of the gear. Otherwise, the countershaft may fall and be damaged.*

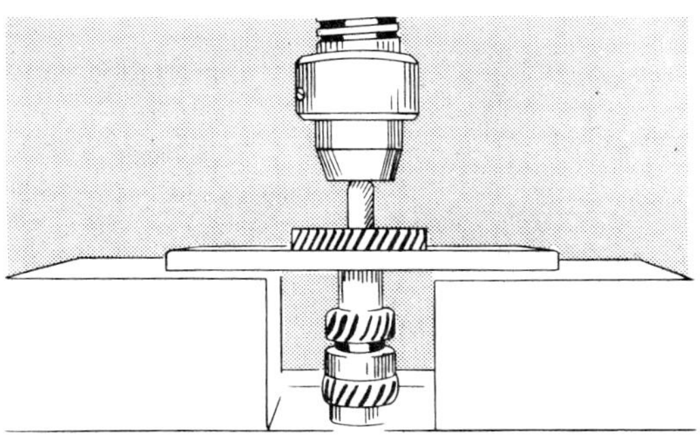

Fig. 5-44. Countershaft being pressed out of T50 transmission's 5th gear.

To assemble:

1. Inspect all components of the countershaft. Replace worn or damaged gears, and replace any ball bearing race that has been removed from the shaft. Replace the roller bearing race if the rollers are galled, flattened, or heat-blued.
2. Lubricate the roller bearing race with SAE 90, API GL-4 gear oil. Then install the roller bearing race on the countershaft so that the large-diameter roller cage is toward the four gears that are integral with the countershaft.

2

> **NOTE —**
> Throughout this assembly procedure, you should lubricate each component thoroughly with SAE 90, API GL-4 gear oil before you install the component on the countershaft.

3. Install the reverse gear on the countershaft so that its teeth are angled in the same directions as the other gear teeth on the countershaft.
4. On five-speed transmissions only, loosely install first the 5th gear and then the rear ball bearing race on the countershaft. Then, with the countershaft assembly supported on a tool that will contact only the inner race of the rear ball bearing race, press the countershaft into the 5th gear and the rear ball bearing.

> **NOTE —**
> As you press the shaft into the gear and the bearing, hold up the roller bearing race and the reverse gear, as indicated in Fig. 5-45.

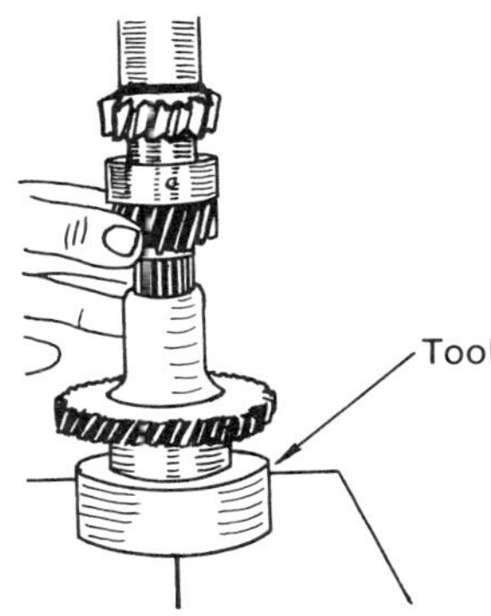

Fig. 5-45. Countershaft being pressed into 5th gear and rear ball bearing race. Notice how reverse gear and roller bearing are held up as shaft is pressed down.

5. By trial and error, select a new countershaft snap ring that will just fill the groove adjacent to the rear ball bearing race (T50 transmissions) or adjacent to the reverse gear (T40 transmissions). Then install the snap ring, making sure that there is no clearance at all between the ring and the gear or the bearing. See Fig. 5-46.

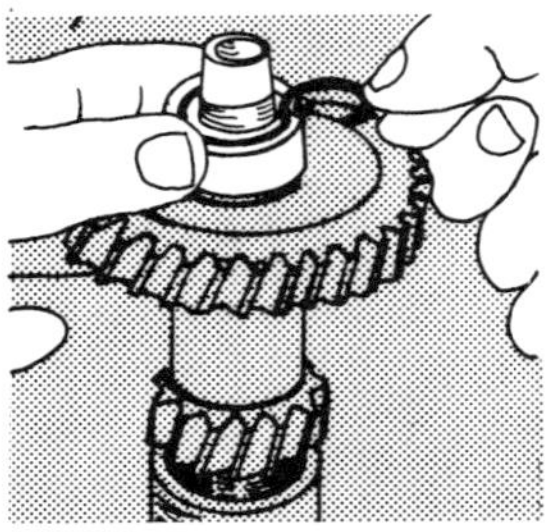

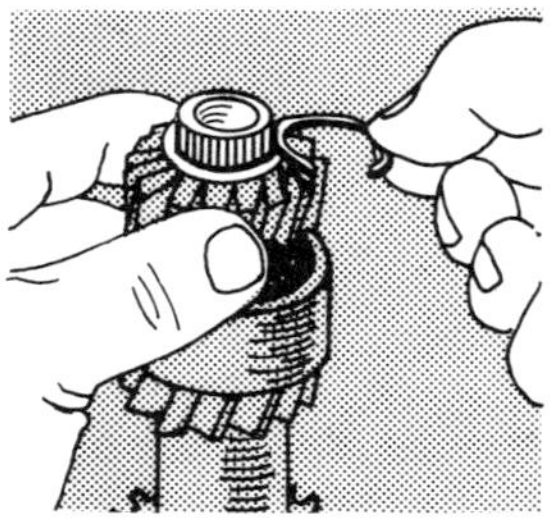

Available snap ring thicknesses (T50)
2.00 mm (.079 in.)
1.80 mm (.071 in.)
1.75 mm (.069 in.)

Available snap ring thicknesses (T40)
1.90 to 1.95 mm (.075 to .077 in.)
1.80 to 1.85 mm (.071 to .073 in.)

Fig. 5-46. Snap ring being tried in groove of T50 countershaft (left) and T40 countershaft (right). Correct ring will fit tightly and permit absolutely no axial movement of gear or bearing.

6. Loosely install a new front ball bearing race on the countershaft. The snap ring groove in the periphery of the bearing should be away from the gears that are integral with the countershaft.
7. Support the countershaft on a tool that will contact only the inner race of the rear ball bearing. Then press the countershaft into the bearing as indicated in Fig. 5-47.

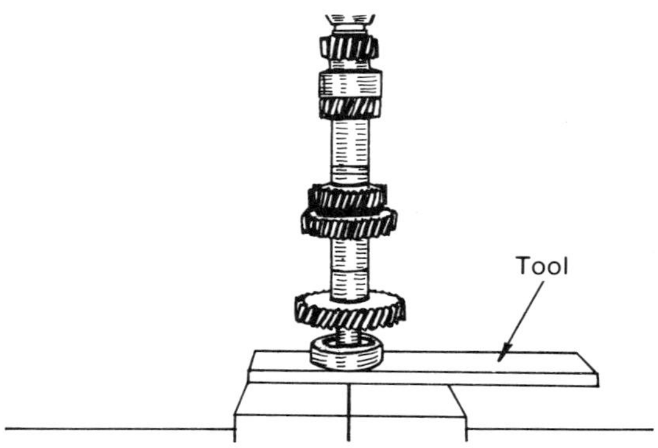

Fig. 5-47. Countershaft being pressed into front ball bearing race.

8. Install the bearing lock plate and the special bolt. Torque the bolt to 40 to 45 Nm (30 to 33 ft. lb.).
9. Install the snap ring in the periphery of the front ball bearing race.

Checking and Repairing Reverse Idler Gear

Inspect the reverse idler gear and replace it as a unit if it has worn thrust surfaces or chipped or broken teeth. Measure the inside diameter of the idler gear's bushing at several points. If at any point the bushing is worn to an inside diameter greater than 16.10 mm (.634 in.), press out the old bushing as indicated in Fig. 5-48.

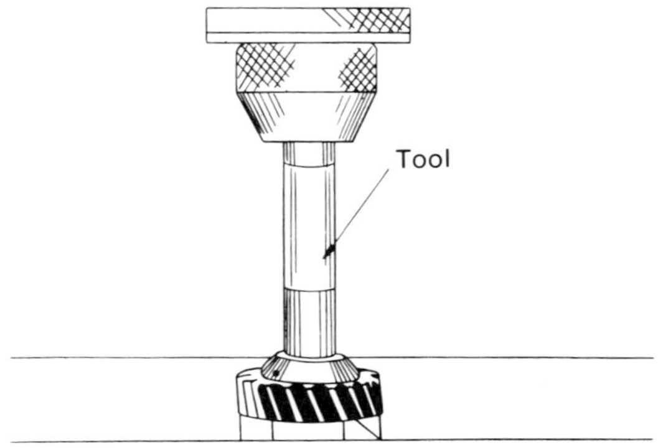

Fig. 5-48. Bushing being pressed out of or pressed into reverse idler gear. Tool shown (Toyota special service tool 09352-10010) fits inside diameter of bushing and has collar that contacts edge of bushing.

Install the new bushing using the same tool that you used to remove the old bushing. Be sure to align the oil holes of the bushing with the oil holes of the gear, as indicated in Fig. 5-49.

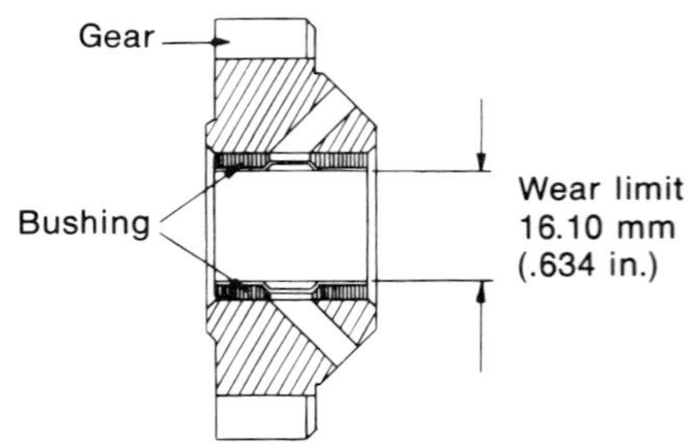

Fig. 5-49. Cross section of reverse idler gear. Notice how oil holes of bushing are lined up with oil holes of gear.

Before you reinstall the reverse idler gear in the transmission case, measure the idler gear's shaft at the point where it is contacted by the idler gear's bushing. Replace the shaft if it has worn to an outside diameter of less than 15.90 mm (.626 in.).

6. CLUTCH AND MANUAL TRANSMISSION TECHNICAL DATA

I. Manual Transmission Tolerances, Wear Limits, and Settings

Designation	Specification	
	With new parts mm (in.)	Wear limit mm (in.)
A. Thrust clearance of gears on output shaft		
1. 1st gear ... axial play	0.150–0.275 (.0059–.0108)	0.50 (.020)
2. 2nd gear ... axial play	0.150–0.250 (.0059–.0098)	0.50 (.020)
3. 3rd gear ... axial play	0.150–0.300 (.0059–.0118)	0.60 (.024)
4. Reverse gear ... axial play	0.200–0.325 (.0079–.0128)	0.60 (.024)
5. 5th gear ... axial play	0.150–0.275 (.0059–.0108)	0.50 (.020)
6. Reverse idler gear ... axial play	0.05–0.50 (.0020–.0197)	1.00 (.040)
B. Available input shaft snap rings		
1. Part No. 90520-30200 ... thickness	1.95–2.00 (.077–.079)	—
2. Part No. 90520-30201 ... thickness	2.00–2.05 (.079–.081)	—
3. Part No. 90520-30202 ... thickness	2.05–2.10 (.081–.083)	—
4. Part No. 90520-30203 ... thickness	2.10–2.15 (.083–.085)	—
5. Part No. 90520-30204 ... thickness	2.15–2.20 (.085–.087)	—
C. Oil clearance of output shaft of 1st, 5th, and reverse gears, measured between needle bearing inner race and gear bore with needle roller bearing race in place between them ... radial play	0.009–0.064 (.0004–.0025)	0.064 (.0025)
D. Bore diameter of gears on output shaft		
1. 1st gear ... inside diameter	—	42.15 (1.659)
2. 2nd and 3rd gears ... inside diameter	—	38.15 (1.502)
3. 5th gear ... inside diameter	—	36.06 (1.420)
4. Reverse gear ... inside diameter	—	42.15 (1.659)
E. Output shaft dimensions		
1. Output shaft journals for 2nd gear and 3rd gear ... outside diameter	—	37.80 (1.488)
2. Output shaft flange thickness ... width	—	4.00 (.157)
3. Output shaft straightness ... bend/runout	—	0.06 (.0024)
F. Oil clearance of output shaft 2nd gear and 3rd gear measured between gear bore and journal of shaft ... radial play	—	0.101 (.0040)
G. Shift fork and clutch gear sleeve		
1. Clearance between side of shift fork and side of groove in sleeve of clutch gear assembly ... clearance	—	1.00 (.040)
2. Groove in sleeve of clutch gear assembly .... maximum permissible width	—	8.50 (.335)
H. Synchronizer rings ... clearance between coupling teeth on gear and synchronizer ring	1.00–2.00 (.040–.080)	0.80 (.031)
I. Available countergear snap rings (T40)		
1. Part No. 90520-21198 ... thickness	1.80–1.85 (.071–.073)	—
2. Part No. 90520-21199 ... thickness	1.90–1.95 (.075–.077)	—
J. Available countergear snap rings (T50)		
1. Part No. 90520-18264 ... thickness	2.00 (.079)	—
2. Part No. 90520-18265 ... thickness	1.80 (.071)	—
3. Part No. 90520-18266 ... thickness	1.60 (.063)	—
K. Reverse idler gear		
1. Reverse idler gear bushing bore ... inside diameter	—	16.10 (.634)
2. Reverse idler gear shaft ... outside diameter	—	15.90 (.626)
L. Available output shaft front snap rings		
1. Part No. 90520-30200 ... thickness	1.95–2.00 (.077–.079)	—
2. Part No. 90520-30201 ... thickness	2.00–2.05 (.079–.081)	—
3. Part No. 90520-30202 ... thickness	2.05–2.10 (.081–.083)	—
4. Part No. 90520-30203 ... thickness	2.10–2.15 (.083–.085)	—
5. Part No. 90520-30204 ... thickness	2.15–2.20 (.085–.087)	—
M. Extension housing		
1. Extension housing bushing ... inside diameter	32.000–32.025 (1.2598–1.2608)	32.075 (1.2628)
2. Extension housing bushing to front universal joint yoke ... clearance	0.009–0.059 (.0004–.0024)	—
3. Extension housing preheating for bushing replacement ... temperature	80°–100°C (176°–212°F)	—

II. Tightening Torques

Location	Designation	Nm	Ft. lb. (In. lb.)
Clutch pedal to mounting bracket	Nut/bolt	30–40	22–30
Clutch hydraulic line to clutch master cylinder	Union	13–15	9.5–11
Clutch master cylinder to car body	Nut	6–10	(53–89)
Fluid reservoir to master cylinder body	Special bolt	20–25	15–18
Clutch slave cylinder to bellhousing	Bolt	10–15	7.5–11
Clutch hydraulic line to slave cylinder	Union	35–40	26–30
Clutch pressure plate assembly to engine flywheel	Bolt	15–20	11–15
Driveshaft to pinion flange of rear axle	Bolt	35–40	26–30
Driveshaft center bearing support to car body	Bolt	35–40	26–30
Extension housing to rear of transmission case	Bolt	40–45	30–33
Retainer for speedometer driven gear to extension housing	Bolt	14–15	10–11
Gearshift assembly housing to extension housing	Bolt	11–15	8–11
Transmission rear mount crossmember to extension housing	Bolt	20–25	15–18
Transmission rear mount crossmember to car body	Bolt	20–25	15–18
Shift return bushing (of gearshift assembly) to return shaft	—	7–9	5–7
Shift return plate (of gearshift assembly) to housing	Lock bolt	10–15	7.5–11
Transmission bellhousing to engine	Bolt	55–65	41–48
Transmission bellhousing to stiffening bracket	Bolt/nut	35–45	26–33
Engine intermediate plate to bottom of bellhousing	Bolt	20	15
Starter to bellhousing and engine	Bolt	55–75	41–55
Exhaust pipe to exhaust manifold	Nut	30–45	22–33
Gear oil drain plug or gear oil filler plug in case	—	30–35	22–26
Reverse idler gear shaft to transmission case	Bolt	12–15	9–11
Shift rod detent cover to right-hand side of transmission case	Bolt	12–15	9–11
Left-hand half of transmission case to right-hand half of transmission case	Bolt	20	15
Back-up light switch in transmission case	—	35–50	26–37
Bellhousing to transmission case	Bolt	35–45	26–33
Gearset on output shaft	Locknut	60–70	44–52
Ball bearing race to front of countershaft	Special bolt	40–45	30–33
Clutch throwout bearing guide sleeve to center of transmission bellhousing	Bolt	12–15	9–11

III. Clutch Tolerances, Wear Limits, and Settings

Designation	Specification
Clutch pedal height (measured from pedal pad to insulation sheet beneath carpet, with pedal up)	169 mm (6 21/32 in.)
Clutch pedal freeplay (1975 through 1977 cars)	20 to 40 mm (25/32 to 1 9/16 in.)
Clutch pedal freeplay (1978 and later cars)	5 to 15 mm (13/64 to 19/32 in.)
Clutch pedal pushrod-to-master cylinder clearance (1975 through 1977 cars only)	2 to 3.5 mm (5/64 to 9/64 in.)
Piston-to-master cylinder bore clearance ... wear limit	0.15 mm (.0059 in.)
Clutch disk lining thickness, measured from surface of either lining to rivet head ... wear limit	0.30 mm (.012 in.)
Throwout bearing guide sleeve outside diameter ... wear limit	32.90 mm (1.295 in.)
Clutch disk runout ... wear limit	0.50 mm (.020 in.)
Diaphragm spring release lever out-of-alignment (can be corrected by bending levers) ... wear limit	0.60 mm (.024 in.)

DRIVESHAFT AND REAR AXLE

Contents

TABLES

Driveshaft and Rear Axle

3

The driveshaft transmits power from the engine/transmission assembly to the rear axle, on which the car's driving wheels are mounted. This arrangement, which is considered conventional, has the advantage of simplifying repairs to the rear axle and the transmission. Because the engine and the transmission are mounted firmly to the car body, and are permitted only slight movement by their bonded rubber mountings, the driveshaft must be designed to accomodate the up-and-down movements of the rear axle. In its basic form, this is accomplished by universal joints at the front and rear ends of the driveshaft. However, two-piece driveshafts with three universal joints are used on some of the cars covered by this Manual. Removal, repair, and installation of both kinds of driveshafts are covered in this section.

The rear axle is mounted on the rear springs and the rear shock absorbers, which constitute the car's rear suspension. This allows the rear axle to move up and down relative to the car body. The up-and-down movement is caused by differences in vehicle load and by road surface irregularities. All repairs to the shock absorbers, the springs, and related parts are covered in **SUSPENSION AND STEERING,** where instructions are also given for removing and installing the rear axle on the car. It is not necessary to remove the rear axle housing for the repairs given in the present section. Repairs related to the rear brakes are described in **BRAKES AND WHEELS.**

Though you may not have the special tools or the experience required to repair the rear axle's final drive and differential, you may be perfectly capable of removing the rear axle as a unit. If so, you can deliver the rear axle to an Authorized Dealer or other qualified repair shop after giving the rear axle a thorough exterior cleaning. You should not, however, do any disassembly work because it will only complicate the repairs.

Please be especially careful in handling and installing the tapered-roller bearings of the final drive, and make all rear axle repairs in clean surroudings. Cover the open ends of the rear axle housing with plastic bags while the axle shafts are out. This will prevent abrasive dust or other foreign matter from entering the housing. If you remove the final drive carrier, you should keep the carrier and the final drive gears in a large plastic bag when you are not working on them so that shop dirt—such as abrasive dust from bench grinders, valve grinding equipment, or body sanding—cannot contact the gears or the bearings. In addition, you should check ahead of time that you have all the necessary tools. Work that is designated by the lack of U.S. equivalents can be carried out correctly only with metric tools and instruments.

1. GENERAL DESCRIPTION

The Corolla 1600 may be equipped with a one-piece or a two-piece driveshaft. The one-piece driveshaft uses two Cardan-type universal joints, and the two-piece driveshaft uses three Cardan-type universal joints. The middle of the two-piece driveshaft is supported by a center bearing that is bolted to the car's underbody. A universal joint, located just behind the center bearing, permits the rear half of the driveshaft to move up and down together with the rear axle. Such a design reduces unsprung weight and minimizes driveline noise.

The Corolla uses two semifloating rear axle shafts. The axles are mounted in a one-piece rear axle housing, which is equipped with a filler plug and a drain plug (Fig. 1-1). The final drive and differential gears are mounted in the final drive carrier, which is bolted to the front of the rear axle housing.

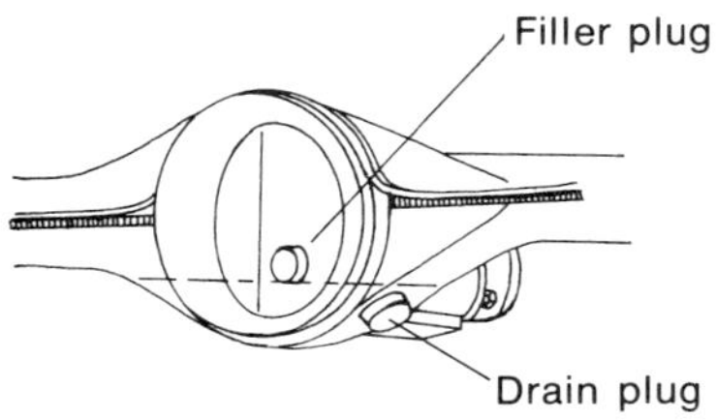

Fig. 1-1. Detail of rear axle, which houses filler plug and drain plug.

The depth of mesh between the ring and pinion gears is controlled by a selective washer between the pinion head and the rear pinion bearing. The ring gear is bolted to the differential assembly, which is supported in the final drive carrier by tapered-roller bearings. The outer ends of the semifloating axle shafts are supported in the ball bearing assemblies.

2. MAINTENANCE

The following three maintenance operations are required at regular mileage intervals. The procedures are covered in **LUBRICATION AND MAINTENANCE.**

1. Checking torque of rear suspension components attached to the rear axle, and checking torque of the driveshaft rear universal joint flange bolts.
2. Checking and, if necessary, correcting the differential oil level.
3. Changing the differential oil.

3. DRIVESHAFT

The Corolla 1600 is equipped with either a one-piece or a two-piece driveshaft. The one-piece driveshaft has two universal joints, and the two-piece driveshaft has three universal joints and a center bearing.

3.1 Removing and Installing Driveshaft

The driveshaft is electronically balanced as a complete assembly during manufacture. Therefore, you must mark all adjacent components before disassembly so that you can reassemble them in their original relationship after the driveshaft has been repaired. If the factory balance is not restored, driveline vibrations will result. Separate procedures are given here for removal and installation of one-piece and two-piece driveshafts (Fig. 3-1).

Fig. 3-1. Driveshaft sectional views.

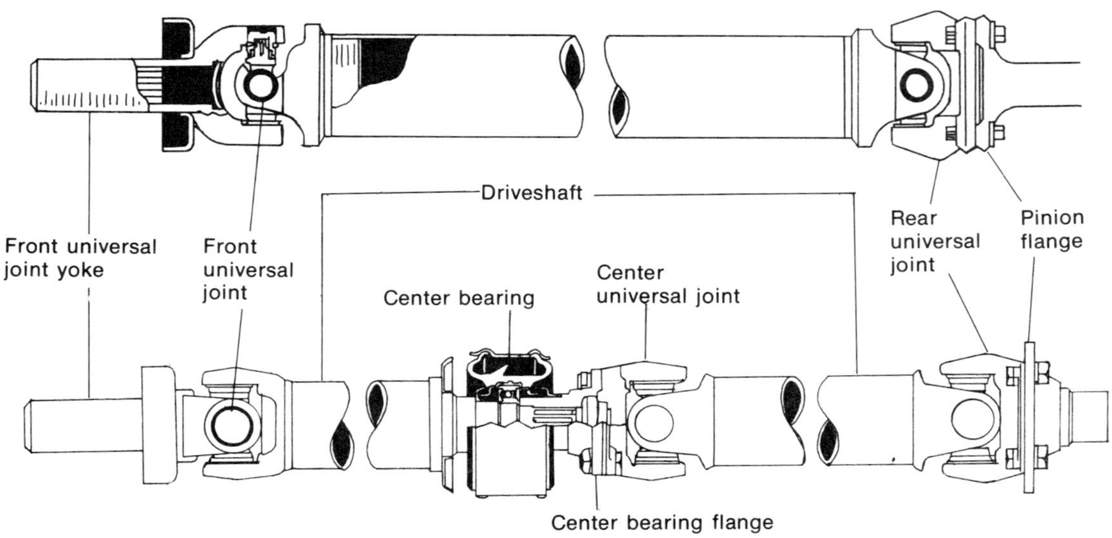

To remove one-piece driveshaft:

1. Raise the car on a hoist or support the car on stands designed for the purpose.
2. Use a center punch or paint to mark adjacent points on the pinion flange and the rear universal joint so that you can reinstall the driveshaft in its original position on the pinion flange (Fig. 3-2).

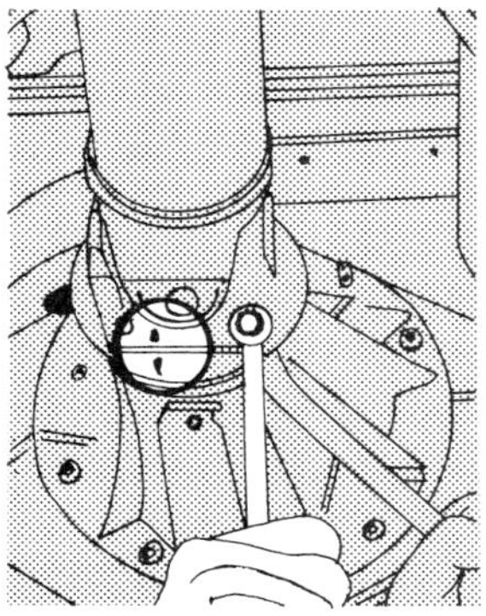

Fig. 3-2. Adjacent marks on pinion flange and rear universal joint.

3. Remove the four bolts and lockwashers that hold the driveshaft rear universal joint to the pinion flange. Then lower the driveshaft and withdraw it from the transmission.

NOTE ——
Unless the rear of the car is raised higher than the front, oil will leak from the transmission. To prevent leakage, you can install an old front universal joint yoke or a clean, lint-free rag.

To install one-piece driveshaft:

1. Wipe clean the front universal joint yoke and inspect it for damage or wear. Then lubricate the polished portion with multipurpose grease.
2. Being careful not to damage the oil seal or the bushing, which are in the rear of the transmission, slide the front universal joint yoke into the transmission. Make sure you engage the splines correctly.
3. Lift the rear of the driveshaft and align the mark that you made on the rear universal joint with the similar mark on the pinion flange.
4. Install the four pinion flange bolts, the lockwashers, and the nuts. Then torque the bolts to 35 to 40 Nm (26 to 30 ft. lb.).
5. Check the transmission oil level (or ATF level) and, if necessary, correct it as described in **LUBRICATION AND MAINTENANCE.** Torque the drain plug and the filler plug to 30 to 35 Nm (22 to 26 ft. lb.).

To remove two-piece driveshaft:

1. Raise the car on a hoist or support the car on stands designed for the purpose.
2. Use a center punch or paint to mark adjacent points on the rear universal joint and the pinion flange so that you can reinstall the driveshaft in its original position on the pinion flange. See Fig. 3-2 given earlier.
3. Remove the two bolts that hold the driveshaft center support bearing to the body. If your car is fitted with a heat insulator shield, it can now be removed separately.
4. Remove the four bolts and lockwashers that hold the rear universal joint to the pinion flange. Then lower the driveshaft and withdraw it as a unit from the transmission.

NOTE ——
Unless the rear of the car is raised higher than the front, oil will leak from the transmission. To prevent leakage, you can install an old front universal joint yoke or a clean, lint-free rag.

To install two-piece driveshaft:

1. Wipe clean the front universal joint yoke and inspect it for damage or wear. Then lightly lubricate the polished portion with multipurpose grease.
2. Being careful not to damage the oil seal or the bushing, which are in the rear of the transmission, slide the front universal joint yoke into the transmission. Make sure you engage the splines correctly.
3. Lift the rear of the driveshaft and align the mark that you made on the rear universal joint with the similar mark on the pinion flange.
4. Install the four pinion flange bolts, the lockwashers, and the nuts. Then torque the bolts to 35 to 40 Nm (26 to 30 ft. lb.).
5. Install the bolts that attach the center bearing to the chassis, but only make them finger-tight. Be sure that for each bolt there are both one spacer washer between the body and the bearing bracket, and one spacer washer between the bracket and the bolt.

6. Before tightening the bolts, check that the bearing bracket is at right angles to the driveshaft. Also check to see that the center line of the bearing is 1 mm ±1 mm (1/32 in. ± 1/32 in.) behind (toward the rear of the car) the center line of the bracket (Fig. 3-3).

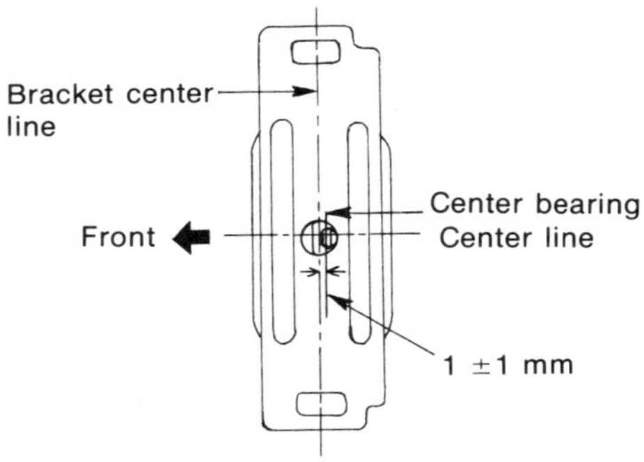

Fig. 3-3. Alignment of center bearing bracket.

7. When you are sure that the center bearing is properly aligned, carefully tighten the bolts to 35 to 40 Nm (26 to 30 ft. lb.).
8. Check the transmission oil level or ATF level and, if necessary, correct it by adding SAE 90 API GL-4 gear oil as described in **LUBRICATION AND MAINTENANCE.** Torque the drain plug and the filler plug to 30 to 35 Nm (22 to 26 ft. lb.).

Removing and Installing Center Bearing

(two-piece driveshaft only)

To remove:

1. Remove the driveshaft. Then make adjacent marks on the center universal joint and the center bearing flange, as shown in Fig. 3-4.

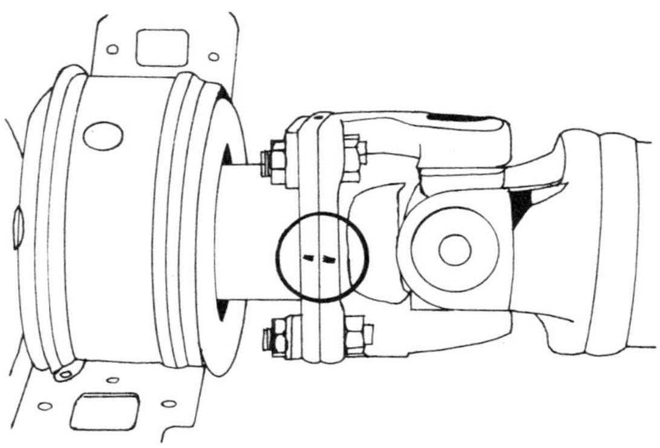

Fig. 3-4. Adjacent marks on bearing flange and center universal joint.

2. Remove the nuts and lockwashers from the four bolts that connect the bearing flange and the center universal joint. Remove the bolts and separate the rear driveshaft segment from the bearing flange.
3. Make paint marks on adjacent areas of the center bearing flange and the threaded end of the front driveshaft segment, as shown in Fig. 3-5. You may need to clean the area before applying the paint.

CAUTION ——
Do not use a center punch to mark the threaded shaft. This can distort the metal and make it difficult to remove the nut from the shaft.

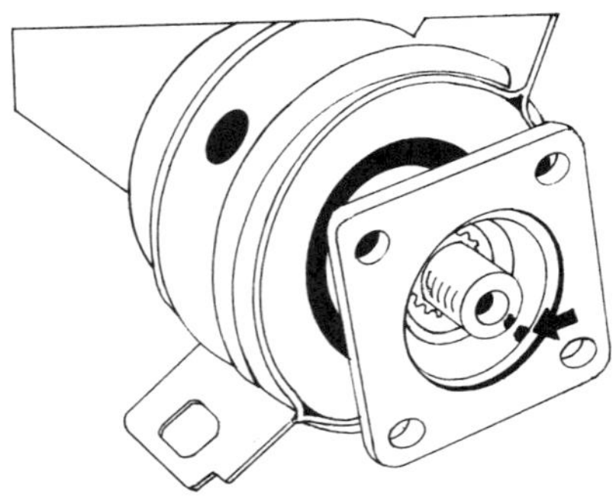

Fig. 3-5. Adjacent marks on bearing flange and shaft.

4. Put the bearing flange in a vise with soft jaw covers. Use a small cold chisel to unstake the large nut that is inside the center bearing flange. Remove the nut and then carefully remove the bearing flange from the splined shaft. You can now separate the center bearing from the front half of the driveshaft.

NOTE ——
If the bearing flange is stuck on the splines and a puller is not available, lightly strike the end of the threaded shaft with a soft hammer, being careful not to deform the shaft or damage the threads.

To install:

1. Slide the center bearing over the threaded end of the front driveshaft half. If you are reinstalling the old bearing, be sure to inspect it for damage or wear, as shown in Fig. 3-6.

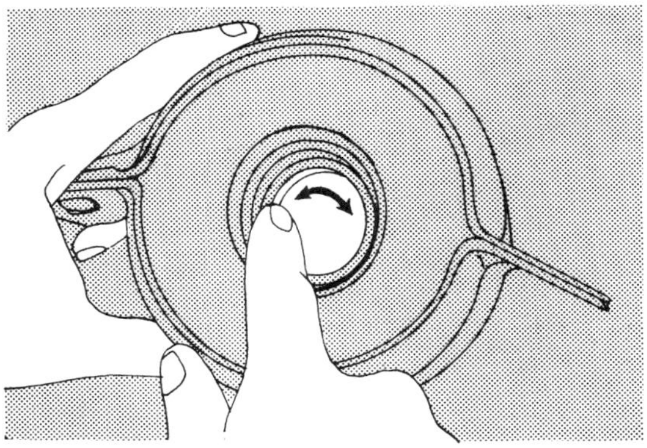

Fig. 3-6. Center bearing being inspected.

2. Coat the splines of the shaft with multipurpose grease. Then reinstall the bearing flange, being careful to align the paint marks on the flange and shaft.
3. Install a new nut and a washer to secure the flange to the shaft. This procedure is best done with the flange mounted in a vise with soft jaws as shown in Fig. 3-7. Torque the nut to 165 to 195 Nm (122 to 144 ft. lb.). Then loosen the nut and retighten it to a torque of 25 to 35 Nm (18 to 26 ft. lb.). Finally, use a center punch to stake the nut, as shown in Fig. 3-8.

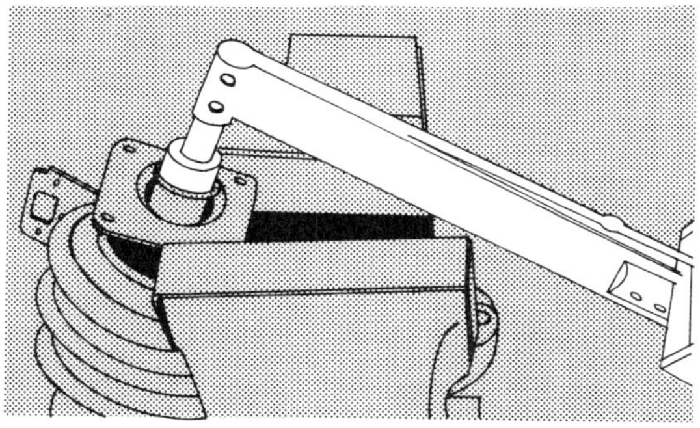

Fig. 3-7. Nut that holds bearing flange to driveshaft being torqued.

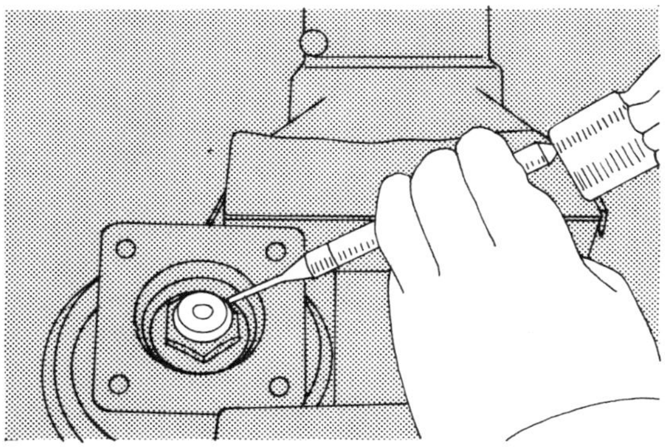

Fig. 3-8. Center punch being used to stake nut.

4. Being careful to align the center punch marks you made, bolt the center universal joint to the bearing flange. Torque the bolts to 20 to 35 Nm (15 to 26 ft. lb.).
5. Install the driveshaft in the car.

Checking Driveshaft for Bending

If your car has driveline vibration that cannot be attributed to bad universal joints, or if it has had under-car damage or been in an engine- or rear axle-displacing collison, you may wish to check the driveshaft for bending.

If you do not have the necessary equipment to perform this measurement, you can have it done by a well-equipped garage or machine shop. 3

To check:

1. Remove the driveshaft.
2. Clean the driveshaft of all dirt, grease, and rust. Pay special attention to the ends and the middle section of the driveshaft, as the cleanliness of these sections will directly affect the accuracy of the measurement.
3. Support the driveshaft on V-blocks on a smooth, level surface, and position a dial indicator with its measuring pin against the driveshaft (see Fig. 3-9). Then zero the gauge. Carefully hand-turn the driveshaft. The maximum allowable bending is 0.25 mm (.010 in.). Maximum allowable runout, therefore, is 0.50 mm (.020 in.).

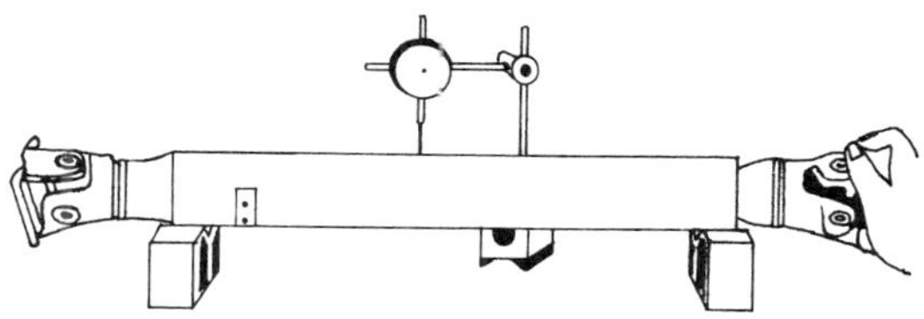

Fig. 3-9. Setup for checking driveshaft for bending.

4. If driveshaft runout exceeds this maximum, and you are sure that dirt or rust deposits are not affecting the results, replace the damaged component.

3.2 Disassembling and Assembling Universal Joints

Before attempting universal joint repairs, you should inspect the driveshaft and read the instructions thoroughly. Acquaint yourself with the component parts illustrated in Fig. 3-10.

1. Dust cover
2. Universal joint yoke
3. Plug
4. Balance piece
5. Driveshaft
6. Universal joint flange yoke
7. Center bearing
8. Bearing flange
9. Bearing cap
10. Snap ring
11. Cross trunion
12. Cross
13. Cross assembly

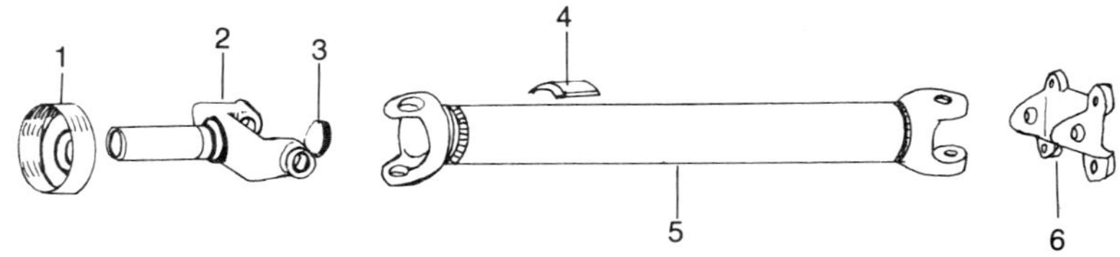

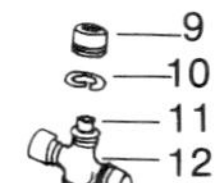

Detail of cross assembly

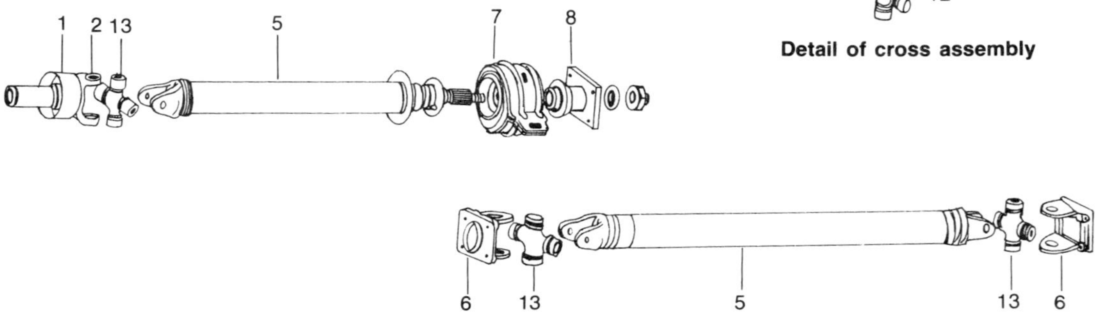

Fig. 3-10. Exploded views of one-piece driveshaft (top) and two-piece driveshaft (bottom).

To disassemble:

1. Remove the driveshaft. Then, using paint or a center punch, mark adjacent points on the universal joint components (Fig. 3-11).

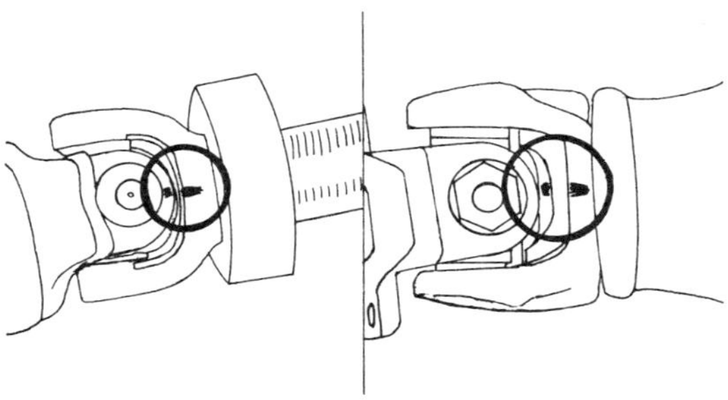

Fig. 3-11. Adjacent marks on universal joint components.

2. Remove the snap rings as shown in Fig. 3-12.

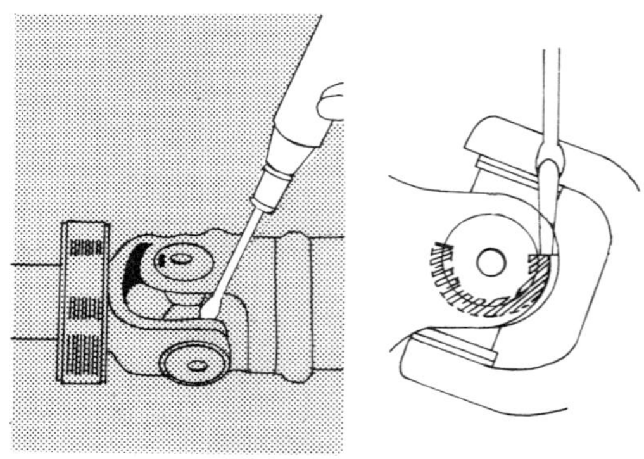

Fig. 3-12. Snap ring being removed.

3. Mount the universal joint assembly in a large vise, using two socket wrenches as shown in Fig. 3-13. The smaller socket wrench should have an outside diameter that is slightly smaller than the bearing bore; the larger should have an inside clearance large enough to receive the bearing cap. Press in one of the bearing caps with the smaller socket so that the opposite bearing cap will be forced out of the yoke and into the larger socket wrench.

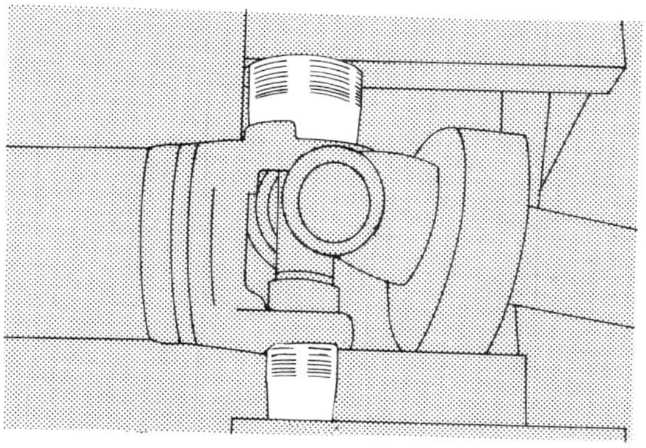

Fig. 3-13. Setup for pressing out bearing caps.

4. Remove the partially exposed bearing cap with a pair of large pliers.
5. Repeat steps 3 and 4 to remove the opposite bearing cap. To do this, you must reverse the socket wrenches and press the cross in the direction opposite to that used to remove the first bearing cap.
6. Remove the yoke from the cross.
7. Repeat steps 3 through 5 to remove the other two bearing caps and the cross from the second yoke of the universal joint.

To assemble:

1. Position the cross in one of the universal joint yokes.
2. Assemble the needle bearings in the bearing caps with enough multipurpose grease to hold them in place.
3. Using the vise and the small socket wrench, press one bearing cap partially into the yoke. Insert the cross trunion into the cap to prevent the needle bearings from being dislodged. Continue to press in the cap until the snap ring can be installed, and then install the snap ring.
4. Install the opposite bearing cap on the yoke. Press in the cap until the snap ring can be installed, and then install the snap ring.

CAUTION —

If you cannot easily press the second cap far enough to uncover the snap ring groove, it is because one or more needle rollers have been dislodged and are caught between the bearing cap and the end of the cross trunion. Do not force the cap in or you will ruin the bearing. Instead, press out the caps and reassemble the needle rollers in their correct locations.

5. Snap rings are available in several thicknesses (see **Table a**). Select rings that will provide less than 0.05 mm (0.002 in.) of axial play. Use new snap rings of the same size on each side. If it is not possible to obtain axial play of less than 0.05 mm (0.002 in.) with snap rings of the same size, a snap ring one size thicker may be used at one side.

Table a. Snap Ring Sizes

Part number	Thickness
90521–29070	2.40 mm (0.0945 in.)
90521–29071	2.45 mm (0.0965 in.)
90521–29072	2.50 mm (0.0984 in.)
90521–29073	2.55 mm (0.1004 in.)

6. With reference to the alignment marks that you made prior to disassembly, position the cross in the second universal joint yoke. Then repeat steps 2 through 5 to complete assembly.
7. Install the driveshaft on the car.

4. REAR AXLE

If it becomes necessary to remove the entire rear axle, do so as described in **SUSPENSION AND STEERING.** Though some of the illustrations show the rear axle removed, you can carry out all of the procedures given here with the rear axle on the car.

3

4.1 Removing and Installing Axle Shaft

Because the rear wheel bearing remains on the axle shaft when the axle shaft is removed, the relatively simple job of axle shaft removal is a prerequisite to the more difficult job of wheel bearing replacement. Refer to Fig. 4-1 for an exploded view of the rear axle shaft and its related components.

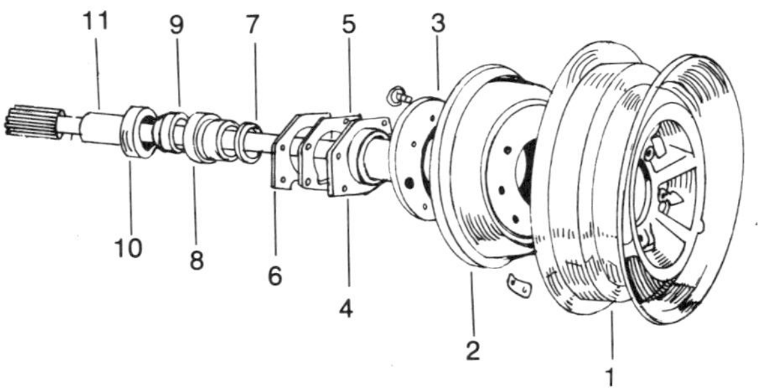

1. Wheel
2. Brake drum
3. Rear axle flange
4. Bearing retainer
5. Retainer gasket
6. Housing gasket
7. Spacer
8. Rear wheel bearing
9. Bearing retaining ring
10. Oil seal
11. Rear axle shaft

Fig. 4-1. Exploded view of rear axle shaft assembly.

To remove:

1. Raise the car until the rear wheel is off the ground. Use a hoist or support the car on stands designed for the purpose. Remove the road wheel.
2. Remove the brake drum as described in **BRAKES AND WHEELS.**
3. Using a socket wrench inserted through the holes in the axle shaft flange as shown in Fig. 4-2, remove the four backing plate mounting nuts.

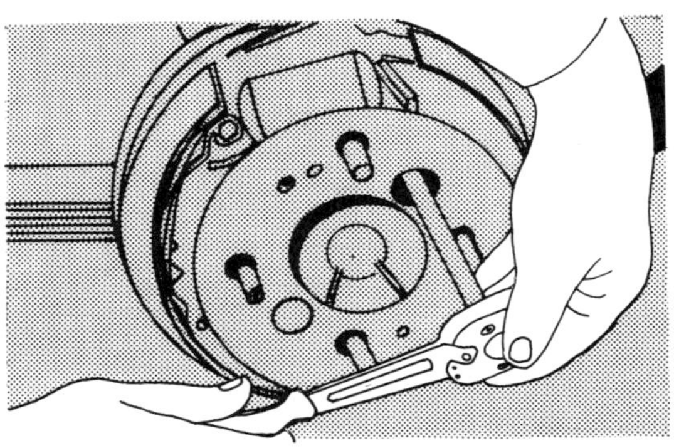

Fig. 4-2. Backing plate nuts being removed.

4. With a slide hammer attached to the axle shaft as shown in Fig. 4-3, pull the rear axle shaft and bearing assembly out of the rear axle housing.

NOTE ——
If you lack a slide hammer, attach a length of chain to the axle flange. Then attach a cement block to the opposite end of the chain. A few sharp jerks on the block should pull the axle out of the housing.

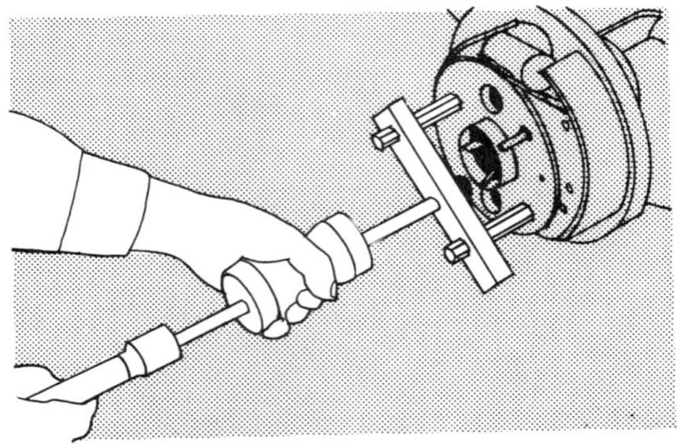

Fig. 4-3. Rear axle shaft being removed.

To install:

1. Carefully wipe clean the splines of the inner end of the axle shaft, then inspect the splines. If they are damaged or deformed, replace the axle shaft.
2. Hand-turn the wheel bearing. If it feels gritty or makes noise, replace the bearing as described under the next heading.
3. Make sure that the axle and the bearings are dirt-free, then insert the axle shaft into the axle housing. Refer to Fig. 4-4 for the correct positions of the housing gasket, the backing plate, the retainer gasket, and the retainer.

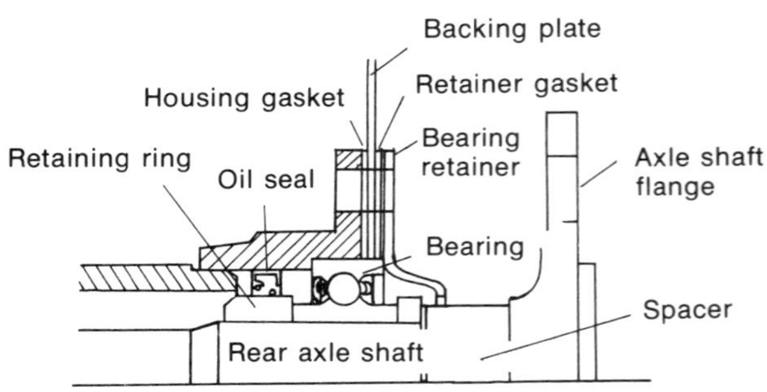

Fig. 4-4. Rear axle shaft assembly.

NOTE ——
If the housing gasket is to be replaced, select the new gasket from **Table b.**

Table b. Available Housing Gasket Thicknesses

Gasket thickness	Backing plate thickness
0.3 mm (.012 in.)	2.36 to 2.48 mm (.0929 to .0976 in.)
0.6 mm (.024 in.)	2.12 to 2.36 mm (.0835 to .0929 in.)

4. Hand-turn the axle shaft until you feel the splines engage those inside the differential sidegear. Then, using a rubber mallet, drive in the axle shaft, being careful that the bearing enters the recess in the axle housing.
5. Torque the backing plate nuts to 60 to 70 Nm (44 to 52 ft. lb.).
6. Install the brake drum and the road wheel.

Replacing Rear Wheel Bearing

The rear wheel bearing is a press fit on the rear axle shaft, and replacement requires special tools and techniques. Read this section carefully to determine whether you have the skills and tools necessary before beginning disassembly.

To remove:

1. Remove the axle shaft as described under the preceding heading. Grind a groove on one side of the bearing retaining ring.
2. Clamp the axle shaft in a vise near the retaining ring, as shown in Fig. 4-5. Then, by driving a cold chisel into the groove that you ground into the ring, expand the ring until you can slip it off toward the splined end of the axle shaft. Cut completely through the ring if necessary.

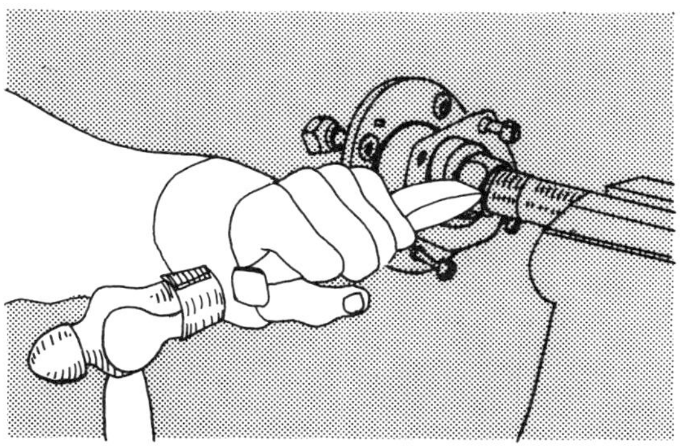

Fig. 4-5. Bearing retaining ring being split so it can be removed from axle shaft.

3. Using a setup similar to the one shown in Fig. 4-6, press the axle shaft out of the rear wheel bearing.

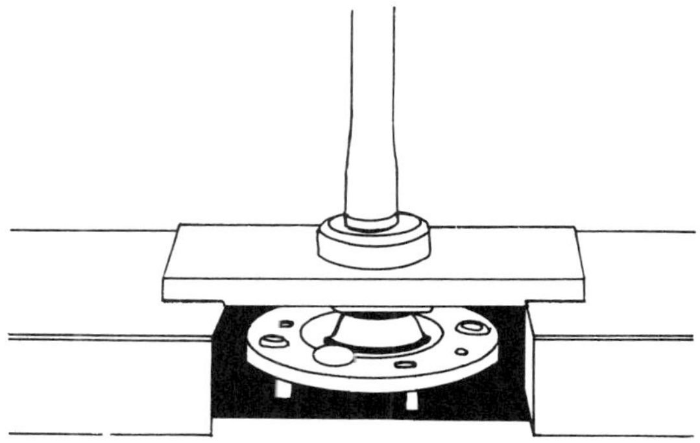

Fig. 4-6. Rear axle shaft being pressed out of rear wheel bearing.

3

NOTE ——
Any automotive machine shop can readily handle the work described in step 3. If you lack both a press and machine shop services, break the outer bearing race by squeezing it in a vise. Pry off the ball race. Then grind through one side of the bearing inner race until it is paper-thin. You will then be able to break the inner race with a cold chisel so that you can slip the race off the axle shaft.

CAUTION ——
Never attempt to remove a bearing by hammering on the splined end of the axle shaft. This will deform the splines, making the axle shaft impossible to install.

To install:

1. Install the bearing retainer on the axle shaft so that its convex side is toward the axle shaft flange. Then install the spacer.
2. Using gear oil, lightly lubricate the axle bore in the inner race of the new rear wheel bearing. Then slip the bearing over the axle shaft.
3. Press the new wheel bearing fully onto the axle shaft. Support the bearing on a plate that contacts only the bearing inner race. Position the press ram

against the axle shaft flange as shown in Fig. 4-7. Then install the retaining ring.

NOTE ——

If you lack both a press and machine shop services, you can simplify the installation of both the wheel bearing and the bearing retaining ring by chilling the axle shaft for one-half hour in a deepfreeze. At the same time, warm the bearing atop a room heat outlet. You can heat the retaining ring by placing it in an oven heated to 150°C (or 300°F). Do not heat the parts with a torch, since doing this could damage them structurally. Without forgetting to install the bearing retainer and spacer, drive on first the bearing and then the retaining ring, using a clean piece of pipe slipped over the axle shaft. Use the pipe as a slide hammer, with the axle shaft supported on a wooden block.

CAUTION ——

Never attempt to install a bearing by hammering on the axle flange. Doing this will deform the flange, making it impossible to install the brake drum.

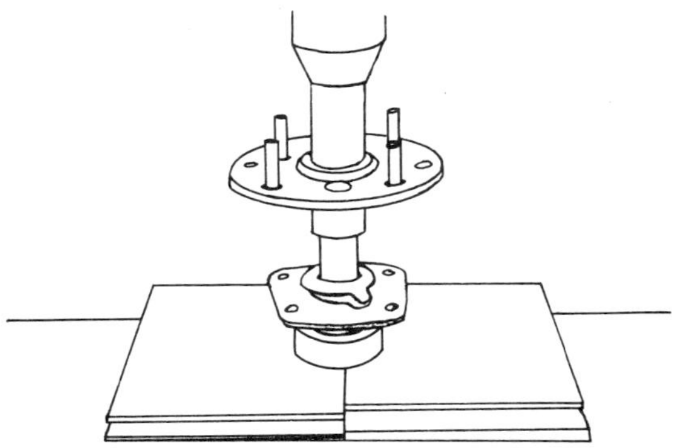

Fig. 4-7. Rear axle shaft being pressed into rear wheel bearing.

4. Wipe clean the mating surfaces of the axle shaft and the bearing retaining ring; neither part should be either degreased or lubricated.
5. Heat the bearing retaining ring to 140° to 160°C (284° to 320°F) in an oven, then install it on the axle shaft. Using a procedure similar to that used in pressing on the wheel bearing, press on the bearing retaining ring until it is in firm contact with the bearing inner race.
6. Install the axle shaft in the rear axle housing.

Replacing Rear Wheel Oil Seal

It is not necessary to replace the rear wheel oil seal routinely when removing the rear axle shaft, although you may wish to inspect it for damage or wear when you have the axle shaft removed.

To remove:

1. Remove the axle shaft as described previously.
2. Using a slide hammer with suitable puller attachment, remove the oil seal as shown in Fig. 4-8.
3. Using solvent and a clean cloth, remove all dirt and oil from the seal recess in the rear axle housing.

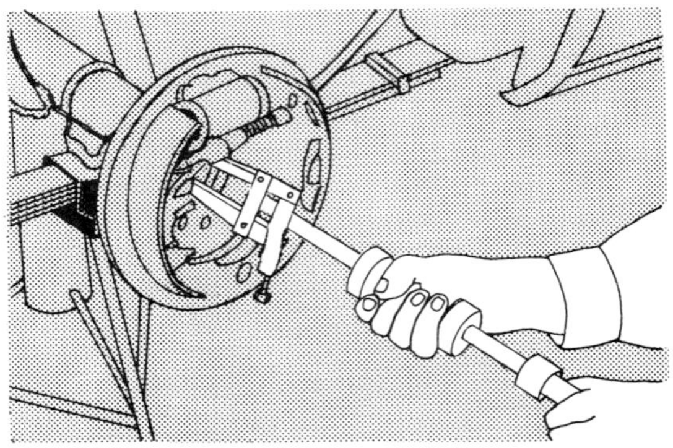

Fig. 4-8. Rear axle bearing oil seal being removed.

To install:

1. Install the new oil seal into the rear axle housing, using a suitable seal driver, as shown in Fig. 4-9. Drive in the oil seal to a depth of 4 mm ($^5/_{32}$ in.).

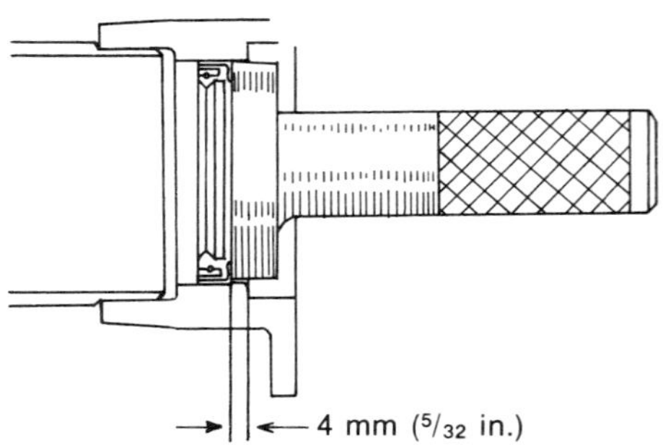

Fig. 4-9. Rear axle bearing oil seal being installed.

2. Apply multipurpose grease to the oil seal and the oil seal lip. Install the rear axle.

4.2 Removing and Installing Pinion Flange

The usual reason for removing the pinion flange is to replace the pinion oil seal. However, if you are making extensive rear axle repairs, you can avoid the need for a special pinion flange holding tool by removing the flange before you disconnect the parking brake or remove the brake drums.

To remove:

1. Using paint or a center punch, make adjacent marks on the pinion flange and the rear universal joint so that you can reinstall the driveshaft in its original position relative to the pinion flange. Then remove the driveshaft as described in **3.1 Removing and Installing Driveshaft.**
2. Using a wire brush, clean all dirt and rust from the exposed threads of the pinion shaft.
3. Either tightly set the parking brake or install a special pinion holding tool as shown in Fig. 4-10. Use a small cold chisel to unstake the nut, then loosen and remove the nut from the pinion shaft.

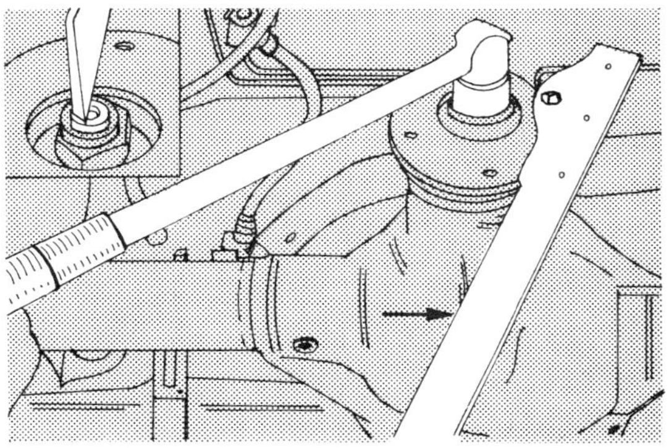

Fig. 4-10. Special tool being used to hold pinion flange stationary while nut is removed. Inset shows technique for loosening staked part of nut with cold chisel.

4. Place a pan beneath the pinion flange to catch the gear oil that will leak out of the rear axle housing after the flange is removed.
5. Using a two-jaw puller, remove the pinion flange from the pinion shaft.

To install:

1. Thoroughly clean the pinion flange. Then inspect the oil seal contact surface on the flange. If the surface is rough or grooved from contact with the seal, replace the flange.
2. Carefully inspect the pinion oil seal. Replace the seal if it is worn, cracked, hard, or otherwise damaged.
3. Using gear oil, lightly lubricate the pinion shaft threads, the contact surface of the nut, and the splines and the oil seal contact surface of the flange, Hand-start the flange on the pinion shaft. Then, using a soft hammer, drive the flange fully into position.
4. Install the washer and a new nut and torque the nut to the minimum torque of 105 Nm (77 ft. lb.). Seat the bearing by hand-turning the flange clockwise and counterclockwise several times.
5. Measure the pinion bearing starting preload with a torque wrench, as shown in Fig. 4-11. Move the torque wrench slowly, and measure the preload within the range of backlash between the drive pinion and the ring gear. Refer to **Table c** for correct preload readings. 3

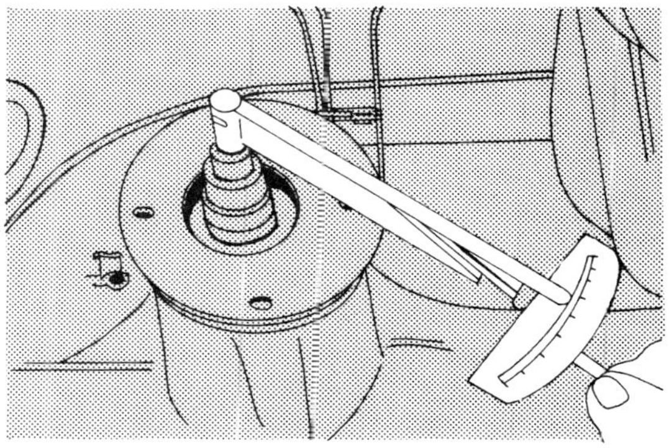

Fig. 4-11. Technique for measuring pinion bearing preload.

Table c. Pinion Bearing Preloads

	162-mm (6.38-in.) differential
New bearings	.98 to 1.56 Nm (or 9.9 to 15.8 cmkg or 8.7 to 13.8 in. lb.)
Used bearings	.05 to .78 Nm (or 0.5 to 7.9 cmkg or .44 to 6.9 in. lb.)
	170-mm (6.7-in.) differential
New bearings	.98 to 1.77 Nm (or 9.9 to 17.9 cmkg or 8.7 to 15.7 in. lb.)
Used bearings	.05 to .88 Nm (or 0.5 to 8.9 cmkg or .44 to 7.8 in. lb.)

6. If the preload is insufficient, continue to tighten the nut in 5° to 10° increments until you obtain the specified starting preload. If you reach the maximum nut-tightening torque of 235 Nm (173 ft.

lb.) without attaining a sufficient starting preload, you must replace the pinion bearing spacer and begin the tightening process again.

CAUTION —

If at any time you tighten the nut so much that the starting preload exceeds the upper limit given previously in **Table c,** *you must install a new pinion bearing spacer and then begin the tightening process again. The spacer is deformable. Once compressed to a shorter length by overtightening of the nut, it will permit drive pinion axial play that may damage the gearset if you reduce the preload merely by loosening the nut without replacing the spacer.*

7. Using a center punch, stake the nut.
8. Refill the rear axle with gear oil as described in **LUBRICATION AND MAINTENANCE.**
9. With careful reference to the marks made prior to removal, install the driveshaft as described in **3.1 Removing and Installing Driveshaft.** Torque the four bolts that hold the driveshaft to the pinion flange to 35 to 40 Nm (26 to 30 ft. lb.). On cars with two-piece driveshafts, torque the bolts that hold the center bearing to the body to 35 to 40 Nm (26 to 30 ft. lb.).

Replacing Pinion Oil Seal

To replace the pinion oil seal, first remove the pinion flange as described under the preceding heading. Then, using a suitable puller as shown in Fig. 4-12, remove the oil seal. If you do not have a puller, you can pry the old oil seal out of the housing with a large, clean screwdriver.

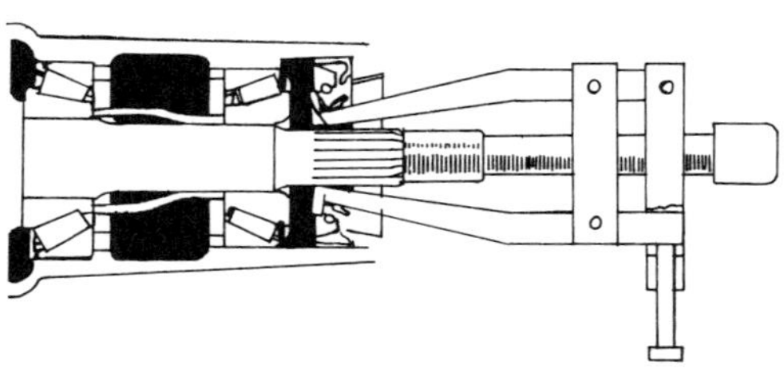

Fig. 4-12. Puller being used to remove pinion oil seal.

To install:

1. Using solvent and a clean cloth, remove all dirt, oil, and old sealer from the seal recess in the rear axle housing.
2. Apply molybdenum grease to the oil seal lip. Using a seal driver, drive in the oil seal as shown in Fig. 4-13.

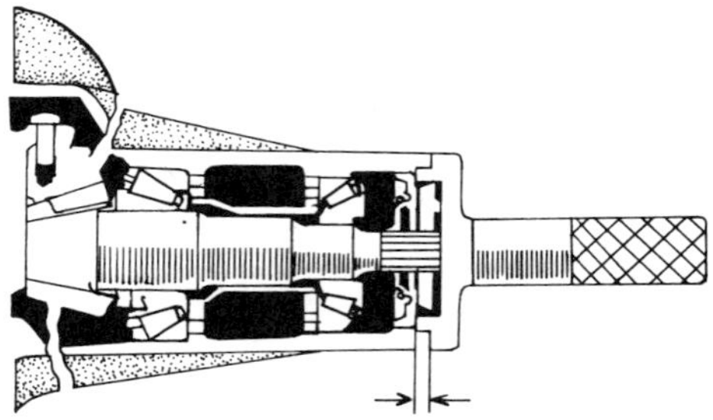

Fig. 4-13. Seal driver being used to install pinion oil seal.

3. Drive in the seal until its face is flush with the housing end face for 162-mm (6.38-in.) differentials. For 170-mm (6.7-in.) differentials, drive in the seal until it is recessed 4 mm ($^5/_{32}$ in.) from the end face. If you are unsure whether yours is a 170-mm (6.7-in.) or a 162-mm (6.38-in.) differential, see **4.4 Disassembling and Assembling Differential.**
4. Install the pinion flange with careful reference to the procedures given under the preceding heading.

4.3 Removing and Installing Ring Gear/Differential Assembly

Before you remove the differential, consult **4.6 Adjusting Mesh of Ring and Pinion Gearset** to determine whether you will have to make precision adjustments following differential repair. If these adjustments are neglected, the rear axle will be noisy and will wear rapidly.

CAUTION —

Please read the instructions thoroughly before you attempt final drive repairs. If you lack the necessary skills or tools, we suggest you leave such work to an Authorized Dealer or other qualified shop. Before taking a removed rear axle in for repair, thoroughly clean its exterior but do not undertake any disassembly.

To remove:

1. Place a pan beneath the rear axle housing, then drain the gear oil.
2. Remove both rear axle shafts as described in **4.1 Removing and Installing Axle Shaft.** Mark each shaft to show whether it is for the left or the right side of the car.
3. Make adjacent marks on the pinion flange and the rear universal joint so that you can reinstall the driveshaft in its original position on the pinion flange. Then remove the driveshaft from the pinion

flange as described in **3.1 Removing and Installing Driveshaft.**

4. Remove the bolts that hold the final drive carrier to the front of the rear axle housing. Then remove the final drive carrier and discard the gasket.

5. Put adjacent marks on both the left and the right bearing caps and on the carrier to prevent interchanging the caps during reassembly.

6. Remove the adjusting ring locks by removing the bolts that attach them to the bearing caps. Then remove the bearing cap mounting bolts and take off the bearing caps. Then remove the adjusting rings.

> *CAUTION* —
> *When removing the bearing caps and adjusting rings, support the differential assembly so that it does not drop and damage any final drive components.*

7. Remove the differential assembly. Tag or mark the left and the right bearing outer races so that you can return them to their original positions during assembly.

8. Measure the pinion bearing starting preload as described in **4.2 Removing and Installing Pinion Flange.** Write down the reading; you will have to refer to it during reassembly.

To install:

1. Liberally lubricate the differential bearings with gear oil. If you are using the original bearings, make sure that you return the left and the right outer races to their original positions. Then install the differential assembly in the final drive carrier.

2. Being careful to maintain backlash between the ring gear and the pinion, install the adjusting rings in their original positions in the threaded saddles. Make sure that the threads align properly.

3. With careful reference to the marks that you made prior to removal, install the bearing caps in their original locations and positions. Insert the bearing cap bolts and tighten them by hand. Verify that each bearing cap fits tightly on the housing. If not, the adjusting ring threads are not aligned. Reposition the threads if necessary, then tighten the bolts until the spring washers just begin to compress.

> **NOTE** —
> If you have replaced the ring and pinion gearset, the final drive carrier, the differential housing, or the drive pinion bearings, you will have to adjust the drive pinion position as described in **4.6 Adjusting Mesh of Ring and Pinion Gearset** before you complete the installation of the ring gear/differential assembly. If you have not replaced any of these parts, you may complete the assembly by following the steps given here.

4. Using a dial indicator and a tool that fits the holes in the adjusting ring, as shown in Fig. 4-14, screw the adjusting ring on the same side as the ring gear until the ring gear has a backlash of about 0.20 mm (.008 in.). Then tighten the adjusting ring on the side opposite the ring gear until the differential bearings are seated. 3

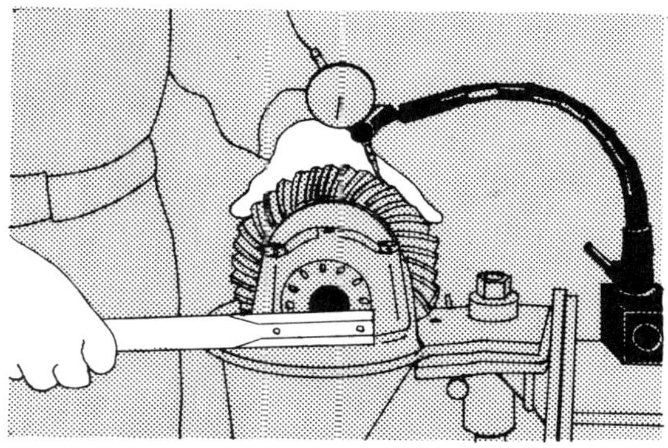

Fig. 4-14. Bearing adjusting ring being tightened to adjust ring gear backlash.

5. Loosen the adjusting ring on the side opposite the ring gear. Retighten the adjusting ring until you just eliminate the ring gear axial play. Then tighten the ring another 1 to 1½ notches.

6. Adjust the backlash to a final setting of 0.13 to 0.18 mm (.005 to .007 in.). Turn the adjusting rings one notch at a time in paired movements (loosen one side one notch and tighten the other side one notch) until you reach the proper setting.

7. Torque the bearing cap bolts to 50 to 70 Nm (37 to 52 ft. lb.) for a 162-mm (6.38-in.) differential and to 70 to 90 Nm (52 to 66 ft. lb.) for a 170-mm (6.7-in.) differential.

8. Use a torque wrench on the pinion flange nut to measure the total starting preload. To determine the proper amount of preload, add the following

numbers to the pinion starting preload that you recorded earlier. For the 162-mm (6.38-in.) differential, add 0.2 to 0.4 Nm or 2 to 4 cmkg or 1.7 to 3.5 in. lb.), and for the 170-mm (6.7-in.) differential, add 0.3 to 0.5 Nm (or 3 to 5 cmkg or 2.6 to 4.3 in. lb.).

NOTE ——
If you measured the pinion starting preload in foot pounds, you can convert to inch pounds by multiplying by 12.

9. If the total starting preload is not within these limits, you must readjust the ring gear/drive pinion backlash. Loosen the bearing cap bolts until the spring washers are just slightly compressed, and then repeat steps 5 through 8.

10. Inspect the contact between the ring gear teeth and the drive pinion teeth by coating the ring teeth with Prussian blue or gear marking compound. Hold the pinion flange steady while you turn the ring gear slowly a few turns in each direction. A correctly centered tooth contact pattern is shown in Fig. 4-15. If necessary, adjust the contact pattern as explained in **4.6 Adjusting Mesh of Ring and Pinion Gearset.**

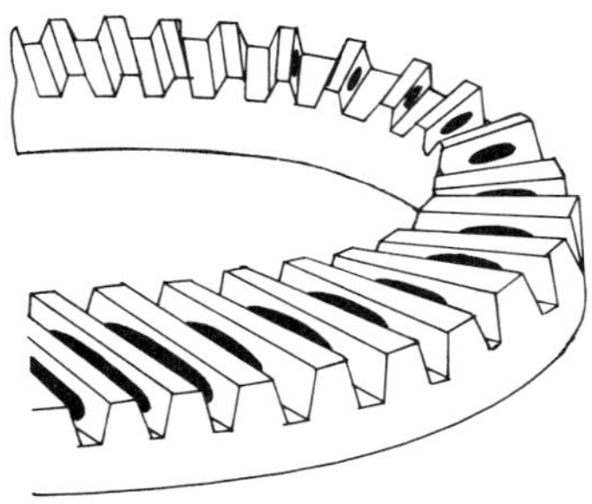

Fig. 4-15. Correct tooth contact pattern. Pattern is elliptical and centered both laterally and vertically on teeth.

11. Select the appropriate lock for each adjusting ring, then install them on the bearing caps as shown in Fig. 4-16. Torque the bolts to 10 to 15 Nm (7.5 to 11 ft. lb.).

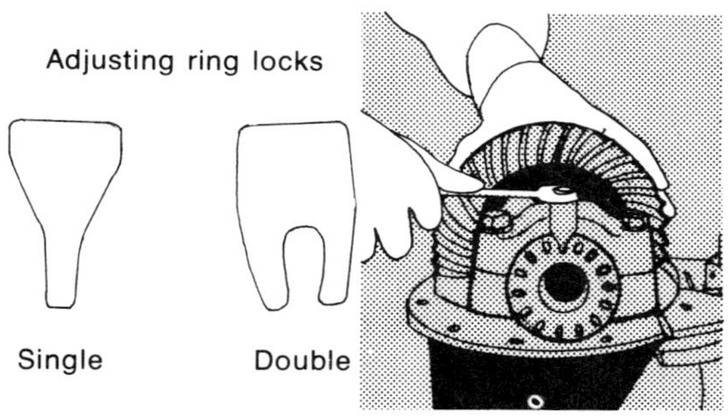

Fig. 4-16. Adjusting ring lock being installed.

12. Using a new gasket, install the final drive carrier on the rear axle housing. Torque the bolts to 25 to 35 Nm (18 to 26 ft. lb.).

13. Install the rear axle shafts as described in **4.1 Removing and Installing Axle Shaft.** Be sure to install each shaft in its original location. Refill the rear axle housing with SAE GL-5 hypoid gear oil as described in **LUBRICATION AND MAINTENANCE.** The capacity of the 162-mm (6.38-in.) differential is 1 liter; the capacity of the 170-mm (6.7-in.) differential is 1.2 liters.

Removing and Installing Differential Bearings

To remove the differential bearings, first remove the ring gear/differential assembly from the rear axle housing, as described under the previous heading. Then, using a two-jaw puller, pull off the bearings as shown in Fig. 4-17. When using the puller, you should cover the axle shaft opening in the differential housing with a plate or a large washer.

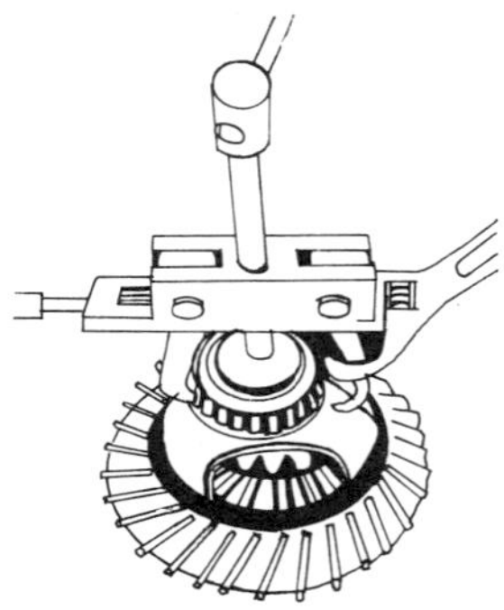

Fig. 4-17. Differential bearing being removed.

NOTE ——
If you intend to reuse the bearings, the puller must grip the inner race only. If the puller contacts the rollers or cage during removal, the bearings cannot be reused. If you have any doubts about the condition of the bearings, replace them with new bearings.

Inspect the bearings before you install them. Replace worn or damaged bearings, or bearings that exhibit galled or heat-blued rollers. Then, using a tool that will apply force only to the bearing's inner race, install the bearings as shown in Fig. 4-18.

Inspect the bearings to make sure that they have not been damaged during installation. Replace damaged bearings. If the bearings are in satisfactory condition, lubricate them liberally with gear oil and install the outer races, being careful not to interchange them. Install the differential assembly in the rear axle housing as described under the previous heading.

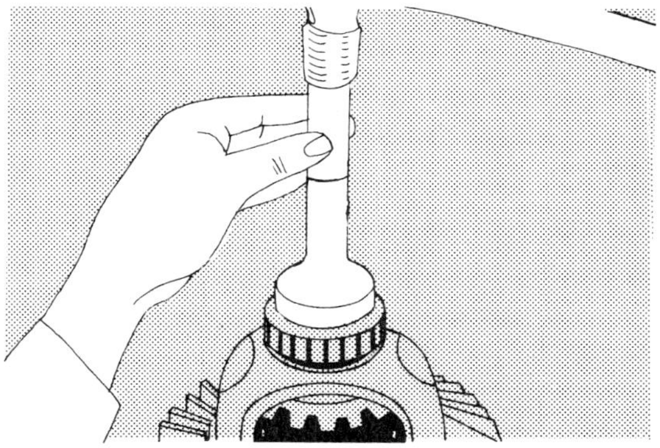

Fig. 4-18. Differential bearing being installed on differential housing.

4.4 Disassembling and Assembling Differential

The Corolla 1600 may be equipped with either of two differential units. A 170-mm (6.7-in.) differential is installed on SR5 models, and a 162-mm (6.38-in.) differential is installed on all other models.

Disassembling and Assembling 170-mm (6.7-in.) Differential

Although individual differential components can be replaced, it is usually best to replace the differential as a unit if it is extensively damaged. Fig. 4-19 is an exploded view of the 170-mm (6.7-in.) differential.

To disassemble:

1. Remove the differential as described in **4.3 Removing and Installing Ring Gear /Differential Assembly.** Remove and mark or tag the left and the right bearing outer races. You need not remove the differential bearings unless you intend to replace them.

> **NOTE ——**
> If you need to remove the ring gear only, do so as described in steps 2 and 3 of this procedure.

2. Clamp the differential housing in a vise. Then loosen the eight ring gear retaining bolts until their heads are about 4 to 6 mm (or ⅛ to ¼ in.) above the surface of the differential housing.

3. Use a rubber mallet to strike the bolt heads, working all around the differential until the ring gear is separated from the differential housing. Remove the bolts and the lockplates, then take off the ring gear.

> ***CAUTION ——***
> *Do not attempt to pry off the ring gear. In doing this, you may scratch the machined surfaces in such a way that the ring gear will have excessive runout when it is reinstalled. If it is necessary to strike the ring gear to remove it completely, use a rubber mallet.*

1. Nut and washer
2. Pinion flange
3. Dust cover
4. Oil seal
5. Oil slinger
6. Front pinion bearing
7. Final drive carrier
8. Pinion bearing spacer
9. Rear pinion bearing
10. Shim (optional for adjusment purposes)
11. Drive pinion selective washer
12. Drive pinion
13. Ring gear
14. Adjusting ring
15. Differential bearing
16. Sidegear selective washer
17. Sidegear
18. Differential pinion
19. Differential pinion shaft
20. Locking pin
21. Differential housing
22. Ring gear lockplate
23. Adjusting ring single lock
24. Adjusting ring double lock
25. Bearing cap

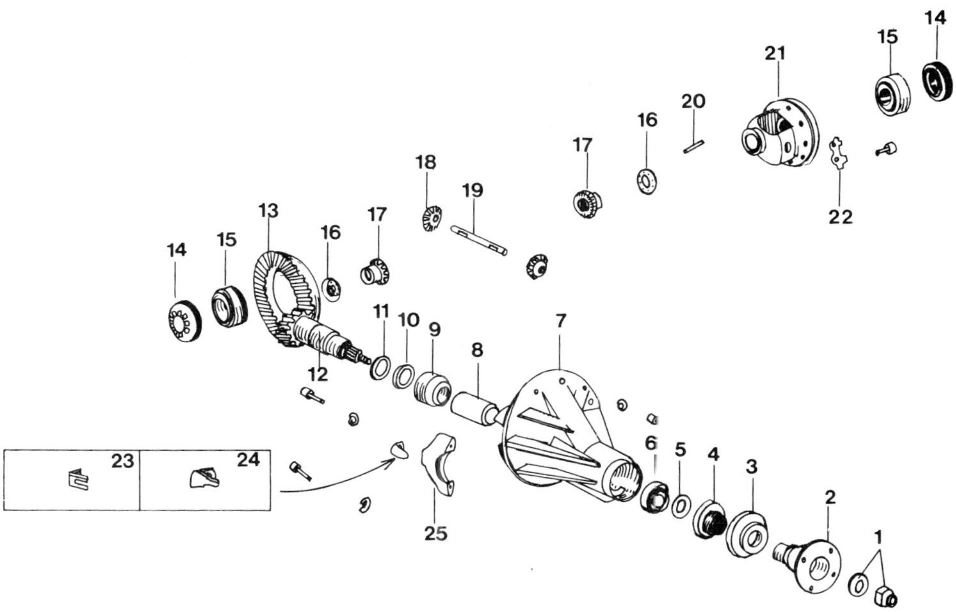

Fig. 4-19. Exploded view of 170-mm (6.7-in.) differential.

4. Using a suitable drift, as shown in Fig. 4-20, drive out the locking pin that secures the differential pinion shaft in the differential housing.

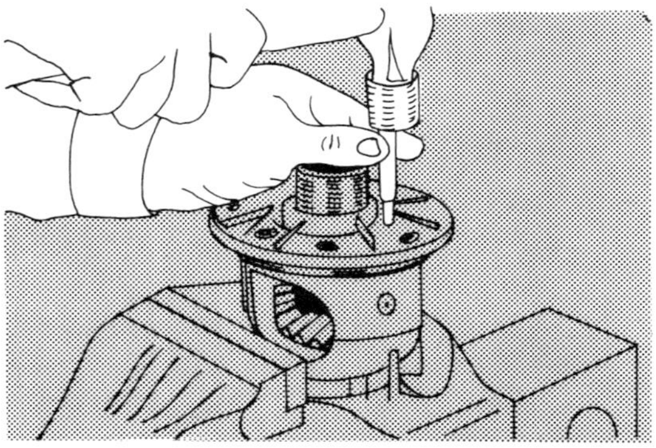

Fig. 4-20. Locking pin being driven out.

5. Drive out the differential pinion shaft. Then remove the differential pinions, the differential sidegears, and the sidegear selective washers from the differential housing.

To assemble:

1. Inspect the gear teeth for burrs or excessive wear and examine all thrust surfaces on the ring gear, the differential pinion shaft, and the sidegear selective washers. Replace worn or damaged parts. Before assembly, use gear oil to lubricate the contact surfaces of the differential pinions, the sidegears, and the differential pinion shaft.

NOTE —

If you replace the ring gear, you must also replace the drive pinion. The ring and pinion gears are manufactured as matched pairs and cannot be replaced individually.

2. Install the sidegear selective washers on the sidegears with the grooved surface of the washer against the gear.

NOTE —

If you have replaced no differential parts, and if no parts are worn, simply install the sidegears with their original selective washers. If parts have been replaced, you may have to use thicker or thinner washers to adjust the sidegear backlash.

3. Install the sidegears in the differential housing.
4. Install the differential pinions. Then, being careful to align the locking pin bores, install the differential pinion shaft in the differential housing.
5. Mount a dial indicator with its gauge pin at a right angle to the sidegear, near the tip of the gear, as shown in Fig. 4-21. Measure the sidegear backlash while holding one differential pinion stationary. If the backlash of either sidegear is outside a range of 0.05 to 0.2 mm (.002 to .008 in.), select a new sidegear selective washer that will bring that sidegear's backlash within the prescribed range.

NOTE —

Sidegear selective washers should be of the same thickness if at all possible. If it is not possible to bring the sidegear backlash within the prescribed range with washers of the same thickness, it is permissible to install a washer that is one size smaller or larger than the other washer.

NOTE —

Six selective washers are available in thicknesses ranging from 0.95 mm (.037 in.) to 1.20 mm (.047 in.), in increments of 0.05 mm (.002 in.).

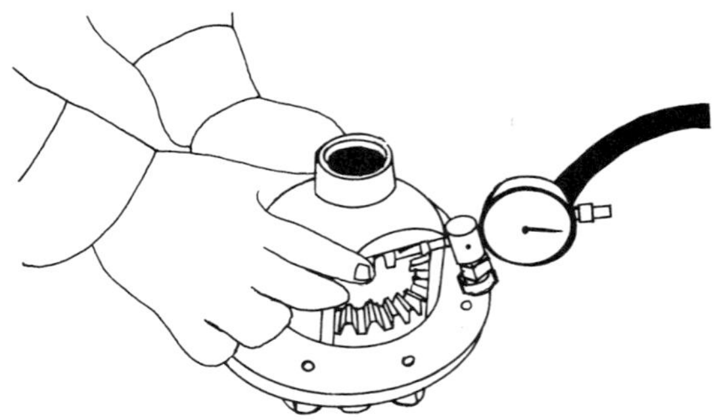

Fig. 4-21. Sidegear backlash being measured.

6. When you have determined that sidegear backlash is correct, drive in the locking pin for the differential pinion shaft. Then use a hammer to peen the hole in the housing case so that the pin is locked in place.
7. If you have removed the ring gear, install centering pins in at least two of the bolt holes. Then heat the ring gear to about 100°C (212°F) in a pan of oil placed in a larger pan of boiling water.

NOTE —

Centering pins can be made from bolts that fit the threads in the ring gear. Grind off the bolt heads and then slot the ends of the pins so that they can be removed or installed with a screwdriver. The pins should be long enough to engage the bolt holes in the differential housing before the ring gear itself contacts the housing.

8. Using gloves or rags so that you do not burn your hands, install the hot ring gear. Hand-press the gear as far as possible onto the housing.
9. Install three or four ring gear bolts with their lockplates until the bolt heads and the plates are in firm contact with the differential housing. Then remove the centering pins and install the remaining bolts and lockplates.
10. Working diagonally, gradually tighten the eight ring gear bolts so that the ring gear is pulled down evenly onto the housing. Then torque the bolts to 90 to 105 Nm (66 to 77 ft. lb.). Use a drift to bend up the lockplates against the bolt heads.
11. If the differential bearings have been removed, install them as described in **4.3 Removing and Installing Ring Gear/Differential Assembly.**

NOTE ——

If you intend to reuse the original bearings, the puller must grip only the inner race during removal. If the puller contacts the rollers or their cage during removal, the bearings cannot be reused. If you have any doubts about the condition of the bearings, replace them.

Disassembling and Assembling 162-mm (6.38-in.) Differential

The 162-mm (6.38-in.) differentials used on cars equipped with manual transmissions have four differential pinions. On cars equipped with automatic transmissions, the 162-mm (6.38-in.) differentials have two differential pinions. Fig. 4-22 is an exploded view of a 162-mm (6.38-in.) differential.

To disassemble:

1. Remove the differential as described in **4.3 Removing and Installing Ring Gear/Differential Assembly.** Remove and mark or tag the left and the right bearing outer races. You need not remove the differential bearings unless you intend to replace them.

NOTE ——

If you need to remove the ring gear only, do so as described in steps 2 and 3 of this procedure.

2. Clamp the differential housing in a vise. Then loosen the eight ring gear retaining bolts until their heads are about 4 to 6 mm (or ⅛ to ¼ in.) above the surface of the differential housing. 3
3. Use a rubber mallet to strike the bolt heads, working all around the differential until the ring gear is separated from the differential housing. Remove the bolts and the lockplates, then take off the ring gear.

CAUTION ——

Do not attempt to pry off the ring gear. In doing this, you may scratch the machined surfaces in such a way that the ring gear will have excessive runout when it is reinstalled. If it is necessary to strike the ring gear to remove it completely, use a rubber mallet.

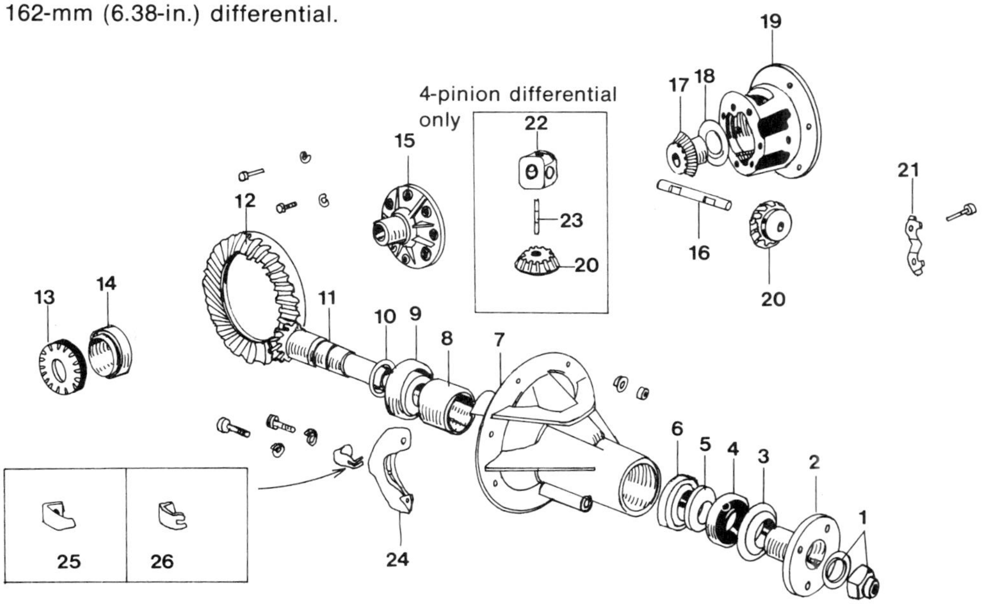

Fig. 4-22. Exploded view of 162-mm (6.38-in.) differential.

1. Nut and washer
2. Pinion flange
3. Dust cover
4. Oil seal
5. Oil slinger
6. Front pinion bearing
7. Final drive carrier
8. Pinion bearing spacer
9. Rear pinion bearing
10. Drive pinion selective washer
11. Drive pinion
12. Ring gear
13. Adjusting ring
14. Differential bearing
15. Differential housing cover
16. Differential pinion shaft
17. Sidegear
18. Sidegear selective washer
19. Differential housing
20. Differential pinion
21. Ring gear lockplate
22. Differential pinion spacer
23. Differential pinion shaft
24. Bearing cap
25. Adjusting ring single lock
26. Adjusting ring double lock

4. Look for adjacent marks on the differential housing and the housing cover. If there are none, use a center punch to make adjacent marks that you can use for reference during reassembly. Remove the eight bolts for the differential housing cover. Then separate the cover from the housing and lift out one sidegear and its selective washer.

5. If you are working on a four-pinion differential, remove the differential pinion shafts, the differential pinion spacer, the four differential pinions, and the second sidegear with its selective washer. See Fig. 4-23.

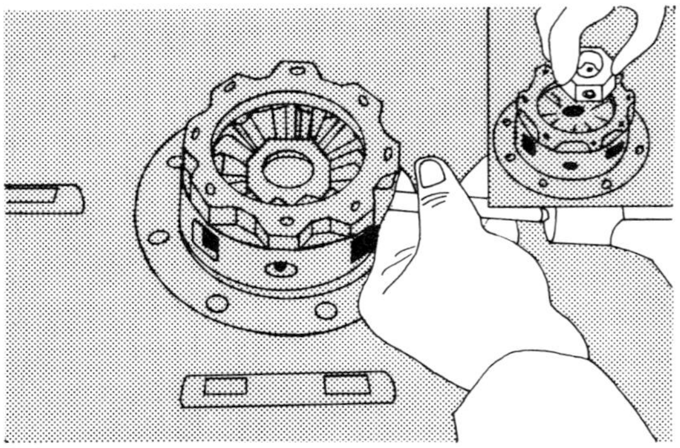

Fig. 4-23. Differential pinion shafts being driven out of four-pinion differential housing.

6. If you are working on a two-pinion differential, drive out the single differential pinion shaft. Then remove the two differential pinions and the second sidegear with its selective washer from the differential housing.

To assemble:

1. Inspect the gear teeth for burrs or excessive wear, and examine all thrust surfaces on the ring gear, the differential pinion shaft(s), and the sidegear selective washers. Replace worn or damaged parts. Before assembly, use gear oil to lubricate the contact surfaces of the differential pinions, the sidegears, and the differential pinion shaft.

   NOTE ——
   If you replace the ring gear, you must also replace the drive pinion. The ring and pinion gears are manufactured as matched pairs and cannot be replaced individually.

2. Install the sidegear selective washers on the sidegears with the grooved surface of the washer against the gear.

   NOTE ——
   If you have replaced no differential parts, and if no parts are worn, simply install the sidegears with their original selective washers. If parts have been replaced, you may have to use thicker or thinner washers to adjust the sidegear backlash.

3. Install one sidegear and its selective washer in the differential housing.

4. Install the differential pinions. In the case of two-pinion differentials, install the differential pinion shaft. In the case of four-pinion differentials, install the differential pinion spacer and the three differential pinion shafts.

   NOTE ——
   The differential pinion shafts are bored at one end and are held in position by pin extensions on the appropriate differential cover bolts. Be careful to align the bore(s) during assembly, and to make sure that you use a bolt with a pin extension to secure each differential pinion shaft.

5. Install the remaining sidegear and its selective washer.

6. Align the reference marks on the differential housing and its cover, then install the cover. Install the eight bolts and washers, making sure that the one bolt with an extension pin (two-pinion differential) or the three bolts with extension pins (four-pinion differential) are properly aligned in the bore(s) of each differential pinion shaft. Then torque the bolts to 25 to 35 Nm (18 to 26 ft. lb.).

7. Mount a dial indicator with its gauge pin at a right angle to the sidegear, near the tip of the gear, as shown in Fig. 4-24. Measure the sidegear backlash while holding one differential pinion stationary. If the backlash of either sidegear is outside a range of 0.02 to 0.2 mm (.001 to .008 in.), select a new sidegear selective washer that will bring that sidegear's backlash within the prescribed range.

   NOTE ——
   Sidegear selective washers should be of the same thickness if at all possible. If it is not possible to bring the sidegear backlash within the prescribed range with washers of the same thickness, it is permissible to install a washer that is one size smaller or larger than the other washer.

   NOTE ——
   Three selective washers are available in the following sizes for cars manufactured through June 1977: 1.50 mm (.059 in.), 1.55 mm (.061 in.), and 1.60 mm (.063 in.). For cars manufactured after June 1977, six selective washers are available, in thicknesses ranging from 1.50 mm (.059 in.) to 1.75 mm (.069 in.), in increments of 0.05 mm (.002 in.).

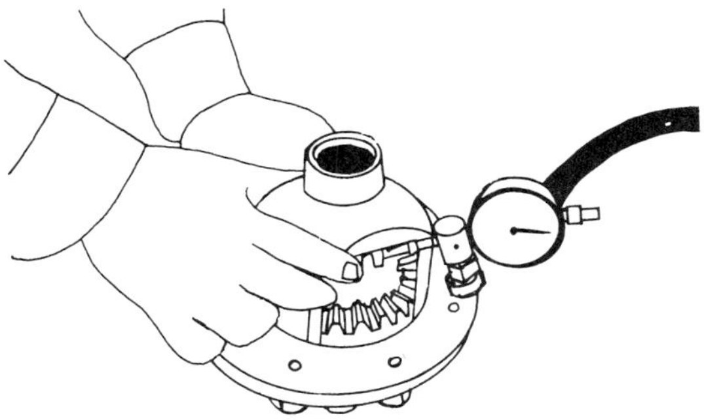

Fig. 4-24. Sidegear backlash being measured.

8. When you have determined that sidegear backlash is correct, drive in the locking pin for the differential shaft. Then use a hammer to peen the hole in the housing so that the pin is locked in place.
9. If you have removed the ring gear, install centering pins in at least two of the bolt holes. Then heat the ring gear to about 100°C (212°F) in a pan of oil placed in a larger pan of boiling water.

> **NOTE ——**
> Centering pins can be made from bolts that fit the threads in the ring gear. Grind off the bolt heads and then slot the ends of the pins so that they can be removed or installed with a screwdriver. The pins should be long enough to engage the bolt holes in the differential housing before the ring gear itself contacts the housing.

10. Using gloves or rags so that you do not burn your hands, install the hot ring gear. Hand-press the gear as far as possible onto the housing.
11. Install three or four ring gear bolts with their lockplates until the bolt heads and the plates are in firm contact with the differential housing. Then remove the centering pins and install the remaining bolts and lockplates.
12. Working diagonally, gradually tighten the eight ring gear bolts so that the ring gear is pulled down evenly onto the housing. Then torque the bolts to 70 to 80 Nm (52 to 59 ft. lb.). Use a drift to bend up the lockplates against the bolt heads.
13. If the differential bearings have been removed, install them as described in **4.3 Removing and Installing Ring Gear/Differential Assembly.**

> **NOTE ——**
> If you intend to reuse the original bearings, the puller must grip only the inner race during removal. If the puller contacts the rollers or their cage during removal, the bearings cannot be reused. If you have any doubts about the condition of the bearings, replace them.

4.5 Removing and Installing Drive Pinion and Pinion Bearings

3

Before you begin disassembly, you should consult **4.6 Adjusting Mesh of Ring and Pinion Gearset** to determine whether you will have to make precision adjustments following repair. If these adjustments are neglected, the rear axle will be noisy and will wear rapidly.

You can remove the drive pinion without disassembling the ring gear/differential assembly, but if the drive pinion is replaced you must also replace the ring gear. The ring and pinion gears are manufactured as matched pairs and cannot be replaced individually.

> ***CAUTION ——***
> *Please read the instructions thoroughly before you attempt final drive repairs. If you lack the necessary skills or tools, we suggest you leave such work to an Authorized Dealer or other qualified shop. Before taking a removed rear axle in for repair, thoroughly clean its exterior but do not undertake any disassembly.*

To remove:

1. Remove the final drive carrier. Then remove the differential. See **4.3 Removing and Installing Ring Gear/Differential Assembly.**
2. Using an appropriate two-jaw puller, remove the front pinion bearing as shown in Fig. 4-25.

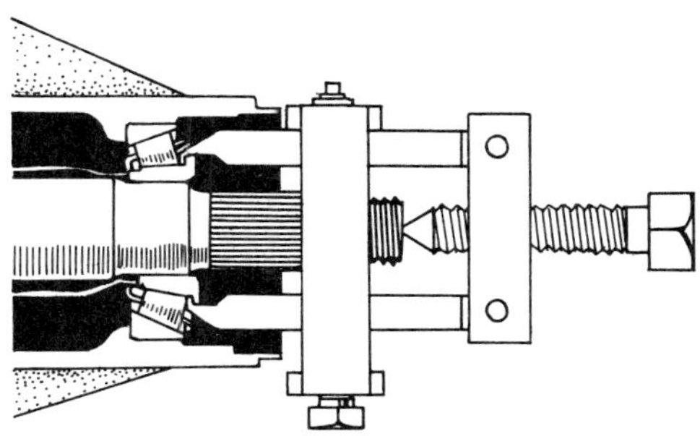

Fig. 4-25. Front pinion bearing being removed.

3. Remove the drive pinion and the pinion bearing spacer from the final drive carrier. The rear pinion bearing will come out with the drive pinion gearshaft when you remove the drive pinion.

To install:

1. Liberally lubricate the pinion bearings with gear oil. Install a new bearing spacer on the drive pinion gearshaft and insert the drive pinion in the rear axle housing as shown in Fig. 4-26.

NOTE ——

If you have replaced the pinion bearings, the final drive carrier, or the ring and pinion gearset, you must make the precision measurements described in **4.6 Adjusting Mesh of Ring and Pinion Gearset** to determine the thickness of the new drive pinion selective washer.

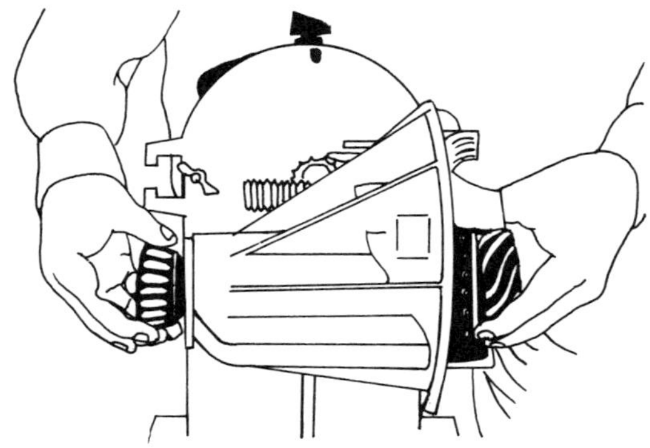

Fig. 4-26. Drive pinion being installed in final drive carrier.

2. Install the front pinion bearing and the oil slinger.
3. Apply molybdenum grease to the oil seal lip. Using a seal driver, as shown in Fig. 4-27, drive in the oil seal. For 162-mm (6.38-in.) differentials, drive in the seal until its face is flush with the housing end face. For 170-mm (6.7-in.) differentials, drive in the seal until it is recessed 4 mm ($^{5}/_{32}$ in.) from the end face.

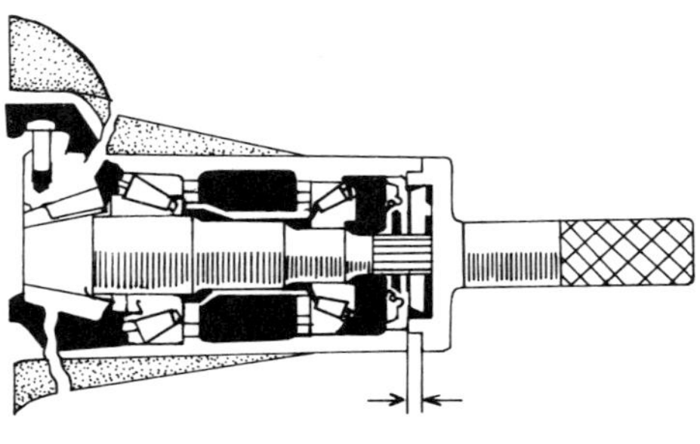

Fig. 4-27. Seal driver being used to install oil seal.

4. Use gear oil to lightly lubricate the drive pinion threads, the contact surface of the nut, and the splines and the oil seal contact surface of the pinion flange. Install the pinion flange, using a tool such as the one shown in Fig. 4-28.

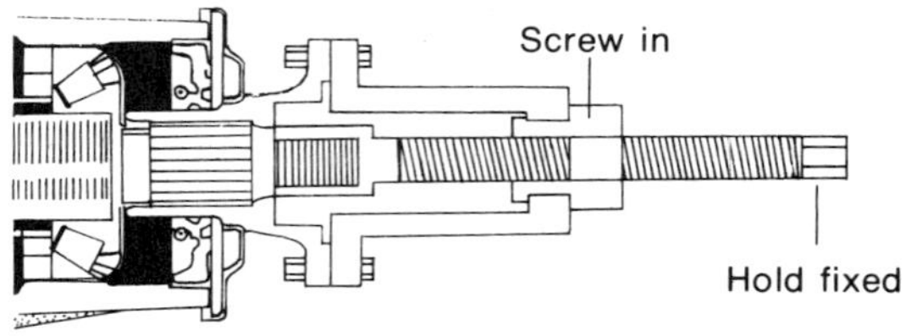

Fig. 4-28. Pinion flange being installed.

5. Hold the flange with an appropriate tool, as shown in Fig. 4-29. Install the washer and a new nut, and torque the nut to the minimum torque of 105 Nm (77 ft. lb.). Then seat the bearing by hand-turning the flange clockwise and counterclockwise several times.

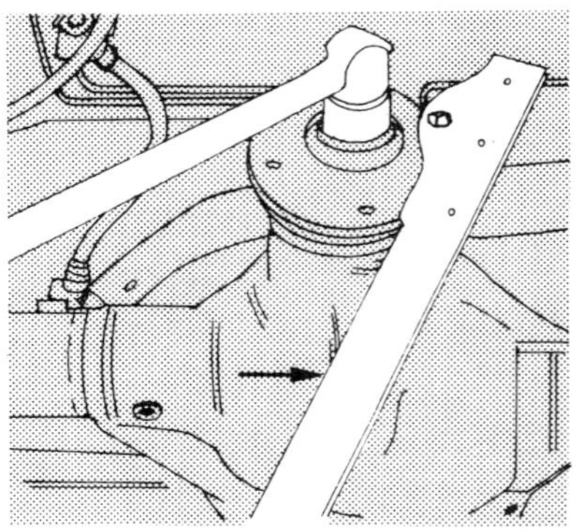

Fig. 4-29. Special tool being used to hold pinion flange stationary while nut is installed.

6. Measure the pinion bearing starting preload with a torque wrench, as shown in Fig. 4-30. Refer to **Table d** for correct preload readings.

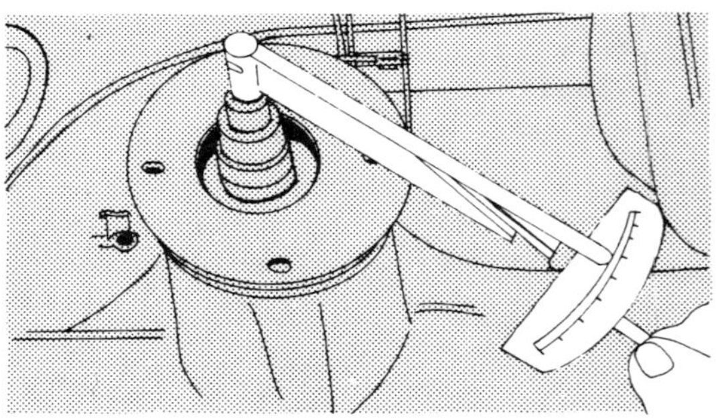

Fig. 4-30. Technique for measuring pinion bearing preload.

Table d. Pinion Bearing Preloads

	162-mm (6.38-in.) differential
New bearings	.98 to 1.56 Nm (or 9.9 to 15.8 cmkg or 8.7 to 13.8 in. lb.)
Used bearings	.05 to .78 Nm (or 0.5 to 7.9 cmkg or .44 to 6.9 in. lb.)
	170-mm (6.7-in.) differential
New bearings	.98 to 1.77 Nm (or 9.9 to 17.9 cmkg or 8.7 to 15.7 in. lb.)
Used bearings	.05 to .88 Nm (or 0.5 to 8.9 cmkg or .44 to 7.8 in. lb.)

7. If the preload is insufficient, continue to tighten the nut in 5° to 10° increments until you obtain the specified starting preload. If you reach the maximum nut-tightening torque of 235 Nm (173 ft. lb.) without attaining a sufficient starting preload, you must replace the pinion bearing spacer and begin the tightening process again.

CAUTION —

If at any time you tighten the nut so much that the starting preload exceeds the upper limit given previously in **Table d**, *you must install a new pinion bearing spacer and then begin the tightening process again. The spacer is deformable. Once compressed to a shorter length by overtightening of the nut, it will permit drive pinion axial play that may damage the gearset if you reduce the preload merely by loosening the nut without replacing the spacer.*

8. When the preload is correct, stake the nut with a center punch.
9. Install the differential as described in **4.3 Removing and Installing Ring Gear/Differential Assembly.**
10. With careful reference to the marks made prior to removal, install the driveshaft as described in **3.1 Removing and Installing Driveshaft.** Torque the four bolts that hold the driveshaft to the pinion flange to 35 to 40 Nm (26 to 30 ft. lb.). On cars with two-piece driveshafts, torque the bolts that hold the center bearing to the body to 35 to 40 Nm (26 to 30 ft. lb.).

Removing and Installing Pinion Bearings

There are two tapered-roller pinion bearings. You must remove the front bearing in order to be able to remove the drive pinion. The rear bearing comes out with the drive pinion gearshaft when you remove the drive pinion.

To remove:

1. Remove the front pinion bearing and the drive pinion as described under the previous heading. Then, using a suitable drift, drive out the front bearing outer race toward the front of the axle housing. Drive out the rear bearing outer race toward the rear of the housing, as shown in Fig. 4-31.

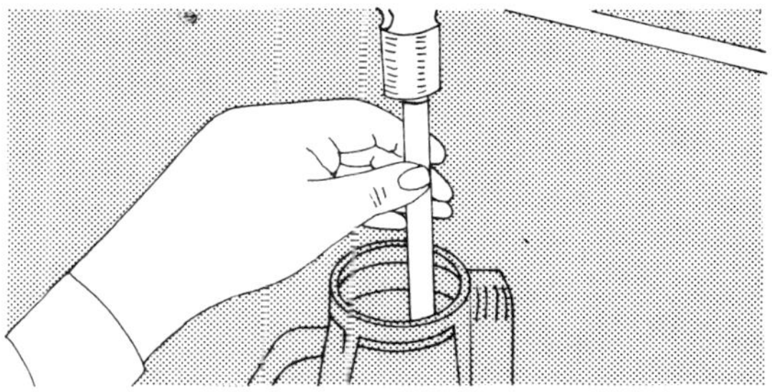

Fig. 4-31. Drift being used to drive out rear pinion bearing outer race.

2. Using a setup such as the one shown in Fig. 4-32, remove the drive pinion rear bearing from the drive pinion gearshaft. Be careful not to damage the pinion selective washer. Then remove the washer from the drive pinion gearshaft.

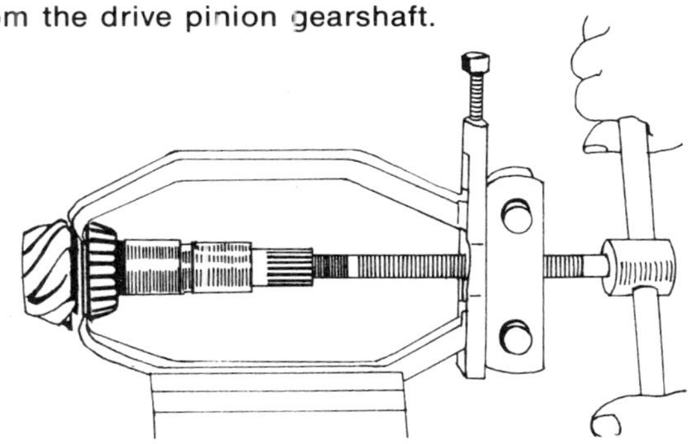

Fig. 4-32. Rear pinion bearing being removed from drive pinion gearshaft.

To install:

1. Using a suitable conical-faced tool, install the pinion bearing outer races in the rear axle housing as shown in Fig. 4-33.

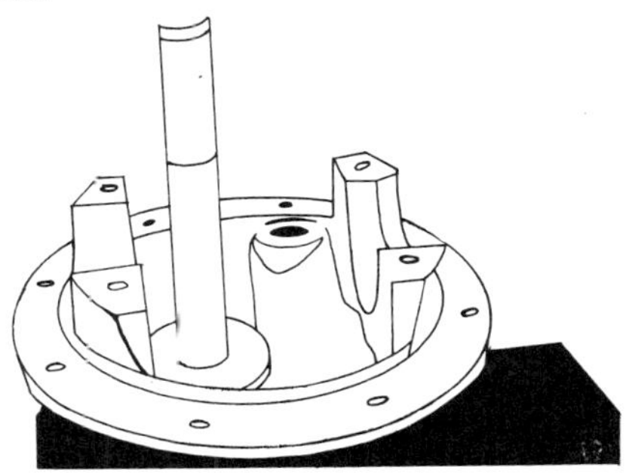

Fig. 4-33. Bearing outer race being installed.

3

2. Install the correct drive pinion selective washer on the drive pinion gearshaft. The chamfered face of the washer must be facing the gear.

> **NOTE** ——
> If you have replaced the pinion bearings, the final drive carrier, or the ring and pinion gearset, you must carry out the precision measurements described in **4.6 Adjusting Mesh of Ring and Pinion Gearset** to determine the width of the drive pinion selective washer. Otherwise you may use the original washer or a new one of the same thickness.

3. Using the setup shown in Fig. 4-34, press the drive pinion into the rear pinion bearing.

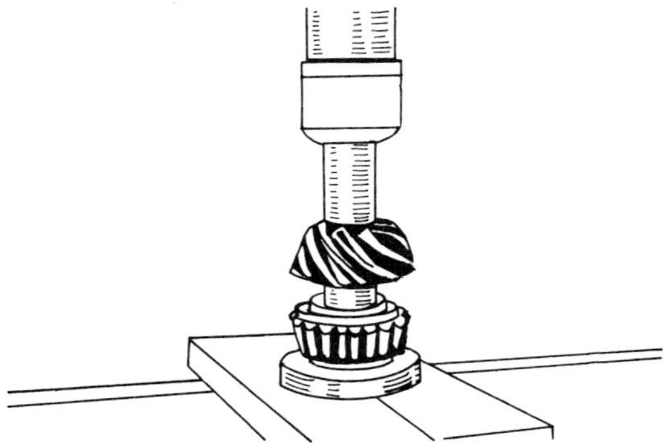

Fig. 4-34. Drive pinion being pressed into rear pinion bearing.

4. Install a new bearing spacer on the drive pinion gearshaft and install the drive pinion as described under the previous heading.

4.6 Adjusting Mesh of Ring and Pinion Gearset

Careful adjustment of the mesh between the ring gear and the drive pinion is essential to ensure long rear axle service and quiet operation. The factors that control the mesh are the pinion position (controlled by the thickness of the pinion selective washer) and the axial position of the ring gear (controlled by the bearing adjusting rings).

The position of the drive pinion must be recalibrated whenever the pinion bearings, the ring and pinion gearset, the final drive carrier, or the differential housing is replaced. This procedure is exacting; it requires Toyota Special Tool 09530–20010 or 09530–20020.

The position of the ring gear must be determined after the drive pinion position is changed and each time the ring gear/differential assembly is installed in the final drive carrier. The procedure requires a tool to turn the bearing adjusting rings and a dial indicator.

Adjusting Pinion Position

The position of the drive pinion is determined by the thickness of the drive pinion selective washer. **Table e** lists the part numbers and thicknesses of the available selective washers. To carry out the measurement, you will need Toyota Special Tool 09530–20010 for a 162-mm (6.38 in.) differential or Special Tool 09530–20020 for a 170-mm (6.7-in.) differential.

To adjust:

1. Attach the dummy pinion head to the dummy pinion with the bolt supplied. Then install the rear pinion bearing on the dummy pinion and insert them into the final drive carrier. Working from the front of the housing, insert the front pinion bearing, and the service tool's collar, flange, and nut.
2. Torque the flange nut to the minimum torque of 105 Nm (77 ft. lb.). Seat the bearing by turning the flange several times in both directions. Measure the bearing preload with a torque wrench as shown in Fig. 4-35. If it is not within the correct range, as previously given in **Table d**, tighten the nut 5° to 10° at a time until you obtain the correct reading.

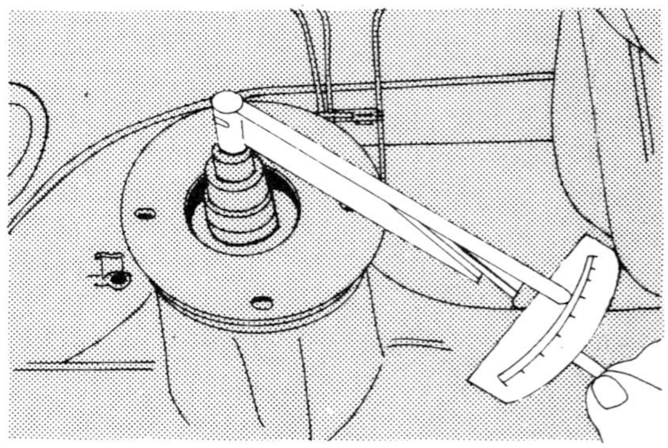

Fig. 4-35. Pinion bearing preload being measured.

3. Put the cylindrical gauge in the differential bearing saddles, install the bearing caps in their proper positions, and torque the bearing cap bolts to 50 to 70 Nm (37 to 52 ft. lb.) for a 162-mm (6.38-in.) differential or to 70 to 90 Nm (52 to 66 ft. lb.) for a 170-mm (6.7-in.) differential. Fig. 4-36 illustrates the complete setup for determining the pinion selective washer thickness.
4. The correct drive pinion selective washer will just fit in the space between the dummy pinion head and the cylindrical gauge. Selective washers are available in thickness increments of .03 mm (.0012 in.). See **Table e** for sizes and part numbers of available washers. An 0.3 mm (.012 in.) shim is also available.

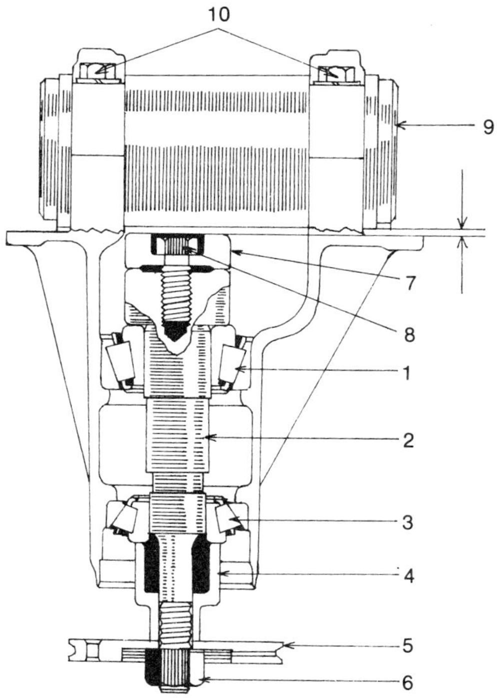

1. Rear pinion bearing
2. Dummy pinion (TST)
3. Front pinion bearing
4. Collar (TST)
5. Flange (TST)
6. Nut (TST)
7. Dummy pinion head (TST)
8. Bolt (TST)
9. Cylindrical gauge (TST)
10. Differential bearing cap

Fig. 4-36. Cylindrical gauge and dummy pinion assembly installed in rear axle housing. Items identified with (TST) are part of Toyota Special Tool.

Table e. Drive Pinion Selective Washers

162-mm (6.38-in.) Differential		170-mm (6.7-in.) Differential	
Part No.	**Thickness mm (in.)**	**Part No.**	**Thickness mm (in.)**
90209–33038	2.52 (.0992)	90201–35435	2.27 (.0894)
90209–33039	2.55 (.1004)	90201–35436	2.30 (.0906)
90209–33040	2.58 (.1016)	90201–35437	2.33 (.0917)
90209–33041	2.61 (.1028)	90201–35396	2.36 (.0929)
90209–33042	2.64 (.1039)	90201–35397	2.39 (.0941)
90209–33043	2.67 (.1051)	90201–35398	2.42 (.0953)
90209–33044	2.70 (.1063)	90201–35399	2.45 (.0965)
90209–33045	2.73 (.1075)	90201–35400	2.48 (.0976)
90209–33046	2.76 (.1087)	90201–35401	2.51 (.0988)
		90201–35402	2.54 (.1000)
		90201–35403	2.57 (.1012)
		90201–35404	2.60 (.1024)
		90201–35438	2.63 (.1035)
		90201–35439	2.66 (.1047)
		90201–35440	2.69 (.1059)

5. When you have determined the correct selective washer size, install the washer on the drive pinion gearshaft with the chamfered face of the washer facing the gear.

6. Using the setup shown in Fig. 4-37, press the drive pinion into the bearing race.

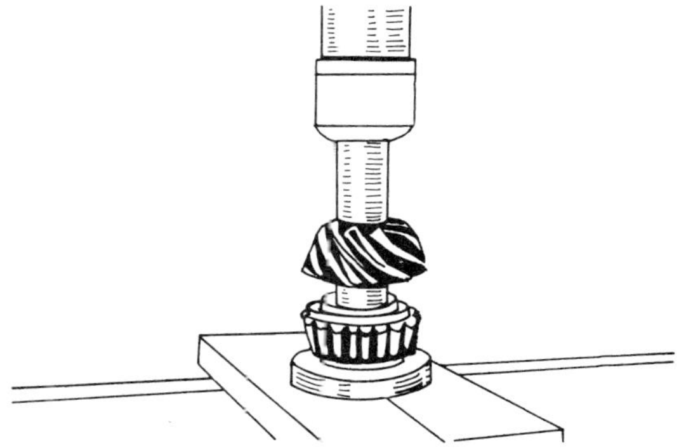

Fig. 4-37. Drive pinion being pressed into rear pinion bearing.

7. Install a new bearing spacer on the drive pinion gearshaft and install the drive pinion as described in **4.5 Removing and Installing Drive Pinion and Pinion Bearings.**

Adjusting Ring Gear Position

The position of the ring gear is controlled by the differential bearing adjusting rings and is adjusted as part of the procedure for installing the ring gear/differential assembly in the final drive carrier. If you have removed the ring gear/differential assembly from the final drive carrier, you should install it according to the procedures and specifications given in **4.3 Removing and Installing Ring Gear/Differential Assembly.** Its position will be correct when the ring gear backlash and the bearing preload are correct.

Checking Mesh of Ring and Pinion Gearset

The mesh of the ring and pinion gearset should be checked whenever differential (final drive) repairs have been performed. It is also a valuable troubleshooting device in trying to locate the cause of rear-end problems.

Coat the ring gear teeth with Prussian blue or gear marking compound. Hold the pinion flange steady while you turn the ring gear slowly a few turns in each direction. The pattern produced should be elliptical and centered on the teeth both laterally and vertically, as shown in Fig. 4-38.

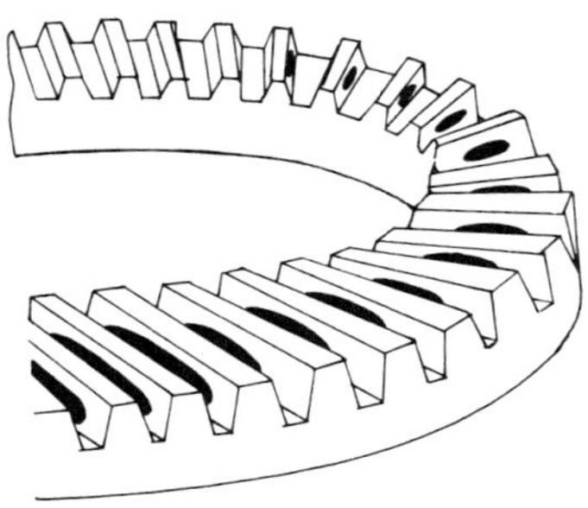

Fig. 4-38. Correct tooth contact pattern. Pattern is elliptical and centered both laterally and vertically on teeth.

Fig. 4-39 illustrates incorrect tooth contact patterns. If the pattern exhibits heel or face contact, adjust the pinion so that it is closer to the ring gear. If the pattern exhibits toe or flank contact, adjust the drive pinion position so that the drive pinion is moved away from the ring gear.

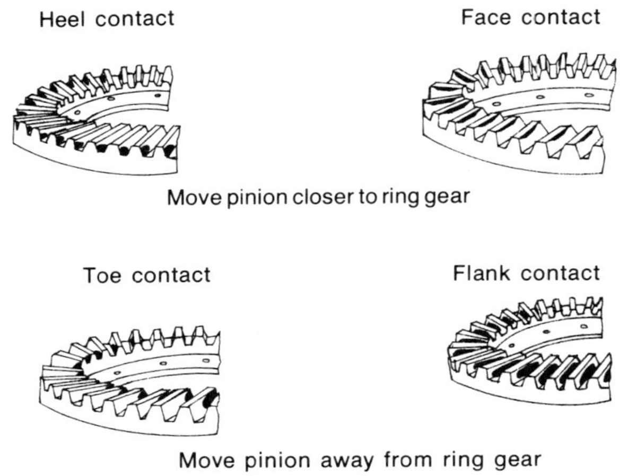

Fig. 4-39. Incorrect tooth contact patterns. If tooth contact pattern is not centered on gear teeth, pinion position must be adjusted. Always adjust ring gear position after adjusting pinion position.

5. DRIVESHAFT AND REAR AXLE TECHNICAL DATA

I. General Data

Ring and pinion gearset backlash	0.13–0.18 mm (.005–.007 in.)
Rear axle oil seal, depth recessed into rear axle housing	4 mm (5/32 in.)
Driveshaft runout . . . maximum permissible	0.50 mm (.020 in.)
Differential sidegear backlash . . . 170-mm (6.7-in.) differential	0.05–0.2 mm (.002–.008 in.)
162-mm (6.38-in.) differential	0.02–0.2 mm (.001–.008 in.)
Oil capacity . . . 170-mm (6.7-in.) differential	1.2 liters (1.3 U.S. quarts, 1.1 Imperial quarts)
162-mm (6.38-in.) differential	1 liter (1.1 U.S. quarts, .9 Imperial quart)
Grade of lubricant . . . above −23°C (−10°F)	SAE 90 API GL-5 hypoid gear oil
. . . below −23°C (−10°F)	SAE 80W or 85W API GL-5 hypoid gear oil
Pinion oil seal, depth recessed into final drive carrier . . . 170-mm (6.7-in.) differential	4 mm (5/32 in.) from housing end face
. . . 162-mm (6.38-in.) differential	flush with housing end face

Available axle ratios		No. of ring gear teeth	No. of pinion teeth
	3.91	43	11
	4.30	43	10
	4.10	41	10
	3.73	41	11

3

II. Tightening Torques

Location	Designation	Nm	Ft. lb.
Rear of driveshaft to pinion flange	nut and bolt	35–40	26–30
Driveshaft center bearing to car body	bolt	35–40	26–30
Center bearing to front half of driveshaft	staked nut	25–35	18–26
Center universal joint to center bearing flange	nut and bolt	20–35	15–26
Rear wheel bearing retainer to rear axle housing	nut and bolt	60–70	44–52
Pinion flange to pinion gearshaft—minimum	staked nut	105	77
—maximum	staked nut	235	173
Differential bearing caps to final drive carrier			
—170-mm (6.7-in.) differential	bolt	70–90	52–66
—162-mm (6.38-in.) differential	bolt	50–70	37–52
Adjusting ring lock to bearing cap	bolt	10–15	7.5–11
Ring gear to differential housing			
—170-mm (6.7-in.) differential	bolt	90–105	66–77
—162-mm (6.38-in.) differential	bolt	70–80	52–59
Final drive carrier to rear axle housing	bolt	25–35	18–26
Rear axle filler plug and drain plug		30–35	22–26

ELECTRICAL SYSTEM

Contents

TABLES

Electrical System

The electrical system is basically an efficient means for transmitting power from the engine to remote parts of the car. It does this with the help of an alternator, which converts some of the engine's mechanical energy into electrical energy. The electrical energy is carried over wires to motors that convert it back into mechanical energy, or to bulbs that convert it into heat and light. The battery in the system supplies electrical power mainly when the engine is not running.

This section of the Manual covers the alternator, the battery, the starter, the lights, wiring, horn, windshield wipers—all the electrical components other than those that make up the engine's ignition system. The ignition system is covered in **ENGINE.** Electrical components that are related to the emission control system are covered in **FUEL AND EXHAUST SYSTEMS.**

Whenever electricity flows through a wire, heat is generated, causing the temperature of the wire to rise. The amount of heat generated is directly proportional to the resistance of the circuit, and to the square of the current flow (amperage). To avoid high temperatures that could damage the insulation of the wiring in the event of an electrical short, fuses are inserted in the car's electrical circuits. Each fuse has an ampere rating marked on it. If the current flow in the circuit exceeds this amperage, with a consequent increase of heat in the wiring and in the fuse, the fuse conductor melts. This shuts off the electrical current in the circuit before the temperature rises high enough to damage the wiring.

In the Toyota Corolla 1600, all electrical circuits other than those required for starting and operating the engine are protected by fuses. To prevent accidental shorts that might blow a fuse or damage wires and electrical components that are not protected by fuses, you should always disconnect the ground cable from the negative post of the battery before working on the electrical system of your car. You should also disconnect the ground cable when you work on the fuel system or make any repair that may allow gasoline to escape from the fuel system. In this way you will remove the possibility that an accidental spark will ignite the spilled fuel.

Some components of the electrical system contain solid state components that can be damaged by excess heat, mechanical shock, or incorrect current polarity. If you lack the skills or the equipment needed for testing and repairing the electrical system, we suggest that you leave this work to an Authorized Dealer or other qualified shop. We especially urge you to consult your Authorized Dealer before attempting repairs on a car still covered by the new-car warranty.

1. GENERAL DESCRIPTION

The components of the electrical system are discussed in detail in later parts of this section. However, brief descriptions of the principal components are presented here for purposes of familiarization.

System Voltage and Polarity

The cars covered by this Manual have a 12-volt, negative-ground electrical system. In other words, the voltage regulator keeps voltage in the system at approximately the 12-volt rating of the battery, and the negative post of the battery is connected directly to the car's chassis.

Battery

The six-cell, 12-volt lead-acid battery is located in the front, left-hand side of the engine compartment. The negative battery post is grounded to the car body by a piece of heavy cable. The positive battery post is connected to the starting system only by a longer piece of heavy cable. A fusible link (two fusible links on some models) connects the positive post to the remaining parts of the electrical system. These fusible links are designed to melt if the current flow rises to a point that might damage the wiring.

Starting System

A reduction-gear starter is used on the cars covered by this Manual. It is located at the left-hand side of the engine, just ahead of the transmission bellhousing. Before power is delivered to the engine's flywheel via the solenoid-engaged starter pinion, the torque of the starter motor is multiplied by reduction gears. This allows the motor to operate at higher speeds, so there is less strain placed on it by cranking the engine in cold weather.

Charging System

The charging system consists of a belt-driven alternator and a regulator. The regulator, a separate component from the alternator, except on some late models, is mounted on the car body, just to the rear of the battery. The alternator is rated at 40 or 50 amperes, depending on the electrical equipment installed on the car, and has a Y-connected three-phase stator winding with full-wave rectification by six silicon diodes. These diodes change the three-phase alternating current produced by the alternator into direct current that is suitable for the 12-volt battery automotive electrical system.

Ignition System

Five different kinds of ignition systems have been used on the cars covered by this Manual. Ignition troubleshooting and repair is covered in **ENGINE.** Radio suppression is by resistance built into the ignition secondary cables.

Wiring

All components of the electrical system (except for the heavy battery cables) have push-on connectors. A system of fuses prevents short circuits or excessive current from damaging the electrical system and wiring.

Lights

The lighting system includes the parking lights, the side marker lights, the turn signals, the back-up lights, the interior lighting, and the sealed beam headlights. The current is switched to the headlights and the taillights by means of a double relay located in the front of the engine compartment, beside the battery.

Heating and Ventilation Fan

The heating and ventilation system includes a three-speed fan. The fan, which is used primarily to assist heating and ventilation while the car is being driven slowly or standing still, is controlled by a dashboard-mounted rotary switch.

Windshield Wipers

The blades of the two-speed windshield wiper system park automatically when the wiper switch is turned off. The wiper switch on the steering column includes a windshield washer control. The washers are supplied with fluid by a motor-driven pump. A rear window wiper and washer are available as optional equipment on some models.

Instruments

All Corolla 1600 cars have a speedometer, a fuel gauge, and an engine coolant temperature gauge. In addition, the liftback and sport coupe models have a tachometer and a clock as standard equipment. SR-5 models have three additional instruments: an ammeter, an oil temperature gauge, and an oil pressure gauge. Except for the hardtop SR-5, which has a charging warning light only, all models have warning lights for low charging system output and for low oil pressure.

2. MAINTENANCE

No routine lubrication of the alternator, the starter, or the other motors is required. However, the following checks are covered in **LUBRICATION AND MAINTENANCE.**

1. Checking the battery
2. Checking the wiring harnesses and connections
3. Checking the seat belt warning system
4. Checking the operation of all lights and switches.

3. BATTERY

Each of the six battery cells contains a set of brown lead oxide positive plates and gray sponge lead negative plates. The cells are connected in series by heavy lead bars and are enclosed in a six-compartment plastic case. The battery case also serves as a tank for the electrolyte—a solution of sulfuric acid diluted with water to a specific gravity of as much as 1.285. (This means that the electrolyte weighs about 1.285 times as much as an equal volume of water.) The battery plates that make up the cells are completely immersed in the electrolyte, and because some of the acid is always in chemical combination with the plates, a specific gravity of 1.285 will not be measured even when the battery is fully charged.

Discharging

The battery does not store electricity. Rather, it produces electrical current by means of a reversible electrochemical reaction. When a circuit is completed between the two battery posts, sulfuric acid from the electrolyte combines with the lead in the plates to produce lead sulfate, releasing a great many electrons in the process.

Charging

The electrochemical reaction by which the battery produces electrical current is reversed when direct current is sent back into the cells. The car's charging system supplies this current. When the discharged battery plates are charged with direct current from an outside source, the lead sulfate in the plates is converted back to its original state, returning sulfuric acid to slution in the electrolyte.

A battery can never be charged to a voltage level in excess of the voltage it can produce electrochemically. As charging proceeds, the battery's voltage builds to a peak called terminal voltage. If charging continues beyond the terminal voltage, the water in the electrolyte begins to decompose into hydrogen and oxygen. This condition is called gassing.

Temperature Effects

Temperature changes modify the battery's efficiency as well as its electrolyte's specific gravity. Low outside temperatures can create slow starting by thickening the engine and transmission oils and by simultaneously reducing the battery power available for running the starter motor. For example, the current-producing capacity of a battery chilled to −15°C (5°F) is only half its capacity at 20°C (68°F).

In addition, there is danger that partly discharged batteries might freeze in cold weather owing to the higher proportion of water in the electrolyte. A frozen battery will produce no current, but it can usually be restored to service if it is thawed slowly. The following list shows the safe low-temperature limits for batteries in various states of charge:

Specific gravity	Freezing point
1.285	−68°C (−90°F)
1.200	−27°C (−17°F)
1.120	−11°C (12°F)

4

3.1 Servicing and Testing Battery

The level of the electrolyte should never be allowed to fall below the tops of the plates in any cell. As water is lost through evaporation and electrolysis, fresh water must be added to maintain the electrolyte's level at the bottoms of the indicator tubes built into the battery filler openings. Use only distilled water to replenish the electrolyte. Water that is not chemically pure may have an adverse effect on battery life and efficiency.

The battery will lose more water in summer than in winter. In very hot weather, it may be necessary to check the electrolyte level as often as once a week. Never overfill the cells. Doing this could cause the electrolyte to boil over during a long daylight drive when the load on the electrical system is light and alternator output is high.

Battery terminals must be tight-fitting and free of corrosion and acid salts. If you notice even a trace of corrosion, disconnect first the ground cable and then the positive cable from the battery posts and clean the posts and the terminal clamps with a battery terminal cleaning tool. After you have cleaned the terminals and tightly installed first the positive cable and then the ground cable on the battery posts, you can spray the terminals and posts with a commercial battery terminal corrosion inhibitor (if the terminals are not protected by the rubber-like plastic applied to them at the factory).

WARNING —

Keep sparks and open flame away from the top of the battery. Hydrogen gas from the battery could explode violently.

Always keep the top of the battery clean. Even a thin layer of dust containing conductive acid salts can cause the battery to discharge. Wash away corrosion and acid salt accumulations with a baking soda solution, being extremely careful that none of this solution enters the cells through the vent holes. Even a drop or two will seriously impair the efficiency of the battery.

You should make periodic battery tests to keep track of the battery's condition. These tests will also help pinpoint the source of suspected battery trouble.

WARNING —
Wear goggles when you work with battery electrolyte, and do not allow the liquid to contact your skin or clothing. Electrolyte is corrosive and can cause severe burns. If it should spill onto your skin, flush the area of contact immediately with large quantities of water. Spilled electrolyte can be neutralized with a strong baking soda solution.

Hydrometer Testing

The simplest tool for testing the battery is a hydrometer, which consists of a glass cylinder with a freely moving float inside. When electrolyte is drawn into the cylinder by squeezing and releasing a rubber bulb, the level to which the float sinks indicates the electrolyte's specific gravity. A specific gravity scale on the float is read at the point where it intersects with the surface of the electrolyte. The more dense the concentration of sulfuric acid in the electrolyte, the less the float will sink and the higher the reading will be. **Table a** lists the specific gravity values for different states of charge at 20°C (68°F), as given by battery manufacturers (based on the chemical make-up of new batteries) and by the car manufacturer (based on the readings obtained from original-equipment batteries in normal service). For every 5°C above 20°C (or 10°F above 68°F), .004 must be added to the hydrometer reading. Subtract .004 for every 5°C below 20°C (or every 10°F below 68°F).

Table a. Specific Gravity of Battery Electrolyte at 20°C (68°F)

Battery manufacturer's standard		Toyota standard	
Specific gravity	**State of charge**	**Specific gravity**	**State of charge**
1.280 to 1.285	Fully charged	1.260	Fully charged
1.240	75% charged	1.210	75% charged
1.200	50% charged	1.160	50% charged
1.160	25% charged	1.110	25% charged
1.120	Fully discharged	1.060	Fully discharged

Voltage Testing

Total battery voltage can be tested with a special voltmeter. The tester should consist of a voltmeter connected in parallel with a test load of approximately 110 amps. The minimum voltage indicated should not be less than 9.6 volts. If total voltage drops below this value during the 5- to 10-second test, the battery is either discharged or sulfated. A sulfated battery is one in which the plates are covered by a layer of lead sulfate that is difficult to reconvert. Sulfating is visible as a gray coating on the plates.

CAUTION —
A discharged battery should be recharged immediately. Otherwise, sulfating will lead to the loss of active plate materials and to reduced battery capacity.

The voltage of an individual cell should not vary from the others by more than 0.2 volts. You can determine this by applying one prong of the tester to the negative battery post, then dipping the other prong into the electrolyte of successive cells, and finally applying it to the positive post (Fig. 3-1). The readings should be 2, 4, 6, 8, 10, and 12 volts. This test should last no more than 10 seconds.

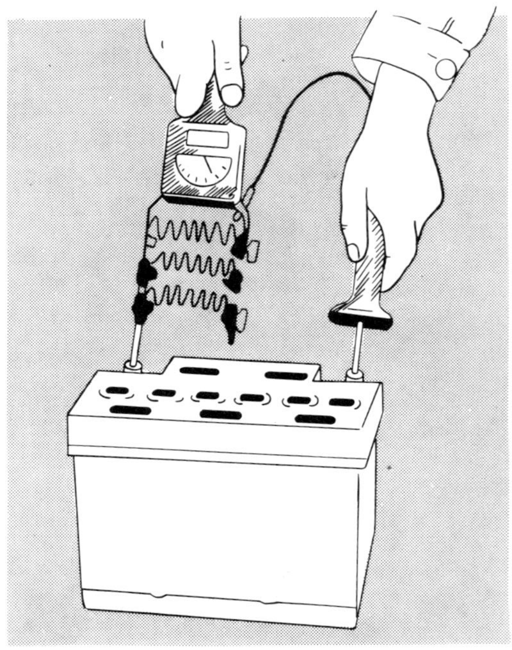

Fig. 3-1. Voltmeter with integral resistance being used to test total voltage of battery.

3.2 Removing and Installing Battery

The battery is fastened in position by a bolt, a nut, and a hold-down clamp (Fig. 3-2). Before removing the hold-down clamp, disconnect first the ground (−) cable and then the positive (+) cable from the battery posts. Remove the nut and the bolt, then—being careful not to let the clamp touch the battery posts—remove the hold-down clamp and lift out the battery.

When installing the battery, clean and install the terminals as described earlier in **3.1 Servicing and Testing Battery.** The battery must be mounted firmly to the body during installation to prevent road shocks and vibration from damaging the plates. However, you should be careful not to overtighten the nut and the bolt for the hold-down clamp because doing this could damage the battery case.

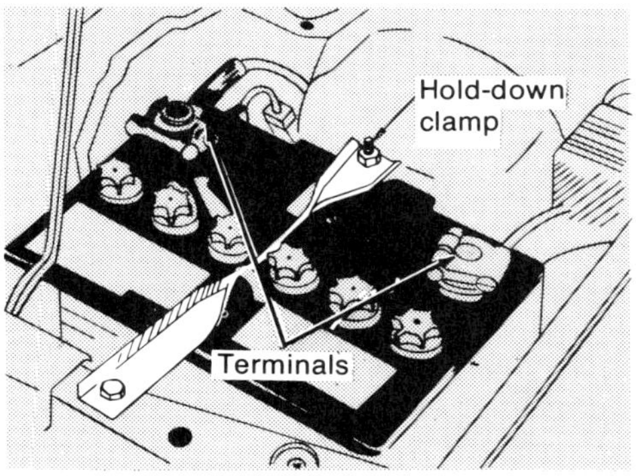

Fig. 3-2. Battery installed, showing hold-down clamp and battery terminals.

3.3 Charging

Normally, a battery should be charged at no more than 10 percent of its rated capacity. For example, a charging current of 6.0 amperes would be used on a battery having 60-Ah (ampere-hours) capacity. However, a current as low as 5 percent of the rated capacity (3.0 amps for a 60-Ah battery) can be used in normal charging and should always be used the first time a new battery is charged.

In normal charging, the battery is considered charged when it is gassing freely and the voltage of each cell has risen to 2.5 to 2.7 volts (about 15 volts for the battery). An hour or so after you have switched off the charging current, use the voltmeter/tester to determine the battery's rest voltage. This should be 2.1 to 2.2 volts per cell, or approximately 12.5 to 13 volts for the battery.

Quick-charging

To save time in an emergency, a higher current can be used to charge batteries that are in good condition. Only sound batteries that are already in service are suitable for quick-charging. Neither factory-new nor sulfated batteries should ever be quick-charged.

WARNING —
Do not boost a sulfated battery at a high charging rate. Doing this could cause the battery to explode.

To quick-charge:

1. Remove the battery caps, then connect a battery charger and voltmeter to the battery. Quick-charge the battery for three minutes at 80 to 90 percent of its rated capacity (48 to 54 amperes for a 60-Ah battery).
2. Observe the voltmeter reading during charging. If the total battery voltage exceeds 15.5 volts, the battery plates are sulfated or worn out and the battery should be replaced.
3. If the total voltage is less than 15.5 volts, test the individual cell voltages. If cell voltages vary by more than 0.1 volt, the battery plates are worn out and the battery should be replaced. If cell voltages are within 0.1 volt, measure the specific gravity and continue quick-charging at 80 to 90 percent of the rated battery capacity (48 to 54 amperes for a 60-Ah battery). Use the following times:

Specific gravity	Period of charge
1.150	1 hour
1.150 to 1.175	45 minutes
1.175 to 1.225	15 minutes
Above 1.225	Slow charge only

WARNING —
Smoking and open flames should not be permitted in a room where batteries are charged. Charging causes excess water in the electrolyte to decompose into hydrogen and oxygen, a dangerously explosive combination of gases.

CAUTION —
Do not store precision tools in a room where batteries are charged. The corrosive fumes generated can severely damage the tools.

4

Storing Battery

A battery that is not in use will gradually discharge itself. At room temperature, it will lose about 1 percent of its remaining capacity per day. The rate of discharge increases with higher temperatures. If the battery is allowed to remain in a partly or fully discharged condition for long periods, it will become badly sulfated and may never be serviceable again. The following procedure is recommended to prevent this from happening in a battery that is to be stored either inside or outside the car.

To store battery:

1. Charge the battery. Check the electrolyte level and the specific gravity, then make corrections as necessary.
2. Store the battery in a cool, dry place.
3. Every six to eight weeks, discharge the battery and recharge it.
4. Before returning the battery to service, charge it with a very low current (not over 3 amps).

4. STARTING SYSTEM

The reduction-type starter used on cars covered by this Manual is an exceptionally high-quality unit. The solenoid-engaged pinion, on a separate shaft parallel to the armature shaft, is driven by the armature through a three-gear reduction gear train. Ball bearings are used at both ends of the armature shaft and at both ends of the pinion shaft, and roller bearings are used for the idler gear.

The starter motor itself is of the multipolar series wound variety with four brushes. The small-diameter armature makes the motor especially suitable for high-rpm operation. A solenoid that is integral with the starter is used to engage the starter's drive pinion with the starter ring gear on the engine's flywheel or drive plate.

To minimize wear and stress on the starter's drive pinion and the starter gear, the solenoid is designed so that it does not switch starting current to the starter motor until the drive pinion has fully engaged the ring gear. Also, the drive pinion is mounted on an overrunning clutch so that if the driver does not immediately release the ignition key as soon as the engine has started, the starter motor will not sustain overspeed damage in being driven by the engine.

4.1 Starting System Troubleshooting

Troubleshooting procedures that are applicable to the starting system appear in **Table b.** The bold numbers in the Remedy column refer to the headings in this section under which the prescribed service and repair procedures are described. If more than one test or probable cause is listed, check them one by one in the order in which they appear.

Table b. Starting System Troubleshooting

Problem	Test and Probable Cause	Remedy
1. Starter does not operate when ignition is turned to start position	Turn lights on for test: a. Lights are out. Loose battery connections or battery run down b. Lights go out when key is moved to starting position. Insufficient current owing to loose battery connections or corroded terminals c. Lights become dim when key is moved to starting position. Battery run down d. Lights stay bright, solenoid operates (clicks). Connect jumper cable between two large terminals of solenoid. Solenoid contacts are faulty if starter runs e. Lights stay bright, solenoid does not operate (car with automatic transmission). Connect jumper cable between terminals on neutral safety switch. If starter can be operated normally, neutral safety switch is defective f. Lights stay bright, solenoid does not operate, neutral safety switch not defective. Connect a jumper cable between large solenoid terminal that receives battery cable and solenoid ST (start) terminal. If starter runs, voltage is not reaching terminal ST when ignition key is turned to its START position	a. Check battery cable terminals. Test battery. Charge if necessary. See **3.1, 3.3.** b. Clean and tighten all battery cable connections See **3.1, 3.2.** c. Charge battery. See **3.3.** d. Replace solenoid. See **4.3.** e. Replace neutral safety switch. See **AUTOMATIC TRANSMISSION.** f. Eliminate open circuits. Replace defective parts. At least 8 volts must be available at terminal ST for the solenoid to operate. See **8.3, 12.**

Table b. Starting System Troubleshooting (continued)

Problem	Test and Probable Cause	Remedy
2. Starter does not operate when battery cable is directly connected with terminal stud that serves starter motor	a. Brushes sticking b. Brushes worn c. Weak spring tension. Brushes do not make contact d. Commutator dirty e. Commutator rough, pitted or burned f. Armature or field coils defective	a. Clean brushes and guides of brush holders. See **4.3.** b. Replace brushes. See **4.3.** c. Replace springs. See **4.3.** d. Clean commutator. See **4.3.** e. Recondition or replace starter motor. See **4.2, 4.3.** f. Recondition or replace starter motor. See **4.2, 4.3.**
3. Starter turns too slowly or fails to turn the engine over	a. Battery run down b. Insufficient current flowing to loose or corroded connections c. Brushes sticking d. Brushes worn e. Commutator dirty f. Commutator rough, pitted, or burned g. Armature or field coils defective	a. Charge battery. See **3.3.** b. Clean battery terminals and cable clamps, tighten connections. See **3.1, 3.2.** c. Clean brushes and guides of brush holders. See **4.3.** d. Replace brushes. See **4.3.** e. Clean commutator. See **4.3.** f. Recondition or replace starter motor. See **4.2, 4.3.** g. Recondition or replace starter motor. See **4.2, 4.3.**
4. Starter makes unusual sounds, cranks engine erratically, or fails to crank	a. Drive pinion defective b. Flywheel or drive plate ring gear defective	a. Replace drive pinion. See **4.3.** b. Replace flywheel or drive plate. See **ENGINE AND CLUTCH.**
5. Drive pinion does not disengage	a. Drive pinion or shaft dirty or damaged b. Solenoid defective	a. Recondition or replace starter motor. See **4.2, 4.3.** b. Replace solenoid. See **4.3.**

4

4.2 Removing and Installing Starter

Because of the starter location, you should remove it by working under the car. Disconnect the battery's negative (−) cable before you raise the car off the ground.

To remove:

1. Disconnect the ground cable from the negative (−) post of the battery. Then raise the car on a hoist or support it on stands designed for the purpose.
2. Disconnect the wires from the starter solenoid.
3. Remove the nuts or the nuts and the bolt(s) that hold the starter to the engine and the transmission bellhousing. Then remove the starter from the car.

Installation is the reverse of removal. Torque the nuts or bolts that hold the starter to the engine and the transmission bellhousing to 55 to 75 Nm (41 to 55 ft. lb.). Clean the terminals of the wires and the cables before you reconnect them to the solenoid.

4.3 Disassembling and Assembling Starter

Fig. 4-1 is an exploded view of the starter, showing the components that are available as replacement parts. If a faulty starter proves to have a number of defects, it is often most economical to replace it with a new or rebuilt starter rather than to attempt repairs. Some tasks, such as reconditioning the armature's commutator, require special tools.

CAUTION —

If you lack the skills, tools, or test equipment needed to repair the starter, we suggest you leave these repairs to an Authorized Dealer or a qualified automotive electrical shop. We especially urge you to consult your Authorized Dealer before attempting repairs on a car still covered by the new-car warranty.

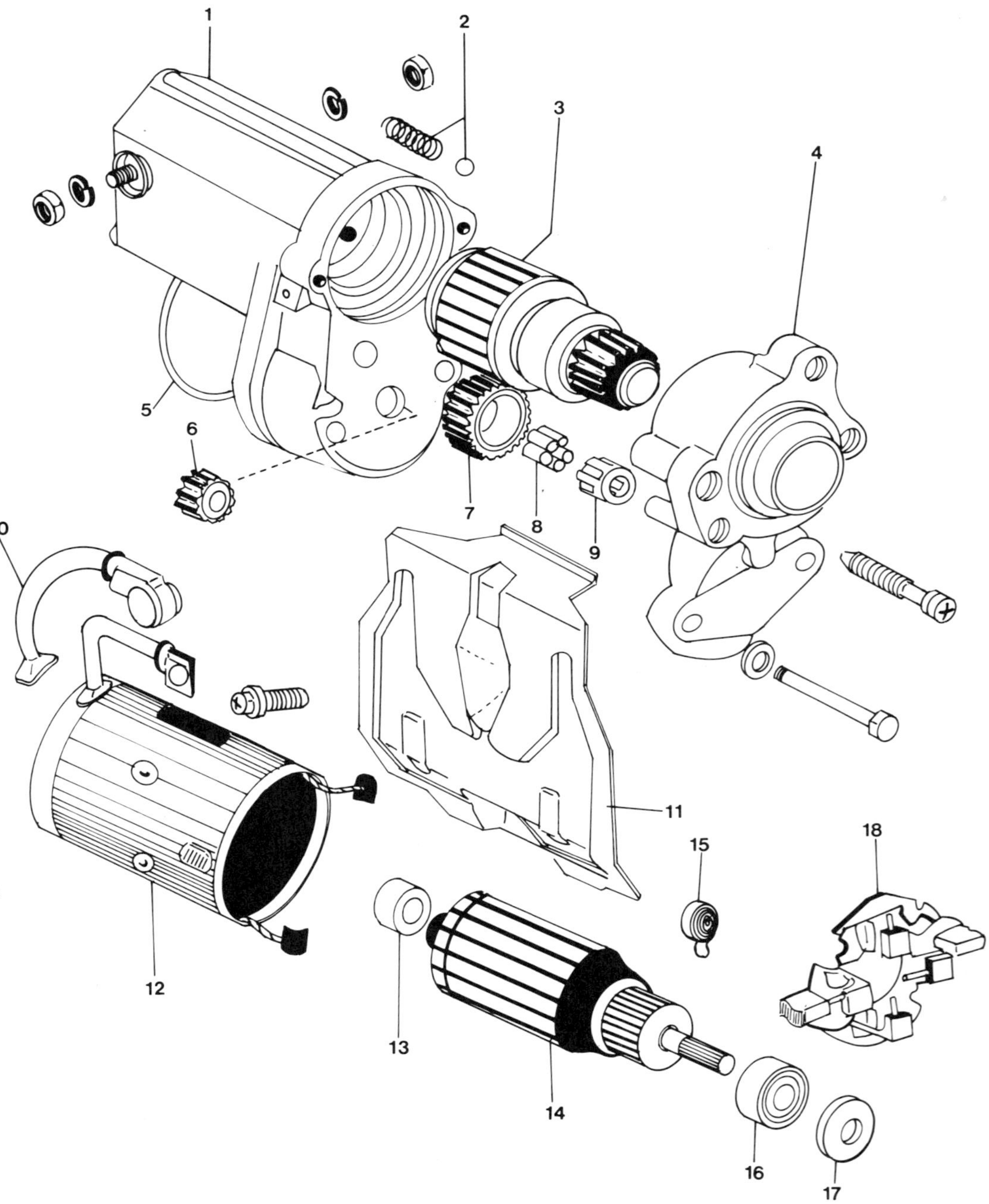

1. Solenoid assembly
2. Spring and ball
3. Overrunning clutch/drive pinion assembly
4. Drive housing
5. O-ring
6. Armature pinion
7. Idler gear
8. Idler gear roller bearings
9. Roller retainer
10. Cable rubber boot
11. Splash cover
12. Field frame assembly
13. Armature bearing
14. Armature
15. Brush spring
16. Armature bearing
17. Felt washer
18. Brush holder assembly

Fig. 4-1. Exploded view of reduction-type starter.

To disassemble:

1. Remove the starter from the car. Remove the splash cover from the starter.
2. Pull back the cable rubber boot, then remove the nut that holds the field frame assembly's cable to the stud on the solenoid assembly. Detach the cable.
3. Remove the two bolts that hold the field frame assembly to the solenoid assembly. Then pull the field frame assembly and the armature off the solenoid assembly as a unit. Remove the O-ring.
4. Remove the two Phillips head screws that hold the drive housing to the solenoid assembly. Then pull the drive housing off the solenoid assembly. Lift out the armature pinion.
5. Pull the overrunning clutch/drive pinion assembly out of the solenoid assembly.
6. To prevent its loss, remove the ball from the pushrod hole of the overrunning clutch/drive pinion assembly (Fig. 4-2).

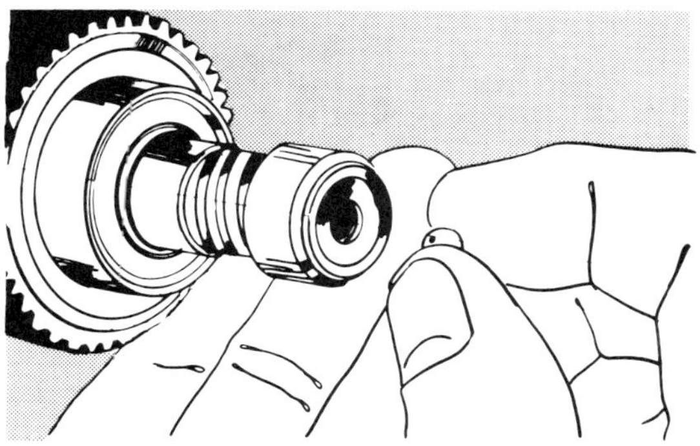

Fig. 4-2. Ball being removed from overrunning clutch/ drive pinion assembly.

7. Using the tip of a screwdriver, lift aside the brush springs so that you can pull the brushes out of the brush holder. Then pull the armature out of the field frame assembly and lift off the brush holder assembly.
8. Being careful not to lose the rollers, remove the idler gear, its roller bearings, and the roller retainer from the stud on the drive housing.

To inspect and assemble:

1. Wipe clean all the parts of the starter.

> ***CAUTION —***
> *Do not wash the armature, the field frame assembly, the solenoid assembly, the sealed ball bearings, or the overrunning clutch/drive pinion assembly in solvent Doing this may damage the insulation of the armature, the solenoid, or the field coils and will destroy the factory-installed lubricants in the bearings and in the overrunning clutch.*

2. If there has been trouble in the starter, make the electrical tests described under the next heading. If necessary, replace the armature, the solenoid assembly, the field frame assembly, or the entire starter.
3. With the armature bearings supported on V-blocks, rotate the commutator against the gauge pin of a dial indicator. If the commutator bars are pitted or if runout exceeds 0.05 mm (.002 in.), machine the commutator on a lathe to make it concentric with the shaft.
4. Using a vernier caliper, measure the diameter of the commutator at several points. If there is more than 0.03 mm (.001 in.) of taper or out-of-round, machine the commutator on a lathe. 4

> **NOTE —**
> The commutator should be machined by an Authorized Dealer or by a qualified automotive machine shop. The commutator diameter must not be reduced to less than 29 mm (1.142 in.). (New commutators are 30 mm (1.181 in.) in diameter.) After the commutator has been turned on a lathe, the insulation strips between the commutator bars must be undercut as indicated in Fig. 4-3.

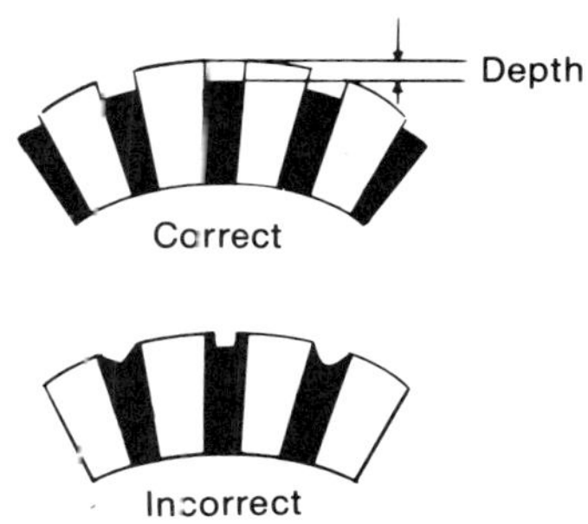

Standard depth of undercut: 0.50 to 0.90 mm (.020 to .035 in.)
Minimum permissible depth: 0.20 mm (.008 in.)

Fig. 4-3. Insulation strips correctly and incorrectly undercut below surface of commutator bars. A special tool is best for this work, but it can be done with a hacksaw blade. Be careful not to narrow the bars.

5. Measure the remaining lengths of each brush. New brushes are 14.5 mm (9/16 in.) long. If any brush has worn to a length of less than 10 mm (3/8

in.), replace either the brush holder or the field frame assembly, depending on the extent to which the brushes of each are worn.

6. Use a pull scale to lift each of the brush springs. New springs should require a tension of from 1445 to 1955 g to lift them. Replace any spring that requires less than 1200 g to lift it.

7. While applying pressure with your fingers, rotate each ball bearing. If the bearing sticks, feels rough, or offers abnormal resistance, replace the bearing.

CAUTION —

The ball bearing races of the overrunning clutch/drive pinion assembly cannot be replaced without the assembly's being replaced as a unit. Removing the bearings from the armature will damage the bearings, so they should not be reinstalled. Before installing an armature bearing, pack its open side (where applicable) with high-melting-point grease. Then position the open side of the bearing away from the armature and drive the bearing on, using a tubular tool that will contact the inner bearing race only.

8. Inspect the drive pinion teeth for chips, wear, and damage. Rotate the pinion as indicated in Fig. 4-4. It should turn freely in a clockwise direction and lock when turned counterclockwise. If you find any fault, replace the overrunning clutch/drive pinion assembly.

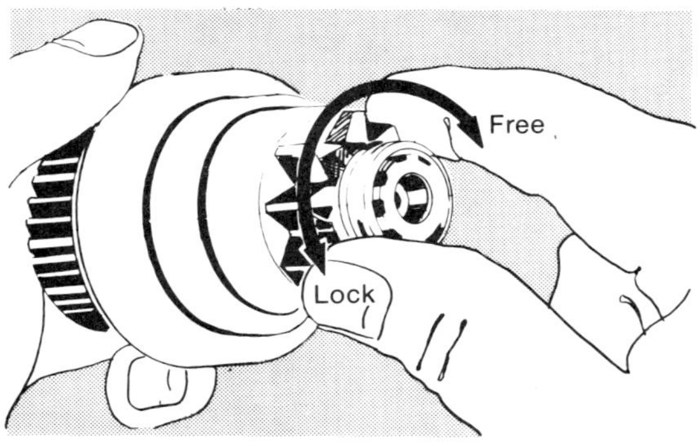

Fig. 4-4. Locking action of overrunning clutch being checked by turning drive pinion.

9. Apply high-melting-point grease to the open side of the armature rear bearing if you have not already done this. Then install the armature in the field frame assembly.

10. Install the brush holder assembly so that its tab engages the notch in the field frame assembly, as indicated in Fig. 4-5.

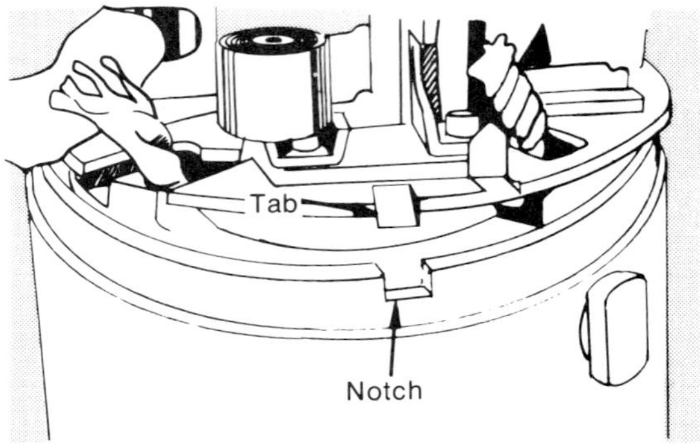

Fig. 4-5. Brush holder assembly being installed on field frame assembly.

11. Install the brushes in the brush holder assembly, then position the brush springs atop the brushes to press the brushes against the commutator.

CAUTION —

Make certain that the lead wires for the positive brushes (which are a part of the field frame assembly) are not grounded by contact with the brush holder assembly. Grounding will cause shorts and poor starter operation, and also can damage the starter electrically.

12. If you removed it previously, install the felt washer on the armature shaft. Install the O-ring on the field frame assembly, then install the field frame assembly and the armature on the solenoid assembly as indicated in Fig. 4-6.

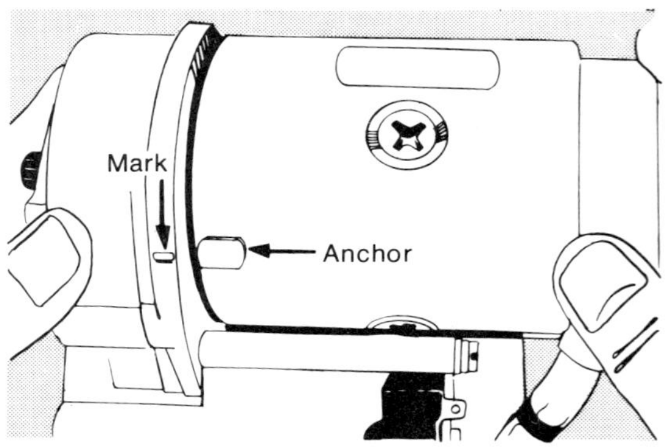

Fig. 4-6. Field frame assembly being installed so that its mounting bolt anchor is aligned with mark on solenoid assembly.

13. Using high-melting-point grease as a lubricant and an adhesive, assemble the idler gear roller bearings and the roller retainer on the stud for the idler gear. Then install the idler gear.

14. Install the armature pinion on the armature shaft.
15. Using high-melting-point grease as an adhesive, place the ball in the hole in the overrunning clutch/drive pinion assembly. Then install the assembly in the solenoid assembly, making sure that the pushrod enters the hole to contact the ball.
16. Lubricate the teeth of the gears with high-melting-point grease. Then install the drive housing. Loosely install the screws and the bolts, tighten the Phillips head screws, and torque the bolts to 25 Nm (18 ft. lb.).
17. Replace the cable rubber boot if it is torn, cracked, or loose-fitting. Then install the cable on the terminal stud of the solenoid assembly and tighten the nut. Position the boot over the terminal.

Testing Disassembled Starter

If the troubleshooting checks given in **4.1 Starting System Troubleshooting** indicate trouble in the armature, the solenoid, or the field coils, you can make further tests after you have removed and disassembled the starter. You can perform several of these tests with a simple battery-powered test light, although an ohmmeter is preferable.

Short circuits in the armature occur when the insulation between the windings breaks down. An armature tester called a growler is used to test for shorts. Growlers are available at most automotive supply stores that offer machine shop service. The shop will test an armature for you at low cost. If the armature is shorted, it must be replaced.

Armature grounds occur when the insulation breaks down and allows the windings to come into electrical contact with the armature laminations or the shaft. It is easy to detect this condition with a battery-powered test light or with an ohmmeter, as shown in Fig. 4-7.

Fig. 4-7. Armature ground test. If testing for continuity between commutator and armature body or shaft produces ohmmeter reading or causes battery-powered test lamp to light, windings are grounded.

Occasionally, carbon dust from the brushes will short an armature. If arcing currect has not permanently damaged the insulation, cleaning with trichloroethylene or a similar solvent will usually cure the short.

To check the armature for open circuits, inspect the commutator bars. Burn marks between the bars indicate that there is an open circuit in the winding coil that is connected to one of the bars. You can also test for open circuits by applying the test probes of an ohmmeter or a battery-powered test light to adjacent bars all around the commutator. There should be electrical continuity among all the bars. If not, there is an open circuit and the armature must be replaced.

To test the field coils for grounded windings, first position the brushes and the field frame assembly cable so that they do not contact the field frame. Then apply one test probe of an ohmmeter or a battery-powered test light to a bolt stud, as indicated in Fig. 4-8, and apply the other test probe to first one brush lead and then the other. If there is continuity—indicated by an ohmmeter reading or the lighting of the test lamp—the field coils are grounded and the field frame assembly must be replaced.

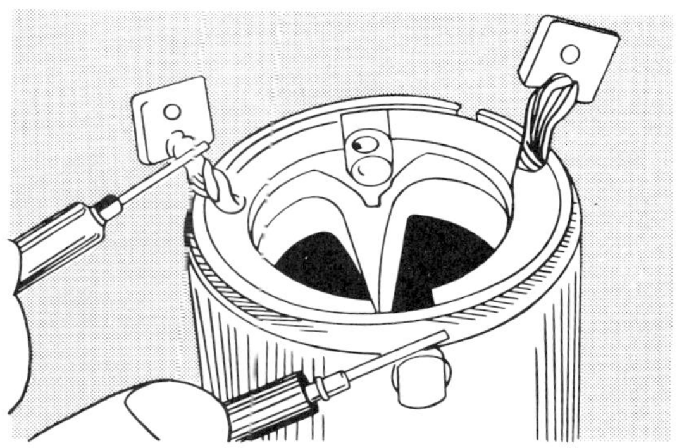

Fig. 4-8. Field coils being tested for grounding.

To test the field coils for open circuits, apply one test probe of an ohmmeter or a battery-powered test light to the field frame assembly's cable. Alternately touch the other test probe to each of the two brushes. You should obtain an ohmmeter reading, or the test lamp should light, each time you touch a brush. If there is no continuity at one or both of the brushes, the field coils have an open circuit and the field frame assembly must be replaced.

Occasionally, carbon dust from the brushes will short an armature. If arcing current has not permanently damaged the insulation, cleaning with trichloroethylene or a similar solvent will usually cure the short.

A minimum of 8 volts must be available at the ST terminal in order to operate the solenoid. However, faulty solenoid windings can cause the starter to operate incorrectly even with greater voltage available. To test the solenoid, carry out the tests indicated in Fig. 4-9, Fig. 4-10, and Fig. 4-11.

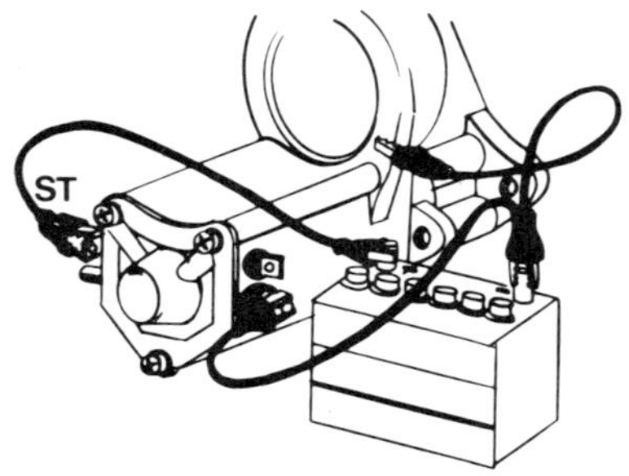

Fig. 4-9. Pull-in test. With solenoid assembly connected to 12-volt battery by jumper cables as shown, plunger should jump out firmly. If not, replace solenoid assembly.

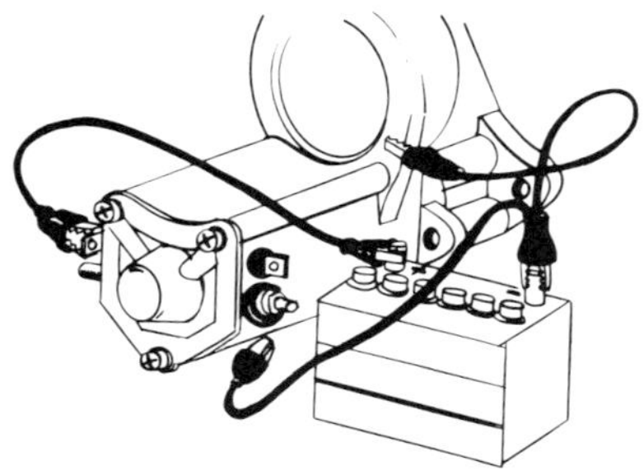

Fig. 4-10. Hold-in test. With one cable disconnected, as shown after pull-in test, plunger should remain jumped out. If not, replace solenoid assembly.

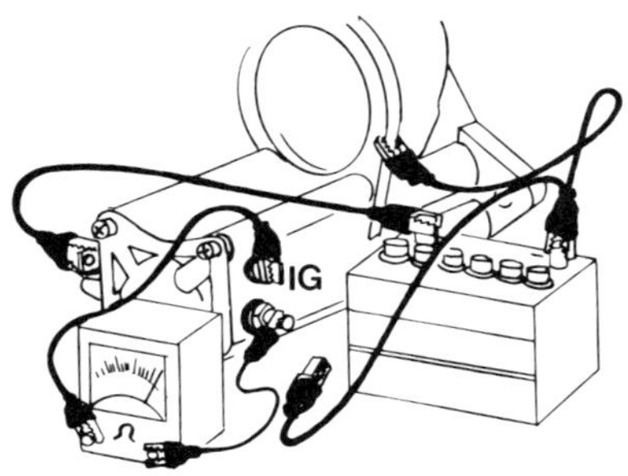

Fig. 4-11. Ignition continuity test. While conducting hold-in test illustrated in Fig. 4-10, use ohmmeter as shown here to check ignition terminal. If there is no continuity, replace solenoid assembly.

Testing Assembled Starter

You can make a basic performance test of the assembled starter as indicated in Fig. 4-12. With the starter running freely (no load), the ammeter should indicate less than 90 amperes with 11.5 volts available at the battery. If you obtain a higher ampere reading, either the starter is binding mechanically or there are shorts in the armature, the field coils, or the brush holder assembly. During this test, the drive pinion speed should be 3500 rpm for starters rated at 1.0 kW or 4000 rpm for starters rated at 1.4 kW.

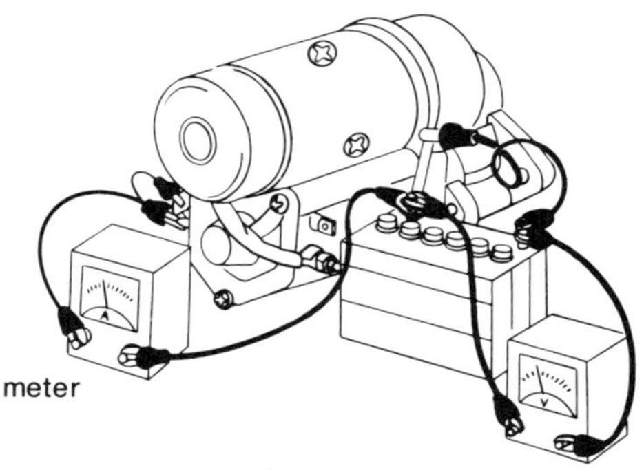

Fig. 4-12. Performance test being made with ammeter and voltmeter while starter runs without load.

5. CHARGING SYSTEM

Two similar alternators are used on the cars covered by this Manual. One is rated at 40 amperes and the other at 50 amperes. The alternator used depends on the electrical equipment that is installed on the car.

The alternator is belt-driven by the same V-belt that drives the water pump. The regulator, which on most cars is an electromagnetic, non-solid state unit, is mounted near the battery on the car body. Some later models have alternators with an integral solid-state regulator. To prevent damage to the alternator and the regulator when you are making tests and repairs, please observe the following precautions:

1. Keep in mind that battery voltage is always present at the alternator's B terminal, and also at the F terminal when the ignition is on.
2. When installing a battery in the car, make certain that the ground cable is connected to the battery's negative (−) post and that the cable that goes to the starter is connected to the battery's positive (+) post.
3. If you connect a battery charger or a booster battery to the battery in the car, make certain that

you connect the negative cable to the battery's negative (−) post and the positive cable to the battery's positive (+) post. Otherwise, the diodes will be damaged—even by momentarily reversed polarity.

4. When charging the battery with a quick-charger, be sure to disconnect not only the battery's negative (−) cable but also the positive (+) cable—in that order. Otherwise, quick-charging will damage the alternator diodes.
5. Never operate the alternator while the battery cables are disconnected. Also, never operate the alternator with its B terminal disconnected. If you must operate the alternator with the B terminal disconnected, disconnect the F terminal also to prevent the N terminal voltage from rising abnormally and burning out the regulator.
6. When adjusting the regulator, be sure to disconnect it first. Otherwise, the contact points of the regulator may short-circuit and fuse together.
7. Do not install a condenser on the alternator's F terminal, as doing this may cause the regulator points to develop metal transfer problems.
8. Never short, bridge, or ground any terminals of the charging system except as specifically described in **5.1 Charging System Troubleshooting.**
9. Do not test the alternator diodes with an outside power source of more than 1.5 volts.
10. When washing the car or cleaning the engine, be careful not to spray water directly onto the alternator. Doing this can damage the diode carrier assembly.

5.1 Charging System Troubleshooting

Charging system trouble is indicated by an alternator warning light or an ammeter that does not function normally, an undercharged battery, or an overcharged battery. Before you proceed with any testing, however, make sure the alternator V-belt is correctly adjusted as described in **5.3 Removing and Installing Alternator.** Visually inspect all electrical connections. The terminals and the connectors must be clean and tight-fitting. Replace wires that have cracked or broken insulation.

If the battery is undercharged or overcharged, you should make the tests described in **5.2 In-car Testing of Alternator and Regulator.** Overcharging is usually indicated by a frequent need to add large quantities of distilled water to the battery electrolyte. Since a worn-out battery will also exhibit a greater-than-normal need for water, make sure that the battery is fully charged and in good condition before you assume that there is trouble in the charging system.

An undercharged battery is usually associated with starting trouble. Again, make sure that the battery is in good condition and capable of accepting a full charge before you blame the charging system. Other causes of a run-down (undercharged) battery are the simultaneous use of a great many electrical accessories for long periods, leaving accessories or lights in operation with the engine stopped, frequent long periods of starter usage, and frequent short-trip driving that does not provide adequate time for the battery to recharge after the starter is operated. Broken or frayed charging system wiring and worn, corroded, or loose battery cable connections will also prevent adequate charging, or increase the time required for the battery to become fully charged.

Alternator noises are usually mechanical in origin, but a high, soft whistling sound may be produced by an alternator that is overcharging because of a faulty regulator or open diode. You may hear the same sound if a shorted diode is placing abnormal electrical strain on the alternator. However, some alternators make this sound when operating normally at maximum output.

Alternator mechanical noises are usually the result of misalignment between the V-belt and the pulley, a loose or broken pulley, worn bearings, or a bent rotor shaft. If you find any of these faults, either replace the faulty parts as described in **5.4 Disassembling and Assembling Alternator** or replace the entire alternator.

5.2 In-car Testing of Alternator and Regulator

A great many different kinds of alternator testers are being sold. If you use an alternator tester, follow the instructions and test procedures given by the tester's manufacturer. In a manual of this kind, it is not possible to cover the operation of so large a variety of proprietary testing equipment.

Fig. 5-1 shows the hook-up for testing alternator output. The ammeter used should have a range of at least 5 amperes discharge to 50 amperes in the charge range. The voltmeter should have a scale of at least 0 to 20 volts. The connections should be made with the engine stopped, as disconnecting the heavy wire from the alternator's B+ terminal with the engine running can burn out the alternator.

CAUTION —

An alternator must never be run with the battery disconnected or the B terminal disconnected. Doing so will severely damage either the alternator or the regulator, or both.

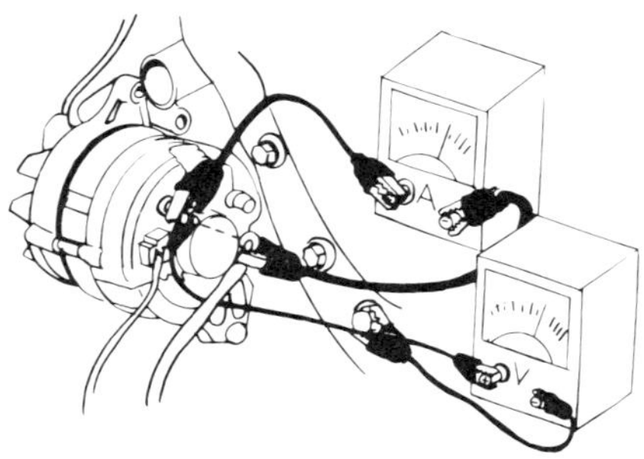

Fig. 5-1. Alternator charging system test. Ammeter is connected in series between alternator's B terminal and wire disconnected from B terminal. Voltmeter positive (+) connection is attached to alternator's B terminal, and voltmeter negative (−) connection is attached to ground on clean, unpainted, metal part of car.

To test:

1. With the engine stopped (alternator stationary), disconnect the battery's negative cable. Then disconnect the wire from the alternator's B terminal and make the test connections. Reconnect the battery's negative (−) cable.
2. Start the engine. Turn on all lights and accessories to place a load on the charging system.
3. With the engine running at approximately 2000 rpm, the ammeter reading should be over 30 amperes with the voltage between 13.8 and 14.8 volts.

   NOTE —

   If the amperage reading is less than specified, it may be because the battery is fully charged or nearly so. Repeat the test after discharging the battery. You can discharge the battery by operating the starter for five to ten seconds with the ignition coil's high-tension cable disconnected to keep the engine from starting.

4. After testing and, if necessary, adjusting the regulator, stop the engine. Then disconnect the battery's negative (−) cable before you remove the instruments and reconnect the wire to the alternator's B terminal. Reconnect the battery.

If the readings are only slightly outside the prescribed ranges, adjust the regulator as described under the next heading. But if charging system output is far above the prescribed range (overcharging), the trouble is probably a faulty regulator. However, test the diodes as described in **5.4 Disassembling and Assembling Alternator** before you replace or adjust the regulator. If any diode is open-circuited, replace the diodes and the diode carrier as a unit. If there is still an overcharge, or if the diodes are not faulty, replace the regulator or adjust it as described under the next heading.

If the charging system output is far below the prescribed range (undercharging), test the diodes as described in **5.4 Disassembling and Assembling Alternator.** If any diode is shorted, replace the diodes and the diode carrier as a unit. If the diodes are not faulty test the stator for grounded coil windings as described in **5.4 Disassembling and Assembling Alternator.** If there are grounded windings, replace the stator or the alternator. If neither the diodes nor the stator windings are faulty, the trouble is in the regulator, which should be replaced.

Adjusting Regulator

(except integral regulator)

You can correct irregularities in charging system output by adjusting the regulator. You should not, however, make haphazard changes in the regulator setting. All adjustments must be carried out with reference to the instrument readings specified under the previous heading.

CAUTION —

If you lack the skills or equipment needed to adjust the regulator, we recommend that you either replace the regulator or leave the adjustment work to an Authorized Dealer or other qualified shop. We especially urge you to consult your Authorized Dealer before attempting adjustments or repairs on a car that is still covered by the new-car warranty.

To adjust:

1. Disconnect the multiple connector from the harness of the regulator. Then take out the two screws and remove the cover from the regulator.
2. Inspect the contact points (Fig. 5-2) for each relay. If any contact is worn, burned, or shows other damage, replace the regulator.

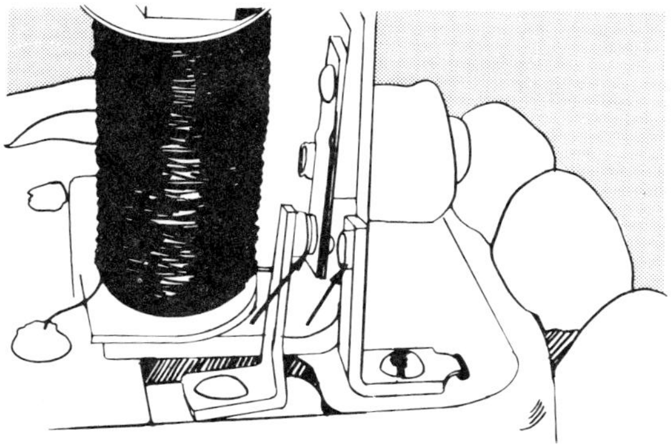

Fig. 5-2. Locations of contact points (arrows). Do not attempt to clean or resurface damaged contacts.

3. If the voltage is too high or too low, adjust the tension of the regulating relay spring as indicated in Fig. 5-3. Bend the spring stop up (increasing spring tension) to increase the voltage output. Bend the spring stop down (decreasing spring tension) to decrease the voltage output.

CAUTION —
Do not make adjustments with the engine running. Before each adjustment, stop the engine, then disconnect the multiple connector from the regulator. Otherwise, there is danger of damaging the regulator or the alternator.

4. If the voltage relay cuts in only after engine speed is very high, or if the voltage relay fails to cut out when the engine is stopped, you can adjust it by the same methods used to adjust the regulating relay. The voltage relay should cut in at between 4.0 and 5.8 volts.

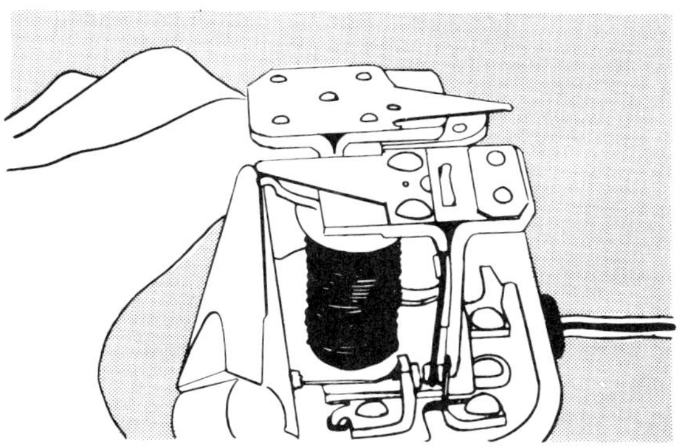

Fig. 5-3. Spring tension of regulating relay being adjusted by bending spring stop with pliers. Voltage relay is in background. Notice orientation of relays to wiring harness.

Removing and Installing Regulator

To remove the regulator, first disconnect the negative (−) cable from the battery. Then remove the two bolts that hold the regulator to the car body. Disconnect the multiple connector for the regulator wiring harness and remove the regulator from the car.

Installation is the reverse of removal. If a radio suppression condenser is installed on one of the regulator mounting bolts, be sure to reinstall it when you reinstall the regulator.

5.3 Removing and Installing Alternator

Because of the location of the alternator, it is easier to accomplish some of the removal steps by working under the car after taking off the splash shield beneath the front of the engine. It will also improve access to the alternator if you remove the battery from the car.

To remove: 4

1. Disconnect the negative (−) cable from the battery.
2. Disconnect the wires from the alternator.
3. Loosen the alternator mounting bolts and also the bolt at the engine end of the alternator adjusting bracket. Push the alternator toward the engine and unhook the V-belt from the alternator pulley.
4. Fully remove the adjusting and mounting bolts, then remove the alternator from the car.

To install:

1. Position the alternator on its lower mounting brackets, then loosely install the lower mounting bolt.
2. Loosely install the alternator's upper mounting bolt. Push the alternator as far as it will go toward the engine. Then install the V-belt on the crankshaft pulley, the water pump pulley, and the alternator pulley.
3. By pulling the alternator away from the engine block, adjust the V-belt tension so that you can depress the V-belt 10 to 13 mm (3/8 to 1/2 in.) at a point midway between the alternator pulley and the water pump pulley. Then tighten the mounting and adjusting bolts.
4. Reconnect the wires to the alternator. Reconnect the battery's negative (−) cable.

CAUTION —
Do not tension the V-belts too tightly. Doing this can cause the alternator bearings or the water pump bearings to fail. Instructions for tensioning all V-belts are given in **LUBRICATION AND MAINTENANCE.**

5.4 Disassembling and Assembling Alternator

Fig. 5-4 is an exploded view of the alternator. The ball bearing races are a press fit on the rotor shaft. Do not reuse bearings that have been removed from the shaft. When installing new bearings, use a press tool that will apply pressure to the inner bearing race only.

> ***CAUTION ——***
>
> *If you lack the skills or tools required to repair the alternator, we suggest you leave these repairs to an Authorized Dealer or other qualified shop. Alternatively, you can replace a faulty alternator with a new or rebuilt alternator. We especially urge you to consult your Authorized Dealer before attempting repairs on a car still covered by the new-car warranty.*

1. Pulley
2. Fan
3. Collar
4. Drive-end frame
5. Felt washer
6. Felt washer cover
7. Ball bearing
8. Bearing retainer plate
9. Spacer ring
10. Snap ring
11. Rotor assembly
12. Ball bearing
13. Stator assembly
14. Lead wire
15. Brush holder assembly
16. Brush spring
17. Brush
18. Positive diode carrier
19. Negative diode carrier
20. Insulator washer
21. Insulator washer
22. Bushing
23. Rectifier-end frame
24. End cover
25. B terminal insulator

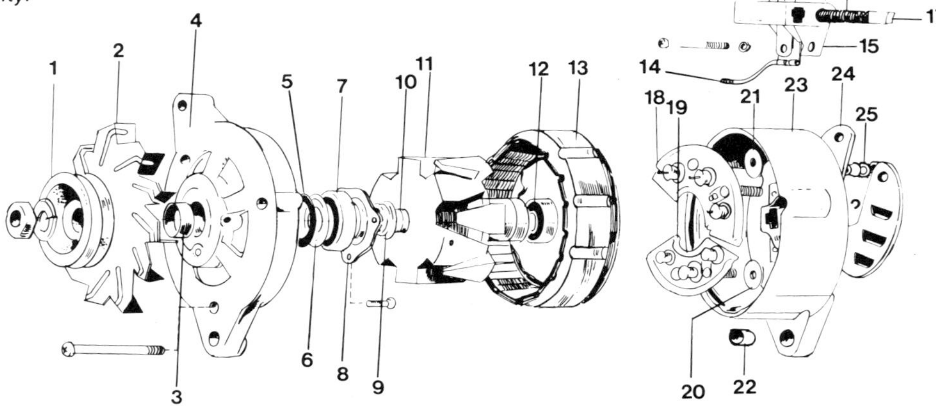

Fig. 5-4. Exploded view of alternator.

The diodes and their carriers must be replaced as a unit. If you replace either of the diode carriers or the stator, you must unsolder the stator wires from the diode carrier and resolder the connections after you have replaced the faulty component. When using the soldering iron, be careful not to overheat the diodes. Overheating will cause the diodes to open-circuit or short.

To disassemble:

1. Disconnect the battery's negative (−) cable. Remove the alternator from the car as described in **5.3 Removing and Installing Alternator.**
2. By inserting a Phillips head screwdriver into the round recesses of the drive-end frame, remove the three long screws that bind the drive-end housing and the rectifier-end housing together on the stator assembly.
3. By inserting two flat-blade screwdrivers into the notches of the drive-end frame, pry the drive-end frame loose from the stator, as indicated in Fig. 5-5. Remove the drive-end frame and the rotor assembly as a unit.

> ***CAUTION ——***
>
> *Be careful not to pry against the stator coil wires, as doing this could severely damage the alternator.*

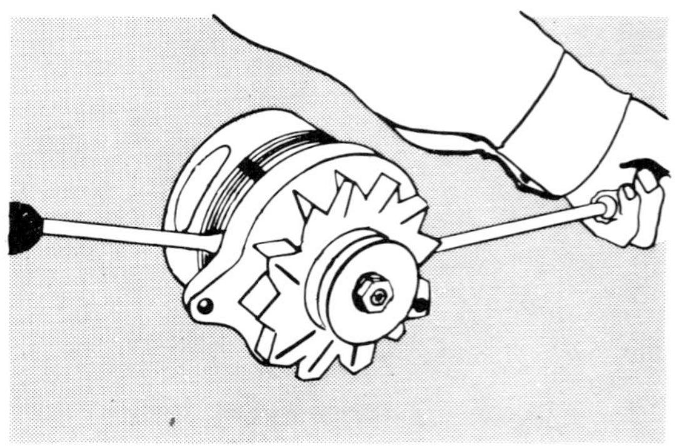

Fig. 5-5. Drive-end frame with rotor attached being pried loose from stator assembly.

4. Clamp the rotor between blocks of wood in a bench vise. Then remove the nut and the lockwasher that are in the center of the pulley.
5. Lift off the collar, the pulley, the fan, and the spacer ring. Then, with the drive-end frame supported on the press bed, press the rotor out of the ball bearing and the drive-end frame as indicated in Fig. 5-6.

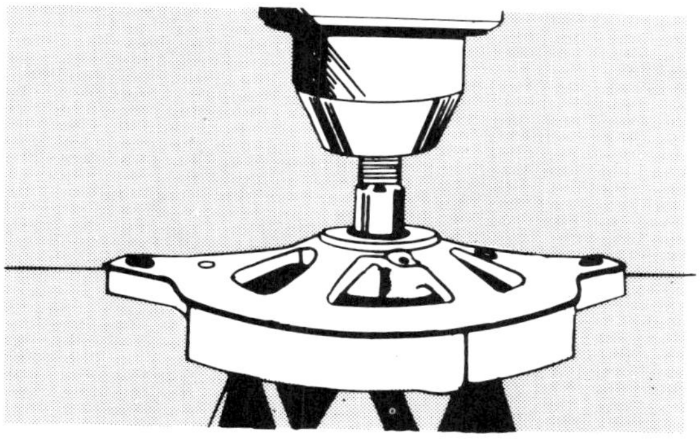

Fig. 5-6. Rotor being pressed out of bearing in drive-end frame.

6. While applying pressure to the outer race, hand-turn the rear ball bearing of the rotor. If it locks, feels rough, or is otherwise faulty, remove it as indicated in Fig. 5-7.

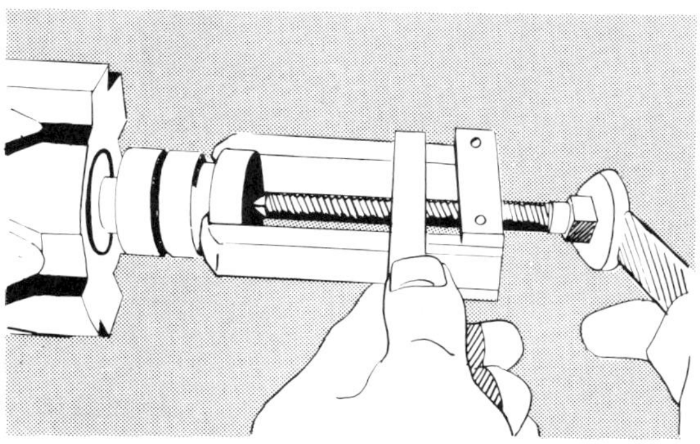

Fig. 5-7. Bearing being removed from rear of rotor.

7. Remove the three Phillips head screws that hold the bearing retainer plate to the drive-end frame. Then remove the plate, the bearing, the felt washer cover, and the felt washer from the drive-end frame.
8. Remove the nuts and the terminal insulators that hold the end cover and the rectifier-end frame to the diode carriers. Remove the two Phillips head screws that mount the brush holder. Then remove the end cover and the rectifier-end frame from the diode carriers, the brush holder, and the stator assembly.
9. Remove the insulator washers from the terminals of the diode carriers.
10. To remove the brush holder assembly, use a small screwdriver to remove the lead wire from the holder. Remove one terminal insulator, then remove the stator coil N terminal from the brush holder.

CAUTION —
Do not remove the brush holder assembly by cutting off or unsoldering the N terminal lead, as this is unnecessary and will increase the time and effort needed to make repairs.

To assemble:

1. Wipe clean the bearings and the electrical parts for the alternator. Wash the end frames and other one-piece, all-metal parts in solvent.

CAUTION —
Do not wash the rotor, the stator assembly, the brush holder assembly, or the bearings in solvent. Doing this may damage the insulation of the electrical components and will destroy the factory-installed grease in the bearings.

2. Inspect the brushes and, if necessary, replace them as described under the next heading. If there have been electrical troubles in the alternator, carry out the tests and repairs described in **5.5 Testing and Repairing Alternator Components.**
3. Reconnect the brush holder assembly to the stator coil N terminal. To do this, leave the brush negative lead terminal unconnected, install the stator coil N terminal in the brush holder (Fig. 5-8), then install one terminal insulator and position the brush negative lead terminal correctly.

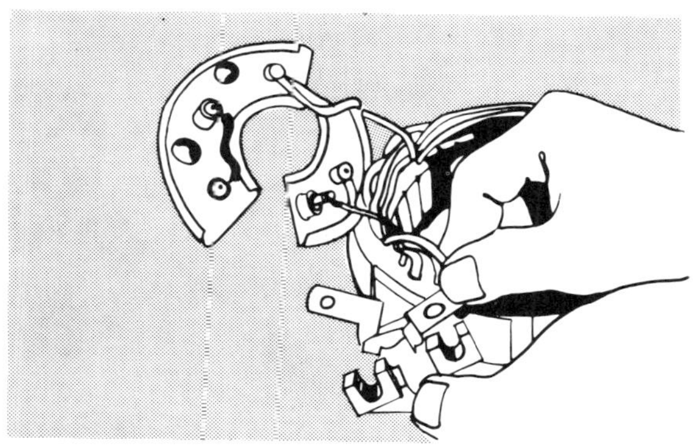

Fig. 5-8. Stator coil N terminal being positioned in brush holder assembly.

4

4. Install a new felt washer in the drive-end frame. Install the felt washer cover, a new ball bearing, and then the bearing retainer plate.

NOTE ——

If the bearing has an open side and is not factory lubricated, pack the bearing with high-melting-point grease.

5. Loosely position the diode carriers, the brush holder assembly, and the stator assembly in the rectifier-end frame. Then, after installing two insulator washers between the positive diode carrier and the frame and the B terminal insulator and the other insulator over the positive diode carrier's retaining bolts, secure the positive diode carrier and the negative diode carrier to the frame with the four nuts.
6. Install the brush holder assembly, being careful not to forget the insulator washer that goes between the brush holder assembly and the rectifier-end frame.
7. If you previously removed it, press a new ball bearing onto the rear of the rotor, using a tool that will exert pressure on the bearing inner race only.

NOTE ——

If the bearing has an open side and is not factory lubricated, pack the bearing with high-melting-point grease.

8. Using a tubular mandrel that will slip over the alternator shaft, press the drive-end frame and bearing onto the rotor.
9. Clamp the rotor between wood blocks in a vise. Install the collar, the fan, the pulley, the lockwasher, and the nut. Then torque the nut to 40 to 50 Nm (30 to 37 ft. lb.).
10. Push in the brushes and insert a wire to keep them in a retracted position, as indicated in Fig. 5-9.

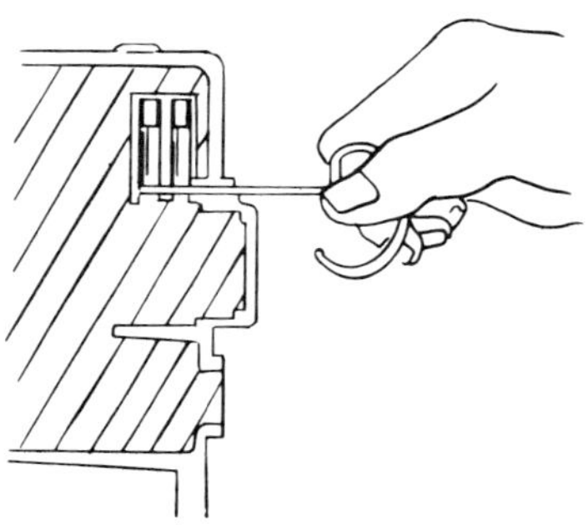

Fig. 5-9. Wire being inserted through access hole in rectifier-end frame to keep brushes retracted.

11. Assemble the drive-end frame and the stator assembly/rectifier-frame end. Install the three screws, then remove the wire installed in step 10 so that the brushes pop out to contact the slip rings of the rotor.

Checking and Replacing Brushes

If the brushes are worn to less than 8.5 mm (11/32 in.) when measured as indicated in Fig. 5-10, replace them. To do this, unsolder the old brush leads from the brush holder and remove the worn-out brushes. Position new brushes in the holder so that they protrude 12.5 mm (½ in.) and no more. Then solder the lead wires as indicated in Fig. 5-10 and cut off the surplus wire.

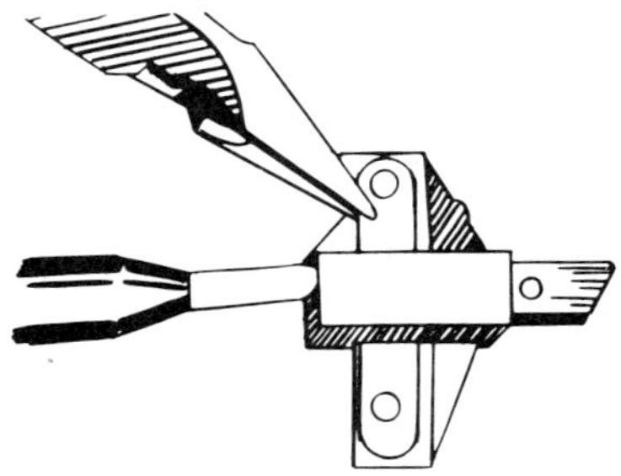

Fig. 5-10. Brush lead being soldered. During soldering, brush should protrude by 12.5 mm (½ in.). Replace brushes if maximum protrusion is 8.5 mm (11/32 in.) or less.

If the old brushes are not worn excessively, check that they move freely in the brush holder. Also check newly installed brushes for free movement. Correct the binding if necessary. To check for shorts, use an ohmmeter to test for continuity between the brushes and between each brush and the brush holder metal parts. Replace the brush holder assembly as a unit if there is continuity, for it indicates a short.

5.5 Testing and Repairing Alternator Components

You can use an ohmmeter or a battery-powered test light to test the rotor's field coil. There should be no electrical continuity when the test probes are applied to the slip rings and to the rotor shaft or the poles (Fig. 5-11). If there is continuity, the field coil is grounded and the rotor must be replaced.

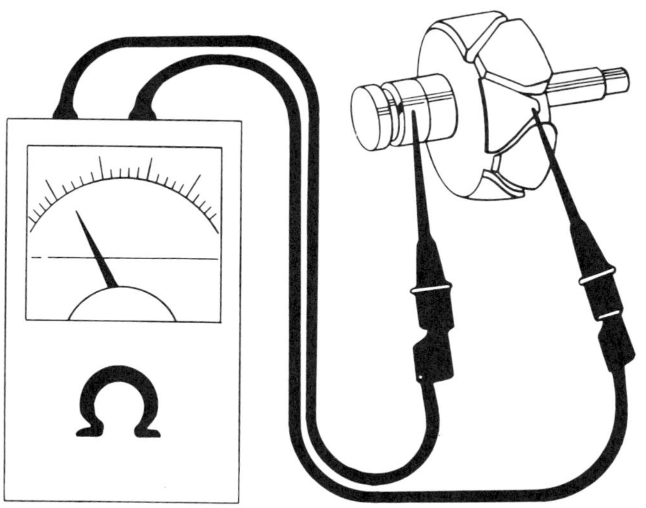

Fig. 5-11. Ohmmeter being used to test rotor for grounded field coil. Poles and shaft should not be in electrical contact with slip rings.

Using an ohmmeter, you can measure the resistance between the slip rings as shown in Fig. 5-12. If the resistance is significantly lower than 4.1 to 4.3 ohms, the field coil is shorted. A battery-powered test light should be dim when the test probes are applied to the slip rings. If there is no continuity, the field coil is burned out. Replace faulty rotors.

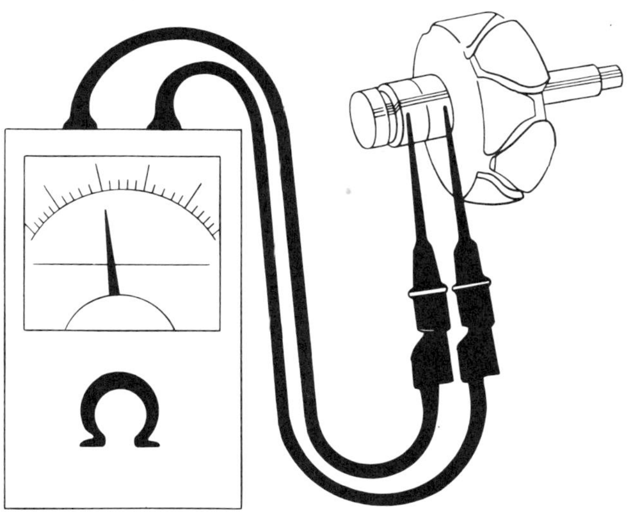

Fig. 5-12. Ohmmeter being used to measure resistance between the two slip rings. Resistance is created by field coil, through which test current must flow.

To check the stator coil insulation, apply an ohmmeter to the stator assembly's N terminal and to the laminations of the stator core. Make sure that the diode carriers are not in contact with the stator core. If there is electrical continuity between the coils and the core, replace the stator assembly.

Additional electrical tests of the stator assembly and the diodes require that the diode carriers be unsoldered from the stator leads. When doing this, be sure to hold the diode leads with a pair of pliers as indicated in Fig. 5-13. Alternatively, install a special heat sink on the diode lead wire. By absorbing heat from the lead wire, the heat sink or pliers will prevent excessive heat from reaching the diode itself. Overheated diodes will open-circuit or short.

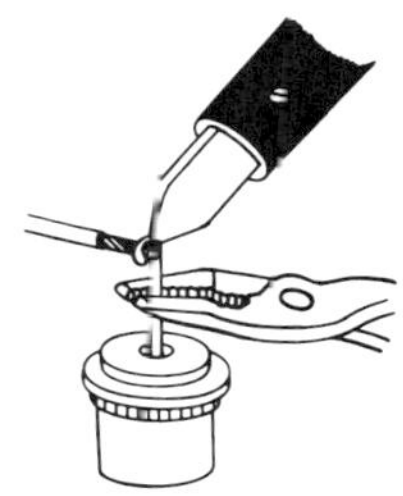

Fig. 5-13. Correct method of soldering or unsoldering connections at diode leads. Pliers are used here as a heat sink to absorb heat before it can reach diode.

4

With the diode carriers unsoldered from the stator assembly, you can test the stator coils for open circuits as indicated in Fig. 5-14. If there is no electrical continuity between any two of the stator coil winding leads, there is an open circuit in the windings. In addition, there should be no electrical continuity between any stator coil winding lead and the laminations of the stator core. Replace faulty stator assemblies.

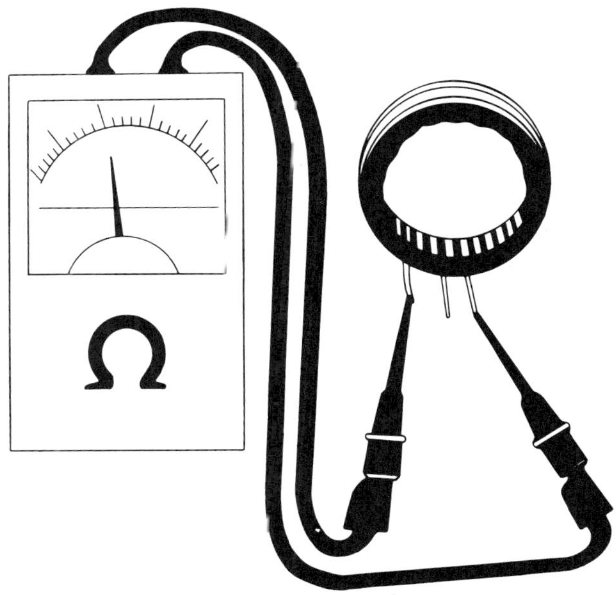

Fig. 5-14. Ohmmeter being used to check continuity through stator coil windings. Battery-powered test light can also be used to make stator continuity tests.

A diode is a kind of transistor that has the unique property of permitting electrical current to flow through it in only one direction. To test the diodes in the alternator's diode carriers, first unsolder the diode carriers from the stator wires as previously described.

Using an ohmmeter or a 1.5-volt battery-powered test light, apply one test probe to the diode lead wire and the other test probe to the diode carrier. Then reverse the positions of the two test probes. The ohmmeter should show a reading (or the test lamp should light) with the test probes in one position but not in the other. If you obtain no reading (or light) in either position, the diode (or diode group) is open-circuited, and the diodes and the diode carrier should be replaced as a unit.

You should also replace the diode carrier if the ohmmeter produces a reading (or the test light comes on) with the test probes in both positions. This is an indication that the diode (or diode group) is shorted.

If either diode group shows continuity in one test probe position but not in the other, it is still possible that an individual diode is faulty. Unsolder each diode lead from its connection with the other diodes, then test the diodes individually as indicated in Fig. 5-15. If one or more diodes show no continuity in either position, replace the diodes and the diode carrier as a unit.

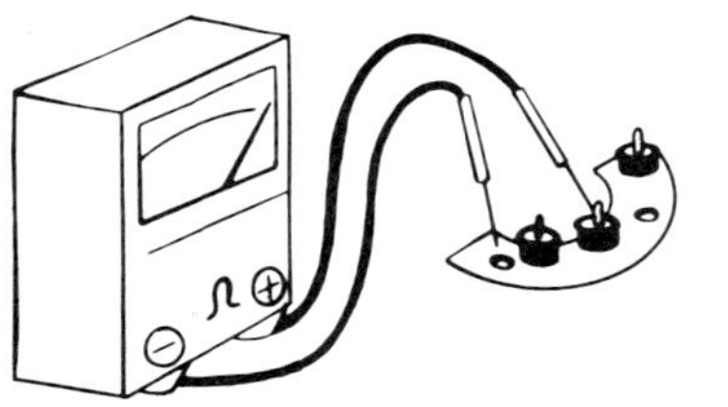

Fig. 5-15. Ohmmeter being used to test diodes individually.

6. TURN SIGNALS AND EMERGENCY FLASHERS

The turn signal switch and the flasher relay are often mistakenly blamed for troubles caused by dirty, corroded, or loose-fitting turn signal bulb contacts. Before you start to troubleshoot either the turn signal switch or the turn signal/emergency flasher relay, be sure that all bulb contacts are clean and tight.

6.1 Turn Signal and Emergency Flasher Troubleshooting

The turn signals and the emergency flashers share the same flasher relay. The flasher relay is labeled in the wiring diagrams that appear elsewhere in this section of the Manual. It is located behind the kick panel to the left of the driver's feet.

The turn signals operate only with the ignition turned on. The emergency flashers operate whether the ignition is on or off. If the emergency flashers work but the turn signals do not, you can be certain that the flasher relay is not faulty. The same is true if the turn signals work but the emergency flashers do not. However, if neither system operates, you should not conclude that the flasher relay is faulty without further troubleshooting.

First check that neither the fuse labeled HORN/STOP nor the fuse labeled TURN/WIPER is burned out; the former protects the emergency flasher circuit and the latter protects the turn signal circuit. Then check that the turn signal bulbs are not burned out, and that the bulb socket contacts are clean and tight. If one bulb is burned out or in poor electrical contact with its socket, the other bulbs may come on without flashing or may flash very slowly. If you find no other fault, and if neither the turn signals nor the emergency flashers will work, replace the flasher relay.

If the turn signals work only on one side, or if the emergency flashers work only on one side of the car or fail to work at all, use the procedure given here to find the malfunction in the switches. With the help of the wiring diagram given for your car, you can also test the wiring from the switches to the other parts of the electrical system to determine whether there is a break in one of the wires.

To test switches:

1. Disconnect the battery's negative (–) cable.
2. By removing the bolts, detach and remove the trim panel beneath the lower end of the steering column cover. Then take out the screws in the recesses and remove the steering column lower cover (Fig. 6-1). This will provide full access to the steering column multiple connector plug.

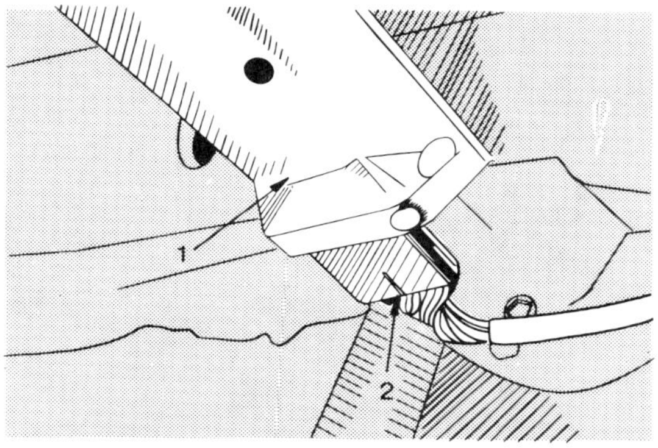

Fig. 6-1. Components to be removed and disconnected prior to testing turn signal and emergency flasher switches. Steering column lower cover is at **1**; multiple connector for wiring is at **2**.

3. By squeezing together the locking levers as indicated in Fig. 6-2, release the multiple connector locks. Then pull apart the multiple connector, disconnecting the switches from the car's electrical system.

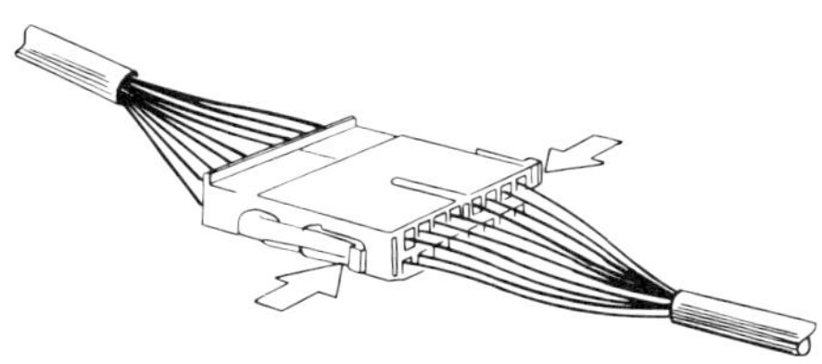

Fig. 6-2. Arrows indicating how locking levers must be squeezed together to disconnect steering column wiring multiple connector.

4. Using Fig. 6-3 as your guide, use an ohmmeter or a battery-powered test light to make continuity tests between different terminals of the multiple connector that is attached to the switches. **Table c** lists the terminals between which there should be continuity in each of the various switch positions. If you find any fault, replace the steering column switch assembly as a unit.

***CAUTION* ——**

When applying the ohmmeter test probes to the multiple connector plug, be very careful not to bend or deform the terminals inside the plug. This could cause difficulty in reconnecting the multiple connector and also electrical system trouble. The safest method for testing is to insert the test probes from the wire side of the plug.

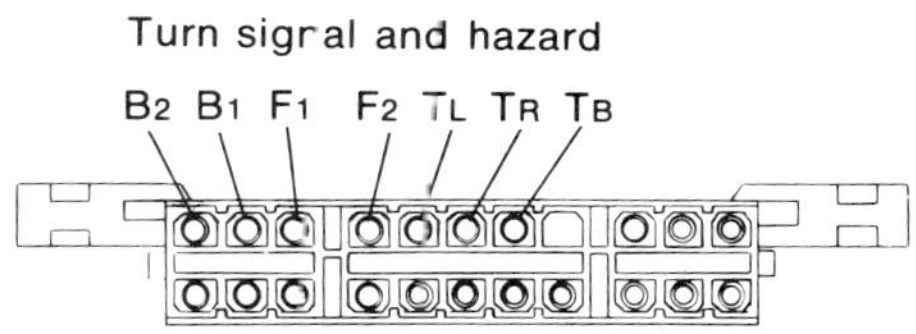

Fig. 6-3. Designations for turn signal and emergency flasher terminals, located in multiple connector plug that is attached to steering column switches. Designations correspond to terminal designations on switches and in wiring diagrams.

Table c. Turn Signal/Emergency Flasher Switch Tests

Switch positions	Terminals between which there should be continuity
Turn signal switch in center (neutral) position—emergency flasher switch OFF	F1 and B1
Turn signal switch in center (neutral) position—emergency flasher switch ON	TL and TB and TR, F2 and B2
Turn signal switch in LEFT-TURN position—emergency flasher switch OFF	TL and TB, F1 and B1
Turn signal switch in RIGHT-TURN position—emergency flasher switch OFF	TB and TR, F1 and B1

5. When testing is complete, reconnect the multiple connector, reinstall the steering column lower cover, and reconnect the battery negative (–) cable.

6.2 Removing and Installing Steering Column Switches

The steering column switch assembly (Fig. 6-4) includes the headlight switch, the turn signal switch, the emergency flasher switch, and the windshield wiper/washer switch. A repair kit is available for repairing the headlight/parking light OFF/ON switch. If there are any other troubles, the entire switch assembly must be replaced as a unit.

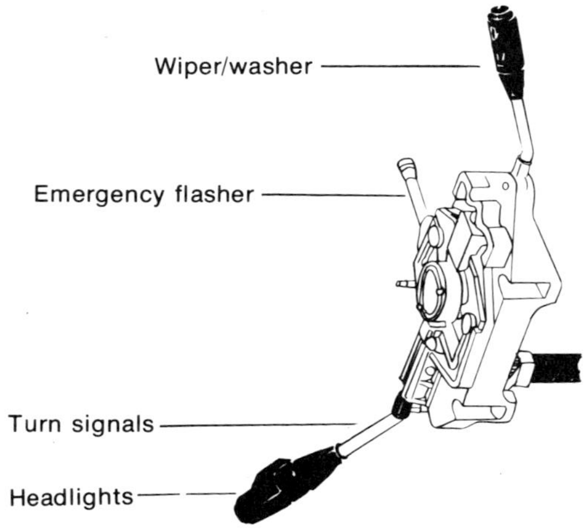

Fig. 6-4. Steering column switch assembly.

To remove:

1. Disconnect the battery's negative cable.
2. On cars with three-spoke steering wheels, remove the steering wheel pad by taking out the screws that are accessible in the spoke cover, behind the steering wheel. On cars with four-spoke steering wheels, carefully pry out the medallion in the center of the wheel. If necessary, consult **SUSPENSION AND STEERING.**
3. Remove the nut that holds the steering wheel to the steering column. Then, using a puller as indicated in Fig. 6-5, pull the steering wheel off the steering column.

> ***CAUTION —***
>
> *Do not attempt to remove the steering wheel by pounding or by using a slide hammer. Any unnecessarily heavy force or shock can damage the steering column bearings and sensitive electrical components.*

4. By taking out the screws in the recesses of the steering column lower cover, remove both the upper and the lower steering column covers.

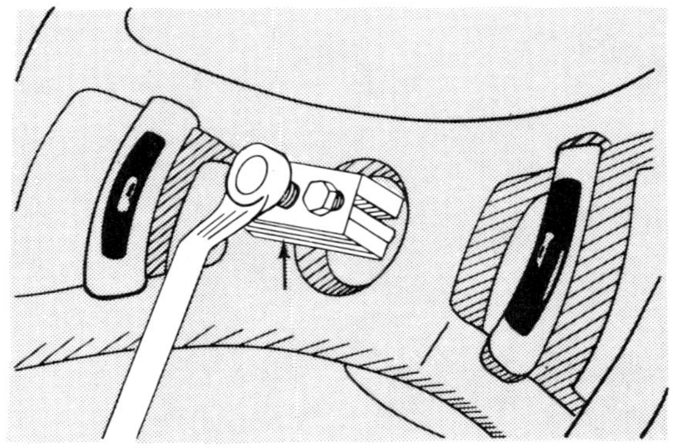

Fig. 6-5. Puller (arrow) being used to remove steering wheel.

5. By squeezing together the locking levers on the multiple connector, pull apart the multiple connector, disconnecting the steering column switches from the car's electrical system. If necessary, refer to Fig. 6-2, given earlier.
6. Remove the screws indicated in Fig. 6-6. Then remove the steering column switch assembly from the steering column.

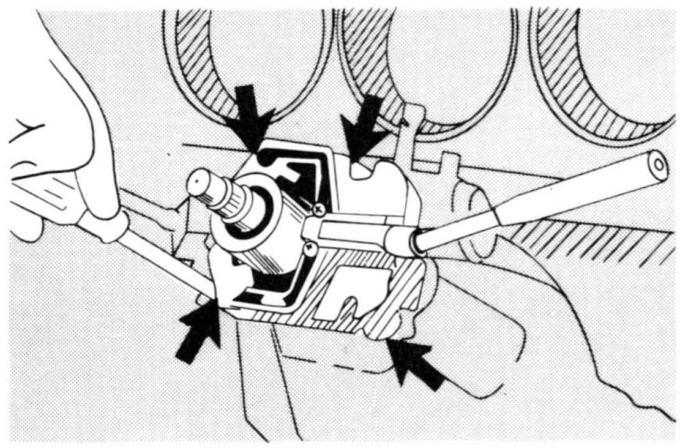

Fig. 6-6. Screws (arrows) that hold steering column switches to ignition/steering column lock assembly.

Installation is the reverse of removal. Make sure that the front wheels are pointed straight ahead when you install the steering wheel. The lower spoke of three-spoke steering wheels should be vertical when the wheel is installed, and the paired spokes of four-spoke steering wheels should be horizontal. Torque the nut for the steering wheel to 35 to 40 Nm (26 to 30 ft. lb.).

> **NOTE —**
>
> If it is necessary to repair the headlight/parking light ON/OFF switch, do the work as described in **8.2 Headlight Switch and Relay.**

6.3 Replacing Turn Signal/Emergency Flasher Relay

The turn signal/emergency flasher relay is located behind the upper part of the kick panel to the left of the driver's feet. To remove the flasher relay, first disconnect the battery's negative (−) cable. Then, working in the passenger compartment, remove the driver's-side kick panel by taking out the plated bolts. Remove the sheet metal screws that hold the flasher relay to the car body, then disconnect the wiring from the relay and remove the relay from the car. Installation is the reverse of removal.

7. WINDSHIELD WIPERS AND WASHERS

The operation of the two-speed windshield wipers and the windshield washers is controlled by a lever on the steering column. The wiper blades park automatically when turned off. The windshield washers are supplied with water by a motor-driven pump.

7.1 Windshield Wiper and Washer Troubleshooting

If the windshield wipers or the windshield washer fail to operate, first check that the fuse labeled TURN/WIPER is not burned out. Sometimes this fuse burns out owing to a temporary overload caused when the wipers are turned on with heavy snow on them. If the fuse is intact, or if the replacement fuse burns out immeidately, further troubleshooting is needed to determine the source of the malfunction.

If the washer motor—including the optional rear window washer—does not run, unplug the wires from the washer motor, which is located in the base of the washer reservoir. Turn on the ignition. Apply the negative test probe of a voltmeter to ground on some clean, unpainted metal part of the car. Then apply the positive test probe alternately to each terminal of the disconnected plug. If no voltage is indicated at either terminal, the wiring from the fuse box to the washer motor is faulty and should be repaired or replaced. If voltage is reaching the plug, keep the positive test probe in contact with the plug's positive current terminal and apply the negative probe to the other plug terminal. Have someone turn on the washer switch. If no current is indicated, the trouble is in the washer switch, and the entire steering column switch assembly should be replaced. If there is current at the plug when the switch is on, but the washer motor does not run when it is connected to the plug, the motor is faulty and should be replaced.

NOTE ——
All the voltmeter tests described under this heading can also be carried out with a test light.

If the windshield wipers fail to operate correctly, unplug the wiring from the wiper motor, which is located just above the washer reservoir in the rear right-hand corner of the engine compartment. Turn on the ignition. Then, using Fig. 7-1 as your guide, check for voltage at the + and − terminals of the disconnected plug. If there is no voltage, the trouble is in the wiring. Test between the − terminal and the battery's positive (+) post. If there is no voltage, the negative wire is faulty. Then test between the + terminal and the battery's negative (−) post. If there is no voltage, the positive wire to the fuse box is faulty.

NOTE ——
All the voltmeter tests described under this heading can also be carried out with a test light.

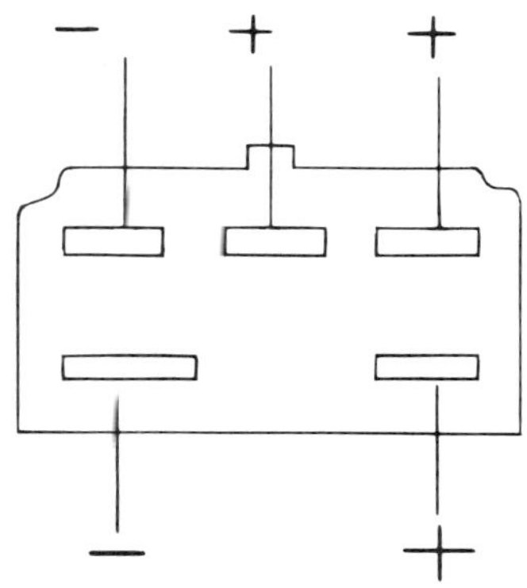

Fig. 7-1. Identification of windshield wiper motor connector plug terminals.

If the windshield wipers operate normally but fail to park correctly when they are switched off, use an ohmmeter or a battery-powered test light to check for continuity between plug terminals +1 and S with the wiper switch turned off. If there is no continuity, the trouble is in the switch or the wiring. If there is continuity, the trouble is in the motor's parking contacts, and the wiper motor should be replaced.

NOTE ——
There is a possibility that the trouble is a worn cam on the motor's driven gear. If so, you can replace the gear as described in **7.3 Removing and Installing Wiper Motors.** If the trouble is caused by dirt, you may be able to correct it by cleaning the contact points.

If there is voltage at the − and + terminals of the plug but the windshield wipers fail to operate or operate at one speed only, apply the voltmeter's negative test probe to the − terminal of the plug and the positive test probe to the +1 terminal of the plug. Voltage should be indicated when the ignition is turned on and the wiper switch put in its low-speed position. Repeat the test with

4

the positive voltmeter probe applied to the plug's +2 terminal and the wiper switch in its high-speed position. With the ignition on, voltage should be indicated. If no voltage is indicated in either of these tests, test the switch as described in the procedure that follows to determine whether it is the switch or the wiring that is faulty. If there is voltage indicated in these tests, the trouble is in the motor.

NOTE ——

If the trouble is in the motor, you may be able to correct it by replacing the brushes and the brush holder as described in **7.3 Removing and Installing Wiper Motors**. Otherwise, replace the motor as a unit.

To test windshield wiper/washer switch:

1. Disconnect the battery's negative (−) cable.
2. By removing the bolts, detach and remove the trim panel beneath the lower end of the steering column cover. Then take out the screws in the recesses and remove the steering column lower cover (Fig. 7-2). Doing this will provide full access to the steering column multiple connector plug.

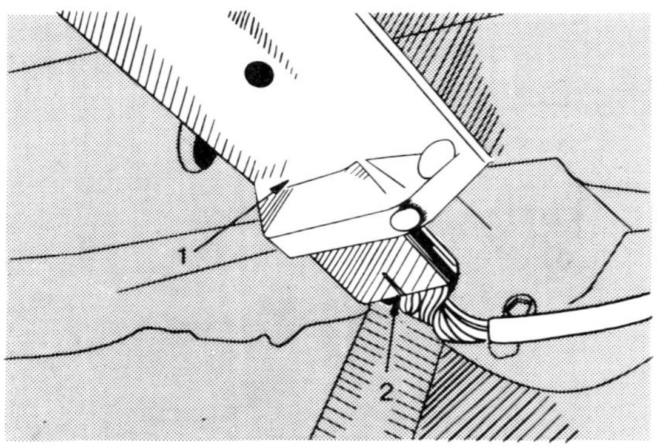

Fig. 7-2. Components to be removed and disconnected prior to testing windshield wiper/washer switch. Steering column lower cover is at **1**; multiple connector for wiring is at **2**.

3. By squeezing together the locking levers as indicated in Fig. 7-3, release the multiple connector locks. Then pull apart the multiple connector, disconnecting the switches from the car's electrical system.
4. Using Fig. 7-4 as your guide, use an ohmmeter or a battery-powered test light to make continuity tests between different terminals of the multiple connector that is attached to the switches. **Table d** lists the terminals between which there should be continuity in each of the various switch positions. If you find any fault, replace the steering column switch assembly as described earlier in **6.2 Removing and Installing Steering Column Switches.**

CAUTION ——

When applying the ohmmeter test probes to the multiple connector plug, be very careful not to bend or deform the terminals inside the plug. This could cause difficulty in reconnecting the multiple connector and also could cause electrical system trouble. The safest method for testing is to insert the test probes from the wire side of the plug.

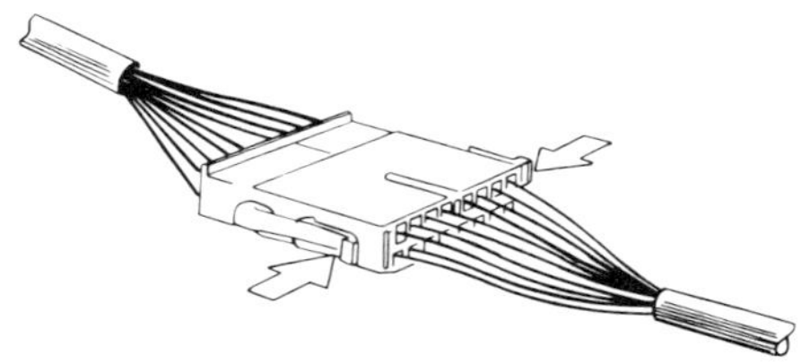

Fig. 7-3. Arrows indicating how locking levers must be squeezed together to disconnect steering column wiring multiple connector.

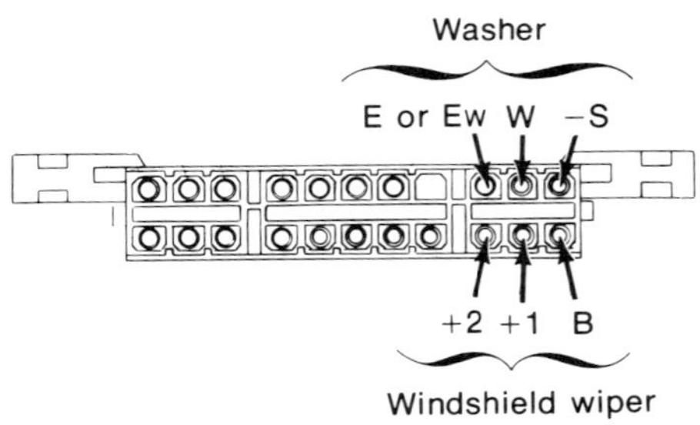

Fig. 7-4. Designations for windshield wiper and washer terminal, located in multiple connector plug that is attached to steering column switches. Designations correspond to terminal designations on switches, on motor, and in wiring diagrams.

Table d. Windshield Wiper/Washer Switch Tests

Switch positions	Terminals between which there should be continuity
Windshield washer switch ON (in any windshield wiper switch position)	W and E (or EW)
Windshield wiper switch OFF	+1 and −S
Windshield wiper switch at low speed	+B and +1
Windshield wiper switch at high speed	+B and +2

5. When testing is complete, reconnect the multiple connector, reinstall the steering column lower cover, and reconnect the battery's negative (−) cable.

Rear Window Wiper Troubleshooting

The rear window wiper motor, which is similar to the windshield wiper motor, is located beneath an access panel inside the rear of the car, near the location for the wiper arm. The motor is grounded by contact with the car body.

To determine whether current is reaching the motor, unplug the wires from the motor. With the ignition turned on and the rear window wiper switch turned off, voltage should be present when a voltmeter or a test light is connected to terminal L of the plug and to ground on some clean, unpainted metal part of the car. If not, the wire that connects terminal L to the switch and the fuse box is faulty. With the switch turned on, voltage should be indicated when the voltmeter or test light is connected to ground and to plug terminal +1. If current is not reaching terminal +1, test the switch as described in the following procedure. If voltage is present, the trouble is in the motor, which should be replaced. Additional help in troubleshooting the system can be obtained from a study of the wiring diagrams.

To test rear window wiper/washer switch:

1. Disconnect the battery's negative (−) cable.
2. Working behind the dashboard, disconnect the wiring harness from the wires attached to the switch.

> **NOTE ——**
> You must make your tests at the connector that remains attached to the switch. To gain access, you may have to remove the switch from the dashboard. Late models have a pop-out rocker switch. To remove the early-type switch, first loosen the setscrew at the bottom of the switch knob, then unscrew the knob by turning it counterclockwise. Then remove the hollow bolt that holds the switch in the dashboard so that you can pull the switch out from behind the dashboard.

3. Using an ohmmeter or a battery-powered test light, make continuity tests at the switch connector. With the washer switch on, there should be continuity between connector terminals E and W. With the wiper switch turned off, there should be continuity between connector terminals S (or −S) and +1. With the wiper switch turned on, there should be continuity between connector terminals B and +1. Replace faulty switches.

7.2 Removing, Servicing, and Installing Wiper Blades and Arms

The windshield wiper blade and the optional rear window wiper blade are easy to remove and install because they are held securely to the wiper arms by screws. To remove a wiper blade, remove the two Phillips head screws that hold it to the wiper arm. Installation is the reverse of removal.

New rubber fillers are available to repair the wiper blades. Although you can replace a rubber filler without removing the wiper blade from the wiper arm, the work is much easier if you remove the blade first. Fig. 7-5 gives the names of the various wiper blade components.

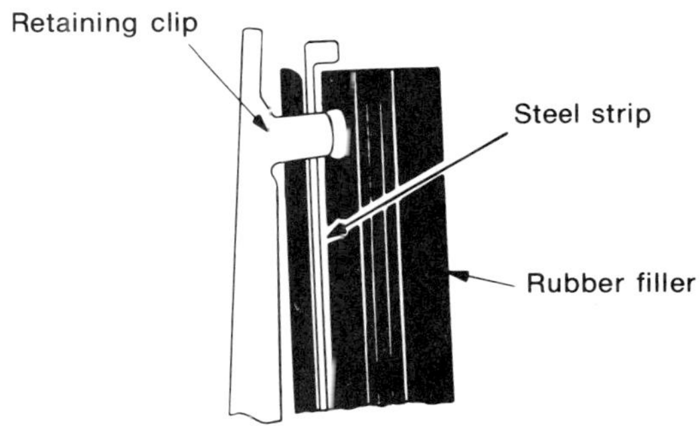

Fig. 7-5. Main wiper blade components involved in rubber filler replacement.

To replace rubber filler:

1. Remove the wiper blade from the wiper arm.
2. Using pliers, tightly compress the steel strip at the point indicated in Fig. 7-6. Then twist one side of the strip out of the retaining clip.

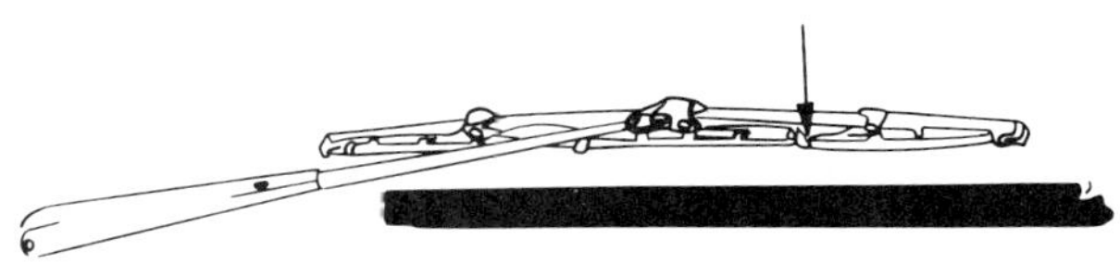

Fig. 7-6. Retaining clip (arrow) from which steel strip and rubber filler should be disengaged by compressing the steel strip.

3. With the free side of the retaining clip resting in the groove with the steel strip, repeat the preceding step to free the other side of the filler and the steel strip from the retaining clip.

4

4. Slide the rubber filler and the steel strip as far as possible toward the end of the wiper blade frame—toward the end that is closest to the retaining clip that has been disengaged. Slide the filler and the steel strip out of the two retaining clips at the opposite end of the blade frame.
5. Slide the steel strip and the rubber filler in the opposite direction to withdraw them from the remaining retaining clip.
6. Spread the steel apart in the middle, then feed both ends of the rubber filler toward the center of the steel strip, pulling the rubber filler out of the middle of the steel strip.
7. Install the new rubber filler in the steel strip, reversing the procedure given in the preceding step. That is, slide each end of the filler from the center of the steel strip outward.
8. Reversing the removal procedure, reinstall the steel strip and the rubber filler in the wiper blade frame. Then install the wiper blade on the arm.

Removing, Installing, and Adjusting Wiper Arms

The wiper arm is held to the wiper shaft by a special nut. When removing the wiper arm, hold it stationary while you remove the nut so that strain will not be placed on the wiper linkage and motor. Fig. 7-7 illustrates the removal of a wiper arm. On 1977 and later rear window wipers and on 1978 and later windshield wipers, the nut is hidden by a plastic cover, which you must pry off before you can remove the nut.

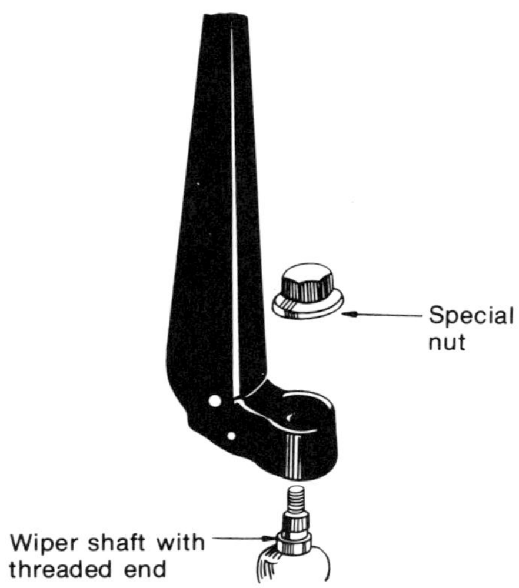

Fig. 7-7. Exploded view of wiper arm and wiper arm nut.

The wiper arms must be adjusted to the correct angles during installation. The wipers can operate correctly in all weather conditions only when the arms are positioned accurately, to the dimensions given in Fig. 7-8. After you have adjusted the angle of the wiper arms, torque the nuts to 7 Nm (5 ft. lb. or 62 in. lb.).

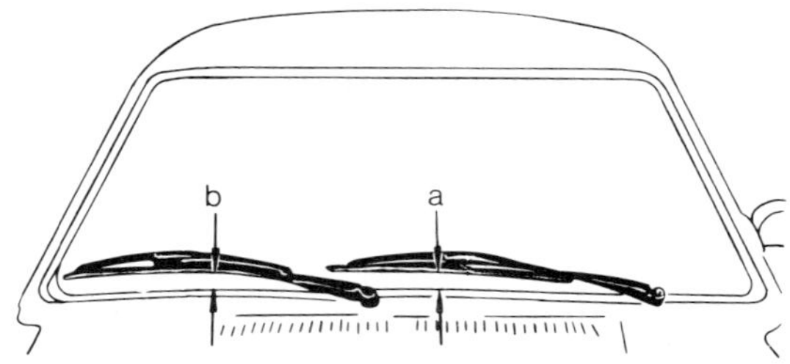

Fig. 7-8. Points where wiper arm adjustment is measured. Distance **b** is 40 mm (1 9/16 in.) and distance **a** is 27 mm (1 1/16 in.), measured from point where glass meets weather seal to center of screws that hold wiper blades to wiper arms.

7.3 Removing and Installing Wiper Motors

The windshield wiper motor is mounted in the rear right-hand corner of the engine compartment, on the firewall. The rear window wiper motor is housed inside the rear lid of the liftback model and inside the trunk of the sport coupe.

To remove windshield wiper motor:

1. Raise the hood. Disconnect the battery's negative cable.
2. Disconnect the multiple connector from the wiper motor.
3. Remove the sheet metal screws that hold the access plate to the firewall. Remove the three bolts that hold the wiper motor to the firewall. See Fig. 7-9.

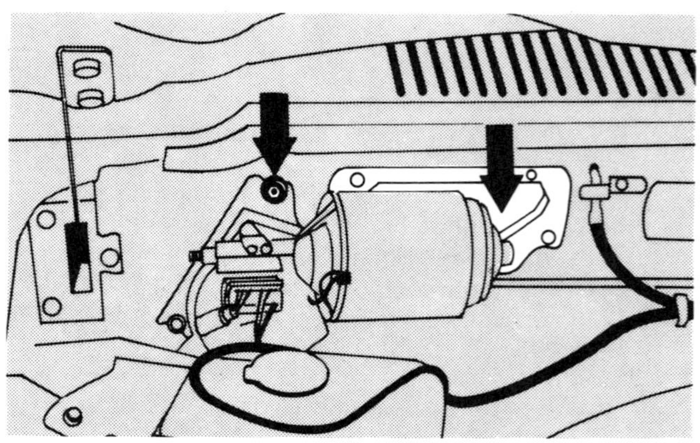

Fig. 7-9. Access plate (right arrow) and one of three motor-mounting bolts (left arrow).

3. Partially withdraw the motor from the firewall. Then, using a screwdriver, carefully pry the wiper operating link off the ball pin on the motor's drive crank. Remove the motor from the car.

To install windshield wiper motor:

1. If you have removed the drive crank, if you are installing a new motor, or if you have disassembled the motor for repairs, adjust the drive crank before you install the motor in the car.

NOTE ——

To adjust the drive crank, you must temporarily reconnect the battery's negative (–) cable and the multiple connector for the motor. Otherwise, the motor will not park correctly. Run the motor for about 3 minutes. Then turn off the windshield wiper switch without disconnecting the multiple connector. The motor will stop in its parking position. Install the drive crank to the angle indicated in Fig. 7-10.

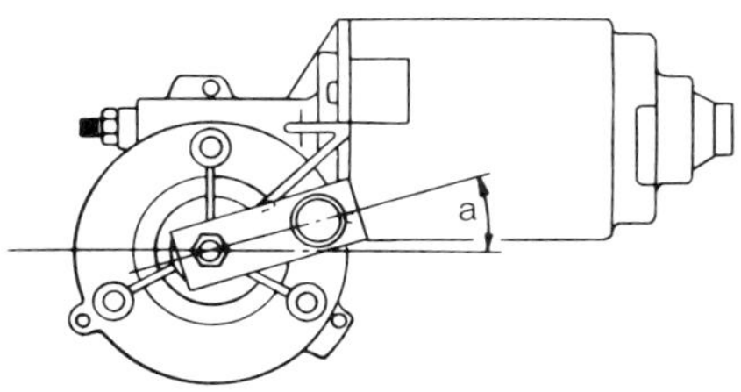

Fig. 7-10. Drive crank correctly installed with motor in parking position. Angle **a** should be 9° to 10°.

2. Position the wiper motor loosely on the firewall, then reconnect the wiper operating link to the motor's drive crank by pressing it onto the ball pin.

3. Loosely install the bolts that hold the wiper motor to the firewall. Using the sheet metal screws, install the access plate.

4. Tighten the wiper motor mounting bolts. Reconnect the multiple connector and the battery's negative (–) cable. Then operate the wipers to make sure that they park correctly.

CAUTION ——

If the wiper blades do not park in the correct positions, the drive crank is not correctly installed on the motor. Do not attempt to correct the problem by repositioning the wiper arms on the wiper shafts, as doing so will place excessive starting loads on the motor, owing to the incorrect drive crank angle.

To remove rear window wiper:

1. Make sure that the rear window wiper arm is in its parked position. Then disconnect the battery's negative (–) cable.

2. Remove the wiper arm as described in **7.2 Removing, Servicing, and Installing Wiper Blades and Arms.** Then remove the nut, the washer, and the seals that hold the wiper shaft bearing in the car body or rear lid. 4

3. Working inside the car, remove the access cover for the rear window wiper motor and frame. Then remove the three bolts that hold the wiper frame to the car body or rear lid and remove the wiper motor and frame as a unit.

CAUTION ——

If for any reason you intend to disassemble the wiper motor or remove it from the frame, mark the positions of all shafts, arms, cranks, gears, and links prior to disassembly. Doing so will enable you to reassemble the rear window wiper parts in their original relationships so that the wiper will park correctly.

Installation is the reverse of removal. Before returning the car to service, be sure to test the operation of the wiper to make sure that it parks correctly.

7.4 Disassembling and Assembling Wiper Motors

Fig. 7-11 is an exploded view of the Nippodenso windshield wipers used on 1975 and later cars; Fig. 7-12 is an exploded view of the Tanaka windshield wiper motor used on 1975 through early 1978 cars; and Fig. 7-13 is an exploded view of the rear window wiper motor. You can use these exploded views as a guide to disassembling and assembling the wiper motors. Some of the components are not available as individual replacement parts. If one of the unavailable components is worn out or damaged, replace the wiper motor as a unit. The wiper linkage is basically similar on all cars covered by this Manual.

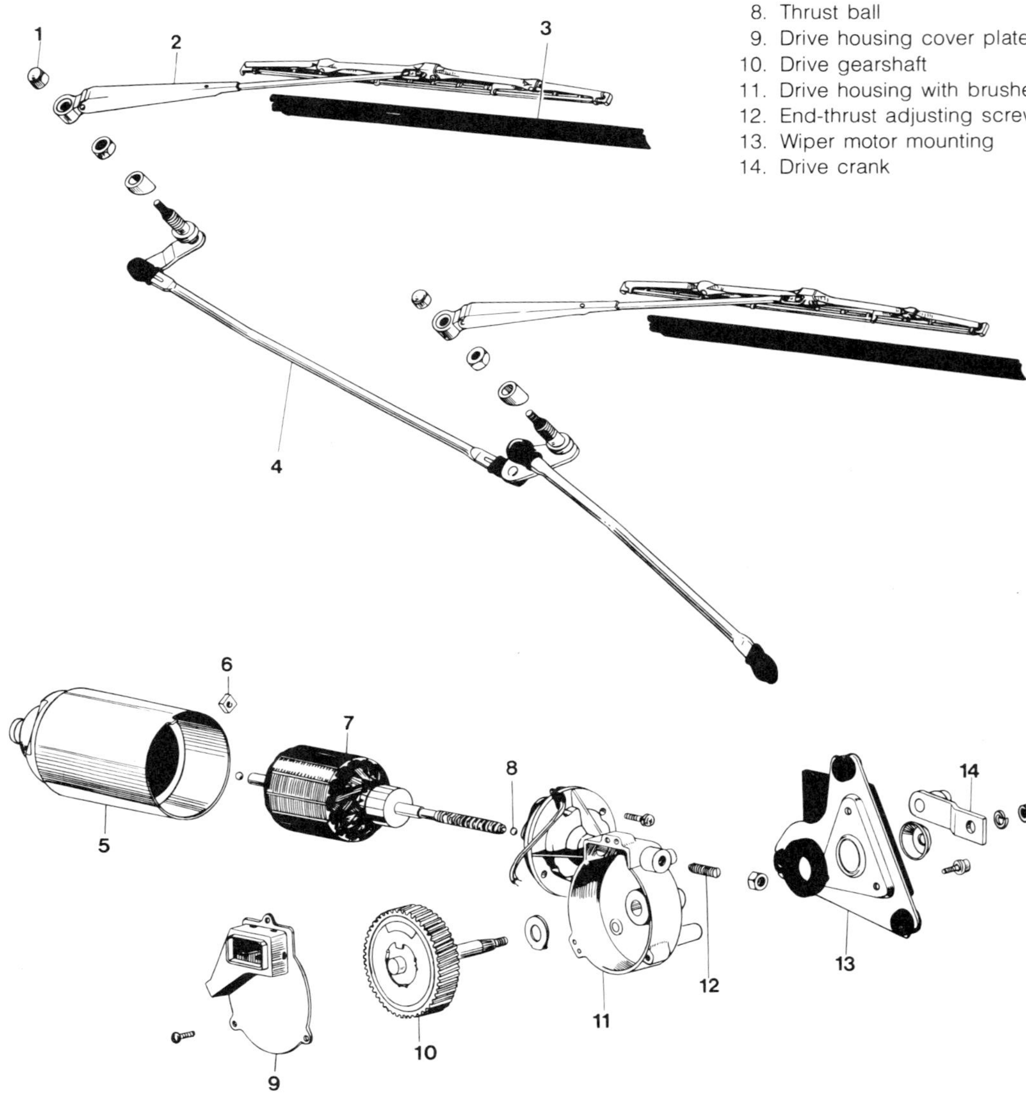

1. Special nut
2. Wiper arm
3. Wiper blade
4. Wiper linkage assembly
5. Motor housing with magnets
6. Housing retaining lug
7. Armature
8. Thrust ball
9. Drive housing cover plate
10. Drive gearshaft
11. Drive housing with brushes
12. End-thrust adjusting screw
13. Wiper motor mounting
14. Drive crank

Fig. 7-11. Exploded view of Nippodenso windshield wiper motor with linkage and blades.

1. Housing retaining lug
2. Motor housing with magnets
3. Armature
4. Thrust ball
5. Drive crank
6. Wiper motor mounting
7. Screw
8. Brush holder
9. Screw
10. Drive shaft
11. End thrust adjusting screw
12. Drive housing
13. Thrust ball
14. Drive gear
15. Gasket
16. Drive housing cover plate

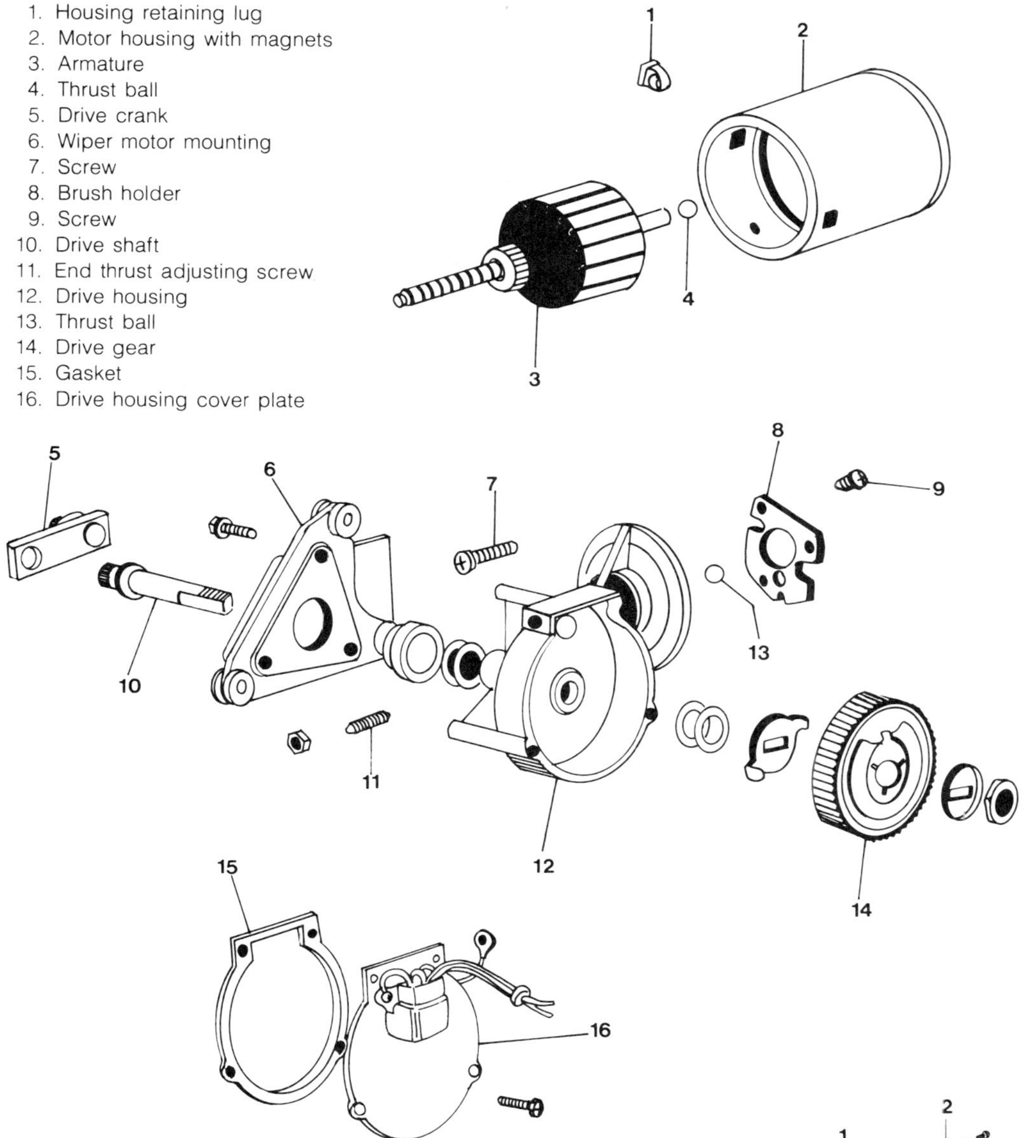

Fig. 7-12. Exploded view of Tanaka windshield wiper motor.

4

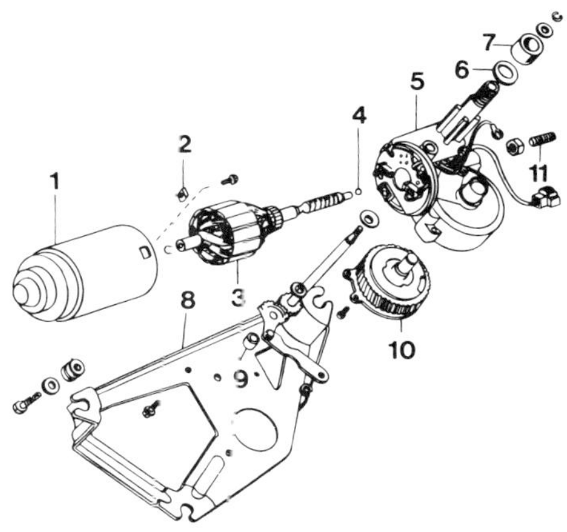

1. Motor housing with magnets
2. Housing retaining lug
3. Armature
4. Thrust ball
5. Drive housing with brushes
6. Washer
7. Weather seal
8. Frame
9. Stop
10. Drive gearshaft
11. End-thrust adjusting screw

Fig. 7-13. Exploded view of rear window wiper motor, which is optional equipment on some cars covered by this Manual.

When assembling a wiper motor, you should adjust the armature's end thrust by turning the end-thrust adjusting screw. To do this, connect the negative (−) post of the battery to the motor's ground wire or drive housing, and connect an ammeter in series between the battery's positive (+) post and the motor's +1 terminal. See Fig. 7-14. Loosen the end-thrust adjusting screw so that the motor runs freely with fewer than 2 amperes. Gradually tighten the screw until the amperage just increases; this increase indicates that the screw is placing a load on the motor. From this position, loosen the adjusting screw only to the point where the amperage falls to its original reading. Then tighten the locknut. If you have adjusted the end thrust correctly, there will be zero clearance between the adjusting screw and the thrust ball, but the screw will place no load on the armature.

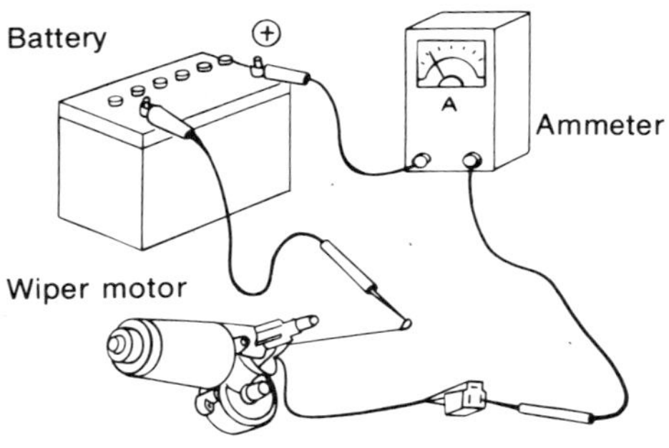

Fig. 7-14. Wiper motor connected to battery so that load on motor can be determined by ammeter readings.

7.5 Windshield Washer and Rear Window Washer

If the windshield washer spray does not strike the glass correctly, you can change the aim by slightly bending the discharge nozzles, which are located in the fresh-air intake slots ahead of the windshield. You can bend the nozzles easily with needle-nose pliers, but be sure that you do not squeeze the tubing so that it becomes flattened or deformed. On rear window washers, you can turn the nozzle one way or the other with your fingers to aim the spray (or use a sewing needle inserted in the jet to adjust the ball position). You can usually clean clogged jets by inserting a sewing needle, as indicated in Fig. 7-15.

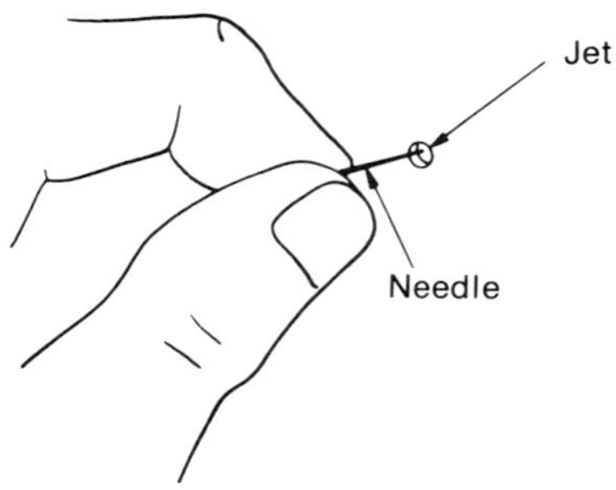

Fig. 7-15. Sewing needle being used to clean clogged washer jet.

To remove the electric pump, first remove the washer reservoir from the car. Then unbolt the pump from the reservoir and pull the pump out of the rubber grommet that is in the bottom of the tank. See Fig. 7-16. To remove the reservoir for the rear window washer, you must first remove the jack carrier, as indicated in Fig. 7-17.

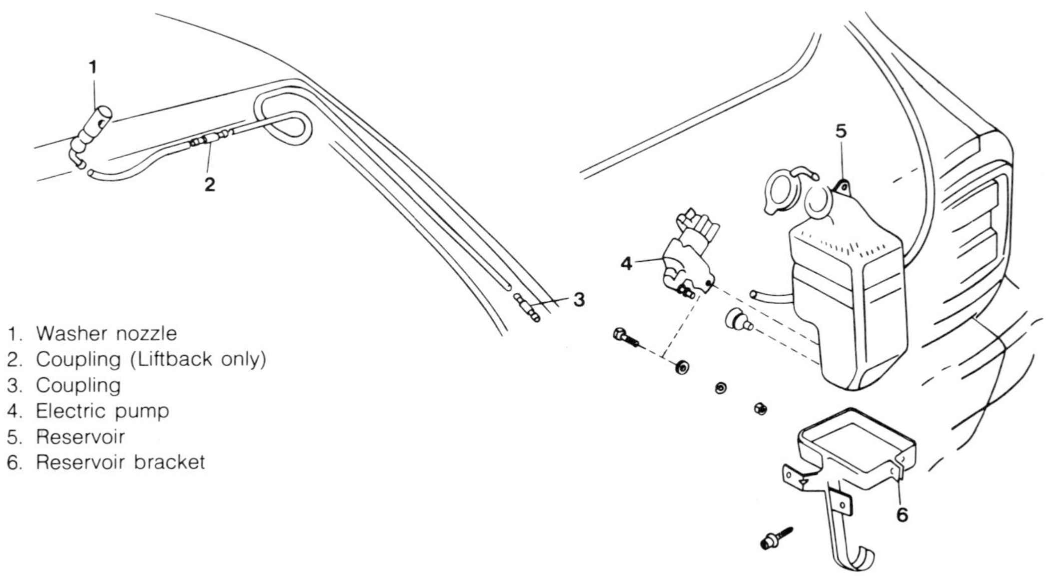

Fig. 7-16. Rear window washer installation.

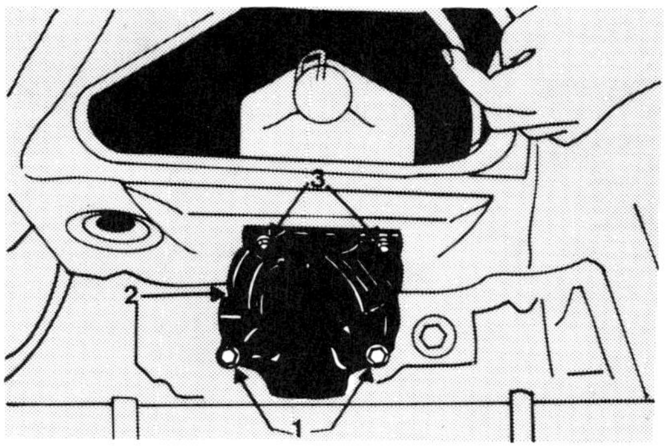

Fig. 7-17. Rear window washer reservoir removal. Remove bolts (**1**) for jack carrier (**2**). Then remove reservoir bracket bolts (**3**). Take out reservoir, detach hose, and then remove reservoir and electric pump from car.

The rear window washer nozzle is a separate component and can be replaced if it is faulty. To remove the discharge tube, first carefully pry off the nozzle, using pads beneath the screwdrivers. Then pry out the discharge tube and detach it from the hose. See Fig. 7-18.

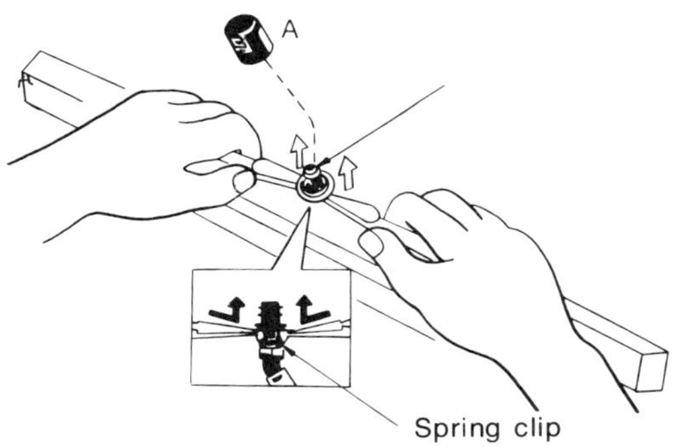

Fig. 7-18. Rear window washer discharge tube being removed. First pry off nozzle (**A**). Then pry out discharge tube (inset).

8. LIGHTS AND SWITCHES

For safety reasons, it is important that all lights on the vehicle be working properly at all times. Correct headlight aim is also necessary for safe night driving. However, since some state governments have restricted headlight adjustment work to state-qualified mechanics, be sure to check your state's motor vehicle laws before you attempt headlight adjustments.

8.1 Removing and Installing Sealed Beam Units and Aiming Headlights

Except on the Liftback and Sport Coupe models, you must remove the radiator grille before you can replace a sealed beam unit. On the Liftback and the Sport Coupe, it is necessary to remove only the headlight trim, as indicated in Fig. 8-1. To remove the grille on other models, open the hood and remove the screws that hold the top of the grille to the front of the body. Then remove the Phillips head screws from the recesses in the front of the grille and remove the grille from the car.

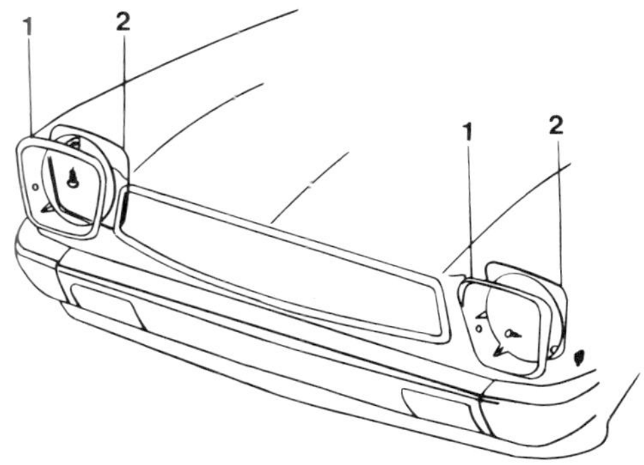

Fig. 8-1. Headlight trim removal. Take out screws, then pull out headlight trim (**1**), being careful not to damage weather seal (**2**).

Once you have removed the grille or the headlight trim, loosen (without removing) the three screws that hold the retaining ring. Then rotate the ring counterclockwise to disengage it from the screw heads and remove it from the car. Pull the sealed beam unit forward and disconnect the wiring harness from the terminals.

CAUTION —

Do not alter the positions of the long headlight adjustment screws indicated in Fig. 8-2. If you do, you will have to readjust the headlight aim.

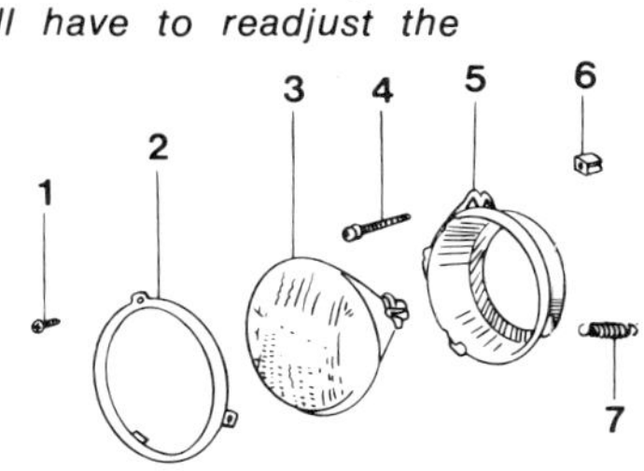

1. Short screw for retaining ring (3)
2. Retaining ring
3. Sealed beam unit
4. Long headlight adjustment screw (2)
5. Sealed beam support ring
6. Threaded lug for adjustment screw (2)
7. Tension spring for support ring

Fig. 8-2. Components of headlight assembly. These parts are attached to headlight mount, which is bolted to body.

When you install a sealed beam unit, be sure that its three glass lugs correctly engage the support ring. Install the retaining ring and then the grille or the headlight trim. It should not be necessary to aim the headlights after you change a sealed beam unit. If you are in doubt, however, check the aim.

Each headlight has two adjusting screws, which are accessible from the front of the car with the grille or the trim still in place. Adjust the vertical aim of each headlight with the top screw; adjust lateral aim with the screw at the side of the headlight.

NOTE —

Check your state laws to determine whether adjustments must be made by a licensed shop. Your state may also have laws that specify aiming different from that described here.

To check and adjust headlight aim:

1. Position the car on a level surface 7.5 m (or 25 ft.) from a vertical wall. Have the fuel tank about half-filled and make certain that the tire pressures are correct.
2. Roll the car back and forth a few yards to settle the suspension. Then have someone sit in the driver's seat, or load the seat with a 70-kg (154-lb.) weight.
3. Turn on the headlights and, if necessary, switch them to low beam. Cover one headlight at a time. The uncovered light's upper and left edges of high intensity should be in the positions shown in Fig. 8-3. If not, adjust the light's position, using the adjustment screws that are accessible from the front of the car. (The headlight trim has holes or channels through which you can insert a Phillips head screwdriver.)

NOTE —

It is unnecessary to adjust the headlight aim on high beam. The high beams will automatically be in adjustment once the low beams are aimed to the correct specifications.

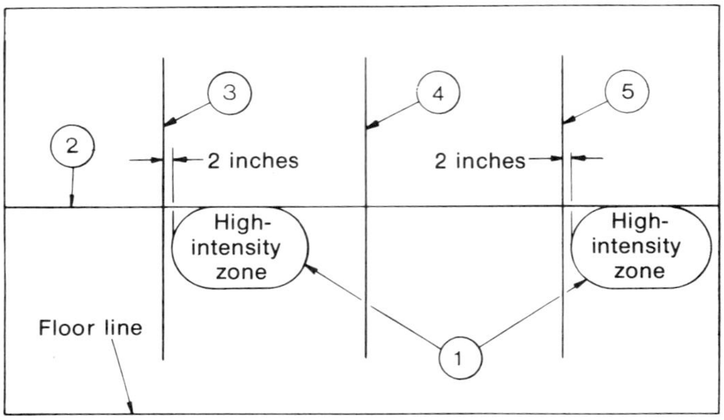

Fig. 8-3. Low-beam aiming target on vertical wall. High-intensity areas are at **1**. Line **2** is at height of headlight centers. Vertical line **4** is vehicle centerline. Vertical lines **3** and **5** are spaced equally on each side of line **4**, and are exactly as far from one another as centers of sealed beam units.

8.2 Headlight Switch and Relay

The headlight switch is built into the end of the turn signal lever on the steering column. This lever also controls the dimming of the headlights. When it is pushed forward, away from the steering wheel rim, the headlights switch to high beam. When the lever is snapped back, the headlights switch to low beam. By pulling the lever back further against spring tension you can flash the high beams on whether the light switch is on or not.

Troubleshooting

If the headlights fail to operate, first check that the fusible link at the battery's positive (+) post is not burned out. If it is, the starter will operate but the rest of the electrical system will not. Locate the short that has overloaded the electrical system and repair it before you replace the fusible link.

The headlights and the taillights are controlled by separate relays. So if the taillights work but the headlights do not, the trouble is in the light control relay, which should be replaced. (The light control relay, located to the left of the battery, contains both the headlight relay and the taillight relay.)

To test the light control relay, turn on the ignition and then turn on the headlight switch. Measured with a voltmeter, approximately 12 volts should be available at relay connector terminals HB and TB when the voltmeter's negative (−) lead is connected to ground on some clean, unpainted metal part of the car and the positive lead is touched first to one of the designated terminals and then to the other (Fig. 8-4). If there is no voltage at terminal TB, either the wiring from the fuse box to the relay is faulty or the fuse marked TAIL is burned out. If there is no voltage at terminal HB, either the wiring between the relay and the battery is faulty or the fusible link is burned out.

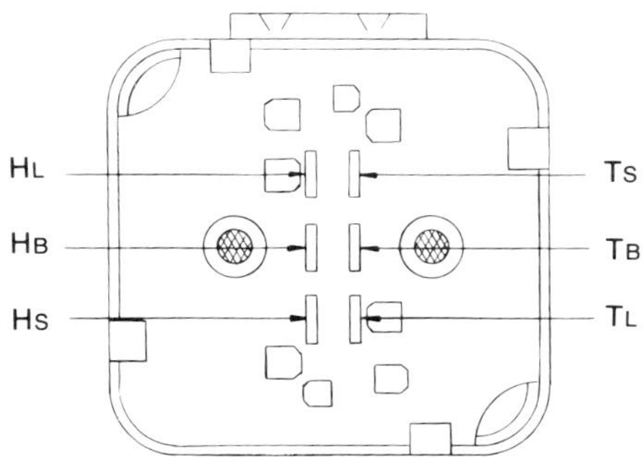

Fig. 8-4. Terminal designations on light control relay. H terminals serve headlights; T terminals serve taillights.

If voltage is reaching the relay, check that the multiple connector is correctly plugged into the relay and that all the terminals are clean and tight-fitting. If the lights still do not function correctly, use a jumper wire to ground first terminal TS and then terminal HS. When the terminal is grounded, the relay should make a clicking sound and the lights should come on. If not, the relay is faulty and should be replaced.

After disconnecting the relay, you can test the coil windings of the relays. With an ohmmeter connected to terminals TB and TS, there should be resistance of approximately 60 ohms. The same should be true if you connect the ohmmeter to terminals HB and HS. If the reading is infinity, the relay coil is open-circuited; if the resistance is considrably less than 60 ohms, the relay coil is shorted. Replace faulty relays.

If you find no trouble in the relay or the positive current supply, test the headlight switch. You can make the tests either with an ohmmeter or with a battery-powered test light.

To test headlight switch:

1. Disconnect the battery's negative (−) cable.
2. By removing the bolts, detach and remove the trim panel beneath the lower end of the steering column cover. Then take out the screws in the recesses and remove the steering column lower cover (Fig. 8-5). This will provide full access to the steering column multiple connector plug.

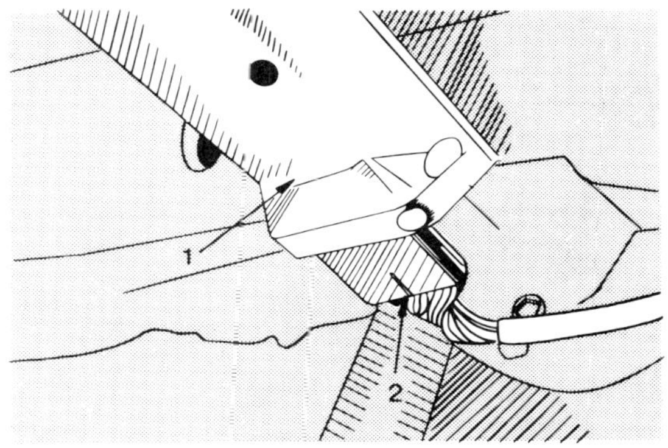

Fig. 8-5. Components to be removed and disconnected prior to testing headlight switch. Steering column lower cover is at **1**; multiple connector for wiring is at **2**.

3. By squeezing together the locking levers as indicated in Fig. 8-6, release the multiple connector locks. Then pull apart the multiple connector, disconnecting the switches from the car's electrical system.

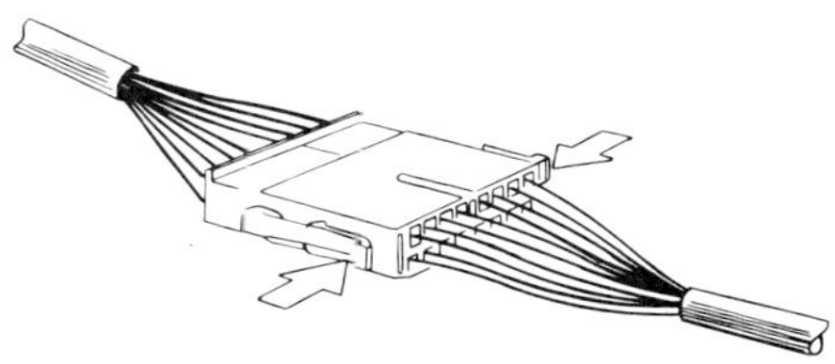

Fig. 8-6. Arrows indicating how locking levers must be squeezed together to disconnect steering column wiring multiple connector.

4

4. Using Fig. 8-7 as your guide, use an ohmmeter or a battery-powered test light to make continuity tests between different terminals of the multiple connector that is attached to the switches. **Table e** lists the terminals between which there should be continuity in each of the various switch positions.

NOTE ——

If you find any fault in the headlight OFF/ON rotary switch, you can repair the switch with a repair kit, as described later. If there is trouble in the dimmer switch, you should replace the steering column switch assembly as described earlier in **6.2 Removing and Installing Steering Column Switches.**

CAUTION ——

In applying the ohmmeter test probes to the multiple connector plug, be very careful not to bend or deform the terminals inside the plug. This could make it difficult to reconnect the multiple connector and also could cause electrical system trouble. The safest method for testing is to insert the test probes from the wire side of the plug.

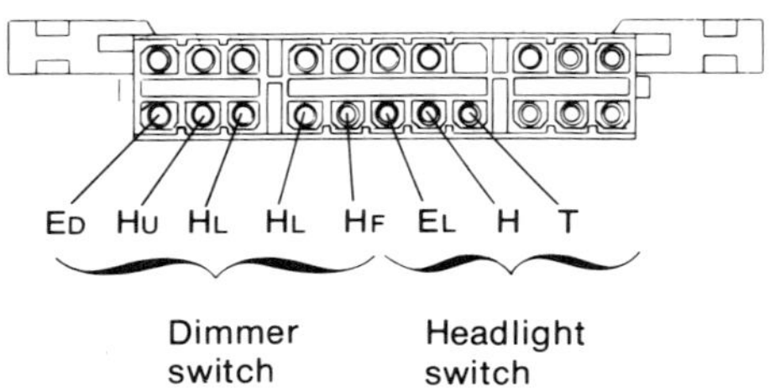

E_D	Ground
H_U	Headlight high (upper) beam
H_L	Headlight low beam
H_F	To light relay terminal H_S
E_L	Ground
H	To light relay terminal H_S
T	To light control relay terminal T_S

Fig. 8-7. Designations for headlight switch and dimmer switch terminals, located in multiple connector plug that is attached to steering column switches.

Table e. Headlight/Dimmer Switch Tests

Switch positions	Terminals between which there should be continuity
Headlight switch OFF	—
Headlight switch ON to first click (parking light position)	T and E_L
Headlight switch ON to second click (headlight position)	T and H and E_L
Headlight switch ON, dimmer switch pushed forward to high beam position	H_U and E_D
Headlight switch ON, dimmer switch in low beam position	H_L and E_D
Dimmer switch lever pulled toward steering wheel (headlight flashing position)	H_U and H_F and E_D

8.3 Replacing Bulbs

Table f lists the replacement bulbs suitable for the cars covered by this Manual. The identification number refers to the circled numbers in the illustrations that follow. To select a replacement bulb, find the illustration that shows how the bulb is replaced. Then find the identification number in the picture that points to the bulb shown. You can then determine the correct replacement bulb from the table by finding the identification number and then writing down the bulb number, which is the number on the bulb itself.

NOTE ——

On cars with an E.S.P. (Electro Sensor Panel), all bulbs in each circuit must be of the same wattage or the E.S.P. will indicate a failure erroneously.

To replace a front turn signal and parking light bulb, remove the screws indicated in Fig. 8-8. Then remove the lens, being careful not to tear the gasket. Remove or install the bulb by pressing it in and turning it counterclockwise to remove it or clockwise to install it. Reinstall the lens, being careful not to overtighten the screws, which could crack the lens.

Table f. Replacement bulbs

Designation	Identification number	Bulb number	Wattage
Front turn signal and parking lights	1	1157	27/8
Front side marker lights	2	194	5
Rear side marker lights (except 1975–76 sedan and coupe)	3	194	5
Rear side marker lights (1975–76 sedan and coupe)	3	67	8
Rear turn signal lights	4	1156	27
Stoplights and taillights	5	1157	27/8
Back-up lights	6	1156	27
License plate lights	7	89	7.5
Interior light	8	12V–10CP	10
Luggage compartment light	9	12V–3CP	5

4

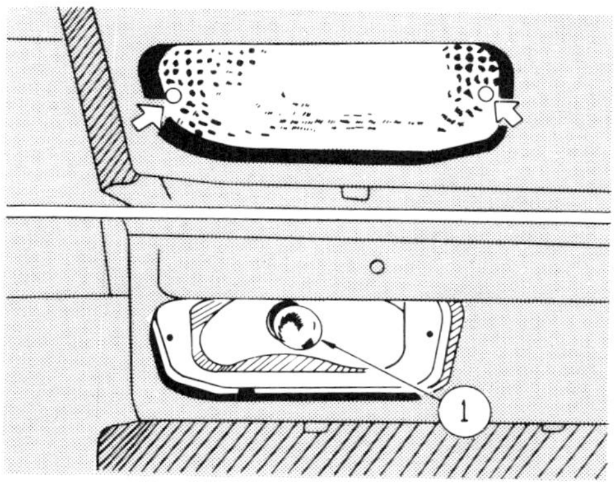

Fig. 8-8. Front turn signal and parking light bulb replacement. Arrows indicate screws that hold lens. Circled numeral is bulb identification number.

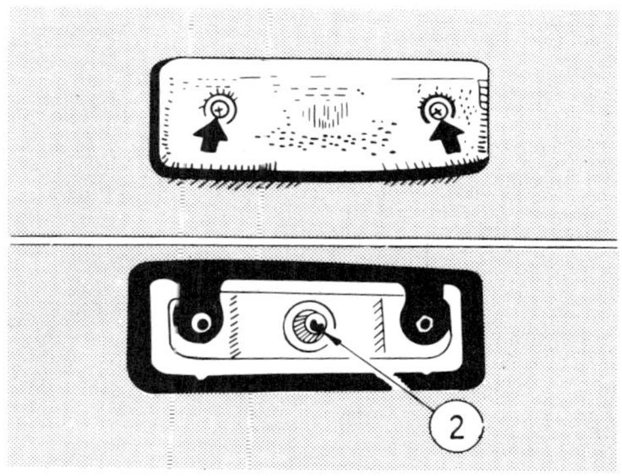

Fig. 8-9. Front side marker light bulb replacement. Arrows indicate screws that hold lens. Circled numeral is bulb identification number.

To replace a front side marker bulb, remove the screws indicated in Fig. 8-9. (Some late model lenses are merely snapped in place and can be pulled out.) Then remove the lens. Press the bulb in and turn it counterclockwise to remove or clockwise to install it. Be careful not to overtighten the screws for the lens, which could crack it.

To replace a rear side marker light bulb, (except on wagon models), open the trunk, tailgate, or rear lid. On liftback models, you must remove the interior trim to gain access to the bulb. Turn the entire bulb holder counterclockwise, then remove it as indicated in Fig. 8-10. Replace the bulb, then reinstall the bulb holder and, if necessary, the interior trim.

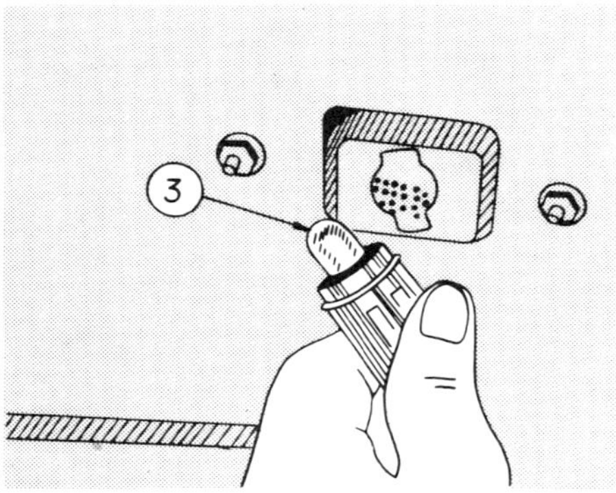

Fig. 8-10. Rear side marker light bulb replacement (except for wagon). Press bulb in to holder and turn counterclockwise to remove or clockwise to install. Circled numeral is bulb identification number.

To replace a rear side marker light bulb on a wagon, remove the screws indicated in Fig. 8-11. Then remove the lens. Press the bulb in and turn it counterclockwise to remove or clockwise to install it. Be careful not to overtighten the screws, which could crack the lens.

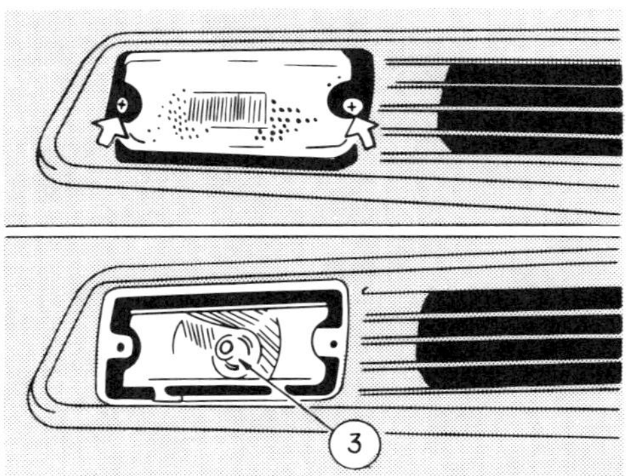

Fig. 8-11. Rear side marker light bulb replacement on wagon. Arrows indicate screws that hold lens. Circled numeral is bulb identification number.

Because of different designs and styling treatments, several different procedures are used for replacing the rear turn signal, stoplight, taillight, and back-up light bulbs. Instructions for each model are given in Fig. 8-12, Fig. 8-13, Fig. 8-14, Fig. 8-15, Fig. 8-16, and Fig. 8-17.

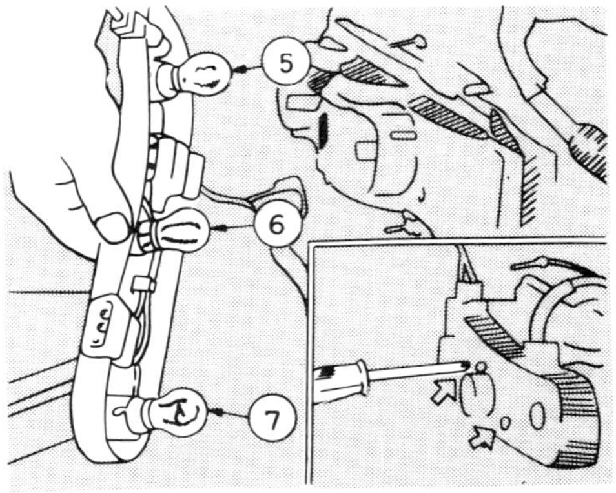

Fig. 8-12. Sedan rear light bulb replacement. Open trunk. Use Phillips screwdriver to remove two screws in recesses indicated by arrows. Then withdraw bulb holder. Press bulb in and turn counterclockwise to remove or clockwise to install. Circled numerals are bulb identification numbers.

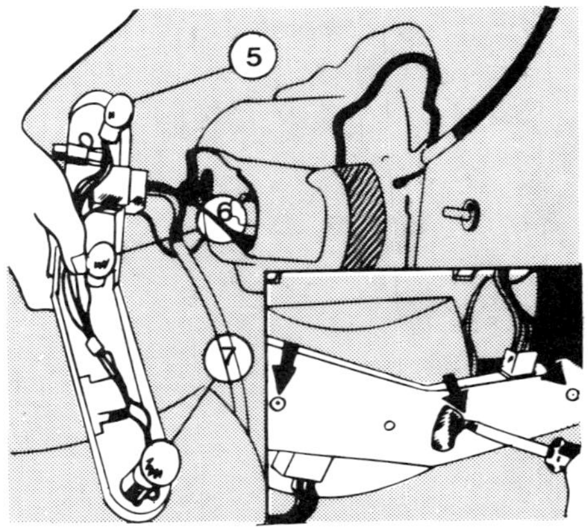

Fig. 8-13. 1975 hardtop rear light bulb replacement. Open trunk. Use Phillips screwdriver to remove three screws in recesses indicated by arrows. Then withdraw bulb holder. Press bulb in and turn counterclockwise to remove or clockwise to install. Circled numerals are bulb identification numbers.

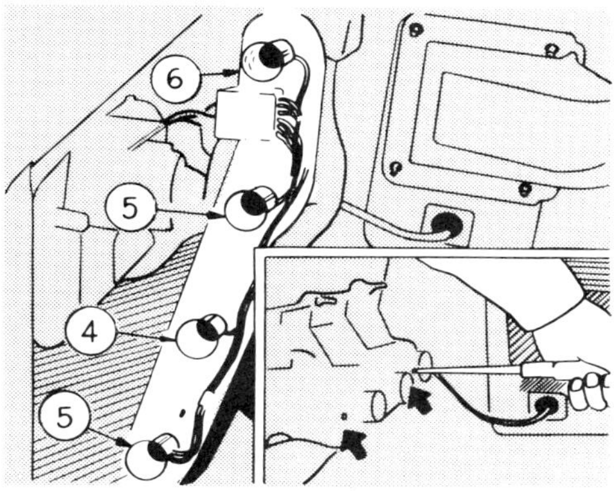

Fig. 8-14. 1976 and later hardtop rear light bulb replacement. Open trunk. Use Phillips screwdriver to remove three screws indicated by arrows and screwdriver. Then withdraw bulb holder. Press bulb in and turn counterclockwise to remove or clockwise to install. Circled numerals are bulb identification numbers.

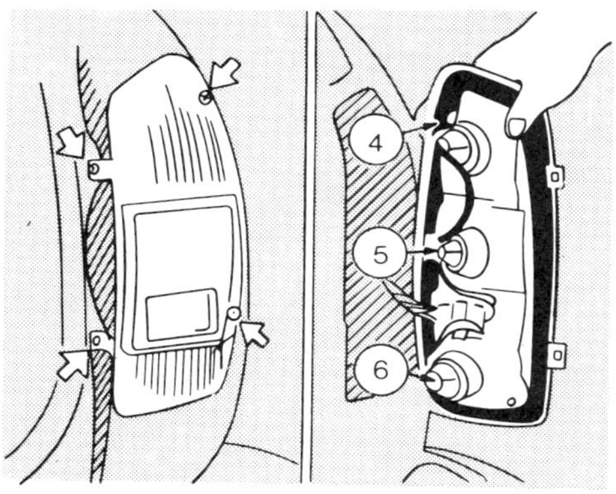

Fig. 8-15. Wagon rear light bulb replacement. Open tailgate. Remove four Phillips head screws indicated by arrows. Remove taillight assembly from fender as indicated. Press bulb in and turn counterclockwise to remove or clockwise to install. Circled numerals are bulb identification numbers.

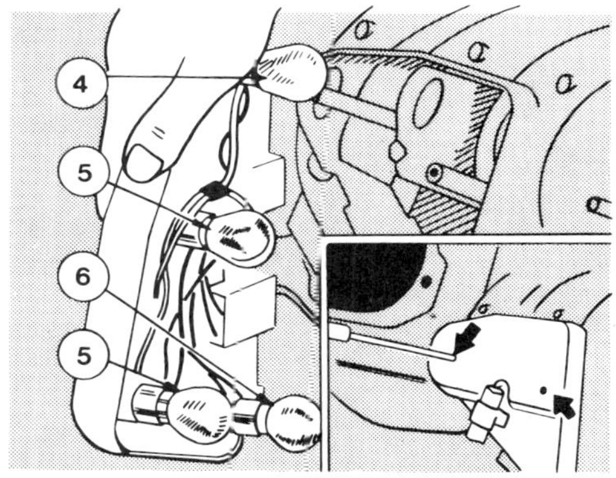

Fig. 8-16. Coupe rear light bulb replacement. Open trunk. Remove two Phillips head screws in recesses indicated by arrows. Press bulb in and turn counterclockwise to remove or clockwise to install. Circled numerals are bulb identification numbers.

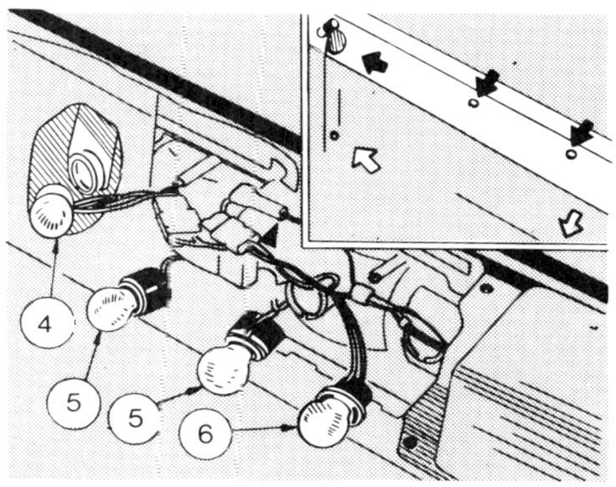

Fig. 8-17. Liftback rear light bulb replacement. Open rear lid. Remove five screws indicated by arrows, then remove interior trim piece. Turn individual bulb holders to release them from light assembly. Press bulb in and turn counterclockwise to remove or clockwise to install. Circled numerals are bulb identification numbers.

To replace the license plate light bulb on a 1975 or 1976 sedan or hardtop, remove the screws indicated by arrows in Fig. 8-18. Remove the lens and cover. Press the bulb counterclockwise for removal or clockwise for installation.

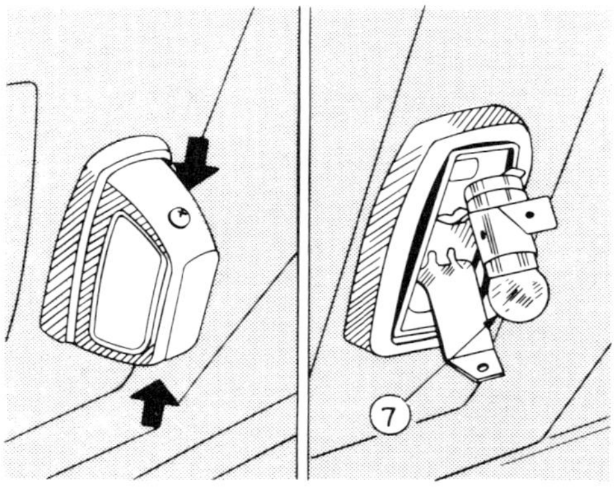

Fig. 8-18. 1975 and 1976 sedan and hardtop license light bulb replacement. Circled numerals are bulb identification numbers.

To replace the license plate light bult on all 1977 and later models other than wagons, you must remove the light assembly from the body as indicated in Fig. 8-19. On liftback models, you must remove the luggage area rear trim for access to the nuts that hold the light assembly to the car. Remove the light assembly, then remove the two Phillips head screws from the rear of the assembly and pull the assembly apart. Press the bulb in, then turn it counterclockwise to remove it or clockwise to install it.

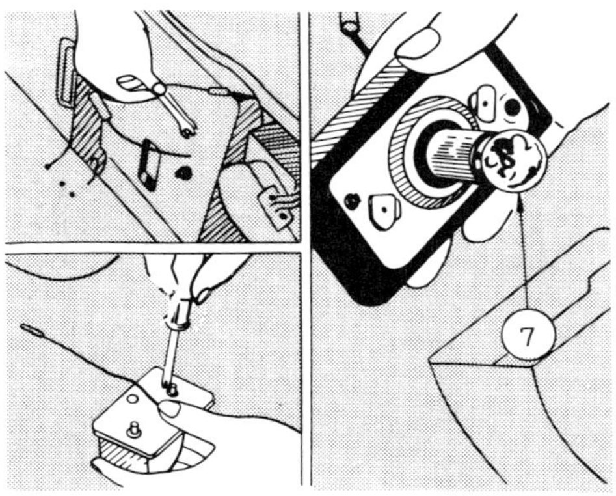

Fig. 8-19. 1977 and later license light bulb replacement (except for wagon). Sedan is shown, but other models are similar. Remove screws to take off lens and cover as indicated in lower left inset. Circled numeral is bulb identification number.

To replace the license plate light bulb on a wagon, open the tailgate. Then take out the screws indicated in Fig. 8-20. Remove the lens. Press the bulb in and turn it counterclockwise to remove it or clockwise to install it. During installation, be careful not to overtighten the screws, which could crack the lens.

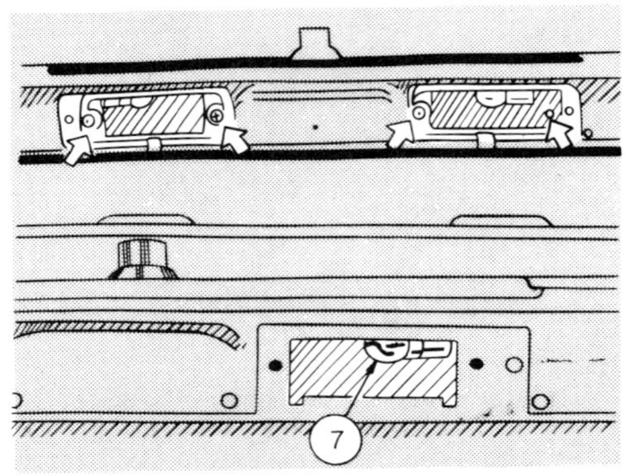

Fig. 8-20. Wagon license light bulb replacement. Arrows indicate screws that hold lens. Circled numeral is bulb identification number.

To replace the interior light bulb, carefully disengage the lens from the light fixture. Pull the double-end bulb straight out (Fig. 8-21) while applying side pressure toward one spring terminal. When you remove or install the bulb, be careful not to bend the spring terminals, as doing this can cause the bulb to fit loosely. Test the bulb operation, then snap the lens in place.

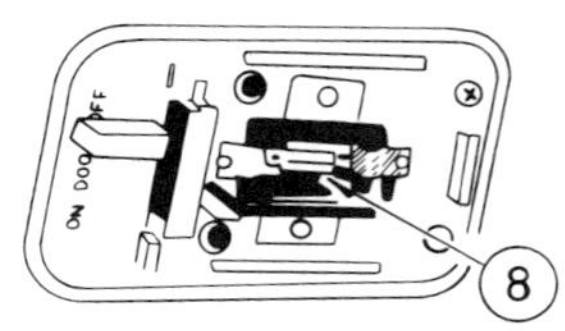

Fig. 8-21. Interior light bulb replacement. Lens is removed in this illustration. Circled numeral is bulb identification number.

To replace the luggage compartment light bulb on liftback models, remove the screws indicated in Fig. 8-22. Remove the lens. Pull the double-end bulb straight out. When you remove or install the bulb, be careful not to bend the spring terminals, as doing this can cause the bulb to fit loosely. During installation, be careful not to overtighten the screws, which could crack the lens.

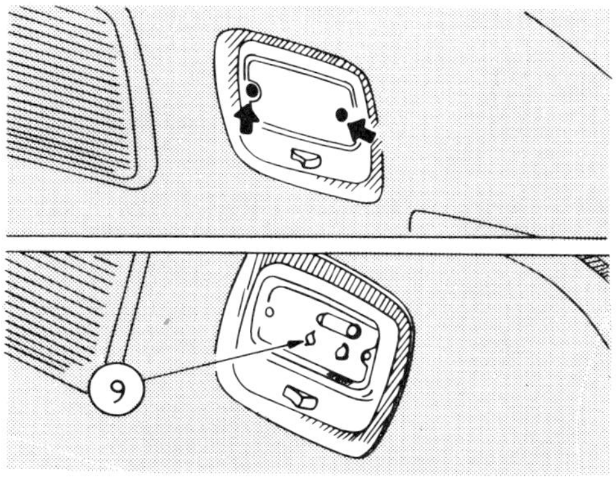

Fig. 8-22. Liftback luggage compartment light bulb replacement. Arrows indicate screws that hold lens. Circled numeral is bulb identification number.

8.4 Switches

Fig. 8-23 gives the locations of the various switches on the car. Other than the ignition switch, which is covered under the next unnumbered heading, the procedures for removing and installing each switch will be apparent once you have obtained access to the switch. The removal and installation of the various interior trim pieces is described in **BODY AND INTERIOR.** However, you can pull out most dashboard switches from behind the dashboard after you have unscrewed their knobs and removed the retaining nut. The removal and installation of the steering column switches is described in **6.2 Removing and Installing Steering Column Switches.**

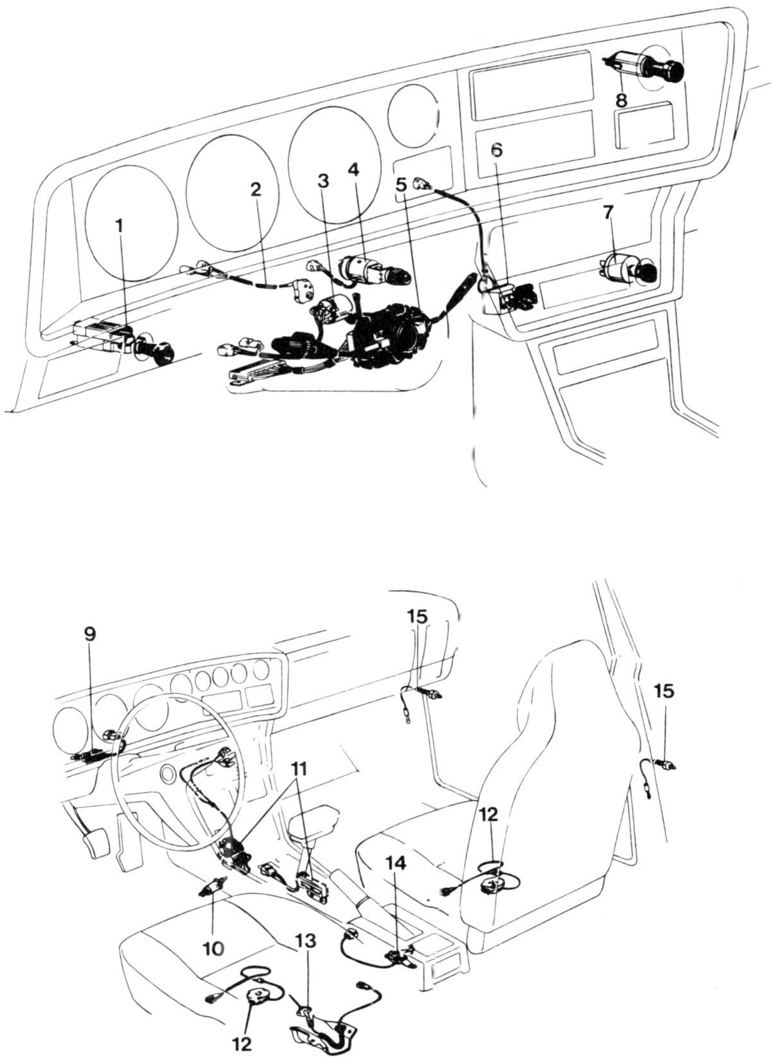

1. Rear window wiper/washer switch (optional)
2. Key warning buzzer switch
3. Ignition switch
4. Rheostat
5. Steering column switch assembly
6. Rear window defogger switch (1975 and 1976)
7. Heater fan switch
8. Cigarette lighter
9. Brake light switch (on pedal bracket)
10. Back-up light switch (manual transmission only)
11. Neutral safety switch (automatic transmission only)
12. Seat switch (early 1975 cars only)
13. Catalytic converter thermo sensor (catalytic converter models only)
14. Parking brake switch
15. Door switch

Fig. 8-23. Locations of switches on car.

Removing and Installing Ignition Switch

You can replace the ignition switch's electrical part without replacing the entire ignition switch/steering column lock assembly. Removal and installation of the lock cylinder and of the lock assembly housing are covered in **SUSPENSION AND STEERING**.

To remove:

1. Disconnect the battery's negative (−) cable.
2. Using a Phillips screwdriver, remove the screws that are in recesses in the steering column lower cover. Then remove the steering column upper cover.
3. Unplug the multiple connector from the wiring that is attached to the ignition switch. Then remove the Phillips head screw indicated in Fig. 8-24 and remove the switch from the car.

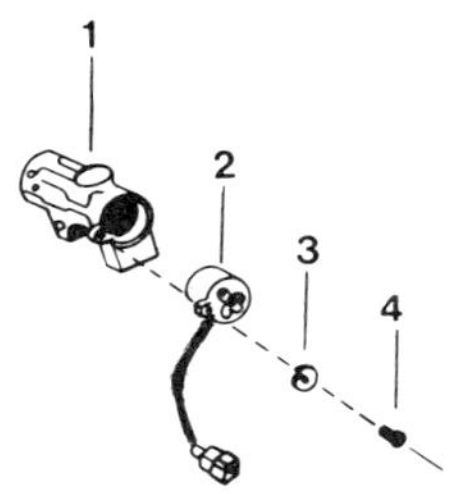

1. Upper half of ignition/steering column lock assembly
2. Ignition switch
3. Lockwasher
4. Phillips head screw

Fig. 8-24. Exploded view of ignition lock and switch, showing installation.

Installation is the reverse of removal. If necessary, you can test the switch for continuity with an ohmmeter, using the wiring diagrams as a guide. Fig. 8-25 identifies the switch terminals. Replace faulty switches.

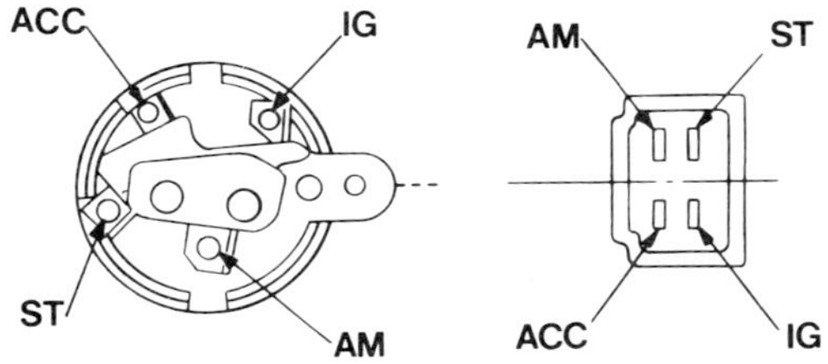

Fig. 8-25. Identification of terminals on ignition switch and multiple connector for switch. Terminal AM is connected to battery at all times via fusible link.

9. HORN AND BUZZER

The horn controls in the steering wheel consist of simple contacts that you can inspect after removing the steering wheel pad (three-spoke wheels) or taking apart the horn control boxes (four-spoke steering wheels). The horn controls on the steering wheel directly control the horn circuit; there is no horn relay.

9.1 Horn Troubleshooting and Adjusting

The horn circuit is protected by a fuse in the fuse box. If the horn fails to operate, check that the fuse is not burned out. If it is, find the short that has caused the overload and repair it before you replace the fuse.

The horn is burned out if there is no electrical continuity between its two terminals. But if damage has not broken continuity, it may still be possible to adjust the horn if it is not working. Typically, if the horn is receiving full battery voltage but makes only a soft clicking sound (or has a poor tone), you can remedy the malfunction by adjustment.

> ***CAUTION —***
> *Do not make needless horn adjustments. Misadjustment can seriously damage the horn.*

To adjust the horn, first remove it from the car by disconnecting its wires and then unbolting it from the body. Then connect an ammeter in series with the horn. That is, positive polarity current for the horn must pass through the ammeter. Make repeated test adjustments by turning the screw that projects from the rear of the horn, off to one side. Strive to obtain the clearest sound with minimum amperage draw.

> ***CAUTION —***
> *Do not turn the adjusting screw while the horn is sounding. Doing this could damage the horn.*

If a suitable ammeter is not available, turn the adjusting screw counterclockwise until there is no sound when current is supplied to the horn. Then turn the screw clockwise very gradually (about ¼ turn at a time) until the horn has a clear tone. After adjustment, seal the adjusting screw with paint to keep the screw in place and prevent the entry of water.

Warning Buzzer

All cars covered by this Manual are equipped with an ignition key warning buzzer that sounds if the ignition key is in the lock when the driver's door is opened. The same buzzer serves the seat belt warning system. The buzzer is located behind the kick panel that is to the left of the driver's feet. If the buzzer functions as a key warning but fails to operate as a seat belt warning, check that current is reaching the seat belt warning relay, which is also behind the left kick panel. If current is reaching the relay when the ignition is on but no current is reaching the buzzer, the relay is faulty and should be replaced. If current is reaching the buzzer but the buzzer does not sound, check that the buzzer is grounded via the seat belt buckle switches when the belts are unbuckled. If you find no fault, the buzzer is faulty and should be replaced. The ignition key warning buzzer switch, located inside the steering column cover, is not a part of the ignition switch, so it can be replaced individually if it is faulty.

10. HEATING AND VENTILATION ELECTRICAL COMPONENTS

You can remove the heater fan without removing the heater from the car. Full removal of the heater is covered in **BODY AND INTERIOR.**

To remove motor:

1. Disconnect the battery's negative cable.
2. Working beneath the dashboard, in the driver's-side footwell, disconnect the heater wiring harness multiple connector indicated in Fig. 10-1.
3. Working in the passenger's-side footwell, detach and remove the right-hand defroster duct.

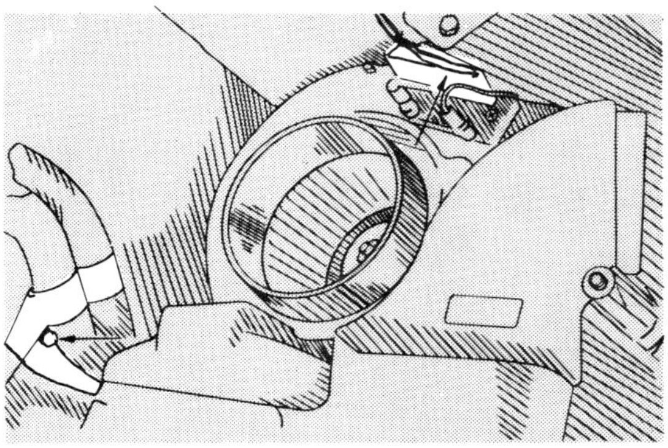

Fig. 10-1. Location of heater wiring harness multiple connector (arrow).

4. Remove the three bolts (Fig. 10-2) that hold the motor and fan to the heater housing. Then remove the blower and fan from the car.
5. If necessary, remove the fan from the motor assembly by taking off the nut.

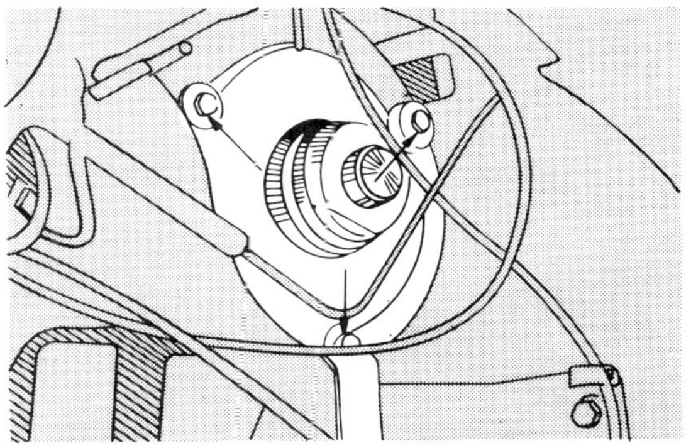

Fig. 10-2. Bolts (arrows) that hold heater motor and fan assembly to heater housing. Bolts are on right-hand side of heater.

4

Installation is the reverse of removal. Replacement parts for the motor itself are not available, so if the motor is faulty you should replace it as a unit. Also replace the gasket that goes between the motor mounting plate and the heater housing if the gasket is torn or otherwise damaged.

If the heater motor fails to operate on one or more speeds, you should test the heater fan switch and the heater control resistor. Fig. 10-3 identifies the terminals of the heater fan switch. After disconnecting the wiring from the switch, you can use an ohmmeter or a battery-powered test light to make continuity tests with the switch in each of its positions.

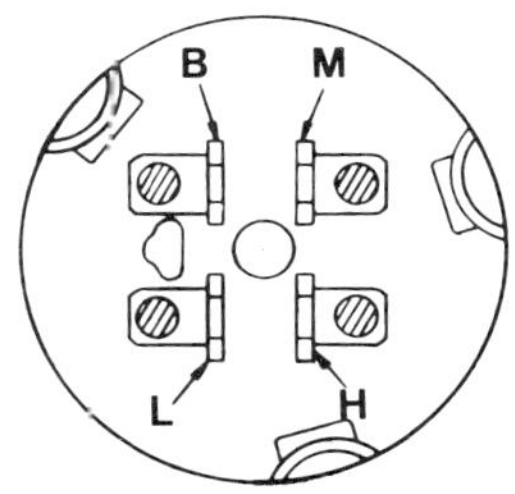

Switch position	Continuity between terminals
OFF	—
I	B and L
II	B and M
III	B and H

Fig. 10-3. Heater fan switch terminal designations and continuity between switch terminals in various switch positions.

You can test heater fan motor control resistor by using an ohmmeter to measure the resistance between the various terminals of the resistor. Fig. 10-4 identifies the resistor terminals and gives the correct resistances. Excessive resistance between terminals B and H indicates a faulty motor. The resistance figures given are approximate, so trouble is indicated by ohmmeter readings that are far from the correct figure.

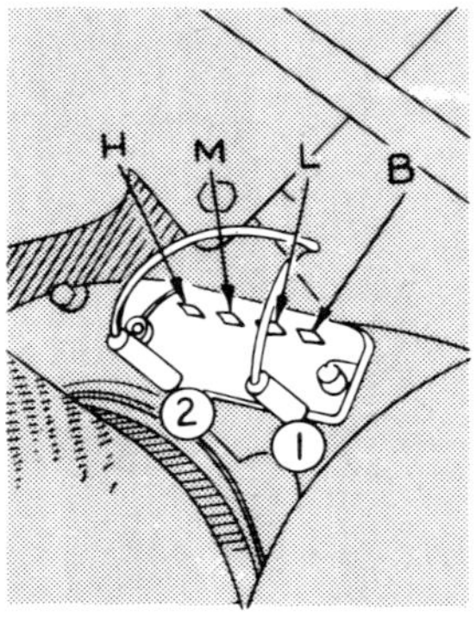

Terminals	Resistance (approximate)
B to H	20 ohms maximum
H to M	1.1 ohms
H to L	2.1 ohms

Fig. 10-4. Designations of terminals on heater fan motor control resistor, and correct resistances between terminals. Replace faulty control resistors.

Heated Rear Window

If the heated rear window fails to work and the indicator light beside the switch does not come on, check whether the dashboard gauges are operating and whether the back-up lights work. If the back-up lights and gauges fail to operate, the fuse marked DEFOG/BACK is burned out. If the fuse is all right and the heated rear window indicator light comes on, the heating grid is probably not operating because of a disconnected wire. If the wiring is not faulty, the trouble is likely to be in the heated rear window relay or in the relay's in-line fuse. (This fuse is held by colored tape to the wiring harness, behind the passenger's-side kick panel on the early models or near the guse box on later models.) Until January 1977, the relay was a rectangular unit located behind the kick panel in the passenger's-side footwell. Later cars have a round relay, which is the lower, rear relay on the relay plate located behind the driver's'side kick panel.

If only the conductive grid is damaged, it is unnecessary to replace the window. Repair material to patch broken circuits is available from Authorized Dealers.

To repair:

1. Apply a strip of masking tape along each edge of the broken conductor.
2. Apply the repair material evenly over the break.
3. Allow the repair to dry for one hour at room temperature. Then remove the tape and test the heating effect.

11. INSTRUMENTS

Electric, thermal-type instruments are used on the cars covered by this Manual. Each instrument cluster has its own printed circuit board, thus eliminating the tangle of wire that used to be found behind automobile dashboards years ago. Each printed circuit board and each instrument is available as a replacement part, so it is possible to repair the instruments without replacing the entire cluster as a unit.

11.1 Replacing Speedometer Cable

The speedometer is driven off the rear of the transmission via a flexible cable. To disconnect the speedometer cable from the speedometer driven gear assembly on the transmission, unscrew the knurled ferrule nut on the cable conduit. To disconnect the cable from the speedometer, use the tip of a small screwdriver to raise the retainer on the side of the cable conduit's end-fixture out of the groove on the speedometer head. Then pull the conduit and the cable off the speedometer.

When installing the cable, check it carefully to see that it has not been kinked and that its conduit has not been flattened. Check also that the ferrule nut is not dented or deformed. Do not lubricate the cable prior to installation. Make sure that the rubber grommet fully engages the hole in the firewall and that the cable has no sharp bends. Be especially careful not to bend the cable sharply or damage it at the point where it comes from under the car into the engine compartment and at the point where it passes through the firewall. Be sure to install the felt gasket and the collar washer correctly when you reconnect the cable to the transmission. See Fig. 11-1.

CAUTION —
The radius of any bend must be at least 150 mm (6 in.). Otherwise the cable will soon break at the bend or become noisy.

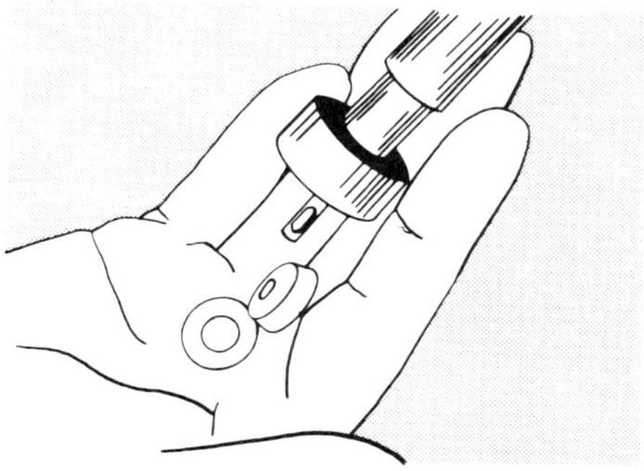

Fig. 11-1. Felt gasket and collar washer, which should be installed in that order inside ferrule nut.

Disassembling and Assembling Speedometer Driven Gear Assembly

Using a 12-mm wrench, you can remove the speedometer driven gear assembly from the transmission's extension housing by removing both the bolt and the retainer. See Fig. 11-2. The speedometer driven gear is nylon and is designed to fail without damaging the speedometer drivegear on the transmission's output shaft if an abnormal load is placed on the cable or the driven gear. Therefore, it is seldom necessary to replace the drivegear as described in **CLUTCH AND MANUAL TRANSMISSION** or in **AUTOMATIC TRANSMISSION** if the speedometer drive is faulty.

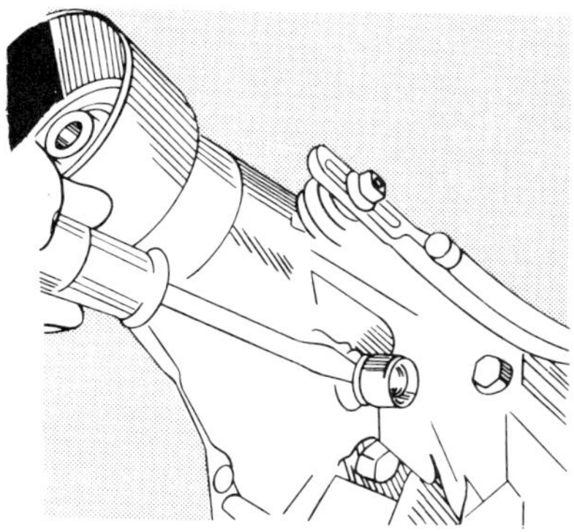

Fig. 11-2. Speedometer driven gear assembly being pried out of transmission extension housing with screwdriver, after removal of bolt and retainer.

Fig. 11-3 is an exploded view of the speedometer driven gear assembly. Disassembly requires only that you withdraw the gearshaft and remove the O-rings. There is little point in pressing out the bushing because no replacement parts other than O-rings are availabe for the assembly. Disassembly, therefore, is mainly for inspection and cleaning. If you discover any wear or damage, replace the driven gear assembly as a unit.

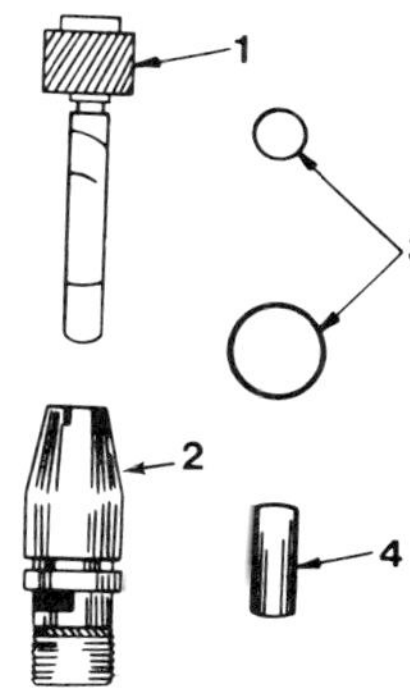

1. Gearshaft
2. Housing
3. O-rings
4. Bushing

Fig. 11-3. Exploded view of speedometer driven gear assembly. Replace worn or damaged O-rings during installation.

4

11.2 Troubleshooting Gauges, Sending Units, and Voltage Stabilizer

All cars covered by this Manual have both a fuel gauge and a coolant temperature gauge. In addition, SR-5 models may have an ammeter, an oil pressure gauge, and an oil temperature gauge. All the gauges are thermo-electrical instruments that require a voltage stabilizer to provide them with current that fluctuates between 2 volts and 7 volts. The voltage stabilizer is integral with the fuel gauge/temperature gauge cluster. SR-5 models have a second voltage stabilizer that is integral with the oil temperature gauge.

Fuel Gauge and Sending Unit Troubleshooting

The fuel gauge is controlled by an electromechanical sending unit in the fuel tank. On some models, the sending unit also includes a sender that causes a warning light to come on when the fuel in the tank has lowered to a level of approximately 5 liters (about 1.3 gallons) or less. Removing the sending unit from the tank requires a special wrench, such as Toyota special service tool 09808–12010, shown in Fig. 11-4.

To remove fuel gauge sending unit:

1. Disconnect the battery's negative cable.
2. Drain as much gasoline as possible from the tank.
3. Disconnect the wiring from the sending unit on the fuel tank. Then, using the special tool shown in Fig. 11-4, unscrew and remove the sending unit. Installation is the reverse of removal.

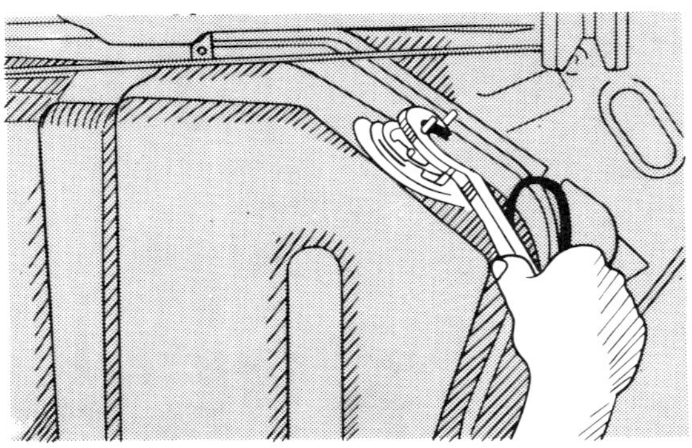

Fig. 11-4. Special tool being used to remove sending unit from tank.

If the fuel gauge never moves from its full position, check whether the coolant temperature gauge indicates overheating. If both gauges are at the top of their scale whenever the ignition is on, the voltage stabilizer is faulty and the gauge cluster should be replaced.

A fuel gauge that never moves from its full position with a normal temperature gauge reading has a grounded control circuit. Disconnect the wires from the sending unit. If the gauge falls from the FULL mark, the trouble is in the sending unit. If it does not, the control wire is grounded somewhere between the sending unit and the gauge.

If the fuel gauge fails to register at all, disconnect the wiring from the sending unit and ground the wire to the fuel gauge on some clean, unpainted metal part of the car. If the fuel gauge moves up to full, the sending unit is faulty or not correctly grounded. If the gauge still fails to move, the gauge or the wire to it is faulty.

Testing Fuel Gauge and Sending Unit Accuracy

With the fuel gauge sending unit removed, you can test its accuracy with an ohmmeter. Fig. 11-5 gives the correct resistance with the sending unit in its full, half-full, and empty positions. Replace faulty sending units.

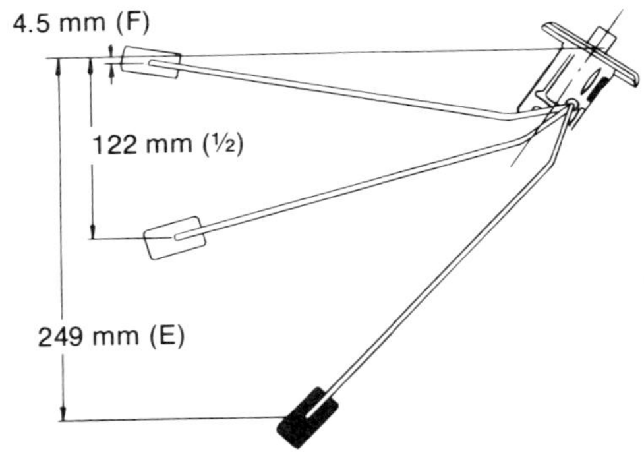

Float position	Resistance
Full (F)	3.0 ohms ±2.1 ohms
Half-full (½)	32.5 ohms ±4.8 ohms
Empty (E)	110 ohms ±7.7 ohms

Fig. 11-5. Float positions and correct resistance readings for fuel gauge sending unit.

On cars that have the fuel level warning light, you can test the warning light sender without removing it from the tank. The level warning light sender consists of a thermistor—a device that varies electrical resistance according to its temperature. See Fig. 11-6.

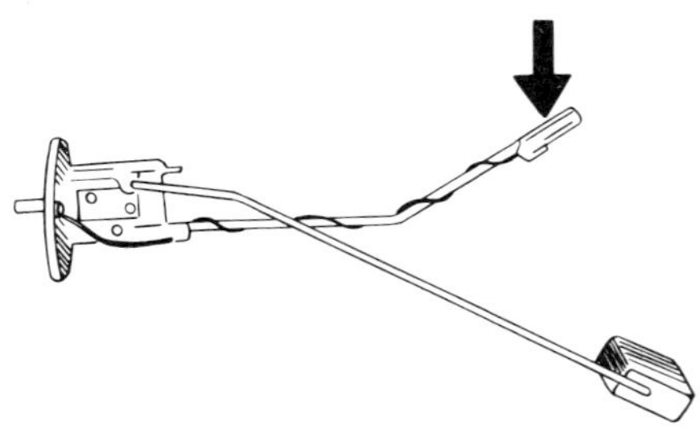

Fig. 11-6. Thermistor (arrow) on sending unit for cars with fuel level warning light.

To test the thermistor, drain as much fuel as possible from the tank. Then connect a voltmeter to the sending unit as indicated in Fig. 11-7. Because the fuel level will be below the level of the thermistor, the thermistor will not be cooled by the fuel, and the voltage should be only 5 to 6 volts because of the increased resistance provided by the warm thermistor. Fill the tank with about 5 liters (or 1.3 gallons) of gasoline. This should immerse the thermistor, thus cooling it, so that the voltage reading will change to 11 to 12 volts. Replace faulty sending units.

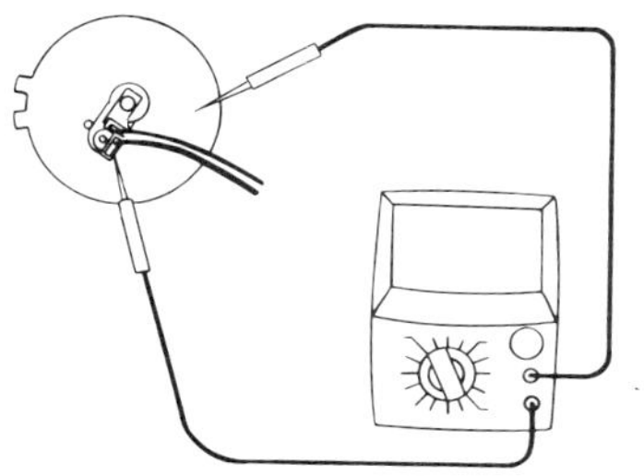

Fig. 11-7. Voltmeter being used to test fuel level warning light thermistor, which is built into fuel gauge sending unit on certain models.

To test the fuel gauge, remove the instrument cluster as described in **11.3 Removing and Installing Instruments.** Temporarily reconnect the wiring to the instrument cluster, making sure that no other disconnected wire is grounded. Then reconnect the battery's negative (−) cable and turn on the ignition. Full battery voltage should be present at terminal A, as given in Fig. 11-8.

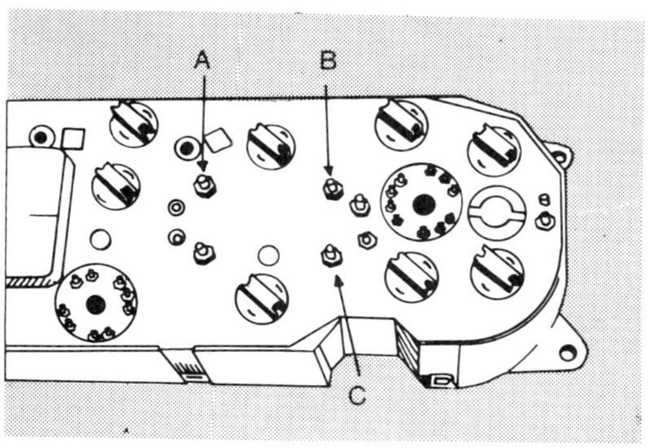

Fig. 11-8. Terminals used in testing fuel gauge and voltage limiter. Terminal A receives 12 volts from fuse marked DEFOG/BACK. Terminal B is fluctuating 2- to 7-volt current from voltage limiter. Terminal C is grounded through fuel gauge sending unit. (Terminal locations vary from one car model to the next, but all three terminals are always connected to fuel gauge.)

If battery voltage is reaching terminal A, measure the voltage at terminal B, as given previously in Fig. 11-8. The voltage should fluctuate constantly between 2 and 7 volts. If not, the voltage limiter is faulty and the fuel gauge should be replaced.

CAUTION ——

When the ignition is first turned on, there will be full battery voltage at terminal B. Do not connect the voltmeter at this time because it may damage the voltage limiter. Wait for at least 10 seconds for the limiter to warm up, and then measure the limited voltage.

If the voltage at terminal B fails to fluctuate, or if there is no voltage or only full battery voltage, disconnect the wiring and use an ohmmeter to measure the resistance between terminals A and C, as given previously in Fig. 11-8. The correct resistance is 55 ohms. If it is considerably more or less, replace the fuel gauge or the gauge cluster.

Testing Coolant Temperature Gauge and Sending Unit

If the coolant temperature gauge is always at the high (hot) end of its range but the fuel gauge is accurate, disconnect the wire from the coolant temperature gauge sending unit. If the gauge falls from its high reading, the sending unit is faulty and should be replaced. If there is no change, either the gauge is faulty or the wire is grounded at some point between the gauge and the sending unit.

If the temperature gauge always remains at the low (cold) end of its scale, disconnect the wire from the coolant temperature sending unit and ground the wire on 4
some clean, unpainted metal part of the engine. The gauge should go all the way to its hot reading, which indicates that the trouble is a faulty sending unit. If the gauge still fails to move, either the gauge is faulty or the wire from the sending unit to the gauge is broken or disconnected at some point.

To test the sending unit for accuracy, connect an ohmmeter as indicated in Fig. 11-9. The resistance should vary with the coolant temperature, as indicated in the illustration. If the resistance readings are considerably different than specified, replace the sending unit.

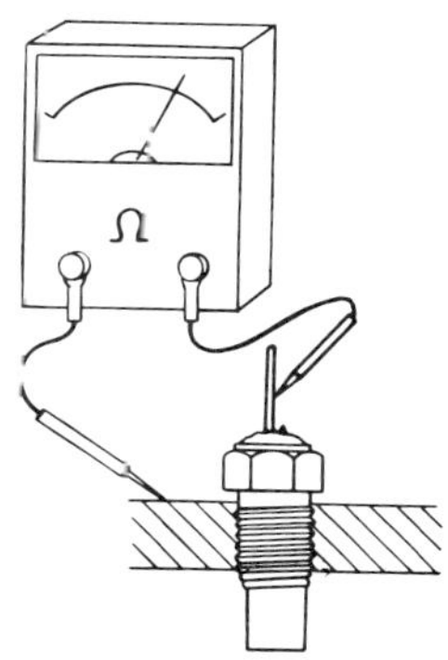

Temperature	Resistance
50°C (122°F)	Approximately 154 ohms
80°C (187°F)	**Approximately 52 ohms**
100°C (212°F)	**Approximately 27.5 ohms**
120°C (248°F)	Approximately 16 ohms

Fig. 11-9. Coolant temperature gauge sending unit resistances at different coolant temperatures. Specifications in bold type are for accuracy testing; other specifications given are for reference only.

Oil Pressure Warning Light Sender Test

If the oil pressure warning light fails to function normally, you can test the sender with an ohmmeter as indicated in Fig. 11-10. With the engine running, there should be 0 ohms resistance (continuity); with the engine stopped, there should be infinite resistance (no continuity). Replace faulty senders.

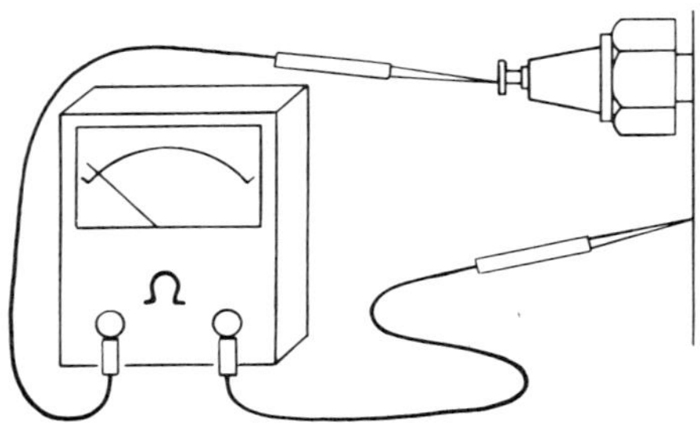

Fig. 11-10. Ohmmeter being used to test oil pressure warning light sender.

Oil Pressure Gauge and Sending Unit Testing

To test the oil pressure gauge sending unit, connect a test light with an approximately 3.4-watt bulb in series between the sending unit and the battery's positive (+) post. With the engine stopped, the light should be out. (When the light is first connected with the engine stopped, the bulb may come on briefly and then go out, which is normal.) Start the engine. The light should begin to flash, the frequency of flashes increasing with the engine speed.

If the sending unit is not faulty, remove the gauge cluster as described in **11.3 Removing and Installing Instruments.** With the multiple connector plugged into the gauge cluster and the battery temporarily reconnected (ignition on), full battery voltage should be available at terminal A, as indicated in Fig. 11-11. Also measure the resistance between terminal A and terminal B with an ohmmeter. The correct resistance is 42 ohms. If there is no battery voltage at terminal A, or if the resistance between terminals A and B is considerably more or less than 42 ohms, replace the oil pressure gauge.

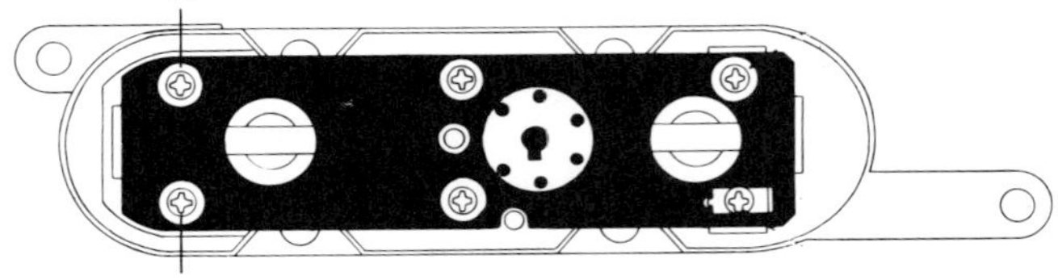

Fig. 11-11. Terminals for oil pressure gauge on back of gauge cluster.

Oil Temperature Gauge and Sending Unit Testing

If the oil temperature gauge is always at the high (hot) end of its range, disconnect the wire from the oil temperature gauge sending unit. If the gauge falls from its high reading, the sending unit is faulty and should be replaced. If there is no change, either the gauge is faulty or the wire is grounded at some point between the gauge and the sending unit.

If the oil temperature gauge always remains at the low (cold) end of its scale, disconnect the wire from the oil temperature gauge sending unit and ground the wire on some clean, unpainted metal part of the engine. The gauge should go all the way to its hot reading, which indicates that the trouble is a faulty sending unit. If the gauge still fails to move, either the gauge is faulty or the wire from the sending unit to the gauge is broken or disconnected at some point.

To test the sending unit for accuracy, connect an ohmmeter as indicated in Fig. 11-12. The resistance should vary with the oil temperature, as indicated in the illustration. If the resistance readings are considerably different than specified, replace the sending unit.

If the sending unit is not faulty, remove the gauge cluster as described in **11.3 Removing and Installing Instruments.** With the multiple connector plugged into the gauge cluster and the battery temporarily reconnected (ignition on), full battery voltage should be available at terminal A, as indicated in Fig. 11-13. The voltage at terminal B should be constantly fluctuating between 2 volts and 7 volts. Also measure the resistance between terminal A and terminal B with an ohmmeter. The correct resistance is 55 ohms. If there is incorrect voltage at terminal A or B, or if the resistance between terminals A and B is considerably more or less than 55 ohms, replace the oil temperature gauge.

CAUTION —

When the ignition is first turned on, there will be full battery voltage at terminal B. Do not connect the voltmeter at this time because it may damage the voltage limiter. Wait for at least 10 seconds for the limiter to warm up, and then measure the limited voltage.

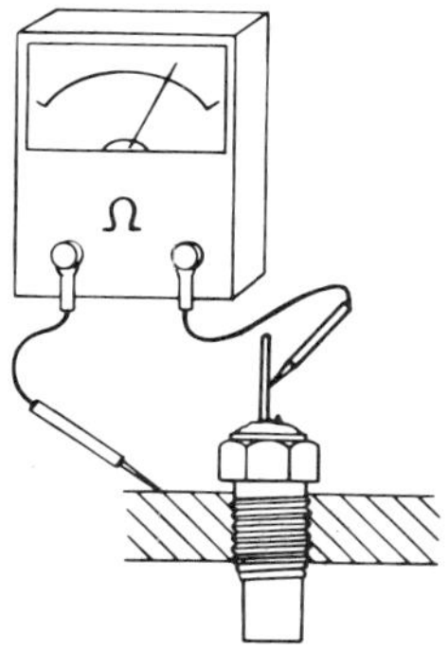

Temperature	Resistance
50°C (122°F)	Approximately 154 ohms
80°C (176°F)	**Approximately 52 ohms**
100°C (212°F)	**Approximately 27.5 ohms**
120°C (248°F)	Approximately 16 ohms

Fig. 11-12. Oil temperature gauge sending unit resistances at different oil temperatures. Specifications in bold type are for accuracy testing; other specifications given are for reference only.

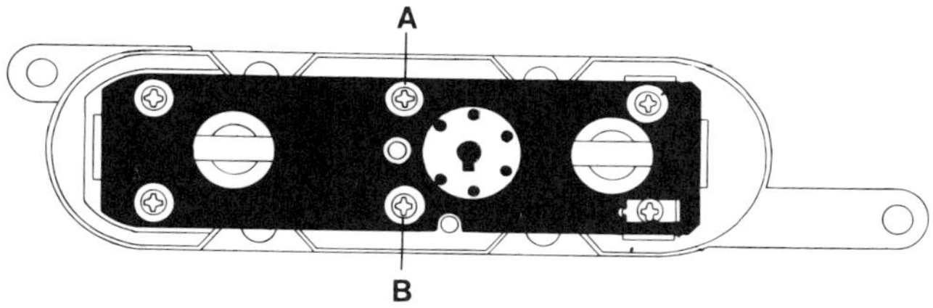

Fig. 11-13. Terminals for oil temperature gauge on back of gauge cluster.

Ammeter Testing

The ammeter is of the shunt type. That is, $^1/_{50}$ of the full current is shunted through the ammeter instead of passing the full current through the gauge. The shunt fusible link is used to carry the main charging system current. See the wiring diagram given later in this section of the Manual.

To test the ammeter, remove the gauge cluster as described in **11.3 Removing and Installing Instruments.** Then connect a battery and an 8-watt bulb as indicated in Fig. 11-14. If the ammeter does not indicate approximately 30 amperes during the test, it is faulty and should be replaced.

CAUTION ——
Never use a bulb of more than 10 watts for this test, and never connect the battery without a bulb. Doing either will burn out the ammeter.

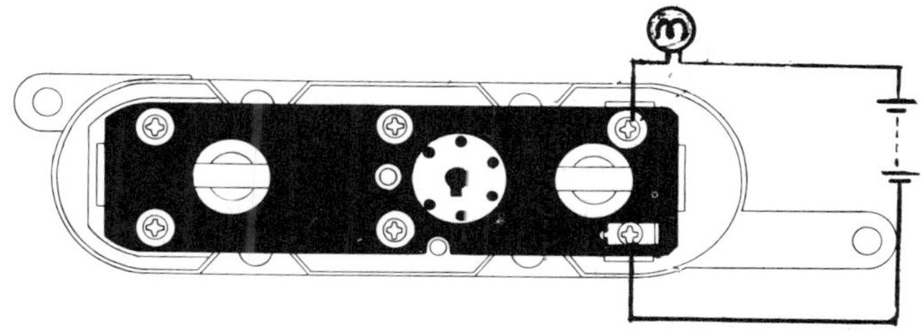

Fig. 11-14. Battery and 8-watt bulb being used to test ammeter.

Tachometer Testing

The tachometer circuit for your car can be determined from the wiring diagrams given elsewhere in this section of the Manual. To test, connect an accurate dwell meter/tachometer as described in **ENGINE.** Set the instrument to measure rpm for a four-cylinder engine. Compare the reading at various engine speeds to the rpm indicated by the dashboard tachometer. If the dashboard tachometer is far off from the reading given by the testing tachometer, the dashboard tachometer is faulty and should be replaced.

CAUTION ——
Do not reverse the battery connections at the tachometer. The tachometer is designed for negative-ground installations and will be damaged if the polarity is reversed. Be careful not to subject the tachometer to heavy shocks, as by dropping it during removal.

11.3 Removing and Installing Instruments

The layout of the dashboard instruments and the various dashboard components varies from model to model. However, the principles illustrated in the procedure that follows apply to all the cars covered by this Manual.

To remove:

1. Disconnect the battery's negative (–) cable.

2. Remove the instrument panel trim by taking out the screws indicated in Fig. 11-15 and, where applicable, Fig. 11-16.

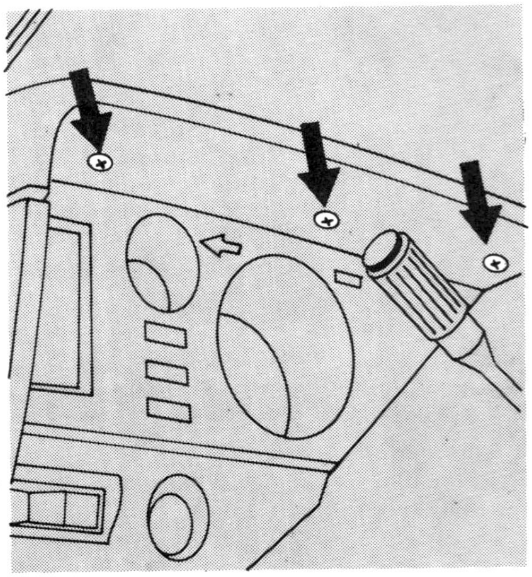

Fig. 11-15. Screws for instrument panel trim that are found above instrument panel of all cars covered by this Manual.

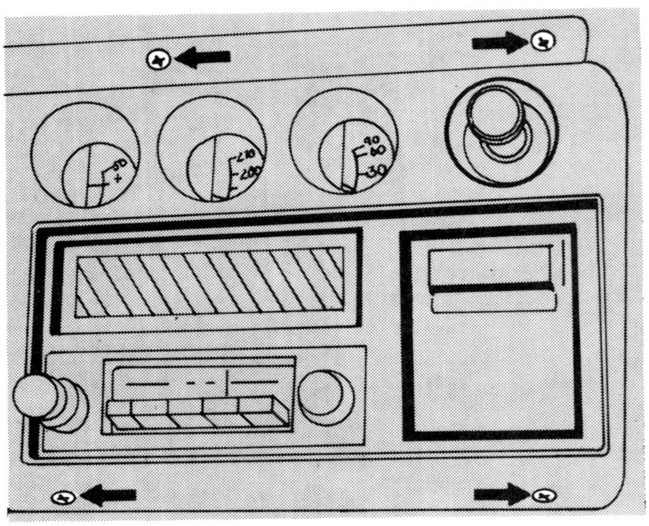

Fig. 11-16. Screws for instrument panel trim above instrument panel center (SR-5 models only).

3. Remove the ashtray and, where applicable, the knobs from the radio and tape player. On applicable models, remove the heater control knobs or fresh-air vent knobs.

4. Remove the instrument panel(s) by raising it slightly to disengage it at the bottom.

5. Reaching up from behind the dashboard, detach the speedometer cable from the speedometer head by raising the retainer on the side of the cable conduit's end-fixture with a small screwdriver and simultaneously pulling the cable and its conduit off the speedometer head.

6. Remove the screws that hold the main instrument cluster, the clock, or the SR-5 gauge cluster to the dashboard assembly. Then pull the cluster partially out of the dashboard so that you can disconnect the multiple connector, the illumination light bulb holders, and other wires from the rear of the cluster.

Installation is the reverse of removal. If you make tests with the battery temporarily reconnected, be sure that no disconnected wire is grounded against the dashboard structure or any other metal part of the car body.

12. WIRING AND FUSES

If you find a fault in one of the wiring harnesses during troubleshooting, it is not advisable to attempt a repair if the trouble is somewhere in the part of the wiring harness that is bound with plastic. In some cases you can make a satisfactory repair by installing a new wire in parallel with the harness, then binding the wire to the harness at intervals with electrical wiring binding strips. If there is extensive wiring damage, or if installing a separate wire will not make a satisfactory repair, replace the wiring harness as a unit.

The best way to install a replacement harness is to start at one end of the old harness, disconnecting it from the components it serves, and then attach the new harness in the same way. Continue working in this manner all along the harness so that the new harness will be installed in the same way as the old one. If you fully remove the old harness and then attempt to install the new one, it is likely that some of the connections or harness bindings will not be installed as neatly or directly as they originally were.

12.1 Replacing Fuses

In addition to the fuses in the fuse box, there are fusible links at the battery (Fig. 12-1) and at the ammeter (on cars that have ammeters). In case of an overload, the fusible links are designed to melt before the wiring is damaged. Always replace these fusible links with new fusible links, which are available from the car manufacturer; never try to repair them or replace them with ordinary wire. Before you replace a fusible link, be sure to correct the cause of the electrical overload.

> ***CAUTION —***
> *The installation of ordinary wire, even as a temporary repair, may cause extensive damage to the electrical system and could start a fire.*

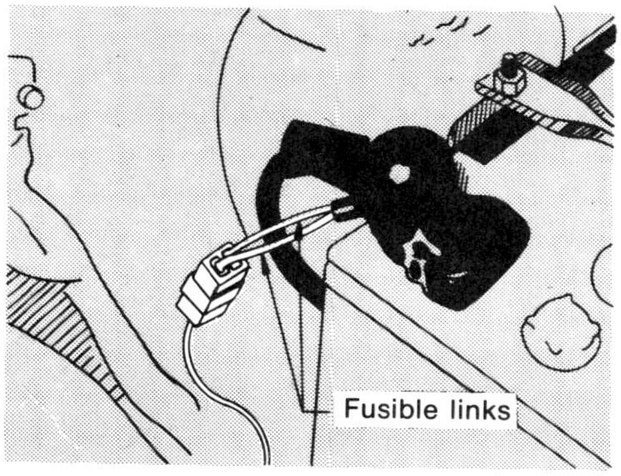

Fig. 12-1. Fusible links at battery's positive (+) post. Because number and colors of fusible links vary on different models, identify links on your car either with owner's manual or with wiring diagrams given in this section of the Manual.

Fig. 12-2 identifies the locations of the fuses in the fuse box. The fuse box is located just ahead of the driver's left knee, beneath the dashboard. All eight fuses are rated at 15 amperes, except on 1977 and later cars which have a 5-amp radio fuse. A spare 15-amp fuse is located inside the cover of the fuse box when the car is delivered.

To install a new fuse, turn off the ignition and the electrical accessories that are served by the burned-out fuse. Pull the cover off the fuse box, top edge first. Pull the old fuse straight out of the clips and push the new fuse straight in; make sure that the new fuse is rated at 15 amps. If the new fuse blows out immediately, there is a problem in the electrical system, which you should locate and correct before installing another fuse.

> ***CAUTION —***
> *Never patch a burned-out fuse with aluminum foil or replace the fuse with wire or a fuse of greater capacity. Doing so can damage the electrical system.*

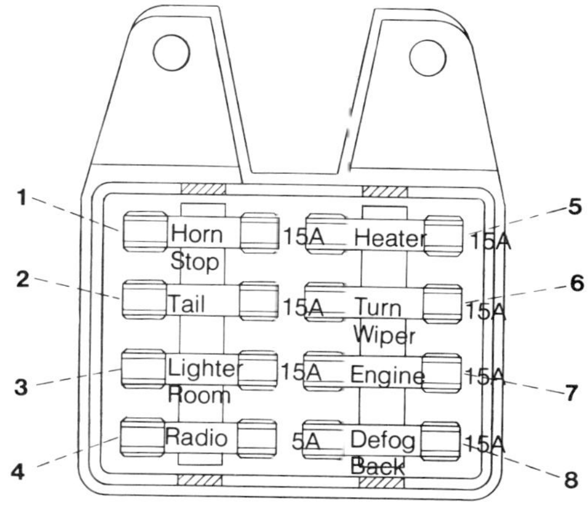

1. Horn, stoplight, emergency flasher warning light
2. Taillights, parking lights, license plate lights, instrument light, heater control lights, ashtray light
3. Interior light, cigarette lighter, clock
4. Radio, tape player, or stereo (15-amp on 1975 and 1976 cars)
5. Heater fan
6. Turn signals, windshield wipers, windshield washer
7. Ignition coil, voltage regulator, fuel cutoff solenoid
8. Heated rear window, instruments, back-up lights

Fig. 12-2. Locations of fuses in fuse box. Words shown in illustration are those printed on cover of fuse box. They identify main components served by individual fuses.

13. WIRING DIAGRAMS

The wiring diagrams given on the following pages are suitable to the cars covered by this Manual. The following abbreviations are used to indicate the colors of the wires:

B=Black
Br=Brown
G=Green
Gr=Grey
L=Light Blue
O=Orange
R=Red
W=White
Y=Yellow

Example: RG indicates a red wire with a green stripe

> ***CAUTION —***
> *Disconnect the battery ground strap before beginning to work on any part of the electrical system.*

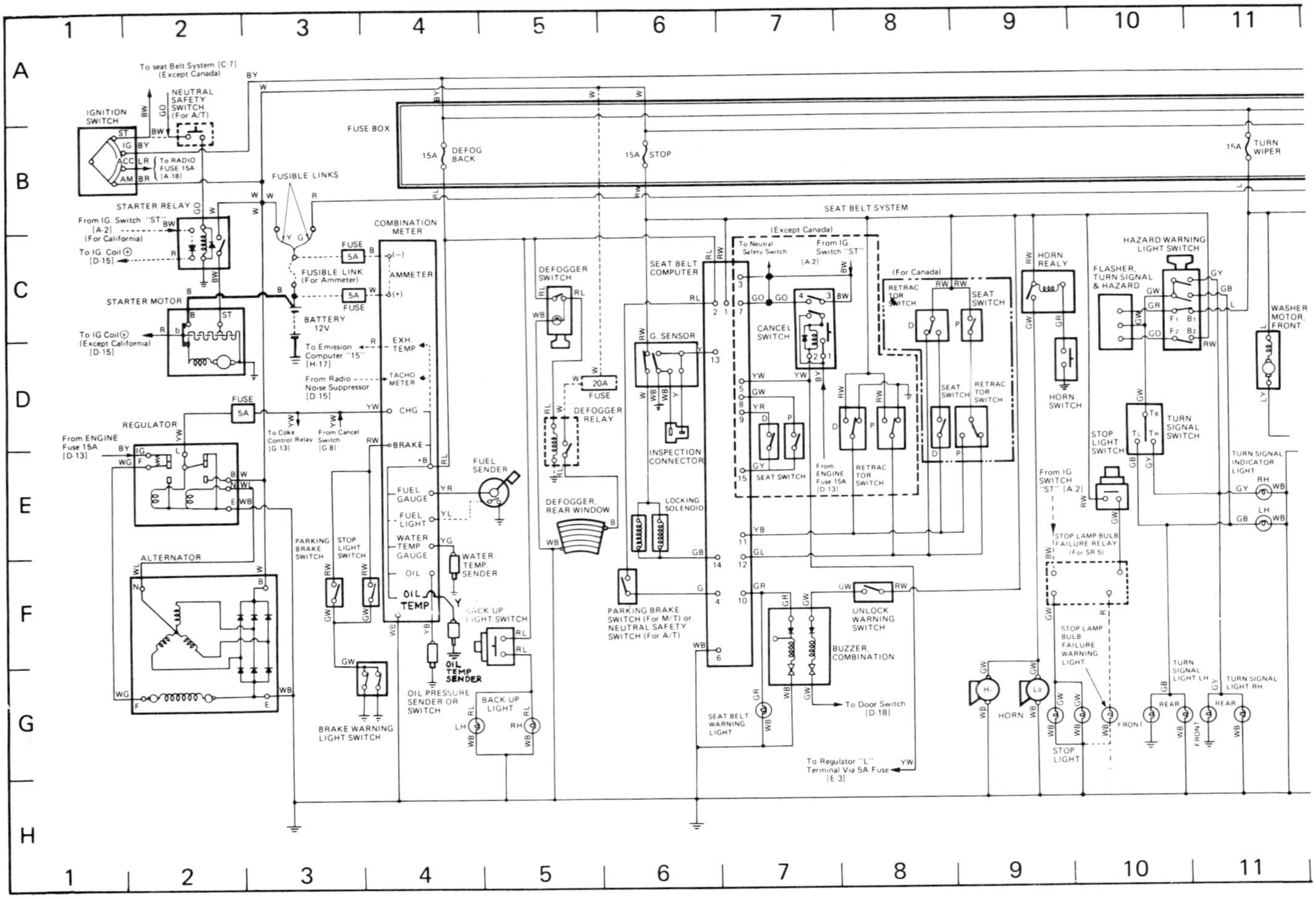

Components	Location
Alternator	F-2
Ammeter	C-4
Automatic choke	G-13
Battery	C-3
Buzzer, combination	F-7
Cigarette lighter	G-19
Clock	F-18
Combination meter	B-4
Defogger, rear window	E-5
Distributor	E-15
Distributor, dual points	D-14
Emission control system	B-16
Emission control computer (except Calif.)	C-16
Emission control computer (Calif.)	E-16
Exhaust temp. warning light (Calif.)	D-4
Inspection connector (Calif.)	G-15
Speed sensor	G-17
Thermo sensor for CCo (Calif.)	F-16
Thermo switch at intake manifold (Calif.)	F-16
Thermo switch at radiator (Calif.)	F-15
Vacuum switching valve (except Calif.)	C-16
Vacuum switching vavle (Calif.)	D-16
Flasher, turn signal and hazard	C-10
Fuel cut solenoid	C-13
Fuel gauge	E-4
Fuel pump (Calif.)	G-14
Fuel pump resistor (Calif.)	F-14
Fuel sender	E-5
Fuse box	B-4
Fuse, external	D-2
Fuse, external (for defogger)	D-5
Fuses, external (for ammeter)	C-3
Fusible links	B-3
Fusible link shunt (for ammeter)	C-3
Horns	G-9
Ignition coil	C-15
Igniter	C-14
Ashtray light	E-20
Automatic transmission indicator light	F-20
Back-up lights, left- and right-hand	G-5
Brake warning light	D-4
Clock light	E-20
Combination meter light	D-20
Discharge warning light	D-4
Fuel remaining warning light (Calif.)	E-4
Headlight, left- and right-hand	G-21
Heater control light	F-20
High beam indicator light	F-22
Interior light	C-19
License plate light	C-21
Low oil pressure warning light	F-4
Parking light, left- and right-hand	G-19
Side marker, front left- and right-hand	G-20
Side marker, rear left- and right-hand	G-20
Spot lamp	F-19
Stop light, left- and right-hand	G-9
Stop lamp bulb failure warning light	G-10
Taillight, left- and right-hand	G-20
Turn signal, left-hand front and rear	G-10
Turn signal, right-hand front and rear	G-11
Turn signal indicator light left-hand and right-hand	E-11
Heater blower motor	E-17
Starter motor	C-2
Windshield washer motor, front	C-11
Windshield washer motor, rear	E-13
Windshield wiper motor, front	E-12
Windshield wiper motor, rear	F-12
Oil pressure gauge	F-4
Oil pressure sender	G-4
Oil temperature gauge	F-4
Oil temperature sender	F-4
Radio	C-18
Radio noise suppressor	D-15
Regulator	E-2
Choke control relay	F-13
Defogger relay	D-5
Fuel pump relay (Calif.)	F-14
Head light and taillight relay	C-21
Horn relay	C-9
Ignition control relay, dual points	D-14
Starter relay	B-2
Stop lamp bulb failure relay	E-10
Seat belt system	B-8
Seat belt buzzer, combination	F-7
Seat belt cancel switch, starter interlock (except Canada)	D-7
Seat belt gravity sensor (deceleration sensor)	D-6

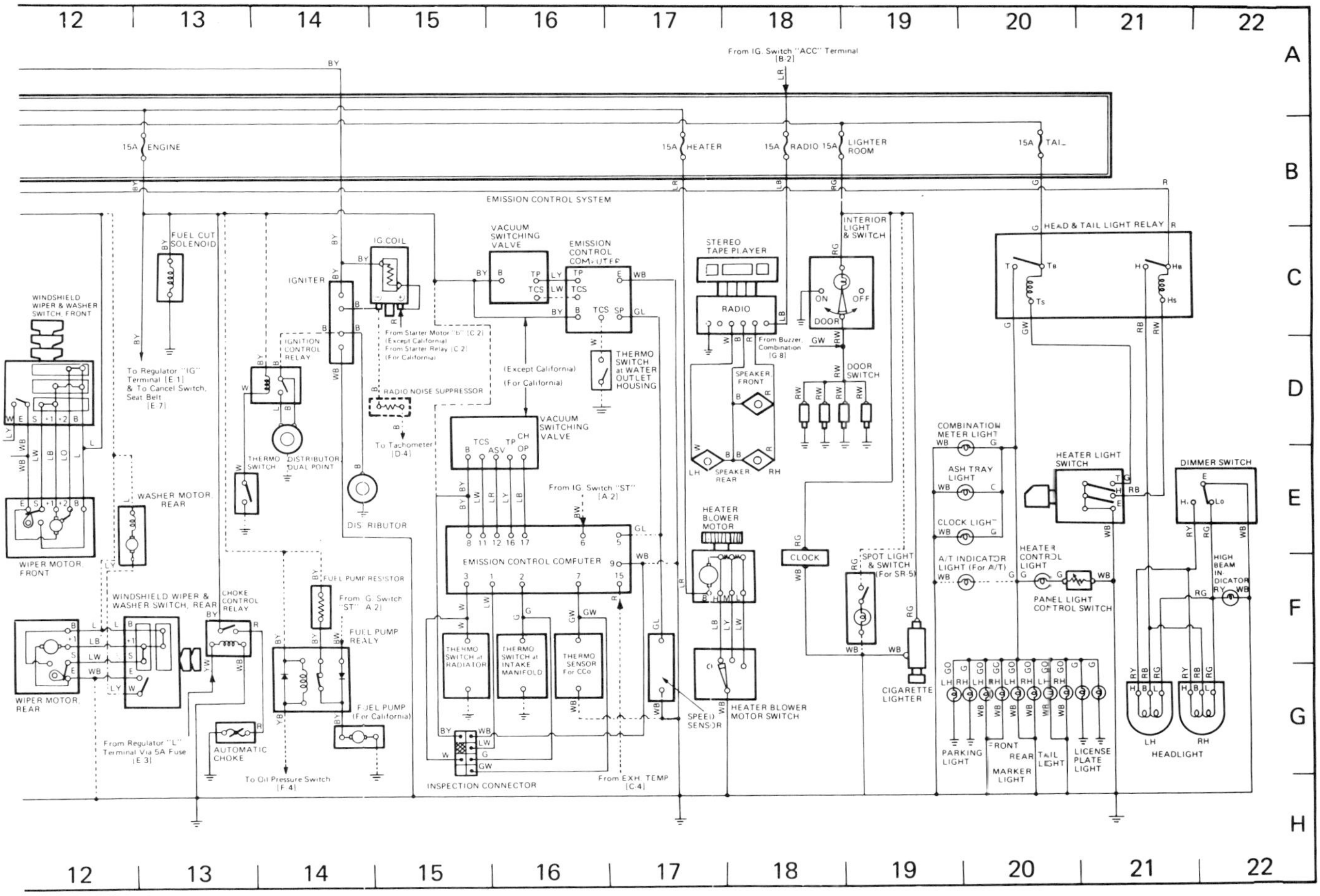

4

Seat belt inspection connector	E–6
Seat belt locking solenoid	E–6
Seat belt parking brake or neutral safety switch	F–6
Retractor switch, driver's side (except Canada)	D–8
Retractor switch, driver's side (Canada)	C–8
Retractor switch, passenger's side (except Canada)	D–8
Retractor switch, passenger's side (Canada)	D–9
Seat belt computer	C–6
Seat belt warning light	G–7
Seat switch, driver's side (except Canada)	E–7
Seat switch, driver's side (Canada)	D–8
Seat switch, passenger's side (except Canada)	E–7
Seat switch, passenger's side (Canada)	C–9
Speaker, front	D–18
Speaker, rear left- and right-hand	E–18
Stereo tape player	C–18
Back-up light switch	F–5
Brake warning light switch	G–4
Defogger switch, rear window	C–5
Dimmer switch	E–22
Door switch	D–19
Hazard warnng light switch	C–10
Headlight switch	E–21
Heater blower motor switch	G–18
Horn switch	D–9
Ignition switch	B–1
Interior light switch	C–19
Neutral safety switch	A–2
Oil pressure switch	G–4
Panel light control switch	F–20
Parking brake switch	F–3
Spot light switch	F–19
Stop light switch	E–10
Stop light switch (for warning light)	F–4
Thermo switch (for dual point)	E–13
Turn signal switch	D–10
Unlock warning switch	F–8
Windshield wiper and washer switch, front	C–12
Windshield wiper and washer switch, rear	F–13
Tachometer	D–4
Water temperature gauge	F–4
Water temperature sender	F–4

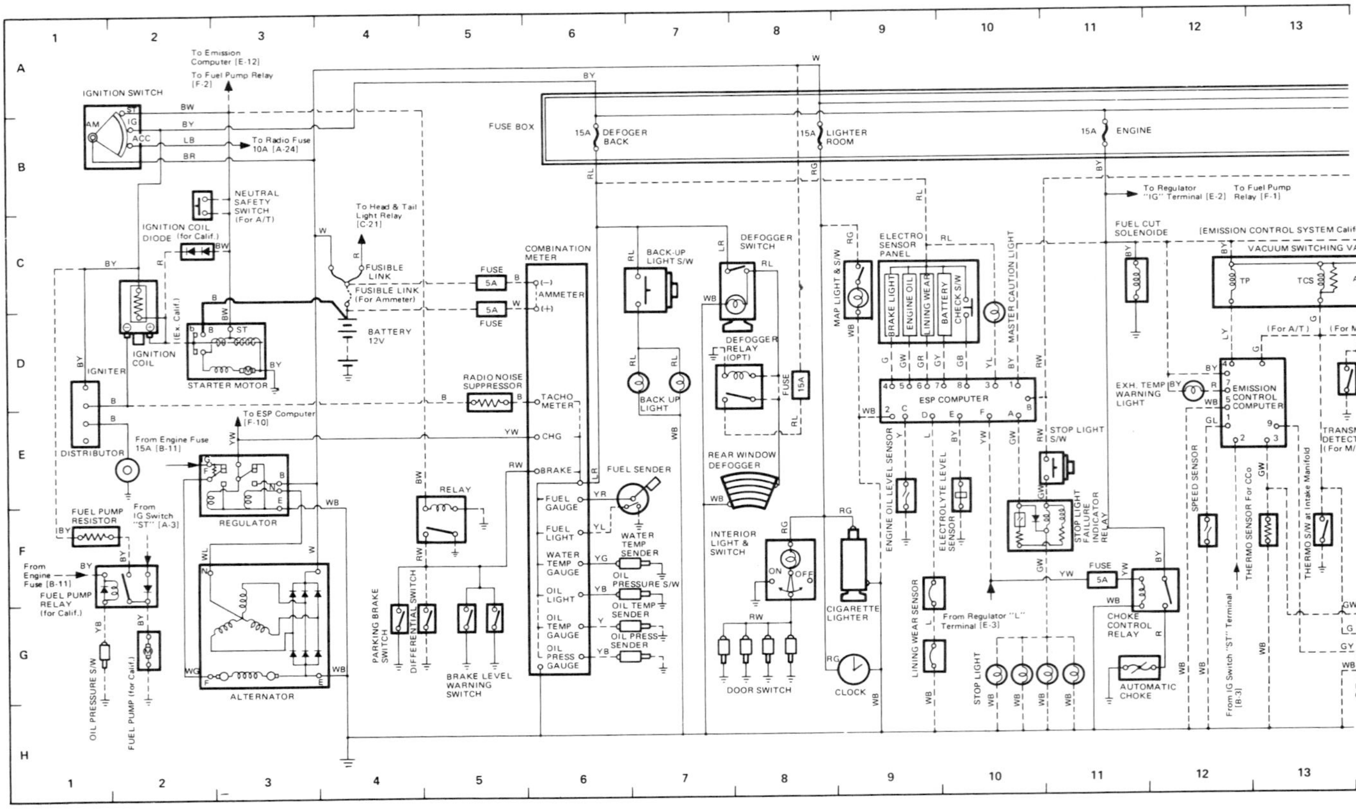

Components	Location
Alternator	G-3
Ammeter	D-6
Antenna	D-25
Automatic choke	G-11
Battery	D-4
Cigarette lighter	G-9
Clock	G-9
Combination meter	C-6
Defogger, rear window	E-8
Distributor	E-1
Emission control computer (Calif.)	D-13
Exhaust temp. warning light (Calif.)	E-12
Inspection connector (Calif.)	G-14
Speed sensor (Calif.)	F-12
Thermo sensor for CCo (Calif.)	F-13
Thermo switch at intake manifold (Calif.)	F-13
Thermo switch at radiator (Calif.)	F-14
Vacuum switching valve (Calif.)	C-13
Emission control computer (not on cars covered by this Manual)	E-15
Speed sensor (not on cars covered by this Manual)	F-15
Thermo switch (not on cars covered by this Manual)	F-15
Vacuum switching valve	C-15
Check switch ESP (for wagon)	D-10
Electro sensor panel ESP (for wagon)	C-9
Electrolyte level sensor ESP (for wagon)	F-10
Engine oil level sensor ESP (for wagon)	F-9
ESP computer (for wagon)	E-9
Lining wear sensor ESP (for wagon)	G-9
Master caution light ESP (for wagon)	D-10
Stop light ESP (for wagon)	G-10
Stop light failure indicator relay ESP (for wagon)	F-11
Stop light switch ESP (for wagon)	F-11
Flasher, turn signal and hazard	C-16
Fuel cut solenoid	C-11
Fuel gauge	E-6
Fuel pump (Calif.)	G-2
Fuel pump resistor (Calif.)	F-1
Fuel sender	E-7
Fuse box	B-5

Components	Location
Fuse, external (for automatic choke)	F-11
fuse, external (for defogger)	D-8
Fuses, external (for ammeter)	C-5
Fusible links	C-4
Fusible link, shunt (for ammeter)	C-4
Horns	F-16
Ignition coil	D-2
Ignition coil diode (Calif.)	C-2
Igniter	D-1
Ashtray lights	E-20
Automatic transmission indicator light	F-20
Back-up light, left- and right-hand	D-7
Brake warning light	E-6
Clock light	E-20
Combination meter light	E-20
Discharge warning light	E-6
Fuel remaining warning light (Calif.)	F-6
Headlight, left- and right-hand	F-22
Heater control light	F-21
High beam indicator light	E-23
Interior light	F-8
License plate light	G-22
Low oil pressure warning light	F-6
Map light (for wagon)	C-9
Parking light, left- and right-hand	G-20
Side marker, front left- and right-hand	G-21
Side marker, rear left- and right-hand	G-21
Stop light, left- and right-hand	G-15
Taillight, left- and right-hand	G-21
Turn signal, left-hand, front and rear	F-17
Turn signal, right-hand, front and rear	F-17
Turn signal indicator, left- and right-hand	H-17
Heater blower motor	C-23
Starter motor	D-2
Windshield washer motor, front	D-18
Windshield washer motor, rear (optional)	F-19
Windshield wiper motor, front	E-19
Windshield wiper motor, rear (optional)	G-19
Oil pressure gauge (for wagon)	G-6
Oil pressure sender (for wagon)	G-7
Oil temperature gauge (for wagon)	G-6

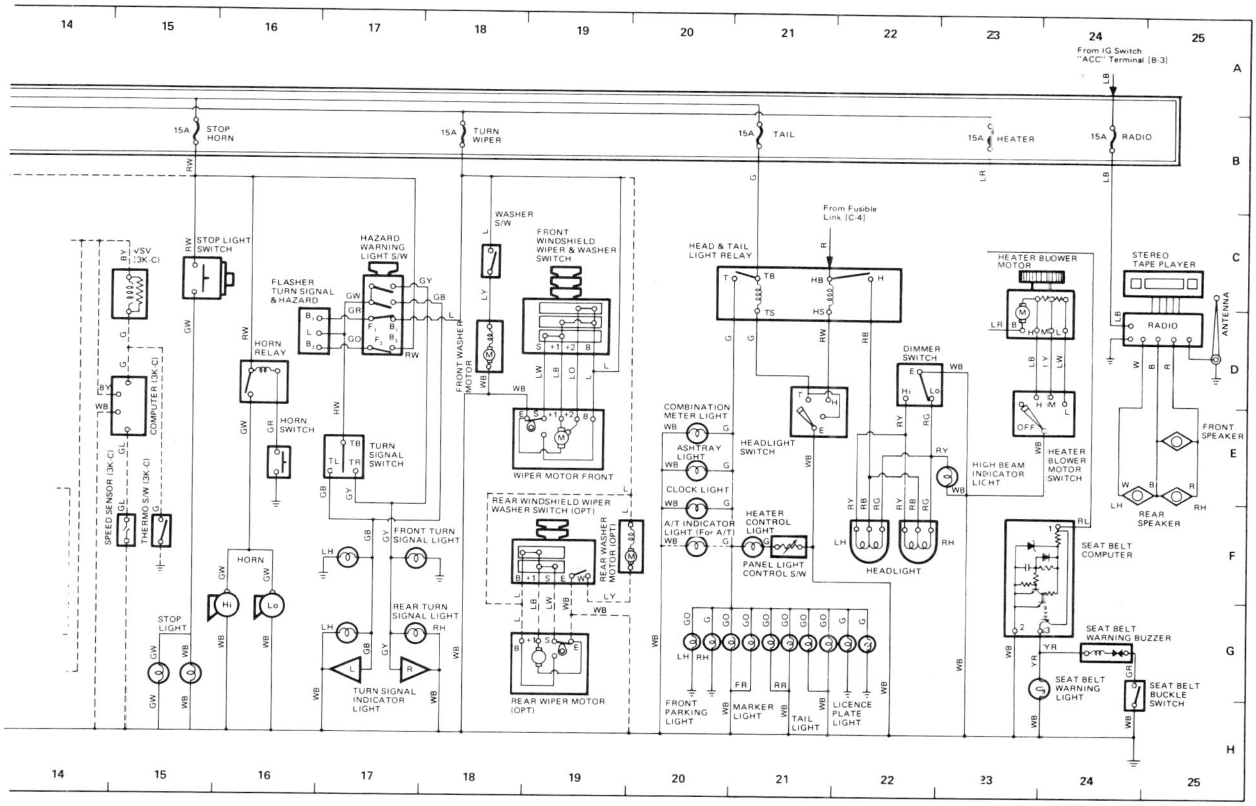

Oil temperature sender (for wagon) F-7
Radio D-25
Radio noise suppressor D-5
Regulator F-3
Choke control relay G-11
Defogger relay (optional) D-8
Fuel pump relay (for Calif.) F-1
Head light and taillight relay C-20
Horn relay D-16
Relay for parking brake light inspection E-5
Seat buckle switch H-25
Seat belt computer F-24
Seat belt warning buzzer G-24
Seat belt warning light H-24
Speaker, front E-25
Speaker, rear, left- and right-hand E-25
Stereo tape player C-25
Back-up light switch C-7
Brake level warning switch G-5
Defogger switch, rear window C-8
Differential switch G-4
Dimmer switch D-22
Door switch G-8
Hazard warning light switch C-17
Headlight switch E-21
Heater blower motor switch E-24
Horn switch E-16
Ignition switch A-1
Interior light switch F-8
Map light switch (for wagon) C-9
Neutral safety switch B-3
Oil pressure switch F-7, G-1
Panel light control switch F-21
Parking brake switch G-4
Stop light switch C-15
Turn signal switch E-17
Windshield wiper and washer switch, front C-19
Windshield wiper and washer switch, rear (optional) F-19
Tachometer D-6
Water temperature gauge F-6
Water temperature sender F-7

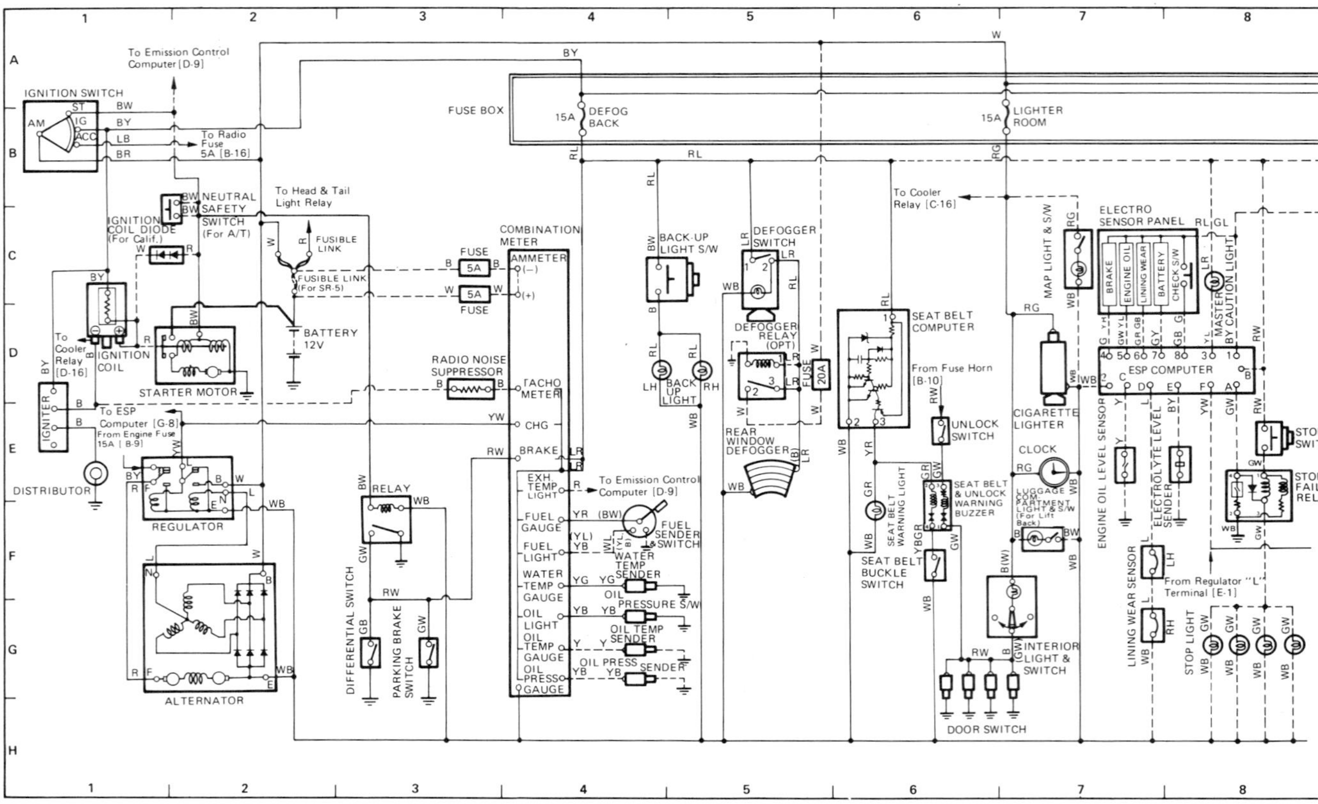

Components	Location
Alternator	G–2
Ammeter (for hardtop SR-5)	C–4
Ammeter (for coupe and liftback, SR-5 only)	C–4
Antenna	F–16
Automatic choke	G–9
Battery	D–2
Cooler idle-up VSV (for cooler)	D–16
Cigarette lighter (for sedan, hardtop, and wagon)	D–7
Cigarette lighter (for coupe and liftback)	D–7
Clock (for sedan, hardtop, and wagon)	F–7
Clock (for hardtop SR-5)	F–7
Clock (for coupe and liftback)	F–7
Combination meter	C–4
Defogger, rear window (for sedan and hardtop)	E–5
Defogger, rear window (for wagon)	E–5
Defogger, rear window (for coupe)	E–5
Defogger, rear window (for liftback)	E–5
Distributor	E–1
Emission control computer	D–9
Exhaust temp. warning light (for sedan, hardtop, and wagon)	F–4
Exhaust temp. warning light (for hardtop SR-5)	F–4
Exhaust temp. warning light (for coupe and liftback)	F–4
Inspection connector	F–10
Speed sensor (for sedan, hardtop, and wagon)	E–9
Speed sensor (for hardtop SR-5)	E–9
Speed sensor (for coupe and liftback)	E–9
Thermo sensor (CCo)	E–9
Thermo switch	E–10
Vacuum switching valve	C–9
Check switch (ESP system for hardtop SR-5)	C–7
Electro sensor panel (ESP system for hardtop SR-5)	C–7
Electrolyte level sensor (ESP system for hardtop SR-5)	E–8
Engine oil level sensor (ESP system for hardtop SR-5)	F–7
ESP computer (ESP system for hardtop SR-5)	D–8
Lining wear sensor, left-hand (ESP system for hardtop SR-5)	F–7
Lining wear sensor, right-hand (ESP system for hardtop SR-5)	G–7
Master caution light (ESP system for hardtop SR-5)	D–8
Stop light, left-hand (ESP system for hardtop SR-5)	G–8
Stop light, right-hand (ESP system for hardtop SR-5)	G–8
Stop light failure indicator relay (ESP system for hardtop SR-5)	E–8
Stop light switch (ESP system for hradtop SR-5)	E–8
Flasher, turn signal and hazard	C–11
Fuel cut solenoid	C–9
Fuel gauge (for sedan, hardtop, and wagon)	F–4
Fuel gauge (for hardtop SR-5)	F–4
Fuel gauge (for coupe and liftback)	F–4
Fuel sender (for sedan and hardtop)	F–4
Fuel sender (for wagon)	F–4
Fuel sender (for coupe)	F–4
Fuel sender (for liftback)	F–4
Fuse box	B–3
Fuse, external (for defogger)	E–5
Fuses, external (for ammeter)	C–3
Fusible links	C–2
Horn, left-hand	D–11
Horn, right-hand	D–11
Ignition coil	D–1
Ignition coil diode (Calif.)	C–2
Igniter	E–1
Ashtray indicator light (for sedan, hardtop, and wagon)	E–13
Ashtray indicator light (for coupe and liftback)	E–13
Automatic transmission indicator light	F–13
Back-up light, left-hand (for sedan and hardtop)	D–5
Back-up light, left-hand (for wagon)	D–5
Back-up light, left-hand (for coupe)	D–5
Back-up light, left-hand (for liftback)	D–5
Back-up light, right-hand (for sedan and hardtop)	D–5
Back-up light, right-hand (for wagon)	D–5
Back-up light, right-hand (for coupe)	D–5
Back-up light, right-hand (for liftback)	D–5
Brake warning light (for sedan, hardtop, and wagon)	E–4
Brake warning light (for hardtop SR-5)	E–4
Brake warning light (for coupe and liftback)	E–4
Clock light	F–13
Combination gauge light (for hardtop SR-5)	G–13
Combination gauge light (for coupe and liftback SR-5)	G–13
Combination meter light (for sedan, hardtop, and wagon)	E–13
Combination meter light (for hardtop SR-5)	E–13
Combination meter light (for coupe and liftback)	E–13
Discharge warning light (for sedan, hardtop, and wagon)	C–4
Discharge warning light (for hardtop SR-5)	C–4
Discharge warning light (for coupe and liftback)	C–4
Fuel remaining warning (sedan, hardtop, and wagon—Calif.)	F–4
Fuel remaining warning light (hardtop SR-5)	F–4
Fuel remaining warning light (coupe and liftback—Calif.)	F–4
Headlight, left-hand	F–14
Headlight, right-hand	F–15
Heater control light (for sedan, hardtop, and wagon)	E–15
Heater control light (for liftback and coupe)	E–15
High beam indicator light (for sedan, hardtop, and wagon)	E–15
High beam indicator light (for hardtop SR-5)	E–15
High beam indicator light (for liftback and coupe)	E–15
Interior light	G–7
Interior light (for hardtop SR-5)	G–7
Luggage compartment light (for liftback)	F–7
License plate light (for sedan, hardtop)	G–14
License plate light (for wagon)	G–14
License plate light (for coupe)	G–14
License plate light (for liftback)	G–14
Low oil pressure warning light (for sedan, hardtop, and wagon)	G–4
Low oil pressure warning light (for liftback and coupe)	G–4
Map light (for hardtop SR-5)	D–7
Parking light, left-hand	G–13
Parking light, right-hand	G–13
Radio indicator light (for sedan, hardtop, and wagon)	F–13
Radio indicator light (for liftback and wagon	F–13
Side marker light, front left-hand	G–13
Side marker light, front right-hand	G–13
Side marker light, rear left-hand (for sedan and hardtop)	G–13
Side marker light, rear left-hand (for wagon)	G–13

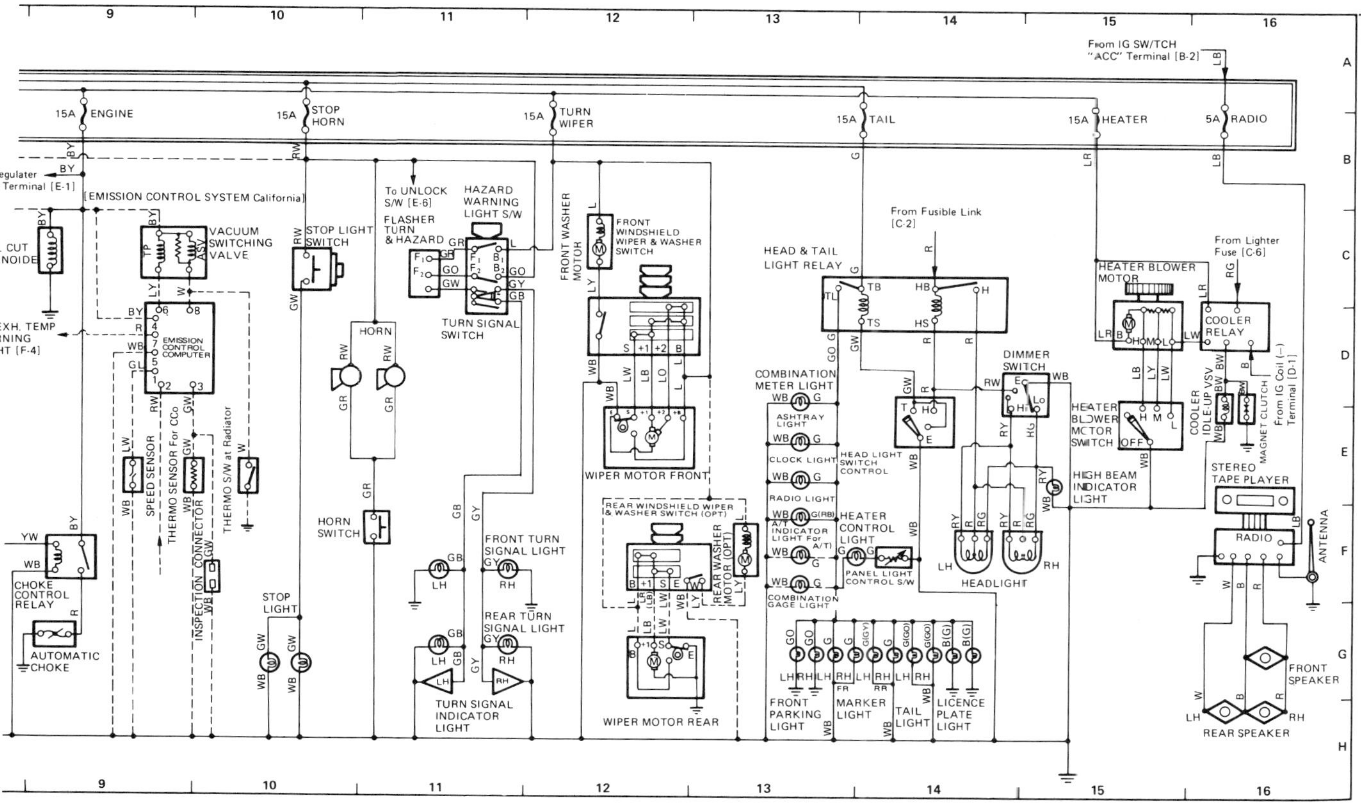

4

Component	Location
Side marker light, rear left-hand (for coupe)	G–13
Side marker light, rear left-hand (for liftback)	G–13
Side marker light, rear right-hand (for sedan and hardtop)	G–13
Side marker light, rear right-hand (for wagon)	G–13
Side marker light, right-hand (for coupe)	G–13
Side marker light, rear right-hand (for liftback)	G–13
Stop light, left-hand (for sedan and hardtop)	G–10
Stop light, left-hand (for wagon)	G–10
Stop light, left-hand (for coupe)	G–10
Stop light, left-hand (for liftback)	G–10
Stop light, right-hand (for sedan and hardtop)	G–10
Stop light, right-hand (for wagon)	G–10
Stop light, right-hand (for coupe)	G–10
Stop light, right-hand (for liftback)	G–10
Taillight, left-hand (for sedan and hardtop)	G–14
Taillight, left-hand (for wagon)	G–14
Taillight, left-hand (for coupe)	G–14
Taillight, left-hand (for liftback)	G–14
Taillight, right-hand (for sedan and hardtop)	G–14
Taillight, right-hand (for wagon)	G–14
Taillight, right-hand (for coupe)	G–14
Taillight, right-hand (for liftback)	G–14
Turn signal, front left-hand	F–11
Turn signal, front right-hand	F–11
Turn signal, rear left-hand (for sedan and hardtop)	G–11
Turn signal, rear left-hand (for wagon)	G–11
Turn signal, rear left-hand (for coupe)	G–11
Turn signal, rear left-hand (for liftback)	G–11
Turn signal, rear right-hand (for sedan and hardtop)	G–11
Turn signal, rear right-hand (for wagon	G–11
Turn signal, rear right-hand (for coupe)	G–11
Turn signal, rear right-hand (for liftback)	G–11
Turn signal indicator light, left-hand (for sedan, hardtop, and wagon)	H–11
Turn signal indicator light, left-hand (for hardtop SR-5)	H–11
Turn signal indicator light, left-hand (for liftback and coupe)	H–11
Turn signal indicator light, right-hand (for sedan, hardtop, and wagon)	H–11
Turn signal indicator light, right-hand (for hardtop SR-5)	H–11
Turn signal indicator light, right-hand (for liftback and coupe)	H–11
Magnet clutch (for cooler, optional)	D–16
Heater blower motor	C–15
Starter motor	D–2
Windshield washer motor, front	C–12
Windshield washer motor, rear (for wagon, optional)	F–13
Windshield washer motor, rear (for liftback, optional)	F–13
Windshield wiper motor, front	E–12
Windshield wiper motor, rear (for wagon, optional)	G–12
Windshield wiper motor, rear (for liftback optional)	G–12
Oil pressure gauge (for hardtop SR-5)	G–4
Oil pressure gauge (for liftback and coupe SR-5)	G–4
Oil temperature sender (for SR-5)	G–4
Radio (for sedan, hardtop, and wagon)	F–14
Radio (for coupe and liftback)	F–14
Radio suppressor (for SR-5)	E–3

Component	Location
Regulator	F–2
Choke control relay	F–9
Cooler relay (optional)	D–16
Defogger relay (optional)	D–5
Headlight and taillight control relay	C–14
Relay (for brake warning light inspection)	F–3
Seat belt buckle switch	D–6
Seat belt warning buzzer	F–6
Seat belt warning computer	D–6
Seat belt warning light (for sedan, hardtop, and wagon)	F–6
Seat belt warning light (for hardtop SR-5)	F–6
Seat belt warning light (for liftback and coupe)	F–6
Speaker, front	G–16
Speaker, front	G–16
Speaker, rear (for sedan and hardtop)	H–16
Speaker, rear (for coupe)	H–16
Speaker, rear (for liftback)	H–16
Stereo tape player	E–16
Back-up light switch	C–5
Defogger, rear window switch (for sedan, hardtop, and wagon)	C–5
Defogger, rear window switch (for coupe and liftback)	C–5
Differential switch	G–3
Dimmer switch	D–14
Door switch, left-hand	G–6
Door switch, right-hand	G–6
Fuel remaining warning switch (for sedan and hardtop)	F–4
Fuel remaining warning switch (for wagon)	F–4
Fuel remaining warning switch (for coupe)	F–4
Fuel remaining warning switch (for liftback)	F–4
Hazard warning light switch	C–11
Headlight control switch	E–14
Heater blower motor switch	E–15
Horn switch	F–11
Ignition switch	A–1
Interior light switch	G–7
Interior light switch (for hardtop SR-5)	G–7
Luggage compartment switch	F–7
Map light switch (for hardtop SR-5)	D–7
Neutral safety switch (for automatic trans.)	C–2
Oil pressure switch	G–4
Panel light control switch (for sedan, hardtop, and wagon)	F–14
Panel light control switch (for coupe and liftback)	F–14
Parking brake switch	G–3
Stop light switch (except hardtop SR-5)	C–10
Turn signal switch	C–11
Unlock warning switch	E–6
Windshield wiper and washer switch, front	D–12
Windshield wiper and washer switch, rear (for wagon, optional)	F–12
Windshield wiper and washer switch, rear (for liftback optional)	F–12
Tachometer (for hardtop SR-5)	E–4
Tachometer (for coupe and liftback SR-5)	E–4
Unlock warning buzzer	F–6
Water temperature gauge (for sedan, hardtop, and wagon)	F–4
Water temperature gauge (for coupe and liftback)	F–4
Water temperature sender	F–4

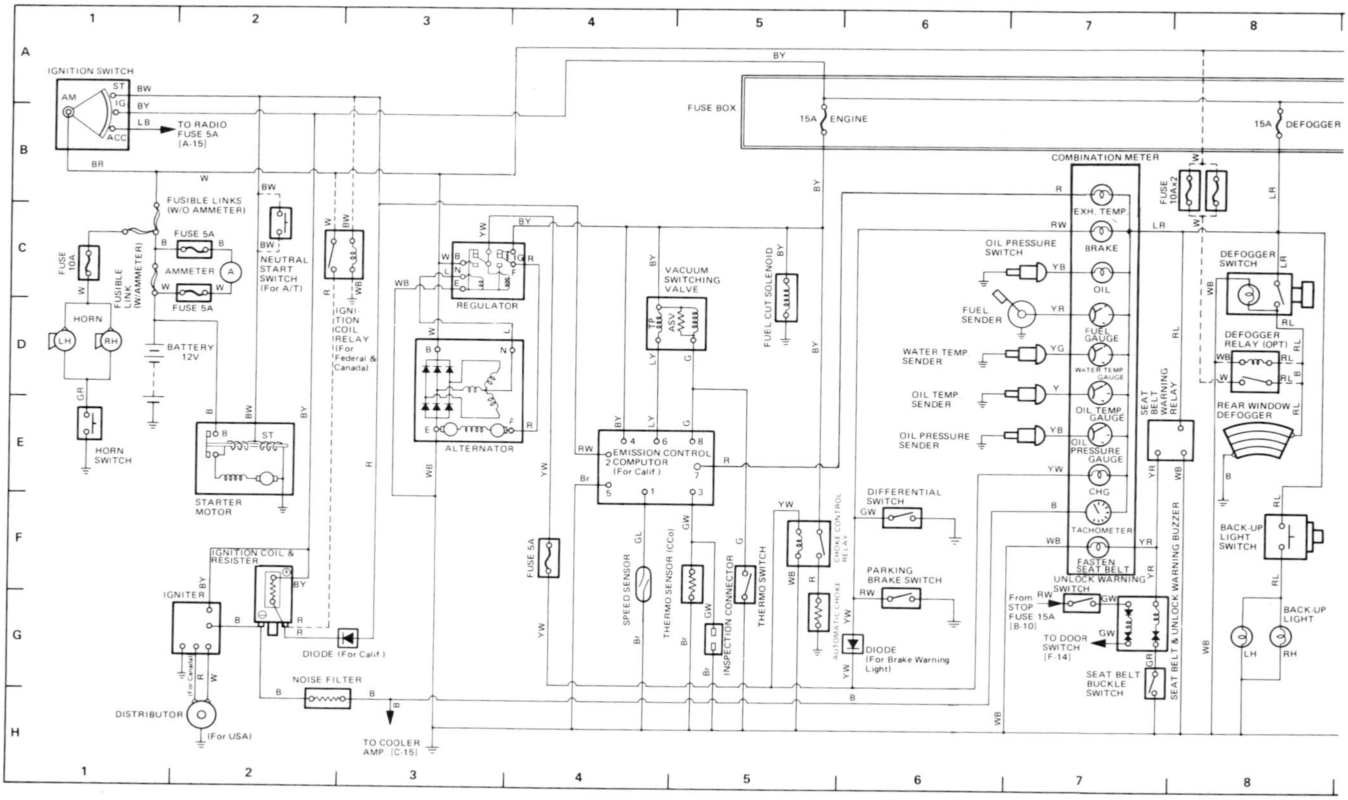

Components	Location
Alternator	E-3
Ammeter (for hardtop, SR-5 only)	C-2
Ammeter (for coupe and liftback SR-5 only)	C-2
Amplifier (for cooler)	C-15
Antenna	F-15
Automatic choke	G-5
Battery	D-2
Cooler idle-up VSV (for cooler)	D-16
Cooler control volume	E-15
Cigarette lighter (for sedan, hardtop, and wagon)	D-13
Cigarette lighter (for coupe and liftback)	D-13
Clock (for sedan, hardtop, and wagon)	E-13
Clock (for hardtop SR-5)	E-13
Clock (for coupe and liftback)	E-13
Combination meter	B-7
Defogger, rear window (for sedan, hardtop, and coupe)	E-8
Defogger, rear window (for wagon)	E-8
Defogger, rear window (for liftback)	E-8
Diode (for ignition coil) (Calif.)	G-2
Diode (for brake warning light)	G-6
Distributor	H-1
Emission control computer	E-4
Exhaust temp. warning light (for sedan, hardtop, and wagon)	C-7
Exhaust temp. warning light (for hardtop SR-5)	C-7
Exhaust temp. warning light (for coupe and liftback)	C-7
Inspection connector	G-5
Speed sensor (for sedan, hardtop, and wagon)	F-4
Speed sensor (for hardtop SR-5)	F-4
Speed sensor (for coupe and liftback)	F-4
Thermo sensor (CCo)	F-5
Thermo switch	F-5
Vacuum switching valve	C-5
Flasher, turn signal and hazard	C-12
Fuel cut solenoid	C-5
Fuel gauge (for sedan, hardtop, and wagon)	D-7
Fuel gauge (for hardtop SR-5)	D-7
Fuel gauge (for coupe and liftback)	D-7
Fuel sender (for sedan, hardtop and coupe)	D-6
Fuel sender (for wagon)	D-6
Fuel sender (for liftback)	D-6
Fuse box	B-5
Fuse (5A) for ammeter	C-2, D-2
Fuse (5A) for charge warning light	F-4
Fuse (5A) for interior light	E-14
Fuse (10A) for horn	C-1
Fuse (10A × 2) for defogger relay	B-8
Fusible links (without ammeter)	C-2
Fusible link (with ammeter)	C-1
Horn, left-hand	D-1
Horn, right-hand	D-1
Ignition coil	F-2
Ignition coil diode (Calif.)	G-3
Ignition coil resistor	F-2
Igniter	G-2
Ashtray indicator light, (for sedan, hardtop, and wagon)	D-10
Ashtray indicator light, (for coupe, liftback)	D-10
Automatic transmission indicator light	E-10
Back-up light, left-hand (for sedan)	G-8
Back-up light, left- and right-hand (for hardtop)	G-8
Back-up light, left-hand (for wagon)	G-8
Back-up light, left-hand (for coupe)	G-8
Back-up light, left-hand (for liftback)	G-8
Back-up light, right-hand (for sedan)	G-8
Back-up light, right-hand (for wagon)	G-8
Back-up light, right-hand (for coupe)	G-8
Back-up light, right-hand (for liftback)	G-8
Brake warning light (for sedan, hardtop, and wagon)	C-7
Brake warning light (for hardtop SR-5)	C-7
Brake warning light (for coupe and liftback)	C-7
Clock indicator light (for coupe and liftback)	D-10
Combination meter indicator light (for hardtop SR-5)	D-10
Combination meter indicator light (for coupe and liftback SR-5)	D-10
Combination meter indicator light (for sedan, hardtop, and wagon)	D-10
Combination meter indicator light (for coupe and liftback)	D-10
Deck room light (for liftback)	E-14
Discharge warning light (for sedan, hardtop, and wagon)	E-7
Discharge warning light (for hardtop SR-5)	E-7
Discharge warning light (for coupe and liftback)	E-7
Headlight, left-hand	E-9
Headlight, right-hand	E-9
Heater control indicator light (for sedan, hardtop, and wagon)	E-10
Heater control indicator light (for liftback and coupe)	E-10
High beam indicator light (for sedan, hardtop, and wagon)	G-9
High beam indicator light (for hardtop SR-5)	G-9
High beam indicator light (for coupe and liftback)	G-9
Interior light	F-13
License plate light (for sedan)	E-10
License plate light (for hardtop)	E-10
License plate light (for wagon)	E-10
License plate light (for coupe)	E-10
License plate light (for liftback)	E-10
Low oil pressure warning light (for sedan, hardtop, and wagon)	C-7
Low oil pressure warning light (for liftback and coupe)	C-7
Parking light, left-hand	G-10
Parking light, right-hand	G-10
Side marker light, front left-hand	F-10
Side marker light, front right-hand	F-10
Side marker light, rear left-hand (for sedan)	F-10
Side marker light, rear left-hand (for hardtop)	F-10
Side marker light, rear left-hand (for wagon)	F-10
Side marker light, rear left-hand (for coupe)	F-10
Side marker light, rear left-hand (for liftback)	F-10
Side marker light, right-hand (for sedan)	F-10
Side marker light, right-hand (for hardtop)	F-10
Side marker light, right-hand (for wagon)	F-10
Side marker light, right-hand (for coupe)	F-10
Side marker light, rear right-hand (for liftback)	F-10
Stop light, left-hand (for sedan)	G-11
Stop light, left- and right-hand (for hardtop)	G-11

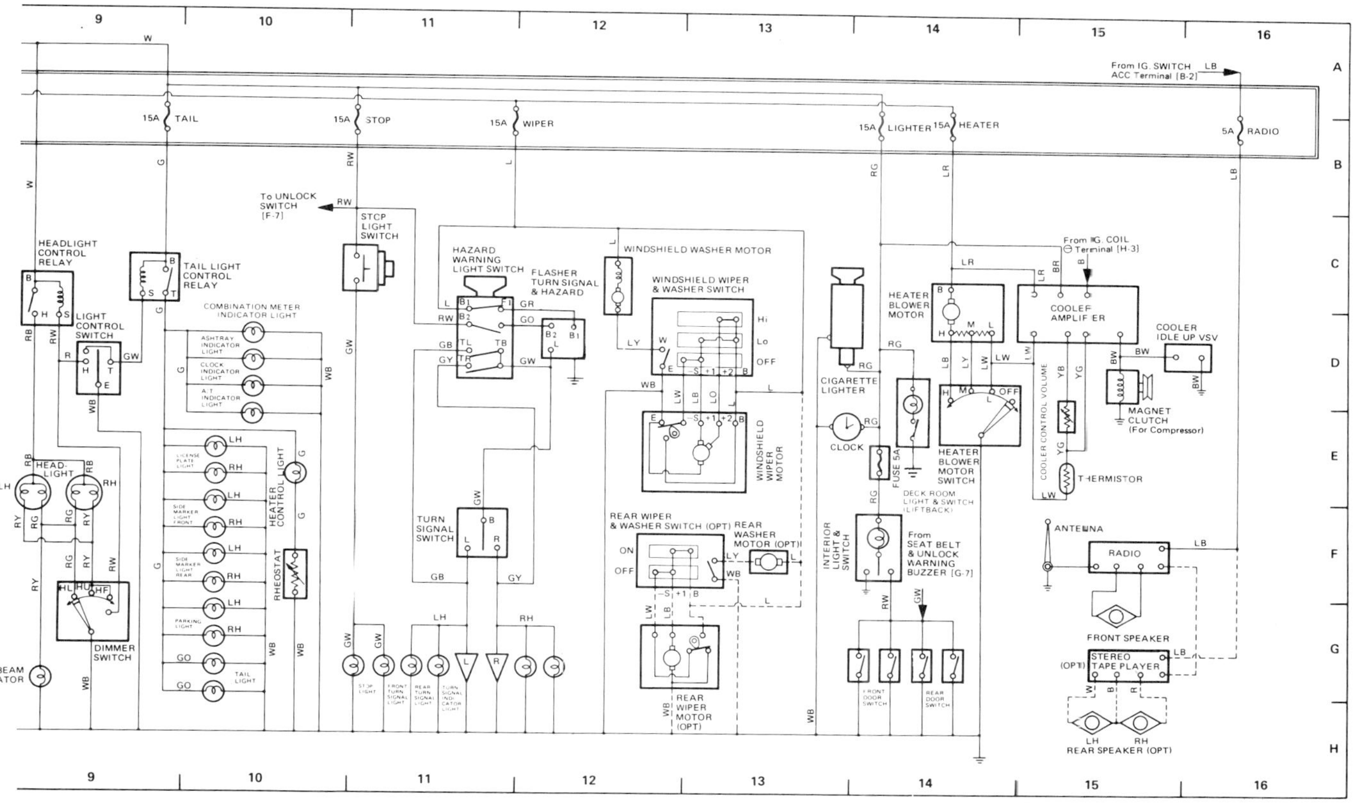

Stop light, left-hand (for wagon)	G–11
Stop light, left-hand (for coupe)	G–11
Stop light, left-hand (for liftback)	G–11
Stop light, right-hand (for sedan)	G–11
Stop light, right-hand (for wagon)	G–11
Stop light, right-hand (for coupe)	G–11
Stop light, right-hand (for liftback)	G–11
Taillight, left-hand (for sedan)	G–10
Taillight, left- and right-hand (for hardtop)	G–10
Taillight, left-hand (for wagon)	G–10
Taillight, left-hand (for coupe)	G–10
Taillight, left-hand (for liftback)	G–10
Taillight, right-hand (for sedan)	G–10
Taillight, right-hand (for wagon)	G–10
Taillight, right-hand (for coupe)	G–10
Taillight, right-hand (for liftback)	G–10
Turn signal light, front left-hand	G–11
Turn signal light, front right-hand	G–12
Turn signal light, rear left-hand (for sedan)	G–11
Turn signal light, rear left-hand (for hardtop)	G–11
Turn signal light, rear left-hand (for wagon)	G–11
Turn signal light, rear left-hand (for coupe)	G–11
Turn signal light, rear left-hand (for liftback)	G–11
Turn signal light, rear right-hand (for sedan)	G–12
Turn signal light, rear right-hand (for hardtop)	G–12
Turn signal light, rear right-hand (for wagon)	G–12
Turn signal light, rear right-hand (for coupe)	G–12
Turn signal light, rear right-hand (for liftback)	G–12
Turn signal indicator light, left-hand (for sedan, hardtop, and wagon)	G–11
Turn signal indicator light, left-hand (for hardtop SR-5)	G–11
Turn signal indicator light, left-hand (for liftback and coupe)	G–11
Turn signal indicator light, right-hand (for sedan, hardtop, and wagon)	G–11
Turn signal indicator light, right-hand (for hardtop SR-5)	G–11
Turn signal indicator light, right-hand (for liftback and coupe)	G–11
Magnet clutch (for compressor)	E–15
Heater blower motor	C–14
Starter motor	E–2
Windshield washer motor	C–12
Washer motor, rear (for wagon, optional)	F–13
Washer motor, rear (for liftback, optional)	F–13
Windshield wiper motor	E–13
Wiper motor, rear (for wagon, optional)	G–13
Wiper motor, rear (for liftback, optional)	G–13
Noise filter	G–2
Oil pressure gauge (for hardtop SR-5)	E–7
Oil pressure gauge (for liftback and coupe SR-5)	E–7
Oil pressure sender	E–6
Oil temperature sender (for SR-5)	D–6
Oil temperature gauge (for hardtop SR-5)	E–7
Oil temperature gauge (for liftback and coupe SR-5)	E–7
Radio (for sedan, hardtop, and wagon)	F–15
Radio (for hardtop SR-5)	F–15
Radio (for coupe and liftback)	F–15

Regulator	D–3
Rheostat (for sedan, hardtop, and wagon)	F–10
Rheostat (for coupe and liftback)	F–10
Choke control relay	F–5
Cooler amplifier relay	C–15
Defogger relay (optional)	D–8
Headlight control relay	C–9
Ignition coil relay (Federal and Canada)	D–3
Taillight control relay	C–9
Seat belt buckle switch	G–7
Seat belt warning buzzer	G–7
Seat belt warning relay	E–7
Seat belt warning light (for sedan, hardtop, and wagon)	F–7
Seat belt warning light (for hardtop SR-5)	F–7
Seat belt warning light (for liftback and coupe)	F–7
Speaker, front	G–15
Speaker, rear left-hand (for sedan, hardtop, and coupe)	H–15
Speaker, rear right-hand (for sedan, hardtop, and coupe)	H–15
Speaker, rear left-hand (for liftback)	H–15
Speaker, rear right-hand (for liftback)	H–15
Stereo tape player	G–15
Back-up light switch (for manual trans.)	F–8
Back-up light switch (for automatic trans.)	F–8
Deck room switch (for liftback)	E–14
Defogger switch, rear window (for sedan, hardtop, and wagon)	C–8
Defogger switch, rear window (for coupe and liftback)	C–8
Differential switch	F–6
Dimmer switch	G–9
Door switch, front left-hand	H–14
Door switch, front right-hand	H–14
Door switch, rear left-hand (for 4-door)	H–14
Door switch, rear right-hand (for 4-door)	H–14
Hazard warning light switch	C–11
Heater blower motor switch	E–14
Horn switch	E–1
Ignition switch	A–1
Interior light switch	F–13
Light control switch	D–9
Neutral start switch (automatic trans.)	C–2
Oil pressure switch	C–7
Parking brake switch	F–6
Stop light switch	C–11
Turn signal switch	F–11
Unlock warning switch	F–7
Windshield wiper and washer switch	C–13
Wiper and washer switch, rear (for liftback and wagon)	F–12
Tachometer (for hardtop SR-5)	F–7
Tachometer (for coupe and liftback SR-5)	F–7
Thermistor	E–15
Unlock warning buzzer	G–7
Water temperature gauge (for sedan, hardtop, and wagon)	D–7
Water temperature gauge (for hardtop SR-5)	D–7
Water temperature gauge (for coupe and liftback)	D–7
Water temperature sender	D–6

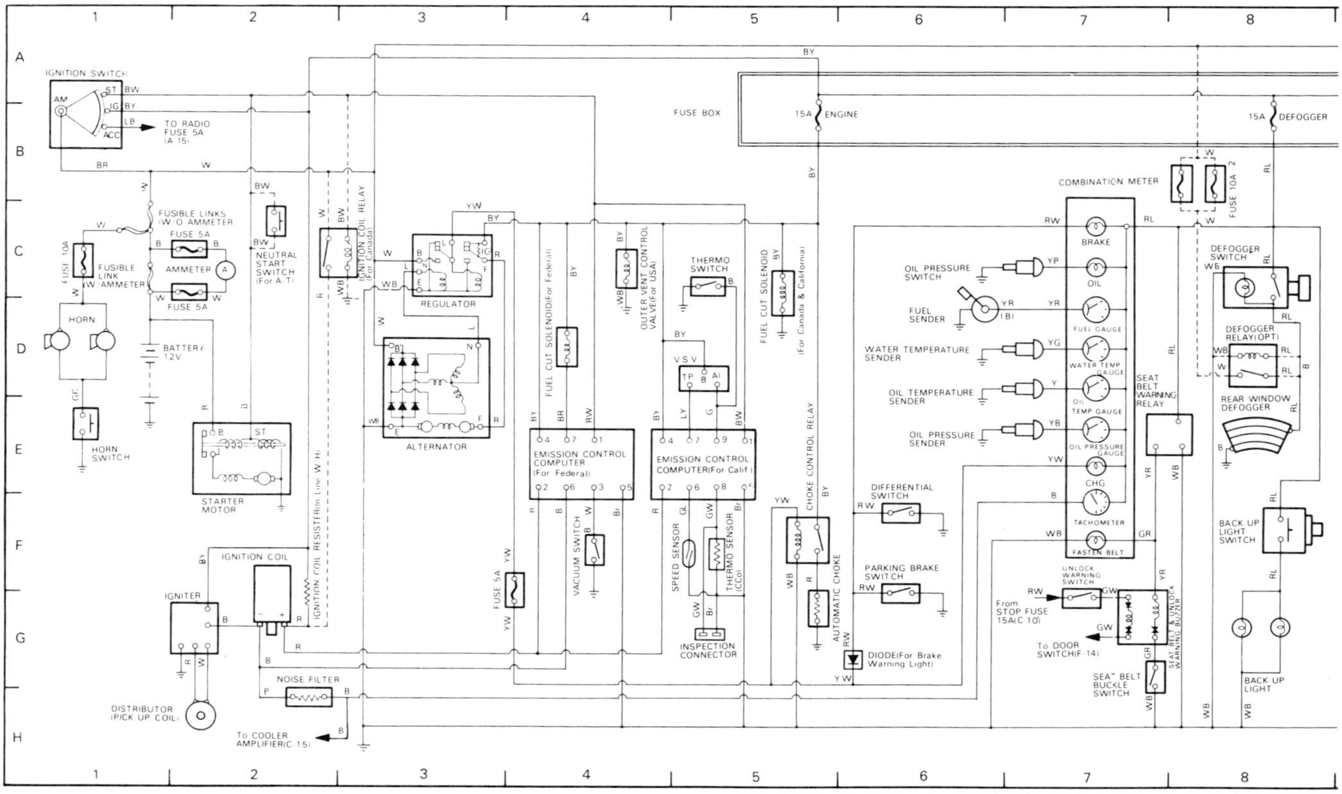

Components	Location
Alternator	E-3
Ammeter (for hardtop, SR-5 only)	C-2
Ammeter (for coupe and liftback, SR-5 only)	C-2
Amplifier (for cooler)	C-15
Antenna	F-15
Automatic choke	G-5
Battery	D-1
Cooler idle-up VSV	C-16
Cooler control volume	E-15
Cigarette lighter (for sedan, hardtop, and wagon)	D-13
Cigarette lighter (for coupe and liftback)	D-13
Clock (for sedan, hardtop, and wagon)	E-13
Clock (for hardtop SR-5)	E-13
Clock (for coupe and liftback)	E-13
Combination meter	B-7
Defogger, rear window (for sedan, hardtop, and coupe)	D-8
Defogger, rear window (for wagon)	D-8
Defogger, rear window (for liftback)	D-8
Diode (for brake warning light)	G-6
Distributor (pick-up coil)	H-1
Emission control computer (Federal)	E-4
Emission control computer (Calif.)	E-5
Inspection connector (Calif.)	G-5
Outer vent control valve (USA)	C-4
Speed sensor (for sedan, hardtop, wagon) (Calif.)	G-5
Speed sensor (for hardtop SR-5) (Calif.)	F-5
Speed sensor (for coupe and liftback) (Calif.)	F-5
Thermo sensor (CCo) (Calif.)	F-5
Thermo switch (Calif.)	C-5
Vacuum switch (Federal)	F-4
Vacuum switching valve (Calif.)	D-5
Flasher, turn signal and hazard	C-12
Fuel cut solenoid (Canada and and Calif.)	C-5
Fuel cut solenoid (Federal)	D-4
Fuel gauge (for sedan, hardtop, and wagon)	D-7
Fuel gauge (for hardtop SR-5)	D-7
Fuel gauge (for coupe and liftback)	D-7
Fuel sender (for sedan, hardtop, and coupe)	D-7
Fuel sender (for wagon)	D-6
Fuel sender (for liftback)	D-6
Fuse box	B-5
Fuse (5A) for ammeter	C-2
Fuse (5A) for charge warning light	G-4
Fuse (5A) for interior light	E-14
Fuse (10A) for horn	C-1
Fuse (10A×2) for defogger relay	B-8
Fusible links (w/o ammeter)	C-1
Fusible link (w/ammeter)	C-1
Horn, left-hand	D-1
Horn, right-hand	D-1
Ignition coil	F-2
Ignition coil resister	G-2
Igniter	G-2
Ashtray indicator light (for sedan, hardtop, and wagon)	D-10
Ashtray indicator light (for coupe and liftback)	D-10
Automatic transmission indicator light	D-10
Back-up light, left-hand (for sedan)	G-8
Back-up light left- and right-hand (for hardtop)	G-8
Back-up light, left-hand (for wagon)	G-8
Back-up light, left-hand (for coupe)	G-8
Back-up light left-hand (for liftback)	G-8
Back-up light, right-hand (for sedan)	G-8
Back-up light, right-hand (for wagon)	G-8
Back-up light, right-hand (for coupe)	G-8
Back-up light, right-hand (for liftback)	G-8
Brake warning light (for sedan, hardtop, and wagon)	C-7
Brake warning light (for hardtop SR-5)	C-7
Brake warning light (for coupe and liftback)	C-7
Clock indicator light (for coupe and liftback)	D-10
Combination meter indicator light (for hardtop SR-5)	D-10
Combination meter indicator light (for coupe and liftback SR-5)	D-10
Combination meter indicator light (for sedan, hardtop, and wagon)	D-10
Combination meter indicator light (for hardtop SR-5)	D-10
Combination meter indicator light (for coupe and liftback)	D-10
Deck room light (for liftback)	D-14
Discharge warning light (for sedan, hardtop, and wagon)	E-7
Discharge warning light (for hardtop SR-5)	E-7
Discharge warning light (for coupe and liftback)	E-7
Headlight, left-hand	E-9
Headlight, right-hand	E-9
Heater control indicator light (for sedan, hardtop, and wagon)	E-10
Heater control indicator light (for liftback and coupe)	E-10
High beam indicator light (for sedan, hardtop, and wagon)	G-9
High beam indicator light (for hardtop SR-5)	G-9
High beam indicator light (for coupe and liftback)	G-9
Interior light	F-14
License plate light (for sedan)	E-10
License plate light (for hardtop)	E-10
License plate light (for wagon)	E-10
License plate light (for coupe)	E-10
License plate light (for liftback)	E-10
Low oil pressure warning light (for sedan, hardtop, and wagon)	C-7
Low oil pressure warning light (for liftback and coupe)	C-7
Parking light, left-hand	G-10
Parking light, right-hand	G-10
Side marker, front left-hand	F-10
Side marker, front right-hand	F-10
Side marker, rear left-hand (for sedan)	F-10
Side marker, rear left-hand (for hardtop)	F-10
Side marker, rear left-hand (for wagon)	F-10
Side marker, rear left-hand (for coupe)	F-10
Side marker, rear left-hand (for liftback)	F-10
Side marker, rear right-hand (for sedan)	F-10
Side marker, rear right-hand (for hardtop)	F-10
Side marker, rear right-hand (for wagon)	F-10
Side marker, rear right-hand (for coupe)	F-10
Side marker, rear right-hand (for liftback)	F-10
Stop light, left-hand (for sedan)	G-11
Stop light, left- and right-hand (for hardtop)	G-11

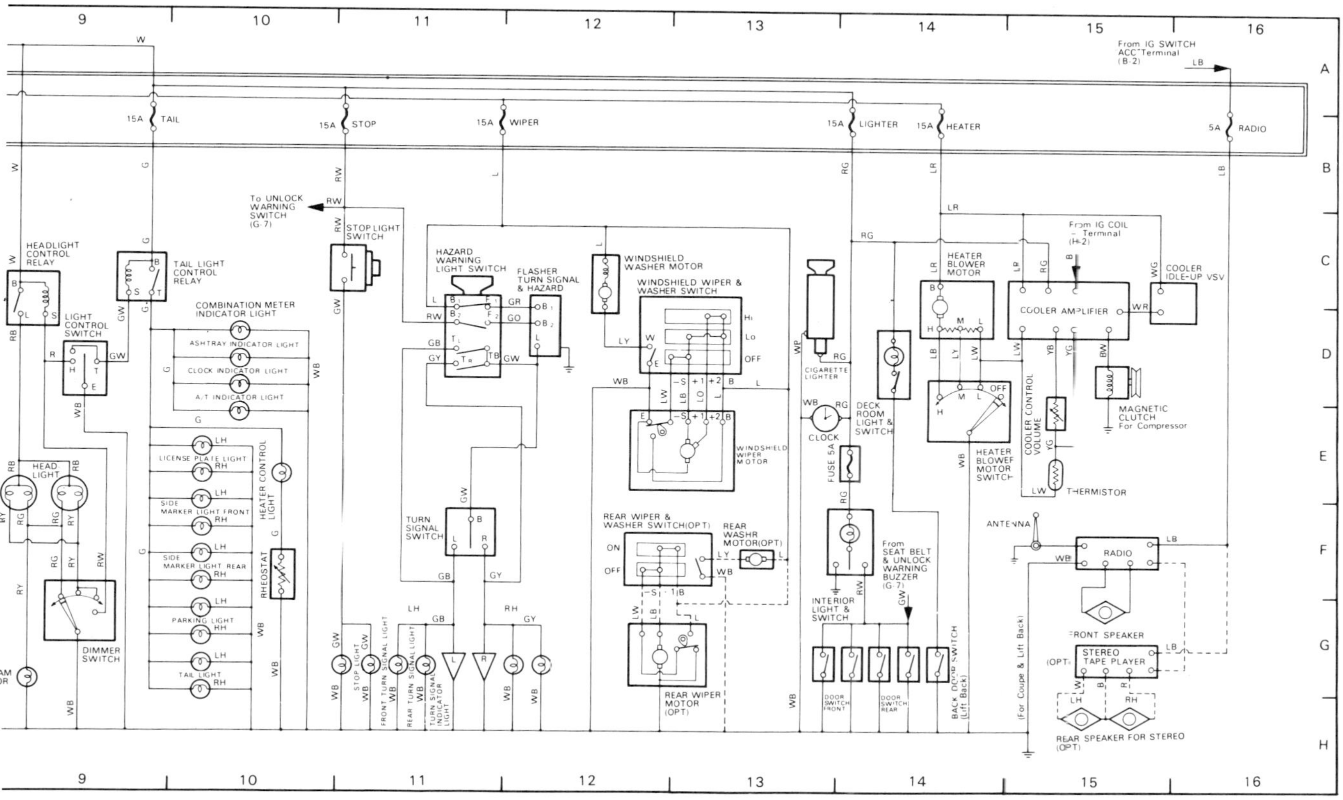

Stop light, left-hand (for wagon)	G-11
Stop light, left-hand (for coupe)	G-11
Stop light, left-hand (for liftback)	G-11
Stop light, right-hand (for sedan)	G-11
Stop light, right-hand (for wagon)	G-11
Stop light, right-hand (for coupe)	G-11
Stop light, right-hand (for liftback)	G-11
Taillight, left-hand (for sedan)	G-10
Taillight, left-hand and right-hand (for hardtop)	G-10
Taillight, left-hand (for wagon)	G-10
Taillight, left-hand (for coupe)	G-10
Taillight, left-hand (for liftback)	G-10
Taillight, right-hand (for sedan)	G-10
Taillight, right-hand (for wagon)	G-10
Taillight, right-hand (for coupe)	G-10
Taillight, right-hand (for liftback)	G-10
Turn signal light, front left-hand	G-11
Turn signal light, front right-hand	G-12
Turn signal light, rear left-hand (for sedan)	G-11
Turn signal light, rear left-hand (for hardtop)	G-11
Turn signal light, rear left-hand (for wagon)	G-11
Turn signal light, rear left-hand (for coupe)	G-11
Turn signal light, rear left-hand (for liftback)	G-11
Turn signal light, rear right-hand (for sedan)	G-12
Turn signal light, rear right-hand (for hardtop)	G-12
Turn signal light, rear right-hand (for wagon)	G-12
Turn signal light, rear right-hand (for coupe)	G-12
Turn signal light, rear right-hand (for liftback)	G-12
Turn signal indicator light, left-hand (for sedan, hardtop, and wagon)	G-11
Turn signal indicator light, left-hand (for hardtop SR-5)	G-11
Turn signal indicator light, left-hand (for coupe and liftback)	G-11
Turn signal indicator light, right-hand (for sedan, hardtop, and wagon)	G-11
Turn signal indicator light, right-hand (for hardtop SR-5)	G-11
Turn signal indicator light, right-hand (for coupe and liftback)	G-11
Magnet clutch (for compressor)	E-15
Heater blower motor	C-14
Starter motor	F-2
Windshield washer motor	C-12
Washer motor, rear (for wagon, optional)	F-13
Washer motor, rear (for liftback, optional)	F-13
Windshield wiper motor	G-13
Wiper motor, rear (for wagon, optional)	G-13
Wiper motor, rear (for liftback, optional)	G-13
Noise filter	G-2
Oil pressure gauge (for hardtop SR-5)	E-7
Oil pressure gauge (for coupe and liftback SR-5)	E-7
Oil pressure sender (for SR-5)	E-6
Oil temperature sender (for SR-5)	D-6
Oil temperature gauge (for hardtop SR-5)	E-7
Oil temperature gauge (for liftback and coupe SR-5)	E-7
Radio (for sedan, hardtop, and wagon)	F-15
Radio (for hardtop SR-5)	F-15
Radio (for coupe and liftback)	F-15
Regulator	D-3
Rheostat (for sedan, hardtop, and wagon)	F-10
Rheostat (for coupe and liftback)	F-10
Choke control relay	E-5
Cooler amplifier relay	C-15
Defogger relay (optional)	D-8
Headlight control relay	C-9
Ignition coil relay (Canada)	C-3
Taillight control relay	C-10
Seat belt buckle switch	G-7
Seat belt warning buzzer	G-7
Seat belt warning relay	D-7
Seat belt warning light (for sedan, hardtop, and wagon)	F-7
Seat belt warning light (for hardtop SR-5)	F-7
Seat belt warning light (for coupe and liftback)	F-7
Speaker, front	G-15
Speaker, rear left-hand (for sedan, hardtop, and coupe)	H-15
Speaker, rear right-hand (for sedan, hardtop, and coupe)	H-15
Speaker, rear left-hand (for liftback)	H-15
Speaker, rear right-hand (for liftback)	H-15
Stereo tape player	G-15
Back-up light switch (manual trans.)	F-8
Back-up light switch (automatic trans.)	F-8
Back door switch (for liftback)	G-14
Deck room switch (for liftback)	E-14
Defogger, rear window switch (for sedan, hardtop, and wagon)	C-8
Defogger, rear window switch (for coupe and liftback)	C-8
Differential switch	E-6
Dimmer switch	G-9
Door switch, front left-hand	G-14
Door switch, front right-hand	G-14
Door switch, rear left-hand (for four-door)	G-14
Door switch, rear right-hand (for four-door)	G-14
Hazard warning light switch	C-11
Heater blower motor switch	E-14
Horn switch	E-1
Ignition switch	A-1
Interior light switch	F-14
Light control switch	D-9
Neutral start switch (for automatic trans.)	C-2
Oil pressure switch	C-6
Parking brake switch	F-6
Stop light switch	C-11
Turn signal switch	F-11
Unlock warning switch	F-7
Windshield wiper and washer switch	C-13
Wiper and washer switch, rear (for liftback and wagon)	F-12
Tachometer (for hardtop SR-5)	F-7
Tachometer (for coupe and liftback SR-5)	F-7
Thermistor (for cooler)	E-15
Unlock warning buzzer	G-7
Water temperature gauge (for sedan, hardtop and wagon)	D-7
Water temperature gauge (for hardtop SR-5)	D-7
Water temperature gauge (for coupe and liftback)	D-7
Water temperature sender	D-6

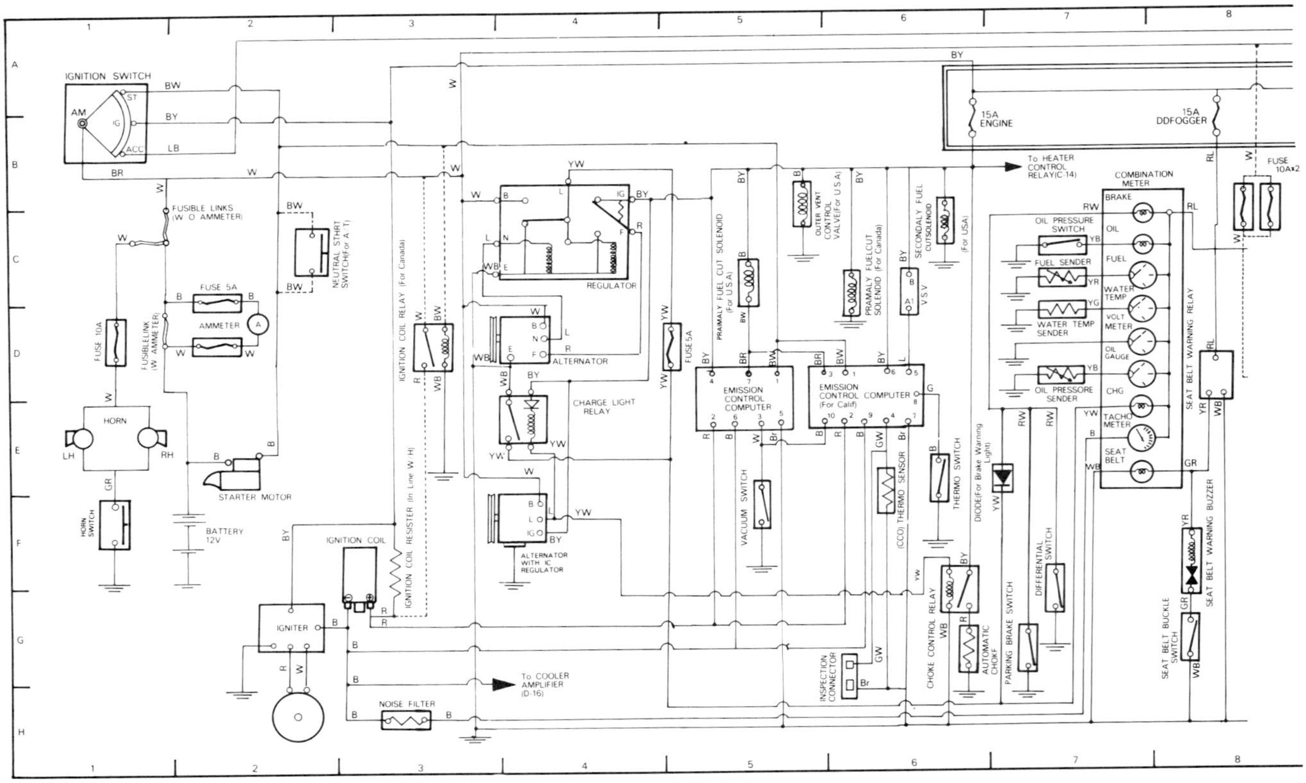

Components	Location
Alternator (with IC regulator)	F-4
Alternator	D-4
Ammeter (for hardtop, SR-5 only)	D-2
Ammeter (for coupe and liftback, SR-5 only)	D-2
Antenna	E-15
Automatic choke	G-6
Battery	F-2
Cooler amplifier	C-15
Cooler idle-up VSV	C-16
Cooler control volume	D-15
Cigarette lighter (for sedan, hardtop, and wagon)	C-13
Cigarette lighter (for coupe and liftback)	C-13
Clock (for sedan, hardtop, and wagon)	E-13
Clock (for hardtop SR-5)	E-13
Clock (for coupe and liftback)	E-13
Combination meter	C-7
Defogger, rear window (for sedan, hardtop, and coupe)	E-8
Defogger, rear window (for wagon)	E-8
Defogger, rear window (for liftback)	E-8
Diode (for brake warning light)	E-7
Distributor (pick-up coil)	H-2
Emission control computer (Federal)	E-5
Emission control computer (Calif.)	E-6
Inspection connector (Calif.)	G-6
Outer vent control valve (USA)	C-5
Thermo sensor (CCo) (Calif.)	E-6
Thermo switch (Calif.)	E-6
Vacuum switch (Federal)	F-5
Vacuum switching valve (Calif.)	C-6
Flasher, turn signal and hazard	C-12
Fuel cut solenoid primary (USA)	C-5
Fuel cut solenoid primary (Canada)	C-6
Fuel cut solenoid secondary (USA)	C-6
Fuel gauge (for sedan, hardtop, and wagon)	C-7
Fuel gauge (for hardtop SR-5)	C-7
Fuel gauge (for coupe and liftback)	C-7
Fuel sender (for sedan, hardtop, and coupe)	C-7
Fuel sender (for wagon)	C-7
Fuel sender (for liftback)	C-7
Fuse box	B-6
Fuse (5A) for ammeter	C-2
Fuse (5A) for charge warning light	D-5
Fuse (5A) for interior light	D-13
Fuse (10A) for horn	D-1
Fuse (10A × 2) for defogger relay	B-8
Fusible links (w/o ammeter)	C-2
Fusible link (w/ammeter)	D-1
Horn, left-hand	E-1
Horn, right-hand	E-1
Ignition coil	F-3
Ignition coil resister	F-3
Igniter	G-2
Ashtray indicator light (for sedan, hardtop, and wagon)	D-10
Ashtray indicator light (for coupe and liftback)	D-10

Components	Location
Automatic transmission indicator light	E-10
Back-up light, left-hand (for sedan)	G-9
Back-up light left- and right-hand (for hardtop)	G-9
Back-up light, left-hand (for wagon)	G-9
Back-up light, left-hand (for coupe)	G-9
Back-up light left-hand (for liftback)	G-9
Back-up light, right-hand (for sedan)	G-9
Back-up light, right-hand (for wagon)	G-9
Back-up light, right-hand (for coupe)	G-9
Back-up light, right-hand (for liftback)	G-9
Brake warning light (for sedan, hardtop, and wagon)	C-7
Brake warning light (for hardtop SR-5)	C-7
Brake warning light (for coupe and liftback)	C-7
Clock indicator light (for coupe and liftback)	D-10
Combination meter indicator light (for hardtop SR-5)	C-10
Combination meter indicator light (for coupe and liftback SR-5)	C-10
Combination meter indicator light (for sedan, hardtop, and wagon)	C-10
Combination meter indicator light (for hardtop SR-5)	C-10
Combination meter indicator light (for coupe and liftback)	C-10
Deck room light (for liftback)	E-13
Discharge warning light (for sedan, hardtop, and wagon)	E-7
Discharge warning light (for hardtop SR-5)	E-7
Discharge warning light (for coupe and liftback)	E-7
Headlight, left-hand	C-9
Headlight, right-hand	C-9
Heater control indicator light (for sedan, hardtop, and wagon)	E-10
Heater control indicator light (for liftback and coupe)	E-10
High beam indicator light (for sedan, hardtop, and wagon)	D-9
High beam indicator light (for hardtop SR-5)	D-9
High beam indicator light (for coupe and liftback)	D-9
Interior light	F-14
License plate light (for sedan)	F-10
License plate light (for hardtop)	F-10
License plate light (for wagon)	F-10
License plate light (for coupe)	F-10
License plate light (for liftback)	F-10
Low oil pressure warning light (for sedan, hardtop, and wagon)	C-7
Low oil pressure warning light (for coupe and liftback)	C-7
Parking light, left-hand	G-10
Parking light, right-hand	G-10
Side marker light, front left-hand	G-10
Side marker light, front right-hand	G-10
Side marker, rear left-hand (for sedan)	H-10
Side marker, rear left-hand (for hardtop)	H-10
Side marker, rear left-hand (for wagon)	H-10
Side marker, rear left-hand (for coupe)	H-10
Side marker, rear left-hand (for liftback)	H-10
Side marker, rear right-hand (for sedan)	H-10
Side marker, rear right-hand (for hardtop)	H-10
Side marker, rear right-hand (for wagon)	H-10
Side marker, rear right-hand (for coupe)	H-10
Side marker, rear right-hand (for liftback)	H-10
Stop light, left-hand (for sedan)	G-11

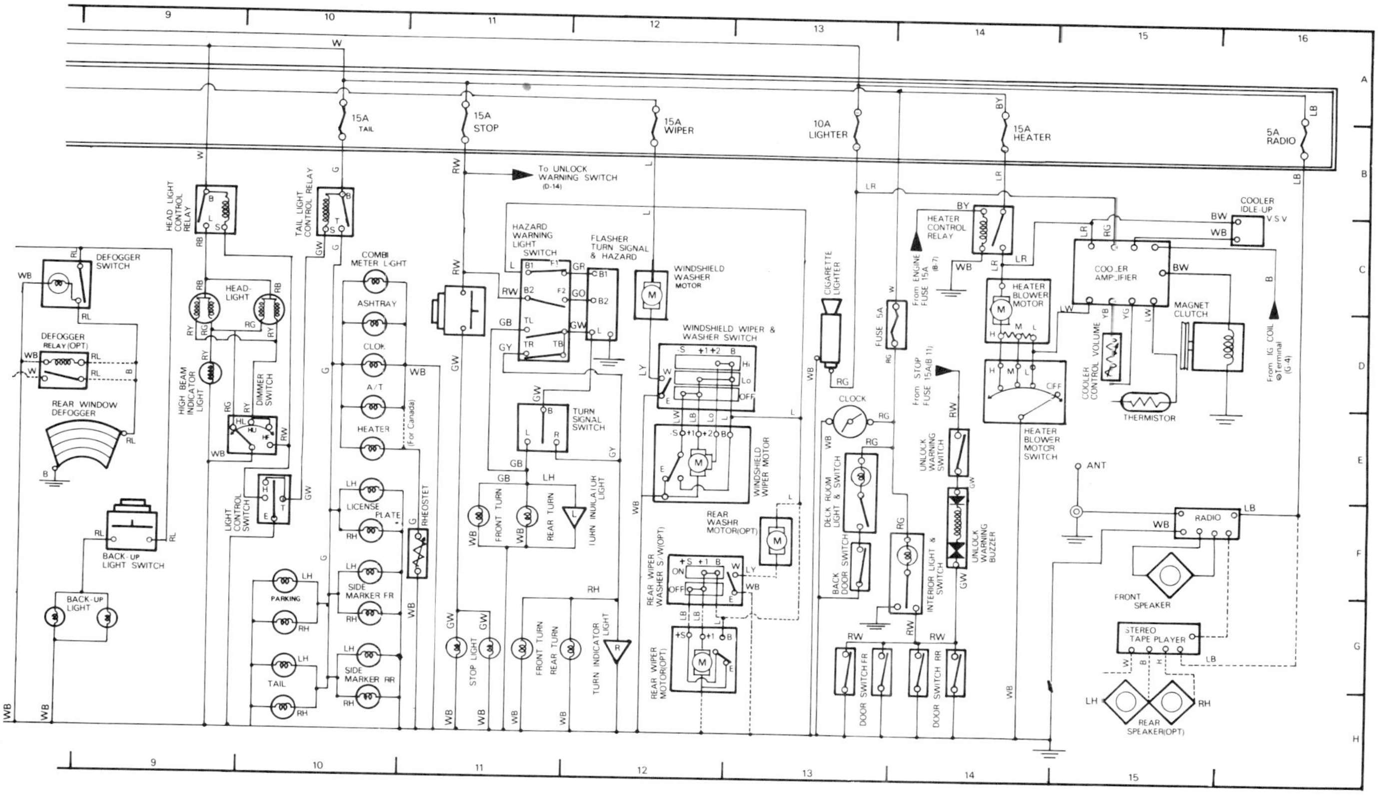

4

Component	Location
Stop light, left- and right-hand (for hardtop)	G-11
Stop light, left-hand (for wagon)	G-11
Stop light, left-hand (for coupe)	G-11
Stop light, left-hand (for liftback)	G-11
Stop light, right-hand (for sedan)	G-11
Stop light, right-hand (for wagon)	G-11
Stop light, right-hand (for coupe)	G-11
Stop light, right-hand (for liftback)	G-11
Taillight, left-hand (for sedan)	H-10
Taillight, left-hand and right-hand (for hardtop)	H-10
Taillight, left-hand (for wagon)	H-10
Taillight, left-hand (for coupe)	H-10
Taillight, left-hand (for liftback)	H-10
Taillight, right-hand (for sedan)	H-10
Taillight, right-hand (for wagon)	H-10
Taillight, right-hand (for coupe)	H-10
Taillight, right-hand (for liftback)	H-10
Turn signal light, front left-hand	F-11
Turn signal light, front right-hand	G-11
Turn signal light, rear left-hand (for sedan)	F-11
Turn signal light, rear left-hand (for hardtop)	F-11
Turn signal light, rear left-hand (for wagon)	F-11
Turn signal light, rear left-hand (for coupe)	F-11
Turn signal light, rear left-hand (for liftback)	F-11
Turn signal light, rear right-hand (for sedan)	G-12
Turn signal light, rear right-hand (for hardtop)	G-12
Turn signal light, rear right-hand (for wagon)	G-12
Turn signal light, rear right-hand (for coupe)	G-12
Turn signal light, rear right-hand (for liftback)	G-12
Turn signal indicator light, left-hand (for sedan, hardtop, and wagon)	F-12
Turn signal indicator light, left-hand (for hardtop SR-5)	F-12
Turn signal indicator light, left-hand (for coupe and liftback)	F-12
Turn signal indicator light, right-hand (for sedan, hardtop, and wagon)	G-12
Turn signal indicator light, right-hand (for hardtop SR-5)	G-12
Turn signal indicator light, right-hand (for coupe and liftback)	G-12
Magnet clutch (for compressor)	D-15
Heater blower motor	C-14
Starter motor	E-2
Windshield washer motor	C-12
Washer motor, rear (for wagon, optional)	F-13
Washer motor, rear (for liftback, optional)	F-13
Windshield wiper motor	E-13
Wiper motor, rear (for wagon, optional)	G-12
Wiper motor, rear (for liftback, optional)	G-12
Noise filter	H-3
Oil pressure gauge (for hardtop SR-5)	D-7
Oil pressure gauge (for coupe and liftback SR-5)	D-7
Oil pressure sender (for SR-5)	D-7
Radio (for sedan, hardtop, and wagon)	F-15
Radio (for hardtop SR-5)	F-15
Radio (for coupe and liftback)	F-15
Regulator	C-4

Component	Location
Rheostat (for sedan, hardtop, and wagon)	F-11
Rheostat (for coupe and liftback)	F-11
Charge light relay	E-4
Choke control relay	G-6
Defogger relay (optional)	D-8
Headlight control relay	C-9
Heater control relay	C-14
Ignition coil relay (Canada)	D-3
Taillight control relay	C-10
Seat belt buckle switch	G-8
Seat belt warning buzzer	F-8
Seat belt warning relay	D-8
Seat belt warning light (for sedan, hardtop, and wagon)	E-7
Seat belt warning light (for hardtop SR-5)	E-7
Seat belt warning light (for coupe and liftback)	E-7
Speaker, front	F-15
Speaker, rear left-hand (for sedan, hardtop, and coupe)	H-15
Speaker, rear right-hand (for sedan, hardtop, and coupe)	H-15
Speaker, rear left-hand (for liftback)	H-15
Speaker, rear right-hand (for liftback)	H-15
Stereo tape player	G-15
Back-up light switch (manual trans.)	F-9
Back-up light switch (automatic trans.)	F-9
Back door switch (for liftback)	F-13
Deck room switch (for liftback)	E-13
Defogger, rear window switch (for sedan, hardtop, and wagon)	C-8
Defogger, rear window switch (for coupe and liftback)	C-8
Differential switch	G-7
Dimmer switch	E-10
Door switch, front left-hand	G-13
Door switch, front right-hand	G-13
Door switch, rear left-hand (for four-door)	G-14
Door switch, rear right-hand (for four-door)	G-14
Hazard warning light switch	C-11
Heater blower motor switch	F-14
Horn switch	F-1
Ignition switch	A-1
Interior light switch	F-14
Light control switch	F-10
Neutral start switch (for automatic trans.)	C-2
Oil pressure switch	C-2
Parking brake switch	G-7
Stop light switch	D-11
Turn signal switch	E-11
Unlock warning switch	E-14
Windshield wiper and washer switch	D-12
Wiper and washer switch, rear (for liftback and wagon)	F-12
Tachometer (for hardtop SR-5)	E-7
Tachometer (for coupe and liftback SR-5)	E-7
Thermistor (for cooler)	D-15
Unlock warning buzzer	F-14
Voltmeter	D-7
Water temperature gauge (for sedan, hardtop and wagon)	D-7
Water temperature gauge (for hardtop SR-5)	D-7
Water temperature gauge (for coupe and liftback)	D-7
Water temperature sender	D-7

Section 5

ENGINE

Contents

TABLES

Engine

The 2T-C four cylinder 1600 OHV engine is front-mounted and water-cooled. It has hemispherical combustion chambers with inclined valves operated by pushrods and rocker arms. The high volumetric efficiency provided by this layout makes possible an ample power output with good fuel economy and a minimum of undesirable exhaust emissions.

The crankshaft is supported in five main bearings and the sides of the cast-iron cylinder block extend well below the crankshaft bearing centerline. The great rigidity and durability inherent in this design is further enhanced by having five bearings to support the camshaft and a unique arrangement of five forged steel supports for the rocker arms and rocker arm shafts.

The cylinder head is a precision aluminum alloy casting with hardened steel valve seats and pressed-in valve guides. The cast aluminum rocker arm cover serves to minimize valve noise and is one of many details that make this engine outstanding in quality and finish. The intake manifold, timing cover, and many other secondary castings are also of high-strength aluminum alloy, and a highly accessible arrangement of external components makes the engine exceptionally easy to service and maintain.

Though the engines of the earlier models are rated at a slightly higher horsepower than those of 1975 and later models, the cars themselves have lost little in the way of performance or economy because of careful attention to such things as weight control, aerodynamics, and gearing. Most of the engine components have remained unchanged during the model years covered by this Manual, and what modifications have been made are generally necessary to accommodate improved kinds of emission controls.

The information in this section of the Manual is intended to serve as a guide to both car owners and professional mechanics. Some of the operations may require special equipment and experience that only a trained mechanic will normally have. If you lack the skills, tools, or a suitable workshop for servicing the engine and clutch, we suggest you leave these repairs to an Authorized Toyota Dealer before attempting any repairs on a car still covered by the new-car warranty.

1. GENERAL DESCRIPTION

Two cross sections of the 1600 OHV engine appear in Fig. 1-1. Notice the hemispherical combustion chambers, the deep bottom end of the cylinder block casting, and the five-main-bearing crankshaft. The camshaft is located high in the block to minimize pushrod length, and drives both the ignition distributor and the oil pump through a single helical gear.

Engine Mounting

The engine and the transmission are supported as a single unit by bonded rubber mountings. Bolts join the engine to the bellhousing of the transmission. Two of three bonded rubber mountings are bolted to the engine, as shown in Fig. 1-1. The third is located on the transmission.

Engine Block

The cylinders of the cast-iron engine block are integral with the block casting and fully exposed on all sides to the coolant that circulates through the water jacket. Oil passages, either cast or drilled into the block casting, provide full pressure lubrication to every bearing and working part of the engine.

Crankshaft and Bearings

The counterweighted crankshaft revolves in five split-shell main bearings. The center bearing shells are not flanged to take crankshaft end thrust; the crankshaft end play is adjustable by means of selectively fitted thrust washers that are inserted on each side of the center bearing. Seals, pressed into lightweight alloy seal carriers, are used at both ends of the crankshaft to prevent oil leakage.

Valve Train

The hemispherical combustion chambers make necessary a very strong and mechanically sophisticated arrangement of the valve gear components. See Fig. 1-1. The forged steel rocker arms, which incorporate adjusting screws for setting the valve clearances, are mounted on steel shafts with cross-braced supports that are anchored to the cylinder head by the cylinder head bolts themselves. The camshaft is crankshaft driven by a double-row roller chain with a hydraulic-type tensioner. In addition to simplifying the valve train geometry, the high position of the camshaft makes it possible to use short tubular pushrods for increased resistance to flexing.

Connecting Rods and Pistons

The three-ring pistons have interference-fit piston pins that are kept in position by being pressed into the connecting rod small ends. The connecting rods are steel forgings. Split-shell bearings are used at the crankshaft end, but because of the interference-fit piston pins there are no bushings in the connecting rod small ends.

Flywheel and Drive Plate

The drive plate, used on cars with automatic transmissions, is mounted on the crankshaft with six steel bolts and held to the torque converter by six other steel bolts. On engines used with manual transmissions, the flywheel is held to the crankshaft by six steel bolts and the clutch pressure plate assembly is mounted on the flywheel with six other steel bolts. Both the flywheel and the drive plate are equipped with ring gears for the starter drive.

Cooling System

Coolant is circulated through the radiator and the engine by a centrifugal-type water pump. On early models the radiator fan is mounted rigidly on the pump shaft, but on most of the later cars the fan is mounted on a viscous drive unit that limits the amount of engine power absorbed in driving the fan. Both the fan and the water pump are crankshaft driven by a V-belt.

Emission Controls

Exhaust emissions are controlled by engine modifications, exhaust gas recirculation (1977 and later models), air injection, (1975 through 1977 models), and a catalytic converter (1975 and later California models, 1977 and later High Altitude models, and all 1978 and later cars sold in the U.S.A. outside California). These systems and the various engine modifications systems are covered in detail in **FUEL AND EXHAUST SYSTEMS.** All cars covered by this Manual have closed positive crankcase ventilation systems on the engine with shuttle-type valves that require periodic inspection and replacement.

Ignition System

On 1975 cars, the ignition is a conventional coil and battery system, although some 1975 models have a dual-point distributor. The 1976 and 1977 models have a breaker point-controlled, transistor-switched electronic ignition system. All 1978 and later cars have a breakerless, fully transistorized ignition.

Lubrication System

A trochoid-type oil pump, driven by the distributor shaft, draws oil through a strainer in the bottom of the oil pan and forces it through a cartridge-type filter and into the engine's oil passages. A pressure relief valve in the pump limits the pressure in the system and a filter bypass valve built into the filter assures lubrication even if the filter is plugged.

Clutch

The engines used with manual transmissions have a dry, single-plate clutch. The operating lever on the transmission's clutch bellhousing is operated by a hydraulic slave cylinder that is linked by a hydraulic line to the pedal-operated clutch master cylinder.

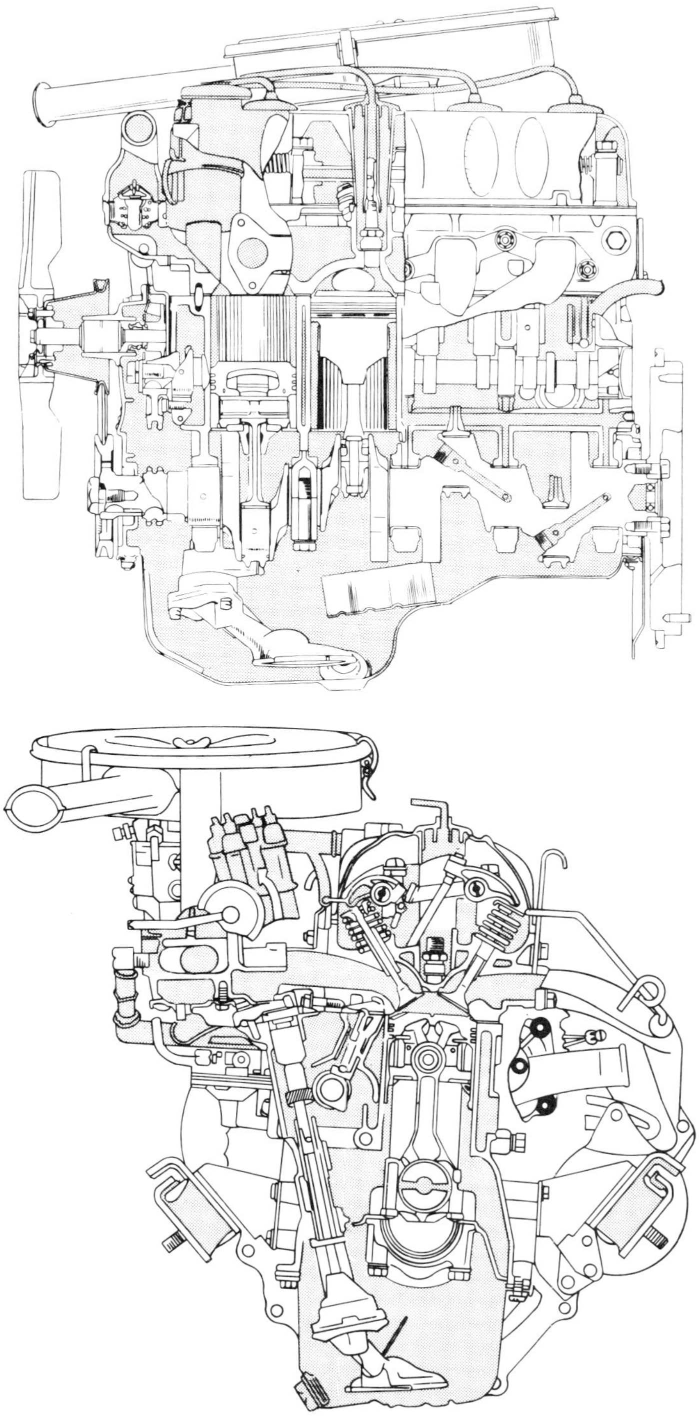

Fig. 1-1. Sectioned views of the 2T-C 1600 engine.

2. MAINTENANCE

The following routine maintenance steps are covered briefly in **LUBRICATION AND MAINTENANCE** or in this section under the headings listed after some of the items.

1. Checking and adjusting valve clearance. **5.2**
2. Checking and adjusting or replacing V-belt(s)
3. Checking engine bolt torques
4. Changing engine oil and filter and checking oil level
5. Checking and replacing coolant
6. Checking cooling system and, if necessary, replacing faulty hoses. **4**
7. Checking and, if necessary, replacing vacuum hoses
8. Checking exhaust system
9. Checking ignition distributor breaker point dwell, then checking and, if necessary, adjusting ignition timing. **3.2**, **3.3**
10. Replacing ignition distributor's breaker points. **3.2**
11. Replacing spark plugs. **3.5**
12. Checking distributor cap, distributor rotor, and spark plug cables and high tension lead. **3.2**, **3.4**
13. Checking ignition distributor's spark advance mechanism. **3.3**
14. Checking spark control systems (described in detail in **FUEL AND EXHAUST SYSTEMS**)
15. Checking and adjusting idle (described in detail in **FUEL AND EXHAUST SYSTEMS**).

3. IGNITION SYSTEM

Because they have a vital influence on performance, fuel economy, and exhaust emissions, all components of the ignition system must be kept in good condition and, where applicable, correctly adjusted to the specifications given in this Manual, the Owner's Manual, or on the engine's emissions decal.

The ignition system has undergone significant changes in each of the model years covered by this Manual. These changes have increased the durability and reliability of the ignition system and have reduced the need for frequent maintenance. The changes are as follows:

1975 models A conventional coil and battery ignition system with a ballast resistor attached to the coil and a dual-breaker point distributor with a simple kind of transistor switching used on certain cars.

1976 models A transistor-switched ignition system that has very low voltage delivered to the distributor's breaker points and a transistorized amplifier, called the igniter, that is mounted on the conventional coil with ballast resistor and handles the actual switching of the ignition's primary current.

1977 models The same system used on the 1976 cars, but with a redesigned igniter unit attached to the conventional coil with ballast resistor.

1978 and later models A breakerless, fully transistorized system with an all-new igniter attached to a special coil that receives current via a resistance wire rather than a ballast resistor; there are no points in the distributor.

3.1 Coil and Igniter

By the process of electrical induction, the coil steps up the primary circuit's 12-volt battery current to as much as 20,000 volts. This high voltage is required to ionize the air in the spark plug gaps so that a spark can jump across them. Despite the painful electrical shock that spark current can produce, its low amperage (current flow) renders it harmless. When you test the spark, you can avoid getting shocks either by wearing rubber gloves or by holding the high tension cable with a spring-type clothespin. A cable with sound insulation, however, is safe to handle. Fig. 3-1 gives a sectional view of an ignition coil.

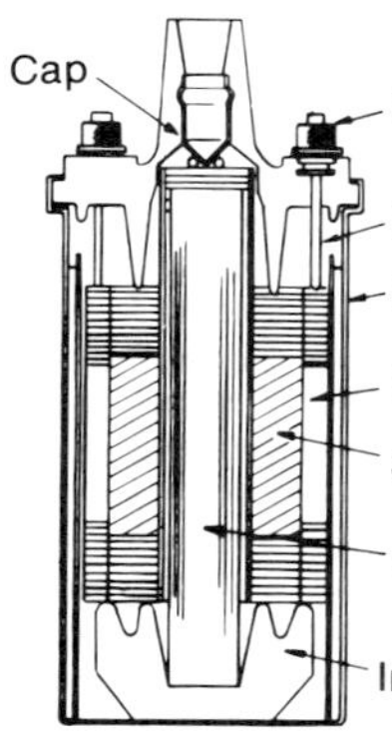

Fig. 3-1. Cross-section of typical ignition coil.

When installing the coil, please be sure you connect the wire from the ignition switch to the positive (+) terminal and the wire from the distributor or the igniter to the negative (−) terminal. Reversing the coil wires will change the polarity of the spark current from positive to negative. Reversed polarity limits the ability of the spark voltage to ionize the air in the spark plug gaps, causing misfiring at high speeds or during hard acceleration.

Keep the coil tower clean and dry and make sure that the rubber boot surrounding the high tension cable is tight-fitting and waterproof. Otherwise, spark current may begin arcing from the high tension terminal to ground or to the negative (−) primary terminal. A short such as this can prevent the engine from running well or even from running at all. The arcing may also burn irreparable carbon tracks into the coil tower.

Ignition coils seldom produce trouble. However, if all the other ignition components are sound and the car still misses or is hard to start, check the coil. First test the battery as described in **ELECTRICAL SYSTEM** to make sure it is not run down. Then disconnect the high tension cable from the center terminal of the distributor cap and hold the cable about 5 mm (3/16 in.) from the engine block. Have someone run the starter while you observe the spark produced. If the spark is weak and yellowish, fires only when the cable is moved close to the engine block, or fails to fire at all, the coil and, where applicable, the igniter should be given a more thorough test.

CAUTION ——

The test described in the preceding paragraph is not recommended for 1978 and later cars with breakerless ignition systems. Inducing abnormal spark pulses can damage the igniter.

Testing 1975 through 1977 Coil and Ballast Resistor

The same coil is used on 1976 and 1977 cars with transistor-switched ignition systems as is used on the 1975 cars with conventional single-point or dual-point ignition systems. The tests described under this heading apply specifically to the 1975 coil but can be used to check 1976 and 1977 coils too. For more comprehensive testing of the 1975 dual-point ignition and the 1976 and 1977 transistor-switched ignitions, please use the tests described under the next heading.

You can use a coil tester, as shown in Fig. 3-2, to perform a coil secondary conductivity test and a capacity test. If a high reading is obtained during a coil secondary conductivity test it indicates either an open secondary circuit or a high secondary circuit resistance. If a low reading is shown, it indicates a short circuit in the secondary winding. The correct secondary conductivity is indicated by a resistance of 6500 to 10,500 ohms.

During a coil capacity test, you should obtain a reading in the "Good" range of the tester's scale. Make the initial tester settings in accordance with the instructions supplied with the tester. If these settings are unknown, make comparison tests with an ignition coil that is known to be in good condition.

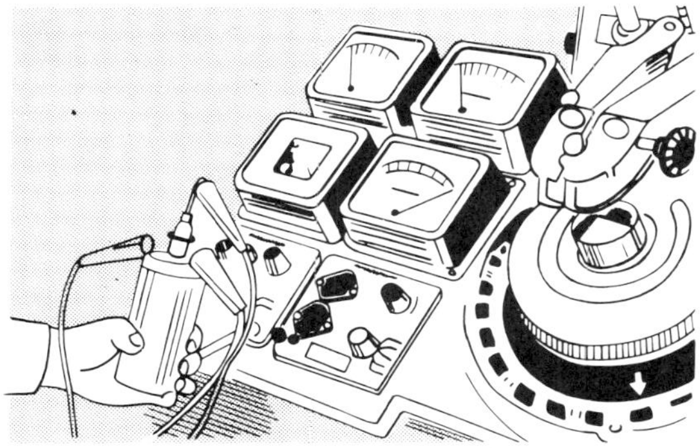

Fig. 3-2. Coil capacity test being made on a complete ignition testing machine that includes a coil tester.

You can also test the ignition coil and the ballast resistor with an ohmmeter. The three coil tests, and their correct readings, are given in Fig. 3-3. Replace coils that

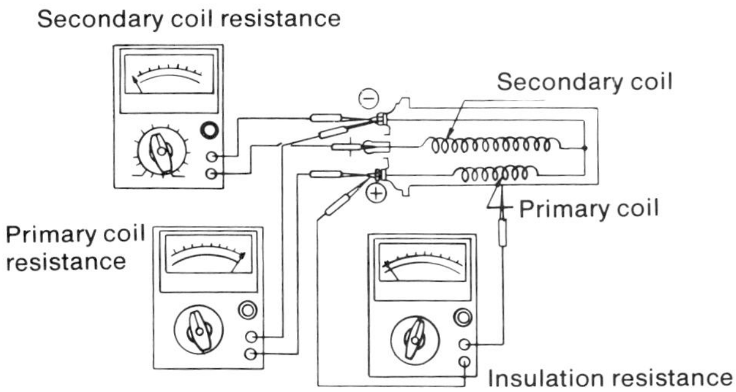

1. Primary coil resistance: 1.3 to 1.5 ohms
2. Secondary coil resistance: 6500 to 10,500 ohms
3. Insulation resistance: Infinite ohms

Fig. 3-3. Ohmmeter tests for 1975 through 1977 ignition coils, with correct ranges of resistance.

do not test within one or more of the correct ranges. Replace ballast resistors that show a resistance greater than 1.3 to 1.7 ohms.

A more reliable test of the insulation resistance can be made with a 500-volt megger (megohmmeter), as shown in Fig. 3-4. With this kind of instrument, the insulation resistance should be above 100. If it is less, replace the coil.

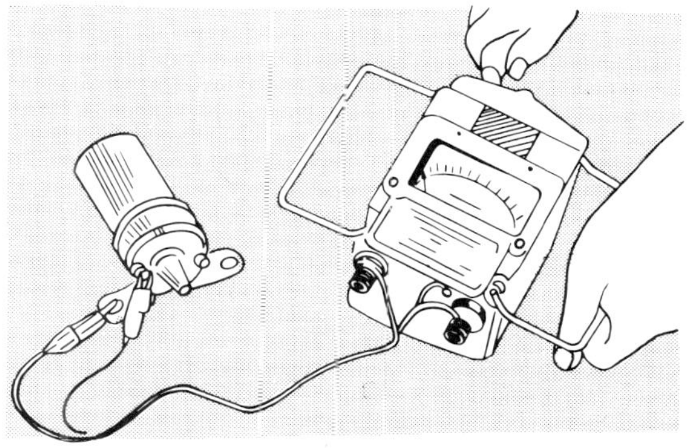

Fig. 3-4. Insulation resistance being tested with megohmmeter.

Testing 1975 Dual-point Ignition System

In this system (Fig. 3-5) the dual-point distributor advances the ignition timing when the engine is cold for the purpose of increasing the engine's torque during warmup. When cold, the thermoswitch is ON. This energizes the ignition relay, disconnecting the main breaker points from the igniter and the ignition coil. The timing is then controlled by the sub-point, which opens about 10° before the main point. During cold operation, the timing at idle is 22° ±3° BTDC (before top dead center). center).

Fig. 3-5. Schematic diagram of 1975 dual-point ignition during cold-engine operation. Circled numerals indicate terminal numbers on relay.

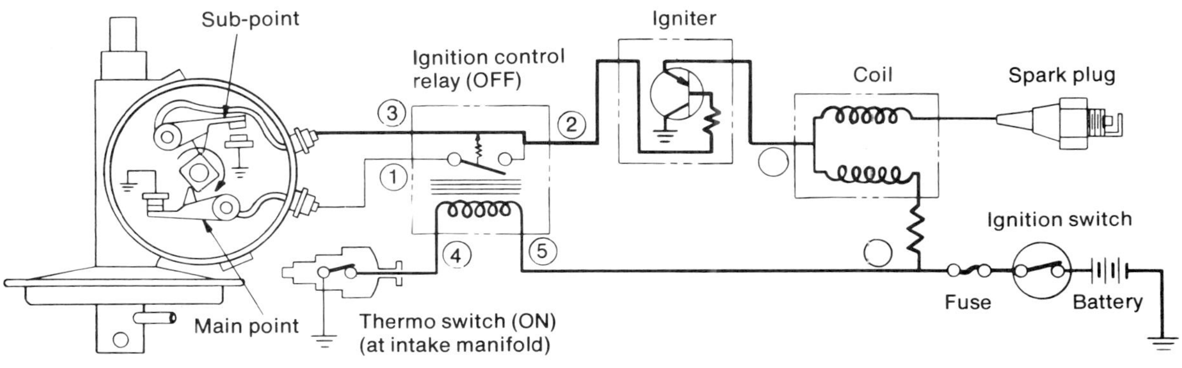

Fig. 3-6 shows the dual-point ignition system after the engine has warmed up. The thermo switch is off, so the relay is no longer energized; the main points are in electrical contact with the igniter and the ignition coil. Under these conditions, the ignition timing at idle is 12° BTDC.

A resistor in the igniter reduces the voltage that passes through the breaker points, thus increasing point life. A transistor in the igniter handles the actual switching ON and OFF of the primary current.

If the timing is inaccurate, or fails to match the design characteristics just described, you can troubleshoot the system as described in **Table a.** This troubleshooting table should also be used if you cannot easily adjust the timing to specifications using the procedure given in **3.3 Adjusting Timing.** The numbers in bold type in the Suggested repairs column indicate the headings in this section of the Manual where you will find information that will help you in making repairs.

Fig. 3-6. Schematic diagram of 1975 dual-point ignition during hot-engine operation. Color code: (L) = light blue, (B) = black, (G) = green, (R) = red, (BY) = black/yellow.

To troubleshoot igniter and ignition control relay:

1. Make sure that the battery is not run down. Check that the igniter is correctly grounded.

2. If there is no spark, or an irregular spark—which could indicate a faulty igniter—disconnect the igniter from both the coil and the ignition control relay. Then, using a jumper wire, connect ignition control relay terminal No. 2 directly to the coil's negative (−) terminal. If there is a good spark with the jumper wire installed, the igniter is faulty and should be replaced.

NOTE ——

If it is necessary to drive the car, the jumper wire can be left in place as an emergency repair.

3. To test the ignition control relay, first disconnect the multiple connector from the relay, which is located on the left-hand side of the engine compartment, just to the rear of the coil. Then use an ohmmeter to make the tests indicated in Fig. 3-7. If there is no electrical continuity between the relay terminals that should be in electrical contact, the relay is faulty and should be replaced.

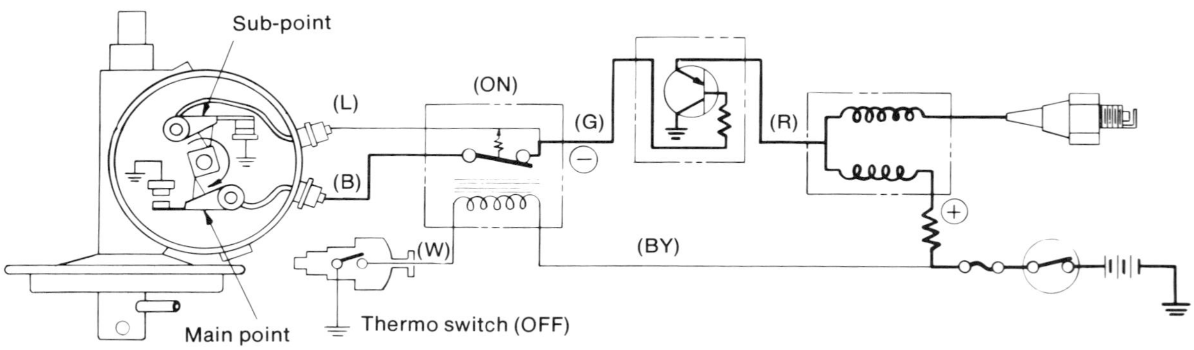

Table a. Dual-point Ignition Troubleshooting

Problem	Probable causes	Suggested repairs
1. Engine cold, timing only close to 22° ±3° BTDC at idle—or engine hot, timing only close to 12° BTDC at idle	Ignition timing out of adjustment	Adjust timing. See **3.3**.
2. Engine cold, timing not close to 22° ±3° BTDC	a. Sub-point dwell incorrect b. Faulty thermo switch c. Ignition control relay faulty d. Ignition timing far out of adjustment	a. Adjust sub-point dwell. See **3.2**. b. Disconnect and ground wire from thermo switch; if timing shifts to 22° ±3° BTDC, thermo switch is faulty and should be replaced. See **4.1**. c. Troubleshoot relay as described later under this heading; replace faulty relays. See **3.1**. d. Adjust ignition timing to specifications. See **3.3**.
3. Engine hot, timing not close to 12° BTDC	a. Main point dwell incorrect b. Faulty thermo switch c. Ignition control relay faulty d. Ignition timing far out of adjustment	a. Adjust main point dwell. See **3.2**. b. Disconnect wire from thermo switch; if timing shifts to 12° BTDC, thermo switch is faulty and should be replaced. See **4.1**. c. Troubleshoot relay as described later under this heading; replace faulty relays. See **3.1**. d. Adjust ignition timing to specifications. See **3.3**.

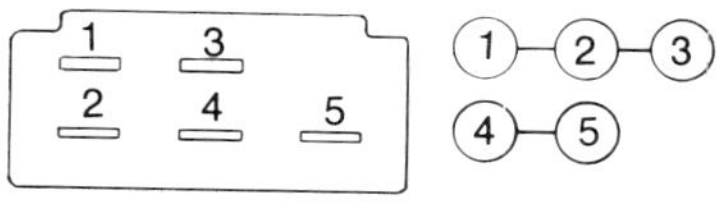

Fig. 3-7. Ignition control relay terminal locations (left). Terminals 1, 2, and 3 should all be in electrical contact with one another and terminals 4 and 5 should be in electrical contact with one another, as indicated in diagrams at right.

4. To test the electromagnetic operation of the relay, energize the relay by connecting terminals 4 and 5 to the battery, as indicated in Fig. 3-8. There should then be electrical continuity between terminals 2 and 3, but no continuity between terminals 1 and 2. Replace relays that do not function correctly.

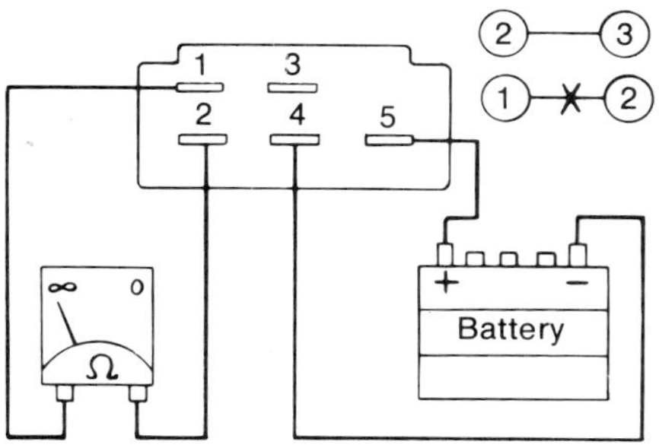

Fig. 3-8. Relay operation being tested. Attach battery's positive (+) terminal to relay terminal 5 and battery's negative (−) terminal to relay terminal 4. Use ohmmeter as indicated to check continuity with relay energized. Diagrams at upper right indicate correct continuity.

Testing 1976 and 1977 Transistor-switched Ignition System

In this system, the distributor breaker point ON and OFF signals cause the transistors inside the igniter to turn the primary current on and off. The advantages of this system are improved engine starting and low speed performance because of the system's capability for maintaining a higher secondary voltage at low speed. In addition, the durability of the distributor's breaker points is greatly improved. Fig. 3-9 shows the ON signal circuit (breaker points closed) and Fig. 3-10 shows the OFF circuit with the breaker points open.

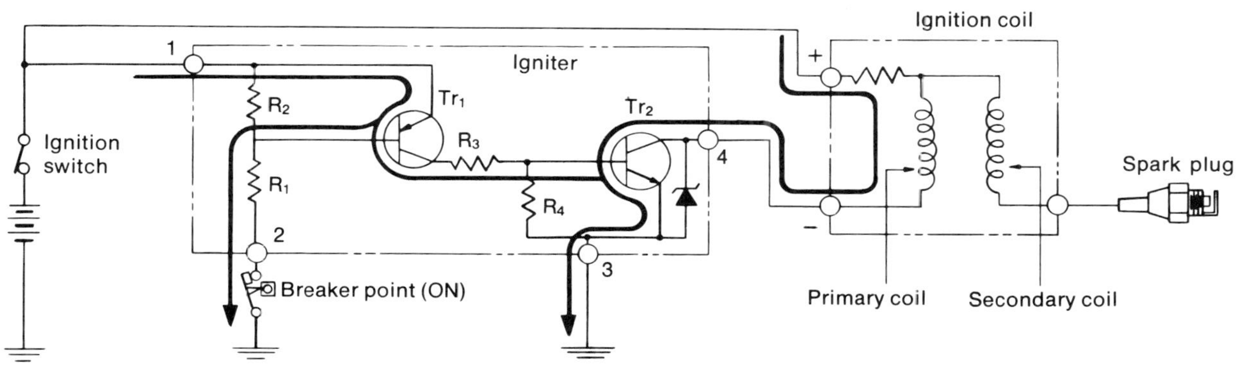

Fig. 3-9. ON circuit, with breaker points closed. Arrows indicate current flow to ground. Left-hand arrow shows low voltage controlled by breaker points as it flows through signal transistor (**Tr_1**). Signal follows heavy line to switching transistor (**Tr_2**), causing current to flow through coil primary winding as indicated by right-hand arrow. Resistances are indicated by **R_1** through **R_4** and numerals **1** and **4** are igniter's terminal numbers.

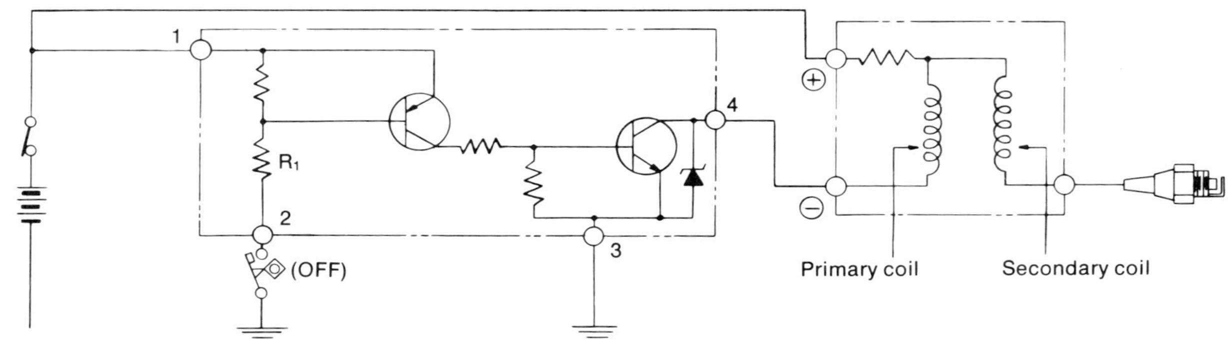

Fig. 3-10. OFF circuit, with breaker points open. No significant current is flowing through any circuit of the igniter, so coil's primary circuit is switched off and a spark is discharged from the coil's secondary circuit. The resistances in the igniter serve to reduce current flow through transistors. Very small current flowing through resistance $\mathbf{R_1}$ and breaker points is so minimal that there is very little arc loss at points.

If poor engine performance and hard starting are believed to be caused by a problem in the igniter, carry out the following procedure to determine whether the trouble is in the igniter, the coil, or some other part of the ignition system.

To troubleshoot:

1. Make sure that the battery is not run down. Check that the igniter is correctly grounded via its terminal No. 3.
2. Disconnect the high tension cable from the center of the distributor cap, then remove the distributor cap from the distributor. Turn on the ignition.
3. Check the position of the breaker points and, if necessary, hand-turn the crankshaft with a wrench placed on the bolt in the center of the crankshaft pulley until the breaker points are closed.
4. Hold the disconnected end of the high tension cable about 5 mm ($^3/_{16}$ in.) from the engine block. Then, using the tip of a screwdriver placed against the movable point arm, open and close the breaker points. If there is a strong blue spark, check for a faulty distributor rotor, distributor cap, spark plug cable, or spark plug. If there is no spark, or a weak yellowish spark, go on to the next step of this procedure.
5. Disconnect the primary wire from the distributor. With the ignition on, hold the high tension cable about 5 mm ($^3/_{16}$ in.) from the engine block. Then, using a jumper wire if necessary, repeatedly ground the disconnected primary wire on a clean, unpainted metal part of the engine, as indicated in Fig. 3-11. If a good spark is produced, but there was a poor spark or no spark in the preceding test, the distributor's breaker points are faulty and should be replaced. If there is still no spark, or a weak spark, continue troubleshooting.

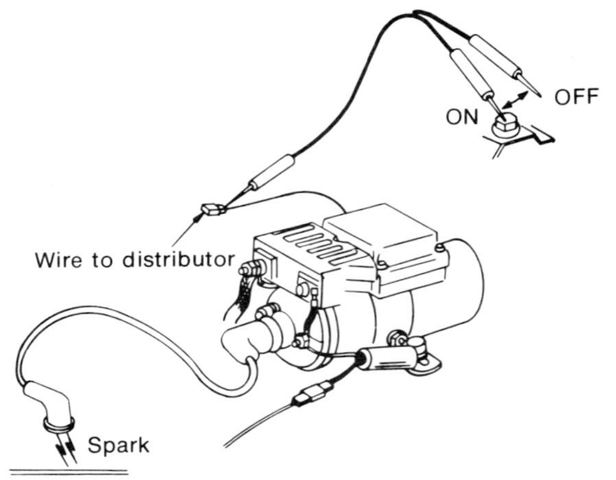

Fig. 3-11. Ignition being tested independently of distributor.

6. With the ignition on, check for voltage at the ballast resistor as shown in Fig. 3-12. If there is no voltage, either the ignition switch or the wiring that connects it to the ballast resistor (or to battery current) is faulty and should be replaced. If there is voltage, continue troubleshooting.

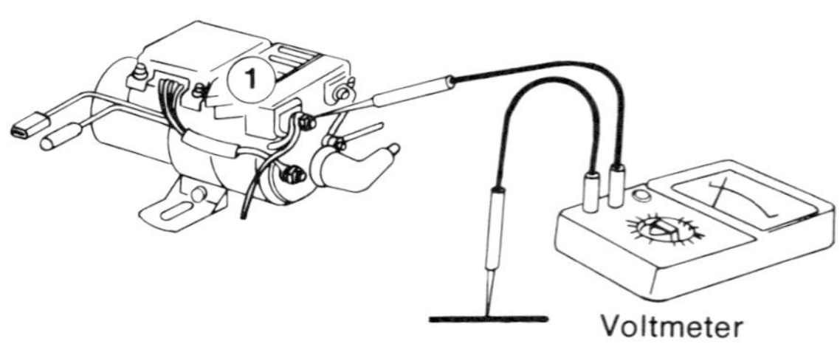

Fig. 3-12. Voltmeter being used to test for voltage at ballast resistor. 1977 igniter is shown, but 1976 test is the same.

7. Disconnect the igniter's No. 4 terminal wire from the coil's negative (−) terminal; disconnect the igniter's No. 1 terminal wire from the ballast resistor. Temporarily install an 0.22 microfarad ignition condenser as shown in Fig. 3-13. Again hold the high tension cable near the engine block, then repeatedly ground the coil's negative (−) terminal with a jumper wire. If there is a good spark, but there was a poor spark or no spark in steps 4 and 5, the igniter is faulty and should be replaced. If there is still a poor spark or no spark, carry out step 8 to determine whether the coil or the ballast resistor is faulty.

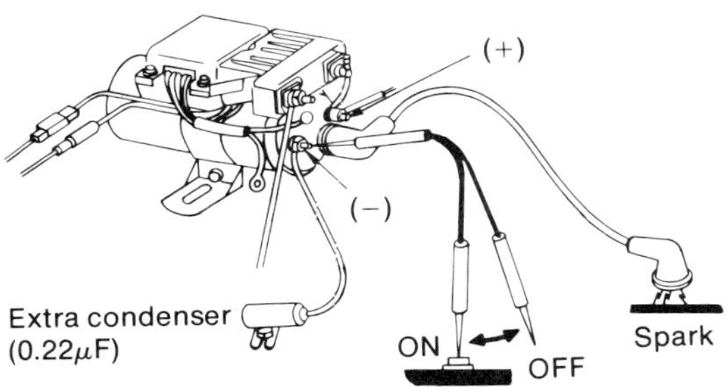

Fig. 3-13. Coil and ballast resistor being tested independently of igniter and distributor. Condenser is 1975 model type and must have its case grounded during test.

8. With the ignition off, or with the coil/ballast resistor/igniter assembly removed from the car, make the ohmmeter tests indicated in Fig. 7-14. Replace the ballast resistor if it does not meet the specifications given for test No. 4; replace coils that do not test within one or more of the correct ranges given in tests Nos. 1, 2, and 3.

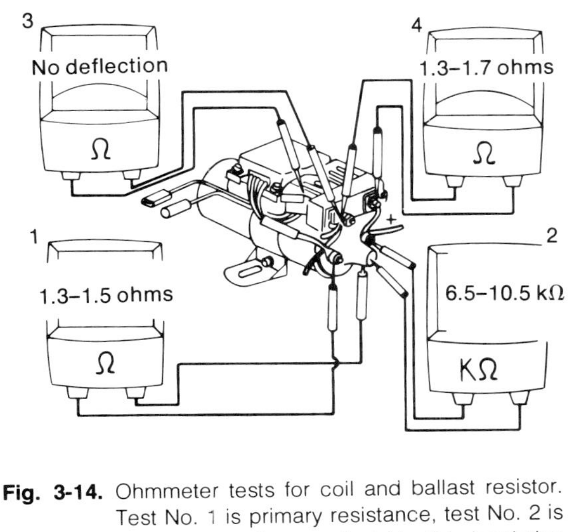

Fig. 3-14. Ohmmeter tests for coil and ballast resistor. Test No. 1 is primary resistance, test No. 2 is secondary resistance, test No. 3 is insulation resistance and test No. 4 is ballast resistance.

In addition to the tests given under this heading, you can test the coil's insulation resistance with a megger (megohmmeter) as described under the preceding heading. During installation of new ignition components, the wires should be connected as indicated either in Fig. 3-15 or in Fig. 3-16. Incorrect connections can damage the igniter. In addition, you should never disconnect the battery while the engine is running. This can damage the transistors of the igniter and can also damage the alternator.

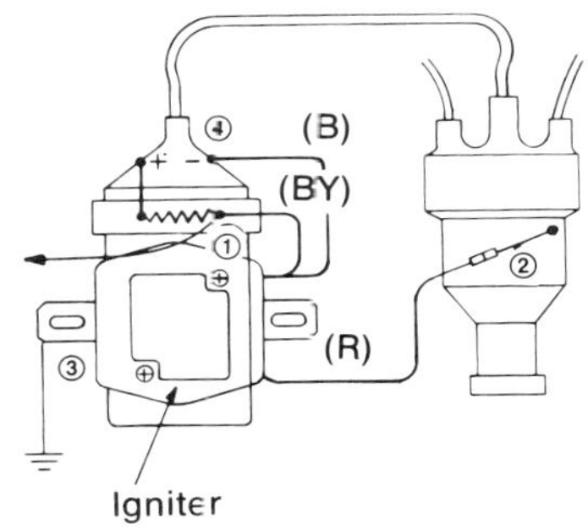

Fig. 3-15. Installation of 1976 igniter. Circled numerals are igniter terminal numbers. (R) is red wire, (B) is black wire, (BY) is black/yellow wire.

5

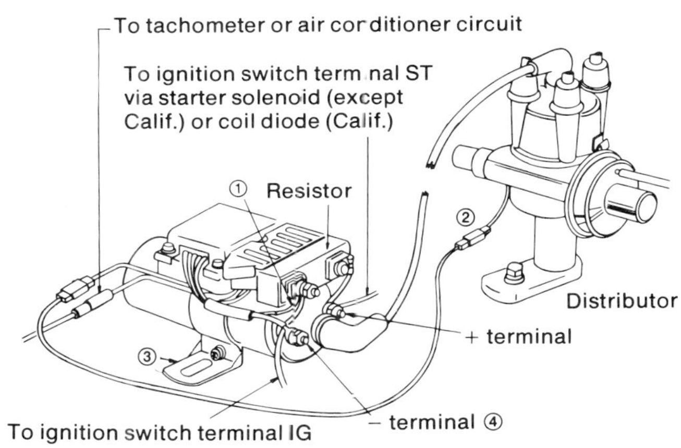

Fig. 3-16. Installation of 1977 igniter. Circled numerals are igniter terminal numbers. Wire for terminal No. 1 is black/yellow. Wires for terminals Nos. 2 and 4 are black.

If, during troubleshooting, an igniter is found to be faulty, you can make an emergency hook-up as shown in Fig. 3-17. By rewiring the ignition to make it a conventional coil and battery system, you will be able to drive the car until a replacement igniter can be obtained.

Testing 1978 and Later Breakerless Ignition System

In this system, the distributor produces its ON and OFF signals by means of an electromagnetic device rather than with mechanically operated breaker points. The signals are amplified and transmitted to a switching transistor that turns the primary current on and off. The advantages of this system are improved engine starting and low speed performance, because of the system's capability for maintaining a higher secondary voltage at low speed. In addition, it completely eliminates any need for periodic gapping or replacement of breaker points. Fig. 3-18 shows the ON signal circuit (no distributor timing rotor tooth aligned with pickup coil) and Fig. 3-19 shows the OFF circuit (timing rotor tooth aligned with pickup coil).

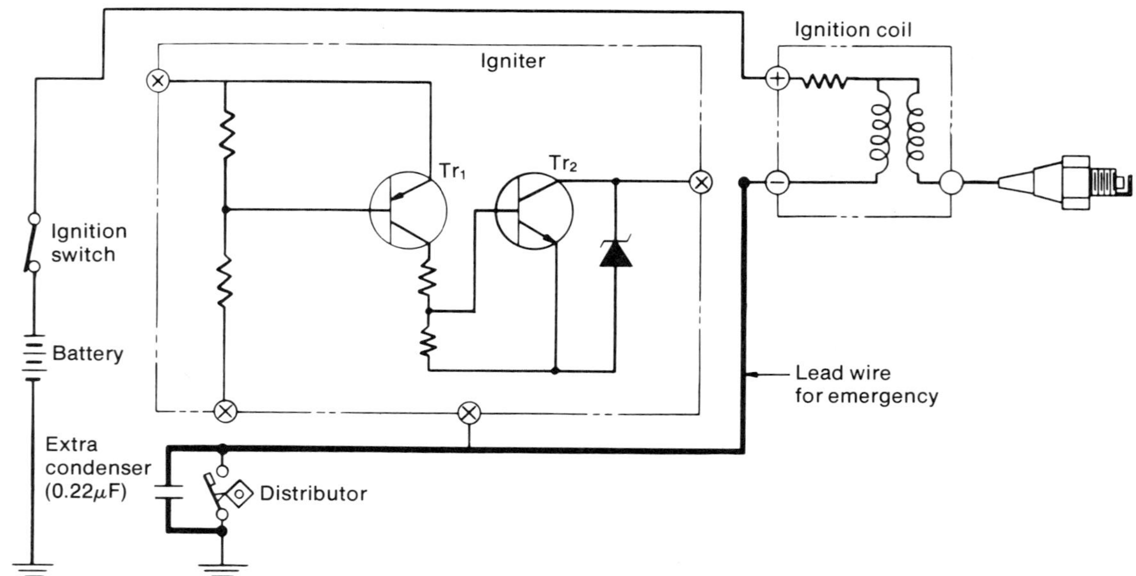

Fig. 3-17. Transistor-switched ignition rewired to make it a conventional coil and battery system. Heavy line indicates temporarily installed jumper wire. Condenser is similar to that used on 1975 cars.

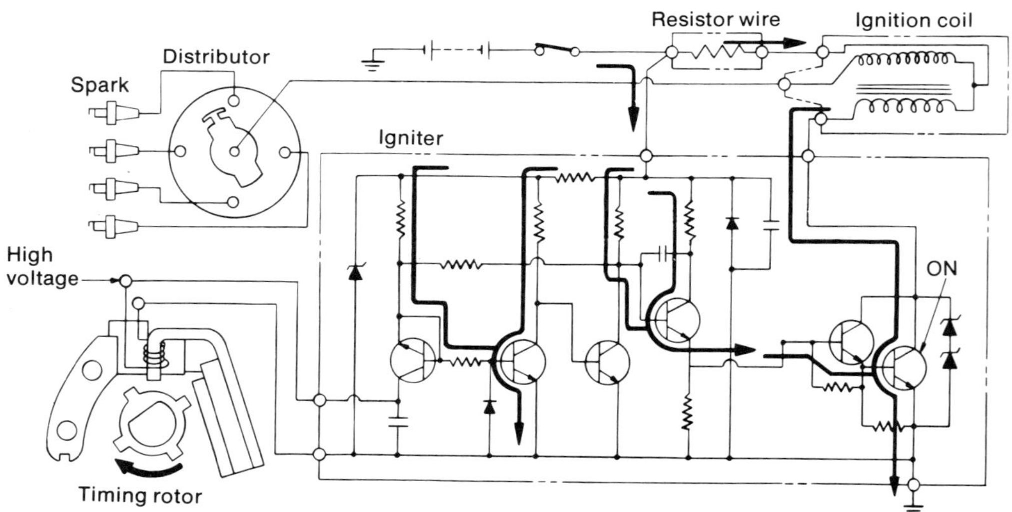

Fig. 3-18. ON: No timing rotor tooth aligned with pickup coil. Pickup coil's generated voltage is high, preventing battery current from flowing toward pickup coil. Current flow through switching transistor energizes ignition coil.

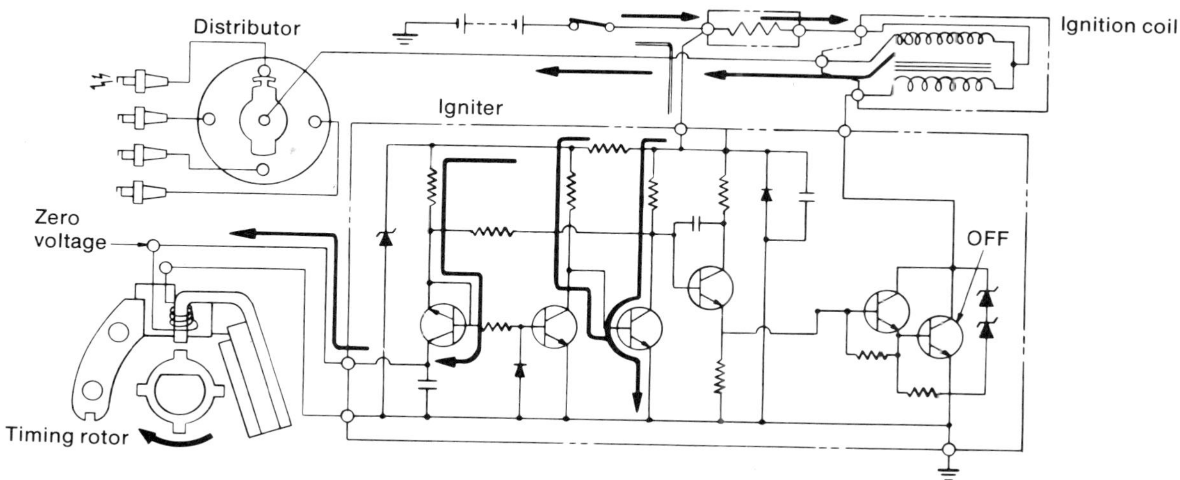

Fig. 3-19. OFF: Timing rotor tooth aligned with pickup coil. Pickup coil generated voltage is zero, allowing battery current to flow toward pickup coil. Center transistor sends current to ground, so switching transistor cuts off primary current to coil—thus releasing high-voltage spark current to distributor.

If poor performance and hard starting are believed to be caused by the igniter or some other part of the breakerless ignition system, you can carry out an overall inspection of the circuit as indicated in Fig. 3-20. These tests may be difficult to understand if you are not familiar with schematic diagrams or the symbols they contain. So instead, you can use the step-by-step troubleshooting procedure given under this heading to determine the location of ignition system faults.

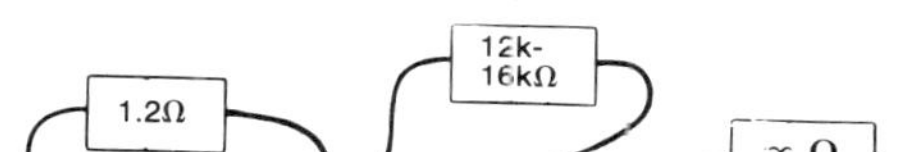

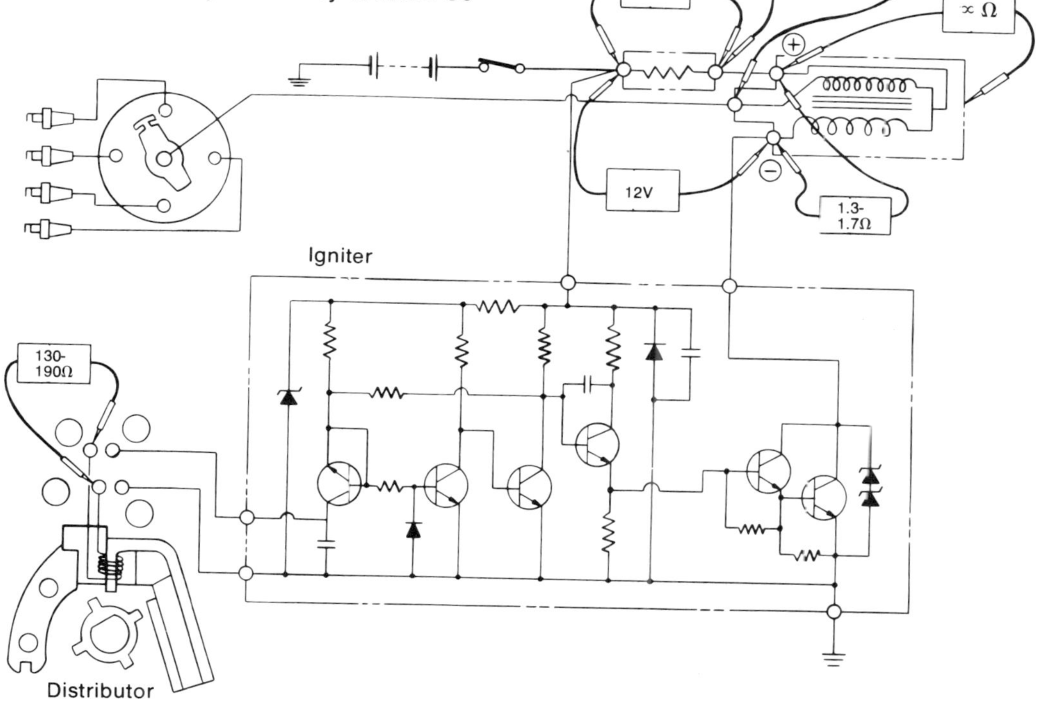

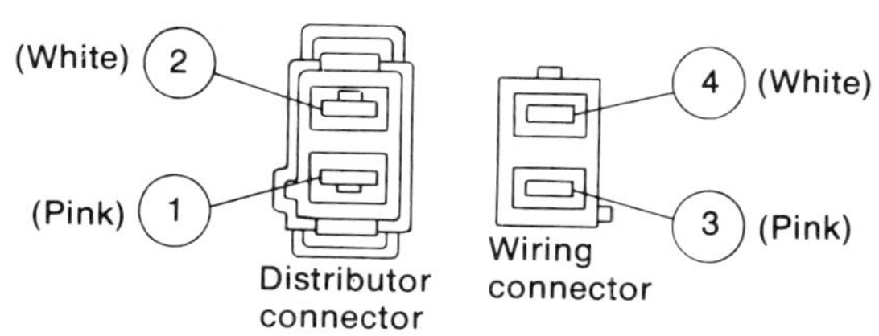

Fig. 3-20. Tests of breakerless ignition system represented schematically. Additional igniter test is given in procedure that follows.

To troubleshoot:

1. Make sure that the battery is not run down. Check that the igniter is correctly grounded.
2. Connect a timing light to the engine. Then either run the starter for a short period of time or start the engine. If the timing light flashes regularly, the trouble is either in the spark plugs or in some system other than the ignition system. If the timing light fails to flash, or flashes irregularly, continue troubleshooting the ignition.

> ***CAUTION ——***
> *The test should be made with a timing light rather than by disconnecting the high-tension cable because it is not recommended that abnormal sparks be created in conjunction with the igniter's solid-state components.*

3. Check the wiring and the wiring connections—with special attention to the cleanliness and tightness of connectors in the ignition system and to the engine's main wiring harness connector, which is located near the right-hand front part of the engine.
4. Check the ignition coil's primary resistance as indicated in Fig. 3-21. If the primary resistance (coil cold) is not between 1.3 and 1.7 ohms, the coil is faulty and should be replaced.

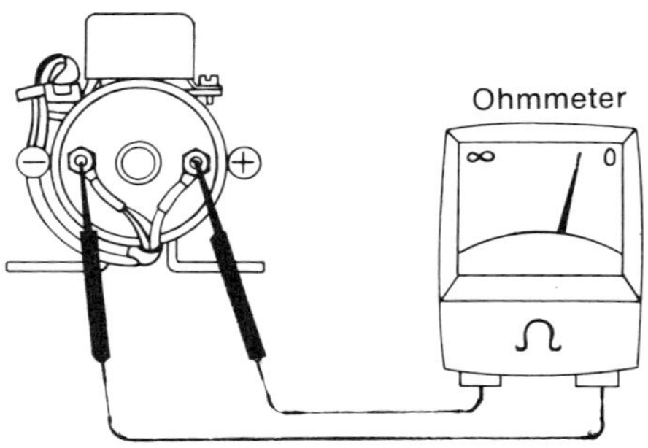

Fig. 3-21. Ignition coil primary resistance being checked with ohmmeter.

5. Check the ignition coil's secondary resistance as indicated in Fig. 3-22. If the secondary resistance (coil cold) is not between 12,000 and 16,000 ohms, the coil is faulty and should be replaced.
6. Check the ignition coil's insulation resistance as indicated in Fig. 3-23. If the insulation resistance is not infinite ohms (no continuity) the coil is faulty and should be replaced.
7. If the preceding tests uncover no faults, disconnect the wiring connector from the igniter, then test the resistance wire at the plug of the wiring harness as indicated in Fig. 3-24. If the resistance exceeds 1.2 ohms (with the wire cold), the resistance wire is faulty and should be replaced. If the resistance is correct, continue troubleshooting.

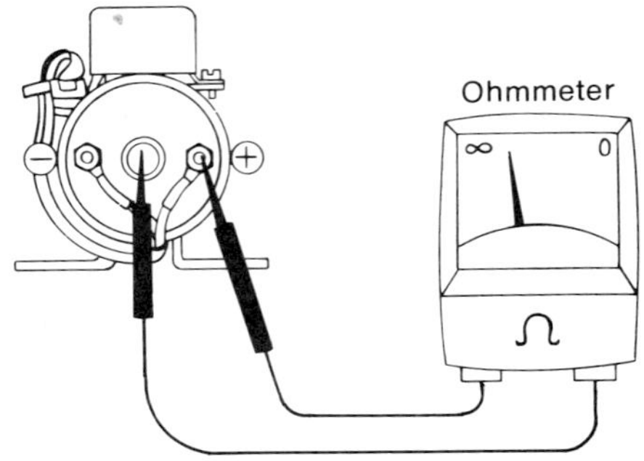

Fig. 3-22. Ignition coil secondary resistance being checked with ohmmeter.

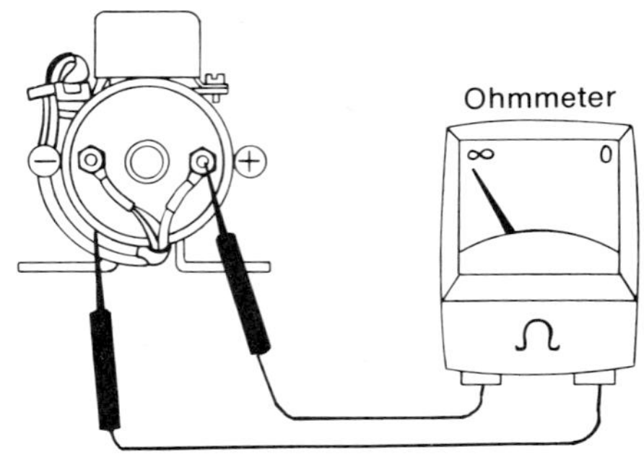

Fig. 3-23. Ignition coil insulation resistance being checked with ohmmeter.

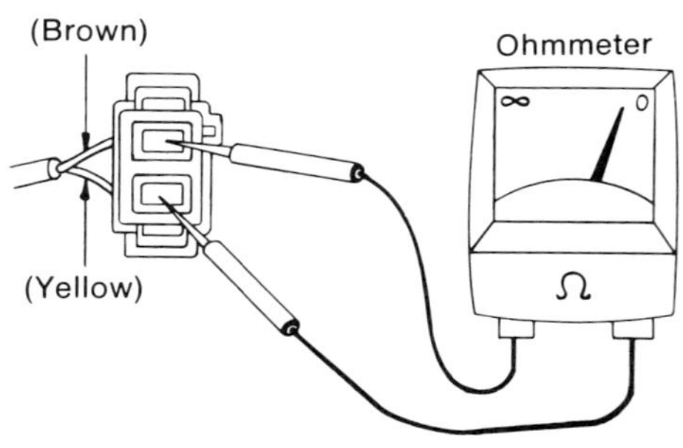

Fig. 3-24. Resistance wire being tested with ohmmeter.

8. Remove the distributor cap. Using a non-magnetic feeler gauge, check the air gap between the timing rotor and the pickup coil, as indicated in Fig. 3-25. If the air gap is not between 0.20 and 0.40 mm (.008 and .016 in.), correct it as described in **3.2 Distributor.** If the air gap is correct, go on to the next troubleshooting step.

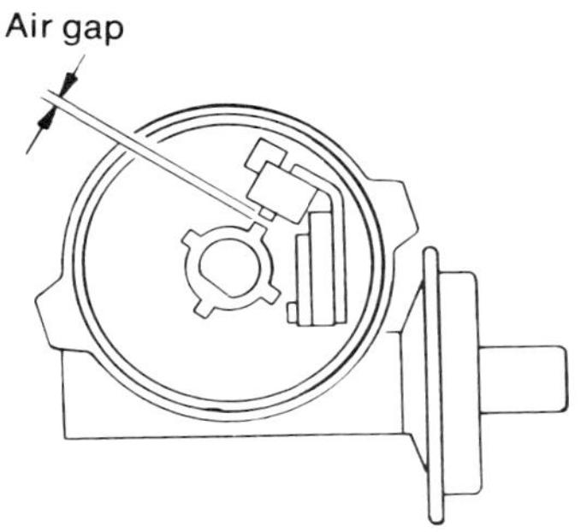

Fig. 3-25. Air gap between timing rotor and core of pickup coil.

9. Disconnect the wiring from the distributor. Then check the pickup coil as indicated in Fig. 3-26. If the resistance at the terminals is not between 130 and 190 ohms, the pickup coil is faulty and the signal generator unit should be replaced. If the resistance is correct, go on to the next step.
10. Turn on the ignition. Then measure the voltage between the ignition coil's negative (−) terminal and the resistor wire terminal as indicated in Fig. 3-27. If there is less than 12 volts (assuming that the battery is not discharged to less than 12 volts), the igniter is faulty and should be replaced. If the voltage is correct, continue troubleshooting.

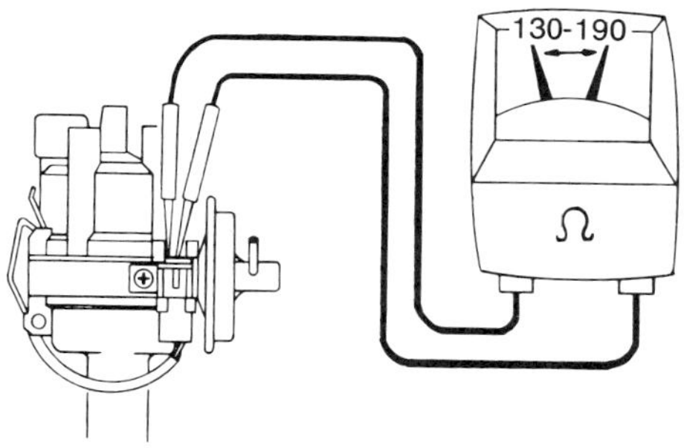

Fig. 3-26. Pickup coil resistance being measured.

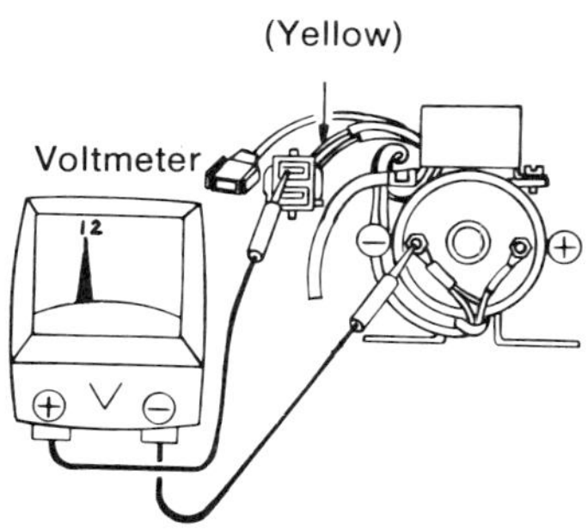

Fig. 3-27. Voltage path through igniter being checked.

11. Set an ohmmeter to its 1X ohms or 10X ohms position. Then—being very careful to connect the positive (+) and negative (−) leads to the distributor connector as shown in Fig. 3-28—use the ohmmeter to create resistance in the signal generator circuit. With the ignition turned on, the voltage between the coil's negative (−) terminal and the resistor wire terminal should fall to nearly zero. If not, the igniter is faulty and should be replaced.

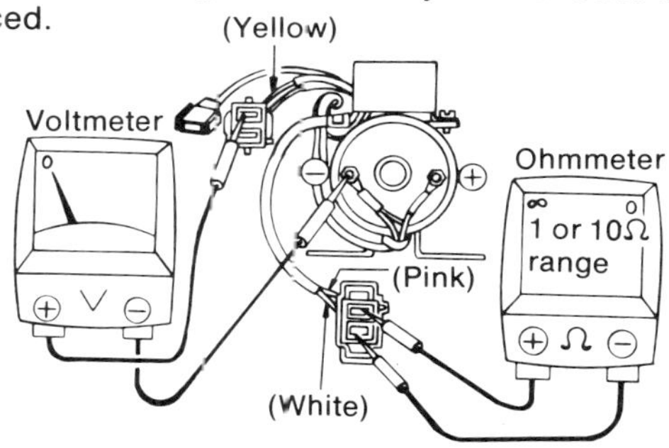

Fig. 3-28. Voltage path through igniter being checked with resistance (supplied by ohmmeter) applied to distributor connector.

3.2 Distributor

Fundamentally, the distributor has been unchanged throughout the model years covered by this Manual. The changes have been to the breaker plate and to the spark advance calibration. The 1975 distributor has either a breaker plate for mounting dual breaker points or a breaker plate for mounting single breaker points. The 1976 and 1977 distributors are single breaker point units, but the contacts themselves are enclosed in a plastic shield that protects them from contamination by dirt and oil.

Beginning with the 1978 models, the breaker plate is not properly a breaker plate at all. Instead, it has been modified to mount the signal generator unit instead of breaker points. However, the vacuum advance works the same—shifting the position of the "breaker" plate to vary the angular relationship of the signal generator's pickup coil core with the teeth of the timing rotor.

Removing and Installing Distributor

Because the elongated hole for the distributor hold-down bolt is in a casting that forms the body of the distributor itself, the possibility for reinstalling the distributor incorrectly is greatly reduced. However, by following the procedure given here, you can be sure that you will not encounter difficulty in timing the engine after the distributor has been reinstalled.

To remove distributor:

1. Remove the distributor cap. Using a wrench on the bolt that is in the center of the crankshaft pulley,

hand-turn the crankshaft clockwise until the V-notch timing mark in the pulley is aligned with the 0° mark of the timing scale cast into the timing cover. See Fig. 3-29.

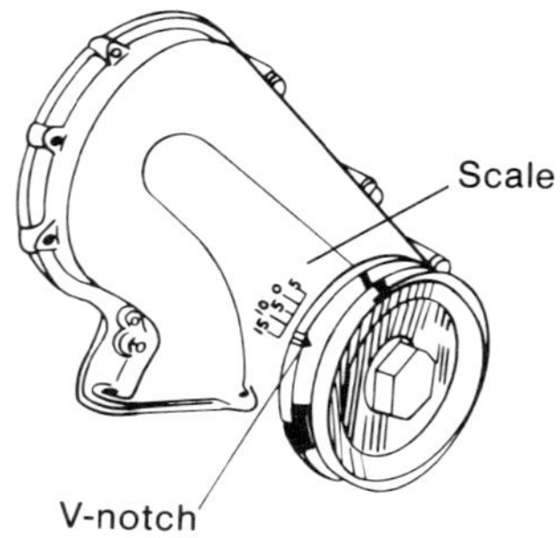

Fig. 3-29. Timing mark and scale on front of engine.

2. Check that the distributor rotor is pointed roughly toward the radiator top hose connection of the engine, as shown in Fig. 3-30. If it is not, turn the crankshaft another full turn until the V-notch is again aligned with the 0° mark of the timing scale—indicating that the No. 1 cylinder is in firing position.

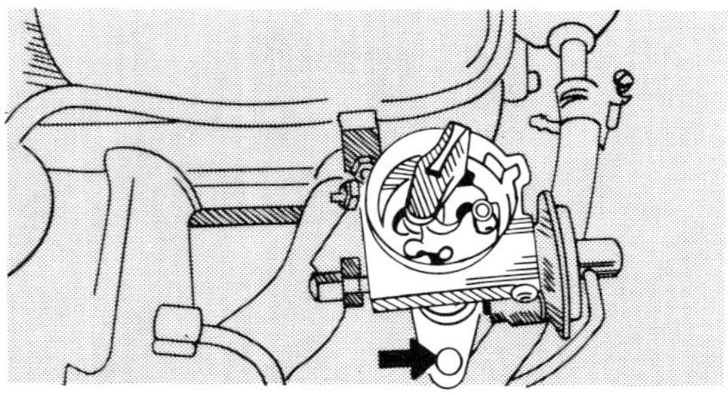

Fig. 3-30. Distributor rotor position with No. 1 cylinder firing point. Arrow indicates distributor hold-down bolt.

3. Make a mark on the edge of the distributor body that is exactly in line with the tip of the distributor rotor. This mark will help you to reinstall the distributor correctly.

> **NOTE ——**
> If you are working on your own car, you may wish to make the mark permanent by filing a small V-notch into the distributor body in line with the rotor tip. Otherwise, make the mark with a waterproof felt-tipped marker.

4. Disconnect the vacuum hose(s) and the electrical wire(s) from the distributor.
5. Remove the hold-down bolt, which was indicated previously in Fig. 3-30. Then lift out the distributor. Cover the opening in the engine block to keep out dirt.

To install:

1. Align the tip of the distributor rotor with the mark you made on the periphery of the distributor body. Notice the position of the oil pump drive dog on the bottom end of the distributor shaft. If the slot in the oil pump driveshaft is not in a similar position when you hold the distributor next to the engine and compare the two components, use a screwdriver to turn the oil pump driveshaft until its slot is aligned approximately with the drive dog on the distributor shaft.

> **NOTE ——**
> Normally, you will not need to reposition the oil pump driveshaft unless the oil pump has been removed or the engine disassembled for major repairs.

2. If the crankshaft was turned while the distributor was out of the engine, hand-turn the crankshaft until the V-notch timing mark on the crankshaft is aligned with the 0° mark on the timing scale and both valves for the No. 1 cylinder are closed.

> **NOTE ——**
> You may have to remove the cylinder head cover as described in **5.1 Removing and Installing Cylinder Head Cover** to check the valve positions. The valves are closed if you can jiggle the rocker arms for both valves of the No. 1 cylinder.

3. Before you install the distributor, hand-turn the distributor shaft until the rotor tip points to a position approximately 26° counterclockwise from the No. 1 cylinder mark that you made on the distributor body prior to distributor removal. If you made no mark, refer to Fig. 3-30, given earlier, and use it as a guide to approximate the correct rotor position.
4. Insert the distributor into the engine, aligning the elongated hole for the hold-down bolt with the bolt hole in the engine block. As the helical gears mesh, the rotor should turn clockwise 26° and the dog on the distributor shaft should engage the slot in the oil pump driveshaft.
5. With the distributor pressed fully into the engine block, check that the rotor tip is aligned with the No. 1 cylinder mark that you made on the distributor body. If not, repeat the installation procedure until the rotor is correctly aligned.
6. Loosely install the hold-down bolt—but tight enough to prevent the distributor body from being easily hand-turned in the engine.
7. Install the vacuum hose(s), the primary wire(s), and the distributor cap. Then start the engine and adjust the ignition timing as described in **3.3 Adjusting Timing** before you torque the hold-down bolt to 15 to 20 Nm (11 to 15 ft. lb.).

Disassembling and Assembling Distributor

A screwdriver and pliers are the only tools required for disassembling the distributor. The distributor shown in Fig. 3-31 is typical of those used in cars covered by this Manual. However, some 1975 cars have dual-point distributors and all 1978 and later models have a breakerless distributor with no points at all.

The distributor cap, the rotor, and the shield plate must be removed for access to the breaker points (or to the signal generator used on 1978 and later cars). To remove the points from a 1975 through 1977 car, first loosen the primary terminal nut on the outside of the distributor, then detach the breaker point assembly's wire from the terminal inside the distributor. Remove the two screws that hold the point assembly (or assemblies) to the breaker plate. On the breakerless distributor introduced on the 1978 models, disconnect the distributor's wires at the signal generator lead wire plug, disengage the lead wire from the distributor body, then remove the two screws that hold the signal generator's pickup coil assembly to the distributor. Remove the points or the signal generator. See Fig. 3-32, Fig. 3-33, or Fig. 3-34.

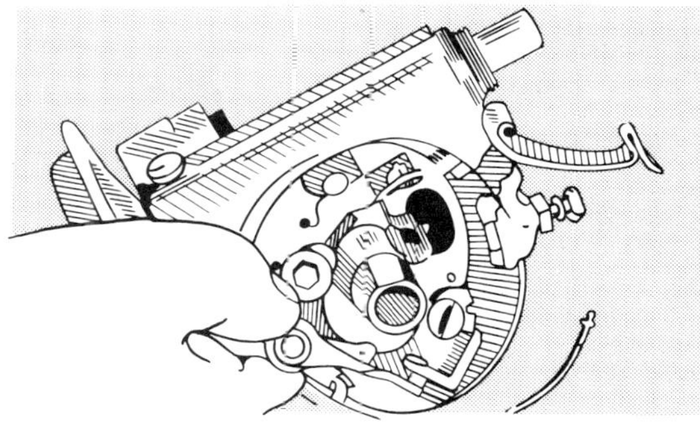

Fig. 3-32. Breaker points being lifted out of distributor.

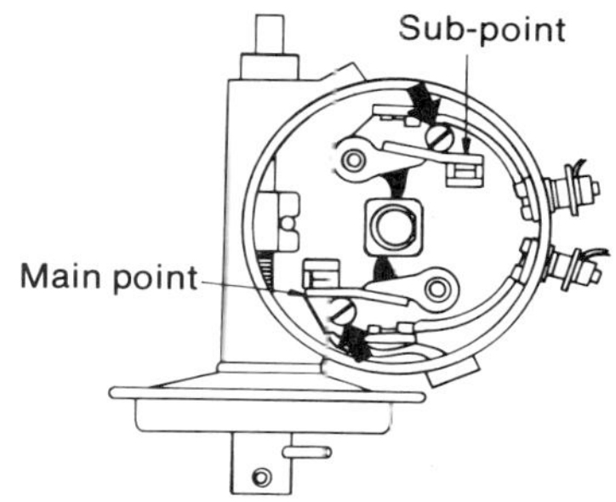

Fig. 3-33. Screws (arrows) that hold breaker point assemblies in dual-point distributor. One screw holds each point assembly.

5

Fig. 3-31. Exploded view of typical distributor. Breaker plate and vacuum advance unit design has been changed from model to model.

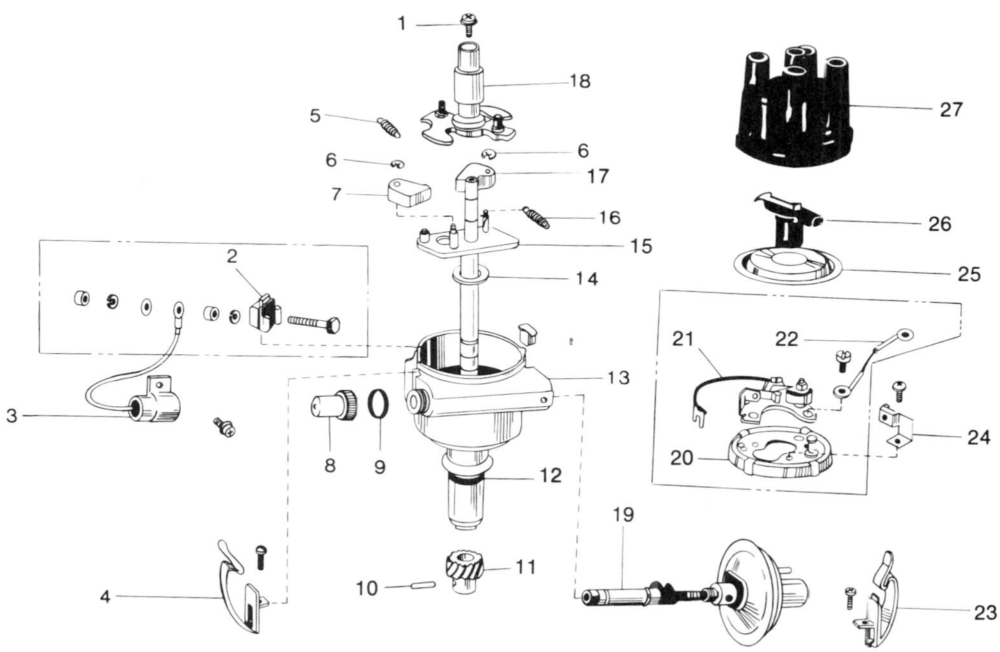

1. Screw for cam assembly
2. Primary terminal subassembly
3. Condenser
4. Cap retainer spring
5. Primary spring
6. E-clip
7. Primary weight
8. Vacuum advance unit cap
9. Rubber washer
10. Pin
11. Drivegear
12. O-ring
13. Distributor body
14. Steel spacer washer
15. Distributor shaft assembly
16. Secondary spring
17. Secondary weight
18. Cam assembly
19. Vacuum advance unit
20. Breaker plate assembly
21. Breaker point assembly
22. Ground wire
23. Cap retainer spring
24. Damping spring with lubricator pad
25. Shield plate with rubber gasket
26. Rotor
27. Distributor cap

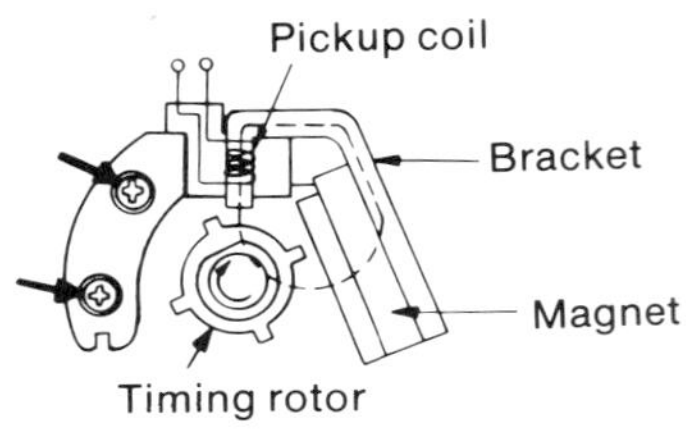

Fig. 3-34. Screws (arrows) that hold signal generator's pickup coil assembly in 1978 and later breakerless distributor. You must also remove the vacuum advance unit's retaining screw in order to free the signal generator plug from the distributor body.

The distributor's breaker points should be replaced and adjusted at the intervals prescribed in **LUBRICATION AND MAINTENANCE.** (The 1978 and later breakerless distributor requires no similar maintenance.) After removing the old point assembly, wipe clean the inside of the distributor. Make sure that the contacts of the new point assembly meet squarely. If the contacts do not meet squarely, carefully bend the stationary contact to align the points. Never bend the movable contact arm since doing this will impair its strength. Also replace the damping spring with lubricating pad if the old pad is hard or deteriorating.

NOTE ——

When you install the damping spring with lubricating pad, the pad should just contact the cam lobes—an interference of 0.10 to 0.40 mm (.004 to .016 in.) is adequate.

After you have installed the new points, lubricate the distributor as indicated in Fig. 3-35. Wipe off any excess lubricants so that they will not be thrown onto the point contacts. Then adjust the breaker points as described

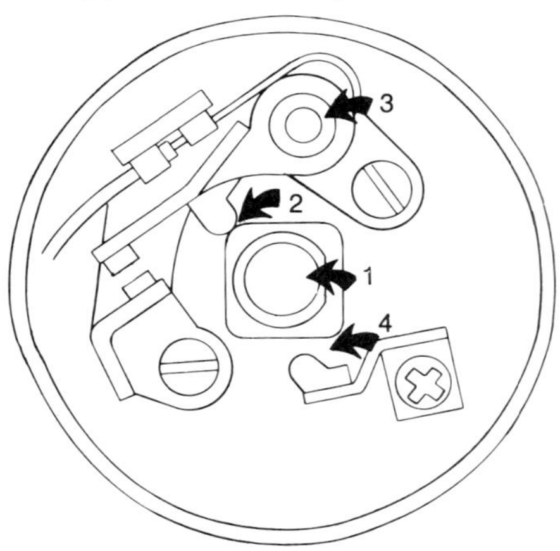

Fig. 3-35. Distributor lubrication. Saturate felt wick (**1**) with engine oil. Apply a small amount of molybdenum grease to the distributor cam and rubbing block (**2**), one drop of engine oil to the breaker point pivot (**3**), and a small amount of molybdenum grease to the lubricating pad (**4**).

under the next unnumbered heading. On the breakerless distributor, you need lubricate only the felt wick. Then adjust the pickup coil's air gap as described under the next unnumbered heading.

NOTE ——

Electrical testing of the pickup coil used in breakerless distributors is covered in **3.1 Coil and Igniter.**

To disassemble distributor completely:

1. Remove the breaker points or the signal generator, as previously described.
2. Remove the vacuum advance unit cap. Remove the vacuum advance retaining screw (Fig. 3-36), then remove the vacuum advance unit from the distributor—disengaging it from the pin on the breaker plate.

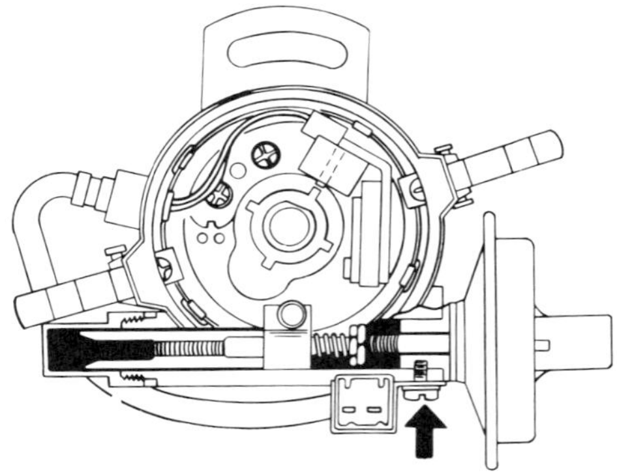

Fig. 3-36. Vacuum advance unit retaining screw (arrow).

3. Remove the two screws that hold the two distributor cap retainer springs to the distributor body. Remove the cap retainer springs, then lift out the breaker plate as indicated in Fig. 3-37.

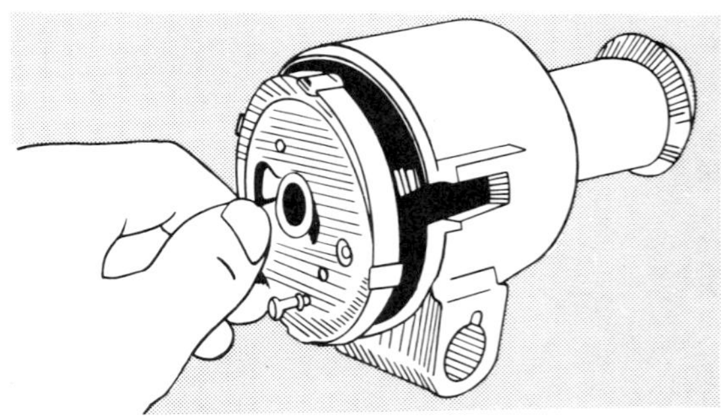

Fig. 3-37. Breaker plate being removed.

4. Using pliers as indicated in Fig. 3-38, remove the primary spring and the secondary spring. Label each spring as you remove it and mark its location so that later you will be able to install it in its correct place.

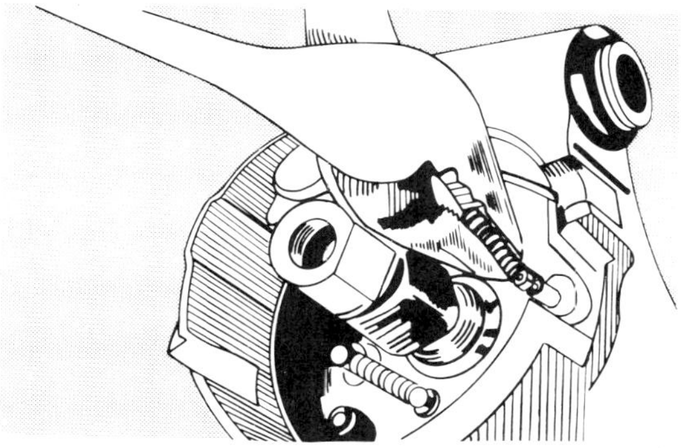

Fig. 3-38. Centrifugal advance mechanism springs being removed.

5. Using a pin or needle, remove the felt wick from the center of the cam assembly. Then remove the screw for the cam assembly and take out the cam assembly as indicated in Fig. 3-39.
6. Remove the E-clips, then remove the centrifugal advance unit weights from the distributor shaft assembly.

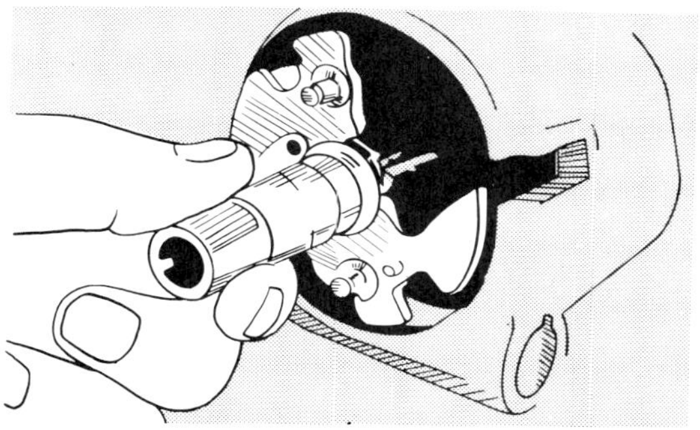

Fig. 3-39. Cam assembly being removed.

7. If further disassembly is required, file the peened ends off the pin for the drivegear. Drive the pin out with a drift, then remove the drivegear and any washers between it and the distributor body. Withdraw the distributor shaft assembly. See Fig. 3-40.

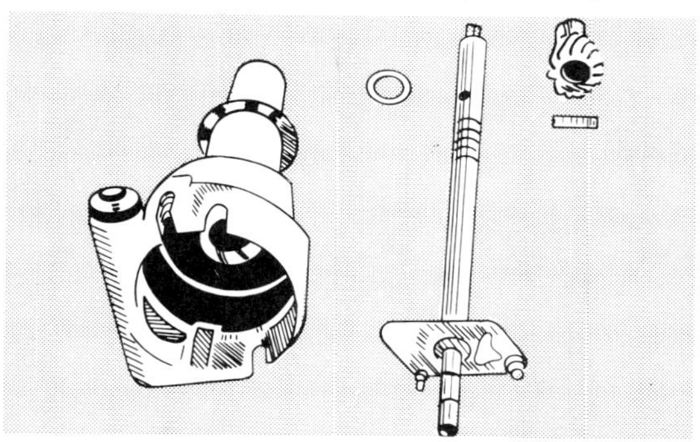

Fig. 3-40. Distributor shaft assembly removed from distributor body. Be careful neither to lose spacer washers located at each end of shaft nor to mix them up.

To inspect:

1. Thoroughly clean in solvent all parts except the breaker points, the condenser, and the vacuum advance unit. Replace visibly worn, damaged, or corroded parts.
2. Roll the shaft on a piece of plate glass or other smooth surface. Replace shafts that are bent more than 0.05 mm (.002 in.).
3. After lightly lubricating the bearings with engine oil, install the distributor shaft assembly in the distributor body. Check the shaft for side play. If the shaft can be shifted from side to side in its bearings, it is probably best to replace the distributor as a unit.
4. Install the distributor shaft assembly in the distributor body with its original spacer washers. Install the drivegear, holding it in position with the old pin or a new un-peened pin. Then measure the shaft's end thrust. If end thrust is not between 0.15 and 0.50 mm (.006 and .020 in.), select new steel spacer washer(s) that will bring the end thrust into the prescribed range.

NOTE ——

The steel spacer washers are available in thicknesses of 2.30 mm, 2.50 mm, 2.70 mm, and 2.90 mm (.091 in., .098 in., .106 in., .114 in.). These washers should always be installed at the upper end of the shaft. You can measure the end thrust of the shaft with a dial indicator, as shown in Fig. 3-41, or by inserting feeler gauges of various thicknesses between the drivegear and the lower end of the distributor body.

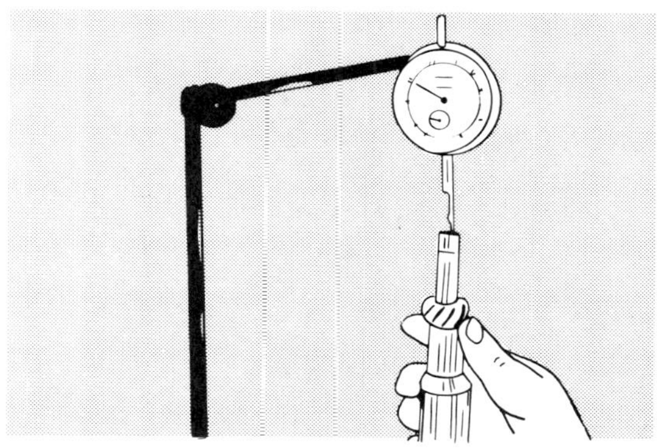

Fig. 3-41. Distributor shaft end thrust being measured with dial indicator.

5. Check the sliding resistance of the breaker plate. Measured with a spring scale, it should require no more than 1 kg (2.2 lb.) to rotate the breaker plate.

Replace breaker plates that are binding. See Fig. 3-42.

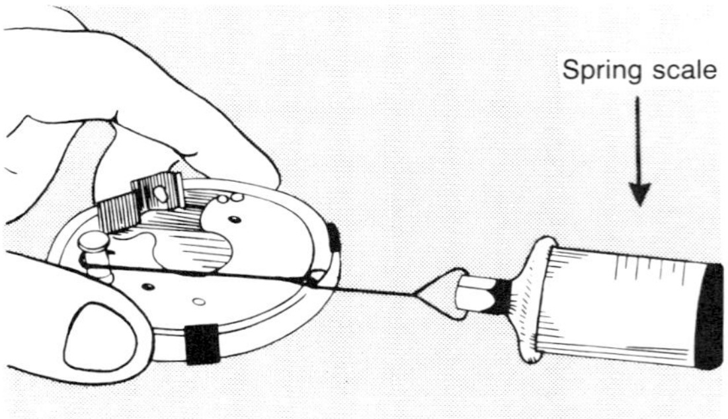

Fig. 3-42. Spring scale (at right) being used to check sliding resistance of breaker plate upper part.

Assembly is the reverse of disassembly. Peen the new pin for the drivegear by clamping it in a vise. Be sure to reinstall the centrifugal advance springs and weights in their original locations. During installation of the breaker plate, the clips indicated in Fig. 3-43 should engage the grooves in the distributor body. Following assembly of the distributor, you should have its advance checked on a distributor testing machine as described in **3.3 Adjusting Timing.**

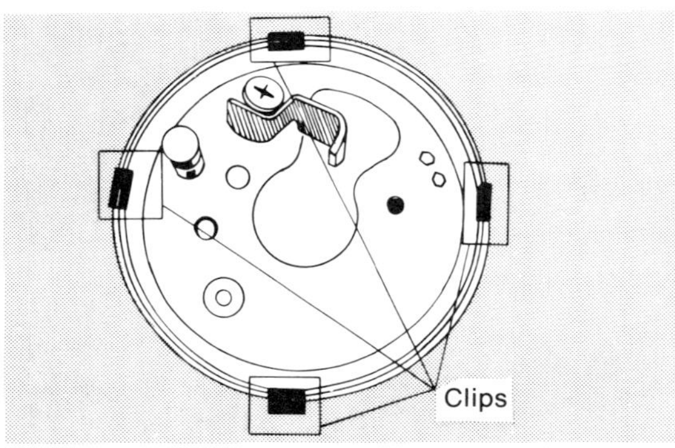

Fig. 3-43. Clips (in boxes) that must engage slots in distributor body.

Adjusting Point Gap or Pickup Coil Air Gap

After you have installed the breaker points or the pickup coil (cars with breakerless ignition), you must adjust the gap(s). A preliminary adjustment can be made with a feeler gauge, but you must always make the final adjustment with a dwell meter.

To adjust (all years):

1. Remove the distributor cap, the rotor, and the shield plate.
2. Using a wrench on the bolt that is in the center of the crankshaft pulley, hand-turn the crankshaft clockwise until the breaker point rubbing block is on a high point on the distributor cam (points wide open). On 1978 and later cars, turn the crankshaft until one tooth of the timing rotor is directly opposite the pickup coil core (Fig. 3-44).

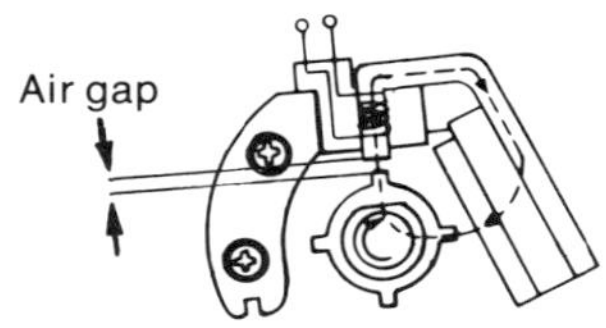

Fig. 3-44. Breakerless ignition distributor in position for air gap adjustment. Tooth of timing rotor is aligned with pickup coil core. Air gap between tooth and coil core is indicated by arrows.

3. To determine whether the breaker points are gapped correctly on 1975 cars only (either single-point or dual-point distributor), use a feeler gauge as indicated in Fig. 3-45. The gap should be between 0.40 and 0.50 mm (.016 and .020 in.). On 1976 and 1977 cars use the feeler gauge as shown in Fig. 3-46; the rubbing block gap should be 0.45 mm (.018 in.). Use a non-magnetic feeler gauge as shown in Fig. 3-47 on cars with breakerless ignition; the air gap should be 0.20 to 0.40 mm (.008 to .016 in.).

CAUTION —

Do not remove the clear plastic contact shield from the 1976 and 1977 breaker points. Do not insert a feeler gauge between the contacts as shown for the 1975 distributor. Because of the low voltage at the 1976 and 1977 points, only a thin film of dirt or oil from a contaminated feeler gauge can prevent current flow and cause misfiring.

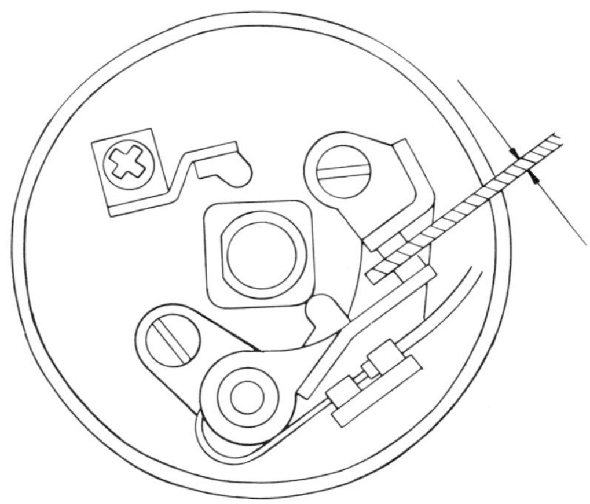

Fig. 3-45. Breaker point gap (arrows) being measured on 1975 car. Gap should be 0.40 to 0.50 mm (.016 and .020 in.) for both single-point and dual-point distributors.

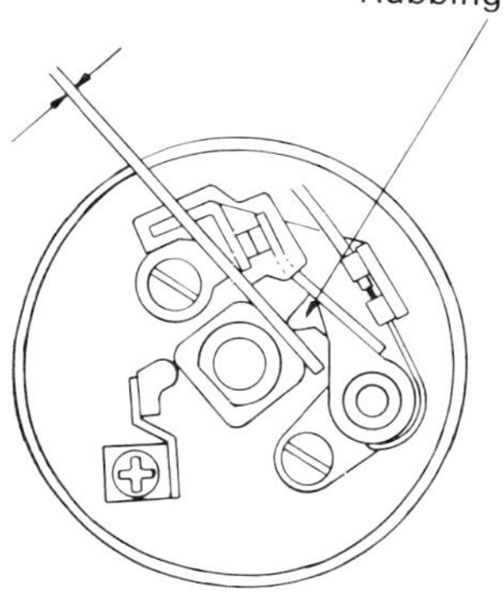

Fig. 3-46. Rubbing block gap being measured on 1976 or 1977 car. Gap should be 0.45 mm (.018 in.).

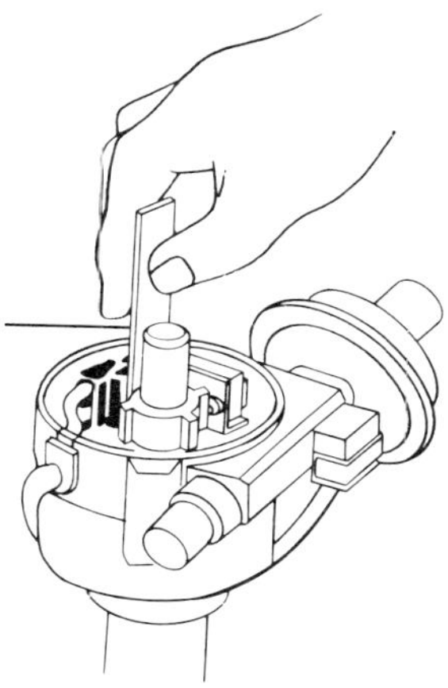

Fig. 3-47. Non-magnetic feeler gauge being used to measure breakerless ignition system air gap. The gap should be between 0.20 and 0.40 mm (.008 and .016 in.).

4. If necessary, loosen the breaker point assembly (or pickup coil assembly) mounting screw(s). Then reposition the breaker point stationary contact or the pickup coil assembly until the point gap or the air gap is within specifications. Tighten the screw(s). If the gap is incorrect when you recheck it, repeat the adjustment.

5. On distributors with breaker points, connect a dwell meter/tachometer. The black clip should be attached to ground on any bare metal part of the engine and the colored clip attached to the negative (−) primary terminal of the coil (single-point distributors) or to the main point primary terminal (the one nearest the vacuum advance diaphragm) on dual-point distributors.

CAUTION —

No further test or adjustment is required on the breakerless ignition distributor used on 1978 and later cars. If you need to connect a tachometer to a 1976 or later ignition system, do not connect it to the distributor. See **3.3 Adjusting Timing.** *On 1975 cars with dual-point distributors, you should disconnect the wire from the thermoswitch on the intake manifold if the engine is not thoroughly warmed up.*

6. Switch the dwell meter to the tachometer position for four-cylinder engines. Make sure that the idle speed is 850 rpm ±50 rpm.

7. Switch the dwell meter to measure dwell. Read the dwell, which should be 50° to 54° for single-point distributors or 57° for dual-point distributors.

NOTE —

Points that have been in service for less than 40,000 km (25,000 mi.) or two years can be retained in service without adjustment so long as dwell is within specifications.

8. If necessary, remove the distributor cap, the rotor, and the shield plate. Then adjust the dwell. To adjust dwell, loosen the breaker point assembly mounting screw(s). Using the tip of a screwdriver engaged in the notch in the stationary contact mounting and the dimples on the breaker plate, move the stationary contact either to widen the gap and decrease dwell, or to narrow the gap and increase dwell.

5

NOTE —

You can run the engine with the starter to check the dwell during adjustment but always make the final check with the engine running.

9. Fully tighten the breaker point assembly mounting screw(s). Then install the shield plate, the distributor rotor, and the cap. Check the dwell at 850 rpm ±50 rpm to make sure that it is within the specified range.

10. Run the engine at about 2000 rpm. The dwell should not vary more than ±1° from the reading obtained at idle. Larger deviations indicate a worn distributor, which should be replaced.

11. On 1975 cars with dual-point distributors, disconnect the wire from the thermo-switch and ground

it as indicated in Fig. 3-48. Then reconnect the dwell meter to the primary terminal for the sub-point. At idle, the dwell for the sub-point should be 50° to 54°. If not, adjust it as previously described, then reconnect the wire to the thermo switch.

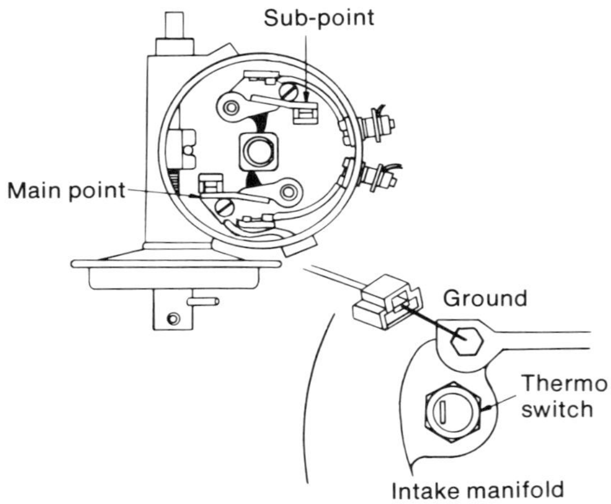

Fig. 3-48. Wire for thermo switch grounded so that dwell of sub-point can be checked.

12. After you have adjusted the dwell to specifications, adjust the ignition timing as described in **3.3 Adjusting Timing.**

3.3 Adjusting Timing

Adjust the timing after you have installed or adjusted the breaker points, after you have adjusted the air gap of a breakerless ignition distributor, or after you have reinstalled the distributor. A change of only 0.10 mm (.004 in.) in the point gap will alter the ignition timing by about 3°.

To adjust timing:

1. Clean the V-notch timing mark on the crankshaft pulley and the timing scale on the front of the engine's timing cover (Fig. 3-49). Touch the V-notch with chalk or white paint to make it more visible.

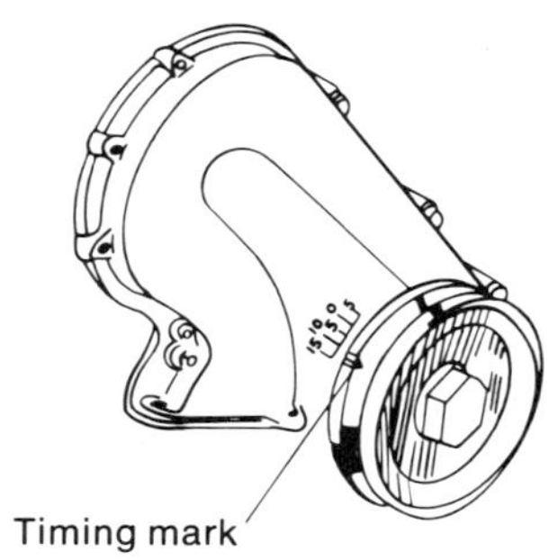

Fig. 3-49. Location of timing mark and timing scale on front of engine.

2. On 1975 through 1977 cars, make sure that the vacuum advance indicator sleeve (sometimes called the octane selector) is at its standard position, as indicated in Fig. 3-50. If necessary, remove the cap and turn the indicator sleeve clockwise or counterclockwise until the annular standard line is flush with the threaded protrusion on the distributor body and the axial standard line is aligned with the standard mark.

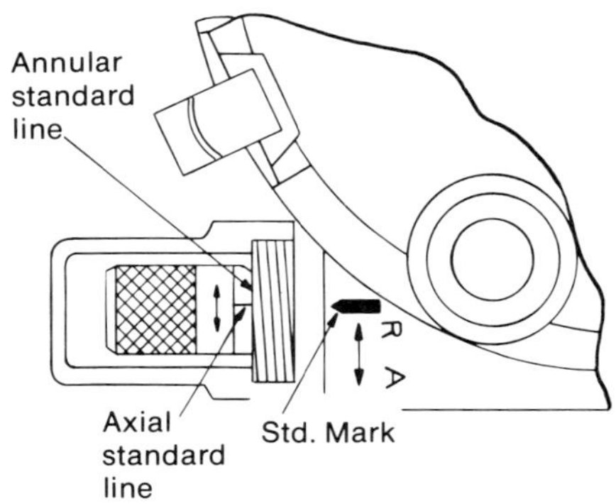

Fig. 3-50. Standard setting for vacuum advance indicator sleeve. Use of this device as an octane selector is impractical on North American models and unnecessary because of standardized fuels.

3. Following the instrument manufacturer's instructions, install a stroboscopic timing light and a tachometer. On 1975 cars with dual-point distributors, disconnect the wire from the thermo switch on the intake manifold (unnecessary if engine is thoroughly warmed up).

CAUTION —
On 1975 cars with dual-point distributors, and on all 1976 and later cars, connect the tachometer's positive (+) lead to the coil's negative (−) terminal, as indicated in Fig. 3-51. Do not connect the tachometer's positive (+) lead to the distributor, which may damage the electronic ignition systems used on these cars.

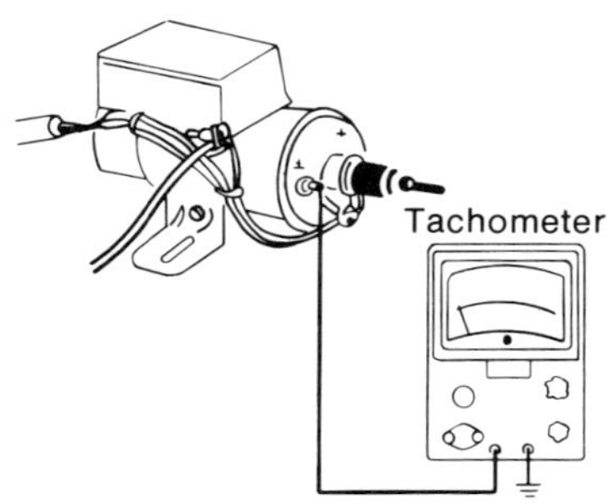

Fig. 3-51. Correct attachment of tachometer to coil of 1978 and later breakerless ignition system.

4. Start the engine and allow it to warm up until the idle stabilizes at 850 rpm ±50 rpm (700 to 900 rpm on 1978 and later high-altitude models). On cars with double-diaphragm vacuum advance units, disconnect and plug the vacuum hose for the secondary (innermost) diaphragm (Fig. 3-52). Keep all other vacuum hoses connected.

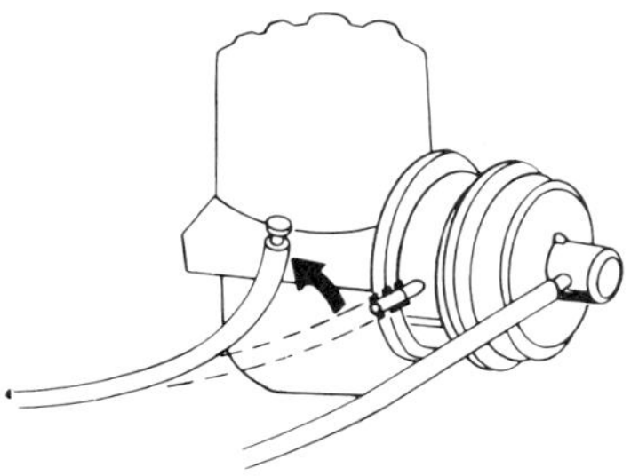

Fig. 3-52. Secondary diaphragm vacuum hose disconnected and plugged on double-diaphragm distributor.

5. Aim the timing light at the timing scale (Fig. 3-53). Except on 1975 cars with dual-point distributors, the V-notch timing mark should be aligned with the 10° BTDC (before top dead center) graduation on the timing scale. On 1975 cars with dual-point distributors, the timing mark should be aligned at 12° BTDC.

NOTE ——

On cars with either manual or automatic transmission, the transmission should be in neutral or "N" and the parking brake firmly set.

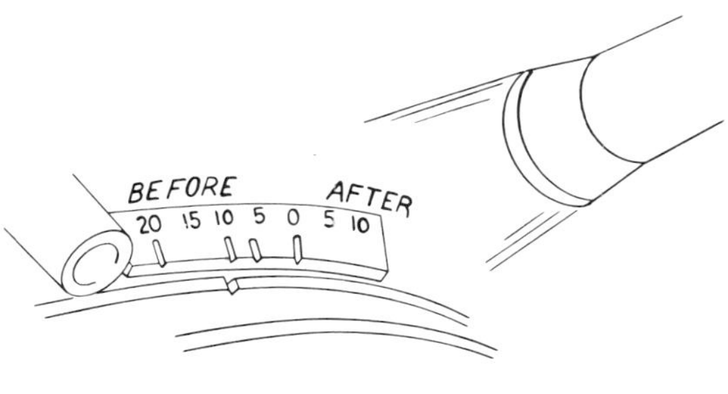

Fig. 3-53. V-notch timing mark as it should appear when illuminated by timing light.

6. If the timing mark is not at 10° BTDC (or 12° BTDC on 1975 cars with dual-point distributors), loosen the distributor hold-down bolt. Then, with the engine idling, hand-turn the distributor body clockwise or counterclockwise until the timing mark, illuminated by the timing light, is correctly aligned with the timing scale.

7. While you hold the distributor in the correct position, tighten the hold-down bolt.

8. Torque the hold-down bolt to 15 to 20 Nm (11 to 15 ft. lb.).

9. On 1975 cars with dual-point distributors, disconnect the wire from the thermo switch on the intake manifold and ground the wire on some clean, unpainted metal part of the engine. The timing mark, illuminated by the timing light, should shift to 22° ±3° BTDC.

NOTE ——

If the timing mark does not shift, troubleshoot the dual-point ignition system as described in **3.1 Coil and Igniter.** If the timing shifts, but is more than 3° above or below 22° BTDC, the sub-point dwell is incorrect and should be adjusted as described in **3.2 Distributor.** Following testing, reconnect the wire to the thermo switch.

10. On cars with double-diaphragm distributors, connect a hose to the secondary diaphragm as indicated in Fig. 3-54. Connect the other end of the hose to the intake manifold tap that is on the right-hand side of the manifold, below the carburetor. With full manifold vacuum thus applied to the secondary diaphragm, the timing mark, illuminated by the timing light, should be at about 20° BTDC. If so, reconnect the regular hose to the distributor.

NOTE ——

This check is for testing the operation of the vacuum advance unit only. Replace vacuum units that do not correctly advance the spark. To test the emission components that control the vacuum supplied to the distributor, see **FUEL AND EXHAUST SYSTEMS.**

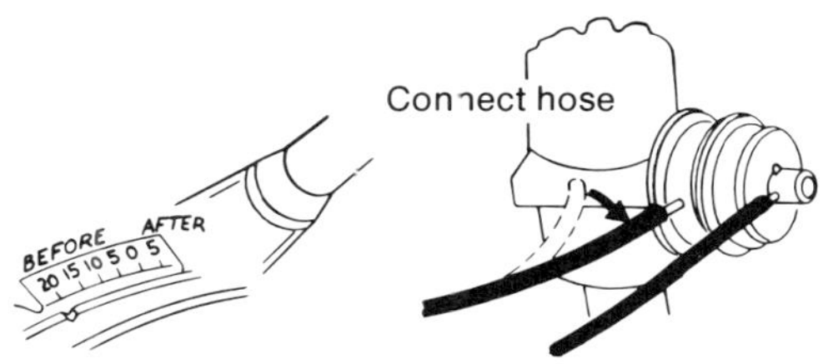

Fig. 3-54. Correct timing at idle with manifold vacuum delivered to secondary diaphragm.

11. On all distributors, connect and disconnect the vacuum hoses with the engine operating at about 2000 rpm while you observe the timing mark with the timing light. The timing mark should shift its position each time vacuum is applied to or removed from the diaphragm connection. If the timing does not shift (and vacuum is present at the hose) the vacuum advance unit is faulty and should be replaced.

12. Disconnect all vacuum hoses from the distributor. Change the engine rpm from 1000 rpm to 2500 rpm and back. The timing mark should appear to move back and forth, as indicated in Fig. 3-55. If it does not, the centrifugal advance mechanism is faulty and the distributor should be disassembled for cleaning and repair.

NOTE —

You can quick-check the centrifugal advance as shown in Fig. 3-56. If the rotor fails to turn or fails to return fully and smoothly, there is trouble in the centrifugal advance mechanism.

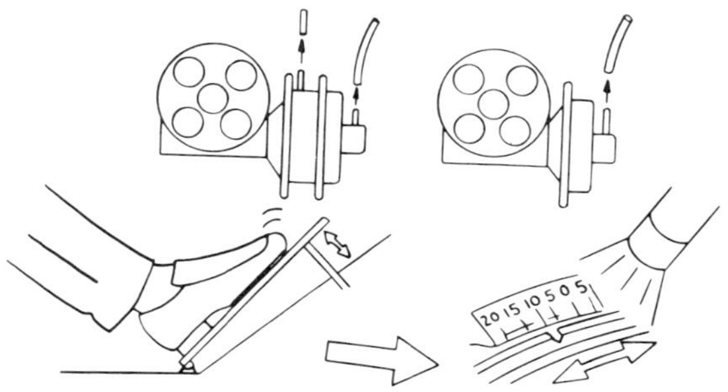

Fig. 3-55. Centrifugal advance being checked. Disconnect vacuum hoses as indicated by single arrows. Move accelerator as indicated by straight double arrow. Large arrow indicates result that should be obtained; timing mark shifts position as indicated by curved double arrow.

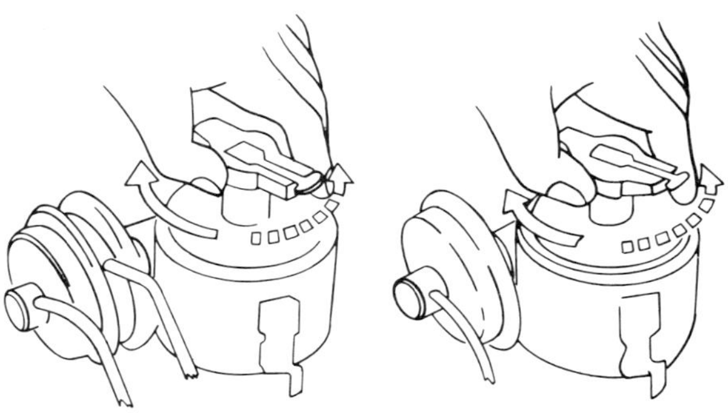

Fig. 3-56. Centrifugal advance quick-check. Hand-turn rotor clockwise and release it. It should return fully and smoothly. Also check for looseness that may indicate screw for cam assembly is loose.

Checking Spark Advance Mechanism

Clean the distributor if dirt or hardened grease is causing the spark advance mechanism to jam, or if the interior of the distributor has become oil soaked. First remove the distributor as described in **3.2 Distributor.** Then, after removing the breaker points or the pickup coil assembly, the condenser (when fitted), and the vacuum advance unit, wash the distributor body assembly thoroughly in clean solvent. Blow the distributor body assembly dry with compressed air.

CAUTION —

Be careful not to direct a strong blast of air into the housing at close range. Doing this could damage the calibrated springs in the centrifugal advance mechanism.

Thoroughly lubricate the distributor shaft and bearings with engine oil by applying the oil to the space between the drivegear and the distributor body. With the distributor body inverted, hand-turn the shaft until the oil has worked its way all along the shaft. The shaft should turn smoothly without binding. Also lubricate the interior distributor parts as described earlier in the procedure for disassembling and assembling the distributor. If necessary, you can remove the breaker plate to gain access to the centrifugal advance.

Tables b, **c**, **d**, and **e** give the spark advance curves used in the distributors of cars covered by this Manual. With the information contained in these tables, a technician who is skilled in the use of a distributor testing machine (Fig. 3-57) can check and, if necessary, adjust the advance curves to exact Toyota specifications.

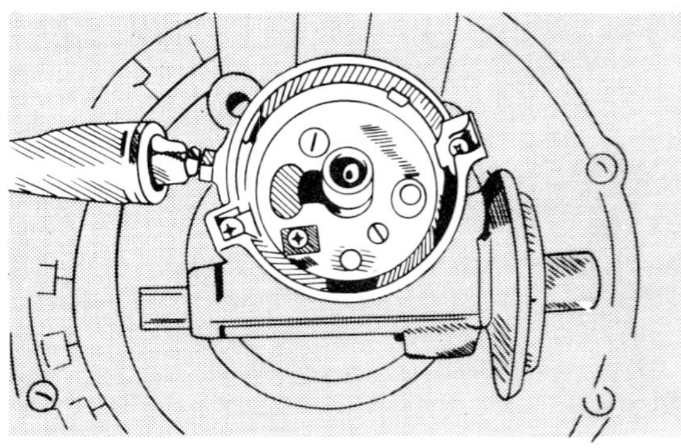

Fig. 3-57. Distributor installed on distributor testing machine.

Table b. Spark Advance Curves for 1975 Model Distributors

Distributor	Centrifugal advance range		Vacuum advance range	
	distributor rpm	degrees	mbar (mm/Hg, in./Hg)	degrees
19100–26110–A	500 1300 2800	advance begins 8.0° 13.0°	120 (90, 3.54) 160 (120, 4.72) 307 (230, 9.06)	advance begins 3.0° 7.0°
19100–26120–A	500 1500 2700	advance begins 7.0° 13.0°	120 (90, 3.54) 160 (120, 4.72) 307 (230, 9.06)	advance begins 3.0° 7.0°
19100–26909 (dual-point distributor)	750 1300 1800	advance begins 7.0° 9.0°	120 (90, 3.54) 160 (120, 4.72) 307 (230, 9.06)	advance begins 3.0° 7.0°

Table c. Spark Advance Curves for 1976 Model Distributors

Distributor	Centrifugal advance range		Vacuum advance range	
	distributor rpm	degrees	mbar (mm/Hg, in./Hg)	degrees
19100–26110–B	500 1300 2800 3000	advance begins 8.0° 13.0° 12.9°	120 (90, 3.54) 160 (120, 4.72) 307 (230, 9.06)	advance begins 3.0° 7.0°
19100–26121–A	650 2600 3000	advance begins 13.0° 12.8°	120 (90, 3.54) 160 (120, 4.72) 307 (230, 9.06)	advance begins 3.0° 7.0°
Double- diaphragm type	500 1300 1900 3000	advance begins 8.0° 10.0° 9.7°	**vacuum applied to main (outermost) diaphragm only**	
			120 (90, 3.54) 267 (200, 7.87)	advance begins 7.0°
			vacuum applied to secondary (innermost) diaphragm only	
			93 (70, 2.76) 200 (150, 5.91)	advance begins 5.0°

Table d. Spark Advance Curves for 1977 Model Distributors

Distributor	Centrifugal advance range		Vacuum advance range	
	distributor rpm	degrees	mbar (mm/Hg, in./Hg)	degrees
19100–26230	550 1200 2100 3000	advance begins 8.0° 12.0° 11.9°	120 (90, 3.54) 160 (120, 4.72) 400 (300, 11.81)	advance begins 3.0° 9.0°
19100–26240 (double- diaphragm type)	550 1200 1650 3000	advance begins 8.0° 10.0° 9.7°	**vacuum applied to main (outermost) diaphragm only**	
			120 (90, 3.54) 200 (150, 5.91) 347 (260, 10.24)	advance begins 4.0° 9.0°
			vacuum applied to secondary (innermost) diaphragm only	
			93 (70, 2.76) 200 (150, 5.91)	advance begins 5.0°

Table e. Spark Advance Curves for 1978 and Later Distributors

Distributor (breakerless)	Centrifugal advance range		Vacuum advance range	
	distributor rpm	**degrees**	**mbar (mm/Hg, in./Hg)**	**degrees**
19100-26280 (Federal specification)	500 876 1400 2700 3000	advance begins 2.1° 6.2° 10.0° 9.8°	147 (110, 4.33) 213 (160, 6.30) 280 (210, 8.27) 347 (260, 10.24) 440 (330, 12.99)	advance begins 4.1° 7.4° 10.0° 13.0°
19100-26231 (California specification)*	550 776 1200 2100 3000	advance begins 2.6° 8.0° 12.0° 11.3°	120 (90, 3.54) 160 (120, 4.72) 293 (220, 8.66) 400 (300, 11.81)	advance begins 3.0° 6.8° 9.0°
19100-26290 (Federal specification, optional double-diaphragm type)	500 876 1400 2060 3000	advance begins 2.1° 6.2° 8.0° 7.3°	**vacuum applied to main (outermost) diaphragm only**	
			147 (110, 4.33) 213 (160, 6.30) 280 (210, 8.27) 347 (260, 10.24) 440 (330, 12.99)	advance begins 3.7° 6.8° 9.2° 12.0°
			vacuum applied to secondary (innermost) diaphragm only	
			267 (200, 7.87) 400 (300, 11.81)	advance begins 5.0°
19100-26261 (Canadian specification)	500 800 1400 2700 3000	advance begins 1.6° 6.2° 10.0° 9.9°	213 (160, 6.30) 280 (210, 8.27) 333 (250, 9.84) 387 (290, 11.42) 440 (330, 12.99) 507 (380, 14.96)	advance begins 4.1° 6.8° 9.0° 10.9° 13.0°
19100-26271 (Canadian specification, optional double-diaphragm type)	500 888 1400 2000 3000	advance begins 2.1° 6.0° 8.0° 7.2°	**vacuum applied to main (outermost) diaphragm only**	
			213 (160, 6.30) 280 (210, 8.27) 347 (260,10.24) 413 (310, 12.20) 480 (360, 14.17) 507 (380, 14.96)	advance begins 3.7° 6.6° 9.1° 11.3° 12.0°
			vacuum applied to secondary (innermost) diaphragm only	
			93 (70, 2.76) 160 (120, 4.72) 200 (150, 5.91)	advance begins 3.3° 5.0°
19100-26241 (double-diaphragm type for high altitude locations	550 776 1200 1650 3000	advance begins 2.6° 8.0° 10.0° 8.9°	**vacuum applied to main (outermost) diaphragm only**	
			120 (90, 3.54) 187 (140, 5.51) 253 (190, 7.48) 320 (240, 9.45) 347 (260, 10.24)	advance begins 3.4° 5.9° 8.2° 9.0°
			vacuum applied to secondary (innermost) diaphragm only	
			93 (70, 2.76) 160 (120, 4.72) 200 (150, 5.91)	advance begins 3.5° 5.0°

*See Table XVI in **12. Engine Technical Data** for Distributor 19100-26232.

3.4 Secondary Circuit

The secondary circuit of the ignition system consists of the distributor rotor, the distributor cap, the spark plug cables, and the high tension cable that links the coil with the distributor cap. Secondary circuit resistance, for radio suppression and reduction of spark plug gap erosion, is built into the spark plug cables and the high tension cable.

In disconnecting the spark plug cables from the spark plugs, firmly grasp the boot and the connector itself, as shown at the top of Fig. 3-58. Do not pull on the cables themselves because this can cause separations in the resistance-type non-metallic conductor.

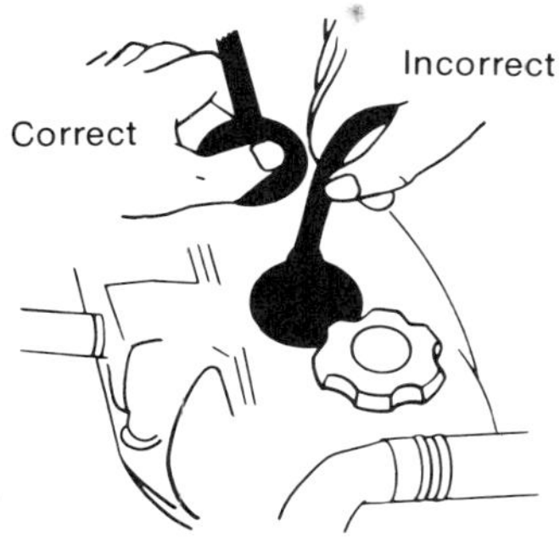

Fig. 3-58. Correct and incorrect methods of disconnecting cables.

You can check the resistance of the spark plug cables and the high tension cable as indicated in Fig. 3-59. New cables should not have a resistance in excess of 16,000 ohms per meter (39⅜ in.). Replace used cables that have a resistance greater than 25,000 ohms per meter (39⅜ in.).

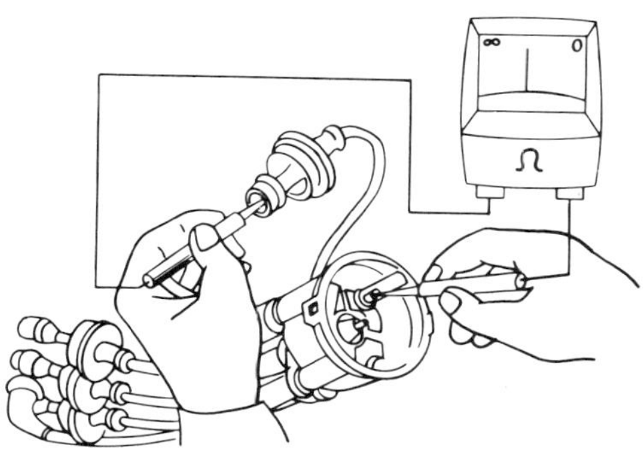

Fig. 3-59. Ohmmeter being used to test cable resistance. Shake each wire as you test it and watch for wide ohmmeter fluctuations that indicate internal breaks in the conductor.

To prevent spark flashover, which could cause irreparable carbon tracks on the distributor cap and rotor, keep the cap and the rotor clean and dry. Also keep the ignition cables clean and replace them when the insulation shows signs of cracking or deterioration. The rubber boots at the coil tower, the distributor cap towers, and the plug connectors must be sound and tight fitting if the secondary circuit is to remain waterproof. Always check for the troubles indicated in Fig. 3-60 during ignition system maintenance or troubleshooting.

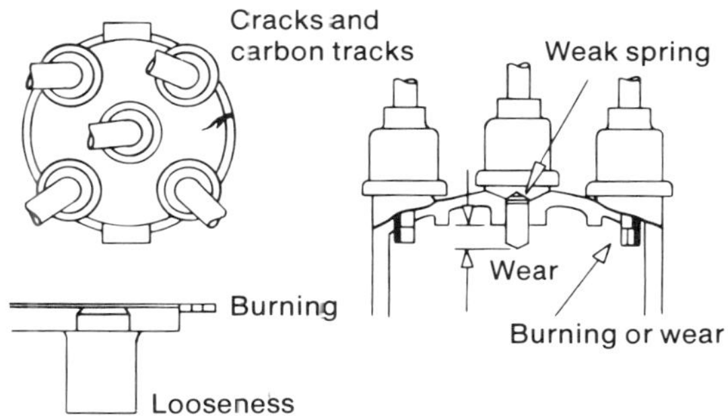

Fig. 3-60. Distributor cap and rotor inspection. Check for faults indicated in illustration.

3.5 Spark Plugs

Replace the spark plugs each 20,000 km (12,500 mi.) on 1975 through 1977 cars; replace the spark plugs each 24,000 km (15,000 mi.) on 1978 and later cars with breakerless ignition systems. If you drive less in a year, replace the spark plugs after twelve months to ensure that deposits will not interfere with efficient spark plug operation. Also, after the mileage intervals and the time period given, the electrodes will have worn to the point that ionization of the spark plug gap is discouraged. 5

Replacement spark plugs must be of the correct heat range and physical dimensions. The plug reach (the length of the threaded portion of the shell) should be 19 mm (¾ in.); the thread diameter should be 14 mm (.550 in.). Suitable spark plugs are listed in **Table f.**

Table f. Suitable Spark Plugs

Brand and designation	Applicable car models
Bosch W175T30	1975 through 1979 USA and Canada
Champion N-10Y	1975 through 1979 USA and Canada
NGK BP5EA NGK BP5ES-L NGK BP5EA-L NGK BP5ES NGK BPR5EA-L NGK BPR5ES	1979 USA only 1975 through 1978 USA, 1975 through 1977 Canada 1977 and 1979 USA, 1977 and 1978 Canada 1978 USA only 1978 and 1979 Canada only 1978 and 1979 Canada only
Nippodenso W16EP Nippodenso W16EX-U Nippodenso W16EPR Nippodenso W16EXR-U Nippodenso W14EX-U Nippodenso W16EPR	1975 through 1978 USA, 1975 through 1977 Canada 1977 through 1979 USA, 1977 Canada 1978 Canada only 1978 and 1979 Canada only 1979 USA only 1979 Canada only

Measure the gaps of new spark plugs and, if necessary, adjust them to 0.80 mm (.032 in.) as shown in Fig. 3-61. In adjusting the gaps, never attempt to bend the center electrode. If you attempt to do this you will break the insulator and render the spark plug unserviceable. If the old spark plugs were difficult to remove, the spark plug holes in the cylinder head should be cleaned with a thread chaser made especially for the job.

During installation, lightly coat the spark plug threads with anti-seize compound or multipurpose grease. If nothing else is available, lubricate the spark plug threads with engine oil. Lubrication will prevent corrosion damage and stuck spark plugs.

CAUTION —
Most anti-seize compounds contain graphite, which must not contact the plug electrodes or insulator. If it does, the graphite could short out the spark plug.

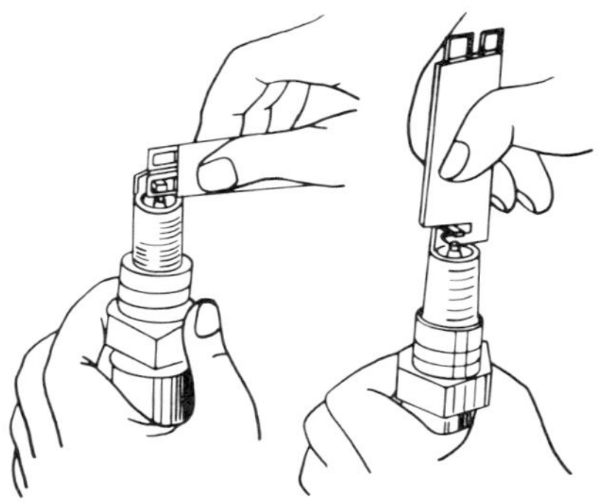

Fig. 3-61. Spark plug being gapped. At left, 0.80-mm (.032-in.) wire-loop spark plug gauge is inserted between center and side electrodes. If gauge is not a good fit in gap, bend side electrode as shown at right until gap is correct.

Start the plug in the cylinder head by hand-holding the spark plug socket. This will give improved feel and help prevent accidental cross-threading. Turn the spark plug in until you feel the gasket contact the cylinder head. Then install a torque wrench on the spark plug socket and torque the plug to 25 to 30 Nm (18 to 22 ft. lb.). If no torque wrench is available, tighten the plug by no more than ¼ turn after its gasket has contacted the cylinder head.

4. COOLING SYSTEM

To maintain the anti-corrosion properties of the coolant, you should use a permanent-type anti-freeze year-round. If coolant must be added, use the same proportion of water to anti-freeze that is already in the cooling system. See **LUBRICATION AND MAINTENANCE** for anti-freeze specifications and mixing proportions.

CAUTION —
Never add cold water or coolant while the engine is hot or overheated. Doing this could crack the engine block or the cylinder head.

4.1 Replacing Hoses

To prevent hose failure and overheating, you should periodically inspect the heater, engine, and radiator hoses. Replace hoses that are hard and cracked, spongy, rotted, or that have a tendency to collapse.

To replace:

1. With the car parked on a level spot, place a receptacle beneath the right-hand side of the radiator to catch the draining coolant. Then remove the radiator cap.

WARNING —
Never remove the radiator cap or drain the coolant while the engine is hot. Doing this could warp the engine block or the cylinder head, or you could burn yourself.

2. On later cars covered by this Manual, pass the hose on the radiator drain tap through the opening in the splash shield so that the hose is directed into the receptacle. On earlier cars, you should remove the splash shield from beneath the radiator if you wish to save the coolant. Otherwise, allow the coolant to run across the splash shield and into the receptacle.

NOTE —
In replacing hoses or removing the thermostat, it is necessary to drain only the radiator. To drain the cooling system completely, also open the drain tap on the left-hand side of the engine block (Fig. 4-1). Catch the coolant in a second receptacle or wait until the radiator is drained, move your receptacle to the left side of the engine, then drain the block.

3. Using a screwdriver, loosen the hose clamps at each end of the hose you must remove. Then slide the clamps toward the center of the hose.
4. Pull the hose off its connections.

Fig. 4-1. Drain taps for coolant. Radiator tap is at left arrow, engine block drain tap is at right arrow.

CAUTION ——

If a radiator hose is stuck to the radiator connection, it is best to cut the old hose off the connection. Prying the hose loose can damage the brass connection or the radiator.

5. Clean bits of old hose and sealer off the connections. The use of sealer during hose installation is optional.
6. Slip the hose clamps onto the hose. Then slide the hose onto its connections.
7. Position the hose clamps so that they are past the beads on the connections, but no nearer than 2.5 mm (1/8 in.) to the ends of the hose. Then tighten the hose clamps just enough to compress the hose firmly around the connections.

CAUTION ——

Overtightening the clamps will cause them to cut into the hose material. This damage may eventually lead to hose failure.

8. Close the radiator drain tap and, when applicable, the engine block drain tap. Then fill the radiator all the way to the base of the filler neck with the mixture of water and permanent-type anti-freeze that is recommended in **LUBRICATION AND MAINTENANCE.**
9. Run the engine for a few minutes with the radiator cap off to clear any air pockets that may have formed during refilling of the system. If necessary, add coolant to top off the radiator, then install the radiator cap.
10. If necessary, add coolant to the coolant reservoir until the level is at the point marked FULL in Fig. 4-2. Install the reservoir cap and double-check that neither the hose you have installed nor the drain taps are leaking.

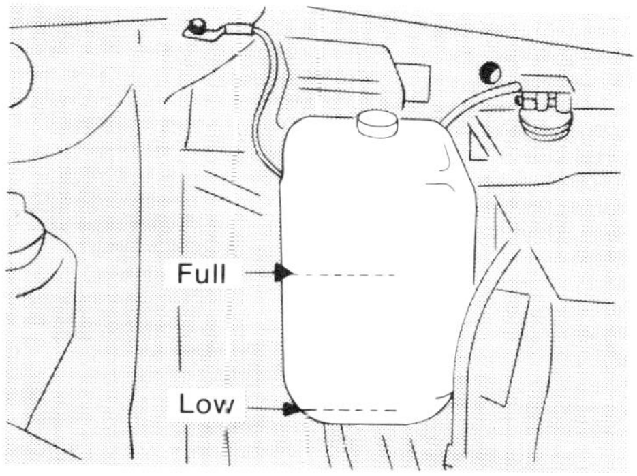

Fig. 4-2. Coolant reservoir in engine compartment. Keep level at point marked FULL.

4.2 Cooling System Troubleshooting

Most cooling system malfunctions not caused by leaks can be traced to a faulty thermostat, a restricted hose, a faulty radiator cap, or a clogged radiator. Clogged radiators and heater cores should be repaired only by an Authorized Dealer or a qualified radiator repair shop.

Virtually all clogged cooling systems are caused by neglect or the addition of substances to the coolant that are not recommended by the car manufacturer. Because radiator repairs are expensive, it is not wise economically to neglect the cooling system in an attempt to save the few dollars that proper maintenance will cost. You will never have to worry about a clogged radiator or heater core if you observe the following precautions: 5

1. To prevent the formation of rust and scale, keep the cooling system filled with an approximate 50% solution of an approved-quality ethylene-glycol permanent-type anti-freeze. Change the anti-freeze solution as recommended in **LUBRICATION AND MAINTENANCE** or by the anti-freeze manufacturer.
2. Never add more than one can of leak sealer to the cooling system as a precaution against leaks. Toyota recommends that you add nothing to the anti-freeze solution. A 'double dose' of leak sealer is especially likely to clog rust-filled, neglected cooling systems.
3. Never fill the radiator from a roadside ditch, a stream, or other water sources that may contain silt and organic material. Do not use water that is alkaline, as this can corrode aluminum.
4. Do not add engine oil to the coolant as a rust preventative. Doing this will encourage the formation of oil sludge in the cooling system and will damage the hoses.

Table g lists possible overheating and underheating symptoms, their probable causes, and suggested repairs. The boldface numbers in the Suggested Repair column refer to the numbered headings in this section where the suggested repairs are described.

Removing, Testing, and Installing Thermostat

To remove the thermostat for testing, drain only the radiator as described in **4.1 Replacing Hoses.** Remove the two bolts that hold the thermostat housing to the front of the cylinder head, then lift up the housing and take out the thermostat as shown in Fig. 4-3.

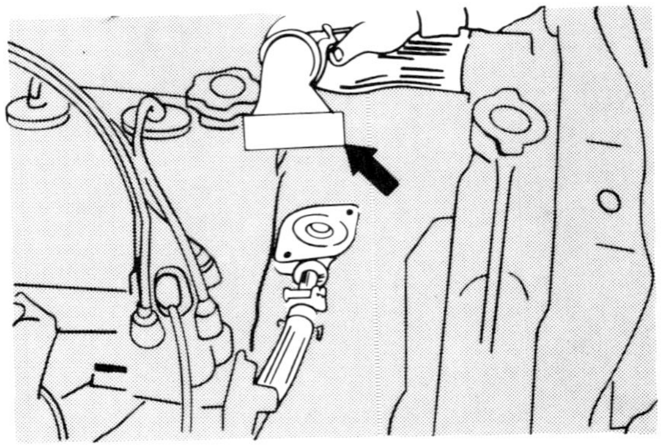

Fig. 4-3. Thermostat housing (arrow) lifted up so that thermostat can be lifted out of recess in front of cylinder head.

Table g. Cooling System Troubleshooting

Symptom	Probable cause	Suggested repair
Inadequate heater output, temperature gauge reads normal	a. Installed position of heater hoses reversed b. Heater hose restricted c. Heater core clogged d. Heater control out of adjustment	a. Install heater hoses correctly. See **4.1**. b. Replace hose. See **4.1**. c. Replace heater core or have core cleaned. See **BODY AND INTERIOR.** d. Adjust control cables. See **BODY AND INTERIOR**.
Inadequate heater output, temperature gauge reads low	Faulty thermostat	Remove and test thermostat. See **4.2**.
Temperature gauge reads low, heater output normal	Faulty temperature gauge or sending unit	Test temperature gauge and sending unit. Replace faulty part. See **ELECTRICAL SYSTEM**.
Engine overheats	a. Low coolant level b. Burst hose c. Radiator hose restricted (lower hose may collapse only at highway speeds) d. V-belt loose or broken e. Faulty thermostat f. Leaking cylinder head gasket or cracked head g. Faulty radiator cap h. Clogged radiator i. Incorrect ignition timing	a. Fill radiator and coolant reservoir. Check cooling system for leaks with pressure tester. See **4.1**, **4.2**. b. Replace hose. Refill radiator and coolant reservoir. See **4.1**. c. Replace hose. See **4.1**. d. Adjust or replace V-belt. See **LUBRICATION AND MAINTENANCE**. e. Remove and test thermostat. Replace if necessary. See **4.1**, **4.2**. f. Look for bubbles in radiator while engine runs at idle. Replace faulty parts. See **5**. g. Test pressure relief valve in cap. Replace faulty cap. See **4.2**. h. Replace radiator or have core cleaned. See **4.3**. i. Adjust ignition timing and check spark advance. See **3.3**.

Check visually whether the thermostat is fully closed at room temperature (Fig. 4-4). If not, it is faulty and must be replaced. Also replace the thermostat if it is closed, but has leaks between the valve and its seat. When you install the thermostat, use a new gasket and torque the bolts to 12 to 15 Nm (9 to 11 ft. lb.).

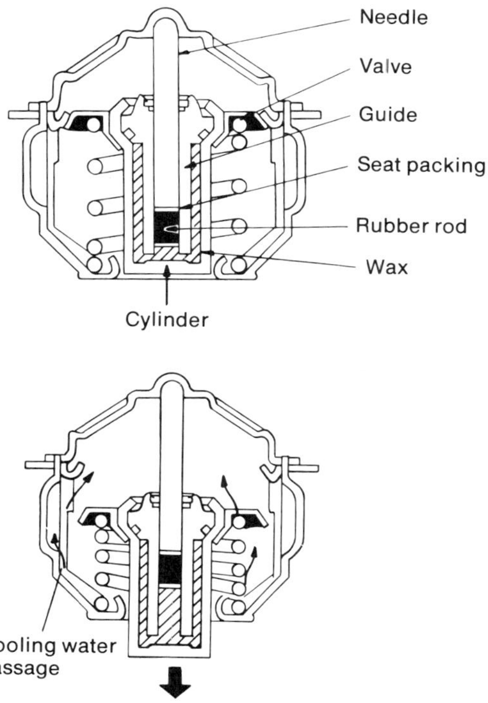

Fig. 4-4. Cross-sections of thermostat in closed (top) and opened (bottom) positions, with components identified.

If the thermostat is closing fully, place it in a pan of cool water (Fig. 4-5) together with a thermometer for measuring the water temperature. Heat the water. A new thermostat for a 1975 or 1976 car should begin to open at 80.5° to 83.5°C (177° to 182°F), and be fully open—cylinder travel 8 mm ($^{5}/_{16}$ in.) or more—at a temperature of 95°C (203°F). A new thermostat for a 1977 or later car should begin to open at 86° to 90°C (187° to 194°F), and be fully open—cylinder travel 8 mm ($^{5}/_{16}$ in.) or more—at a temperature of 100°C (212°F). Replace thermostats that do not meet these specifications.

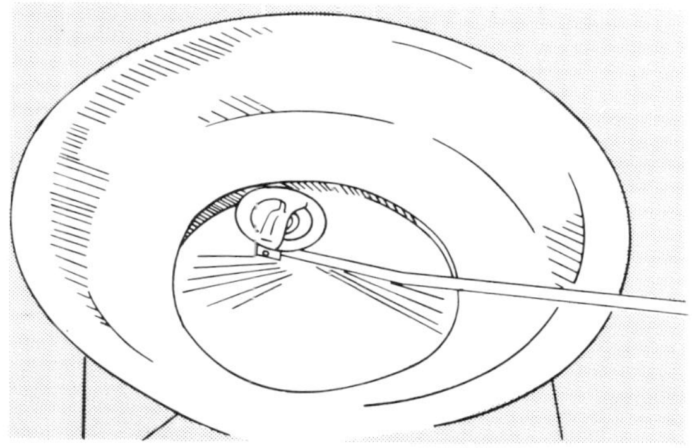

Fig. 4-5. Thermostat placed in pan of water for test.

Pressure Testing Radiator Cap and Cooling System

Various kinds of cooling system pressure testers are available. In carrying out pressure tests, follow the instructions supplied by the instrument's manufacturer and use a procedure that is suitable to the tester's design.

When tested as shown in Fig. 4-6, the pressure relief valve in the radiator cap should maintain a seal up to a pressure of 0.9 bar (13 psi). Replace caps that release pressure below the 0.6-bar (8.5-psi) wear limit. Fig. 4-7 shows the operation of the cap's pressure relief valve.

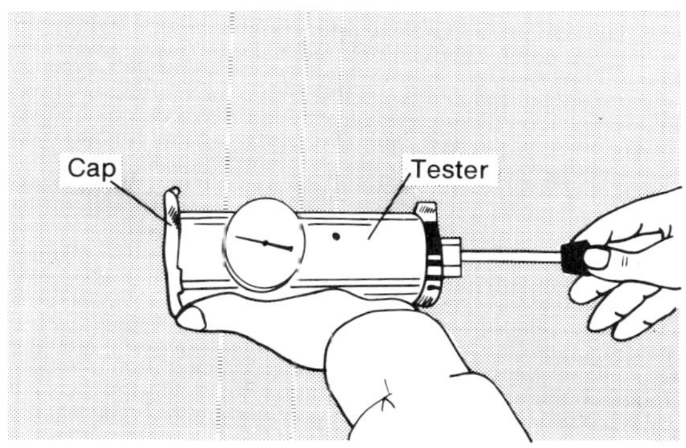

Fig. 4-6. Radiator cap being checked with pressure tester.

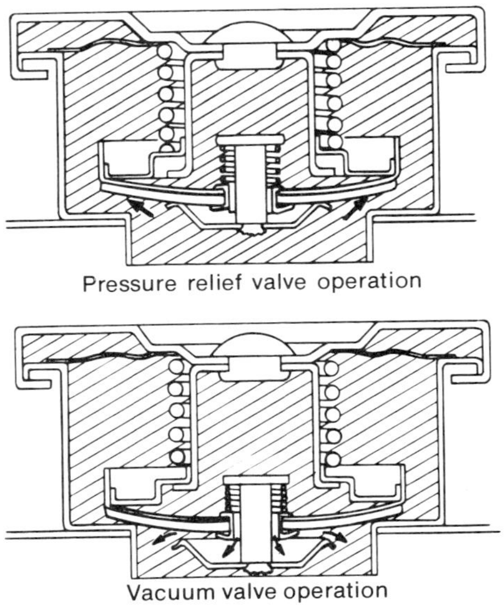

Fig. 4-7. Cross-section of radiator cap that shows operation of pressure relief valve.

To pressure-test the cooling system, pump the pressure up to 0.9 bar (13 psi). Observe the gauge on the pressure tester pump. The gauge should not indicate a pressure loss during a two-minute waiting period. If it does, there are leaks in the system that should be shown by the seepage of coolant.

> ***CAUTION —***
> *Never pump the pressure above 0.9 bar (13 psi)—the maximum pressure permissible for the radiator cap's relief valve. Exceeding this pressure could burst the radiator.*

4.3 Removing and Installing Radiator

On cars with air conditioning, the condenser for the air conditioning system is ahead of the radiator and is held by the same bolts. During removal of the radiator, do not loosen any of the connections to the air conditioning condenser.

To remove radiator:

1. Drain the radiator and disconnect the radiator hoses as described in **4.1 Replacing Hoses.**

> ***CAUTION —***
> *Never remove the radiator cap or drain the coolant while the engine is hot. Doing this could warp the engine block or the cylinder head, or you could burn yourself. If a radiator hose is stuck on the radiator connection, it is best to cut the old hose off the connection and later replace the hose. Prying the hose loose can damage the brass connection or the radiator.*

2. Detach the overflow line from the radiator's filler neck. If so equipped, disconnect and plug the automatic transmission ATF cooler lines from the radiator. This job can be done more easily if you first remove the splash shield from beneath the radiator.
3. Remove the four radiator mounting bolts—two at each side of the radiator. Then lift the radiator straight up and out of the car as indicated in Fig. 4-8.

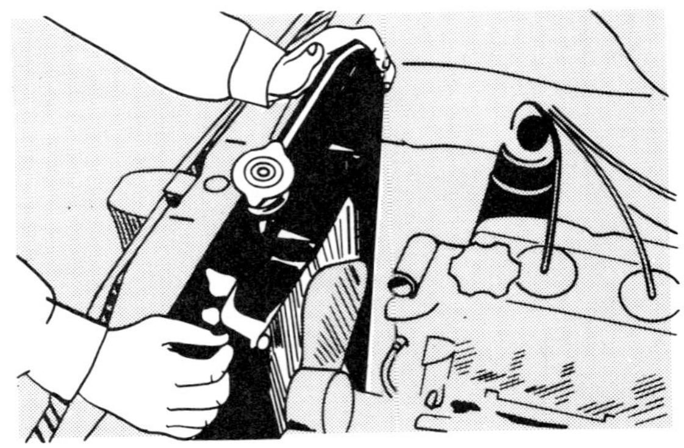

Fig. 4-8. Radiator being removed.

To install:

1. Thoroughly inspect the radiator for signs of leakage and physical damage. Re-solder any cracks between the ends of the radiator core and the top and bottom tanks. Straighten bent cooling fins as indicated in Fig. 4-9.

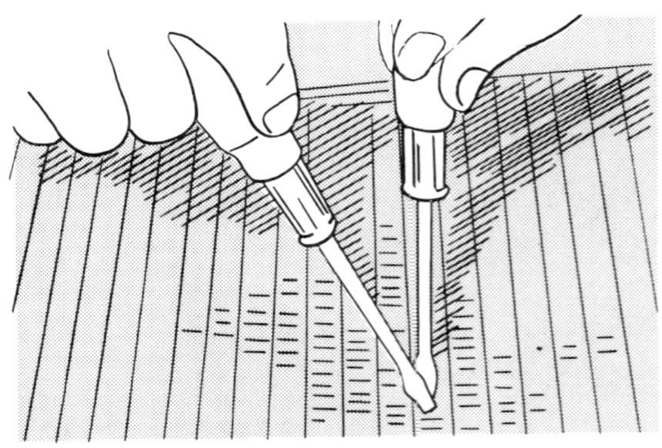

Fig. 4-9. Damaged radiator cooling fins being straightened so that they will not obstruct airflow.

2. Check the radiator interior for obvious accumulations of rust and dirt. If clogging exceeds 20% of the entire radiating area, either replace the radiator or turn it over to a qualified radiator shop for cleaning and reconditioning. These shops are also able to repair leaks in radiator tubes. **Table h** gives the overall specifications for the radiator.

Table h. Radiator Specifications

	Manual Trans.	Automatic Trans.
Fin type	Corrugated	Corrugated
Radiation quantity	14,500 kcal/hr	17,000 kcal/hr
Opening pressure	0.9 bar (13 psi)	0.9 bar (13 psi)
Cooling water capacity	2.1 liter (2.2 qts)	2.0 liter (2.1 qts)
Dry weight	3.8 kg (8.4 lbs.)	4.3 kg (9.5 lbs.)
Core dimensions (hgt × wdth × th)	325 × 418 × 32 mm (12.79 × 16.46 × 1.26 in.)	

3. Install the radiator in the car. Torque the mounting bolts to 15 to 20 Nm (11 to 15 ft. lb.), remounting the condenser for the air conditioning system on cars that are so equipped.
4. On cars with automatic transmissions, lubricate the ATF cooler lines with clean ATF before you reconnect them to the radiator. Torque the fittings to 1.5 to 2.5 Nm (13 to 22 in. lb.).
5. Reconnect the overflow line to the radiator's filler neck. Then install the radiator hoses and refill the cooling system as described in **4.1 Replacing Hoses.** Position the hose clamps so that they are past the beads on the connections, but no nearer than 2.5 mm (1/8 in.) to the ends of the hoses. Then tighten the hose clamps just enough to compress each hose firmly around its connections.

> ***CAUTION —***
> *Overtightening the clamps will cause them to cut into the hose material. This damage may eventually lead to hose failure.*

6. With the engine running, check the system for coolant leaks. Where applicable, also check for ATF leaks. Check and, if necessary, correct the transmission's ATF level on cars that have automatic transmissions.
7. If no leaks are found, reinstall the splash pan if you have removed it.

4.4 Removing and Installing Water Pump

The water pump can be removed and replaced if it is faulty. Alternatively, the old water pump can be removed and rebuilt with new seals and working parts as described in **4.5 Reconditioning Water Pump.**

To remove:

1. Drain the coolant from the radiator and the engine block as described in **4.1 Replacing Hoses.**
2. Loosen the bolts for the alternator adjusting bracket. Loosen the alternator mounting bolts. Then push the alternator toward the engine and slip the V-belt off the alternator pulley.
3. On cars with viscous drive fans, remove the nuts that hold the fan drive spacer/adaptor and the V-belt pulley to the water pump's pulley mounting flange. Then remove the fan, viscous drive, and spacer/adaptor as a unit. Remove the V-belt pulley, leaving the belt on the crankshaft pulley.
4. On cars without viscous drive fans, remove the bolts that hold the fan and the V-belt pulley to the water pump's pulley mounting flange. Then remove the fan and the V-belt pulley, leaving the belt on the crankshaft pulley.
5. Detach the two small hoses and the radiator top hose from the water pump. Then remove the five nuts or bolts that hold the water pump to the engine.

> **NOTE —**
> If you find it difficult to remove the small hose that is on the passenger's side of the car, you can loosen the hose clamp and then pull the pump off the hose as you remove the pump from the engine.

6. Remove the water pump, pulling it forward out of the engine.

Installation is the reverse of removal. Use new gaskets during installation, and insert one mounting bolt as shown in Fig. 4-10 to keep the gaskets aligned with the pump body and the pump rear plate. Working diagonally, torque the bolts or nuts to 12 to 15 Nm (9 to 11 ft. lb.). Install the radiator as described in **4.3 Removing and Installing Radiator,** then install the hoses and refill the cooling system as described in **4.1 Replacing Hoses.** Adjust the V-belt as described in **LUBRICATION AND MAINTENANCE.**

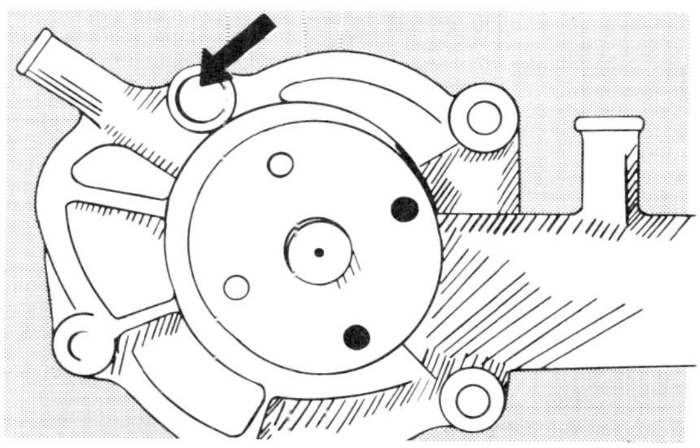

Fig. 4-10. Bolt (arrow) being used to hold gaskets in alignment during pump installation.

5

4.5 Reconditioning Water Pump

Fig. 4-11 is an exploded view of the water pump. Each of the components in the illustration is available as a replacement part, with item 7 being included in the seal set. There is also a rotor set available that includes the rotor, the seal set, and the gasket.

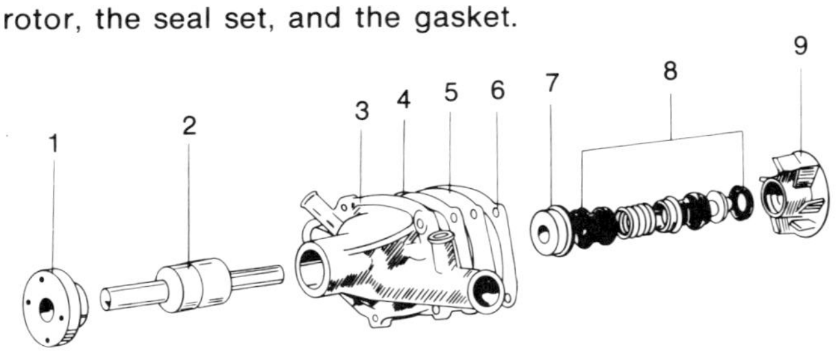

1. Pulley mounting flange
2. Bearing with shaft
3. Water pump body
4. Pump body gasket
5. Pump rear plate
6. Mounting gasket
7. Shaft seal cover
8. Seal set
9. Rotor

Fig. 4-11. Exploded view of water pump.

To disassemble:

1. Remove the nuts or the bolts that hold the fan assembly and the V-belt pulley to the pulley mounting flange. Then remove the pulley and the fan.
2. Mount the water pump—front side up—in a vise with soft jaws. Then, using a puller as shown in Fig. 4-12, pull the pulley mounting flange off the shaft. Turn the pump over and repeat the operation as shown in Fig. 4-13 to pull the rotor off the shaft.
3. Remove the water pump rear plate and the gasket. Then remove the seal set from the shaft seal cover.
4. Heat the water pump body to about 75° to 80°C (167° to 176°F). Then, using a repair press and the special tools indicated in Fig. 4-14, press the bearing with shaft out of the pump body.

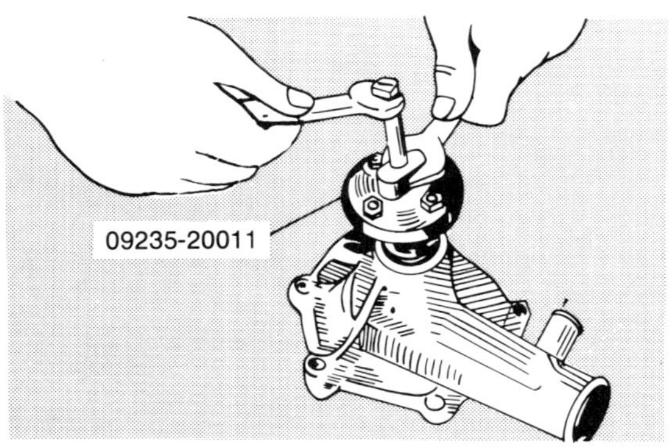

Fig. 4-12. Special puller being used to remove pulley mounting flange.

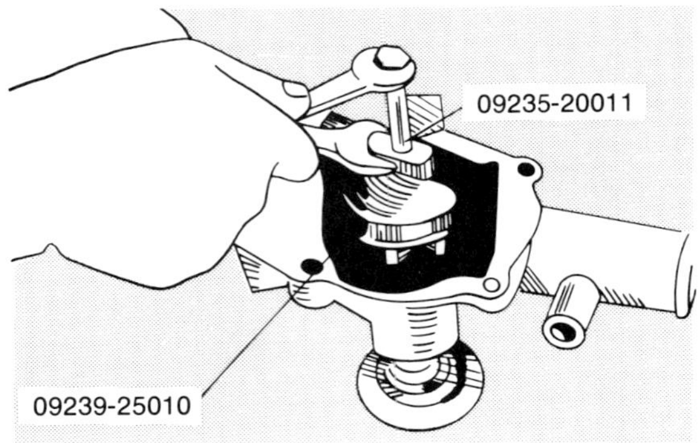

Fig. 4-13. Special puller being used to remove rotor.

CAUTION —

Once removed, the bearing with shaft is no longer serviceable and must be replaced.

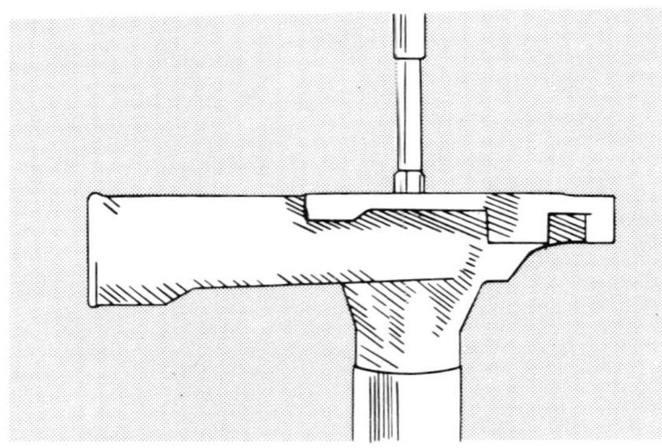

Fig. 4-14. Special tool being used to press bearing with shaft out of water pump body.

To inspect and recondition:

1. Inspect all parts for cracks, wear, and damage. Replace faulty parts. If the pump body itself is faulty, it is advisable to replace the pump as a unit.
2. Thoroughly clean the water pump body and remove the shaft seal cover. Then heat the pump body to approximately 75° to 85°C (167° to 185°F). Using the special tool indicated in Fig. 4-15, press in a new bearing with shaft until the bearing is flush with the front of the pump body as shown in the illustration.
3. Install the shaft seal cover. Then install the seal set in the seal cover—without installing the seal component that is closest to the rotor.
4. Insert the rearmost component of the seal set in the recess in the rotor. Then install the pump body gasket and the pump rear plate on the pump body.

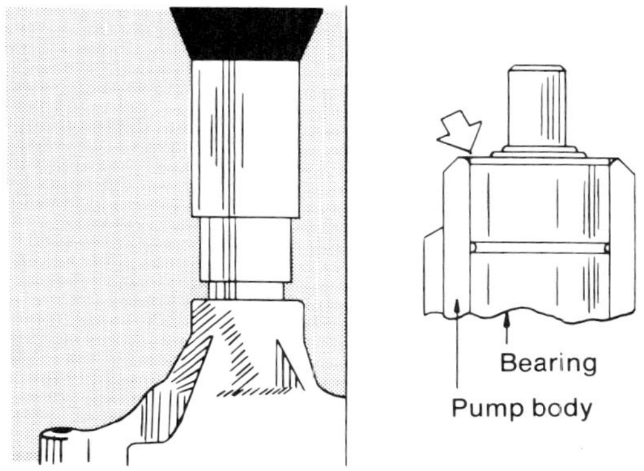

Fig. 4-15. Special press tool being used to install new bearing with shaft. Press bearing in until flush with body at point indicated by arrow.

5. Apply a small amount of silicone lubricant or water pump lubricant to the seal surfaces. Then carefully press the rotor onto the shaft (Fig. 4-16) until the clearance between the rotor and the water pump rear plate is 0.50 mm (.020 in.).

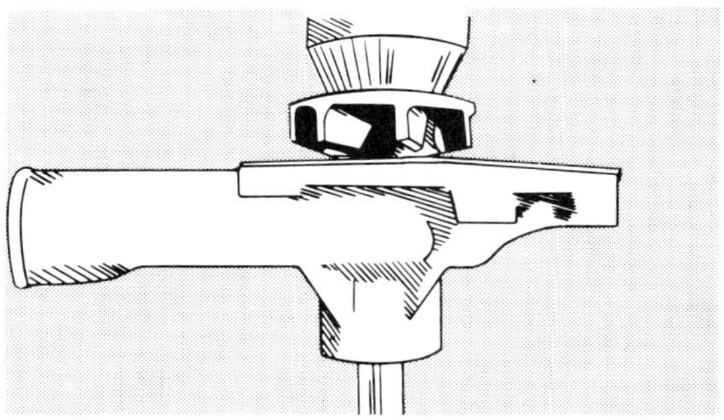

Fig. 4-16. Rotor being pressed onto shaft. Check rotor clearance with feeler gauge inserted between rotor and rear plate.

6. Using the special tool indicated in Fig. 4-17, press on the pulley mounting flange until the shaft projects 7.5 mm (about .30 in. or 19/64 in.) from the front of the flange.

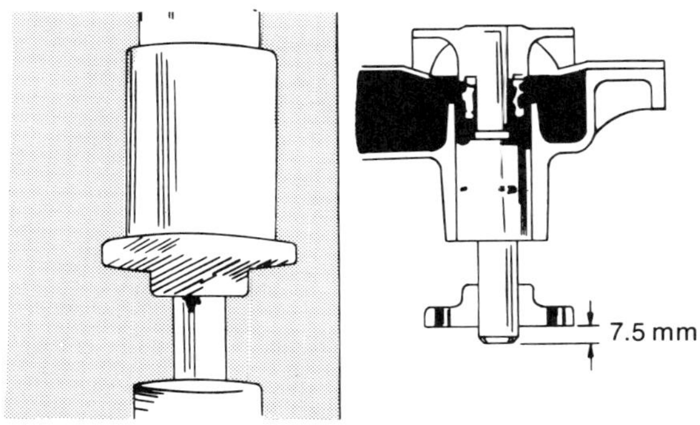

Fig. 4-17. Special press tool being used to press pulley mounting flange onto water pump shaft (left). Correct position of flange is indicated at right.

5. VALVES, MANIFOLDS, AND CYLINDER HEAD

The cylinder head and the manifolds can be removed from the engine without first removing the engine from the car. Be sure to use fender covers and take ample care to avoid damaging the paint or body metal with either scratches or dents or with spilled oil and other foreign matter.

5.1 Removing and Installing Cylinder Head Cover

The cylinder head cover, sometimes called the rocker arm cover, must be removed before you can adjust the valve clearances. The cover must also be taken off before you remove the cylinder head.

To remove cylinder head cover:

1. Remove the distributor cap. Disconnect the spark plug cables from the spark plugs and disconnect the high tension cable from the ignition coil. See Fig. 5-1.

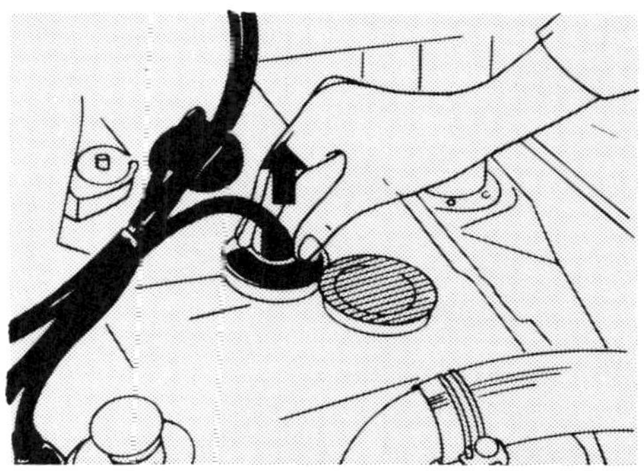

Fig. 5-1. Spark plug cable being disconnected. Grasp the boot and plug connector; do not pull on the cable itself.

2. Disengage the three clips that hold the periphery of the air cleaner cover to the air cleaner body. Remove the wing nut and washer from atop the air cleaner, lift off the cover, and take out the filter element. See Fig. 5-2.

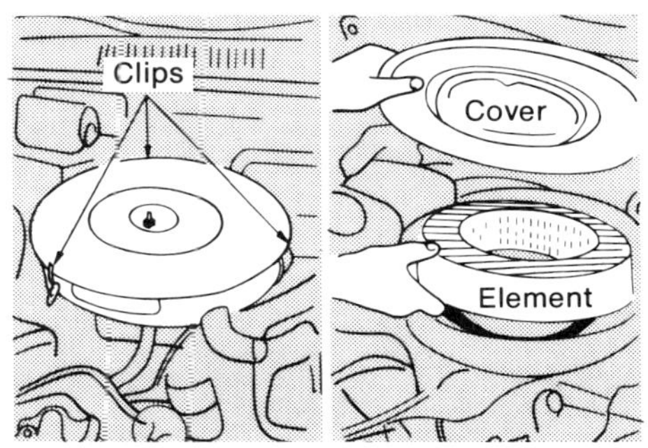

Fig. 5-2. Air cleaner cover clips (left) and air cleaner filter element (right).

5

3. Pull the (black) air injection dump hose and the (black) air injection intake hose off the connections on the underside of the air cleaner body.
4. Pull the PCV (positive crankcase ventilation) valve out of the rear of the cylinder head cover and disengage its (red) hose from the side clip and the bottom clip of the air cleaner body. Pull the PCV intake hose off the connection at the front of the cylinder head cover.
5. Using a 10-mm wrench, remove the two bolts and flat washers that hold the air cleaner body to the cylinder head cover.
6. Disengage the throttle cable conduit from the clip on the air cleaner body. Pull the air cleaner's vacuum line off the connection at the intake manifold tap, then lift off the air cleaner body—carefully disengaging it from the intake air preheating duct atop the exhaust manifold stove.
7. Using a 10-mm socket wrench and a suitable extension, remove the six bolts that hold the cylinder head cover to the cylinder head. Then lift off the cylinder head cover, being careful not to lose any of the ring-shaped spark plug recess gaskets.

To install:

1. Inspect the cylinder head cover gasket and the ring-shaped spark plug recess gaskets. Replace broken, cracked, or hardened gaskets.
2. Position the ring-shaped gaskets on the spark plug bosses of the cylinder head so that the flanges of the gaskets are downward, overlapping the bosses. Install the large gasket on the cylinder head cover's periphery so that its tabs engage the notches in the cover. Do not use sealer on any of these gaskets.
3. Position the cylinder head cover atop the cylinder head. By looking down into the spark plug recesses of the cover, check that no ring-shaped gasket has been accidentally displaced.
4. Install the six bolts that hold the cylinder head cover to the cylinder head. Working diagonally, torque the bolts in stages to 4 to 5 Nm (35 to 44 in. lb.).
5. Loosely position the air cleaner body on the carburetor and the rocker arm cover—carefully engaging the intake air preheating duct that is atop the exhaust manifold stove. Then connect the air cleaner's vacuum line to the intake manifold tap.
6. Install the PCV valve in the rear of the cylinder head cover, then engage its hose with the side clip and the bottom clip of the air cleaner body.
7. Engage the throttle cable conduit in the clip on the air cleaner body. Install the flat washers and the bolts that hold the air cleaner body to the rocker arm cover. Working alternately, torque the bolts in stages to 2 to 3 Nm (18 to 27 in. lb.).
8. Reconnect the two (black) air injection hoses to the connections on the underside of the air cleaner body.
9. Install the air cleaner filter element in the air cleaner body. Then install the cover so that the arrow on the cover is aligned with the arrow on the air cleaner body's intake air duct. See Fig. 5-3.

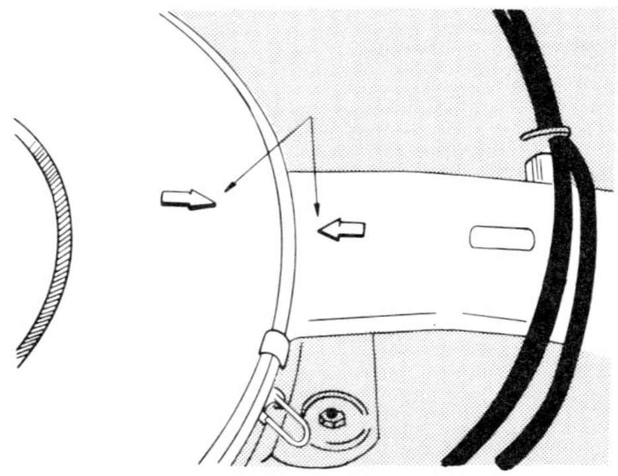

Fig. 5-3. Arrows that should be aligned during installation of air cleaner cover.

10. Install the washer, then install the wing nut finger-tight. Engage the three clips that hold the air cleaner cover to the air cleaner body.
11. Install the distributor cap on the ignition distributor.
12. Install the high tension cable on the ignition coil. Reconnect the spark plug cables to the spark plugs, being careful not to damage the rubber boots.

5.2 Adjusting Valves

For best performance and minimum noise and wear, the valves should be kept adjusted to specification at all times. Because there may be cylinder-to-cylinder variations between hot and cold valve clearances, the valves should always be adjusted with the engine hot.

To adjust valves:

1. Operate the vehicle until the oil temperature is about 50°C (122°F) and the coolant is at full operating temperature—about 88°C (190°F).
2. Stop the engine. Remove the cylinder head cover as described in **5.1 Removing and Installing Cylinder Head Cover.** (This should require no more than 15 minutes even for an inexperienced mechanic, so the engine will not have time to cool appreciably.)

3. Using a wrench on the bolt that is in the center of the crankshaft pulley, hand-turn the crankshaft until the timing mark on the crankshaft pulley is at 0°. Check that the distributor rotor is pointing roughly toward the radiator top hose connection on the engine. This indicates the firing point for the No. 1 cylinder.
4. Check the clearances of half the valves by inserting the correct feeler gauge between each rocker arm and the tip of the valve stem. Use an 0.20-mm (.008-in.) feeler gauge to check the clearances of the intake valves for cylinders No. 1 and No. 2; use an 0.33-mm (.013-in.) feeler gauge to check the clearances of the exhaust valves for cylinders No. 1 and No. 3. See Fig. 5-4.

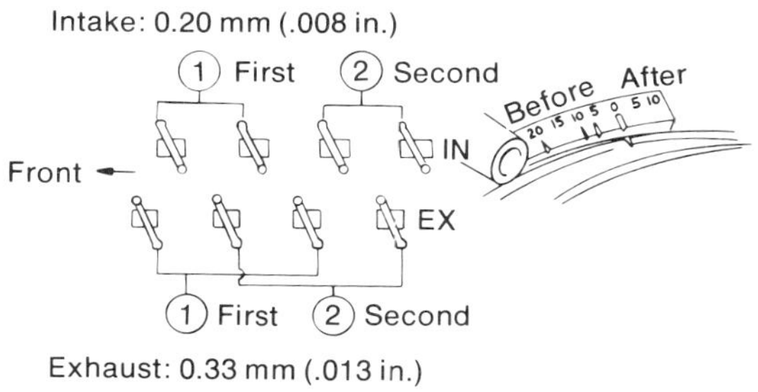

Fig. 5-4. Valves fully closed and in position for clearance check with timing mark at 0°. Rocker arms indicated by circled numerals **1** are for valves to be checked with cylinder No. 1 in position to fire. Rocker arms indicated by circled numerals **2** are for valves to be checked with cylinder No. 4 in position to fire.

5. If the correct feeler gauge fails to enter the gap between the rocker arm tip and the valve stem, or if it fits loosely within the gap, loosen the rocker arm's adjusting screw locknut. Then turn the adjusting screw one way or the other until the clearance produces moderate drag on the feeler gauge. See Fig. 5-5. When the adjustment is correct, hold the adjusting screw stationary while you tighten the locknut.

NOTE ——

Do not overtighten the locknuts; a torque of 10 Nm (7.5 ft. lb.) is sufficient. If you lack experience in adjusting the valves, it is advisable to use go/no-go stepped feeler gauges. These gauges have a thin tip and a thicker blade. To check an 0.20-mm (.008-in.) clearance, use a feeler gauge with an 0.18-mm (.007-in.) tip and an 0.22-mm (.009-in.) blade. The tip should easily enter the gap but the blade should not go in at all. Always recheck the clearance after you have tightened the locknut.

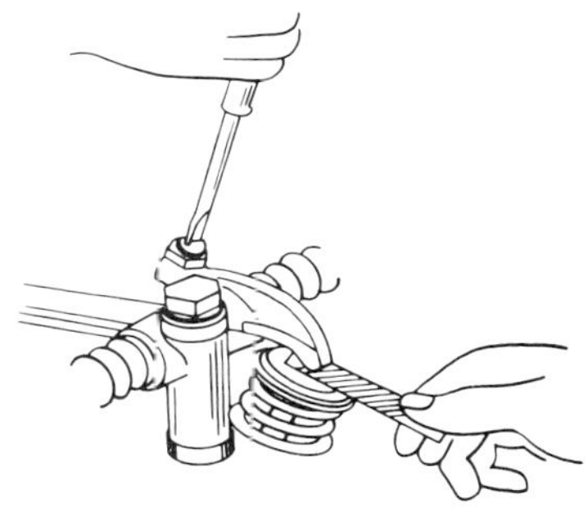

Fig. 5-5. Valve clearance being adjusted. Feeler gauge is inserted between tip of rocker arm and tip of valve stem while adjusting screw is turned with screwdriver.

6. Using a wrench on the bolt that is in the center of the crankshaft pulley, hand-turn the crankshaft one complete turn clockwise, so that the timing mark on the pulley again lines up with the 0° mark, but the distributor rotor is pointing in the opposite direction from the radiator top hose connection on the front of the cylinder head. This is the approximate firing point for the No. 4 cylinder.
7. Check the clearances of the other half of the valves. Use an 0.20-mm (.008-in.) feeler gauge to check the clearances of the intake valves for cylinders No. 3 and No. 4; use an 0.33-mm (.013-in.) feeler gauge to check the clearances of the exhaust valves for cylinders No. 2 and No. 4. See Fig. 5-4, given earlier.
8. If necessary, correct the valve clearances using the adjustment technique described in step 5. Then install the cylinder head cover as described in **5.1 Removing and Installing Cylinder Head Cover.**

5.3 Removing and Installing Cylinder Head and Manifolds

Though both the intake manifold and the exhaust manifold can be removed with the cylinder head installed on the engine, it is easier to remove the intake manifold after the cylinder head is removed in circumstances where both the head and the manifolds must be removed. On 1977 and later cars, which have the entire exhaust manifold enclosed in a heat stove that prevents easy removal of the exhaust manifold, you can also leave the exhaust manifold installed on the head during cylinder head removal. If care is taken not to dent the stove, the exhaust manifold can be left in place on the head during most common cylinder head service operations.

To remove cylinder head and manifolds:

1. Drain the coolant from the radiator as described in **4.1 Replacing Hoses.** It is unnecessary to drain all of the coolant from the engine block.
2. Disconnect the radiator top hose from the thermostat housing. Disconnect the heater hose from the left rear of the cylinder head; disconnect the hose that connects the head with the intake manifold and the hose that connects the front of the head with the water pump.

   NOTE ——
   Also disconnect and dismount the second heater hose if it passes over the exhaust manifold and is attached to the cylinder head by a bracket.

3. Disconnect the wire from the water temperature gauge sending unit at the front of the cylinder head. Then disconnect the ground wire from the right rear of the cylinder head.
4. Remove the EGR (exhaust gas recirculation) valve from the front of the cylinder head on cars that have the valve.
5. Working under the car, unbolt the clamp and disconnect the exhaust pipe from the exhaust manifold. Then disconnect the air injection line from the manifold at the union beneath the exhaust manifold.
6. Remove the air cleaner and the cylinder head cover as described in **5.1 Removing and Installing Cylinder Head Cover.**
7. Remove the ignition distributor as described in **3.2 Distributor.**
8. Disconnect the throttle cable from the carburetor and the intake manifold.
9. Disconnect the fuel line from the carburetor. Disconnect the vacuum lines that are connected to the carburetor and the intake manifold.

   CAUTION ——
   Label each vacuum line as you disconnect it so that later you will be able to reinstall it on its correct connection. In some cases the vacuum hose connections do not correspond fully to the diagram on the hood and to other illustrations.

10. If you intend to remove the exhaust manifold, remove the nuts, then pull the manifold and its gasket off the studs on the cylinder head. On 1977 and later cars, you must first remove the nuts for the heat stove cover and remove the cover and its gasket for access to the manifold nuts. See Fig. 5-6.

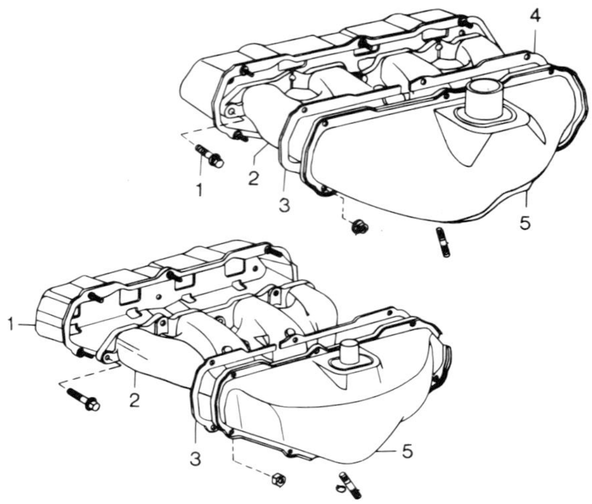

1. Inner heat stove insulator
2. Exhaust manifold
3. Gasket
4. Gasket
5. Outer heat stove insulator

Fig. 5-6. Exploded view of 1977 and later exhaust manifold with sealed heat stove.

11. Loosen each cylinder head bolt a little at a time in the sequence given in Fig. 5-7, repeating the sequence until all ten bolts are completely loose. Then remove the bolts and lift off the rocker arm shaft assembly.

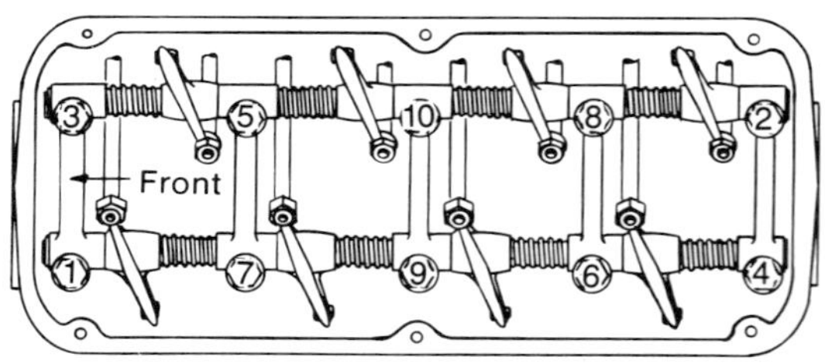

Fig. 5-7. Sequence for loosening cylinder head bolts.

12. Begin the disassembly of the rocker arm shaft assembly as indicated in Fig. 5-8, and continue until all components are laid out in order as shown in Fig. 5-9. It is a good precaution to mark each rocker arm according to cylinder order and whether it is the intake or the exhaust rocker arm.

    CAUTION ——
    Three kinds of supports are used, and these too should be kept in order. Be especially careful not to interchange the intake rocker arm shaft with the exhaust rocker arm shaft.

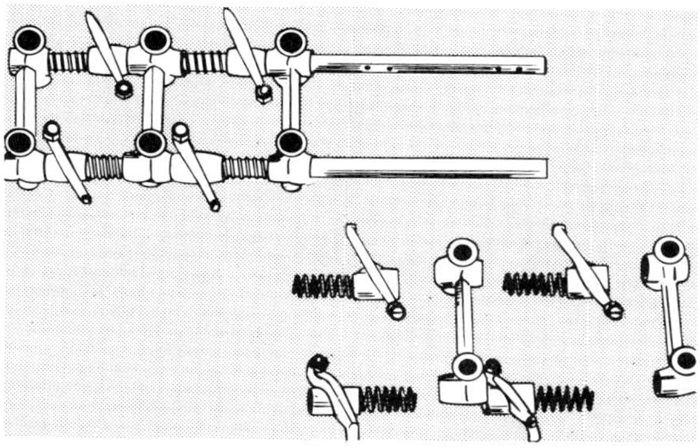

Fig. 5-8. Rocker arms, supports, springs, and shafts being disassembled.

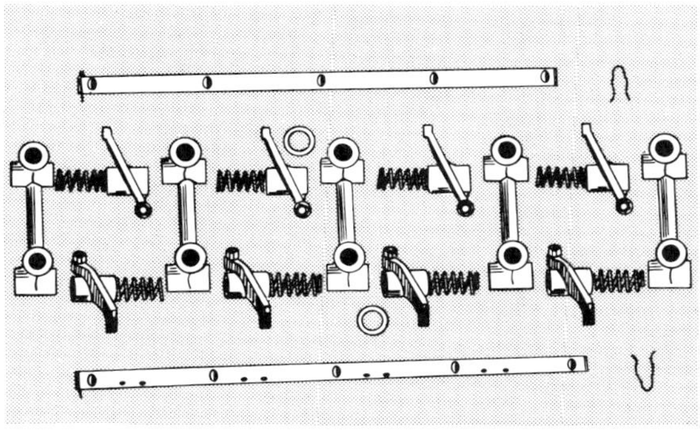

Fig. 5-9. Components of rocker arm assembly laid out in assembled relationship. Keeping parts in this arrangement will greatly simplify reassembly.

13. Remove the pushrods, keeping them in order so that later you will be able to reinstall them in their original locations.

NOTE ——

A convenient way to keep the pushrods in order is to push them through a piece of wood or cardboard in which you have made eight holes. If necessary, you can number the holes to identify the location of each pushrod in the engine.

14. Lift off the cylinder head as shown in Fig. 5-10, leaving the intake manifold (and perhaps the exhaust manifold) attached. Then, with the head on the workbench, remove the nuts and take the intake manifold and its gasket off the cylinder head.

CAUTION ——

If the exhaust manifold is kept on the head, be careful not to dent the stove. You must lift the head straight up because of the alignment pins between the head and the block.

Fig. 5-10. Cylinder head being lifted off with intake manifold attached. Because of the close clearance and the likelihood of damage to the cap, it is recommended that the ignition distributor be removed beforehand.

15. Using a magnetic tool or expanding tip pliers, remove the cam followers from the engine block. Wipe clean each cam follower as you remove it, then number it with a waterproof felt-tipped marker so that later it can be reinstalled in its original location.

5

To install:

1. Thoroughly clean the cylinder head.

CAUTION ——

Do not use a metal scraper or a power-driven wire brush to clean the combustion chambers or gasket sealing surfaces. Doing this can gouge the aluminum, which could cause the gaskets to leak or leave scratches in the combustion chambers that could become "hot spots". Instead, use solvent to soften dirt, combustion chamber deposits, dried sealer, and material torn from the old gaskets. Then remove this foreign matter with a wooden or plastic scraper.

2. Thoroughly clean the gasket sealing surface of the engine block. Then clean the threads in the head bolt holes.

NOTE ——

To keep out dirt, stuff clean rags into the cylinder bores and seal all water and oil passages with tape. After you have cleaned the sealing surface of the block, use a thread-cutting tap or thread chaser to clean the bolt holes. It is extremely important that all oil and debris be removed from the bottoms of the holes whether you have cleaned the threads or not. See Fig. 5-11.

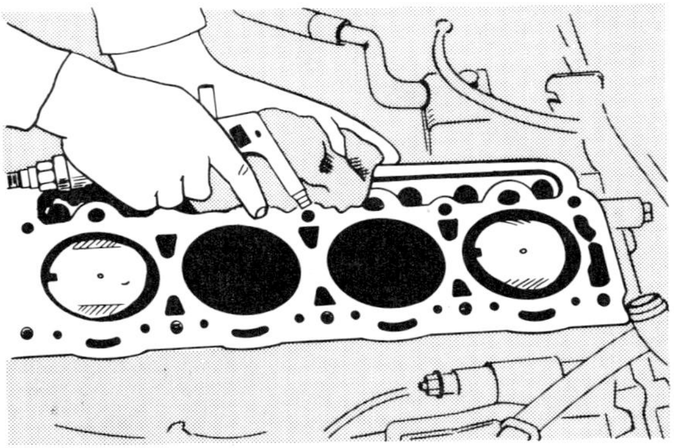

Fig. 5-11. Oil and dirt being blown out of bolt holes with compressed air.

3. Check the cylinder head for warping. To do this, lay a straightedge lengthwise across the sealing surface of the head as shown in Fig. 5-12. You should not be able to insert an 0.06-mm (or .0025-in.) feeler gauge between the sealing surface and the straightedge at any point. Repeat the check with the straightedge positioned in each of the locations indicated in Fig. 5-13.

NOTE ——

If an 0.06-mm (or .0025-in.) feeler gauge can be inserted at any point, either replace the cylinder head or take it to an automotive machine shop where the head can be milled or ground to obtain a true surface.

4. If you have removed the manifolds, or if there has been any indication of leakage, check the manifold gasket surfaces for damage and warping as shown in Fig. 5-14. Use the same procedure to check the manifold gasket surfaces of the cylinder head. If either a manifold or the head is faulty, have the head or the manifold ground or milled to obtain a true surface.

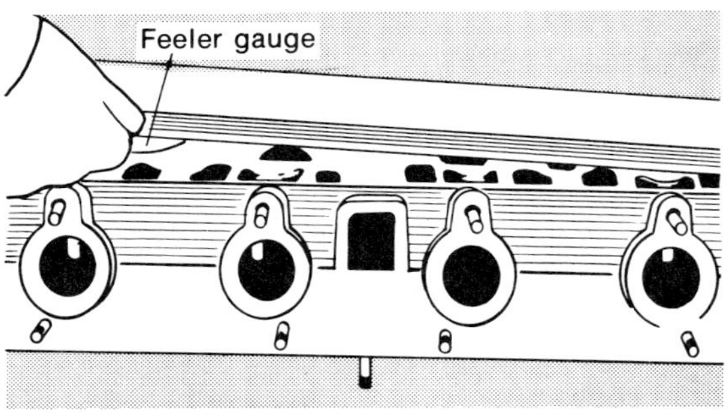

Fig. 5-12. An 0.06-mm (or .0025-in.) feeler gauge being used to check cylinder head for warping. 0.05 mm (.002 in.) is the maximum allowable distortion.

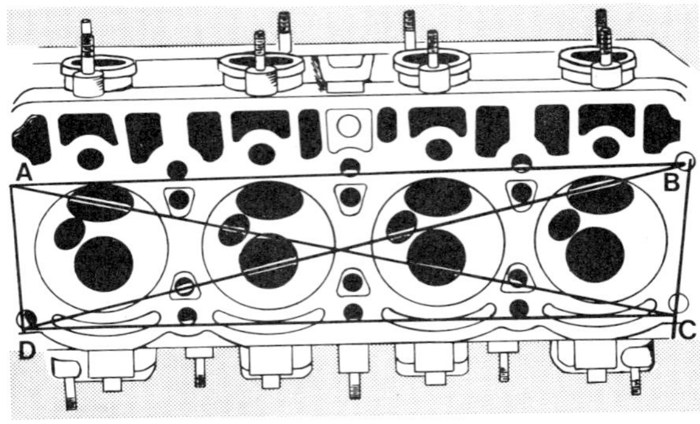

Fig. 5-13. Positions for straightedge during check for cylinder head warping. Place straightedge along lines AB, DC, AC, DB, AD, and BC.

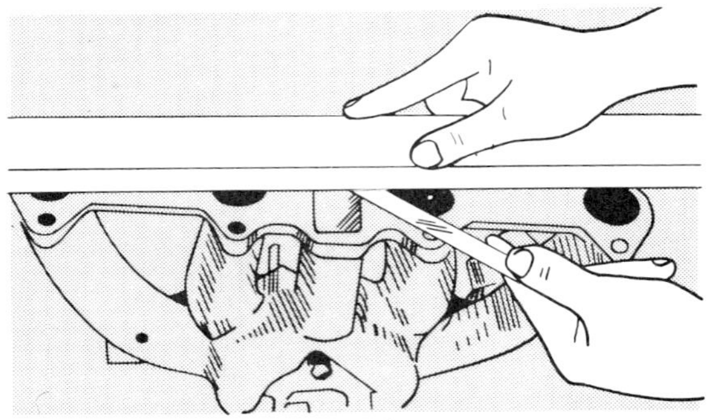

Fig. 5-14. Intake or exhaust manifold gasket surface being checked for warping. Place straightedge at one diagonal and then the other. 0.20 mm (.008 in.) is maximum allowable distortion.

5. If there has been trouble that might indicate cylinder head structural damage, such as leaks between the oil passages and the coolant passages, compression leaks between combustion chambers, or leaks between the combustion chambers and the water jacket, the cylinder head should be checked for cracks and damage both visually and with a flaw detector such as the Zyglo® process. A hydraulic pressure test of the head's water jacket should show no leakage within a 3-minute time period at a pressure of 4 bar (58 psi).

6. Using the procedure you used for the head, check the engine block for warping. Warped blocks can also be milled or ground but the engine must be removed and completely disassembled beforehand.

7. Measure each cam follower and its bore as shown in Fig. 5-15. Subtract the cam follower's diameter from the bore diameter to obtain the clearance, which should be 0.02 to 0.03 mm (.0008 to .0012 in.) with new parts. If the clearance exceeds the 0.10-mm (.004-in.) wear limit, install the oversize valve lifters listed in **Table i.**

NOTE ——

If necessary, you can use a brake cylinder hone to enlarge the bores in the block slightly to accept the oversize cam followers. However, this work should not be done unless the engine block has been removed and stripped of all working parts so that it can be thoroughly cleaned after the honing.

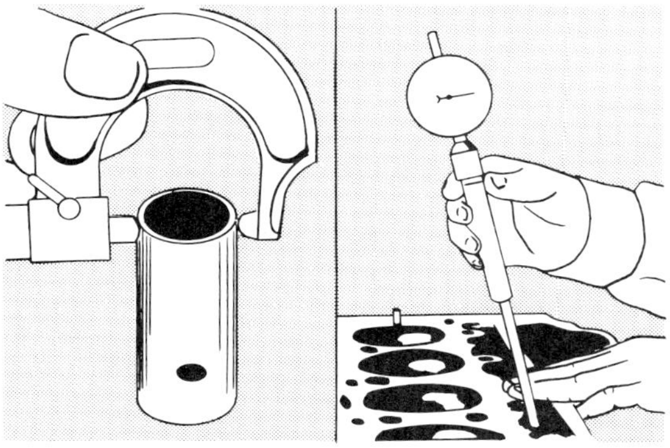

Fig. 5-15. Micrometer being used (left) to measure cam follower diameter; bore gauge being used (right) to measure cam follower bore in engine block.

Table i. Cam Follower and Bore Dimensions

Size	Cam follower outside diameter in mm (in.)	Bore in engine block inside diameter in mm (in.)
Standard	22.179 to 22.199 (.8732 to .8739)	22.200 to 22.221 (.8740 to .8748)
0.05-mm (.002-in.) oversize	22.229 to 22.249 (.8752 to .8759)	22.250 to 22.271 (.8760 to .8768)

8. Lightly lubricate each cam follower with assembly lubricant or multipurpose grease, then install it in its bore. Used cam followers must be returned to their original bores.
9. Using a thread-cutting die, clean the cylinder head bolt threads. Do not use a power-driven wire brush, which could distort the threads. Replace damaged or distorted bolts. Then coat the threads and the undersides of the bolt heads with anti-sieze compound.
10. Place a new cylinder head gasket atop the engine block so that the alignment pins engage the gasket and the holes in the gasket are aligned with those in the block. If one surface of the new gasket is marked TOP, install the gasket with that side up.

CAUTION ——

Never reinstall a cylinder head gasket that has previously been compressed by tightening the cylinder head bolts. Once compressed, these gaskets lose their resilience and will not produce a reliable seal if reused.

11. If previously removed, install the intake manifold on the cylinder head with a new gasket. Torque the nuts to 20 to 25 Nm (15 to 18 ft. lb.). Then lower the cylinder head onto the engine block as shown in Fig. 5-16.

CAUTION ——

Do not allow the cylinder head to slide about on the block unsupported. Doing this will cause the alignment pins to gouge and damage the head. It will be easier to lower the head straight down onto the alignment pins if you temporarily install wooden dowels 200 mm long and 10 mm in diameter (or 8 in. long and 3/8 in. in diameter) in two of the block's outermost bolt holes. The head will be guided onto the alignment pins by the dowels, which can be pulled out after the head is in place.

5

Fig. 5-16. Cylinder head being lowered onto engine block.

12. Roll each pushrod on a piece of glass or other smooth surface to detect bending. Replace any pushrod that is bent or has dents or damaged ends. Then lightly lubricate the pushrod's ends with assembly lubricant or multipurpose grease and install it ball-end first in its original location in the engine.
13. Position the rocker arm assembly atop the cylinder head, then loosely install all ten head bolts to hold it in place.

14. Measure the rocker arm shafts and the rocker arm bores as indicated in Fig. 5-17. Subtract the outside diameter of the shaft from the inside diameter of the rocker arm bore in order to determine the clearance. If the clearance is not between 0.02 and 0.04 mm (.0008 and .0016 in.), replace the rocker arm, the shaft, or both—depending on the extent to which each part is worn.

NOTE ——
The outside diameter of a new shaft is 15.97 to 15.99 mm (.6287 to .6295 in.). The inside diameter of a new rocker arm's bore is 16.00 to 16.02 mm (.6299 to .6307 in.).

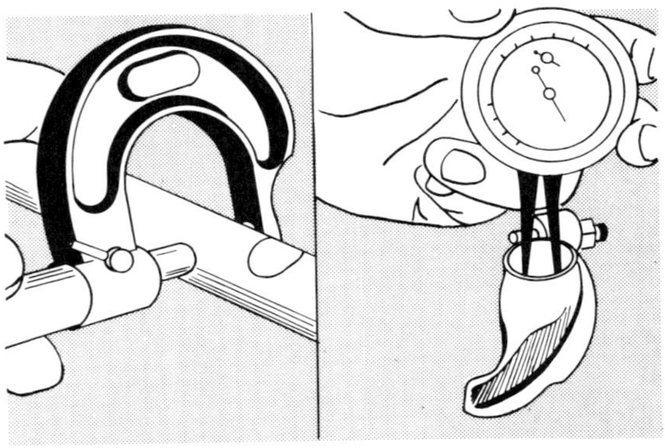

Fig. 5-17. Micrometer being used (left) to measure rocker arm shaft diameter; bore gauge being used (right) to measure bore in rocker arm.

15. After washing the components of the rocker arm assembly in solvent, blow out all oil passages with compressed air. Inspect each rocker arm for a worn or deformed ball tip on its adjusting screw and for pockets worn into the tip that contacts the valve stem. Replace worn adjusting screws. Replace rocker arms that have deep pockets worn into their tips. (Minor wear can be corrected with an oilstone.)

16. Reassemble the rocker arm shaft assembly. Then position it atop the cylinder head and loosely install all ten head bolts.

NOTE ——
During assembly, first insert both shafts in the No. 1 support, which has a letter F on it that must be toward the front of the engine when installed. See Fig. 5-18. The oil hole in the exhaust rocker arm shaft must be at the front as shown. Next install the exhaust rocker arm for the No. 1 cylinder, its spacer spring, the intake spacer spring, and the intake rocker arm for the No. 1 cylinder—in that sequence. Slide the No. 2 support onto the shafts and continue to assemble the remaining components in a similar pattern. The supports are identified in Fig. 5-19.

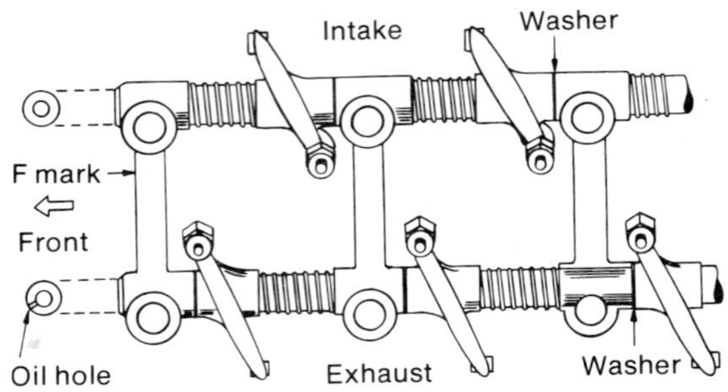

Fig. 5-18. Relationship of shafts to front support and positions of rocker arms and springs. Washers are used only at center (No. 3) support brace in positions shown.

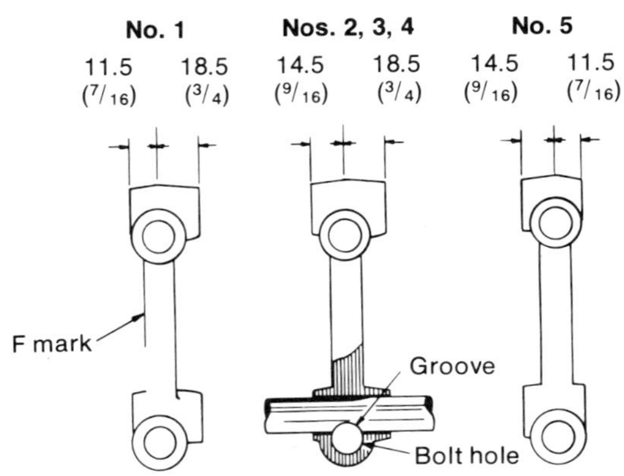

Fig. 5-19. Identification of supports. Dimensions are given in mm (in.).

17. Following the sequence given in Fig. 5-20, torque the head bolts to 20 to 25 Nm (15 to 18 ft. lb.). Go over the sequence a second time torquing the bolts to 55 to 60 Nm (41 to 44 ft. lb.), then a third time, torquing the bolts to 85 to 90 Nm (63 to 66 ft. lb.).

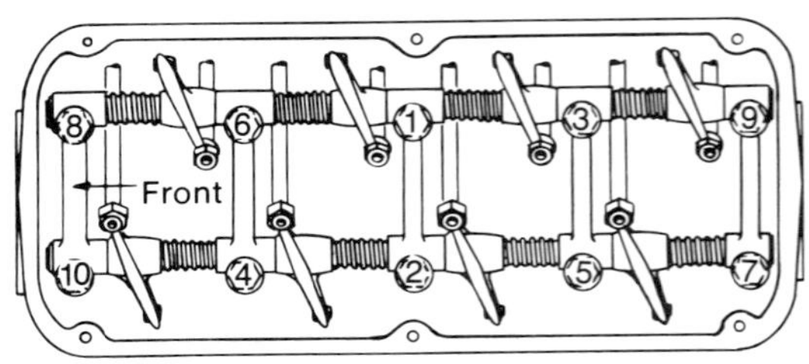

Fig. 5-20. Head bolt tightening sequence.

18. If previously removed, install the exhaust manifold with a new gasket. Torque the nuts to 30 to 45 Nm (22 to 33 ft. lb.). Then, when necessary, install the heat stove with a new gasket between its halves.

19. Reconnect the vacuum lines with reference to the labels you attached during removal and to the diagrams given in this Manual and on the car itself.
20. Reconnect the fuel line and the throttle cable to the carburetor as described in **FUEL AND EXHAUST SYSTEMS.**
21. Install the ignition distributor as described in **3.2 Distributor.** Then adjust the valve clearances (engine cold) to 0.18 mm (.007 in.) for the intake valves and 0.30 mm (.012 in.) for the exhaust valves. If necessary, consult **5.2 Adjusting Valves**—but do not use the hot setting specifications at this time.
22. Install the cylinder head cover and the air cleaner as described in **5.1 Removing and Installing Cylinder Head Cover.**
23. Working under the car, reconnect the exhaust pipe to the exhaust manifold, torquing the nuts to 30 to 45 Nm (22 to 33 ft. lb.). Then reconnect the air injection line at the union on the manifold.
24. Reinstall the EGR valve at the front of the cylinder head on cars that have the valve. If necessary, consult **FUEL AND EXHAUST SYSTEMS.**
25. Reconnect the wire to the temperature gauge sending unit. Reconnect the ground wire to the left rear of the cylinder head.
26. Reconnect all coolant hoses. Then refill the cooling system as described in **4.1 Replacing Hoses.**
27. Start the engine and allow it to warm up until, after driving, the oil temperature is about 50°C (122°F) and the coolant is at full operating temperature—about 88°C (190°F). Then stop the engine and carefully adjust the valve clearances to 0.20 mm (.008 in.) for the intake valves and 0.33 mm (.013 in.) for the exhaust valves, as described in **5.2 Adjusting Valves.**

5.4 Disassembling and Assembling Cylinder Head

Fig. 5-21 is an exploded view of the cylinder head, showing the relationship of the valves, valve springs, and valve guides to the other components of the valve train. You should not completely disassemble the cylinder head in one continuous operation. Instead, disassemble the head in stages, following the sequence given here, so that you can make various checks and measurements at each stage of disassembly. By doing this, you will be able to determine which parts can be reused and which parts require reconditioning or replacement.

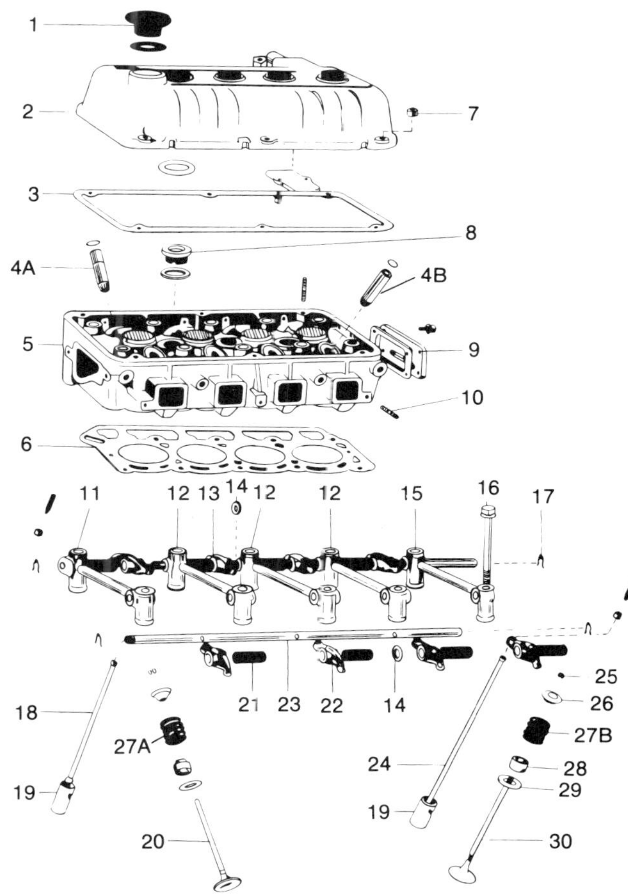

1. Oil filler cap
2. Cylinder head cover
3. Cylinder head cover gasket
4A. Intake valve guide (4)
4B. Exhaust valve guide (4)
5. Cylinder head
6. Cylinder head gasket
7. Nut (6)
8. Threaded plug (3)
9. Cylinder head rear plate
10. Manifold mounting stud (13)
11. Support No. 1
12. Support Nos. 2, 3, and 4
13. Intake rocker arm (4)
14. Center support washer (2)
15. Support No. 5
16. Cylinder head bolt (10)
17. Spring wire end clip (4)
18. Intake pushrod (4)
19. Cam follower (8)
20. Intake valve (4)
21. Spacer spring (8)
22. Exhaust rocker arm (4)
23. Rocker arm shaft (2)
24. Exhuast pushrod (4)
25. 2-piece valve lock (8 pair)
26. Valve spring retainer (8)
27A. Intake valve spring (4)
27B. Exhaust valve spring (4)
28. Valve stem oil seal (8)
29. Valve spring seat (8)
30. Exhaust valve (4)

Fig. 5-21. Exploded view of cylinder heads.

To disassemble and inspect cylinder head:

1. Remove the cylinder head as described in **5.3 Removing and Installing Cylinder Head and Manifolds.** Then, using a waterproof felt-tipped marker, write the cylinder number on the head of each valve so that it can be returned to its original location if it is reusable.

2. Using a C-type valve spring compressing tool, as shown in Fig. 5-22, pull down each valve spring retainer—compressing the valve spring until the 2-piece valve lock is uncovered.
3. Remove the valve lock halves from the valve stem. Gradually release the spring tension and remove the compressing tool. Then remove the valve spring retainer, the valve spring, the valve stem oil seal, and the valve spring seat.
4. Remove the valve from the cylinder head. Then repeat the entire operation, removing all eight valves from the head.

***CAUTION* —**

If the valve lock grooves in the valve stem are burred, file them smooth before you remove the valve. If a burred stem is forced into the valve guide, the guide will be ruined.

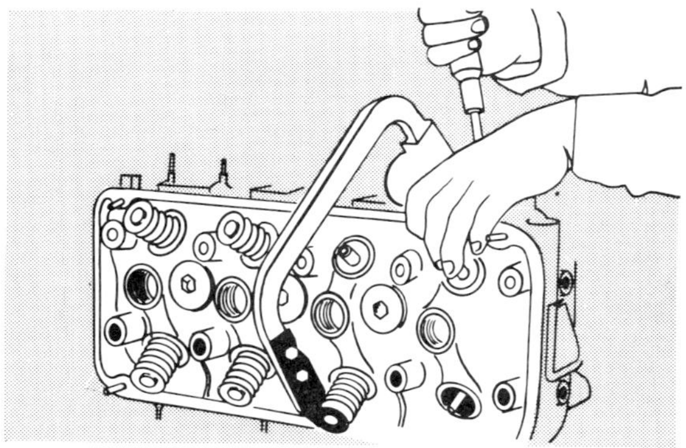

Fig. 5-22. Valve spring being compressed with C-type valve spring compressing tool.

5. Thoroughly clean all cylinder head components.

***CAUTION* —**

Do not use a metal scraper or a power-driven wire brush to clean the combustion chambers or gasket sealing surfaces. Doing this can gouge the aluminum, which could cause the gaskets to leak, or leave scratches in the combustion chambers that could become "hot spots". Instead, use solvent to soften dirt, combustion chamber deposits, dried sealer, and material torn from old gaskets. Then remove this foreign matter with a wooden or plastic scraper.

6. Using a micrometer, as shown in Fig. 5-23, measure the diameter of each valve stem at the point where it contacts the valve guide. Write down the measured diameter of any valve that does not conform to the new-part diameters given in the illustration.

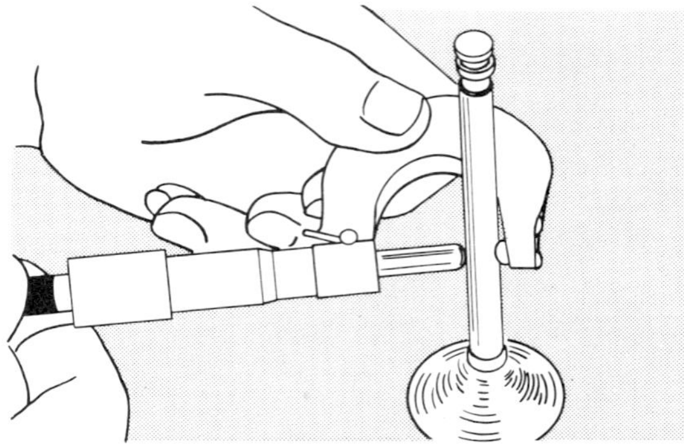

Valve stem diameters

Intake: 7.970 to 7.985 mm (.3138 to .3144 in.)
Exhaust: 7.965 to 7.980 mm (.3136 to .3142 in.)

Fig. 5-23. Valve stem diameter being measured.

7. Using a bore gauge, as shown in Fig. 5-24, measure the inside diameter of each valve guide. Write down the measured inside diameter of any valve guide that does not conform to the new-part diameter given in the illustration.

Valve guide inside diameter

Intake and exhaust: 8.01 to 8.03 mm (.3154 to .3161 in.)

Fig. 5-24. Inside diameter of valve guide being measured. Write down largest measured diameter, which will usually be obtained near the top of the bore.

8. If you have written down a measured diameter for any valve or valve guide, subtract the diameter of the valve stem from the inside diameter of its guide to obtain the clearance. If the clearance for an intake valve stem exceeds an 0.08-mm (.003-in.) wear limit, or if the clearance for an exhaust valve exceeds an 0.10-mm (.004-in.) wear limit, replace both the valve and the valve guide.
9. To determine whether the original valve springs can be reused, check them for squareness and measure their tensions with a valve spring tester as shown in Fig. 5-25. Replace springs that do not conform to the specifications given in **Table j.**

NOTE —

If you do not have a spring tester, have the springs tested by your Authorized Dealer or by a qualified automotive machine shop.

Table j. Valve Spring Specifications

Description	Specification
Maximum permissible deviation from squareness	1.9 mm (.075 in.)
Normal free height	42.1 mm ($1^{21}/_{32}$ in.)
Installed height	37.7 mm ($1^{31}/_{64}$ in.)
Pressure required to compress new spring to installed height	26.3 kg (58.0 lb.)
Minimum acceptable pressure required to compress used spring to installed height	24.3 kg (53.6 lb.)

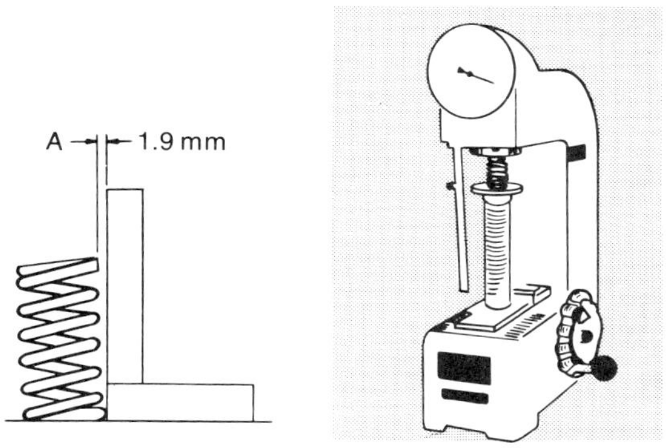

Fig. 5-25. Valve spring being checked for squareness (left) with machinist's square positioned on surface plate. Check dimension **A** with a feeler gauge. At right is valve spring tester with spring in place.

10. Inspect the valve seats and the valve facings as described in **5.5 Reconditioning Valves and Valve Seats.** If necessary, recondition (grind) the seats and the facings.

To replace valve guides:

1. To remove a worn or damaged valve guide, first break off its upper part as indicated in Fig. 5-26.
2. Before driving out the remainder of the old valve guide or driving in a new valve guide, heat the cylinder head to 80° to 100°C (176° to 212°F) either in boiling water or in an oven. Then, using special tool 09201-60011 shown in Fig. 5-27, drive the broken-off guide out toward the combustion chamber.
3. With the head heated to 80° to 100°C (176° to 212°F), drive in the new valve guide as shown in Fig. 5-27. Continue driving in the guide until it protrudes 17 mm (or $^{43}/_{64}$ in.) from the top of the head.

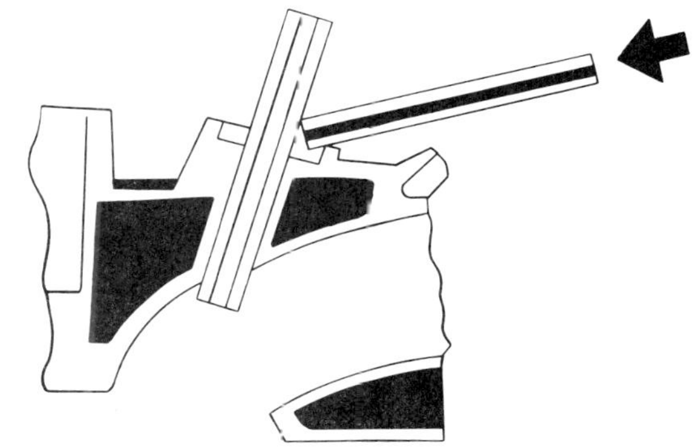

Fig. 5-26. Top of valve guide being broken off. Position a brass drift as shown, then strike it sharply with a hammer as indicated by the arrow.

NOTE —

Always drive in the new guide from the top toward the combustion chamber, just as you drove out the old guide. If the new guide drives in easily—or requires little effort to drive out once the head has cooled—install an oversize guide in its place. The outside diameter of standard guides is 13.04 to 13.05 mm (.5134 to .5138 in.). The outside diameter of oversize valve guides is 13.09 to 13.10 mm (.5154 to .5157 in.). To simplify installing the guide to the correct depth, scribe a line on the guide that is 17 mm (or $^{43}/_{64}$ in.) from the top. 5

4. Measure the inside diameter of any newly installed valve guide, as previously shown in Fig. 5-24. If it is undersize, enlarge its inside diameter with a hone or a reamer until it provides the correct clearance with its valve. See Fig. 5-27.

NOTE —

The standard clearance for intake valve stems/guides is 0.025 to 0.060 mm (.0010 to .0024 in.). The standard clearance for exhaust valve stems/guides is 0.030 to 0.065 mm (.0012 to .0026 in.)

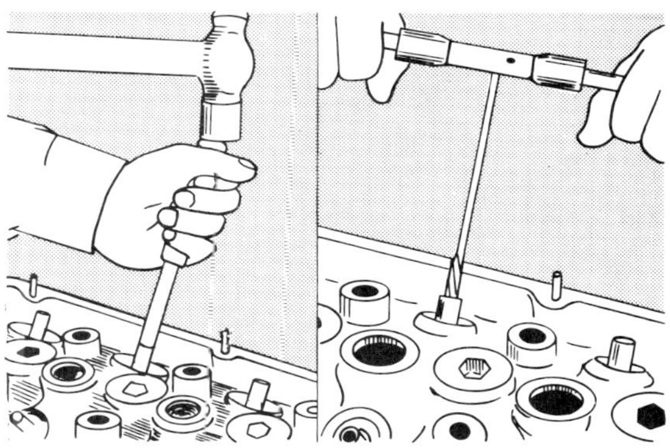

Fig. 5-27. New valve guide being driven in (left) using special too 09201-60011. At right new guide is being reamed to obtain the correct clearance with its valve. Lubricate the reamer with cutting oil during the reaming operation.

5. To ensure that the valve seats are concentric with the new valve guides, reface the seats as described in **5.5 Reconditioning Valves and Valve Seats.**

To reassemble cylinder head:

1. If you have removed any of the three threaded plugs in the top of the head, or if you have removed the cylinder head rear plate, install these parts with new gaskets. Torque the threaded plugs to 30 to 40 Nm (22 to 30 ft. lb.) and torque the bolts for the rear plate to 4 to 5 Nm (35 to 44 in. lb.).
2. Lubricate the valve stems with engine oil. Then, with reference to the numbers marked on the valves during removal, install each valve in its original location.
3. Install the spring seat. Install the oil seal atop the valve guide. Then install the spring and the spring retainer. See Fig. 5-28.

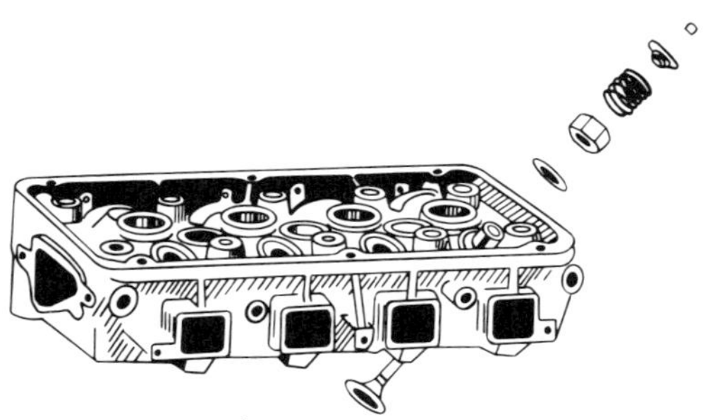

Fig. 5-28. Exploded view of valve and related components.

4. Install the C-type valve spring compressing tool. Push down the spring retainer, compressing the valve spring until you can install the two-piece valve lock in the grooves of the valve stem. Then gradually release the spring tension, making sure that the valve lock halves are correctly engaged in the valve stem grooves and in the tapered bore of the valve spring retainer.
5. When all valves and valve components have been installed, install the cylinder head as described in **5.3 Removing and Installing Cylinder Head and Manifolds.**

5.5 Reconditioning Valves and Valve Seats

Carefully inspect used valves in order to determine whether they are suitable for reuse. Worn valve seats can usually be reconditioned. In reconditioning valves and seats, follow a procedure suitable to the valve and seat resurfacing machines that you have. Alternatively, have worn valves and seats refaced by an Authorized Dealer or a qualified automotive machine shop.

To inspect and recondition used valves:

1. Discard any valve with damaged valve lock grooves or with a stem that has been warped or galled by seizure.
2. Using a motor-driven wire brush, remove the combustion chamber deposits from the valves.
3. Examine the part of the valve facing that contacts the valve seat for pits, burns, and other signs of wear. Recondition slightly worn facings as shown in Fig. 5-29. If the damage to a valve is too extensive to be corrected by machine-grinding, replace the valve.

CAUTION —

Do not grind the stem end more than 0.50 mm (.020 in.). New intake and exhaust valves are 109.00 mm (4.291 in.) long. Replace any valve that is less than 108.50 mm (4.272 in.) after its worn stem tip has been ground true. Because of the extreme conditions under which exhaust valves operate, many experienced mechanics routinely replace any exhaust valve that has been in service for 40,000 km (25,000 mi.) or more.

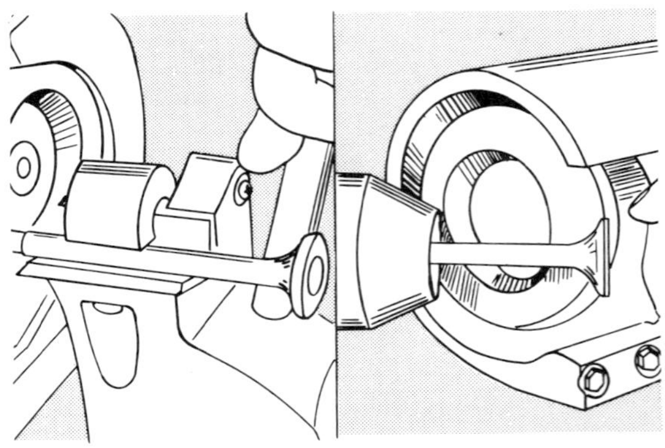

Fig. 5-29. Reusable valve being reconditioned. At right, valve facing is being ground to 45° angle (both intake and exhaust valves). At left, stem is being ground in order to correct wear caused by contact with rocker arm.

4. After you have refaced valves by machine grinding, the remaining margin must not be less than the minimum specified in Fig. 5-30. Discard any valve that has an irregular margin after machine-grinding—a condition that indicates a warped valve.

NOTE —

If for any reason you replace a valve, it is recommended that you replace the valve guide also. See **5.4 Disassembling and Assembling Cylinder Head.**

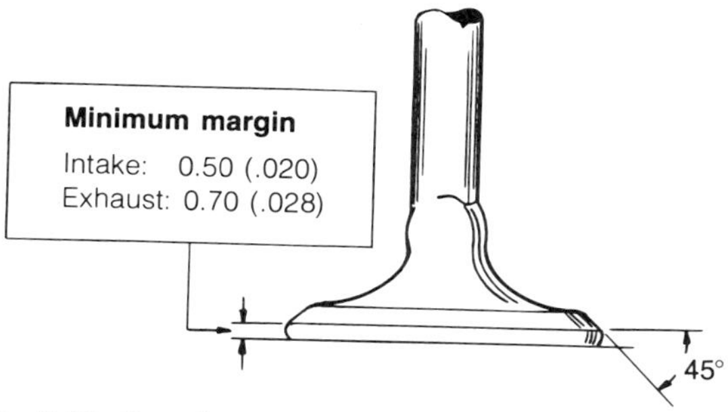

Fig. 5-30. Seat face angle and minimum margin for refaced valves given in mm (in.).

To inspect and reface valve seats:

1. If any valve seat is cracked or so badly gas-cut that it cannot be refaced to the specified dimensions, replace the cylinder head.
2. If inspection has shown that the valve guides are no longer serviceable (see **5.4 Disassembling and Assembling Cylinder Head**), replace the guides before you recondition the valve seats.
3. Lightly coat the valve facing with Prussian blue, then insert the coated valve into the valve seat. Applying light pressure, rotate the valve about a quarter turn. Remove the valve and check the seat contacting position on the valve facing, which will be shown by an area where the coating has been rubbed off. See Fig. 5-31.

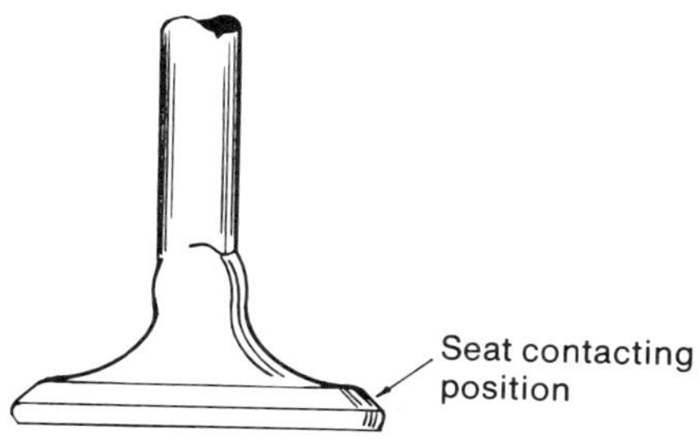

Fig. 5-31. Seat contacting position marked on new or refaced valve. Seat should contact center of valve facing.

4. If the seat contacting position is centered on the valve facing, mark the seat's contact area equally on both its top and bottom edges so that it can be narrowed to 1.20 to 1.60 mm (.047 to .063 in.). If the seat contacting position is not centered on the valve facing, mark off the 1.20-mm to 1.60-mm (.047-in. to .063-in.) contact area at a point on the seat that will center it on the valve facing.
5. Whether you use a hand-operated seat cutter (Fig. 5-32) or a power-driven seat grinder, make sure that the tool pilot fits the valve guides with little or no play.

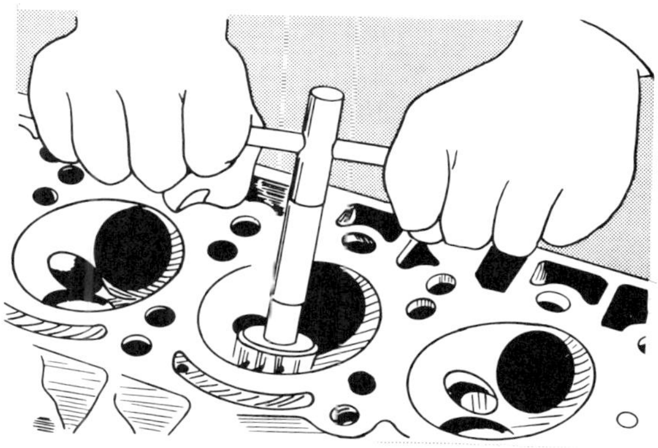

Fig. 5-32. Valve seat being refaced with hand-operated cutter.

6. Using a 30° seat cutter or a 30° grinding stone, narrow the seat from the top until you reach the marked upper edge for the new contact area. See Fig. 5-33. Use a 65° cutter or stone to narrow the seat from the bottom.

CAUTION —
Do not neglect narrowing the valve seats to specifications. Overly wide seats produced by using only a 45° cutter or stone tend to trap carbon particles and other deposits.

5

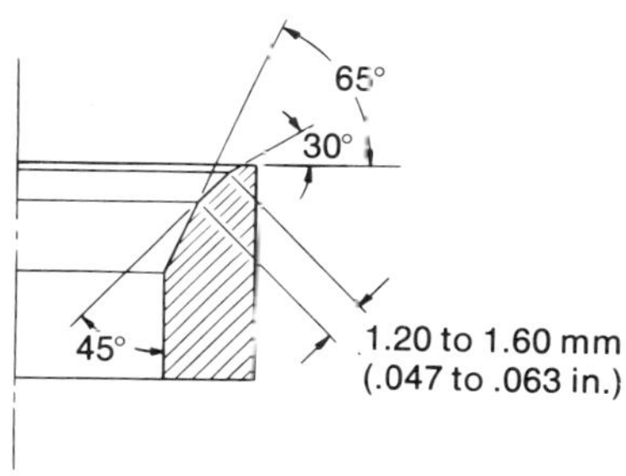

Fig. 5-33. Finished dimensions for valve seat. Cut 30° angle first; cut 65° angle second. When finished, 45° contact area of the seat should be 1.20 to 1.60 mm (.047 to .063 in.) wide.

7. Lightly cut or grind to 45° the contact area of the valve seats. Remove no more metal than is necessary to erase wear and pitting—the less metal removed, the better.
8. Lightly lap the valves into their seats as described in the following procedure.

To hand-lap valves and seats:

1. Lubricate the valve stem with engine oil. Coat the valve seat contact facing with a small amount of valve grinding compound (available from automotive supply stores).
2. Using a suction cup tool as shown in Fig. 5-34, turn the valve clockwise and counterclockwise against the seat. Lift the valve off the seat every few turns in order to avoid cutting concentric grooves into the seat.

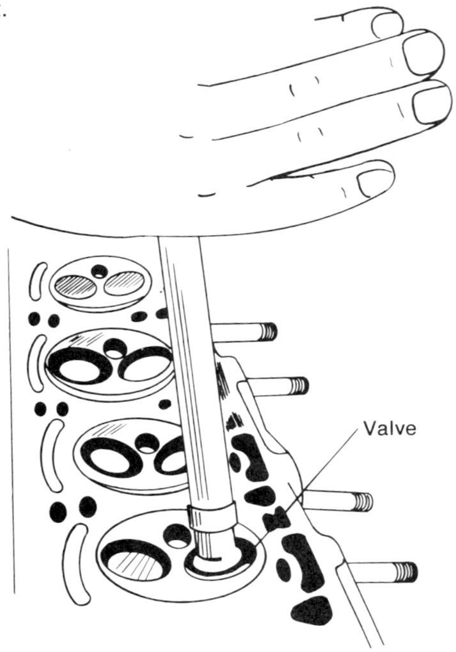

Fig. 5-34. Suction cup tool used to turn valve against seat.

3. Clean away every trace of grinding compound. Inspect the valve and the seat. There should be a uniform dull gray band completely around the valve facing and the seat contact area.
4. To check the valve seating, lightly coat the valve facing with Prussian blue. Then install the valve. While applying light pressure to the valve, rotate the valve about a quarter turn against its seat.
5. Remove the valve and examine the contact pattern. If the seating is correct, the valve will leave an even coating of Prussian blue on the seat. If it does not, either the valve is warped and must be replaced or the seat must be reconditioned with greater care.

6. LUBRICATION SYSTEM

Oil pressure for the lubrication system is supplied by a trochoid-type oil pump that is located inside the engine's crankcase. The oil from the pump passes through a full-flow oil filter before it reaches the moving parts of the engine. Instructions for replacing the oil filter are given in **LUBRICATION AND MAINTENANCE.** Full oil pump output and pressure specifications are given in **12. Engine and Clutch Technical Data.**

Fig. 6-1 is a diagram of the lubrication system with a chart that shows the flow of oil from one component to the next. This chart can be valuable in troubleshooting an engine that has been damaged by loss of oil pressure to one or more components. For example, a noisy timing chain caused by loss of oil pressure to the timing chain tensioner should prompt you to inspect the chain and its sprockets for abnormal wear before reassembling the engine after correcting the blockage of the tensioner's oil passage. Similarly, noisy rocker arms caused by a lack of

Fig. 6-1. Oil flow in the Toyota 2T-C engine.

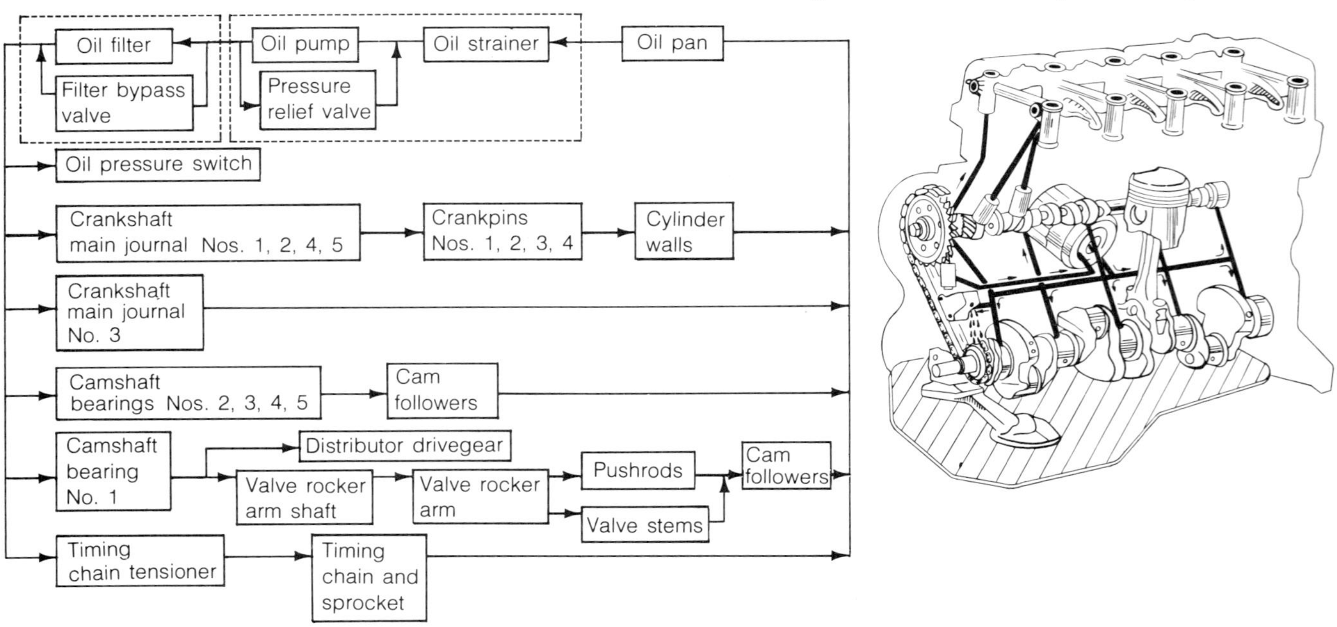

lubrication should lead you to disassemble the cylinder head and inspect the valve stems and the valve guides even though the basic fault can be corrected merely by cleaning the oil passage inside the rocker arm shafts.

The bypass valve is integral with the oil filter and permits oil to bypass the filter and reach the engine's bearings in the event that the filter becomes plugged. Whenever the pressure in the system exceeds a predetermined level, the pressure relief valve in the pump opens to return oil to the crankcase. By doing this, the pressure relief valve prevents over-pressurization of the system, which could increase oil consumption or burst the filter. The oil pressure gauge, its sending unit, and the oil pressure warning light switch are covered in **ELECTRICAL SYSTEM** in conjunction with the dashboard instruments.

6.1 Removing, Checking, and Installing Oil Pump

Fig. 6-2 is an exploded view of the oil pump. Because the pump is inside the crankcase, you must remove the oil pan before you can remove the pump. The instructions given here should be followed preparatory to any repair that requires removal of the oil pan.

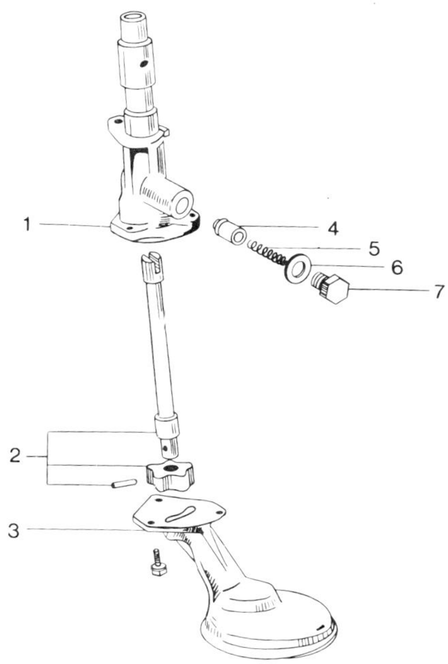

1. Oil pump body
2. Rotor set (includes driven rotor)
3. Oil pickup
4. Pressure relief valve plunger
5. Pressure relief valve spring
6. Pressure relief valve gasket
7. Pressure relief valve plug

Fig. 6-2. Exploded view of oil pump. Pin holds drive rotor to shaft. Driven rotor, which cannot be seen in illustration, is located inside pump body and is easily removable.

To remove and inspect oil pump:

1. Place a receptacle of at least six liters (or six quarts) capacity beneath the engine. Then remove the oil drain plug and allow the engine oil to drain into the receptacle. If necessary, consult **LUBRICATION AND MAINTENANCE.**
2. Remove the nuts that hold the side engine mounts to the front suspension crossmember.
3. Raise the car on a hoist or support it on stands designed for this purpose. Then remove the splash shield that is beneath the engine.
4. Remove the two U-shaped clamps that hold the front suspension's stabilizer bar to the body. Then unbolt the ends of the stabilizer bar from the track control arms and remove the bar from the car. If necessary, consult **SUSPENSION AND STEERING.**
5. Remove the bolts that hold the oil pan to the engine, then lower the pan as far as possible. If the pan is stuck in place with sealer, tap the sides of the pan with a rubber mallet to break the pan free with a tilting motion.
6. Remove the pump's mounting bolt as shown in Fig. 6-3.

5

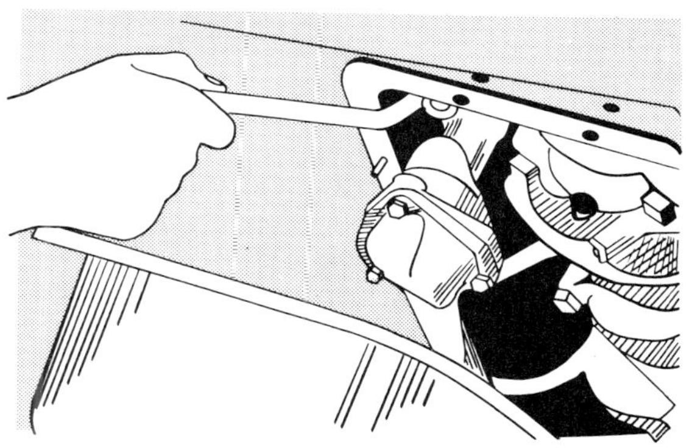

Fig. 6-3. Oil pump mounting bolt being removed after oil pan is lowered.

7. Place a jack beneath the bellhousing, then raise the engine until you can remove the oil pump and the oil pan simultaneously. See Fig. 6-4.

> ***CAUTION —***
> *Do not raise the engine so far that a strain is placed on the radiator hoses, as doing this could damage the radiator. Also, be careful that the cooling fan does not strike the shield mounted above it. If you have difficulty pulling the oil pump downward out of the engine block, remove the ignition distributor as described in* **3.2 Distributor.** *Then use a long brass drift to drive the oil pump out from above.*

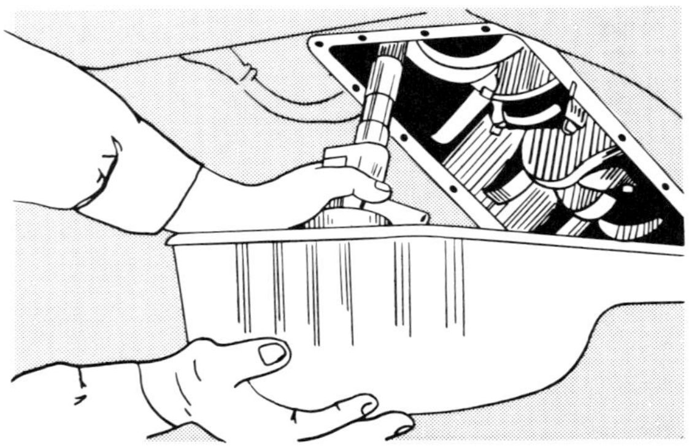

Fig. 6-4. Oil pump and oil pan being removed from engine. Pump must be pulled downward out of engine block.

8. Remove the three bolts that hold the oil pickup to the oil pump body. Then remove the oil pump's rotor set and shaft. Remove the pressure relief valve plug, its gasket, the spring, and the plunger. See Fig. 6-5.

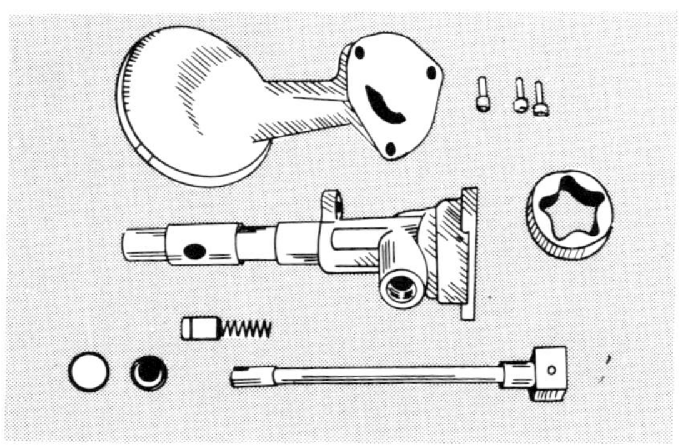

Fig. 6-5. Oil pump disassembled.

9. Wash the parts in solvent. Then inspect the top end of the pump shaft. Replace the shaft and rotor set if there is visible wear at the bearing or if the drive slot is damaged.

10. Install the driven rotor and the drive rotor in the oil pump body, aligning the punch marks as shown later in the assembly and installation procedure. Then use feeler gauges of various thicknesses in order to determine the tip clearance. If tip clearance exceeds the 0.25-mm (.010-in.) wear limit, replace the rotor set. See Fig. 6-6.

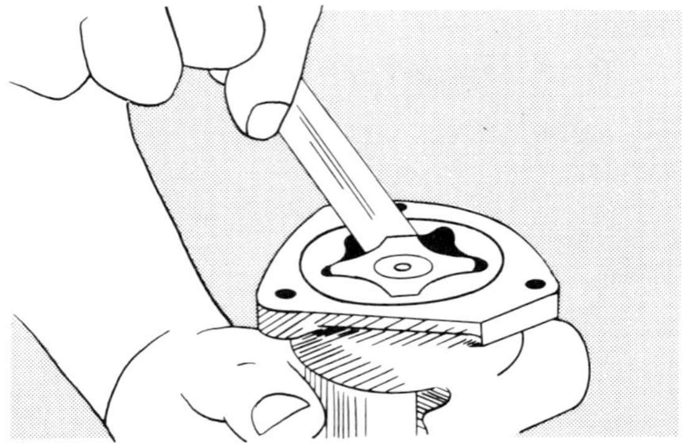

Fig. 6-6. Tip clearance being measured with feeler gauge. Rotors must be positioned as shown. With new parts, the tip clearance should be between 0.04 and 0.16 mm (.0016 and .0063 in.).

11. Place a straightedge across the face of the pump body and the rotors as shown in Fig. 6-7. Then use feeler gauges of various thicknesses in order to determine the side clearance between the rotor set and the straightedge. If the side clearance exceeds the 0.15-mm (.006-in.) wear limit, replace the rotor set.

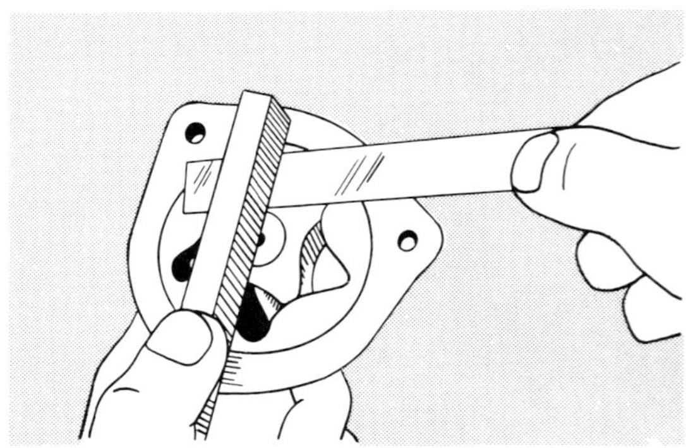

Fig. 6-7. Rotor side clearance being measured. With new parts the clearance should be between 0.03 and 0.09 mm (.0012 and .0035 in.).

12. Use feeler gauges of various thicknesses to determine the clearance between the driven rotor and the oil pump body. See Fig. 6-8. If the clearance exceeds the 0.25-mm (.010-in.) wear limit even with a new rotor set, replace the oil pump as a unit.

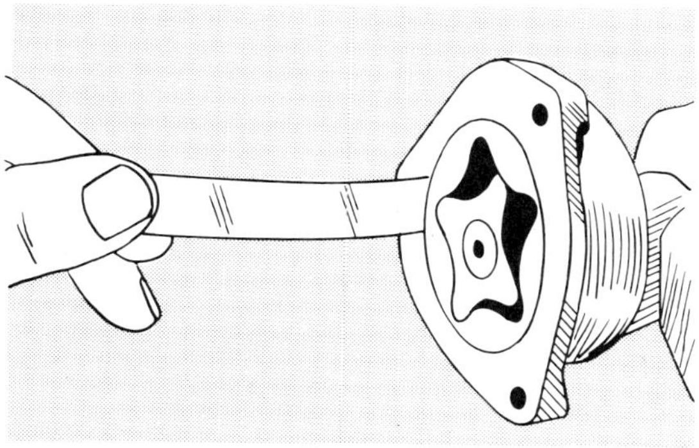

Fig. 6-8. Clearance between driven rotor and pump body being measured. With new parts the clearance should be 0.10 and 0.16 mm (.0039 to .0063 in.).

13. Inspect the pressure relief valve components (Fig. 6-9). The plunger should be a good fit with the valve bore and be free of scoring or wear. The spring should be neither weakened nor damaged. Replace faulty parts.

NOTE ——
The free height of a new spring is 47 mm ($1^{55}/_{64}$ in.). It should require a pressure of 5.99 to 6.59 kg (13.2 to 14.52 pounds) to compress the spring to its installed height of 36.80 mm ($1^{29}/_{64}$ in.). A weak spring will cause lowered oil pressure.

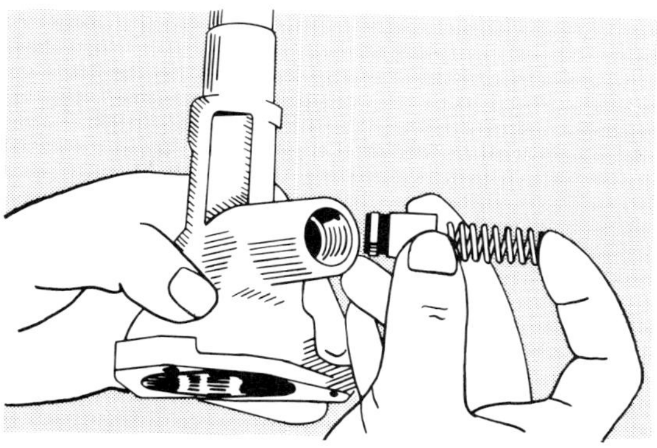

Fig. 6-9. Pressure relief plunger and spring being inspected.

To assemble and install:

1. Lubricate the rotor set and the shaft with engine oil, then install them in the pump body as indicated in Fig. 6-10.
2. Install the pressure relief valve plunger and its spring. Then install the gasket and the plug.
3. Install the oil pickup, torquing the bolts to 5 to 7 Nm (44 to 62 in. lb.).
4. Immerse the oil pickup in a pan of clean engine oil. Then, using a screwdriver, turn the pump shaft clockwise and see that oil comes out through the discharge hole as shown in Fig. 6-11. Repeat the test with the discharge hole blocked by your thumb. The shaft should at first become difficult to turn and then be stopped by hydrostatic lock. If the pump fails to operate correctly, either its internal clearances are excessive or it has been incorrectly assembled.

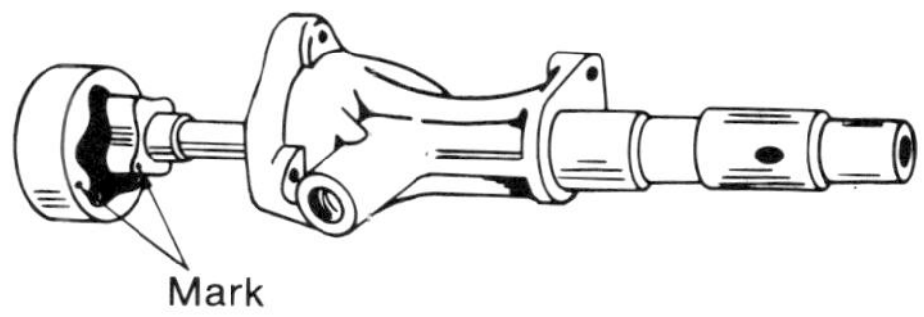

Fig. 6-10. Rotor set being installed. Punch marks should be aligned in order to guarantee smooth rotation of the pump components.

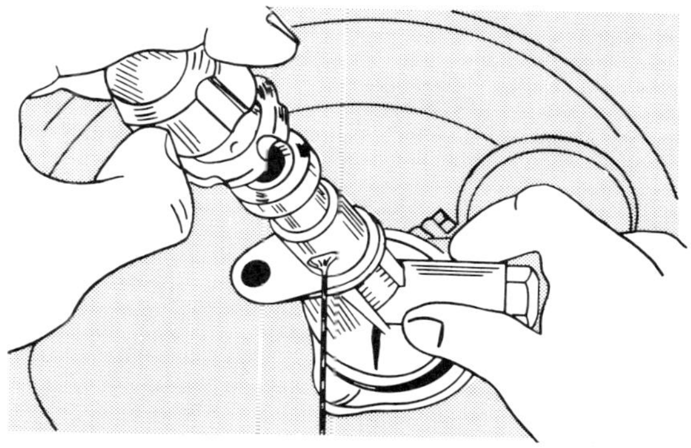

Fig. 6-11. Simple oil pump function check. Notice oil coming out of discharge hole.

5. Simultaneously install the oil pan and the oil pump beneath the engine, inserting the oil pump into the engine block. Install the pump mounting bolt to a torque of 20 to 25 Nm (15 to 18 ft. lb.).
6. After applying sealer to both sides of a new oil pan gasket at the points indicated in Fig. 6-12, position the gasket atop the pan. Then lift the pan up to contact the engine and loosely install the bolts.

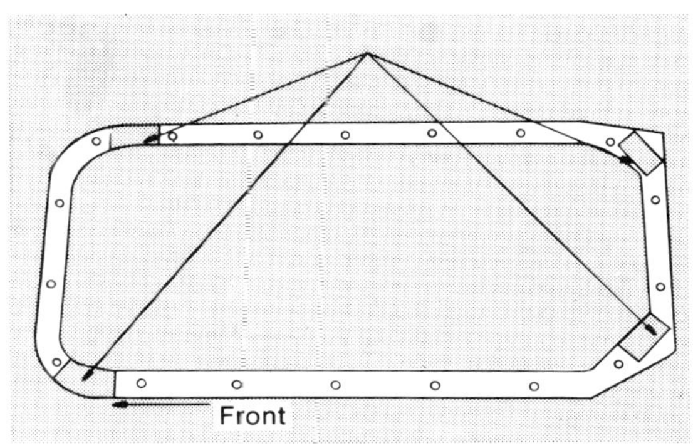

Fig. 6-12. Points at which sealer should be applied to new oil pan gasket.

7. Working diagonally, torque the oil pan bolts in stages to 3 to 4 Nm (27 to 35 in. lb.).
8. Gradually lower the jack, carefully guiding the engine mount studs into the holes. Then install the washers and the nuts to a torque of 30 to 40 Nm (22 to 30 ft. lb.).
9. Install the stabilizer bar. Torque the nuts for the bolts that hold the ends of the bar to the track control arms to 15 to 20 Nm (11 to 15 ft. lb.) for the first nut and 10 to 15 Nm (7.5 to 11 ft. lb.) for the jam nut. Torque the bolts for the U-shaped clamps to 10 to 15 Nm (7.5 to 11 ft. lb.).
10. Install the splash shield beneath the engine. Install the oil drain plug.
11. Lower the car to the ground. Then refill the crankcase with oil as described in **LUBRICATION AND MAINTENANCE.**

7. Removing and Installing Engine

Though it is possible to remove the oil pan and the cylinder head so that the pistons and connecting rods can be removed and installed with the engine in the car, more extensive engine reconditioning should be performed only with the engine removed. The procedure for removing the engine from a car with an automatic transmission is somewhat different from the procedure for removing the engine from a car with a manual transmission. These differences are noted in the instructions.

To remove engine:

1. Disconnect the battery ground cable.
2. Remove the radiator cap. Place a receptacle beneath the radiator for catching the draining coolant. On cars with a hose attached to the radiator tap, direct the hose into the receptacle. Then open the drain tap and allow the coolant to drain.

WARNING —

Never remove the radiator cap or drain the coolant while the engine is hot. Doing this could warp the engine block or the cylinder head, or you could burn yourself.

3. Once the radiator has drained, move the receptacle to a point beneath the left side of the engine. Then drain the coolant from the engine block by taking out the plug in the drain tap. The tap is located on the block casting between the No. 1 and the No. 2 cylinders.
4. While the coolant is draining, mark the positions of the hood hinges on the hood panel. Then take out the bolts (Fig. 7-1) that hold the hood to one hinge. Have someone support that side while you unbolt the hinge from the opposite side. Working together, remove the hood from the car toward the front.

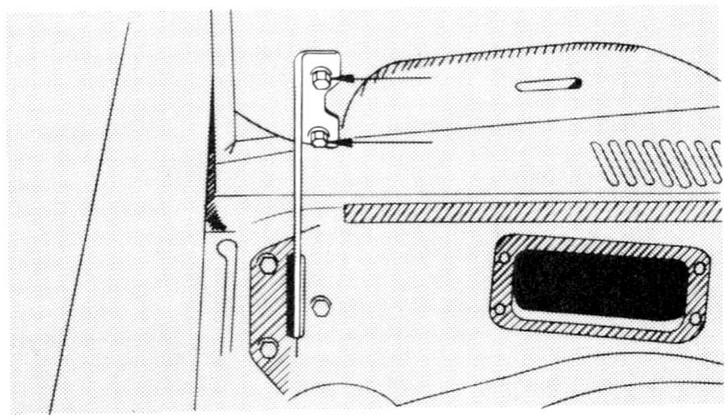

Fig. 7-1. Bolts (arrows) that hold hood to hinge. By marking hinge position on hood, you will simplify realignment of hood during installation.

5. Remove the radiator as described in **4.3 Removing and Installing Radiator.** Remove the radiator hoses from their connections on the engine.

NOTE —

On cars with automatic transmissions, dismount the ATF (automatic transmission fluid) lines from any brackets on the engine after disconnecting the lines from the radiator.

6. If the car is equipped with air conditioning, dismount the air injection pump and the air pump stay from the air conditioning compressor. Disconnect the hoses from the air pump and remove the air pump from the car. On cars without air conditioning, remove the air pump by dismounting it from its bracket, leaving the bracket attached to the engine.

NOTE —

If the car is equipped with air conditioning, dismount the compressor and the lines as described in the next 3 steps. If the car is not equipped with air conditioning, continue the procedure beginning with step 10.

7. Remove the nuts and bolts that hold all refrigerant lines and hoses to the car body. Disconnect the compressor's electrical wire. See Fig. 7-2.

CAUTION —

Do not loosen or disconnect any of the refrigerant hose connections. If you do, it will make necessary costly and time-consuming air conditioning repairs.

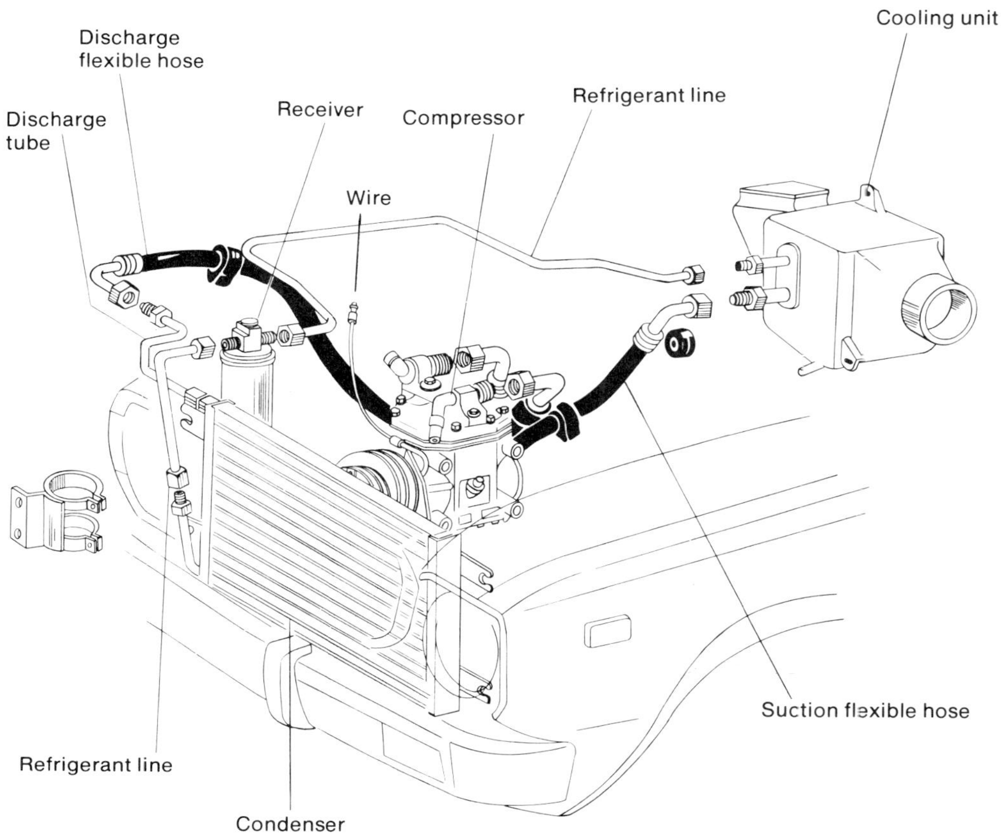

Fig. 7-2. Air conditioning components. Be sure to disconnect the electrical wire for the magnetic clutch of the compressor.

5

8. Place a padded cover atop the left front fender. Arrange a stand beside the left front fender upon which the air conditioner compressor can be placed.
9. Remove the V-belts. Unbolt the air conditioner compressor's mounting bracket from the cast compressor mount on the engine. Then, keeping the hoses attached, lift the compressor out of the engine compartment and support it on the stand beside the left front fender.

CAUTION ——

Do not let the compressor hang by the hoses. Doing this can damage the hoses and cause leaks.

10. Disconnect the heater hoses from the engine. Disconnect the wiring from the alternator.
11. Remove the air cleaner together with the distributor cap and ignition cables. If necessary, consult **5.1 Removing and Installing Cylinder Head Cover.** Disconnect the distributor's primary wire from the ignition coil.
12. Disconnect the wires from the water temperature and oil pressure gauge (or warning light) sending units.
13. Disconnect any and all vacuum hoses that connect the engine to emission control components mounted on the body, labeling each hose so that later you can install it in its original location.
14. Disconnect the engine's wiring harness from the car wiring harness at the round multiple connector located near the front right-hand part of the engine. Unbolt the battery ground cable from the engine block at a point near the alternator.

15. Disconnect the carburetor's fuel return line and the fuel pump intake line. These lines can be disconnected by releasing the hose clamps and slipping the fuel hoses off the metal lines to the right of the engine.

16. Disconnect the accelerator cable from the carburetor. Dismount the accelerator cable's conduit from the bracket. On cars that have the clutch hydraulic hose attached to the engine, dismount the hose bracket.

17. Disconnect the ground wire that joins the rear of the cylinder head to the car body, detaching it at the firewall.

18. Slightly raise the car on a lift or support it on stands designed for the purpose. Then, working under the car, unbolt the clamp and disconnect the exhaust pipe from the exhaust manifold. Unbolt and remove the splash pan that is beneath the engine.

19. Remove the nuts that hold the engine's flexible side mountings to the front suspension crossmember.

20. Working in the engine compartment, attach an engine hoist with suitable tackle to the lifting hooks provided at the left front and the right rear of the cylinder head. Then slightly raise the engine/transmission assembly until the studs on the engine's side mountings are just free of the supports on the front suspension crossmember.

21. Remove the upper bolts that hold the engine to the transmission's bellhousing.

22. Install a jack beneath the transmission, then raise the jack until the transmission is firmly supported.

23. Working beneath the car, disconnect the wires and the battery positive (+) cable from the starter solenoid. Unbolt the starter from the engine, then withdraw it from the bellhousing.

NOTE ——
You can leave the starter lying atop the suspension crossmember and the steering tierods.

24. On cars with automatic transmissions, remove the rubber plug from the intermediate plate where it covers the front of the bellhousing. See Fig. 7-3.

25. On cars with automatic transmissions, use a wrench on the bolt that is in the center of the crankshaft pulley to hand-turn the crankshaft, thus positioning each of the six torque converter-to-drive plate bolts for removal as shown in Fig. 7-4.

26. Remove the remaining bolts that hold the engine to the transmission bellhousing.

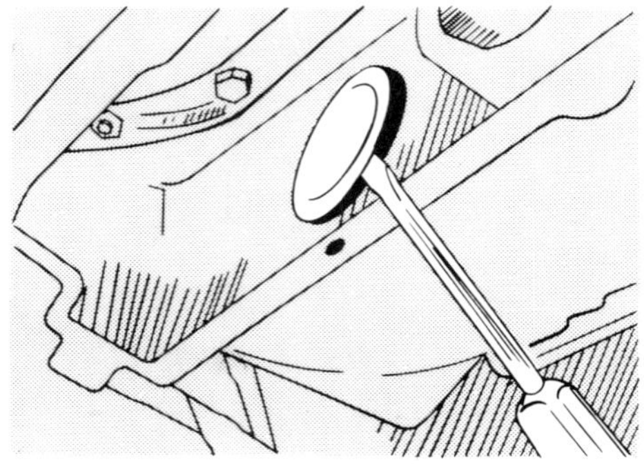

Fig. 7-3. Rubber plug being pried out of intermediate plate on car with automatic transmission.

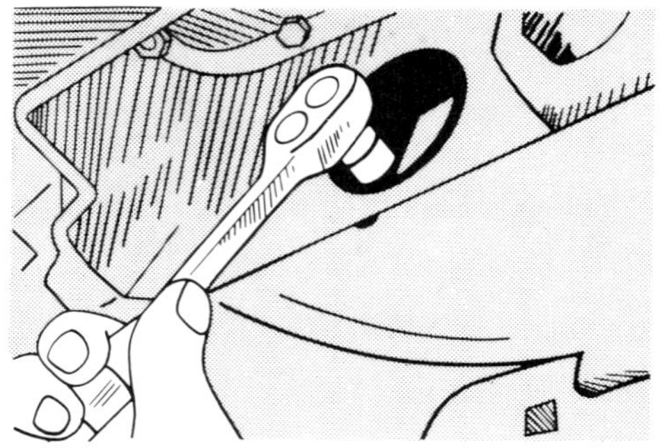

Fig. 7-4. Torque converter-to-drive plate bolt being removed. Turn crankshaft six times to place each bolt in position for removal.

27. On cars with manual transmissions, pull the engine forward so that the transmission input shaft slides out of the splines in the clutch. On cars with automatic transmissions, pull the engine forward, making sure that the torque converter does not slide off its support on the transmission.

CAUTION ——
At no time should you allow the weight of the engine or the transmission to be supported by the manual transmission's input shaft or by the automatic transmission's torque converter. Doing this can damage the transmission's oil seal, bearings, shaft, or the torque converter.

28. Using the lifting tackle, lift the engine upward out of the car. On cars with automatic transmissions, immediately tie a piece of wire across the mouth of the bellhousing to prevent the torque converter from sliding off its support and falling out of the bellhousing.

29. Move the engine away from the car and drain the oil from the oil pan.

To install:

1. With all necessary engine servicing or repairs completed, raise the engine on the lifting tackle and suspend it over the engine compartment.
2. Using multipurpose grease as an adhesive, install the large intermediate plate over the dowels on the rear of the engine block and press the plate against the block. Remove the wire used to hold torque converters on automatic transmissions.
3. Carefully position the engine in the engine compartment. Then move the engine rearward until it is correctly positioned against the bellhousing. On cars with manual transmissions, the transmission's input shaft must enter the splines of the clutch driven plate and the spigot on the shaft must enter the pilot bearing in the center of the crankshaft. If necessary, hand-turn the crankshaft in order to mesh the clutch and input shaft splines.

> ***CAUTION ——***
>
> *On cars with automatic transmissions, the torque converter's pilot must enter the recess in the center of the engine's crankshaft. The alignment of the engine and the transmission must be perfect in order to engage the pilot correctly. If you attempt to force the engine onto the converter, you will probably damage the torque converter.*

4. Install the bolts that hold the engine to the bellhousing finger-tight. Remove the jack from beneath the transmission, then gradually lower the engine onto its mounts—carefully guiding the studs on the flexible mountings into the holes in the front suspension crossmember. Install the nuts on the mounts to a torque of 30 to 40 Nm (22 to 30 ft. lb.).
5. Loosely install the starter. Then torque the bolts that hold the engine and the starter to the bellhousing to 55 to 75 Nm (41 to 55 ft. lb.).
6. Remove the engine lifting tackle. Then, if previously lowered, raise the car on a hoist or support it on stands designed for the purpose.
7. On cars with automatic transmissions, install the bolts that hold the torque converter to the engine's drive plate. Torque the bolts to 15 to 20 Nm (11 to 15 ft. lb.), then install the rubber plug in the intermediate plate.
8. Reconnect the wires and the battery positive (+) cable to the starter solenoid. Reconnect the exhaust pipe to the exhaust manifold, torquing the nuts to 30 to 45 Nm (22 to 33 ft. lb.).
9. Reconnect the ground cable to the engine block. Reconnect the wires to the alternator.
10. On cars that have the clutch hydraulic line attached to the engine, reinstall the brackets for the line. Then install the splash pan beneath the engine.
11. Reconnect the engine's wiring harness to the car wiring harness at the round multiple connector.
12. Reconnect the carburetor's fuel return line and the fuel pump intake line
13. Reconnect the accelerator cable and its conduit to the carburetor and the bracket. Adjust the cable as described in **FUEL AND EXHAUST SYSTEMS.**
14. Reconnect the ground wire at the left rear of the cylinder head to the car's firewall.
15. Reconnect the heater hoses. Loosely install the radiator hoses on their connections on the engine.
16. Reconnect all vacuum hoses with careful reference to the labels you placed on them during removal, the vacuum hose diagram on the car, and the diagrams in the **FUEL AND EXHAUST SYSTEMS** section of this Manual.
17. Reconnect the wires to the water temperature and oil pressure gauge or warning light sending units.
18. Install the air cleaner together with the distributor and ignition cables. Reconnect the distributor's primary wire to the ignition coil. If necessary, consult **5.1 Removing and Installing Cylinder Head Cover.**
19. On cars with air conditioning, reinstall the compressor on the engine. On all cars, reinstall the air injection pump and reconnect its hoses. Then install and adjust the V-belts as described in **LUBRICATION AND MAINTENANCE.** Reattach all refrigerant hoses and lines to the car body.
20. Install the radiator and, where applicable, remount the air conditioning system condenser as described in **4.3 Removing and Installing Radiator.** Tighten the hose connections both on the radiator and on the engine. On cars with automatic transmissions, remount the ATF lines.
21. Install the hood with careful reference to the marks made during removal. Consult **BODY AND INTERIOR** if it is necessary to realign the hood.
22. Refill the engine and the radiator with coolant as described in **4.1 Replacing Hoses.** Reconnect the battery's ground cable.

8. TORQUE CONVERTER AND DRIVE PLATE

Cars equipped with automatic transmissions have a drive plate rather than a conventional flywheel. The torque converter is held to the drive plate by six bolts that are taken out when the engine is removed. Torque converter repair and replacement are covered in **AUTOMATIC TRANSMISSION.**

8.1 Removing and Installing Drive Plate

If you must disassemble the engine, remove the drive plate before you remove the crankshaft. The starter ring gear is an integral part of the drive plate assembly. If the gear is faulty, replace the drive plate.

To remove:

1. If you have not removed the engine, remove the driveshaft as described in **DRIVESHAFT AND REAR AXLE.** Then remove the transmission as described in **AUTOMATIC TRANSMISSION.** Mark the drive plate so that you can install it in the exact original position on the crankshaft.
2. Install a drive plate holding fixture (a dog that engages the starter ring gear teeth) on the engine. Alternatively, use coathanger wire to bind a bolt hole in the drive plate to a bolt hole in the engine block's transmission mounting flange.
3. Pry the locking tabs of the bolt lock plates away from the bolt heads. Then remove the six bolts that hold the drive plate to the crankshaft. Remove the drive plate.

To install:

1. If the crankshaft oil seal is leaking, replace the seal as described in **11.1 Replacing Crankshaft Oil Seals.**
2. With reference to the marks made prior to removal, install the drive plate on the crankshaft. Loosely install the six bolts together with two new bolt lock plates.
3. Reinstall the drive plate holding fixture, or again bind the drive plate in place with heavy wire. Then, working diagonally, torque the six bolts in stages to 58 to 60 Nm (43 to 44 ft. lb.). Bend the tabs on the bolt lock plates over to keep the bolts from loosening.
4. Check the drive plate for runout as described in **AUTOMATIC TRANSMISSION.** Measured at the starter ring gear, runout should not exceed 0.20 mm (.008 in.).
5. Remove the wire or the holding fixture. Then reinstall the engine or reinstall the transmission and the driveshaft.

9. FLYWHEEL AND CLUTCH

The flywheel and the clutch assembly remain on the crankshaft when you remove the engine from the car. The clutch release bearing and related parts stay in the transmission bellhousing. If you have not removed the engine, but need to remove the flywheel, first remove the driveshaft as described in **DRIVESHAFT AND REAR AXLE.** Then remove the transmission, the clutch pressure plate assembly, and the clutch driven plate as described in **CLUTCH AND MANUAL TRANSMISSION.**

9.1 Removing, Checking, and Installing Flywheel

Fig. 9-1 is an exploded view of the flywheel and related parts. If you have removed the engine, remove the clutch pressure plate assembly and the clutch driven plate as described in **CLUTCH AND MANUAL TRANSMISSION.** If you must disassemble the engine, remove the flywheel before you remove the crankshaft. The starter ring gear is not an integral part of the flywheel and can be replaced separately, as described in **9.2 Replacing Starter Ring Gear.**

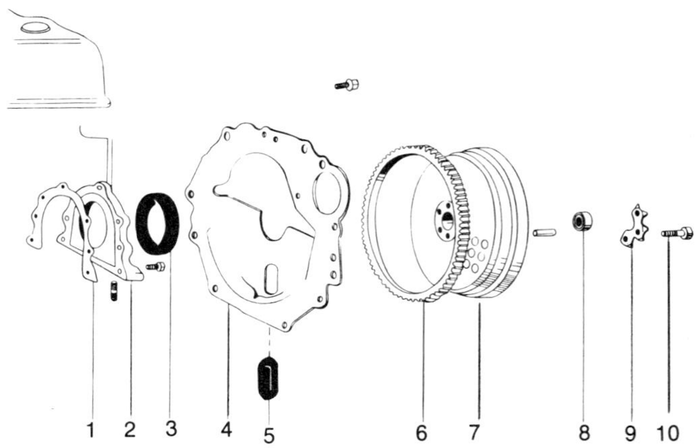

1. Oil seal carrier gasket
2. Oil seal carrier
3. Crankshaft rear oil seal
4. Intermediate plate
5. Rubber plug (cars with automatic transmissions only)
6. Starter ring gear
7. Flywheel
8. Pilot bearing
9. Bolt lock plate (2)
10. Bolt (6)

Fig. 9-1. Exploded view of flywheel and related parts.

To remove flywheel:

1. Install a flywheel holding fixture (a dog that engages the starter ring gear teeth) on the engine. Alternatively, use coathanger wire to bind a partially installed clutch mounting bolt in the flywheel to one of the bolt holes in the engine block's transmission mounting flange.
2. Place a mark on the end of the crankshaft, in the area between the pilot bearing and the center hole

of the flywheel, and an adjacent mark on the flywheel itself. This will ensure that later you can reinstall the flywheel in its original position on the crankshaft.

3. Pry the locking tabs of the bolt lock plates away from the bolt heads.
4. Remove the six bolts that hold the flywheel to the crankshaft—supporting the flywheel firmly as the last bolt is removed. Remove the flywheel.

> ***WARNING —***
> *Wear gloves when you handle the flywheel, as frequently there are sharp edges on the starter ring gear which are caused by wear.*

To install:

1. If the crankshaft oil seal is leaking, replace the seal as described in **11.1 Replacing Crankshaft Oil Seals.**
2. Inspect the clutch friction surface of the flywheel for wear, cracks, and grooves. With the crankshaft removed, you can check the friction surface for runout as shown in Fig. 9-2. Runout should not exceed a wear limit of 0.10 mm (.004 in.). Minor defects may be correctable by regrinding or machining at a specialty shop. If the flywheel is unserviceable, replace it.

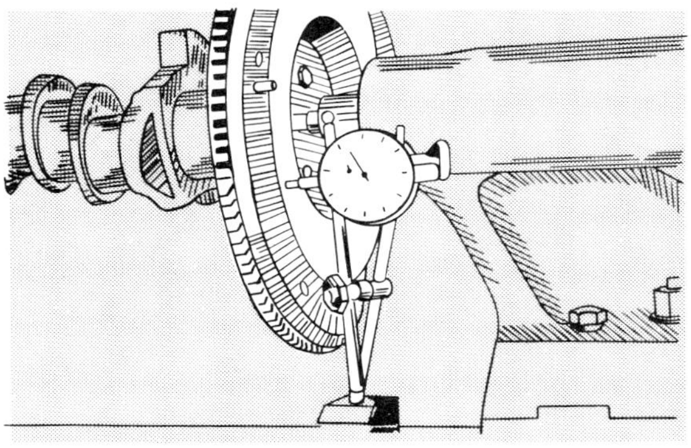

Fig. 9-2. Flywheel being checked for runout by turning it between centers with dial indicator gauge pin in contact with clutch friction surface.

3. Inspect the starter ring gear. If it is cracked, badly worn, or otherwise damaged, you can replace it as described in **9.2 Replacing Flywheel Starter Ring Gear,** or you can replace the entire flywheel as a unit.
4. With reference to the marks made prior to removal, install the flywheel on the crankshaft. Loosely install the six bolts together with two new lock plates.
5. Reinstall the flywheel holding fixture, or again bind the flywheel in place with heavy wire. Then, working diagonally, torque the six flywheel bolts in stages to 58 to 60 Nm (43 to 44 ft. lb.) as shown in Fig. 9-3. Bend the tabs on the bolt lock plates over to keep the bolts from loosening.

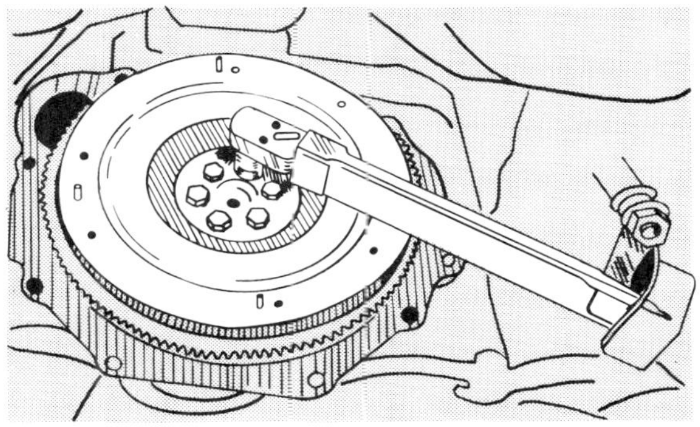

Fig. 9-3. Flywheel bolts being torqued.

6. Remove the wire or the holding fixture. Then reinstall the engine or reinstall the transmission and the driveshaft.

9.2 Replacing Flywheel Starter Ring Gear

The starter ring gear can be replaced only on flywheels. If a drive plate has a faulty starter ring gear, you should replace the entire drive plate.

To replace:

1. Clamp the flywheel in a vise with soft jaws. Then drill one or more holes through the faulty starter ring gear at a point between two of the gear teeth. See Fig. 9-4.
2. Use a cold chisel as shown in Fig. 9-4 to split the ring gear.

> ***WARNING ——***
> *Place a heavy cloth over the ring gear for protection against flying fragments. It is especially important to wear goggles to protect your eyes from fragments as the ring gear is split. Do not attempt to press off or drive off the faulty gear, as this will damage the flywheel and increase the possibility of injury by flying chips.*

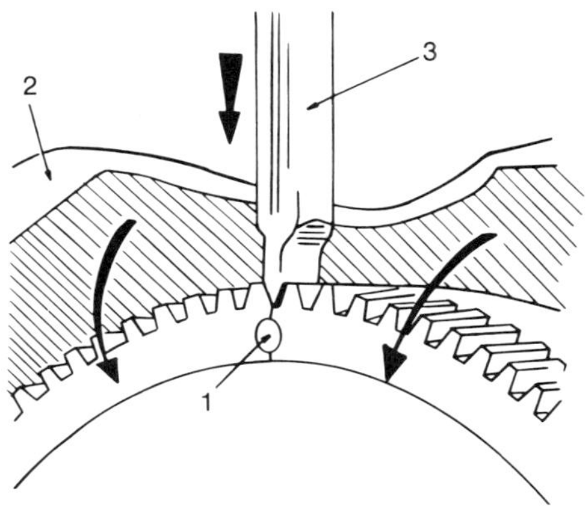

Fig. 9-4. Ring gear being split. Drilled hole is at **1**, the protective cloth at **2**, and cold chisel at **3**. Fold cloth over gear as indicated by curved arrows, then drive cold chisel down as indicated by straight arrow.

3. Remove the cloth and the broken gear. Remove the flywheel from the vise and clean any dirt or rust off its ring gear seating area.

To install:

1. Heat the new ring gear to a temperature of 160° to 200°C (320° to 392°F) in an oven with temperature control.

> ***CAUTION ——***
> *You can heat the gear with a torch if you place the ring gear on a bed of fire bricks and then play the flame in a circular motion onto the bricks about 40 mm (or 1½ in.) from the inside of the gear. Alternatively, you can place the gear on a steel plate and direct the torch at the plate's underside. Polish a section of the gear and heat it only until the polished section begins to approach a dark blue. A temperature in excess of 290°C (550°F) will cause the gear to wear rapidly in service.*

2. Pre-heat two pairs of pliers so that they will not chill the hot gear. Put on a pair of heavy gloves.
3. Using the pre-heated pliers, pick up the heated ring gear and quickly install it on the flywheel so that it is fully in contact with the shoulder.

> ***CAUTION ——***
> *Do not quench the heated gear either with water or oil. Unless the ring gear is allowed to cool naturally and away from drafts, it will break or become distorted. Do not attempt to reposition an incorrectly installed or distorted gear using pressure, as doing this is likely to break the gear.*

10. PISTONS, PISTON RINGS, AND CONNECTING RODS

The components of the piston/connecting rod assembly for one cylinder of the engine are shown in Fig. 10-1. Though it is possible to remove the cylinder head and the oil pan so that the connecting rods and pistons can be removed and installed with the engine in the car, that procedure is advisable mainly for the purpose of inspecting and, if necessary, replacing the connecting rod bearings. Any work that requires grinding or machining—such as removing the top-cylinder ridges or honing the cylinder bores—should be done with the engine removed and disassembled. Otherwise, abrasive dirt and metal particles will remain in the engine, causing bearing damage and rapid wear.

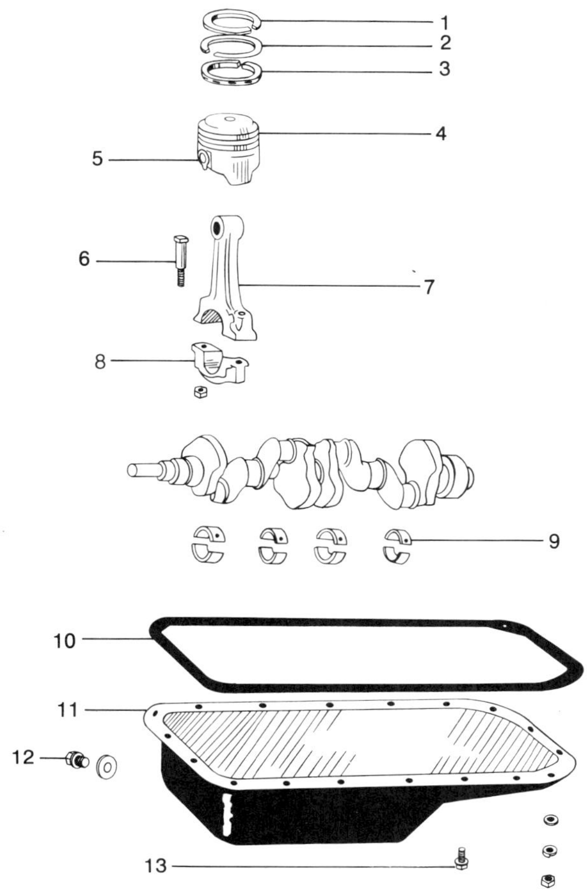

1. Upper compression ring
2. Lower compression ring
3. Oil scraper ring
4. Piston
5. Piston pin
6. Connecting rod bolt
7. Connecting rod
8. Connecting rod cap
9. Connecting rod bearing
10. Oil pan gasket
11. Oil pan
12. Oil drain plug
13. Oil pan bolt with washer

Fig. 10-1. Components of piston/connecting rod assembly. Oil pan and gasket must be removed for access to the connecting rod big end bolts and nuts.

10.1 Removing, Checking, and Installing Pistons, Piston Rings, Connecting Rods, and Connecting Rod Bearings

Because the pistons, the connecting rods, and many of their related parts must be reinstalled in their original locations and positions, you should mark the parts as you remove them. Replacement parts must be selected with careful reference to the cylinder bore, the original part, and to the other parts in the piston/connecting rod assembly.

To remove, check, and install:

1. Unless you are replacing connecting rod bearings only, or are removing the piston and connecting rod for inspection purposes only, remove the engine as described in **7. Removing and Installing Engine.**
2. Remove the cylinder head as described in **5.3 Removing and Installing Cylinder Head and Manifolds.** Remove the oil pan and the oil pump as described in **6.1 Removing, Checking, and Installing Oil Pump.**
3. Mark the cylinder number on the crown of each piston so that the piston/connecting rod assemblies can be reinstalled in their original cylinders.
4. Remove the connecting rod nuts. One at a time, remove the connecting rod caps from the connecting rods. Then, using a wooden hammer handle, as shown in Fig. 10-2, push each piston/connecting rod assembly away from the crankshaft and out through the top of the cylinder.

CAUTION —
If the engine block has pronounced top-cylinder ridges, remove them with a cylinder ridge reamer before you remove the pistons. Otherwise, the piston rings and pistons may be damaged during removal. A top-cylinder ridge is a band of unworn cylinder wall that remains above the part of the cylinder that has been worn to a larger diameter by contact with the piston rings.

5

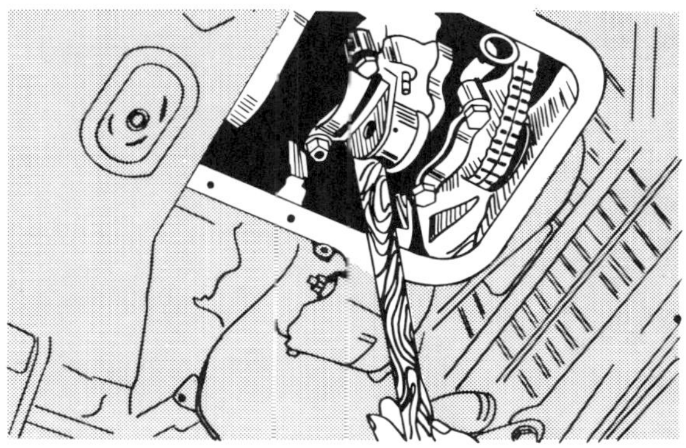

Fig. 10-2. Piston/connecting rod assembly being pushed upward out of cylinder block with wooden hammer handle.

5. As soon as you remove each piston/connecting rod assembly, mark the cylinder number on both the rod cap and the connecting rod. This will ensure that these parts are not accidentally interchanged with those of other cylinders.

6. Using special mandrels (Fig. 10-3) and a repair press, press the piston pins out of the piston/connecting rod assemblies as shown in Fig. 10-4. Number each pin as it is removed, or temporarily reinsert it into its own piston, so that later you can reinstall each pin in its exact original location.

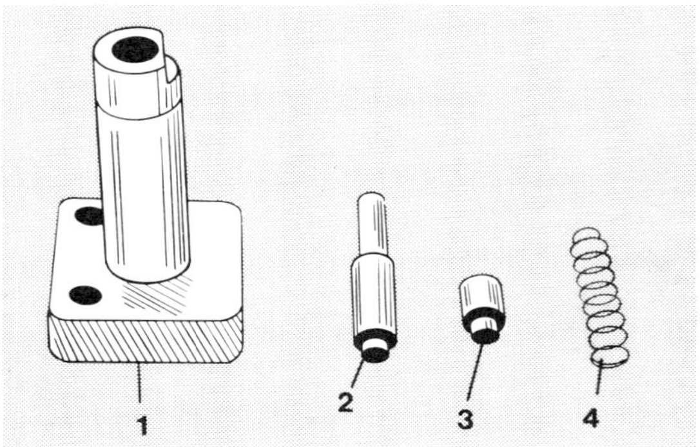

1. Mandrel body
2. Long mandrel
3. Short mandrel
4. Spring

Fig. 10-3. Piston pin removing and installing mandrel set, Special Service Tool 09221–25011.

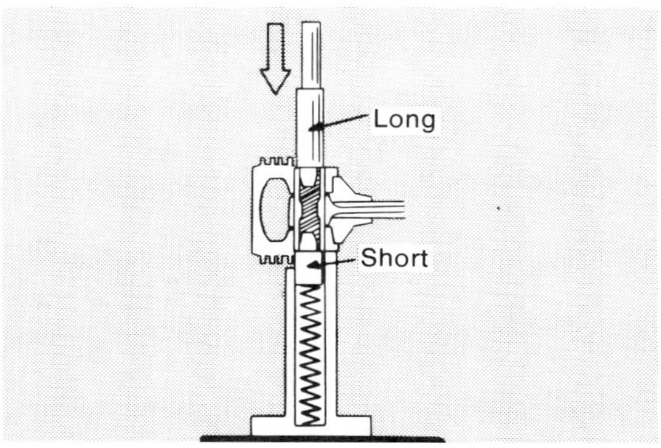

Fig. 10-4. Piston pin being driven out using special mandrels. Short mandrel is inserted atop spring in mandrel body; long mandrel is driven downward by repair press (arrow). Use press and mandrels to press pin completely out in one smooth operation.

7. Using a micrometer, check each piston for wear as shown in Fig. 10-5. Measure the piston at right angles to the piston pin at a point approximately 11 mm ($^7/_{16}$ in.) from the lower edge of the oil scraper ring groove. Write down the measured diameter of each piston.

NOTE ——

During factory assembly, the pistons are selectively fitted to the honed diameters of the cylinders and marked accordingly. See Fig. 10-6. Therefore, a new standard-diameter piston can measure from 84.94 to 84.99 mm (3.3441 to 3.3461 in.). During repair, only one replacement piston is available, so it is not possible to use the cylinder diameter marks or the piston diameter marks as a guide for selecting new pistons.

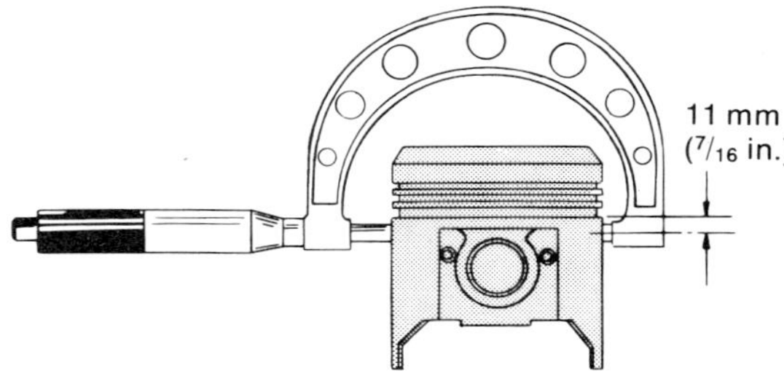

Fig. 10-5. Piston diameter being measured.

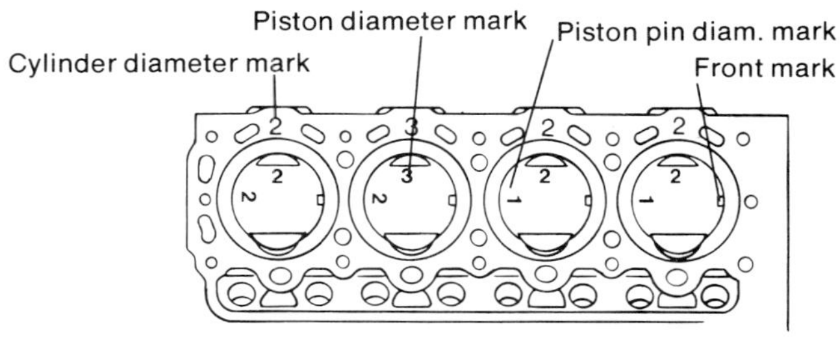

Standard size pistons

Grade 1: 84.94 to 84.95 mm (3.3441 to 3.3445 in.)
Grade 2: 84.95 to 84.96 mm (3.3445 to 3.3449 in.)
Grade 3: 84.96 to 84.97 mm (3.3449 to 3.3453 in.)
Grade 4: 84.97 to 84.98 mm (3.3453 to 3.3457 in.)
Grade 5: 84.98 to 84.99 mm (3.3457 to 3.3461 in.)

Piston pins

Grade 1: 22.00 mm (.8661 in.)
Grade 2: 22.01 mm (.8665 in.)

Fig. 10-6. Grade markings on factory-installed pistons.

8. Using a dial indicator device, as shown in Fig. 10-7, determine the cylinder diameters and the degree of wear.

NOTE ——

When checking the cylinder bores, make your measurements at three points throughout each cylinder and at right angles to one another, as indicated in the right-hand side of the illustration. Variations of less than 0.02 mm (.0008 in.) in cylinder diameter can be corrected by honing, as described in later steps of this procedure. If, however, the bore diameter of a cylinder exceeds one or more of the wear limits given in **Table k**, the cylinder must be rebored and honed to accept a new oversize piston.

9. Write down the largest bore diameter measurement you obtain for each of the cylinders. Normally, this will be measured in the thrust direction as given in Fig. 10-7.

Table k. Cylinder Bore Wear Limits

Dimension	Wear limit
Cylinder bore wear beyond the standard 85.00- to 85.05-mm bore diameter	0.20 mm (.008 in.)
Difference in bore diameter between one cylinder and any other	0.05 mm (.002 in.)
Maximum permissible taper or out-of-round	0.02 mm (.0008 in.)

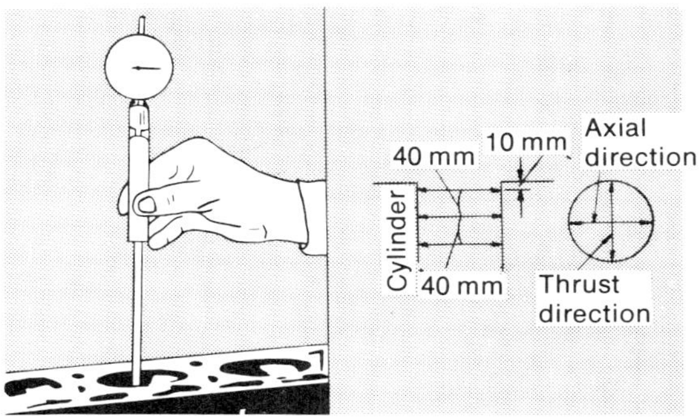

Fig. 10-7. Cylinder bore being measured with a special dial indicator. Diagrams at right show points at which measurements should be made. The given dimensions, 10 mm and 40 mm, are equal to 3/8 in. and 1 9/16 in. respectively.

10. Compute the clearance between the original pistons and their cylinders. To do this, subtract the measurements obtained in step 7 from the measurements obtained in step 8. With new parts, the clearance should be 0.05 to 0.07 mm (.002 to .003 in.).

11. If the piston clearance exceeds 0.07 mm (.003 in.), but the cylinders are not worn beyond their standard diameter, you may be able to correct the wear by installing new standard replacement pistons. Cylinder and piston dimensions for both standard and oversize pistons are given in **Table l.**

12. If the piston clearance exceeds the upper clearance limit because of cylinder wear, or if the cylinders are scored, then the cylinders must be rebored and honed to accept new pistons from one of the available oversize ranges. This work can be done by your Authorized Dealer or by a qualified automotive machine shop. The machinist should have the new pistons on hand so that the cylinders can be honed to precise clearances.

13. Check the fit of the piston pins in their original pistons. The pins should be a light push fit at room temperature. This corresponds to a clearance of about 0.008 to 0.016 mm (.0003 to .0006 in.). If the pin falls out of the piston, or the clearance exceeds a wear limit of 0.020 mm (.0008 in.), replace both the piston and the pin.

14. If little force was required to press a piston pin out of the piston/connecting rod assembly, carefully measure the outside diameter of the piston pin at the point where it is an interference fit with the connecting rod small end. Then measure the inside diameter of the connecting rod small end bore. With both parts at 20°C (68°F), the bore in the connecting rod should be at least 0.020 mm (.0008 in.) smaller than the diameter of the pin for a reliable interference fit. If the fit is not tight enough, replace the connecting rod.

15. Remove the piston rings. If the rings are to be reused, be careful not to break them. Used rings must always be reinstalled in their original grooves on their origina pistons.

16. Being careful not to gouge metal from the pistons, use a tool such as the one shown in Fig. 10-8 to remove carbon and other deposits from the ring grooves of used pistons.

> **NOTE ——**
> If the lower ring lands have high "steps" worn into them, replace the piston.

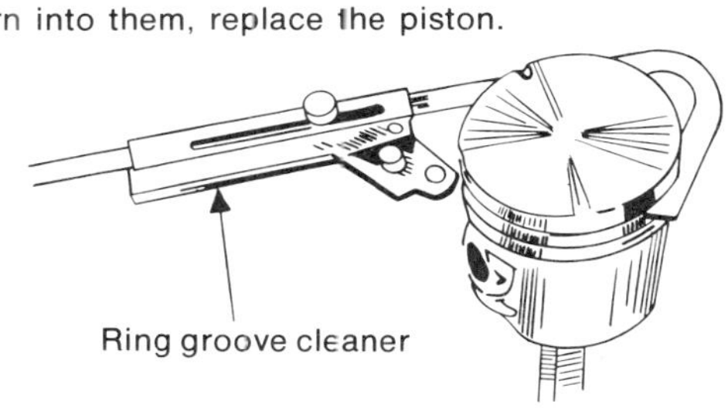

Fig. 10-8. Piston ring grooves being cleaned.

Table l. Piston and Cylinder Diameters

Repair stage	Piston diameter mm (in.)	Cylinder bore diameter mm (in.)
Standard dimension	84.94 to 84.99 (3.3441 to 3.3461)	85.00 to 85.05 (3.3465 to 3.3484)
0.25 mm (.010 in.) oversize	85.19 to 85.24 (3.3539 to 3.3559)	85.25 to 85.30 (3.3563 to 3.3583)
0.50 mm (.020 in.) oversize	85.44 to 85.49 (3.3638 to 3.3657)	85.50 to 85.55 (3.3661 to 3.3681)
0.75 mm (.030 in.) oversize	85.69 to 85.74 (3.3736 to 3.3756)	85.75 to 85.80 (3.3760 to 3.3779)
1.00 mm (.040 in.) oversize	85.94 to 85.99 (3.3835 to 3.3854)	86.00 to 86.05 (3.3858 to 3.3878)

17. If you intend to install new piston rings, obtain the correct ring set for the diameter of the cylinder bores. Then, whether you are installing new or used rings, use feeler gauges of various sizes to determine the side clearance of all the piston rings as shown in Fig. 10-9.

NOTE ——
The piston ring side clearances should be in the ranges given in the illustration. If you install new piston rings, make certain that the side clearance is not less than specified. If there is too little clearance, either replace the piston or have the grooves reconditioned by your Authorized Dealer or a qualified automotive machine shop.

Piston ring side clearances

Upper compression ring:	0.020 to 0.060 mm (.0008 to .0024 in.)
Lower compression ring:	0.050 to 0.055 mm (.0020 to .0022 in.)
Oil scraper ring:	Snug fit all around piston

Fig. 10-9. Piston ring side clearance being measured. Insert feeler gauge between piston ring and one of piston lands, then roll ring around piston, checking clearance with gauge. Roll modern formed steel oil scraper rings without feeler gauge to check for snug fit. Old-style cast-iron oil scraper rings can have 0.020 to 0.060 mm (.0008 to .0024 in.) side clearance.

18. Using the piston as a tool, push each piston ring into its cylinder. Then measure the ring gap as shown in Fig. 10-10. If the cylinder has not been rebored, push the ring to the narrowest (least worn) part of the cylinder, which is usually about 15 mm (5/8 in.) from the bottom of the bore.

NOTE ——
The piston ring end gaps should be in the ranges given in the illustration. If the gap is too large, the rings either are worn excessively or are not the correct rings for the bore diameter and should be replaced. If the gaps are too narrow, enlarge them with a fine file.

Piston ring end gaps

Upper compression ring:	0.20 to 0.40 mm (.008 to .016 in.)
Lower compression ring:	0.10 to 0.30 mm (.004 to .012 in.)
Oil scraper ring:	0.20 to 0.50 mm (.008 to .020 in.)

Fig. 10-10. Piston ring end gap being measured with feeler gauge.

19. Using a tool such as the one shown in Fig. 10-11, install the piston rings on the pistons.

CAUTION ——
The code letter and number are punched on the piston ring's upper surface, which must always be installed so that it is toward the piston crown. The correct installed positions of the rings are shown in Fig. 10-12.

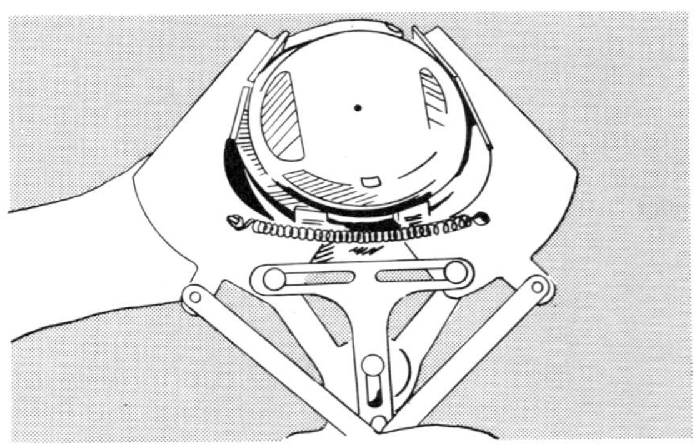

Fig. 10-11. Piston ring being installed.

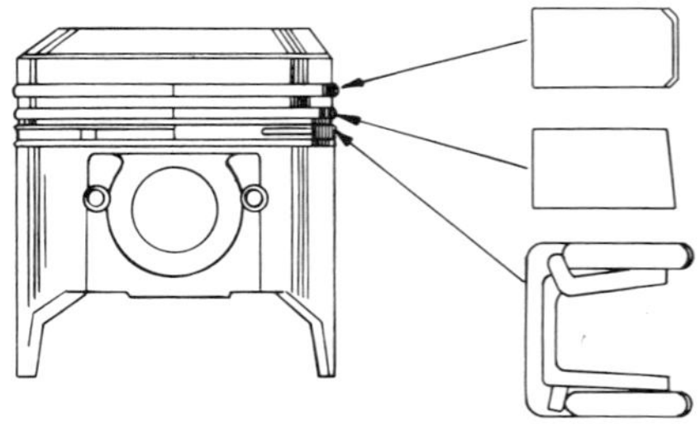

Fig. 10-12. Correct positions for piston rings in piston.

20. Using some kind of connecting rod aligning equipment, such as that shown in Fig. 10-13, check each connecting rod for bend and twist. If the bend or twist exceeds the limits given in the illustration, straighten the rod until it meets the specifications.

NOTE ——
This work can be done by your Authorized Dealer or by a qualified automotive machine shop. If the original connecting rod bearing has failed, or if its overlay is wiped out in two opposing locations, check also that the big end bore is concentric.

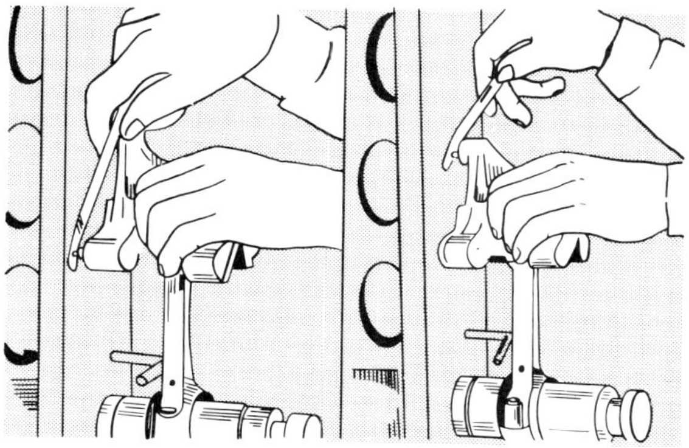

Maximum permissible bend: 0.05 mm per 100 mm (.002 in. per 4 in.)
Maximum permissible twist: 0.05 mm per 100 mm (.002 in. per 4 in.)

Fig. 10-13. Connecting rod alignment being checked. Big end is bolted to mandrel; 3-point V-block is placed on dummy piston pin. With one of V-block points against surface plate, bend or twist is measured by inserting feeler gauges of various thicknesses between other two V-block points and surface plate.

21. Position the connecting rod in its correct piston so that the mating marks are aligned as indicated in Fig. 10-14. Then, with the piston pin and the connecting rod at 20°C (68°F), press in the pin as shown in Fig. 10-15.

NOTE ——
If you replace a piston or a connecting rod, it should be no more than 10g lighter or heavier than any other rod or piston in the engine. The weights can be adjusted to fit a 10g range by grinding a small amount of metal off the interior of the heavy piston(s) or off the rough edge surfaces of the connecting rod big ends.

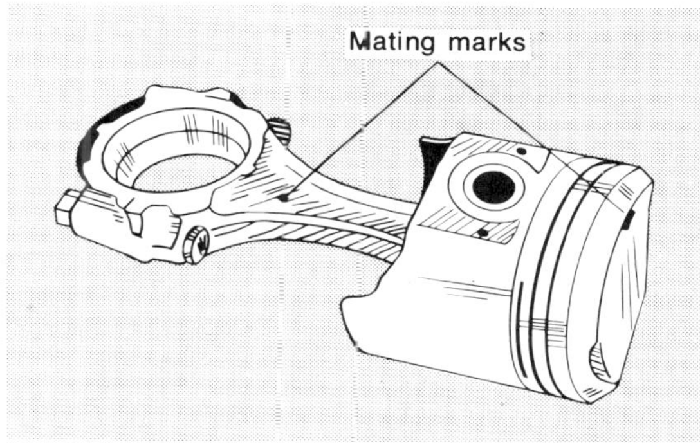

Fig. 10-14. Notch in piston crown and ( ) mark on connecting rod big end correctly positioned on same side of assembly.

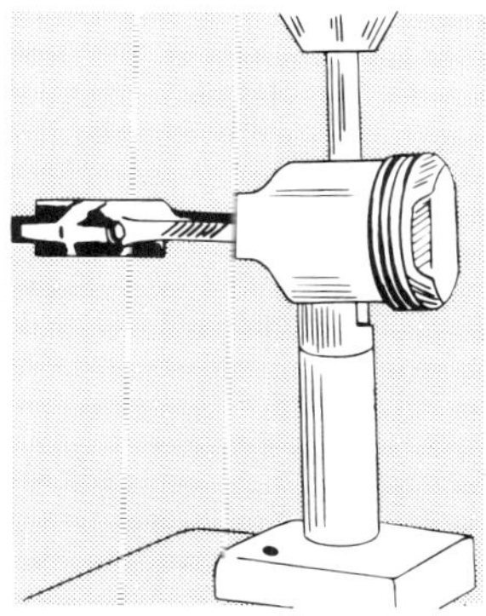

Fig. 10-15. Piston pin being pressed in. Details of tool setup appear earlier in Fig. 10-4. Press pin into assembly in one smooth operation until pin is just below upper surface on piston.

22. If the cylinders have not been rebored, but you are installing new piston rings, inspect the cylinders to see whether there are top-cylinder ridges. Remove top-cylinder ridges with a cylinder ridge reamer. Then—whether there were ridges or not—lightly hone the cylinder bores with a hone that has fine (220-grit) stones. Move the spinning hone smoothly in and out of the bore to produce a fine cross-hatch pattern on the cylinder walls.

NOTE ——
A top-cylinder ridge is a band of unworn cylinder wall that remains above the part of the cylinder that has been worn to a larger diameter by contact with the piston rings. If the ridge is not removed, the new upper compression ring will strike the ridge, breaking the ring and damaging the piston. The object of honing the cylinder is to remove "glaze" that could keep the new rings from seating. In breaking the glaze, remove as little metal as possible.

5

23. Thoroughly clean the engine block with detergent and water to remove metal particles and abrasive dust. Then install the crankshaft, the camshaft, and their bearings and seals. (See **11. Crankshaft and Camshaft**).

CAUTION —
Do not bore or hone the cylinders with the moving parts installed in the engine. Abrasive dust on these components cannot be thoroughly cleaned off and will cause rapid bearing and piston ring wear. Do not clean the block with kerosene or other oily solvents because they tend to carry abrasive dust into the pores of the metal.

24. Hand-turn the crankshaft until the crankpin for the No. 1 cylinder is at bottom dead center.
25. Thoroughly lubricate the No. 1 cylinder bore and the piston rings of the No. 1 cylinder's piston with engine oil only. Stagger the ring gaps as indicated in Fig. 10-16. Then install a piston ring compressor and fully compress the rings.

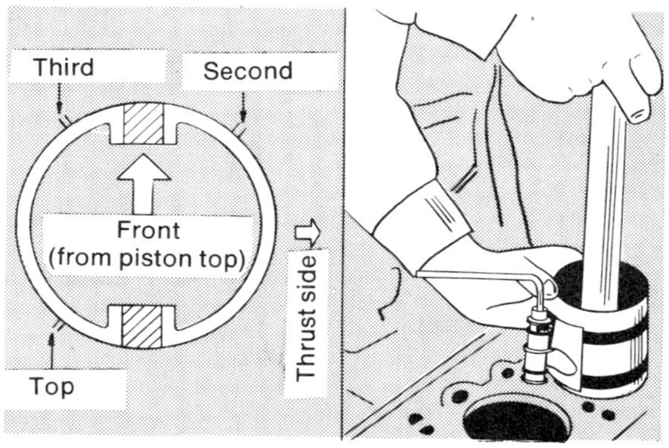

Fig. 10-16. Piston rings being staggered and compressed. Right-hand side of illustration shows piston being pushed out of ring compressor and into cylinder.

26. If previously removed, install the connecting rod bearing shells in the connecting rod and the connecting rod cap. Make sure that the anti-rotation tabs on the bearing shells engage the notches in the rod and the cap. Do not install the cap on the rod.
27. Install the piston/connecting rod assembly in the No. 1 cylinder until the piston ring compressor band contacts the engine block. The notch in the piston, indicated earlier in Fig. 10-14, should be toward the front of the engine.
28. Being careful to guide the connecting rod bolts over opposite sides of the crankpin, use a wooden hammer handle as previously shown in Fig. 10-16 to tap the piston out of the ring compressor and into the cylinder. Then use the hammer handle to press the piston down in the cylinder until the connecting rod bearing is seated squarely on the crankshaft journal.

CAUTION —
Check the progress of the connecting rod as you press the piston toward the crankshaft. The rod bearing or the crankshaft will be damaged if you drive them together at an angle.

29. Loosely install the connecting rod cap. Using the same procedure you used on the No. 1 cylinder, install the piston/connecting rod assembly of the No. 4 cylinder. Then hand-turn the crankshaft 180° and install the piston/connecting rod assemblies of the No. 2 and No. 3 cylinders.
30. One at a time, remove the connecting rod caps. Then place a piece of Plastigage® (available at automotive supply stores) on the crankpin. Do not lay the Plastigage across the crankpin's oil hole. See Fig. 10-17.

NOTE —
Use green Plastigage, which measures clearances from 0.025 to 0.076 mm (.001 to .003 in.). In checking used bearings or new bearings installed in high-mileage engines, it may be necessary to use red Plastigage, which measures clearances from 0.050 to 0.150 mm (.002 to .006 in.).

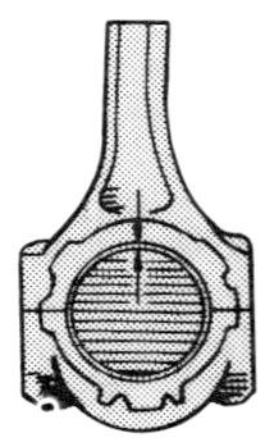

Fig. 10-17. Correct position (arrow) for Plastigage with engine installed in car. With engine removed and inverted, place Plastigage between crankpin and connecting rod cap.

31. Install the connecting rod cap. Working alternately, gradually torque the nuts to 40 to 50 Nm (30 to 37 ft. lb.), then remove the nuts and the connecting rod cap.

NOTE —
Torquing the nuts will compress and flatten the Plastigage, which you will measure to determine the connecting rod bearing clearance. Do not turn the crankshaft as you

NOTE (cont.) ——

compress the Plastigage. Doing this will spread the Plastigage and cause inaccurate measurement.

32. To determine the bearing clearance, compare the flattened Plastigage to the scale that is printed on the edge of the Plastigage package. Read the clearance printed adjacent to the scale band that has the same width as the flattened Plastigage strip (Fig. 10-18).

NOTE ——

Used bearings must be installed in their original positions in their original connecting rods. New bearings must be installed so that their anti-rotation tabs engage the notches in the connecting rod and rod cap. If the clearance is at or near the wear limit given in the illustration, check the crankshaft as described in **11.2 Removing, Checking, and Installing Crankshaft and Main Bearings.** Then replace the bearings.

CAUTION ——

Use solvent to remove the flattened Plastigage. Scraping off the Plastigage could damage the connecting rod bearings.

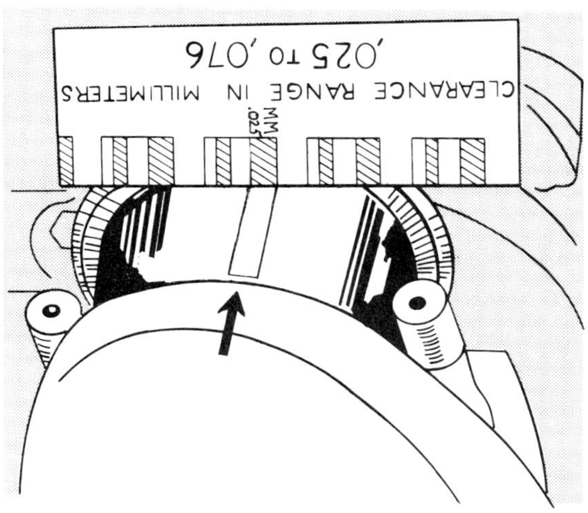

Clearance: 0.024 to 0.048 mm (.0009 to .0019 in.)
Wear limit: 0.08 mm (.0031 in.)

Fig. 10-18. Flattened Plastigage being measured to determine connecting rod bearing clearance.

33. If the bearing clearance is correct, lightly coat the connecting rod bearing shells and the crankpin with assembly lubricant or with a thin coating of multipurpose grease.

CAUTION ——

Modern thin-wall bearings of the kind used in Toyota engines (Fig. 10-19) are made up of several very thin layers and depend on direct contact with a perfectly round connecting rod big end to keep clearances accurate. These bearings must never be adjusted by using shims or by scraping, nor should they be ground down with sandpaper. Always use Plastigage® to determine whether clearances are correct.

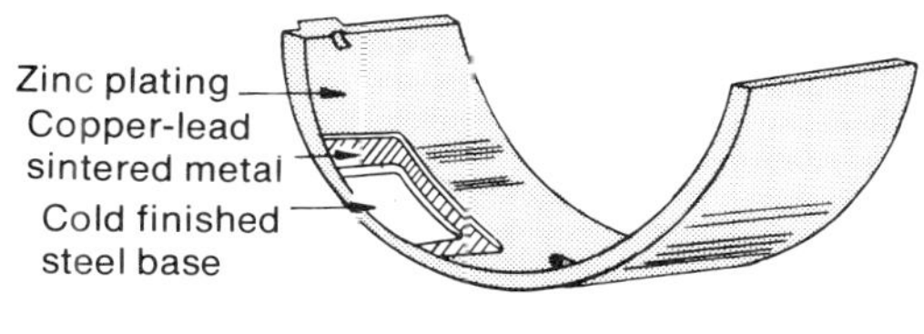

Fig. 10-19. Cutaway view of modern thin-wall bearing shell of kind used in Toyota engines.

34. Install the connecting rod caps. Working alternately, gradually torque the connecting rod nuts of each rod to 40 to 50 Nm (30 to 37 ft. lb.).

35. Using feeler gauges of various thicknesses, determine the connecting rod bearing axial play. To do this, push each connecting rod as far as possible toward one side of the crankpin. If you can insert an 0.27-mm (.0105-in.) feeler gauge between the opposite side of the journal and the connecting rod (Fig. 10-20), the clearance is excessive. 5

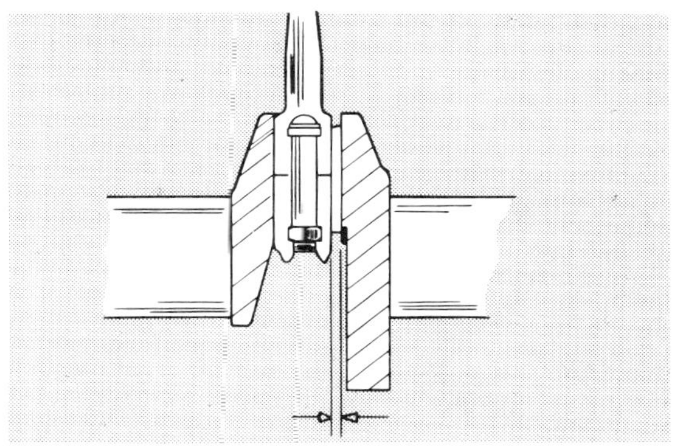

Fig. 10-20. Connecting rod side clearance, which is equal to the rod's axial play.

NOTE ——

With new parts the clearance should be between 0.16 and 0.26 mm (.0063 and .0102 in.). Excessive clearance can be corrected by installing new bearings, a new crankshaft, a new connecting rod, or all three—depending on the extent to which any of these parts is worn.

36. Install the oil pump and the oil pan as described in **6.1 Removing, Checking, and Installing Oil Pump.** Install the cylinder head as described in **5.3 Removing and Installing Cylinder Head and Manifolds.** Then install the engine, if previously removed, as described in **7. Removing and Installing Engine.**

11. CRANKSHAFT AND CAMSHAFT

The crankshaft's front and rear oil seals can be replaced with the engine installed. However, you can replace the rear oil seal only after you have removed the transmission. See **CLUTCH AND MANUAL TRANSMISSION** or **AUTOMATIC TRANSMISSION.** You must remove the engine if you intend to remove the crankshaft from the engine block.

The timing sprockets, the timing chain, and the camshaft can be removed and installed with the engine in the car. The camshaft bearings cannot be replaced with the engine installed.

11.1 Replacing Crankshaft Oil Seals

The crankshaft's front oil seal can be replaced with the engine in the car. However, the seal can also be replaced with the front oil seal carrier removed during more extensive disassembly of the engine.

To replace crankshaft front oil seal:

1. Remove the radiator as described in **4.3 Removing and Installing Radiator.**

   WARNING —
   Never remove the radiator cap or drain the coolant while the engine is hot. Doing this could warp the engine block or the cylinder head, or you could burn yourself.

2. Remove the V-belt(s). See **4.4 Removing and Installing Water Pump.**
3. Using a wrench, as shown in Fig. 11-1, remove the bolt that is in the center of the crankshaft pulley.
4. Using a puller as shown in Fig. 11-2, remove the pulley from the crankshaft.

   CAUTION —
   Use an adaptor plug in the center of the crankshaft so that the puller will not damage the crankshaft threads.

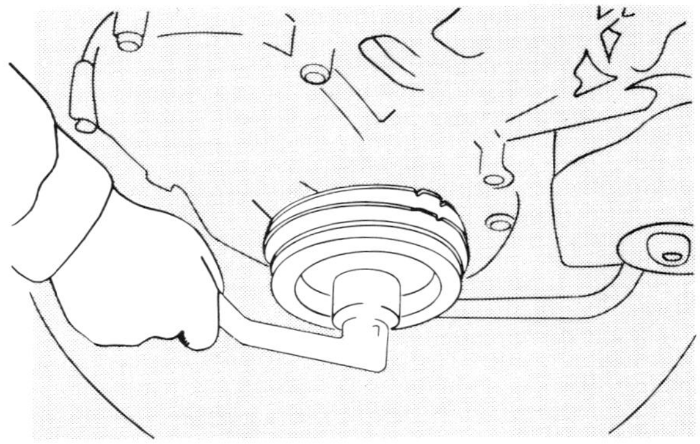

Fig. 11-1. Bolt being removed from center of crankshaft pulley.

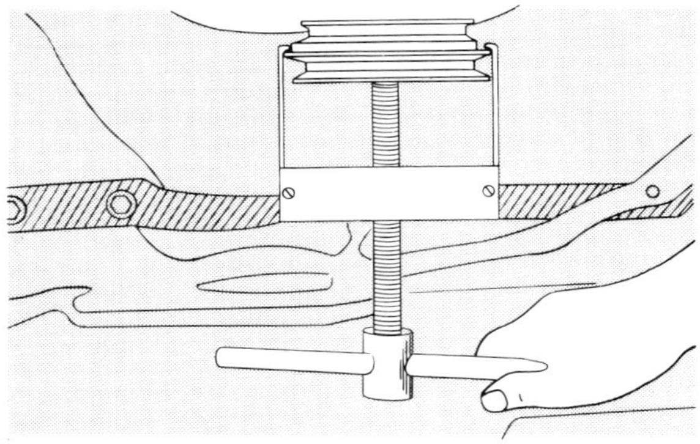

Fig. 11-2. Crankshaft pulley being removed. Use a puller that is suitable to the kind of pulley on the car.

5. Using a tool such as the one shown in Fig. 11-3, pull the old oil seal out of the timing cover.

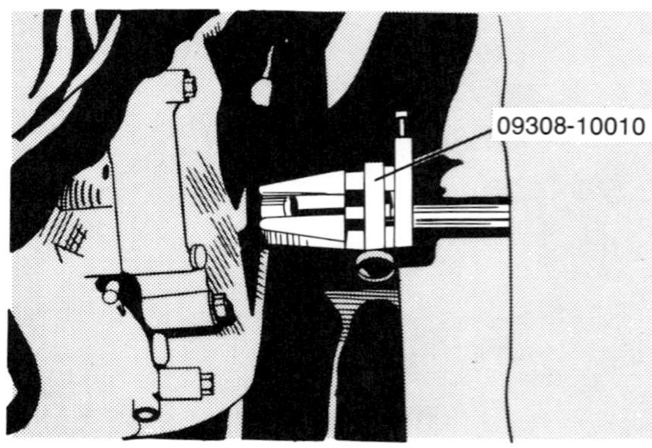

Fig. 11-3. Front oil seal being removed. If you pry out the seal instead of using the tool shown, be careful not to scratch or deform the light alloy timing cover or—especially—the polished seal contact area of the crankshaft.

6. Using solvent and a wooden scraper to avoid damage to the aluminum, thoroughly clean the seal

recess. Then drive in a new seal with the seal's closed surface outermost, as indicated in Fig. 11-4.

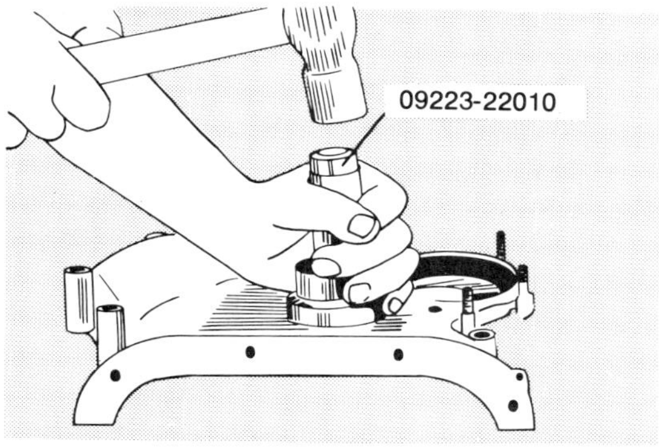

Fig. 11-4. Oil seal being driven into recess. Timing cover is shown removed in this illustration.

7. Reinstall the V-belt(s) to the correct tension, as described in **4.4 Removing and Installing Water Pump.** Reinstall the radiator as described in **4.3 Removing and Installing Radiator.** Then refill the radiator and the engine with coolant.

To replace crankshaft rear oil seal:

1. Remove the transmission as described in either **CLUTCH AND MANUAL TRANSMISSION** or in **AUTOMATIC TRANSMISSION.**
2. Remove the flywheel as described in **9.1 Removing, Checking, and Installing Flywheel** or remove the drive plate as described in **8.1 Removing and Installing Drive Plate.**
3. Remove the large intermediate plate that is between the engine and the transmission.
4. Using an awl, punch two holes in the crankshaft rear oil seal. The holes should be 180° apart. Then install sheet metal screws in the holes as shown in Fig. 11-5.

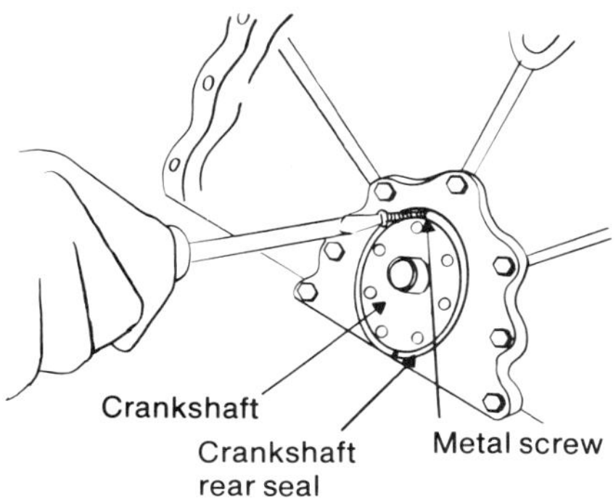

Fig. 11-5. Sheet metal screw being installed in crankshaft rear oil seal.

5. Use a large screwdriver to pry against one of the screw heads, or pull on it with a claw hammer, thereby partially extracting the seal from its recess. For a fulcrum point, place a small block of wood between the screwdriver or the hammer and the engine block. With the seal pried loose, grasp the two sheet metal screws with two pairs of pliers and pull the seal from its recess.

> ***CAUTION —***
> *Be careful not to scratch the seal contact area of the crankshaft. Doing this will cause the new seal to wear rapidly and produce an oil leak.*

6. Clean any old sealer or other debris from the seal recess. If the seal has been leaking, carefully inspect the crankshaft. If the crankshaft is deeply grooved in the area that contacts the seal, replace the crankshaft.
7. Lightly lubricate the seal lip and the crankshaft with multipurpose grease so that the seal will slip easily over the crankshaft. Then hand-start the new oil seal into the seal recess with the closed side of the seal outermost.
8. Using a tool such as the one shown in Fig. 11-6, drive the seal fully into the recess.

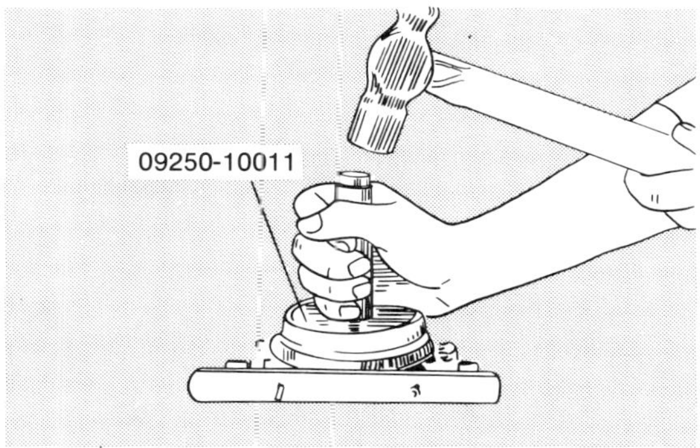

Fig. 11-6. Oil seal being driven into crankshaft rear oil seal carrier. Carrier is shown removed in this illustration.

9. Install the flywheel or the drive plate, then install the transmission.

5

11.2 Removing, Checking, and Installing Crankshaft and Main Bearings

Fig. 11-7 illustrates the removal of the crankshaft, the crankshaft bearings (main bearings), the camshaft, and the camshaft bearings. In removing the crankshaft, both crankshaft oil seal carriers must be removed from the engine block.

Though the main bearing shells are identical, you must always reinstall used bearing shells in their original locations. Similarly, the main bearing caps must always be reinstalled on their original bearing saddles.

To remove, check, and install:

1. Remove the engine. Remove the pistons and connecting rods as described in **10.1 Removing, Checking, and Installing Pistons, Piston Rings, Connecting Rods, and Connecting Rod Bearings.**
2. Remove the flywheel and clutch as described in **9.1 Removing, Checking, and Installing Flywheel** or remove the drive plate as described in **8.1 Removing and Installing Drive Plate.** Then remove the rear oil seal carrier.
3. Remove the bolt that is in the front end of the crankshaft. Then, using a puller that is suitable to the kind of pulley on the engine, remove the pulley from the crankshaft.

   CAUTION ——
   Use an adaptor plug in the center of the crankshaft so that the puller will not damage the crankshaft threads.

4. Remove the timing cover.
5. Remove the camshaft drive sprockets and timing chain as a unit. See **11.3 Removing, Checking, and Installing Camshaft, Camshaft Drive, and Camshaft Bearings.**

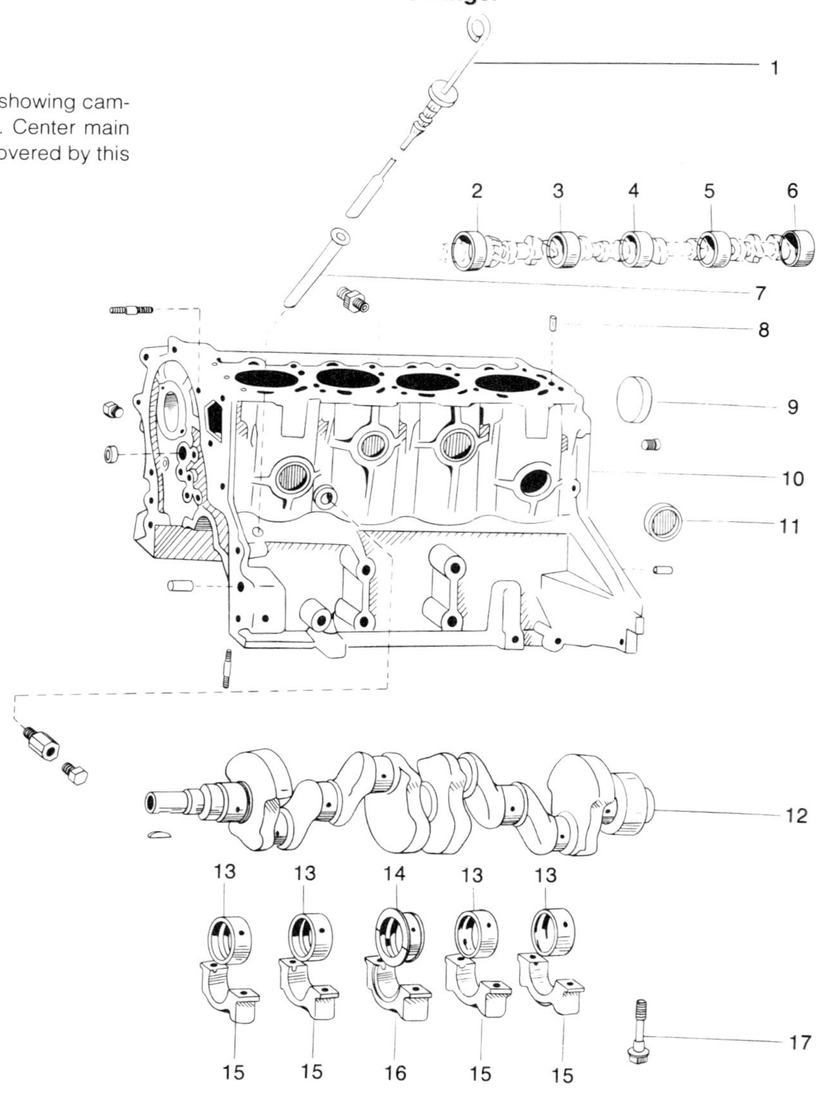

Fig. 11-7. Exploded view of engine block, showing camshaft, crankshaft, and bearings. Center main bearing is not flanged on cars covered by this Manual.

1. Engine oil dipstick assembly
2. Camshaft bearing No. 1
3. Camshaft bearing No. 2
4. Camshaft bearing No. 3
5. Camshaft bearing No. 4
6. Camshaft bearing No. 5
7. Dipstick guide tube
8. Cylinder head alignment pin (2)
9. Camshaft bore core plug
10. Engine block
11. Water jacket core plug
12. Crankshaft
13. Crankshaft bearing Nos. 1, 2, 4, 5
14. Crankshaft bearing No. 3 (cars covered by this Manual have thrust washers instead of bearing shells with integral flanges)
15. Main bearing cap Nos. 1, 2, 4, 5
16. Main bearing cap No. 3
17. Main bearing cap bolt (10)

6. With the engine block inverted on an engine repair stand or clamped upside down on a workbench, remove the bolts from the main bearing caps, remove the caps and bearings, then lift out the crankshaft.

NOTE ——
The main bearing caps are factory-numbered. If you intend to reuse the bearings, mark the bearing numbers on the backs of the bearing shells as you remove them from the caps and the main bearing saddles.

7. Using a micrometer, measure the crankshaft's main bearing journals and crankpins as shown in Fig. 11-8. Then compare the measurements with the dimensions given in **Table m.** So that you can be certain the journals and crankpins are not worn to a taper, make duplicate measurements at opposite ends of each crankpin or journal. To determine out-of-round, make a second pair of measurements at a point 90° from the initial measurements.

NOTE ——
If the bearing surfaces are round or scored, tapered, exceed the limit for maximum out-of-round, or have worn to such a degree that the connecting rod or the bearing clearances exceed the wear limit even with new bearings, the crankshaft must be either replaced or reconditioned. A specialty shop can recondition your worn crankshaft to one of the undersizes listed in **Table m.**

8. To check the crankshaft for bending and runout, install the crankshaft between centers as shown in Fig. 11-9. Mount a dial indicator so that its gauge pin is against the center main bearing journal. Then rotate the crankshaft once and observe the runout range shown by the dial indicator. If runout exceeds 0.06 mm (.0024 in.), which could indicate a bend of 0.03 mm (.0012 in.) or more, either replace the crankshaft or have it straightened by a specialty shop.

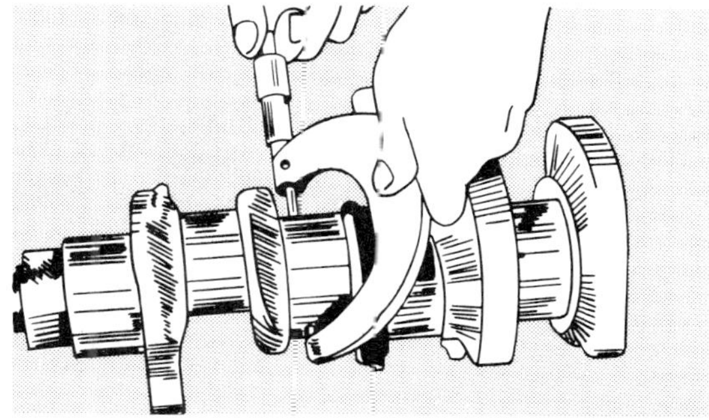

Fig. 11-8. Crankshaft journal diameter being checked with micrometer.

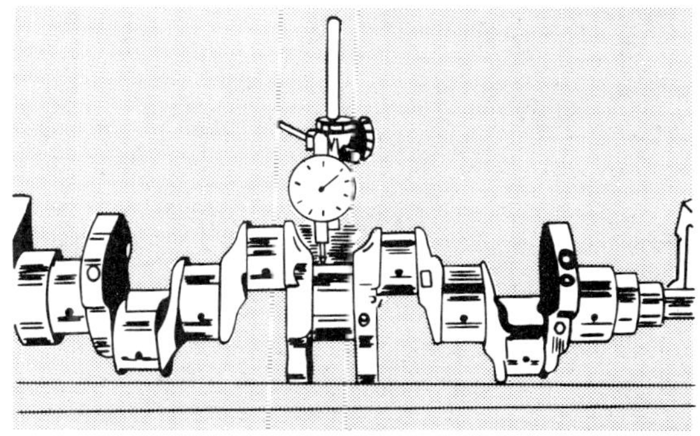

Fig. 11-9. Crankshaft being checked for runout or bending.

9. Using the original bearings, original-size replacement bearings, or undersize main bearings—depending on the condition of the crankshaft as determined in step 7—install the upper main bearing shells (with oil holes) in the bearing saddles of the engine block. Make certain that the bearing saddles are clean and that the anti-rotation tabs engage the notches in the saddles.

10. Place the crankshaft in the engine block. Install the lower main bearing shells in the bearing caps.

11. Cut pieces of Plastigage® to match the lengths of the main bearing journals. Place the pieces of

5

Table m. Crankshaft Journal and Crankpin Sizes

Sizes	Crankshaft main bearing journal: diameter in mm (in.)	Crankshaft main bearing journal: maximum out-of-round or taper in mm (in.)	Crankshaft crankpin: diameter in mm (in.)	Crankshaft crankpin: maximum out-of-round or taper in mm (in.)
Original	57.976 to 58.000 (2.2825 to 2.2835)	0.01 (.0004)	47.976 to 48.000 (1.8888 to 1.8898)	0.01 (.0004)
Undersize I 0.25 mm (.010 in.)	57.74 to 57.75 (2.2732 to 2.2736)	0.01 (.0004)	47.74 to 47.75 (1.8795 to 1.8799)	0.01 (.0004)
Undersize II 0.50 mm (.020 in.)	57.49 to 57.50 (2.2634 to 2.2638)	0.01 (.0004)	47.49 to 47.50 (1.8697 to 1.8701)	0.01 (.0004)
Undersize III 0.75 mm (.030 in.)	57.24 to 57.25 (2.2535 to 2.2539)	0.01 (.0004)	47.24 to 47.25 (1.8598 to 1.8602)	0.01 (.0004)

Plastigage on the journals, being careful to avoid the oil holes in the crankshaft.

12. One at a time, install each main bearing cap and torque the bolts to about 25 Nm (or about 20 ft. lb.), then remove the bearing cap.

NOTE ——
The torque given is for checking purposes only and is not the final torque. Torquing the nuts will compress and flatten the Plastigage, which you will measure to determine the main bearing clearance. Do not turn the crankshaft as you compress the Plastigage. Doing this will spread the Plastigage and cause inaccurate measurement.

13. To determine the bearing clearance, compare the flattened Plastigage to the scale that is printed on the edge of the Plastigage package. Read the clearance printed adjacent to the scale band that has the same width as the flattened Plastigage strip (Fig. 11-10).

NOTE ——
Used bearings must be installed in their original positions in the engine. New bearings must be installed so that their anti-rotation tabs engage the notches in the bearing saddles and caps. If the clearance is at or near the wear limit given in the illustration, even with new bearings, you should either replace the crankshaft or have it reconditioned by a specialty shop to accept one of the standard undersize bearing ranges given earlier in **Table m.**

CAUTION ——
Use solvent to remove the flattened Plastigage. Scraping off the Plastigage could damage the main bearings.

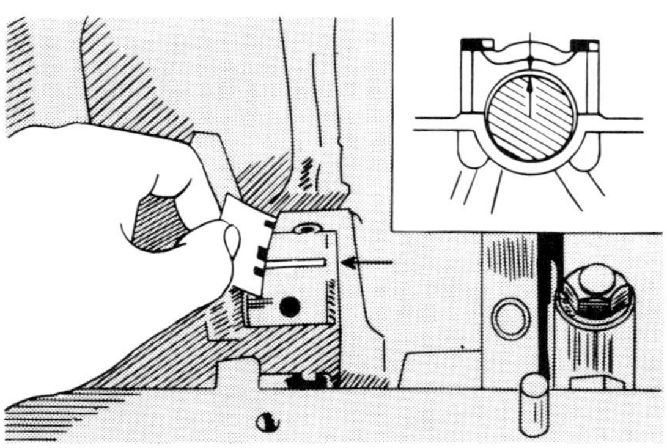

Clearance: 0.024 to 0.048 mm (.0009 to .0019 in.)
Wear limit: 0.08 mm (.0031 in.)

Fig. 11-10. Flattened Plastigage being measured to determine main bearing clearance. Insert shows correct position for Plastigage (arrow).

14. If the bearing clearance is correct, lightly coat the main bearing shells and journals with assembly lubricant or a thin coating of multipurpose grease.

CAUTION ——
Modern thin-wall bearings of the kind used in Toyota engines (Fig. 11-11) are made up of several very thin layers and depend on direct contact with a perfectly round bearing bore to keep clearances accurate. These bearings must never be adjusted by using shims or by scraping, nor should they be ground down with sandpaper. Always use Plastigage® to determine whether clearances are correct.

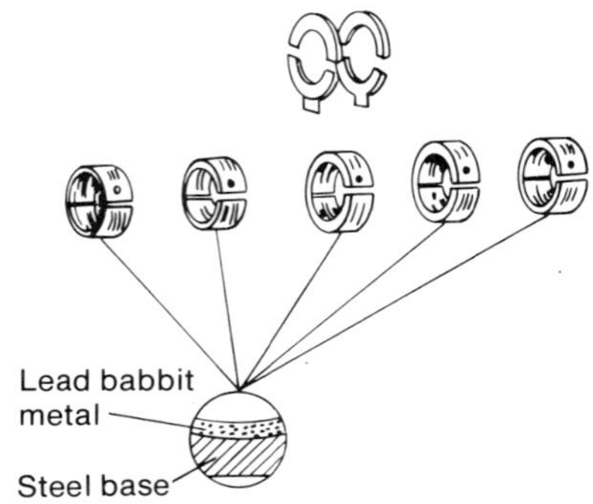

Fig. 11-11. Detail of main bearing construction. Notice also the two-piece thrust washers that are used to control crankshaft axial play. These are used in place of the flanged center main bearings found in some early engines of the kind used in cars covered by this Manual.

15. Install the center (No. 3) main bearing together with the crescent-shaped thrust washers shown previously in Fig. 11-11. Use the standard-size thrust washers and torque the bolts for the main bearing cap to about 25 Nm (or about 20 ft. lb.).

NOTE ——
The torque given is for checking purposes only and is not the final torque. The oil grooves in the thrust washers should be toward the thrust surfaces on the crankshaft and the tabs on the lower halves of the thrust washers should engage the notches in the center main bearing cap.

16. Push the crankshaft as far as it will go toward the rear of the engine. Then, using feeler gauges of various thicknesses, measure the axial play clearance between the thrust surface of the crankshaft's center journal and the rear thrust washer. See Fig. 11-12.

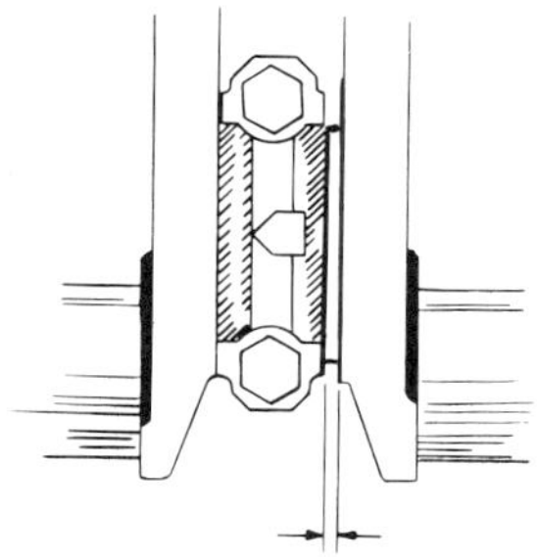

Fig. 11-12. Crankshaft axial play being measured (dimension indicated between arrows).

17. With new standard-size thrust washers, the axial play should be between 0.07 and 0.18 mm (.003 and .007 in.). If the clearance exceeds the 0.30-mm (.012-in.) wear limit, select oversize thrust washers from **Table n** that will bring the crankshaft axial play within the prescribed range.

Table n. Crankshaft Thrust Washer Dimensions

Size	Thickness of individual washers mm (in.)
Standard	2.440 to 2.490 (.0961 to .0980)
0.125 mm (.005 in.) oversize	2.503 to 2.553 (.0985 to .1005)
0.250 mm (.010 in.) oversize	2.565 to 2.615 (.1010 to .1030)

18. Remove the center main bearing cap and apply assembly lubricant or a thin coating of multipurpose grease to the thrust washers. Then loosely install all five main bearings and caps, making sure that the arrows on the caps point toward the front of the engine and that each numbered cap is in its correct location.

19. Following the sequence given in Fig. 11-13, torque the bolts for the main bearing caps to about 25 Nm (or about 20 ft. lb.). Go over the sequence a second time, torquing the bolts to about 55 Nm (or about 40 ft. lb.), then a third time to bring the bolts up to their final torque of 75 to 85 Nm (55 to 63 ft. lb.).

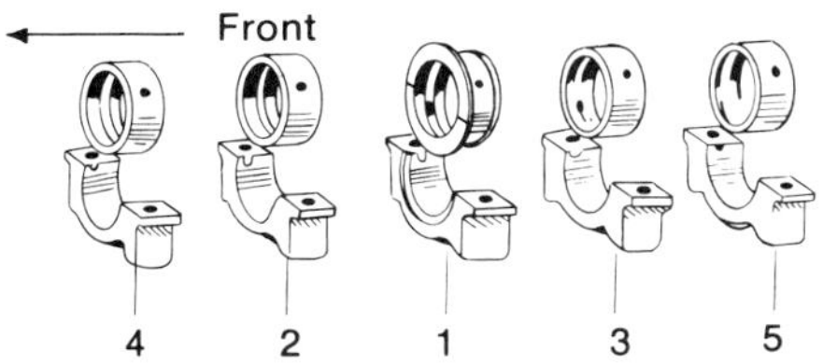

Fig. 11-13. Sequence in which main bearings should be torqued.

20. Install the camshaft drive sprockets and timing chain with careful reference to the instructions given in **11.3 Removing, Checking, and Installing Camshaft, Camshaft Drive, and Camshaft Bearings.**

21. Using new gaskets, install the timing cover and the crankshaft rear oil seal carrier, torquing the bolts to 12 to 15 Nm (9 to 11 ft. lb.).

22. Install the pistons and connecting rods as described in **10.1 Removing, Checking and Installing Pistons, Piston Rings, Connecting Rods, and Connecting Rod Bearings**. Install the flywheel and clutch as described in **9.1 Removing, Checking, and Installing Flywheel** or install the drive plate as described in **8.1 Removing and Installing Drive Plate.**

23. Install the crankshaft pulley. Torque the bolt to 40 to 55 Nm (30 to 41 ft. lb.). Then install the engine.

5

11.3 Removing, Checking, and Installing Camshaft, Camshaft Drive, and Camshaft Bearings

Fig. 11-14 illustrates the removal of the camshaft drive and the camshaft. These components can be removed and installed with the engine in the car if you first remove the cylinder head. The camshaft bearings can be inspected and replaced only with the engine removed.

To remove camshaft drive and camshaft:

1. Remove the radiator as described in **4.3 Removing and Installing Radiator.**

   WARNING —
   Never remove the radiator cap or drain the coolant while the engine is hot. Doing this could warp the engine block or the cylinder head, or you could burn yourself.

2. If you intend to inspect or replace the camshaft bearings, remove the engine as described in **7. Removing and Installing Engine.** If you intend to remove the camshaft with the engine installed, remove the grille and the hood lock brace so that the camshaft can be pulled out through the front of the body. See **BODY AND INTERIOR.**

3. Remove the water pump as described in **4.4 Removing and Installing Water Pump.**

4. Using a wrench, as shown in Fig. 11-15, remove the bolt that is in the center of the crankshaft pulley.

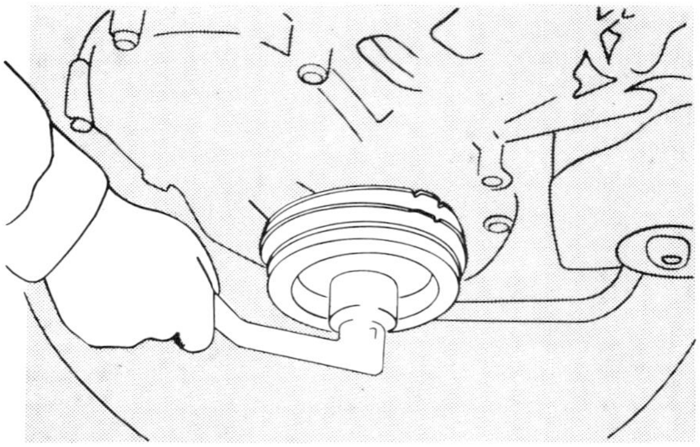

Fig. 11-15. Bolt being removed from center of crankshaft pulley.

5. Using a puller, as shown in Fig. 11-16, remove the pulley from the crankshaft.

Fig. 11-14. Exploded view of camshaft and camshaft drive, including timing cover.

1. Timing cover
2. Timing cover gasket
3. Bolt
4. Retaining washer
5. Bolt
6. Camshaft thrust plate
7. Camshaft
8. Bolt
9. Crankshaft pulley
10. Crankshaft front oil seal
11. Woodruff key
12. Camshaft sprocket
13. Woodruff key
14. Crankshaft sprocket
15. Timing chain
16. Timing chain tensioner assembly
17. Timing chain damper

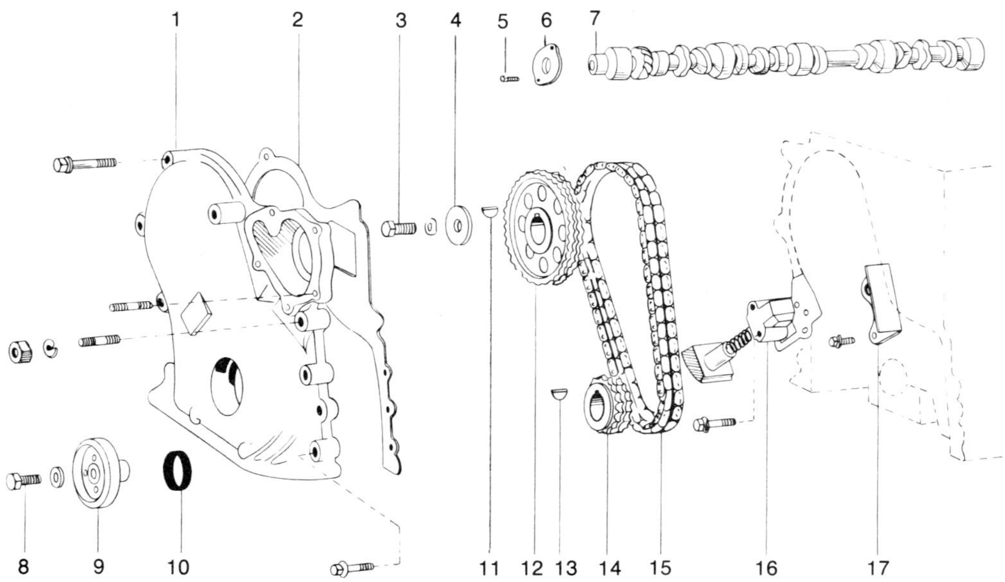

CAUTION ——
Use an adaptor plug in the center of the crankshaft so that the puller will not damage the crankshaft threads.

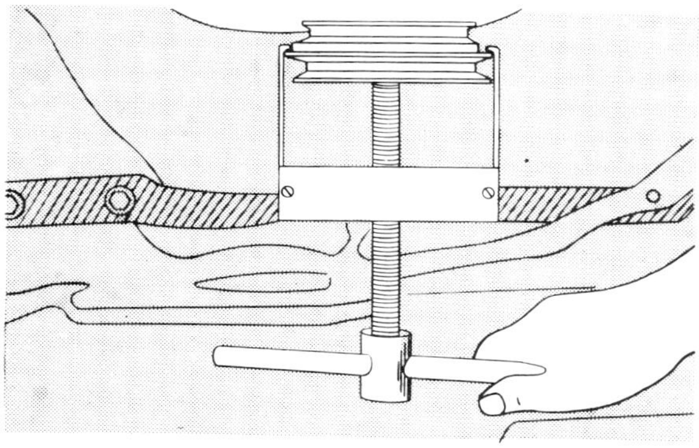

Fig. 11-16. Crankshaft pulley being removed. Use a puller that is suitable to the kind of pulley on the car.

6. Remove the front four bolts that hold the oil pan to the timing cover. Fully loosen the remaining oil pan bolts, then pull the pan down at the front. See **6.1 Removing, Checking, and Installing Oil Pump.**

CAUTION ——
The oil pan gasket is installed with sealer on both of its surfaces, so carefully insert a thin knife blade to separate the pan gasket from the timing cover and the engine block.

7. Remove the bolts that hold the timing cover to the front of the engine block. Then, by tapping the timing cover with a rubber or plastic mallet, drive it forward and off the alignment pins.

NOTE ——
The bolts that hold the timing cover to the engine block also support the bracket for the V-belt idler pulley on cars with air conditioning or the bracket for the air injection pump on cars without air conditioning. Remove the idler pulley or suspend the dismounted air pump from the car body with a stiff wire hook.

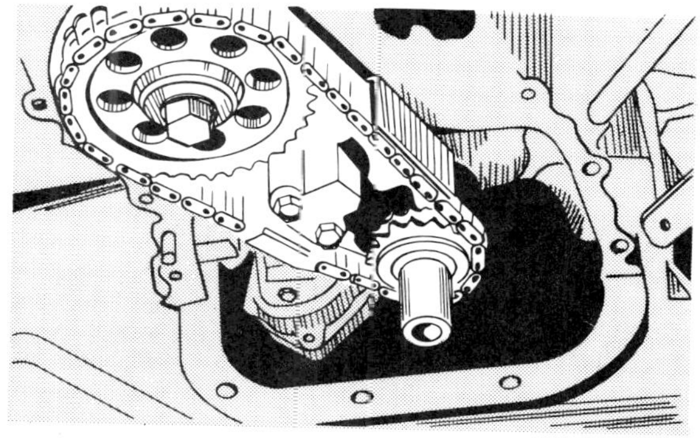

Fig. 11-17. Camshaft drive with timing cover removed.

8. Attach a spring scale to the slipper pad of the timing chain tensioner plunger. With the plunger pulled out of its cylinder under a tension of 10 kg (22 lb.), measure the gap indicated in Fig. 11-18. If the gap is 13.50 mm (.532 in.) or more, carefully inspect the tensioner assembly, the chain, the sprockets, and the damper prior to reinstallation and replace any component that is worn or damaged.

5

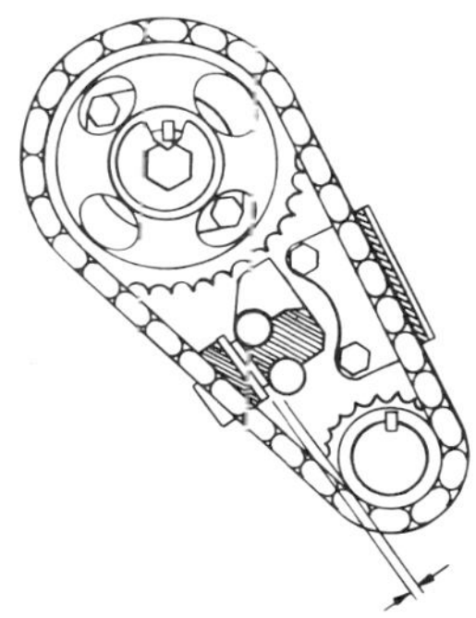

Fig. 11-18. Gap (arrows) between timing chain tensioner plunger and timing chain tensioner cylinder body being measured.

9. Remove the timing chain tensioner assembly and its backing plate. Remove the timing chain damper.
10. Remove the bolt that is in the center of the camshaft together with the spring washer and the retaining washer. Then remove the timing chain and sprockets as a unit, being careful that the Woodruff keys do not fall into the oil pan.
11. Remove the cylinder head as described in **5.3 Removing and Installing Cylinder Head and Manifolds.**

12. Remove the ignition distributor as described in **3.2 Distributor.** Remove the fuel pump as described in **FUEL AND EXHAUST SYSTEMS.**
13. Using a magnetic tool or expanding-tip pliers, carefully lift out each cam follower, wipe it dry, and then number it with a waterproof felt-tip marker so that the lifter can later be reinstalled in its original location.
14. If the engine is installed in the car, remove the gearshift lever on cars with manual transmissions or disconnect the selector linkage from the manual valve lever on cars with automatic transmissions. See **CLUTCH AND MANUAL TRANSMISSION** or **AUTOMATIC TRANSMISSION.** With the transmission lightly supported by a jack, unbolt the transmission rear mount crossmember from the car body. Then gradually lower the rear of the engine/transmission assembly as far as necessary for camshaft removal.

NOTE ——
On some car models you may also have to unbolt the exhaust system or detach the exhaust pipe from its supports. Also disconnect the speedometer cable if it is likely to be placed under any strain by lowering the rear of the engine/transmission assembly.

15. Remove the camshaft thrust plate. Then, being very careful not to scratch the camshaft bearings with the cam lobes, withdraw the camshaft from the engine block as shown in Fig. 11-19.

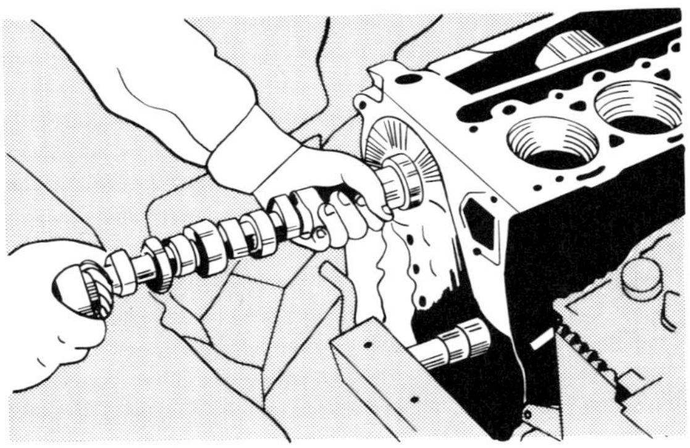

Fig. 11-19. Camshaft being withdrawn from front of engine block.

To inspect camshaft drive and camshaft:

1. Remove the plunger from the cylinder body of the timing chain tensioner assembly, as indicated in Fig. 11-20.
2. Determine the minimum thickness of the plunger's slipper pad as shown in Fig. 11-21. If the remaining thickness is less than 12.5 mm (.492 in.), or if the plunger is scored or visibly worn, replace the plunger.

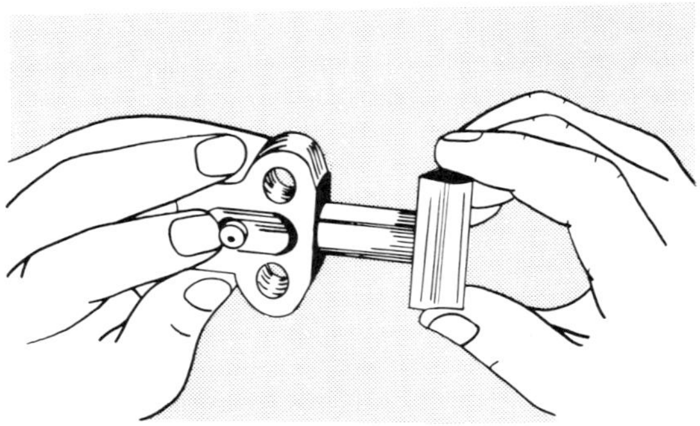

Fig. 11-20. Plunger being removed from cylinder body of timing chain tensioner assembly.

NOTE ——
It is normal for the slipper pad to become grooved owing to contact with the chain links. However, you should replace the plunger if there is wear other than grooves, when the grooves have become so deep that the rollers are striking the pad, or when the remaining thickness measured at the grooves is less than 12.5 mm (.492 in.). Under no circumstances should you dress the surface of the pad to restore a smooth surface as doing this will accelerate pad wear.

3. Lightly oil the plunger, then temporarily install it in the cylinder body without the spring. Cover the two oil holes in the cylinder body with your fingertips. Pull the plunger out and release it. If sufficient vacuum is not generated to pull the plunger back into the cylinder body, the tensioner assembly is worn out and should be replaced.
4. Measure the timing chain damper as shown in Fig. 11-21. Replace the damper if its minimum remaining thickness is less than 5.00 mm (.197 in.), or if it is so grooved that the rollers are striking the pad.

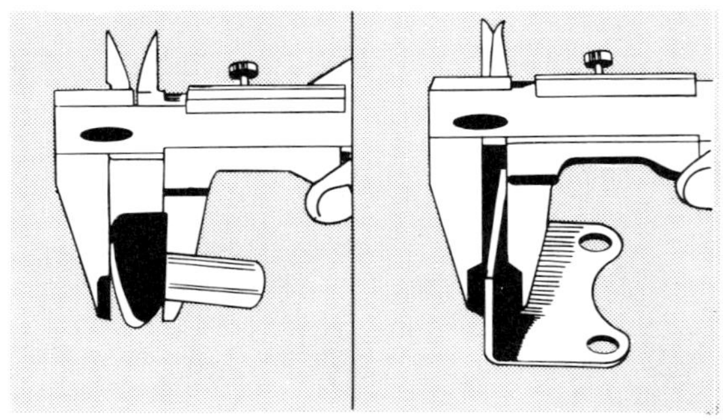

Fig. 11-21. Minimum remaining thickness of tensioner plunger slipper pad (left) and timing chain damper pad (right) being measured with vernier caliper.

5. Inspect the timing chain and replace it if it is

cracked, damaged, visibly worn—or if, under a tension of 5 kg (11 lb.), its length is greater than 291.40 mm (11.472 in.). See Fig. 11-22.

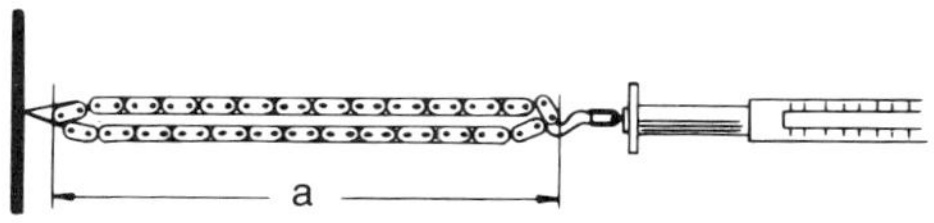

Fig. 11-22. Timing chain being checked for stretching. With spring scale (at right) indicating 5 kg (11 lb.), dimension **a** (measured to surfaces of rollers) should not exceed 291.40 mm (11.472 in.).

6. Wrap an unworn timing chain around the crankshaft sprocket, then measure the outside diameter at the chain rollers as indicated in Fig. 11-23. Replace the sprocket if the diameter is 59.40 mm (2.339 in.) or less.

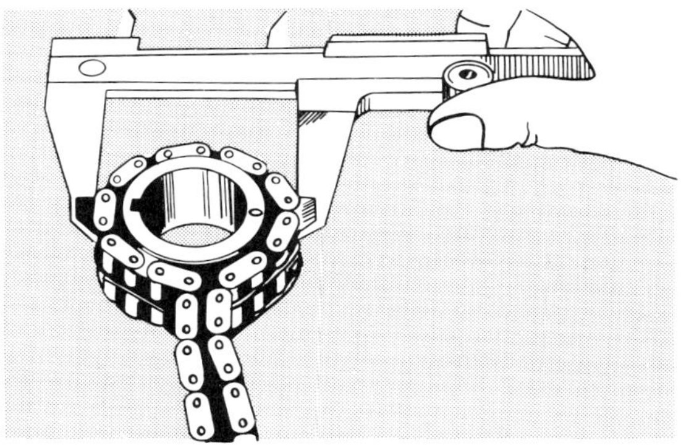

Fig. 11-23. Crankshaft sprocket wear being measured with timing chain seated on sprocket.

7. Wrap an unworn timing chain around the camshaft sprocket, then measure the outside diameter at the chain rollers as indicated in Fig. 11-24. Replace the sprocket if the diameter is 113.80 mm (4.480 in.) or less.

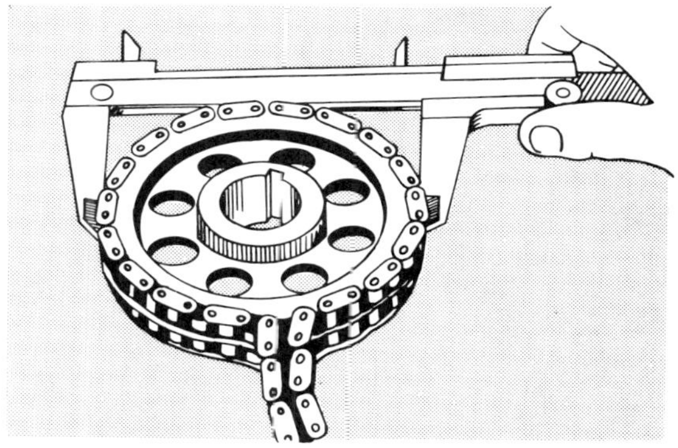

Fig. 11-24. Camshaft sprocket wear being measured with timing chain seated on sprocket.

8. Using a micrometer or a vernier caliper, measure the height and the width of each cam lobe, as indicated in Fig. 11-25. Replace the camshaft if the heights are not uniformly within the range of dimensions given in the illustration, or if the widths are not uniform owing to wear.

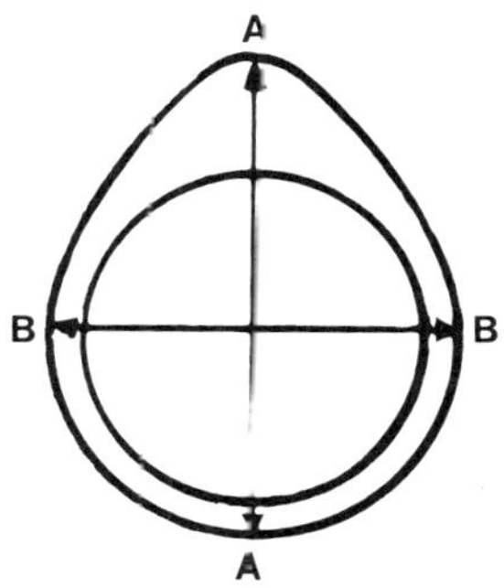

Cam lobe height

Intake (all models):	38.36 to 38.46 mm (1.5102 to 1.5142 in.)
Exhaust (1975 only):	38.29 to 38.39 mm (1.5075 to 1.5114 in.)
(1976 and later):	38.25 to 38.35 mm (1.5059 to 1.5098 in.)

Fig. 11-25. Cam lobe height (dimension **A**) and width (dimension **B**). Difference between these two dimensions is cam lift.

9. Using a micrometer or a vernier caliper, measure the diameters of all five camshaft journals and compare the readings to the dimensions given in **Table o.** Replace or recondition worn camshafts.

NOTE —

Measure each journal at two points 90° apart first at one end and then at the other in order to detect taper and out-of-round, neither of which should exceed 0.02 mm (.0008 in.). If the journals are tapered, out-of-round, or worn to less than the minimum diameter given for each journal, either replace the camshaft or have the journals reground to one of the undersizes given in the table. Then install 0.125-mm (.005-in.) or 0.250-mm (.010-in.) undersize bearings in the engine block as described later in the procedure for inspecting and replacing camshaft bearings.

10. Install the camshaft between centers, then position the gauge pin of a dial indicator against the center journal as shown in Fig. 11-26. Rotate the camshaft once. If the dial indicator shows a total runout of 0.06 mm (.0024 in.) or more (which equals a bend of 0.03 mm (.0012 in.) or more), either replace the camshaft or have it straightened by a specialty shop.

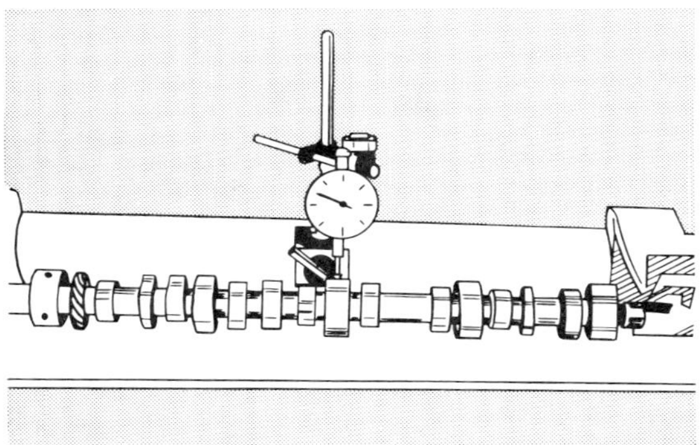

Fig. 11-26. Camshaft being checked for bending.

11. Install the camshaft thrust plate, the Woodruff key, and the camshaft sprocket on the front of the camshaft. With a tool engaged in the holes of the sprocket to keep it from turning, install the retaining washer, the spring washer, and the bolt. Torque the bolt to 70 to 105 Nm (52 to 77 ft. lb.).

12. Using feeler gauges of various thicknesses, determine the clearance between the thrust plate and the No. 1 camshaft journal as shown in Fig. 11-27. If the clearance exceeds the wear limit given in the illustration, replace the camshaft, the thrust plate, or both—depending on the extent to which each component is worn.

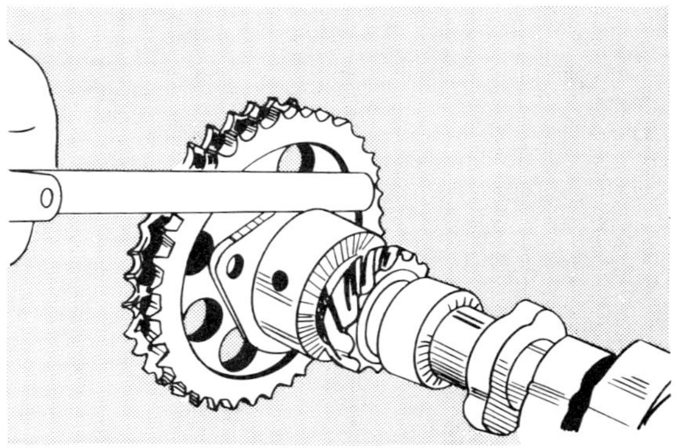

Fig. 11-27. Feeler gauge being used to measure clearance between camshaft thrust plate and No. 1 camshaft journal.

To install camshaft and camshaft drive:

1. Remove the camshaft sprocket if previously installed. Lubricate the camshaft journals, the cam lobes, the oil pump/distributor drivegear, and the fuel pump eccentric with assembly lubricant or with a thin coating of multipurpose grease. Then, being careful not to scratch the bearings, insert the camshaft into the engine block as shown in Fig. 11-28.

Table o. Camshaft Journal Standard and Undersize Finishing Dimensions

Bearing size	Outside diameter in mm (in.)				
	No. 1	No. 2	No. 3	No. 4	No. 5
Standard	46.459 to 46.475 (1.8291 to 1.8297)	46.209 to 46.225 (1.8192 to 1.8199)	45.959 to 45.975 (1.8094 to 1.8100)	45.709 to 45.725 (1.7996 to 1.8002)	45.459 to 45.475 (1.7897 to 1.7904)
0.125-mm (.005-in.) undersize	46.340 to 46.350 (1.8244 to 1.8248)	46.090 to 46.100 (1.8146 to 1.8150)	45.840 to 45.850 (1.8047 to 1.8051)	45.590 to 45.600 (1.7949 to 1.7953)	45.340 to 45.350 (1.7850 to 1.7854)
0.250-mm (.010-in.) undersize	46.215 to 46.225 (1.8195 to 1.8199)	45.965 to 46.975 (1.8096 to 1.8494)	45.715 to 45.725 (1.7998 to 1.8002)	45.465 to 45.475 (1.7900 to 1.7904)	45.215 to 45.225 (1.7801 to 1.7805)

NOTE ——

If you are installing a new camshaft, it is advisable to install new cam followers as well. The wear pattern on used cam followers may cause accelerated wear on the new cam lobes. The cam followers should also be replaced if their clearances with the bores in the engine block exceed the wear limit given in **5.3 Removing and Installing Cylinder Head and Manifolds.**

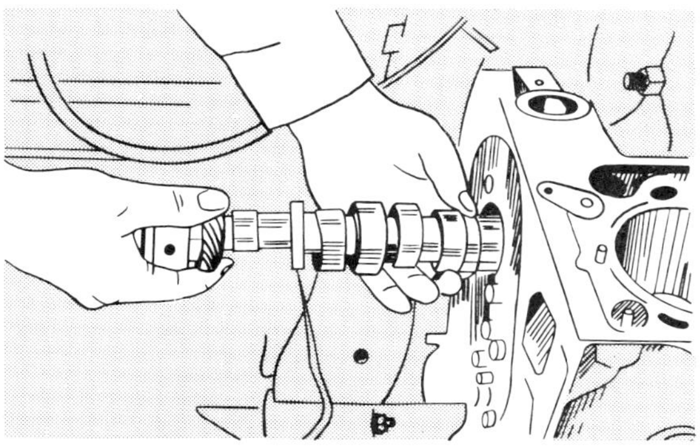

Fig. 11-28. Camshaft being inserted into engine block.

2. Install the camshaft thrust plate so that its timing mark points up, as shown in Fig. 11-29. Torque the bolts to 10 to 15 Nm (7.5 to 11 ft. lb.).
3. Position the camshaft and the crankshaft so that the keyways are pointed up. The camshaft's keyway should be aligned with the timing mark on the thrust plate and the pistons of cylinders Nos. 1 and 4 should be at top dead center. Install the Woodruff keys in the keyways.
4. Assemble the camshaft sprocket, the timing chain, and the crankshaft sprocket so that the timing marks on the chain are aligned with the Toyota marks on the sprockets. See Fig. 11-29. Then install simultaneously the sprockets and the chain on the camshaft and the crankshaft.
5. Install the retaining washer and the spring washer. Then install the bolt in the center of the camshaft, torquing it to 70 to 105 Nm (52 to 77 ft. lb.).
6. Lubricate the timing chain and the sprockets. Install the timing chain damper, torquing its bolts to 10 to 15 Nm (7.5 to 11 ft. lb.).
7. Reassemble the timing chain tensioner assembly and fill it with engine oil. Then install the tensioner assembly and its backing plate, torquing the bolts to 10 to 15 Nm (7.5 to 11 ft. lb.).
8. Replace the crankshaft oil seal in the timing cover as described in **11.1 Replacing Crankshaft Oil Seals.**

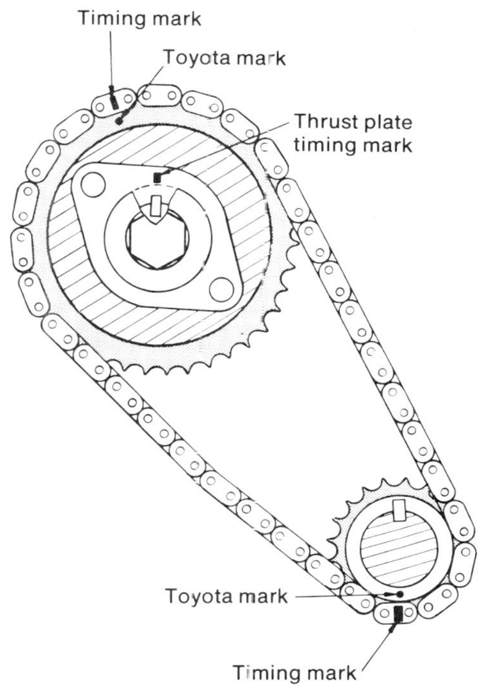

Fig. 11-29. Positions of timing marks and Toyota marks when sprockets and timing chain are correctly installed.

9. Using a new gasket, install the timing cover. Working diagonally, gradually torque the bolts to 12 to 15 Nm (9 to 11 ft. lb.).
10. Apply sealer to the oil pan gasket at the points indicated in Fig. 11-30 and at any place where the gasket was damaged by removal of the timing cover. Then install the oil pan bolts to a torque of 3 to 4 Nm (27 to 35 in. lb.).

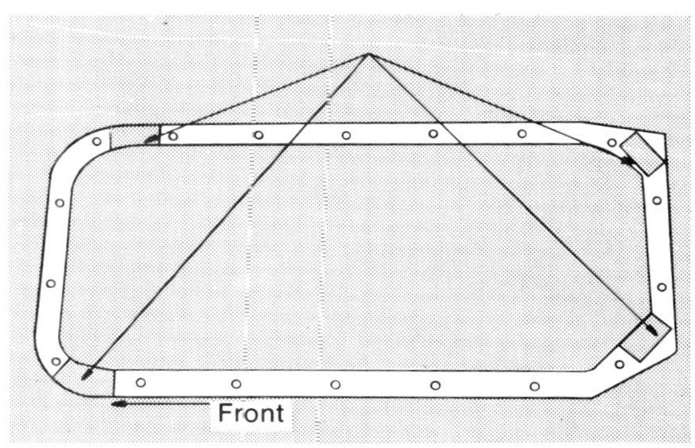

Fig. 11-30. Points where sealer must be applied to oil pan gasket

11. Install the crankshaft pulley. Torque the bolt to 40 to 55 Nm (30 to 41 ft. lb.).

12. Install the water pump and the V-belt(s) as described in **4.4 Removing and Installing Water Pump.**
13. Install the cam followers. Used cam followers must be installed in their original locations. Install the cylinder head as described in **5.3 Removing and Installing Cylinder Head and Manifolds.**
14. Install the ignition distributor as described in **3.2 Distributor.** Install the fuel pump as described in **FUEL AND EXHAUST SYSTEMS.**
15. If previously removed, install the engine as described in **7. Removing and Installing Engine.** Then install the radiator and refill the cooling system as described in **4.3 Removing and Installing Radiator.** If the engine has not been removed, bolt the transmission rear mount crossmember to the car body, then install the gearshift lever on cars with manual transmissions or reconnect the selector linkage to the manual valve on cars with automatic transmissions. Install any removed body parts.

To inspect and replace camshaft bearings:

1. Remove the camshaft drive and the camshaft as previously described—fully removing the oil pan as described in **6.1 Removing, Checking, and Installing Oil Pump.**
2. Visually inspect the camshaft bearings. Replace bearings that are fused, burned, or have their overlays wiped out.
3. Using a telescope gauge (snap gauge) and a micrometer, or other suitable measuring tool, determine the inside diameters of the camshaft bearings. Write down your measurements.
4. Check the camshaft journal diameters as described previously in the procedure for checking the camshaft drive and the camshaft. Subtract the diameter of each journal from the inside diameter of its bearings. With new parts the clearance should be 0.025 to 0.066 mm (.0010 to .0026 in.). If the clearance is 0.10 mm (.004 in.) or more, replace the camshaft bearings.

NOTE ——

If the camshaft journal diameters are worn to less than the minimum diameters given previously in **Table o,** either replace the camshaft or have it reground to accept undersize bearings as described previously in the procedure for inspecting the camshaft drive and the camshaft.

5. To replace the camshaft bearings, first use a long drift inserted through the engine block to drive out the camshaft bore core plug that is in the rear of the engine block.
6. Assemble special tool 09215–25010 in the engine block without components 6, 7, and 9. See Fig. 11-31. Components 4, 5, and 8 should be positioned inside bearings No. 1, No. 2, and No. 5 with their flanges in contact with the rear edges of the bearings. Components 1, 2, and 3 should project from the front of the block.

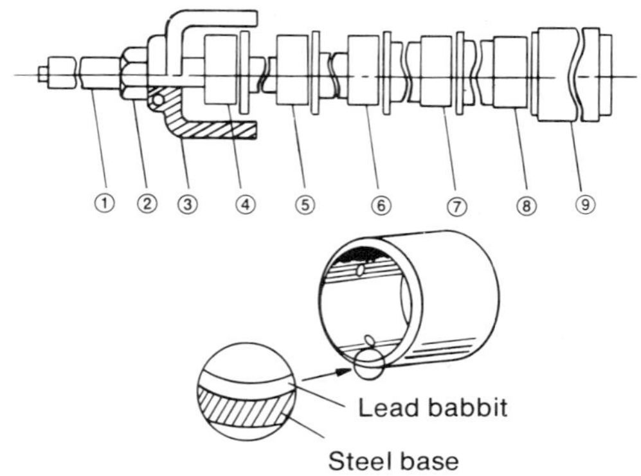

Fig. 11-31. Special tool for pulling camshaft bearings out of engine block and installing new bearings. Inset shows cross-section of camshaft bearing.

7. Using one wrench on the spindle (component 1) to hold it stationary, use a second wrench to tighten the nut (component 2) on the special tool, thereby pulling bearings No. 1, No. 2, and No. 5 out toward the front of the engine block. See Fig. 11-32.

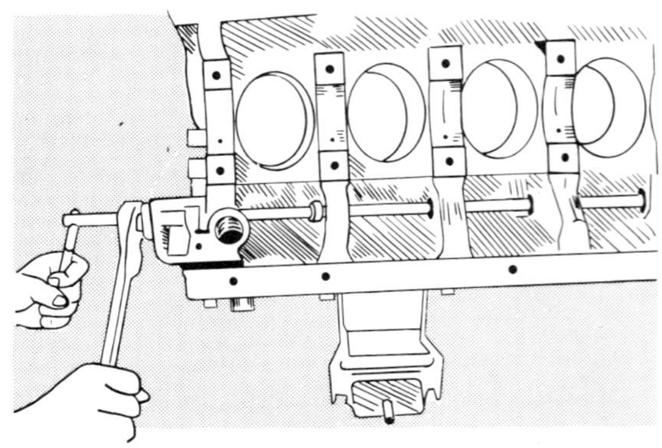

Fig. 11-32. Bearings No. 1, No. 2, and No. 5 being removed.

8. Reassemble special tool components 1, 2, 3, and 6 so that components 1, 2 and 3 project from the rear of the block. See Fig. 11-33. Component 6 should be inside bearing No. 3 with the flange against the front edge of the bearing.
9. Pull bearing No. 3 out of its bore toward the rear. Then detach the spindle (component 1) from component 6. Leave component 6 and bearing No. 3 inside the engine block.

10. By inserting it through the No. 3 bearing bore of the engine block, attach component 5 of the special tool to the spindle (component 2). Insert component 5 in bearing No. 4 with its flange against the bearing's front edge.

11. Using the special tool, pull bearing No. 4 out to the rear. Then repeat the operation, pulling component 6 and bearing No. 3 out through the No. 4 bearing bore of the engine block.

CAUTION —

Once removed, used bearings should not be reinstalled. Removed bearings are likely to be distorted.

12. Install the new bearings one at a time. Component 9, the installation guide, should be in position on the special tool during installation of each bearing. See Fig. 11-33. Components 1, 2, and 3 should be at the front of the engine block and each bearing should be pulled into the block from rear to front in the sequence No. 1, No. 2, No. 3, No. 4, and No. 5.

CAUTION —

Before you begin pulling each bearing into its bore, the oil hole in the bearing must be perfectly aligned with the oil hole in the bearing bore of the engine block. Otherwise the bearing will not be correctly aligned and will fail owing to inadequate lubrication.

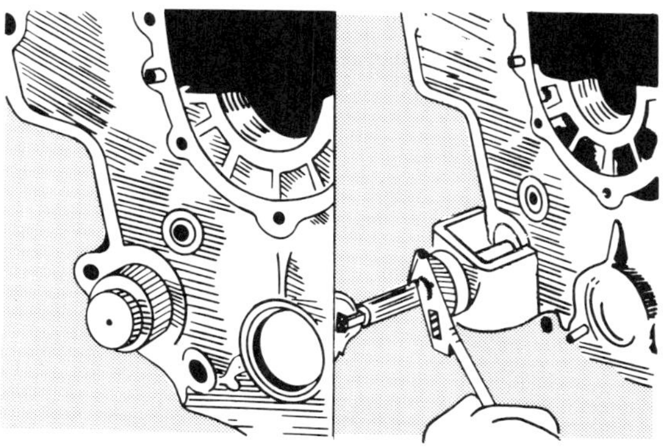

Fig. 11-33. Special tool positions at rear of engine block. At right spindle, nut, and claw project from rear of block for removal of No. 3 and No. 4 bearings. At left, installation guide (component 9) is positioned in core plug bore to ensure correct alignment of spindle with bearing bore axis.

13. Coat the periphery of a new core plug with sealer. Then, using an appropriate driving tool, drive in the new plug—convex side first—until the rim of the plug is just flush with the surface of the engine block. If the plug is driven in further, it may prevent installation of the camshaft.

14. Coat the bearings with assembly lubricant or with a thin coating of multipurpose grease. Then install the camshaft and camshaft drive as described in the preceding procedure.

12. ENGINE TECHNICAL DATA

I. Ignition Coil and Ballast Resistance

Model years	Designation	Specification
1975 through 1977	Coil capacity Coil primary resistance Coil secondary resistance (continuity) Coil insulation resistance Coil insulation resistance (tested with 500-volt megger) Ballast resistor	Reading in coil tester's "Good" range 1.3 to 1.5 ohms 6500 to 10,500 ohms Infinite ohms Above 100 1.3 to 1.7 ohms
1978 and later	Coil primary resistance Coil secondary resistance Coil insulation resistance Resistor wire (ballast)	1.3 to 1.7 ohms (cold) 12,000 to 16,000 ohms (cold) Infinite ohms 1.2 ohms (cold)

II. Spark Plugs and Gap

Brand and designation	Applicable car models
Bosch W175T30	1975 through 1979 USA and Canada
Champion N-10Y	1975 through 1979 USA and Canada
NGK BP5EA NGK BP5ES-L NGK BP5EA-L NGK BP5ES NGK BPR5EA-L NGK BPR5ES	1979 USA only 1975 through 1978 USA, 1975 through 1977 Canada 1977 and 1979 USA, 1977 and 1978 Canada 1978 USA only 1978 and 1979 Canada only 1978 and 1979 Canada only
Nippodenso W16EP Nippodenso W16EX-U Nippodenso W16EPR Nippodenso W16EXR-U Nippodenso W14EX-U Nippodenso W16EPR	1975 through 1978 USA, 1975 through 1977 Canada 1977 through 1979 USA, 1977 Canada 1978 Canada only 1978 and 1979 Canada only 1979 USA only 1979 Canada only
Gap	All models: 0.80 mm (.032 in.)

III. Basic Tune-up Specifications

Designation	Specification
Side deflection of V-belts at correct tension of	
10 kg (22 lb.) .... between water pump pulley and alternator pulley	8 to 12 mm (5/16 to 15/32 in.)
.... between air pump pulley and crankshaft pulley	13 to 18 mm (1/2 to 23/32 in.)
.... between air pump pulley and air conditioner compressor	10 to 14 mm (3/8 to 9/16 in.)
...... between crankshaft pulley and air conditioner compressor	11 to 14 mm (7/16 to 9/16 in.)
Battery specific gravity at 20° C (68°F)	1.250 to 1.270
Engine oil capacity .... with filter change	4.4 liters (4.6 U.S. qt., or 3.9 Imperial qt.)
.... without filter change	3.5 liters (3.7 U.S. qt., or 3.1 Imperial qt.)
Coolant capacity .... manual transmission, including heater	7.8 liters (8.2 U.S. qt., or 6.9 Imperial qt.)
.... automatic transmission, including heater	7.7 liters (8.1 U.S. qt., or 6.8 Imperial qt.)
Spark plug type	Please see Table II
Spark plug gap	0.80 mm (.032 in.)
Secondary cable resistance .... new	16,000 ohms per meter (39⅜ in.)
.... wear limit	25,000 ohms per meter (39⅜ in.)
1975 dual-point distributor dwell .... main point	57°
.... sub-point	50° to 54°
1975 through 1977 single-point distributor dwell	50° to 54°
1978 and later breakerless distributor air gap	0.20 to 0.40 mm (.008 to .016 in.)
1975 dual-point distributor timing .... (at sub-point, engine coild)	22° ±3°BTDC at 850 rpm ±50 rpm
.... (at main point, engine hot)	12° BTDC at 850 rpm ±50 rpm
1975 through 1977 single-point distributor timing	10° BTDC at 850 rpm ±50 rpm
1978 and later breakerless distributor timing .... (except high altitude)	10° BTDC at 850 rpm ±50 rpm
.... (high altitude)	10° BTDC at 700 to 900 rpm, innermost vacuum hose disconnected and plugged
Firing order	1—3—4—2
Valve clearances (hot) .... intake valve	0.20 mm (.008 in.)
.... exhaust valve	0.33 mm (.013 in.)
Compression pressure for 1975 and 1976 engines .... normal	12 bar (171 psi)
.... wear limit	10 bar (142 psi)
Compression pressure for 1977 engine .... normal	10.5 bar (149 psi)
.... wear limit	8.5 bar (121 psi)
Compression pressure for 1978 and later California and high altitude models .... normal	more than 11.5 bar (164 psi)
.... wear limit	8.5 bar (121 psi)
Compression pressure for 1978 and later Federal and Canadian models .... normal	12 bar (171 psi)
.... wear limit	9 bar (128 psi)
Idle speed	850 rpm ±50 rpm
CO content, fast idle speed, throttle positioner speed, and other carburetor adjustments	Please refer to **FUEL AND EXHAUST SYSTEMS** or to the engine's emissions decal

IV. Cooling System

Component	Designation	Specification
Radiator	Fin type	Corrugated
	Radiation quantity (manual transmission)	14,500 kcal/hour
	Radiation quantity (automatic transmission)	17,000 kcal/hour
	Water capacity (manual transmission)	2.1 liters (2.2 U.S. quarts)
	Water capacity (automatic transmission)	2.0 liters (2.1 U.S. quarts)
	Dry weight (manual transmission)	3.8 kg (8.4 lb.)
	Dry weight (automatic transmission)	4.3 kg (9.5 lb.)
	Core dimensions (height × width × thickness)	325 × 418 × 32 mm (12.79 × 16.46 × 1.26 in.)
Radiator cap	Pressure release rating/maximum permissible pressure	0.9 bar (13 psi)
	Minimum permissible release pressure	0.6 bar (8.5 psi)
Thermostat	1975 and 1976 .... Begins opening	80.5° to 83.5°C (177° to 182°F)
	.... Fully open (cylinder travel 8 mm or 5/16 in.)	95°C (203°F)
	1977 and later .... Begins opening	86° to 90°C (187° to 194°F)
	.... Fully open (cylinder travel 8 mm or 5/16 in.)	100°C (212°F)

V. Camshaft and Valve Gear

Designation	Specification
Camshaft journal-to-bearing clearance	New: 0.025 to 0.066 mm (.0010 to .0026 in.) Wear limit: 0.10 mm (.0004 in.)
Camshaft journal diameters—No. 1	46.459 to 46.475 mm (1.8291 to 1.8297 in.)
No. 2	46.209 to 46.225 mm (1.8192 to 1.8199 in.)
No. 3	45.959 to 45.975 mm (1.8094 to 1.8100 in.)
No. 4	45.709 to 45.725 mm (1.7996 to 1.8002 in.)
No. 5	45.459 to 45.475 mm (1.7897 to 1.7904 in.)
Available camshaft bearing undersizes	0.125 mm (.005 in.) and 0.250 mm (.010 in.) See **11.3 Removing, Checking, and Installing Camshaft, Camshaft Drive, and Camshaft Bearings** for standard and undersize camshaft journal finishing dimensions.
Camshaft journal maximum taper or out-of-round	0.02 mm (.0008 in.)
Camshaft maximum permissible runout at center bearing with camshaft mounted between centers	0.06 mm (.0024 in.)
Camshaft maximum bending	0.03 mm (.0012 in.)
Cam lobe height	Intake (all models): 38.36 to 38.46 mm (1.5102 to 1.5142 in.) Exhaust (1975 only): 38.29 to 38.39 mm (1.5075 to 1.5114 in.) Exhaust (from 1976): 38.25 to 38.35 mm (1.5059 to 1.5098 in.)
Maximum permissible length of timing chain, measured at rollers, with chain under a tension of 5 kg (11 lb.)	291.40 mm (11.472 in.)
Minimum permissible diameter of crankshaft sprocket with chain wrapped around it, measured at rollers	59.40 mm (2.339 in.)
Minimum permissible diameter of camshaft sprocket with chain wrapped around it, measured at rollers	113.80 mm (4.480 in.)
Maximum protrusion of hydraulic timing chain tensioner plunger with timing chain pulled out under a tension of 10 kg (22 lb)	13.50 mm (.532 in.)
Minimum remaining thickness of timing chain tensioner plunger's slipper pad, measured at thinnest point	12.50 mm (.492 in.)
Minimum remaining thickness of timing chain damper's pad, measured at thinnest point	5.00 mm (.197 in.)
Cam follower outside diameter	Standard: 22.179 to 22.199 mm (.8732 to .9739 in.) 0.05-mm (.002-in.) oversize: 22.229 to 22.249 mm (.8752 to .9759 in.)
Cam follower bore in engine block	Standard: 22.200 to 22.221 mm (.8740 to .8748 in.) 0.05-mm (.002-in.) oversize: 22.250 to 22.271 mm (.8760 to .8768 in.)
Cam follower-to-cam follower bore clearance	New: 0.02 to 0.03 mm (.0008 to .0012 in.) Wear limit: 0.10 mm (.004 in.)
Rocker arm bore-to-rocker arm shaft clearance	0.02 to 0.04 mm (.0008 to .0016 in.)
Rocker arm shaft outside diameter	15.97 to 15.99 mm (.6287 to .6295 in.)
Rocker arm inside diameter	16.00 to 16.02 mm (.6299 to .6307 in.)
Valve spring normal free height	42.1 mm ($1^{21}/_{32}$ in.)
Valve spring installed height	37.7 mm ($1^{31}/_{64}$ in.)
Valve spring maximum permissible deviation from squareness	1.9 mm (.075 in.)
Pressure required to compress new valve spring to installed height	26.3 kg (58.4 lb.)
Minimum acceptable pressure required to compress used valve spring to installed height	24.3 kg (53.6 lb.)

5

VI. Connecting Rod and Bearing

Designation	Specification
Maximum permissible connecting rod bend or twist	0.05 mm per 100 mm (.002 in. per 4 in.)
Maximum permissible weight difference between any two connecting rods in engine	10 g
Connecting rod bearing-to-crankpin clearance with new parts	0.024 to 0.048 mm (.0009 to .0019 in.)
Connecting rod bearing-to-crankpin clearance wear limit	0.08 mm (.0031 in.)
Connecting rod big end side clearance with new parts	0.16 to 0.26 mm (.0063 to .0102 in.)
Connecting rod big end side clearance wear limit	0.27 mm (.0105 in.)
Available connecting rod bearing undersizes (see crankshaft and bearings table for crankpin sizes)	0.25, 0.50, and 0.75 mm (.010, .020, and .030 in.)
Minimum interference fit between piston pin and connecting rod small end bore, measured with both parts at 20°C (68°F)	0.02 mm (.0008 in.)

VII. Pistons and Piston Rings

Designation	Specification
Standard piston diameter (measured 90° to piston pin bore, at a point 11 mm (7/16 in.) below lower edge of oil scraper ring groove	84.94 to 84.99 mm (3.3441 to 3.3461 in.)
Piston grades used during engine manufacture (replacement pistons are not available by grade) . . . Grade 1	84.94 to 84.95 mm (3.3441 to 3.3445 in.)
Grade 2	84.95 to 84.96 mm (3.3445 to 3.3449 in.)
Grade 3	84.96 to 84.97 mm (3.3449 to 3.3453 in.)
Grade 4	84.97 to 84.98 mm (3.3453 to 3.3457 in.)
Grade 5	84.98 to 84.99 mm (3.3457 to 3.3461 in.)
Maximum permissible weight difference between any two pistons in engine	10g
Piston-to-cylinder bore clearance with new parts	0.05 to 0.07 mm (.002 to .003 in.)
Piston-to-cylinder bore clearance wear limit	0.07 mm (.003 in.)
Piston ring end gaps . . . Upper compression ring	0.20 to 0.40 mm (.008 to .016 in.)
Lower compression ring	0.10 to 0.30 mm (.004 to .012 in.)
Oil scraper ring	0.20 to 0.50 mm (.008 to .020 in.)
Piston ring side clearances . . . Upper compression ring	0.020 to 0.060 mm (.0008 to .0024 in.)
Lower compression ring	0.050 to 0.055 mm (.0020 to .0022 in.)
Formed steel oil scraper ring	Snug fit all around piston
Old-style cast oil scraper ring	0.020 to 0.060 mm (.0008 to .0024 in.)
Piston pin diameter (divided into two grades during piston manufacture)	22.00 to 22.01 mm (.8661 to .8665 in.)
Piston-to-piston pin clearance	A light push fit at room temperature, or a measured clearance of 0.008 to 0.016 mm (.0003 to .0006 in.)
Piston-to-piston pin clearance wear limit	Pin falls out of piston at room temperature, or a measured clearance over 0.02 mm (.0008 in.)
Piston pin installing temperature	Piston pin, piston, and connecting rod at 20°C (68°F)

VIII. Crankshaft and Bearings

Designation	Specification
Maximum permissible crankshaft runout (measured at center main bearing with crankshaft rotated between centers)	0.06 mm (.0024 in.)
Maximum permissible crankshaft bend (measured at center main bearing, one-half of maximum permissible runout)	0.03 mm (.0012 in.)
Crankshaft axial play with new parts	0.07 to 0.18 mm (.003 to .007 in.)
Maximum permissible crankshaft axial play	0.08 mm (.0031 in.)
Available crankshaft thrust washers, to control axial play . . . Standard	2.440 to 2.490 mm (.0961 to .0980 in.)
0.125 mm (.005 in.) oversize	2.503 to 2.553 mm (.0985 to .1005 in.)
0.250 mm (.010 in.) oversize	2.565 to 2.615 mm (.1010 to .1030 in.)
Maximum permissible journal or crankpin taper or out-of-round	0.01 mm (.0004 in.)
Main bearing-to-journal clearance with new parts	0.024 to 0.048 mm (.0009 to .0019 in.)
Maximum permissible main bearing-to-journal clearance	0.08 mm (.0031 in.)
Crankshaft journal standard diameter	57.976 to 58.000 mm (2.2825 to 2.2835 in.)
Crankshaft journal diameters for available main bearing undersizes . . . 0.25-mm (.010-in.) undersize	57.74 to 57.75 mm (2.2732 to 2.2736 in.)
0.50-mm (.020-in.) undersize	57.49 to 57.50 mm (2.2634 to 2.2638 in.)
0.75-mm (.030-in.) undersize	57.24 to 57.25 mm (2.2535 to 2.2539 in.)
Crankpin standard diameter	47.976 to 48.000 mm (1.8888 to 1.8898 in.)
Crankpin diameters for available connecting rod bearing undersizes . . . 0.25-mm (.010-in.) undersize	47.74 to 47.75 mm (1.8795 to 1.8799 in.)
0.50-mm (.020-in.) undersize	47.49 to 47.50 mm (1.8697 to 1.8701 in.)
0.75-mm (.030-in.) undersize	47.24 to 47.25 mm (1.8598 to 1.8602 in.)

IX. Flywheel and Drive Plate

Designation	Specification
Maximum permissible flywheel runout, measured at clutch friction surface	0.10 mm (.004 in.)
Temperature to which new flywheel starter ring gear must be heated just prior to installation (Starter ring gear cannot be replaced separately on drive plate)	160° to 200°C (320° to 392°F)
Maximum permissible ring gear runout, measured at starter ring gear	0.20 mm (.008 in.)

X. Valves and Valve Guides

Designation	Specification
Valve clearance (measured with engine hot)	Intake: 0.20 mm (.008 in.) Exhaust: 0.33 mm (.013 in.)
Valve clearance (measured with engine cold—use only during engine assembly work)	Intake: 0.18 mm (.007 in.) Exhaust: 0.30 mm (.012 in.)
Valve overall length	New: 109.00 mm (4.291 in.) Wear limit: 108.50 mm (4.272 in.)
Maximum permissible amount to be ground from stem tip during repair	0.50 mm (.020 in.)
Minimum permissible margin after machine grinding	Intake: 0.50 mm (.020 in.) Exhaust: 0.70 mm (.028 in.)
Valve facing angle	45°
Valve stem diameter	Intake: 7.970 to 7.985 mm (.3138 to .3144 in.) Exhaust: 7.965 to 7.980 mm (.3136 to .3142 in.)
Valve stem-to-valve guide clearance (with new valves and guides)	Intake: 0.025 to 0.060 mm (.0010 to .0024 in.) Exhaust: 0.030 to 0.065 mm (.0012 to .0026 in.)
Valve stem-to-valve guide clearance (wear limit)	Intake: 0.08 mm (.003 in.) Exhaust: 0.10 mm (.004 in.)
Valve guide inside diameter	8.01 to 8.03 mm (.3154 to .3161 in.)
Valve guide outside diameter	Standard: 13.04 to 13.05 mm (.5134 to .5138 in.) Oversize: 13.09 to 13.10 mm (.5154 to .5157 in.)
Valve guide removal and installation temperature	Cylinder head heated to 80° to 100°C (176° to 212°F)
Valve guide installed protrusion above top surface of cylinder head	17 mm (or 43/6 in.)

XI. Ignition Distributor and Secondary Cables

Model year and Distributor type	Designation	Specification
All models and types	Spark plug cable and high tension cable resistance Maximum permissible bending of distributor shaft Distributor shaft end thrust Force required to rotate breaker plate Engine speed during dwell and ignition timing tests Spark advance curves	16,000 ohms per meter (39⅜ in.) when new 25,000 ohms per meter (39⅜ in.) wear limit 0.05 mm (.002 in.) 0.15 to 0.50 mm (.006 to .020 in.) 1 kg (2.2 lb.) maximum 850 rpm ±50 rpm Please see tables given in **3.3 Adjusting Timing**
1975 dual-point	Preliminary point gap setting Main point dwell Sub-point dwell Ignition timing (engine cold) Ignition timing (engine hot)	0.40 to 0.50 mm (.016 to .020 in.) 57° 50° to 54° 22° ±3° BTDC (sub-point timing) 12° BTDC (main point timing)
1975 single-point	Preliminary point gap setting Dwell Ignition timing	0.40 to 0.50 mm (.016 to .020 in.) 50° to 54° 10° BTDC
1976 and 1977 shielded point	Preliminary rubbing block gap setting Dwell Ignition timing	0.45 mm (.018 in.) 50° to 54° 10° BTDC
1978 and later breakerless	Pickup coil resistance Pickup coil/timing rotor air gap Ignition timing	130 to 190 ohms 0.20 to 0.40 mm (.008 to .016 in.) 10° BTDC

XII. Cylinder Head and Manifolds

Designation	Specification
Maximum permissible cylinder head warpage at combustion chamber surface	0.05 mm (.002 in.)
Maximum permissible cylinder head warpage at manifold surfaces	0.20 mm (.008 in.)
Maximum permissible manifold warpage at gasket surface	0.20 mm (.008 in.)
Valve seat contact surface width	1.20 to 1.60 mm (.047 to .063 in.)
Valve seat contact surface angle	45°
Valve seat outer chamfer angle (used to narrow contact surface)	30°
Valve seat inner chamfer angle (used to narrow contact surface)	65°
Maximum permissible water jacket leakage	No leakage in a 3-minute period at a pressure of 4 bar (58 psi)

XIII. Lubrication System

Designation	Specification
Type of oil pump	Distributor-driven trochoid
Delivery capacity and minimum permissible pressure at 300 pump shaft rpm with SAE 30 oil at 100°C (212°F)	1.7 liters per minute at 2 bar (1.8 U.S. quarts per minute at 28 psi)
Delivery capacity and minimum permissible pressure at 3000 pump shaft rpm with SAE 30 oil at 100°C (212°F)	24.0 liters per minute at 3 bar (25.4 U.S. quarts per minute at 43 psi)
Oil pressure measured at engine's oil pressure switch or sending unit hole ... idle speed	More than 0.8 bar (11.4 psi)
... 2000 crankshaft rpm	3.5 to 4.5 bar (49.8 to 64.0 psi)
... 5000 crankshaft rpm	4.0 to 5.0 bar (56.9 to 71.1 psi)
Pressure at which pressure relief valve begins to open	3.6 to 4.4 bar (51 to 63 psi)
Pressure at which pressure relief valve is fully open	5.9 to 7.1 bar (84 to 101 psi)
Pressure relief valve spring free height	47 mm (1 55/64 in.)
Pressure relief valve spring installed height	36.80 mm (1 29/64 in.)
Pressure needed to compress pressure relief valve to installed height	5.99 to 6.59 kg (13.21 to 14.53 lb.)
Oil pump inner rotor tip clearance with new parts	0.04–0.16 mm (.0016 to .0063 in.)
Oil pump inner rotor tip clearance wear limit	0.25 mm (.010 in.)
Oil pump rotor side clearance (from rotors to pickup flange) with new parts	0.03 to 0.09 mm (.0012 to .0035 in.)
Oil pump rotor side clearance wear limit	0.15 mm (.006 in.)
Oil pump driven rotor-to-housing clearance with new parts	0.10 to 0.16 mm (.0039 to .0063 in.)
Oil pump driven rotor-to-housing clearance wear limit	0.25 mm (.010 in.)
Oil filter specification	Full-flow with built-in bypass valve

XIV. Engine Block

Designation	Specification
Maximum permissible engine block warpage at cylinder head gasket surface	0.05 mm (.002 in.)
Standard cylinder bore diameter	85.00 to 85.05 mm (3.346 to 3.348 in.)
Maximum permissible wear beyond standard bore diameter	0.20 mm (.008 in.)
Maximum permissible difference in bore diameter between one cylinder and any other cylinder in the engine	0.05 mm (.002 in.)
Maximum permissible cylinder bore taper or out-of-round	0.02 mm (.0008 in.)
Cylinder diameters for available piston oversizes ... 0.25 mm (.010 in.) oversize	85.25 to 85.30 mm (3.3563 to 3.3583 in.)
... 0.50 mm (.020 in.) oversize	85.50 to 85.55 mm (3.3661 to 3.3681 in.)
... 0.75 mm (.030 in.) oversize	85.75 to 85.80 mm (3.3760 to 3.3779 in.)
... 1.00 mm (.040 in.) oversize	86.00 to 86.05 mm (3.3858 to 3.3878 in.)

XV. Tightening Torques

Location	Designation	Nm	Ft. lb.
Ignition distributor to engine block (hold-down bolt)	bolt	15–20	11–15
Spark plug in cylinder head	spark plug	25–30	18–22
Radiator to car body	bolt	15–20	11–15
Thermostat housing to cylinder head	bolt	12–15	9–11
Water pump to timing cover	bolt or nut	12–15	9–11
Valve adjusting screw locknut	locknut	10	7.5
Intake manifold to cylinder head	nut or bolt	20–25	15–18
Cylinder head to engine block	bolt	85–90	63–66
Exhaust manifold to cylinder head	nut	30–45	22–33
Exhaust pipe to exhaust manifold	nut	30–45	22–33
Large threaded plug in top of cylinder head	socket-head plug	30–40	22–30
Oil pump to engine block	bolt	20–25	15–18
Side engine mount to suspension crossmember	nut	30–40	22–30
End of front stabilizer bar to track control arm	first nut	15–20	11–15
	jam nut	10–15	7.5–11
Stabilizer bar U-shaped clamp to car body	bolt	10–15	7.5–11
Engine block to bellhousing	bolt	55–75	41–55
Starter to engine and bellhousing	bolt	55–75	41–55
Torque converter to drive plate	bolt	15–20	11–15
Drive plate to crankshaft	bolt	58–60	43–44
Flywheel to crankshaft	bolt	58–60	43–44
Connecting rod cap to connecting rod	nut	40–50	30–37
Main bearing cap to engine block	bolt	75–85	55–63
Timing cover to engine block	bolt	12–15	9–11
Crankshaft rear oil seal carrier to engine block	bolt	12–15	9–11
Crankshaft pulley to crankshaft	bolt	40–55	30–41
Camshaft thrust plate to engine block	bolt	10–15	7.5–11
Camshaft sprocket to camshaft	bolt	70–105	52–77
Timing chain tensioner to engine block	bolt	10–15	7.5–11
Timing chain damper to engine block	bolt	10–15	7.5–11
Thermo switch in radiator (when fitted)	switch	30–35	22–26
Location	**Designation**	**Nm**	**In. lb.**
ATF line to radiator	union	1.5–2.5	13–22
Cylinder head cover to cylinder head	bolt	4–5	35–44
Air cleaner body to cylinder head cover	bolt	2–3	18–27
Cylinder head rear plate to rear of cylinder head	bolt	4–5	35–44
Oil pickup to oil pump body	bolt	5–7	44–62
Oil pan to engine block	bolt	3–4	27–35

XVI. Spark Advance Curves for 1979 California-only Distributor

Distributor	Centrifugal advance range		Vacuum advance range	
(breakerless)	distributor rpm	degrees	mbar (mm/Hg, in./Hg)	degrees
19100–26232 (California specification)	500	advance begins	107 (80, 3.16)	advance begins
	824	2.3°	155 (116, 4.57)	3.5°
	1350	7.5°	227 (170, 6.69)	7.5°
	3000	6.1°	307 (230, 9.06)	11.0°
			400 (300, 11.81)	14.0°

Section 6

FUEL AND EXHAUST SYSTEMS

Contents

6

TABLES

Fuel and Exhaust Systems

The fuel system handles five main tasks necessary for proper engine operation: (1) it provides storage space for the gasoline; (2) it includes the components necessary for delivering gasoline to the engine; (3) it is responsible for admitting the correct amount of filtered air to the engine; (4) it incorporates a carburetor for mixing fuel and air in precisely controlled proportions and a manifold for delivering this mixture to the cylinders; and (5) it modifies the density of the incoming air so that the combustion process does not produce an excess of undesirable exhaust emissions. Also covered in this section of the Manual are all the emission controls, including those that operate electrically or control the spark advance.

The Corolla carburetor is a dual-venturi, progressive opening carburetor. That is, the primary venturi's throttle valve is directly controlled by the accelerator pedal, and it is the only throttle valve in operation during normal driving. During acceleration to high speeds, and during high-speed cruising, the secondary venturi's throttle valve also opens. Because the operation of the second venturi is limited to periods of high power demand, greater fuel economy is obtained during normal driving, when the power needed is either light or moderate.

On all models, the carburetor has a built-in automatic choke operated by a thermostatic spring, which closes the choke valve when the engine is cold. When the engine is started and begins to run, an electric heating element warms the thermostatic spring. As the spring warms, it opens the choke valve. For fuel economy and emissions reasons, the choke system has one or more other opening devices, which can override the thermostatic spring and open the choke valve when operating conditions make this necessary.

The carburetor is mounted atop a cast aluminum intake manifold, which is held to the engine's cylinder head by nuts and bolts. This manifold is heated by an integral water jacket, through which a portion of the engine's coolant is circulated. The heated manifold aids fuel vaporization during cold weather operation.

Because many of the repairs and tune-up procedures described in this section of the Manual have a direct influence on exhaust emissions, you should not undertake these jobs unless you have all the prescribed equipment available. If you lack the skills, the special equipment, or the tools for servicing and adjusting the fuel system, we suggest you leave these repairs to an Authorized Dealer or other qualified shop. We especially urge you to consult your Authorized Dealer before attempting repairs on a car still covered by the new-car warranty.

1. GENERAL DESCRIPTION

As noted earlier, the fuel system may conveniently be divided into five subsystems, each with a separate function. For brevity, these will be called fuel storage, pump and lines, air cleaner, carburetor, and emission controls.

Fuel Storage

The fuel tank is housed in the front of the trunk on sedan, hardtop, and sport coupe models. On the wagon and the liftback, the fuel tank is mounted under the car, beneath the rear cargo area. Except for the wagon model, which has a 47-liter (12.4-U.S. gallon or 10.3-Imperial gallon) tank, all models have a nominal fuel capacity of 50 liters (13.2 U.S. gallons or 11.0 Imperial gallons). All 1977 and later cars have the small fuel filler that will accept only pump nozzles for unleaded gasoline, whether or not the car has a catalytic converter.

The fuel tank is equipped with a sending unit for the fuel gauge. On certain models, the sending unit also contains a thermistor for the dashboard-mounted fuel level warning light. The tanks are equipped with drain plugs and with connections for a sealed evaporative emission control system. The fuel filler cap has no vent that would allow gasoline fumes to escape to the atmosphere.

Pump and Lines

The fuel pump is a mechanical diaphragm-type pump, which is operated by an eccentric on the engine's camshaft. Although all the pumps have a similar overall design, they differ in some details from one car model to the next. Thus, when you replace the fuel pump, it is important to obtain a new pump that is the correct one for the particular car model.

Air Cleaner

The air cleaner is similar on all cars covered by this Manual. It has a round main housing, mounted atop the carburetor, with an air intake tube that extends toward the left-hand side of the engine. The main housing contains a ring-shaped, dry-type, pleated-paper air filter. The air intake contains a thermostatically controlled flap for the intake air preheating system. Beginning with the 1978 models, a separate pleated-paper, dry-type air filter is installed beneath a cover at the rear of the air cleaner's main housing. This filter is for the air suction emission control system.

Carburetor

The cars covered by this Manual are equipped with Aisan two-venturi carburetors. With this design, one throttle valve is used for mid-range operation. This gives good economy and throttle response with a minimum of exhaust emissions. At full load, a second throttle valve opens, too.

Fig. 1-1 shows the operating stages of the dual-venturi carburetor. Once the primary throttle valve has opened beyond a predetermined point, the secondary throttle valve is able to open to a degree that is proportional to engine vacuum. This avoids the hesitation that might occur if both throttle valves were fully opened at low speed on an engine tuned for maximum fuel economy and minimum exhaust emissions.

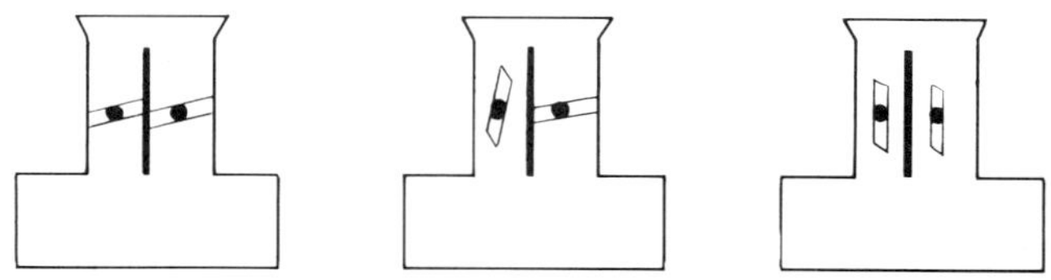

Fig. 1-1. Stages of dual-venturi carburetor operation. Secondary throttle valve is opened by vacuum chamber attached to carburetor.

Emission Controls

Approximately twenty-five different emission control systems or devices are used on the cars covered by this Manual. Not all cars have the same controls, however. You can determine which emission controls are on the car by checking its emissions decal, located in the engine compartment. You can identify the abbreviations—EGR, for example—along with their correct systems and devices by consulting the table given in **8. Emission Control Systems.**

2. MAINTENANCE

The following routine maintenance steps are covered briefly in **LUBRICATION AND MAINTENANCE** or in this section, under the headings listed after some of the items.

1. Servicing air cleaner.
2. Replacing fuel filter.
3. Checking exhaust emission controls. **8.4**
4. Replacing catalytic converter. **8.2**
5. Checking PCV (positive crankcase ventilation) system, and replacing PCV valve. **8.1**
6. Checking evaporative emission control system, and replacing charcoal canister. **8.3**
7. Adjusting idle speed and idle mixture. **5.1**
8. Adjusting fast idle speed. **5.1**

9. Checking throttle positioner system. **8.4**
10. Checking exhaust pipe, muffler, and brackets. **9**
11. Replacing fuel tank cap gasket.

3. FUEL TANK

If you must remove the fuel tank to clean or repair it, it is important that you install the connections leading to the tank correctly, without kinks, and in their original locations. Errors can lead to fuel starvation, a collapsed fuel tank, or the improper venting of fumes.

3.1 Removing and Installing Fuel Tank

To avoid the hazard of spilled fuel, the tank should be as nearly empty as possible during removal. Remove surplus fuel by unscrewing the drain plug from the bottom of the tank. Removal and testing of the fuel gauge sending unit is described in conjunction with instruments in **ELECTRICAL SYSTEM.**

> ***WARNING —***
> *Disconnect the battery ground cable. Do not smoke or work near heaters or other fire hazards. Have a fire extinguisher handy.*

Because the tanks and their locations are different on sedan, hardtop, or coupe, and wagon or liftback models, two removal procedures are given under this heading. Please choose the procedure that applies to your car.

To remove tank from sedan, hardtop, or coupe:

1. To remove fuel from the tank, carefully pry out the rubber shielding plug that is accessible under the car. Then place a receptacle for catching the draining fuel beneath the car. Using a suitable socket wrench, remove the drain plug from the tank and allow the fuel to drain.

> ***WARNING —***
> *Disconnect the battery ground strap. Do not smoke or work near heaters or other fire hazards. Have a fire extinguisher handy. If the tank contains more than five gallons, it is safer to remove the bulk of the gasoline with a siphoning device inserted into the fuel filler before removing the plug from the bottom of the tank.*

2. Open the trunk. Take out the screws and remove the fiberboard protector panel from the front of the trunk.
3. Disconnect the wire(s) from the fuel gauge sending unit.
4. Detach the ventilation hoses from the fuel tank, attaching tags to the disconnected hoses so that you will be able to reconnect them in the correct locations.
5. Loosen the clamp that holds the fuel filler hose to the neck of the tank. Then detach the hose from the tank.
6. Detach the fuel pickup hose from the tank, then plug the hose to prevent leakage and the entry of foreign matter.
7. Remove the bolts that hold the tank's mounting flange to the body. Then remove the tank through the trunk opening.

Installation is the reverse of removal. Use new hose clamps for the ventilation hoses, and replace any hose that is cracked, that leaks, or that does not fit tightly. Be careful not to install the pickup hose, the filler hose, or any ventilation hose in a twisted position. No hose should be bent so sharply that it may collapse.

To remove tank from liftback or wagon:

1. To remove fuel from the tank, place a receptacle for catching the draining fuel beneath the rear of the car. Then, using a suitable socket wrench, remove the drain plug from the tank and allow the fuel to drain.

> ***WARNING —***
> *Disconnect the battery ground strap. Do not smoke or work near heaters or other fire hazards. Have a fire extinguisher handy. If the tank contains more than five gallons, it is safer to remove the bulk of the gasoline with a siphoning device inserted into the fuel filler before removing the plug from the bottom of the tank.*

2. Loosen the clamp that holds the fuel filler hose to the neck of the tank. Then detach the hose from the tank.
3. Place a box, wood blocks, or some other support beneath the tank so that the tank can be lowered 50 to 75 mm (or 2 to 3 in.) after you dismount it from the car body. Then, on liftback models, unbolt and remove the two tank mounting straps. On wagons, remove the bolts that hold the tank's mounting flange to the body. Lower the tank onto the support.
4. Disconnect the wire(s) from the fuel gauge sending unit.
5. Detach the ventilation hoses from the fuel tank,

attaching tags to the disconnected hoses so that you will be able to reconnect them in the correct locations.

6. Detach the fuel pickup hose from the tank, then plug the hose to prevent leakage and the entry of foreign matter.
7. Remove the tank from beneath the car, being careful not to lose any of the rubber or plastic cushions that insulate the tank from the car body. Make a note of the locations of all such cushions so that you can reinstall them in their correct positions.

Installation is the reverse of removal. Use new hose clamps for the ventilation hoses, and replace any hose that is cracked, that leaks, or that does not fit tightly. Be careful not to install the pickup hose, the filler hose, or any ventilation hose in a twisted position. No hose should be bent so sharply that it may collapse.

Fuel Gauge Sending Unit and Fuel Pickup

The removal, installation, and testing of the fuel gauge sending unit is covered in **ELECTRICAL SYSTEM.** Only the fuel pickup is discussed here.

At the end of the fuel pickup, which is integral with the fuel gauge sending unit, there is a wire gauze filter. To remove this filter, remove the sending unit from the fuel tank as shown in **ELECTRICAL SYSTEM.** (On liftback models you must first remove the fuel tank to gain access to the sending unit.) You can then detach the filter from the pickup tube. Installation is the reverse of removal.

3.2 Removing and Installing Filler Pipe and Hose

To remove the fuel filler hose, which connects the fuel tank neck with the filler pipe, first remove fuel from the tank until the fuel level is below the level of the filler hose connections. Then remove the large hose clamps from each end of the filler hose so that you can remove the hose. Installation is the reverse of removal.

> ***WARNING ——***
> *Disconnect the battery ground strap. Do not smoke or work near heaters or other fire hazards. Have a fire extinguisher handy.*

To remove the filler pipe, first remove the filler hose as just described. Take off the filler cap. Then remove the four Phillips head screws that hold the filler pipe and related components to the car body. (The screws are normally concealed by the fuel filler cap.) Before you reinstall the filler pipe on the car body, make sure that you have replaced any damaged gaskets or sealing pieces.

4. FUEL PUMP AND LINES

The fuel pump is mounted on the engine. It is a mechanical pump, operated by an eccentric on the engine's camshaft. The stroke of the pump is determined by the thicknesses of the two gaskets and the insulating spacer that go between the pump and the engine block. Thus it is important that you install the correct gaskets and insulating spacer.

Troubleshooting Fuel Supply Problems

The fuel pump troubles that are most likely to affect engine performance adversely are incorrect fuel pump pressure and inadequate output volume. Before you test the pump for inadequate pressure and volume, make sure that the car's fuel starvation symptoms are not being caused by clogging in the fuel filter (or in the wire gauze filter on the end of the fuel pickup in the tank). Also, before you assume that excessive pump pressure is causing flooding, make sure that the carburetor's float valve is not leaking and that the carburetor float is not cracked or pinholed and filled with gasoline.

To test pump:

1. Remove the air cleaner. See **6.1 Removing and Installing Carburetor.**
2. Detach the fuel inlet line from the carburetor. Then, using appropriate fittings, attach a pressure gauge to the disconnected line and to the carburetor. For output volume testing, install an outlet hose that will deliver fuel to a graduated container. See Fig. 4-1.

> ***WARNING ——***
> *Do not disconnect any live electrical wires in the engine compartment. Do not smoke or work near heaters or other fire hazards. Have a fire extinguisher handy.*

3. Start the engine and operate it at an idle. Bleed the line connected to the pressure gauge. Using the equipment shown in Fig. 4-1, you can bleed the gauge connection by releasing the hose restrictor until fuel begins flowing into the container. Then close the restrictor.

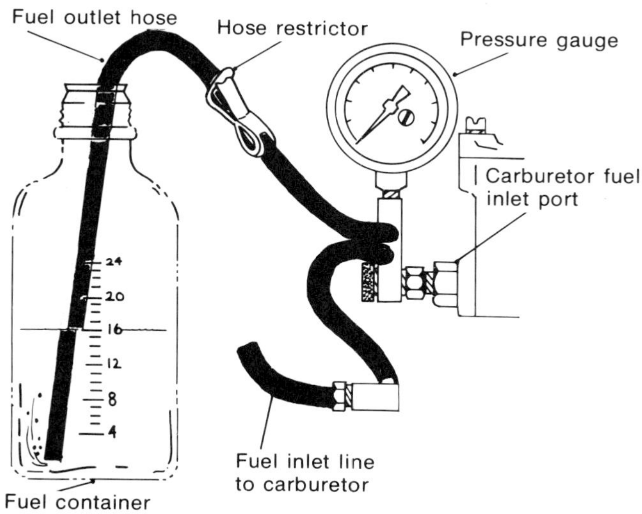

Fig. 4-1. Typical pressure and capacity test hookups. Inlet line from pump is normally attached to carburetor's fuel inlet port.

4. Allow the pressure to stabilize. The gauge should read 0.20 to 0.30 bar (2.8 to 4.3 psi). If the pressure is not within specifications—and if neither the fuel lines nor the filter is restricted—replace the pump.
5. If the pressure is within specifications, measure the pump's output volume. Operate the engine at 3000 rpm. Open the hose restrictor for 30 seconds. Within that period, the pump should discharge at least 450 cm^3 (about 15¼ oz.) into the fuel container.
6. If the pump fails to produce adequate volume, repeat the test using an auxiliary fuel supply rather than the car's own fuel tank. If the volume is within specifications, look for a restriction in the fuel supply line or for a fault in the fuel tank ventilation system that is not permitting air to enter the tank. If the outlet volume remains low with the auxiliary fuel supply, replace the pump.
7. To test the pump's suction, you can attach a vacuum gauge to the fuel supply line that leads from the tank to the pump. (You can easily detach this line from the fuel filter outlet.) The suction, while running the starter, should be about 300 mm/Hg (11.8 in./Hg). Replace faulty fuel pumps.

4.1 Removing and Installing Fuel Pump

The fuel pump is located on the right-hand side of the engine block, almost directly below the carburetor. Replacement parts for the fuel pump are not widely available; and because repairs can be time-consuming, it is usually best to replace any faulty pump. Although the fuel pumps shown in the illustrations may differ slightly from the fuel pump installed on your car—in the number of fuel line unions, for example—the removal procedure is the same.

To remove:

1. Loosen the hose clamps that hold the fuel lines to the fuel pump unions. Then detach from the pump the inlet hose, the outlet hose and, where applicable, the return hose. Attach tags, if necessary, to help you reinstall the lines on the correct unions.

> ***WARNING ——***
>
> *The fuel in the pump lines may be under some pressure and will spurt out when you disconnect the lines. Disconnect the battery's negative (−) cable before you begin work. Do not smoke or work near heaters or other fire hazards. Have a fire extinguisher handy. Remove the fuel filler cap to release any pressure in the tank.*

2. Remove the two bolts that hold the fuel pump to the engine.
3. Remove the fuel pump (Fig. 4-2), its gaskets, and the insulating spacer. Discard the gaskets.

6

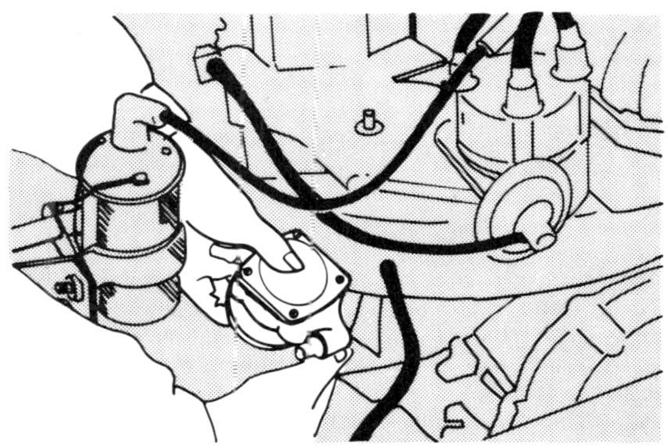

Fig. 4-2. Fuel pump being removed. Because of emission control hoses on some models, it may be easier to remove pump from beneath car. On cars with air injection, disconnect one air hose from the air pump for access to the fuel pump.

Installation is the reverse of removal. Be sure to install new gaskets on each side of the insulating spacer. Torque the bolts to 15 to 20 Nm (11 to 15 ft. lb.). Use new hose clamps to reconnect the fuel lines. After starting the engine, check that there are neither oil leaks past the gaskets nor fuel leaks at the unions.

Cleaning and Replacing Fuel Lines

Replace a damaged steel fuel line with a new steel line rather than repairing it, such as by straightening, soldering, or welding it. If you replace a fuel hose, you should use new hose clamps at points where the hose is attached to metal lines or connections.

Replace fuel hoses if they are clogged or restricted. Steel lines should be cleared with compressed air if they are obstructed by dirt. Use solvent to flush loose foreign matter from the lines. Replace lines that are rusted internally or clogged by rust.

4.2 Disassembling and Assembling Fuel Pump

Fig. 4-3, Fig. 4-4, and Fig. 4-5 are exploded views of the various kinds of fuel pumps. You can use these illustrations as guides for disassembling and assembling the pumps. Only the components named in the illustrations are available as replacement parts; therefore disassembly beyond that indicated in these exploded views will serve no practical purpose. If you find faults that cannot be repaired with the parts available, replace the fuel pump as a unit.

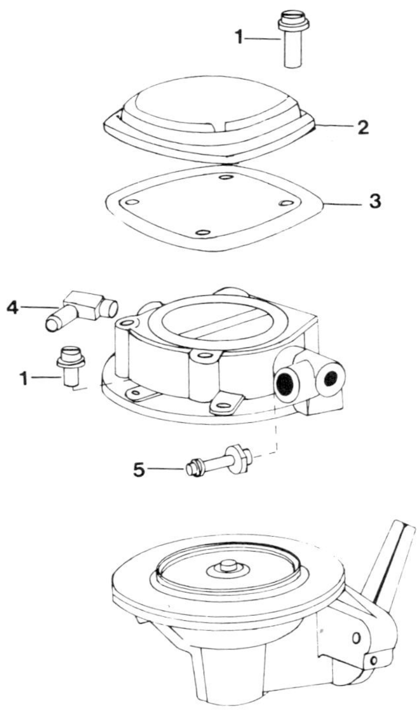

1. Screw
2. Cover
3. Gasket
4. Angled union
5. Straight union

Fig. 4-3. Exploded view of fuel pump used on 1975 and 1976 cars.

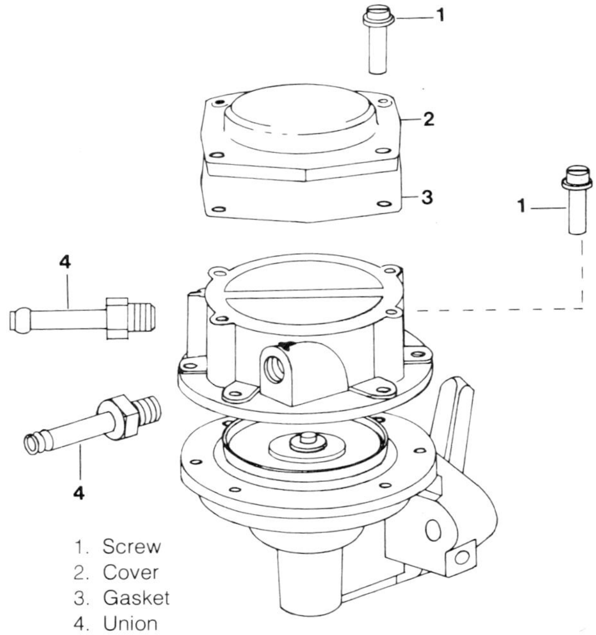

1. Screw
2. Cover
3. Gasket
4. Union

Fig. 4-4. Exploded view of fuel pump used on 1977 and later Canadian cars and on 1977 and early 1978 U.S. models (except California and high-altitude models). Pump used on late 1978 and all 1979 U.S. models is similar, but only unions are available as replacement parts.

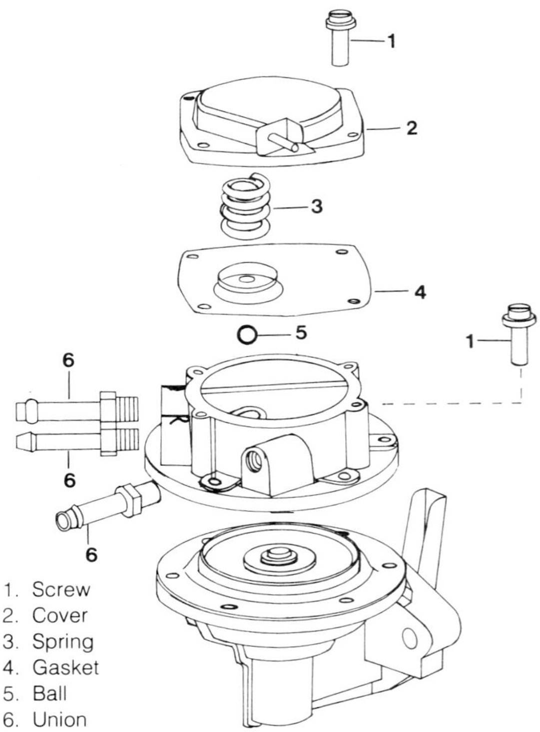

1. Screw
2. Cover
3. Spring
4. Gasket
5. Ball
6. Union

Fig. 4-5. Exploded view of fuel pump used on 1977 and later California and high-altitude models.

5. ADJUSTING CARBURETOR

Fig. 5-1 shows where various carburetor adjustments should be made. During routine maintenance, it should be necessary to adjust only the idle speed and the fuel mixture. Adjust the choke, the fast idle, and the throttle positioner only when a check determines that adjustment is necessary.

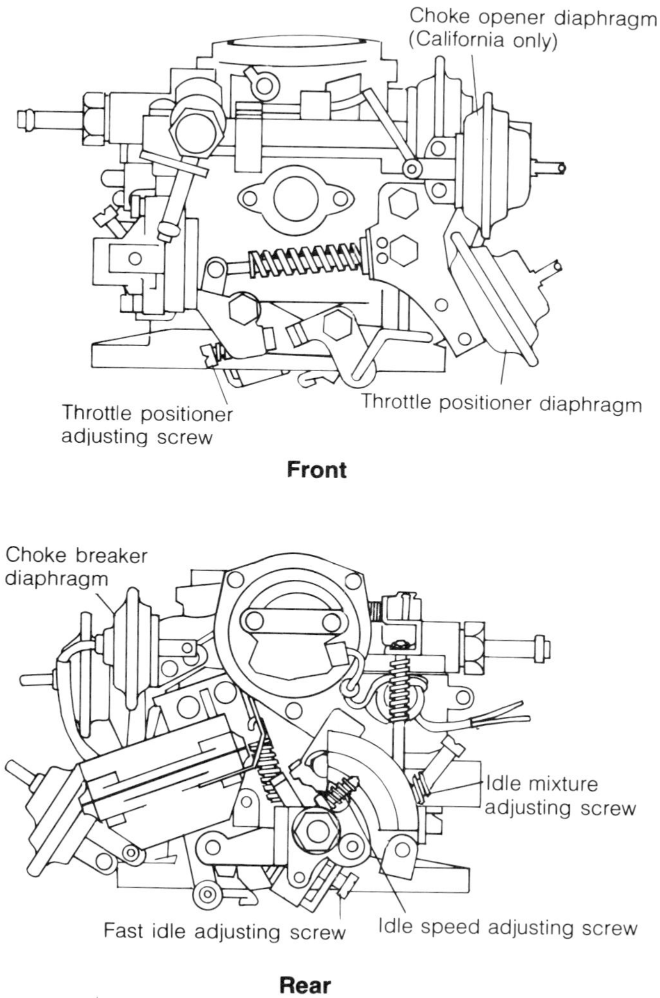

Fig. 5-1. Front and rear views of carburetor, showing locations of adjusting screws.

5.1 Adjusting Idle Speed and Idle Mixture

Adjusting the carburetor should be the last step in a tune-up, as nearly every other tune-up adjustment will alter the engine's idle speed or the idle mixture required for proper operation. Similarly, when you troubleshoot the engine, always eliminate other possible trouble sources before you make any changes in the carburetor adjustments.

Because even minor carburetor adjustment changes influence exhaust emissions, carburetor adjustment should follow the procedure given here. Professional mechanics should check their state's laws to determine whether state authorization is required for a shop to make adjustments that influence exhaust emissions.

> ***CAUTION —***
> *If you lack the skills, tools, or test equipment for adjusting the carburetor, we suggest you leave these adjustments to an Authorized Dealer or other qualified shop.*

To adjust:

1. Start the engine and allow it to reach its normal operating temperature. Make sure that the choke valve is fully open, that the ignition timing is correct, that all vacuum lines are connected, and that the air cleaner is installed.
2. Place the transmission in neutral and turn off all accessories, such as the headlights, the heater, and the air conditioning.
3. With the engine idling, check that the fuel level is about even with the dot, which is in the center of the sight glass located in the front of the carburetor. See Fig. 5-2.

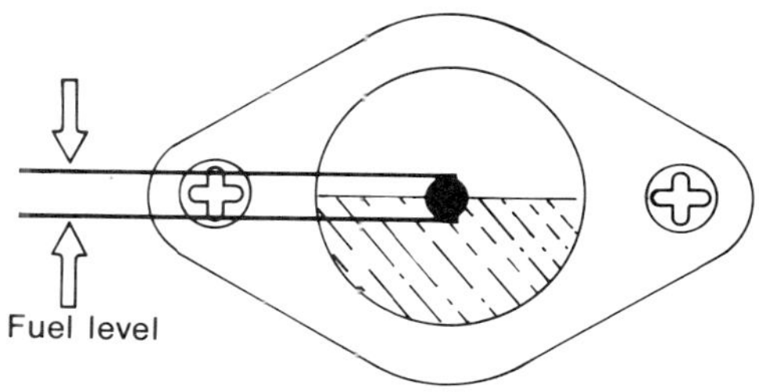

Fig. 5-2. Correct fuel level with engine at idle. Fuel level in carburetor float bowl should be in range indicated between arrows.

4. If the fuel level is not correct, correct the float level or replace the float valve as described in **6.1 Removing and Installing Carburetor.**
5. Connect a tachometer to the engine.

> **NOTE —**
> During routine maintenance, you need not adjust the idle speed or the idle mixture if the idle speed is 850 rpm ± 50 rpm and if the engine is running satisfactorily.

6. If adjustment is necessary, and if plastic limiter caps are installed on the idle speed adjusting screw and the idle mixture adjusting screw, remove the caps as indicated in Fig. 5-3.

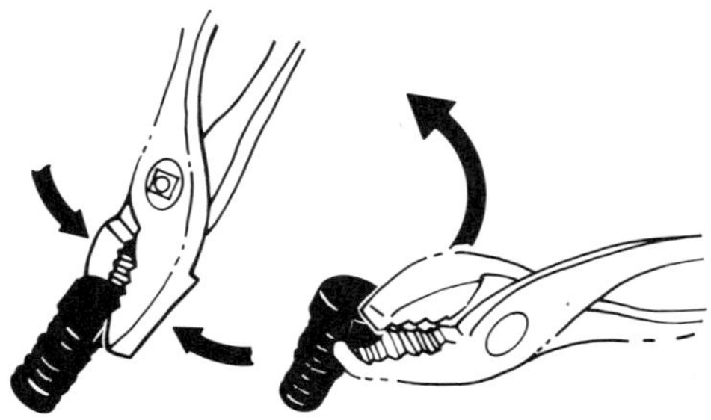

Fig. 5-3. Limiter cap being removed from adjusting screw. First squeeze cap, as indicated at left, to crack it. Then twist off cracked cap, as indicated at right.

7. By turning the idle mixture adjusting screw (Fig. 5-4), obtain the fastest possible idle speed.

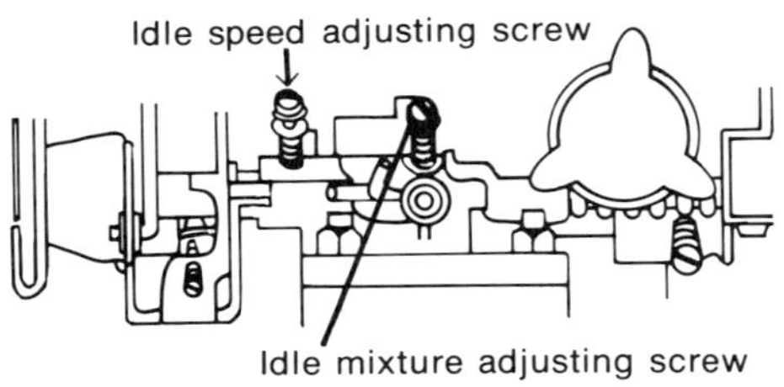

Fig. 5-4. Locations of idle speed adjusting screw and idle mixture adjusting screw, seen from right-hand side of carburetor.

8. By turning the idle speed adjusting screw, adjust the engine speed to the rpm given in **Table a.**

Table a. Idle Speeds prior to Final Mixture and Speed Adjustment

Car model	Temporary idle speed
1975 and 1976 models	930 rpm
1977, except Calif. and high-altitude models 1977 Calif. and high-altitude models	930 rpm 910 rpm
1978 and later Canadian models 1978 and later U.S. except Calif. and high-altitude models 1978 and later Calif. and high-altitude models	930 rpm 920 rpm 910 rpm

9. Repeat step 7 and step 8 until turning the idle mixture adjusting screw will not increase the idle speed above the rpm given in **Table a.** Then go on to step 10.

10. By gradually turning the idle mixture adjusting screw clockwise, adjust the idle speed to 850 rpm.

NOTE —
This is the lean drop method for setting the idle speed and mixture, which is necessary for low exhaust emissions. Do not adjust the final idle speed by turning the idle speed adjusting screw.

11. Install new blue plastic limiter caps on the adjusting screws, as indicated in Fig. 5-5.

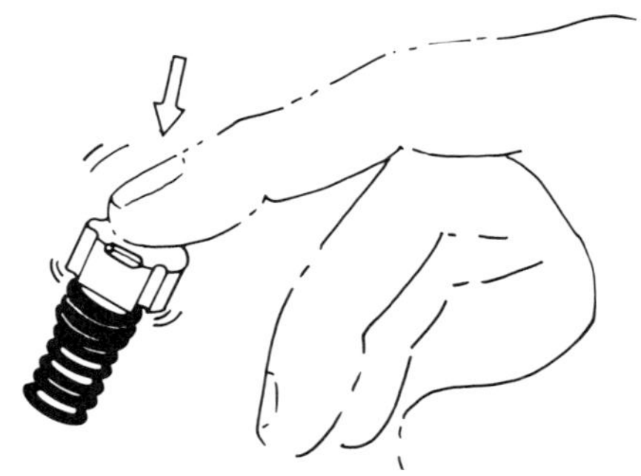

Fig. 5-5. New limiter cap being snapped onto adjusting screw. Press on as indicated by arrow.

Checking Emissions with Exhaust Gas Analyzer

The test described under this heading is used to determine whether hydrocarbon and carbon monoxide emissions conform to state or city regulations. You can also use this test to diagnose trouble in the emission controls or to check the accuracy of your idle mixture and idle speed adjustments.

CAUTION —
You should never attempt to adjust the idle mixture using an exhaust gas analyzer. Adjust it only using the lean drop method described earlier. If, after repeated adjustments, the car fails to conform to local emissions standards, find and correct faults in the ignition system, the engine itself, or the emission controls. Then use the lean drop method to adjust the idle mixture and idle speed.

To check:

1. Allow the engine to warm to its normal operating temperature. The choke should be fully open, the air cleaner installed, all accessories switched off, and all vacuum hoses properly connected.
2. Make sure that the ignition timing is set correctly. If necessary, consult **ENGINE.**
3. With the engine idling, check that the fuel level in the carburetor's float bowl is about even with the dot in the sight glass.
4. Insert the test probe of the exhaust gas analyzer at least two feet into the tailpipe. Make sure that the analyzer is properly prepared and calibrated.
5. With the engine idling and the transmission in neutral, measure the hydrocarbon and carbon monoxide levels.

   NOTE ——
   Use the exhaust gas analyzer as its manufacturer suggests in the directions supplied with the instrument. After beginning the test, wait at least one minute before you take readings. The entire measurement procedure should be completed within three minutes.

6. If hydrocarbon or carbon monoxide emissions exceed the prescribed levels, adjust the idle mixture by using the lean drop method already described.

   NOTE ——
   If you find that adjusting the mixture by using the lean drop method fails to bring emissions within the prescribed range, disconnect the air injection system by detaching the vacuum hose from the system's air switching valve. Also, on 1978 and later cars, detach the air suction hose from the air cleaner and plug the disconnected hose. See **8.4 Exhaust Emission Controls.** With these systems disconnected, the carbon monoxide level should be lower than 4.5% and the hydrocarbon concentration should be lower than 800 parts per million. If hydrocarbon emissions are considerably higher, troubleshoot the engine, using **Table b** as your guide. After making necessary repairs, repeat the test with the air injection system and, where applicable, the air suction system connected.

Checking and Adjusting Fast Idle Speed

You can use the procedure given here to determine whether the fast idle speed is correct. Make the adjustment described in step 3 only if the fast idle speed is above or below the prescribed rpm.

Table b. Analyzer Reading Diagnosis

Hydrocarbon level	Carbon monoxide level	Symtoms	Possible causes
High	Normal	Rough idle	a. Fouled, shorted, or incorrectly gapped spark plugs b. Faulty or misconnected spark plug cables c. Cracked, carbon-tracked distributor cap or other distributor fault d. Incorrect ignition timing e. Exhaust valves leaking f. Low compression owing to worn or damaged engine parts
High	Low	Rough idle, fluctuating hydrocarbon reading	a. Leaking or disconnected vaccum hose b. Leaking intake manifold or manifold gasket c. Leaking cylinder head gasket d. Idle mixture excessively lean, causing misfiring
High	High	Rough idle, black smoke coming from exhaust	a. Clogged air filter in air cleaner b. Clogged positive crankcase ventilation valve or hose c. Excessively rich mixture caused by faulty choke, incorrect carburetor float level, or carburetor internal leaks

To check and adjust:

1. With the engine stopped, remove the air cleaner as described in **6.1 Removing and Installing Carburetor.** Disconnect and plug the hose that is attached to the choke opener diaphragm (when fitted). See Fig. 5-6. Also plug the vacuum hose that leads to the air cleaner.

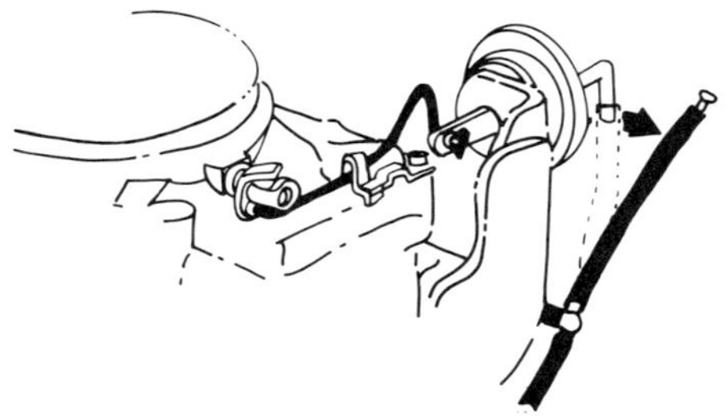

Fig. 5-6. Vacuum hose for choke opener diaphragm being disconnected and plugged. This diaphragm is found on California and high-altitude models through 1977 and on all U.S. models from 1978.

2. While holding the throttle valve slightly open (Fig. 5-7), close the choke valve. Release the throttle valve to hold the choke valve closed. Then, without touching the accelerator pedal, start the engine.

NOTE ——
Moving the accelerator pedal will permit the choke to open. The choke must remain closed throughout this procedure.

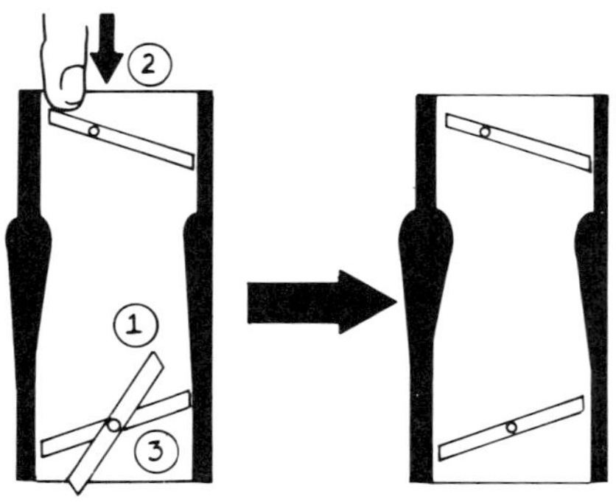

Fig. 5-7. Choke valve being closed. Open throttle valve as at **1**, close choke as indicated by black arrow at **2**, then allow throttle valve to close as at **3**. Choke and throttle should then remain closed as indicated to right of white arrow.

3. If the fast idle is not in the ranges given in **Table c**, adjust it as indicated in Fig. 5-8.

Table c. Fast Idle Rpm

Car model	Fast idle speed (choke closed)
1975 and 1976, except Calif. models 1975 and 1976 Calif. models	3000 rpm ±200 rpm 2700 rpm ±200 rpm
1977 U.S., except Calif. and high-altitude models 1977 Canadian, Calif. and high-altitude models	3400 rpm ± 200 rpm 3000 rpm ± 200 rpm
1978 and later U.S., except Calif. and high-altitude models 1978 and later Calif. and high-altitude models 1978 and later Canadian models	3200 rpm ±200 rpm 3000 rpm ±200 rpm 3400 rpm ± 200 rpm

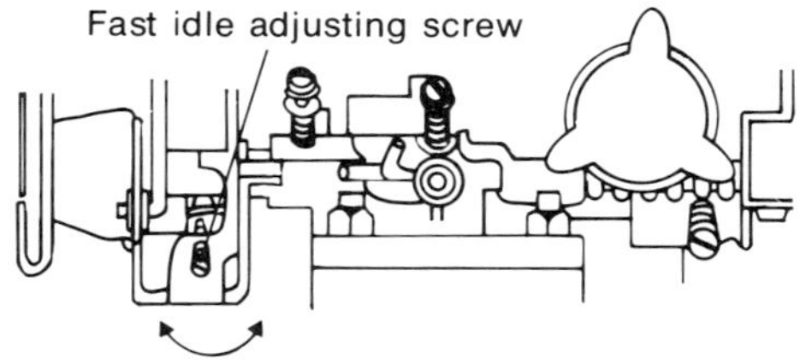

Fig. 5-8. Fast idle adjusting screw being turned (double arrow) to set fast idle to rpm prescribed in **Table c.**

4. On cars that have a choke opener diaphragm, reconnect the vacuum hose (Fig. 5-9). The fast idle speed should drop to approximately 1500 rpm. If not, either the choke opener diaphragm or its linkage is faulty and should be replaced.

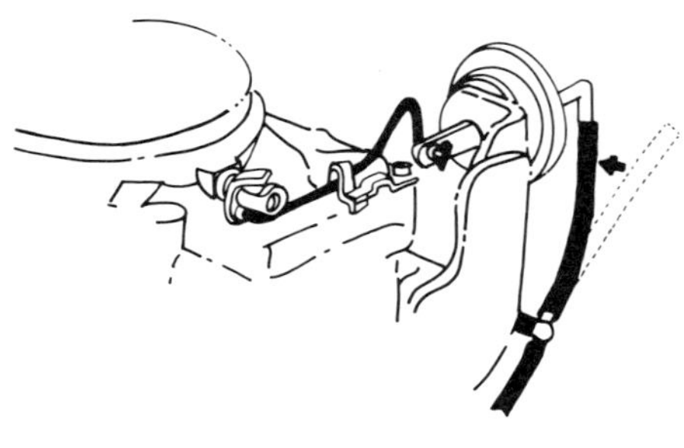

Fig. 5-9. Vacuum hose being reconnected to choke opener diaphragm.

Adjusting Throttle Positioner

You can use the checking and adjusting procedure given here to make sure that the throttle positioner adjusting screw is correctly set during carburetor adjustment. A procedure for checking the throttle positioner system's operation is given in **8.4 Exhaust Emission Controls.**

To adjust:

1. If you have installed a new throttle positioner diaphragm or a new throttle positioner linkage, check that the adjusting screw contacts the metal pad of the bellcrank at approximately the pad's center. If not, you can slightly bend the link that connects the diaphragm to the bellcrank in order to obtain good contact.
2. With the engine idling at its normal operating temperature, disconnect the vacuum hose from the throttle positioner diaphragm, which was identified in Fig. 5-1.
3. Open and release the throttle. Instead of returning to idle, the engine should run at the rpm given in **Table d.** If not, adjust the rpm to the correct range by turning the throttle positioner adjusting screw (Fig. 5-10).

Table d. Engine Rpm with Throttle Positioner Engaged

Car model	Engine speed with throttle positioner engaged
1975 and 1976 with manual trans.	1500 rpm ±100 rpm
1975 and 1976 with automatic trans.	1400 rpm ±100 rpm
1977 U.S. with manual trans.	1400 rpm ±100 rpm
1977 U.S. with automatic trans.	1200 rpm ±100 rpm
1977 Canadian with manual trans.	1500 rpm ±100 rpm
1977 Canadian with automatic trans.	1400 rpm ±100 rpm
1978 and later California and high-altitude with manual trans.	1400 rpm ±100 rpm
1978 and later California and high-altitude with automatic trans.	1200 rpm ±100 rpm
1978 and later Canadian with manual trans.	1400 rpm ±100 rpm
1978 and later Canadian with automatic trans.	1200 rpm ±100 rpm

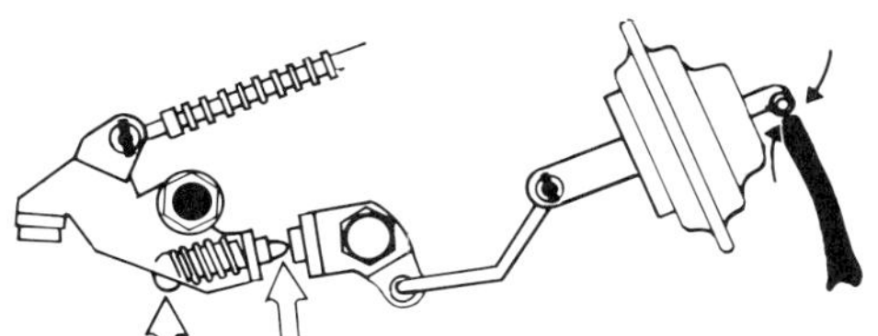

Fig. 5-10. Throttle positioner adjusting screw and related parts. Bellcrank that screw contacts may be shaped differently on some models. On all models, screw must contact metal pad on bellcrank squarely.

6. REPAIRING CARBURETOR

Most individual components for the carburetor are available as replacement parts. In addition, there are rebuilding kits that contain complete sets of gaskets and other "soft" parts.

Two possible carburetor conditions could make it necessary to rebuild the carburetor. First, foreign matter may be clogging the tiny air and fuel passages inside the carburetor. Dirt that is visible on the outside of the carburetor or that is visible when you look into the carburetor's air intake should not be considered an indication that the carburetor needs rebuilding—unless the engine is operating poorly owing to a carburetor fault.

The second condition that might make it advisable to rebuild the carburetor is air and fuel leakage caused by worn parts or damaged gaskets and seals. These problems are usually a source of trouble only after considerable time and mileage. If the throttle shafts or parts of the carburetor linkage are badly worn, it is best, either to replace the entire throttle body assembly or to replace the carburetor rather than to rebuild the old carburetor.

6.1 Removing and Installing Carburetor

If the carburetor must be replaced, it is important that the new carburetor have the same part number as the original or that the new carburetor be the correct replacement for the car model you are servicing. See **10. Fuel System Technical Data.** Always obtain replacement carburetors and carburetor parts with reference to the carburetor part number and the car model number.

6

To remove:

1. Disconnect the battery's negative (−) cable. Disconnect the spark plug cables from the spark plugs (Fig. 6-1). Disengage the cables for cylinders No. 3 and No. 4 from the plastic retainer atop the air cleaner's air intake tube.

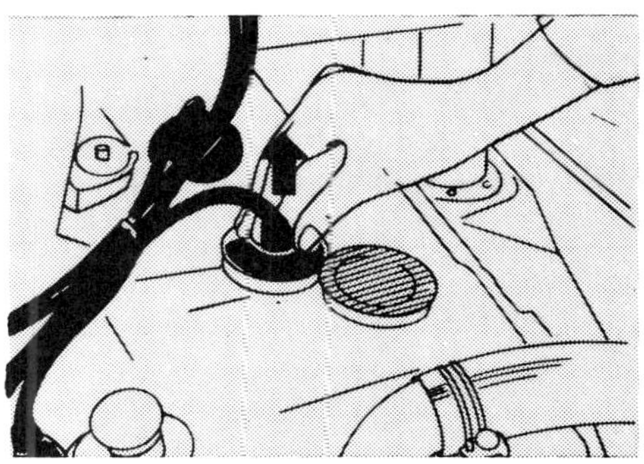

Fig. 6-1. Spark plug cable being disconnected. Grasp boot and plug connector; do not pull on cable itself.

2. Disengage the three clips that hold the periphery of the air cleaner cover to the air cleaner body. Remove the wing nut and washer from atop the air cleaner, lift off the cover, and take out the filter element. See Fig. 6-2.

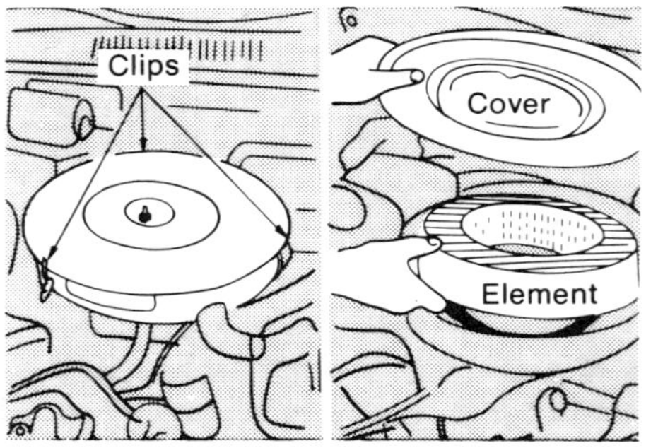

Fig. 6-2. Air cleaner cover clips (left) and air cleaner filter element (right).

3. Pull the (black) air injection dump hose and the (black) air injection intake hose off the connections on the underside of the air cleaner body. Detach the (red) PCV (positive crankcase ventilation) hose from the side clip and the bottom clip of the air cleaner body. On 1978 and later cars, disconnect the air suction hose.
4. Using a 10-mm wrench, remove the two bolts and flat washers that hold the air cleaner body to the cylinder head cover. On certain 1978 and later cars, loosen the nut or bolt that holds the air cleaner's front support bracket to the engine.
5. Disengage the throttle cable conduit from the clip on the air cleaner body. Pull the air cleaner's vacuum line off the connection at the intake manifold tap, then lift off the air cleaner body, carefully disengaging it from the intake air preheating duct atop the exhaust manifold stove.
6. By grasping the cable quadrant of the carburetor's throttle valve shaft, fully open the primary throttle valve so that there is slack in the cable. Pull the slack cable away from the quadrant until the cable is aligned with the slot. Then pull the cable's pivot pin out of its hole, guiding the cable itself out through the slot and detaching it from the carburetor.
7. Detach the electrical wire(s) from the carburetor's automatic choke and the solenoid valve(s).
8. Disconnect the vacuum hoses and the fuel hoses from the carburetor. Plug the fuel hoses with pencils or golf tees to prevent fuel leakage. Mark the hoses so that you will be able to reinstall them in the correct locations.

***WARNING* ——**

Disconnect the battery's negative (−) cable. Do not smoke or work near heaters or other fire hazards. Have a fire extinguisher handy.

9. Remove the four nuts from the studs that hold the carburetor to the intake manifold. Remove the carburetor and the gasket.

Installation is the reverse of removal. Use a new gasket between the carburetor and the intake manifold and torque the nuts to 20 to 25 Nm (15 to 18 ft. lb). After you have reconnected the accelerator cable, adjust it as described in **7.1 Removing and Installing Accelerator Cable.** Align the arrows as indicated in Fig. 6-3 when you install the air cleaner cover. Then torque the bolts that hold the air cleaner to the cylinder head cover, working alternately and in stages, to 2 to 3 Nm (18 to 27 in. lb.).

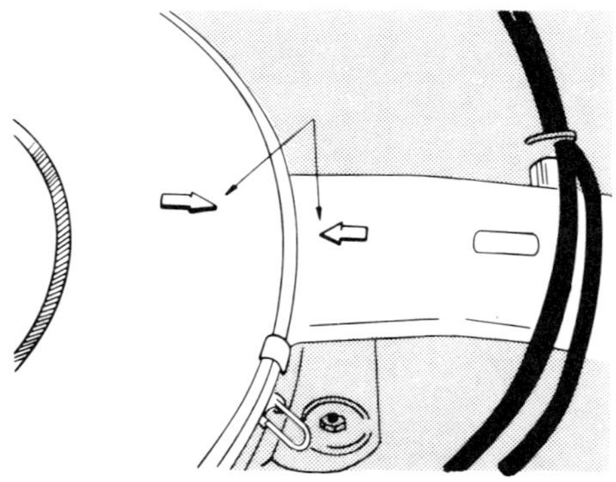

Fig. 6-3. Arrows that should be aligned during installation of air cleaner cover.

6.2 Disassembling and Assembling Carburetor

Fig. 6-4, Fig. 6-5, Fig. 6-6, Fig. 6-7, Fig. 6-8, and Fig. 6-9 show the carburetor disassembled. Follow this basic disassembly sequence when you disassemble the carburetor:

1. Dismount the various vacuum diaphragm units, including the vacuum unit for the secondary throttle valve.
2. Remove the carburetor upper part from the carburetor body. (In doing this, you should completely remove the accelerator pump lever.)
3. Remove the power valve, the float, and the float valve from the carburetor upper part. Then disassemble the automatic choke assembly.
4. Remove the screw-held external components from the carburetor body.

5. Detach the carburetor body from the carburetor's throttle valve housing assembly.
6. Remove the various jets and adjustment screws from the carburetor body, including the solenoid valve(s).
7. Remove the needle valves and the linkage components from the throttle valve housing.

CAUTION ——

We do not recommend that you try to disassemble the throttle valves and shafts. The screws that hold the throttle valves to the shafts are peened and are likely to strip or break if you try to remove them. The throttle valves, the throttle valve shafts, and the screws are not available as individual replacement parts.

Assembly is the reverse of disassembly. Obtain new gaskets or a rebuilding kit and install the components that the kit contains. With the exception of the choke thermostatic spring, the diaphragms, and any plastic parts, wash all old parts in lacquer thinner, acetone, or a commercial carburetor cleaner.

WARNING ——

Do not smoke or work near heaters or other fire hazards. Have a fire extinguisher handy. The cleaning agents are highly inflammable.

Blow out all jets, valves, and drillings with compressed air. Do not clean them with pins or pieces of wire, which could upset the precise calibration of these parts. During assembly, make the checks and adjustments described under the nine unnumbered headings that follow. After you have installed the rebuilt carburetor, carry out the adjustments described in **5. Adjusting Carburetor.** Do not install plastic limiter caps on the idle mixture adjusting screw or the idle speed adjusting screw until you have completed these adjustments.

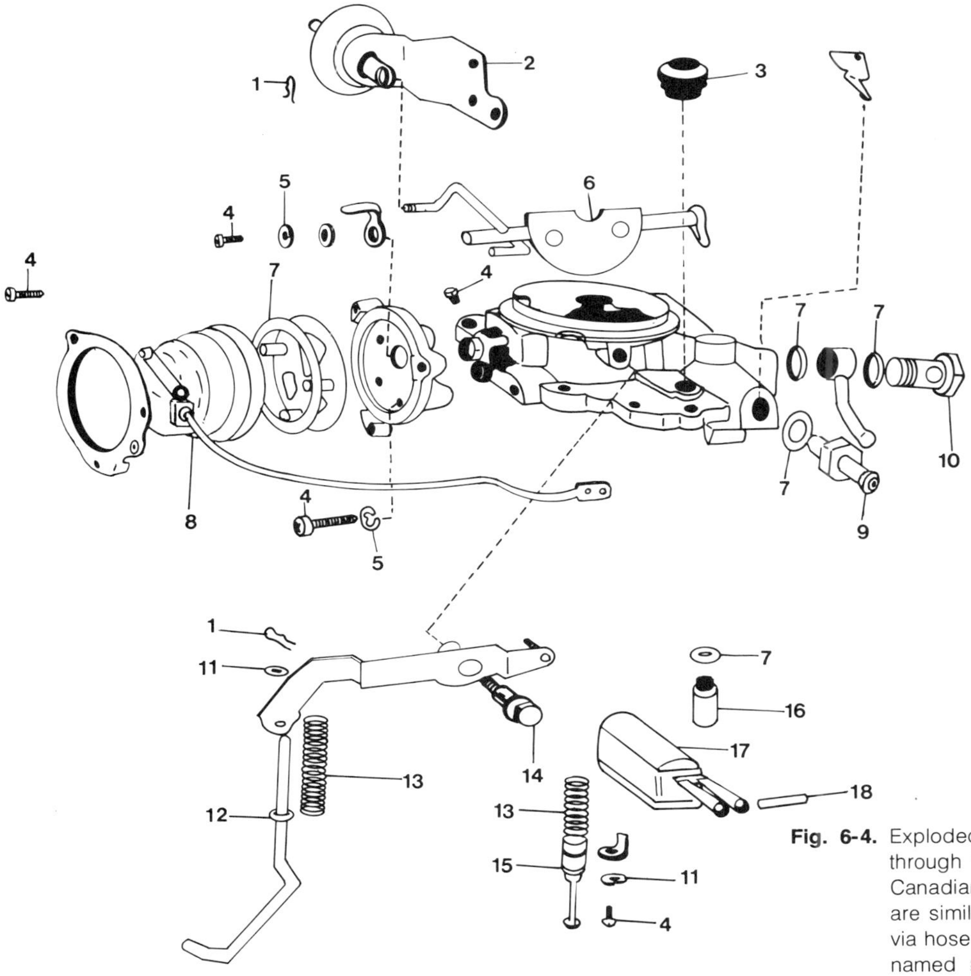

1. Clip
2. Choke breaker
3. Rubber boot
4. Screw
5. Lockwasher
6. Choke valve
7. Gasket
8. Choke heating element assembly
9. Union
10. Union bolt
11. Washer
12. Rod
13. Spring
14. Special bolt
15. Power valve
16. Float needle valve
17. Float
18. Pin

Fig. 6-4. Exploded view of carburetor upper part (1975 through 1976 U.S. models and 1977 and later Canadian models). Earlier Canadian models are similar but have choke heated by engine via hose instead of electric heat. Components named are those available as replacement parts.

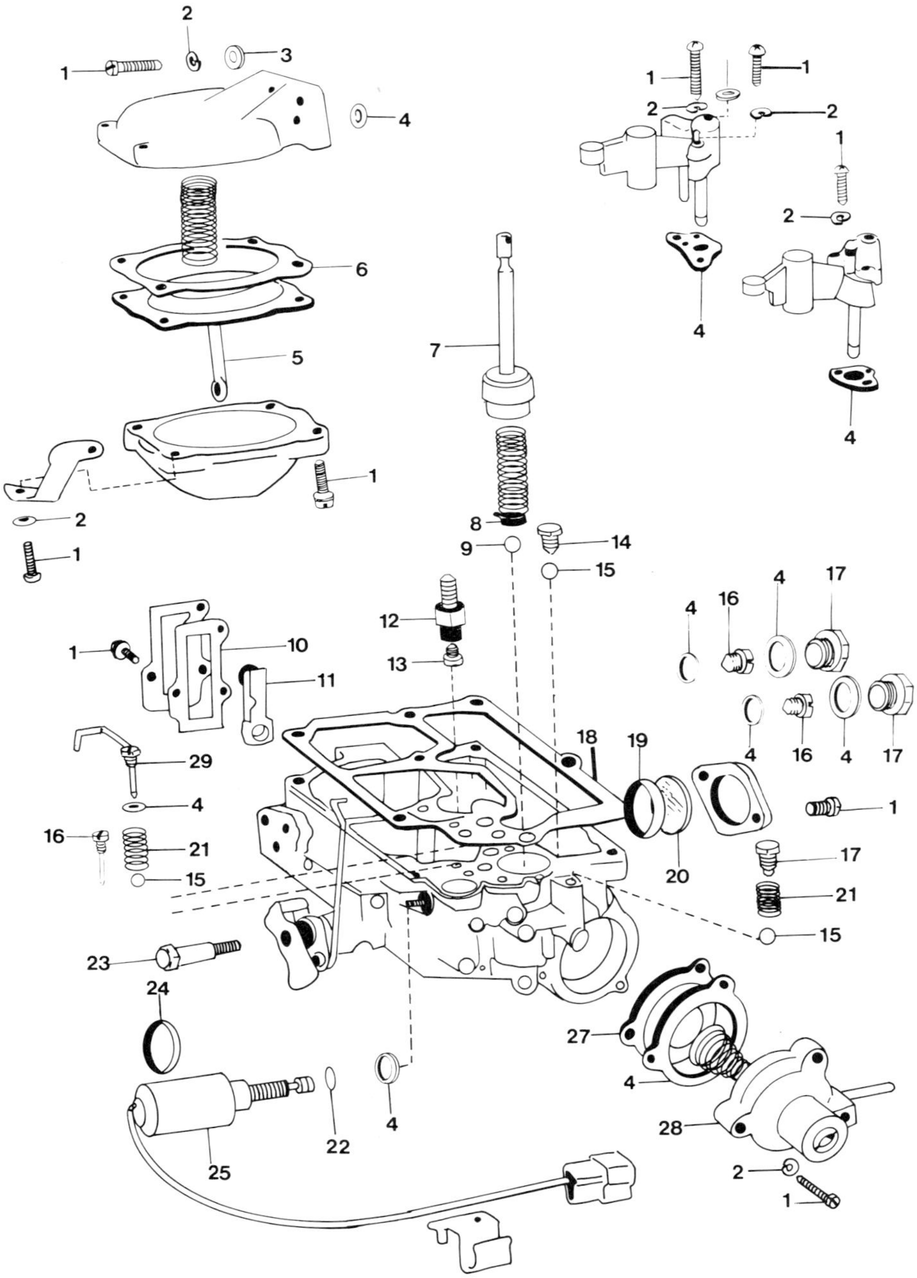

1. Screw
2. Lockwasher
3. Flat washer
4. Gasket
5. Diaphragm
6. Gasket
7. Accelerator pump plunger
8. Spring retainer
9. Ball valve
10. Gasket
11. Thermostatic valve
12. Valve
13. Jet
14. Plug
15. Ball valve
16. Jet
17. Plug
18. Float bowl gasket
19. Seal
20. Sight glass
21. Spring
22. O-ring
23. Special bolt
24. Seal
25. Solenoid valve
26. AAP pump
27. Diaphragm
28. AAP cover
29. Accelerator pump jet

Fig. 6-5. Exploded view of carburetor body (1975 through 1976 U.S. models and 1977 and later Canadian models). Earlier Canadian models do not have auxiliary acceleration pump diaphragm. Components named are those available as replacement parts.

1975 and 1976 California cars

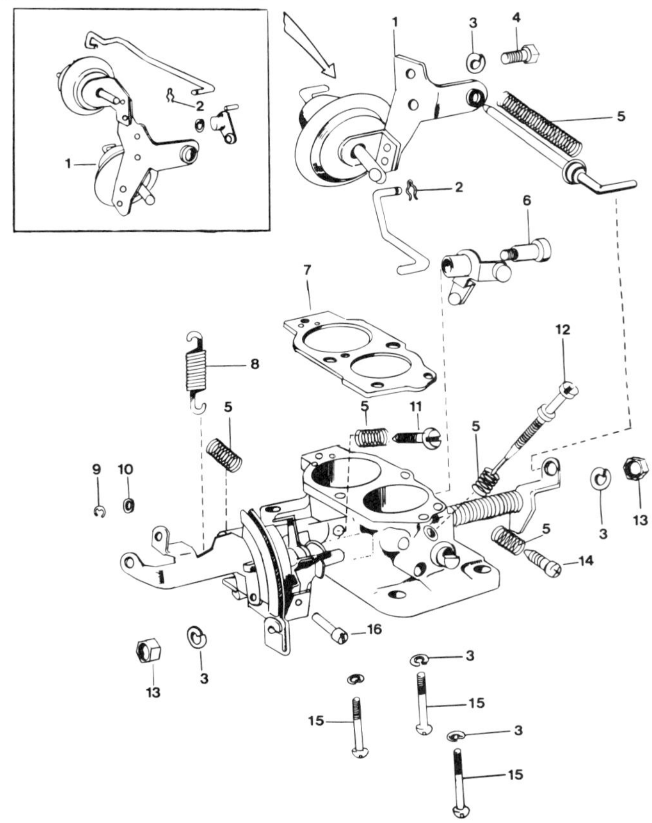

1. Throttle positioner
2. Clip
3. Lockwasher
4. Bolt
5. Spring
6. Special bolt
7. Gasket
8. Throttle return spring
9. Retainer
10. Washer
11. Idle speed adjusting screw
12. Idle mixture adjusting screw
13. Nut
14. Throttle positioner adjusting screw
15. Screw
16. Fast idle adjusting screw

Fig. 6-6. Exploded view of throttle valve housing assembly and related parts (1975 through 1976 U.S. models and 1977 and later Canadian models). Earlier Canadian models are similar. Components named are those available as replacement parts.

6

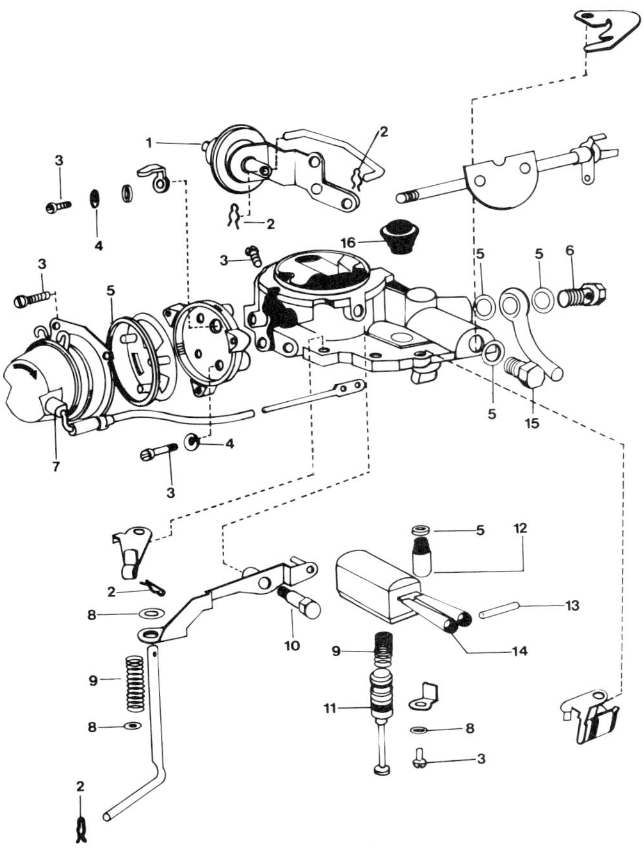

1. Choke breaker
2. Clip
3. Screw
4. Lockwasher
5. Gasket
6. Union bolt
7. Choke heating element assembly
8. Washer
9. Spring
10. Special bolt
11. Power valve
12. Float needle valve
13. Pin
14. Float
15. Plug
16. Rubber boot

Fig. 6-7. Exploded view of carburetor upper part (1977 and later U.S. models). Components named are those available as replacement parts.

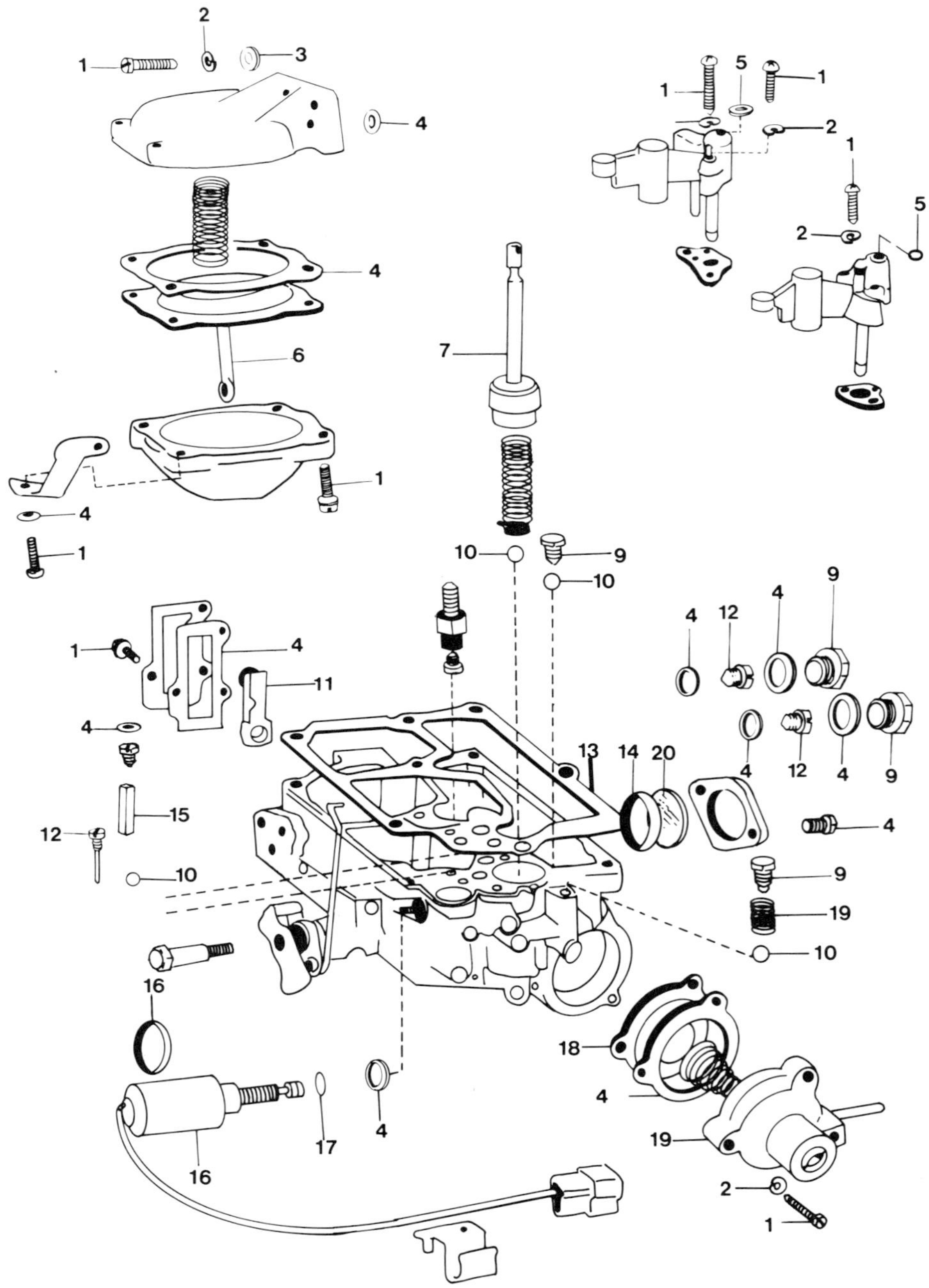

1. Screw
2. Lockwasher
3. Flat washer
4. Gasket
5. O-ring (high-altitude only)
6. Diaphragm
7. Accelerator pump plunger
8. Spring retainer
9. Plug
10. Ball valve
11. Thermostatic valve
12. Jet
13. Float bowl gasket
14. Seal
15. Weight
16. Solenoid valve
17. O-ring
18. AAP pump diaphragm
19. AAP pump cover
20. Sight glass

Fig. 6-8. Exploded view of carburetor body (1977 and later U.S. models). Components named are those available as replacement parts.

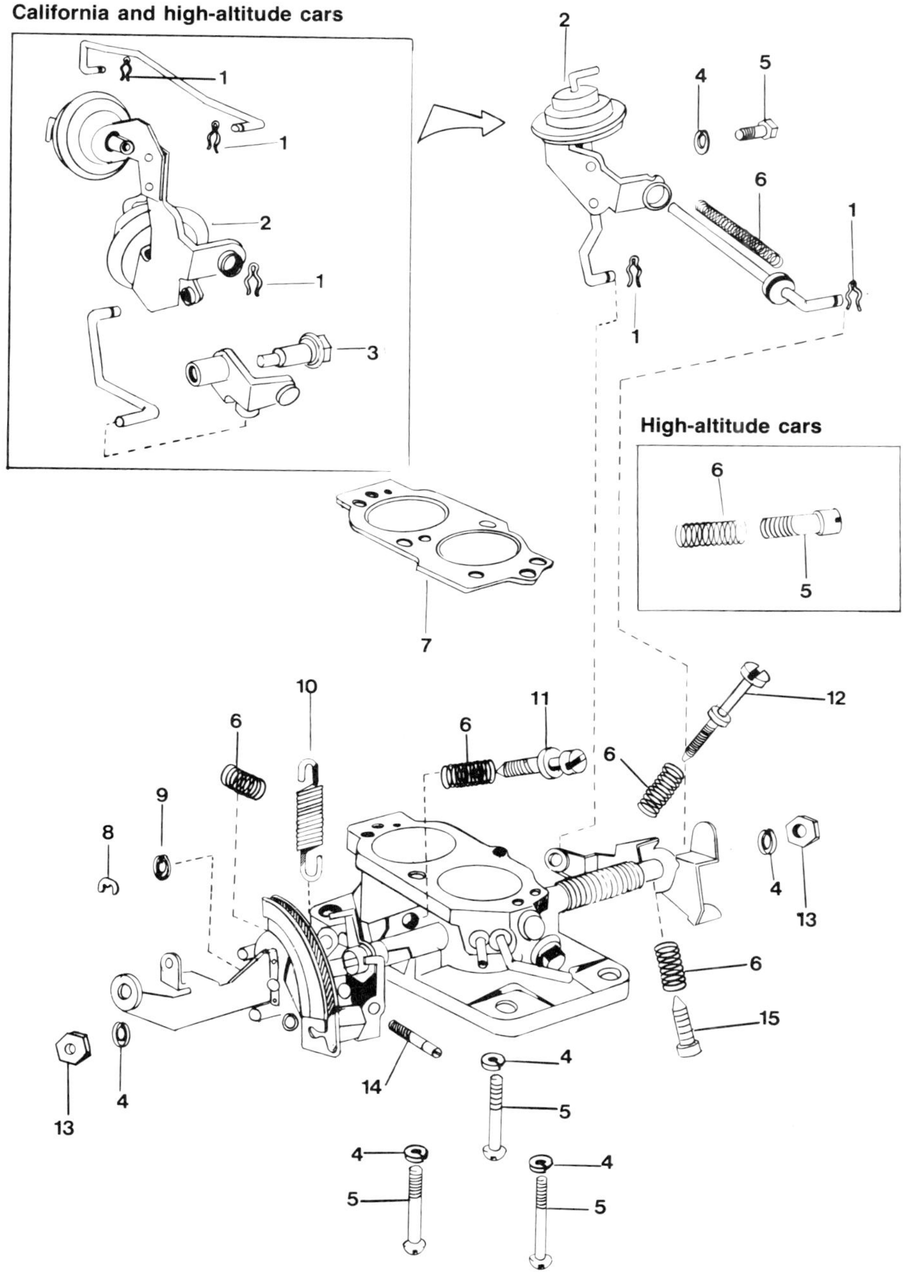

1. Clip
2. Throttle positioner
3. Special bolt
4. Lockwasher
5. Screw
6. Spring
7. Gasket
8. Retainer
9. Washer
10. Throttle return spring
11. Idle speed adjusting screw
12. Idle mixture adjusting screw
13. Nut
14. Fast idle adjusting screw
15. Throttle positioner adjusting screw

Fig. 6-9. Exploded view of throttle valve housing assembly and related parts (1977 and later U.S. models). Components named are those available as replacement parts.

Installing, Checking, and Adjusting Automatic Choke

You can check the automatic choke's electrical heating element by connecting an ohmmeter or a battery-powered test light to the wire and to the thermostatic spring housing. If the element is heating correctly, there should be continuity (that is, the ohmmeter should read zero ohms or the test lamp should light). In addition, you can connect the heating element to the car's battery to make sure that the element is heating correctly. Check that the thermostatic spring is not deformed or damaged (Fig. 6-10). Replace faulty components.

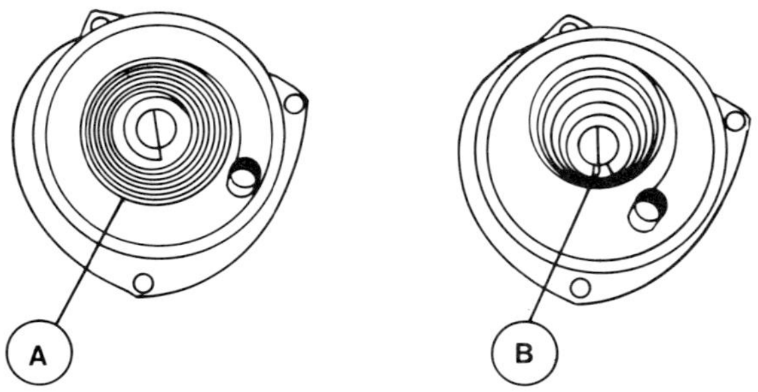

Fig. 6-10. Correctly centered thermostatic spring (**A**) and distorted spring (**B**). Replace entire housing if spring is damaged or deformed.

When installing the automatic choke, insert the end of the choke valve operating lever into the loop or tabs on the thermostatic spring end. Install the housing so that the index mark on the thermostatic spring housing is aligned with the central index mark on the carburetor's choke mounting plate (Fig. 6-11.) Then, at an ambient temperature of no more than 25°C (77°F), open the choke valve fully and release it. If the thermostatic spring is in good condition and correctly installed, the choke valve will close completely. Automatic choke system troubleshooting and routine maintenance checks are covered in **8.4 Exhaust Emission Controls.**

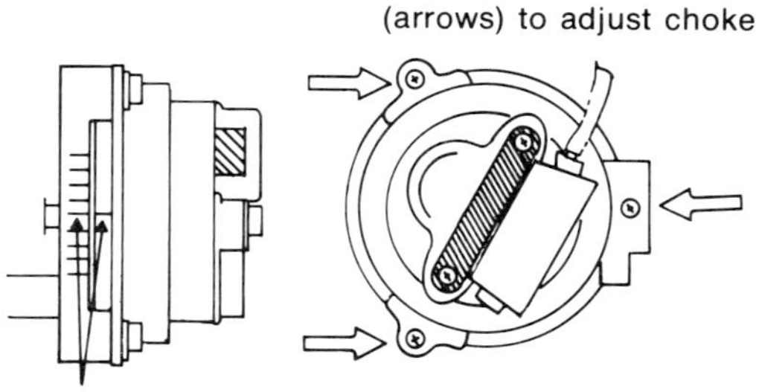

Fig. 6-11. Automatic choke adjustment. Align index marks as shown at left. Then tighten screws indicated at right.

Adjusting Throttle Valve Gaps

During assembly of the carburetor, you should check and, if necessary, adjust the throttle valve gaps. First, check that both the primary throttle valve and the secondary throttle valve are at 90° to the carburetor's mounting flange when they are fully open (Fig. 6-12). Also check that when the throttle valves are fully closed their movement is limited by the external stops and not by the throttle valves coming into contact with the bores of the throttle valve housing. When the throttle valves are fully closed, the primary throttle valve should be at a 7° angle to the bore axis, and the secondary throttle valve at a 20° angle to the bore axis. If necessary, bend the projections on the throttle valve shaft levers to adjust the open and closed gaps.

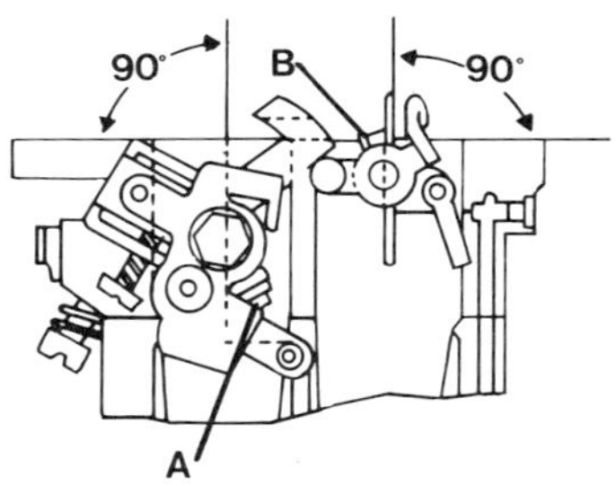

Fig. 6-12. Angles (90°) for primary throttle valve (**A**) and secondary throttle valve (**B**) in fully open positions.

To adjust the secondary throttle valve's kick-up gap, move the primary throttle valve to a position between 62° open and wide open. In this position (Fig. 6-13), the tab on the secondary throttle valve shaft lever will lie against the kick-up projection on the primary throttle valve shaft lever. With the secondary throttle valve thus kicked up, you should just be able to insert a 0.20-mm (.008-in.) round-wire feeler gauge between the secondary throttle valve and the bore of the carburetor's throttle valve housing. If necessary, bend the tab on the secondary throttle valve shaft lever to obtain the correct clearance.

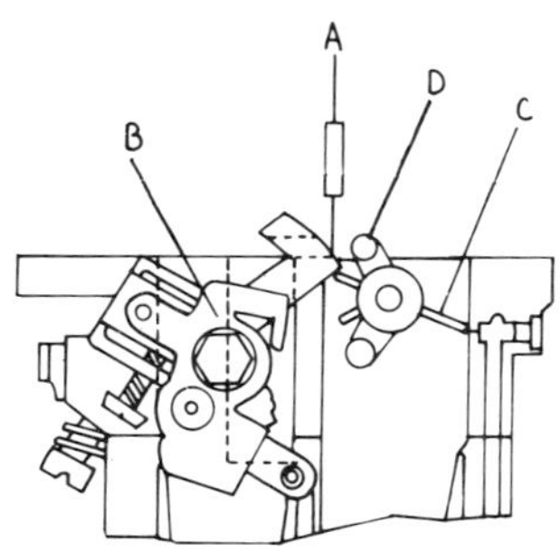

Fig. 6-13. Secondary throttle valve kick-up gap being checked with round-wire feeler gauge (**A**). Primary throttle valve is at **B**, secondary throttle valve at **C**. Bend tab at **D** to make adjustments.

Adjusting Fast Idle Linkage

This adjustment is to be made, if necessary, during assembly of the carburetor. You should make the final fast idle adjustment with the carburetor installed on the engine, as described in **5. Adjusting Carburetor.**

Fully close the choke valve and hold it in that position. Then turn the fast idle adjusting screw (Fig. 6-14) until the primary throttle valve gap is 1.10 mm (.043 in.) when measured with a round-wire feeler gauge inserted between the primary throttle valve and the bore of the throttle valve housing.

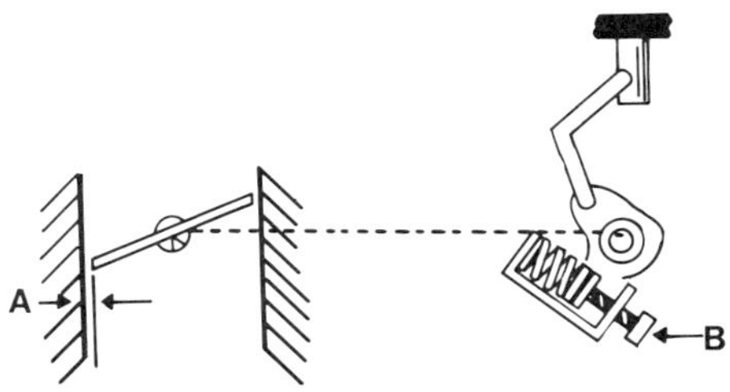

Fig. 6-14. Fast idle gap being measured (**A**). Adjusting screw is at **B**.

Adjusting Mechanical Choke Unloader

During carburetor assembly, you should check the adjustment of the mechanical choke unloader. You can also check the adjustment for maintenance or troubleshooting purposes with the carburetor installed. However, both the engine coolant and the choke's electrical heating element must be completely cold.

First check that the automatic choke is correctly adjusted, as described under an earlier unnumbered heading. Then check that the choke valve closes fully when the accelerator pedal is pressed and released. If the choke valve does not close fully, repair or replace either the choke linkage or the thermostatic spring. With the choke valve fully closed and the engine stopped, fully open the primary throttle valve. The mechanical unloader should open the choke valve to an angle of 47° from horizontal (Fig. 6-15). If not bend the tab on the throttle valve shaft lever so that you obtain the correct choke valve angle.

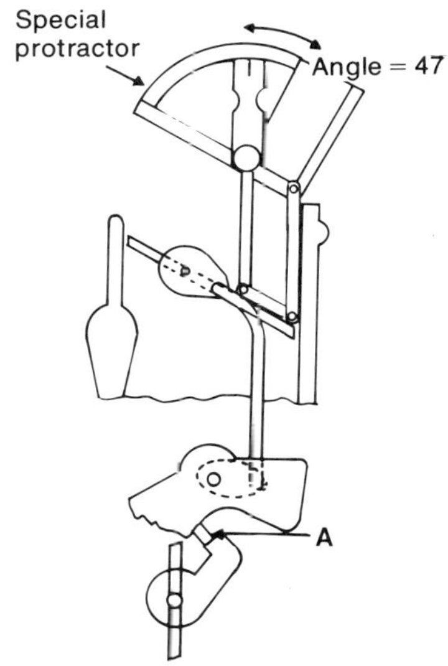

Fig. 6-15. Adjustment of choke mechanical unloader being checked. Special protractor is used to measure angle of choke valve. Bend tab at **A** to make adjustments.

Adjusting Carburetor Float Level

(1975 through 1977 cars)

You can adjust the carburetor's float level by bending the tabs indicated in fig. 6-16. When correctly adjusted, the float should maintain the fuel level in the carburetor's float bowl at the center of the sight glass.

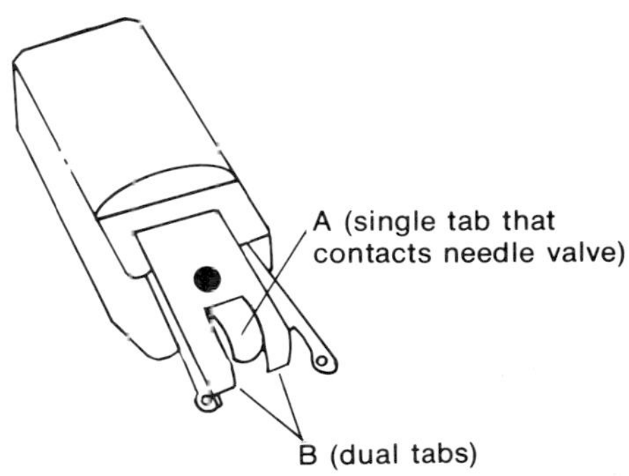

Fig. 6-16. Tabs that can be bent to adjust float level. Tab **A** determines upward limit of float travel, and hence fuel level. Tabs **B** determine lower limit of float travel.

6

To adjust the fuel level, hold the carburetor upper part in an inverted position with the float and the needle valve assembly installed. Then measure the gap between the float tip and the carburetor upper part (Fig. 6-17). If the gap is not 3.50 mm (.138 in.) on 1975 and 1976 cars or 6.00 mm (.236 in.) on 1977 cars, you should adjust the gap to this specification by bending tab **A**, shown previously in Fig. 6-16.

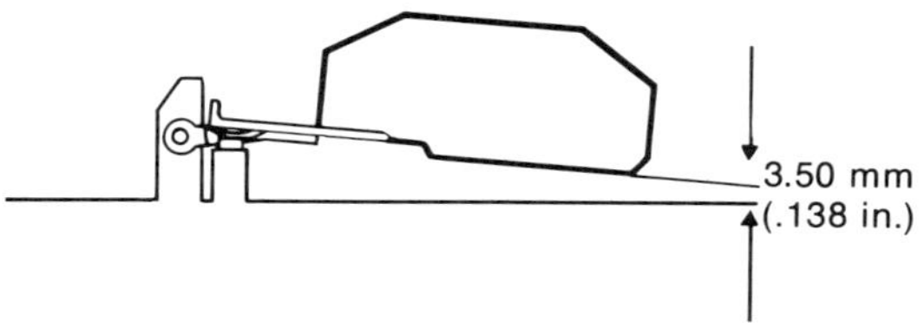

Fig. 6-17. Gap from float tip to carburetor upper part being measured with float in fully up position. Gasket for carburetor upper part should not be in place.

To adjust the lower limit of float travel, keep the carburetor upper part inverted so that the needle valve remains seated. Then lift the float as indicated in Fig. 6-18 so that the dual tabs contact the stop. With the float in this position, measure the gap between tab **A** (the single tab) and the needle valve. If necessary, adjust the gap to 1.20 mm (.047 in.) by bending tabs **B** (the dual tabs).

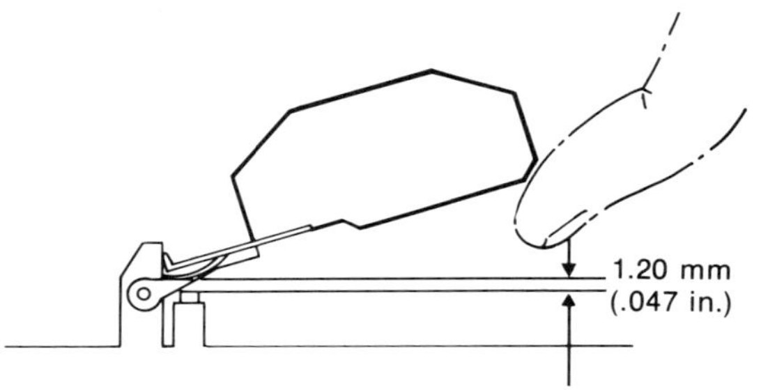

Fig. 6-18. Gap between needle valve and single tab of float being measured with float in fully down position.

Adjusting Carburetor Float Level

(1978 and later cars)

The carburetor's float level should be adjusted to maintain the fuel level in the carburetor's float bowl at the center of the sight glass. To do this, hold the carburetor upper part in an inverted position with the float and the needle valve assembly installed. Then measure the gap between the projection on the float and the carburetor upper part (Fig. 6-19). If the gap is not 6.50 mm (.256 in.), you should adjust the gap to this specification by bending the float hinge at the point indicated in the illustration.

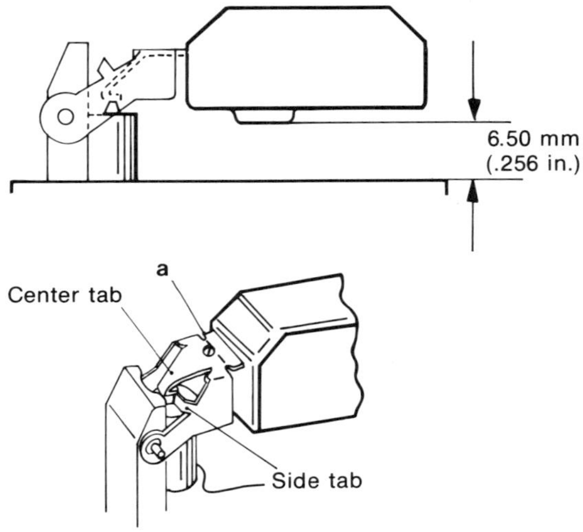

Fig. 6-19. Gap from projection on float to carburetor upper part being measured (top). Gasket for carburetor upper part should not be in place. If necessary, adjust gap by bending hinge at point **a** (bottom).

To adjust the lower limit of float travel, keep the carburetor upper part inverted so that the needle valve remains seated. Then lift the float, as indicated in Fig. 6-20, so that the tab on the side of the hinge contacts the stop. With the float in this position, measure the gap between the hinge's center tab and the needle valve. If necessary, adjust the gap to 1.20 mm (.047 in.) by bending the tab on the side of the hinge. Under no circumstances should you adjust the gap by bending the center tab.

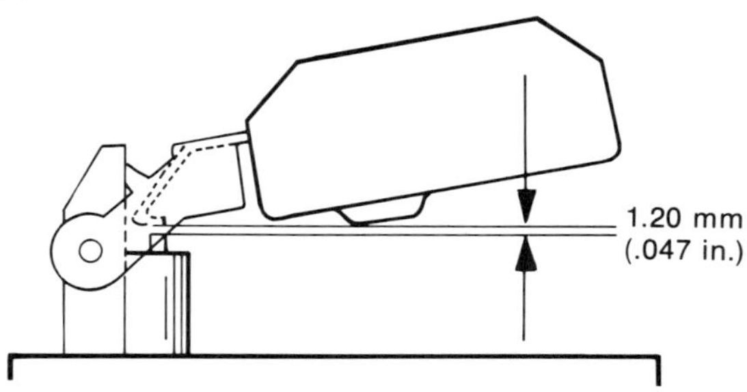

Fig. 6-20. Gap between center tab and needle valve being measured with float in fully down position. Side tab and center tab are identified in Fig. 6-19, given earlier.

Adjusting Accelerator Pump

After you have assembled the carburetor, you should carefully check the stroke of the accelerator pump—especially if you have installed any new components in the accelerator pump linkage. You may have altered the stroke unintentionally by installing slightly thicker or thinner gaskets between the carburetor body and the carburetor upper part or between the carburetor body and the throttle valve housing. Measured at the center of the pump piston pin, the total pump stroke should be 5 mm (.197 in. or 13/64 in.). Adjust the stroke by bending the connecting link at the point indicated in Fig. 6-21.

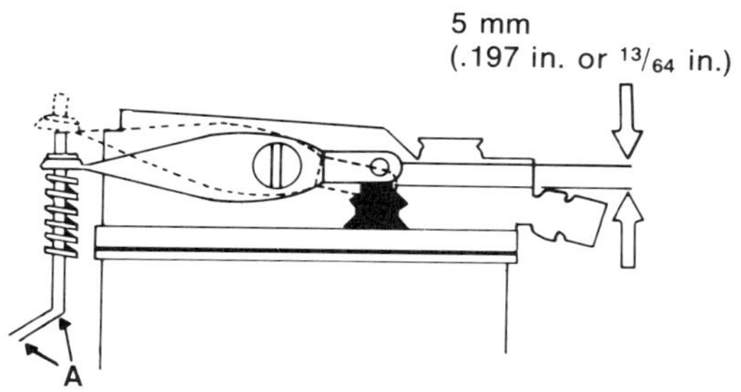

Fig. 6-21. Accelerator pump adjustment. Measure stroke at center of pump piston pin (right). Make adjustments by increasing or decreasing angles of bends at **A**.

Checking Electromagnetic Cutoff Valve
(solenoid valve)

The electromagnetic cutoff valve(s) can be checked while installed. Turn on the ignition without starting the engine, then disconnect the wire from the terminal of each electromagnetic cutoff valve. Touch the wire to the terminal several times. The valve should make a clicking sound each time contact is made. With an electromagnetic cutoff valve removed, you can check it by connecting it to the battery with jumper wires.

Presetting Idle Mixture Adjusting Screw

When you are assembling the carburetor, or after you have installed a replacement carburetor on the engine, you should make a preliminary setting of the idle mixture adjusting screw so that the engine will start and idle satisfactorily. After the engine has warmed up, you can make the final adjustment as described in **5. Adjusting Carburetor.**

To preset the idle mixture adjusting screw (Fig. 6-22), first turn the screw clockwise, screwing it in until it just contacts its seat. From this position, turn the screw counterclockwise 2⅝ turns (2½ turns on 1979 and later cars).

CAUTION —

Do not turn the screw clockwise so tightly that it is forced against its seat. Doing this can deform the tip of the screw, making accurate adjustment impossible.

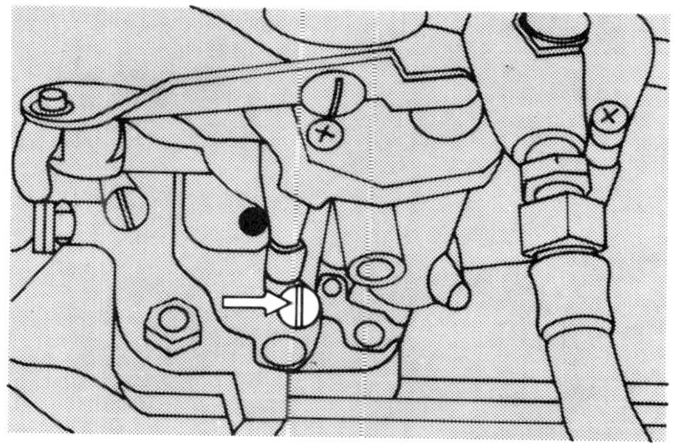

Fig. 6-22. Location of idle mixture adjusting screw (arrow).

7. ACCELERATOR PEDAL AND LINKAGE

Fig. 7-1 and Fig. 7-2 show the accelerator pedals and cables used on the cars covered by this Manual. The cable itself should not be lubricated. Replace it if it binds or is in any other way faulty.

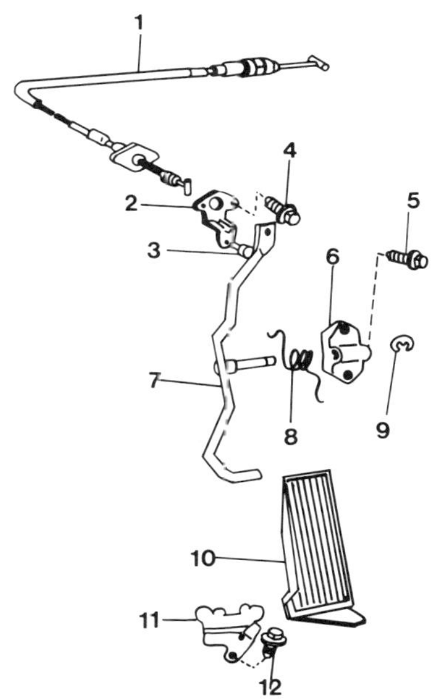

1. Cable
2. Conduit retainer
3. Cushion
4. Bolt
5. Bolt
6. Bracket
7. Pedal lever
8. Return spring
9. Retainer
10. Pedal pad
11. Mounting bracket
12. Bolt

Fig. 7-1. Exploded views of accelerator pedals and cables used on 1975 and 1976 cars.

6

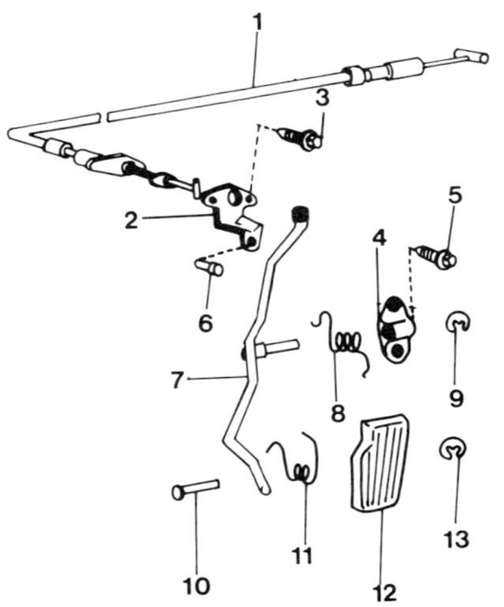

1. Cable
2. Conduit retainer
3. Bolt
4. Bracket
5. Bolt
6. Cushion
7. Pedal lever
8. Return spring
9. Retainer
10. Pin
11. Pad spring
12. Pedal pad
13. Retainer

Fig. 7-2. Exploded views of accelerator pedals and cables used on 1977 and later cars.

7.1 Removing and Installing Accelerator Cable

The pivot pin (or other end fitting on the accelerator cable) is factory-installed and cannot be removed. You should replace cables as a unit if they are in any way faulty or damaged.

To remove:

1. Working beneath the dashboard, disengage the retainer on the cable end from the eye in the pedal lever. Then detach the cable from the lever, removing it to the right so that the cable comes out through the slot in the eye.
2. Remove the two bolts that hold the cable conduit retainer to the firewall. Remove the cable conduit retainer, slipping it over the end of the cable.
3. Working in the engine compartment, remove the air cleaner as described in **6.1 Removing and Installing Carburetor.**
4. By grasping the cable quadrant of the carburetor's throttle valve shaft, fully open the primary throttle valve so that there is slack in the cable. Pull the slack cable away from the quadrant until the cable is aligned with the slot. Then pull the cable's pivot pin out of its hole, guiding the cable itself out through the slot and detaching it from the carburetor.
5. Loosen the two adjusting nuts that hold the cable conduit to the bracket on the carburetor. Then disengage the cable conduit from the bracket.
6. Working inside the car, remove the cable and its conduit by pulling it out through the firewall and into the passenger compartment.

Installation is the reverse of removal. Following installation, adjust the cable as described under the next heading.

Adjusting Accelerator Cable

Have someone hold the accelerator fully to the floor. By turning the two adjusting nuts that hold the cable conduit to the bracket on the carburetor, adjust the position of the cable conduit until the primary throttle valve is almost wide open (about 0.50 mm, or .020 in., clearance between the throttle stop and the throttle valve lever). Tighten the nuts against the bracket to hold the cable conduit in this position, then check to make sure there is still clearance between the throttle stop and the throttle valve lever. In this way, you will keep the cable from being strained when the accelerator is pressed to the floor, which could cause the cable to break.

> **NOTE ——**
> See **AUTOMATIC TRANSMISSION** if you need to check or adjust the throttle cable used on cars with automatic transmissions.

7.2 Removing and Installing Accelerator Pedal

On 1975 and 1976 cars, the pedal pad itself is a separate part that you can pull away from the pedal lever and snap off the ball-pins on its mounting bracket. You can remove the mounting bracket from the floor by taking out the bolts. On 1977 and later cars, you can remove the pedal pad from the pedal lever by removing the retainer from the pin and then pulling the pin out of the pedal pad, the spring, and the pedal lever.

To remove pedal lever assembly as a unit:

1. Working beneath the dashboard, disengage the retainer on the cable end from the eye in the pedal lever. Then detach the cable from the lever, removing it to the right so that the cable comes out through the slot in the eye.
2. If necessary, fold down the carpet to gain access to the pedal lever bracket's mounting bolts.
3. Remove the bolts that hold the pedal lever bracket to the firewall. Then remove the accelerator pedal lever assembly from the car.

Installation is the reverse of removal. Following installation, adjust the accelerator cable as described under the preceding heading.

8. EMISSION CONTROL SYSTEMS

Because slightly different models of Corolla cars sold during a model year may have different emission controls, it is impossible to make an accurate list of the emission controls used on your particular car. You can determine which controls have been installed by checking the emissions decal located in the engine compartment. The following abbreviations are used:

AAP—Auxiliary Acceleration Pump System
AI—Air Injection System
AS—Air Suction System
CB—Choke Breaker System
CCo—Catalytic Converter
EGR—Exhaust Gas Recirculation System
EVAP—Evaporative Emission Control System
HAC—High-altitude Compensation System
HAI—Heated Air Intake System
HIC—Hot Idle Compensation System
MC—Mixture Control System
PCV—Positive Crankcase Ventilation System
SC—Spark Control System
TCS—Transmission Controlled Spark System
TP—Throttle Positioner System

8.1 Positive Crankcase Ventilation System (PCV)

All cars covered by this Manual are equipped with a closed positive crankcase ventilation (PCV) system. The filtered air drawn into the crankcase for ventilation purposes is taken from the bottom of the engine's air cleaner by a hose connected to the front, right-hand side of the cylinder head cover. Ventilating air and crankcase fumes are drawn out of the engine through a PCV valve located in the rear, upper part of the cylinder head cover. These fumes are conducted from the valve through a hose into the intake manifold so that the fumes will be burned along with the fuel/air mixture entering from the carburetor.

You can quick-check the PCV system with the engine idling. Pull the PCV valve out of the cylinder head cover and observe the engine rpm either on the dashboard tachometer or on a dwell meter/tachometer. Then seal the end of the PCV valve with your thumb. If the PCV valve is not clogged, the engine speed will have dropped by about 50 rpm.

To inspect and service:

1. Pull the PCV valve out of the cylinder head cover. Detach its hose from the connection on the intake manifold and the clip on the bottom of the air cleaner body. Remove the hose and the PCV valve from the car, then detach the hose from the valve.
2. Attach a clean piece of hose to the end of the PCV valve that is normally inserted into the cylinder head cover. Then blow air through the valve as indicated in Fig. 8-1. If air does not pass through the valve readily, the valve is faulty and should be replaced.

WARNING —
Do not put the dirty PCV valve hose into your mouth and do not suck air through the PCV valve. Petroleum residues are harmful to health and in some cases poisonous.

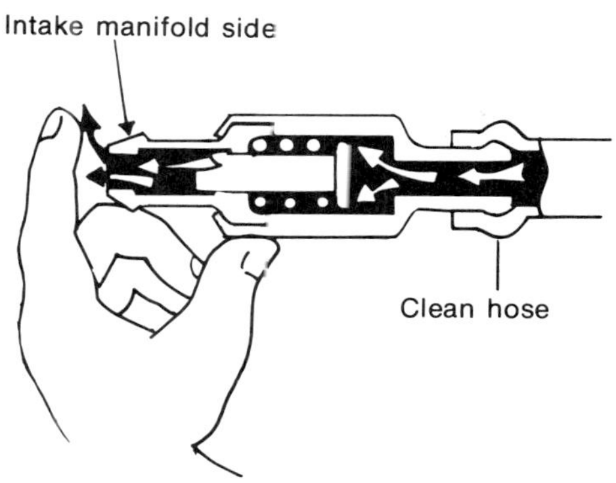

Fig. 8-1. Air being blown through PCV valve from end that is normally inserted into cylinder head cover.

6

3. Attach the clean hose to the opposite end of the PCV valve, as indicated in Fig. 8-2. The valve should close when you blow into it, preventing air from passing through. Replace leaking PCV valves.

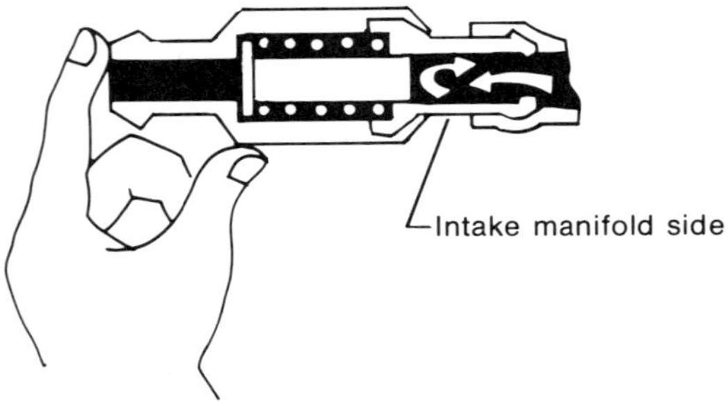

Fig. 8-2. Valve closed, preventing passage of air from intake manifold end to cylinder head cover end.

4. Remove the PCV hose that connects the bottom of the air cleaner body to the front of the cylinder head cover. Then clean the hoses and the valve with solvent, scrubbing the hoses with a long brush. Replace kinked or leaking hoses.
5. Reinstall the hoses and the PCV valve. Visually inspect the hoses, the connections, and the gaskets for leakage, especially at the points indicated in Fig. 8-3. Replace loose-fitting hoses and damaged gaskets, and tighten loose screws or bolts where applicable.

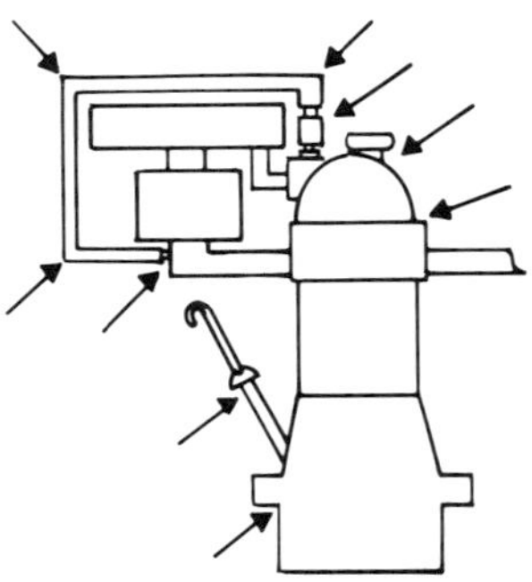

Fig. 8-3. Points at which you should check for PCV system leakage. Leaks at oil pan, oil dipstick, oil filler, and cylinder head cover will allow entry of dusty, unfiltered air and permit escape of oil vapors and crankcase fumes.

8.2 Catalytic Converter (CCo)

The catalytic converter is located beneath the car, approximately beneath the driver's seat. On 1975 through 1977 models with catalytic converters, an exhaust temperature thermo sensor is in the catalytic converter, which is attached to an exhaust temperature warning light on the instrument panel. Beginning with the 1978 models, the thermo sensor is found only on cars with catalytic converters that are sold in California or in high-altitude areas. Instead of being attached to a warning light, the sensor on 1978 and later cars is designed to cut off the air injection system if the catalytic converter begins to overheat, exceeding 750°C (1382°F). Many cars with no catalytic converters have front mufflers that resemble a catalytic converter and are equipped with small fuel fillers, which will accept only the small pump nozzles used to dispense unleaded gasoline. Thus the best way to determine whether your car has a catalytic converter is to check for the abbreviation CCo on the emissions decal located in the engine compartment.

To inspect:

1. Inspect the exhaust system. Repair all leaks and loose connections, especially around clamps. Replace rust-weakened, cracked, or damaged exhaust system components.

> ***WARNING —***
> *Catalytic converters generate very high heat and can remain hot enough to burn you or to ignite combustible materials half an hour or more after the engine has been stopped.*

2. Inspect the exterior of the catalytic converter. If you find any dent that is more than 20 mm ($^{25}/_{32}$ in.) deep, replace the catalytic converter. See Fig. 8-4.

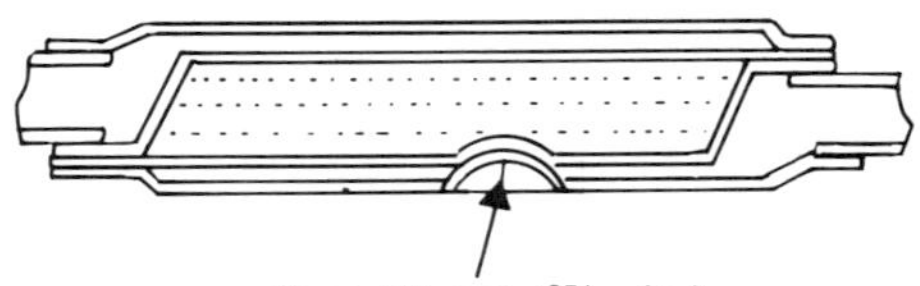

Fig. 8-4. Cross-section of catalytic converter, showing how deep dents can obstruct gas flow and damage catalytic element.

3. Shake the catalytic converter as indicated in Fig. 8-5. If you can distinctly hear loose matter rattling inside, replace the catalytic converter.

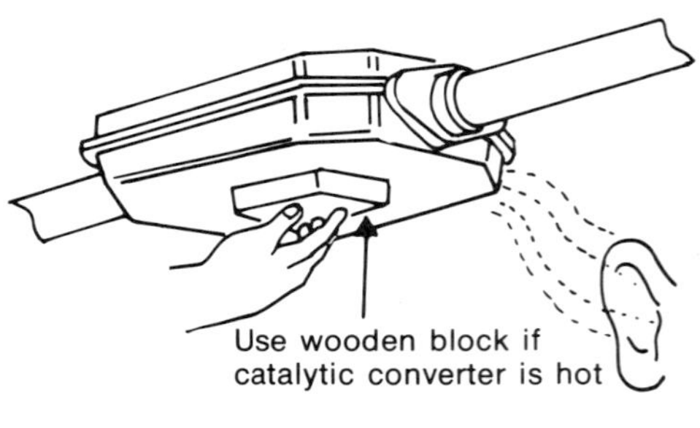

Fig. 8-5. Catalytic converter being shaken to check for rattles that indicate loose, broken, or disintegrating catalytic element.

4. Inspect the heat shield between the catalytic converter and the car body (Fig. 8-6). Replace heat shields that are missing, deformed, or badly rust damaged. Make sure there is adequate clearance at all points between the catalytic converter and the heat shield.

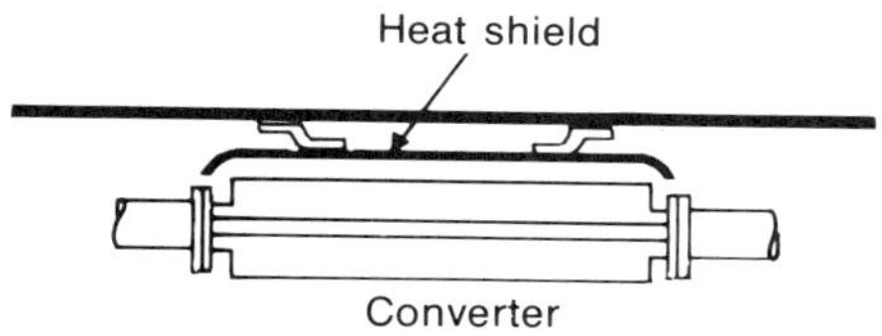

Fig. 8-6. Location of heat shield above catalytic converter. Notice approximate clearance between shield and converter.

5. To test the thermo sensor, disconnect its lead wires at the multiple connector beneath the driver's seat, being careful to pull only on the connector halves and not on the wires themselves. Connect an ohmmeter to the thermo sensor's lead wires as indicated in Fig. 8-7. Then start the engine and observe the ohmmeter as the catalytic converter warms up.

   NOTE ——
   On 1975 through 1977 cars, the ohmmeter should begin with a high resistance reading, then fall to 430 ohms as the catalytic converter's temperature increases to 920°C (1688°F). On 1978 or later cars (California and high-altitude models only), the resistance should be between 2000 and 200,000 ohms after idling and warm-up. Replace temperature sensors that indicate low resistance when cold or that do not change to lower resistance as they are heated.

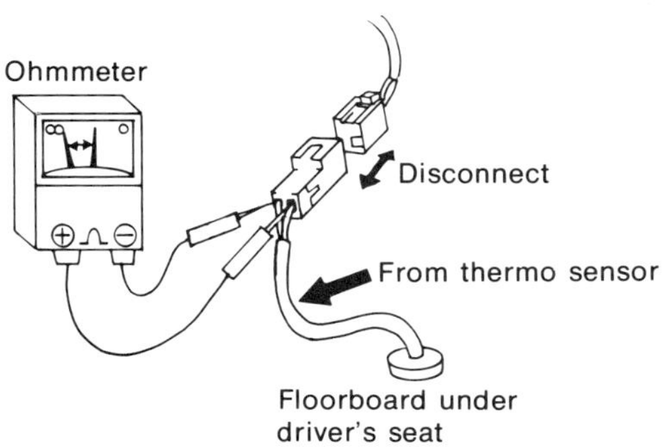

Fig. 8-7. Ohmmeter being used to test thermo sensor.

6. To test the warning light on a car that has one, connect a jumper wire to the service connector as indicated in Fig. 8-8. The warning light bulb is faulty if it does not light.

   NOTE ——
   If it is apparent that the catalytic converter is overheating, check the air suction (AS) system or the air injection (AI) system, whichever is applicable to the car. On cars with a catalytic converter warning light, the computer wiring could be at fault if the light stays on after you start a cold engine.

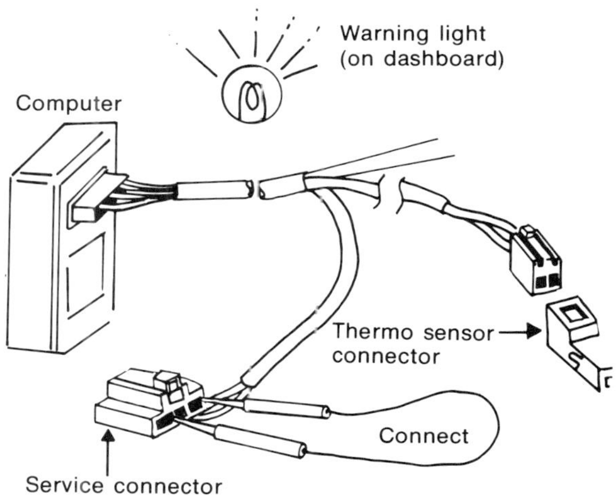

Fig. 8-8. Catalytic converter warning light being tested.

To replace:

1. Working beneath the driver's seat, disconnect the multiple connector for the catalytic converter's thermo sensor, being careful to pull on the connector halves themselves and not on the wiring. Then remove the rubber grommet from the floorboard so that you will be able to pull the wires and the connector out from under the car.

   NOTE ——
   The 1978 and later cars sold outside California and high-altitude areas do not have thermo sensors in their catalytic converters.

2. Raise the car on a hoist or support it on stands designed for the purpose.
3. Make sure that the catalytic converter is cool enough to handle. If not, allow it to cool before you continue working.

4. Remove the bolts that hold the catalytic converter to the exhaust system (Fig. 8-9). Then, while supporting the catalytic converter, unhook the rubber rings and remove the catalytic converter and its gaskets from the car, pulling the thermo sensor wire out of the car's floorboard where applicable.

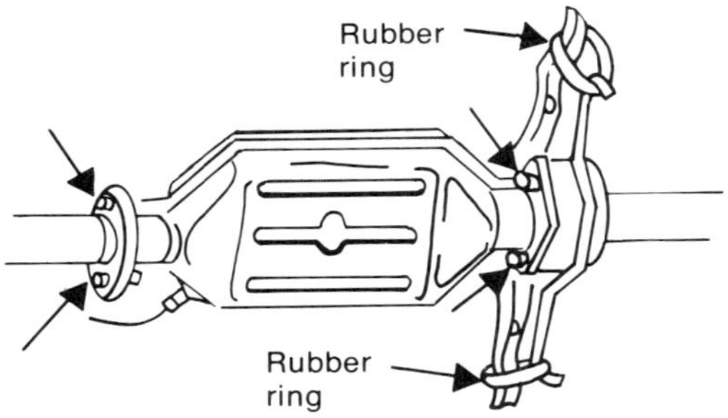

Fig. 8-9. Bolts (arrows) and rubber rings that hold catalytic converter to exhaust system and to car body.

5. If the catalytic converter has a thermo sensor, hold the converter so that the thermo sensor is up. Then remove the bolts for the thermo sensor and remove the sensor and its gasket as indicated in Fig. 8-10.

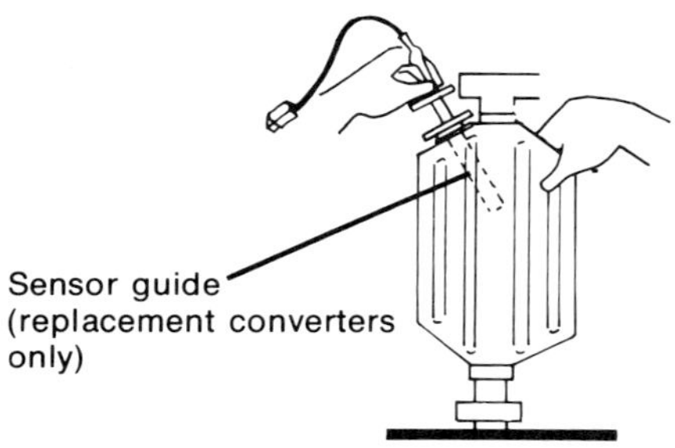

Fig. 8-10. Thermo sensor being removed or installed. During insertion into replacement catalytic converter, sensor should enter plastic guide as indicated.

Installation is the reverse of removal. Use new gaskets at all points. Torque the bolts for the thermo sensor to 4 to 6 Nm (35 to 53 in. lb.). Torque the bolts that hold the catalytic converter to the exhaust system to 35 to 45 Nm (26 to 33 ft. lb.). Replace the rubber rings and the grommet for the thermo sensor wire if these parts are in poor condition. Make sure that the thermo sensor wire is not excessively tight, twisted, or caught on parts that will rub through the insulation as the exhaust system moves or vibrates.

8.3 Evaporative Emission Control (EVAP) System

A great many different hookups for the evaporative emission control (EVAP) system have been used, with different components designed for particular models. For example, six slightly different systems were used for the 1978 model year alone.

In many 1975 cars and in all 1976 through 1978 California and high-altitude models, the vacuum supply is routed through the vacuum switching valve (Fig. 8-11 and Fig. 8-12). The vacuum switching valve, which also determines when vacuum reaches the throttle positioner and the air injection system's air suction valve on California and high-altitude cars, is controlled by a speed sensor, which is built into the car's speedometer. A solid state computer analyzes the signal from the speed sensor, thereby determining how fast the car is moving and turning the vacuum switching valve on and off at appropriate times for low emissions.

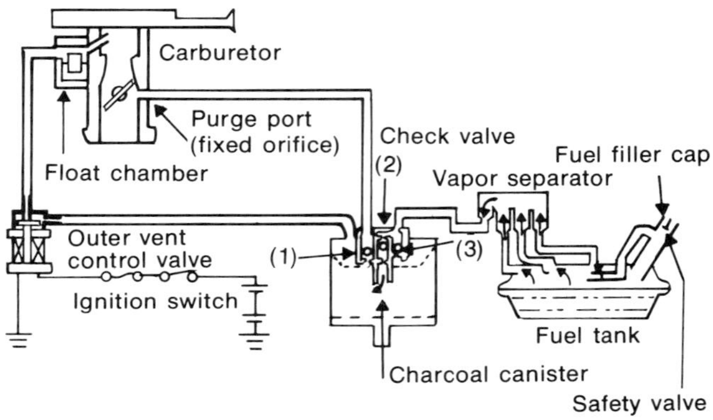

Fig. 8-11. Typical 1978 and later evaporative emission control system for cars that meet 1978 federal and 1979 U.S. air pollution standards. Vapor separator is used only on liftback and wagon. Outer vent control valve system is not used on 1975 through 1977 cars.

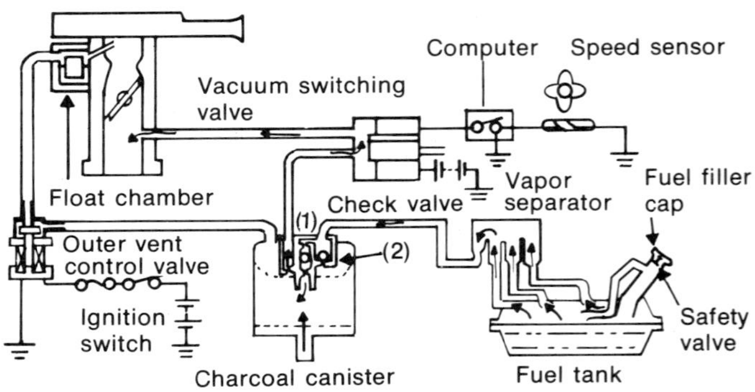

Fig. 8-12. Typical 1978 evaporative emission control system for cars sold in California and in high-altitude areas. Vapor separator is used only on liftback and wagon. Outer vent control valve system is not used on 1975 through 1977 cars; all 1979 and later cars have system shown in Fig. 8-11.

To inspect and repair:

1. Visually inspect the fuel vapor lines, the fuel tank, and all related parts. Replace kinked, leaking, or loose-fitting hoses. Replace the fuel tank if it is cracked, leaking, or deformed. Replace deformed or damaged fuel filler cap gaskets, and make sure that the filler cap's safety valve is not stuck—especially if the fuel tank has been deformed by collapsing.

   NOTE ——
   The vapor separator and vapor line(s) may pass through the fuel tank cover or behind the interior trim panels at the rear of the car. If there has been trouble in the evaporative emission control system, you should remove the trim and inspect the hoses in these areas as well.

2. Inspect the charcoal filter canister and replace it if it is cracked, deformed, or otherwise damaged.
3. Detach the hoses from the charcoal filter canister, attaching tags to the disconnected hoses or making a note of their locations so that you will be able to reconnect them in the correct locations.
4. On 1975 cars, blow air at 3.0 bar (or 40 psi) into connection **A**, as given in Fig. 8-13. With connection **B** sealed, air should flow freely and without resistance from connection **C**. If the flow is restricted, or if charcoal particles are expelled from connection **C**, replace the canister. Install the canister and connect the hose.

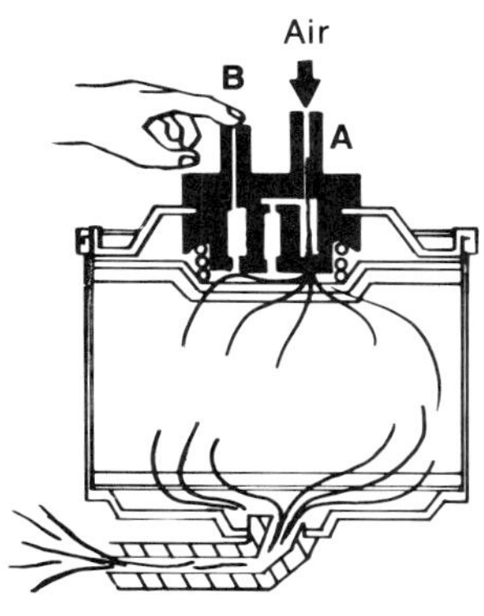

Fig. 8-13. Identification of connections on 1975 charcoal filter canister.

5. On 1976 and 1977 cars, blow air at 3.0 bar (or 40 psi) into connection **A**, as given in Fig. 8-14. Air should flow freely and without resistance from connections **B** and **C**. Then blow air into connection **B**. Neither air nor charcoal particles should exit through connection **A** or connection **C**.

   NOTE ——
   If you find a fault, replace the canister. If you find no fault, clean the canister by blowing air at 3.0 bar (or 40 psi) into connection **A** while closing connection **B** with your finger. Then reinstall the canister and reconnect the hoses.

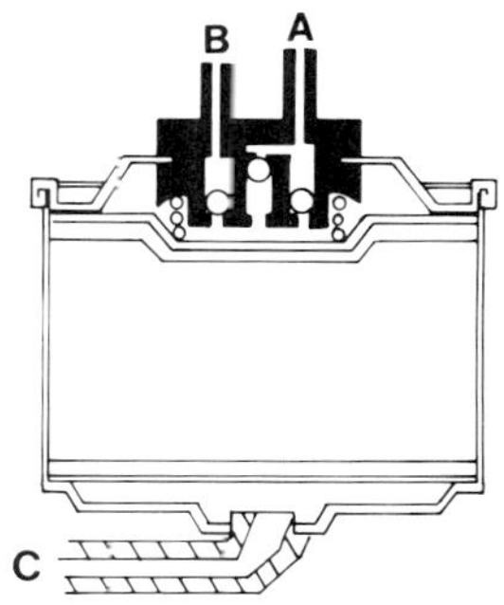

Fig. 8-14. Cross-section of 1976 and 1977 charcoal filter canister, identifying connections **A**, **B**, and **C**. On California and high-altitude models, connection **C** may be straight.

6. On 1978 and later cars, blow air at 3.0 bar (or 40 psi) into connection **A**, as given in Fig. 8-15. Air should flow freely and without resistance from connections **B** and **C**. Repeat the test by blowing air into connection **B**. On 1978 California models, air should flow from the other connections without resistance, but no air should pass through on other 1978 models and on all 1979 and later models.

   NOTE ——
   If you find a fault, replace the canister. If you find no fault, clean the canister by blowing air at 3.0 bar (or 40 psi) into connection **C** while closing connections **A** and **B** with your fingers. Replace the canister if charcoal particles emerge from connection **D**.

   CAUTION ——
   Under no circumstances should you attempt to clean the canister for any model year by washing it in solvent.

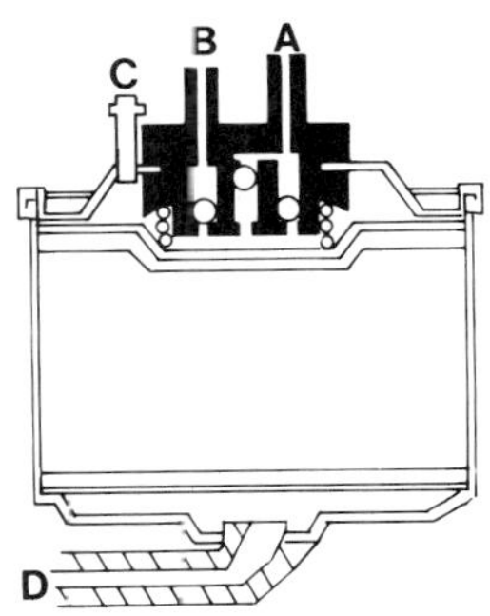

Fig. 8-15. Cross-section of 1978 and later charcoal filter canister, identifying connections **A**, **B**, **C**, and **D**. On 1978 California models, check valve assembly has only two ball valves.

7. On 1978 and later models only, disconnect the hoses from the outer vent control valve. Check that the valve is open when the ignition switch is off (Fig. 8-16). Then check that the valve is closed with the ignition switch on. If the valve does not operate correctly, check the fuse and the wiring connections. Replace the valve if you find no electrical fault. Otherwise, correct the electrical fault, recheck the valve, and reconnect the hoses.

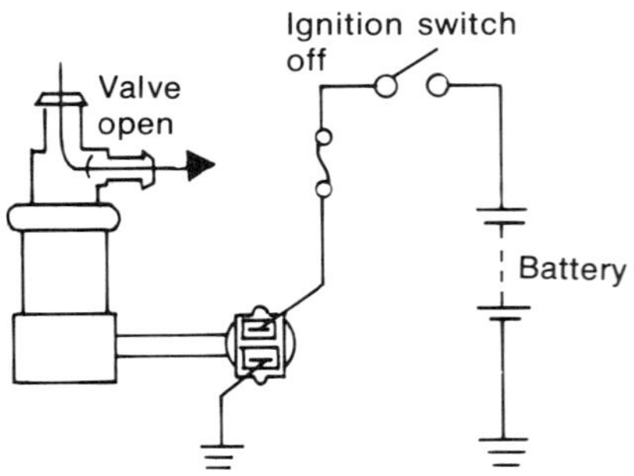

Fig. 8-16. Outer vent control valve in open position with ignition off. With ignition on, air should not flow through as indicated by arrow.

8. On cars with a vacuum switching valve, connect a vacuum gauge to the purge hose, using a T-fitting that has an orifice no more than 1 mm (.040 in.) in diameter in the connection for the canister's hose. See Fig. 8-17. Place the gauge inside the car. If the vacuum readings are not correct at the speeds given in the illustration, test the speed sensor and the vacuum switching valve as described in the next two procedures. If the readings are correct, remove the gauge and reconnect the hose.

NOTE ——
If the vacuum switching valve fails to function correctly in this test, but neither the vacuum switching valve, the speed sensor, nor the wiring prove to be faulty, replace the computer.

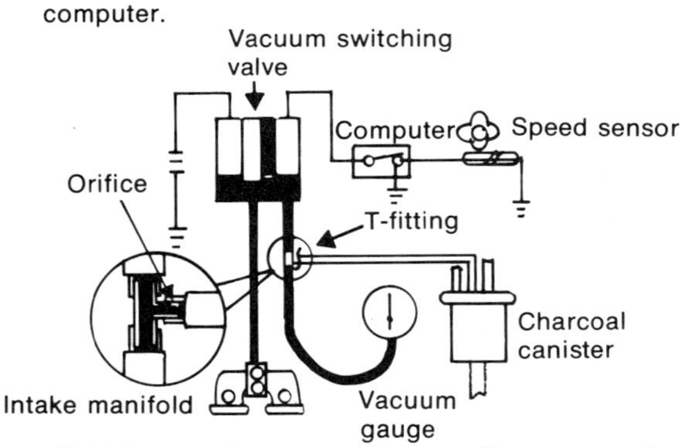

Vehicle speed	Vacuum reading
Below 11 kph (7 mph)	0 or nearly 0
Above 26 kph (16 mph)	Manifold vacuum

Fig. 8-17. Vacuum gauge hookup used to check whether vacuum switching valve is operating. Manifold vacuum depends on accelerator position.

9. On pre-1978 cars that have a check valve in the line from the tank or the vapor separator to the charcoal filter canister, you can test the check valve by blowing through it. Replace the check valve if it does not function correctly or if it is cracked or otherwise damaged.

NOTE ——
The check valve should open after initial resistance when you blow into it from either the tank side or the canister side. If there is no initial resistance, or if no air passes through, replace the valve. During installation, be careful not to reconnect the valve in its reversed position.

WARNING ——
Attach a clean hose to the removed check valve during the test, and do not suck air through the valve. Petroleum residues are harmful to health and in some cases poisonous.

To test speed sensor:

1. Check the speed sensor connections on the rear of the speedometer to see that they are properly installed and tight-fitting.
2. Jack up one rear wheel only. It must be off the ground. Chock the front wheels to keep the car from rolling, then release the parking brake and place the transmission in neutral.
3. By pulling on the connector itself and not on the wires, unplug the multiple connector from the computer, which is located beneath the left-hand end of the dashboard, on the cowl side (Fig. 8-18).

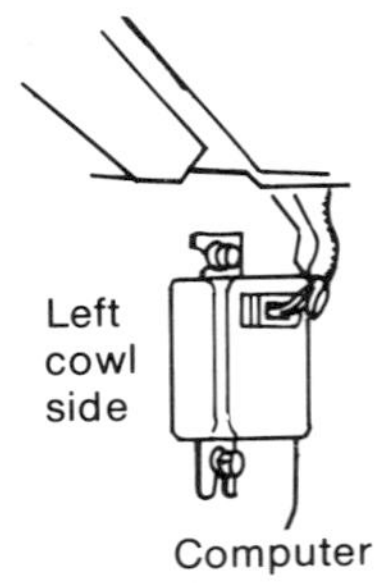

Fig. 8-18. Location of computer on left cowl side. Notice multiple connector for wiring.

4. Connect an ohmmeter to the detached multiple connector as indicated in Fig. 8-19, inserting the test probe from the rear of the connector as shown. Then hand-turn the rear wheel while you observe the ohmmeter. The ohmmeter needle should deflect constantly, indicating that the reed switch of the speed sensor is opening and closing correctly. If not, the speedometer is faulty and should be replaced, unless you find a wiring fault.

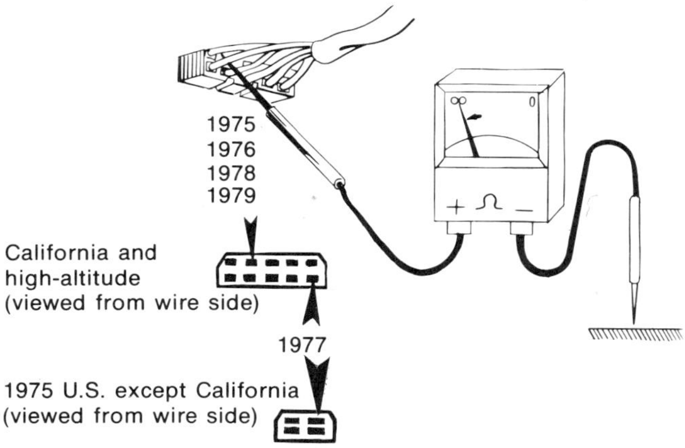

Fig. 8-19. Ohmmeter hookup used to test operation of speed sensor. Reinstall multiple connector following test.

To test vacuum switching valve:

1. Disconnect the vacuum switching valve's multiple connector from the car's wiring harness. Touch one test probe of an ohmmeter to the case of the valve, then touch the other test probe to each of the wiring terminals, as indicated in Fig. 8-20. If there is electrical continuity between any terminal and the valve case, the valve is faulty and should be replaced.

   NOTE ——
   The vacuum switching valve is located in the right-hand side of the engine compartment, about straight out from the carburetor. The number of terminals will be different on earlier models.

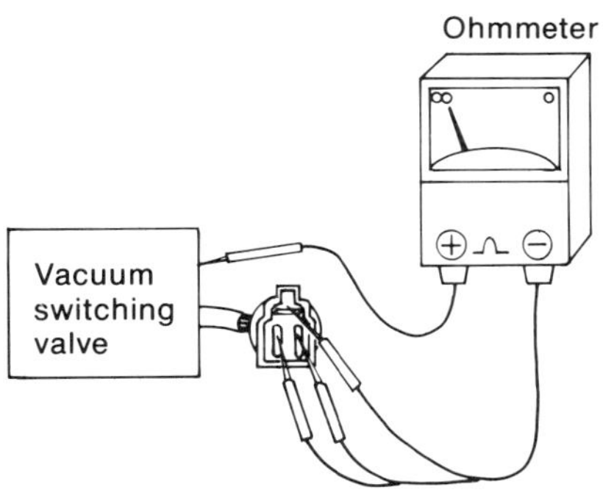

Fig. 8-20. Vacuum switching valve being tested for internal grounds (1977 and later connector shown).

2. Using the ohmmeter as indicated in Fig. 8-21, measure the resistance between the positive (+) terminal and each of the negative (−) terminals. With the valve at room temperature, the resistance should be between 48 and 60 ohms. If infinite ohms are indicated, the vacuum switching valve has an open circuit. A lower reading indicates internal shorts. Replace faulty valves.

   NOTE ——
   Some early models have only two terminals—one positive and one negative. Others may have four or five terminals, the top, center one being positive. Measure resistance between it and each of the other terminals.

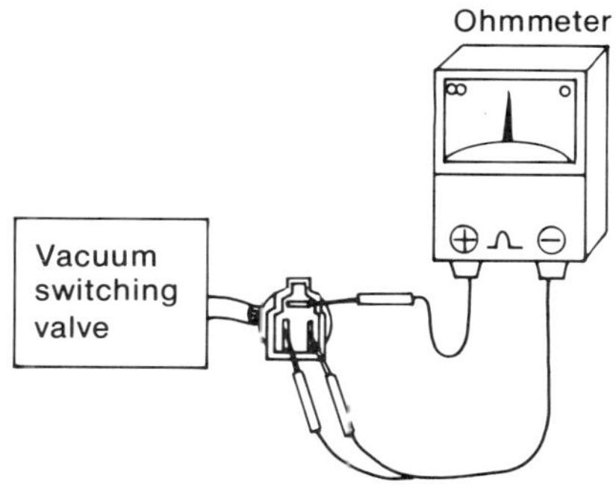

Fig. 8-21. Vacuum switching valve being tested for open circuits and internal shorts (1977 and 1978 connector shown).

3. If you found no electrical fault with the ohmmeter, disconnect the vacuum hoses from the vacuum switching valve, marking the hoses for correct reinstallation. Use a length of clean hose to blow through the ports indicated in Fig. 8-22. If these ports are not open and interconnected, the valve is faulty and should be replaced.

   NOTE ——
   The hookup shown is for the 1977 and 1978 connector plug. On 1975 and 1976 cars, connect the top center terminal to the battery's positive (+) post and the remaining terminals to the battery's negative (−) post.

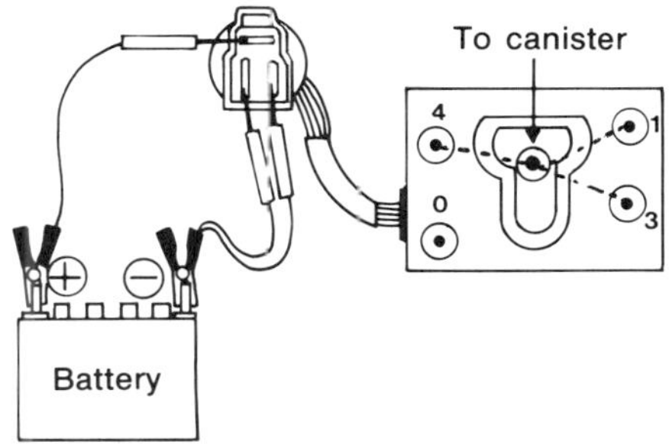

Fig. 8-22. Vacuum ports (1977 and 1978) that should be open and interconnected with vacuum switching valve energized. On 1975 cars (not shown), canister port should be interconnected with **1**, **3** and **6**; **04** and **4** should be connected with one another, and so should **07 and 7**. On 1976 cars (not shown), canister port should be interconnected with **1**, **3**, and **4**. Ports **5** and **6** should also be connected with one another.

4. With reference to Fig. 8-22, given previously, disconnect the jumper wire from the battery's positive (+) post. On 1977 and 1978 cars, vacuum connections **4** and **0** should be open and connected with one another, and so should **1** and **3**. Replace faulty valves.

> **NOTE ——**
> On 1975 cars, the canister port should be interconnected with **4** and **7**; **1** and **3** should be connected with one another, and so should **5** and **6**. On 1976 cars, the canister port should be interconnected with **6** only; **1** and **3** should be connected with one another, and so should **0** and **4**.

8.4 Exhaust Emission Controls

The emission controls used on the 1977 Canadian cars are the same as those introduced on the 1976 Canadian models. To determine which emission controls are present on a given car sold either in the U.S.A. or in Canada, you should check the emissions decal located in the engine compartment. Then, using the table of abbreviations given earlier in **8. Emission Control Systems,** determine which of the following unnumbered headings apply to the car. Some systems, such as the spark delay system, do not have a standard abbreviation used on the decal. Therefore, if an abbreviation is not given in one of the unnumbered headings, you may have to compare the test and the illustrations given under that heading with the equipment on the car to determine whether the system or device is present.

Throttle Positioner (TP) System

(all 1975 cars and 1976 California cars)

In this throttle positioner system, shown schematically in Fig. 8-23, the vacuum switching valve supplies atmospheric pressure instead of manifold vacuum to the throttle positioner diaphragm whenever the car exceeds approximately 26 kph (16 mph). This allows the spring in the throttle positioner diaphragm to set the positioner so that the carburetor's throttle valve will not close fully if the accelerator is released. At lower speeds, manifold vacuum pulls back the diaphragm, permitting the throttle valve to close so that the engine idles normally.

To check and repair:

1. Visually check all wiring and hoses to determine their conditions. Replace cracked, loose-fitting or kinked hoses. Make sure that all electrical terminals are clean and tight-fitting.
2. Check and, if necessary, adjust the throttle positioner as described in **5.1 Adjusting Idle Speed and Idle Mixture.**
3. While driving the car at approximately 50 kph (or 30 mph), either depress the clutch or place the automatic transmission's selector lever at **N**. Release the accelerator and gradually apply the brakes. The engine should idle at about 1200 to 1500 rpm until the vehicle speed falls below approximately 11 kph (7 mph), at which speed the idle should drop to about 850 rpm.

> **NOTE ——**
> If the throttle positioner fails to function correctly in the preceding test, troubleshoot the vacuum switching valve and (if you find no fault in the vacuum switching valve) the speed sensor and the computer. See **8.3 Evaporative Emission Control (EVAP) System.** If vacuum is reaching the throttle positioner diaphragm but the diaphragm is not operating as it should, replace the diaphragm unit.

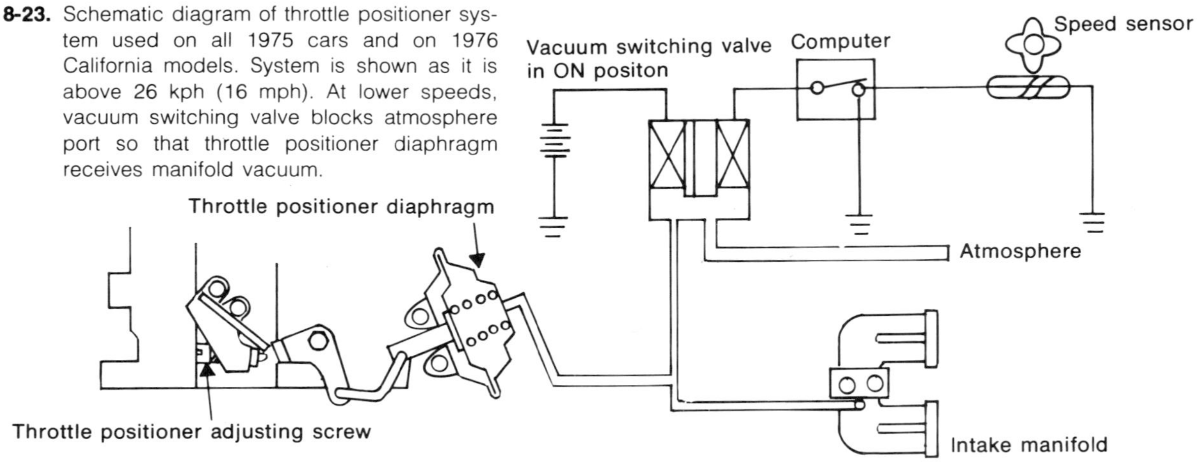

Fig. 8-23. Schematic diagram of throttle positioner system used on all 1975 cars and on 1976 California models. System is shown as it is above 26 kph (16 mph). At lower speeds, vacuum switching valve blocks atmosphere port so that throttle positioner diaphragm receives manifold vacuum.

Throttle Positioner (TP) System

(1979 and later California cars, 1978 and later Canadian cars, and 1976 and 1977 U.S. cars sold outside California and high-altitude areas)

In this throttle positioner system, shown schematically in Fig. 8-24 and Fig. 8-25, the throttle positioner diaphragm prevents immediate closing of the throttle valve during deceleration. The degree and rate of closing depends on the vacuum level supplied to the throttle positioner diaphragm by a vacuum control valve and a vacuum transmitting valve. In general, the only maintenance required is to adjust the system and then visually check its operation by accelerating the engine and then releasing the throttle. If the throttle positioner cannot be adjusted, returns the engine to idle immediately, or does not allow the engine to return to idle, you can troubleshoot the system using the procedure given here.

NOTE ——
Because of its influence on intake manifold vacuum, the ignition timing must be correct for the throttle positioner to work properly. If the visual check indicates a malfunction, first set the timing as described in **ENGINE.** Next, adjust the idle speed and mixture and then the throttle positioner as described in **5.1 Adjusting Idle Speed and Idle Mixture.** Finally, repeat the visual check.

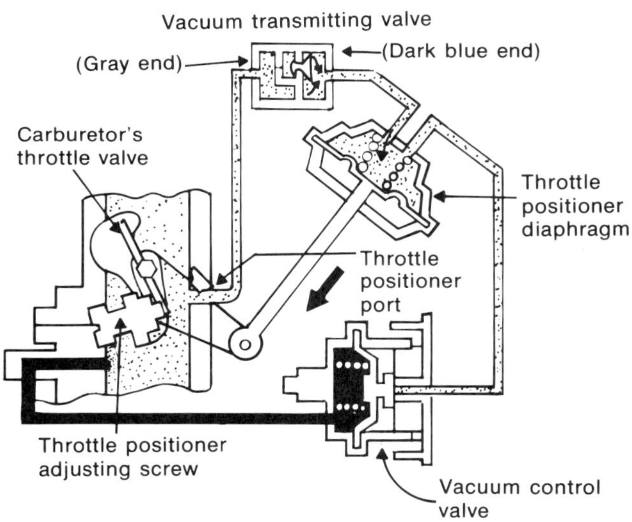

Fig. 8-24. Throttle positioner system (except 1979 and later California cars) during normal driving at highway speeds. Because carburetor's throttle valve is open, air at about atmospheric pressure reaches throttle positioner diaphragm via vacuum transmitting valve. Spring moves diaphragm and pushrod fully out (arrow) to position that prevents full closing of throttle valve.

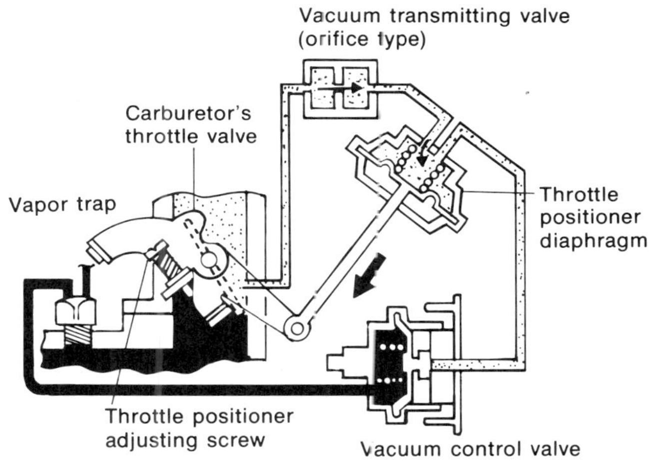

Fig. 8-25. Throttle positioner system for 1979 and later California cars during normal driving at highway speeds. System is essentially same as that shown in Fig. 8-24, but has orifice-type vacuum transmitting valve and vapor trap on manifold connection.

To test and repair:

1. Visually check the hoses and the vacuum transmitting valve. Replace cracked, loose-fitting, or kinked hoses. Make sure that the dark blue end of the vacuum transmitting valve is toward the throttle positioner diaphragm and replace the vacuum transmitting valve if it is cracked or otherwise damaged.
2. Check and, if necessary, adjust the throttle positioner as described in **5.1 Adjusting Idle Speed and Idle Mixture.**
3. With the engine idling, disconnect the vacuum sensing hose from the throttle positioner dia-

6

phragm (Fig. 8-26). The diaphragm's pushrod should move out so that the engine runs faster. If not, the throttle positioner linkage is binding or the throttle positioner diaphragm is faulty and should be replaced.

4. Check that vacuum is present at the disconnected hose. If not, check that the throttle positioner port of the carburetor is not clogged. If the vacuum transmitting valve is clogged or otherwise faulty, replace it.
5. Reconnect the vacuum transmitting valve's hose to the throttle positioner diaphragm (Fig. 8-26). The diaphragm's pushrod should move in gradually so that the engine returns to its normal idle. If not, pinch shut the hose between the diaphragm and the vacuum control valve. If the engine returns to idle, there is a leak in the vacuum control valve's hoses, the vacuum control valve, or the throttle positioner diaphragm. Replace faulty components.

NOTE ——

On Canadian models, it should take the engine from 2 to 6 seconds to return to idle after the hose is reconnected. On 1976 and 1977 U.S. models, it should take 6 to 15 seconds, and, on 1979 and later California models, it should take 1.5 to 5 seconds. If the time is incorrect, replace the vacuum transmitting valve or, if this does not correct the trouble, the throttle positioner diaphragm.

6. During routine maintenance, or when throttle positioner problems remain after you complete the preceding steps, check the vacuum control valve's filter. To do this, remove the vacuum control valve, then take off its filter cover and withdraw the filter (Fig. 8-27). Clean the filter with compressed air, or replace it if it is damaged. When you reinstall the vacuum control valve, make sure that you insert the correct connection into the intake manifold hose.
7. To troubleshoot the vacuum control valve, use a T-fitting as indicated in Fig. 8-28 to connect a vacuum gauge to the hose between the intake manifold and the vacuum control valve.
8. While the engine is idling at about 850 rpm, pinch shut the hose between the vacuum transmitting valve and the throttle positioner diaphragm. Then increase the engine speed until the vacuum gauge falls below approximately 560 mm/Hg (22 in./Hg). If the throttle positioner diaphragm's pushrod moves out, as it would if the hose were not pinched, the vacuum control valve is faulty and should be replaced.

NOTE ——

Before you replace the vacuum control valve, check that vacuum is reaching it from the intake manifold. If necessary, clean the vacuum fitting on the manifold.

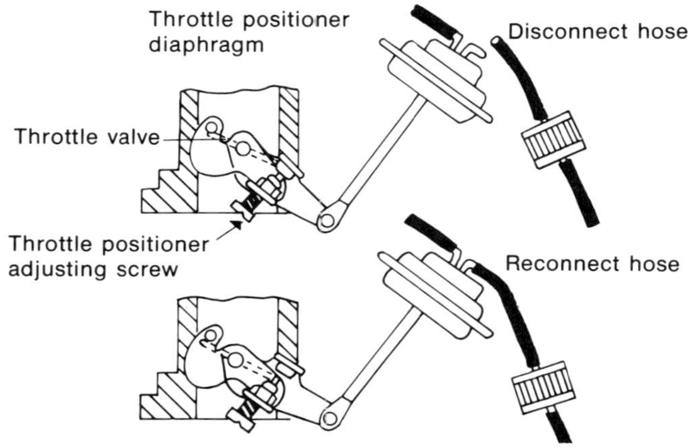

Fig. 8-26. Throttle positioner operation being checked. At top, pushrod moves out (arrow) when vacuum transmitting valve's hose is disconnected from diaphragm—allowing entry of air at atmospheric pressure (curved arrow). At bottom, pushrod moves in (arrow) when hose is reconnected.

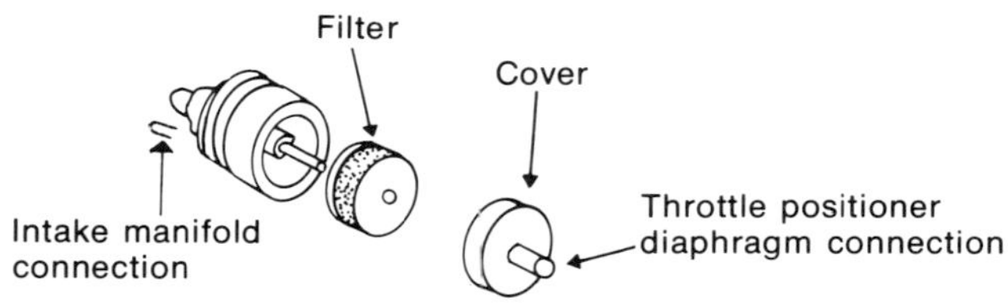

Fig. 8-27. Filter removed from vacuum control valve.

9. Keeping the hose pinched, either release the throttle or accelerate the engine and then release the throttle so that the vacuum gauge indicates a reading above 580 mm/Hg (22.8 in./Hg) on 1979 and later cars or above 550 mm/Hg (21.7 in./Hg) on earlier cars. If the throttle positioner diaphragm's pushrod fails to move out, the vacuum control valve is faulty and should be replaced.

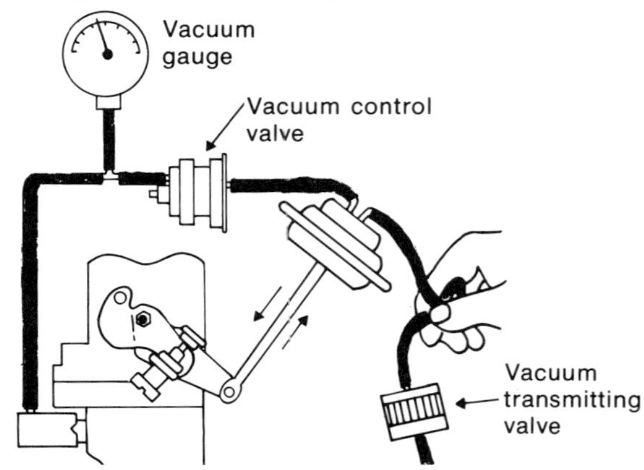

Fig. 8-28. Vacuum control valve being checked. Pinch hose as indicated. Pushrod should move out (arrow **A**) when vacuum is above specified reading. Pushrod should stay in (arrow **B**) when vacuum is below specified reading.

Throttle Positioner (TP) System

(1977 and 1978 California and high-altitude models)

Beginning with the 1978 models, cars sold outside California and high-altitude areas do not have a throttle positioner system. As on earlier California and high-altitude models, the throttle positioner system used on 1977 and 1978 models is controlled by vehicle speed. As shown in Fig. 8-29, the vacuum switching valve supplies atmospheric pressure taken from the evaporative emission control's charcoal filter canister to the throttle positioner diaphragm whenever the car exceeds approximately 26 kph (16 mph). This allows the spring in the throttle positioner diaphragm to set the positioner so that the carburetor's throttle valve will not close fully if the accelerator is released. At speeds below 11 kph (7 mph), the vacuum switching valve closes the port leading to the charcoal canister. Thus manifold vacuum pulls back the diaphragm, permitting the throttle valve to close so that the engine idles normally.

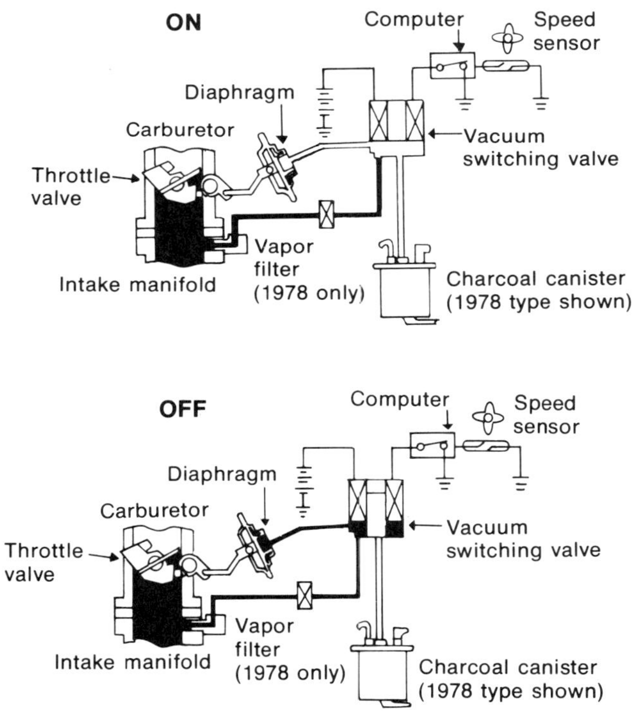

Fig. 8-29. Schematic diagrams of throttle positioner system used on 1977 and 1978 California and high-altitude models. At top, system is shown with accelerator released at speed above 26 kph (16 mph). At bottom, system is shown below 11 kph (7 mph) when manifold vacuum causes positioner to allow throttle to close fully.

To check and repair:

1. Visually check all wiring and hoses to determine their conditions. Replace cracked, loose-fitting or kinked hoses. Make sure that all electrical terminals are clean and tight-fitting.
2. Start the engine and allow it to warm up. If the engine does not idle at approximately 850 rpm, adjust the speed as described in **5.1 Adjusting Idle Speed and Idle Mixture,** making sure that the throttle positioner is not engaged at idle.
3. With the engine idling, disconnect the vacuum hose from the throttle positioner diaphragm (Fig. 8-30). Then speed up the engine to about 2500 rpm and release the throttle valve. The throttle positioner should engage as indicated, preventing the throttle valve from fully closing.

NOTE ——

If the throttle positioner diaphragm's pushrod moves in correctly but the bellcrank does not contact the throttle positioner adjusting screw squarely, bend the link that connects the pushrod to the bellcrank to center it. This is usually necessary only after you have installed a new throttle positioner diaphragm or linkage. If the pushrod has not moved out, engaging the throttle positioner, check the linkage for binding and, if you find no fault, replace the throttle positioner diaphragm. If the engine speed with the throttle positioner engaged is not between 1100 and 1300 rpm (automatic transmissions) or between 1300 and 1500 rpm (manual transmissions), adjust the throttle positioner as described in **5.1 Adjusting Idle Speed and Idle Mixture.**

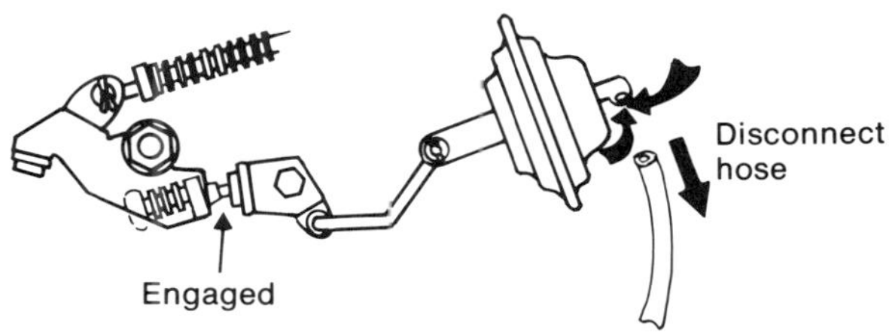

Fig. 8-30. Throttle positioner correctly engaged.

4. Make sure that vacuum is present at the hose you disconnected from the throttle positioner diaphragm. If no vacuum is present, troubleshoot the speed sensor, the computer, and the vacuum switching valve as described in **8.3 Evaporative Emission Control (EVAP) System.**

5. Reconnect the vacuum hose to the throttle positioner diaphragm. The throttle positioner diaphragm's pushrod should move in, releasing the throttle positioner and allowing the throttle valve to close fully (Fig. 8-31).

NOTE ——

If the throttle position diaphragm's pushrod moves in correctly but the bellcrank does not move far enough to become disengaged from the adjusting screw, adjust the bellcrank position by bending the link that connects the pushrod to the bellcrank. This is usually necessary only after you have installed a new throttle positioner diaphragm or linkage.

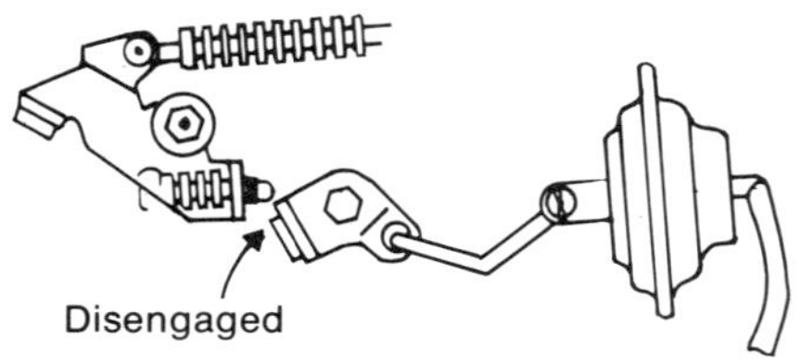

Fig. 8-31. Throttle positioner disengaged with engine idling and car standing still.

Spark Delay System

(1975 and 1976 only, except California)

Fig. 8-32 is a schematic view of the spark delay system. When the engine is cold and the thermostatic vacuum switching valve is open, vacuum from the carburetor reaches the ignition distributor's vacuum advance directly—via the hoses connected to the thermostatic vacuum switching valve. After the engine has warmed up so that the coolant is above 60°C (140°F), the thermostatic vacuum switching valve closes. Then vacuum can reach the distributor only by way of the vacuum transmitting valve. The vacuum transmitting valve delays the action of vacuum on the distributor's vacuum advance, preventing rapid changes in spark timing and thereby reducing exhaust emissions.

To test and repair:

1. Visually check that no hose is damaged or disconnected and that the vacuum transmitting valve is connected correctly and is not cracked or otherwise damaged. Replace faulty components.
2. Detach the distributor's vacuum line from the thermostatic vacuum switching valve. Pinch shut the other vacuum hose connected to the distributor, then suck on the disconnected hose. If the vacuum advance indicator sleeve fails to move in and out, the ignition distributor is faulty and should be checked and repaired as described in **ENGINE.**
3. Make sure that the engine's coolant temperature is below 35°C (95°F). Reconnect the hose to the thermostatic vacuum switching valve, then start the engine. Accelerate and decelerate the engine while you observe the vacuum advance indicator sleeve on the distributor. With the engine cold, the indicator sleeve should move in and out immediately in response to changes in manifold vacuum. After the coolant has reached 60°C (140°F), the indicator sleeve should no longer move in response to vacuum changes. If you find any fault, replace the thermostatic vacuum switching valve.

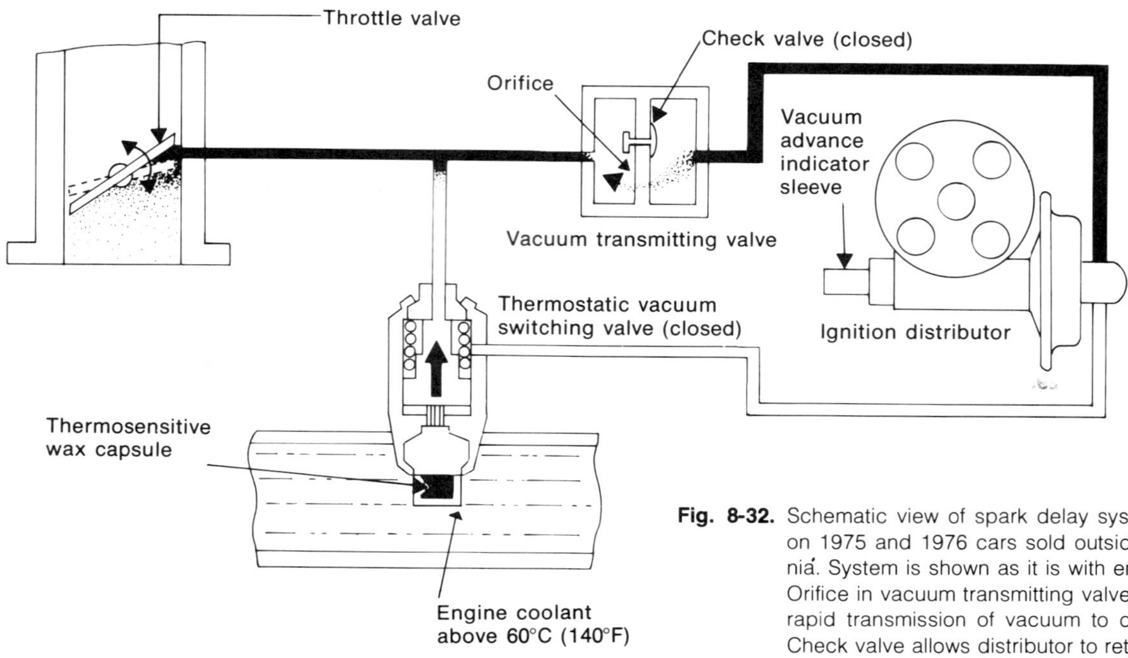

Fig. 8-32. Schematic view of spark delay system used on 1975 and 1976 cars sold outside California. System is shown as it is with engine hot. Orifice in vacuum transmitting valve prevents rapid transmission of vacuum to distributor. Check valve allows distributor to retard spark quickly.

4. With the engine idling and the coolant temperature above 60°C (140°F), pinch shut the vacuum hose at the point indicated in Fig. 8-33. Then increase the engine speed to a steady 2000 rpm. Release the pinched hose. The vacuum advance indicator sleeve should not begin to move for 4 to 12 seconds. If it moves sooner, the vacuum transmitting valve is faulty or installed backward and should be either replaced or reinstalled correctly.
5. Operate the engine at a steady 2000 rpm until the vacuum advance indicator sleeve has moved in and assumed a stable position with the coolant temperature above 60°C (140°F). When the throttle is released, the indicator sleeve should move out immediately as the engine returns to idle. If not, the vacuum transmitting valve is faulty and should be replaced.

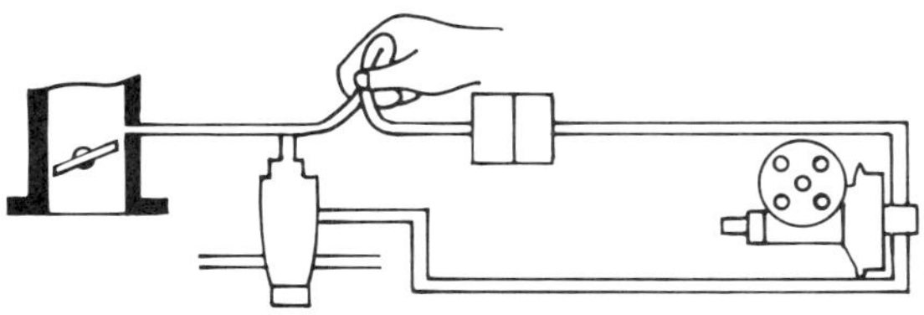

Fig. 8-33. Vacuum hose pinched in preparation for test of vacuum transmitting valve.

Mixture Control (MC) System

(1977 and later California and high-altitude models with manual transmissions)

Fig. 8-34 is a schematic view of the mixture control system. When the engine is operating at a steady speed, the mixture control valve is closed. During sudden deceleration, when intake manifold vacuum increases, the mixture control valve's diaphragm is pulled downward, opening the valve and allowing air to enter the engine's intake manifold. After a few seconds, vacuum in both chambers of the mixture control valve is equalized by an interchange of air through the valve's balancing port. This closes the valve so that air no longer enters the intake manifold.

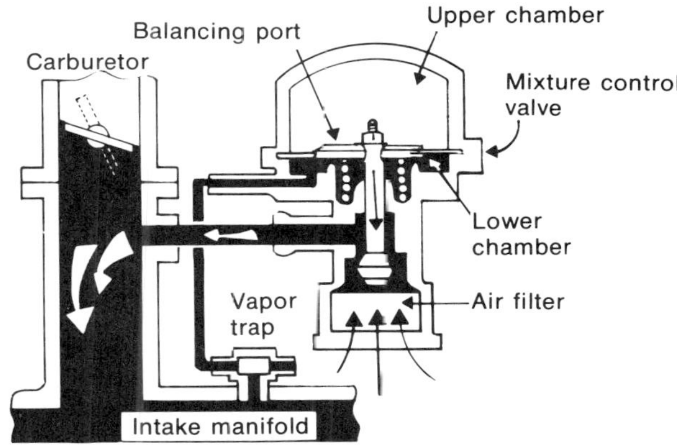

Fig. 8-34. Schematic view of mixture control system. In this diagram, car is decelerating at closed throttle. High intake manifold vacuum has opened mixture control valve, allowing fresh air from valve's air filter to enter manifold (arrows).

To test and repair:

1. Visually inspect all hoses and connections, looking for cracks, leaks, or damage. Replace faulty components.
2. Start the engine and allow it to idle.
3. Disconnect and plug the vacuum line (Fig. 8-35). If you feel vacuum at the mixture control valve's air filter, the mixture control valve is faulty and should be replaced.

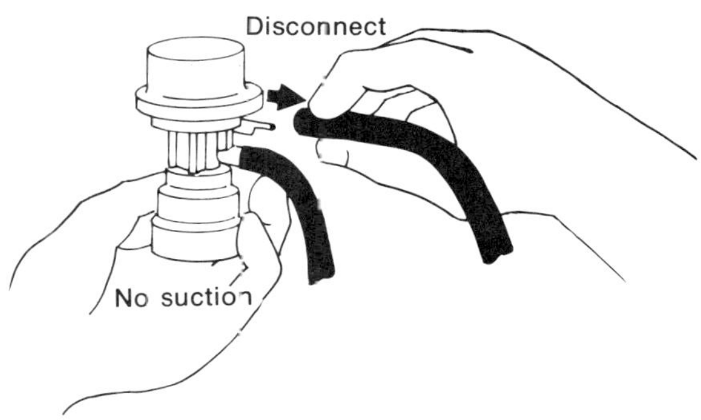

Fig. 8-35. Mixture control valve being tested. When you place your hand over bottom of valve, you should feel no suction while vacuum line is disconnected.

4. Reconnect the vacuum line. If you do not feel suction momentarily as the line is connected, the mixture control valve is faulty and should be replaced.

NOTE ——

If your hand does not fully cover the bottom of the mixture control valve, air entering the intake manifold at idle will cause the engine to run roughly or stall. This is normal.

6

Transmission Controlled Spark (TCS) System

(1975 and 1976 California and high-altitude models only)

Fig. 8-36 is a schematic diagram of the transmission controlled spark system. On 1975 cars, the ignition distributor's vacuum advance is cut off whenever the engine coolant is 5°C (41°F) or above. Even after warming up, the vacuum advance is turned on again at higher speeds—above appoximately 65 kph (40 mph) for cars with manual transmissions or 105 kph (65 mph) for cars with automatic transmissions. On 1976 cars, the ignition distributor's vacuum advance is cut off whenever the engine coolant is between 47°C and 105°C (117°F and 221°F). Even after warming up, the vacuum advance is turned on again when a car with a manual transmission is in 4th gear and, where applicable, 5th gear, or when a car with an automatic transmission is at a speed above 105 kph (65 mph).

To test and repair 1975 system:

1. Visually inspect all hoses and wiring. Replace cracked, loose-fitting, or kinked hoses. Make sure that all wires have clean, tight connections.
2. Allow the car to sit outside until the coolant temperature is below 4°C (or 40°F). If this is not possible owing to warm weather, disconnect the wires from the thermo switches and then ground the disconnected wires on some clean, unpainted metal parts of the engine.
3. Start the engine and immediately (before the coolant begins to warm up) accelerate it and decelerate it several times while you observe the vacuum advance indicator sleeve of the ignition distributor. If the indicator sleeve fails to move in and out, troubleshoot the ignition distributor and the thermo switches.

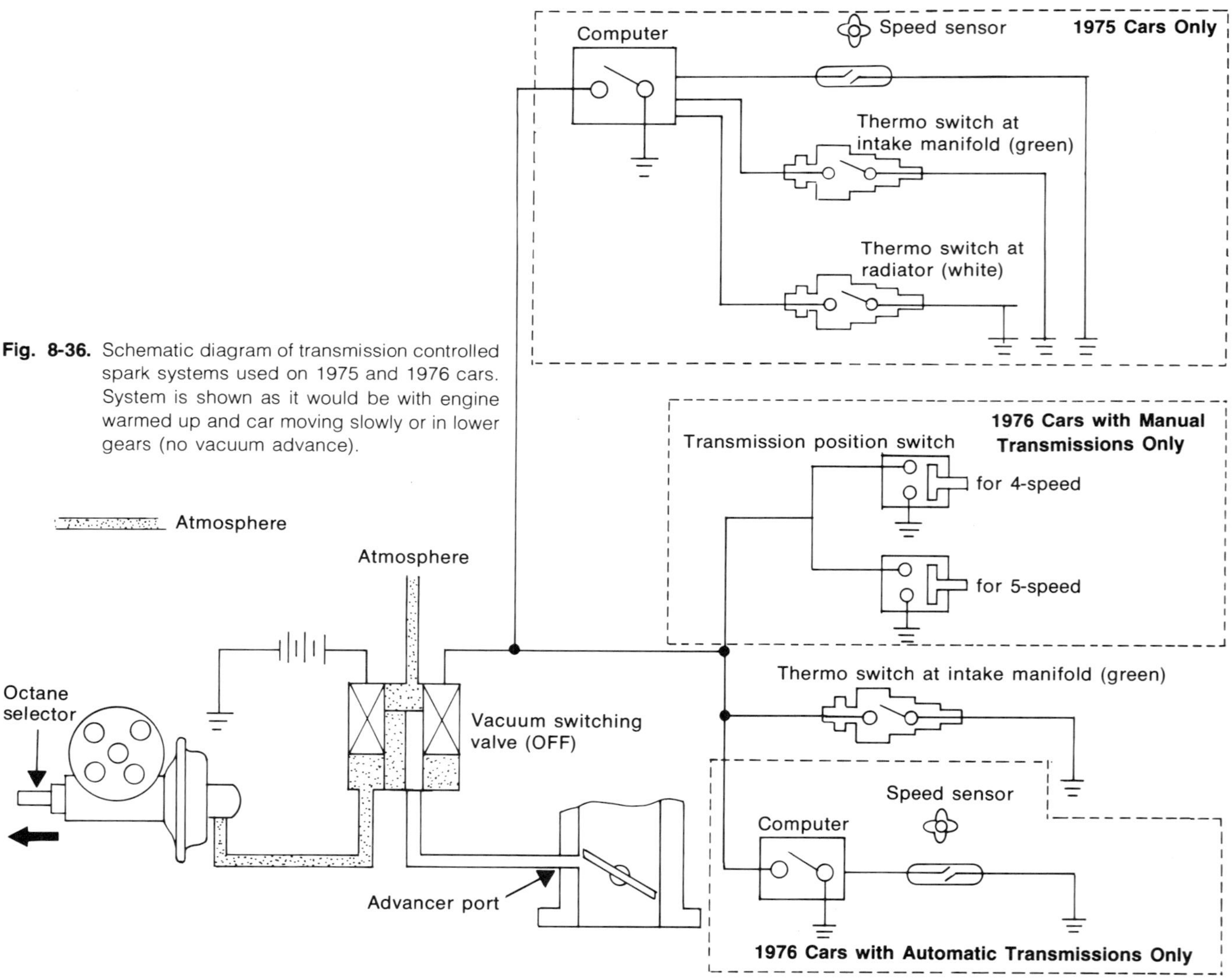

Fig. 8-36. Schematic diagram of transmission controlled spark systems used on 1975 and 1976 cars. System is shown as it would be with engine warmed up and car moving slowly or in lower gears (no vacuum advance).

NOTE —

To troubleshoot the distributor, first disconnect the vacuum hose from its vacuum advance unit. If vacuum is present at the hose, check the vacuum advance as described in **ENGINE.** If there is no vacuum at the hose, disconnect and ground the wires for each thermo switch one at a time. If vacuum is present when the wire is grounded, replace the faulty thermo switch. If, because of warm weather, you have already grounded a thermo switch wire, you should check the thermo switches separately, as described later in this procedure. Should grounding the wires fail to produce vacuum, carry out the test described in the next step.

4. If no vacuum is obtained at the ignition distributor in the preceding tests, disconnect the wiring from the vacuum switching valve. If vacuum is then available at the distributor, the computer is faulty and should be replaced. If there is still no vacuum, replace the vacuum switching valve.

NOTE —

The computer is located beneath the dashboard, on the left cowl panel. The vacuum switching valve is on the left-hand side of the engine compartment.

5. If you have previously disconnected any wires, reconnect them. Allow the engine to warm up. Then accelerate and decelerate the engine while you observe the vacuum advance indicator sleeve, which should not move. If it moves, disconnect the wires of the thermo switches one at a time. If disconnecting a wire prevents the indicator sleeve from moving as you change engine speeds, the disconnected thermo switch is faulty and should be replaced.

NOTE —

If disconnecting one or both thermo switches fails to keep the vacuum advance indicator sleeve from moving, first check the wiring and the fuses and replace faulty electrical components. See **ELECTRICAL SYSTEM.** If you find no electrical fault, test the vacuum switching valve as described in **8.3 Evaporative Emission Control (EVAP) System,** and replace it if it is faulty. If you find no fault, replace the computer.

6. Turn off the engine. Disconnect the ignition distributor's vacuum hose from the vacuum switching valve and connect a vacuum gauge in its place. Put the vacuum gauge in the passenger compartment and then road-test the car (Fig. 8-37). If the vacuum gauge does not change readings at the speeds given in the illustration, there is trouble in the speed sensor or in the computer.

NOTE —

If necessary, test the speed sensor as described in **8.3 Evaporative Emission Control (EVAP) System.** Replace faulty speedometers. If you discover no speed sensor fault, the trouble is in the computer, which should be replaced.

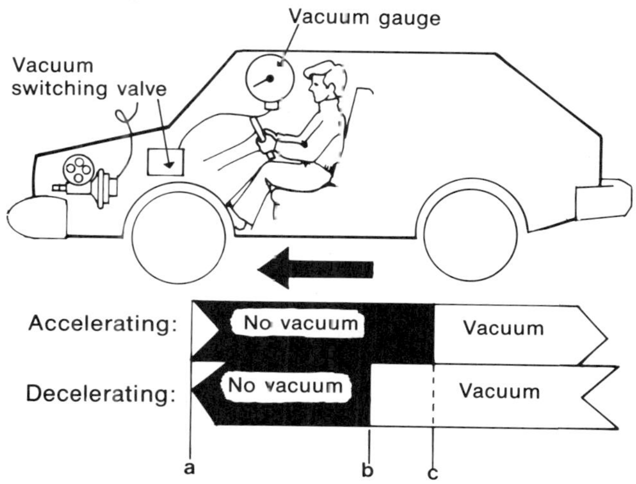

Manual transmission: a = car standing still
b = 65 ±5 kph (40 ±3 mph)
c = 32 ±5 kph (20 ±3 mph)

Automatic transmission: a = car standing still
b = 105 ±5 kph (65 ±3 mph)
c = 73 ±5 kph (45 ±3 mph)

Fig. 8-37. Vacuum switching speeds being checked. First accelerate car. With engine warmed up, there should be no vacuum until you reach speed **b**. Then decelerate. Vacuum should cut off at speed **c**. If traffic conditions or speed laws prevent highway testing, make test on chassis dynamometer or with rear wheels off ground and front wheels firmly chocked.

7. If, because of warm weather, you could not check the thermo switches as part of the earlier tests, test them as indicated in Fig. 8-38 if there is a possibility that either is faulty. Replace faulty thermo switches.

> ***WARNING —***
> *You must drain the cooling system as described in* **ENGINE** *before you remove the thermo switches. Do not drain the coolant while the engine is hot because doing this could damage the engine or cause you to burn yourself.*

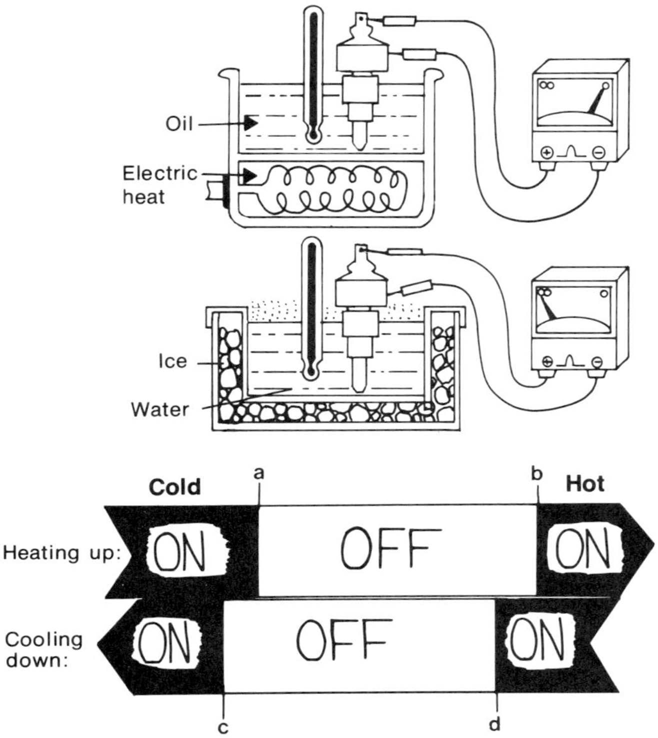

Thermo switch on radiator: a = 13° ± 5°C (55° ± 9°F)
(white, marked 13/105) b = 105° ± 5°C (221° ± 9°F)
c = 98°C (208°F) minimum
d = 6°C (43°F) minimum

Thermo switch on manifold: a = 60° ± 5°C (140° ± 9°F)
(green, marked 60B) b — not applicable
c — not applicable
d = 48°C (118°F) minimum

Fig. 8-38. Thermo switches being tested. After first cooling switches to below temperature **a**, heat to temperatures **a** and **b**, checking continuity through switch with ohmmeter or battery-powered test light. Then cool to temperatures **c** and **d**, again making sure that switch is on or off at correct temperatures.

To test and repair 1975 system:

1. Visually inspect all hoses and wiring. Replace cracked, loose-fitting, or kinked hoses. Make sure that all wires have clean, tight connections.

2. Allow the car to sit until the engine's coolant temperature is below 43°C (110°F).

3. Start the engine and, before the coolant begins to warm up, accelerate it and decelerate it several times while you observe the vacuum advance indicator sleeve of the ignition distributor. If the indicator sleeve fails to move in and out, troubleshoot the ignition distributor and the thermo switches.

> **NOTE —**
> To troubleshoot the distributor, first disconnect the vacuum hose from its vacuum advance unit. If vacuum is present at the hose, check the vacuum advance as described in **ENGINE.** If there is no vacuum at the hose, disconnect and ground the wire for the thermo switch, which is on the intake manifold. If vacuum is present when the wire is grounded, replace the faulty thermo switch. If there is still no vacuum and the wiring and fuses are not at fault (see **ELECTRICAL SYSTEM**), you should replace the transmission position switch on cars with manual transmissions. On cars with automatic transmissions, carry out the test described in the next step.

4. If, on a car with an automatic transmission, no vacuum is obtained at the ignition distributor in the preceding tests, disconnect the wiring from the vacuum switching valve. If vacuum is then available at the distributor, the computer is faulty and should be replaced. If there is still no vacuum, replace the vacuum switching valve.

> **NOTE —**
> The computer is located beneath the dashboard, on the left cowl panel. The vacuum switching valve is on the left-hand side of the engine compartment.

5. If you have previously disconnected any wires, reconnect them. Allow the engine to warm up. Then accelerate and decelerate the engine while you observe the vacuum advance indicator sleeve, which should not move. If if moves, disconnect the wire from the thermo switch. If this prevents the indicator sleeve from moving as you change engine speeds, the thermo switch is faulty and should be replaced.

6. On cars with manual transmissions, have someone depress the clutch and engage 4th or 5th gear. Accelerate and decelerate the engine. If the vacuum advance indicator sleeve fails to move in and out, replace the transmission position switch.

7. Turn off the engine. On cars with automatic transmissions only, disconnect the ignition distributor's vacuum hose from the vacuum switching valve and connect a vacuum gauge in its place. Put the vacuum gauge in the passenger compartment and then road test the car (Fig. 8-39). If the vacuum gauge does not change readings at the speeds given in the illustration, there is trouble in the speed sensor or in the computer.

NOTE ——

Test the speed sensor as described in **8.3 Evaporative Emission Control (EVAP) System.** Replace faulty speedometers. If you discover no speed sensor fault, the trouble is in the computer, which should be replaced.

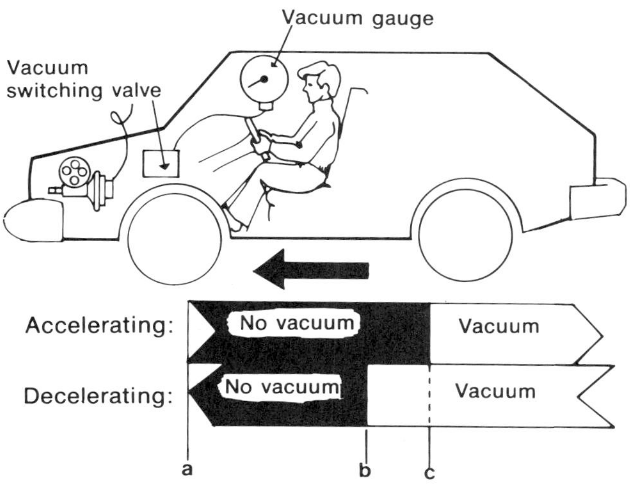

a = car standing still
b = 105 ± 5 kph (65 ± 3 mph)
c = 89 $\pm ^{0}_{6}$ kph (55 $\pm ^{0}_{4}$ mph)

Fig. 8-39. Vacuum switching speeds being checked. First accelerate car. With engine warmed up, there should be no vacuum until you reach speed **b**. Then decelerate. Vacuum should cut off at speed **c**. If traffic conditions or speed laws prevent highway testing, make test on chassis dynamometer or with rear wheels off ground and front wheels firmly chocked.

Spark Control (SC) System

(1977 and later California and high-altitude models only)

The spark control (SC) systems described under this heading replace the transmission controlled spark system used on the 1975 and 1976 cars. The function of the spark control system is to delay the operation of the ignition distributor's vacuum advance whenever the temperature of the intake manifold rises above 35°C (95°F) on 1977 models or above 44°C (111°F) on 1978 and later models. Fig. 8-40 is a schematic view of the system with the intake manifold cold. The center orifice of the thermostatic vacuum transmitting valve is open, allowing manifold vacuum to act immediately on the distributor's vacuum advance. After the manifold has warmed up, the bimetallic valve deflects so that its center plug closes the center orifice; vacuum reaches the distributor only via the metering orifice, slowing the vacuum advance's response to increases in manifold vacuum. If manifold vacuum decreases rapidly, as when the accelerator is suddenly pressed to the floor, the check valve deflects, opening the check valve orifice so that the spark will retard immediately.

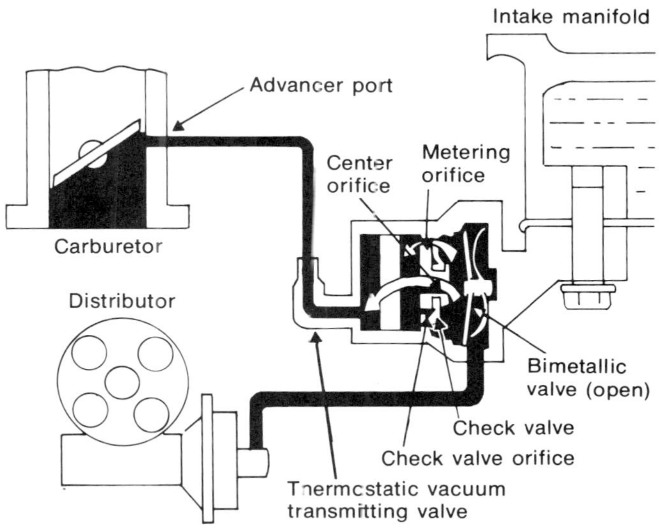

Fig. 8-40. Schematic diagram of spark control system. Thermostatic vacuum transmitting valve is shown with manifold cold. When manifold is hot, center orifice is closed by plug in center of bimetallic valve.

To test and repair 1977 system:

1. Visually inspect all hoses. Replace any that is cracked, loose-fitting, or kinked.
2. If necessary, allow the car to stand until the coolant temperature is below 35°C (95°F).
3. If the car has a double-diaphragm distributor and is built to high-altitude specifications, pinch shut the vacuum hose to the secondary diaphragm (Fig. 8-41). If the car is built to cold weather specifications, disconnect and plug this hose.
4. Start the engine and, before the coolant begins to warm up, accelerate and decelerate the engine while you observe the distributor's vacuum advance indicator sleeve. If the indicator sleeve fails to move in and out as the engine is accelerated and

decelerated (Fig. 8-41), troubleshoot the ignition distributor and the thermostatic vacuum transmitting valve.

> **NOTE** —— Check the distributor's vacuum advance as described in **ENGINE.** If the vacuum advance is not working because no vacuum is reaching it, check whether the advancer port of the carburetor is clogged. If it is not clogged, the thermostatic vacuum transmitting valve is faulty and should be replaced.

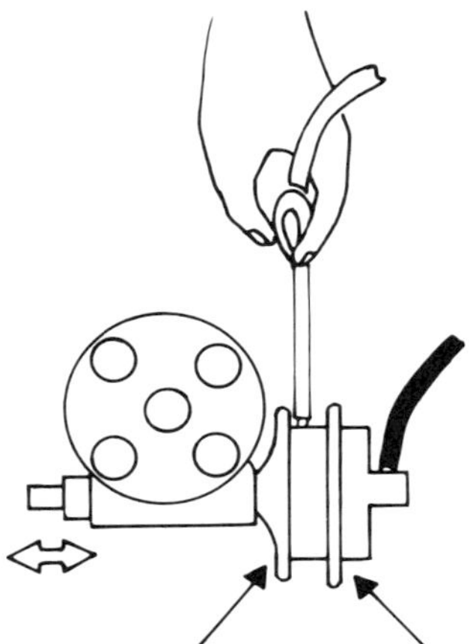

Fig. 8-41. Vacuum advance indicator sleeve moving in and out (double arrow) as engine is speeded and slowed. On high-altitude models, pinch hose to secondary diaphragm as shown.

5. Allow the engine to warm up so that the temperature of the intake manifold is above 35°C (95°F). If the car has a double-diaphragm distributor, keep the hose to the secondary diaphragm pinched or disconnected and plugged as in step 3.

6. With the engine idling, pinch shut the hose that connects the thermostatic vacuum transmitting valve to the carburetor. Increase the engine speed to a steady 3000 rpm, then release the hose (Fig. 8-42). If the vacuum advance indicator sleeve fails to start moving within the time limits given in the illustration, the thermostatic vacuum transmitting valve is faulty and should be replaced.

> **NOTE** —— When replacing the thermostatic vacuum transmitting valve, be sure you have obtained the correct part. Valves for California and high-altitude models are green; valves for other models are yellow. Before you remove the valve, allow the engine to cool. If the engine is cold and the radiator cap is kept

> **NOTE (cont.)** —— installed, almost no coolant will leak from the bolt hole when you remove the valve. Immediately reinstall the bolt to prevent leakage and, when you reinstall the valve, apply waterproof sealer to the bolt threads.

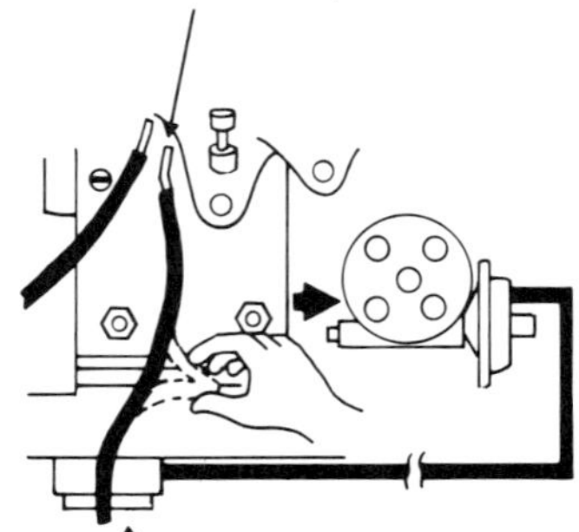

Time limits
California and high-altitude cars: 2 to 6 seconds
All other cars: 6 to 16 seconds

Fig. 8-42. System being checked with engine hot. Pinch hose at idle, increase engine speed to steady 3000 rpm, then release hose. After correct delay, indicator sleeve should begin to move as indicated by arrow.

7. Keeping the engine at 3000 rpm after the vacuum advance indicator sleeve has pulled in, disconnect the vacuum hose from the distributor (the main or outer, hose on double-diaphragm distributors). If the vacuum advance indicator sleeve does not move in immediately, the thermostatic vacuum transmitting valve is faulty and should be replaced.

To test and repair 1978 and later systems:

1. Visually inspect all hoses. Replace any that is cracked, loose-fitting, or kinked.

2. If necessary, allow the car to stand until the coolant temperature is below 30°C (86°F). If this is not possible, owing to warm weather, test the system by removing the thermostatic vacuum transmitting valve and checking it as described at the end of this procedure.

3. With the engine cold, disconnect the vacuum hose from the ignition distributor and connect the hose to a vacuum gauge.

4. Start the engine and, before the coolant warms up, check that the vacuum gauge indicates manifold vacuum at 3000 rpm. If not, check that the carburetor's advancer port is not clogged. If the port is clear, the thermostatic vacuum transmitting valve is faulty and should be replaced.

5. Allow the engine to warm up until the intake manifold temperature is above 44°C (111°F). Then accelerate the engine to 3000 rpm and keep it there. If the vacuum gauge does not change from a low reading to a high reading after a delay of from 1 to 3 seconds, the thermostatic vacuum transmitting valve is faulty and should be replaced.
6. Hold the engine at 3000 rpm until the vacuum gauge indicates manifold vacuum, then suddenly allow the engine to return to idle. If the vacuum gauge does not immediately fall to zero, the thermostatic vacuum transmitting valve is faulty and should be replaced.

> **NOTE ——**
> When replacing the thermostatic vacuum transmitting valve, be sure you have obtained the correct part, which is brown. Before you remove the valve, allow the engine to cool. If the engine is cold and the radiator cap is kept installed, almost no coolant will leak from the bolt hole when you remove the valve. Immediately reinstall the bolt to prevent leakage and, when you reinstall the valve, apply waterproof sealer to the bolt threads.

7. Even if you find no fault in the hoses, the advancer port, or the thermostatic vacuum transmitting valve, there still might be trouble in the distributor's vacuum advance unit. Therefore check the vacuum advance as described in **ENGINE** before you judge the spark control system to be in good condition.

If, owing to warm weather, it is not possible to check the thermostatic vacuum transmitting valve as described in the preceding procedure, remove the valve as described earlier in the **NOTE.** With the valve cooled below 30°C (86°F) (you can apply ice or put it in a refrigerator), when you blow air into either of its vacuum connections, the air should pass freely through the valve and out the other connection. Then hold the valve's mounting lug in boiling water until the aluminum part of the valve is heated to above 44°C (111°F). With the valve hot, when you blow air into the plastic connection, a large amount of air should flow from the metal connection. When you blow air into the metal connection, only a small amount of air should flow from the plastic connection. If the valve fails any of these three tests, replace it.

Exhaust Gas Recirculation (EGR) System

(1977 and later models only)

Nitrogen in the air is oxidized in the cylinders of an engine when combustion takes place at high pressures and high temperatures, resulting in oxides of nitrogen, a major air pollutant in exhaust gases. Because a portion of the exhaust gases is introduced into the fresh mixture going to the cylinders, combustion flame peaks are lowered and the formation of oxides of nitrogen is reduced. The purpose of the exhaust gas recirculation (EGR) system is to introduce spent exhaust gases into the engine's induction system only under high temperature/high pressure combustion chamber conditions, thereby reducing the formation of oxides of nitrogen. At other times, the system stops the recirculation of exhaust gases in order to prevent poor running and inefficient use of fuel.

Fig. 8-43 is a schematic view of the EGR system used on 1977 models sold outside California and high-altitude areas. In this system, manifold vacuum reaches the EGR system whenever the carburetor's throttle valve is moved off its fully closed position, uncovering the EGR port. However, when the engine is cold, there is insufficient vacuum to open the EGR valve because air enters the vacuum lines via the bimetallic vacuum switching valve and the carburetor's thermostatic valve case. (The thermostatic valve itself is not part of the EGR system.) When the coolant temperature rises above 50°C (122°F), the bimetallic vacuum switching valve closes, blocking the entry of air from the carburetor, and allowing manifold vacuum to open the EGR valve so that exhaust gases are recirculated. There is no exhaust gas recirculation at idle, when the throttle valve blocks the EGR port, nor at wide-open throttle and low vehicle speeds when manifold vacuum is low.

6

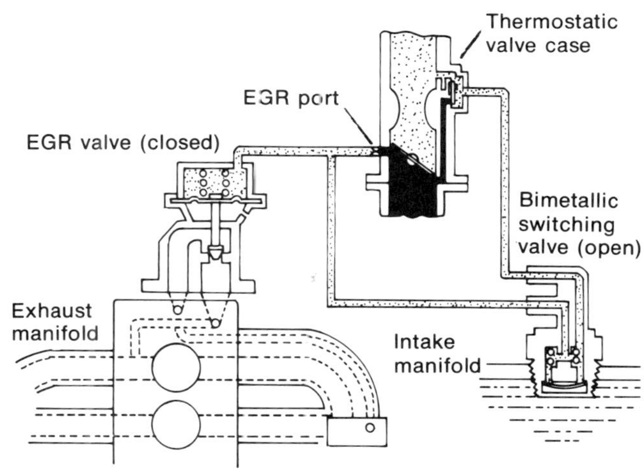

Fig. 8-43. Schematic view of EGR system used on 1977 cars sold outside California and high-altitude areas. System is shown at moderate engine speed with engine cold. Bimetallic vacuum switching valve closes when engine warms up, blocking entry of air from carburetor.

To test and repair 1977 system only
(except California and high-altitude cars):

1. Visually inspect all hoses. Replace any that is cracked, loose-fitting, or kinked.
2. If necessary, allow the car to stand outside until the coolant temperature is below 50°C (122°F).
3. Disconnect the EGR vacuum supply hose from the carburetor's EGR port, then connect it to the intake manifold's vacuum tap as indicated in Fig. 8-44.

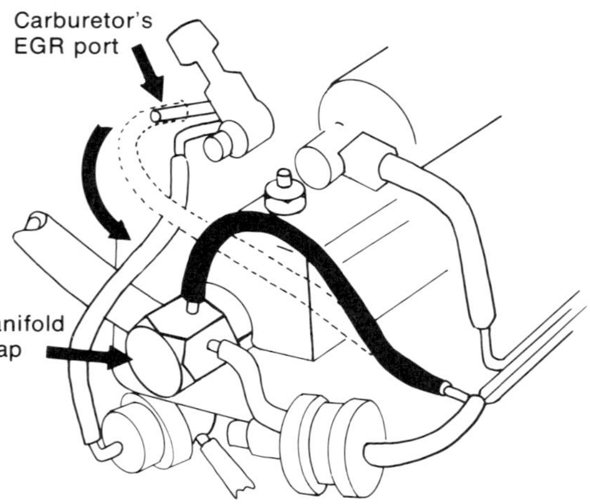

Fig. 8-44. EGR vacuum supply hose temporarily connected to vacuum tap on intake manifold.

4. With the engine cold and the vacuum hose reconnected to the intake manifold as previously described, start the engine and allow it to idle.

NOTE ——

If the engine fails to start, fails to run, or runs very roughly at idle, disconnect and plug the vacuum hose connected to the EGR valve. (The EGR valve is located on the front of the engine's cylinder head, beside the upper radiator hose connection.) If the engine still fails to start and idle, either something unrelated to the EGR valve is causing trouble, or else the EGR valve is faulty and should be replaced. If the engine does start and idle normally, the bimetallic vacuum switching valve is faulty and should be replaced. The correct bimetallic vacuum switching valve is blue.

5. With the engine cold and idling, pinch shut the hose between the bimetallic vacuum switching valve and the carburetor's thermostatic valve case (Fig. 8-45). If the engine does not die or idle roughly, the EGR valve is faulty and should be replaced.

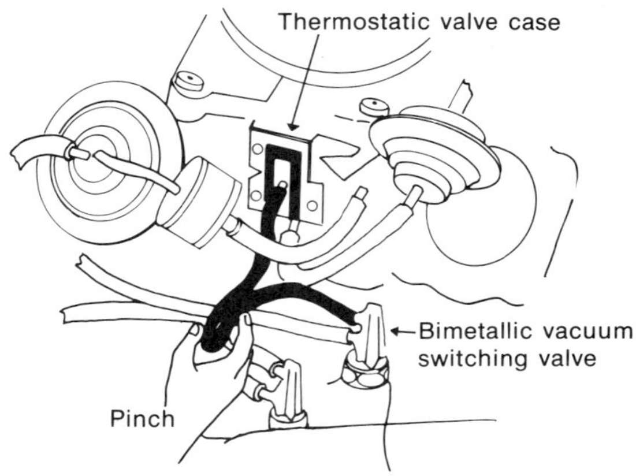

Fig. 8-45. Hose being pinched shut between bimetallic vacuum switching valve and thermostatic valve case.

6. Release the pinched hose. Then allow the engine to warm up to a coolant temperature above 50°C (122°F). The engine should begin to idle roughly as the bimetallic vacuum switching valve closes. If not, stop the engine, try to restart it, and then allow it to idle. If the engine starts and idles normally instead of stalling, the bimetallic vacuum switching valve is faulty and should be replaced.
7. Disconnect the EGR vacuum supply hose from the intake manifold vacuum tap and reconnect the hose to its correct location on the carburetor's EGR port.

Fig. 8-46 is a schematic view of the EGR system used on 1977 California and high-altitude models and on all 1978 and later cars. In this system, manifold vacuum can reach the EGR system only when the engine's coolant temperature is above 50°C (122°F) on 1977 cars or 54°C (129°F) on 1978 and later cars—the temperature at which the bimetallic vacuum switching valve opens. Once the engine has warmed up, vacuum reaches the EGR valve and opens the valve whenever the carburetor's throttle valve is moved off its fully closed position (which uncovers the EGR port). When the pressure of the exhuast gases falls in the EGR valve's constant pressure chamber, a spring in the EGR vacuum modulator opens the modulator's valve. This allows air to enter, and the consequent loss of vacuum closes the EGR valve. Thus exhaust gas recirculation is cut off when exhaust gas pressure is low—an indication that cylinder pressures and temperatures are also low. Because the EGR system is cut off when it is not needed to reduce pollutants, fuel is used more efficiently.

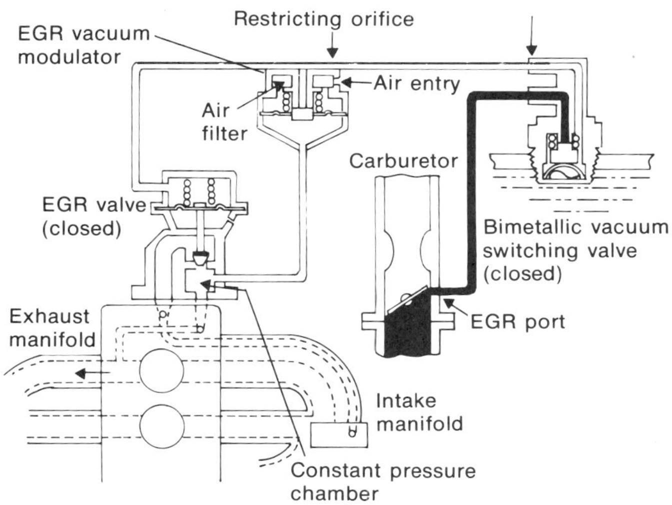

Fig. 8-46. Schematic view of EGR system used on 1977 California and high-altitude models and on all 1978 and later cars. System is shown at moderate engine speed with engine cold. Bimetallic vacuum switching valve closes, blocking vacuum to system until engine has warmed up.

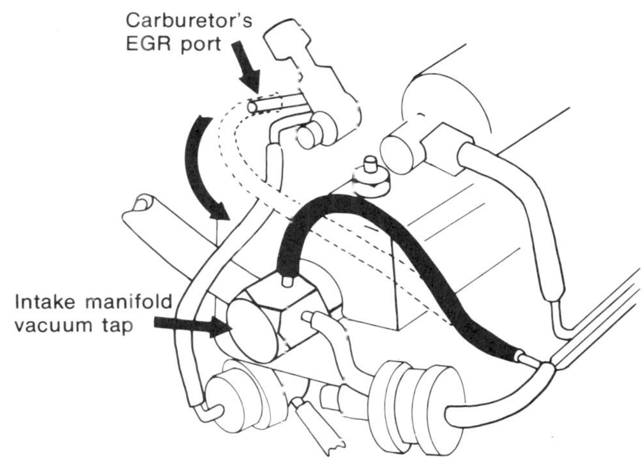

Fig. 8-47. EGR vacuum supply hose temporarily connected to vacuum tap on intake manifold.

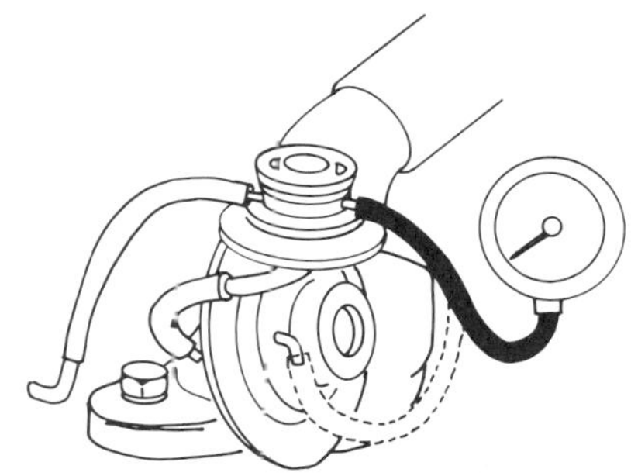

Fig. 8-48. EGR valve's vacuum hose connected to vacuum gauge.

6

To test and repair 1977 and later systems
(except 1977 cars sold outside California and high-altitude areas):

1. Visually inspect all hoses. Replace any that is cracked, loose-fitting, or kinked.
2. If necessary, allow the car to stand outside until the coolant temperature is below 50°C (122°F) on 1977 cars or 40°C (105°F) on 1978 and later cars.
3. Remove the cap from the EGR vacuum modulator, which is located atop the EGR valve on the front of the engine's cylinder head, beside the connection for the radiator top hose. Inspect and clean the modulator's air filter, then reinstall the filter and the cap. If the filter is faulty, replace the modulator as a unit.
4. Disconnect the EGR vacuum supply hose from the carburetor's EGR port, then connect it to the intake manifold's vacuum tap as indicated in Fig. 8-47.
5. Disconnect the vacuum hose from the EGR valve and then connect it to a vacuum gauge, as indicated in Fig. 8-48.
6. With the engine cold, start the engine and allow it to idle. If the engine refuses to start or to keep running at idle, either there is trouble outside the EGR system, or else the EGR valve is faulty and should be replaced.
7. Check that the vacuum gauge indicates no vacuum while the engine is cold and running. If vacuum is indicated, the bimetallic vacuum switching valve is faulty and should be replaced. The correct replacement valve is blue.
8. Allow the engine to warm up to a coolant temperature above 54°C (129°F). If the vacuum gauge does not indicate manifold vacuum at a steady 2000 rpm, disconnect the vacuum hose leading to the EGR vacuum modulator to see whether vacuum is present. If there is no vacuum, the bimetallic vacuum switching valve is faulty and should be replaced. If there is vacuum, the EGR vacuum modulator is faulty and should be replaced.
9. Maintaining the engine speed at 2500 rpm, disconnect the vacuum hose from the vacuum gauge and connect the hose to its normal location on the EGR valve. The engine speed should drop by about 200 rpm. If there is no change in the rpm as you connect the hose, the EGR valve is faulty and should be replaced.

Air Suction (AS) System

(1978 and later cars sold in the U.S. outside California and high-altitude areas)

The air suction (AS) system, shown schematically in Fig. 8-49, introduces air into the exhaust ports of the No. 2, No. 3, and No. 4 cylinders when the engine is warm and there is low pressure in the exhaust port. The air promotes the burning of residual carbon monoxide and hydrocarbon emissions in the exhaust system.

To check and repair:

1. Visually inspect all hoses. Replace any that is cracked, loose-fitting, or kinked.
2. If necessary, allow the car to stand outside until its coolant temperature is below 6°C (43°F).
3. Disconnect the air suction hose from the engine's air cleaner, then start the engine. With the engine cold to the extent specified in the preceding step, there should be no operating noise at the disconnected hose. If there is noise, the bimetallic vacuum switching valve is faulty and should be replaced. The correct replacement valve is green.

   NOTE ——
   If, because of warm weather, you cannot cool the engine sufficiently for the preceding test, you will have to check the bimetallic vacuum switching valve separately, as described at the end of this procedure.

4. Allow the engine to warm up. Check that operating noises can be heard at the disconnected hose. If you hear no noise, disconnect both vacuum hoses from the air suction valve. If you still hear no operating noise, the air suction valve is faulty and should be replaced. If disconnecting the vacuum hoses does produce noise at the air suction hose, then the bimetallic vacuum switching valve is faulty and should be replaced.
5. With the engine warm and idling, disconnect the vacuum hose that leads from the bimetallic vacuum switching valve to the vacuum transmitting valve (Fig. 8-50). Operating noises from the air suction hose should stop immediately. Reconnect the vacuum hose. After a few seconds' delay, operating noise should resume at the air suction hose. If there is no delay, the vacuum transmitting valve is faulty and should be replaced.

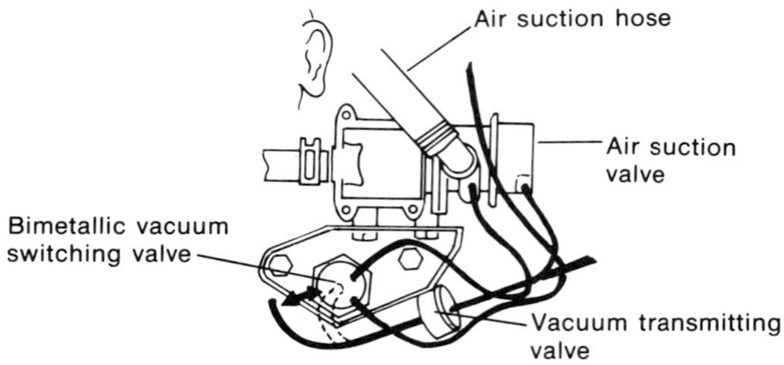

Fig. 8-50. Vacuum hose being disconnected and reconnected (double arrow) to check delay operation of vacuum transmitting valve.

If the system failed to operate correctly in the tests just described and the tests did not pinpoint the faulty component, you can check the system components individually. To test the bimetallic vacuum switching valve, remove it from the engine. Then connect a hose as indicated in Fig. 8-51 so that you can blow air through the valve. With the valve cooled by ice to a temperature below 6°C (43°F), air should pass through as indicated in the illustration. With the valve heated in hot water to a temperature above 17°C (63°F), no air should pass through the valve. Replace faulty valves.

Fig. 8-49. Schematic view of air suction system with engine cold. Air suction valve opens, permitting air from air cleaner to be drawn into exhaust manifold during low-pressure pulsations in manifold.

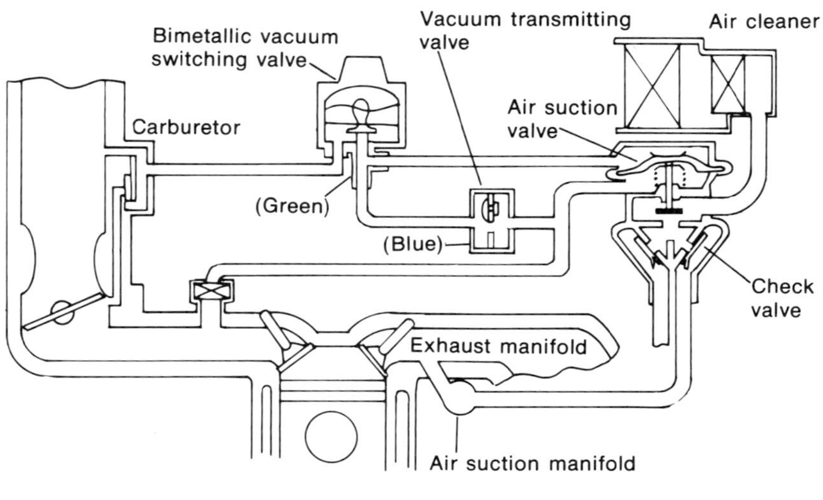

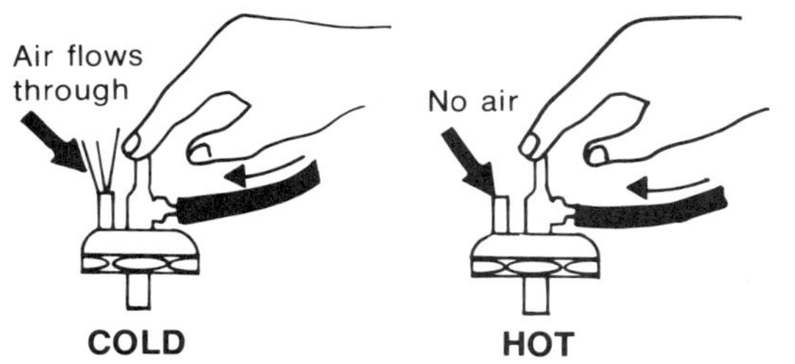

Fig. 8-51. Bimetallic vacuum switching valve being tested. Blow air into valve as indicated by arrow.

To test the vacuum transmitting valve after you have removed it from the car, blow air through it from the dark-colored end. A large amount of air should flow through the valve. When you blow into the light-colored end, only a small amount of air should flow through. If the valve is faulty, replace it.

To test the air suction valve separately, apply vacuum to connection **A**, as given in Fig. 8-52. Then blow air into connection **B**. If air passes through and emerges at connection **C**, the air suction valve is faulty and should be replaced. Repeat the test with no vacuum applied at connection **A**. Air should pass freely from connection **B** to connection **C**—but when air is blown into connection **C**, no air should flow through to connection **B**. Replace the air suction valve if it fails either test.

The air suction system's air filter, located on the side of the engine's air cleaner, should be checked whenever you discover trouble in the air suction system. This work is described in **LUBRICATION AND MAINTENANCE**, which covers routine inspection, cleaning, and replacement of the filter.

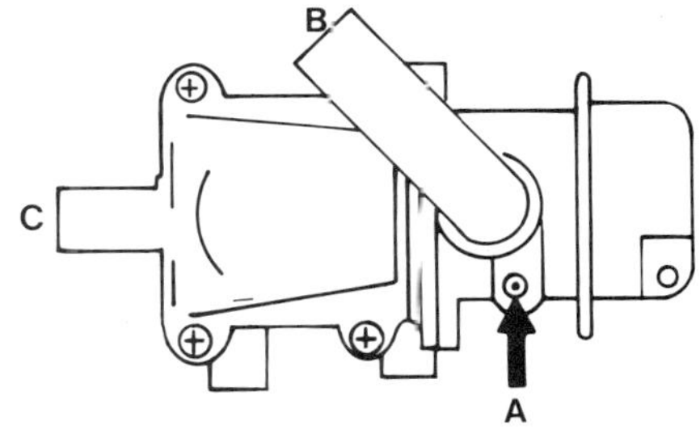

Fig. 8-52. Connections **A**, **B**, and **C** of air suction valve, as referred to in preceding text.

Air Injection (AI) System

(except 1978 and later cars sold outside California and high-altitude areas)

Fig. 8-53 and Fig. 8-54 are schematic diagrams of the air injection systems used on the cars covered by this Manual. A thorough check of the system requires that each component be tested separately. You can make a quick check by disconnecting the hose from the check valve with the engine idling to see that air comes from the disconnected hose. On California and high-altitude models, the engine must be warmed up and the catalytic converter not overheated.

Fig. 8-53. Schematic diagram of air injection system used on 1975 through 1977 cars sold outside California and high-altitude areas. Connection indicated by dotted lines is found on 1975 and 1976 cars only.

6

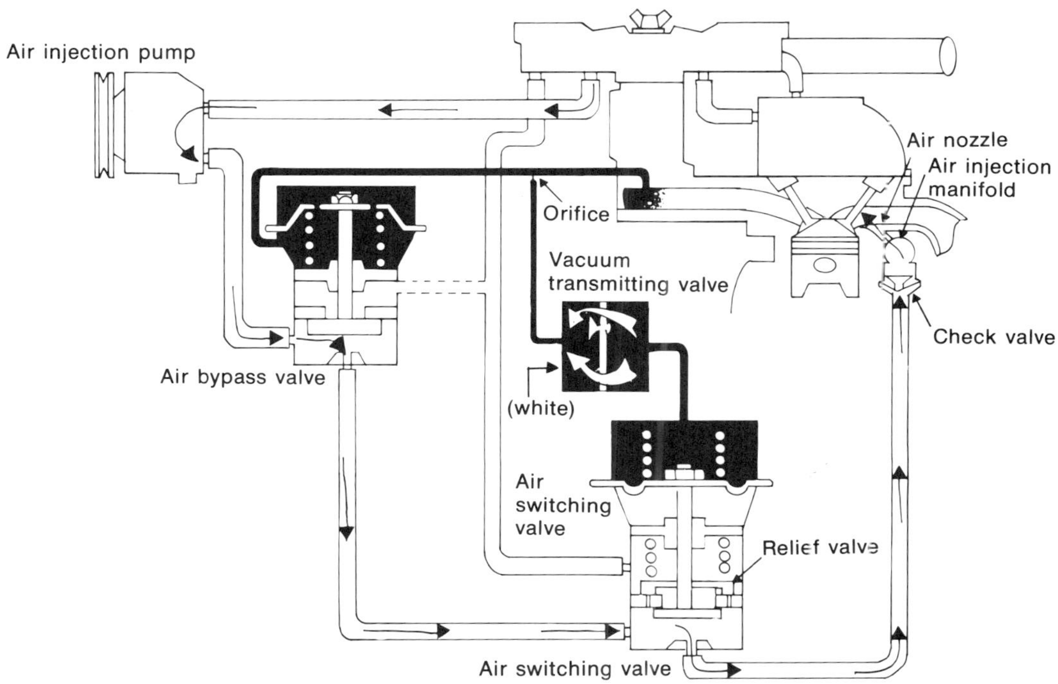

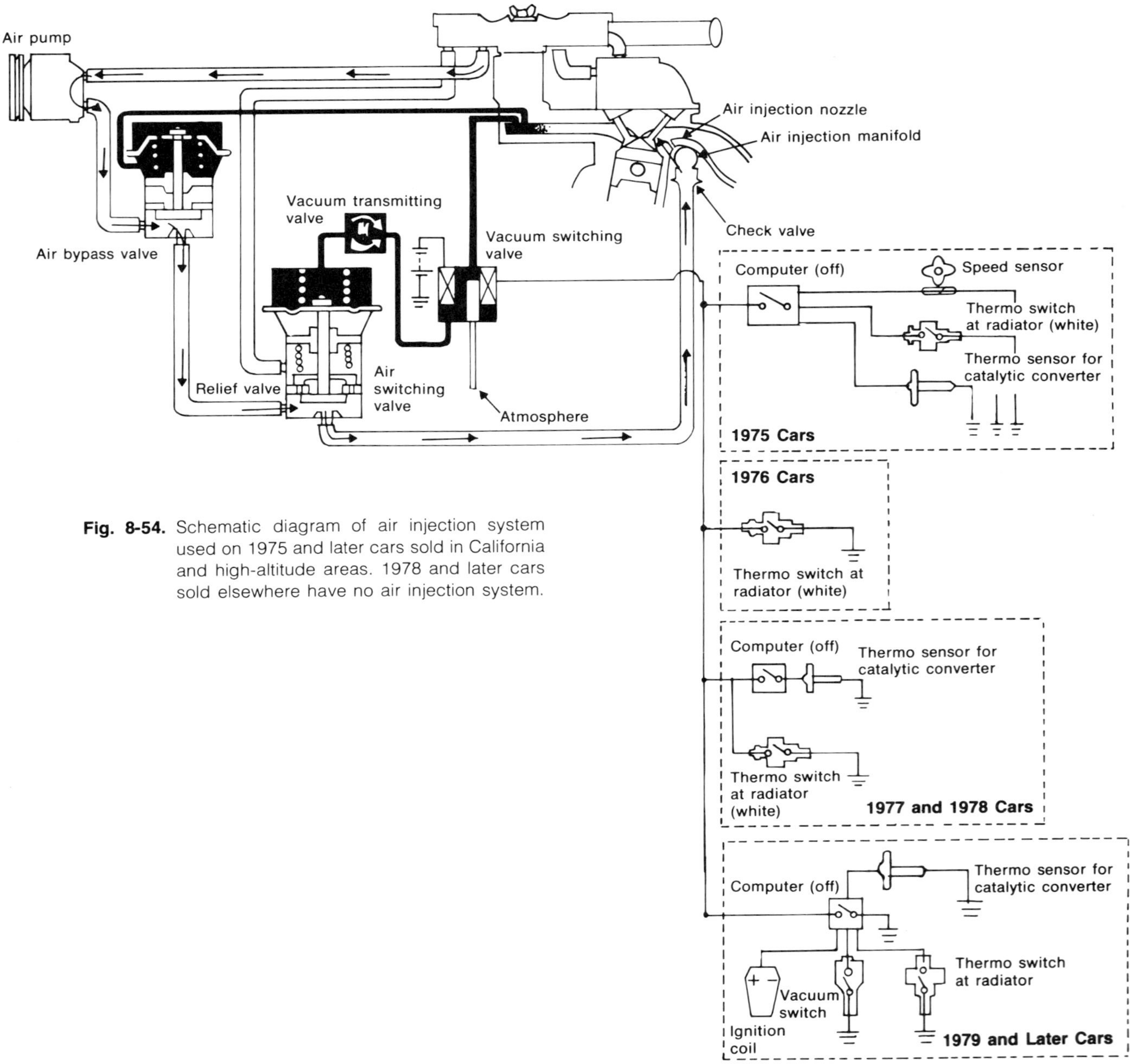

Fig. 8-54. Schematic diagram of air injection system used on 1975 and later cars sold in California and high-altitude areas. 1978 and later cars sold elsewhere have no air injection system.

To check thoroughly:

1. Visually inspect all hoses, tubes, and electrical wires. Replace any that is cracked, loose-fitting, or otherwise faulty.
2. Visually inspect the V-belt for the air pump. Replace it if it is cracked, deformed, worn, or otherwise damaged or deteriorating.
3. Check the tension of the air pump's V-belt and, if necessary, adjust the belt tension(s). See **LUBRICATION AND MAINTENANCE.**

> ***CAUTION —***
> *When adjusting the air pump's belt tension, move the air pump by inserting a large screwdriver between the pin and the cast iron cover of the pump. Never attempt to move the air pump by prying against its die-cast alloy housing. Doing this will deform the housing and ruin the pump. See Fig. 8-55.*

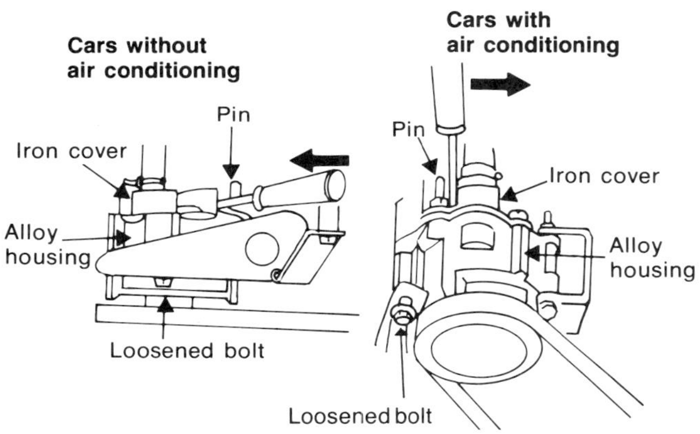

Fig. 8-55. Air pump being moved to adjust V-belt tension. Illustrations show screwdriver correctly inserted between pin and cast iron cover.

4. Start the engine. If any abnormal noise comes from the air pump, replace the pump.
5. To test the pump's output, detach the air outlet hose from the air bypass valve. Then insert a tester such as the one shown in Fig. 8-56, into the disconnected hose. With the engine running at 1800 rpm, the tester should give a reading in the "satisfactory" range. If not, replace the air pump.

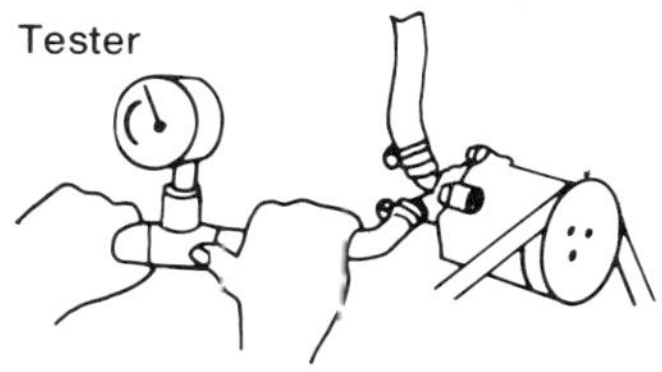

Fig. 8-56. Air pump output being measured. Tester shown is Toyota Special Tool 09258-14010 with a 4.90-mm (.193-in.) diameter bleed orifice installed. If you use another tester, follow its manufacturer's instructions.

6. Reconnect the pump's outlet hose to the air bypass valve. Then, with the engine idling, disconnect the vacuum sensing hose from the air bypass valve (Fig. 8-57). Reconnect the vacuum sensing hose. Air should come out of the bypass hoses temporarily, as indicated in the illustration. If not, replace the air bypass valve.

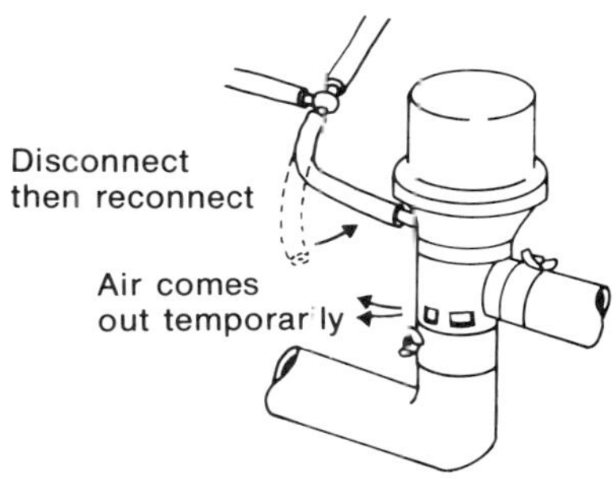

Fig. 8-57. Air bypass valve being tested. Air should come out of holes temporarily as vacuum hose is reconnected.

7. To test the vacuum transmitting valve, blow into its dark-colored end. A large amount of air should flow freely through the valve. When you blow into the light-colored end, only a small amount of air should flow through. Replace the vacuum transmitting valve if it is faulty in either test.

8. Disconnect the air hose from the check valve, as indicated in Fig. 8-58. Insert the tester in the disconnected hose, closing its bleed orifice with your fingertip. Gradually increase the engine speed to the point where the air switching valve's relief valve opens and air comes out of the relief hose (on 1975 and 1976 cars, you must disconnect the relief hose from the air cleaner). If the pressure at which the relief valve opens is not between 0.19 and 0.46 bar (2.7 and 6.5 psi) on 1975 through 1978 cars or between 0.29 and 0.34 bar (4.1 and 4.8 psi) on 1979 and later cars, the air switching valve is faulty and should be replaced.

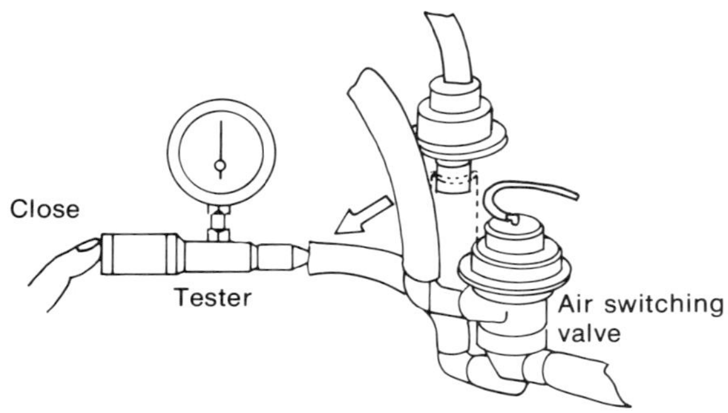

Fig. 8-58. Air switching valve's relief valve being tested. Detach hose from check valve as indicated by arrow. Relief valve should open at correct pressure.

9. Remove the tester and reconnect the air hose to the check valve, but for the moment do not reconnect the relief hose to the air cleaner on 1975 or 1976 cars. Temporarily disconnect the small vacuum hose from the top of the air switching valve. If air does not begin flowing from the air switching valve's relief hose, the air switching valve is faulty and should be replaced. Reconnect all disconnected hoses.

10. To inspect the check valve, disconnect its hose and then unscrew the check valve from the tube that leads to the air injection manifold. Air blown into the check valve's threaded end should close the valve so that no air flows from the hose connection. Air blown into the hose connection should open the valve and flow from the threaded connection. If the check valve fails either test, replace it.

11. To test the thermo switch on California and high-altitude models, check the continuity at different temperatures with an ohmmeter, as indicated in Fig. 8-59. Replace faulty thermo switches.

***WARNING* ——**

You must drain the cooling system as described in **ENGINE** *before you remove the thermo switch. Do not drain the coolant while the engine is hot because doing this could damage the engine or cause you to burn yourself.*

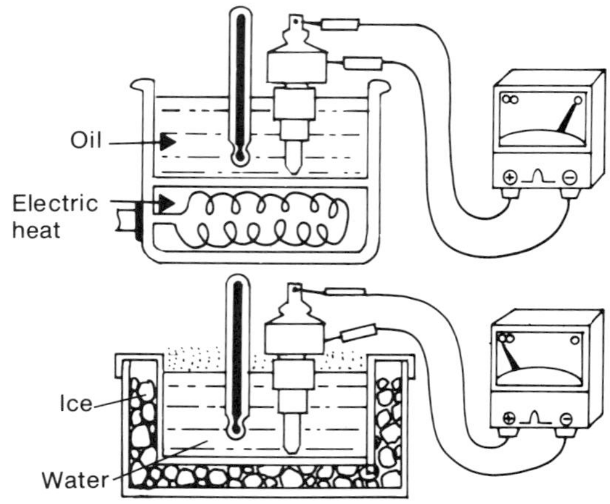

Fig. 8-59. Thermo switch being tested. There should be electrical continuity through switch when cooled below 6°C (43°F). There should be no continuity between 13° and 98°C (55° and 208°F) on 1975 and 1976 cars or between 18° and 98°C (65° and 208°F) on 1977 and later cars. Above this range there should again be continuity.

12. On 1975 California and high-altitude models, and on 1977 and later California and high-altitude models, test the catalytic converter's thermo sensor as described in **8.2 Catalytic Converter (CCo).** Except on 1979 and later California cars, test the vacuum switching valve, the computer, and, where applicable, the speed sensor as described in **8.3 Evaporative Emission Control (EVAP) System.** Replace faulty components.

13. On 1979 and later California cars only, remove the vacuum switching valve from the car if you wish to test it. (This vacuum switching valve is different from that used on earlier models.) Then carry out the tests described in the next four steps.

14. Connect the positive (+) post of the car's battery to terminal **A** and the negative (−) post of the battery to terminal **B**, as given in Fig. 8-60. Then blow air into connection **1**. Air should flow freely from connection **2**, but no air should flow from connection **3**. Replace faulty vacuum switching valves.

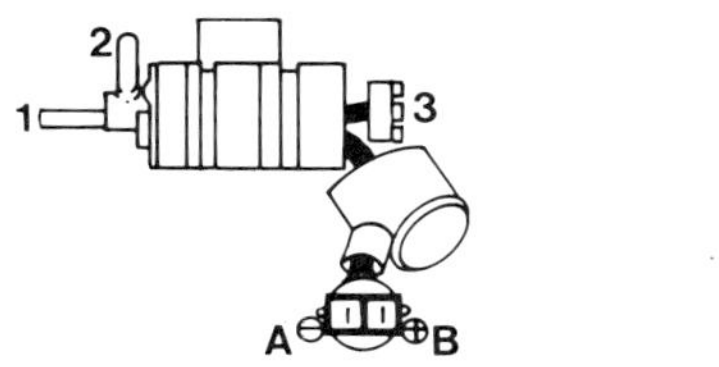

Fig. 8-60. Identification of electrical terminals and hose connections on vacuum switching valve introduced on 1979 California cars. Notice how rubber cap has been pulled off to uncover filter at connection **3**.

15. Disconnect the battery. Then blow air into connection **2**, as given previously in Fig. 8-60. Air should flow from connection **3**, but no air should flow from connection **1**. Replace faulty vacuum switching valves.
16. To test the vacuum switching valve for grounded windings, connect one test probe of an ohmmeter or a battery-powered test light to terminal **B**. Touch the other test probe to the metal body of the vacuum switching valve. If there is electrical continuity (that is, if the ohmmeter indicates 0 ohms or if the test light comes on), the vacuum switching valve is faulty and should be replaced.
17. To test the vacuum switching valve for open circuits, connect the ohmmeter to terminals **A** and **B**. If the resistance is not between 48 and 60 ohms with the windings cold, replace the vacuum switching valve.

Choke Breaker (CB) System

This system is designed to open the choke slightly as soon as the engine is started. In addition to reducing unburned hydrocarbons in the exhaust, the choke breaker system saves fuel and improves cold running. The choke breaker is nothing more than a vacuum diaphragm supplied with vacuum from the intake manifold. The diaphragm is connected by a pullrod to the choke valve.

To inspect the operation of the choke breaker, start the engine while the engine is cold. Disconnect the vacuum hose from the choke breaker diaphragm as indicated in Fig. 8-61. The choke linkage should move slightly in the choke-closed direction. Vacuum should pull the choke slightly open again when you reconnect the hose. Replace the diaphragm if you find any fault.

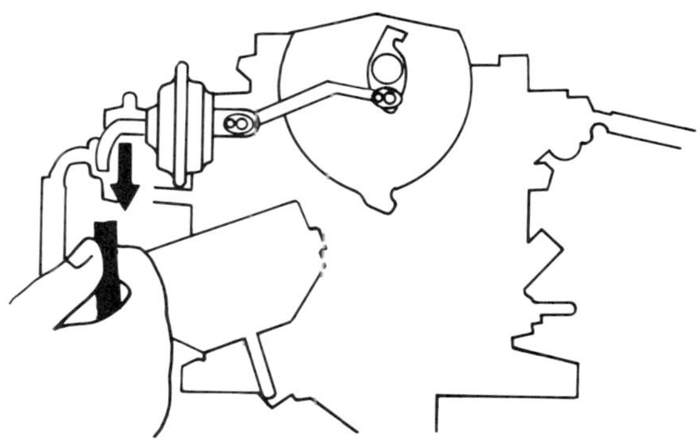

Fig. 8-61. Choke breaker being tested. Diaphragm should move out, as indicated by horizontal arrow, when vacuum hose is detached, as indicated by vertical arrow.

6

Electrically Heated Automatic Choke System

All cars covered by this Manual have similar electrical circuits for the electrically heated automatic choke system. The only differences are in the choke control relays (Fig. 8-62). A positive temperature coefficient thermistor, which is a ceramic semiconductor using barium titanate as its main constituent, is built into the choke heating element assembly. The resistance of this thermistor increases with elevated temperature. Its purpose in the circuit is to limit the electricity consumed in keeping the choke open once the choke's bimetallic spring has been thoroughly warmed.

You can make a simple test of the electrically heated automatic choke system by starting the engine and then, with the engine's air cleaner removed, watching to see that the choke valve opens and that the housing for the bimetallic spring heats. If it does not heat, unplug the wiring connector for the choke, then measure the resistance through the choke heating element and thermistor as indicated in Fig. 8-63. If there is no continuity, or if the resistance is not between 7.5 and 10.0 ohms, the choke heating element is faulty and the entire choke housing assembly should be replaced. If you find no trouble, use a voltmeter or a test light to determine whether voltage is reaching the connector while the engine is running. (The engine must be running, turning the alternator, in order for the choke control relay to be energized so that it completes the circuit from the ignition switch to the automatic choke.) If there is no voltage, and if the alternator or its regulator is not faulty, check the fuse marked ENGINE in the fuse box. Then, if the fuse is not blown, test the choke control relay as described in the following procedures.

NOTE ——

On some 1975 cars there is an in-line fuse located in the engine compartment, beneath the coolant overflow reservoir. This fuse is in series with the alternator warning light and the choke control relay. Check this fuse, if present, before you test the choke control relay.

Fig. 8-62. Schematic diagram of electrically heated choke circuit. Positive temperature coefficient thermistor is shown schematically at **A**. Insets show alternative choke control relay circuits. 1977 relay has diode in parallel with relay winding, whereas 1978 and later relays have resistor.

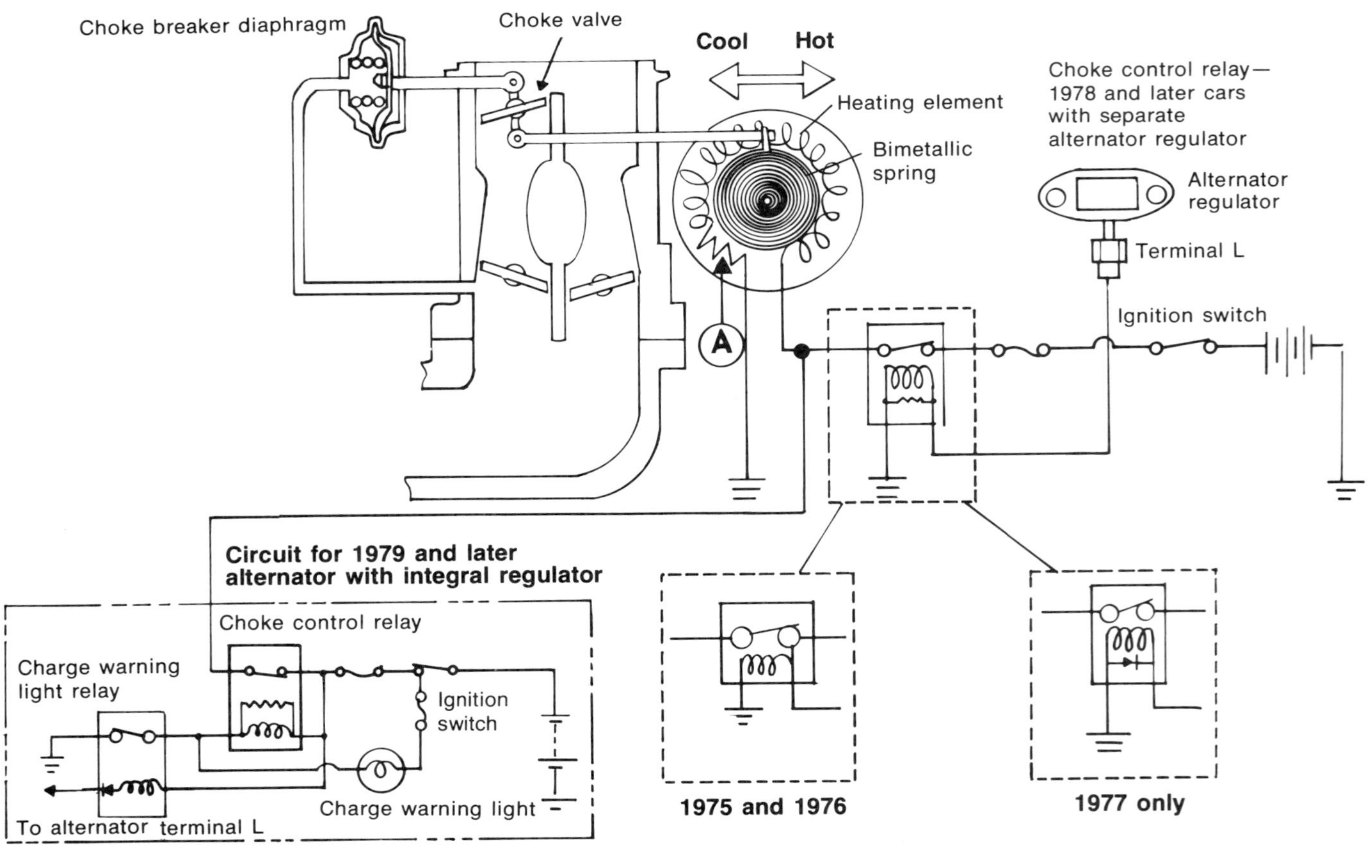

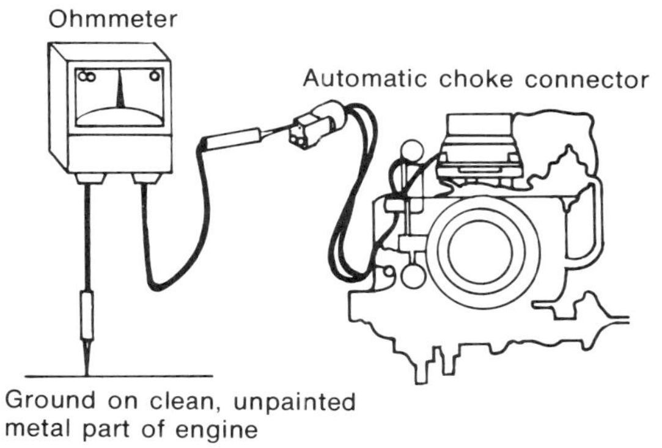

Fig. 8-63. Resistance being measured through choke heating element and thermistor.

To test 1975 and 1976 relay:

1. Turn off the ignition. Either remove the choke control relay from the car or disconnect its multiple connector from the car's wiring harness. (The choke control relay is located beneath the dashboard, on the cowl panel to the right of the passenger's feet; it is the upper left relay mounted on the bracket.)

NOTE ——

If the relay plugs into a socket instead of having wires and a multiple connector attached to it, use the test described in the next (1977) procedure.

2. Using an ohmmeter or a battery-powered test light, check for electrical continuity between the relay's multiple connector terminals **A** and **B**, as indicated in Fig. 8-64. If there is continuity, replace the relay.
3. Connect a 12-volt battery to relay terminals **C** and **D** as indicated in Fig. 8-64. Repeat the continuity test at terminals **A** and **B**, as shown. There should now be continuity. If not, replace the relay.

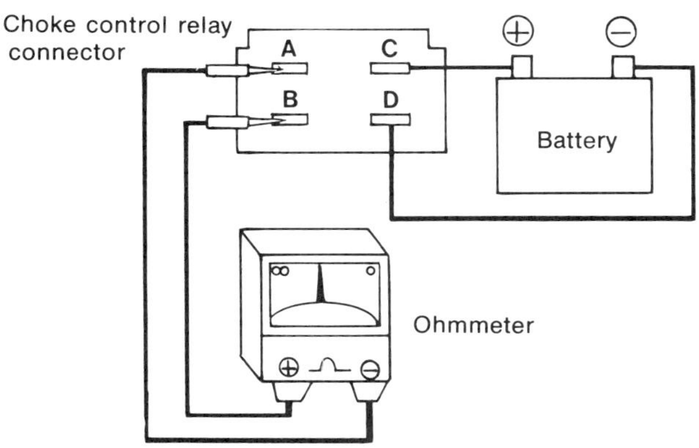

Fig. 8-64. Tests being made at multiple connector attached to choke control relay. There should be continuity from terminal **A** to terminal **B** with battery connected to terminals **C** and **D**, but no continuity when battery is not connected.

To test 1977 relay:

1. Turn off the ignition. Remove the relay. To do this, unplug it from its socket and then dismount it from the bracket that is beneath the dashboard, on the cowl panel to the right of the passenger's feet. The choke control relay is the upper left relay mounted on the bracket.

NOTE ——

If the relay is not in this location, the car was probably manufactured after January 1, 1977. If this is the case, use the test described in the next (1978 and later) procedure.

2. Using an ohmmeter, as indicated in Fig. 8-65, measure the resistance between relay terminals **E** and **L**. If the resistance is not between 70 and 90 ohms, replace the relay.
3. Repeat the test described in step 2, but reverse the position of the ohmmeter's test probes so that the negative probe is applied to relay terminal **E** and the positive probe applied to relay terminal **L**. If the resistance is not approximately 20 ohms, replace the relay.

NOTE ——

The tests described in steps 2 and 3 will determine whether the diode and the relay windings are in good condition. The tests are not valid for a relay that has no diode.

6

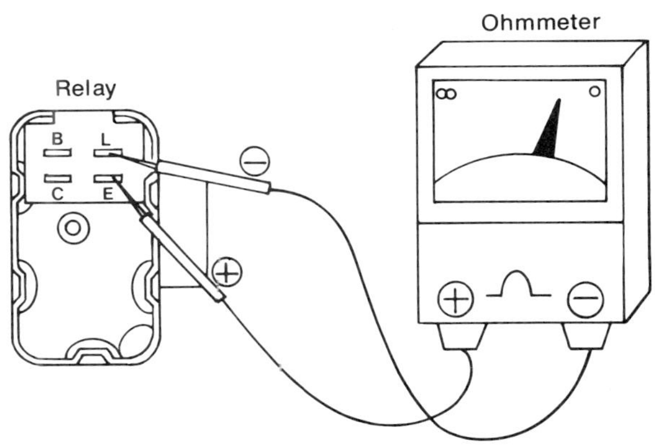

Fig. 8-65. Resistance being measured through diode and relay winding. With negative probe on terminal **L** and positive probe on terminal **E**, resistance should be 70 to 90 ohms. With probes reversed, resistance should be about 20 ohms.

4. Using an ohmmeter or a battery-powered test light, check for electrical continuity between relay terminals **B** and **C**, as indicated in Fig. 8-66. If there is continuity, replace the relay.

5. Connect a 12-volt battery to relay terminals **L** and **E** as indicated in Fig. 8-66. Repeat the continuity test at terminals **B** and **C**, as shown. There should be continuity. If not, replace the relay.

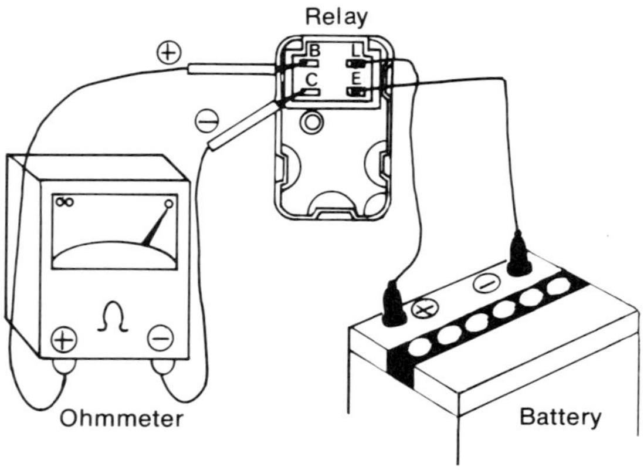

Fig. 8-66. Tests being made at relay terminals. There should be continuity from terminal **B** to terminal **C** with battery connected to terminals **L** and **E**, but no continuity when battery is not connected.

To test 1978 and later relay:

1. Turn off the ignition. Remove the relay from the car by unplugging it from its socket.

NOTE ——
On cars with a separate alternator regulator, the relay is located at the point indicated in Fig. 8-67. Late 1977 cars also have this relay in this position. On cars with a regulator that is integral with the alternator, the relay is located at the point indicated in Fig. 8-68.

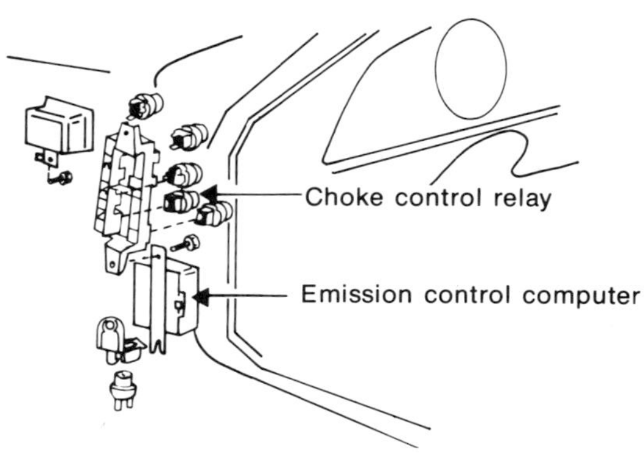

Fig. 8-67. Location of choke control relay used on late-model cars with separate alternator regulators.

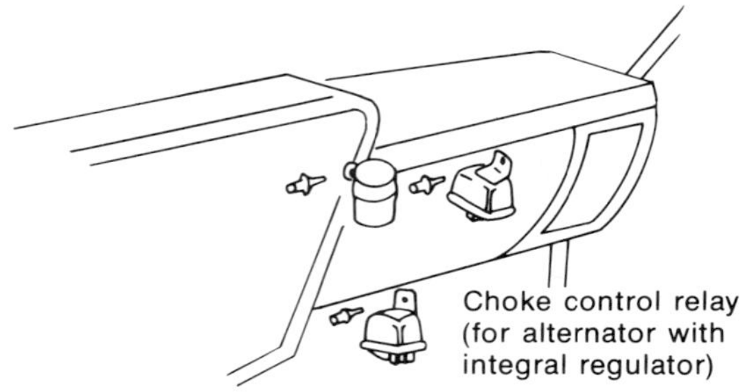

Fig. 8-68. Location of choke control relay used on 1979 and later cars with integral alternator regulators.

2. On cars with separate alternator regulators, use an ohmmeter, as indicated in Fig. 8-69, to measure the resistance between relay terminals **1** and **2.** If the resistance is not between 48 and 80 ohms, replace the relay.

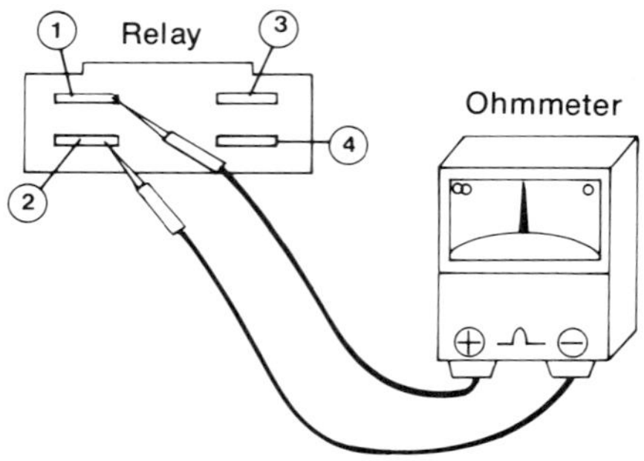

Fig. 8-69. Resistance being measured through relay winding and resistor, which is in parallel with winding.

3. On cars with separate alternator regulators, connect a 12-volt battery to relay terminals **1** and **2**, as indicated in Fig. 8-70. Then, using an ohmmeter or a battery-powered test light, check for continuity between relay terminals **3** and **4**. If there is no continuity, replace the relay.

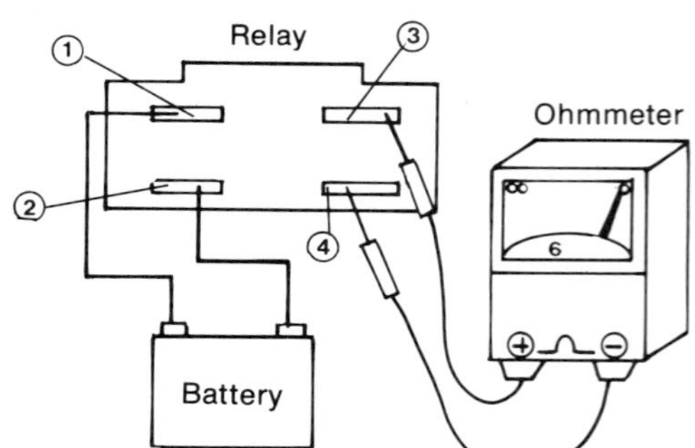

Fig. 8-70. Continuity test being made at relay terminals. There should be continuity from terminal **3** to terminal **4** with battery connected to terminals **1** and **2**.

4. On cars with alternators that have integral regulators, use an ohmmeter to measure the resistance between relay terminals **1** and **2**, as given in Fig. 8-71. If the resistance is not between 60 and 120 ohms, replace the relay. Also replace the relay if the resistance between terminals **3** and **4** is not zero ohms.

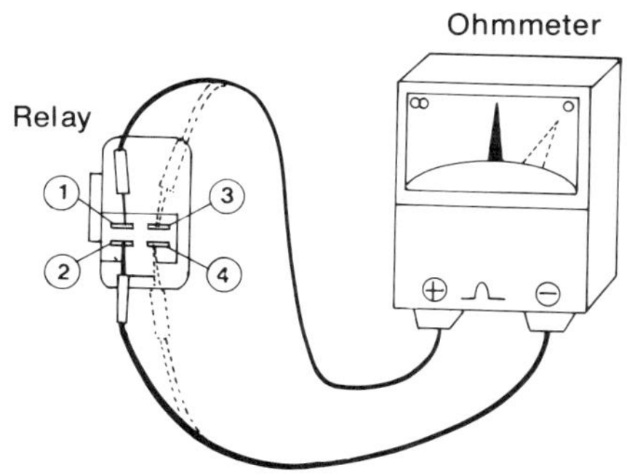

Fig. 8-71. Resistance being measured at relay terminals.

5. On cars with alternators that have integral regulators, connect a 12-volt battery to relay terminals **1** and **2**, as indicated in Fig. 8-72. Then, using an ohmmeter or a battery-powered test light, check for electrical continuity between terminals **3** and **4**. If there is continuity with the relay energized, the relay is faulty and should be replaced.

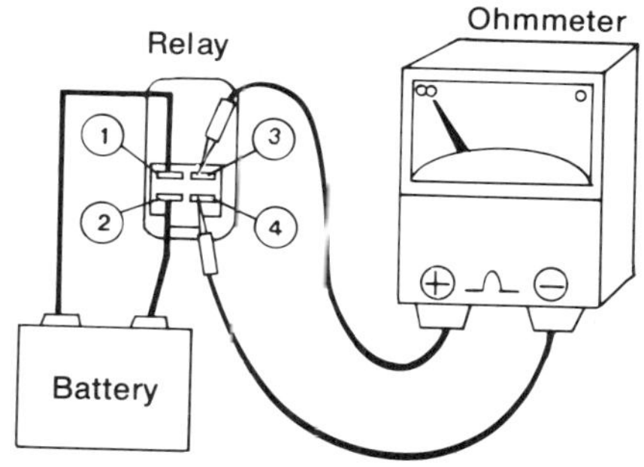

Fig. 8-72. Relay being checked for continuity while energized by battery.

Choke Opener System

The choke opener system forcibly opens the choke when the engine has warmed, regardless of the temperature of the automatic choke's heating element and bimetallic spring. In addition to preventing excessive hydrocarbon emissions, this device saves fuel and, by lowering the fast idle speed, reduces stress on the engine. Fig. 8-73, Fig. 8-74, and Fig. 8-75 show the choke opener systems used on the cars covered by this Manual.

Fig. 8-73. Choke opener system used on 1975 California and high-altitude models. System is shown in its ON position, which opens choke valve.

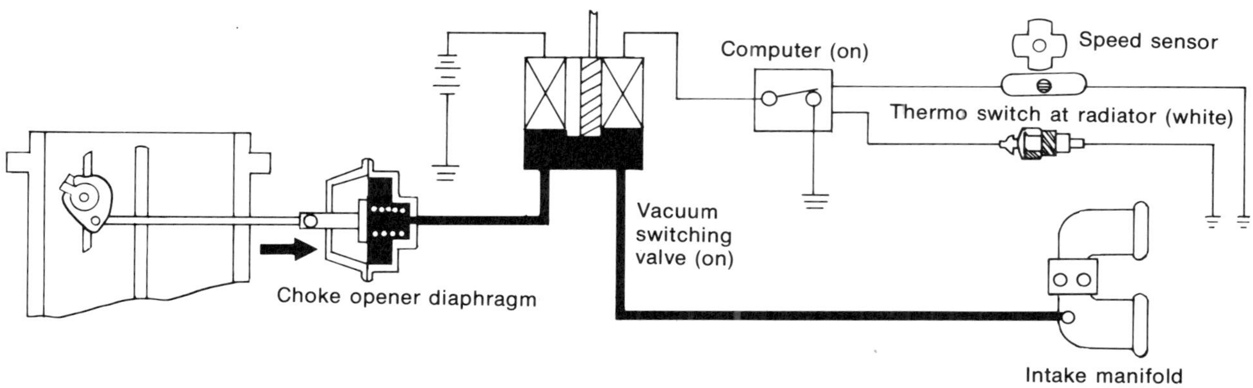

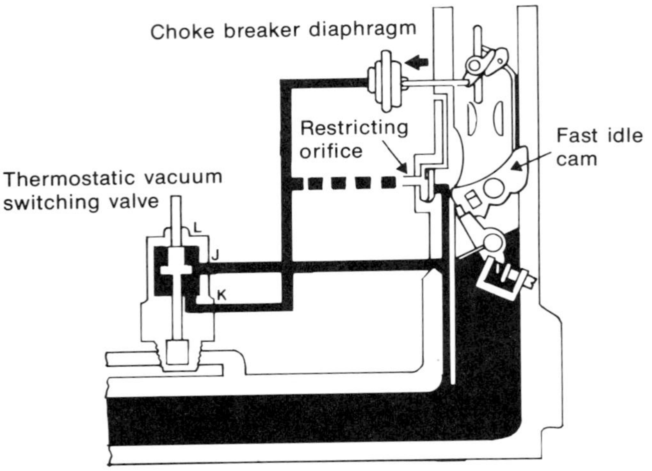

Fig. 8-74. Choke opener system used on 1976 and 1977 California and high-altitude models, and on all 1978 U.S. models. Connection shown by dashed line is not used on 1976 and 1977 cars. System is shown in its ON position, which opens choke valve.

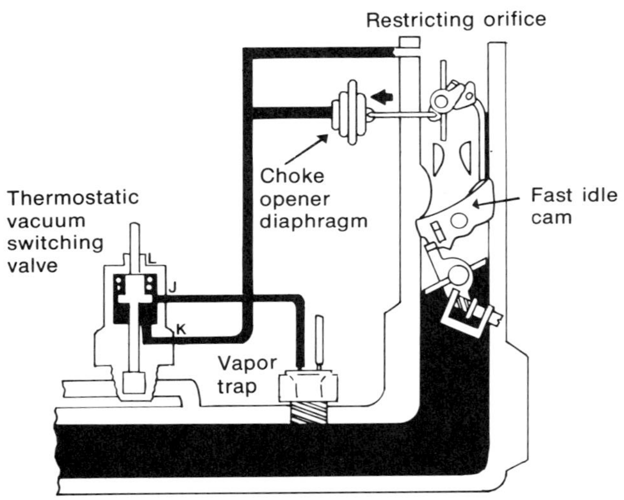

Fig. 8-75. Choke opener system used on 1979 and later U.S. models.

To test 1975 system:

1. Disconnect the vacuum hose from the choke opener diaphragm. Connect a long hose to the disconnected hose so that you can put a vacuum gauge inside the car where the driver can see it.

2. Start the engine and allow it to warm up. The vacuum gauge should indicate no vacuum while the car is standing still.

3. Gradually accelerate the warmed-up car to a speed of approxiamtely 32 kph (20 mph). At between 13 and 23 kph (8 and 14 mph), the vacuum should come on, then go off again as the vehicle slows to about 21 to 27 kph (13 to 16 mph).

NOTE ——
If you find any trouble when you carry out step 2 or step 3 of this procedure, test the vacuum switching valve and the speed sensor as described in **8.3 Evaporative Emission Control (EVAP) System.** Also test the thermo switch (white) on the radiator as indicated in Fig. 8-76. Replace faulty components.

WARNING ——
You must drain the cooling system as described in **ENGINE** *before you remove the thermo switch. Do not drain the coolant while the engine is hot because doing this could damage the engine or cause you to burn yourself.*

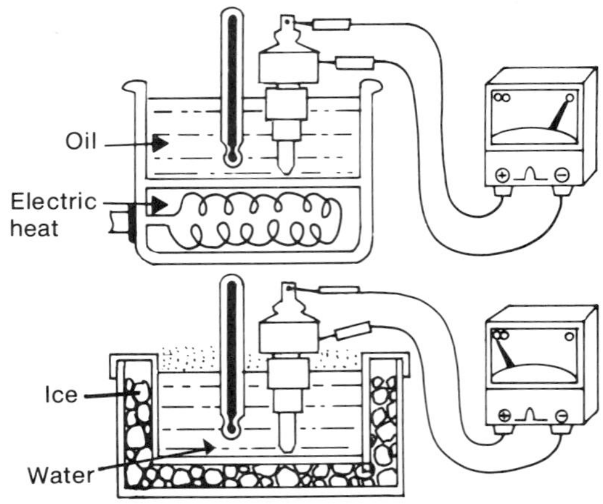

Fig. 8-76. Thermo switch being tested. There should be electrical continuity through switch when cooled below 6°C (43°F). Between 13° and 98°C (55° and 208°F), there should be no continuity. Above this range there should again be continuity.

To test 1976 and later systems:

1. Allow the car to stand outside until the coolant temperature is below 35°C (95°F).

2. Start the engine with the air cleaner removed so that you can observe the choke opener diaphragm. Disconnect the vacuum hose from the choke opener diaphragm.

3. With the coolant temperature below the range specified in step 1, reconnect the vacuum hose.

The choke opener linkage should not move. If the diaphragm pulls in, moving the linkage, the thermostatic vacuum switching valve is faulty and should be replaced.

4. Allow the engine to warm up. Disconnect the vacuum hose from the choke opener diaphragm. If there is no vacuum at the disconnected hose, replace the thermostatic vacuum switching valve. If there is vacuum, reconnect the hose. If the diaphragm fails to pull in, moving the choke opener linkage, the diaphragm is faulty and should be replaced.

NOTE ——

If you find no trouble but if engine operation suggests that the choke is being pulled open at too low or too high an engine temperature, check the thermostatic vacuum switching valve as indicated in Fig. 8-77. Replace the valve if it fails to open or close at the temperatures given in the illustration. Always apply waterproof sealer to the threads of the thermostatic vacuum switching valve when you reinstall it in the engine.

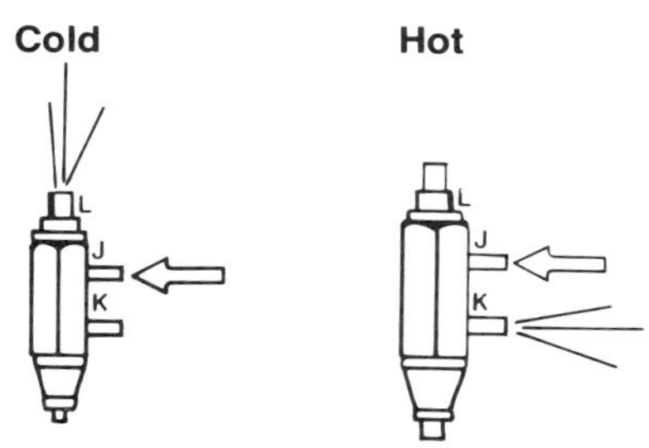

Temperature at which **J** is connected to **L**
(1976 through 1978): 35°C (95°F)
(1979 and later): 50°C (122°F)
Temperature at which **J** is connected to **K**
(all years): 65°C (149°F)

Fig. 8-77. Thermostatic vacuum switching valve tests. Blow air into connection **J** (arrow) with valve in water heated to low temperature and then to high temperature as given above. Air should emerge at correct connection.

Auxiliary Acceleration Pump (AAP) System

If the carburetor's acceleration pump were set to deliver adequate fuel for good acceleration while the engine is cold, it would supply surplus fuel during acceleration with the engine hot. In addition to wasting fuel, this would result in increased hydrocarbon emissions in the exhaust. Therefore the acceleration pump is set to deliver adequate fuel for good acceleration only with the engine warmed up. To ensure good acceleration at low engine temperatures, the auxiliary acceleration pump (AAP) system supplies additional fuel. The system is shown schematically in Fig. 8-78.

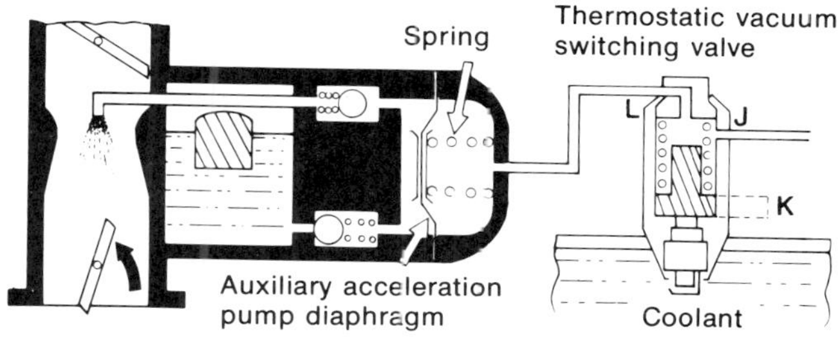

Fig. 8-78. Schematic view of auxiliary acceleration pump system, shown with engine cold. When throttle valve is opened (curved arrow at left), manifold vacuum falls, allowing spring-loaded diaphragm to force additional fuel to acceleration pump discharge tube. At warmer temperatures, vacuum is shut off by thermostatic vacuum switching valve and system no longer functions. Connection **K** for choke opener system is on later models only.

To check and repair system:

1. Allow the car to stand until the coolant temperature is below 35°C (95°F).
2. Start the engine with the air cleaner removed.
3. Pinch shut the vacuum hose that connects the auxiliary acceleration pump on the carburetor to the thermostatic vacuum switching valve (Fig. 6
8-79), then stop the engine.

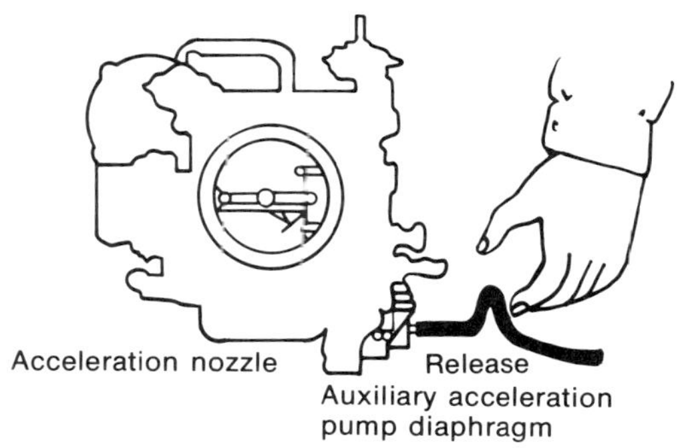

Fig. 8-79. Hose for auxiliary acceleration pump being pinched and released.

4. Look into the carburetor throat, then release the pinched hose. Fuel should spray from the acceleration nozzle of the acceleration pump discharge tube.
5. If no fuel sprays from the acceleration nozzle in the preceding step, disconnect the hose from the diaphragm. If there is no vacuum present with the engine running—and if the coolant temperature is below that specified in step 1—then the thermostat-

ic vacuum switching valve is faulty and should be replaced.

> **NOTE —**
> Always apply waterproof sealer to the threads of the thermostatic vacuum switching valve when you install the valve in the engine.

6. If there is vacuum at the disconnected hose, allow the engine to idle. Reconnect and disconnect the hose to the diaphragm. If the engine fails to change rpm each time vacuum is applied to the auxiliary acceleration pump diaphragm, the trouble is in the diaphragm or related parts of the carburetor. See **6. Repairing Carburetor.**
7. Allow the engine to warm up. Again pinch shut the vacuum hose that connects the auxiliary acceleration pump to the thermostatic vacuum switching valve. Then stop the engine.
8. Look into the carburetor throat, then release the pinched hose. If fuel sprays from the acceleration nozzle, the thermostatic vacuum switching valve is faulty and should be replaced. A thorough test of the valve is described under the preceding unnumbered heading.

Heated Air Intake (HAI) System and Hot Idle Compensation (HIC) System

Fig. 8-80 shows the components of the heated air intake/hot idle compensation system used on the 1979 models. The hot idle compensation (HIC) system is not used on 1975 through 1978 cars.

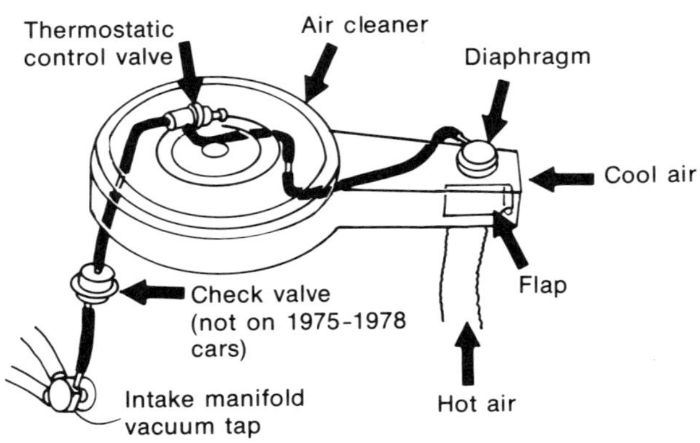

Fig. 8-80. Phantom view of air cleaner, showing components of heated air intake system. Beginning with 1979 models, check valve is used as shown here. Also, thermostatic control valve is designed to admit air to intake manifold in quantities that vary with air temperature.

In operation, the heated air intake (HAI) system supplies warmed air to the carburetor in cold weather and allows cool air to enter the carburetor whenever under-hood temperatures rise above a predetermined level. This improves driveability with the lean fuel/air mixtures needed for correct exhaust emission control and also prevents carburetor icing, which could cause rough running and fuel waste when temperatures are near the freezing point.

To check and repair heated air intake system:

1. Make sure that the vacuum hoses are tight-fitting, correctly installed, and in good condition.
2. By removing the wing nut and releasing the three clamps, take off the cover of the air cleaner. If necessary, cool the thermostatic control valve with ice or compressed air so that its temperature is below 30°C (86°F).
3. Start the engine. At idle, the flap in the air cleaner's intake air duct should be up, in the position that will admit hot air to the carburetor from the stove on the exhaust manifold.
4. If the flap is not up at idle in the preceding step, disconnect the vacuum hose from the diaphragm. If there is no vacuum at the disconnected hose, the thermostatic control valve is faulty and should be replaced. If there is vacuum, check that the flap can be moved by hand. If it is not binding, the trouble is in the diaphragm, which should be replaced.
5. On 1979 and later cars only, temporarily disconnect the vacuum hose for the heated air intake system from the vacuum tap on the intake manifold. The flap should remain up. If not, the thermostatic control valve is faulty and should be replaced.
6. On 1979 and later cars only, temporarily remove the check valve from the hoses. When you blow into the white end of the check valve, air should flow through. When you blow into the black end of the check valve, no air should pass through. Replace faulty check valves.
7. Reinstall the cover on the air cleaner, making sure to align the arrow on the cover with the arrow on the air cleaner's intake air duct. If necessary, consult **6.1 Removing and Installing Carburetor.**
8. Allow the engine to warm up. Check to see that the flap goes down, opening the cool air passage. If not, the thermostatic control valve is faulty and should be replaced.

To test and repair hot idle compensation system (1979 and later cars only):

1. Remove the thermostatic control valve from the air cleaner.
2. If necessary, cool the control valve to below 30°C (86°F). No air should flow from connection **A** to connection **C** with connection **B** sealed. See Fig. 8-81.

> ***CAUTION —***
> *In cooling or heating the thermostatic control valve, use the setup shown in the illustration. To avoid damage and malfunctioning, be careful that no water enters the valve.*

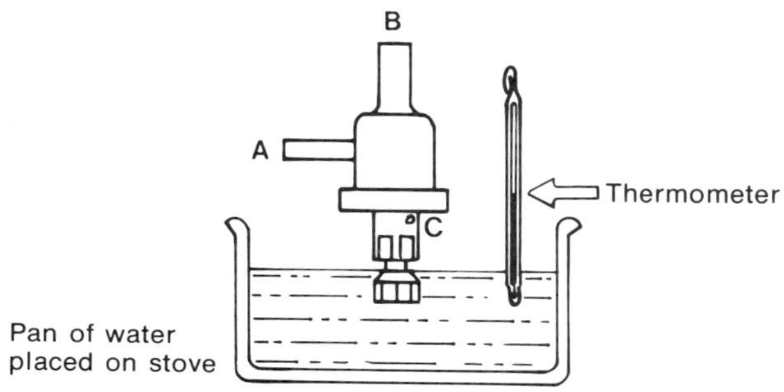

Fig. 8-81. Thermostatic control valve being heated or cooled by water. Do not immerse valve farther than shown here. When cold, no air should flow from connection **C** when you blow into connection **A** and seal connection **B**.

3. Heat the water to 40°C (104°F). With the valve at this temperature, air should flow from connection **C** when you seal connection **B** and blow into connection **A**.
4. Heat the water to between 40°C and 70°C (104°F and 158°F). With the valve at any point in this temperature range, a small amount of air should flow from connection **C** when you seal connection **A** and blow into connection **B**.
5. Heat the water to a temperature above 80°C (176°F). With the valve above this temperature, a large amount of air should flow from connection **C** when you seal connection **A** and blow into connection **B**. If the thermostatic control valve fails this or any preceding test, replace it.

High-altitude Compensation (HAC) System

(1977 and later high-altitude models only)

Fig. 8-82 and Fig. 8-83 show the high-altitude compensation (HAC) systems that are used on cars covered by this Manual. The high-altitude compensation valve contains double aneroid capsules. These capsules expand at the lower atmospheric pressures encountered at high altitudes, thereby closing a valve that at low altitudes introduces air into the vacuum line that serves the ignition distributor's vacuum advance secondary diaphragm. This causes the spark to advance farther whenever intake manifold vacuum is high, improving driveability and increasing fuel economy. The system is desirable because of the lean fuel/air mixtures and lower cylinder pressures used in emission-controlled engines.

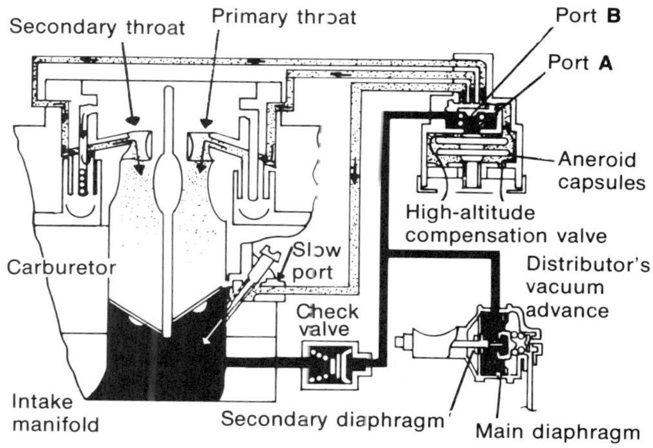

Fig. 8-82. Schematic view of high-altitude compensation system used on 1977 and 1978 cars. At low altitudes, port **A** is open and port **B** closed. Above 1219 m (4000 ft.), port **A** is closed and port **B** open, adding spark advance supplied by secondary diaphragm to that provided by main diaphragm and centrifugal advance mechanism.

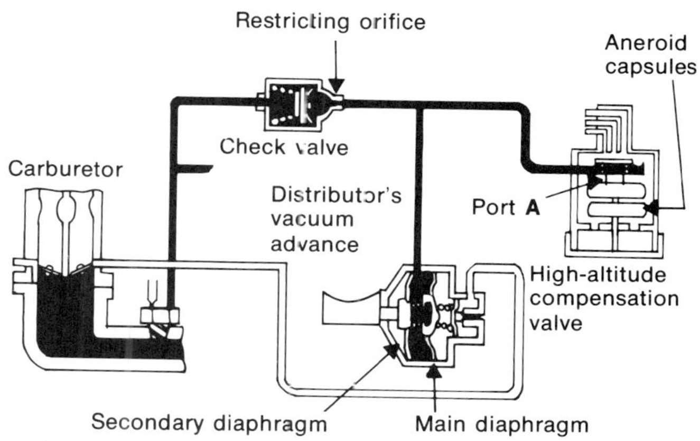

Fig. 8-83. Schematic view of high-altitude compensation system used on 1979 and later cars. At low altitudes, below 783 m (2570 ft.), port **A** is open so that air is admitted. Above 1198 m (3930 ft.), port **A** is closed, adding spark advance supplied by secondary diaphragm to that provided by main diaphragm and centrifugal advance mechanism.

Before you can test the high-altitude compensation system, you must determine whether the high-altitude compensation valve is in its high-altitude or low-altitude position. Usually, you can determine this by knowing your actual altitude above sea level. However, at altitudes near 1220 m (4000 ft.), variations in barometric pressure may change the valve's position with changes of weather, so you must check the valve itself. To do this, blow into any one of the three connections at the top of the valve (disconnect a hose, or remove a plastic cap on 1979 and later cars). If air exits through the valve's filter (Fig. 8-84), the valve is in its high-altitude position. If no air comes out, the valve is in its low-altitude position.

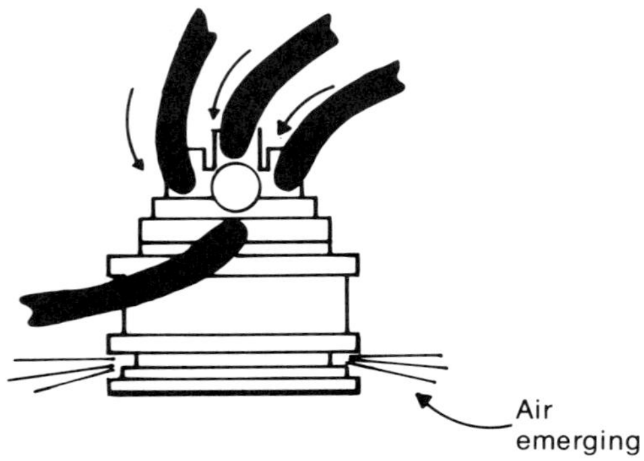

Fig. 8-84. Position of high-altitude compensation valve being checked. Blow into one of top connections (arrows). If air emerges at points shown, valve is in high-altitude position.

To test and repair at low altitude:

1. Using the procedure given in **ENGINE,** check that the ignition timing is correctly set to 10° BTDC (before top dead center).
2. With the engine idling, pinch shut the hose between the high-altitude compensation valve and the T-fitting (Fig. 8-85).
3. With the hose pinched, aim the timing light at the engine's timing scale and crankshaft pulley. The timing should be approximately 20° BTDC.

   NOTE ——

   If the timing does not advance to about 20° BTDC with the hose pinched, check and if necessary adjust, repair, or replace the ignition distributor as described in **ENGINE.** If you find no fault in the hoses or the distributor, remove the high-altitude compensation valve. Carefully remove its cover. Clean the air filters and visually inspect the valve. If you find any fault, replace the high-altitude compensation valve.

4. Remove the check valve from the vacuum hoses. When you blow into the white end, air should flow through the check valve. When you blow into the black end, the valve should close, preventing air from passing through. Replace faulty check valves.

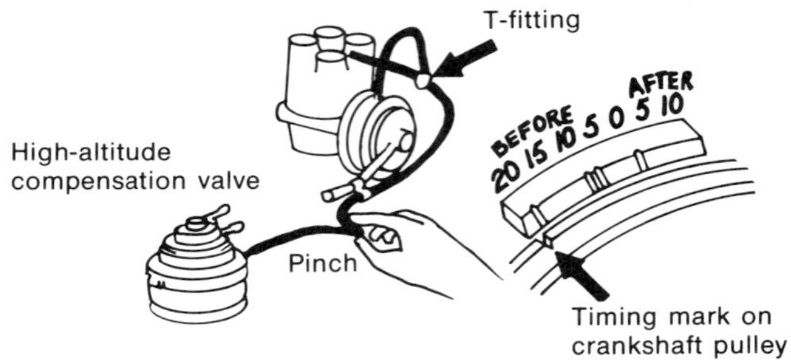

Fig. 8-85. Spark advanced to 20° BTDC with hose pinched.

To test and repair at high altitude:

1. With the engine idling at 800 to 900 rpm, aim a timing light at the timing scale and the crankshaft pulley on the front of the engine. The timing should be at approximately 20° BTDC (before top dead center). If necessary, consult **ENGINE.**
2. Disconnect the vacuum hose from the distributor's secondary diaphragm. The timing should be 10° BTDC. If not, adjust the timing as described in **ENGINE,** then repeat step 1.

   NOTE ——

   If the timing is incorrect in either step 1 or step 2, check and if necessary adjust, repair, or replace the ignition distributor as described in **ENGINE.** If you find no fault in the hoses or the distributor, remove the high-altitude compensation valve. Carefully remove its cover. Clean the air filters and visually inspect the valve. If you find any fault, replace the high-altitude compensation valve.

3. Disconnect the vacuum hose from the black end of the check valve, then plug the hose. If the timing fails to stay at about 20° BTDC for more than one minute, the check valve is faulty and should be replaced.

Deceleration Fuel Cutoff System

(1978 and later cars)

Fig. 8-86 is a schematic view of the deceleration fuel cutoff system. This system controls the operation of the first electromagnetic cutoff valve on the carburetor. During deceleration, this system cuts off the flow of fuel to the carburetor's idle circuit to prevent afterburning in the exhaust system. This afterburning not only wastes fuel but also can overheat the catalytic converter.

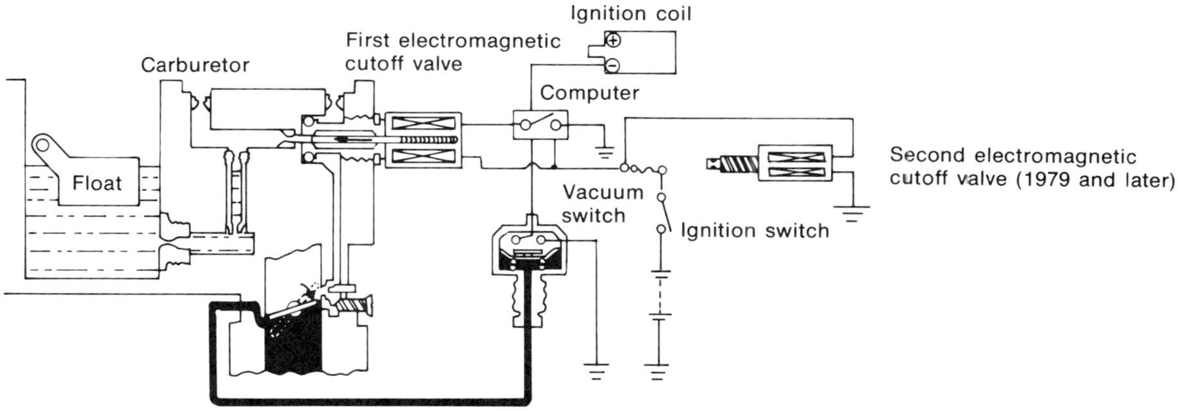

Fig. 8-86. Deceleration fuel cutoff system shown schematically. Manifold vacuum, acting on vacuum switch, supplies computer with engine load information.

To test and repair:

1. Start the engine. It should run smoothly and idle normally.
2. With the engine idling, pinch shut the vacuum hose that leads to the vacuum switch. (The vacuum switch is located on the right-hand side of the engine compartment.) Gradually increase the engine speed to 2500 rpm. Between 2000 and 2500 rpm, the engine should run slightly rough and occasionally misfire.

CAUTION —

Make this test and the test described in step 4 quickly to avoid damaging the catalytic converter.

3. Release the pinched hose. Allow the engine to idle, then again increase its speed to 2500 rpm. The engine should run smoothly and normally.
4. Disconnect the wire from the electromagnetic cutoff valve by pulling apart the multiple connector for the carburetor wiring. The engine should begin idling roughly. Immediately reconnect the wire.

NOTE —

If you find no fault when you carry out the preceding steps, the system is operating correctly. If you find any fault, test the individual components of the system as described in the procedure steps that follow.

5. Test the first electromagnetic cutoff valve as indicated in Fig. 8-87. If the valve fails to click each time you connect or disconnect the battery, replace it.

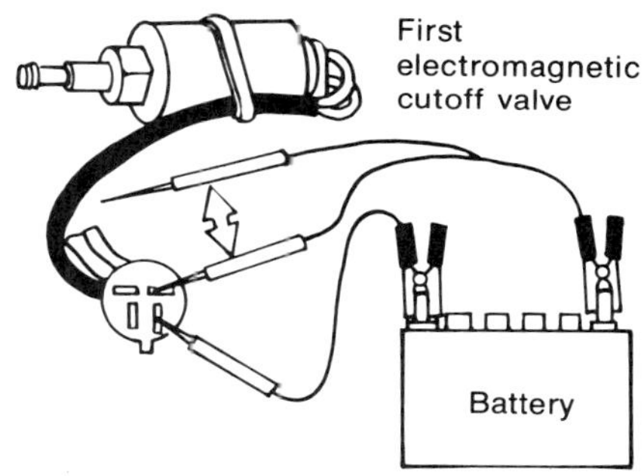

Fig. 8-87. First electromagnetic cutoff valve being tested. Valve should click each time battery is connected or disconnected (double arrow). Valve need not be removed for test.

6. Using an ohmmeter or a battery-powered test light, check for electrical continuity between the terminal of the vacuum switch and the vacuum switch body. With the engine stopped, there should be continuity. With the engine idling, there should be no continuity. Replace faulty vacuum switches.

6

Double Vacuum Advance System

An ignition distributor with a double vacuum advance unit is used on some cars other than those with the high-altitude option or the spark control (SC) system. On these cars, the system is called the double vacuum advance system. This system is used primarily on 1976 and later cars sold in Canada and in cold climate areas outside California, if improves the cold-engine driveability of emission-controlled engines, and it makes more efficient use of the added fuel supplied to the engine during cold operation. Fig. 8-88, Fig. 8-89, and Fig. 8-90 give schematic views of the different double vacuum advance systems.

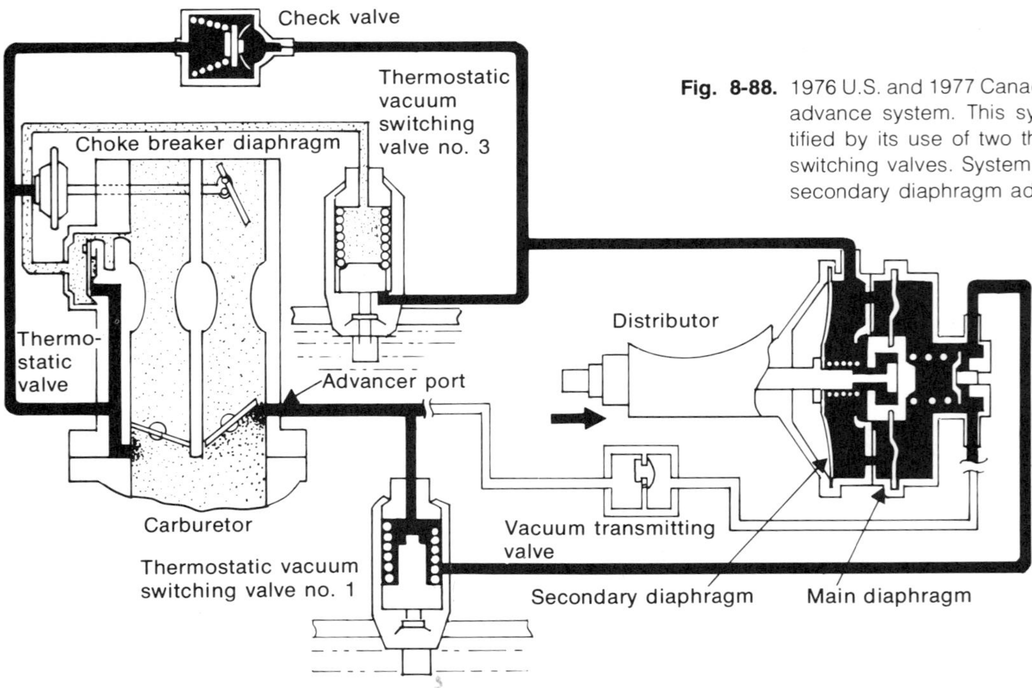

Fig. 8-88. 1976 U.S. and 1977 Canadian double vacuum advance system. This system can be identified by its use of two thermostatic vacuum switching valves. System is shown cold, with secondary diaphragm advanced.

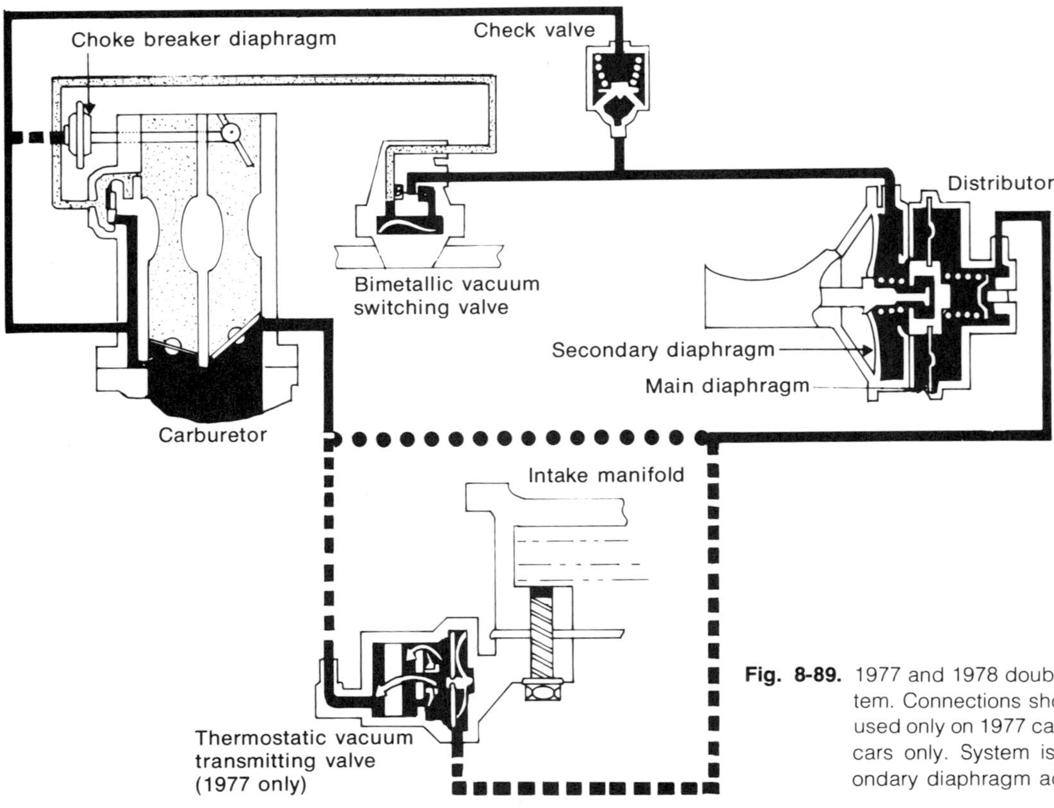

Fig. 8-89. 1977 and 1978 double vacuum advance system. Connections shown as dashed lines are used only on 1977 cars. Dotted line is for 1978 cars only. System is shown cold, with secondary diaphragm advanced.

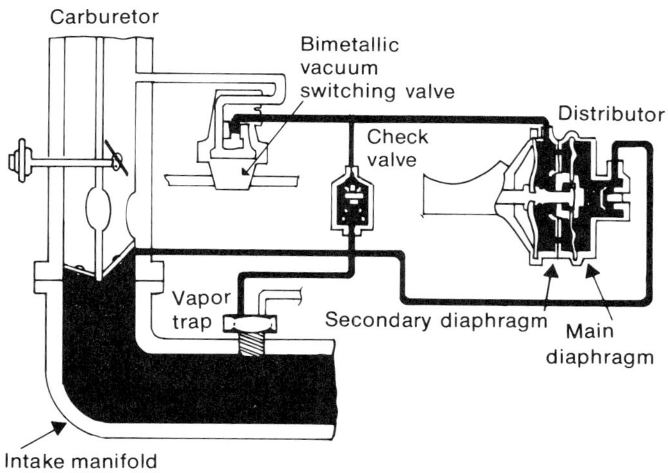

Fig. 8-90. 1979 and later double vacuum advance system. System is shown cold, with secondary diaphragm advanced.

To test and repair system:

1. If necessary, allow the car to stand until the engine's coolant temperature is below 27°C (81°F). Connect a timing light, as described in **ENGINE,** to check the ignition timing.
2. Start the engine and allow it to idle. The ignition timing should be approximately 20° BTDC (before top dead center).
3. Disconnect the vacuum hose from the black end of the check valve. The ignition timing should stay at about 20° BTDC for one minute or more. Reconnect the hose.
4. Allow the engine to warm up. The ignition timing should be 10° BTDC at idle. If the timing has shifted by about 10°, but is not at 10° BTDC, the double vacuum advance system is all right, but the ignition timing needs to be adjusted as described in **ENGINE.**

> **NOTE ——**
> If you find no fault during the preceding tests, the system is operating correctly. If you find any fault in the double vacuum advance system, first check the distributor's vacuum advance as described in **ENGINE.** If necessary, adjust, repair, or replace the vacuum advance or the distributor. If the trouble persists after you check the distributor, test the individual components of the system as described in the steps that follow.

5. To test the cold operation of the thermostatic vacuum switching valves (1976 U.S. cars and 1977 Canadian cars), try blowing air through each valve with the engine coolant below 35°C (95°F). Air should pass freely through thermostatic vacuum switching valve No. 1 (located on the intake manifold), but no air should pass through valve No. 3 (located on the connection for the radiator's top hose, above the thermostat). Replace faulty valves.
6. To test the hot operation of the thermostatic vacuum switching valves (1976 U.S. cars and 1977 Canadian cars), try blowing air through each valve with the engine coolant above 60°C (140°F). Air should pass freely through thermostatic vacuum switching valve No. 3 (on the radiator hose connection), but no air should pass through valve No. 1 (on the manifold). Replace faulty valves.
7. To test the check valve, disconnect it from its hoses. Air should pass through freely when you blow into the white end, but the valve should seal and prevent air from passing through when you blow into the black end. Replace faulty valves.
8. To test the bimetallic vacuum switching valve, remove it from the engine, then connect a hose to one of its connections so that you can blow air through the valve. With the valve cooled to a temperature below 20°C (68°F) on 1977 models or below 30°C (86°F) on 1978 and later models, no air should pass through the valve. With the valve heated to above 20°C (68°F) on 1977 models or above 44°C (111°F) on 1978 and later models, air should pass freely through the valve. Replace faulty valves.

> **NOTE ——**
> When you install a thermostatic vacuum switching valve or a bimetallic vacuum switching valve, apply waterproof sealer to the threads.

9. To test the thermostatic vacuum transmitting valve on 1977 cars, use the procedure given in conjunction with the spark control (SC) system under an earlier unnumbered heading. Replace faulty valves as described in that procedure.

6

9. EXHAUST SYSTEM

Because of the large number of different exhaust systems and exhaust system components used on the cars covered by this Manual, it is not possible to give step-by-step instructions for their replacement. Instead, a few general directions that apply to all systems will be given. A careful inspection of the old system prior to its removal should be your guide for the correct installation of a replacement system.

On certain models, such as the one illustrated in Fig. 9-1, it is necessary to remove the transmission mount crossmember partially in order to remove or install the front exhaust pipe. Catalytic converter removal and installation is covered separately in **8.2 Catalytic Converter (CCo).**

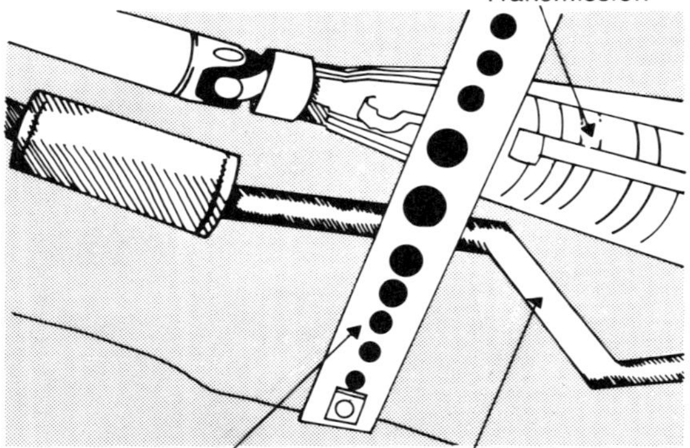

Fig. 9-1. Location of components mentioned in procedure that follows.

To remove transmission rear mounting:

1. Remove the gearshift lever as described in **CLUTCH AND MANUAL TRANSMISSION.** On cars with automatic transmissions, detach the rod from the transmission's selector lever.
2. Raise the car on a hoist or support it on stands designed for the purpose.
3. Unbolt the front exhaust pipe from the engine's exhaust manifold.
4. Unbolt the clamp, then disconnect the rear end of the front exhaust pipe from the rest of the exhaust system.
5. Remove the exhaust pipe support bracket and allow the detached pipe to rest atop the transmission rear mounting.
6. Place a jack beneath the transmission, then raise the jack to support the engine/transmission assembly.
7. Unbolt the outer ends of the transmission mount crossmember from the car body. Then, using the jack, lower the transmission and the crossmember so that you can remove the exhaust pipe.

Installation is the reverse of removal. Torque the nuts that hold the front exhaust pipe to the exhaust manifold to 30 to 45 Nm (22 to 33 ft. lb.). Torque the bolts that hold the transmission mount crossmember to the car body to 20 to 25 Nm (15 to 18 ft. lb.).

General Rules for Exhaust System Replacement

To obtain the correct replacement components for your car, you should be prepared to give certain information to the parts department. First, you should know the model year and, if possible, the approximate month when the car was manufactured. Be sure that you know the body style (hardtop, sport coupe, or liftback, for example) and the model number. You can find the model number on the vehicle identification plate in the engine compartment; it is preceded by the letters TE. It is also important to know whether the car was originally built to particular local standards—whether it is a California model or a Canadian model, for example. Lastly, you can avoid mistakes by giving the old exhaust system a visual examination so that you will be familiar with the correct parts for the car. If you are in doubt, it may help to take the old part for comparison with the replacement part. Please observe the following general rules:

1. Always use new gaskets at all points when you install new exhaust system components or reinstall old components following repairs.
2. Do not tighten any clamps or mounting bolts until you have loosely installed the entire system on the car and then aligned it so that no part of the system will contact any other part of the car.
3. Be especially careful to use new ring gaskets and to align carefully the joints where ring gaskets are used. See Fig. 9-2.

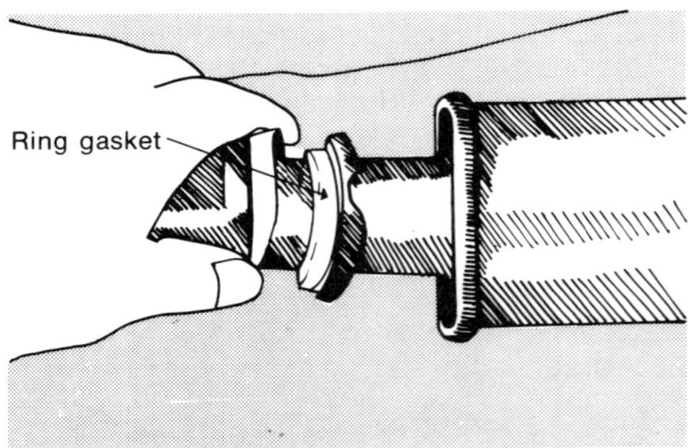

Fig. 9-2. Exhaust system joint with ring gasket being assembled. Conical seats for gasket must be smooth, and no part should be dented or otherwise deformed. Light application of grease to gasket will help it seat correctly when clamping bolts are tightened.

4. In aligning the system, make sure that any rubber rings used to support the system hang straight and are not under abnormal strain. Replace rubber components that are deteriorating or are in any way damaged or deformed.

5. Use new bolts and clamps in assembling the exhaust system. Otherwise there is danger that they will break during installation.

6. With the system carefully aligned, tighten all mounting bolts and clamps. Normally it should not be necessary to torque any nut or bolt to more than 20 to 25 Nm (15 to 18 ft. lb.).

7. After completing the installation, start the engine and check for leakage. Correct any leaks before returning the car to service.

8. Drive the car over railroad tracks or some other irregular surface and isten for noises that may be caused by the exhaust system striking some part of the suspension or the car body. If you have aligned the system carefully, you should not need to make any corrections.

10. FUEL SYSTEM TECHNICAL DATA

I. Carburetor Adjustment, Assembly, and Repair Data

Description	Specification
Float levels—raised position (1975, 1976)	3.50 mm (.138 in.)
—raised position (1977)	6.00 mm (.236 in.)
—raised position (1978 and later)	6.50 mm (.256 in.)
—lowered position (all models)	1.20 mm (.047 in.)
Accelerator pump stroke	5.00 mm (.197 in.)
Throttle valve angle (measured from bore)—fully opened	90°
—primary, fully closed	7°
—secondary, fully closed	20°
Secondary throttle valve touch angle (measured from bore)	57°
Primary throttle valve kick-up gap (measured between throttle valve and carburetor body)	0.20 mm (.008 in.)
Secondary throttle valve kick-up angle (measured from bore)	64° to 90°
Fast idle clearance for primary throttle valve (measured between throttle valve and carburetor body)	1.10 mm (.043 in.)
Primary throttle valve angle with throttle positioner engaged (measured from bore)	
—1975 and 1976	16°
—1977 and later with manual transmission	16°
—1977 and later with automatic transmission	15°
Choke valve mechanical unloader angle (measured from horizontal)	47°
Choke valve angle with choke breaker pulled in (measured from horizontal)—1975 and 1976	—
—1977	38°
—1978, Canada only	38°
—1978, U.S. only	39°
—1979	39°
Choke valve angle with choke opener pulled in (measured from horizontal)	
—1975	—
—1976	47° 3′
—1977, California and high-altitude only	67° 30′
—1978	78°
—1979	77°
Idle mixture adjusting screw preliminary setting—through 1978	screwed out 2⅝ turns
—from 1979	screwed out 2½ turns

II. Carburetor Part Numbers

Cars to which carburetor is suited	Part Number for carburetor
1975 cars sold outside California with manual transmissions	21100-26356
1975 cars sold outside California with automatic transmissions	21100-26360
1975 California cars with manual or automatic transmissions	21100-26370
1976 cars sold outside California with manual or automatic transmissions	21100-26362
1976 California cars with manual transmissions	21100-26391
1976 California cars with automatic transmissions	21100-26372
1977 cars sold outside California and high-altitude areas with manual transmissions	21100-26510
1977 cars sold outside California and high-altitude areas with automatic transmissions	21100-26520
1977 California cars with manual or automatic transmissions	21100-26393
1977 high-altitude cars with manual or automatic transmissions	21100-26600
1978 U.S. cars sold outside California and high-altitude areas with manual or automatic transmissions	21100-26800
1978 California cars with manual or automatic transmissions	21100-26395
1978 U.S. high-altitude cars with manual or automatic transmissions	21100-26602
1978 Canadian cars with manual transmissions	21100-26511
1978 Canadian cars with automatic transmissions	21100-26521
1979 U.S. cars sold outside California with manual or automatic transmissions	21100-26802
1979 California cars with manual or automatic transmissions	21100-26397
1979 Canadian cars with manual transmissions	21100-26512
1979 Canadian cars with automatic transmissions	21100-26522

Section 7

BRAKES AND WHEELS

Contents

7

TABLES

Brakes and Wheels

The dual-circuit hydraulic foot brakes operate on all four wheels. The foot pressure required to operate the brakes is reduced by a vacuum-powered servo between the pedal and the master cylinder. All Corolla models covered by this Manual have floating-caliper front disc brakes and rear drum brakes. The hand-operated parking brake operates on the rear wheels only.

A dual-chamber master cylinder provides operating pressure to both brake circuits. The system is so designed that leaks in one circuit cannot affect the other circuit. One circuit operates the front wheel brakes, and the other operates the rear wheel brakes. An electrical warning system causes a red warning indicator on the instrument panel to light if hydraulic pressure is too low in either brake circuit. If you see this light while you are driving, it is imperative that the brake system be given a thorough check, even though braking action may still seem satisfactory. Complete loss of pressure in one of the brake circuits will cause the pedal to fall closer to the floor during braking and will result in abnormally long stopping distances. 7

Because safe vehicle operation depends very heavily on the brakes, all brake system service and repair work should be carried out with extreme cleanliness, careful attention to specifications, and proper working procedures. All necessary information is given here, although some of the operations that are described may be of practical value only to professional mechanics. If you lack the skills, the special tools, or a clean workshop for servicing the brake system, we suggest you leave these repairs to an Authorized Dealer or other qualified shop. We especially urge you to consult your Authorized Dealer before attempting repairs on a car still covered by the new-car warranty.

The pages devoted to wheels and tires should have practical interest to all drivers, whether they service their own cars or not. Often, abnormal tire wear or poor vehicle handling is the direct result of improperly fitted tires, incorrectly inflated tires, or driving practices that damage the tires. Thus, following the advice offered here will not only save you money but will also make your driving safer.

1. GENERAL DESCRIPTION

Fig. 1-1 is a simplified schematic diagram of the dual-circuit brake system. Each chamber of the dual-chamber master cylinder is connected to one of the circuits. The front chamber of the master cylinder operates the front wheel brakes, and the rear chamber of the master cylinder operates the rear wheel brakes. Each circuit can operate independently of the other, and each chamber of the master cylinder has its own brake fluid reservoir.

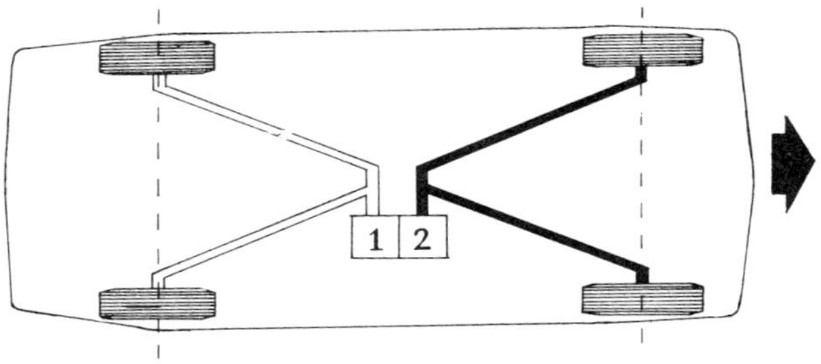

Fig. 1-1. Simplified schematic diagram of dual-circuit brake system. Arrow indicates front of car.

Master Cylinder and Hydraulic Lines

The master cylinder generates the hydraulic pressure used to operate the brakes. It is connected to the wheel cylinders by the brake lines and hoses. When you depress the brake pedal, a rod transmits the movement to a valve inside the vacuum-powered brake servo. Depending on the movement of the valve, engine vacuum acts on the servo piston. The piston is connected to a pushrod that moves the master cylinder pistons. The system fails safe, so, if the servo ceases to function, you can still apply the foot brakes. The pedal pressure required will, however, be somewhat greater than normal.

Calipers and Wheel Cylinders

The rear drum brake wheel cylinders are rigidly mounted with dual opposed pistons. When hydraulic pressure is applied to the cylinder, the pistons move outward—applying mechanical pressure to the brake shoes. Four slightly different front disc brake calipers have been used on the cars covered by this Manual. All are floating-caliper single-piston designs. For the purposes of servicing and repair work; the main difference between one kind of caliper and another is the part number.

Brake Warning System

The main hydraulic lines from the master cylinder chambers are connected to a pressure differential warning actuator. This device turns on the brake warning light if the pressure in one brake circuit is lower than that in the other.

Parking Brake

The cable-operated parking brake works on the rear wheels only. The hand lever, centrally located between the front seats, is held or released by a ratchet.

2. MAINTENANCE

You should perform the following routine maintenance operations at the times or mileages listed in **LUBRICATION AND MAINTENANCE.** You can find instructions for doing these jobs in this section under the headings listed after each maintenance operation.

1. Checking brake fluid level and, if necessary, adding fluid. **9.1**
2. Checking brake pedal height and travel. **5.2**
3. Checking brake pad thickness and brake lining thickness. **7.1, 8.1**
4. Checking rear brake drum condition. **8.1**
5. Checking condition of brake lines hoses. **6**
6. Checking operation of brake servo. **5**
7. Checking and, if necessary, adjusting parking brake lever travel. **10.1**
8. Lubricating and adjusting front wheel bearings. **11.4, 11.5.**

3. BRAKE TROUBLESHOOTING

Table a lists brake problems, probable causes, and suggested remedies. The numbers in bold type in the Remedy column refer to the numbered headings in this section of the Manual under which the suggested repairs are described.

Table a. Brake Troubleshooting

Problem	Probable Cause	Remedy
1. Pedal goes all the way to floor, or nearly so, in braking	a. Rear brakes require adjustment b. Automatic adjuster faulty c. No fluid or low fluid	a. Operate parking brake lever repeatedly (with foot brakes released) so that automatic adjuster functions. b. Repair or clean and lubricate automatic adjusters. See **8.2**. c. Find and repair leaks. Fill and bleed system. See **9**.
2. Low pedal even after rear brake adjustment and bleeding	Master cylinder faulty	Replace or rebuild master cylinder. See **4.1**, **4.2**.
3. Pedal spongy or brakes work only after pedal is pumped	a. Insufficient fluid in reservoir b. Air in system c. Master cylinder faulty	a. Find and repair leaks. Fill and bleed system. See **9**. b. Check for leaks and bleed system. See **9**. c. Replace or rebuild master cylinder. See **4.1**, **4.2**.
4. Braking action decreases after rear brakes have been adjusted	a. Brake lines leaking b. Faulty wheel cylinder	a. Tighten connections or fit new lines and hoses. See **6**. b. Replace or rebuild faulty cylinder. See **8.3**, **8.4**.
5. Brakes drag or overheat	a. Compensating port of master cylinder blocked b. Brake servo pushrod misadjusted c. Brake pedal binding, return spring weak, or brake pedal height misadjusted d. Parking brake misadjusted e. Automatic adjuster faulty f. Distorted brake shoe or cracked brake lining g. Sticking caliper piston or wheel cylinder piston h. Brake line restricted	a. Clean and rebuild master cylinder. See **4.1**, **4.2**. b. Adjust brake servo pushrod. See **5.1**. c. Check pedal for free movement; check that pedal height is correct and that return spring keeps pedal against stop. See **5.2**. d. Adjust parking brake. See **10.2**. e. Check and, if necessary, repair automatic adjusters. See **8.2**. f. Check and, if necessary, replace brake pads or brake shoes. See **7.1**, **8.1**. g. Check and, if necessary, repair or replace brake caliper or wheel cylinder. See **7.3**, **8.4**. h. Check and, if necessary, replace brake line. See **6.1**.
6. Brakes inefficient despite high pedal pressure	a. Oil, grease, or brake fluid on linings b. Brake linings distorted, glazed, of wrong composition, or distorted c. Leaking vacuum hose to brake servo d. Servo diaphragm leaking e. Sticking caliper piston or wheel cylinder piston f. Poor seal between servo and master cylinder g. Check valve in vacuum hose faulty h. Brake line restricted	a. Clean drums or discs. Replace linings, replace oil seals, or correct fluid leaks. See **7.1**, **8.1**. b. Check and, if necessary, replace brake pads or brake shoes. See **7.1**, **8.1**. c. Replace hose or tighten hose clamps. See **5.1**. d. Replace or repair servo. See **5.1**. e. Check and, if necessary, repair or replace brake caliper or wheel cylinder. See **7.3**, **8.4**. f. Replace seal. Check piston rod for damage and, if necessary, replace it. See **4.1**. g. Replace faulty check valve. See **5.1**. h. Check and, if necessary, replace brake line. See **6.1**.
7. Brakes chatter and tend to grab	a. Linings worn b. Brake drum or brake disc scored or distorted c. Brake linings oily, distorted, glazed, or worn d. Disc brake pad sticking e. Brake servo faulty	a. Check and, if necessary, replace brake pads or brake shoes. See **7.1**, **8.1**. b. Recondition or replace brake drum or disc. See **7.4**, **8.1**. c. Check and, if necessary, replace brake pads or brake shoes. See **7.1**, **8.1**. d. Replace brake pads, or clean caliper so that pads do not stick. See **7.1**. e. Replace or repair servo. See **5.1**.
8. Drum brakes squeak	a. Unsuitable or badly fitted linings b. Brake linings dirty c. Backing plates distorted d. Brake shoe return springs weak e. Poor lining contact patter owing to shoe distortion	a. Fit new linings correctly. See **8.2**. b. Clean brakes. See **8.1**. c. Check backing plates for distortion and fit new parts if necessary. See **8.1**, **8.5**. d. Fit new return springs. See **8.2**. e. Align shoes with backing plate, with 0.20 mm (.008 in.) clearance at lining ends and contact across full width. See **8.2**.

(continued on next page)

Table a. Brake Troubleshooting (cont.)

Problem	Probable Cause	Remedy
9. Disc brakes squeak	a. Unsuitable pads b. Spreader spring faulty or missing c. Pad guide surfaces dirty or rusted d. Pads dirty or glazed e. Lining loose on pad	a. Fit new pads. See **7.1**. b. Install new spreader spring. See **7.1**. c. Clean pads and calipers. See **7.1**. d. Clean or replace pads. See **7.1**. e. Replace pads. See **7.1**.

4. MASTER CYLINDER

The master cylinder is mounted on the vacuum-powered brake servo, inside the engine compartment. Two brake fluid reservoirs, which can be replaced separately, are mounted atop the brake master cylinder.

4.1 Removing and Installing Master Cylinder

The master cylinder is mounted on two studs (four studs on some early models). In removing or installing the master cylinder, be careful not to bend any of the brake lines or damage the union nuts that hold the lines to the master cylinder.

To remove:

1. Using a clean syringe, remove the brake fluid from the reservoirs. Discard the fluid.

   WARNING —
   Do not start a siphon with your mouth or spill fluid onto the car. Brake fluid is both poisonous and damaging to paint.

2. Disconnect the brake lines from the master cylinder. On 1975 and 1976 cars that have them, disconnect the wires from the pressure switches of the master cylinder.
3. Remove the nuts that hold the master cylinder to the vacuum-powered brake servo. Then remove the master cylinder from the car. Discard the old gasket that is between the master cylinder and the servo, and also the rubber seal that surrounds the end of the master cylinder.

To install:

1. Install a new gasket on the studs of the brake servo. Install a new rubber seal (called a boot in the factory parts list) in the groove on the end of the master cylinder.

   NOTE —
   If you have replaced or rebuilt either the master cylinder or the brake servo, you must adjust the master cylinder pushrod, which is inside the servo, before you install the master cylinder. See **5.1 Removing and Installing Brake Servo.**

2. Position the master cylinder on the servo. Then, while you hold the master cylinder loosely in position, screw the brake line union nuts into the master cylinder by a few turns.
3. Install the nuts that hold the master cylinder to the brake servo. Torque the nuts to a maximum of 15 Nm (11 ft. lb.). (Overtightening the nuts may damage the brake servo.)
4. Torque the brake line union nuts to 14 to 15 Nm (10 to 11 ft. lb.).
5. If necessary, reconnect the wires to the pressure switches.
6. Fill the brake fluid reservoirs with new, unused brake fluid that meets the DOT-3 standard. Then bleed the entire brake system as described in **9.2 Bleeding Brakes.**
7. Make sure that the pedal travel is not excessive. See **5. BRAKE PEDAL AND BRAKE SERVO.** Also check that the pedal does not feel spongy—which could indicate that the bleeding operation needs to be repeated. Then road-test the car to check the brake operation, making sure that the pedal effort is correct, that the brakes do not drag, and that the brake warning light does not come on during braking.

4.2 Rebuilding Master Cylinder

When you rebuild the brake master cylinder, always use all the parts in the repair kit in order to prevent wear and leakage.

> ***WARNING —***
> *Rebuilding the master cylinder requires skill, special tools, and perfectly clean working conditions. Because the master cylinder has a vital influence on safe vehicle operation, you should not attempt to repair a master cylinder that has a worn cylinder bore or other physical damage.*

To disassemble:

1. Remove the master cylinder as described in **4.1 Removing and Installing Master Cylinder.** Remove the gland nut that holds each reservoir, then remove the reservoirs. See Fig. 4-1.
2. Where applicable, remove the pressure switches. Then, with the master cylinder in a vise that has soft jaws, push in the pistons as indicated in Fig. 4-2 while you remove the stop bolt.

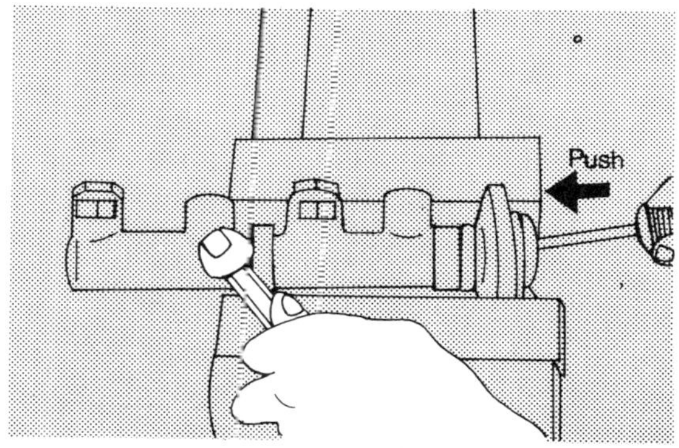

Fig. 4-2. Stop bolt being removed. Piston No. 2 (innermost piston) should be pushed out of contact with bolt

Fig. 4-1. Exploded view of master cylinder. This illustration is typical of all master cylinders used on cars covered by this Manual, without being identical to any in physical shape.

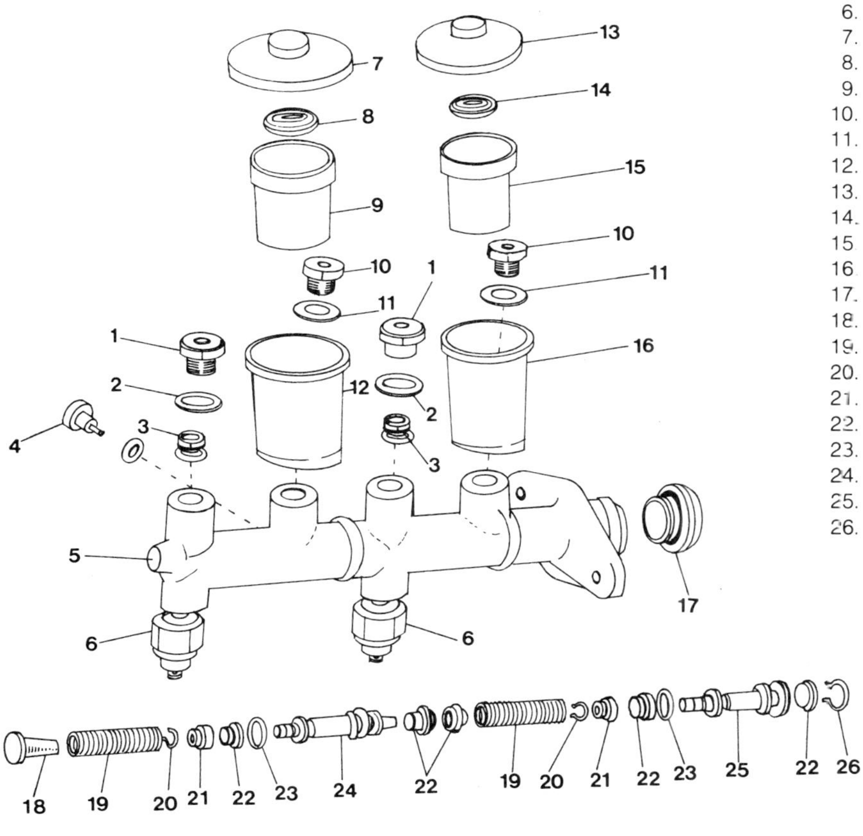

1. Fluid outlet plug
2. Gasket
3. Check valve assembly
4. Stop bolt
5. Master cylinder body
6. Pressure switch (early cars only)
7. Cap for front fluid reservoir
8. Float for front fluid reservoir
9. Strainer for front fluid reservoir
10. Gland nut for reservoir
11. Gasket
12. Front fluid reservoir
13. Cap for rear fluid reservoir
14. Float for rear fluid reservoir
15. Strainer for rear fluid reservoir
16. Rear fluid reservoir
17. Rubber seal
18. Piston stop
19. Spring
20. Small snap ring
21. Spring seat
22. Piston cup
23. Piston cup spacer
24. Piston No. 2
25. Piston No. 1
26. Large snap ring

3. Remove the fluid outlet plugs, their gaskets, and the check valve assemblies.
4. Push piston No. 1 in slightly. Then use snap ring pliers as indicated in Fig. 4-3 to remove the large snap ring.

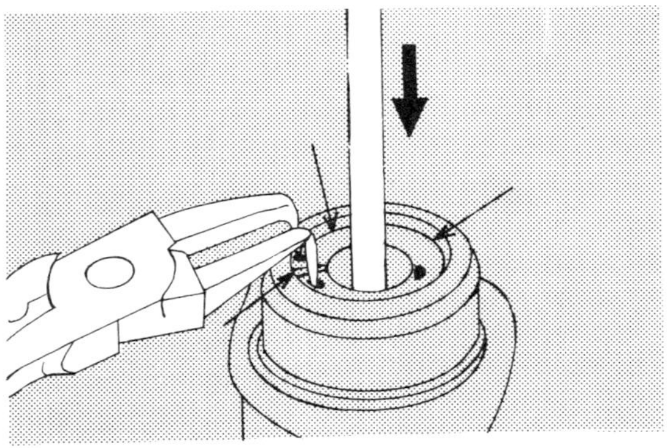

Fig. 4-3. Large snap ring being removed. Use rod or screwdriver to push in piston (arrow).

5. Withdraw the piston No. 1 assembly and its spring. Then, by tapping the cylinder on a piece of soft wood or by injecting compressed air, remove the remaining components from inside the master cylinder.
6. Carefully inspect the bore of the master cylinder. If the bore is scored, corroded, or in any way damaged, replace the entire master cylinder.

You can use a brake cylinder hone to remove minor scratches and hardened deposits from the cylinder. When using the hone, lubricate the stones with brake fluid only—never with mineral oil or kerosene. While the hone is spinning, move it in and out of the bore rapidly to achieve an even polish over the entire cylinder wall.

After honing, check the fit between the new pistons and the cylinder bore. If the clearance exceeds 0.10 mm (.004 in.), replace the entire master cylinder. You can measure the clearance by inserting a feeler gauge between the piston and the cylinder wall. However, a brake cylinder bore measuring tool or a snap (telescope) gauge and micrometer are preferable tools.

WARNING —
After honing the master cylinder, clean any burrs from the compensating ports and other holes in the side of the cylinder. Otherwise, the burrs may damage the piston cups.

To assemble:

1. Thoroughly clean the master cylinder with new, unused brake fluid that meets the DOT-3 standard.

WARNING —
Never wash brake parts in gasoline or other petroleum-base solvents. Such solvents are damaging to rubber parts in the system.

2. Make sure the repair kit contains all the necessary new seals, cups, and pistons. See Fig. 4-1, given earlier.
3. Check that there is no foreign matter on the new parts. If necessary, wash the parts in new, unused brake fluid that meets the DOT-3 standard.
4. Install the piston cups and related parts on the pistons.
5. Using brake cylinder paste, or a silicone grease specifically labeled as suitable for use as a brake cylinder lubricant, lightly coat the pistons and the cups at the points indicated in Fig. 4-4. Alternatively, you can fully lubricate the cylinder bore, the pistons, and the cups with new, unused brake fluid that meets the DOT-3 standard.

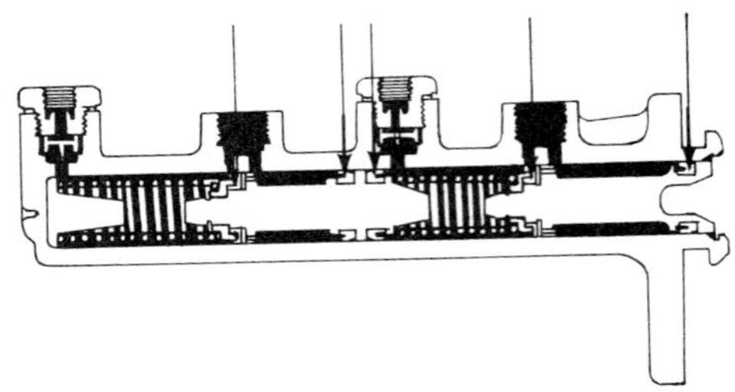

Fig. 4-4. Points (arrows) at which brake cylinder paste or suitable silicone grease should be applied.

NOTE —
Brake cylinder paste or a silicone grease suitable for brake cylinders is the preferred form of lubrication for brake cylinder repair. Use brake fluid as a substitute only if you are unable to reach an Authorized Dealer or an automotive supply store. Brake cylinders will give longer service when lubricated with brake cylinder paste or a suitable silicone grease than when lubricated by brake fluid alone.

6. Hold the master cylinder with its closed end down. Install the piston stop, large end first. Then install the first spring and the piston No. 2 assembly, pushing it as far as possible into the cylinder.

7. Using a rod or a screwdriver, push in piston No. 2 against spring tension until its primary (single) cup is well past the hole for the front reservoir. Then install the stop bolt and its gasket to a torque of 5 to 10 Nm (3.5 to 7.5 ft. lb. or 44 to 89 in. lb.).

> ***CAUTION —***
> *Be sure the stop screw hole is clear. If it is blocked by the piston, you will damage the piston when you install the screw. When correctly installed, the point of the screw will enter the space between the primary (single) cup seat and the secondary (double) cups at the rear of the piston.*

8. Using Fig. 4-1, given earlier, as your guide, install the remaining master cylinder internal components. Then install the large snap ring.
9. Install the check valve assemblies. Then install the fluid outlet plugs and their gaskets, torquing the plugs to 40 to 50 Nm (30 to 37 ft. lb.). Where applicable, install the pressure switches to a torque of 20 Nm (15 ft. lb.).
10. Install the reservoirs, torquing the gland nuts to 20 to 30 Nm (15 to 22 ft. lb.). Then install the remaining parts of the reservoir assemblies.
11. Install the new rubber seal on the end of the master cylinder, so that the closed side of the seal will be toward the servo. Install the master cylinder as described in **4.1 Removing and Installing Master Cylinder.**

5. BRAKE PEDAL AND BRAKE SERVO

As a part of routine maintenance, you should check the brake pedal height and travel as well as the operation of the brake servo. The pedal height and pedal reserve travel dimensions, together with the procedures for adjusting them, are given in **5.2 Removing and Installing Brake Pedal.**

To check brake servo:

1. Stop the engine. Then depress the brake pedal several times, waiting five seconds between applications. If the pedal travel changes noticeably each time you apply the brakes, the brake servo is faulty.
2. With the brake pedal fully depressed, start the engine. The pedal should move down slightly as the engine starts. If not, the servo is faulty, there is a leak in the vacuum line to the servo, or the check valve in the vacuum line is faulty and should be replaced.
3. With the engine idling, allow the pedal to rise, then depress it fully and stop the engine. Keep a uniform pressure on the pedal; it should neither rise nor fall lower. If it does, either the master cylinder or the brake servo is faulty.
4. Run the engine for about a minute with the brake pedal up, then turn off the engine. Depress the brake pedal firmly several times in rapid succession. The pedal travel should decrease with each application of the brakes.

If you are in doubt about the brake servo's operation, compare it with the operation of a servo known to be in good condition on a similar car.

5.1 Removing and Installing Brake Servo

The vacuum-powered brake servo is very durable and seldom causes trouble. If you must remove the servo, it is usually best to remove first the master cylinder and then the servo.

To remove:

1. With the engine stopped, apply the brakes repeatedly to bleed air into the servo, so that no partial vacuum remains.
2. Remove the master cylinder as described in **4.1 Removing and Installing Master Cylinder.** Alternatively, you can disconnect the brake lines and, where applicable, the wires from the master cylinder—and then remove the servo with the master cylinder attached.
3. Working beneath the dashboard, detach the brake pedal return spring from the pedal arm. Disconnect the brake servo's pushrod from the brake pedal arm by removing the wire clip from the clevis pin and then removing the clevis pin.
4. Working beneath the dashboard, remove the four nuts that hold the brake servo to the car body and to the brake pedal mounting bracket. Then, from outside the car, remove the servo by taking it out into the engine compartment.

To install:

1. Loosely position the servo on the car's firewall. Then, working inside the car, beneath the dashboard, install the washers and the nuts that hold the servo to the car body and to the pedal mounting bracket. Torque the nuts to a maximum of 15 Nm (11 ft. lb.). (Overtightening the nuts may damage the brake servo.)
2. Especially if you have replaced or repaired either the brake servo or the brake master cylinder, check the

master cylinder pushrod clearance as described in the next two steps.

3. Position Toyota special tool 09737-00010 on the master cylinder as indicated in Fig. 5-1. Then, with the tool body against the gasket, push the measuring slide in until its rounded end just contacts the master cylinder piston.

NOTE ——
If you cannot obtain the special measuring tool, you can check the dimensions for piston depth and pushrod projection with a depth micrometer or a vernier caliper and gauge blocks. The procedure for using these precision tools will be evident to a person experienced in their uses.

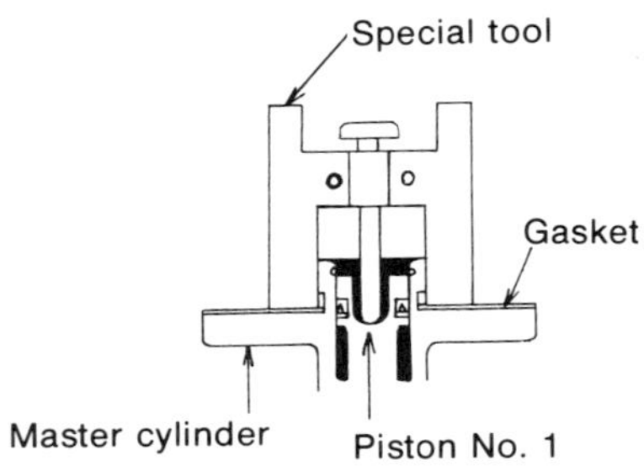

Fig. 5-1. Depth of piston No. 1 being determined with special tool.

4. Apply the opposite end of the special tool to the servo, as indicated in Fig. 5-2. If the head of the measuring slide does not just touch the rounded end of the acorn bolt, adjust the acorn bolt's position until the measuring slide just touches it.

NOTE ——
If you are not using the special tool, you must adjust the pushrod's length by turning the acorn bolt until the clearance between the rounded end of the acorn bolt and the master cylinder's piston No. 1 is 0.10 to 0.50 mm (.004 to .020 in.).

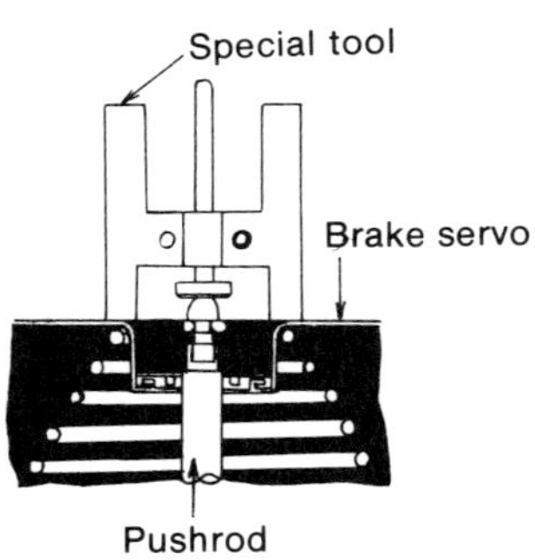

Fig. 5-2. Pushrod clearance being checked with special tool. Brakes may bind and overheat if clearance is not correct.

5. Install the master cylinder as described in **4.1 Removing and Installing Master Cylinder.** Torque the master cylinder mounting nuts to a maximum of 15 Nm (11 ft. lb.). (Overtightening the nuts may damage the brake servo.) Torque the brake line union nuts to 14 to 15 Nm (10 to 11 ft. lb.).

6. Working beneath the dashboard, reconnect the brake servo's pushrod to the brake pedal arm by installing the clevis pin and the wire clip. Reconnect the pedal return spring to the pedal arm.

7. Check and, if necessary, adjust the brake pedal height and reserve travel as described in **5.2 Removing and Installing Brake Pedal.**

Testing Vacuum Check Valve

A check valve in the middle of the vacuum hose connects the brake servo with the engine's intake manifold. The purpose of this valve is to prevent an engine backfire from producing pressure rather than vacuum in the brake servo's vacuum chamber.

To test the vacuum check valve, remove it from the vacuum line. Blow into the valve from the end toward the servo. Air should pass through. Blow into the valve from the end toward the engine. The valve must seal and prevent the passage of air. When you reinstall or replace the check valve, be sure to install it in the correct direction. If there is an arrow on the valve, the arrow should point toward the brake servo.

5.2 Removing, Installing, and Adjusting Brake Pedal

Fig. 5-3 is an exploded view that illustrates the removal of the brake pedal and related components. To remove the pedal, first remove the pedal return spring. Remove the wire clip and the clevis pin for the pushrod and detach the pushrod from the pedal arm. Remove the pedal mounting bolt, then remove the pedal and disassemble the bushing and the collars.

Installation is the reverse of removal. Replace the bushing or any collar, pin, or bolt that is worn. Worn pedal pads and pedals with worn bearing bores should likewise be replaced. Apply a thin coating of multipurpose grease to the bushing before you install it. Torque the nut for the pedal mounting bolt to 30 to 40 Nm (22 to 30 ft. lb.). After you have reconnected the pedal return spring, check and, if necessary, adjust the brake pedal height and reserve travel as described in the procedure that follows.

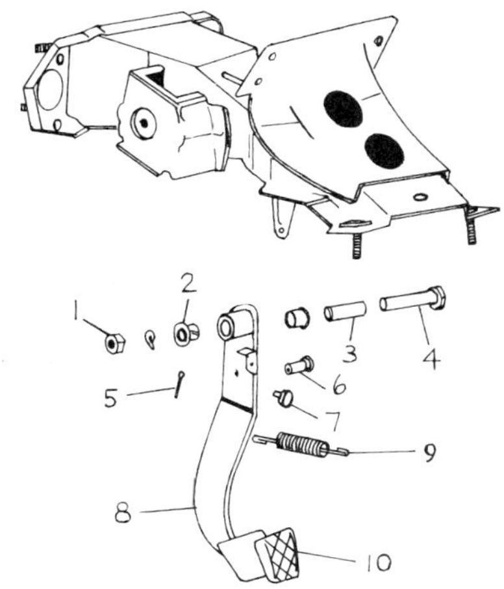

1. Nut
2. Collar (2)
3. Bushing
4. Bolt
5. Wire clip
6. Clevis pin
7. Stop cushion
8. Pedal
9. Pedal return spring
10. Pedal pad

Fig. 5-3. Exploded view of brake pedal and related components.

To adjust brake pedal:

1. Measure the pedal height (Fig. 5-4). If it is not 169 mm ($6^{21}/_{32}$ in.), loosen the locknuts for the brake light switch. Turn the switch one way or the other until the pedal height is correct, then tighten the locknuts.
2. Measure the pedal freeplay (Fig. 5-4) by lightly pressing down on the pedal pad with your fingertips until you feel working resistance. If the freeplay is not between 3 and 6 mm (⅛ and ¼ in.), loosen the locknut for the clevis. Turn the brake servo pushrod one way or the other until the freeplay is correct, then tighten the locknut.
3. Press down the brake pedal as far as it will go, then measure the pedal reserve travel (Fig. 5-4). If it is 85 mm (3⅜ in.) or less, there is trouble in the brake system. See **3. Brake Troubleshooting.**

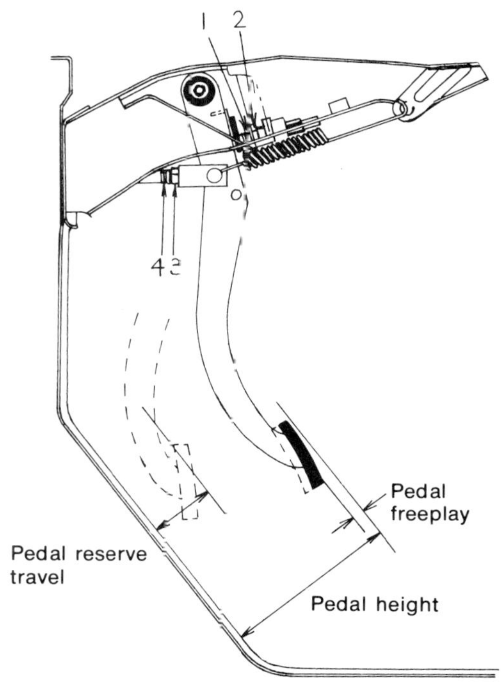

1. Front locknut for brake light switch
2. Rear locknut for brake light switch
3. Locknut for servo pushrod clevis
4. Servo pushrod

Fig. 5-4. Brake pedal adjustments and dimensions.

6. BRAKE LINES AND HOSES

When you inspect the brake lines and hoses during brake system troubleshooting or during routine maintenance, you should have a good light source available. A mirror will help you inspect the hoses, because all sides of the hoses should be examined carefully. When you check the front wheel brakes, turn the wheels fully to the left or the right. This will improve visibility and will also help reveal damage on the outsides of the hoses. Look for the following defects:

1. Physically damaged hoses and lines
2. Rounded-off or worn hose and line unions
3. Cracked hoses or lines
4. Swollen or deformed hoses
5. Corroded brake lines
6. Fluid leakage at connections
7. Loose or broken retainers for hoses and lines
8. Twisted, stretched, or kinked hoses
9. Hoses and lines in contact with sharp edges, moving parts, the exhaust system, or other compo-

nents that might damage the hoses and lines through contact

10. Lines that are not centered in their rubber grommets.

6.1 Removing and Installing Brake Lines

You can obtain replacement brake lines from your Authorized Dealer. The unions are factory-installed on the replacement lines, and the lines themselves are preformed to the correct shapes for immediate installation.

To remove brake line:

1. Unscrew the unions on the line ends (Fig. 6-1).
2. Remove the spring steel clips or screw-held brackets that hold the line to the car body.
3. Remove the brake line from the car.

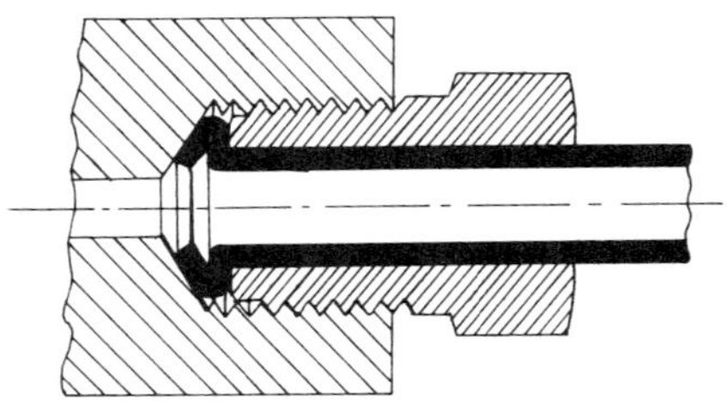

Fig. 6-1. Cross-section of brake line union. Notice double flare that holds union on tubing.

To install brake lines:

1. Route the new line so that it follows the routing of the old line.
2. Lubricate the flared ends of the brake lines with brake fluid, then insert the unions and torque them to 14 to 15 Nm (10 to 11 ft. lb.).

   NOTE ——
   Use a properly fitting wrench, such as a flare nut wrench, to avoid rounding off the union.

3. Carefully install the clips to hold the new line.
4. Bleed the brakes as described in **9.2 Bleeding Brakes.**

WARNING ——
When you install brake lines, be very careful not to dent, flatten, or bend the tubing enough to collapse it. The resulting restriction can upset brake balance and will create stress points in the tubing that may later cause it to crack. Never attempt to straighten a bent or dented brake line.

6.2 Removing and Installing Brake Hoses

Because they are flexible, brake hoses are much more subject to wear than brake lines. Therefore you should inspect them very carefully every time you carry out routine maintenance procedures, and replace them if they are faulty.

To remove:

1. Remove the road wheel if the hose is connected to a brake caliper or rear wheel cylinder.
2. Unscrew the union that holds the hose to the brake line or other brake system component.
3. If necessary, remove the spring steel hose clip from the body or suspension component. Then pull the hose off the line, caliper, wheel cylinder, or other component and plug the line if it is connected to the master cylinder.
4. Unscrew the hose at its opposite end.

To install:

1. Obtain a new hose of the correct length with the correct end fittings.

WARNING ——
If the hose is too long, it may rub the wheel or moving suspension parts. If it is too short, it could break when drawn tight by wheel travel or steering movements. In either case, partial brake failure could result. Hoses must never be painted, and they can be damaged by grease, oil, gasoline, or kerosene. Brake hoses that bulge or appear oil-soaked or cracked must be replaced immediately.

2. Install the hose, following the removal steps in reverse. The hose must hang down and be free of twists.
3. Torque the hose ends to 25 to 30 Nm (18 to 22 ft. lb.).
4. Check the hose position and the routing in all steering and suspension travel positions.

7. FRONT BRAKES

All the cars covered by this Manual are equipped with front disc brakes. The brake calipers are mounted at the leading edges of the discs and may be one of four kinds, depending on the car model and year. Faulty calipers must always be replaced with calipers of the same kind, and replacement parts must be the correct ones for the calipers on the vehicle.

7.1 Removing and Installing Brake Pads

Some of the cars covered by this Manual have an electrical brake pad wear indicator system. If the car is not equipped with this system, you should replace the pads when the friction material has worn to a remaining thickness of no less than 1 mm (about $^3/_{64}$ in.). Measure the pads at their points of greatest wear. If you are conducting routine maintenance, replace the pads if it is likely that they will wear to the minimum permissible thickness before the next regular maintenance check.

To remove:

1. Remove the front road wheel.
2. Using a pry bar inserted between the caliper and the suspension strut, pry the caliper outward—thus pushing the caliper piston as far as possible into its cylinder. See Fig. 7-1.

NOTE ——
Pushing in the piston will make it easier to remove the cylinder. As you push in the piston, brake fluid will be forced back into the reservoir. Therefore first remove some fluid to prevent the front reservoir from overflowing.

WARNING ——
Do not start a siphon with your mouth or spill fluid on the car. Brake fluid is both poisonous and damaging to paint.

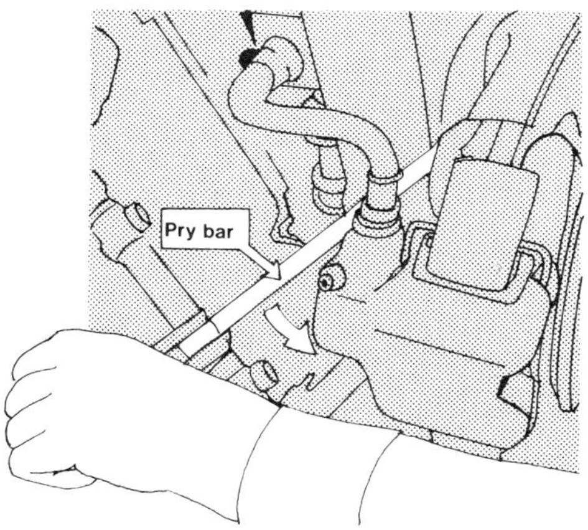

Fig. 7-1. Prying caliper's cylinder outward (curved arrow) to push in piston.

3. Using pliers or an awl, pull out the two small cotter pin-like clips that hold the upper guide and also the two small cotter pin-like clips that hold the lower guide (Fig. 7-2).

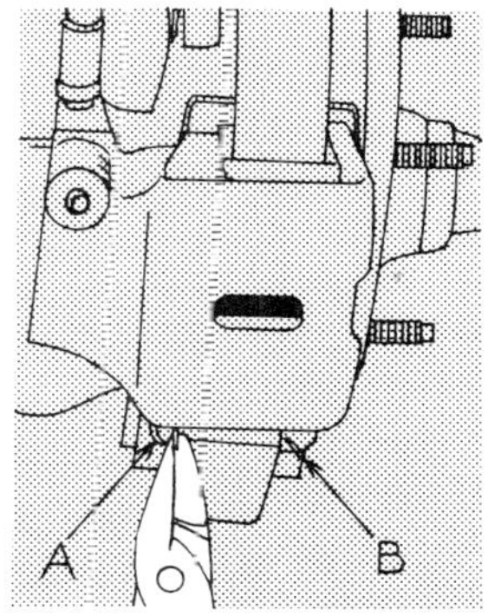

Fig. 7-2. Pliers being used to pull clip (**A**) out of guide (**B**). There are four clips, two for upper guide and two for lower guide.

4. Remove the upper and lower guides, pressing them out with the tip of a screwdriver, if necessary. See Fig. 7-3.

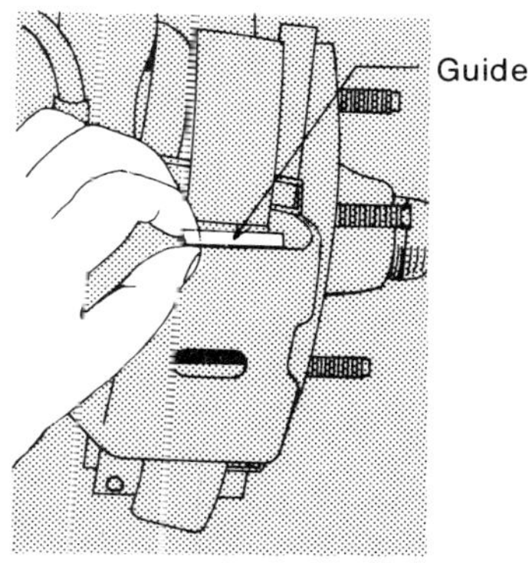

Fig. 7-3. Guide being removed from caliper.

7

5. By pulling out at the top of the cylinder assembly and angling the bottom inward (Fig. 7-4), disengage the cylinder assembly from the caliper frame. Then remove the cylinder assembly by pulling it forward and off the disc and the pads.

> ***CAUTION —***
> *Once you have removed the cylinder assembly, you should suspend it from the suspension spring with a stiff wire hook, Allowing the cylinder to hang by the brake hose may damage the hose. Place a wooden block inside the cylinder assembly to hold in the piston. If you have trouble pulling the cylinder assembly off the pads and the disc, again press the piston into the cylinder as described earlier in step 2.*

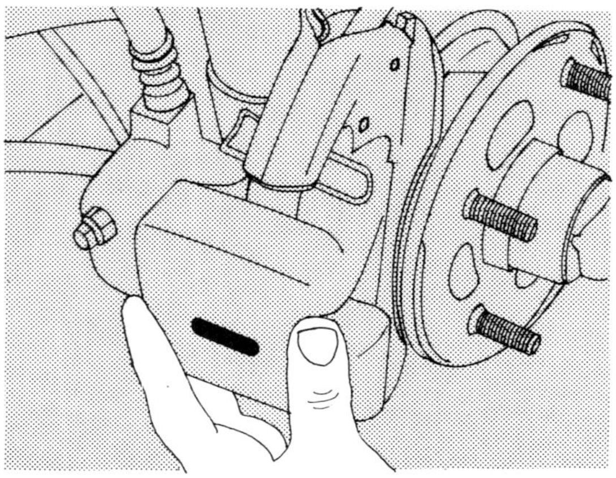

Fig. 7-4. Cylinder assembly being pulled off brake pads and brake disc.

6. Using a screwdriver, remove the brake pads (Fig. 7-5).

> ***WARNING —***
> *If you plan to reuse the pads, mark each pad and its original position in the caliper. Changing the locations of used pads will result in uneven braking.*

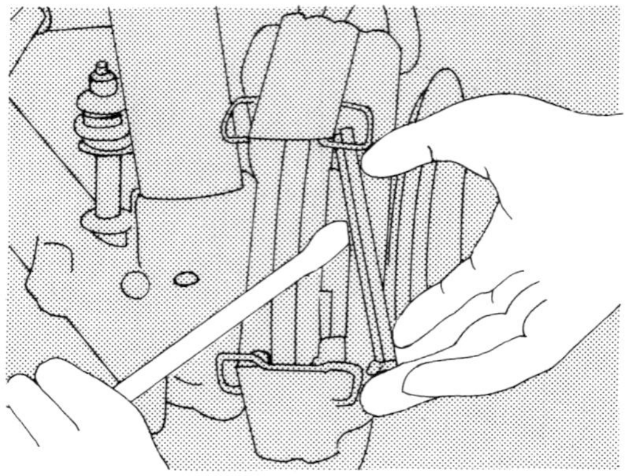

Fig. 7-5. Brake pad being removed.

To install:

1. Inspect the cylinder support springs, the guides, the clips, and (where applicable) the pad support plates. If any part is worn, cracked, deformed, or badly corroded, replace it.
2. Scrape clean the pad seating and sliding surfaces in the caliper frame and inside the cylinder assembly. Then blow out the dirt with compressed air.
3. Check the rubber dust seal for the piston. The seal must not be cracked, hard, or swollen. If necessary, replace the seal, which you can do without detaching the cylinder from the brake hose. See **7.3 Repairing Brake Caliper.**
4. Check the brake disc for wear as described in **7.4 Brake Disc.** If necessary, replace or recondition the disc.
5. Install the pads in the caliper frame, making sure they are firmly seated against the disc. On calipers that have them, be sure to install the pad support plates. (The pad support plates are identified in **7.3 Repairing Brake Caliper.**)

> ***WARNING —***
> *Install used pads in the positions you marked for them earlier. If the pads are in the wrong locations, or bind in the caliper, uneven braking will result.*

6. Using Plastilube®, or some similar disc brake lubricant specifically labeled as suitable for use on disc brake components, lubricate the sliding surfaces of the cylinder body, the caliper frame, the guides, and the guide plates.

> ***WARNING —***
> *Use a suitable lubricant only. Incorrect lubricants may melt owing to the heat produced by braking and flow onto the pads or the disc. This can greatly increase stopping distances.*

7. Press the piston fully into the cylinder, then install the cylinder assembly over the pads and the disc, engaging the cylinder body correctly in the caliper frame.
8. Install the upper and lower guides. Then install the cotter pin-like clips to hold the guides in place.
9. Install the road wheel. Torque the lug nuts to 90 to 120 Nm (66 to 89 ft. lb.).
10. Check the level of the brake fluid in the front reservoir. If necessary, add fresh fluid that meets the DOT-3 standard.
11. Before driving the car, depress the brake pedal several times while the car is stationary to ensure that the pads are seated against the disc.

7.2 Removing and Installing Brake Caliper

To remove the brake caliper, first remove the brake pads as described in **7.1 Removing and Installing Brake Pads.** Then unscrew the brake hose from the caliper's cylinder assembly and seal the hose with a clean brake bleeder dust cap to prevent fluid leakage. To remove the caliper frame from the suspension strut and splash shield, remove the two bolts and their lockwashers. Then take the caliper frame off the strut.

Installation is the reverse of removal. Torque the bolts that hold the caliper frame to the splash shield and suspension strut to 60 to 70 Nm (44 to 52 ft. lb.). Lubricate the threads of the brake hose with brake fluid, then install the hose in the cylinder assembly to a torque of 25 to 30 Nm (18 to 22 ft. lb.). After you have reinstalled the brake pads and related parts as described in **7.1 Removing and Installing Brake Pads,** depress the brake pedal several times before you drive the car. This will ensure that the pads are seated against the disc.

7.3 Repairing Brake Caliper

Fig. 7-6 is an exploded view of a typical Corolla 1600 disc brake caliper. Both the caliper cylinder body and the caliper frame can be replaced individually, as can the piston and other parts shown. Do not hone worn cylinders. Replace the cylinder body if the cylinder bore is worn, or if the original cylinder body is in any way faulty.

7

Fig. 7-6. Exploded view of typical brake caliper.

1. Brake caliper assembly
2. Caliper mounting bolt
3. Splash shield mounting bolt
4. Splash shield
5. Brake bleeder dust cap
6. Bleeder valve
7. Cylinder body
8. Piston
9. Piston seal
10. Dust seal
11. Dust seal retaining ring
12. Guide plate
13. Clip (4)
14. Guide
15. Cylinder support ring
16. Caliper frame
17. Pad
18. Pad support plate

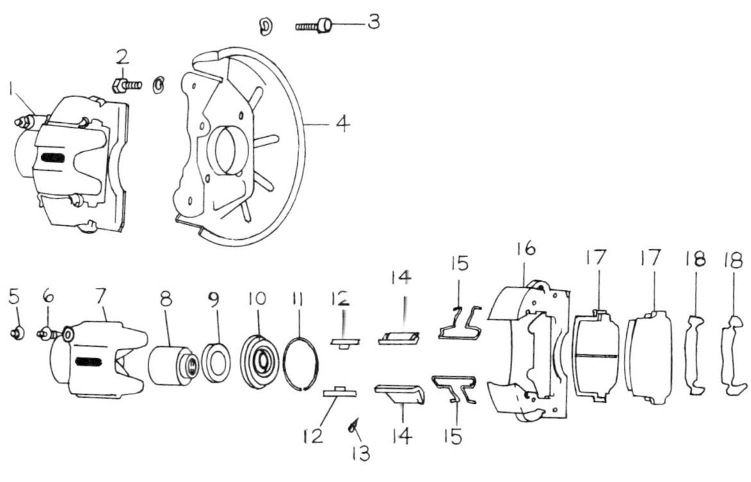

To repair:

1. Remove the bleeder valve and pour out the fluid.
2. Remove the dust seal retaining ring and then the dust seal.
3. Place a hardwood block inside the cylinder body to catch the piston. Then, to expel the piston from the cylinder, inject compressed air as indicated in Fig. 7-7.

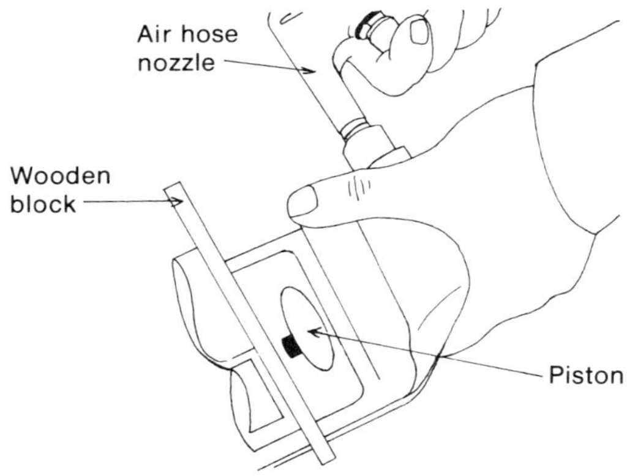

Fig. 7-7. Piston being removed. Notice hardwood block used to catch piston. If piston is allowed to fly out uncontrolled, it is likely to be damaged.

4. Using a plastic knitting needle, carefully pry the piston seal out of the annular groove inside the cylinder. See Fig. 7-8.

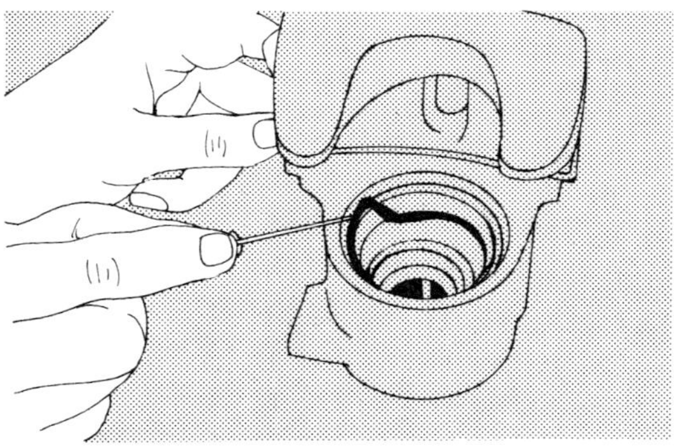

Fig. 7-8. Piston seal being removed from annular groove inside cylinder.

5. Clean all parts with brake fluid only. Check all parts for wear. If the cylinder is worn, scored, or otherwise damaged, replace the cylinder body. Do not hone the cylinder.

NOTE ——
The caliper frame requires cleaning only. If it is in any way faulty, replace it.

6. Lightly coat the piston and the piston seal with brake cylinder paste or a silicone grease that is specifically labeled as suitable for use in brake cylinders.

WARNING ——
Never clean or lubricate brake parts with petroleum-base substances, as they will damage rubber parts of the system and cause early brake failure.

7. Using a plastic knitting needle so that you will not accidentally scratch the cylinder bore, carefully install the piston seal in the annular groove inside the cylinder.
8. Install the piston in the cylinder body. You will probably need to squeeze the piston and the cylinder together in a vise to push the piston past the piston seal. To do this, use a hardwood block between one vise jaw and the outer end of the piston. Press in the piston fully.
9. Install the dust seal. Then lock it in place by installing the retaining ring.
10. Loosely install the bleeder valve.

7.4 Brake Disc

Although four slightly different brake calipers are used on the cars covered by this Manual, all models use the same brake disc. The brake disc is separate from the front wheel hub. Nevertheless, the hub and the disc must be removed as a unit and then disassembled.

Checking Brake Disc

You should check the brake discs for wear each time you do repair work on the front brakes. Replace the discs if they are scored with sharp ridges, worn irregularly, or cracked. Also replace brake discs that have worn down, or have been machined, to a thickness of less than 9 mm (.354 in. or $^{23}/_{64}$ in.). New brake discs are 10 mm (.394 or $^{25}/_{64}$ in.) thick.

Check the discs for excessive runout. If a low-speed front-end shimmy goes away when you release the brakes, excessive brake disc runout is probably the cause of the shimmy.

To measure runout:

1. Remove the front road wheel.
2. Install a dial indicator so that its gauge pin contacts the disc (Fig. 7-9). Then zero the dial indicator.

3. Slowly hand-turn the brake disc to check the runout. The maximum allowable runout is 0.15 mm (.006 in.). If the brake disc runout exceeds this specification, replace or recondition the brake disc.

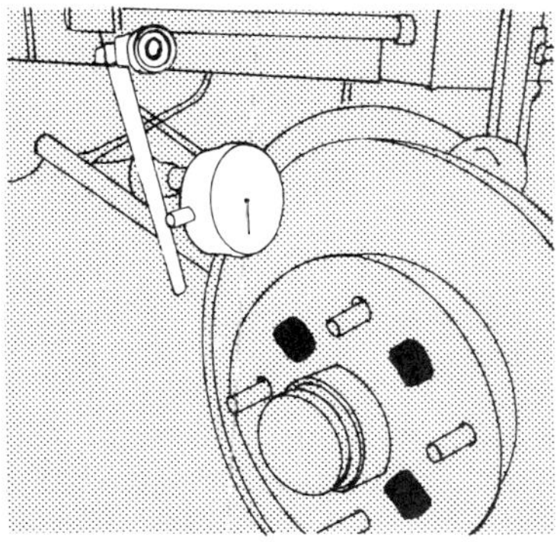

Fig. 7-9. Dial indicator being used to measure brake disc runout.

Removing and Installing Brake Disc

Even though it is possible to unbolt the brake caliper frame from the suspension strut, and then remove the caliper as a unit (after first prying the cylinder assembly outward to push in the piston), it will be easier to reinstall the caliper if you first remove the cylinder assembly and the pads. Usually, you will want to disassemble the caliper anyway—in order to clean and, if necessary, repair it or replace the pads.

To remove disc:

1. Remove the road wheel. Then remove the brake caliper as described in **7.2 Removing and Installing Brake Caliper.**

CAUTION —
Always remove the brake caliper. Never try to remove the disc by using force. Force may damage the caliper mounting frame or the brake disc.

2. Remove the dust cap from the front wheel hub. Remove the cotter pin, the wheel bearing nut lock, and the wheel bearing adjusting nut. See Fig. 7-10.
3. Being careful not to get dirt into the wheel bearing lubricant, carefully remove the wheel bearing thrust washer and the outer wheel bearing's inner race, which includes the caged roller bearings. Store the bearing race in a clean, dust-free location.
4. Pull the brake disc and the wheel hub off the wheel spindle as a unit, being careful that the threaded end of the spindle does not damage the hub's bearing races or the inner grease seal.

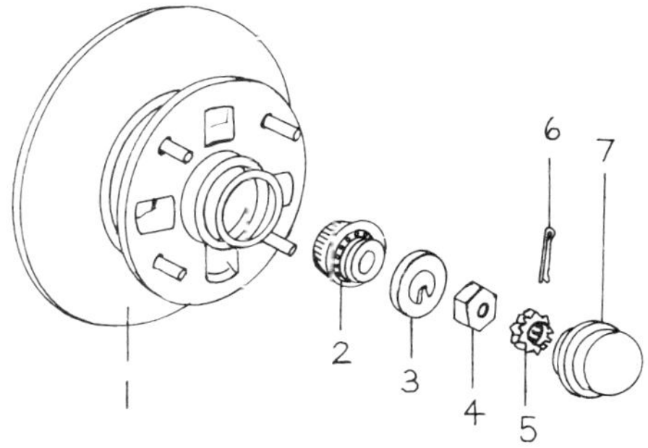

1. Wheel hub/brake disc assembly
2. Outer wheel bearing
3. Thrust washer
4. Wheel bearing adjusting nut
5. Nut lock
6. Cotter pin
7. Dust cap

Fig. 7-10. Exploded view of parts that hold wheel hub on wheel spindle.

5. Take out the four bolts that hold the brake disc to the wheel hub. Then remove the disc.

Installation is the reverse of removal. The mating surfaces of the hub and the brake disc must be absolutely clean and free of all nicks and burrs. Otherwise, there will be disc runout that can cause brake lockup and brake pedal pulsation. Torque the bolts that hold the disc to the hub to 45 to 50 Nm (33 to 37 ft. lb.).

Be careful not to get grease on the brake disc. If necessary, wash the disc with solvent before you install the brake caliper. If the grease seal in the hub is faulty, or if you need to replace or repack the front wheel bearings, do this work as described in **11.5 Servicing and Replacing Front Wheel Bearings.** After you have installed the disc and hub on the wheel spindle, adjust the front wheel bearings with careful attention to the instructions given in **11.4 Adjusting Front Wheel Bearings.**

7

Reconditioning Brake Disc

You should check the brake discs for wear whenever you make brake repairs. Replace discs that have worn below the minimum thickness, are scored with sharp ridges, or are cracked. If a disc's thickness is less than 9 mm (.354 in. or 23/64 in.), replace it. If the disc has not worn to the minimum thickness, you can recondition it. Recondition discs that have thickness variations or runout in excess of 0.15 mm (.006 in.), observing the following restrictions:

1. The minimum allowable thickness after rework is 9 mm (.354 in. or 23/64 in.).

CAUTION —
Under no circumstances should you rework the brake discs to a lesser thckness. Although the disc itself is not significantly weakened by being thinner, bear in mind that a thinner disc

CAUTION (cont.)—
causes the piston to travel farther out in its cylinder. This may severely damage the calipers and pistons.

2. After you have reworked a brake disc, its thickness should not vary by more than 0.02 mm (.0008 in.), measured at several locations on the disc.
3. The brake disc must be reworked equally on both sides to prevent squeaking, chattering, or brake pedal pulsations.
4. Brake disc must be reworked in a special machine designed for the task.
5. The maximum allowable runout of reworked brake discs is 0.15 mm (.006 in.).

7.5 Removing and Installing Brake Disc Splash Shield

To remove the brake disc splash shield, you must first remove the brake disc as described in **7.4 Brake Disc.** You will then notice that the splash shield is held to the suspension strut by four bolts, which you can remove so that you can take off the splash shield.

If the splash shield is bent, rusted, or otherwise damaged, replace it. Several kinds of splash shields are used on the cars covered by this Manual, depending on which brake caliper is fitted. Thus it is best to take the old splash shield with you when seeking a replacement.

Position the splash shield on the suspension strut so that the cutout for the brake caliper is at the front of the strut. Then install the bolts to a torque of 30 to 35 Nm (22 to 26 ft. lb.). Reinstall the brake disc, the brake caliper, and the road wheel.

8. REAR BRAKES

The rear drum brakes are self-adjusting and normally require no adjustment. The self-adjuster mechanism operates each time the parking brake is applied.

8.1 Removing and Installing Brake Drum

You must remove the brake drum in order to inspect the rear brake linings. You must also remove it before you can make any brake repair.

To remove:

1. Loosen, but do not remove, the rear wheel lug nuts. Release the parking brake. Then raise the car on a hoist or support it on stands designed for the purpose. If you raise the rear wheels only, chock the front wheels to prevent the car from rolling.
2. Remove the road wheel.
3. Remove the two bolts that hold the brake drum to the rear axle flange. Then remove the brake drum.

NOTE —
If the drum is badly worn, you may have to back off the brake adjuster's star wheel before you can pull the drum off the brake shoes. See **8.2 Removing and Installing Brake Shoes.**

Installation is the reverse of removal. Make sure that there is no dirt on the mating surfaces of the brake drum and the axle shaft flange. Lightly lubricate the threads of the brake drum bolts with multipurpose grease to make future removal easier. After you have loosely installed the road wheel and lowered the car to the ground, set the parking brake and torque the wheel lug nuts to 90 to 120 Nm (66 to 89 ft. lb.).

Reconditioning Brake Drum

Check the brake drums whenever new linings are installed. Taper, scoring, or other wear should, if possible, be corrected on a special machine by an Authorized Dealer or a qualified automotive machine shop. Both rear drums must be machined to the same dimensions. The linings should be ground to the new radius with a special machine by an Authorized Dealer or other qualified shop. Unless the linings are radiused to fit the reconditioned drums, uneven or ineffective braking may result. When you recondition the drums, their inside diameters should not be increased to more than 230.60 mm (9.079 in.). New brake drums have an inside diameter of 228.60 mm (9.000 in.). Replace brake drums that cannot be reconditioned.

8.2 Removing and Installing Brake Shoes

Fig. 8-1 is an exploded view of a rear brake assembly, which identifies the components involved in the removal and installation of the brake shoes. Notice especially the plug and the slot in the brake backing plate. It may be necessary to insert a screwdriver or a brake adjusting tool through this slot in order to back off the star wheel of the brake adjuster.

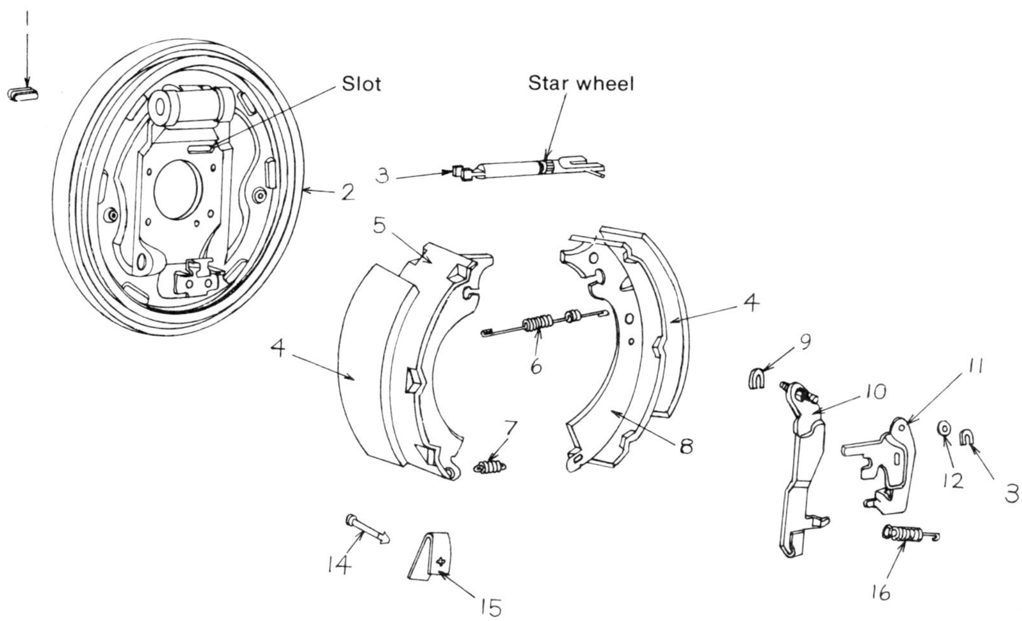

1. Plug for adjuster slot
2. Brake backing plate
3. Brake adjuster
4. Brake lining (bonded to shoe)
5. Front brake shoe
6. Return spring
7. Anchor spring
8. Rear brake shoe
9. C-clip
10. Parking brake lever
11. Automatic adjuster lever
12. Shim
13. C-clip
14. Shoe retaining pin (4)
15. Shoe retaining spring clip (4)
16. Adjuster lever tension spring

Fig. 8-1. Exploded view of brake shoes and related parts.

To remove:

1. Remove the brake drum as described in **8.1 Removing and Installing Brake Drum.**

NOTE ——
If the drum is badly worn, you may have to back off the brake adjuster's star wheel before you can pull the drum off the shoes. To do this, take the plug out of the brake backing plate. Then insert a screwdriver and push the automatic adjuster lever away from the star wheel (position **1** in Fig. 8-2). Next, push the bottom of the star wheel away from you (position **2** in Fig. 8-2). Repeat these two steps until you have moved the brake shoes far enough from the drum for the drum to be removed.

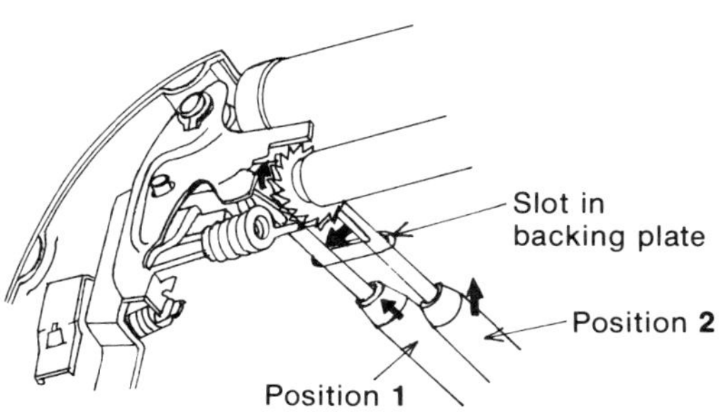

Fig. 8-2. Screwdriver being used to back off brake adjuster star wheel. Push adjuster lever away from star wheel (position **1**), then rotate bottom of star wheel away from you (position **2**).

2. Pull forward the parking brake lever that is on the rear brake shoe, then disconnect the cable from the lever.
3. Check the wheel cylinder for sticking pistons by having someone slowly depress the brake pedal while you watch to see whether the brake shoes move out the same distance at a uniform rate.

NOTE ——
Insert two screwdrivers behind the backing plate flange. Press them against the shoes to limit their travel. Also lift the wheel cylinder boot to check for fluid leakage. If the cylinder is sticking or leaking, or if the bleeder valve is rusted tight, rebuild or replace the cylinder.

4. Remove the four shoe-retaining spring clips and the four shoe-retaining pins.
5. Using pliers, detach the return spring from the rear shoe. This spring is under tension.

NOTE ——
To prevent the wheel cylinder pistons from coming out owing to residual pressure in the hydraulic lines, snap a strong rubber band around the wheel cylinder to hold the pistons in.

6. Remove the adjuster lever tension spring. Remove the brake adjuster.
7. Slide the shoes down off the anchor piece at the bottom of the brake backing plate, then remove the shoes and the anchor spring.

7

To install:

1. Inspect the brake linings. Replace the brake shoes if the linings have at any point worn to a remaining thickness of 1 mm (.040 in.) or less. New linings are 5 mm (.197 in.) thick. Make sure that the same kind of brake linings are used at both rear wheels.

> ***WARNING —***
> *Using linings of different size or composition on opposite sides of the car can cause dangerously uneven braking.*

2. Inspect the brake drum and compare its diameter to the specifications given in **8.1 Removing and Installing Brake Drum.** If necessary, recondition or replace the drum.
3. Disassemble the adjuster and clean the threads. Lubricate the threads with a nonmelting grease, such as zinc oxide grease, then reassemble the adjuster.

> **NOTE —**
> You should also apply a thin coat of nonmelting grease to the shoe contact surfaces of the brake backing plate, to the slots of the anchor piece, and to the slots of the adjuster ends.

4. If you have replaced the brake shoes, remove the C-clip (Fig. 8-3) so that you can remove the shim, the parking brake lever, and the automatic adjuster lever from the old rear brake shoe.

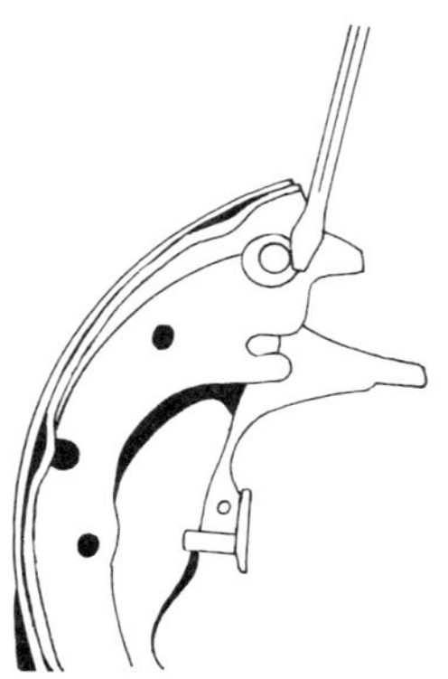

Fig. 8-3. C-clip being removed so that parking brake lever and automatic adjuster lever can be removed from old rear brake shoe.

5. Install the parking brake lever, the automatic adjuster lever, and the shim on the new rear brake shoe. Then, using feeler gauges of various thicknesses, determine clearance **A**, as given in Fig. 8-4. If the clearance is not between 0.00 and 0.35 mm (.0000 and .0138 in.), select a new shim that will correct the clearance from the list given in the illustration.

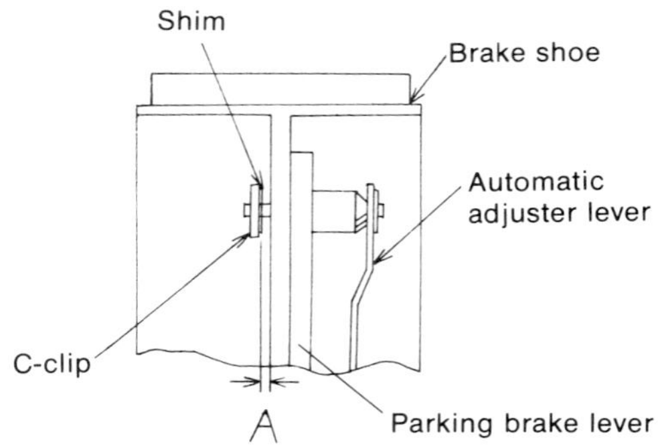

Available shim thicknesses	Part No.
0.30 mm (.012 in.)	90564–08150
0.60 mm (.024 in.)	90564–08151
0.90 mm (.035 in.)	90564–08152
0.20 mm (.008 in.)	90564–08172
0.40 mm (.016 in.)	90564–08173
0.50 mm (.020 in.)	90564–08174

Fig. 8-4. Cross-section of rear brake shoe, showing correct installation of parking brake and automatic adjuster levers. If clearance **A** is not correct, add or subtract shims until it is.

6. Reconnect the brake shoes using the anchor spring. Then position the bottom ends of the shoes on the anchor piece of the brake backing plate.

> **NOTE —**
> The brake shoe containing the parking brake lever must be installed at the edge of the backing plate that is toward the rear of the car.

7. With the brake adjuster set at its shortest length, install the brake adjuster between the shoes. Then install the return spring. Remove the rubber band from the wheel cylinder pistons.
8. Install the four shoe-retaining pins and the four shoe-retaining spring clips.
9. Install the adjuster lever tension spring. Reconnect the parking brake cable to the lever on the rear brake shoe. Check that the adjuster lever correctly engages the star wheel of the brake adjuster.
10. As nearly as you can, center the shoes on the brake backing plate. Then install the brake drum and its bolts.
11. Adjust the rear brakes either by repeatedly applying and releasing the parking brake, or by inserting a screwdriver as shown earlier in Fig. 8-2.

> **NOTE —**
> To adjust the brakes with a screwdriver, lever the side of the star wheel closest to the brake backing plate upward—moving the shoes

NOTE (cont.) ——

outward until they contact the drum. Depress the brake pedal from time to time to keep the shoes centered in the drum. Then back off the adjuster just enough so that, when you hand-turn the brake drum, the shoes do not rub against it.

8.3 Removing and Installing Wheel Cylinder

To remove a wheel cylinder, first carry out the procedure for removing the brake shoes as given under the preceding heading. Using a flare nut wrench, detach the brake line (Fig. 8-5). Then take out the bolts that hold the wheel cylinder to the brake packing plate and remove the cylinder.

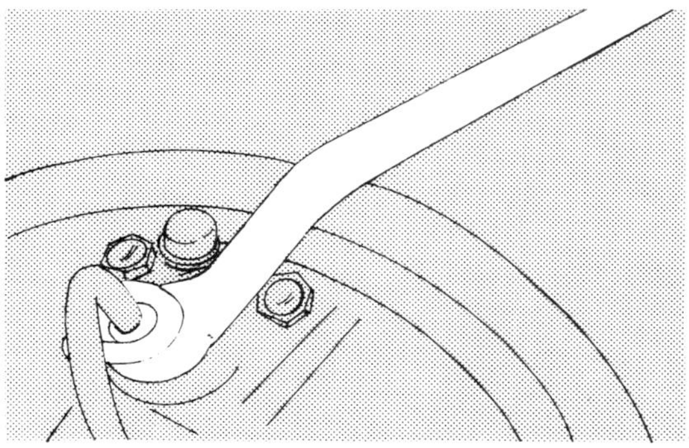

Fig. 8-5. Flare nut wrench being used to detach brake line from wheel cylinder at rear of backing plate.

Installation is the reverse of removal. If you are replacing the wheel cylinder, please notice that cylinders for the left rear wheel are not the same as those for the right rear wheel. Torque the cylinder mounting bolts to 10 to 11 Nm (7.5 to 8 ft. lb.). Torque the brake line union to 14 to 15 Nm (10 to 11 ft. lb.). Install the brake shoes and the brake drums as described in **8.2 Removing and Installing Brake Shoes.** Then bleed the rear brakes as described in **9.2 Bleeding Brakes.**

8.4 Rebuilding Wheel Cylinder

Because replacement wheel cylinders are inexpensive, it is usually more economical to replace them as a unit. However, repair kits are available. Other than a very light honing to remove tarnish or gummy deposits, no machine work should be done.

Fig. 8-6 shows the components of a rear wheel cylinder. You can hand-press the internal parts out of the housing once the boots are removed. Remove the brake line union seat by pulling it out with a bolt extractor. Clean all parts with brake fluid only.

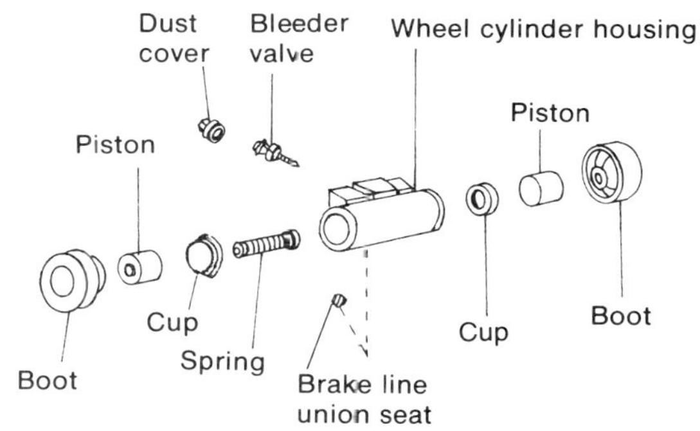

Fig. 8-6. Exploded view of rear brake wheel cylinder.

Check the cylinder for wear. Do not machine or hone metal from the cylinder bore. A new piston, lubricated with brake fluid, must be an airtight fit. If it is not, replace the cylinder.

NOTE ——

Vacuum should keep a new piston (lubricated with brake fluid) from falling out of the cylinder when the bleeder valve and brake line holes are sealed, and when you cover the opposite end of the cylinder with your thumb.

Lightly coat the pistons and the piston seals with brake cylinder paste or a silicone grease that is specifically labeled as suitable for use in brake cylinders. Assemble the cylinder, making sure that the cups are positioned as shown in Fig. 8-7.

WARNING ——

Never clean or lubricate brake parts with petroleum-base substances, as they will damage rubber parts of the system and cause early brake failure.

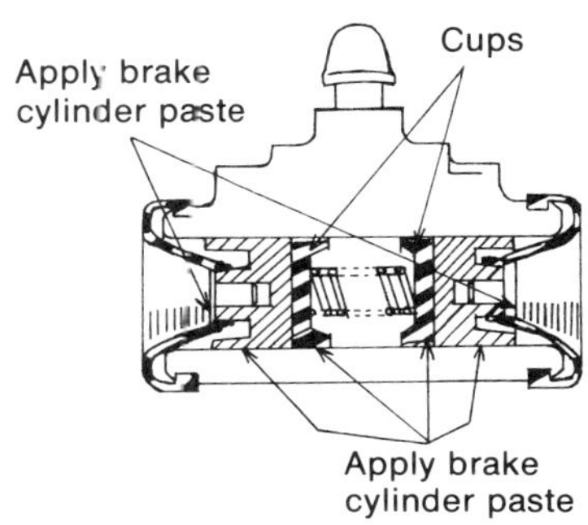

Fig. 8-7. Cross-section of wheel cylinder, showing correct position of cups and points where lubrication is needed.

8.5 Removing and Installing Backing Plate

To remove the brake backing plate, first remove the brake drum, the brake shoes, and the brake cylinder as described under the first three of the four preceding headings. Then remove the axle shaft and rear wheel bearing assembly as described in **DRIVESHAFT AND REAR AXLE.** Detach the parking brake cable conduit from the backing plate, then remove the backing plate from the rear axle housing.

Installation is the reverse of removal. Torque the nuts and bolts for the wheel bearing retainer to 60 to 70 Nm (44 to 52 ft. lb.). Torque the brake line union to 14 to 15 Nm (10 to 11 ft. lb.). Then bleed the brakes as described in **9.2 Bleeding Brakes.**

9. BRAKE FLUID

Add more brake fluid to the brake system when you service or bleed it. The quality of the new brake fluid is important. Using a brake fluid that does not conform to the DOT-3 standard can cause brake failure, premature wear, or erratic operation.

Once you have removed brake fluid from the brake system, never reuse it—even if it is new fluid that has been expelled during bleeding, or fluid removed from the master cylinder during front brake pad replacement. Never introduce any fluid into the brake system other than new, unused brake fluid that meets the DOT-3 standard.

9.1 Changing Brake Fluid

Although the car manufacturer does not specify that the Corolla's brake fluid needs to be changed at any particular time or mileage, many car care experts advise such a change every two years in the interest of longer life for the hydraulic components of the brake system. Brake fluid tends to absorb moisture from the air, and water can initiate corrosion. Water can also cause the fluid to boil when the brakes are used very hard. Because the brake calipers surround the friction linings, they pick up a great deal of heat from them. Thus it is particularly important that the brake systems of vehicles with disc brakes have a fluid with a high boiling point.

To change:

1. Attach suitable hoses to the bleeder valves for draining the fluid into containers.
2. Open the rear wheel bleeder valves and pump the pedal until fluid ceases to flow from them.
3. Open the front brake caliper bleeder valves and pump the pedal until fluid ceases to flow from them. Then close all four bleeder valves.
4. Fill the fluid reservoir with new, unused brake fluid that conforms to the DOT-3 standard. Then bleed the brakes as described under the next heading.

9.2 Bleeding Brakes

Whenever possible, bleed the brakes with a pneumatic pressure bleeder of the kind used in an Authorized Dealer's service department. Connect the device to the brake fluid reservoirs. The bleeder fills the system with fluid under pressure and will complete the job in a very short time. Simply open the bleeder valve, quickly depress and slowly release the pedal several times, and then close the bleeder valve. A fluid receptacle supplied with the bleeding device must be installed on the wheel being bled.

For car owners, the pumping method of bleeding the brakes is the most practical, even though it requires two people. Have your helper sit in the car to pump the brake pedal. You will then be free to move from wheel to wheel to perform the actual bleeding.

To bleed by pumping:

1. Fully fill the fluid reservoirs with brake fluid that conforms to the DOT-3 standard.
2. Take the dust cap off the bleeder valve at the right-hand front wheel. Slip a 4-mm (5/32-in.) I.D. hose over the bleeder valve and submerge the other end in a clear glass jar partially filled with clean brake fluid. The jar must be clear so that you can see air bubbles coming out of the hose.
3. Open the bleeder valve a half-turn. Have your helper slowly depress the brake pedal until it reaches the floor and keep it there while you close the bleeder valve.
4. Have your helper slowly release the pedal until it is completely up. Repeat the preceding step until no more air bubbles emerge from the hose.
5. Torque the bleeder valve to from 7 Nm (5 ft. lb.) to no more than 10 Nm (7.5 ft. lb.). Replace the dust cap.
6. Repeat the entire bleeding procedure on the other three wheels in the sequence left front, right rear, left rear.

NOTE ——

Refill the reservoir after bleeding each wheel cylinder. If the system contains a great deal of air, or if you are changing the brake fluid, you will have to add more fluid once or twice while you bleed each wheel cylinder. Never let the reservoir empty completely, or you will have to start bleeding the brakes all over again.

CAUTION —
Do not allow brake fluid to come in contact with painted surfaces. Brake fluid contains a solvent that is damaging to most finishes.

WARNING —
Do not use soft drink bottles or other food containers to store brake fluid or to bleed the brakes. Brake fluid is poisonous.

9.3 Flushing Brake System

Never use anything but brake fluid to flush the brake system. Alcohol must not be used since it will destroy residual lubrication and will encourage the accumulation of water in the system.

NOTE —
Do not rely on flushing alone to clean a brake system contaminated by dirt or rust. To remove all foreign matter, you must disassemble the system and clean the parts individually.

10. PARKING BRAKE

You should check the parking brake lever travel during routine maintenance at the mileage prescribed in **LUBRICATION AND MAINTENANCE.** To do this, count the clicks while you slowly pull up the parking brake lever without depressing its release button. The parking brake adjustment is correct if you hear four to six double clicks before you can pull the lever up no further.

10.1 Adjusting Parking Brake

Because the rear wheel brakes are self-adjusting, and because disc brakes of the kind used on the front wheels do not require adjustment, it is not usually necessary to adjust the parking brake. If an excessive number of clicks are required to apply the parking brake firmly, you should first check the rear brake adjustment and then inspect the parking brake cables for stretching or damage before you decide that a parking brake adjustment is necessary.

To adjust:

1. Check the rear brake adjustment as described in **5.2 Removing and Installing Brake Pedal.** If necessary, adjust the rear brakes as described in **8.2 Removing and Installing Brake Shoes.** If the automatic adjusters are not functioning, clean and repair them as described under the same heading.
2. Inspect the parking brake cables for breakage, damaged conduits, and stretching. If only one cable is stretching, you will notice that the parking brake cable equalizer is not at an approximate 90° angle to the car's center line. If necessary, replace damaged cables as described under the next heading.
3. Remove the rear part of the console that is between the two front seats. To do this, untie the parking brake lever boot, remove the four screws that hold the console to the floor, then lift the rear part of the console at its front end and remove it toward the front of the car—sliding it off over the parking brake lever. If necessary, consult **BODY AND INTERIOR.**
4. Loosen the adjusting nut cap by several turns. See Fig. 10-1.

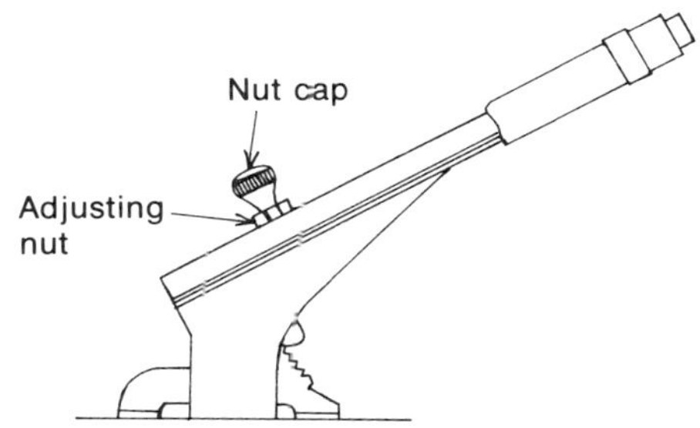

Fig. 10-1. Parking brake adjusting nut, located on end of primary cable, atop parking brake lever.

5. By turning the adjusting nut one way or the other, lengthen or shorten the primary cable until, when you fully apply the parking brake, the number of clicks required is in the correct range.
6. While holding the adjusting nut stationary, screw the nut cap down as tightly as you can with your fingers against the adjusting nut.
7. Reinstall the rear part of the console.

NOTE —
If for any reason you need to adjust the parking brake warning light switch, which is beneath the parking brake lever, simply loosen the nuts on the switch, then reposition the switch until the light comes on as soon as you pull the parking brake lever upward. Tighten the nuts to hold the switch in this position.

7

10.2 Removing and Installing Parking Brake Lever and Cables

Fig. 10-2 is an exploded view of the parking brake lever and its cables. The components shown are available as replacement parts. The parking brake lever itself, however, is also available as a complete new assembly.

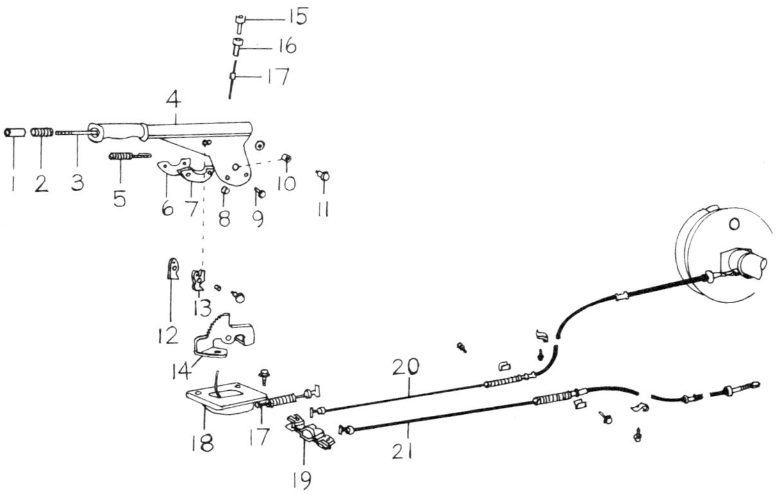

1. Release button
2. Compression spring
3. Release rod
4. Parking brake lever
5. Tension spring for pawl No. 2
6. Cable guide support
7. Cable guide
8. Spacer for guide pin (2)
9. Guide pin (2)
10. Spacer for pivot pin
11. Lever pivot pin
12. Ratchet pawl No. 1
13. Ratchet pawl No. 2
14. Ratchet sector
15. Adjusting nut cap
16. Adjusting nut
17. Primary cable
18. Mounting boot
19. Equalizer
20. Right secondary cable
21. Left secondary cable

Fig. 10-2. Exploded view of parking brake lever and cables.

To remove:

1. Remove the rear part of the console that is between the two front seats. To do this, untie the parking brake lever boot, remove the four screws that hold the console to the floor, then lift the rear part of the console at its front end and remove it toward the front of the car—sliding it off over the parking brake lever. If necessary, consult **BODY AND INTERIOR.**
2. Fully remove the adjusting nut cap and the adjusting nut.
3. Working beneath the car, pull the primary cable slightly rearward, then detach it from the equalizer.
4. Remove the bolts that hold the parking brake lever assembly and its mounting boot to the floorboard. Then take the lever assembly out upward, together with the primary cable.
5. Separate the primary cable from the parking brake lever assembly and, if necessary, replace the cable.

Installation is the reverse of removal. If you need to repair the parking brake lever, do so as described under the next unnumbered heading. After you reinstall the handle and the primary cable, adjust the parking brake as described in **10.1 Adjusting Parking Brake.**

Disassembling and Assembling Parking Brake Lever

You can use the procedure here to repair the parking brake lever. Alternatively, you can replace the entire parking brake lever assembly as a unit.

To disassemble:

1. Remove the parking brake lever as described in the previous procedure.
2. Using a 6-mm (or ¼-in.) drill or a small abrasive stone chucked in an electric drill, drill out or grind off the peened part of the parking lever's pivot pin. Then knock out the pin with a pin punch. Detach the lever from the ratchet sector.
3. Using a procedure similar to that described in the preceding step, drill out or grind off the peened part of the pin for the ratchet pawls. If you must replace the cable guide or the cable guide support, also drill or grind the pins that hold them.
4. Unscrew the release button from the end of the release rod. Remove the compression spring. Then remove the release rod, the pawls, and the tension spring for pawl No. 2 from the lever.
5. Disassemble the pawls, the tension spring, and the release rod.

To assemble:

1. Assemble the release rod and the ratchet pawls as indicated in Fig. 10-3. You can use multipurpose grease as an adhesive to hold the pawls and the spacer for the pawl pin in place.

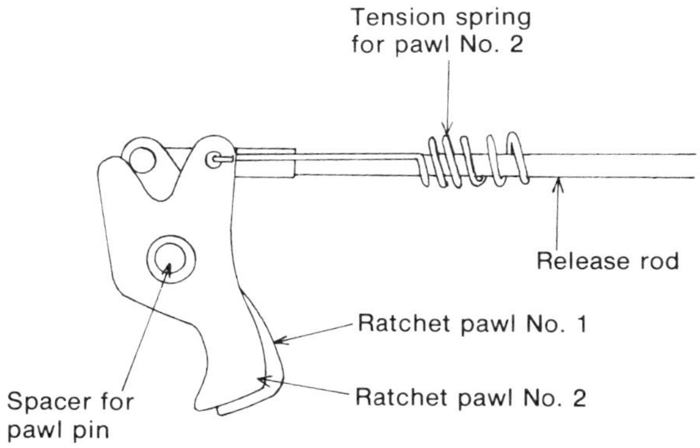

Fig. 10-3. Release rod and pawls correctly assembled.

2. Install the release rod and pawl assembly inside the parking brake lever so that the spacer is aligned with the hole for the pawl pin. Loosely install a new pawl pin.
3. Correctly insert the ratchet sector into the lever. Install the spacer and the washer, and then insert a new pivot pin.
4. If necessary, install the cable guide, the cable guide support, the spacers for the guide pins, and two new guide pins. Using a pin punch or other suitable tool, peen or stake the ends of the guide pins, the pivot pin, and the pawl pin (Fig. 10-4).

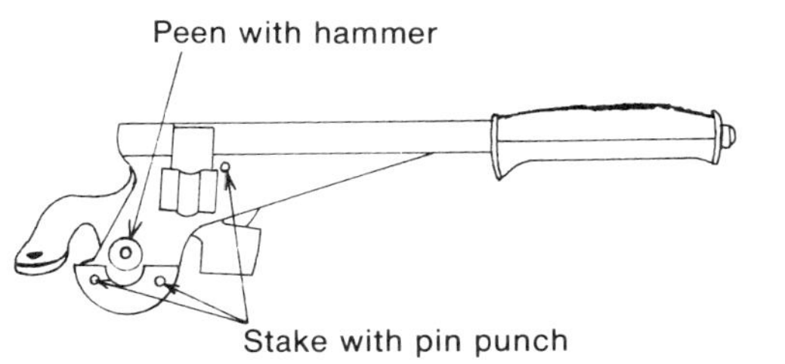

Fig. 10-4. Pins that are to be peened or staked during assembly of parking brake lever.

5. Install the parking brake lever in the car as described in the previous procedure.

Removing and Installing Secondary Cable

You can replace each of the two secondary cables individually. They are not identical, so it is important that you obtain the correct replacement part for the cable you are replacing.

To remove:

1. Remove the rear part of the console that is between the two front seats. To do this, untie the parking brake lever boot, remove the four screws that hold the console to the floor, then lift the rear part of the console at its front end and remove it toward the front of the car—sliding it off over the parking brake lever. If necessary, consult **BODY AND INTERIOR.**
2. Fully remove the adjusting nut cap. Then unscrew the adjusting nut as far as possible without removing it from the end of the primary cable. If necessary, consult Fig. 10-1 and Fig. 10-2, given earlier.
3. Remove the guide grommet for the secondary cable you are replacing from the bracket at the rear of the equalizer. Then detach the front end of the secondary cable from the equalizer.
4. Remove the clamps or clips that hold the cable conduit to the underside of the car body.
5. Remove the brake drum and the brake shoes. See **8.2 Removing and Installing Brake Shoes.**
6. Using a screwdriver as indicated in Fig. 10-5, detach the cable conduit from the brake backing plate. Then remove the cable and its conduit from the car.

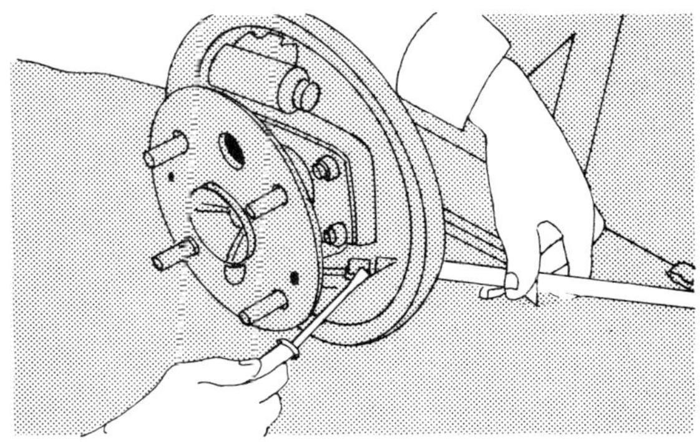

Fig. 10-5. Secondary cable conduit being detached from brake backing plate.

Installation is the reverse of removal. Following installation, adjust the parking brake as described in **10.1 Adjusting Parking Brake.**

7

11. WHEELS AND TIRES

Tires are subject to many stresses. If they are to perform as intended, they must be inflated to specifications and correctly balanced. Properly maintained, the factory-installed tires will provide long service with comfort and safety. However, they must never be kept in service when worn out or damaged by accidents or careless driving.

The front wheel bearings, covered under two of the following headings, will often be serviced and adjusted while front brakes are being repaired. For this reason, the bearings have been covered in this section of the Manual. The rear wheel bearings are not commonly serviced during rear brake repairs. For information concerning the replacement of the rear wheel bearings, please refer to **DRIVESHAFT AND REAR AXLE.**

11.1 Checking Wheels

The SR-5 models are factory-equipped with 5J×13 four-hole, pressed steel wheels. Other models have 4.5J×13 four-hole, pressed steel wheels. You should inspect the wheel lug nuts and torque them to 90 to 120 Nm (66 to 89 ft. lb.) at regular intervals. Loose wheel lug nuts may cause noise, shimmy, and vibration. They may also create elongated holes that render the wheel unserviceable. The wheel lug circle has a diameter of 115 mm (4½ in.).

It is important that you keep the wheels clean on both the inside and the outside surfaces. Otherwise, stones, grease, and hardened mud may cause wheel and tire imbalance. Replace wheels that have lateral runout in excess of 1.15 mm (.045 in.) or raidal runout (out-of-round) in excess of 0.75 mm (.030 in.). Excessive runout will cause shimmy or wobble that will eventually damage the wheel bearings. Also replace any wheel that has a rough or dented rim, which could cause air to leak from the tires.

11.2 Tire Specifications and Inflation Pressures

Radial tires are either optional or standard factory-installed equipment on nearly all cars covered by this Manual. Bias-ply tires are standard only on basic models of the sedan and on some early station wagon models. Many owners have replaced the original tires with better-quality or larger radial tires that are standard on other Corolla models. When replacing the factory-installed tires, you should select a kind of tire that is recommended for your Corolla by the tire manufacturer. You should, however, select radial tires in preference to tires having any other kind of construction.

There is less friction between the ply layers in radial tires, so they generate less heat. This makes them especially suitable for long-distance, high-speed driving. They also do not heat so much when carrying heavy loads. Their rigid tread improves wet-weather traction and, because a rigid tread has less rolling resistance, it also helps reduce gasoline consumption.

Winter Tires

Although they are inferior to regular tires for dry-road wear and handling, winter (mud and snow) tires can greatly improve operation on snowy or slushy roads. Studded winter tires improve traction on icy surfaces, but they can be damaged by fast driving on dry roads and they themselves may damage some road surfaces. You should use them only if icy conditions predominate throughout the winter months. Also check you local vehicle laws, which may restrict the use of studded tires in your area. Regardless of the kind of winter tires you use, they should be of radial-ply construction if the other tires on the car are radials, or of bias-ply construction if the other tires are bias-ply. The use of bias-ply winter tires on the rear of the car in combination with radial tires on the front can produce especially dangerous handling characteristics.

Tire Pressures

It is essential to safety that you always maintain the recommended inflation pressures and stay within the load limits for the car and for the tires on it. For reliable vehicle control, always maintain the specified pressures. Accidents have been caused by service station personnel who inflate tires by guesswork rather than with careful reference to the car manufacturer's specifications. Wise drivers check their tire pressures personally.

The tire size, application, and inflation pressure table given here is based on information published by Toyota Motor Sales Co., Ltd., for the 1979 models. These data correspond to data given for 1975 through 1978 models in other Toyota Service Specifications books. If the specifications given here differ in any way from those given in your car's Owner's Manual or in the tire pressure chart inside the glove compartment, use the specifications from the Owner's Manual or the chart in the glove compartment. Please consult your Authorized Dealer if you have any question concerning these specifications. For continuous driving at speeds above 120 kph (75 mph), inflate the tires to 0.3 bar (4 psi) above the pressure(s) given in **Table b.**

Radial tires will appear underinflated at the correct recommended pressures. This is normal, so do not inflate the tires beyond the recommended pressures, and under

Table b. Tire Sizes, Applications, and Inflation Pressures

Tire size	Car model	Vehicle load condition	Inflation pressure in bar (psi)	
			Front wheels	Rear wheels
165S × or 6.45S × 13 Bias-ply, 4-ply rating	Sedan	All, up to tire or vehicle capacity	1.7 (24)	1.7 (24)
	Station wagon	Up to four occupants	1.7 (24)	1.7 (24)
		Up to tire or vehicle capacity	1.7 (24)	2.0 (28)
165SR × 13 Radial-ply	Sedan and coupe	All, up to tire or vehicle capacity	1.7 (24)	1.7 (24)
	Station wagon	Up to four occupants	1.7 (24)	1.7 (24)
		Up to tire or vehicle capacity	1.7 (24)	2.0 (28)
	Liftback	All, up to tire or vehicle capacity	1.8 (26)	1.8 (26)
175/70SR × 13	Liftback SR-5	All, up to tire or vehicle capacity	1.7 (24)	1.7 (24)
185/70SR × 13	Hardtop SR-5 Coupe SR-5	All, up to tire or vehicle capacity	1.7 (24)	1.7 (24)

no circumstances inflate a tire to a pressure in excess of the maximum inflated pressure marked on the tire.

CAUTION —
You should measure and correct tire pressure only when the tire is cold (car parked for at least one hour). Otherwise, the pressure measurements will be inaccurate. It is normal for a "hot" tire to exceed the specified pressure. Do not release air from a "hot" tire.

Normal Tire Wear

The original equipment tires on your Corolla have built-in tread wear indicators. These indicators are molded into the bottoms of the tire tread grooves. The indicators eventually appear as the result of normal wear. They are about 13 mm (½ in.) wide in visible bands when the tire tread depth gets down to 1.5 mm (1/16 in.).

When these indicators appear in two or more adjacent grooves of a tire tread, as shown in Fig. 11-1, replace the tire. It is recommended that you replace tires well before the indicators are as visible as shown. Worn tires cannot grip even a dry road surface properly and are almost completely ineffective on a wet road surface.

WARNING —
Do not assume that a tire is sound merely because the tread wear indicators have not yet appeared. Always check for cuts, cracks, rubber separation, and internal damage. Normal wear is only one factor in determining tire serviceability.

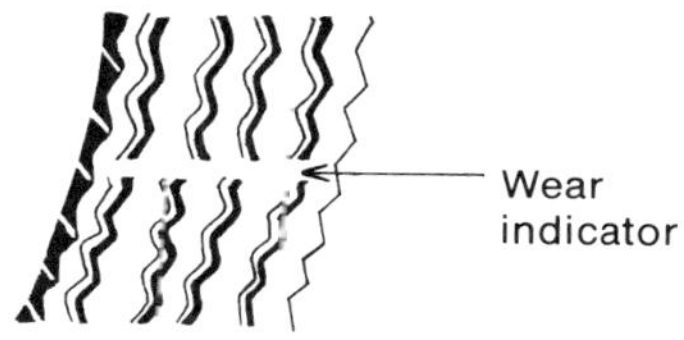

Fig. 11-1. Tread wear indicator showing on worn-out tire.

For best all-around handling, always replace all four tires at the same time. If this is not possible, replace both tires on one axle. Do not combine radial tires with conventional (bias-ply or bias-belted) tires. Do not combine tires of different sizes or tread patterns.

WARNING —
Break in new tires by driving at moderate speeds for the first 100 to 160 km (60 to 100 miles). New tires do not have full traction when first installed.

Normal tire wear is accelerated by higher speeds. Wear at a constant 55 kph (or 35 mph) is only about a third of that produced at a constant 110 kph (or 70 mph)—not half, as might seem logical.

Weather also affects normal tire wear. Hot weather is the most damaging; and, when heat is combined with high speeds and underinflation, tire structure is seriously endangered. Cold weather prolongs tire life; so does wet weather, which reduces the friction between tire and road.

7

Tire Rotation

Although tire rotation is not included as a part of routine maintenance, Toyota recommends that, in the interest of improved tire life, the tires be rotated each 10,000 km (6,000 mi.). You can obtain the greatest life from the factory-installed tires if you include the spare wheel in the rotation pattern. If you intend to keep the car past the time when the original tires wear out, you may, however, choose to rotate the tires without using the spare. By doing this, you will need to buy only three new tires, keeping the best of the old tires for a spare. The correct rotation patterns for both bias-ply (or bias-belted) and for radial tires are given in Fig. 11-2.

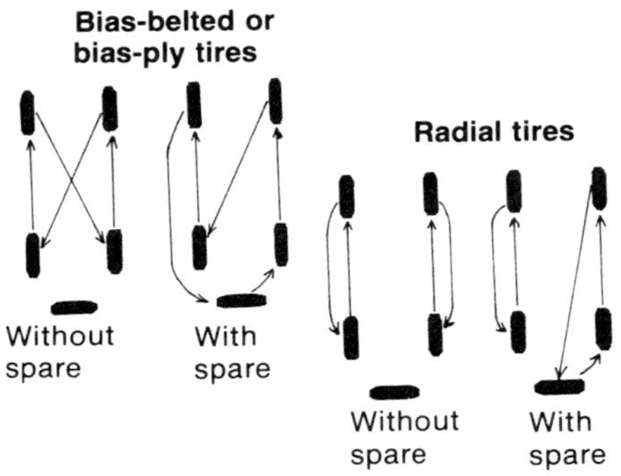

Fig. 11-2. Correct tire rotation patterns. Please notice that you should not interchange radial tires from one side of car to other. If you do, it may cause a period of accelerated wear or lead to internal tire faults.

11.3 Removing and Installing Road Wheel

Even though you may have changed tires many times before, the following procedure includes several helpful steps that you will want to use in servicing your car. Other helpful instructions can be found in the Owner's Manual supplied with the car.

To remove:

1. Make sure that the car is on level ground and that the parking brake is applied.
2. Loosen the wheel lug nuts a half-turn each, but do not remove them yet.
3. Raise the wheel with a jack or raise the vehicle on a hoist. If you use the emergency jack supplied with the car, make sure that you correctly position the jack beneath the vehicle and that you chock the wheel diagonally opposite the wheel you are lifting.
4. When the wheel to be removed has cleared the ground, unscrew the lug nuts. Then remove the wheel from the car.

NOTE ——
If the wheel has been dynamically balanced while installed on the car, you should reinstall it in its original position on the wheel lugs. Mark one of the lugs with chalk and mark an adjacent part of the wheel before you remove the wheel from the car.

Installation is the reverse of removal. Install the wheel lug nuts finger-tight, lower the car to the ground, then torque the nuts to 90 to 120 Nm (66 to 89 ft. lb.) in the sequence given in Fig. 11-3.

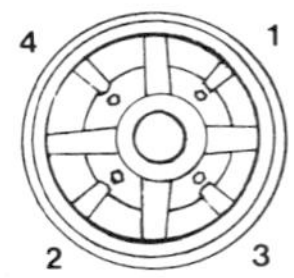

Fig. 11-3. Tightening sequence for wheel lug nuts.

11.4 Adjusting Front Wheel Bearings

Each front road wheel is mounted on its respective front hub and brake disc assembly. Inside each front hub are two opposed tapered roller bearings. A grease seal is installed at the inner end of the hub to prevent the wheel bearing lubricant from leaking out onto the brake disc. The entire hub, disc, and bearing assembly is held on the front wheel spindle by an adjusting nut, a nut lock, and a cotter pin.

Adjust the front wheel bearings if the wheel is loose on the spindle or if the wheel does not rotate freely with the brake pads removed. You should check the adjustment if the bearings are making noise or if the steering seems affected when you apply the brakes. You should also lubricate and then adjust the bearings at the mileage or time intervals prescribed in **LUBRICATION AND MAINTENANCE.**

To adjust:

1. Remove the front road wheels as described in **11.3 Removing and Installing Road Wheel.**
2. Pry off the wheel hub dust cover.
3. Wipe the excess grease from the end of the spindle, then remove the cotter pin and the stamped steel nut lock.
4. Loosen the wheel bearing adjusting nut by approximately three turns. Then, being careful not to get grease on the brake disc, pull the disc outward and then push it inward to force the brake pads away from the disc.

NOTE ——

If, because of new pads or residual pressure in the hydraulic lines, you cannot move the pads away from the disc, temporarily remove the brake pads as described in **7.1 Removing and Installing Brake Pads.**

5. Turn the adjusting nut clockwise until it is finger-tight. Then install a torque wrench on the adjusting nut.
6. While rotating the wheel hub alternately clockwise and counterclockwise to settle the bearings, gradually torque the adjusting nut to 25 to 30 Nm (18 to 22 ft. lb.).
7. Without rotating the wheel hub, loosen the adjusting nut until you can turn it by hand. Then, gripping the socket wrench (without a handle) in your hand, tighten the adjusting nut as much as possible. See Fig. 11-4.

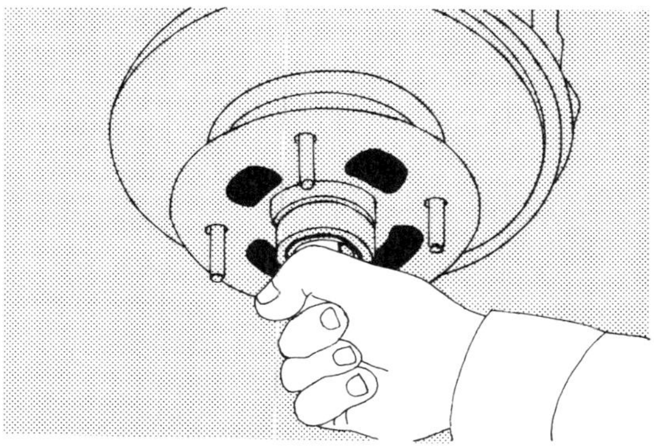

Fig. 11-4. Adjusting nut being tightened.

8. With a spring scale as shown in Fig. 11-5, a pull of 300 to 700 g (about 11 to 24 oz.) should be required to rotate the wheel hub. If more or less pull is required, slightly loosen or tighten the adjusting nut until the pull required is in the correct range.

NOTE ——

You must either remove the brake pads or push them away from the disc during this test.

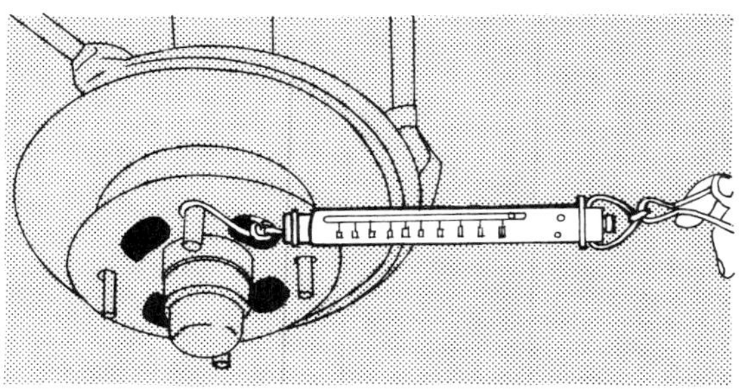

Fig. 11-5. Bearing preload being measured with spring scale attached to wheel lug nut.

9. Without moving the adjusting nut, install the nut lock so that the castellations do not cover the cotter pin hole. You may have to reposition the nut lock on the adjusting nut
10. Install a new cotter pin and bend the ends of the cotter pin around the castellated flange of the nut lock (Fig. 11-6). Reinstall the dust cap.

Fig. 11-6. Nut lock and cotter pin correctly installed. Dashed line indicates position of adjusting nut.

11. Check that the wheel hub turns easily; if not, the bearings may be adjusted too tightly, or they may require lubrication or replacement. If the bearings are rough-turning or noisy, you should definitely service and inspect them as described in **11.5 Servicing and Replacing Front Wheel Bearings.**
12. If necessary, reinstall the brake pads. Then, even if you only pressed the pads away from the disc, pump the brake pedal several times before you drive the car so that the brake pads will firmly contact the brake discs.

11.5 Servicing and Replacing Front Wheel Bearings

If adjusting the bearings fails to eliminate looseness or rough and noisy operation, you should remove, clean, inspect, and relubricate the front wheel bearings. You should also do this work as a part of routine maintenance at the mileage or time intervals prescribed in **LUBRICATION AND MAINTENANCE.** Replace the bearing races if they are in any way worn or damaged.

7

To service:

1. Remove the road wheel, then remove the brake caliper as described in **7.2 Removing and Installing Brake Caliper.**
2. Pry off the wheel hub dust cover.
3. Wipe the excess grease from the end of the spindle, then remove the cotter pin and the stamped steel nut lock.
4. Remove the wheel bearing adjusting nut. Remove the flat thrust washer and the outer wheel bearing's inner race, which includes the caged roller bearings. Store the bearing race in a clean, dust-free location or place it in a clean pan of kerosene.

5. Pull the brake disc and the wheel hub off the spindle as a unit.
6. Working at the inner side of the wheel hub, pry out and discard the old grease seal. Remove the inner bearing race, which includes the caged roller bearings. Store the bearing race in a clean, dust-free location or place it in a clean pan of kerosene. Fig. 11-7 shows the relative positions of the wheel bearing components.
7. Carefully clean the inner bearing races with kerosene, then dry them with compressed air.

> ***CAUTION —***
> *Do not use solvents such as gasoline, because they remove all lubrication. Also, do not let blasts of compressed air spin the races, as rapid movement can damage unlubricated bearings. It is important that you clean all the old grease not only from the bearing races but also from the hub's interior and the stub axle. Lithium-base grease is not compatible with sodium-base grease. If the two kinds are present in the same hub and bearing assembly, the bearings may fail owing to inadequate lubrication.*

8. Clean the interior of the wheel hub and inspect the outer bearing races. If either outer race is worn, burred, rough, or heat-blued, remove it as shown in Fig. 11-8. Drive in a new race as shown in Fig. 11-9.
9. Pack the inner bearing's inner race with multipurpose grease or with a wheel bearing grease that is intended for use with disc brakes. If you lack a pressure bearing lubricator, place some grease in your palm, then thrust the bearing race into the grease repeatedly so that the rollers turn each time. Continue until all parts of the bearing are coated with grease.

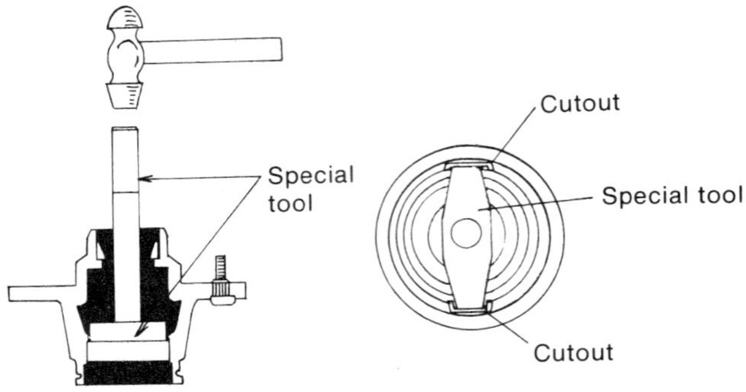

Fig. 11-8. Bearing outer race being driven out of hub (left) with special tool that enters cutouts inside hub (right).

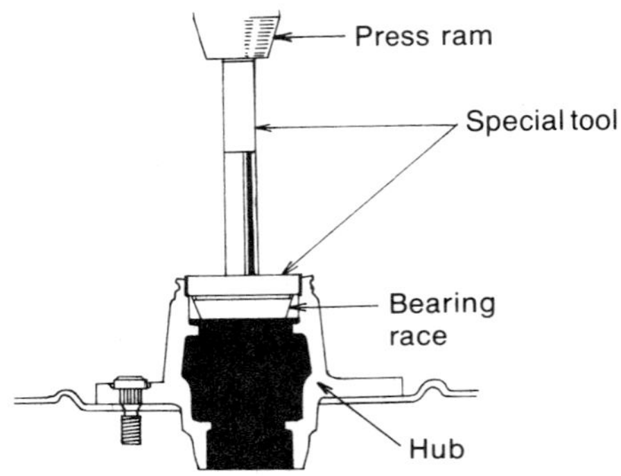

Fig. 11-9. Bearing outer race being pressed into hub. This work can be done at low cost by most automotive machine shops.

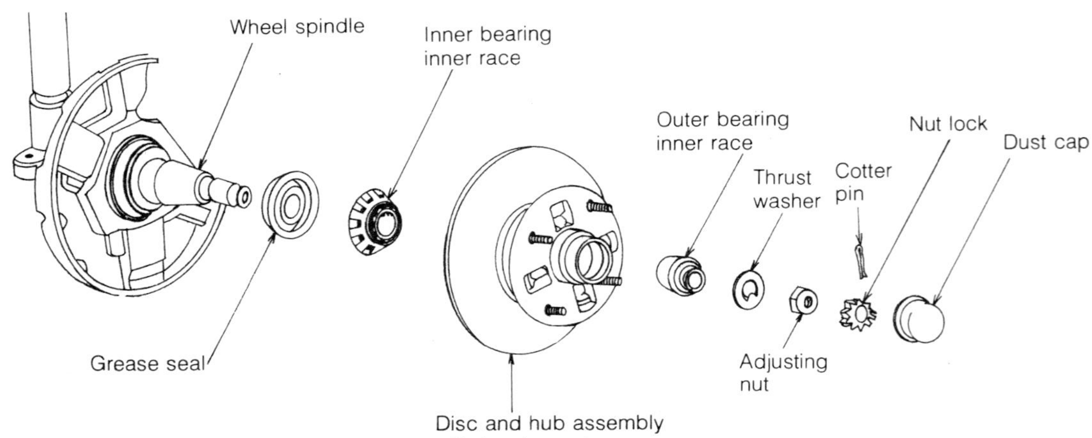

Fig. 11-7. Wheel bearings and related parts.

10. Insert the inner race into the brake drum. Then press a new grease seal into place.
11. Pack the inside of the hub with the same grease you used in step 9. Add the lubricant only until the grease is flush with the inside diameters of both bearing outer races.

> ***WARNING —***
> *Do not completely fill the hub with grease. If you do, expansion caused by heat will force grease past the grease seal and onto the brake disc, resulting in a dangerous brake condition.*

12. Thoroughly clean the spindle. Then, to prevent corrosion, lightly coat the spindle with the same grease you used in step 9.
13. Carefully slide the disc and hub assembly onto the spindle, being careful not to damage the grease seal on the spindle's sharp threads.
14. Pack the outer bearing's inner race with the same grease you used in step 9. Then carefully slide it onto the stub axle and into the hub.
15. Install the thrust washer and the adjusting nut. Tighten the nut until the bearings just contact their outer races.
16. Before you install the brake caliper, adjust the bearings as described in **11.4 Adjusting Front Wheel Bearings.** Then install the brake caliper as described in **7.2 Removing and Installing Brake Caliper.** Torque the caliper mounting bolts to 60 to 70 Nm (44 to 52 ft. lb.). Torque the wheel lug nuts to 90 to 120 Nm (66 to 89 ft. lb.).

11.6 Balancing Wheels and Tires

Wheels that are out of balance cause abnormal tire wear and constitute a driving hazard. Unbalanced wheels bounce, tramp, and wobble. The faster you drive, the more dangerous these wheel vibrations are.

Wheel imbalance is always more evident, and usually more dangerous, on the front wheels. Fig. 11-10 shows the condition that static balancing of the wheel and tire can detect. The effect of such imbalance is shown in the right-hand part of the illustration.

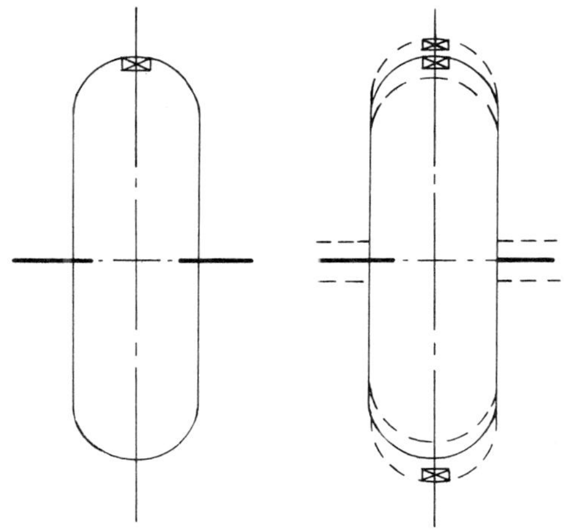

Fig. 11-10. Imbalance that can be cured by static balancing. Vibration of spinning wheel is shown at right.

Fig. 11-11 shows the kind of imbalance that only dynamic balancing can detect. Although the wheel is in perfect static balance, the concentrations of mass are not in line with one another or with the tire centerline. The wheel wobbles sideways when it spins, as shown in the right-hand side of the illustration. This causes deep wear in the form of cupped areas on the tread. Check that the wheel lateral runout does not exceed 1.15 mm (.045 in.) and that radial runout (out-of-round) does not exceed 0.75 mm (.030 in.) before dynamically balancing the wheel. Replace the wheel if it does.

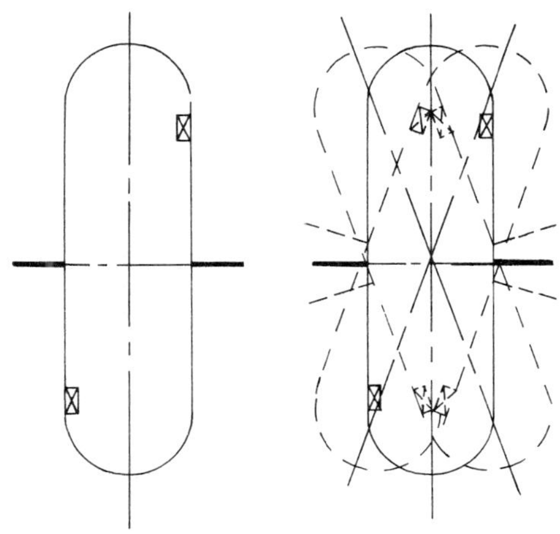

Fig. 11-11. Imbalance that can be cured only by dynamic balancing. Vibration of spinning wheel is shown at right.

7

12. Brakes and Wheels Technical Data

I. Tightening Torques

Location	Designation	Nm	Ft. lb.
Brake master cylinder to brake servo	nut	15 max.	11 max.
Brake line ends	flare nut	14–15	10–11
Brake hose end to union	—	25–30	18–22
Master cylinder piston stop bolt in master cylinder housing	special bolt	5–10	3.5–7.5
Fluid outlet plug in master cylinder housing	special plug	40–50	30–37
Pressure switch in master cylinder housing	—	20	15
Fluid reservoir to master cylinder housing	gland nut	20–30	15–22
Brake servo to car body	nut	15 max.	11 max.
Brake pedal to pedal housing	nut and bolt	30–40	22–30
Road wheel to front wheel hub or rear axle flange	lug nut	90–120	66–89
Front disc brake caliper to splash shield and suspension strut	bolt	60–70	44–52
Front brake disc to front wheel hub	bolt	45–50	33–37
Front disc brake splash shield to suspension strut's wheel spindle	bolt	30–35	22–26
Rear brake wheel cylinder to brake backing plate	bolt	10–11	7.5–8
Rear wheel bearing retainer and brake backing plate to rear axle housing	nut and bolt	60–70	44–52
Brake bleeder valve in caliper or wheel cylinder	—	10	7.5

II. Tolerances, Wear Limits, and Settings

Designation	New part mm (in.)	Wear limit mm (in.)
A. Master cylinder and brake servo		
1. Master cylinder/master cylinder piston . . . . . clearance	—	0.10 (.004)
2. Servo's master cylinder pushrod/master cylinder piston . . . . . clearance	0.10–.50 (.004–.020)	—
3. Brake pedal . . . . . height above floor when all the way up	169 (6 21/32)	—
. . . . . freeplay	3–6 (1/8–1/4)	—
. . . . . reserve travel (height above floor when depressed)	85 (3 3/8) minimum	—
B. Front disc brakes		
1. Brake disc . . . . . thickness	10 (.394 or 25/64)	9 (.354 or 23/64)
. . . . maximum allowable runout or thickness variation before rework	—	0.15 (.006)
. . . . . maximum allowable runout or thickness variation after rework		0.02 (.0008)
2. Brake pad . . . . . thickness	—	1.0 (.040)
C. Rear drum brakes		
Brake shoe . . . . . lining thickness	5 (.197)	1.0 (.040)
. . . . . clearance between shim for parking brake lever and rear brake shoe	0.00–0.35 (.0000–.0138)	—
D. Road Wheel . . . . . maximum allowable lateral runout	—	1.15 (.045)
. . . . . maximum allowable radial runout (out-of-round)	—	0.75 (.030)
. . . . . bolt hole circle diameter	115 (4½)	—

Section 8

SUSPENSION AND STEERING

Contents

Suspension and Steering

The Toyota Corolla has strut-type independent front wheel suspension. The struts, with their built-in hydraulic shock absorbers, are similar in many respects to the landing wheel struts used on commercial airliners. In addition to providing excellent steering and handling, the system has the combined advantages of compact size and comparatively light weight.

The front suspension has fixed-rate coil springs, one at each front wheel. The springs are installed concentrically over the upper parts of the struts, and can be removed for replacement of the spring or the strut itself. This work, as well as that of rebuilding the shock absorbers, which are integral with the struts, requires special tools, experience, and clean shop conditions. If you do not have access to a suitable workshop, or if you lack the skills or tools necessary for strut repairs (or for repairs to the rear suspension or the steering) we suggest you leave these repairs to an Authorized Dealer or other qualified shop. We especially urge you to consult an Authorized Dealer before attempting any repairs on a car still covered by the new-car warranty.

The steering gearbox is of the recirculating ball type. Replacement parts are available for many of its internal components, so it is possible to rebuild the gearbox in order to correct normal wear. The gearbox can also be adjusted. This work, however, should always be done with the steering gearbox removed from the car. Power steering is not available as an option on the Toyota Corolla.

The rear suspension is by multiple-leaf springs and a tubular hydraulic shock absorber at each rear wheel. There is no anti-roll bar, Panhard rod, or track arm on the rear axle, so the axle is located only by the springs. Two U-bolts hold the rear axle housing to each spring, and the springs are approximately parallel to the road in order to control roll-steer. Removal and installation of the rear axle housing is covered in this section of the Manual. Please see **DRIVESHAFT AND REAR AXLE** for all repairs to the driving components of the rear axle.

Tire wear and vehicle handling qualities are good indicators of the condition of the front suspension and of the steering system. However, before assuming that the struts or the steering requires repair or adjustment, make sure that the front tires are correctly inflated, that different tire size or tread patterns are not on the front wheels, and that the front wheels have been accurately balanced. These checks and adjustments are described in **BRAKES AND WHEELS.**

1. GENERAL DESCRIPTION

The Corolla's strut front suspension consists of two vertically-mounted shock absorbers surrounded by large coil springs. Each front wheel is located laterally by a track control arm. Fore and aft wheel location is controlled by strut bars and not by the stabilizer bar.

The rear suspension is by semielliptical multiple-leaf springs and double-acting tubular hydraulic shock absorbers. The mounting points of both the front and the rear suspension systems are rubber insulated in order to minimize the transmission of road noise and vibration to the car body.

The recirculating ball steering gearbox is mounted on the left-hand chassis box-member of the body. At the opposite side of the car is an idler arm which is matched in length to the pitman arm on the steering gearbox. A steering relay rod connects these two arms, and equal-length steering tie rods extend from each end of the relay rod to the steering arm on each wheel spindle.

Front Suspension Struts

Each strut consists of a large hydraulic shock absorber assembly housed in a tube with an integral steering knuckle. Around the tube is a concentric coil spring. The strut assembly also includes the upper strut mounting and a number of smaller parts. The suspension's upward travel is limited by a rubber buffer at the top of the strut's piston rod. Downward movement is limited by a rubber rebound stopper inside the shock absorber.

Front Track Control Arms, Stabilizer Bar, and Strut Rods

The two track control arms locate the suspension struts laterally. There is no provision for adjusting front wheel camber. The outer ends of the track control arms have integral ball joints that are attached by large nuts on their ball studs to the steering arms. The steering arms are bolted to the wheel spindles of the suspension struts.

The stabilizer bar provides anti-roll stabilization; it does not serve to locate the suspension struts longitudinally, as on a "pure" MacPherson strut suspension. Instead, the struts are located longitudinally by two strut rods. Although the lengths of the strut rods control the front wheels' caster angles, there is no provision for adjustment. New parts should be installed if wear or accident damage has produced incorrect camber or caster.

Rear Springs and Shock Absorbers

The four-leaf (five-leaf on station wagons) semielliptical springs can be disassembled for cleaning and replacement of parts other than the leaves themselves. The front ends of the springs are mounted on the body. The rear ends are suspended on shackles. Two U-bolts hold each spring to the rear axle housing.

The tubular, double-acting hydraulic shock absorbers are installed between the U-bolt plates below the springs and reinforced mounting points on the car body. On station wagons, the lower ends of the shock absorbers are mounted behind the rear axle, whereas on other models they are mounted ahead of the rear axle. By being in front of or behind the axle, instead of atop it, the shock absorbers assist in limiting rear axle windup during braking or acceleration.

Steering

The recirculating ball steering gearbox is so named because, instead of the steering worm's operating a gear sector directly, a separate rack, or ball nut, travels along the worm and meshes with the gear sector, which turns the pitman arm. Between the worm and the ball nut are steel balls, which can endlessly recirculate in the spiral grooves of the ball nut and the worm. Thus, the mechanism is nearly frictionless in operation and far less subject to wear.

2. MAINTENANCE

Because of the extensive use of rubber mountings in the suspension and steering systems, only a few maintenance operations must be carried out after a specified mileage or period of service. These operations are listed below and are covered briefly in **LUBRICATION AND MAINTENANCE** or under the listed heading in this section of the Manual.

1. Checking torque of front and rear suspension bolts. **7**
2. Checking for abnormal steering looseness
3. Lubricating front suspension lower ball joints
4. Inspecting front suspension lower ball joints and dust covers
5. Lubricating front suspension upper support bearings
6. Inspecting steering wheel and steering linkage
7. Checking and, if necessary, correcting steering gearbox oil level.

3. FRONT WHEEL ALIGNMENT

Only front wheel toe is adjustable. Caster angle, wheel camber, and steering axis inclination are determined by the manufactured dimensions of the suspension parts, so damaged parts must be replaced to correct these alignment factors. The following preparatory steps are essential to accurate alignment measurements:

1. Have the car on a level surface.
2. Inflate the tires to specifications and unload the car except for the spare wheel and a full fuel tank. Then jounce the car several times and let it settle into its normal position.
3. Check the adjustment of the front wheel bearings and if necessary adjust them. See **BRAKES AND WHEELS.**
4. Make sure that there is no play in the tie rod ends, the relay rod ends, or the bearings for the idler arm. Make sure that the steering gearbox and the idler arm assembly are not loose on the car body.

3.1 Checking and Adjusting Front Wheel Toe

The Toyota Corolla is designed to operate with a small amount of toe-in. This means that the front edges of the two front tires are slightly closer together than the rear edges. You can measure and adjust front wheel toe with a track gauge. Different degrees of toe-in are used with bias-ply tires and with radial-ply tires, so check which kind of tire is installed before making any adjustment.

To check toe:

1. Turn the steering to its center position (front wheels pointing straight ahead and steering wheel spokes horizontal).

   NOTE ——

   If the steering wheel spokes are not horizontal when the wheels are pointed straight ahead, check the toe with the front wheels straight ahead. Then correct the steering wheel position as described later, at the end of the procedure for adjusting toe.

2. Adjust the height of the track gauge to match the height of the wheel hubs.
3. By positioning the track gauge pointers against the inner rear edges of the tire treads, measure the distance between the tire rear edges. Mark the measuring points on each front tire with chalk. This allows you to make measurements between the same two points after you roll the car ahead a half-turn of the wheels.
4. Roll the car ahead until the chalk marks on the wheels are at wheel hub height on the fronts of the wheels. Then measure between the chalk marks on the tires and compare the measurements to that obtained with the measuring points at the rears of the wheels.
5. The measurement made between the front edges of the wheels should be less than that measured at the rear edges, by 2 to 4 mm ($^5/_{64}$ to $^5/_{32}$ in.) on cars with bias ply tires or 0 to 2 mm (0 to $^5/_{64}$ in.) on cars with radial ply tires. If not, adjust the toe.

   NOTE ——

   If you are using alignment equipment that measures tire slip angles to determine toe, the sideways slippage should be 0 to 3 mm (0 to ⅛ in.) in 1 m (3 ft. 4 in.) of forward travel. This and the specifications given for track gauges apply only with the wheels in their straight-ahead position. The specifications for camber angle, caster angle, and steering axis inclination—some of which may be measured with the wheels turned—are given in **7. Suspension and Steering Technical Data.** With the help of optical alignment equipment, this additional data can be used to detect worn or damaged steering and suspension parts.

To adjust toe:

1. Loosen the clamp bolts on each of the two tie rods. (The tie rods are connected at their inner ends to the steering relay rod, and at their outer ends to the steering arms on the front suspension struts.) See Fig. 3-1.

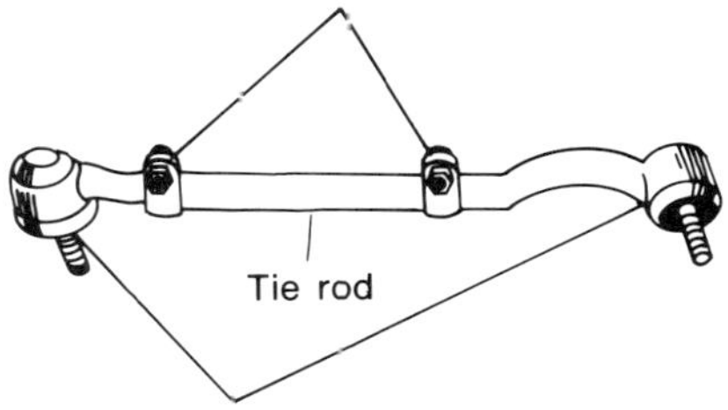

Fig. 3-1. Components of tie rod. Both tie rods on car are adjustable

8

2. Correct the toe by turning the two tie rods by equal amounts and in the same direction. See Fig. 3-2.

NOTE ——
You must turn the tie rods equally in order to keep the steering wheel centered. If one or both adjusting sleeves is frozen by rust to the tie rod ends, first apply penetrating oil that contains a rust solvent, tapping the tie rod lightly with a hammer to assist the penetration of oil between the treads. If this fails to free the tie rod, wipe away surplus oil and then moderately heat the threaded parts of the tie rod with a torch, tapping the tie rod lightly to break the corrosion. Should this fail to free the tie rod, replace the tie rod and tie rod ends as a unit. Also replace any tie rod that has been damaged or deformed by your attempts to free it.

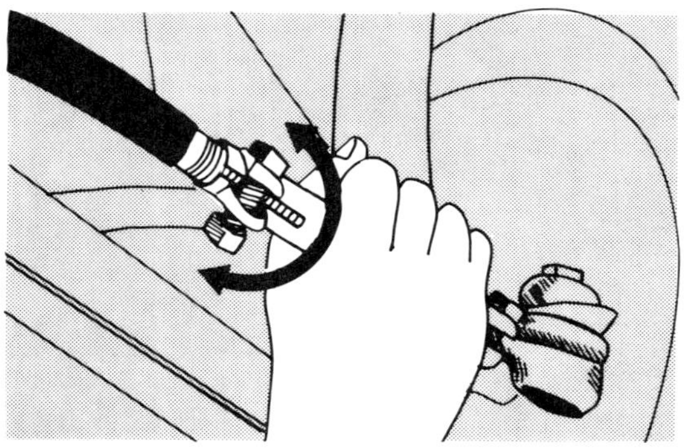

Fig. 3-2. Tie rod being turned after clamp bolts have been loosened.

3. When the toe is correct, torque the clamp bolts to 15 to 20 Nm (11 to 15 ft. lb.).

CAUTION ——
To prevent wear and strain on the tie rod end ball joints, position the inner tie rod end at a 90° angle to the outer tie rod end before you tighten the clamp bolts.

If the steering wheel is not centered while you are driving straight ahead on a level surface, center it by turning one tie rod in one direction and the other by exactly the same number of turns in the opposite direction. This procedure will move the steering wheel without moving the front wheels or changing the toe.

CAUTION ——
Never center the steering wheel either by altering its position on the steering column or by moving the column on the steering gearbox worm shaft. Doing this leaves the real fault uncorrected and could result in dangerous steering characteristics.

3.2 Adjusting Steering Lock

Steering lock—the maximum angle to which the front wheels can be turned—can be adjusted if necessary. The angles given in the following procedure are for reference only. The steering lock should be adjusted so that neither front tire contacts a fixed part of the car when turned fully to the right or fully to the left. Wider tires, which are sometimes specified as a replacement for the tires originally installed on the car, may require a correction in the steering lock adjustment.

To adjust steering lock:

1. Using an alignment gauge that can be placed beneath the front wheels, and which will indicate in degrees the angles to which the front wheels are turned, measure the steering lock angles with the steering wheel turned fully to the left.
2. If necessary, adjust the angle of the left front wheel to 37° to 39° as indicated in Fig. 3-3. Then check that the angle of the right front wheel is between 29° 25′ and 33° 25′, which is an indication that the toe is correctly adjusted and that there is neither distortion nor excessive wear in the steering linkage or front suspension.

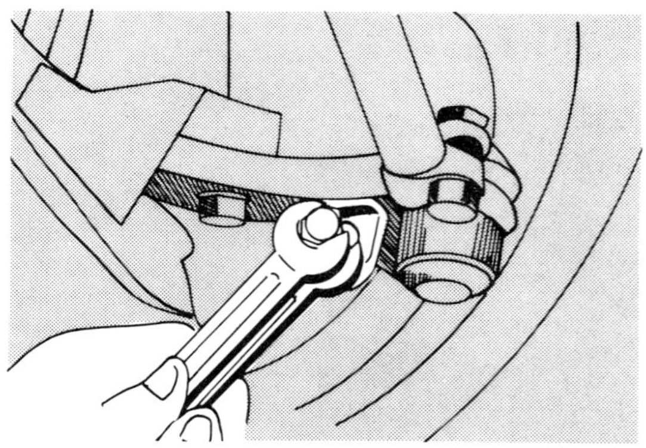

Fig. 3-3. Steering lock being adjusted. Remove adjusting bolt cover. Use one wrench to loosen locknut. Adjust by turning bolt. Then, while holding adjusting bolt stationary, retighten locknut and install bolt cover.

3. Measure the steering lock angles with the steering wheel turned fully to the right. If necessary, adjust the angle of the right front wheel to 37° to 39°. Then check that the angle of the left front wheel is between 29° 25′ and 33° 25′. If the angle of the outer wheel is incorrect in a right or left full-lock turn, replace worn or damaged components of the steering and suspension systems.

4. FRONT SUSPENSION

Owing to its small number of components, it is easy to remove and install the front suspension. For good handling, accurate steering, and maximum tire life, worn ball joints and rubber bushings should be replaced promptly. Bent front suspension components should always be replaced, not straightened or welded. Heating the parts or bending them back to their original shapes will seriously weaken them structurally. Fig. 4-1 is an exploded view of the front suspension.

1. Strut bar bracket
2. Stabilizer bar
3. Stabilizer bar bushing
4. Stabilizer bar bracket
5. Bolt
6. Retainer plate for stabilizer bar buffers
7. Stabilizer bar buffers
8. Spacer
9. Reinforcement plate for stabilizer bar buffers
10. Upper bearing dust cover
11. Nut
12. Nut
13. Lock washer
14. Suspension strut upper bearing assembly
15. Dust seal
16. Upper spring seat
17. Dust cover
18. Buffer seat
19. Strut buffer
20. Spring
21. Suspension strut assembly
22. Nut
23. Retainer plate for strut bar bushing
24. Strut bar rubber bushings
25. Spacer
26. Strut bar
27. Bushing for track control arm
28. Mounting plate with captive nut
29. Bolt
30. Lock washer
31. Nut
32. Lock washer
33. Bolt
34. Cotter pin
35. Castellated nut
36. Steering arm
37. Ball joint dust seal
38. Retaining ring for dust seal
39. Track control arm with ball joint
40. Nut
41. Jam nut

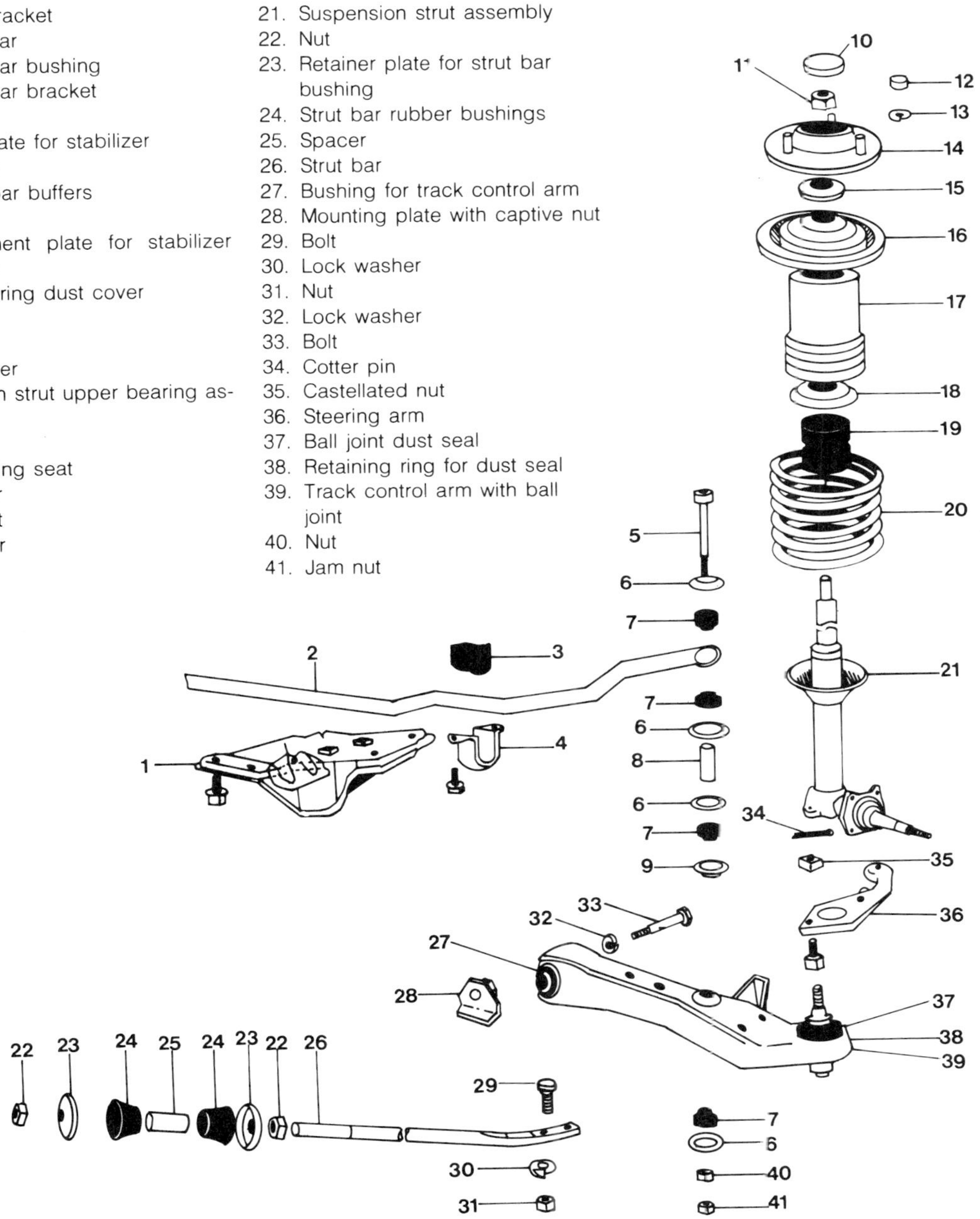

Fig. 4-1. Exploded view of front suspension.

8

4.1 Removing and Installing Strut Bar

Though it may appear that the nuts on the front ends of the strut bars can be used to correct errors in front wheel alignment, this should not be done. The position-locating nut on each strut bar should be kept at the prescribed distance from the front end of the strut bar, and if the wheel alignment is incorrect it should be returned to specifications by the replacement of worn or damaged front suspension and steering components.

To remove strut bar:

1. Raise the car on a hoist or support the front end on stands designed for the purpose.
2. Place a jack beneath the track control arm or the front wheel, then raise the track control arm just enough so that the strut bar bushings are not under strain. Doing this will prevent the track control arm from being distorted, as it would be if the suspension moved down during strut bar removal.
3. Remove the nuts, bolts, and lock washers that hold the rear end of the strut bar to the front suspension's track control arm.
4. Remove only the front nut from the strut bar. Then take out the strut bar toward the rear. Remove the bushings and their retainer plates.

> *CAUTION —*
> *Do not remove the position-locating (rear) nut from the strut bar unless absolutely necessary. The nut is staked in position on the strut bar and may be damaged by removal.*

To install:

1. Inspect the rubber bushings. Check the strut bar for bending or other damage. Repalce worn or damaged components.
2. Using Fig. 4-2 as your guide, install the rubber bushings, the strut bar, and related components in the strut bar bracket. Loosely install the front nut.
3. Using the bolts, the lock washers, and the nuts, attach the strut bar to the front suspension's track control arm. Torque the nuts to 45 to 55 Nm (33 to 41 ft. lb.).
4. If for any reason you have removed the position-locating nut or altered its position, set it to the dimension indicated in Fig. 4-2, then stake it in place using a center punch. torque the front nut to 80 to 110 Nm (59 to 81 ft. lb.).

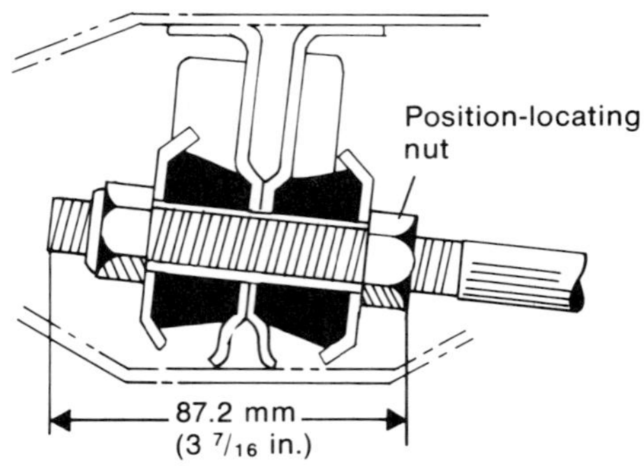

Fig. 4-2. Components at front of strut bar correctly installed. Position-locating nut should be staked in place after it has been positioned 87.2 mm (3 7/16 in.) from front end of strut bar.

5. Remove the jack from beneath the wheel or the track control arm. Lower the car to the ground. Check and if necessary adjust the front wheel toe as described in **3.1 Checking and Adjusting Front Wheel Toe.**

4.2 Removing and Installing Stabilizer Bar

You need not fully remove the stabilizer bar in order to replace its rubber buffers, which are the parts most likely to wear or deteriorate. The stabilizer bar should be removed and replaced if it is broken or distorted. Welding or straightening a faulty stabilizer bar will weaken it structurally and could result in dangerous vehicle handling.

To remove:

1. Raise the car on a hoist, or support the front end on stands designed for the purpose.
2. Remove the splash shield that is beneath the front of the engine.
3. Remove the jam nut from the bottom of the bolt that holds one end of the stabilizer bar to one of the track control arms. Then remove the nut and the bolt.
4. Repeat step 3 on the opposite end of the bar. Remove and disassemble the rubber buffers, the retainer plates, and the spacers.
5. If you must fully remove the stabilizer bar, first remove the bolts that hold the stabilizer bar brackets and bushings to the strut bar brackets. Carry out the next two steps before attempting to remove the stabilizer bar.

6. Place a jack beneath the track control arm or one front wheel, then raise the track control arm just enough so that the strut bar bushings are not under strain, and so that downward movement of the suspension while the strut bar is being unbolted will not distort the track control arm.
7. Working on the side that you have supported with a jack, as described in the preceding step, unbolt the strut bar from the track control arm. Then unbolt the strut bar bracket from the car body and remove the strut bar and its bracket as a unit.
8. Remove the stabilizer bar, taking it out toward the side from which you have removed the strut bar.

To install:

1. Inspect the stabilizer bar, its rubber buffers, and related components. Replace faulty parts.
2. Loosely position the stabilizer bar on the car. Then install the strut bar and strut bar bracket. Torque the bolts for the strut bar bracket to 35 to 40 Nm (26 to 30 ft. lb.). Torque the bolts that hold the strut bar to the track control arm to 45 to 55 Nm (33 to 41 ft. lb.).
3. Install the stabilizer bar bushings and brackets. Torque the bolts that hold the brackets to 10 to 15 Nm (7.5 to 11 ft. lb.).
4. Using Fig. 4-3 as your guide, assemble one set of stabilizer bar buffers, their retainer plates, the spacer, the bolt, and the nuts. Torque the first nut to 15 to 20 Nm (11 to 15 ft. lb.). Then, while holding the first nut stationary, torque the jam nut to 10 to 15 Nm (7.5 to 11 ft. lb.).

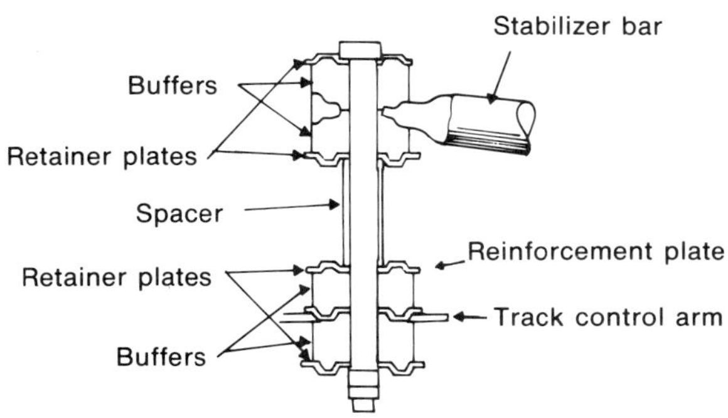

Fig. 4-3. Correct assembly of buffers which connect stabilizer bar to track control arm.

5. Remove the jack. Reinstall the splash shield beneaththe front of the engine.
6. Lower the car to the ground. Check and, if necessary, adjust the front wheel toe as described in **3.1 Checking and Adjusting Front Wheel Toe.**

4.3 Removing and Installing Track Control Arm

The front suspension ball joint is integral with the track control arm. If you must replace a ball joint, because it is worn or damaged, you must replace the track control arm and the ball joint as a unit.

To remove:

1. Raise the car on a hoist or support is on stands designed for the purpose.
2. Remove the road wheel.
3. Remove the two bolts that hold the bottom of the strut suspension assembly's wheel spindle to the steering arm. Then pry the steering arm downward off the strut, moving the strut aside and away from the track control arm. See Fig. 4-4.

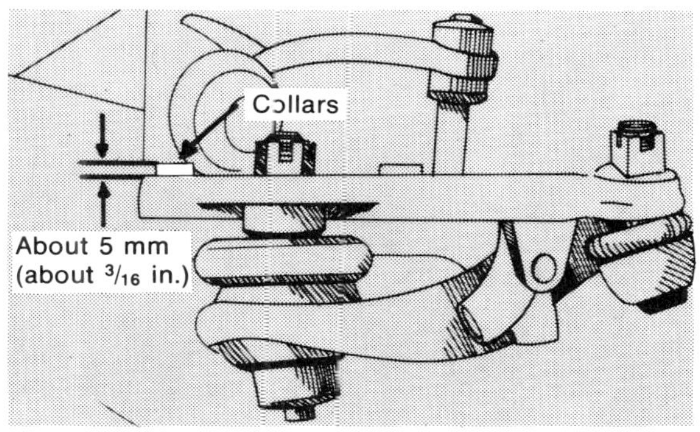

Fig. 4-4. Collars (one at arrow) and nut on ball joint stud that project up into strut's wheel spindle. Track control arm must be pried down so that collars disengage and you can swing strut aside over ball joint stud.

4. Remove the cotter pin. Then remove the castellated nut that holds the outer tie rod end's ball stud in the steering arm. Using a puller as indicated in Fig. 4-5, press the tie rod end's ball stud out of the steering arm.

CAUTION ——
Do not hammer out the ball stud. Doing this can damage the tie rod end or ruin its threads, making the tie rod end unserviceable.

5. Remove the jam nut from the bottom of the bolt that holds the stabilizer bar to the track control arm. Then remove the nut and the bolt. See Fig. 4-5.
6. Unbolt the strut rod from the track control arm. See Fig. 4-5.

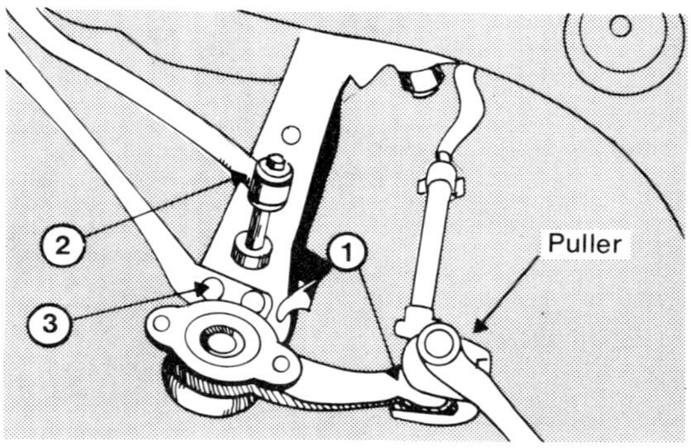

Fig. 4-5. Components to be detached from track control arm. Tie rod end is at **1** with puller (arrow) being used to press tie rod end ball stud out of steering arm. Bolt for stabilizer bar is at **2**. One of two bolts for strut bar is at **3**.

7. Remove the bolt that holds the track control arm to the front suspension crossmember (Fig. 4-6). Then remove the track control arm from the car.

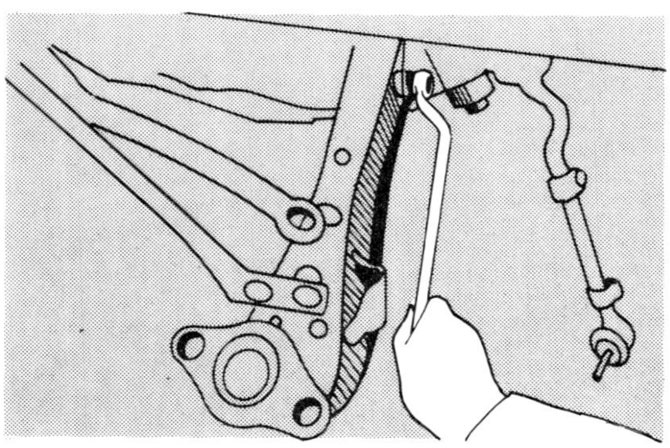

Fig. 4-6. Track control arm being unbolted from front suspension crossmember.

8. To remove the steering arm, first clamp the steering arm in a vise, making sure that the vise jaws do not deform the hole for the tie rod end's ball stud. Then remove the cotter pin and the castellated nut. Use a puller as shown in Fig. 4-7 to remove the steering arm from the ball joint stud.

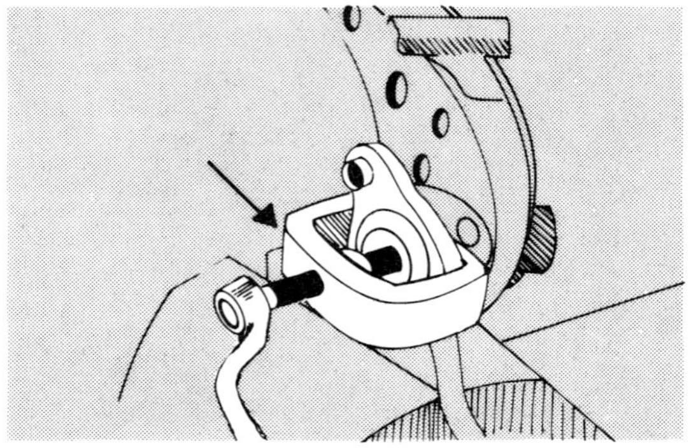

Fig. 4-7. Steering arm being pulled off track control arm's ball joint stud using special puller (arrow). Conventional gear puller can also be used.

To install:

1. Inspect the track control arm. If necessary, replace the ball joint dust seal or the bushings as described under the next heading. If the track control arm is in any way damaged or distorted, or if the ball joint is no longer serviceable, replace the track control arm as a unit.
2. If necessary, press collars into the bolt holes of the steering arm. Each collar should project about 5 mm (or about $^{3}/_{16}$ in.) above the upper surface of the arm. Wipe clean the ball joint stud. Then insert the ball stud into the steering arm.
3. With the steering arm clamped in a vise, install the castellated nut to a torque of 80 to 90 Nm (59 to 66 ft. lb.). If necessary, advance the nut to uncover the cotter pin hole, then install a new cotter pin.
4. Install the track control arm on the front suspension crossmember. Then install the bolt and the mounting plate with captive nut. Torque the bolt to 80 to 90 Nm (59 to 66 ft. lb.).
5. Reconnect the strut bar to the track control arm, torquing the nuts and bolts to 45 to 55 Nm (33 to 41 ft. lb.).
6. Reconnect the stabilizer bar to the track control arm. Install the first nut to a torque of 15 to 20 Nm (11 to 15 ft. lb.). Then install the jam nut to a torque of 10 to 15 Nm (7.5 to 11 ft. lb.). If necessary, consult **4.2 Removing and Installing Stabilizer Bar.**
7. Pull down the track control arm. Guide the suspension strut's wheel spindle down onto the collars of the steering arm. Install the bolts through the centers of the collars, torquing the bolts to 80 to 90 Nm (59 to 66 ft. lb.).

8. Install the road wheel. Torque the wheel lugs to 90 to 120 Nm (66 to 89 ft. lb.). Lower the car to the ground, then check and, if necessary, adjust the front wheel toe as described in **3.1 Checking and Adjusting Front Wheel Toe.**

Repairing Track Control Arm

The suspension ball joint cannot be replaced separately. If it is faulty, replace the track control arm as unit.

To replace the ball joint dust seal, first clean thoroughly the outside of the dust seal and all nearby parts of the track control arm. Pry off the retaining ring for the dust seal as indicated in Fig. 4-8, then pull the dust seal off the ball joint.

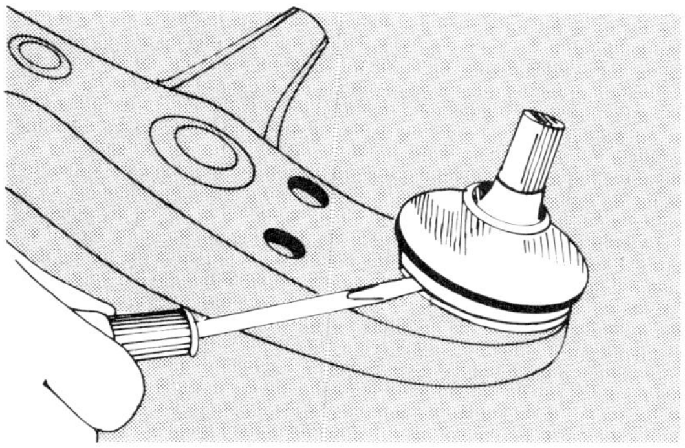

Fig. 4-8. Retaining ring for ball joint dust seal being pried off.

Before installing the new dust seal, apply molybdenum grease to the seal at points **A** and **B** as indicated in Fig. 4-9. Then install the dust seal so that the vent (item **C** in Fig. 4-9) is toward the rear of the car. Using wire or a new retaining ring, attach the lower end of the dust seal to the ball joint socket—being careful that you do not install a wire so tightly that it cuts into the rubber. Lubricate the ball joint with molybdenum grease that meets specification NLGI No. 1 or No. 2 before you return the car to service. See **LUBRICATION AND MAINTENANCE.**

To replace the track control arm bushings, press out the old bushings as indicated in Fig. 4-10. The large socket wrench should be big enough so that the bushing will enter it easily. The small socket wrench should be somewhat smaller than the outside diameter of the bushing, but must contact the outermost (metal) part of the bushing.

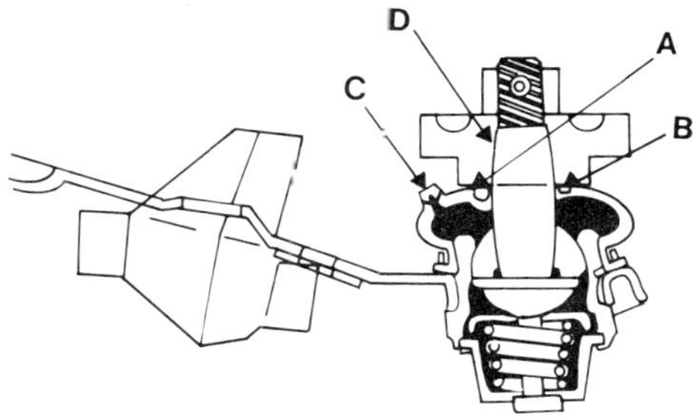

Fig. 4-9. Cross-section of suspension ball joint. Upper lips (**A** and **B**) of dust seal should be lubricated before you install seal. Vent (**C**) goes to rear. Surface **D** should be wiped clean of grease before steering arm is installed.

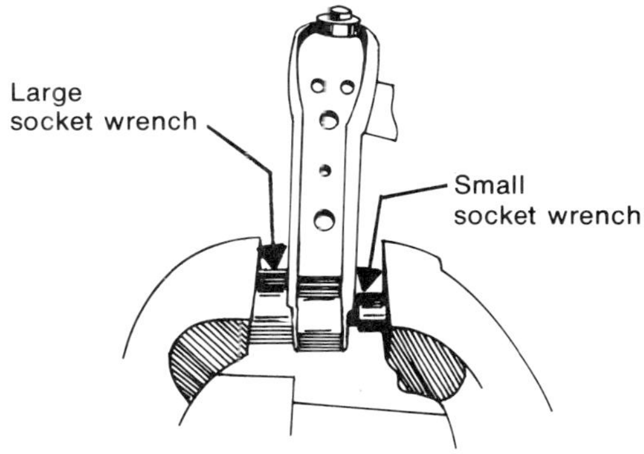

Fig. 4-10. Bushings being pressed out of, or into, track control arm.

To press in the new bushings, make sure that the small socket wrench bears against the outermost (metal) part of the bushing. There must be no oil or grease on either the bushing or in the bore of the track control arm. Press in the bushing as shown earlier in Fig. 4-10. The bushing must be pressed in from the front of the track control arm until the collar on the bushing assembly contacts the arm.

8

4.4 Removing and Installing Suspension Strut

It is best to remove the suspension strut with the brake assembly left on. If you wish to remove any part of the brake assembly separately, follow the instructions given in **BRAKES AND WHEELS.**

To remove suspension strut:

1. Raise the car on a hoist or support it on stands designed for the purpose. Remove the road wheel.

2. Thoroughly clean the brake line union that joins the brake hose on the strut to the steel brake line. Then disconnect the hose from the line and the mounting plate on the car body, as shown in Fig. 4-11. Quickly plug the steel line with a clean brake bleeder dust cap in order to prevent fluid leakage and the ingress of dirt.

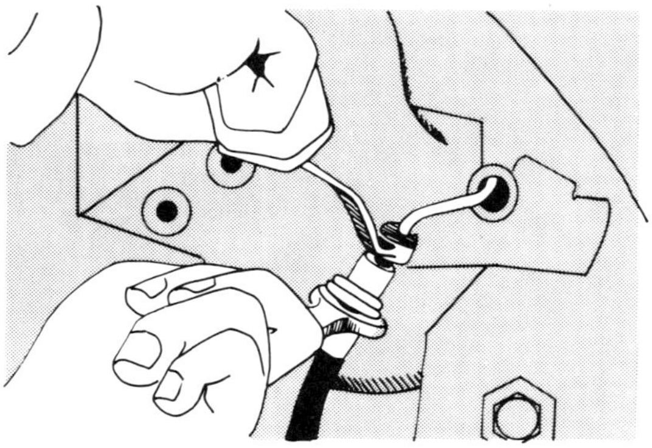

Fig. 4-11. Brake hose of strut being detached from brake line.

3. On cars that are equipped with an electronic brake pad wear indicator, disconnect the wires on the brake caliper from the car's wiring harness by separating the multiple connector.
4. Working inside the engine compartment, remove the three nuts that hold the suspension strut's upper bearing assembly to the car body. See Fig. 4-12.

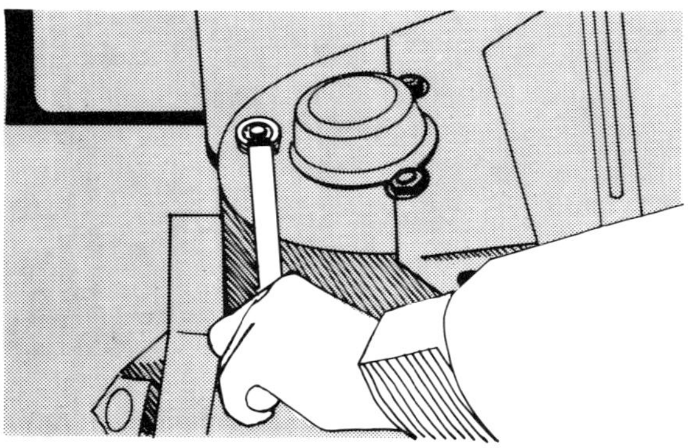

Fig. 4-12. Suspension strut being unbolted from car body.

5. Remove the two bolts that hold the suspension strut's wheel spindle to the steering arm. Pull down the track control arm so that you can disengage the strut from the collars on the steering arm and swing the strut aside. Then pull the strut downward and out of the car. See Fig. 4-13.

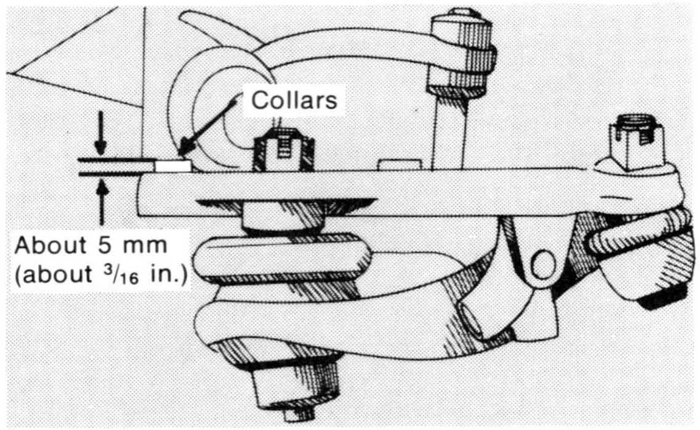

Fig. 4-13. Collars (one at arrow) and nut on ball joint stud that project up into strut's wheel spindle. Track control arm must be pried down so that collars disengage and you can swing strut aside over ball joint stud.

6. Clamp the strut in a vise as indicated in Fig. 4-14. Then remove the brake components. If necessary, consult the procedures given for removing each component in **BRAKES AND WHEELS.**

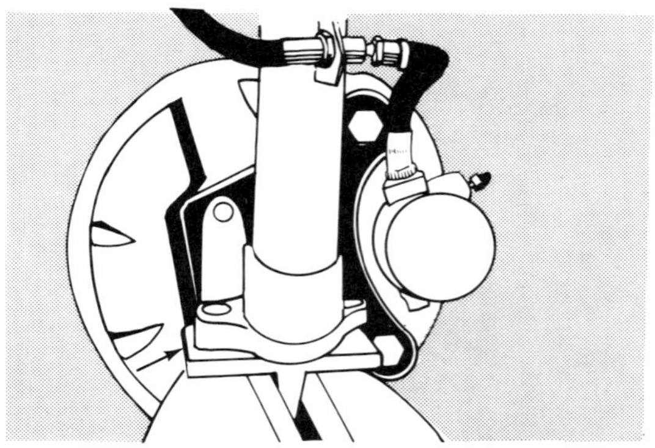

Fig. 4-14. Special holder (arrow) bolted to suspension strut so that strut can be held in vise. A similar tool can be made from two small sections of angle iron.

To install:

1. Install the brake components using the torque specifications, the lubricants, and the wheel bearing adjusting procedure given in **BRAKES AND WHEELS.**
2. Check that the collars on the steering arm project by about 5 mm (or about $^{3}/_{16}$ in.). See Fig. 4-14, given earlier.
3. Loosely position the strut on the car, guiding the three studs on its upper bearing assembly through the three holes in the car body, and then guiding the lower end down over the collars on the steering arm. Loosely install the two bolts that hold the strut's wheel spindle to the steering arm.

4. Install the nuts and the lock washers that hold the strut's upper bearing assembly to the car body. Torque the nuts to 20 to 30 Nm (15 to 22 ft. lb.).
5. Torque the two bolts that hold the strut's wheel spindle to the steering arm to 80 to 90 Nm (59 to 66 ft. lb.).
6. If necessary, reconnect the wires for the brake pad wear indicator.
7. Lightly lubricate the threads with clean brake fluid, then reconnect the brake hose to the brake line and the mounting.
8. Lower the car to the ground. Then bleed the brakes as described in **BRAKES AND WHEELS.**

4.5 Disassembling and Assembling Suspension Strut

If the wheel spindle is in good condition and if the outer shell of the strut is not bent, dented, or severely corroded, you can rebuild the strut's internal shock absorber using the procedure given under this heading. A separate procedure is given for removing and installing the spring. Some shock absorbers are cartridge-type units. On these, all of the internal parts can be replaced simply by removing the old shock absorber cartridge and installing a new one. Other shock absorbers can be rebuilt by replacing individual components or by replacing all of the internal components with those included in a rebuilding kit.

If the strut's outer shell or its wheel spindle has been physically damaged, you should replace the suspension strut as a unit. The wheel spindle cannot be removed from the strut.

To remove spring:

1. With the strut mounted in a vise (see Fig. 4-14, given earlier), compress the spring using a suitable spring compressor (Fig. 4-15).

   ***WARNING* ——**

   Be sure that you use a suitable spring compressor and that it is correctly installed on the spring. Do not attempt to compress the spring with makeshift equipment. If an even slightly compressed spring should suddenly fly loose from the spring compressor, it could injure you severely.

2. Remove the upper bearing dust cover. Insert a screwdriver into a hole in the upper spring seat to prevent it from turning. Then remove the nut from the piston rod as indicated in Fig. 4-16.
3. Remove the suspension strut upper bearing assembly, the dust seal, the upper spring seat, the piston rod's dust cover, the spring, the buffer seat, and the strut buffer.

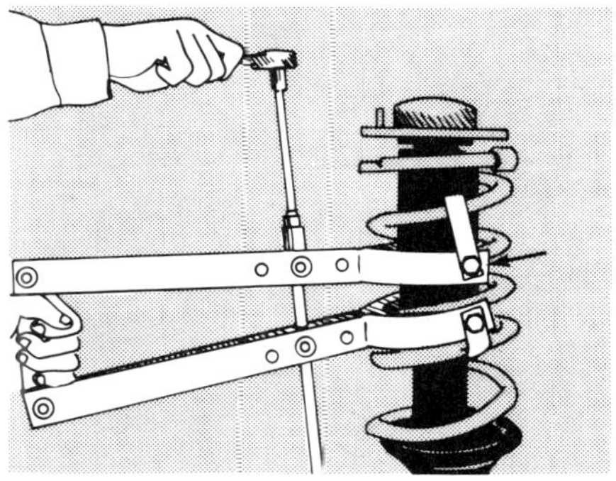

Fig. 4-15. Special spring compressor (arrow) being used to compress spring on suspension strut.

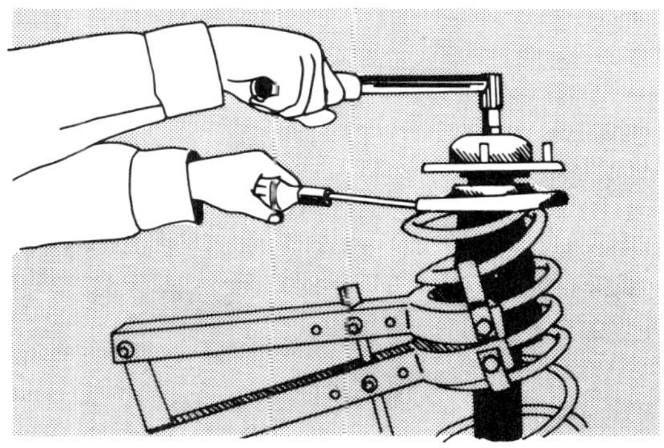

Fig. 4-16. Nut being removed from piston rod while upper spring seat is held stationary with screwdriver.

To install spring:

1. Install the strut buffer and the buffer seat on the piston rod—using a new buffer if the original buffer is worn or damaged.
2. Position the spring on the suspension strut—making sure that it is correctly seated on the strut's lower spring support. Install the piston rod's dust cover, the upper spring seat, the dust seal, and the upper bearing assembly. See Fig. 4-17.

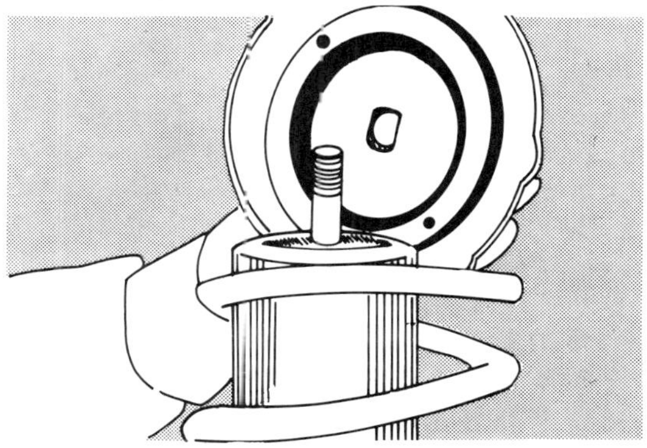

Fig. 4-17. Upper spring seat being installed. Flat sides of elongated hole must engage flats on piston rod.

3. While holding the upper spring seat (and thus the piston rod) stationary with a screwdriver, as you did during disassembly, install the nut on the piston rod to a torque of 45 to 50 Nm (33 to 37 ft. lb.). Install the upper bearing dust cover.
4. Hand-turn the upper spring seat until it is correctly aligned with the upper end of the spring. Then, while guiding the spring into its upper seat, gradually loosen the spring compressor.
5. Remove the spring compressor. Remove the suspension strut from the vise.

To rebuild shock absorber:

1. Remove the suspension strut and take off the brake components. Then remove the spring and related parts as described in the preceding procedure.

NOTE ——
Before you decide to go to the trouble and expense of rebuilding the shock absorber, check the condition and the physical dimensions of the wheel spindle. If possible, you should have the spindle crack-tested by the Magnaflux® process. Do not rebuild a strut that has a cracked, worn, or damaged wheel spindle.

2. With the lower end of the strut clamped in a vise (see Fig. 4-14, given earlier), use Toyota special tool 09728-14010 as indicated in Fig. 4-18 to remove the gland nut from the top of the strut tube.

NOTE ——
On later cars the special tool may not be necessary because the gland nut has a conventional hexagonal shape.

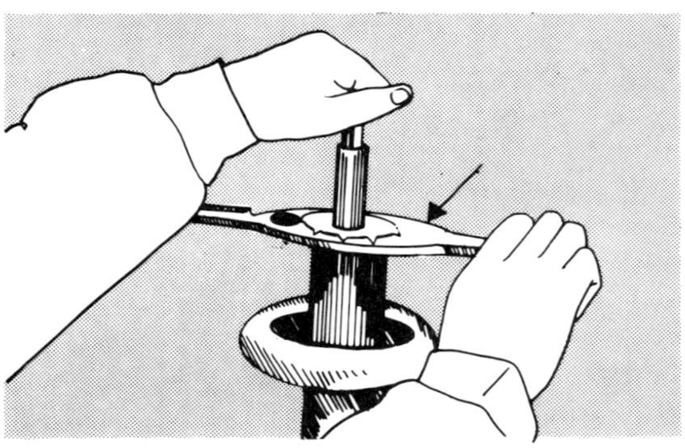

Fig. 4-18. Gland nut being removed from around piston rod using special tool (arrow). Be careful not to damage oil seal which is inside nut.

3. Using a darning needle, pick out the seal shown in Fig. 4-19.
4. Carefully pull out the piston rod and the rod guide as shown in Fig. 4-19. Then take out the cylinder. Remove the strut from the vise, and pour out the fluid.

NOTE ——
If you are rebuilding a strut that has a cartridge-type shock absorber, remove the entire cartridge by pulling on the piston rod. Then thoroughly clean the interior of the strut's shell. Install the new cartridge-type shock absorber and reassemble the strut as described beginning with step 22.

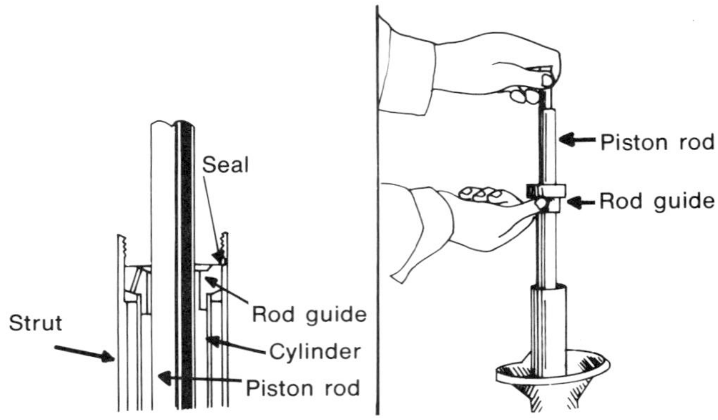

Fig. 4-19. Piston rod and rod guide being removed. First pick out seal indicated at left with darning needle. Then pull out piston rod and rod guide as shown at right.

5. Using a wooden dowel about 450 mm (about 18 in.) long, drive out the base valve, which is a press-fit in the bottom of the cylinder. See Fig. 4-20.

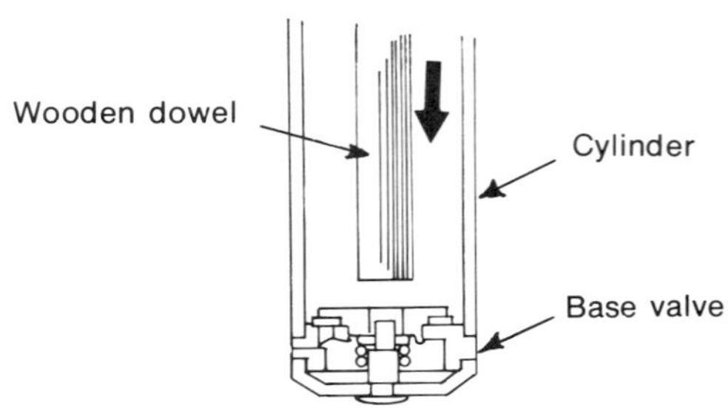

Fig. 4-20. Wooden dowel being inserted in cylinder (arrow) so that dowel can be used to drive out base valve, which is a press-fit.

6. Using screwdrivers inserted into the slots in the side of the base valve, pry the base valve from the base valve case. See Fig. 4-21.
7. Clamp the flats on the upper end of the piston rod in a vise that has soft jaws. Alternatively, clamp the flats between pieces of sheet aluminum.

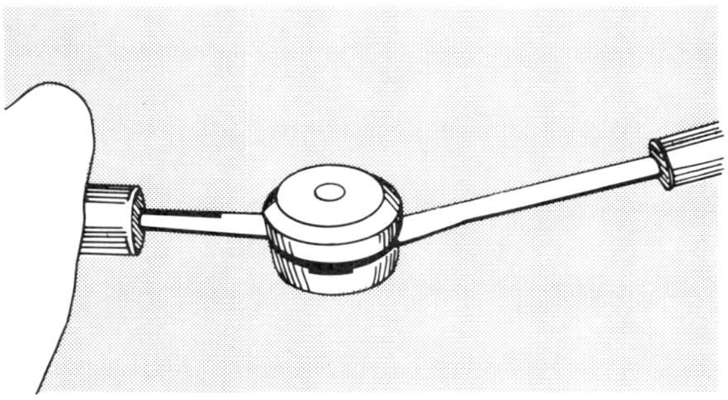

Fig. 4-21. Screwdrivers being used to pry base valve out of base valve case.

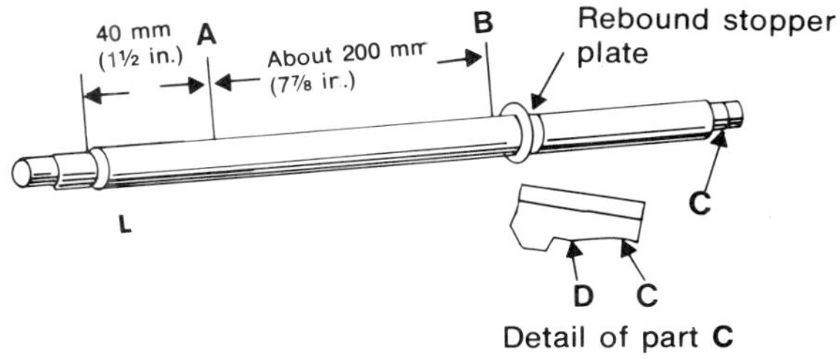

Fig. 4-23. Piston rod being inspected. There must be no wear between points **A** and **B**, which mark contact area for rod guide and gland-nut seal. Threads are at **C**. Surface **D** is for piston valve and must not be worn.

8. Remove the piston nut. Then remove the components indicated in Fig. 4-22.

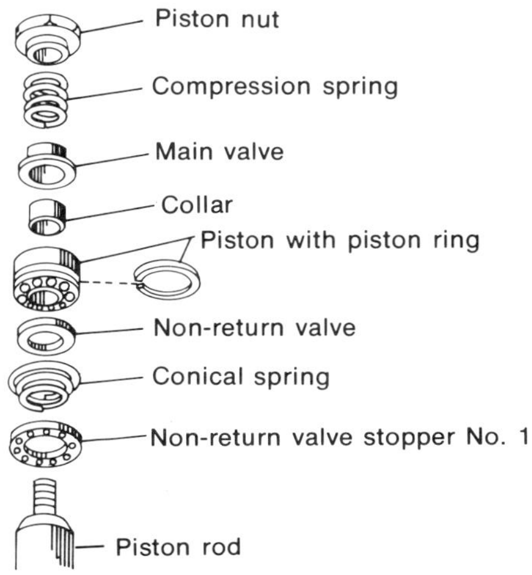

Fig. 4-22. Exploded view showing piston components removed from piston rod.

9. Carefully inspect the piston rod. The surface from **A** to **B**, as given in Fig. 4-23, must be absolutely smooth and not worn at any point to a diameter of less than 21.90 mm (.8622 in.). Even a small injury, such as pitted plating, on this surface could cause fluid leakage. Make sure that the threads (**C** in Fig. 4-23) for the piston nut and the piston valve contact surface (**D** in Fig. 4-23) are in flawless condition.

NOTE —

If a cartridge-type replacement shock absorber is not available for the strut, you can either replace individual parts (after inspecting the original parts to determine which ones are faulty) or replace the entire piston rod, the piston assembly, and all related parts with a rebuilding kit. Fluid is not included in this kit and must be obtained separately.

10. Make sure that the piston rod is not bent. You can do this by rolling it on a flat surface, such as a sheet of plate glass, or you can support the ends of the rod on V-blocks, then rotate it against the gauge pin of a dial indicator positioned at the middle of the rod. The runout should not exceed 0.30 mm (.0118 in.).

11. Carefully inspect the piston. Neither the contact surface for the non-return valve nor the contact surface for the main valve should be in any way worn or damaged. The piston should not be worn to an elliptical shape or to a diameter of less than 31.80 mm (1.2519 in.).

12. Inspect the remaining parts of the piston assembly and replace any that is worn or damaged. It is advisable to replace any piston ring that is worn so that it tapers toward its ends or has a conspicuous gap when placed inside the cylinder.

NOTE —

Measured at the point where the piston slides into the cylinder, the inside diameter of the cylinder should not exceed 32.23 mm (1.2689 in.). Replace faulty cylinders.

13. Inspect the base valve components indicated in Fig. 4-24. The contact surface for the sub-valve must be free of all wear or damage. The valve guide pin must not be loose where it is staked or peened to the base valve case.

8

1. Conical spring
2. Non-return valve
3. Sub-valve
4. Main base valve
5. Sub-valve contact surface
6. Staking or peening that holds guide

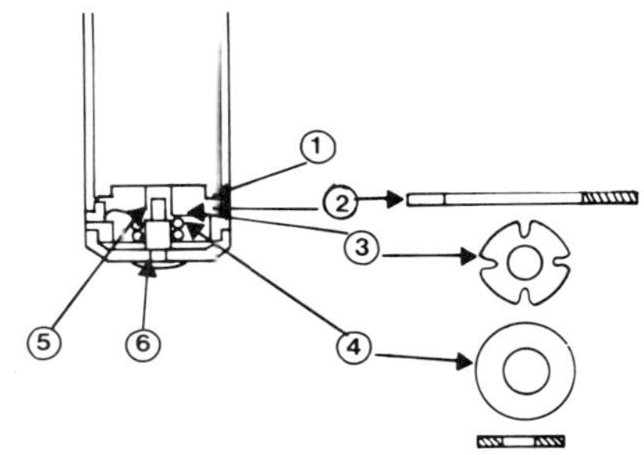

Fig. 4-24. Components of base valve assembly. Replace base valve as a unit if any part is distorted, corroded, or otherwise damaged.

14. Check the cylinder for bending. To do this, either roll it on a flat surface, such as a sheet of plate glass, or support its ends on V-blocks and rotate the cylinder against the gauge pin of a dial indicator located at the middle of the cylinder. The runout should not exceed 0.10 mm (.0039 in.). Replace bent, scored, or dented cylinders.

15. Measure the inside diameter of the bushing inside the rod guide. The bushing should not be eccentric, scored, or worn to an inside diameter greater than 22.35 mm (.8799 in.). Replace worn rod guides as a unit.

16. If the shock absorber was leaking around the piston rod, or if the oil seal inside the gland nut is hard, cracked, or deformed, pry out the old oil seal. Then, using a vise and Toyota special tool 09742-14010 as indicated in Fig. 4-25, press in a new oil seal.

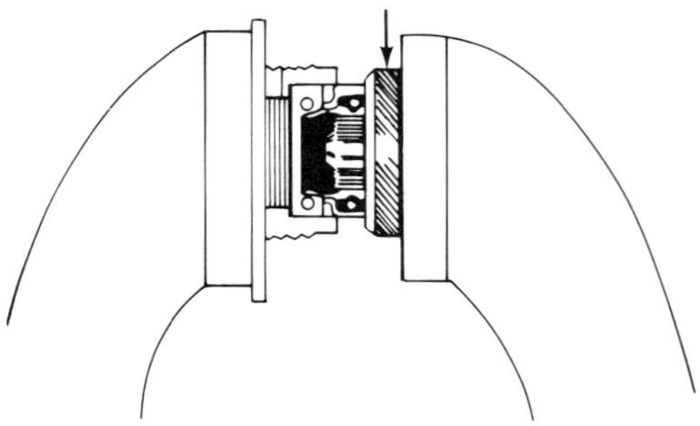

Fig. 4-25. Oil seal being pressed into gland nut using special tool (arrow).

17. Assemble the piston components on the piston rod in the order previously given in Fig. 4-22, loosely installing the piston nut.

18. With the flats on the upper end of the piston rod clamped between pieces of aluminum or in a vise with soft jaws, carefully set the position of the non-return valve into the center of the non-return valve stopper. Then, using a completely clean socket wrench, torque the piston nut to 20 to 30 Nm (15 to 22 ft. lb.).

19. Using a sharp punch, stake the piston nut at four places as indicated in Fig. 4-26.

20. Press the base valve into its case. Then, using a soft hammer, drive the base valve assembly into the cylinder. See Fig. 4-27.

21. Lubricate the piston with fluid (see step 23). Then, being very careful not to damage or break the piston ring, insert the piston rod into the cylinder—piston-end first.

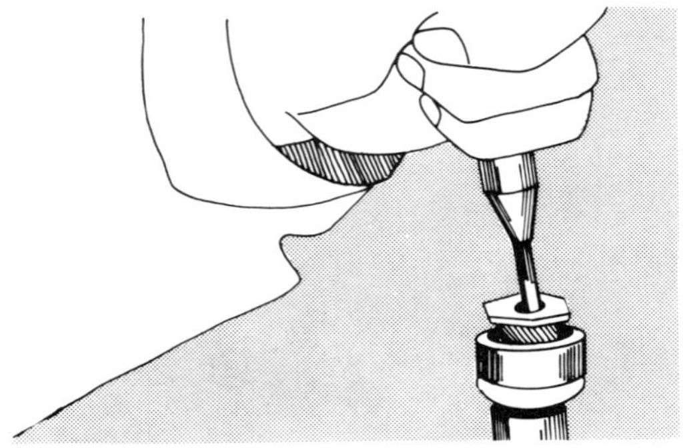

Fig. 4-26. Piston nut being staked to piston rod.

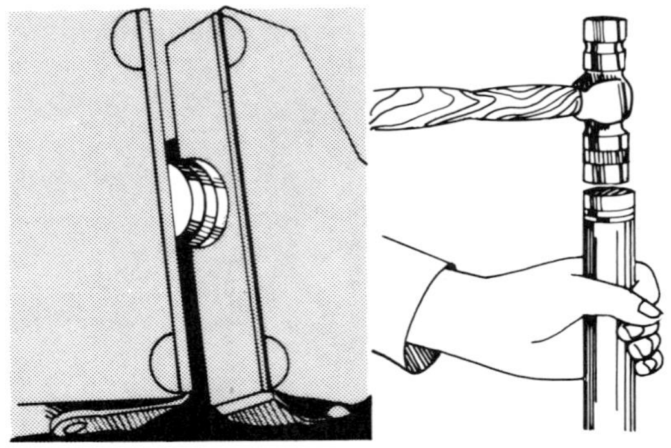

Fig. 4-27. Left: vise being used to press base valve into its case. **Right**: soft hammer being used to drive base valve assembly into cylinder.

22. Insert the cylinder together with the piston rod into the strut's outer shell. Alternatively, on cars that are so-equipped, insert an entire new cartridge-type shock absorber into the shell, then go on to step 26.

23. Push the piston rod fully down into the cylinder. Fill the strut's shell with 315 ml or cm³ (19.2 in.³ or 10¾ oz.) of either Dexron® or Type F automatic transmission fluid (ATF). If necessary, pull up the piston rod in order to draw fluid into the cylinder.

24. Lubricate the rod guide bushing with ATF. Then insert the rod guide in the strut's shell—pushing the guide down over the piston rod so that it enters the cylinder correctly.

25. Lubricate a new rod guide seal with fluid. Then, using a blunt, smooth tool, press the seal into the gap formed between the top of the rod guide and the strut's shell.

26. Apply a light coating of multipurpose grease to the lip of the oil seal in the gland nut. Pull the piston rod up by about 80 to 90 mm (about 3³⁄₁₆ to 3½ in.). Being very careful not to damage the oil seal, slip the gland nut down over the piston rod and hand-start it in its threads. See Fig. 4-28.

NOTE —

One way to avoid damaging the oil seal is to wrap the upper part of the piston rod with a single layer of plastic electrical tape. This will cover all sharp edges, and allow the seal to slide down smoothly onto the rod.

27. Using an appropriate wrench, as shown in Fig. 4-28, torque the gland nut to 125 to 145 Nm (92 to 107 ft. lb.), keeping the piston rod pulled up 80 to 90 mm (about 3$^3/_{16}$ to 3½ in.) as in the preceding step.

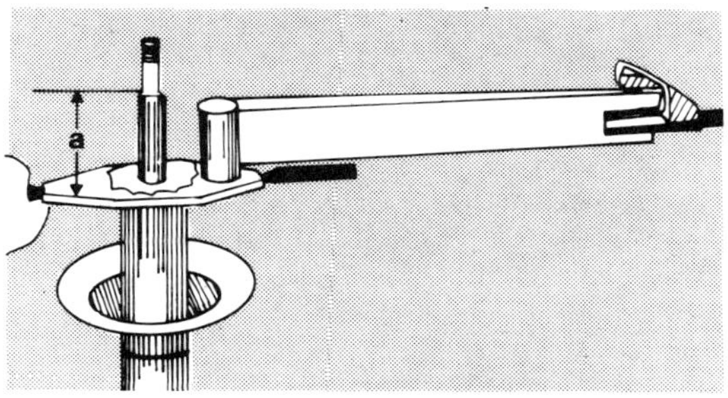

Fig. 4-28. Gland nut being installed and torqued. Dimension **a** is 80 to 90 mm (about 3$^3/_{16}$ to 3½ in.).

28. Install the spring and related parts as described in the preceding procedure. Then install the suspension strut on the car.

4.6 Removing and Installing Front Suspension Crossmember

If the front suspension crossmember is deformed or damaged, it may upset the front wheel alignment. You can check the crossmember against the dimensions given in Fig. 4-29. If the crossmember is deformed or damaged, replace it. Unless you are a skilled body repairman or metal fabricator, you should not attempt to bend the old crossmember back to its original shape or to weld it if it is broken.

To remove:

1. Working in the engine compartment, remove the nuts that hold the engine mounts to the front suspension crossmember.
2. Place a steel bar or a length of two-by-four lumber across the front of the engine compartment so that its ends rest solidly on the part of the body that is contacted by the hood when the hood is closed. Then, using a chain or strong rope, tie the front engine-hoisting hook tightly to the steel bar or the two-by-four. Alternatively, you can support the front of the engine with a jack.

Fig. 4-29. Critical dimensions of front suspension crossmember. (Dimensions given are in millimeters with inch equivalents in parentheses.)

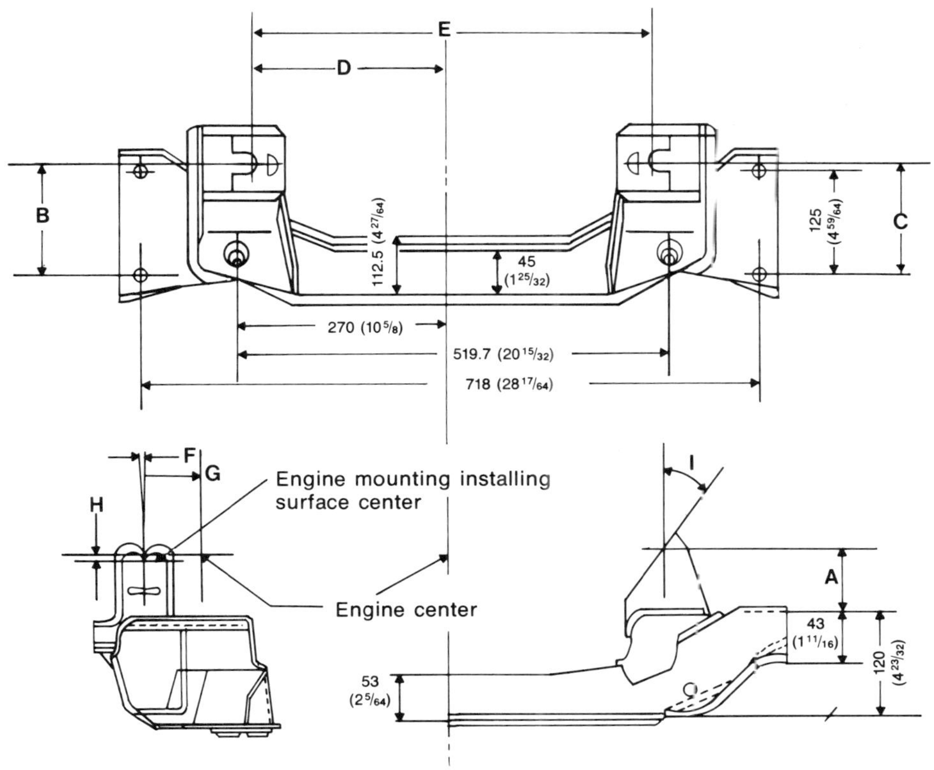

A = 56.6 mm (2$^7/_{32}$ in.)
B = 129 mm (5$^5/_{64}$ in.)
C = 129 mm (5$^5/_{64}$ in.)
D = 220 mm (8$^{21}/_{32}$ in.)
E = 453 mm (17$^{53}/_{64}$ in.)
F = 3° 10′
G = 60 mm (2$^{23}/_{64}$ in.)
H = 1.5 mm ($^1/_{16}$ in.)
I = 45°

3. Raise the car on a hoist or support it on stands designed for the purpose. Remove the splash shield that is beneath the front of the engine.
4. Remove the bolts that hold the inner ends of the front suspension's track control arms to the front suspension crossmember. Carefully lower the arms from the crossmember so that the ball joints will not be damaged.
5. Unbolt the outer ends of the front suspension crossmember from the car body. Then lower the crossmember and remove it from the car.

To install:

1. If the old crossmember is in any way damaged, replace it.
2. Install the front suspension crossmember on the car body. Torque the bolts to 45 to 50 Nm (33 to 37 ft. lb.).
3. Reattach the track control arms to the front suspension crossmember. Torque the bolts to 80 to 90 Nm (59 to 66 ft. lb.).
4. Install the splash shield beneath the engine.
5. Lower the car to the ground. Install the nuts that hold the engine mounts to the front suspension crossmember. Torque the nuts to 30 to 40 Nm (22 to 30 ft. lb.).
6. If previously installed, remove the engine support device (the bar or the two-by-four).

5. REAR SUSPENSION

Removal and installation of the rear axle is described in **5.3 Removing and Installing Rear Axle.** It is not necessary, however, to remove the axle from the car for most rear axle repairs. Rear axle repairs are described in **DRIVESHAFT AND REAR AXLE.**

5.1 Checking and Replacing Rear Shock Absorbers

Rear shock absorbers cannot be repaired or serviced and should be replaced if faulty. You can quickly check the shock absorbers by grasping the rear bumper and jouncing the car vigorously. When you let go, the car should rebound only once and then settle into its normal attitude. If the car continues to rock or bob, the shock absorbers are worn. Excessive bobbing on the highway also signals defective shock absorbers. Badly worn shock absorbers often make knocking noises when the car is driven.

You can hand-check a removed shock absorber by extending and compressing it while holding it in its installed position. It should operate smoothly and with uniform resistance throughout its entire stroke. If possible, compare the used shock absorber with a new one. New shock absorbers that have been in storage may have to be pumped several times before they reach full efficiency.

An adequate supply of fluid is placed in the shock absorbers during manufacture to compensate for small leaks. Minor traces of fluid are acceptable if the shock absorber still functions efficiently. To ensure good handling, it is best to replace both shock absorbers on the axle at the same time.

To replace:

1. Raise the car on a hoist or support it on stands designed for the purpose. If you raise the rear wheels only, chock the front wheels to prevent the car from rolling.
2. Unbolt the lower end of the shock absorber. See Fig. 5-1.

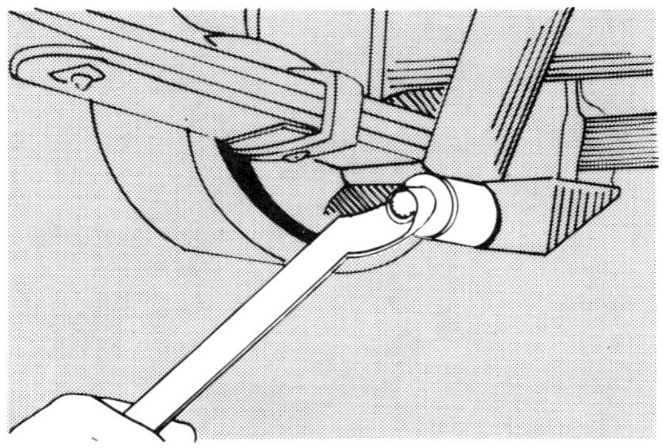

Fig. 5-1. Lower end of shock absorber being unbolted from U-bolt seat for rear spring.

3. Except on station wagon models, remove the rear seat. Then, using two wrenches as indicated in Fig. 5-2, remove the nuts that hold the shock absorber piston rod to the car body. Remove the shock absorber.

NOTE ——
Remove the upper nut while you hold the lower nut stationary. Then hold the piston rod stationary by installing a wrench on the rod flats while you remove the lower nut.

4. Working beneath station wagon models, remove the three bolts that hold the shock absorber upper mounting to the car body (Fig. 5-2). Then remove the shock absorber and detach it from the upper mounting.

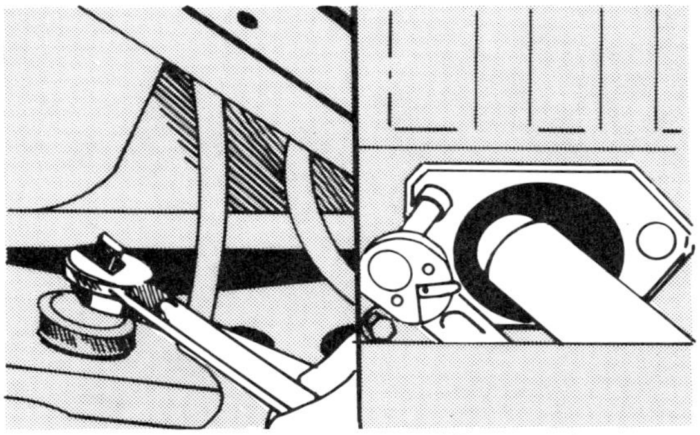

Except wagon Wagon only

Fig. 5-2. Left: upper end of shock absorber being unbolted (except wagon). **Right**: shock absorber upper mounting being unbolted from underside of station wagon.

5. Check the shock absorber as described earlier under this heading. If the shock absorber is in any way faulty, replace it.
6. Inspect the shock absorber mounting components. Replace any that is worn, corroded, or otherwise damaged.
7. Making sure that you install the mounting components in their correct positions (Fig. 5-3), attach the upper end of the shock absorber to its upper mounting (wagon) or to the car body (except wagon). Tighten the lower nut until the piston rod is held firmly—but do not greatly compress the rubber cushions. Then hold the lower nut stationary while you torque the upper nut to 20 to 30 Nm (15 to 22 ft. lb.).
8. On station wagons only, install the upper mounting on the car body. Torque the bolts to 15 to 20 Nm (11 to 15 ft. lb.).
9. Making sure that you install the mounting components in their correct positions (Fig. 5-3), attach the lower end of the shock absorber to the spring's U-bolt seat. Torque the bolt to 20 to 30 Nm (15 to 22 ft. lb.).
10. Lower the car to the ground. Except on station wagons, install the rear seat.

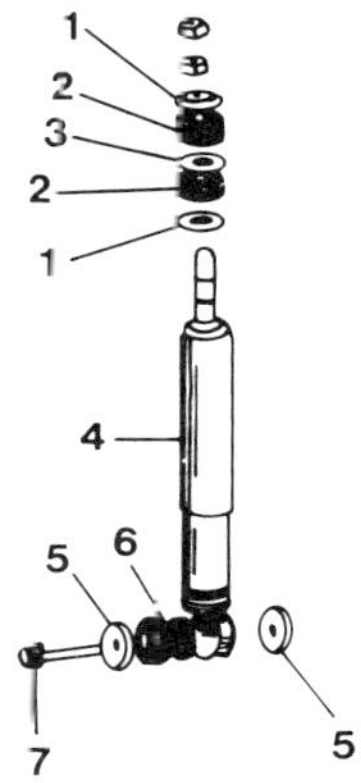

1. Retainer plate for shock absorber cushion
2. Shock absorber cushion
3. Reinforcement plate for shock absorber cushion
4. Rear shock absorber
5. Washer for shock absorber bushing
6. Shock absorber bushing
7. Bolt

Fig. 5-3. Exploded view giving installed positions of shock absorber mounting components.

5.2 Removing and Installing Rear Spring

Fig. 5-4 is an exploded view of a rear spring and its mounting components. Normally, the rear springs need to be disassembled only for cleaning and replacing the silencer pads. Individual spring leaves are not available as replacement parts. A used spring leaf can be installed if it is in good condition. But if a good used leaf is unavailable, the entire spring should be replaced if it is sagging or has one or more broken leaves.

> ***WARNING —***
> *Clamp the spring near its center in a vise while you remove the spring clips and the center bolt. Otherwise there is a possibility that the spring might fly apart and injure you. With the bolt and clips removed, gradually loosen the vise until no spring tension remains, then remove the spring leaves from the vise and separate them.*

To remove spring:

1. Raise the car on a hoist, or support it on stands designed for the purpose, so that the rear wheels are off the ground and the rear springs are unloaded. If you raise the rear wheels only, chock the front wheels to prevent the car from rolling. Remove the road wheel.
2. Remove the bolt that holds the lower end of the shock absorber to the U-bolt seat. If necessary, consult Fig. 5-1, given earlier.

Fig. 5-4. Exploded view of rear spring mounting components and rear springs.

1. Rear spring assembly
2. Differential carrier bumper
3. U-bolt
4. Rear spring rebound stop
5. Spring pad retainer
6. Nut
7. Lock washer
8. Spring shackle outer plate
9. Bushings
10. Spring shackle
11. Bolt
12. Spring bracket pin
13. Bushings
14. U-bolt seat
15. Nut with lock washer for U-bolt
16. Rear spring center bolt
17. Rear spring main (No. 1) leaf
18. Rear spring silencer pad
19. Rear spring No. 2 leaf
20. Rear spring No. 3 leaf
21. Rear spring No. 4 leaf
22. Rear spring No. 1 clip
23. Round head rivet
24. Rear spring No. 2 clip
25. Round head rivet
26. Spacer
27. Nut
28. Rear spring No. 5 left
29. Rear spring No. 3 clip

3. Remove the four nuts and lock washers that hold the U-bolts to the U-bolt seat. See Fig. 5-5.

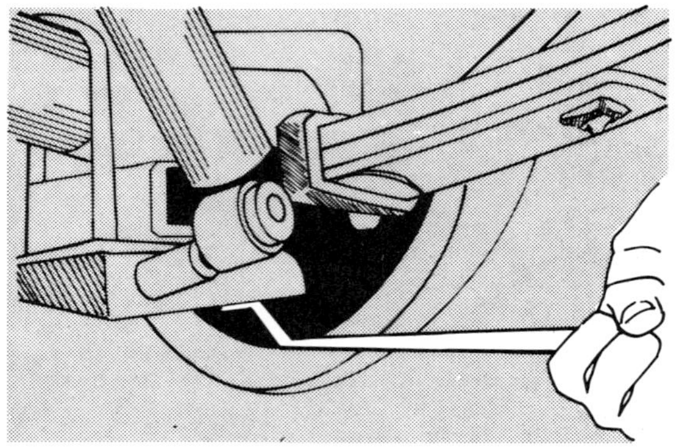

Fig. 5-5. Nut being removed from U-bolt. Notice how shock absorber has been pulled away from boss on U-bolt seat.

4. Remove the U-bolts, the U-bolt seat, the spring pad retainer and related parts.
5. Support the rear axle with a stand or a jack, lifting it free of the spring.

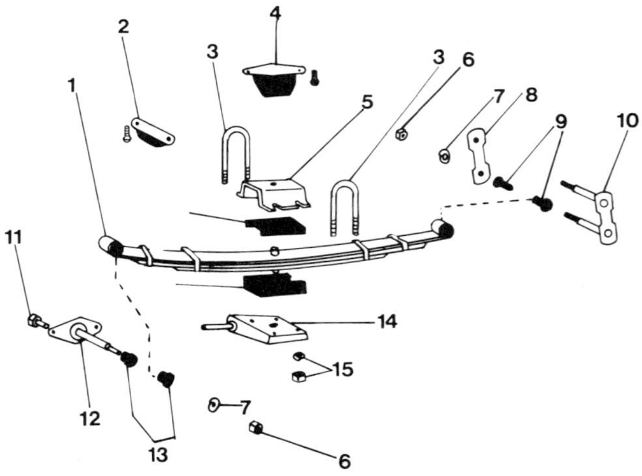

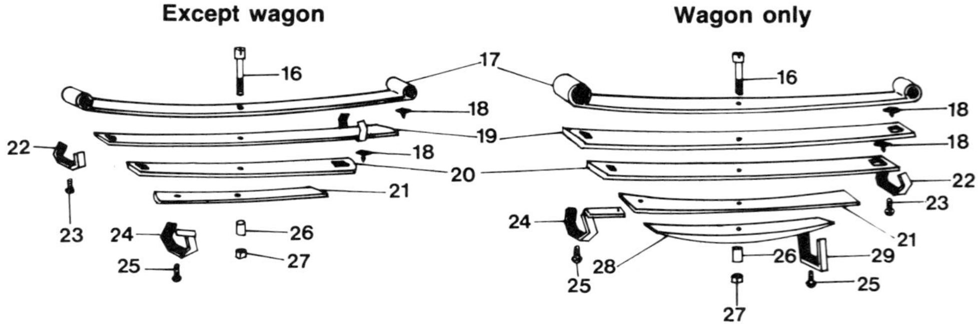

6. Remove the nuts and the lock washers that hold the spring shackle outer plate to the pins of the spring shackle. Then pry the shackle out of the eye at the rear of the spring's main leaf and out of the bracket on the body. See Fig. 5-6.
7. Remove the nut and the lock washer from the end of the spring bracket pin. Remove the two bolts that hold the spring bracket pin to the bracket. Then pry out the spring bracket pin as indicated in Fig. 5-6 and remove the spring from the car.

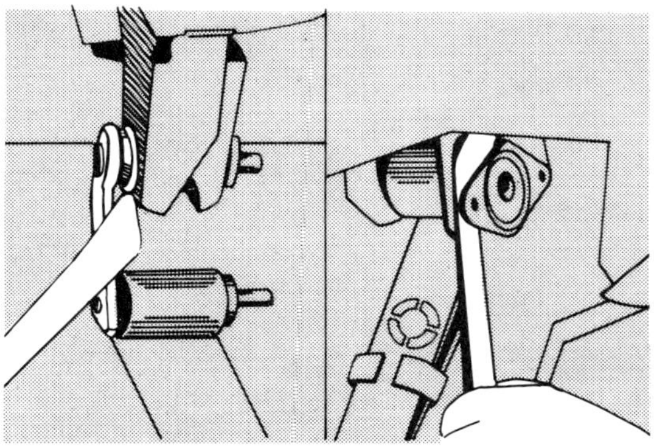

Fig. 5-6. Left: spring shackle being pried out of spring and bracket on body. **Right**: spring bracket pin being pried out of bracket. Be careful not to lose or damage bushings or deform threads.

Installation is the reverse of removal. Inspect all parts and replace any that is worn, corroded, or otherwise damaged. Torque the bolts that hold the spring bracket pin to the bracket to 10 to 15 Nm (7.5 to 11 ft. lb.). Torque the nut for the bracket pin to 45 to 50 Nm (33 to 37 ft. lb.). Torque the nuts that hold the spring and the shackle outer plate to the rear spring shackle to 45 to 50 Nm (33 to 37 ft. lb.). Carefully align the center bolt's head with the hole in the rear axle's spring mounting, then install the U-bolts and related parts. Torque the nuts for the U-bolts to 35 to 45 Nm (26 to 33 ft. lb.). Torque the bolt for the shock absorber to 20 to 30 Nm (15 to 22 ft. lb.). Torque the wheel lugs to 90 to 120 Nm (66 to 89 ft. lb.).

5.3 Removing and Installing Rear Axle

You can repair the working parts of the rear axle without removing the rear axle from the car. This work is described in **DRIVESHAFT AND REAR AXLE.** The procedure given here is for removing the complete rear axle assembly from the car. Some steps in the procedure may be unnecessary if you have already removed the working parts from the rear axle.

To remove:

1. Raise the car on a hoist or support it on stands designed for the purpose. If you raise the rear wheels only, chock the front wheels to prevent the car from rolling.
2. Using a file or a center punch, mark adjacent points on the rear axle's pinion flange and the rear universal joint so that the driveshaft can be reinstalled in its original position on the pinion flange. Then remove the driveshaft as described in **DRIVESHAFT AND REAR AXLE.**
3. Remove both rear road wheels.
4. Detach the parking brake cables from the parking brake equalizer, which is beneath the car and just to the rear of the handbrake lever location. If necessary, consult **BRAKES AND WHEELS.**
5. Disconnect the rear of the brake hose that connects the rear brake hydraulic line to the 3-way union on the rear axle. Quickly plug the disconnected hose with a clean brake bleeder dust cap to prevent fluid leakage and the ingress of dirt.
6. Unbolt the rear shock absorbers at their lower ends. Remove the U-bolts and related parts that hold the rear springs to the rear axle. Then, with the rear axle supported solidly on stands or a floor jack with an axle adaptor, detach the rears of both springs from the car body by removing the shackles. If necessary, consult **5.2 Removing and Installing Rear Spring.**
7. Remove the rear axle from the car.

To install:

1. Position the rear axle beneath the rear of the car. Then reinstall the rear springs on their shackles, reattach the rear axle to the rear springs, and reconnect the lower ends of the shock absorbers. Use the procedures and the torque specifications given in **5.2 Removing and Installing Rear Spring.**
2. Reconnect the brake hose to the rear axle. Reconnect the parking brake cables to the equalizer. Then adjust the parking brake and bleed the rear brake circuit as described in **BRAKES AND WHEELS.**
3. With careful reference to the marks which you made prior to removal, install the driveshaft as described in **DRIVESHAFT AND REAR AXLE.** Torque the bolts that hold the driveshaft to the pinion flange to 35 to 40 Nm (26 to 30 ft. lb.). On cars with two-piece driveshafts, torque the bolts that hold the center bearing to the car body to 35 to 40 Nm (26 to 30 ft. lb.).
4. Install the road wheels. Torque the lugs to 90 to 120 Nm (66 to 89 ft. lb.). Then lower the car to the ground.

6. STEERING

Fig. 6-1 gives a horizontal cross section of the recirculating ball steering gearbox used on cars covered by this Manual. Because of annual changes, different gearbox suppliers, and product improvement modifications, not all of the steering gearboxes found on Corolla 1600s are identical. The basic design and the operating principles, however, are the same.

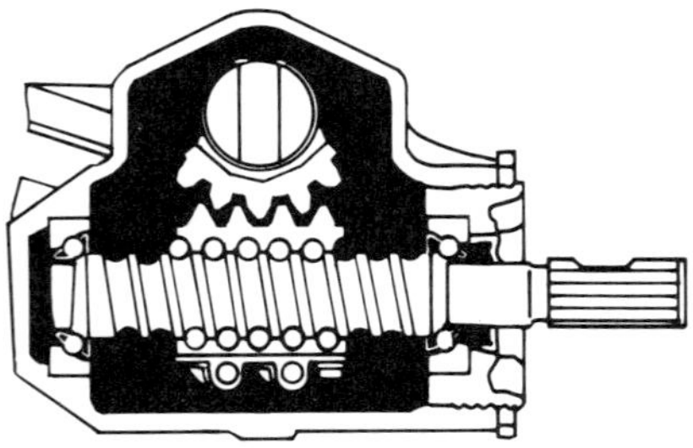

Fig. 6-1. Horizontal cross section of recirculating ball steering gearbox. Notice shape of groove in worm, which matches profile of balls. Balls recirculate between worm and ball nut as steering wheel is turned, causing ball nut to travel along worm and move gear sector shaft on which pitman arm is mounted.

6.1 Replacing Tie Rod Ends and Tie Rod End Dust Seals

Tie rod end dust seals are sometimes torn or pulled loose by driving in deep, crusted snow, driving over fallen branches, or by other road hazards. Once the dust seal is leaky, dirt and water can enter the tie rod end's ball joint, causing it to wear. Therefore, you should replace damaged or deteriorating dust seals immediately and, in the interest of safety and tire tread life, replace loose, worn, or damaged tie rod ends when these parts are inspected during routine maintenance.

To repair or replace tie rod end:

1. Raise the car on a hoist or support it on stands designed for the purpose.
2. If you are to replace a tie rod end or remove a tie rod end for repair, loosen the clamp bolt for that tie rod end.
3. Remove the cotter pin, then remove the castellated nut that holds the tie rod end stud to the steering arm or to the steering relay rod.
4. Use a tool such as the one shown in Fig. 6-2 to press the tie rod end's ball stud out of the steering arm or the relay rod.

CAUTION ——

Do not hammer out the tie rod ends. Doing this will ruin the threads and make reinstallation impossible.

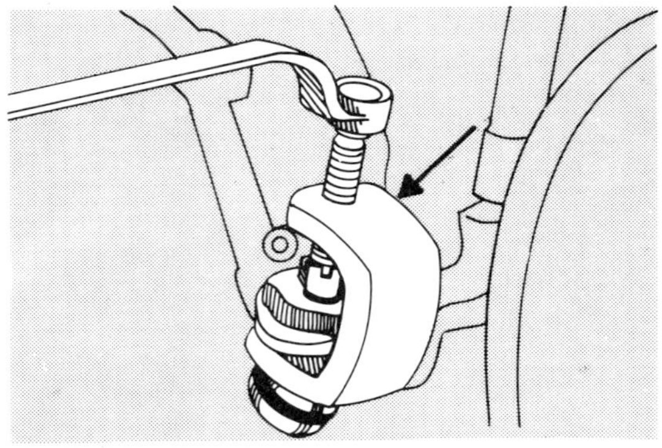

Fig. 6-2. Tie rod end removing tool (arrow) being used to press tie rod end's ball stud out of steering arm.

5. Counting carefully the number of turns required, grip the tie rod end and unscrew it from the tie rod.

NOTE ——

It is not necessary to remove the tie rod end in order to replace the dust seal as described in the next four steps.

6. If it is necessary to replace the dust seal, thoroughly clean the outside of the tie rod end to prevent road dirt from entering the tie rod end when the dust seal is removed.
7. Pry the dust seal retaining ring (or wire) out of the groove, then remove the old dust seal from the tie rod end. See Fig. 6-3.
8. Install the new dust seal—making sure that you do not press it down onto the ball stud so far that it slips off the taper and assumes a sunken-in look. See Fig. 6-3.

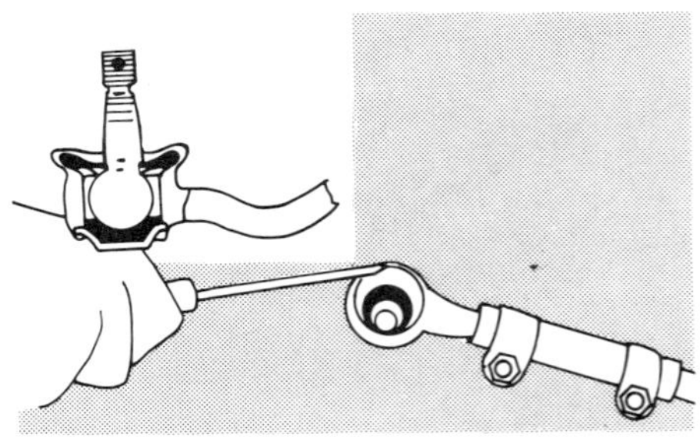

Fig. 6-3. Dust seal retaining ring being pried out. Insert gives cross-section of tie rod end with incorrectly installed dust seal. Seal should not be sunken in as shown, but should be seated on the long taper of the ball stud.

9. With the dust seal correctly installed, secure it to the tie rod end with a new retaining ring or with wire.

10. If you have fully removed the tie rod end, screw it into the tie rod using the same number of turns as were required to remove it.
11. Install the tie rod end's ball stud in the steering arm or the relay rod. Torque the castellated nut to 55 to 65 Nm (41 to 48 ft. lb.). Advance the nut, if necessary, to uncover the cotter pin hole. Then install a new cotter pin.
12. Lower the car to the ground. Then check and adjust the front wheel toe as described in **3.1 Checking and Adjusting Front Wheel Toe.**
13. With the toe correctly adjusted, make sure that the ball studs of the two tie rod ends on the tie rod are at 90° to one another. Then torque the clamp bolts to 15 to 20 Nm (11 to 15 ft. lb.).

6.2 Removing and Installing Steering Gearbox

The recirculating ball steering gearbox should be removed from the car for repairs or adjustment. It cannot be correctly adjusted while it is installed. Adjustment and repair are covered in **6.4 Disassembling and Assembling Steering Gearbox.**

To remove gearbox:

1. Raise the car on a hoist or support it on stands designed for the purpose.
2. Fully remove the clamp bolt that holds the steering column's flexible coupling to the steering gearbox worm shaft. See Fig. 6-4.

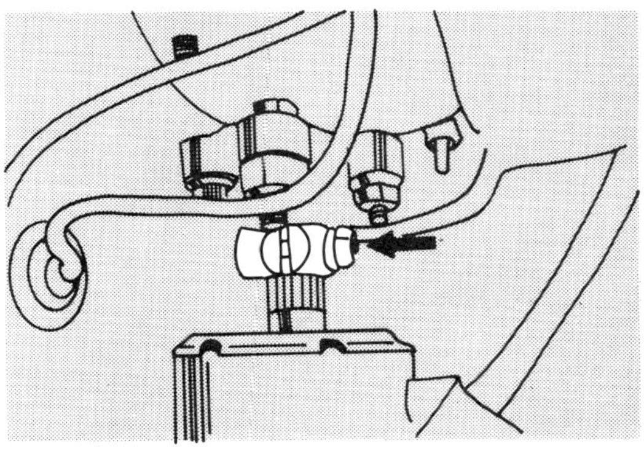

Fig. 6-4. Clamp bolt (arrow) that holds steering column's flexible coupling to worm shaft of steering gearbox.

3. Remove the cotter pin, then remove the castellated nut that holds the pitman arm's ball stud to the steering relay rod. Using a tool such as the one indicated in Fig. 6-5, press the pitman arm's ball stud out of the relay rod.

CAUTION ——
Do not hammer out the ball stud, which will ruin its threads and make reinstallation impossible. Do not hammer on the relay rod because this can bend or damage it.

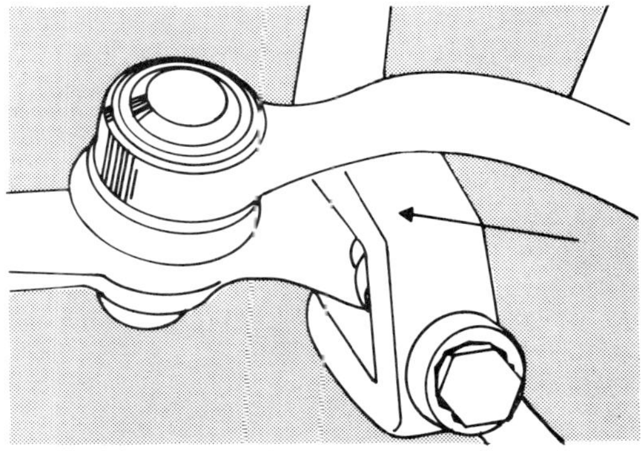

Fig. 6-5. Special tool being used (arrow) to press pitman arm ball stud out of relay rod.

4. Remove the nuts, the lock washers, the flat washers, and the bolts that hold the steering gearbox to the car body. Then pull the steering gearbox's worm shaft out of the steering column's flexible coupling and remove the gearbox, taking it out from beneath the car.

To install:

1. If necessary, repair or adjust the steering gearbox as described in **6.4 Disassembling and Assembling Steering Gearbox.**
2. Position the steering gearbox on the car body, guiding the gearbox's worm shaft into the flexible coupling of the steering column. Install the bolts. Install first a flat washer, then a lock washer, and finally a nut on each bolt. Torque the nuts to 40 to 50 Nm (30 to 37 ft. lb.).
3. Install the steering relay rod on the ball stud of the steering gearbox's pitman arm. Install the castellated nut to a torque of 60 to 65 Nm (44 to 48 ft. lb.). Advance the nut, if necessary, to uncover the cotter pin hole, then install a new cotter pin.
4. Make sure that the front wheels are pointed straight ahead; check that the steering wheel spokes are horizontal (the steering column lock will hold the wheel in this position).
5. Moving the front wheels or the steering wheel by as little as possible, align the recess in the steering gearbox's worm shaft with the clamp bolt hole in the steering column's flexible coupling. Then in-

8

stall the clamp bolt to a torque of 25 to 30 Nm (18 to 22 ft. lb.). See Fig. 6-6.

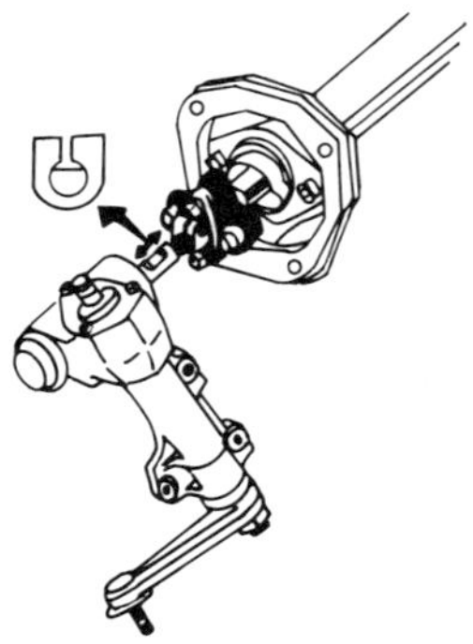

Fig. 6-6. Recess in worm shaft correctly aligned (inset) with bolt hole in flexible coupling.

6. Lower the car to the ground. Then check and, if necessary, adjust the steering lock as described in **3.1 Checking and Adjusting Front Wheel Toe.**

6.3 Removing and Installing Steering Linkage

The steering linkage consists of the two tie rods, the steering relay rod, and the idler arm. An exploded view of these components is given in Fig. 6-7. If you need only repair or replace a tie rod end, do so as described in **6.1 Replacing Tie Rod Ends and Tie Rod End Dust Seals.**

To remove linkage:

1. Raise the car on a hoist or support it on stands designed for the purpose.
2. Remove the cotter pin, then remove the castellated nut that holds the steering gearbox's pitman arm to the steering relay rod. Using a tool such as the one indicated in Fig. 6-8, press the pitman arm's ball stud out of the relay rod.

> ***CAUTION —***
> *Do not hammer out the ball stud, which will ruin its threads and make reinstallation impossible. Do not hammer on the relay rod because this can bend or damage it.*

3. Unbolt the idler arm assembly from the car body.

1. Cotter pin
2. Castellated nut
3. Tie rod end dust seal
4. Dust seal retainer ring
5. Outer tie rod end
6. Tie rod clamp
7. Tie rod
8. Clamp bolt
9. Lock washer
10. Nut
11. Inner tie rod end
12. Idler arm pivot
13. Idler arm pivot dust seal
14. Bushing
15. Idler arm
16. Lock ring
17. Idler arm dust seal
18. Bushing
19. Idler arm pivot dust seal
20. Flat washer
21. Self-locking nut
22. Steering relay rod
23. Nut
24. Lock washer
25. Flat washer
26. Idler arm assembly
27. Bolt

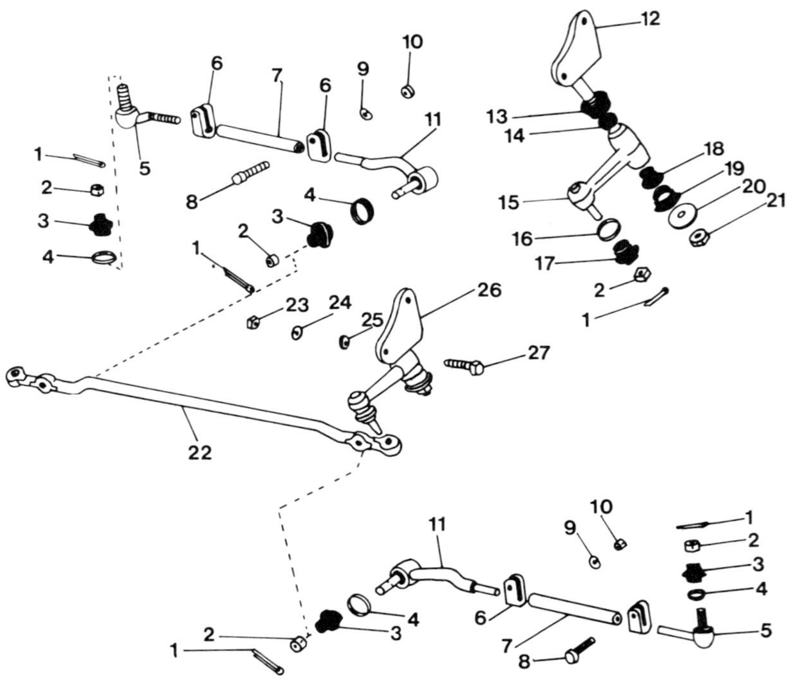

Fig. 6-7. Exploded view of steering linkage.

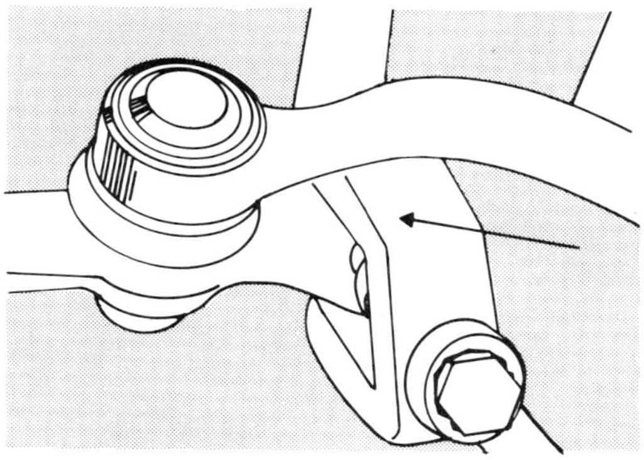

Fig. 6-8. Special tool being used (arrow) to press pitman arm ball stud out of relay rod.

4. Remove the cotter pins, then remove the castellated nuts that hold the two outer tie rod ends to the steering arms. Use a tool such as the one shown in Fig. 6-9 to press the tie rod end's ball studs out of the steering arms. Remove the steering linkage from the car.

> ***CAUTION —***
> *Do not hammer out the tie rod ends. Doing this will ruin the threads and make reinstallation impossible.*

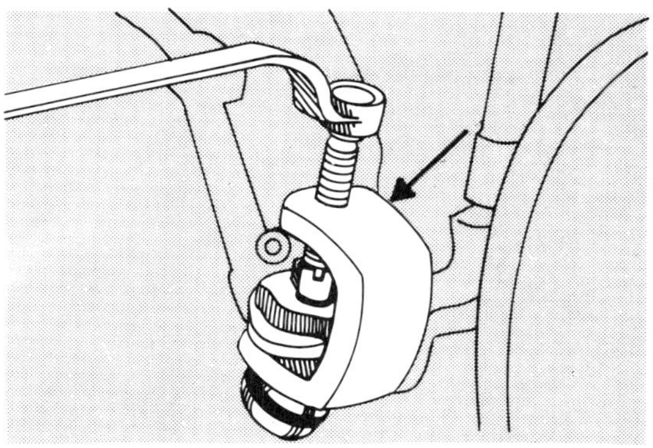

Fig. 6-9. Tie rod end removing tool (arrow) being used to press tie rod end's ball stud out of steering arm.

5. Clamp the relay rod in a vise. Remove the cotter pin, then take off the castellated nut that holds the idler arm's ball stud to the relay rod.
6. Remove the cotter pins, then take off the castellated nuts that hold the inner tie rod ends to the relay rod.
7. Using a tool such as the one shown previously in Fig. 6-8, press the ball studs of the inner tie rod ends and the idler arm out of the steering relay rod.

> ***CAUTION —***
> *Do not hammer out the ball studs. Doing this will ruin the threads and make reinstallation impossible.*

Installation is the reverse of removal. Before reassembling the linkage components, thoroughly clean them and replace any that is worn, corroded, bent, or in any way damaged. After you have loosely assembled the linkage, loosely install it on the car. Then torque the nuts that hold the idler arm assembly to the car body to 40 to 50 Nm (30 to 37 ft. lb.). Torque the castellated nut on the pitman arm's ball stud and on the idler arm's ball stud to 60 to 65 Nm (44 to 48 ft. lb.). Torque the castellated nuts for the tie rod ends to 55 to 65 Nm (41 to 48 ft. lb.). Advance all castellated nuts, if necessary, to uncover the cotter pin holes. Then install new cotter pins.

After you have lowered the car to the ground, check and adjust the front wheel toe as described in **3.1 Checking and Adjusting Front Wheel Toe.** With the toe correctly adjusted, make sure that the ball studs of each tie rod's ends are at 90° to one another. Then torque the clamp bolts to 15 to 20 Nm (11 to 15 ft. lb.).

Inspecting Linkage and Repairing Idler Arm

If the car has been in a collision, or if the steering linkage has been bent or subjected to any heavy impact, it is recommended that the idler arm, the steering relay rod, and the steering gearbox's pitman arm be checked for cracks by the Magnaflux® process. Pitman arm removal and inspection is described in **6.4 Disassembling and Assembling Steering Gearbox.** Replace cracked parts, and replace any part that is damaged or deformed. If you replace a tie rod or the tie rod ends, screw both tie rod ends into each tie rod by an equal 8
number of turns before you install the tie rods on the car. Tie rod end repair is described in **6.1 Replacing Tie Rod Ends and Tie Rod End Dust Seals.**

To repair idler arm:

1. Remove the idler arm assembly. Clamp its pivot in a vise. Check the play as indicated in Fig. 6-10. If the play exceeds 2.33 mm (.092 in.), the bushings should be replaced during repair.

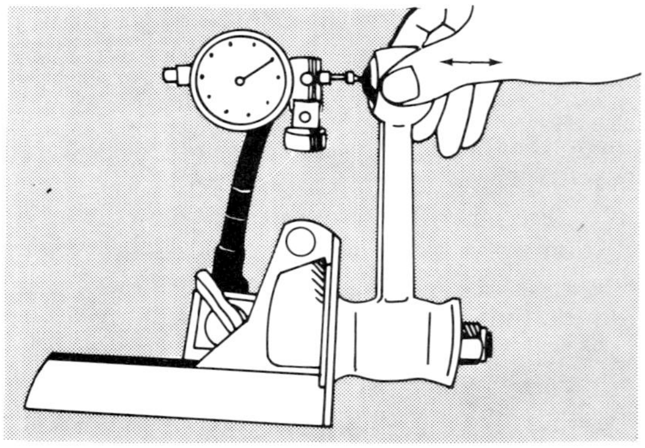

Fig. 6-10. Dial indicator being used to check idler arm play. Play is combined rocking play and axial play. This inspection should be made prior to disassembly.

2. Remove the self-locking nut and the flat washer. Then remove the idler arm from the pivot and take out the bushings. See Fig. 6-11.

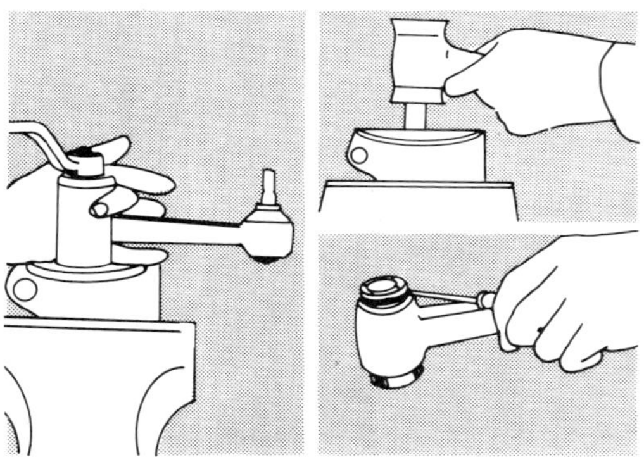

Fig. 6-11. Idler arm being disassembled. **Left**: self-locking nut being removed. **Top roght**: idler arm being removed from pivot. **Bottom right**: bushings being pried out of idler arm.

3. If you have any suspicion that the idler arm may have been weakened, have it checked for cracks by a process such as Magnaflux®. Then install new bushings and dust seals, lubricate all working surfaces with multipurpose grease, and loosely assemble the idler arm with new dust seals. See Fig. 6-12.

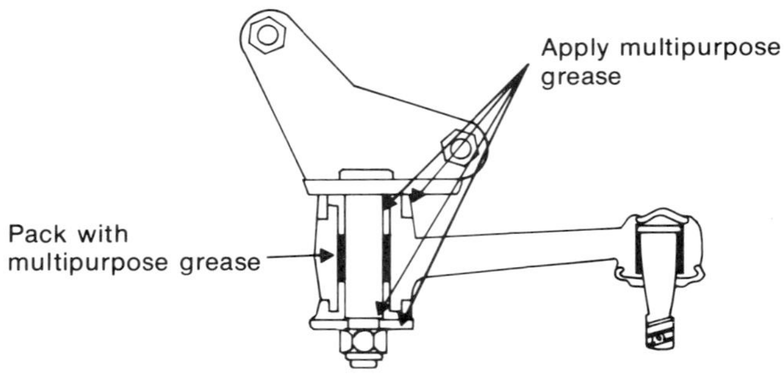

Fig. 6-12. Cross-section of correctly assembled idler arm, showing points which should be lubricated with multipurpose grease during assembly.

4. Install a new self-locking nut on the pivot, making sure that you have installed either an unworn flat washer or a new flat washer. (If a new self-locking nut cannot be obtained, install the old nut with Loctite®.) Torque the self-locking nut to 60 to 65 Nm (44 to 48 ft. lb.). Then install the idler arm assembly on the linkage or on the car.

6.4 Disassembling and Assembling Steering Gearbox

Fig. 6-13 gives exploded views of the recirculating ball steering gearbox. You should not disassemble the worm from the ball nut and balls. If you do, you will have difficulty in reinstalling the loose ball bearings, which must be fed carefully into the assembly and in some cases stuck into place with multipurpose grease during assembly. If there is play between the worm and the ball nut, you should replace the steering gearbox or the worm/ball nut assembly as a unit, depending on the extent to which other parts of the gearbox are worn.

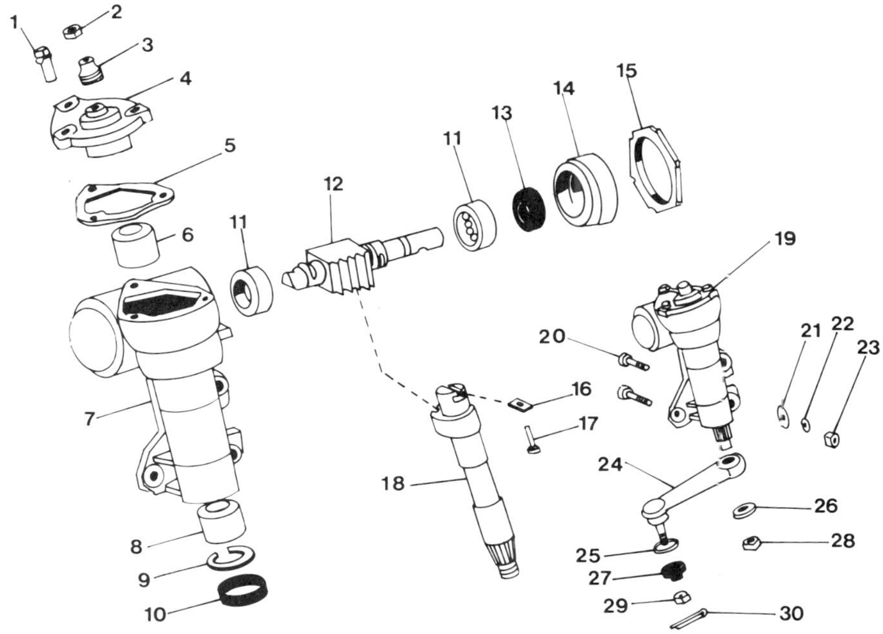

1. Cover bolt
2. Sector shaft adjustment locknut
3. Breather plug
4. Cover
5. Cover gasket
6. Upper needle bearing assembly
7. Gearbox housing
8. Lower needle bearing assembly
9. Snap ring
10. Oil seal
11. Ball bearing
12. Worm/ball nut assembly
13. Oil seal
14. Worm bearing adjusting screw
15. Locknut
16. Sector shaft thrust washer
17. Sector shaft adjustment screw
18. Sector shaft
19. Steering gearbox assembly
20. Mounting bolt (3)
21. Flat washer
22. Lock washer
23. Nut
24. Pitman arm
25. Retaining ring for dust seal
26. Lock washer
27. Dust seal
28. Self-locking nut
29. Cotter pin
30. Castellated nut

Fig. 6-13. Exploded view of recirculating ball steering gearbox.

To disassemble gearbox:

1. Clamp the steering gearbox in a vise. Remove the self-locking nut from the lower end of the sector shaft.
2. Check whether there are matching marks on the pitman arm and the sector shaft. If not, scribe a mark on the pitman arm and another on the end of the sector shaft so that later you will be able to reinstall the pitman arm in its exact original position on the sector shaft.
3. Using a puller, as indicated in Fig. 6-14, remove the pitman arm from the sector shaft.
4. Loosen the sector shaft adjustment locknut. Remove the bolts that hold the cover to the gearbox housing. Then, using a screwdriver to turn the sector shaft adjustment screw clockwise, raise the cover and its gasket away from the housing.

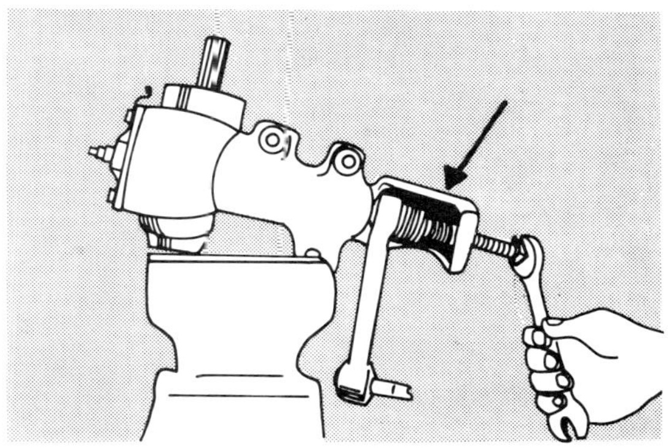

Fig. 6-14. Puller (arrow) being used to remove pitman arm from sector shaft of steering gearbox.

8

5. Hold the sector shaft in position while you pour the oil out of the gearbox. Then remove the sector shaft as indicated in Fig. 6-15.

> ***CAUTION —***
> *If the lower end of the sector shaft is rusted or covered by hardened dirt, clean the shaft before you withdraw it. Otherwise, the needle bearings may be damaged. Under no circumstances should you remove and disassemble the needle bearing races if you intend to reuse them. If the sector shaft, either the needle bearing race, or the gearbox housing is in any way faulty, these parts should be replaced as a unit. The bearings and the sector shaft are not available as individual replacement parts.*

Fig. 6-15. Sector being removed. Once removed, you can take off the locknut, then unscrew the cover from the adjustment screw.

6. Using a suitable wrench, remove the locknut for the worm bearing adjusting screw. Then, using a special wrench such as Toyota special tool 09616-30011, remove the worm bearing adjusting screw (Fig. 6-16).

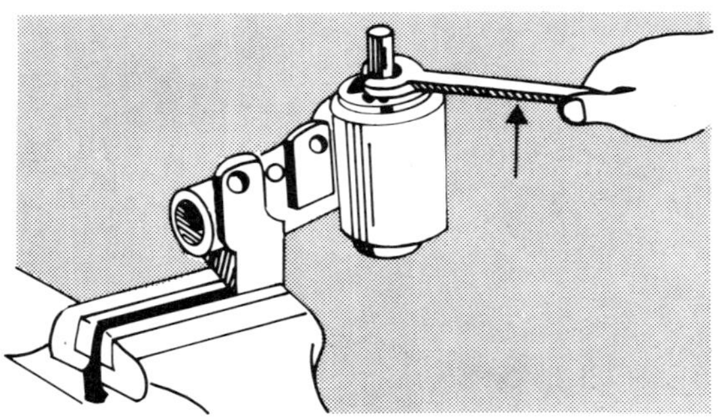

Fig. 6-16. Worm bearing adjusting screw being removed with special wrench (arrow).

7. Remove the worm/ball nut assembly and its bearing inner races as a unit.

> ***CAUTION —***
> *Do not remove the ball nut from the worm because you will be unable to reinstall it. If the assembly is in any way defective, replace it as a unit.*

To inspect and assemble:

1. Check the condition of the oil seals. Replace either seal if it is hardened, cracked, worn, or in any way faulty.
2. Check that the ball nut turns smoothly and without play on the worm shaft. Replace the worm/ball nut assembly if it is any way faulty.
3. Inspect the ball bearings for the worm. If the balls are galled, corroded, flattened, or fail to move freely, replace the ball bearing races.
4. Inspect the sector shaft (Fig. 6-17). If the gear teeth are worn, or if the bearing surfaces are worn or galled, replace the gearbox housing together with the needle roller bearings and the sector shaft.

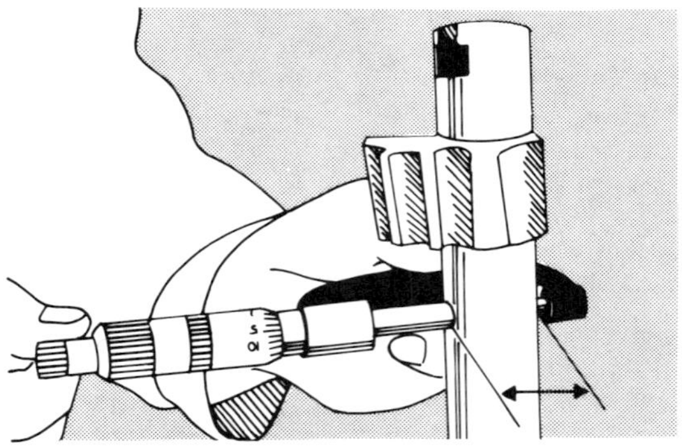

Fig. 6-17. Diameter of sector shaft bearing surface being measured. New shaft has outside diameter of 27.976 to 27.993 mm (1.1014 to 1.1021 in.). Standard inside diameter of bearings is 28.000 to 28.025 mm (1.1024 to 1.1033 in.). If either shaft or bearing is worn so that clearance exceeds 0.049 mm (.0019 in.), replace the shaft, the bearings, and the gearbox housing as a unit.

5. Using feeler gauges of various thicknesses, determine the clearance between the head of the sector shaft adjustment screw and the sector shaft, making your measurement at the point indicated in Fig. 6-18 If the clearance exceeds 0.05 mm (.002 in.), select a thicker sector shaft thrust washer from the list given in Fig. 6-18. and install it between the screw head and the sector shaft.
6. If the ball bearings require replacement, remove them as indicated in Fig. 6-19. Then press in the new ball bearings with a tool that will contact only the bearings' outer races.

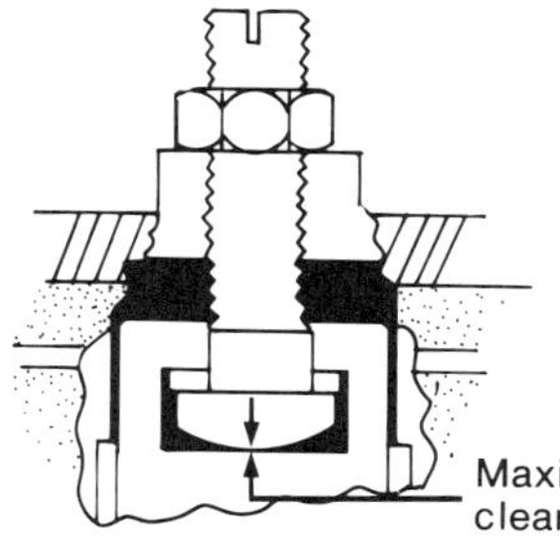

Available thrust washers

Part No.	Thickness
45352-12010	2.00 mm (.079 in.)
45352-12020	2.04 mm (.080 in.)
45352-12030	2.08 mm (.082 in.)
45352-12040	2.12 mm (.083 in.)
45352-12050	2.16 mm (.085 in.)
45352-12060	2.20 mm (.087 in.)

Fig. 6-18. Point at which clearance should be measured between head of adjustment screw and sector shaft. If necessary, choose thicker thrust washer from above list.

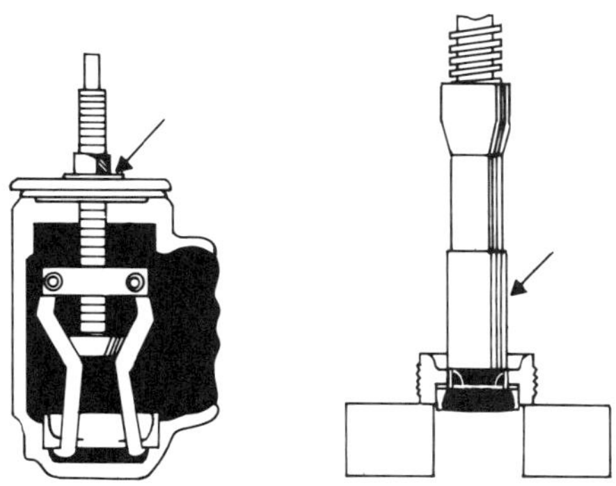

Fig. 6-19. Ball bearing outer races being removed. **Left**: puller with extracting screw and plate (arrow) being used to withdraw bearing race from gearbox housing. **Right**: press mandrel being used to press oil seal and bearing race simultaneously out of worm bearing adjusting screw.

7. Install new oil seals using suitable seal drivers. Apply multipurpose grease to all working parts of the steering gearbox and to the lips of the oil seals. Install the worm/ball nut assembly, its bearings, the worm bearing adjusting screw, and its locknut. For the moment, do not fully tighten the adjusting screw or install the sector shaft.

8. Using the special wrench, gradually tighten the worm bearing adjusting screw, turning the worm frequently in order to settle the bearings correctly. Continue tightening the adjusting screw until the correct preload is obtained. See Fig. 6-20 and Fig. 6-21.

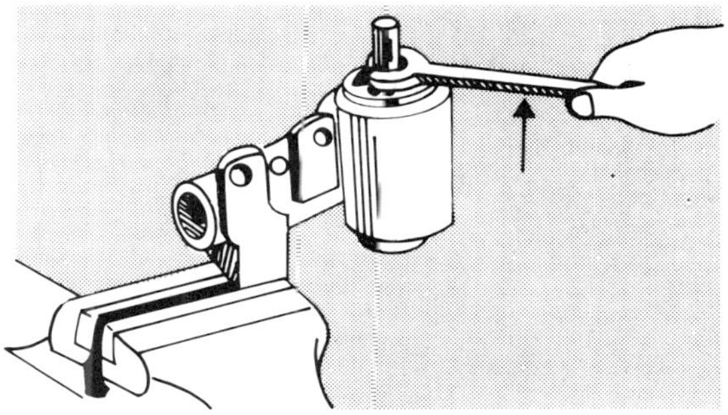

Fig. 6-20. Special wrench (arrow) being used to tighten worm bearing adjusting screw.

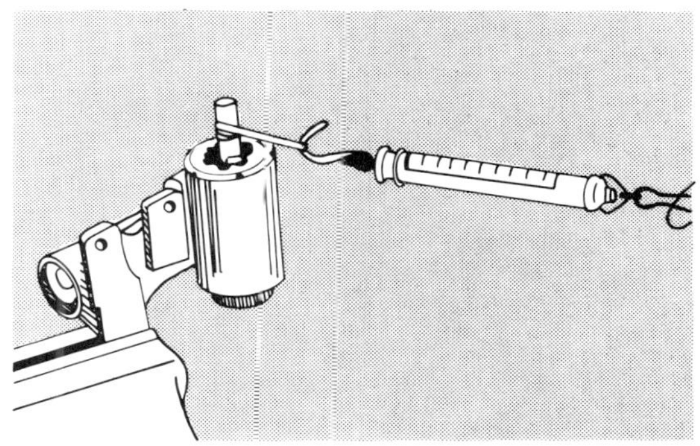

Fig. 6-21. Ball bearing preload being measured. Wrap string around serrations of worm and attach spring scale as indicated. It should require a tension of 4.0 to 6.0 kg (8 lb. 13 oz. to 13 lb. 3 oz.) to rotate worm. Turn worm bearing adjusting screw one way or the other until preload is correct.

9. When the ball bearing preload is correct, hold the worm bearing adjusting screw stationary while you torque the locknut to 14 to 15 Nm (10 to 11 ft. lb.). Then recheck the preload to make sure that it remains within the correct range.

10. Hand-turn the worm shaft until the ball nut is centered on the worm. Then install the sector shaft. Install the cover gasket and the cover. Torque the cover bolts to 15 to 20 Nm (11 to 15 ft. lb.).

11. Again attach the string and the spring scale to the worm shaft. Gradually tighten the sector shaft adjustment screw until the overall preload is correct. See Fig. 6-22.

NOTE ——

The ball nut should be centered on the worm before each check of the overall preload.

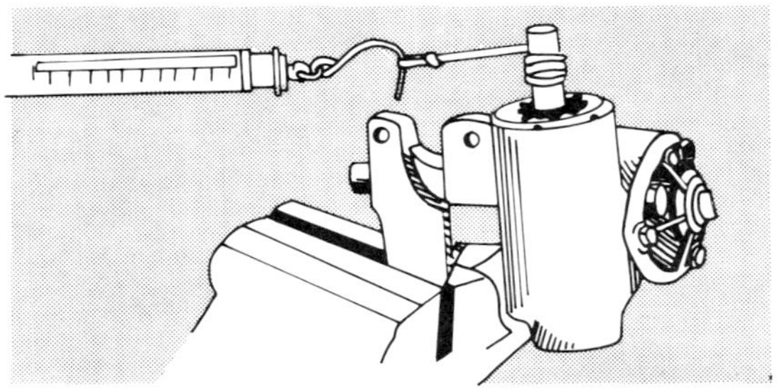

Fig. 6-22. Overall preload being measured. It should require a tension of 8.0 to 11.0 kg (17 lb. 10 oz. to 24 lb. 3 oz.) to rotate worm. Turn sector shaft adjustment screw one way or the other until overall preload is correct.

12. Loosely install the pitman arm on the sector shaft. Center the ball nut on the worm, then check for play at the pitman arm as indicated in Fig. 6-23. There should be no play at the pitman arm when the pitman arm is within 5° in either direction from the centered position.

NOTE ——

If you cannot eliminate play by turning in the sector shaft adjustment screw, you have either assembled the gearbox incorrectly or reinstalled a part that is excessively worn.

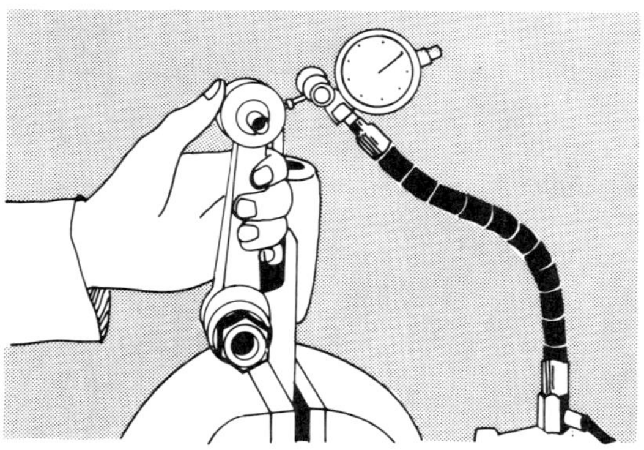

Fig. 6-23. Dial indicator being used to check for play at pitman arm with steering centered.

13. With all adjustments correct, hold the sector shaft adjustment screw stationary while you torque its locknut to 20 to 30 Nm (15 to 22 ft. lb.).

14. Install the pitman arm on the sector shaft so that the matching marks you made prior to disassembly are aligned. Then, while supporting the pitman arm so that an excessive load is not placed on the internal parts, install the self-locking nut to a torque of 125 to 135 Nm (92 to 100 ft. lb.).

15. Refill the steering gearbox with 230 to 250 ml or cm^3 (7¾ to 8½ oz.) of SAE 90 gear oil.

6.5 Removing and Installing Steering Wheel and Steering Column

You can use the instructions given here for removing and installing the steering wheel by using only steps 1 through 3 of the removal procedure and steps 7 through 9 of the installation procedure. The entire procedure should be used if the steering column must be removed and installed.

To remove:

1. Disconnect the battery's negative cable.

2. On cars with three-spoke steering wheels, and no medallion in the center, remove the steering wheel pad by taking out the screws (Fig. 6-24) that are accessible in the spoke cover, behind the steering wheel. Alternatively, you can carefully pry out the medallion. On cars with four-spoke steering wheels, carefully pry out the medallion in the center of the wheel.

3. Remove the nut that holds the steering wheel to the steering column. Then, using a puller as indicated in Fig. 6-25, pull the steering wheel off the steering column.

CAUTION ——

Sometimes you can pull the wheel off by hand, using rocking motions, after first loosening the nut by two or three turns. But do not attempt to remove the steering wheel by pounding or with a slide hammer. Any unnecessarily heavy force or shock can damage the steering column bearings and sensitive electrical components.

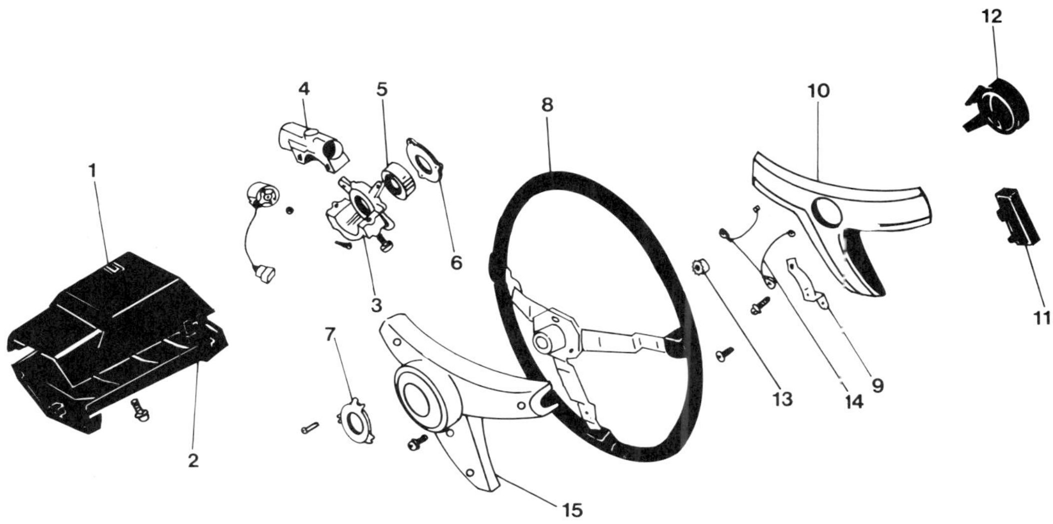

1. Steering column upper cover
2. Steering column lower cover
3. Column lock and bearing holder
4. Column lock housing
5. Ball bearing
6. Bearing retainer
7. Horn contact ring
8. Steering wheel
9. Horn button plate
10. Steering wheel pad
11. Horn button
12. Medallion
13. Column nut
14. Electrical wire for horn buttons
15. Spoke cover

Fig. 6-24. Exploded view of three-spoke steering wheel and related components. Steering column cover and steering lock/ignition lock assembly are same with four-spoke wheel.

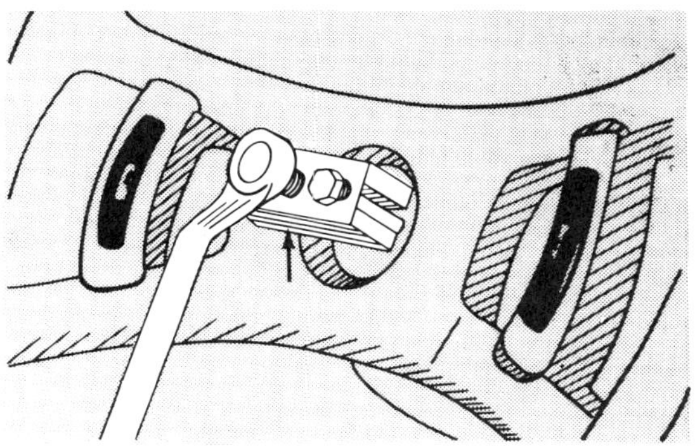

Fig. 6-25. Puller (arrow) being used to remove steering wheel.

4. By taking out the screws in the recesses of the steering column lower cover, remove both the upper and the lower steering column covers.

5. By squeezing together the locking levers on the multiple connector, pull apart the multiple connector, disconnecting the steering column wiring from the car's electrical system. If necessary, consult **ELECTRICAL SYSTEM.**

6. Remove the screws indicated in Fig. 6-26. Then remove the steering column switch assembly from the steering column in order to protect the switches from accidental damage during steering column removal.

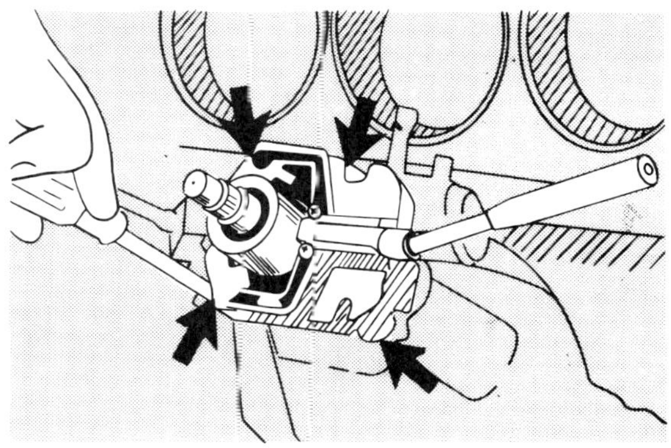

Fig. 6-26. Screws (arrows) that hold the steering column switches to ignition/steering column lock assembly

8

7. Working in the engine compartment, fully remove the clamp bolt that holds the steering column's flexible coupling to the steering gearbox worm shaft. See Fig. 6-27.

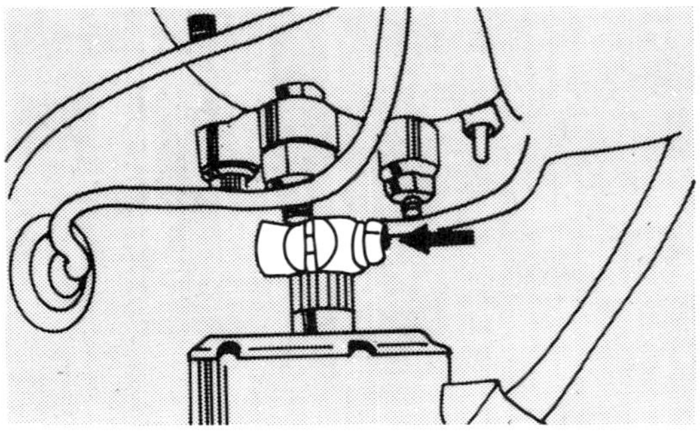

Fig. 6-27. Clamp bolt (arrow) that holds steering column's flexible coupling to worm shaft of steering gearbox.

8. Partially remove the carpet that is behind the brake and clutch pedals, rolling it down from the top after you detach it. Then remove the four bolts indicated in Fig. 6-28.

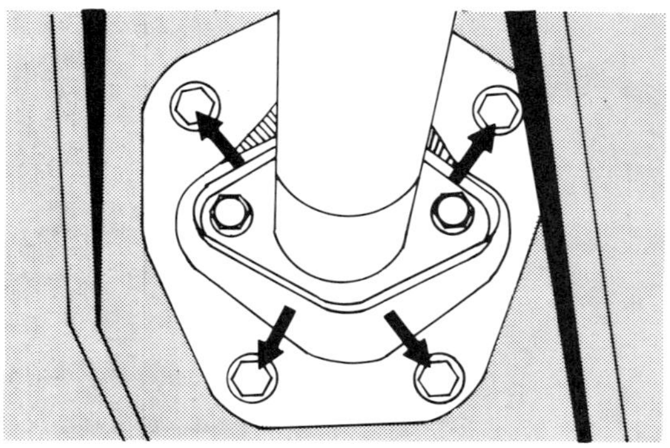

Fig. 6-28. Bolts (arrows) that hold steering column hole cover to car's floorboard.

9. Remove the bolts and the nuts (Fig. 6-29) that hold the steering column's break-away bracket to the bottom of the dashboard structure. Then remove the steering column, pulling it up into the passenger compartment.

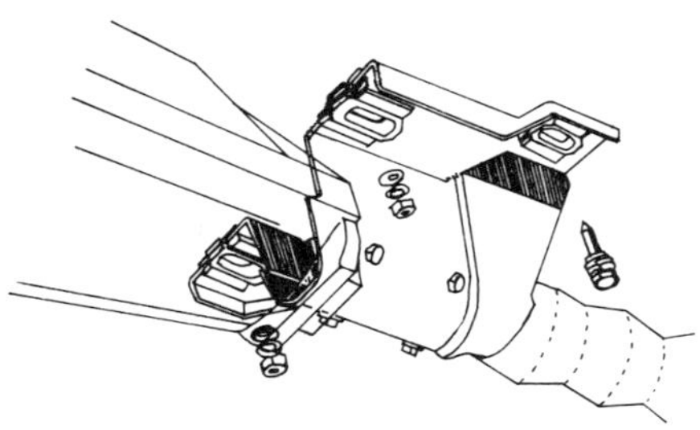

Fig. 6-29. Exploded view of bolts and nuts that hold break-away bracket to dashboard structure.

To install:

1. If necessary, disassemble the steering column for repairs and then reassemble it. See **6.6 Disassembling and Assembling Steering Column.** Replace the gasket for the steering column hole if the old gasket is in any way damaged or deteriorating.
2. Install the steering column in the car, guiding it down onto the worm shaft of the steering gearbox. Loosely install the nuts and the bolts for the break-away bracket in order to hold the column in place.
3. Make sure that the front wheels are pointed straight ahead. Align the clamp bolt hole in the steering column's flexible coupling with the recess in the steering gearbox's worm shaft (Fig. 6-30). Install the clamp bolt to a torque of 25 to 30 Nm (18 to 22 ft. lb.).

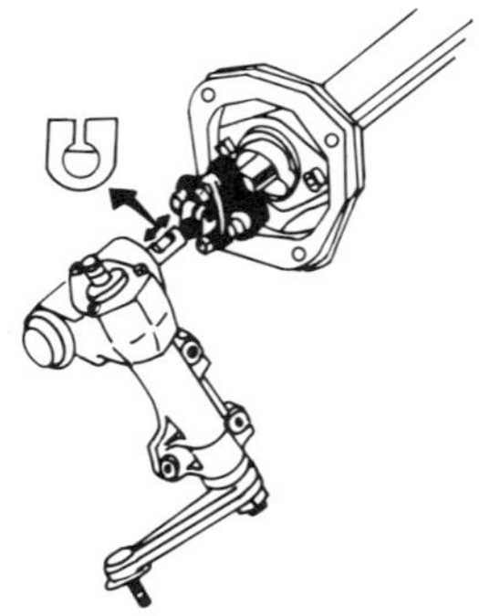

Fig. 6-30. Recess in worm shaft correctly aligned (inset) with bolt hole in flexible coupling.

4. Torque the nuts and the bolts for the break-away bracket to 35 to 45 Nm (26 to 33 ft. lb.). Using the four bolts, install the steering column hole cover and its gasket on the car's floorboard. Then reinstall the carpet.
5. Install the steering column switches. Reconnect the multiple connector for the steering column wiring.
6. Using the screws, install the steering column upper and lower covers.
7. After making sure that the car's front wheels are pointed straight ahead, install the steering wheel so that its spokes are horizontal. (The lower spoke of a three-spoke steering wheel should be vertical.) Torque the steering column nut that holds the steering wheel to 35 to 40 Nm (26 to 30 ft. lb.).
8. On cars with three-spoke steering wheels, either install the medallion or install the steering wheel pad using the spoke cover and the screws. On cars with four-spoke steering wheels, carefully reinstall the medallion.
9. Reconnect the battery's negative cable.

6.6 Disassembling and Assembling Steering Column

Fig. 6-31 is an exploded view of the steering column assembly. This steering column is a telescopic kind that has steel balls between its inner and outer components. If the steering column has been collapsed or deformed by impact, you should replace it with a new steering column assembly. Do not under any circumstances repair one of these columns after it has been collapsed.

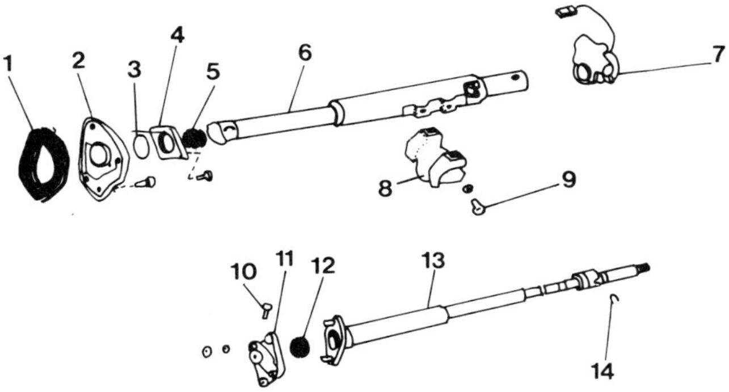

1. Hole cover gasket
2. Steering column hole cover
3. O-ring
4. Cover plate
5. Dust seal
6. Steering column tube
7. Ignition/steering lock assembly
8. Break-away bracket
9. Bolt for column tube
10. Clamp bolt
11. Flexible coupling
12. Plug
13. Steering column
14. Snap ring

Fig. 6-31. Exploded view of steering column assembly.

To disassemble:

1. After removing the screws, take off the bearing retainer. (If necessary, consult Fig. 6-24, which appears earlier.) Then remove the snap ring (Fig. 6-32).

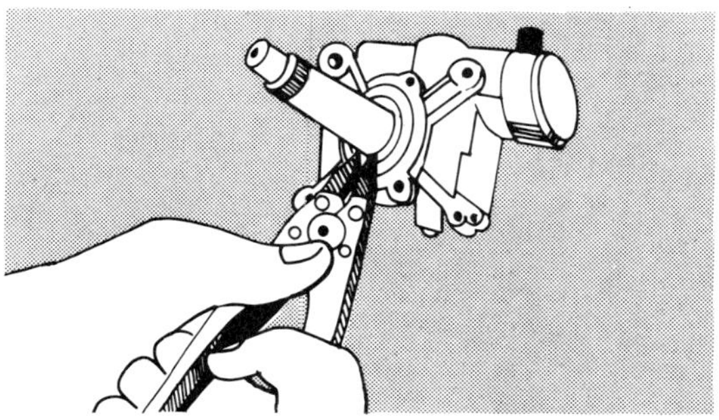

Fig. 6-32. Snap ring being removed.

2. To remove the ignition/steering lock assembly, first remove the lock cylinder as indicated in Fig. 6-33. Then, after drilling a 3-mm to 4-mm (or 3/8-in. to 5/32-in.) diameter hole in each shear bolt, use a bolt extractor to remove the shear bolts so that you can take off the lock assembly. See Fig. 6-34.

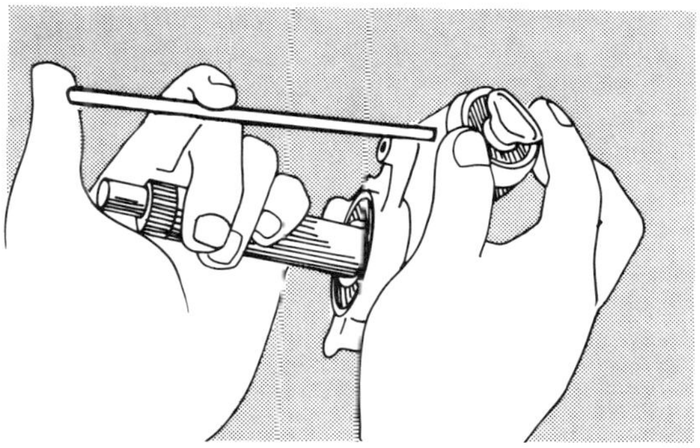

Fig. 6-33. Lock cylinder being removed. Insert key and turn ignition switch to its **ACC** position. While pressing down stop with stiff wire as indicated, use key to pull lock cylinder out of housing.

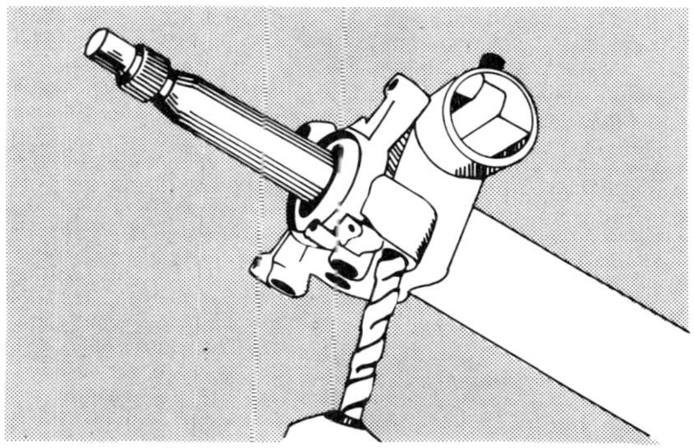

Fig. 6-34. Hole being drilled into shear bolt so that bolt can be removed with bolt extractor. There are two shear bolts to be removed.

3. Take out the bolts and remove the break-away bracket from the column tube.
4. Pull the steering column out of the steering column tube (Fig. 6-35). Then remove the dust seal.

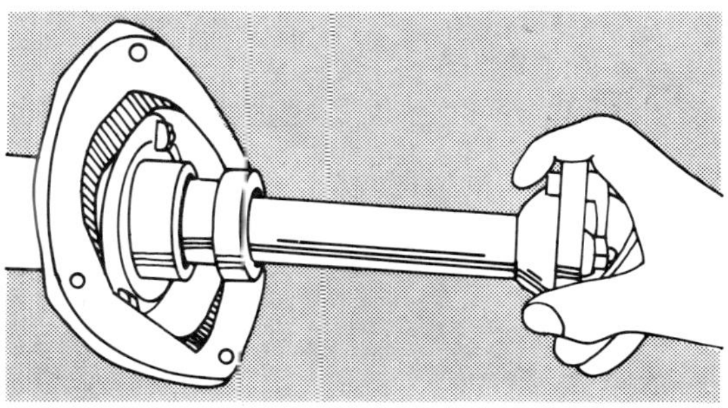

Fig. 6-35. Steering column being withdrawn from column tube. Notice dust seal at arrow.

5. If necessary, remove the flexible coupling from the steering column.
6. Remove the bolts that hold the cover plate to the steering column hole cover. Then, twisting the column tube to disengage the slot of the tube from the tab of the hole cover, remove the tube from the cover and the hole cover.

To assemble:

1. Inspect all parts and replace any that is broken, worn, deformed, or otherwise damaged.
2. If necessary, reinstall the flexible coupling on the steering column.
3. Loosely assemble the cover and the steering column hole cover on the column tube. Lubricate the inside and the outside of the dust seal with multipurpose grease. Then insert the column through the dust seal and into the column tube.
4. Engage the slot of the column tube with the tab of the hole cover as indicated in Fig. 6-36. Then bolt the cover plate to the steering column hole cover.

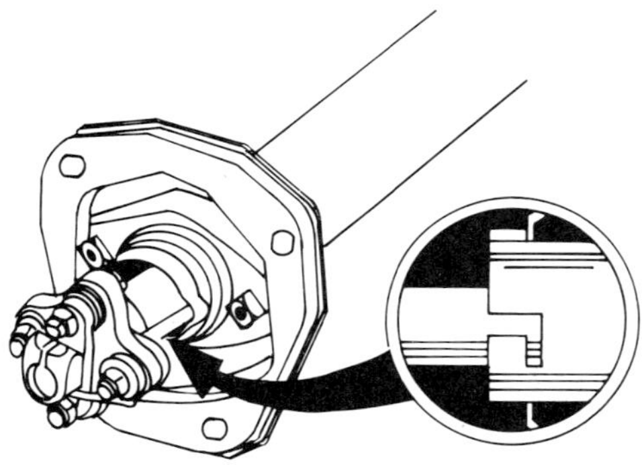

Fig. 6-36. Tab correctly engaged in slot (inset).

5. Using the bolts, install the break-away bracket on the column tube. Torque the bolts to 35 to 45 Nm (26 to 33 ft. lb.).
6. If necessary, pack multipurpose grease into the ball bearing. If the bearing is being replaced, drive it out of the ignition/steering lock housing. Then drive in a new bearing (Fig. 6-37) until the bearing's upper face if flush with the housing.
7. Loosely assemble the ignition/steering lock assembly on the steering column. Install two new shear bolts—but do not tighten them so much that their heads shear off. (The bolt heads shear off at a torque of about 15 to 20 Nm (11 to 15 ft. lb.).)

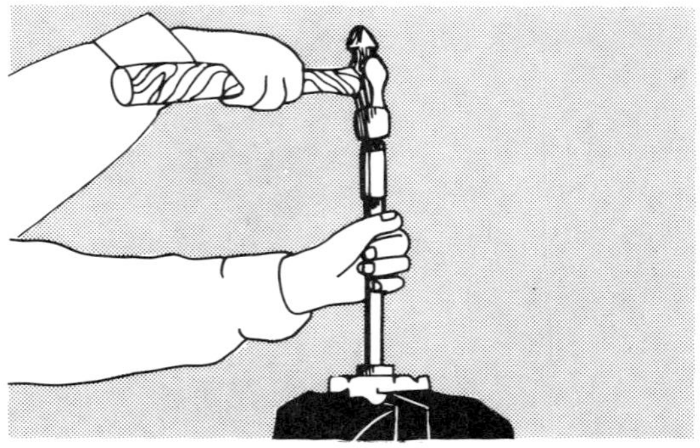

Fig. 6-37. Ball bearing being driven into ignition/steering lock housing. Tool should contact only bearing outer race.

8. If necessary, use a screwdriver to position the lock as indicated in Fig. 6-38. With the key in the lock cylinder, insert the cylinder so that the key is aligned with the **ACC** mark on the bezel. The lock cylinder should engage the lock and snap into place.

Fig. 6-38. Left: lock correctly positioned (arrow). **Right**: key and cylinder correctly positioned for installation.

9. Install the snap ring on the upper end of the column, then install the bearing retainer.
10. Test the operation of the ignition/steering lock. If necessary, loosen the shear bolts slightly and reposition the lock housing until the lock operates smoothly. Then tighten the shear bolts until their heads shear off.

7. SUSPENSION AND STEERING TECHNICAL DATA

I. Tightening Torques

Location	Designation	Nm	Ft. lb.
Tie rod to tie rod end	clamp and clamp bolt	15 to 20	11 to 15
Front suspension strut bar to track control arm	nut and special bolt	45 to 55	33 to 41
Front suspension strut bar to strut bar bracket on car body	nut at front end only	80 to 110	59 to 81
Strut bar bracket to car body	bolt	35 to 40	26 to 30
Stabilizer bar bracket to strut bar bracket	bolt	10 to 15	7.5 to 11
Stabilizer bar to track control arm	first nut only	15 to 20	11 to 15
	jam nut only	10 to 15	7.5 to 11
Suspension ball joint stud to steering arm	castellated nut	80 to 90	59 to 66
Track control arm to front suspension crossmember	bolt	80 to 90	59 to 66
Steering arm to suspension strut	bolt	80 to 90	59 to 66
Road wheel to wheel hub or rear axle flange	lug nut	90 to 120	66 to 89
Front suspension strut upper bearing assembly to piston rod of strut	nut	45 to 50	33 to 37
Front suspension strut upper bearing assembly to car body	nut	20 to 30	15 to 22
Piston to front suspension strut piston rod	special piston nut	20 to 30	15 to 22
Gland nut in top of front suspension strut tube	gland nut	125 to 145	92 to 107
Front suspension crossmember to car body	bolt	45 to 50	33 to 37
Engine mounts to front suspension crossmember	nut	30 to 40	22 to 30
Upper end of rear shock absorber piston rod to car body or, on station wagon, to shock absorber upper mounting	upper nut (jam nut) only	20 to 30	15 to 22
Station wagon upper rear shock absorber mounting to car body	bolt	15 to 20	11 to 15
Rear shock absorber lower end to U-bolt seat on rear axle	bolt	20 to 30	15 to 22
Rear spring bracket pin to bracket on car body	bolt (for flange)	10 to 15	7.5 to 11
	nut (for pin end)	45 to 50	33 to 37
Rear spring and shackle outer plate to shackle	nut	45 to 50	33 to 37
Rear spring to rear axle	nut for U-bolt	35 to 45	26 to 33
Driveshaft rear universal joint to pinion flange of rear axle	bolt	35 to 40	26 to 30
Driveshaft center bearing to car body (where applicable)	bolt	35 to 40	26 to 30
Tie rod end to steering arm or to relay rod	castellated nut	55 to 65	41 to 48
Steering gearbox to car body	nut and bolt	40 to 50	30 to 37
Relay rod to pitman arm	castellated nut	60 to 65	44 to 48
Steering column flexible coupling to worm shaft of steering gearbox	clamp bolt	25 to 30	18 to 22
Steering idler arm assembly to car body	nut	40 to 50	30 to 37
Relay rod to idler arm	casellated nut	60 to 65	44 to 48
Idler arm to idler arm pivot	self-locking nut	60 to 65	44 to 48
Steering gearbox worm bearing adjusting screw to gearbox housing	locknut	14 to 15	10 to 11
Steering gearbox cover to steering gearbox housing	bolt	15 to 20	11 to 15
Steering gearbox sector shaft adjustment bolt to cover	locknut	20 to 30	15 to 22
Steering gearbox pitman arm to sector shaft	self-locking nut	125 to 135	
Steering column break-away bracket to steering column tube or to dashboard structure	bolt or nut	35 to 45	26 to 33
Steering wheel to steering column	nut	35 to 40	26 to 30
Ignition/steering lock housing to steering column	shear bolts	tighten until heads shear off—about 15 to 20 Nm (about 11 to 15 ft. lb.)	

II. Front Wheel Alignment Specifications

Toe in—with bias-ply tires	2 to 4 mm (5/64 to 5/32 in.)
—with radial-ply tires	0 to 2 mm (0 to 5/64 in.)
Side slip	0 to 3 mm (0 to 1/8 in.) in 1 m (3 ft., 4 in.) of forward travel
Wheel camber	1° ±30′
Caster angle	1° 50′ ±30′
Maximum difference in wheel camber and caster angle between wheels	30′
Steering axis inclination	7° 50′ ±30′
Steering lock (maximum turning angle)—inside wheel	37° to 39°
—outside wheel	29° 25′ to 33° 25′

III. Tolerances, Wear Limits, and Settings

Designation	New installation mm (in.)	Wear limit mm (in.)
1. Front suspension		
a. Fixed location of position-locating nut (rear nut) on strut rod	87.2 (3 7/16) from rear face of nut to front end of strut rod	—
b. Projection of collars that align bolt holes of steering arm with bolt holes of suspension strut	about 5 (3/16) above top surface of steering arm	—
2. Suspension strut shock absorber components		
a. Piston rod ... outside diameter	21.90 (.8622)	—
... runout (on V-blocks)	—	0.30 (.0118)
b. Shock absorber piston ... outside diameter	—	31.80 (1.2519)
c. Shock absorber cylinder ... inside diameter	—	32.23 (1.2689)
... runout (on V-blocks)	—	0.10 (.0039)
d. Piston rod guide bushing ... inside diameter	—	22.35 (.8799)
e. Refill quantity ... shock absorber fluid	315 ml or cm³ (19.2 in.³ or 10¾ oz.)	—
3. Steering linkage		
a. Idler arm bearing ... combined rocking play and axial play	—	2.33 (.092)
4. Steering gearbox		
a. Sector shaft bearing surfaces ... outside diameter	27.976–27.993 (1.1014–1.1021)	27.976 (1.1014)
b. Sector shaft needle bearings ... inside diameter	28.000–28.025 (1.1024–1.1033)	28.025 (1.1033)
c. Sector shaft to needle bearing ... clearance	0.007–0.049 (.0003–.0019)	0.049 (.0019)
d. Sector shaft ... axial play	—	0.05 (.002)
e. Available thrust washers ... to adjust sector shaft axial play		
Part No. 45352–12010	2.00 (.079)	—
Part No. 45352–12020	2.04 (.080)	—
Part No. 45352–12030	2.0 (.082)	—
Part No. 45352–12040	2.12 (.083)	—
Part No. 45352–12050	2.16 (.085)	—
Part No. 45352–12060	2.20 (.087)	—
f. Pitman arm ... play with steering centered	—	5°
g. Steering wheel ... play with steering centered	—	20 (¾) at rim
h. Worm bearing preload (see Fig. 6-21 in text)	4.0 kg (8 lb. 13 oz.)–6.0 kg (13 lb. 3 oz.)	—
i. Overall preload (see Fig. 6-22 in text)	8.0 kg (17 lb. 10 oz.)–11 kg (24 lb. 3 oz.)	—
j. Refill quantity ... SAE 90 gear oil	230–250 ml or cm³ (7¾–8½ oz.)	—

Section 9

BODY AND INTERIOR

Contents

Body and Interior

The Toyota Corolla cars have unit construction steel bodies that are exceptionally strong and light. Their lightness contributes greatly to the outstanding performance and fuel economy that these cars deliver. Because very few screws and bolts are used to assemble the body, there is little opportunity for annoying rattles to develop. A quiet ride is further ensured by the sound-dampening materials used and the sound-dampening qualities of the carpeting and interior trim.

The floor plate, which comprises three subassemblies welded together, is not the same on all models, so the station wagon, for example, is distinct in construction from the other Corollas. In addition, the liftback and sports coupe share few body parts with the sedan, the hardtop, and the station wagon. Therefore, in obtaining replacement parts from a salvage yard, professional body repair technicians should carefully select those body sections that may be needed to repair a damaged Corolla.

On the cars covered by this Manual, the bumpers, the hood, the luggage compartment lid (or tailgate), the doors, the front fenders, the grille, and the exterior trim are held to the body shell by screws, bolts, or other removable fasteners. Thus all these parts can be replaced with the aid of ordinary hand tools. The rear fenders, the rear body panels, and other parts of the body shell itself can be replaced only by cutting away the damaged parts and then butt welding a new fender or a new panel to the body. This work should be done by someone with training and experience in auto body repair. If you lack the skills, the tools, or a suitable workshop for auto body repairs and adjustments, we suggest that you leave this work to an Authorized Dealer or other qualified shop.

Also covered in this section of the Manual are the seats and the seat belts, the ventilation and heating system, and the removal of the dashboard panels that give access to the instruments. Repairs related to the gauges and the instrument clusters are covered in **ELECTRICAL SYSTEM.** For information on the care and maintenance of the carpeting, the seat upholstery, and other interior appointments, we recommend that you refer to **LUBRICATION AND MAINTENANCE,** or to the Owner's Manual supplied with the car.

1. GENERAL DESCRIPTION

The Corolla body is a unit construction steel assembly consisting of the car's floor pan, roof, and other body panels. The front fenders, the doors, the trim, the hood, and the rear lid (or the tailgate) are bolted to the body and are easily removable for replacement or repair.

Doors and Windows

Each door is attached to the body by two hinges. The hinges and the lock striker plates can be shifted on the body to adjust the positions of the doors in their openings.

The windshield and the rear window are held in place by a one-piece weatherstrip (rubber seal). The door windows can be fully raised or lowered. Except on the liftback, the rear quarter windows of two-door models can be raised and lowered. The rear quarter windows on the liftback open outward. Most cars covered by this Manual have an electrically heated rear window that can be kept warm to prevent fogging.

Hood, Tailgate, and Rear Lid

The front hood is hinged at the cowl. It can be opened only after it is unlocked from inside the car. A metal support is mounted in the front of the engine compartment to hold the hood in its open position. Except on the liftback, the rear lid is mounted on spring-loaded hinges, which hold the lid open after it is raised. The liftback's rear lid is mounted on two upward-opening hinges attached to the car roof. This lid is supported in its open position by two gas-filled dampeners. The station wagon tail gate is also mounted on two upward-opening hinges but a pair of torsion bars connected to the hinges are used to hold the tailgate open after it is raised.

Seats and Interior

The front seats are individually mounted and can be moved forward or backward. The angle of the seatbacks is also adjustable. Locks built into the seatbacks keep them upright even during hard braking. A foot-operated seatback release allows the passenger seatback to be unlocked and folded forward for exiting from the back seat.

The rear seat cushion is readily removable for access to the rear seat belt mountings. The station wagon rear seat can be folded forward and the backrests folded down to create a large cargo area. Liftback rear seat backrests can be individually folded forward to provide additional cargo space.

Seat belts and seat belt mounting points are provided for each passenger. The seat belts are designed to move freely during normal driving but to lock during sudden deceleration or changes of direction.

Heating and Ventilation

Fresh air is admitted to the car through an opening in the cowl at the base of the windshield. Air from the car's interior is exhausted through vents in the rear quarter pillars. Controlled amounts of incoming air can be admitted to the passenger compartment through two vents in the outer ends of the dashboard and two vents near the center of the dashboard.

A three-speed fan can be used to create a flow through the ventilation system while the car is moving slowly or standing still. The ventilating air that comes through the defroster vents, the floor vents, and the vents in the center of the dashboard can be heated. It is also possible to block incoming air, and to heat and recirculate the air in the car.

2. MAINTENANCE

The following maintenance operations, which should be performed at the correct mileage intervals, are covered in **LUBRICATION AND MAINTENANCE,** or in this section of the Manual under the heading listed.

1. Checking torque of the seat and the seat belt mounting bolts. **10.1**
2. Checking and, if necessary, adjusting the operation of the hood lock. **4.1**
3. Checking and, if necessary, adjusting the operation of the door locks. **6.5, 7.5**
4. Checking and, if necessary, adjusting the operation of the luggage compartment, tailgate, or rear lid lock. **7.5**
5. Checking and, if necessary, adjusting the operation of the seat adjusters and the seat back locks. **10.2.**

3. BUMPERS AND GRILLE

The bumpers on the various Corolla models covered by this Manual are essentially the same. To meet federal regulations, Corolla front and rear bumpers incorporate a bumper reinforcement and are supported on energy-absorbing mountings.

3.1 Removing and Installing Grille

Except on liftback and sport coupe models, open the hood and remove the screws that hold the top of the grille to the front of the body. On all models, remove the Phillips head screws from the recesses in the front of the grille, then remove the grille by pulling it out forward.

Installation is the reverse of removal. Be sure that all parts are properly aligned before you tighten the screws that attach the grille to the body.

3.2 Removing and Installing Bumpers

The front and rear bumpers are mounted on silicone-filled shock absorbers (Fig. 3-1). The shock absorbers are bolted to mounting brackets, which are bolted to the body. If only part of the bumper assembly needs to be replaced, you may be able to do so without removing the bumper assembly from the car.

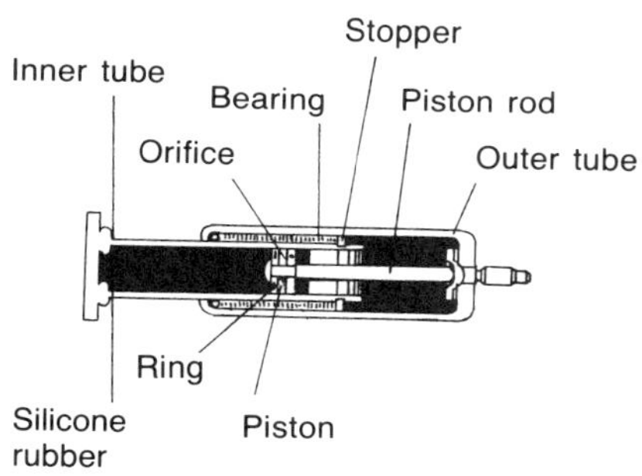

Fig. 3-1. Section view of bumper shock absorber. Shock absorber should return to original condition after being compressed. If not, replace it.

To remove:

1. Disconnect the battery ground strap. Then disconnect the wires for the bumper-mounted parking lights (front bumper) only.
2. Remove the two bolts that attach each bumper shock absorber to its mounting brackets. Then remove the bumper assembly together with the shock absorbers.
3. The bumper assembly can be separated into its individual components for repair. If you separate the bumper from the reinforcement member by removing the central bolt and nut and the bolts along the bottom edge of the bumper, you can gain access to the bolts that attach the shock absorbers to the reinforcement. See Fig. 3-2 for an exploded view of the front and rear bumper assemblies.

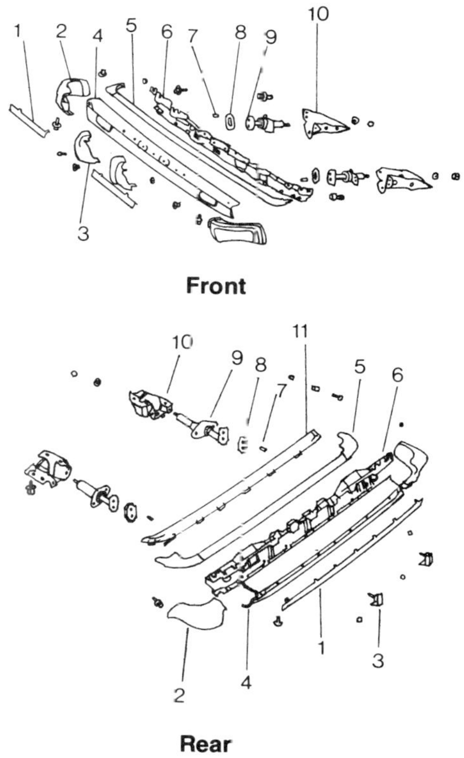

1. Pad
2. Extension
3. Guard
4. Bumper
5. Filler
6. Reinforcement
7. Spacer
8. Mounting plate
9. Shock absorber
10. Mounting bracket
11. Stone deflector

Fig. 3-2. Exploded view of front and rear bumper assemblies.

Installation is the reverse of removal. Lubricate the threads of the nuts, bolts, and screws before you install them.

4. FRONT BODY

The removal and installation of the bumpers, the front fenders, the hood, and similar components do not require a thorough knowledge of automobile body repair. For the most part, you can do the work with ordinary hand tools.

4.1 Removing, Installing, and Adjusting Hood and Hood Lock

If you remove the hood, make sure that you properly align it when you reinstall it. If misaligned, it may rattle or leak.

To remove hood:

1. Open the hood. If you plan to reinstall the hood, carefully mark the locations of the hinges on the hood so that you can reinstall the hood in its exact original location.
2. Remove from one of the hinges the two hood bolts that hold the upper arm of the hinge to the hood (Fig. 4-1).

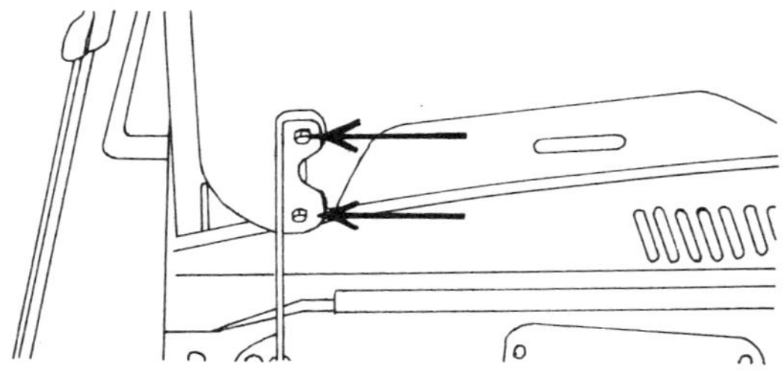

Fig. 4-1. Bolts (arrows) that attach hood to hinge.

3. While someone holds the unbolted side, remove the two upper hood bolts from the other hinge.
4. Working with your helper, lift the hood up and off toward the front of the car.

To install and adjust hood:

1. Using all four bolts, loosely install the hood on its hinges. Reposition the hood by moving its bolts in the elongated bolt holes until the hinges are in the positions you marked for them prior to removal. If you are installing a new hood, align it with the body so that the gap is even all around and the hood lock engages correctly. Then tighten the bolts.
2. If the hood is not flush with the body, adjust its vertical position. Loosen the hinge mounting bolts (Fig. 4-2) to adjust the height of the hood at its rear edge. Adjust the height at the front by raising or lowering the rubber stops mounted on the body at the front corners (Fig. 4-3).

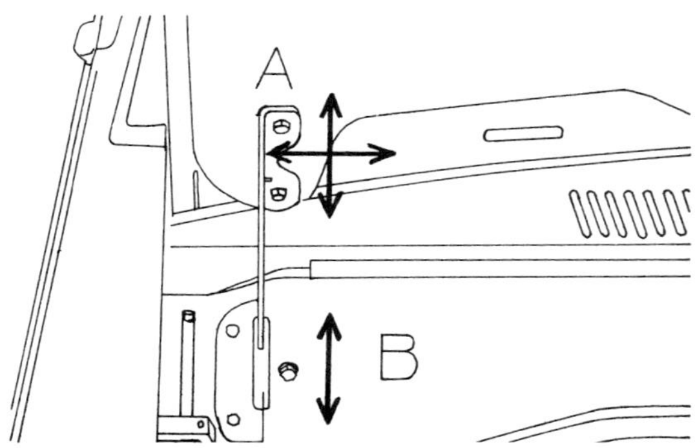

Fig. 4-2. Loosen bolts at **A** to adjust gap between hood and body. Loosen bolts at **B** to adjust height of hood at rear edge.

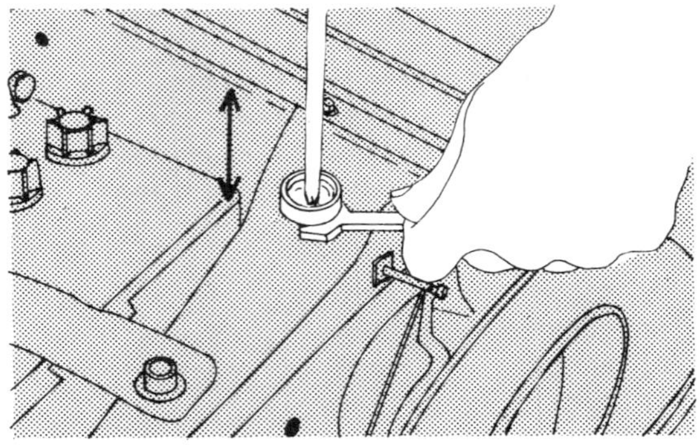

Fig. 4-3. Rubber stops being raised or lowered to adjust height of hood at front edge.

3. After adjusting the heights of the hood, check the hood lock for proper engagement. If necessary, adjust it as described under the next heading.

To remove hood lock:

1. Raise the hood and prop it open. Remove the two bolts that hold the hood lock to the front body panel.
2. Disconnect the release cable from the lock, then remove the lock from the car.

Installation is the reverse of removal. Adjust the position of the cable at the point where it is attached to the lock so that the lock catch retracts fully when you pull the hood release control lever.

After you install the hood and adjust its position, you may need to adjust the lock assembly (Fig. 4-4). If the hood fails to lock, or will lock only if you slam it down hard, raise the lock assembly. If the hood rattles or does not come close to the level of the front fenders, lower the lock assembly. Also, check the lateral adjustment of the hood lock. If the striker is to the left or right of the opening in the hood lock, move the lock accordingly.

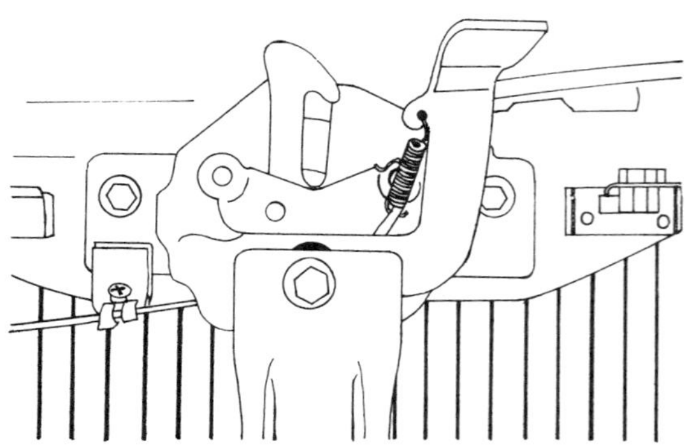

Fig. 4-4. Hood lock assembly.

4.2 Removing and Installing Front Fenders and Lower Front Body Panel

The front fenders are bolted onto the body and can be removed and installed with common hand tools. The rear fenders are welded onto the body and can be replaced only by an experienced body repair technician.

To remove front fender:

1. Disconnect the battery ground strap. Then disconnect the wires for the front sidemarker light.
2. Remove the grille and the front bumper as described in **3. Bumpers and Grille.**
3. Refer to Fig. 4-5 for the locations of the ten bolts and three screws that attach the fender to the body. Open the door and remove the threaded fastener that attaches the fender at its upper rear corner. Then remove the two threaded fasteners that attach the fender at its lower rear corner. Then remove the five threaded fasteners at the front of the fender.

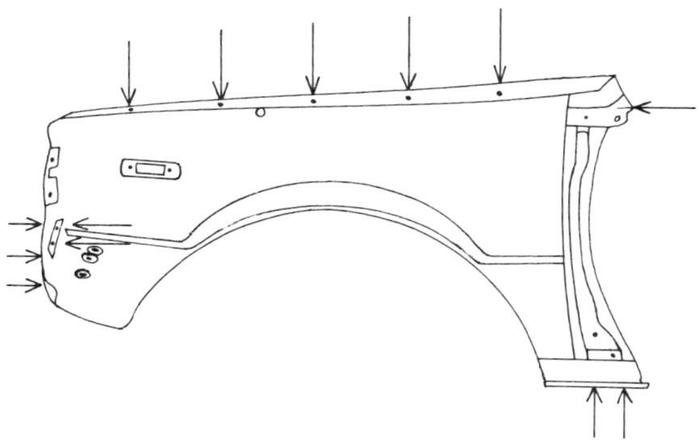

Fig. 4-5. Locations (arrows) of bolts and screws that attach fender to body.

4. Raise the hood. Loosen, but do not remove, the five bolts that hold the top of the fender to the body. Pull out the lower edge of the fender until it is 13 to 25 mm (½ to 1 in.) away from the body. This will break away the undercoating, if applicable, and allow you to check that you have removed all screws or bolts other than those at the top edge of the fender.

> ***CAUTION —***
> *If the fender does not pull away with a moderate amount of effort, make sure you have not overlooked one or more of the mounting screws or bolts. Excessive force will damage the fender.*

5. Supporting the fender so that it does not bend of its own weight, remove the remaining mounting bolts that hold the top of the fender to the body and take off the fender.

Installation is the reverse of removal. Loosely install the bolts and the screws and adjust the gap between the fender and the door and between the fender and the hood. When the fender is properly aligned, tighten the mounting bolts and the screws. Fully undercoat new fenders. If you are reinstalling the original fender, renew the undercoating along the joint between the body and the fender, over the heads of the mounting bolts, and wherever the original undercoating was chipped or scratched during removal.

To remove lower front body panel:

1. Remove the grille and the front bumper as described in **3. Bumpers and Grille.**
2. Remove the four bolts and the six screws that attach the lower front body panel to the body. (See Fig. 4-6.) On liftback and sport coupe models, you need remove only two central bolts and one bolt and one screw at each fender joint. Then remove the panel from the body.

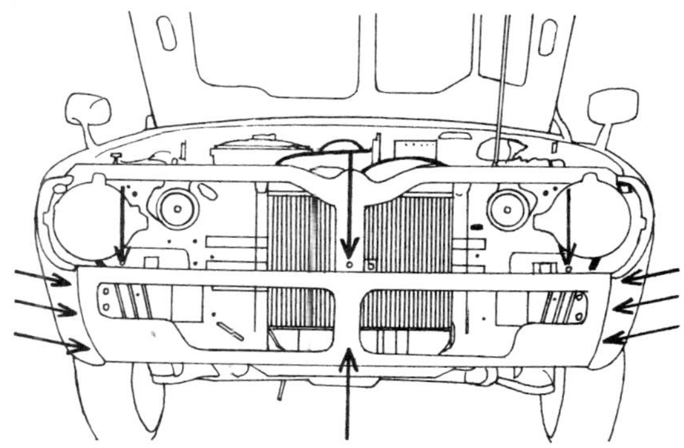

Fig. 4-6. Typical locations (arrows) of fasteners that attach lower front body panel to body.

Installation is the reverse of removal. Loosely install the bolts and the screws and adjust the gap between the panel and the fenders. Then tighten the fasteners. Fully undercoat new panels. If you are reinstalling the original panel, renew the undercoating along the joints between the panel and the fenders, over the heads of the mounting bolts, and wherever the original undercoating was chipped or scratched during removal.

5. REAR BODY

If you remove the luggage compartment lid, it is important that you properly align the lid when you reinstall it. If misaligned, it may rattle or leak.

5.1 Removing, Installing, and Adjusting Luggage Compartment Lid, Hinges, and Lock

Fig. 5-1 is an exploded view of the luggage compartment lid and related parts. You can remove the luggage compartment lid without removing the hinges.

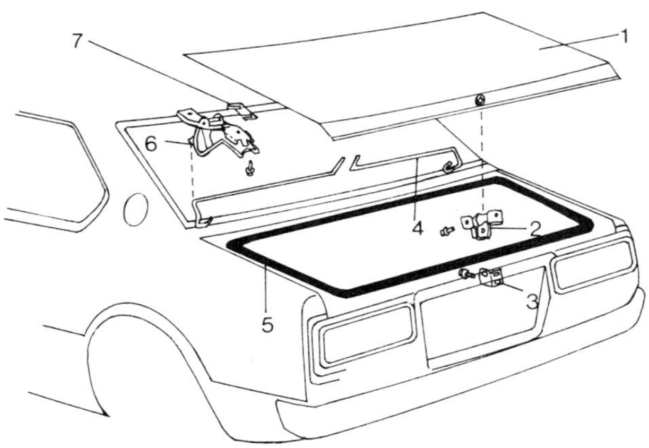

1. Luggage compartment lid
2. Lock assembly
3. Lock striker
4. Torsion bar
5. Weatherstrip
6. Hinge
7. Hinge spacer

Fig. 5-1. Luggage compartment lid and related parts.

Removing and Installing Luggage Compartment Lid

Mark the hinge positions on the lid inner panel to help you align the lid with the body during installation. Unbolt the lid from one hinge, then support the lid with one hand while you unbolt the lid from the second hinge. Then remove the lid from the car.

Before installing the lid, check the condition of the rubber weatherstrip. If necessary, glue or replace it. (Remove all the old trim cement with solvent so that the new weatherstrip will adhere properly.) Carefully align the hinges with the marks you made earlier. Install the hinge spacers and the bolts. Then tighten the bolts. Carefully close the lid and check its alignment with the body. There should be equal space at each side and at the front of the lid. If not, make minor adjustments by loosening the hinge bolts and sliding them in the elongated bolt holes.

To remove hinges:

1. Remove the luggage compartment lid as described under the previous heading.
2. Use a screwdriver to remove the cranked end of the torsion bar from the hinge arm. See Fig. 5-2.

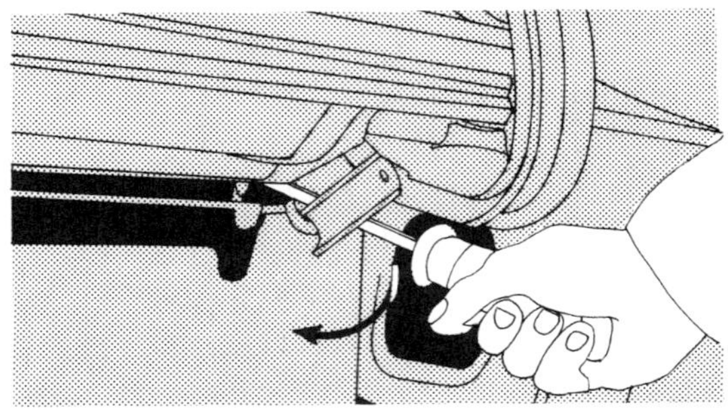

Fig. 5-2. Luggage compartment lid torsion bar being removed from hinge arm.

3. Remove the bolts and the washers that hold the hinge to the body. Then remove the hinge from the car.

Installation is the reverse of removal. Bolt the hinges to the body and connect the torsion bar to the hinge arms. With the hood and the hinge spacers in position, loosely install the bolts that attach the lid to the hinges. Be careful to align the hinges with the marks you made earlier. Then tighten the bolts. Carefully close the lid and check its alignment with the body. There should be equal space at each side and at the front of the lid. If not, make minor adjustments by loosening the hinge-to-lid bolts and sliding them in the elongated bolt holes.

Removing, Installing, and Adjusting Luggage Compartment Lock

To remove the lock, open the trunk. Use a pair of pliers to release the retainer, as shown in Fig. 5-3. This will allow you to pull the cylinder out of the lock assembly. After you have done so, remove the two bolts that hold the latch to the trunk lid and take off the latch.

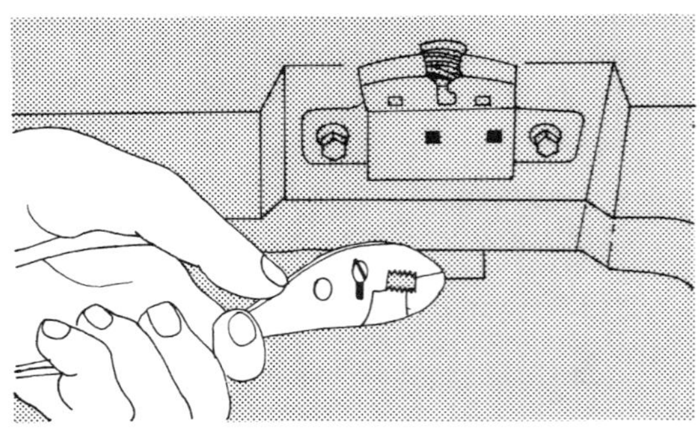

Fig. 5-3. Luggage compartment lock retainer being released.

Installation is the reverse of removal. Following installation, you may need to adjust the lock striker's position (Fig. 5-4). If the lid fails to lock, or will lock only if you slam it down hard, raise the striker. If the lid does not contact the weather seal all around, if it rattles, or if it does not close to the level of the rear fenders, lower the striker on the panel brace. You can adjust the striker position by loosening the bolts and moving the striker on its elongated bolt holes. Tighten the bolts and check the lid closing frequently during the course of adjustments. When the lid closes correctly, fully tighten the bolts.

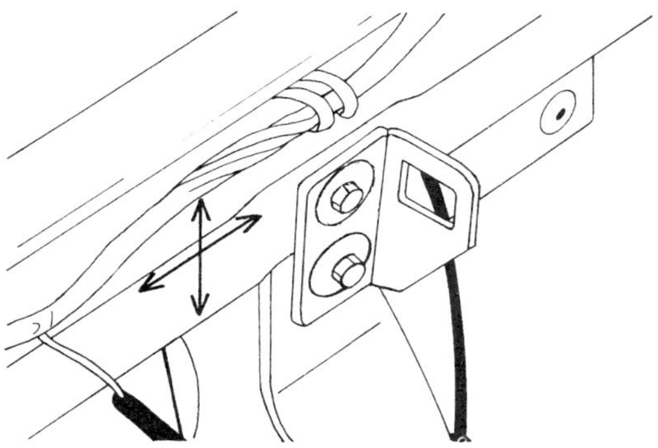

Fig. 5-4. Adjust lock striker's position by loosening two mounting bolts and moving striker on elongated bolt holes as indicated by arrows.

5.2 Removing, Installing, and Adjusting Rear Quarter Window

The Corolla two-door models have two kinds of rear quarter windows. The hardtop has a fully retractable rear quarter window, whereas the liftback and sport coupe models have hinged rear quarter windows.

Removing, Installing, and Adjusting Retractable Rear Quarter Window

The operating mechanism of the retractable rear quarter window differs from the mechanism of the door-mounted windows. Fig. 5-5 is an exploded view of the retractable rear quarter window assembly.

1. Front upper stop
2. Guide
3. Regulator
4. Clip
5. Lower stop
6. Handle
7. Snap ring
8. Escutcheon
9. Front corner weatherstrip
10. Glass holder bracket with followers
11. Spacer
12. Window
13. Weatherstrip
14. Rear upper stop
15. Stop pad

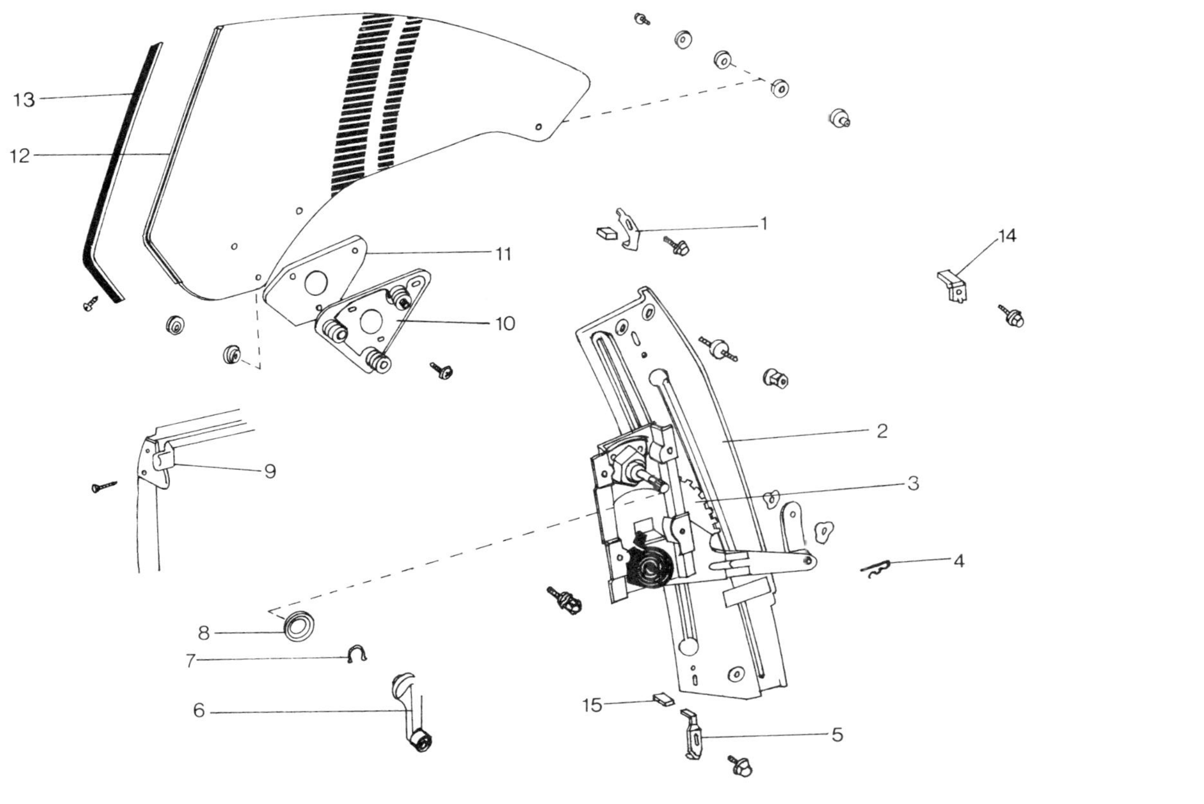

Fig. 5-5. Retractable rear quarter window assembly.

To remove:

1. Remove the rear seat as described in **10.3 Removing and Installing Rear Seat.** Remove the seat belt retractor as described in **10.1 Removing and Installing Seat Belts.**
2. Remove the snap ring that attaches the handle to its shaft, and then remove the quarter window handle and the escutcheon.
3. Remove the two trim panel retainers and the screw that attaches the trim panel at its top front corner. Then remove the trim panel.
4. Remove the two Phillips head screws that attach the rubber belt molding to the body. Then remove the molding (Fig. 5-6).

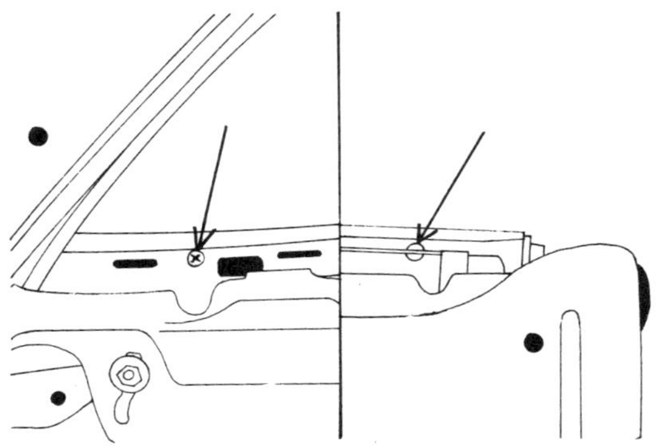

Fig. 5-6. Phillips head screws (arrows) that attach rubber belt molding to body.

5. Peel the covering from the access cutout. Remove the clip that attaches the regulator arm to the follower on the glass holder bracket (Fig. 5-7). Then separate the arm from the follower.

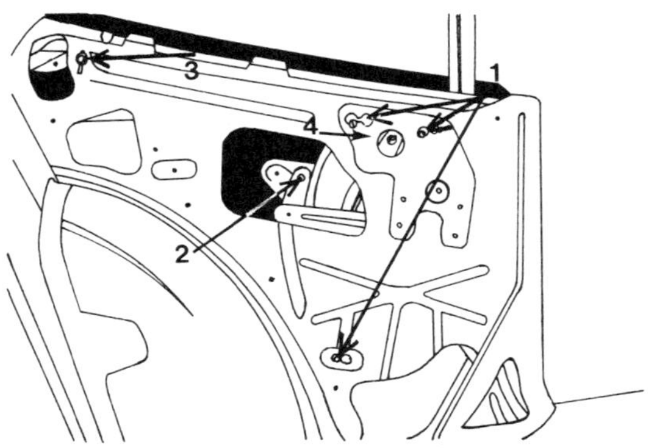

1. Slotted studs (3)
2. Clip
3. Rear upper stop
4. Front upper stop

Fig. 5-7. Slotted studs and other components to be taken out during removal of window and guide.

6. Mark the body panel to record the positions of the three slotted studs, which will simplify reassembly. Then use a screwdriver to hold the studs stationary while you remove the nuts with a wrench. You should now be able to remove the glass and guide as a unit.
7. If necessary, separate the guide from the glass holder bracket by withdrawing the bracket's followers from the holes at the end of the slots in the guide.
8. If you are replacing the glass, remove the glass holder bracket and its spacer by removing the three screws. Also remove the round bumper for the rear upper stop from the lower rear edge of the glass.

To install:

1. If you have replaced the glass, attach the glass holder bracket and its spacer to the glass. Mount the round bumper at the lower rear corner of the glass.
2. Attach the window to the guide by installing the bracket's followers in the slots of the guide.
3. Install the window and guide assembly, and loosely tighten the three nuts on the slotted studs, using the marks you made earlier to help you position the studs. Then tighten the three nuts with a wrench while you hold the studs stationary with a screwdriver.
4. Connect the regulator arm to the window bracket follower using one special washer on each side of the arm. Then install the clip. Reinstall the front and rear upper stops, making sure that the stop pads are installed and in good condition.
5. Before installing the trim panel, temporarily install the handle and wind the window up and down to check for smooth operation. Make sure that the window retracts fully and that there are no gaps between it and the weatherstrip, the rubber molding, or the door window. If the window needs to be adjusted, do so before continuing reassembly, using the instructions given under the next unnumbered heading. If you are satisfied that the window is correctly adjusted, continue with step 6.
6. Replace the cover over the access cutout. Install the rubber belt molding and tighten the two Phillips head screws that hold it in place.
7. Put the trim panel in place and tighten the screw that holds it to the body at its top front corner. Then press the two trim panel retainers in place.
8. Place the handle escutcheon over the shaft, install the snap ring on the handle, then install the handle by pushing it onto the shaft.

9. Replace the seat belt retractor as described in **10.1 Removing and Installing Seat Belts.** Replace the rear seat as described in **10.3 Removing and Installing Rear Seat.**

Adjusting Rear Quarter Window

The position of the rear quarter window is controlled by the front and rear upper stops, the lower stop, and the three slotted studs. You can adjust the window by varying their positions.

To adjust:

1. Remove the rear seat as described in **10.3 Removing and Installing Rear Seat.** Remove the seat belt retractor as described in **10.1 Removing and Installing Seat Belts.**
2. Remove the snap ring that attaches the window handle to its shaft, and then remove the quarter window handle and the escutcheon.
3. Remove the two trim panel retainers and the screw that attaches the trim panel at its top front corner. Then remove the trim panel.
4. Remove the two Phillips head screws that attach the rubber belt molding to the body. Then remove the molding.
5. Peel the covering from the access cutout. Reinstall the window handle and wind the window all the way up. If there is a uniform gap between the top of the window and the body, adjust the window by loosening the lockscrews on the front and the rear upper stops and moving them in equal amounts in the direction indicated by the arrows in Fig. 5-8. If the glass is tilted, adjust its position by loosening and moving only the rear upper stop.

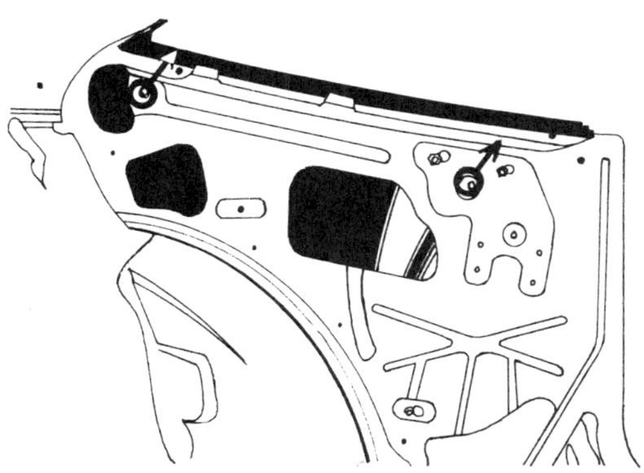

Fig. 5-8. Upper stops (circled) which control maximum window height.

6. If the fit of the window at the top of the frame is correct, make sure there is no gap between the quarter window and the door window. Also see whether there is any front-to-rear play in the window. If either of these conditions exist, correct it by adjusting the positions of the three slotted studs (Fig. 5-9).

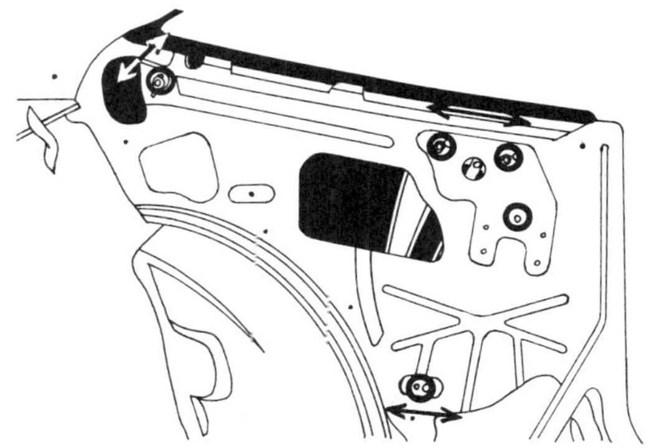

Fig. 5-9. Slotted studs that control position of guide. Move them in directions indicated to close gap at front of window or to eliminate front-to-rear play.

7. Make sure that the quarter window and the door window are flush and that there are no gaps between the glass and the rubber molding. If any of these conditions exist, adjust the lateral position of the glass by loosening the locknuts and then adjusting the slotted studs in or out with a screwdriver (Fig. 5-10).

NOTE ——

If you do not adjust the three slotted studs an equal number of turns in the same direction, you will alter the window's vertical position.

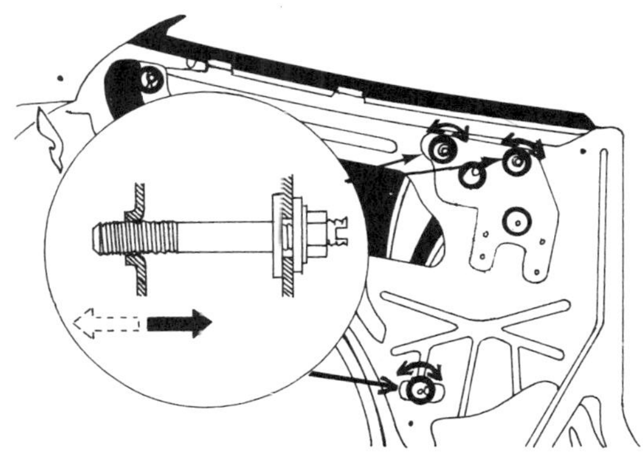

Fig. 5-10. Slotted studs which can be turned clockwise or counterclockwise to vary window's lateral position.

8. See whether you can roll the window completely down into the quarter panel. If the top of the window protrudes when you roll it down all the way, loosen the lower stop (Fig. 5-11) and move it toward the bottom of the car.

NOTE ——

The lower stop is located near the lower slotted stud. If no access hole provides direct access to the lower stop, you can use another adjacent access hole to adjust it.

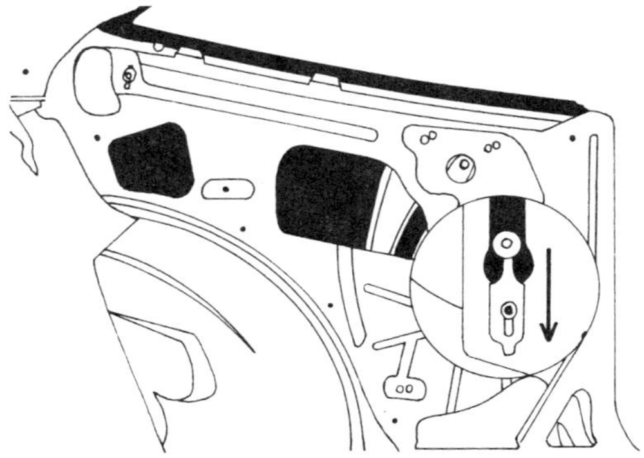

Fig. 5-11. Detail of lower stop.

9. When the window is correctly adjusted, replace the cover over the access cutout. Install the rubber belt molding, if it was removed, and tighten the two Phillips head screws that hold it in place.
10. Put the trim panel in place, and tighten the screw that holds it to the body at its top front corner. Then press the two trim panel retainers in place.
11. Place the handle escutcheon over the shaft, install the snap ring on the handle, then install the handle by pushing it onto the shaft.
12. Replace the seat belt retractor as described in **10.1 Removing and Installing Seat Belts.** Replace the rear seat as described in **10.3 Removing and Installing Rear Seat.**

Removing and Installing Window Regulator

You need not remove the rear quarter window in order to remove the window regulator. If you have already removed the quarter window and guide, proceed to step 5.

To remove:

1. Remove the rear seat as described in **10.3 Removing and Installing Rear Seat.** Remove the seat belt retractor as described in **10.1 Removing and Installing Seat Belts.**
2. Remove the snap ring that attaches the window handle to its shaft, and then remove the quarter window handle and the escutcheon.
3. Remove the two trim panel retainers and the screw that attaches the trim panel at its top front corner. Then remove the trim panel.
4. Peel the covering from the access cutout. Remove the clip that attaches the regulator arm to the window bracket follower, then separate the arm from the follower.
5. Holding the stud stationary with a screwdriver, use a wrench to remove the nut from each slotted stud.
6. Remove the four bolts that attach the regulator to the body panel (Fig. 5-12). Then remove the regulator through the access cutout.

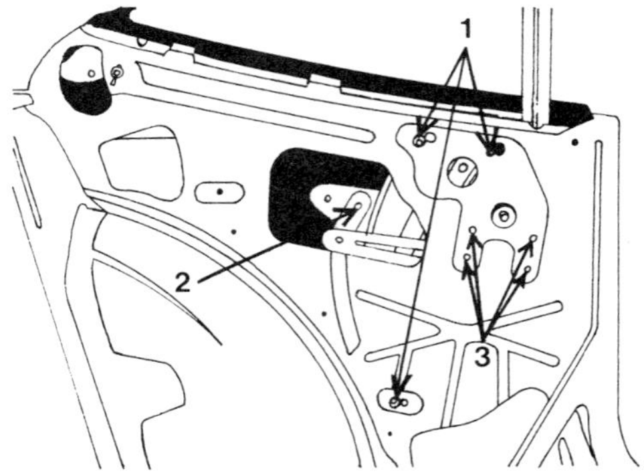

1. Slotted studs (3)
2. Regulator arm clip
3. Regulator bolts (4)

Fig. 5-12. Fasteners related to window regulator removal.

To install:

1. Install the regulator with the arm facing toward the rear of the car. Tighten the four bolts that hold it in place.

NOTE ——

If you have removed the window and guide assembly, complete the installation by following the procedure given in **Removing, Installing, and Adjusting Retractable Rear Quarter Window.** If you did not remove the window and guide assembly, proceed with step 2.

2. Install the nuts on the three slotted studs. Holding the studs stationary with a screwdriver, use a wrench to tighten the nuts.
3. Connect the regulator arm to the window bracket follower, using one special washer on each side of the arm. Then install the clip.

NOTE ——

Before installing the trim panel, temporarily install the handle and wind the window up and downto check for smooth operation. Make sure that the window retracts fully and that there are no gaps between it and the weatherstrip, the rubber molding, or the door window. If the window needs to be adjusted, do so before continuing reassembly, using the instructions given in **Adjusting Rear Quarter Window.** If you are satisfied that the window is correctly adjusted, continue with step 4.

4. Replace the cover over the access cutout. Put the trim panel in place, and tighten the screw that holds it to the body at its top front corner. Then press the two trim panel retainers in place.
5. Place the handle escutcheon over the shaft, install the snap ring on the handle, then install the handle by pushing it onto the shaft.
6. Replace the seat belt retractor as described in **10.1 Removing and Installing Seat Belts.** Replace the rear seat as described in **10.3 Removing and Installing Rear Seat.**

Removing and Installing Hinged Rear Quarter Window

The design of the rear quarter window used on the liftback and the sport coupe models allows it to be easily removed and installed. Fig. 5-13 is an exploded view of the hinged rear quarter window assembly.

To remove:

1. Remove the two Phillips head screws that attach the window latch to the body. Then support the window and remove the Phillips head screw that attaches each flexible hinge to the body. Remove the window by carefully sliding the hinges through the slots in the rubber molding.
2. If you intend to install a new window, remove the screws and mounting hardware that attach the latch and the hinges to the glass.

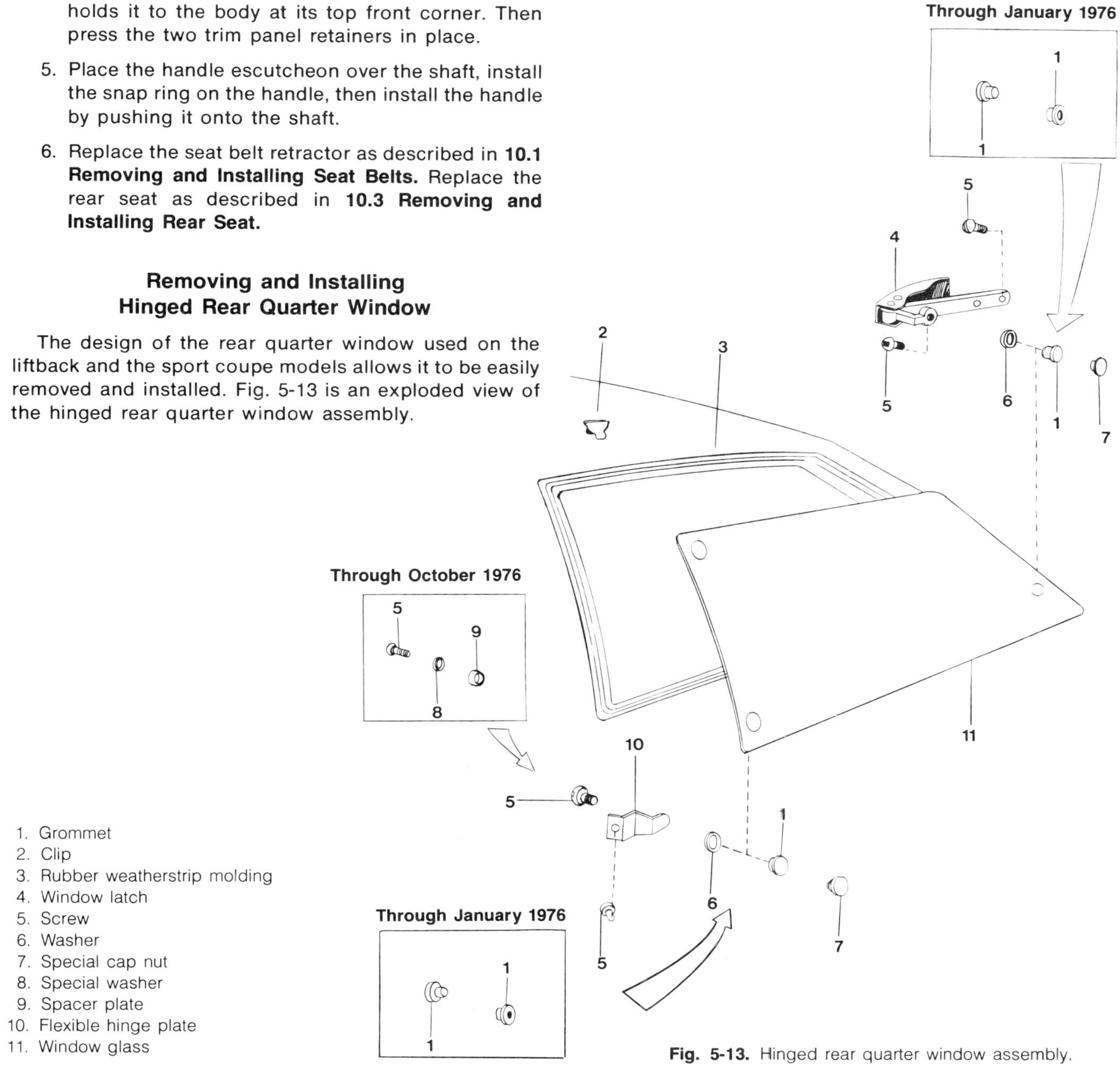

Fig. 5-13. Hinged rear quarter window assembly.

9

Installation is the reverse of removal. If you have installed a new window, install the flexible hinges and the latch on the glass before attaching the hinges and the latch to the body. When sliding the flexible hinges through the slots in the rubber molding, be careful not to tear or damage the rubber. After tightening the screws, check that the window opens and closes smoothly, and that it fits snugly when closed.

6. FRONT DOOR

You can adjust or repair the front door, its hinges, and its window and lock mechanisms. This work can be done without special tools or techniques.

6.1 Removing and Installing Front Door Interior Trim and Glass

All the various Corolla models covered by this Manual have similar regulator mechanisms to raise and lower the front window. However, the regulators are linked to the window glass in different ways. On sedans, the regulator attaches to a channel that supports the glass. On hardtop, sport coupe, and liftback models, the glass is bolted to the regulator's glass holder plates. Fig. 6-1 shows the two basic kinds of front door window assemblies and Fig. 6-2 shows the front door components.

Fig. 6-1. Front door window assemblies.

1. Weatherstrip
2. Channel
3. Stop
4. Regulator arm
5. Regulator
6. Escutcheon
7. Clip
8. Window handle
9. Retainer
10. Glass holder plate (front)
11. Glass holder plate (rear)
12. Regulator bracket

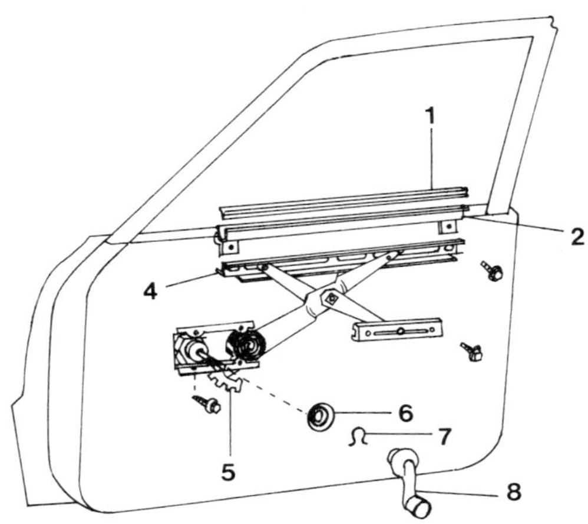

Sedan

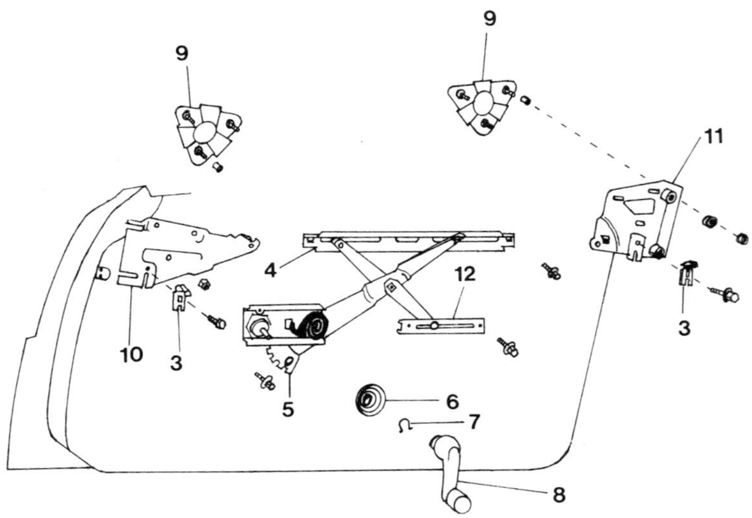

Hardtop, Liftback, and Sport Coupe

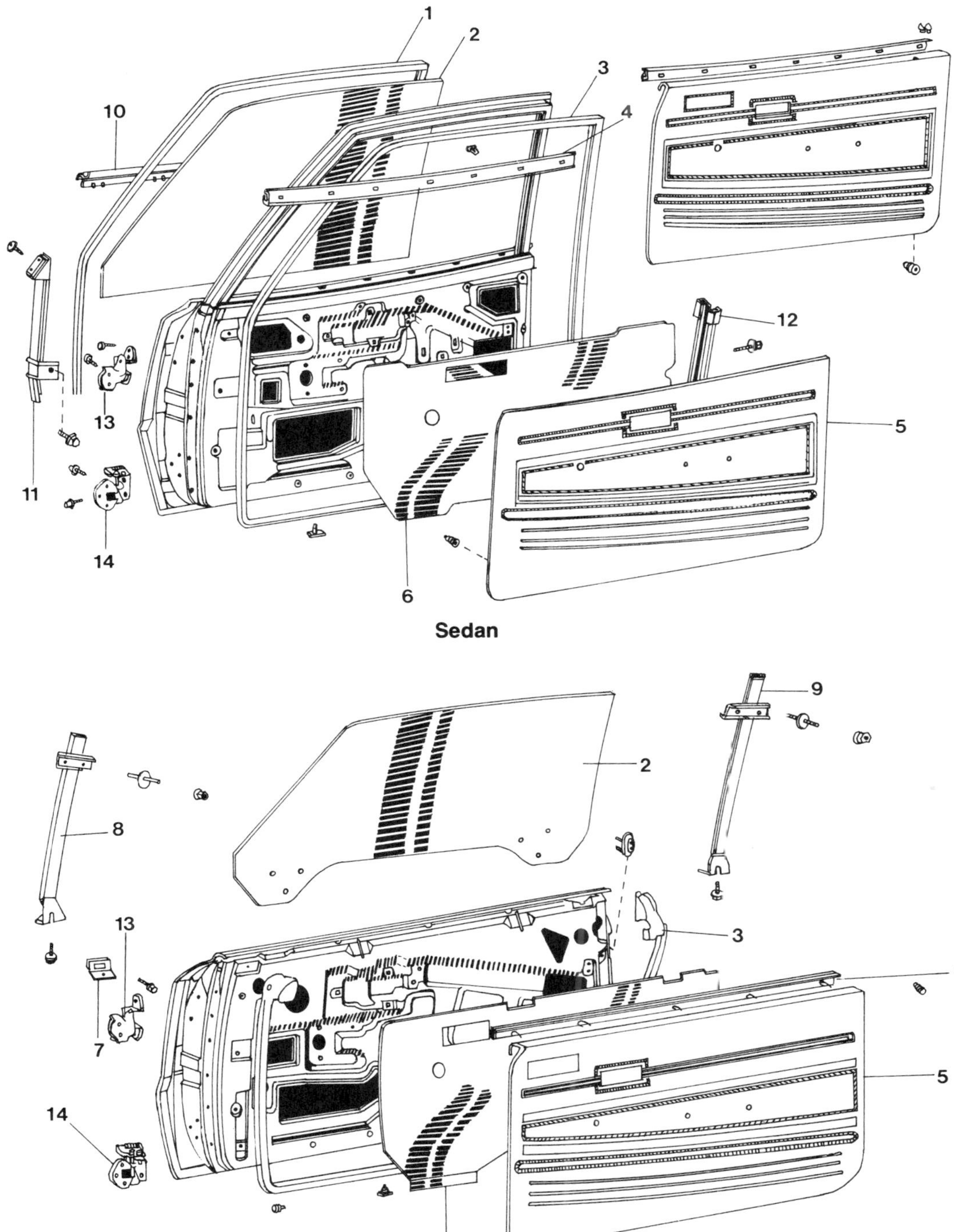

1. Glass guide
2. Glass
3. Weatherstrip
4. Inner weatherstrip
5. Trim panel
6. Access hole cover
7. Inner cushions
8. Front window guide
9. Rear window guide
10. Outer weatherstrip
11. Front support
12. Rear support
13. Upper hinge
14. Lower hinge

Fig. 6-2. Front door components.

To remove front door interior trim:

1. Use a screwdriver to pry off the clip that holds the window handle on its shaft; then remove the window handle and the escutcheon.
2. Remove the liner from behind the inside door handle by taking out the single Phillips head screw that is in the hollow of the liner.
3. Remove the armrest by taking out the two Phillips head screws that hold it to the door.
4. Carefully pull out the trim retainers that attach the trim panel to the door, then remove the panel.
5. Remove the access hole cover, which is attached to the door with adhesive and tape, by peeling it from the door.

To install front door interior trim:

1. Attach the access cover to the door by applying trim cement and tape at the locations shown in Fig. 6-3.

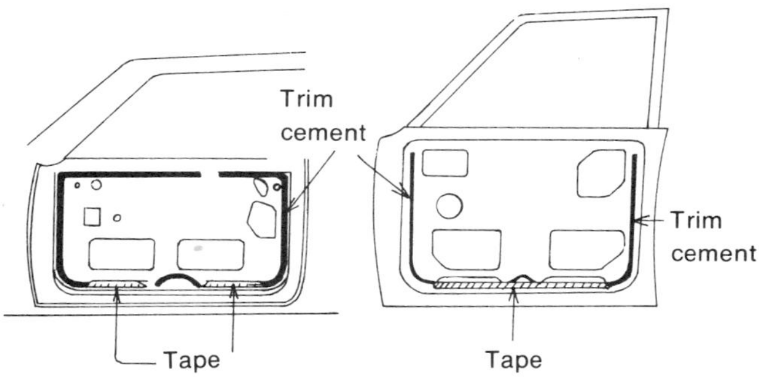

Fig. 6-3. Access cover tape and cement locations.

2. Install the trim panel by pushing the trim retainers into their receptacles in the door panel. Hold the edge of the receptacle with a screwdriver while you push in on the retainer.
3. Install the window handle escutcheon and the window handle. The handle should be angled 45° from the vertical toward the front of the car when the window is rolled up. When the handle is correctly positioned, temporarily remove it, install the clip, then reinstall the handle.
4. Using the Phillips head screws, install the armrest and the door handle liner.

To remove sedan front door window:

1. Wind the window down to its lowest position. Remove the interior trim as described under the previous heading.
2. Remove the two bolts that attach the regulator arm to the channel (Fig. 6-4). Then remove the glass from the door, leaving the channel attached.

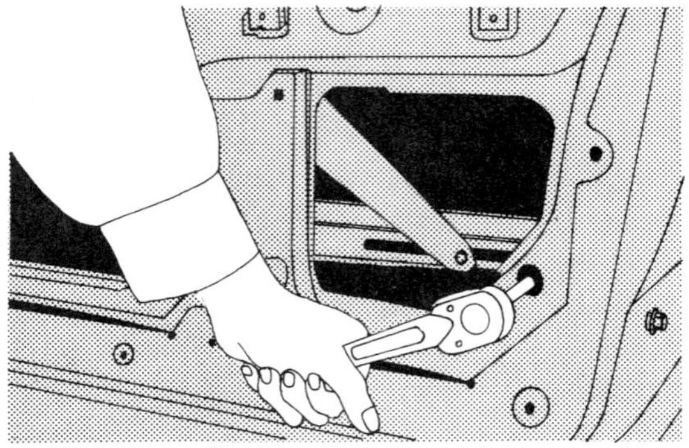

Fig. 6-4. Regulator arm being unbolted from channel.

3. If you intend to install new glass, remove the channel from the glass with a screwdriver or a similar tool. Then remove the weatherstrip.

To install sedan front door window:

1. If you have removed the channel, put the weatherstrip on the glass and lubricate it with soapy water. Using a soft-faced hammer, tap the channel over the weatherstrip. When correctly installed, the front edge of the channel should be 251.5 mm (9⅞ in.) from the front lower corner of the glass.
2. Mount the window assembly in the door. Attach the regulator arm to the channel and tighten the two bolts.
3. Install the front door interior trim as described earlier.

To remove front door window (hardtop, liftback, and sport coupe):

1. Remove the front door interior trim as described earlier. Unscrew the attaching screws and remove the rubber belt molding from the top edge of the door.
2. So that you can reinstall them in their original positions, mark the position of the two stops (Fig. 6-5), that are mounted on the glass holder plates. Careful replacement of the stops will simplify adjustment of the window position after installation.
3. Remove the two bolts that attach the regulator arm to the front and rear glass holder plates (see Fig. 6-6). Then remove the window assembly from the door.
4. If you are installing new glass, remove the retainers and the glass holder plates from the glass.

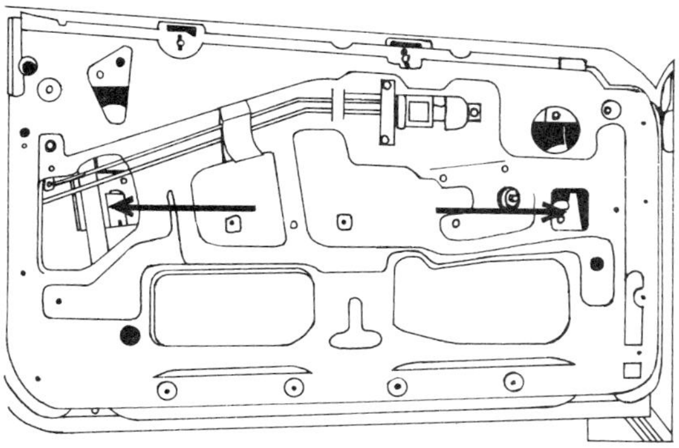

Fig. 6-5. Window stop locations (arrows).

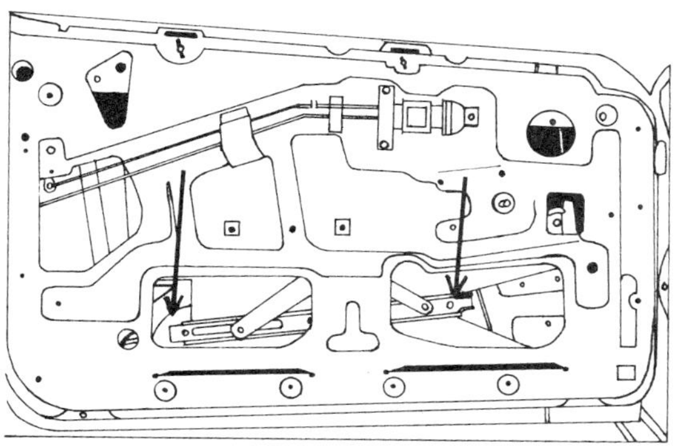

Fig. 6-6. Bolts (arrows) that hold regulator arm to glass holder plates.

To install front door window (hardtop, liftback, and sport coupe):

1. If you are installing new glass, fasten the retainers and the glass holder plates to the glass.
2. Mount the window assembly in the door. Attach the regulator arm to the glass holder plates and tighten the two bolts.
3. Install the two stops in their original locations on the glass holder plates.

> **NOTE ——**
> Temporarily install the window handle and wind the window up and down to check for smooth operation. Make sure that the window retracts fully and that there are no gaps between it and the weatherstrip, the rubber molding, or the door frame. If the window needs to be adjusted, do so before you go on to step 4. The adjustment instructions are given in **6.2 Removing, Installing, and Adjusting Front Door Window Regulator.**

4. Install the rubber belt molding. Then replace the interior trim as described earlier.

6.2 Removing, Installing, and Adjusting Front Door Window Regulator

You can remove and install the window regulator without removing the front door window. If you wish to remove the window also, do so as described in **6.1 Removing and Installing Front Door Interior Trim and Glass.**

To remove:

1. Wind the window down to its lowest position. Remove the interior trim and the access cover as described in **6.1 Removing and Installing Front Door Interior Trim and Glass.**
2. On hardtop, liftback, and sport coupe models, mark the positions of the two stops, and then remove them from the glass holder plates. See Fig. 6-7.

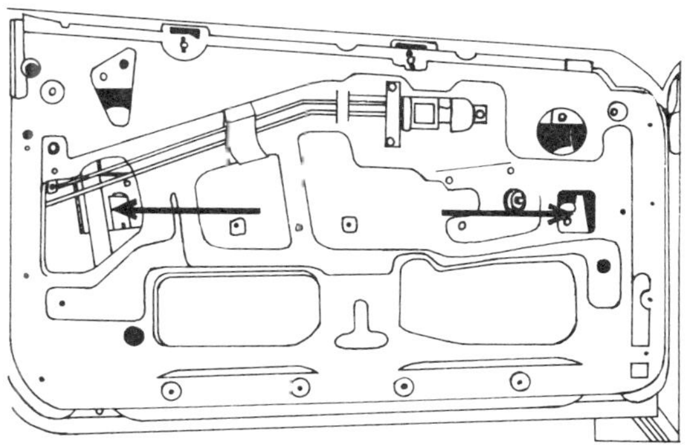

Fig. 6-7. Window stop locations (arrows).

3. Remove the two bolts that attach the regulator arm to the channel on sedans (Fig. 6-8), and to the glass holder plates on hardtops, liftbacks, and sport coupes (Fig. 6-9).

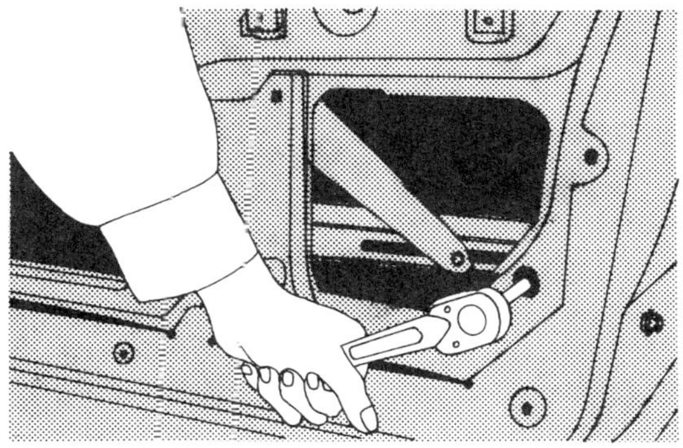

9

Fig. 6-8. Regulator arm being unbolted from channel (sedan only).

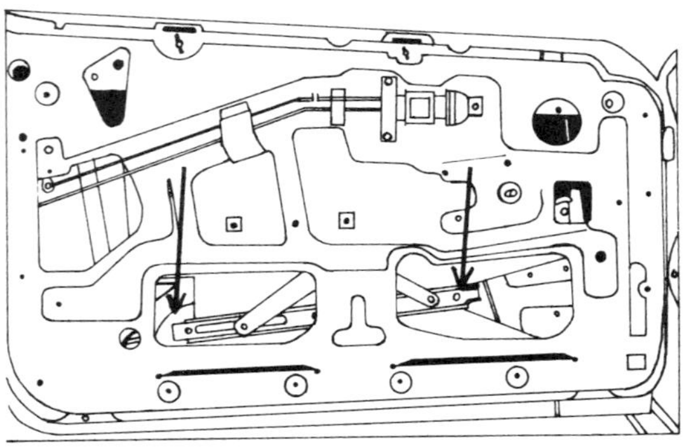

Fig. 6-9. Bolts that hold regulator arm to glass holder plates (arrows) (hardtop, liftback, and sport coupe).

4. On hardtops, sport coupes, and liftbacks, mark the positions of the two bolts that hold the regulator bracket to the door. Then, on all models, remove the six bolts that attach the regulator and the regulator arm to the door (Fig. 6-10). Remove the regulator assembly through the access hole.

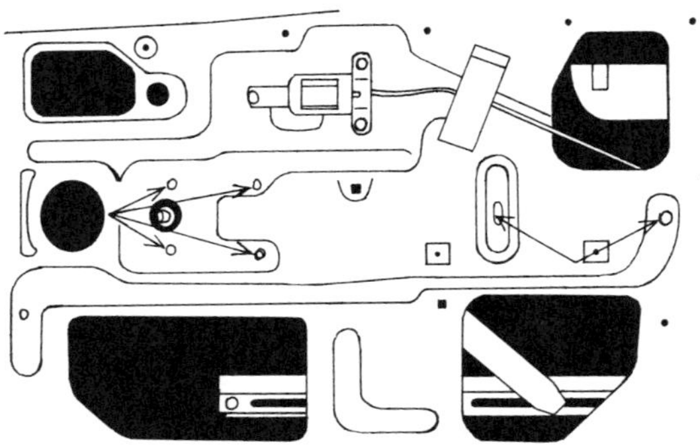

Fig. 6-10. Bolts (arrows) that attach regulator to door.

To install and adjust (sedan only):

1. Inspect the regulator for damage or wear. If necessary, lubricate the spring and the sliding parts with multipurpose grease.
2. Install the regulator and tighten the four bolts that hold it to the door. The two bolts that attach the regulator bracket to the door should remain finger-tight.
3. Lower the window 30 to 60 mm ($1\frac{3}{16}$ to $2\frac{3}{8}$ in.). Adjust the position of the regulator bracket so that it is horizontal (Fig. 6-11). Then tighten the two bolts that hold it in place.
4. Attach the regulator arm to the window channel and tighten the two bolts that hold it in place.
5. Install the interior trim as described previously.

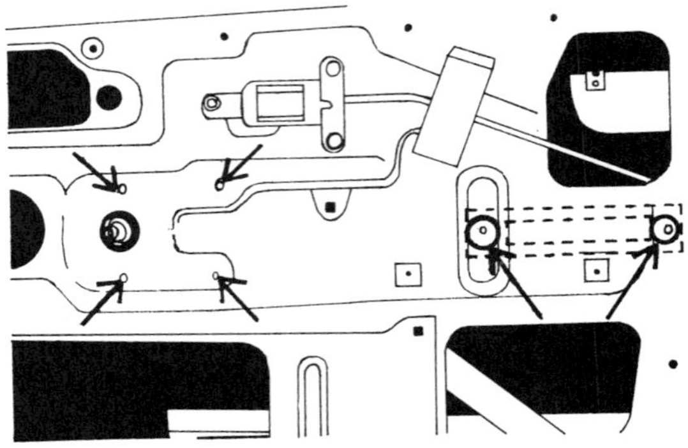

Fig. 6-11. Four bolts (left) that hold regulator to door and two bolts (right) that hold regulator bracket (dotted lines) to door. Regulator bracket must be horizontal for correct window adjustment.

To install and adjust (hardtop, liftback, and sport coupe):

1. Inspect the regulator for damage or wear. If necessary, lubricate the spring and the sliding parts with multipurpose grease.
2. Install the regulator, loosely installing the six bolts that hold it. Tighten the four bolts that hold the main body of the regulator to the door. Position the two remaining bolts in the locations you marked for them before disassembly, then tighten them.
3. Attach the regulator arm to the two glass holder plates and tighten the two bolts that hold it in place.
4. Temporarily install the window handle and wind the window all the way up. If there is a uniform gap at the top and the front of the window, adjust the window by loosening the two stops (Fig. 6-12) and moving them toward the bottom of the door. Move both stops an equal amount to avoid tilting the window. Tighten the bolts that hold the stops, then see whether the problem has been corrected.

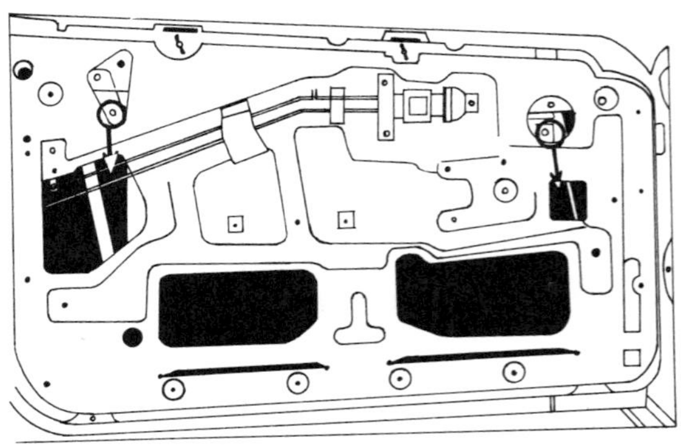

Fig. 6-12. Window position stops (circled). Move equally in direction indicated to maintain uniform gap at top and front of window.

5. With the window wound all the way up, see whether there is a gap at the front edge of the window. To eliminate any gap, loosen the nuts on the four slotted studs (Fig. 6-13) while you hold the studs stationary with a screwdriver. Move the studs toward the front of the door until the gap at the front of the window is eliminated. Then, holding the studs stationary with a screwdriver, tighten the four nuts.

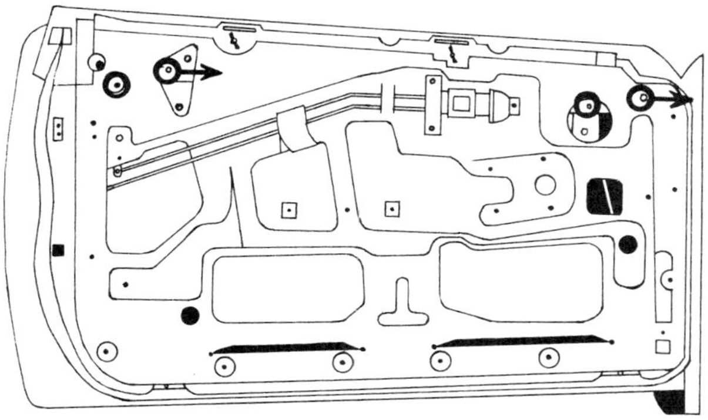

Fig. 6-13. Four slotted studs (circled) that control position of window guides. Move equally in direction indicated to eliminate gap at front of window.

6. If there is a gap at the top edge with the window wound all the way up, loosen the nuts on the slotted studs while you hold the studs stationary with a screwdriver. Also loosen the two stops. Move the slotted studs toward the rear of the door and the stops toward the bottom of the door a sufficient amount to eliminate the gap. Then tighten the bolts and recheck the window adjustment.

7. If the glass is tilted, adjust it by changing the position of the regulator bracket. First loosen the two bolts that hold the bracket (Fig. 6-14). Then adjust the positions of the bracket until the tilt of the glass is eliminated and tighten the bolts.

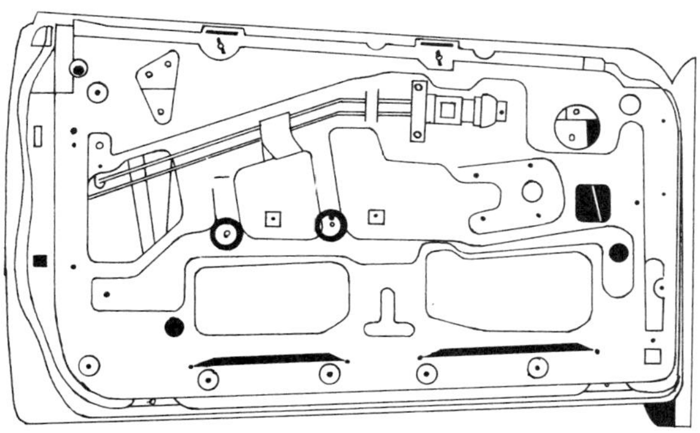

Fig. 6-14. Two bolts (circled) that hold regulator bracket to door.

8. See whether the glass makes good contact with the weatherstrip. If the glass is too far toward the inside or the outside of the door, you can adjust its lateral position by turning the slotted studs.

NOTE ——

To make this adjustment, loosen the nuts sufficiently to allow the studs to be turned in or out with a screwdriver. Also loosen the two bolts on the bottom edge of the door (Fig. 6-15) so that the supports are free to move. Turn all four studs the same amount in the same direction. When the window's lateral position is correct, hold the studs stationary with a screwdriver while you tighten the locknuts with a wrench. Then tighten the two bolts at the bottom of the door. If this adjustment produces a gap at the top of the window, eliminate the gap by repositioning the two stops toward the bottom of the door.

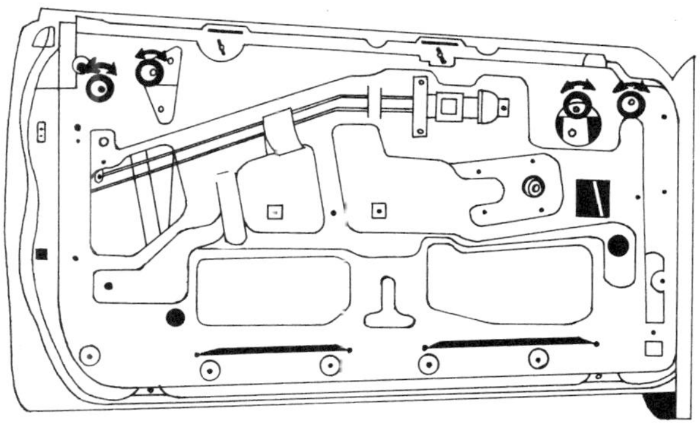

Fig. 6-15. Four slotted studs (circled) at top of door panel and two bolts at bottom edge of door, which control position of window supports.

9. Check the window for excessive front-to-rear play. To correct excessive play, loosen the four nuts on the slotted studs, then move the studs toward the center of the door. Once the window is correctly adjusted, you should tighten the nuts on the slotted studs while holding the studs stationary with a screwdriver.

9

10. If there is side-to-side play, eliminate it by loosening the two bolts that hold the two inner cushions (Fig. 6-16). Move the bolts and the inner cushions until the window is correctly adjusted, then tighten the bolts.

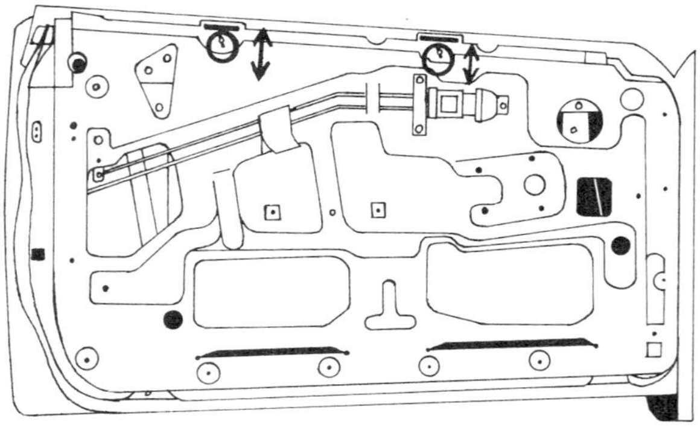

Fig. 6-16. Bolts (circled) that are loosened to adjust inner cushions.

11. When the window is correctly adjusted, replace the interior trim panel as described in **6.1 Removing and Installing Front Door Interior Trim and Glass.**

6.3 Checking and Adjusting Front Door Hinges

The door hinges are adjustable. You should adjust their positions if the door is not correctly aligned with the body, or if the door does not close correctly.

To check and adjust:

1. Check the condition of the hinges. If the hinge pin is loose because of wear or damage, replace the hinge assembly.
2. Check the space between the door and the door aperture in the body. If the gap is not uniform, adjust the hinges as described in the next three steps.
3. Loosen the five bolts that attach the hinges to the door. Correctly position the door in the aperture, then tighten the bolts.
4. If the door is not flush with the body, adjust it by loosening the five bolts that attach the hinges to the body. Correct the alignment of the door and then tighten the bolts.
5. If the door alignment is correct but the door does not close completely, adjust the position of the striker as described in **6.5 Removing, Installing, and Adjusting Front Door Lock System.**

6.4 Removing and Installing Front Door

If you plan to reinstall the same door, mark the location of the hinges on the door before removal, to help you realign the door later.

To remove:

1. Support the door solidly so that the upper hinge will not be bent or broken by the door's weight when you unbolt the lower hinge.
2. Remove the three bolts that hold the lower hinge to the door.
3. Keeping the door supported, remove the three bolts that attach the upper hinge to the door. Remove the door from the car.

To install:

1. Inspect the rubber weatherstrip around the door. If it is cracked or deformed, replace it.

NOTE ——
Before replacing a weatherstrip, clean away all the old adhesive with solvent. Install the new weatherstrip with trim cement.

2. If you are reinstalling the original door, mount the hinges with reference to the marks you made earlier. If you are installing a new door, do not fully tighten the hinge mountings until you have aligned the door.
3. Position the door in the door opening so that it contacts the weatherstrip evenly all around. After the door is aligned, tighten the five bolts that attach the hinges to the door.

6.5 Removing, Installing, and Adjusting Front Door Lock System

To carry out all the following procedures, you must first remove the door trim panel and the access hole cover as described in **6.1 Removing and Installing Front Door Interior Trim and Glass.** Refer to Fig. 6-17 for an exploded view of the front door release and lock assembly.

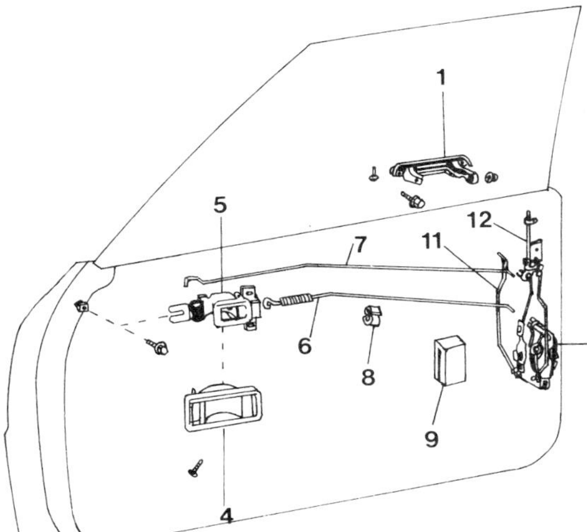

Two-door

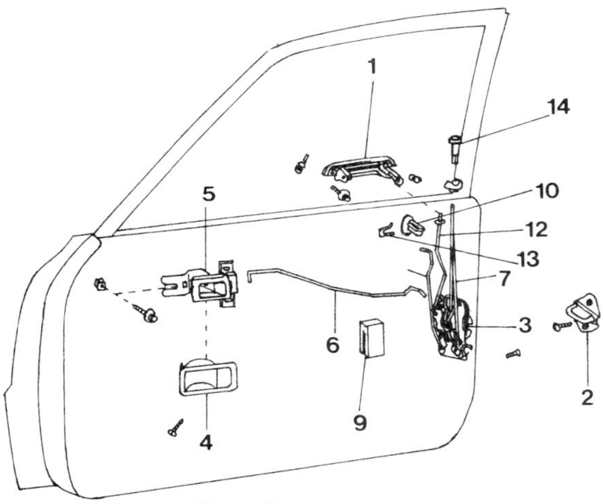

Four-door

1. Outside door handle
2. Striker
3. Lock
4. Handle liner
5. Inside door handle
6. Pullrod
7. Lockrod
8. Clip
9. Silencer
10. Lock cylinder
11. Cylinder rod
12. Handle rod
13. Cylinder clamp
14. Lock button

Fig. 6-17. Front door release and lock assembly.

To remove front door lock:

1. Remove the clips that attach the four operating rods to the lock mechanism, and remove the rods.
2. Remove the bolt at the lower rear corner of the door (refer to Fig. 6-18).
3. Remove the four Phillips head screws and remove the door lock from the door.

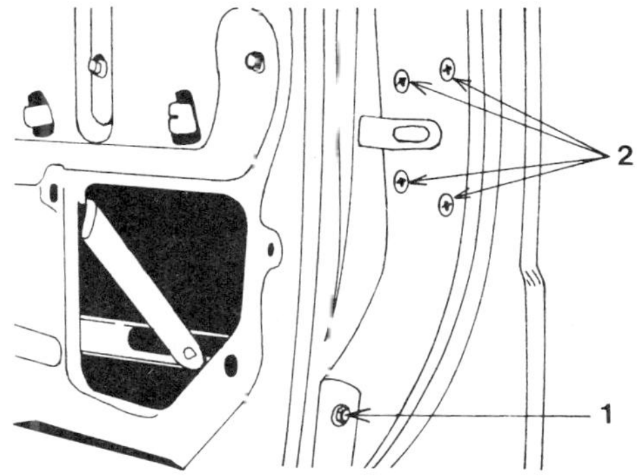

Fig. 6-18. Bolt (**1**) and four screws (**2**) that hold lock to door.

Installation is the reverse of removal. Before installation, inspect the door lock for smooth operation and, if necessary, lubricate the sliding parts with multipurpose grease. After installation, replace the access hole cover and the interior trim panel as described in **6.1 Removing and Installing Front Door Interior Trim and Glass.**

To remove outside front door handle:

1. By reaching up inside the door and removing the bushing from the threaded adjuster at the end of the rod, disconnect the handle rod from the outside door handle.
2. Remove the two Phillips head screws that hold the door handle to the door panel.
3. Remove the handle from the door.

To install and adjust outside front door handle:

1. Position the door handle and tighten the two Phillips head screws that hold it to the door panel.
2. Before connecting the handle rod, adjust its free-play. Because of the elongated hole at its lower end, which connects to the lock, the rod has a range of up-and-down movement. Allow it to drop to its lowest position. Then adjust the threaded connector so that, when connected to the door handle, the rod is 0.5 to 1.0 mm (.02 to .04 in.) above this lowest position.
3. Connect the handle rod to the door handle and reinstall the bushing on the threader adjuster.
4. Replace the access hole cover and the trim panel as described in **6.1 Removing and Installing Front Door Interior Trim and Glass.**

To remove lock cylinder:

1. Remove the connector that holds the cylinder rod to the back of the door lock cylinder.
2. Slide out the clamp that holds the lock cylinder in place.
3. Insert the key, then remove the lock cylinder.

Installation is the reverse of removal. Install the lock cylinder and the clamp. Then attach the cylinder rod to the cylinder. Replace the access hole cover and the trim panel as described in **6.1 Removing and Installing Front Door Interior Trim and Glass.**

To remove inside front door handle:

1. Disconnect the pullrod from the lock assembly. On two-door models, disconnect the lockrod from the lock assembly.
2. Remove the three Phillips head screws that hold the door handle to the door panel (Fig. 6-19).
3. Remove the handle assembly.

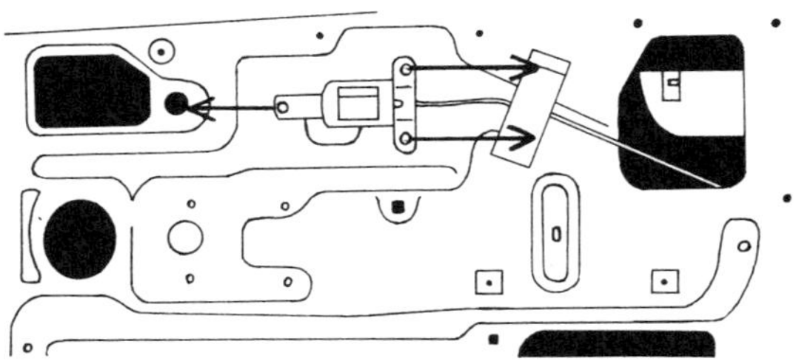

Fig. 6-19. Inside door handle mounting screws (arrows).

To install and adjust inside front door handle:

1. Loosely install the handle assembly using the three Phillips head screws.
2. Connect the pullrod to the lock assembly. On two-door cars, also connect the lockrod to the lock assembly.
3. Slide the handle assembly toward the front of the door until you feel increased resistance from the lock mechanism. Then move the handle assembly 0.5 to 1.0 mm (.02 to .04 in.) toward the rear of the door and tighten the screws.
4. Replace the access hole cover and the trim panel as described in **6.1 Removing and Installing Front Door Interior Trim and Glass.**

Adjusting Front Door Striker

If the door does not close flush with the body, or if the lock is not correctly aligned with the striker, you can adjust the striker's position. To do this, loosen the two Phillips head screws that hold the striker to the body. Then adjust the striker so that the lock does not hit it off center and so that the door is flush with the body when it is closed. If the door lock does not make contact with the striker because the rear of the door is too low, correct the door position by adjusting the hinges as described in **6.3 Checking and Adjusting Front Door Hinges.**

7. REAR DOOR

You can adjust or repair the rear door, its hinges, and its window and lock mechanisms without special tools or techniques.

7.1 Removing and Installing Rear Door Interior Trim and Glass

The rear door window is raised and lowered by a single regulator arm, instead of the dual scissors-like regulator arms that operate the front door. The regulator arm is attached to a channel that supports the window glass. Fig. 7-1 and Fig. 7-2 give exploded views of the rear door window assembly and the rear door.

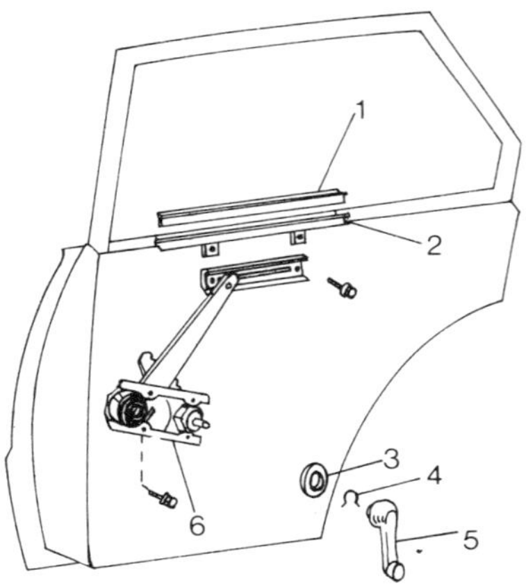

1. Weatherstrip
2. Channel
3. Escutcheon
4. Clip
5. Window handle
6. Regulator

Fig. 7-1. Rear door window assembly.

1. Outer weatherstrip
2. Glass
3. Glass guide
4. Quarter window glass
5. Quarter window weatherstrip
6. Rear door
7. Divider
8. Weatherstrip
9. Inner weatherstrip
10. Access hole cover
11. Trim panel
12. Upper hinge
13. Lower hinge

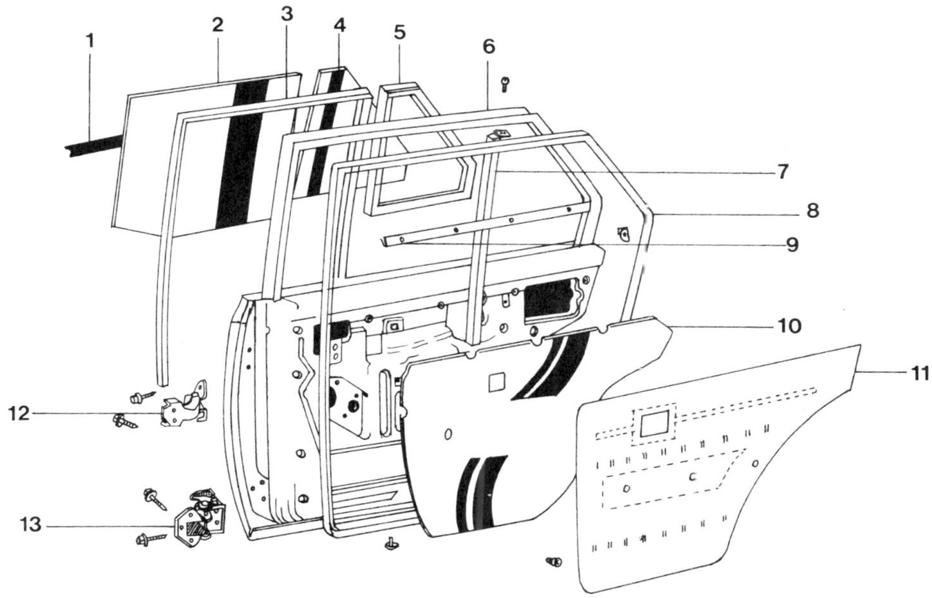

Fig. 7-2. Rear door components.

To remove rear door interior trim:

1. Use a screwdriver to pry off the clip that holds the window handle on its shaft; then remove the window handle and the escutcheon.
2. Remove the liner from behind the inside door handle by taking out the single Phillips head screw that is in the hollow of the liner.
3. Remove the armrest by taking out the two Phillips head screws that hold it to the door.
4. Carefully pull out the trim retainers that attach the trim panel to the door, then remove the panel.
5. Remove the access hole cover, which is attached to the door with adhesive and tape, by peeling it from the door.

To install rear door interior trim:

1. Attach the access cover to the door by applying trim cement and tape at the locations shown in Fig. 7-3.

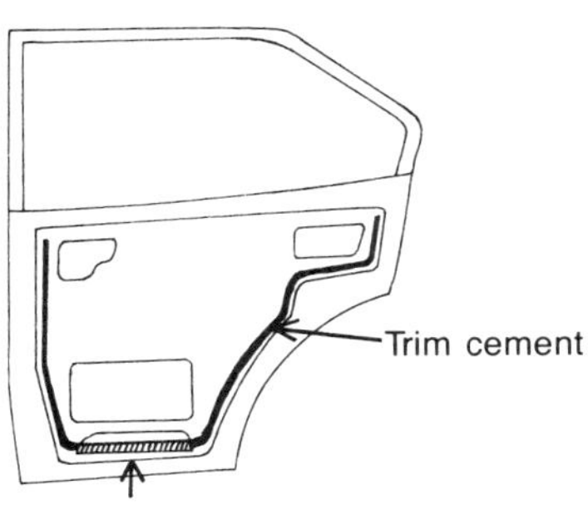

Fig. 7-3. Access cover tape and cement locations.

2. Install the trim panel by pushing the trim retainers into their receptacles in the door panel. Hold the edge of the receptacle with a screwdriver while you push in on the retainer.
3. Install the window handle escutcheon and the window handle. The handle should be angled 45° below horizontal toward the rear of the car when the window is rolled up. When the handle is correctly positioned, remove it temporarily, install the clip, then reinstall the handle.
4. Using the Phillips head screws, install the armrest and the door handle liner.

To remove rear door window:

1. Wind the window down to its lowest position. Remove the interior trim as described under the previous heading.
2. Remove the two bolts that attach the regulator arm to the channel (Fig. 7-4). Then remove the glass from the door, leaving the channel attached.

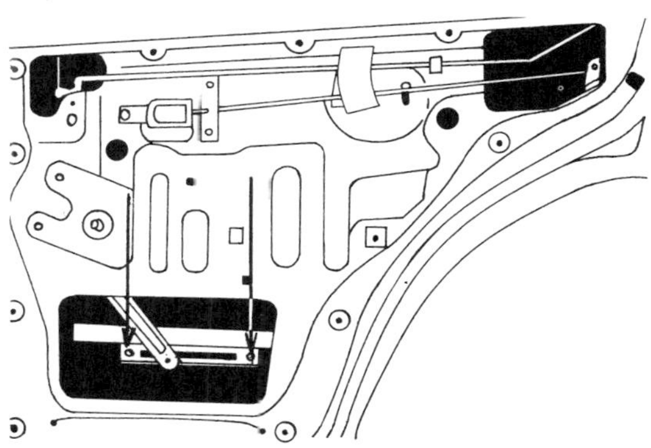

Fig. 7-4, Bolts (arrows) that attach regulator arm to channel.

9

3. If you intend to install glass, remove the channel from the glass with a screwdriver or a similar tool. Then remove the weatherstrip.

To install rear door window:

1. If you have removed the channel, put the weatherstrip on the glass and lubricate it with soapy water. Using a soft-faced hammer, tap the channel over the weatherstrip. When correctly installed, the front edge of the channel should be 115.5 mm (4½ in.) from the front lower corner of the glass.
2. Mount the window assembly in the door. Attach the regulator arm to the channel and tighten the two bolts.
3. Install the rear door interior trim as described earlier.

To remove rear door quarter window glass:

1. Remove the interior trim and the rear door trim as described in **7.1 Removing and Installing Rear Door Interior Trim and Glass.**
2. Peel back the weatherstrip to expose the screw that attaches the divider to the window frame (Fig. 7-5). Remove the screws.

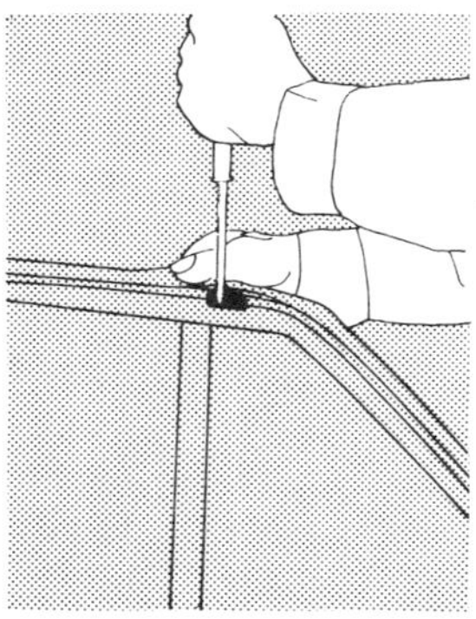

Fig. 7-5. Screw that attaches top of divider to window frame being removed.

3. Remove the bolt that holds the base of the divider to the door. Remove the divider, then pull out the quarter window glass toward the front of the door.

Installation is the reverse of removal. Install the quarter window, the divider, and the screw and bolt that hold the divider in place. Replace the access hole cover and trim panel as described in **7.1 Removing and Installing Rear Door Interior Trim and Glass.**

7.2 Removing and Installing Rear Door Window Regulator

You can remove and install the window regulator without removing the rear door window. If you wish to remove the window also, do so as described in **7.1 Removing and Installing Rear Door Interior Trim and Glass.**

To remove:

1. Wind the window down to its lowest position. Remove the interior trim and the access hole cover as described in **7.1 Removing and Installing Rear Door Interior Trim and Glass.**
2. Remove the two bolts that attach the regulator arm to the channel (Fig. 7-6).

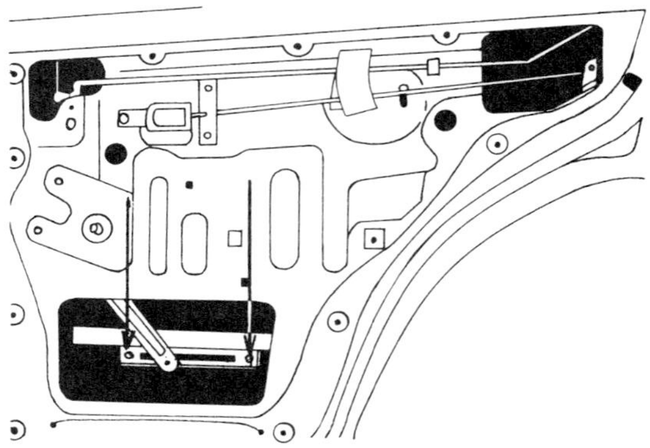

Fig. 7-6. Bolts (arrows) that attach regulator arm to channel.

3. Remove the four bolts that attach the regulator to the door (Fig. 7-7). Then remove the regulator through the access hole.

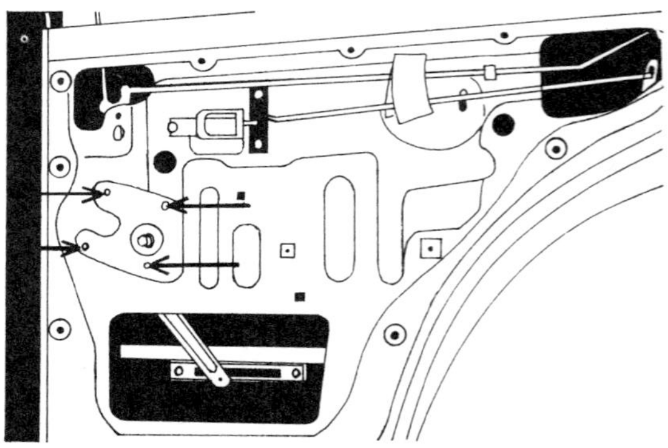

Fig. 7-7. Bolts (arrows) that attach regulator to door.

To install:

1. Inspect the regulator for damage or wear. If necessary, lubricate the spring and the sliding parts with multipurpose grease.
2. Install the regulator and tighten the four bolts that hold it to the door.
3. Attach the regulator arm to the window channel and tighten the two bolts that hold it in place.
4. Install the interior trim as described previously.

7.3 Checking and Adjusting Rear Door Hinges

The door hinges are adjustable. You should adjust their positions if the door is not correctly aligned with the body, or if the door does not close correctly.

To check and adjust:

1. Check the condition of the hinges. If the hinge pin is loose because of wear or damage, replace the hinge assembly.
2. Check the space between the door and the door aperture in the body. If the gap is not uniform, adjust the hinges as described in the next three steps.
3. Loosen the five bolts that attach the hinges to the door. Correctly position the door in the aperture, then tighten the bolts.
4. If the door is not flush with the body, adjust it by loosening the five bolts that attach the hinges to the body. Correct the alignment of the door and then tighten the bolts.
5. If the door alignment is correct but the door does not close completely, adjust the position of the striker as described in **7.5 Removing, Installing, and Adjusting Rear Door Lock System.**

7.4 Removing and Installing Rear Door

If you plan to reinstall the same door, mark the location of the hinges on the door before removal to help you realign the door later.

To remove:

1. Support the door solidly so that the upper hinge will not be bent or broken by the door's weight when you unbolt the lower hinge.
2. Remove the three bolts that hold the lower hinge to the door.
3. Keeping the door supported, remove the two bolts that attach the upper hinge to the door. Remove the door from the car.

To install:

1. Inspect the rubber weatherstrip around the door. If it is cracked or deformed, replace it.

> **NOTE ——**
> Before replacing a weatherstrip, clean away all the old adhesive with solvent. Install the new weatherstrip with trim cement.

2. If you are reinstalling the original door, mount the hinges with reference to the marks you made earlier. If you are installing a new door, do not fully tighten the hinge mountings until you have aligned the door.
3. Position the door in the door opening so that it contacts the weatherstrip evenly all around. After the door is aligned, tighten the five bolts that attach the hinges to the door.

7.5 Removing, Installing, and Adjusting Rear Door Lock System

To carry out all the following procedures, you must first remove the door trim panel and the access hole cover as described in **7.1 Removing and Installing Rear Door Interior Trim and Glass.** Refer to Fig. 7-8 for an exploded view of the rear door release and lock assembly.

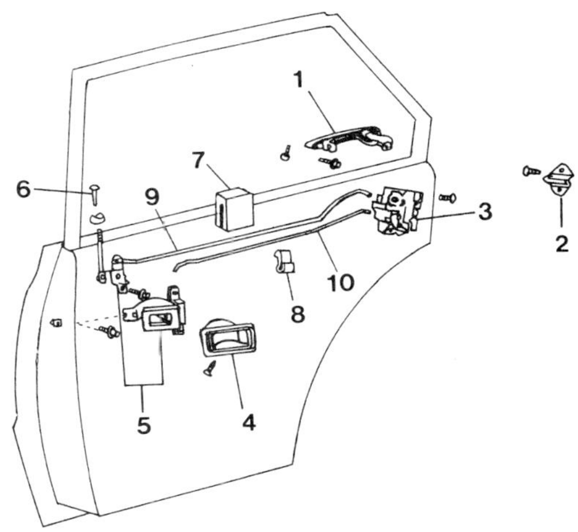

1. Outside door handle	6. Lock button
2. Striker	7. Silencer
3. Lock	8. Clip
4. Handle liner	9. Lockrod
5. Inside door handle	10. Pullrod

Fig. 7-8. Rear door release and lock assembly.

9

To remove rear door lock:

1. Remove the clips that attach the lockrod and the pullrod to the lock mechanism, and remove the rods.
2. Remove the three Phillips head screws that hold the door lock in position.
3. Disengage the lock assembly from the outside door handle mechanism, then remove the lock from the door.

Installation is the reverse of removal. Before installation, inspect the door lock for smooth operation and, if necessary, lubricate the sliding parts with multipurpose grease. After installation, replace the access hole cover and the interior trim panel as described in **7.1 Removing and Installing Rear Door Interior Trim and Glass.**

To remove outside rear door handle:

1. Remove the door lock as described under the preceding heading.
2. Remove the two Phillips head screws that hold the door handle to the door panel.
3. Remove the handle from the door.

Installation is the reverse of removal. Replace the access hole cover and the trim panel as described in **7.1 Removing and Installing Rear Door Interior Trim and Glass.**

To remove inside rear door handle:

1. Disconnect the pullrod from the lock assembly.
2. Remove the three Phillips head screws that hold the door handle to the door panel (see Fig. 7-9).
3. Remove the inside door handle from the door.

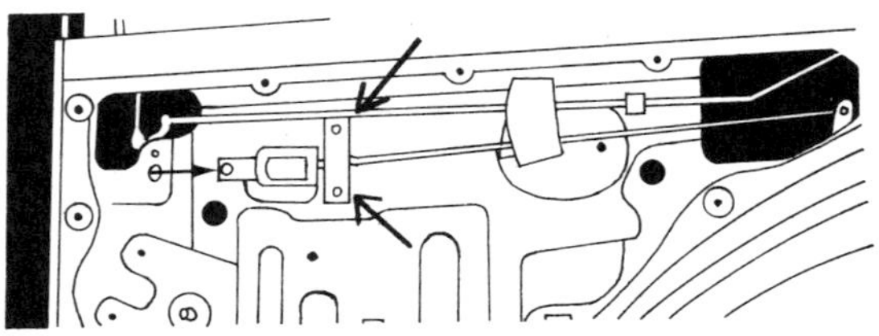

Fig. 7-9. Inside rear door handle mounting screws (arrows).

To install and adjust inside rear door handle:

1. Loosely install the handle assembly using the three Phillips head screws.
2. Connect the pullrod to the lock assembly.
3. Slide the handle assembly toward the front of the door until you feel increased resistance from the lock mechanism. Then move the handle assembly 0.5 to 1.0 mm (.02 to .04 in.) toward the rear of the door and tighten the screws.
4. Replace the access hole cover and the trim panel as described in **7.1 Removing and Installing Rear Door Interior Trim and Glass.**

Adjusting Rear Door Striker

If the door does not close flush with the body, or if the lock is not correctly aligned with the striker, you can adjust the striker's position. To do this, loosen the two Phillips head screws that hold the striker to the body. Then adjust the striker so that the lock does not hit it off center and so that the door is flush with the body when it is closed. If the door lock does not make contact with the striker because the rear of the door is too low, correct the door position by adjusting the hinges as described in **7.3 Checking and Adjusting Rear Door Hinges.**

8. WINDSHIELD AND REAR WINDOW

To avoid scratching the glass, use only liquid cleaners to clean the windows. Do not use steel wool, abrasives, dry paper, or dry cloth.

8.1 Removing and Installing Windshield

Cover the hood and the cowl with a cloth when you work on the windshield. This will help prevent accidental damage to the body.

To remove:

1. Remove the windshield wiper arms and the interior rear view mirror. To protect it from accidental damage, remove the radio antenna if it is mounted on the windshield pillar.
2. Remove the windshield corner moldings and the windshield moldings as described under **9.1 Removing and Installing Exterior Trim Moldings.**
3. Use a screwdriver to break the weatherstrip loose from the body (Fig. 8-1). Be careful not to scratch the finish with the screwdriver.
4. Working inside the car at the top edge of the windshield, use a screwdriver to push the weatherstrip around the metal body lip and through the space between the windshield and the body. See Fig. 8-2.

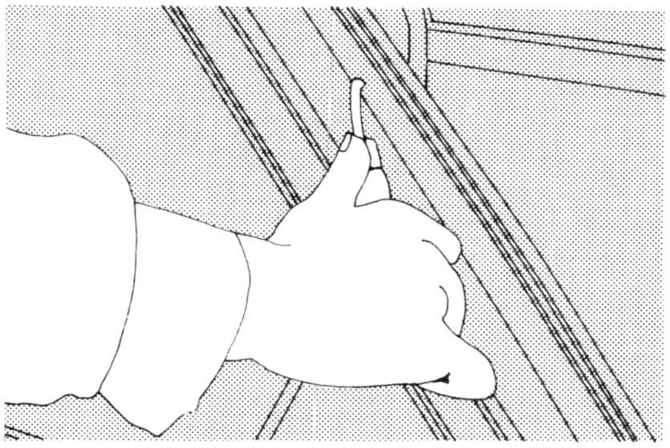

Fig. 8-1. Weatherstrip being separated from body.

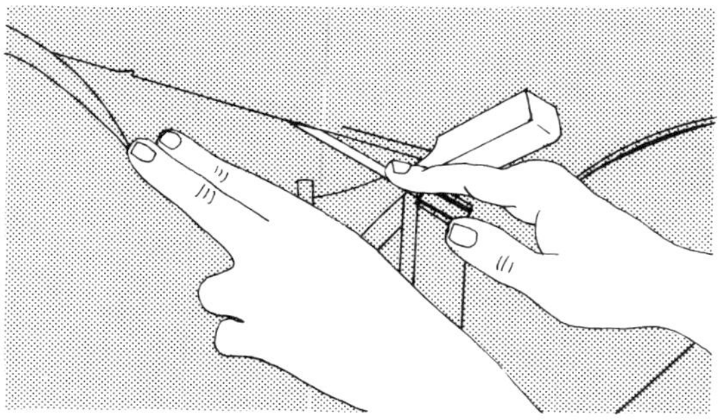

Fig. 8-2. Using screwdriver to push weatherstrip outside of car.

5. Push the glass toward the outside as you continue to work the weatherstrip toward the outside. Push out the glass and the weatherstrip as a unit. Be careful to apply even pressure to the glass as you press it out; a glass installer's suction gripper is helpful for this job.

CAUTION —
If you are replacing the glass because it is broken, remove all traces of hardened sealer and shattered glass from the weatherstrip and the window aperture. Otherwise, the new window may leak.

To install:

1. Reinstall the weatherstrip around the periphery of the glass. You can use the original weatherstrip if it is in good condition, but it is good practice to replace the weatherstrip whenever possible.

2. Insert a glass installer's drawcord into the groove in the weatherstrip that will fit over the edge of the body. Make a loop in the cord at the top and a crossover at the bottom (Fig. 8-3).

NOTE —
You should lubricate the weatherstrip and the body surfaces with soapy water or a silicone spray to facilitate the installation of the glass and the weatherstrip.

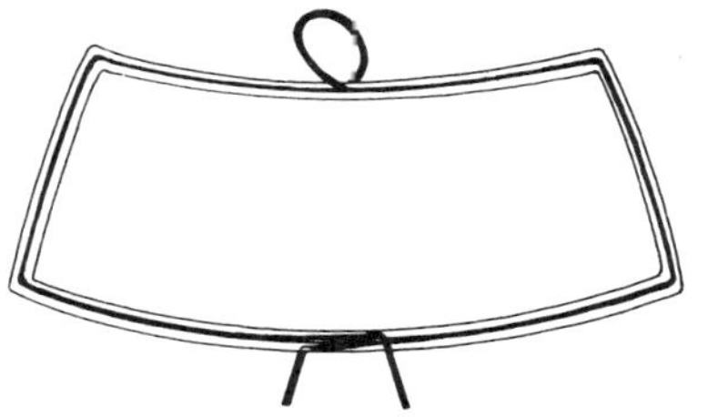

Fig. 8-3. Drawcord correctly inserted in weatherstrip groove.

3. Position the glass and the weatherstrip in the window aperture with the cord ends inside the car. Then, applying pressure to the outside of the glass, pull out the cord so that the weatherstrip is made to overlap the body (Fig. 8-4).

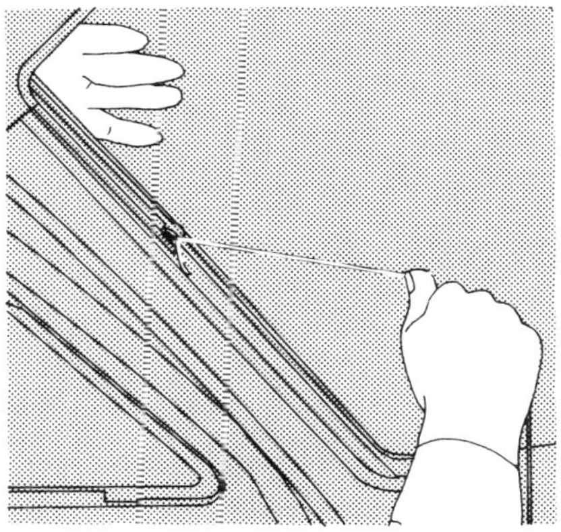

Fig. 8-4. Drawcord being pulled out while pressure is applied to outside of glass.

4. Lightly tap the outer surface of the glass with the palm of your hand to make sure that the glass is fully seated in the aperture.

9

5. To protect the glass and the body from being accidentally marred by sealer, cover the areas adjacent to the weatherstrip with masking tape. Then, working from the outside, apply sealer (Toyota part No. 08704–00020) between the weatherstrip and the body and between the weatherstrip and the glass (Fig. 8-5).

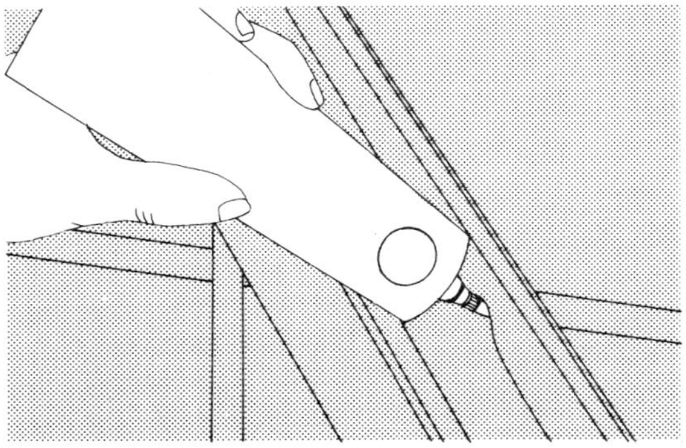

Fig. 8-5. Weatherstrip sealer being applied.

6. Remove any excess sealer from the weatherstrip. Then remove the masking tape from the glass and the body.
7. Using a weatherstrip-lip positioning tool when necessary, install the windshield molding as shown in Fig. 8-6.

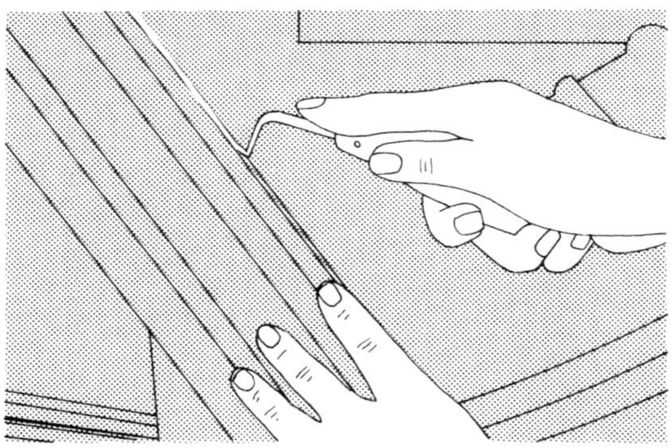

Fig. 8-6. Using weatherstrip-lip positioning tool to install windshield molding.

8. Install the windshield wiper arms, the radio antenna, and the interior rear view mirror.

8.2 Removing and Installing Rear Window

(all models, including station wagon)

The procedures for removing and installing the rear window are nearly identical to the procedures for removing and installing the windshield. When removing an electrically heated rear window, you must first disconnect the two spade terminal connectors. When installing a station wagon rear window, you must insert the weatherstrip wedge into the weatherstrip before applying the weatherstrip sealer. This procedure is easier if you have a tool similar to the one shown in Fig. 8-7. Be sure to reconnect the wiring if the window is electrically heated.

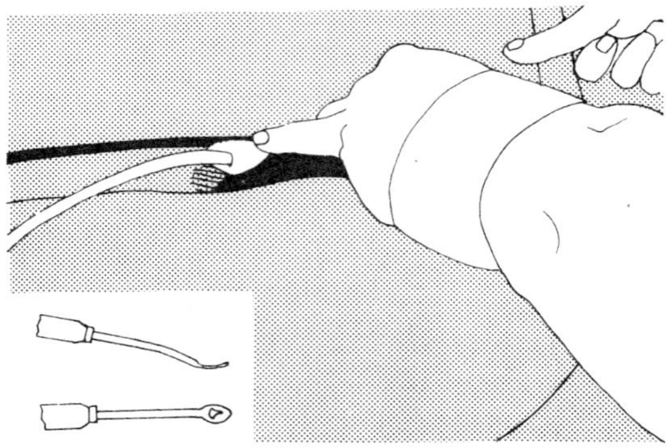

Fig. 8-7. Weatherstrip wedge being installed with special tool shown in insert.

9. EXTERIOR AND INTERIOR TRIM

This section discusses the removal and installation of exterior trim panels and moldings. Also included are the instrument panel, the dashboard, the headliner, and the side trim.

9.1 Removing and Installing Exterior Trim Moldings

Handle the moldings with care when you remove or install them. These moldings can easily be damaged by the application of force.

To remove the rear windshield or rear window moldings, remove the four corner moldings with a screwdriver or a similar tool (Fig. 9-1). Then remove the side moldings.

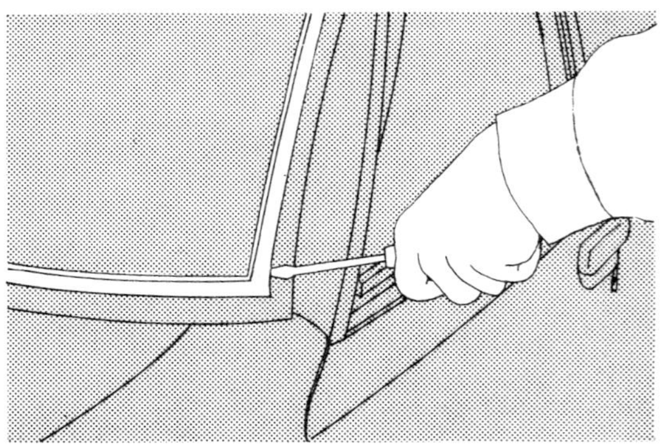

Fig. 9-1. Using a screwdriver to remove windshield corner molding.

To install, use a weatherstrip-lip positioning tool to push the molding into the groove in the weatherstrip (Fig. 9-2). Lubricating the weatherstrip with soapy water may make the job easier.

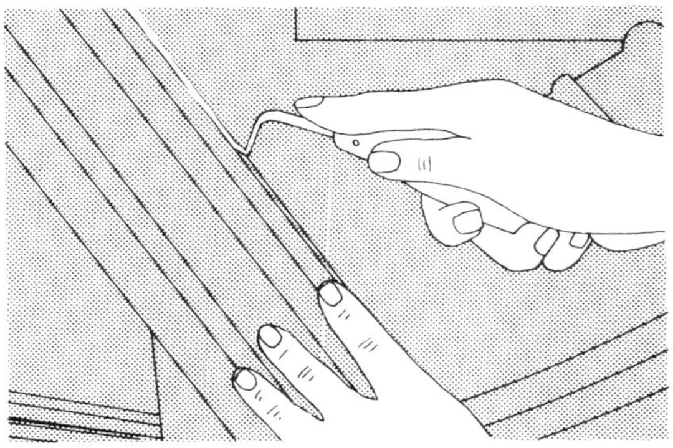

Fig. 9-2. Using weatherstrip-lip positioning tool to install windshield molding.

To remove beltline molding:

1. To remove the front door's beltline molding, begin with step 3 of this procedure. To remove the rear door's beltline molding, first remove the rear door's trim panel as described in **7.1 Removing and Installing Rear Door Interior Trim and Glass.**
2. Remove the divider and the rear quarter window as described in **7.1 Removing and Installing Rear Door Interior Trim and Glass.**
3. Loosen the screw indicated in Fig. 9-3.

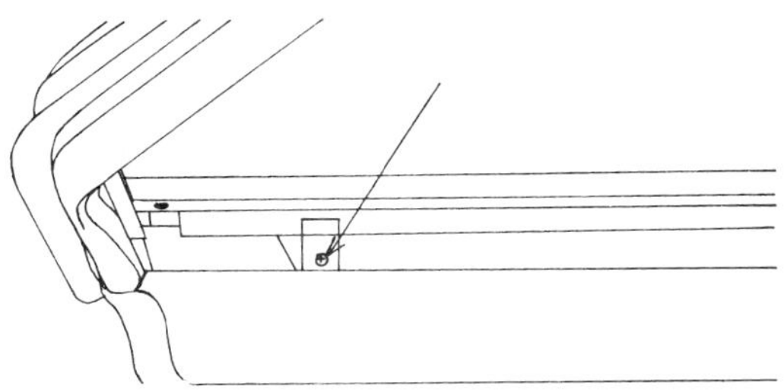

Fig. 9-3. Molding retainer screw (arrow).

4. Using a screwdriver, carefully pry the molding away from the body panel.

Installation is the reverse of removal. When you install the beltline molding, press the molding retainers into the holes in the door panel carefully.

To replace drain channel molding:

1. Remove the molding by pressing it up and off the drain channel.
2. Scrape any excess adhesive off the drain channel, then clean the drain channel with solvent.
3. Apply trim cement to the hollow of the drain channel molding, as indicated in Fig. 9-4—using 30- to 40-mm (about 1½-in.) strips of cement spaced about 100 mm (about 4 in.) apart. Leave the last 100 mm (about 4 in.) at each end of the molding cement-free.

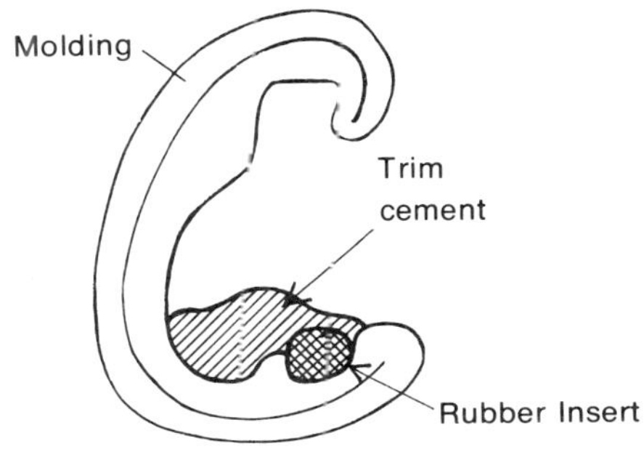

Fig. 9-4. Cross-section of drain channel molding. Apply trim cement to hollow of molding, as shown.

4. Press the molding down over the tip of the drain channel. If the rubber insert in the molding has hardened, you may have trouble pressing the molding fully into place. In this case, you should make an installing tool (Fig. 9-5) from a piece of scrap metal to help you press on the molding.

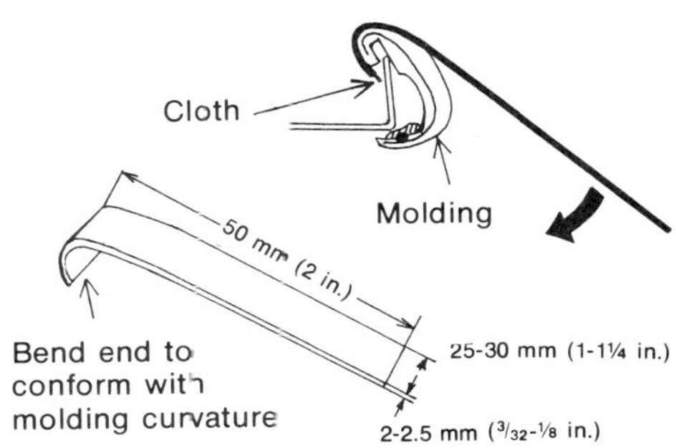

Fig. 9-5. Molding installing tool. In using this tool, cover it with cloth insert as shown, and be careful not to damage the molding.

9

To remove rear ventilator:

1. Remove the rear pillar trim by taking out the three attaching screws and the three button retainers.
2. Remove the single mounting screw that holds the ventilator to the body interior. (Fig. 9-6).

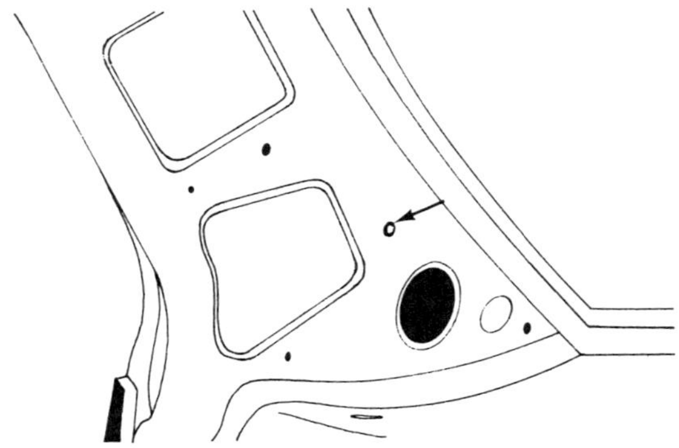

Fig. 9-6. Ventilator mounting screw (arrow).

3. Working inside the trunk, remove the two nuts indicated in Fig. 9-7. Then remove the ventilator.

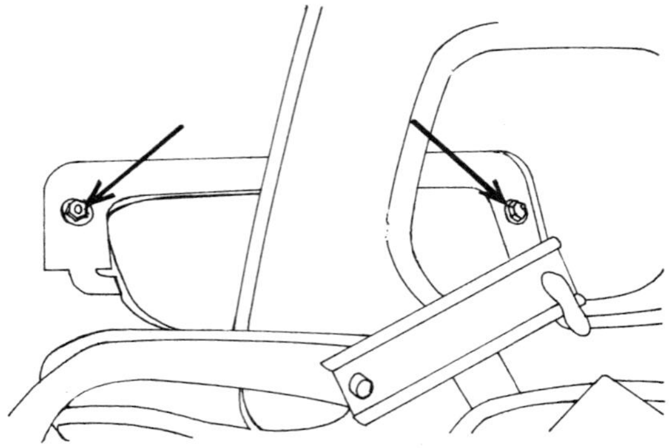

Fig. 9-7. Rear ventilator mounting nuts (arrows).

9.2 Removing and Installing Interior Trim

Fig. 9-8 illustrates typical interior trim components—including the two different kinds of headliners used in the cars covered by this Manual. The layout of the interior trim panels may vary from model to model, but the principles given in the procedures apply to all.

1. Front pillar trim
2. Door pillar trim
3. Kick panel
4. Trunk divider
5. Package shelf trim
6. Rear pillar trim
7. Station wagon quarter trim
8. Station wagon quarter board

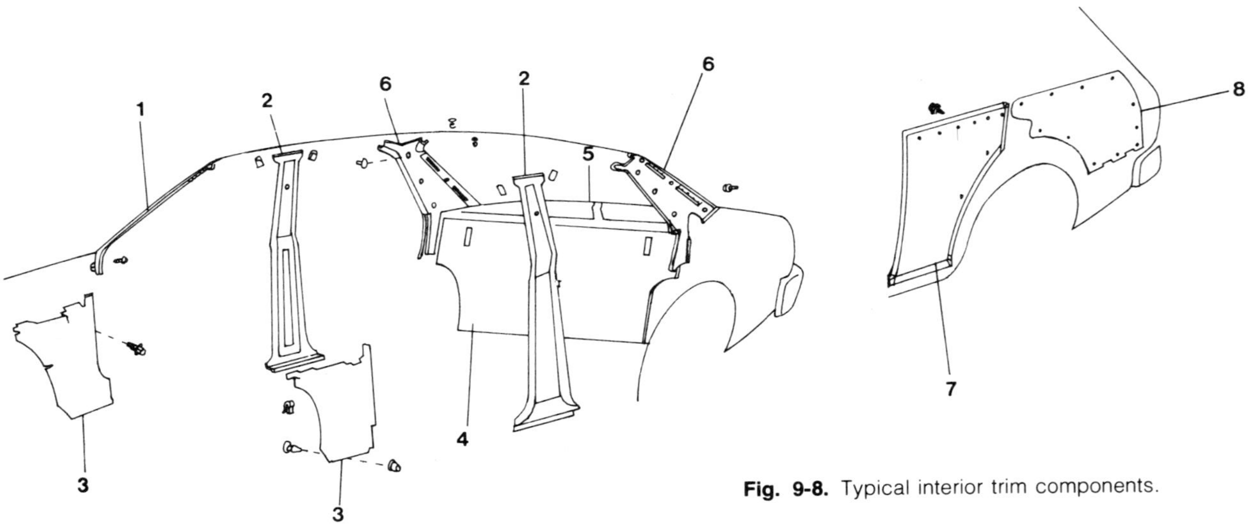

Fig. 9-8. Typical interior trim components.

To remove kick panel:

1. If necessary, remove the package tray by taking out the bolts that attach the tray to the firewall, the dashboard, and the kick panel.
2. Take out the single bolt that holds the kick panel to the body (Fig. 9-9).
3. Pull out the two retainers at the base of the kick panel (Fig. 9-9). Pull the panel away from the body.

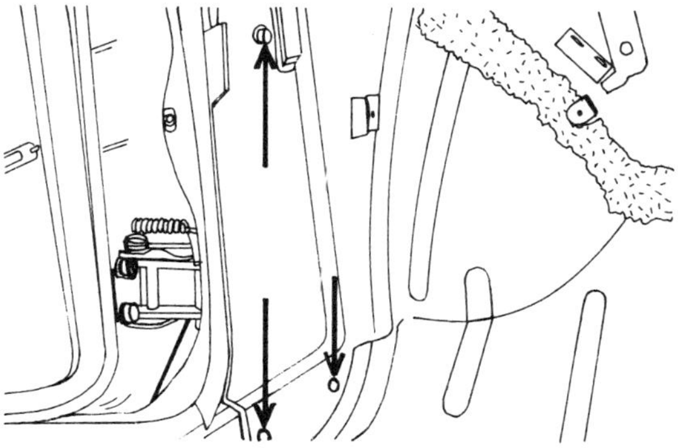

Fig. 9-9. Kick panel mounting bolt (top arrow) and retainers (bottom arrows).

Installation is the reverse of removal. Press the retainers firmly in place before you tighten the mounting bolt.

To remove rear pillar trim:

1. On four-door models, open the rear doors and remove the upper mounting screws from the door apertures' trim plates.
2. Check whether, as on most models, you need to remove the rear seat in order to remove the rear pillar trim. For example, see whether the seat back blocks access to the lower part of the pillar trim. If so, remove the rear seat as described in **10.3 Removing and Installing Rear Seat.**
3. Pry out the three button retainers. Then remove the three mounting screws and the trim piece. See Fig. 9-10.

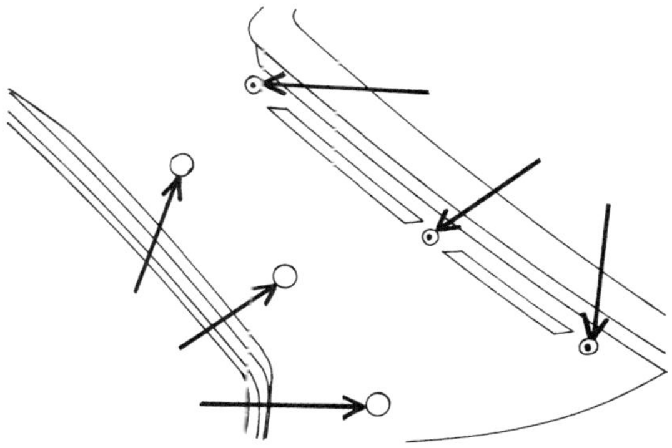

Fig. 9-10. Rear pillar trim retainer buttons (left arrows) and mounting screws (right arrows).

Installation is the reverse of removal. You may find it easier to locate the three button retainers in their mounting holes if you install them before you replace the three mounting screws.

9

Instrument Panel and Console

Fig. 9-11 is an exploded view of the dashboard and the instrument panel. The layout of the instruments and the various dashboard components varies from model to model. Nevertheless, the principles illustrated in the procedures that follow apply to all the cars covered by this Manual.

To remove instrument panel:

1. Disconnect the battery's negative (−) cable.
2. Remove the instrument panel trim by taking out the three screws indicated in Fig. 9-12 and, where applicable, the two screws indicated in Fig. 9-13.
3. Remove the ashtray and, where applicable, the knobs and the nuts from the radio and tape player. On applicable models, remove the heater control knobs or fresh air vent knobs.

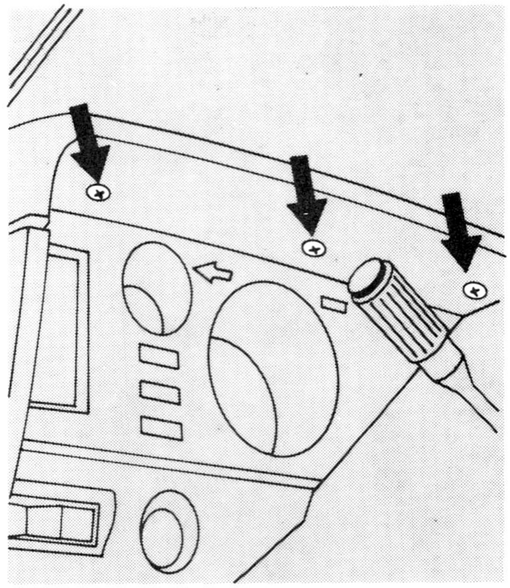

Fig. 9-12. Screws (arrows) for instrument panel trim, found above instrument panel of all cars covered by this Manual.

1. Dashboard
2. Brace
3. Reinforcement
4. Box
5. Ashtray bracket
6. Ashtray
7. Glove compartment
8. Glove compartment door
9. Instrument panel
10. Ventilating duct
11. Ventilation control panel

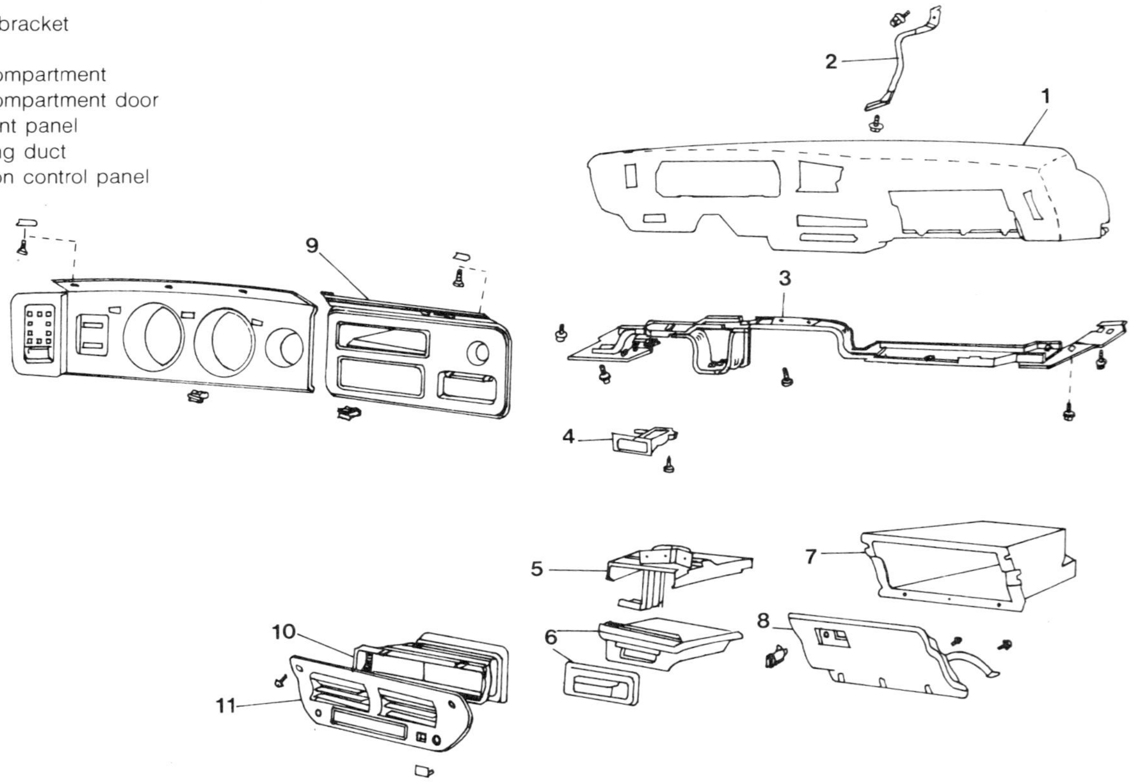

Fig. 9-11. Exploded view of dashboard and instrument panel.

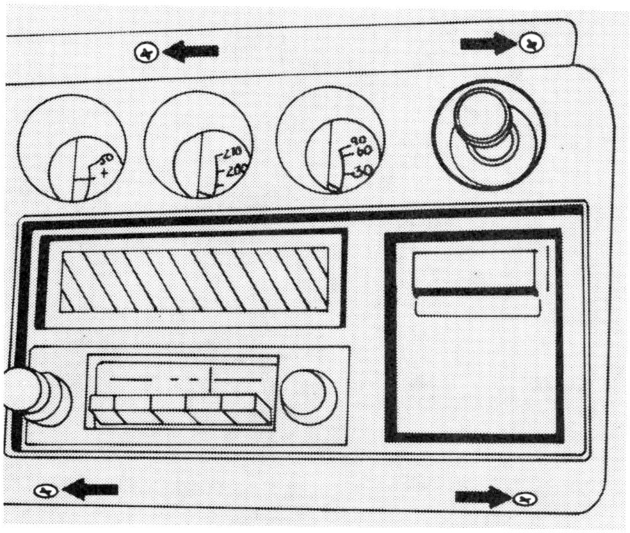

Fig. 9-13. Screws (arrows) for instrument panel trim, found above instrument panel center. Panel illustrated is used only on SR-5 models.

4. Remove the instrument panel(s) by raising it slightly to disengage it at the bottom.
5. Reaching up from behind the dashboard, use a small screwdriver to detach the speedometer cable from the speedometer head by slightly raising the retainer on the side of the cable conduit's end fixture; simultaneously pull the cable and its conduit off the speedometer head.
6. Remove the screws that hold the main instrument cluster, the clock, or the SR-5 gauge cluster to the dashboard assembly. Then pull the cluster partially out of the dashboard so that you can disconnect the multiple connector, the illumination light bulb holders, and other wires from the rear of the cluster.

To remove console:

1. Remove the knobs from the heater and ventilation controls. On models with a removable panel, take out the two Phillips head screws and remove the panel. Then remove the four screws and the nut that attach the control assembly to the console.
2. Remove the two Phillips head screws from the base of the tray located to the rear of the shift lever. These screws connect and anchor the front and rear sections of the console at the point where the sections meet.
3. Remove the Phillips head screws located on each side of the rear console section, near the floor. Untie the parking brake handle's boot. Then pull the rear section of the console off over the parking brake handle.
4. Remove the two screws indicated in Fig. 9-14 and the two corresponding screws on the opposite side of the console.

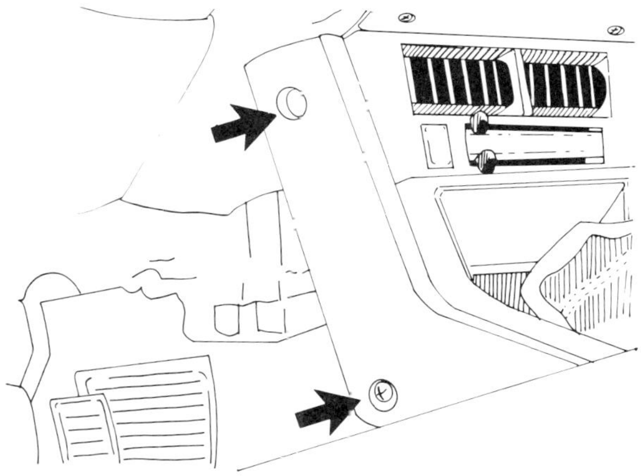

Fig. 9-14. Console mounting screws (arrows).

5. Remove the shift knob. Then remove the console by sliding it up and over the gearshift lever.

To remove dashboard:

1. Remove the instrument panel and the console as described in the preceding procedures.
2. Remove the six glove compartment mounting screws indicated in Fig. 9-15.

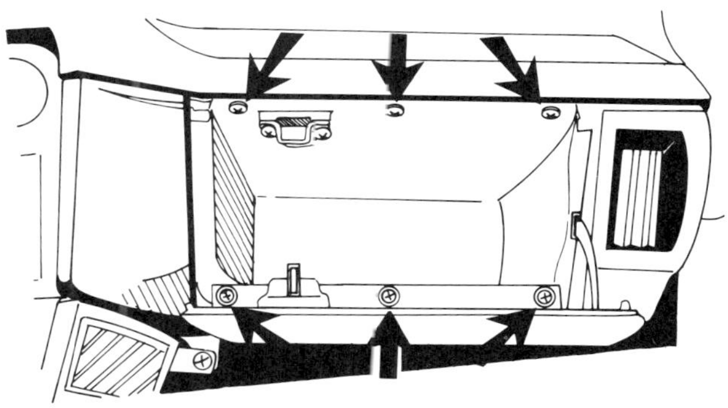

Fig. 9-15. Glove compartment mounting screws (arrows).

9

3. On models that are so equipped, remove the package tray.
4. If applicable, detach the heater control mechanism from the dashboard.
5. If applicable, remove the choke control mounting bolt.
6. Remove the padded surround for the dashboard. To do this, remove the bolt and the Phillips head

screw at each end of the dashboard. Then remove the bolt at the far right edge of the instrument panel. See Fig. 9-16.

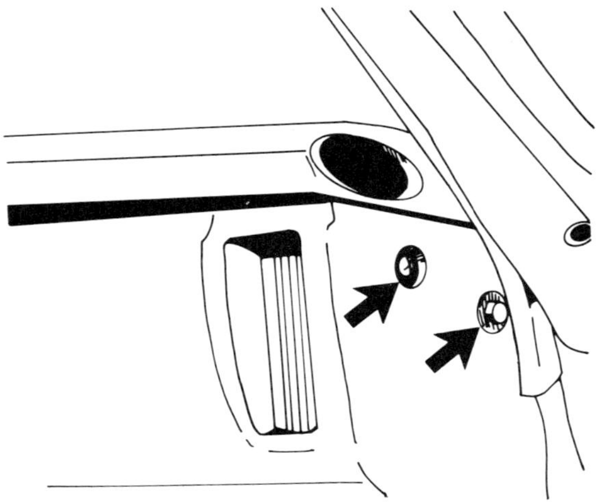

Fig. 9-16. Mounting bolt and screw (arrows) for dashboard padded surround.

7. Remove the trim piece below the steering column. Then remove the bolts and the nuts (Fig. 9-17) that hold the steering column's break-away bracket to the bottom of the dashboard. Lower the steering wheel and column.

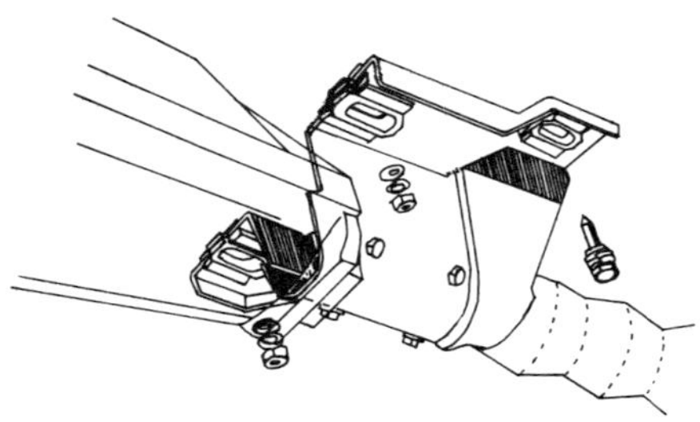

Fig. 9-17. Exploded view showing bolts and nuts that hold break-away bracket to dashboard structure.

8. Working under the dashboard, remove the cowl-to-dashboard brace(s).
9. Separate the reinforcement from the dashboard. To do this, remove the four bolts at the bottom edge of the dashboard.
10. Remove the mounting bolts that hold the dashboard to the cowl (Fig. 9-18).

Installation is the reverse of removal. Torque the steering column break-away bracket bolts and nuts to 35 to 45 Nm (26 to 33 ft. lb.).

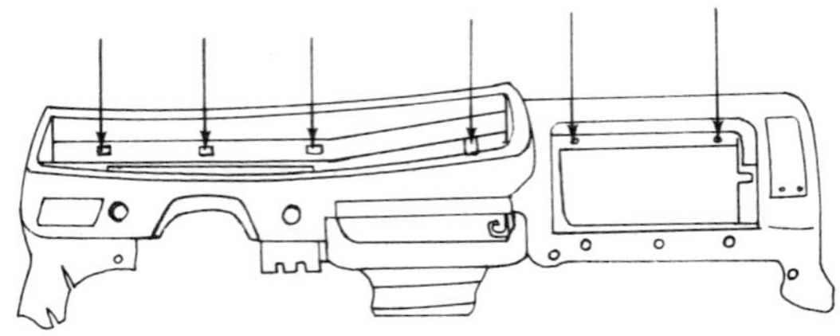

Fig. 9-18. Dashboard-to-cowl mounting bolt locations (arrows).

9.3 Removing and Installing Headliner and Side Trim

Two kinds of headliners have been installed in the cars covered by this Manual. Some models are equipped with one-piece molded headliners, whereas others have cloth headliners hung on wire supports. Fig. 9-19 gives an exploded view of each kind of headliner.

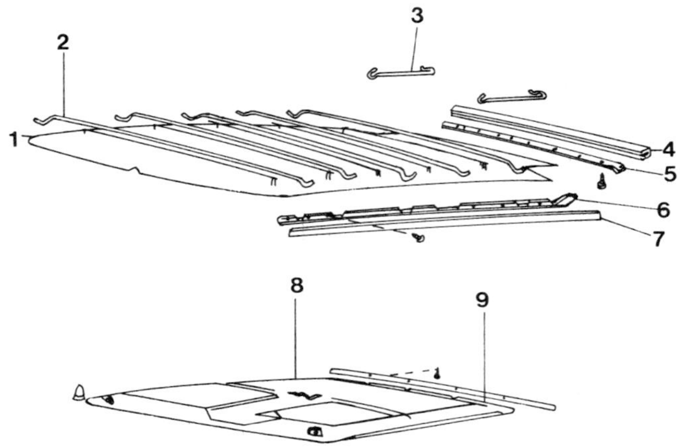

1. Cloth headliner
2. Support wire
3. Hook
4. End trim
5. End retainer
6. Side retainer
7. Side trim
8. Molded headliner
9. End trim

Fig. 9-19. Exploded views of cloth headliner (top) and molded headliner (bottom).

Molded Headliner

You can remove and install the molded headliner without special tools and techniques, but be sure to handle it carefully to avoid damaging it during removal or installation.

To remove:

1. Remove the sun visors, the sun visor holders, and the rear view mirror.
2. Disconnect the battery's negative (–) cable. Then remove the interior light.

3. Remove the rear seat as described in **10.3 Removing and Installing Rear Seat.**
4. Remove the front pillar trim pieces by taking out the screws. Then remove the rear pillar trim pieces by taking out the three screws and three button retainers.
5. Remove the screws that hold the headliner end trim in place and remove the trim.
6. Carefully remove the side trim by prying the clips from their recesses in the body (Fig. 9-20).
7. Remove the headliner and side trim as a unit, carefully prying them away from the body so that the clips compress as indicated by the arrows in Fig. 9-20.

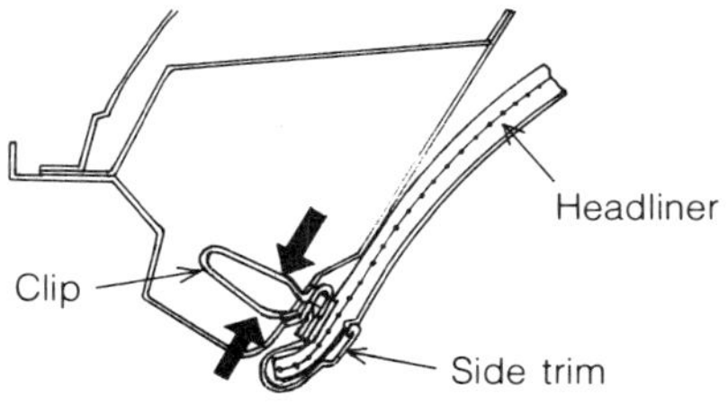

Fig. 9-20. Cross-section view showing how clips hold headliner.

Installation is the reverse of removal. When pushing the clips into place, be careful not to damage the side trim or the headliner.

Cloth Headliner

The removal and installation of the cloth headliner are complex tasks that include the removal and reinstallation of the windshield and, except on wagons, the rear window. The cloth headliner must be installed carefully. Otherwise, it will be wrinkled or will not fit well at the edges. The procedures given here are for a station wagon, but the principles illustrated apply to other models as well.

To remove:

1. Remove the sun visors, the sun visor holders, and the rear view mirror, by removing their mounting screws.
2. Remove the windshield as described in **8.1 Removing and Installing Windshield.**
3. Disconnect the battery's negative (−) cable. Then remove the interior light.
4. Remove the assist handles and the coat hooks by taking out their mounting screws. Remove the rear hinge covers as described in **11.1 Removing, Installing, and Adjusting Station Wagon Tailgate.**
5. Remove the side and end trim pieces.
6. Pull the headliner away from its attachment points at the sides, the windshield, and rear body flanges.
7. Flex the centers of the support wires upward so that you can disengage the ends of the support wires from their sockets. Then remove the headliner and the support wires as a unit.

To install:

1. If you are installing a new headliner, install the support wires of the old headliner in the sleeves of the new headliner—transferring them one at a time so that each wire is in the same relative position.
2. Remove the rear and side retainers. Install double-sided adhesive tape on the windshield flange and on the side and rear retainers (Fig. 9-21). For the moment, do not peel the paper from the exposed side of the tape.
3. Use the screws to attach the side retainers and the rear retainer to the body panels.

Fig. 9-21. Headliner adhesive tape installed. Windshield flange is at **1**, rear retainer at **2**, and side retainer at **3**.

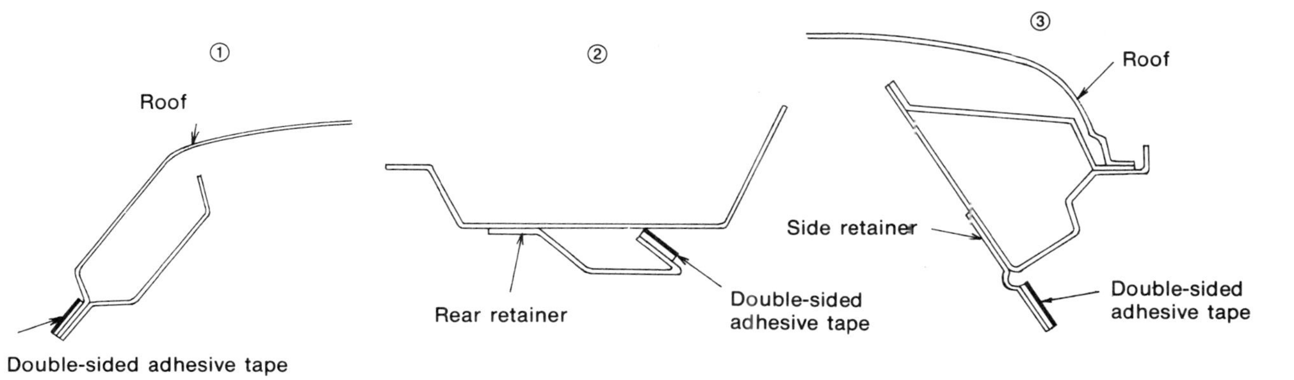

4. Install the two mounting hooks in position at the rear of the headliner, as shown in Fig. 9-22. Then insert the hooks into the holes in the upper rear body panel.

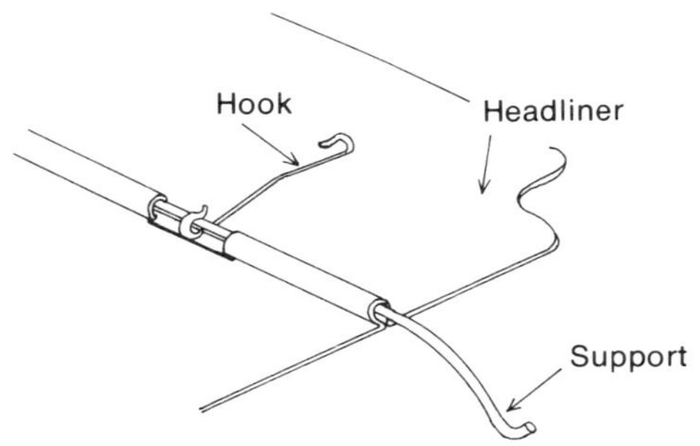

Fig. 9-22. Headliner mounting hook in position at rear of headliner.

5. Working from the rear toward the front of the car, install the headliner wire supports in their sockets.
6. Peel the paper from the double-sided tape that is on the windshield flange. Working from the center of the flange, pull the headliner as tight as possible and position it on the windshield flange.
7. Peel the paper from the tape on the rear retainer. Working from the center, position the headliner on the rear retainer.

   NOTE ——
   Make sure that you keep the headliner smooth and wrinkle-free as you pull it over the retainer. You should push the headliner down and over the saw-tooth portion of the retainer to keep it firmly in place.

8. Trim off the excess headliner material, then hand-press the rear trim piece into place.
9. Peel the paper from the tape on the side retainers. Position the headliner firmly against the tape, working as before to avoid wrinkles.
10. Trim off the excess headliner material at the sides. Then reinstall the side trim pieces.
11. Install the windshield as described in **8.1 Removing and Installing Windshield.**
12. Using your fingertips to feel through the headliner, locate the opening for the interior light. Then cut an opening for the light in the headliner. Connect the light to the wires, and install the light in the car.
13. Install the sun visors, the sun visor holders, the rear view mirror, the assist handles, the coat hooks, and the rear hinge covers.
14. Reconnect the battery's negative (–) cable.

   NOTE ——
   You may be able to remove some wrinkles that appear after installation by heating the headliner with an infrared heat lamp. Be careful not to melt or scorch the fabric.

10. SEATS AND SEAT BELTS

For safety while driving, the seat belts should be maintained in good condition at all times. Never clean the belts with anything other than mild soap and water. Replace frayed or cut belts, and belts that have been in use during an accident.

10.1 Removing and Installing Seat Belts

Do not attempt to repair faulty seat belt retractors. Doing this may prevent them from locking correctly in a collision. Always replace faulty retractors as a unit.

To remove front seat belts:

1. If the car is equipped with a retractor cover on the floor-mounted retractor, remove the screw and separate the cover from the retractor.
2. On two-door cars (Fig. 10-1), take out the bolt that holds the floor-mounted retractor and separate the retractor from the car body. On four-door cars and station wagons (Fig. 10-2), remove the seat belt lower anchor by removing its mounting bolt. Then remove the bolt that holds the retractor and separate the retractor from the door pillar body.
3. Carefully pry the plastic cap from the relay bracket. Then unbolt the relay bracket from the pillar and remove the belts.
4. If you wish to also remove the seat belt lock assembly, unbolt the seat belt lock from the front seat. Then disconnect the wire for the seat belt warning system and remove the lock assembly.

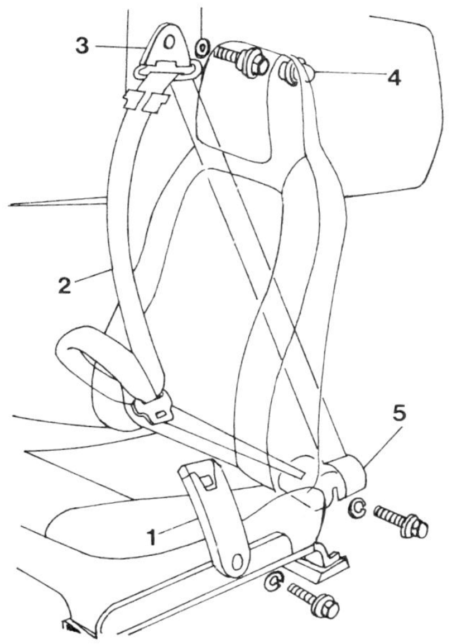

1. Lock assembly
2. Seat belt
3. Relay bracket
4. Cap
5. Retractor assembly

Fig. 10-1. Front seat belt components (two-door cars).

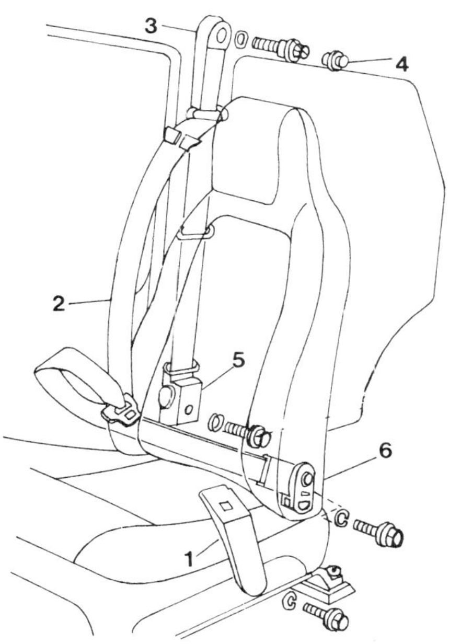

1. Lock assembly
2. Seat belt
3. Relay bracket
4. Cap
5. Retractor
6. Lower anchor

Fig. 10-2. Front seat belt assembly (four-door cars and station wagons).

To install front seat belts:

1. If previously removed, install the seat belt lock assembly. Torque the mounting bolt to 20 to 45 Nm (15 to 33 ft. lb.). Reconnect the wire for the seat belt warning system.
2. Install the relay bracket and torque the mounting bolt to 20 to 45 Nm (15 to 33 ft. lb.).
3. On four-door cars and station wagons, install the seat belt lower anchor and torque the mounting bolt to 20 to 45 Nm (15 to 33 ft. lb.). Then bolt the retractor to the body pillar, torquing the bolt to 20 to 45 Nm (15 to 33 ft. lb.). On two-door cars, install the floor-mounted retractor and torque the mounting bolt to 20 to 45 Nm (15 to 33 ft. lb.).
4. If the car is equipped with a retractor cover, install the cover and tighten the screw.

NOTE ——
When correctly installed, the belts should lie flat without twists when they are worn. Make sure that the retractor cover is correctly positioned and that the belt does not rub the edges of the cover.

To remove rear seat belts:

1. Remove the rear seat cushion as described in **10.3 Removing and Installing Rear Seat.**
2. Remove the bolts that attach the seat belt ends to the body. Usually there is one mounting bolt per belt, although some cars have two bolts. See Fig. 10-3.

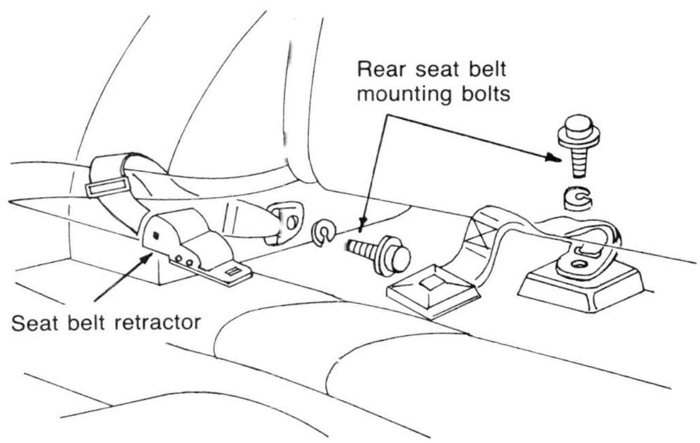

Fig. 10-3. Rear seat belt assembly.

9

3. Remove the seat belts and their integral retractors.

Installation is the reverse of removal. Install the mounting bolts and washers, torquing the bolts to 20 to 45 Nm (15 to 33 ft. lb.). Then install the rear seat cushion as described in **10.3 Removing and Installing Rear Seat.**

10.2 Removing and Installing Front Seats

The front seats slide on tracks that are bolted to the car's floor. You can easily remove the front seat and its tracks as a unit for repair or replacement.

To remove:

1. Adjust the seat to its rearmost position. Then remove the mounting bolt from the front end of each seat track (Fig. 10-4).
2. Adjust the seat to its forward position. Remove the mounting bolt from the rear end of each seat track (Fig. 10-4).

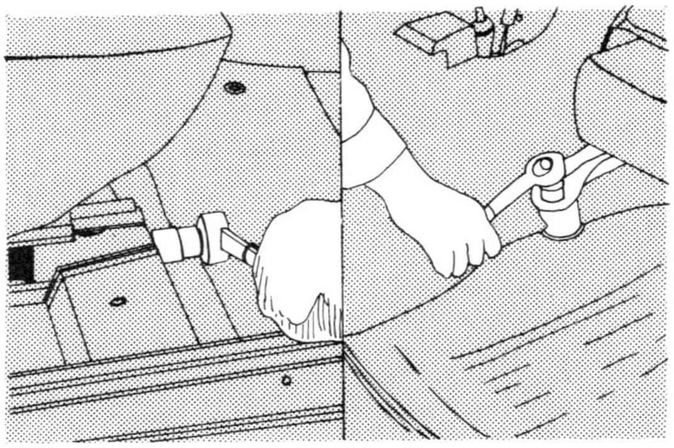

Fig. 10-4. Front seat tracks being unbolted from floor mounting points. Front bolt is at left; rear bolt is at right.

3. Take out the front seat and its tracks as a unit.

Installation is the reverse of removal. Check the track mechanism for smooth operation; if necessary, lubricate it with multipurpose grease. Position the seat in the car and install the two rear mounting bolts. Move the seat to its rearmost position, then install the two front mounting bolts. Torque the mounting bolts to 30 to 55 Nm (22 to 41 ft. lb.).

Disassembling and Assembling Front Seats

The front seat assembly can be disassembled into its component parts. It is easiest, but not always necessary, first to remove the seat from the car. Fig. 10-5 is an exploded view of the front seat assembly.

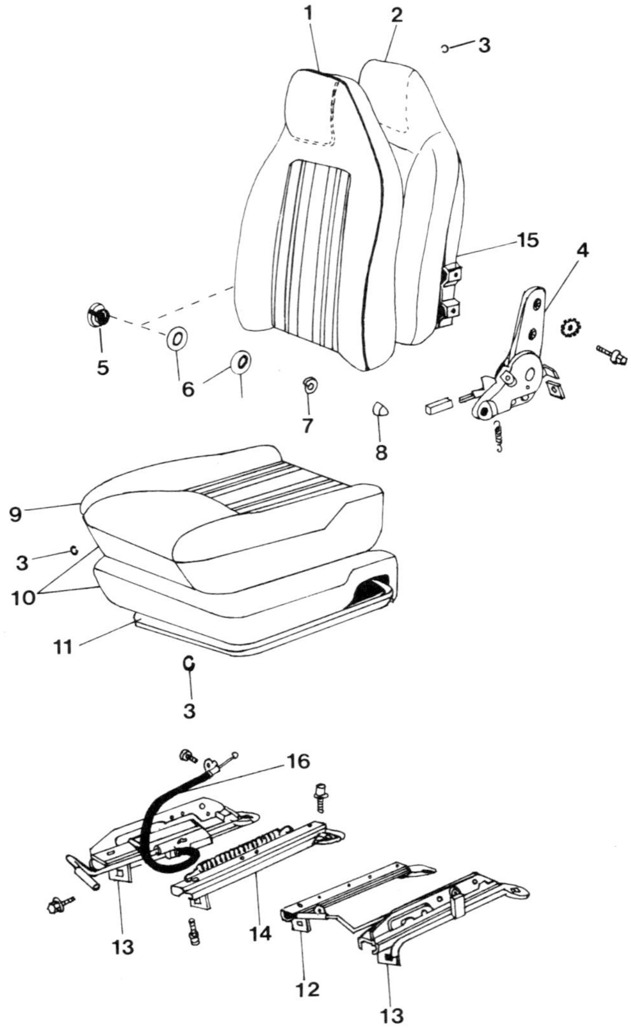

1. Backrest covering
2. Backrest
3. Clip
4. Backrest positioner
5. Bushing
6. Washer (2)
7. Spring washer
8. Acorn nut
9. Seat cushion covering
10. Seat cushion
11. Seat frame
12. Driver's seat outer track
13. Inner track (2)
14. Passenger's seat outer track
15. Backrest frame
16. Foot release cable

Fig. 10-5. Front seat components.

To disassemble:

1. If you are disassembling the passenger's seat, first disconnect the end of the foot release cable from the pedal.
2. To remove the seat backrest from the seat cushion, loosen and remove the acorn nut and its washers from the side of the seat opposite the back positioner.
3. While supporting the seat backrest, loosen and remove the two bolts and washers that attach the back frame to the backrest positioner. Then remove

the seat backrest. If you wish to separate the backrest positioner from the seat cushion, remove the two remaining bolts and washers.

4. To separate the tracks from the base frame, you must remove the two bolts that attach each track to the base frame. On the passenger's seat, you may also have to remove the cable clamp that is bolted to the base frame.

To assemble:

1. Install and tighten the four bolts that attach the seat tracks to the seat frame. Be careful not to interchange the inner and outer tracks. If necessary, connect the cable clamp to the base frame of the passenger's seat.
2. If you removed the backrest positioner entirely, first install the two bolts that attach it to the seat frame. Hold the seat backrest in position while you install the two bolts that attach the backrest positioner to the backrest frame. Tighten all four bolts.
3. Install the washers and the acorn nut. Tighten the acorn nut, and then check that the backrest moves smoothly.
4. Connect the foot release cable to the release pedal on the passenger's seat.

10.3 Removing and Installing Rear Seat

Most cars covered by this Manual have fixed rear seats. The exceptions are the station wagon, which has a one-piece folding rear seat, and the liftback, which has individual folding rear seat backrests.

To remove fixed rear seat:

1. Remove the two bolts that are located below the front edge of the seat cushion, near the floor.
2. Push the rear seat cushion toward the back of the car. Then pull up on its front edge, and remove it from the car.
3. Remove the two bolts that are located at the lower outside corners of the seat backrest. Then pull the rear seat back up and forward to separate it from the body.

Installation is the reverse of removal. Before you install the two bolts at the lower corners of the seat back, make sure the rear seat backrest is firmly attached where its top rear edge meets the body. Then slide the seat cushion back and down until it is locked in position. Install and tighten the two bolts that hold it in place.

To remove station wagon rear seat:

1. Fold the rear seat cushion into the forward position. Remove the two bolts that attach the hinge to the bottom of the seat cushion (Fig. 10-6). Remove the seat cushion from the car.

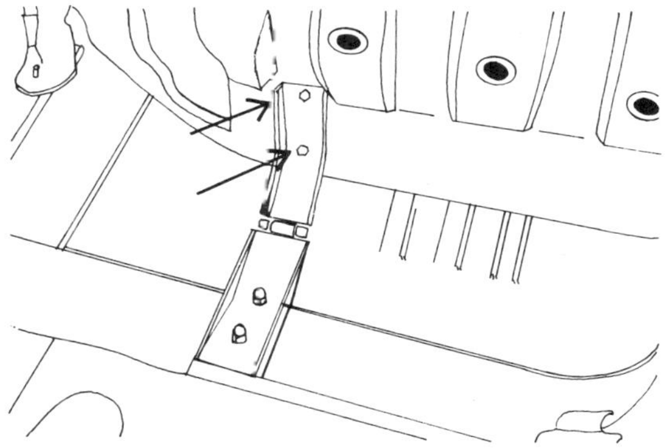

Fig. 10-6. Station wagon rear seat cushion hinge. Bolts indicated by arrows attach seat cushion to hinge.

2. Release the seat backrest and fold it forward. Remove the screws and the cover plate from atop each bushing (Fig. 10-7) on the two pin-and-bushing hinges located at the lower corners of the seat backrest.

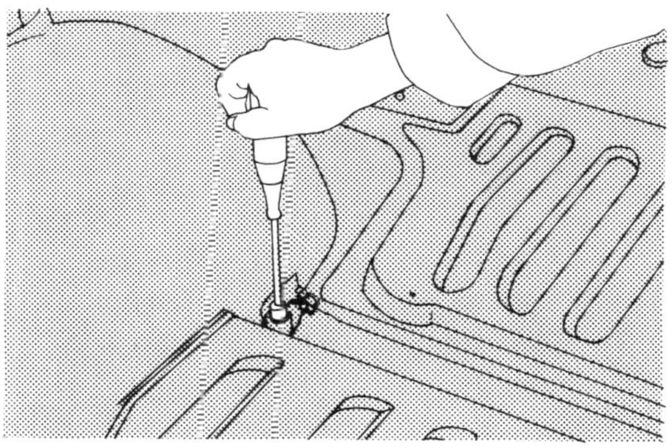

Fig. 10-7. Station wagon rear seat backrest hinge being removed.

3. Remove the seat backrest from the car. Be careful not to lose the bushings for the hinge pins.

Installation is the reverse of removal. Make sure the bushings are installed on the pivot pins, then position the seat backrest in the car. Install the cover plates and tighten the two screws that hold each plate atop its hinge bushing. Attach the seat cushion to its hinges and tighten the two bolts. With the seat backrest locked upright, fold the base into a normal seating position.

9

To remove liftback rear seat:

1. Remove the two bolts that are located below the front edge of the seat cushion, near the floor.
2. Push the seat cushion toward the back of the car and pull up on its front edge. Remove the cushion from the car by pulling it forward.
3. Release the seat backrest locks and fold the seat backrests forward. Remove the screws and the cover plate from atop each bushing (Fig. 10-8) on the pin-and-bushing hinges located at the outside lower corner of each seat backrest.

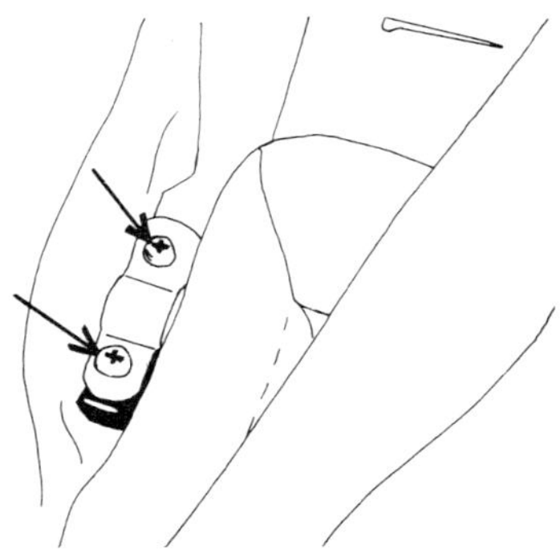

Fig. 10-8. Liftback rear seat backrest hinge (arrows indicate mounting screws).

4. Slide each seat backrest forward and out of the central hinge bracket shown in Fig. 10-9. Then remove the seat backrests from the car.

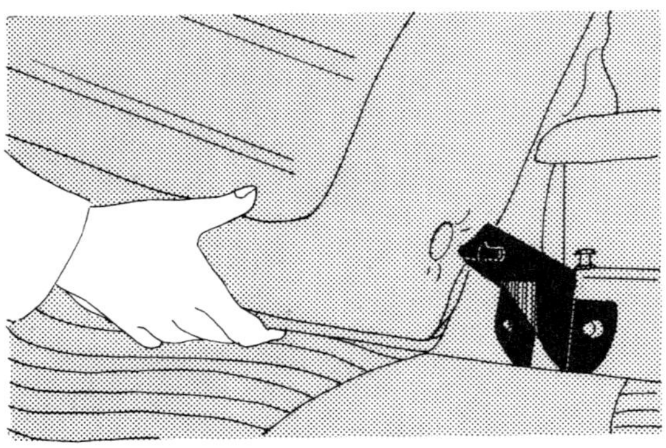

Fig. 10-9. Central hinge bracket for liftback rear seat backrests.

To install liftback rear seat:

1. Put the pin of one of the seat backrests in position in the central hinge bracket. With the bushing in place on the other pin, put the seat backrest in place and install the cover plate and screws. Repeat this procedure for the other seat backrest.
2. Install the seat cushion by sliding it back and down until it is locked in position.
3. Install and tighten the two bolts that hold the rear seat cushion in place.

11. STATION WAGON AND LIFTBACK COMPONENTS

The procedure for removing and installing rear windows is given in **8. Windshield and Rear Window.** The procedures for removing and installing the station wagon and liftback rear seats are given in **10. Seats and Seat Belts.**

11.1 Removing, Installing, and Adjusting Station Wagon Tailgate

Fig. 11-1 is an exploded view of the station wagon tailgate assembly. You can remove the tailgate without removing the tailgate hinges. If you want to remove the hinges, you should have a special tool for removing the tailgate hinge torsion bars.

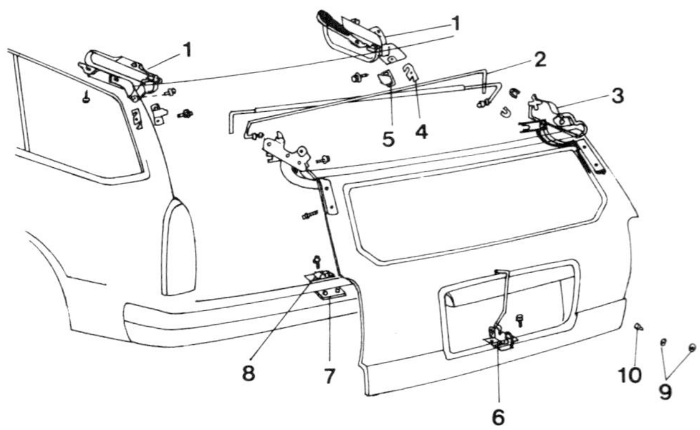

1. Hinge cover
2. Torsion bar
3. Hinge
4. Spacer
5. Upper stop
6. Lock
7. Shim
8. Lock striker
9. Washer
10. Lower stop

Fig. 11-1. Station wagon tailgate components.

To remove tailgate:

1. Open the tailgate and disconnect the wire for the license plate light. If the window is electrically heated, or has a rear wiper/washer, you should also disconnect the wires and, where applicable, the washer hose.
2. Remove the four screws from each hinge cover, then take off the hinge covers.
3. Remove the two mounting bolts from one of the hinges. Have someone support the unbolted side of the tailgate while you remove the two mounting bolts from the other hinge.

   NOTE ——
   If you intend to reinstall the original tailgate, mark the positions of the hinges before removal to facilitate adjustment after reinstallation.

4. Working with your helper, lift the tailgate up and off toward the rear of the car.

To install tailgate:

1. Before installing the tailgate, check the condition of the rubber weatherstrip. If necessary, reglue or replace it.

   NOTE ——
   Before replacing a weatherstrip, clean away all the old adhesive with solvent. Install the new weatherstrip with trim cement.

2. With the tailgate firmly supported, install and tighten the four bolts that attach the tailgate to the hinges.
3. If you are installing a new tailgate, make sure that the gap is even all around and that the lock engages properly. See the tailgate adjustment procedures given on the next page.
4. Position the hinge covers and install the four screws that hold each cover in place.
5. Reconnect the license plate light wire, and if applicable, the wire for the electrically heated rear window.

To remove hinge:

1. Remove the headliner end trim and peel back enough of the headliner to expose the torsion bars for the hinges.
2. Remove the tailgate.
3. Use Toyota special tool 09804–13020, or a similar tool, to release each torsion bar at the end that is not attached to the hinge (Fig. 11-2). Then remove the torsion bars.

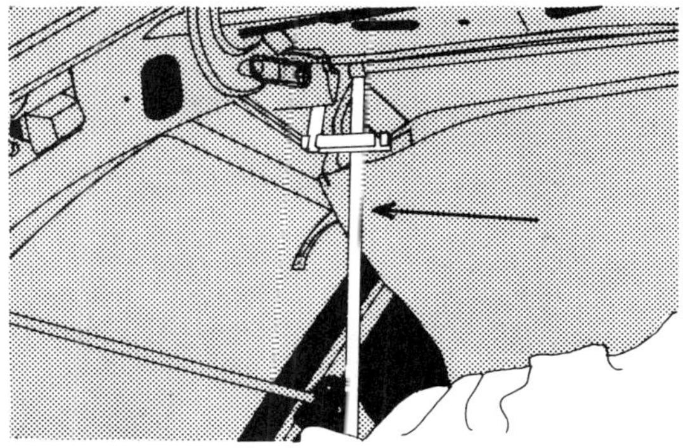

Fig. 11-2. Using special tool (arrow) to remove tailgate hinge torsion bar.

4. Remove the two bolts that hold each hinge to the body (Fig. 11-3). If you intend to reinstall the same hinges, mark their positions on the body before removal to facilitate adjustment after reinstallation.

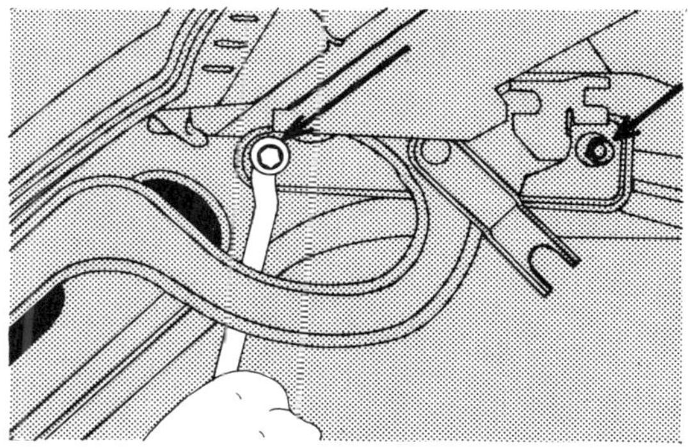

Fig. 11-3. Tailgate hinge mounting bolts (arrows).

Installation is the reverse of removal. If you are reinstalling the same hinges, line them up with the marks you made earlier. If the hinges operate stiffly or squeak, lubricate the pivot points with multipurpose grease.

9

To adjust tailgate:

1. Check the gap between the tailgate and the body. If it is uneven, loosen the four bolts that attach the tailgate to the hinges. Adjust the position of the tailgate so that the gap is uniform, then tighten the bolts.
2. Close the tailgate and see whether the tailgate is flush with the lip of the body. If it is not, open the tailgate and loosen the four hinge mounting bolts (Fig. 11-4). Adjust the position of the hinges until the tailgate is uniformly flush with the body. Then tighten the hinge mounting bolts.

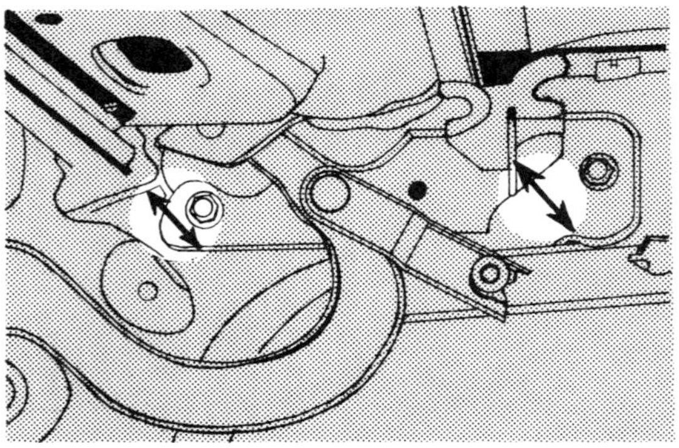

Fig. 11-4. Tailgate being adjusted for flush fit with body. Move one way or other in directions indicated by double arrows.

3. Check the lock operation by opening and closing the tailgate several times. If necessary, adjust the position of the striker plate (Fig. 11-5). The striker plate can be moved forward or backward, and its up and down position can be varied by the use of 1-mm (.040-in.) shims.

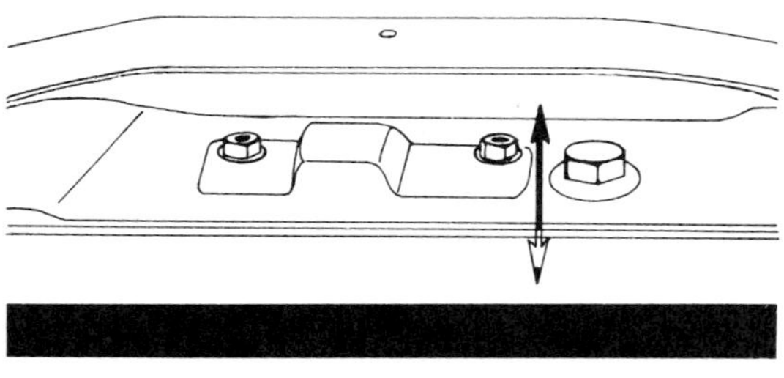

Fig. 11-5. Tailgate striker plate, which can be adjusted in direction indicated by arrows. Position can be raised or lowered by use of shims.

4. Check the tailgate stops for correct contact. You can adjust the lower stops (Fig. 11-6) and the upper stops (Fig. 11-7) to position the tailgate and prevent rattles. Spacers in 2.3-mm (.091-in.) and 1.0-mm (.040-in.) thicknesses are available for adjusting the positions of the stops.

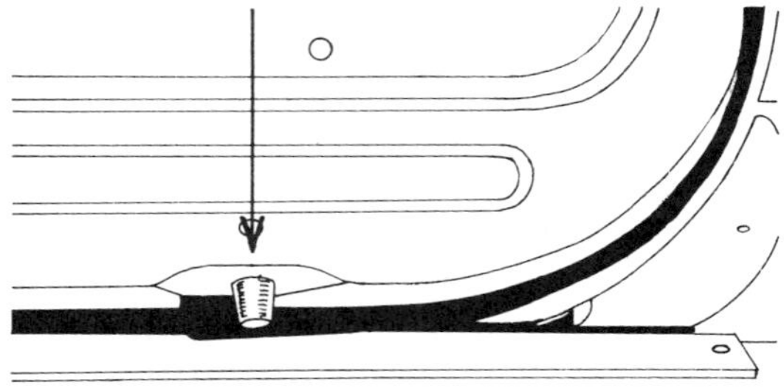

Fig. 11-6. Tailgate lower stop (arrow).

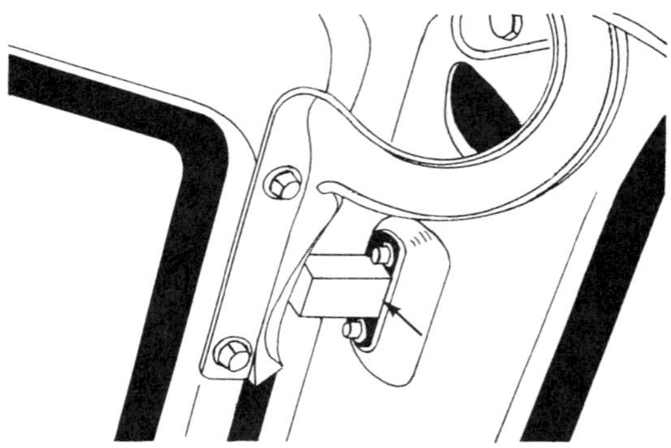

Fig. 11-7. Tailgate upper stop.

11.2 Removing and Installing Liftback Rear Lid

Fig. 11-8 is an exploded view of the liftback rear lid assembly. You can remove the rear lid without removing either the hinges or the dampers. It is possible to remove and replace the dampers without removing the rear lid.

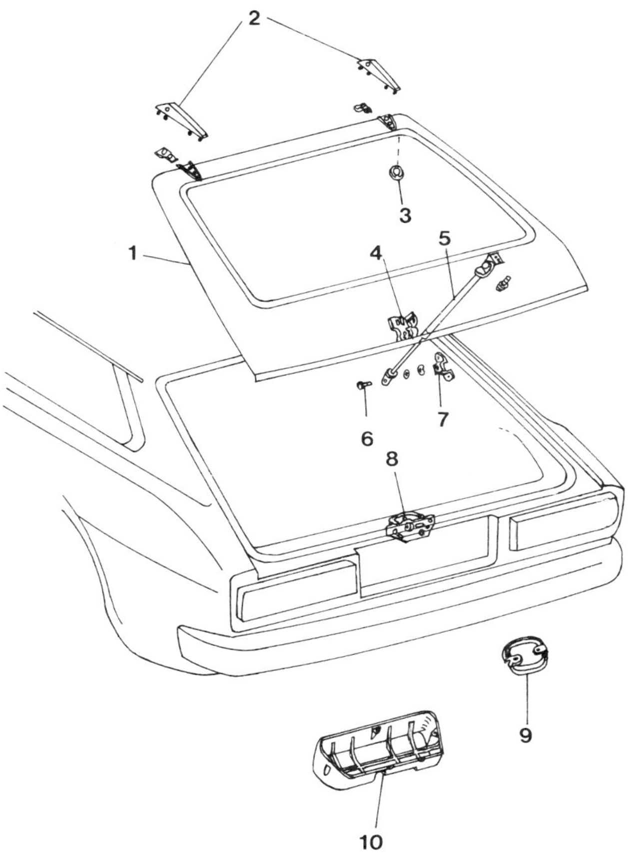

1. Rear lid
2. Hinges
3. Hinge cover
4. Lock
5. Damper
6. Bolt
7. Bracket
8. Striker assembly
9. Hole cover
10. Trim board

Fig. 11-8. Liftback rear lid components.

To remove:

1. Open the rear lid. Remove the two mounting bolts that attach the upper end of each damper to the lid.
2. If you intend to replace one or both dampers, remove the mounting bolt that attaches the lower end of each damper to the bracket mounted on the body. If you do not intend to replace either damper, you can leave them attached to the body.

> ***WARNING* —**
> *Do not disassemble the dampers. They contain inert gas under pressure. To avoid injuring yourself or others, dispose of faulty dampers properly by drilling a 2- to 3-mm (about ⅛-in.) hole at the end opposite the piston rod, which will allow gas to escape. When drilling the hole, wear gloves and a suitable face shield because oil and drill cuttings may be forcibly expelled when the*

> ***WARNING (cont.)* —**
> *gas is released. If you cannot or do not want to perform this operation, take used dampers to your Authorized Dealer for disposal.*

3. Disconnect the window washer hose and the wires for the electrically heated rear window or the rear window wiper, if the car is so equipped.
4. Remove the two rubber hinge covers from the upper inside surface of the lid, so that you can gain access to the lid hinge mounting nuts.
5. Have someone support the rear lid while you remove the two nuts from each lid hinge. When you have removed all four nuts, separate the lid from the hinges and lift it off the rear of the car.
6. If you want to replace one or both hinges, remove the headliner end trim and peel back enough of the headliner to expose the hinge mounting nuts. Remove the two nuts, then take off the hinge and mounting pad.

Installation is the reverse of removal. Center the lid in the body opening before you tighten the hinge mounting nuts. If you are installing a new lid, you may have to adjust the position of the lock striker plate once the lid is correctly positioned.

9

12. HEATING AND VENTILATION

Fig. 12-1 is an exploded view of the heating and ventilation system. Not pictured are the fresh air vents, which are located at each end of the dashboard.

You can remove the heater fan without removing the heater from the car. This procedure is given in **ELECTRICAL SYSTEM.** You can also remove the heater valve separately. Close the heater valve before you remove it. If you remove only the heater valve, you need not drain the coolant; simply disconnect and plug the hoses.

To remove heater assembly:

1. Drain the engine coolant as described in **ENGINE.**
2. Working under the hood, loosen the clamps and disconnect the two heater hoses at the firewall. You should also disconnect the battery ground strap.
3. Working inside the car under the dashboard, remove the air intake duct and the two heater defroster ducts from the heater. See Fig. 12-2.
4. Remove the knobs from the blower switch and the ventilation and heating controls. On some models, you can remove the heater control panel (Fig. 12-3) after you take out the two screws in the panel's upper corners. On other models, the panel is integral with the console and must be removed with the console as a unit. If so, remove the console as described in **9.2 Removing and Installing Interior Trim.**

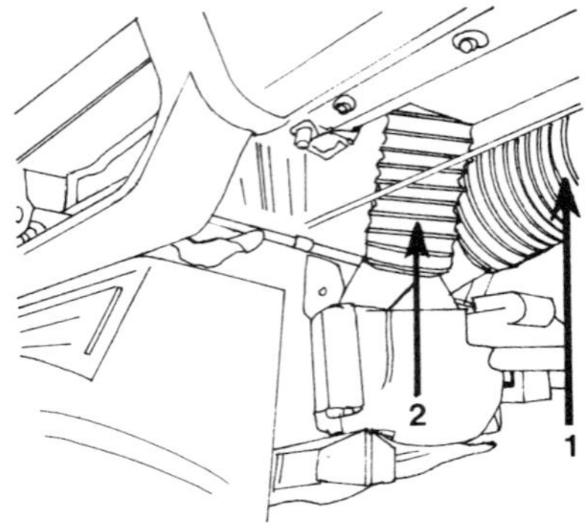

Fig. 12-2. Heater air intake duct (**1**) and defroster duct (**2**).

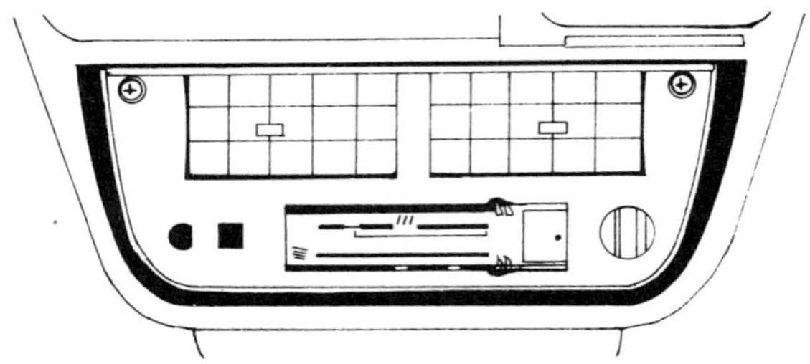

Fig. 12-3. Heater control panel. Remove screws at upper corners to remove panel, or remove console and panel as unit if there are no screws.

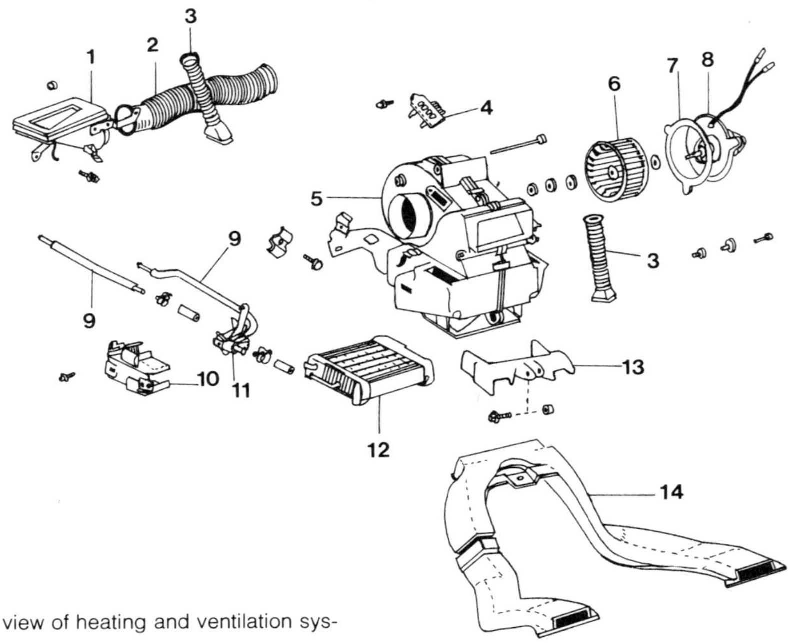

1. Air inlet
2. Air duct
3. Defroster duct (2)
4. Control resistor
5. Housing
6. Fan
7. Gasket
8. Fan motor
9. Water hose
10. Valve cover
11. Heater valve
12. Heat exchanger
13. Cover
14. Rear air duct

Fig. 12-1. Exploded view of heating and ventilation system.

5. Now that the control mechanism is exposed, take out its four mounting screws, but do not disconnect the cables. Later, the control mechanism, the cables, and the heater will be removed as a unit.
6. Working under the dashboard, disconnect the heater wiring harness multiple connector. Remove the long mounting bolt and nut at the top of the heater and the two mounting bolts on each side of the heater at the firewall. See Fig. 12-4.

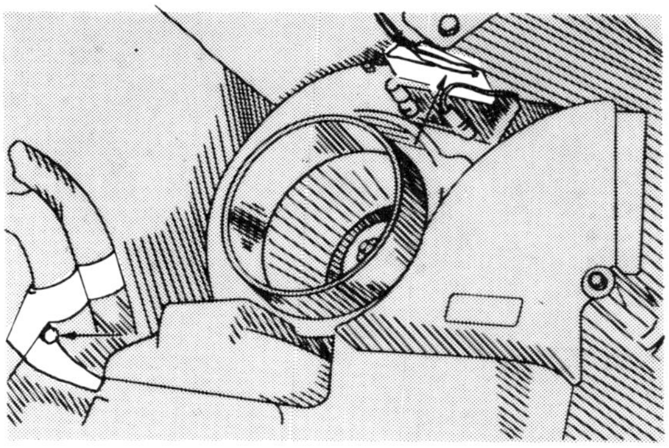

Fig. 12-4. Heater mounting bolts (top and left arrows). Third mounting bolt is on firewall on other side of heater. Wiring harness multiple connector is near top mounting bolt.

7. Detach all ducts from the heater. Pull the water hoses free from the hole in the firewall. Then remove the heater assembly from the car.

Installation is the reverse of removal. When you install the heater control mechanism, make sure the cables and controls operate smoothly. Remember to connect the heater wiring harness multiple connector and the battery ground strap, and to replace any engine coolant that has been lost.

13. BODY DIMENSIONS

The illustrations in this section give the basic body dimensions. Using them as a guide, you can check a vehicle that has been in an accident or otherwise damaged for twisting or misalignment. You can also use the measurements as a standard to follow during body repairs. Units of measurement are in millimeters, with inches in parentheses.

Fig. 13-1. Sedan body dimensions.

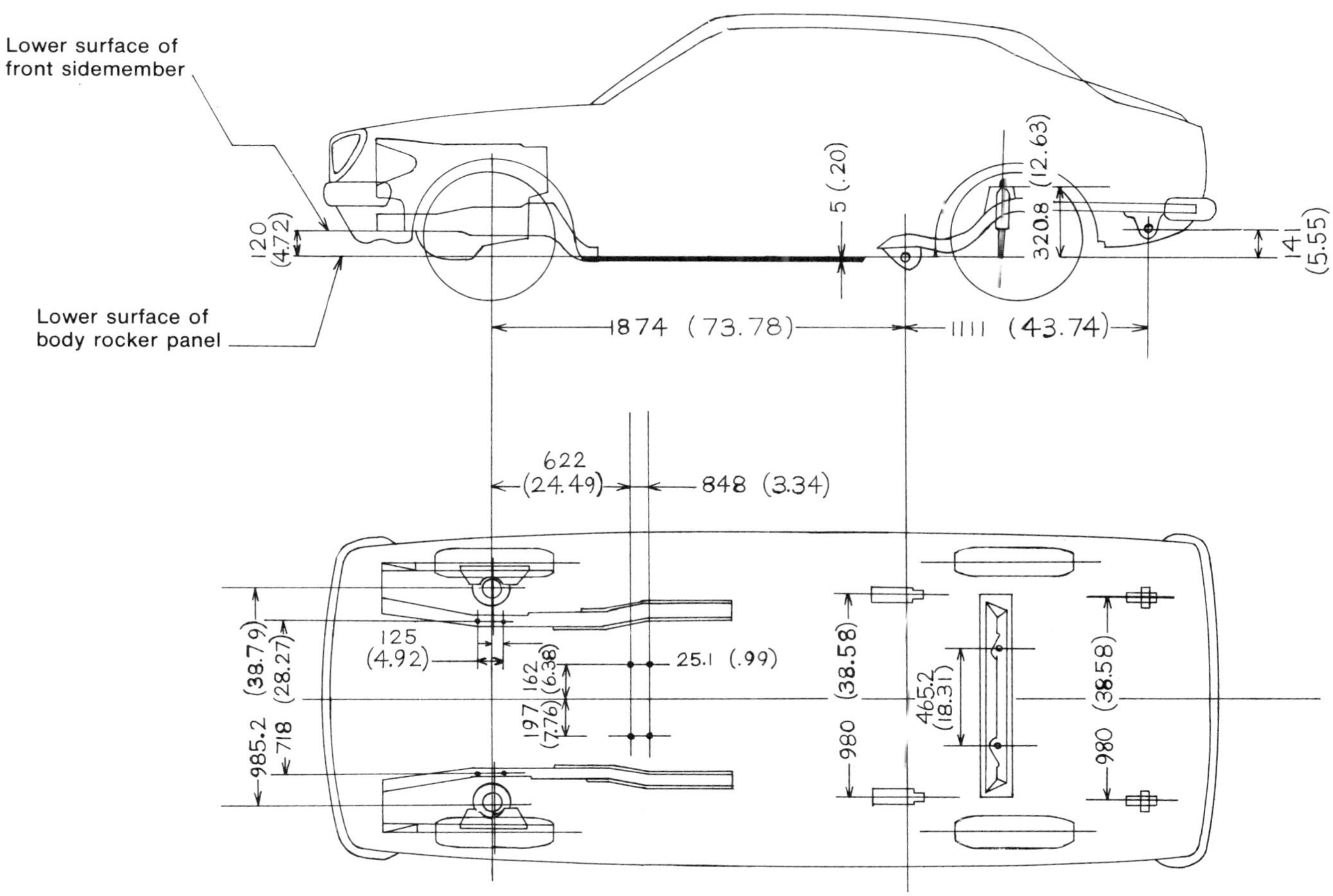

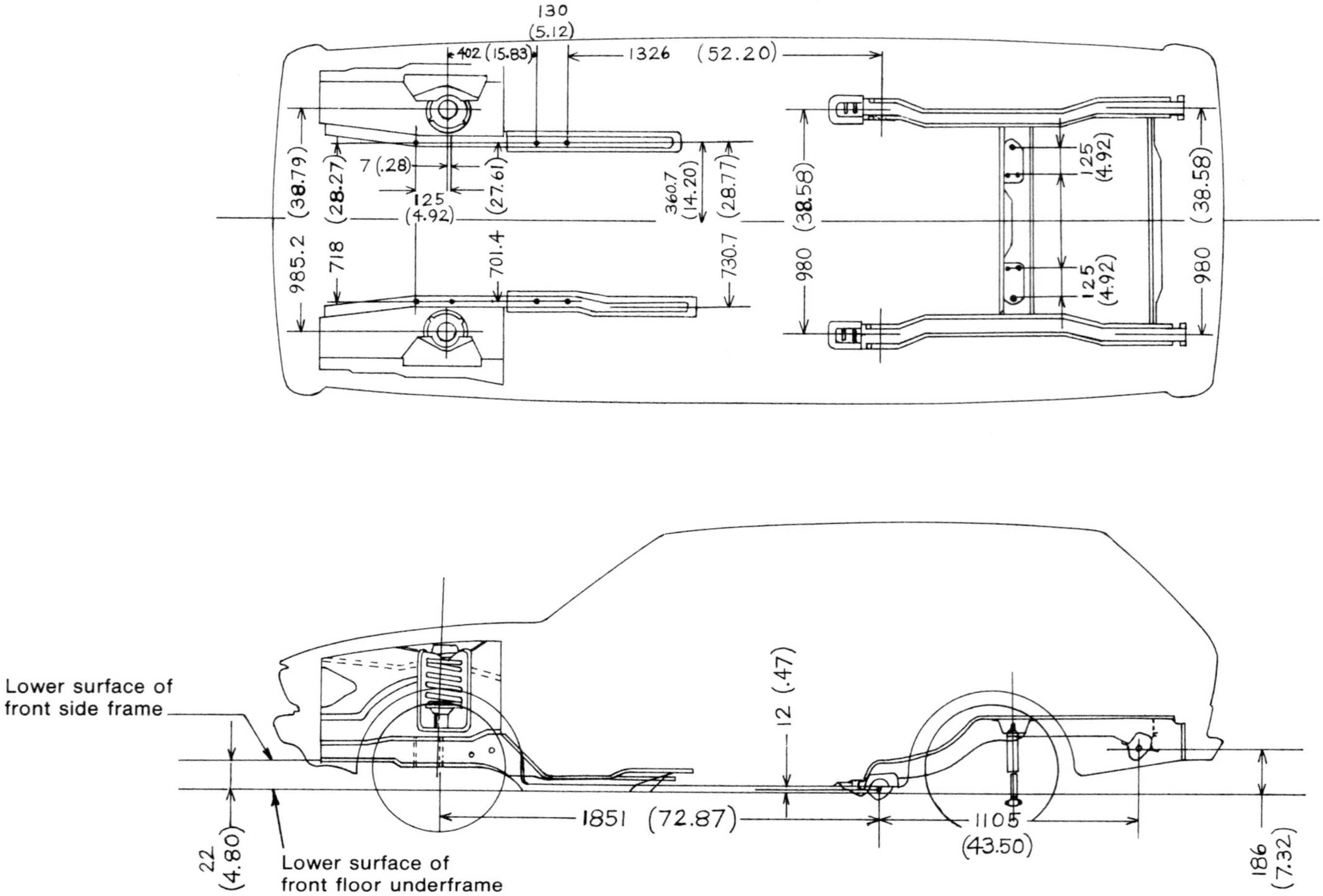

Fig. 13-2. Station wagon body dimensions.

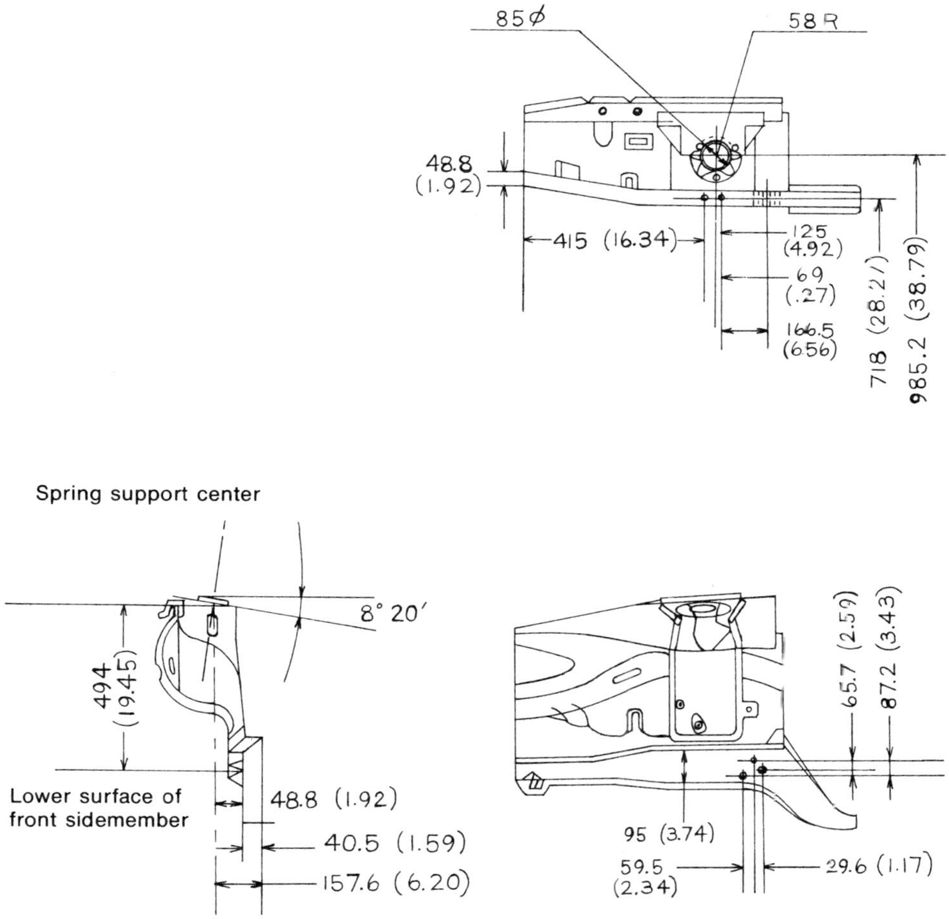

Fig. 13-3. Front fender apron dimensions.

Section 10

LUBRICATION AND MAINTENANCE

Contents

TABLES

Lubrication and Maintenance

The service life of your Corolla depends on the kind of maintenance it receives. The Owner's Manual originally supplied with the car contains valuable information concerning correct car maintenance, and that information should be used in conjunction with this Manual. Because several model years are covered in this Manual, some of the procedures described may not apply to your car. If you are in doubt, always take the Owner's Manual as your guide.

Some maintenance procedures, such as oil change service, require no special tools and can be carried out by almost all car owners, regardless of their mechanical experience. Certain other diagnosis and maintenance operations, however, require tools and equipment specifically designed for those operations. Wheel alignment checks, ignition timing, and emission control checks are a few examples. If you lack the skills, the tools, or a suitable workshop for performing any of the service steps described, we suggest you leave this work to an Authorized Dealer or other qualified shop. We especially urge you to consult your Authorized Dealer before attempting any repairs on a car still covered by the new-car warranty.

Many of the service operations that are required at a specific mileage or time interval are made with the engine cold, whereas many others are made with the engine hot. Most of these service operations are related to checks of the various emission controls. Before you begin carrying out any engine, ignition, fuel system, and emission control checks, you will find it helpful if you go over the various procedures given in this Manual and mark those that on your particular model need to be done with the engine cold and those that need to be done with the engine warmed up. By doing this, you will be able first to conduct the tests that are to be done with the engine cold, then those that are to be made during warm-up, and finally those that are done with the engine at full operating temperature.

1. LUBRICANTS

The lubricants used in your Toyota Corolla have a vital influence on its operation. Use only name brand oils labeled "For Service SE". Automatic transmission fluid (ATF) should be labeled "Type F". The hypoid oil used in the rear axle must meet specification API/GL5, whereas the gear oil used in the manual transmissions must meet specification API/GL4. The API/GL4 oil for the transmission lacks some of the anti-friction additives used in the API/GL5 oil for the rear axle. If used in the transmission, these anti-friction additives may cause the synchronizer rings to slip and result in clashing gear changes. No supplementary additives should be used in the engine oil, the transmission oil or ATF, or in the hypoid oil for the rear axle. Experience has shown that name brand lubricants of the correct specification and viscosity meet all operating needs of the engine, the transmission, and the rear axle.

Oil viscosity must be suitable to climatic conditions. Viscosity is a term used to describe how readily a liquid flows. High viscosity oils seem thicker and pour more slowly at room temperature than do low viscosity (thinner) oils. When heated, however, oil loses some of its viscosity. A high viscosity oil heated to 90°C (200°F) may pour as readily as a low viscosity oil at room temperature. If an oil has too low a viscosity, it will not maintain an adequate lubricating film between moving parts. A thin, low viscosity oil may maintain this film at low temperatures but become so much thinner after it has warmed up that it leaves the engine parts unprotected.

It might seem that a high viscosity oil is all that is necessary to lubricate an engine properly. Unfortunately, this is not true. If a high viscosity oil is used during cold weather, it will become so thick and resistant to flow that it cannot properly circulate and reach the parts of the engine requiring lubrication. A thick, high viscosity oil will also become so gummy in cold weather that the starter cannot turn the engine fast enough to start it. The proper viscosity oil will remain fluid enough after the engine has cooled to permit easy starting, yet after the engine has reached operating temperature will retain sufficient viscosity to maintain an adequate lubricating film.

Single-grade engine oils, such as SAE 30, were formerly recommended for high-temperature use because even when thinned by heat adequate viscosity remained for good lubrication. The new high standard for engine oils that conform to the API (American Petroleum Institute) ratings has, however, made multi-grade oils suitable for use at all temperatures. Car owners will find that high-quality multi-grade oils with the correct API ratings for their cars offer many advantages in convenience, performance, and economy.

For example, a single-grade oil may have to be discarded after a short period of service owing to the early arrival of winter temperatures. A multi-grade oil, suitable for both summer and winter temperatures, can be left in the engine until the normal oil change mileage has been reached. This feature of multi-grade oils can save the expense of oil changes necessitated by climatic conditions, and also conserve natural resources.

By becoming familiar with the oil recommendations, you can be sure that the oil you buy is the correct kind for your car. Inferior lubricants, no matter how attractively priced, are not a good investment; using the wrong oil will greatly shorten the service life of your Corolla.

Oil Viscosities

The viscosity grade of oil is designated by an SAE (Society of Automotive Engineers) standard number. An oil designated SAE 40 has a higher viscosity (greater resistance to flow) than an oil designated SAE 30. Multi-grade oils have an extended viscosity range and can be used in place of a number of single-grade oils. For example, an SAE 10W-30 oil is suitable for use within a range of temperatures that would require three different single-grade oils in order to cover it (SAE 10W, SAE 20W/20, and SAE 30). **Table a** lists the correct oil viscosity for Corolla 1600 engines under specific climatic conditions. The SAE viscosity number of the oil should be selected for the lowest anticipated temperature at which engine starting will be required, and not for the temperature at the time of the oil change. Because the temperature ranges of the different oil grades overlap, brief variations in outside temperatures are no cause for alarm.

Table a. Oil Viscosity Specifications

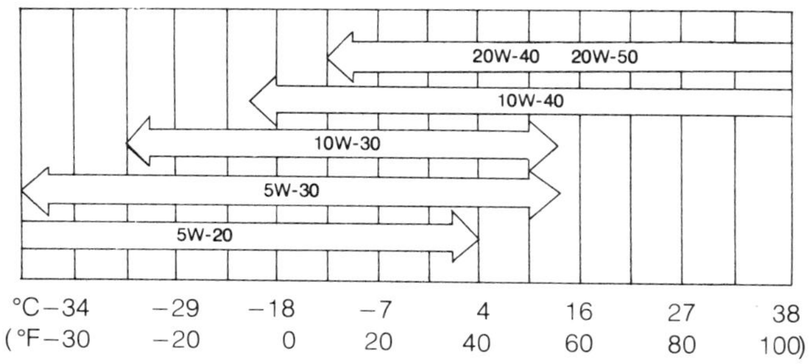

CAUTION —

Avoid high-speed, long distance driving when using SAE 5W-20 oil—especially if the outside temperature rises above the limits given for this lubricant. If you anticipate continuous operation that will impose maximum loads on the engine, or if you expect to drive at sustained speeds above 100 kph (60 mph), use a 5W-30 or 10W-30 oil. Under these conditions, the engine will run at higher temperatures and SAE 5W-20 may be inadequate to maintain a proper lubricating film between the moving parts of the engine.

The viscosity of gear oil is also designated by SAE numbers. Use SAE 90 API/GL4 oil in manual transmissions. Use SAE 90 API/GL5 oil in the rear axle. If the outside temperature in your area regularly falls below 0°C (32°F), use SAE 80W-90 multi-grade gear oil in the transmission.

Greases

Several kinds of grease are used for the lubrication of automobile chassis and driveline parts. Multipurpose grease (lithium grease) has a wider temperature tolerance range than ordinary grease and should be used for most lubrication purposes on your Corolla. The additives in multipurpose grease give it increased pressure resistance and anticorrosion capabilities. It is suitable for use both in plain bearings and in roller bearings. Molybdenum grease is lithium grease with a friction-reducing molybdenum disulfide additive. It is used in the front suspension ball joints and at a number of other points, as designated in certain repair procedures in this Manual. Dry stick lubricants can be used on the hood locks and on the sliding surfaces of the door striker plates. The battery terminals, if not encased in rubber-like plastic, should be coated with either silicone spray or petroleum jelly.

2. MAINTENANCE SCHEDULES

The maintenance schedules given in **Table b** should be followed carefully even if your Corolla is not being serviced by an Authorized Dealer. The second column of the table tells where each maintenance job is covered in this Manual. For example, the first operation listed in the table, checking and adjusting valve clearance, is covered in Section 5 (**ENGINE**) under heading 5.2 (Adjusting Valves). The fourth operation listed in the table, changing engine oil and filter and checking the oil level, is covered in Section 10 (**LUBRICATION AND MAINTENANCE**) under heading 3 (Oil Change Service).

Key for Table b

★ = 10,000—30,000—50,000—70,000 km (6,000—19,000—31,000—44,000 mi.) (or at 6—18—30—42 months if you drive less than the prescribed distance in that period of time)

○ = 20,000—40,000—60,000—80,000 km (12,500—25,000—37,500—50,000 mi.) (or at 12—24—36—48 months if you drive less than the prescribed distance in that period of time)

□ = 12,000—36,000—60,000—84,000 km (7,500—22,500—37,500—52,500 mi.) (or at 6—18—30—42 months if you drive less than the prescribed distance in that period of time)

● = 24,000—48,000—72,000—96,000 km (15,000—30,000—45,000—60,000 mi.) (or at 12—24—36—48 months if you drive less than the prescribed distance in that period of time)

■ = each 40,000 km (25,000 mi.) (or at each 24 months if you drive less than the prescribed distance in that period of time)

☆ = each 48,000 km (30,000 mi.) (or at each 24 months if you drive less than the prescribed distance in that period of time)

◆ = each 80,000 km (50,000 mi.) (or at each 48 months if you drive less than the prescribed distance in that period of time)

◇ = each 96,000 km (60,000 mi.) (or at each 48 months if you drive less than the prescribed distance in that period of time)

Table b. Scheduled Maintenance Operations

Maintenance operation	Where operation is covered in Manual	1975 through 1977 cars	1978 and later cars
Checking and adjusting the engine valve clearance	Section 5 Heading 5.2	○	●
Checking and adjusting or replacing the engine V-belt(s) (replace at every second maintenance interval)	Section 10 Heading 4.1	○	●
Checking the engine bolt torques	Section 10 Heading 4.2	1st 1600 km (1000 mi.) or 1st month only	1st 1600 km (1000 mi.) or 1st month only
Changing the engine oil and oil filter and checking the oil level	Section 10 Heading 3	★ ○	□ ●
Replacing the engine coolant	Section 10 Heading 4.3	■	☆
Checking the cooling system and, if necessary, adding coolant and replacing faulty hoses	Section 5 Heading 4	○	●
Checking and, if necessary, replacing the vacuum hoses	Section 10 Heading 5.5	○	●
Checking the exhaust system for leaks	Section 10 Heading 5.1	○	●
Checking the ignition distributor breaker point dwell, then checking and, if necessary, adjusting the ignition timing	Section 5 Heading 3.2	○	● check timing only
Replacing the ignition distributor's breaker points	Section 5 Heading 3.2	■	[NA]
Replacing the spark plugs	Section 5 Heading 3.5	○	●
Checking the distributor cap, distributor rotor, and spark plug cables and high-tension lead	Section 5 Headings 3.2, 3.4	○	●
Checking the ignition distributor's spark advance mechanism	Section 5 Heading 3.2	○	●
Checking the spark control systems	Section 6 Heading 8.4	○	●

Table b. Scheduled Maintenance Operations (continued)

Maintenance operation	Where operation is covered in Manual	1975 through 1977 cars	1978 and later cars
Servicing the air cleaner	Section 10 Heading 4.5	○	●
Replacing the air filter element(s)	Section 10 Heading 4.5	■	☆
Replacing the fuel filter	Section 10 Heading 4.6	■	☆
Checking the exhaust controls	Section 6 Heading 8.4	○	●
Checking and, if necessary, replacing the catalytic converter	Section 6 Heading 8.2	○	●
Checking the PCV (positive crankcase ventilation) system	Section 6 Heading 8.1	○	●
Replacing the PCV (positive crankcase ventilation) valve	Section 6 Heading 8.1	■	☆
Checking the evaporative emission control lines	Section 6 Heading 8.3	○	●
Checking the evaporative emission control canister	Section 6 Heading 8.3	■	☆
Replacing the evaporative emission control charcoal filter canister	Section 6 Heading 8.3	◆	◇
Adjusting the engine idle speed and idle mixture	Section 6 Headings 5.1, 5.2	○	●
Adjusting the engine fast idle speed	Section 6 Heading 5.1	○	●
Checking the throttle positioner system	Section 6 Heading 5.3	○	●
Checking the exhaust pipe, muffler, and brackets for correct installation	Section 6 Heading 9	○	●
Replacing the fuel tank cap gasket	Section 10 Heading 6.4	■	☆
Checking and, if necessary adjusting the clutch pedal freeplay	Section 2 Heading 3.1	★ ○	□ ●
Checking the clutch master cylinder fluid level, and adding fluid if necessary	Section 10 Heading 4.7	★ ○	□ ●
Checking and, if necessary, correcting the manual transmission oil level	Section 10 Heading 5.3	★ ○	□ ●
Changing the manual transmission oil	Section 10 Heading 5.3	■	☆
Checking the ATF (automatic transmission fluid) level and condition and, if necessary, adding ATF	Section 10 Heading 5.2	★ ○	□ ●
Replacing the ATF (automatic transmission fluid)	Section 10 Heading 5.2	■	☆
Checking that the kickdown operates correctly during a road test and, if necessary, adjusting the throttle cable	Section 1 Headings 4.1, 4.2	★	□
Checking the torque of the rear suspension components attached to the rear axle, and checking the torque of the driveshaft rear universal joint flange bolts	Section 10 Heading 5.5	○	●
Checking and, if necessary, correcting the differential oil level	Section 10 Heading 5.4	★	□
Changing the differential oil	Section 10 Heading 5.4	■	☆
Checking the brake fluid level and, if necessary, adding fluid	Section 7 Heading 9.1	★ ○	□ ●

10

(continued on next page)

Table b. Scheduled Maintenance Operations (continued)

Maintenance operation	Where operation is covered in Manual	1975 through 1977 cars	1978 and later cars
Checking the brake pedal height and travel	Section 7 Heading 5.2	★ ○	□ ●
Checking the brake pad thickness and the brake disc condition	Section 7 Heading 7.1	★ ○	□ ●
Checking the brake lining thickness and brake drum condition	Section 7 Heading 8.1	○	●
Checking the condition of brake lines and hoses	Section 7 Heading 6	★ ○	□ ●
Checking the operation of the brake servo	Section 7 Heading 6	★ ○	□ ●
Checking and, if necessary, adjusting the parking brake lever travel	Section 7 Heading 10.1	★ ○	□ ●
Lubricating and adjusting the front wheel bearings	Section 7 Headings 11.4, 11.5	■	☆
Checking the torque of the front and rear suspension bolts	Section 8 Heading 7	○	●
Lubricating the front suspension lower ball joints	Section 10 Heading 5.7	■	☆
Inspecting the front suspension lower ball joints and dust covers	Section 10 Heading 5.7	★ ○	□ ●
Lubricating the front suspension upper support bearings	Section 10 Heading 4.8	■	☆
Inspecting the steering wheel (for excessive play) and the steering linkage (for looseness)	Section 10 Heading 5.6	★ ○	□ ●
Checking and, if necessary, correcting the steering gearbox oil level	Section 10 Heading 4.9	★ ○	□ ●
Checking the battery	Section 10 Heading 3	weekly	weekly
Checking the wiring harness and connections	Section 10 Heading 4.10	○	●
Checking the seatbelt warning system	Section 10 Heading 6.2	○	●
Checking the operation of all lights and switches	Section 10 Heading 6.3	○	●
Checking the torque of the seat and the seatbelt mounting bolts	Section 9 Heading 10.1	○	●
Checking and, if necessary, adjusting the operation of the door locks	Sections 9 & 10 Headings 6.5, 7.5 & 6.1	○	●
Checking and, if necessary, adjusting the operation of the hood lock	Sections 9 & 10 Headings 4.1 & 6.1	○	●
Checking and, if necessary, adjusting the operation of the luggage compartment, tailgate, or rear lid lock	Sections 9 & 10 Headings 7.5 & 6.1	○	●
Checking and, if necessary, adjusting the operation of the seat adjusters and the seat back locks	Sections 9 & 10 Headings 10.2 & 6.1	○	●
Checking the seatbelt retractor emergency lockup	Section 10 Heading 6.2	○	●

3. OIL CHANGE SERVICE

While you are changing the oil, it is wise to check the battery electrolyte as described in **ELECTRICAL SYSTEM.** First test the specific gravity of the electrolyte with a hydrometer. Then, if necessary, add distilled water in order to bring the electrolyte level above the cell separators, or to the bottom of the filler tubes on batteries that are so equipped. You should make this check weekly. An excessive need for water indicates either a battery that is nearing the end of its useful service life or trouble in the charging system.

3.1 Changing Engine Oil

The oil should be drained from the engine while it is hot. Drive the car to a level place and stop the engine. Drain the oil by placing a pan of at least 6-liter (or 6-quart) capacity beneath the engine. Then remove the oil drain plug from the engine's oil pan and allow the oil to drain into the collecting pan. You can also change the oil filter, as described under the next heading, while the oil is draining.

Carefully inspect the drain plug's gasket and replace if it is cracked or deteriorating. When the flow has diminished to one drop per minute, reinstall the drain plug. Tighten the plug securely, but to no more than about 30 Nm (22 ft. lb.). Then, if you have changed the oil filter, refill the crankcase with 4.4 liters (4.6 U.S. quarts, 3.9 Imperial quarts) of oil labeled "For Service SE". If you have not changed the oil filter, you will need only 3.5 liters (3.7 U.S. quarts, 3.1 Imperial quarts) of this oil.

NOTE ——

Always make a final check of the oil level after the engine has been run long enough to fill the filter and has been stopped long enough for oil to drain down off internal engine parts. Check the dipstick to make sure that the level is correct before you drive the car. See Fig. 3-1.

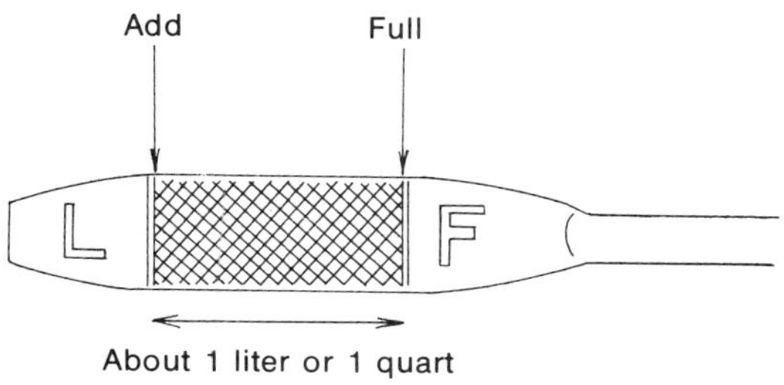

Fig. 3-1. Engine oil dipstick. After change, oil should be at full mark (**F**). Always maintain oil level in roughened part of dipstick, adding oil when level falls to (**L**) end of rough part.

Replacing Oil Filter

The oil filter is located on the right-hand side of the engine block. To change the filter, place a drip pan beneath the filter location. Then, using an oil filter wrench, turn the filter counterclockwise until it is off the engine. To avoid a serious leak, make sure that the old filter's gasket is not left sticking to the engine block. Coat the gasket of the new filter with engine oil, then screw on the filter as tightly as you can using your bare hand only.

After you have refilled the engine with oil, run the engine until the new filter is filled and under pressure. Check visually for leaks around the filter. Stop the engine and, after waiting for the oil to drain down off the engine's internal parts, recheck the oil level.

4. ENGINE COMPARTMENT MAINTENANCE OPERATIONS

Because the automatic transmission fluid dipstick is located in the engine compartment, you should check the ATF level before you raise the car on a hoist. Instructions for checking the ATF level are given in **5.2 Checking and Correcting ATF Level.**

4.1 Checking and Adjusting or Replacing Engine V-belt(s)

First, check the V-belts visually. If a belt is oil-soaked, cracked, or worn so much that it contacts the bottom of any pulley groove, replace the belt. To check whether the belt tension is correct, press the belt(s) at the points indicated in Fig. 4-1. If you use a belt tester, press against each belt with a force of 10 kg (22 lb.).

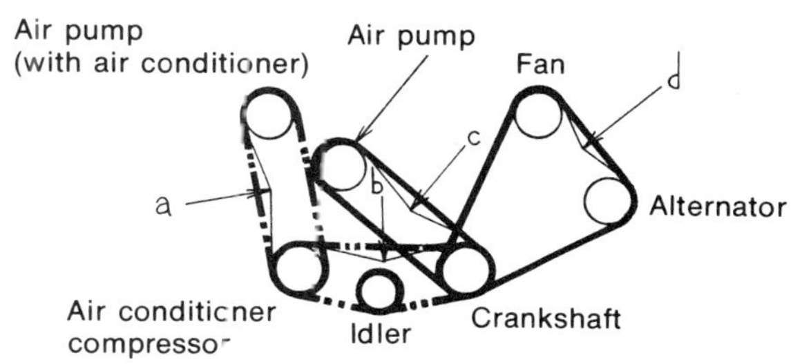

Point **a**: 10 to 14 mm (3/8 to 9/16 in.)
Point **b**: 11 to 14 mm (7/16 to 9/16 in.)
Point **c**: 13 to 18 mm (1/2 to 11/16 in.)
Point **d**: 8 to 12 mm (5/16 to 15/32 in.)

Fig. 4-1. Points at which you should press against V-belts to check tension. Correct depression dimensions are given for each point. 10

You can adjust the belt tension by loosening the adjusting bolt and the mounting bolt for either the alternator, the air injection pump, or the idler pulley (on cars with air conditioners). By moving each of these components to tighten or loosen its V-belt, obtain the correct tension. Then retighten the bolts.

> ***CAUTION —***
> *Overtightening a belt can cause pulleys to break and bearings to fail. In adjusting the air pump's belt tension, move the air pump by inserting a large screwdriver between the pin and the cast-iron cover of the pump. Never attempt to move the air pump by prying against its die-cast alloy housing. Doing this will deform the housing and ruin the pump. See Fig. 4-2.*

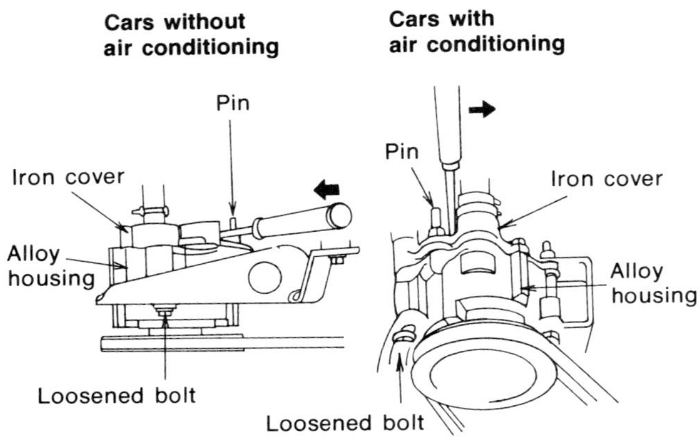

Fig. 4-2. Air pump being moved to adjust V-belt tension. Illustrations show screwdriver correctly inserted between pin and cast-iron cover.

The V-belts should be replaced each 40,000 km (25,000 mi.) on 1975 through 1977 cars or each 48,000 km (30,000 mi.) on 1978 and later cars. Loosen the adjusting bolts and the mounting bolts for the alternator, the air injection pump, and the idler pulley (on cars with air conditioners). Move these components to loosen the belts fully and remove the belts from the pulleys. Install the new belts, then adjust their tensions as previously described.

4.2 Checking Engine Bolt Torques

Normally, the engine bolt torques are checked by the dealer who does the 1600-km (1000-mi.) or 1-month maintenance check of the vehicle. No further checks are specified by the car manufacturer. However, to prevent leaking gaskets, it is wise to check the bolt torques at subsequent maintenance intervals as well. You should never exceed the torques given in the technical data section of **ENGINE.** Doing this can damage parts and gaskets. If there is a leak even though the bolt torque is correct, the gasket should be replaced.

4.3 Replacing Engine Coolant

The coolant for the engine should be replaced each 40,000 km (25,000 mi.) on 1975 through 1977 cars or each 48,000 km (30,000 mi.) on 1978 and later cars. If you do not drive this far in a two-year period, replace the coolant every twenty-four months.

Place a drain pan beneath the radiator and beneath the left-hand side of the engine block. Then open the drain tap on the bottom of the radiator and the drain tap on the left-hand side of the engine block. Remove the radiator cap and allow the coolant to drain.

> ***WARNING —***
> *Do not drain the coolant with the engine hot. This could warp the cylinder head or the engine block, or you could burn yourself.*

Thoroughly flush the cooling system with clean water. When this has fully drained, close the drain taps. Then refill the radiator with a mixture of clean, non-alkaline, phosphate-free water and a phosphate-free, permanent-type anti-freeze with an integral rust inhibitor. The proportion of permanent-type anti-freeze to water will vary according to the lowest temperatures expected in your climatic area, so you should follow the mixing instructions given on the container by the anti-freeze manufacturer. The minimum percentage of anti-freeze recommended by Toyota is 50%, which will give freezing protection down to approximately −37°C (−34°F). Toyota does not recommend that you use any supplemental additives in the coolant, and you should bear in mind that hard water and any substance that is alkaline or contains phosphates will damage the cylinder head and other aluminum components of the engine and the cooling system.

When the radiator is nearly filled, momentarily remove one of the thermo switches from the thermostat housing/EGR valve mounting at the front of the cylinder head so that coolant flows out, thus releasing trapped air that could keep hot coolant from opening the thermostat. Start the engine and allow it to idle—continuing to add coolant each time the level in the radiator falls until the system is filled. Then install the radiator cap tightly and fill the coolant reservoir. Check the drain taps for leakage and, if necessary, tighten them.

4.4 Checking and Replacing Vacuum Hoses

To check the vacuum hoses and their connections, look for loose-fitting and misconnected hoses. The correct locations for the hoses can be determined from the vacuum hose layout decal on the underside of the hood. Replace vacuum lines that are cracked, bent sharply enough to collapse themselves, or are in any other way damaged. You should include in this check the vapor lines for the evaporative emission control system, which are beneath the fuel tank cover and the body interior's left rear quarter trim panel of liftback models or the right rear quarter trim panel of station wagon models.

4.5 Servicing Air Cleaner and Replacing Air Filter Element(s)

Though their operating principles are identical, several different kinds of air cleaners are used on the cars covered by this Manual. All the dust that is present in the air drawn into the engine is trapped and retained by the pleated paper filter element(s) in the air cleaner.

To service:

1. Release the clips that hold the cover to the air cleaner body. Remove the wing nut that is in the center of the cover, then lift the cover off the air cleaner body.
2. Lift out the ring-shaped pleated paper filter element.
3. If you have removed the filter element for inspection and cleaning only, first tap the element lightly on a hard surface to knock off all loose dust. Then, using low-pressure compressed air, blow dust from the element as indicated in Fig. 4-3.

> ***CAUTION —***
> *Never wash the filter element in solvent or blow it off with a powerful blast of high-pressure compressed air. This can ruin the filter. Replace filters that are excessively dirty, oily, or damaged. (Oil on the filter element may indicate trouble in the positive cranckcase ventilation (PCV) system, such as a stuck or clogged PCV valve.) After cleaning off dust, hold the filter up to a bright light and check for cracks in the pleats. If any crack or hole is found, replace the filter element.*

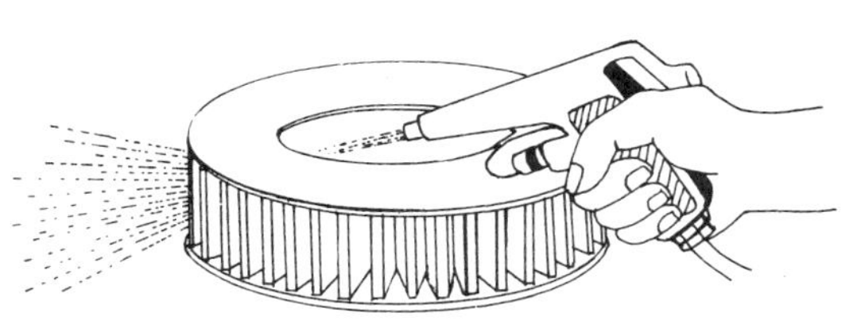

Fig. 4-3. Low-pressure compressed air being used to blow dust off filter element. Blow first from inside as shown, then blow dust off outside.

4. Before installing either a new or a used filter element, wipe clean the air cleaner housing using a lightly oiled, lint-free cloth.
5. Install the filter element and the cover—making sure that the arrow on the cover is aligned with the arrow on the air cleaner body's intake air duct.
6. On cars with an air suction (AS) emission control system, remove the AS filter from the side of the air cleaner as indicated in Fig. 4-4.

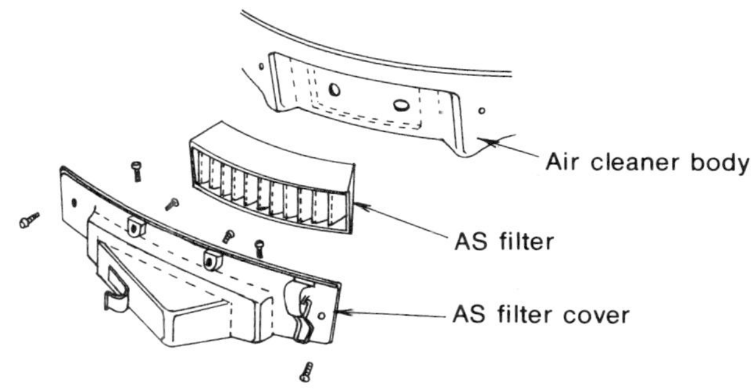

Fig. 4-4. Air suction filter element being removed. Detach hose(s) from AS filter cover, then remove screws and take cover off air cleaner body.

7. Clean and inspect the AS filter as you did the ring-shaped filter. The AS filter does not require routine replacement, but should be replaced if it is in any way damaged or unserviceable.
8. Reinstall the AS filter element and its cover, then reconnect the hose(s).

4.6 Replacing Fuel Filter

The fuel filter is located on the right-hand side of the firewall in the engine compartment, near the windshield wiper motor. To replace the filter, first disengage it from the clip that holds it to the firewall. Then, while squeezing together the tabs of the spring-steel hose clamps, detach the hoses from the fuel filter. Install the new filter as indicated in Fig. 4-5—with careful reference to the arrow on the filter.

> ***CAUTION —***
> *Fuel will be expelled when you detach the hoses from the filter. Turn off the engine. Do not smoke or work near heaters or other fire hazards. Have a fire extinguisher handy. To minimize fuel loss, briefly open and close the fuel tank filler cap so that pressure is released from the tank.*

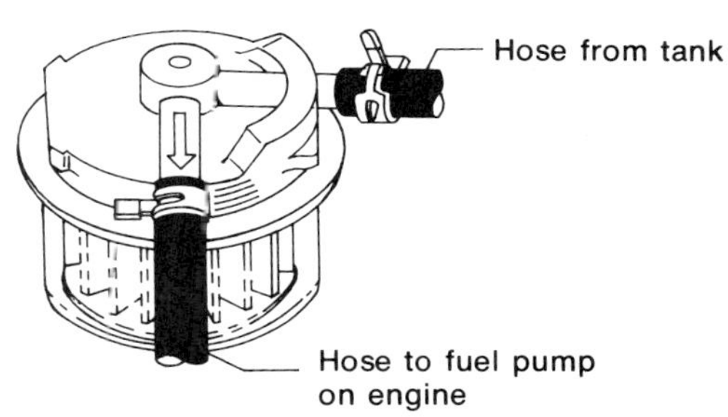

Fig. 4-5. Correct installation of fuel filter. Notice that connection with arrow is for hose that goes to fuel pump on engine.

4.7 Clutch Master Cylinder

Because the reservoir for the clutch master cylinder is translucent, you can check the level of the hydraulic fluid without removing the cap (Fig. 4-6). To add fluid, carefully snap off the cap. You need not remove the float from inside the reservoir. If the level is low, add brake fluid that meets the DOT-3 standard. Then snap on the cap.

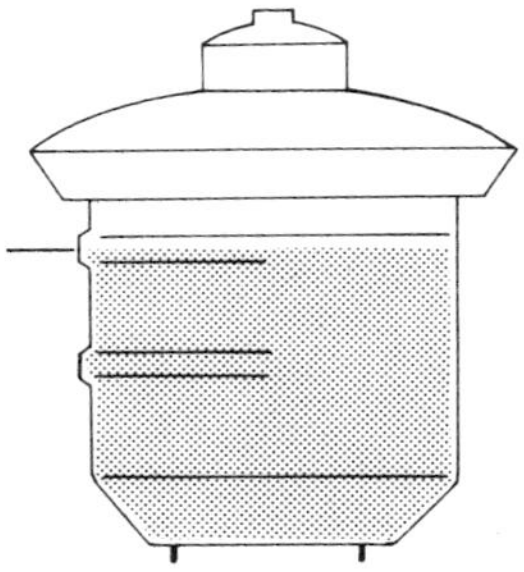

Fig. 4-6. Fluid level at full mark on translucent reservoir.

4.8 Lubricating Suspension Strut Support Bearings

To check the quantity of multipurpose grease in the front suspension strut upper support bearings, remove the caps as indicated in Fig. 4-7. If necessary, add multipurpose grease that meets standard NLGI No. 2. If there is water or other foreign matter in the grease, clean out the old grease and then refill the bearings with new multipurpose grease that meets standard NLGI No. 2.

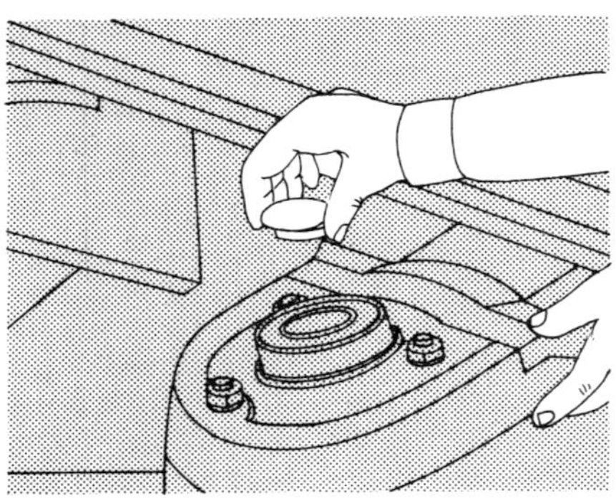

Fig. 4-7. Multipurpose grease being checked in suspension support bearing.

4.9 Steering Gearbox Oil Level

It is unnecessary to replace the oil in the steering gearbox. Oil should be added, however, if the level is low. Replace or repair steering gearboxes that are leaking. To check the level, remove the filler plug. Then measure the distance from the filler hole to the oil level as indicated in Fig. 4-8. If the distance from the top of the filler hole to the oil is greater than 21 to 36 mm ($^{13}/_{16}$ to $1\frac{3}{8}$ in.), add SAE 90 gear oil to bring the level into the correct range.

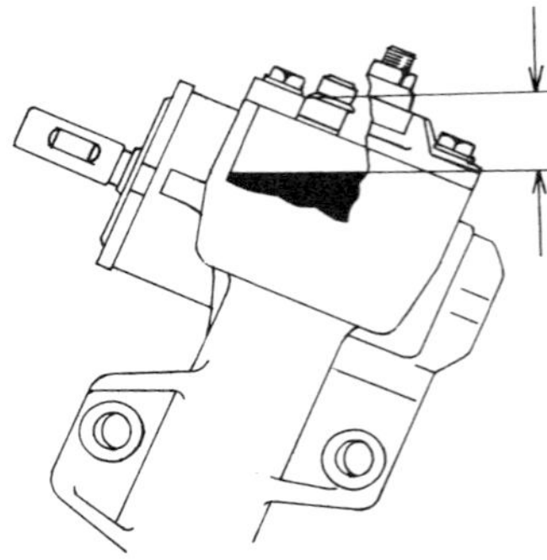

Fig. 4-8. Steering gearbox oil level being checked. Distance between arrows should be 21 to 36 mm ($^{13}/_{16}$ to $1\frac{3}{8}$ in.).

4.10 Wiring Harnesses and Connections

Most of the car's wiring harnesses pass through the engine compartment. You should, however, make the same checks on the wiring harnesses and wiring connections that are inside the passenger compartment and in the luggage compartment. Look especially for loose-fitting and partially-disconnected connections. Replace or repair wiring harnesses that have cracked and deteriorating insulation, or that have been damaged by fire, overheating, electrical shorts, spilled oil, or through contact with mechanical parts or hard objects.

5. UNDER-CAR MAINTENANCE OPERATIONS

Except for checking the level of the automatic transmission fluid (ATF), which should be done with the car on the ground, the maintenance operations described under the next seven numbered headings should be done with the car raised on a hoist. Alternatively, you can support the car on stands designed for the purpose.

> ***WARNING —***
> *Never work beneath a car that is supported solely by a jack. There is a very real danger that the jack may fail or accidentally release, allowing the car to fall.*

5.1 Checking Exhaust System

Momentarily cover the tailpipe opening with a pad of rags while the engine is running. Hissing sounds coming from underneath the car indicate leakage. Darker or lighter areas around joints in the system may indicate escaping gases. Check that the exhaust pipe and muffler mountings are secure and that the rubber parts of the mountings are in good condition.

5.2 Checking and Correcting ATF Level

(automatic transmission only)

The dipstick for the ATF in the automatic transmission is inserted into the ATF filler tube on the left-hand side of the engine (Fig. 5-1). The dipstick is attached to the cap for the ATF filler tube. The level can be checked with the ATF either hot or cold, as indicated in the illustration. The ATF is considered to be cold if the car has not been driven for eight or more hours; it is considered to be hot if the car has been driven for at least 15 km (or 10 mi.).

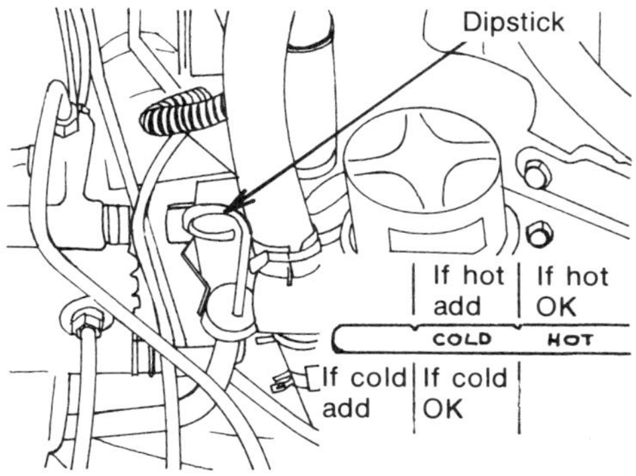

Fig. 5-1. Location of ATF dipstick and ATF filler tube. Inset shows dipstick's ATF level markings and indicates their uses in checking level of either hot or cold ATF.

To check the ATF level, hot or cold, start the engine. Then, with the brakes firmly applied, move the selector lever through all its positions from P through L, finally returning the lever to P. Remove the dipstick while the engine is idling. If the level is low, add Type F ATF using a funnel inserted into the filler tube. Be careful not to overfill the transmission, which can result in ATF foaming and transmission trouble. If, when you wipe clean the dipstick, the ATF smells burned, or if there are specks of metal or friction lining material in the ATF, the ATF may need to be replaced or the transmission repaired. See the troubleshooting information given in **AUTOMATIC TRANSMISSION.**

Changing ATF

The task of changing the ATF should normally be done at the mileage specified in **2. Maintenance Schedules.** You should, however, change the ATF earlier if it is dirty or contaminated, or if the car is used under severe conditions such as trailer towing, stop-and-go driving, or extended mountain driving.

To change the ATF, warm the transmission up thoroughly by driving at least 15 kilometers or 10 miles. Then stop the engine and place a receptacle for catching the draining ATF beneath the transmission. Remove the drain plug and allow the ATF to drain.

NOTE ——

Though Toyota does not specify that the ATF pan of the transmission and the pickup screen for the transmission's ATF pump should be cleaned when you change the ATF, many experienced mechanics do this whenever the ATF is changed. If you decide to clean the pan and screen, be sure to use a new ATF pan gasket and do not torque the pan bolts to more than 4 to 5 Nm (35 to 44 in. lb.).

When you have drained as much ATF as possible from the transmission, reinstall the drain plug to a torque of 15 to 20 Nm (11 to 15 ft. lb.). Then with the engine stopped, pour in 2.4 liters (2.5 U.S. quarts or 2.1 Imperial quarts) of Type F ATF. (If the transmission has just been repaired, so that there is no ATF remaining in the torque converter or the pump, you will need 6.3 liters (6.7 U.S. quarts or 5.7 Imperial quarts) of Type F ATF to refill the transmission.)

CAUTION ——

Do not tow the car or run the engine while there is no ATF in the transmission. This could ruin the transmission bearings.

Start the engine. Then check the ATF level and, if necessary, add ATF as described previously. Be especially sure not to overfill the transmission.

5.3 Checking and Changing Transmission Oil

(manual transmission only)

The gear oil in the manual transmission should be kept at the lower edge of the filler hole in the side of the transmission case. The level is correct if oil just barely drips from the hole with the plug removed, or if you can feel the oil with your fingertip just below the edge of the filler hole. Add the correct kind of gear oil, if necessary, through the filler hole. See **1. Lubricants.** Torque the filler plug to 30 to 35 Nm (22 to 26 ft. lb.). See Fig. 5-2.

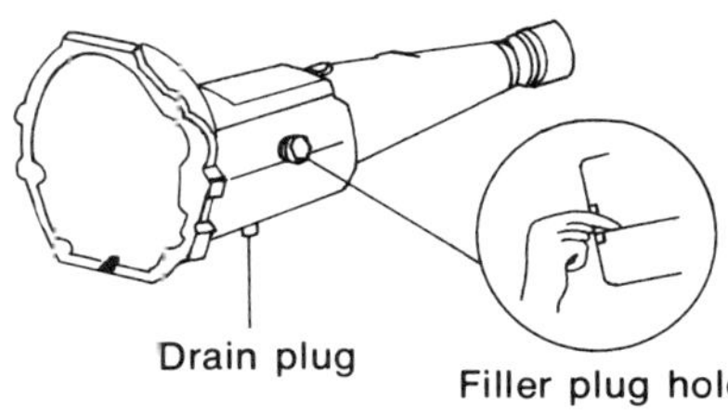

Fig. 5-2. Locations of drain and filler plugs for manual transmission. Inset shows method for checking oil level.

10

To replace the manual transmission's gear oil, first drive the car until the transmission is warmed up. Then place a drain pan beneath the transmission and remove the drain plug, allowing as much gear oil as possible to drain out.

Install the drain plug to a torque of 30 to 35 Nm (22 to 26 ft. lb.). Then, through the filler plug hole, pump into both 4-speed and 5-speed transmissions 1.5 liters (1.6 U.S. quarts or 1.4 Imperial quarts) of the gear oil specified in **1. Lubricants.** With the gear oil level at the bottom of the filler hole, install the filler plug to a torque of 30 to 35 Nm (22 to 26 ft. lb.).

> **NOTE ——**
> In some areas of the country, gear oil is available in quart-size plastic squeeze bottles that are suitable for home use. If you cannot find the correct grade of gear oil in a small quantity, obtain some in your own container from a garage or service station that has the correct grade in their pump. You can put the oil in at home using an oil syringe or a turkey baster that has a length of oil-proof hose slipped over its end.

5.4 Checking and Changing Rear Axle Oil

The gear oil in the rear axle should be kept at the lower edge of the filler hole (Fig. 5-3). The level may be considered satisfactory if you can feel the oil with your fingertip just below the edge of the filler hole. Add the correct kind of gear oil, if necessary, through the filler hole. See **1. Lubricants.** Torque the filler plug to 30 to 35 Nm (22 to 26 ft. lb.).

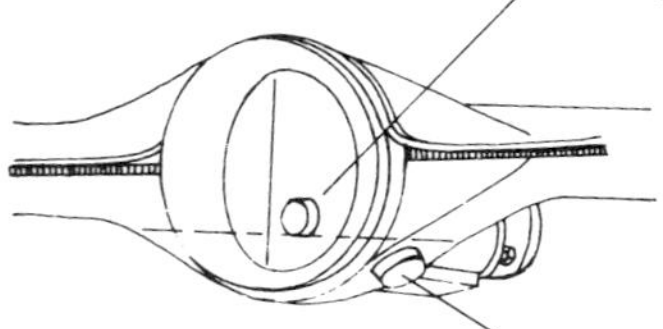

Fig. 5-3. Locations of drain plug and filler plug on rear axle.

To replace the rear axle's gear oil, first drive the car until the rear axle is warmed up. Then place a drain pan beneath the rear axle and jack up the left rear wheel and support it on a stand so that oil will flow toward the drain plug hole. Remove the drain plug and allow as much oil as possible to drain out.

Lower the left rear wheel to the ground and then install the drain plug to a torque of 20 to 35 Nm (22 to 26 ft. lb.). Then, through the filler plug hole, pump into the axle used on SR-5 models 1.2 liters (1.3 U.S. quarts or 1.1 Imperial quarts) of the gear oil specified in **1. Lubricants.** The rear axle used on models other than the SR-5 requires only 1.0 liter (1.1 U.S. quarts or 0.9 Imperial quart) of the same kind of gear oil. With the gear oil level at the bottom of the filler hole, install the filler plug to a torque of 30 to 35 Nm (22 to 26 ft. lb.).

5.5 Checking Rear Axle Bolt Torques

When you check the torques of the rear suspension components attached to the rear axle, you should use the specifications given in the Technical Data of **SUSPENSION AND STEERING.** The bolts that hold the driveshaft rear universal joint to the rear axle's pinion flange shouid be torqued to 35 to 40 Nm (26 to 30 ft. lb.).

5.6 Checking for Abnormal Steering Looseness

Measured at the steering wheel rim (Fig. 5-4) the maximum permissible freeplay (under light finger pressure) should be no more than 20 mm (about ¾ in.) with the car's front wheels pointed straight ahead. If the play exceeds this amount slightly, you can probably correct it by adjusting the steering gearbox as described in **SUSPENSION AND STEERING.** A great deal of excessive play is abnormal, and is an indication that you should inspect the steering linkage carefully. To do this, observe the steering gearbox's pitman arm, the idler arm, the relay rod, and the tie rods while someone moves the steering wheel from side to side. There should be no play whatsoever in the ball joints of the tie rod ends, the pitman arm, or the idler arm. Nor should there be play in the bushings of the idler arm or the steering gearbox's sector shaft. If any fault is found, repair or replace the faulty component as described in **SUSPENSION AND STEERING.**

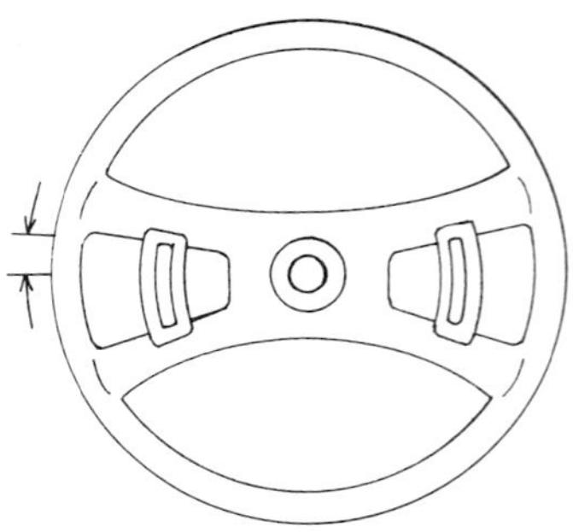

Fig. 5-4. Steering wheel freeplay (arrows) being checked. Rock the wheel slowly, using only very light finger pressure.

5.7 Inspecting and Lubricating Front Suspension Lower Ball Joints

The front suspension lower ball joints are integral with the track control arms of the front suspension . So if the ball joints are worn out, or are in any way faulty, you should replace the track control arms.

To check the ball joints for looseness, raise the rear of the car on a hoist or with a jack, then lower the rear axle onto stands designed to support a car. Make sure that the front wheels are pointed straight ahead and that the front wheel you are not checking is firmly chocked. Raise the other front wheel and place beneath it a block of wood 180 to 200 mm (7 to 8 in.) in height, then lower the wheel onto the block until the front coil spring is about half loaded. Place additional stands beneath the body for safety. There should be little or no play in the ball joint when the track control arm is moved up and down. If there is excessive play, replace the track control arm as described in **SUSPENSION AND STEERING.**

You should also inspect the rubber dust seal of each suspension ball joint. If it is cracked, deteriorating, or in any way worn or damaged, replace the dust seal as described in **SUSPENSION AND STEERING.**

Lubricating Ball Joints

In addition to lubricating the front suspension lower ball joints at the intervals prescribed in **2. Maintenance Schedules,** you should lubricate them whenever you discover that a damaged dust seal has allowed moisture or dirt to enter. If the amount of dirt is considerable, it is usually best to replace the track control arm because wear has probably taken place and it is difficult to force all dirt out by injecting grease into the ball joint.

To lubricate a ball joint, remove the plug and install a grease fitting (Fig. 5-5). Then, using a grease gun, pump in molybdenum grease that meets standard NLGI No. 1 or NLGI No. 2. Slowly pump in grease until clean grease issues from the vent in the ball joint's dust seal, then wipe away all expelled grease. Do not fill the ball joint too rapidly because this may force the dust seal off the ball joint or cause the seal to burst. Replace or reinstall the dust seal as described in **SUSPENSION AND STEERING** if there is any grease leakage around the seal.

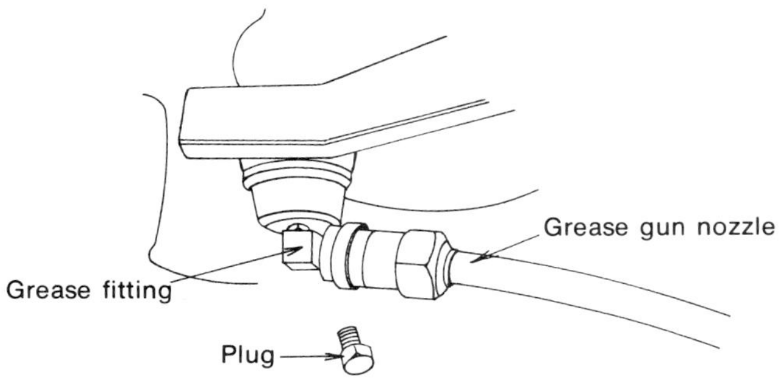

Fig. 5-5. Grease gun attached to grease fitting installed in ball joint. Notice that plug has been removed. After lubricating ball joint, remove grease fitting and reinstall plug.

6. BODY AND INSIDE-VEHICLE MAINTENANCE OPERATIONS

There are only a few routine maintenance steps for the body and interior of your car, but they are important steps. Especially make sure that the driving controls are in good working order before you take the car on a road test following servicing.

6.1 Body Lubrication

Lubricate the door locks and the lock cylinders with lock lubrication. The body hinges, the hood latch, the auxiliary hood catch, and the door checks should be lubricated with SAE 30 or SAE 40 engine oil or with polyethylene grease. Lubricate the door hinges with engine oil. Use polyethylene or multipurpose grease on the seat runners, the seat back pivots, and the trunk (or tailgate or rear lid) latch. If any latch, lock, or seat adjustment fails to work correctly, adjust it as described in **BODY AND INTERIOR.**

6.2 Seat Belt Inspection

The seat belts should be kept clean. If cleaning is necessary, wash the belts with a mild soap solution without removing them from the car. Do not bleach or dye the seat belts or use any other cleaning agents. They may weaken the webbing.

Carefully check the condition of the webbing while you are cleaning the belts or the interior of the car. Frayed or damaged belts should be replaced. Also check that the belts operate correctly and are correctly installed. The "Fasten Seat Belts" notice should be illuminated and the buzzer should sound as soon as the engine is started. Then both the light and the buzzer should turn off after the correct delay. If necessary, troubleshoot the system using the wiring diagrams given in **ELECTRICAL SYSTEM.**

To check the seat belt emergency lockup devices in the retractors, drive the car at about 40 kph (25 mph) with a passenger in the car to check the belt for the right-hand front seat. On a deserted roadway or in an empty parking lot where it will be safe to make the test, apply the brakes firmly—stopping the car as quickly as possible without locking the wheels. The belt retractors should lock up, preventing the seat belts from pulling out of the retractors. If the retractors fail to lock up in a fast stop, replace the retractors.

6.3 Checking Lights and Switches

Turn on each light switch, including the turn signals, the back-up lights (by engaging reverse or R), and the brake lights (by depressing the pedal). Have someone check that the lights come on. If any light or switch is faulty, troubleshoot and repair it using the information and wiring diagrams given in **ELECTRICAL SYSTEM.**

6.4 Replacing Fuel Filler Cap Gasket

To prevent the escape of gasoline and fumes, the fuel filler cap gasket should be replaced at the intervals prescribed in **2. Maintenance Schedules.** Remove the old gasket by pulling it off or cutting it. Then install the new gasket by hand, making sure that it is positioned on the cap as shown in Fig. 6-1.

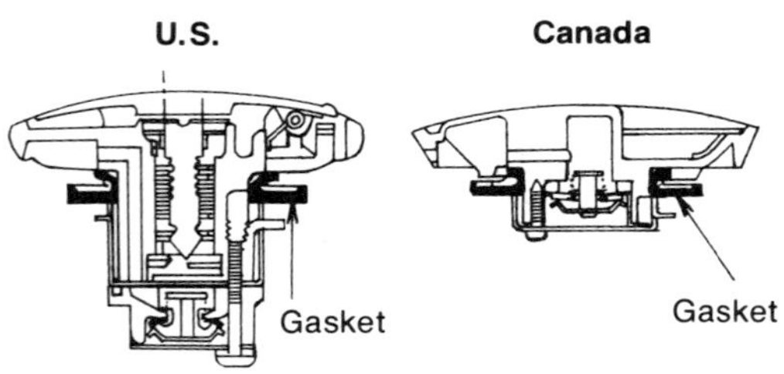

Fig. 6-1. Gaskets correctly installed on U.S. and Canadian fuel filler caps.

7. BASIC CAR CARE

The brief guide given here will help you keep your car looking as good as it runs. Though not included in the maintenance schedules, the steps described are those recommended by most car manufacturers for basic car care.

7.1 Body Preventive Maintenance

Clean debris from the body drain holes, including any holes in the bottoms of the doors. If there are foam plastic strips in these holes, do not remove the strips. Make sure that there are no "mud packs" built up in the fenders owing to dirt and water thrown up by the wheels.

Door weatherstrips should be lubricated with silicone spray or with talcum powder. If any weatherstrip is loose, clean away the old cement. Then reglue the weatherstrip with trim cement (available from automotive supply stores).

7.2 Care of Car Finish

The longer dirt is left on the paint, the greater the risk of damaging the glossy finish, either by scratching or simply by the chemical effect dirt particles have on the painted surface.

Washing

Never wash the car in direct sunlight. Beads of water not only leave spots when dried rapidly by the sun's heat, but act as tiny magnifying glasses that burn spots into the finish. Use plenty of water, a car-wash soap, and a soft sponge.

Begin by spraying water over the dry car to remove all loose dirt. Then apply lukewarm soapy water. Rinse the car after sponging off the soapy water, using plenty of clear water under as little pressure as possible. Wipe the car dry with a chamois or soft terrycloth towel to prevent water-spotting.

Waxing

For a long-lasting, protective, and glossy wax finish, apply a hard wax, such as Classic Car Wax, after the car has been washed and dried. Waxing is not needed after every washing, and a more effortless shine can be obtained by using a pre-softened wax, a liquid wax, or a car-wash liquid containing wax. You can tell when waxing is required by looking at the finish while it is wet. If the water coats the paint in smooth sheets instead of forming beads that roll off, waxing is in order.

Polishing

Use paint polish only if the finish assumes a dull look after long service. You can use polish on the car's brightwork to remove tar spots and tarnish, but afterwards apply a coat of wax to protect the clean plating.

Washing Chassis

The best time to wash the underside of the car is just after it has been driven in the rain. Spray the chassis with a powerful jet of water to remove dirt and deicing salt that may have accumulated there.

Special Cleaning

Tar spots can be removed with tar remover. Never use gasoline, kerosene, nail polish remover, or other unsuitable solvents. Insect spots also respond to tar remover. A bit of baking soda dissolved in the wash water will facilitate their removal. This method can also be used to remove spotting from tree sap.

The windshield wiper blades can be removed periodically and scrubbed with a hard bristle brush and alcohol or a strong detergent solution to remove debris. The windows themselves can be cleaned with a sponge and warm water, then dried with a chamois or soft towel. If you use commercial window washing preparations, make certain they will not damage automotive finishes.

7.3 Care of Interior

Clean the carpet with a vacuum cleaner or whisk broom. Dirt spots can usually be removed with lukewarm soapy water. Use spot remover for grease and oil spots. Do not pour the liquid directly on the carpet, but dampen a clean cloth and rub carefully, starting at the edge of the spot and working inward. Do not use gasoline, naptha, or other inflammable substances to clean the carpeting.

Upholstery and Trim

Use a dry foam cleaner. Grease or paint spots can be removed by wiping with a cloth soaked with this cleaner. Use the same cleaner, applied with a soft cloth or brush, on the headliner and side trim panels. For cloth covered seat areas, use the techniques described previously for cleaning the carpeting.

7.4 Tires and Accessories

Never use tar remover, gasoline, or any other petroleum-based substance for cleaning tires. These liquids damage rubber. Whitewall tires can be cleaned with tire sidewall cleaner. Rubber paints, commonly sold as tire dressing, are largely cosmetic.

Accessories

Most chrome-plated accessories can be polished and waxed along with the rest of the car's bright trim. The radio antenna should be lubricated only if hardened grease and collected dirt are interfering with raising or lowering the antenna. Do not use abrasive polish or cleaners on aluminum trim or accessories. They will destroy the mirror-like shine of anodized surfaces.